Winfield Scott.

GENERAL-IN-CHIEF OF THE ARMIES OF THE UNITED STATES.

(at the period of his commanding in Mexico.)

From the original Picture by Chappel, in the possession of the Publishers

Johnson Fry & Co. Publishers New York.

NEW YORK.

JOHNSON, FRY & COMPANY,

27 BEEKMAN STREET.

BATTLES

OF

THE UNITED STATES,

BY SEA AND LAND:

EMBRACING THOSE OF THE

REVOLUTIONARY AND INDIAN WARS,

THE WAR OF 1812, AND THE MEXICAN WAR:

WITH IMPORTANT OFFICIAL DOCUMENTS.

BY HENRY B. DAWSON,

MEMBER OF THE NEW YORK HISTORICAL SOCIETY, ETC.

Illustrated with numerous highly-finished Steel Engravings,

INCLUDING BATTLE SCENES AND FULL-LENGTH PORTRAITS,—FROM ORIGINAL PAINTINGS

BY ALONZO CHAPPEL.

IN TWO VOLUMES.—VOL. II.

NEW YORK:

JOHNSON, FRY, AND COMPANY,

27 BEEKMAN-STREET.

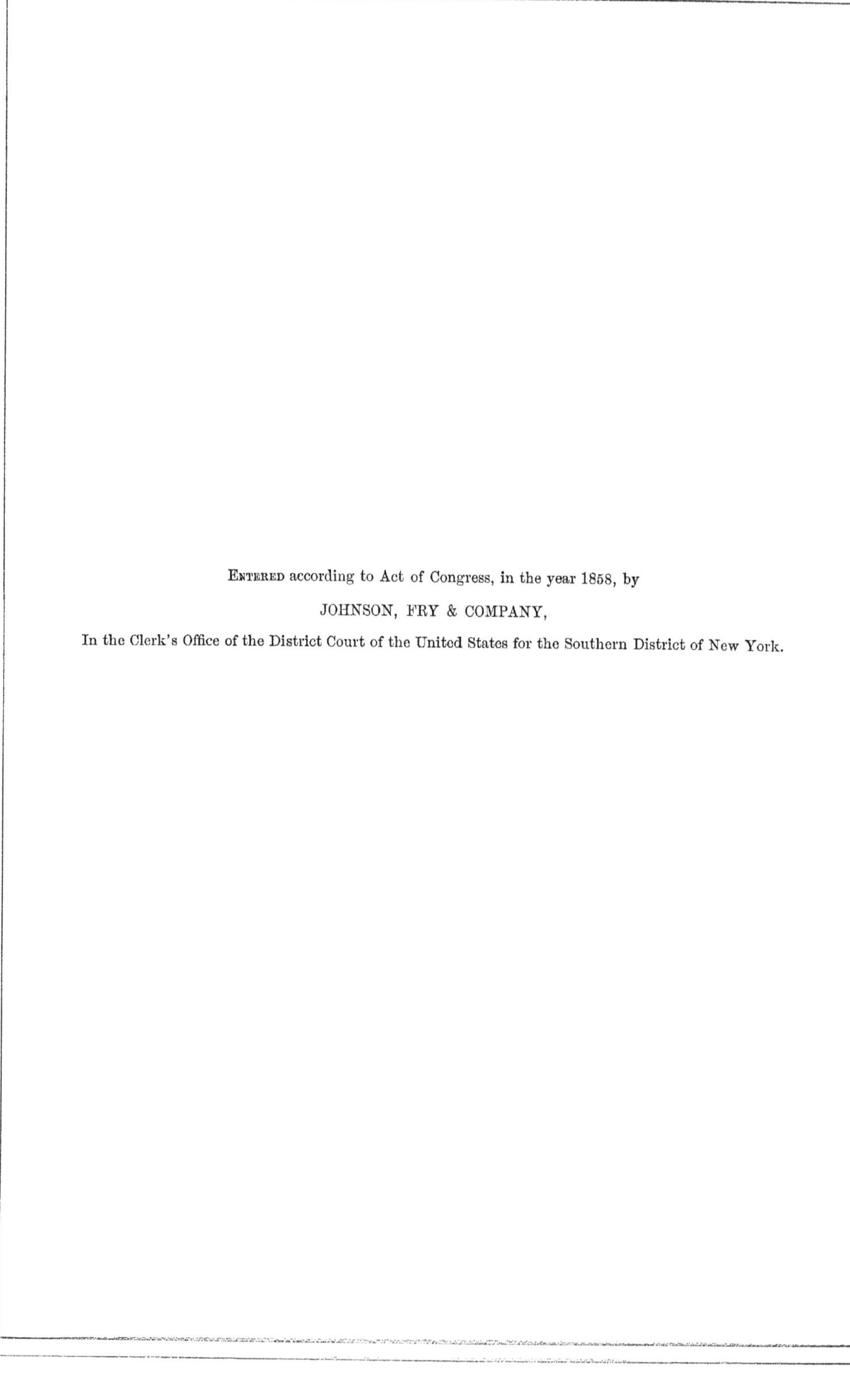

CONTENTS OF VOLUME II.

CONTENTS TO VOLUME II.

BATTLES

OF

THE UNITED STATES.

BOOK II.

THE INDIAN, FRENCH, AND ALGERINE WARS, THE WAR OF 1812, AND THE MEXICAN WAR.

1790–1847.

CHAPTER I.

September and October, 1790.

THE DEFEAT OF GENERAL HARMAR.

Among the many difficulties which the new government of the United States had to encounter, in the earlier days of General Washington's administration, none was more annoying than the disaffection of the Indian tribes which then inhabited the Northwestern Territory, which had, even at that early day, attracted the attention of the older States. While the Confederacy was yet governed by the Congress of the United States, under the "Articles of Confederation," the tide of emigration had flowed in that direction; and the foundations had been laid for those mighty Commonwealths, which, in our day, exercise so great an influence over the destinies of our country. Without stopping to inquire what causes produced these troubles, which, from their complicity, would require more space than can be devoted to the subject in this chapter, suffice it to say, that, at an early day, Brevet Brigadier-general Josiah Harmar had been ordered to this part of the country;[1] and that, with a respectable force of regulars, he had occupied, and fortified, the sites now occupied by the cities of Cincinnati[1] (*Fort Washington*) and Marietta (*Fort Harmar*).[2]

The troubles still continuing, and the grievances of the settlers demanding reparation, in December, 1789, General Harmar, with three hundred men, moved down to Fort Washington,—where Major Doughty and one hundred and forty men were stationed,—and preparations were made to chastise the offenders.[3] Notwithstanding the efforts which were made, however, it was not until the thirtieth of September, 1790, that a movement could be made,[4] when General Harmar,—who had remained in camp, on the southern bank of the Ohio, opposite Fort Washington,[5] and had been strengthened by the arrival of Colonel John Hardin, of Kentucky, and Major James Paul, of Pennsylvania, with eleven hundred and thirty-three volunteers from Kentucky, Western

---

[1] It appears to be disputed whether or not Gen. Harmar was in the Territory before the accession of Gen. Washington to the Presidency. Mr. Atwater (*History of Ohio, first ed.*, p. 132) says he "had been ordered to this frontier *by the old Congress*, and he was here at a very early day;" and Chief-justice Marshall (*Life of Washington*, v. p. 359) agrees with him; while Mr. S. Wilkeson (*American Pioneer*, i. p. 205) maintains that he was appointed by the new government.

[1] Burnett's Notes, pp. 54, 55; Atwater's Ohio, p. 132.

[2] Burnett's Notes, p. 43; Hildreth's Pioneer Hist. of the Ohio Valley, p. 213.—[3] Burnett's Notes, pp. 99–101; Atwater's Ohio, p. 133; Butler's Kentucky, p. 191; Marshall's Kentucky, i. p. 362.—[4] Burnett's Notes, p. 102; Atwater's Ohio, p. 133; Marshall's Ky., i. p. 363; Marshall's Washington, v. p. 359.—[5] Atwater's Ohio, p. 133.

Virginia, and Pennsylvania,[1] — taking with him three hundred and twenty regulars,[2] crossed the Ohio River, struck into the old Indian war-path, and marched to the villages on the head-waters of the Little Miami,[3] near where Fort Wayne now stands. The march was conducted in good order, and the standing corn was destroyed;[4] after which the expedition, striking across the woods, marched towards the towns on the Great Miami, where Piqua now stands.[5]

When the expedition had reached the place where Loramie's Ferry now is, and where it had encamped for the night, three Indians were seen and pursued; one of whom was taken prisoner, while the others escaped.[6] From this prisoner information was obtained that the inhabitants of the villages were unapprised of the approach of the expedition, that no reinforcements had come in, and that they were quarrelling among themselves;[7] and, evidently forgetting that this information was not to be depended on, and that the two scouts who had escaped would convey full information of the approach and the strength of the expedition, General Harmar resolved to send forward a detachment, under Colonel Hardin, to attack and destroy the village.[8] Accordingly six hundred volunteers, including fifty regulars,[9] moved forward, by

[1] Atwater's Ohio, pp. 133, 134; Marshall's Ky., i. p. 362; Marshall's Washington, v. p. 359.—[2] Marshall's Ky., i. p. 363; Marshall's Washington, v. p. 359.

[3] Atwater's Ohio, p. 134; Burnett's Notes, p. 102.

[4] Marshall's Ky., i. p. 363.—[5] Atwater's Ohio, p. 134; Burnett's Notes, p. 102.—[6] Atwater's Ohio, p. 134.

[7] Burnett's Notes, p. 103.—[8] Marshall's Washington, v. p. 359; Atwater's Ohio, p. 134; Burnett's Notes, p. 103.

[9] Burnett's Notes, p. 103; Marshall's Washington, v. p. 359.

forced marches;[1] and, on the second day of its march,[2] the detachment reached the villages.[3] With great forethought—worthy of more enlightened warriors — the Indians had removed their women and children to places of greater safety; burned their wigwams; and, with the exception of a small party of observation, had retired into the woods.[4]

The main body of the army moved slowly forward, over roads which were constructed by itself;[5] and, four days after the villages had been occupied by Colonel Hardin, General Harmar reached them.[6] A week was spent among the ashes of the settlements, and the hidden stores of the savages, including not less than twenty thousand bushels of corn, were discovered and destroyed;[7] while, emulous of renown, General Harmar disgraced himself, as General Sullivan had done in New York, by cutting down or girdling the fine orchards with which the settlements were surrounded.[8]

Without being contented with this complete, and, almost bloodless, accomplishment of the purposes for which the expedition had been organized, General Harmar appears to have been ambitious of still greater exploits; and, forgetful of the peculiar character of his troops, he sent out three several detachments in pursuit of the enemy.

The first, composed of three hundred men,[9] under Colonel Trotter, returned

[1] Burnett's Notes, p. 103; Atwater's Ohio, p. 134.

[2] Atwater's Ohio, p. 134.—[3] Ibid.; Marshall's Washington, v. p. 359; Burnett's Notes, p. 103.—[4] Marshall's Washington, v. p. 359; Atwater's Ohio, p. 134.—[5] Burnett's Notes, p. 103; Atwater's Ohio, p. 134.—[6] Atwater's Ohio, p. 134.—[7] Burnett's Notes, p. 103.—[8] Ibid.—[9] Ibid.

to the camp on the same day on which it left it, after killing two Indians.[1] With some insinuations against the prudence of Colonel Trotter, the same party was again detached, under Colonel Hardin.[2] When this officer had marched six miles from the camp he fell into an ambuscade which had been prepared for him;[3] when the Kentuckians, who led the militia, in the column,[4] with the greatest cowardice, "ran away and threw down their arms, without firing scarcely a single gun,"[5] and left the handful of regulars—thirty in number—to oppose the enemy single-handed and alone.[6] Notwithstanding the overpowering force of the enemy, the little party maintained its ground until twenty-three of the number had fallen, when the remainder fled, and reached the camp in safety.[7]

After remaining at the villages a day or two longer, and discovering that the enemy was gradually concentrating his strength around the encampment, General Harmar considered it prudent to retire to Fort Washington, without farther pursuing the objects which had originally led to the expedition.[8] But in this the General's wonted imprudence did not forsake him. Without considering the character and strength of his enemy, on the second day of his march, he detached Colonel Hardin, with three hundred volunteers[9] and sixty regulars, under Major Wyllys,[10] with orders to return to the villages, and bring the enemy to an action. When this detachment reached the confluence of the St. Joseph's and St. Mary's rivers, it divided into three columns, each of whom speedily encountered considerable bodies of Indians, and a series of severe, but unsuccessful, actions ensued, in which the enemy was the victor; Major Wyllys, Lieutenant Frothingham, and fifty of the regulars, and nine officers and about one hundred militiamen, being among the slain.[1]

The army moved by slow and easy marches to Fort Washington, where the militia were dismissed; and General Harmar, after proceeding to the seat of government, resigned his command.[2]

The loss of the regulars, in this affair, was seventy-three killed, besides the wounded; that of the militia was ninety-eight killed and ten wounded.[3]

This expedition, without any apparent reason, was claimed as a victory by the commanding General, on the ground "that any battle in which the Indians might lose a considerable number of men, would be fatal to them, although a still greater loss should be sustained by the Americans, because the savages did not possess a population from which they could replace the warriors who had fallen;"[4] yet it is proper to remark that the Court of Inquiry which was appointed to investigate the matter, acquitted the General with honor.[5] In that inquiry it was found that the militia were very badly equipped; that

[1] Burnett's Notes, p. 103.—[2] Ibid.—[3] Marshall's Ky., i. p. 363; Atwater's Ohio, p. 134.—[4] Marshall's Washington, v. p. 359.—[5] Order Book of Gen. Harmar.

[6] Marshall's Washington, v. p. 360.—[7] Marshall's Ky., i. p. 363.—[8] Ibid., p. 364.—[9] Marshall's Washington, v. p. 360.—[10] Marshall's Ky., i. p. 364.

[1] Marshall's Washington, v. pp. 361, 362.—[2] Burnett's Notes, p. 104; Marshall's Ky., p. 365.—[3] Ibid.

[4] Marshall's Washington, v. pp. 362, 363.

[5] Ibid.; Marshall's Ky., i. p. 366.

their arms were very bad and out of repair; that the men themselves were unfit for service and insubordinate; that the heavy loss was occasioned by the ignorance, imbecility, insubordination, and defective equipment of the militia, and not to any defect of capacity or bravery, in the commanding General, or in the officers who served under him;[1] and, although General Harmar's name has come down to us in association with a "defeat," there is but little doubt that the mischief was really produced by causes over which the General had not, and could not exercise the least possible control.

DOCUMENT.

GENERAL HARMAR'S DISPATCH TO THE SECRETARY OF WAR.

HEAD-QUARTERS, FORT WASHINGTON, *November* 4, 1790.

Sir:—I have the honor to inform you, that on the 30th of September I marched with three hundred and twenty federal troops, and eleven hundred and thirty-three militia—total, fourteen hundred and fifty-three; after encountering a few difficulties, we gained the Miami village. It was abandoned before we entered it, which I was very sorry for. The villanous traders would have been a principal object of attention. I beg leave to refer you to my orders, which are inclosed. The substance of the work is this: our loss was heavy, but the head-quarters of iniquity were broken up. At a moderate computation, not less than one hundred, or one hundred and twenty warriors were slain, and three hundred log-houses and wigwams burned. Our loss, about one hundred and eighty. The remainder of the Indians will be ill off for sustenance. Twenty thousand bushels of corn, in the ears, were consumed, burned, and destroyed by the army, with vegetables in abundance. The loss of Major Wyllys and Lieutenant Frothingham, of the federal troops, and a number of valuable militia officers, I sincerely lament.

The brave Lieutenant Denny is my adjutant. It will afford me great satisfaction to know that some mark of honor will be shown to him—his long and faithful services merit it. There is a vast deal of business in this western world. If there is no impropriety in giving me an aid-de-camp, I wish him to be the person.

In my next dispatches I shall enter into the minutiæ of business, and give you a particular description of each day's march, with all the occurrences, observations, &c., &c.

I have the honor to be, sir, with perfect esteem, your most humble and obedient servant,

J. Harmar,
Lieut.-Col. 1st U. S. Regt.

The Hon. Maj.-Gen. Knox, Secretary at War.

Return of the killed and wounded upon the expedition against the Miami Towns, under the command of Brigadier-general Harmar.

HEAD-QUARTERS, FORT WASHINGTON, *November* 4, 1790.

Killed.—*Federal Troops.*—One major, one lieutenant, seventy-three rank and file. *Militia.*—One major, three captains, two lieutenants, four ensigns, ninety-eight rank and file.

Wounded.—*Federal Troops.*—Three rank and file. *Militia.*—Two lieutenants, one ensign, twenty-five rank and file.

Killed.—*Federal Troops.*—Major Wyllys, Lieutenant Frothingham. *Militia.*—Major Fontaine; Captains Sharp, Scott, and McMurtrey; Lieutenants Clark and Rogers; Ensigns Bridges, Higgens, Sweet, and Threlheld.

Wounded.—Lieutenants Sanders and Worley, and Ensign Arnold.

E. Denny, *Lieut and Adjt.*

J. Harmar.

[1] Burnett's Notes, pp. 104, 105.

CHAPTER II.

November 4, 1791.

THE DEFEAT OF GENERAL St. CLAIR.

The expedition under General Harmar was closely followed by the most desperate efforts of the savages to harass and destroy the neighboring settlements, in which the enemy felt the want of those provisions which had been then destroyed. In these predatory attacks the enemy received the countenance and support of the British authorities; and British subjects, more savage even than the Indians, not unfrequently led the latter on their errands of destruction.[1]

In January, 1791, the President (*General Washington*) laid before the Senate of the United States "a statement relative to the frontiers, which had been submitted to him by the Secretary for the Department of War," "relying upon its wisdom to make such arrangements as might be essential for the preservation of good order, and the effectual preservation of the frontiers."[2] Three days afterwards he transmitted a second message,[3] with intelligence received by him from General Rufus Putnam, in which not only the audacity of the enemy, but the weakness of the settlements, was fully detailed.[1] The Federal Congress promptly authorized the President to raise a corps of volunteers for the immediate relief of the settlements; while, for permanent service, an army of three thousand men, the number asked for,[2] of which Governor Arthur St. Clair, to whom the rank of Major-general was assigned, as the commander, was afterwards placed in command.

The volunteers, under General Scott, marched on the twenty-third of May, and between that time and the fourteenth of June, they had destroyed several villages, with large quantities of provisions, peltry, &c.; killed thirty-two and captured fifty-seven warriors; and returned to the settlements without losing a single man, and with only four wounded.[3]

A second volunteer force, led by Colonel Wilkinson, was also similarly successful; and it also had returned to Fort Washington without serious loss.[4]

In the mean time General St. Clair, and his second in command, General Butler, had been actively engaged in

---

[1] N. Y. Journal, No. 2614, Saturday, Nov. 16, 1791;

[2] President's Message, in the Jour. of the Senate, Monday, Jan. 24, 1791. I find no reference to the message in the House Journal, and suppose, therefore, that it was not sent to that body.

[3] President's Message, in the Jour. of the Senate and the House, Thursday, Jan. 27, 1791.

[1] Burnett's Notes on the Northwest, p. 114.

[2] "An Act for raising and adding another regiment to the military establishment of the United States, and for making further provision for the protection of the frontiers." Approved March 3, 1791.

[3] Burnett's Notes, pp. 115–118; N.Y. Journal, No. 2582, Saturday, Aug. 6, 1791.

[4] Burnett's Notes, pp. 118–121.

preparing for the campaign; yet the enlistments proceeded so slowly, and the appointments which had been provided were so scanty, that, although the first of July had been appointed for the opening of the campaign,[1] it was several weeks after that date before any of the new levies reached Fort Washington, the appointed place of rendezvous.[2] The ammunition for the campaign had also to be made up; the gun-carriages had to be renewed; an armory for the repair of arms had to be erected; and stores had to be collected for the forts which it had been designed to establish in the enemy's country. Nearly all the arms required repairs; tools, kegs for cartridges, boxes for fixed ammunition, splints for the wounded, and bells for the horses had to be made on the spot, by such artificers as could be selected from the recruits, after they reached Fort Washington.[3] In addition to these difficulties, the supplies were insufficient; and, in the latter part of August, not more than two thirds of the requisite force had come in, compelling the General to seek the assistance of volunteers from Kentucky, to complete his force.[4]

With these difficulties to contend with, about the first of September, 1791, Colonel Darke was ordered to move, with the greater part of the troops then at Fort Washington, to the Great Miami; and, on the site of Hamilton, Butler County, Ohio, to build a stockade-fort, which would serve as a

[1] St. Clair's Narrative, p. ix.—[2] Adj.-Gen. Sargent's Diary, pp. 6–8.—[3] St. Clair's Narrative, pp. 10–13.

[4] St. Clair's Narrative, p. 9; Adj.-Gen. Sargent's Diary, Sept. 5, 1791.

deposit for provisions, and, at the same time, form the first link in the chain of works which General St. Clair designed to construct.[1]

The fort having been so far completed as to be ready to receive and afford shelter for a garrison, on the thirtieth of September, the General returned to Fort Washington "to forward the preparations of the campaign," leaving General Butler in command, with orders to push forward still farther in the enemy's country.[2]

On the fourth of October the army left Fort Hamilton;[3] and, on the thirteenth of that month, having advanced forty-five miles, and a proper place presenting itself for another post, the army halted and encamped, and proceeded to erect another fort.[4] This post—which is about six miles south of the present town of Greenville, in Darke County, Ohio—was called Fort Jefferson,[5] and so vigorously were the men employed that on the twenty-fourth of October it was in such forwardness that the garrison, composed of ninety men, which was detached to occupy it, could readily complete it.[6]

On that day (*October 24th*) the army moved six miles, when it halted to await the arrival of provisions.[7] The force, including the First regiment, was

[1] Burnett's Notes, p. 122; Adj.-Gen. Sargent's Diary, Sept. 6 to Sept. 11.—[2] Adj.-Gen. Sargent's Diary, Oct. 1 to Oct. 9.—[3] Ibid., Oct. 4; Burnett's Notes, pp. 122, 123; Gen. St. Clair's Narrative, p. 15.—[4] Adj.-Gen. Sargent's Diary, Oct. 13, 14; Gen. St. Clair's Narrative, p. 18. Judge Burnett (*Notes*, p. 123) supposes the army *halted* on the 24*th October*.—[5] Atwater's Hist. of Ohio, p. 137.

[6] Adj.-Gen. Sargent's Diary, Oct. 24; Gen. St. Clair's Narrative, p. 18.—[7] Adj.-Gen. Sargent's Diary, Oct. 24, 25; Gen. St. Clair's Dispatch, Nov. 1, 1791; Gen. St. Clair's Narrative, p. 18.

now reduced, by the withdrawal of the detachments for the forts, to less than two thousand effective men;[1] the country through which the expedition had to pass was a dense forest, through which roads had to be cut for the passage of the artillery, baggage, and stores;[2] the provisions had become so scarce that the army had been reduced to short allowance;[3] and the enemy had began to show himself and oppose the progress of the army.[4] Add to this a spirit of insubordination among the volunteers, a large number of whom deserted, with the expressed determination of seizing a convoy of flour which was then on its way to the army;[5] and General St. Clair was obliged to detach the First regiment of United States troops, under Major Hamtramck, to protect the flour, and, if possible, to bring the deserters back to their duty.[6]

Under these circumstances the progress of the army was necessarily slow; and on the afternoon of the third of November it encamped on the eastern bank of a small stream, which was supposed to have been the St. Mary's, one of the main branches of the Maumee.[7] It was afterwards found to be a branch of the Wabash,—near the site of Fort Recovery, in Mercer County, Ohio,[1]—about ninety-seven miles from Fort Washington, and about twenty from the Miami Towns, which was the point of the projected attack on the enemy.[2]

The site of the encampment was "a small rising ground, descending gradually in front to a stream," already referred to, "of fifty feet wide, and fordable at this time."[3] On this ground, in accordance with general orders, the army encamped in two lines—the first, under General Butler, composed of Patterson's New Jersey Volunteers on the right, Clarke's Pennsylvanians in the centre, and Butler's Pennsylvanians on the left; and the second, under Lieutenant-colonel Darke, composed of Second United States regiment, on the right, Gaither's Marylanders in the centre, and Beddinger's Virginians on the left. Four pieces of artillery were posted between the centre and the left wing of each of these lines; Captain Truman's troop of Kentucky horse, and Captain Faulkner's company of riflemen, guarded the right flank, and Captain Snowden's troop of horse the left flank; a camp-guard of two officers and fifty-four men; a picket of a captain and thirty men; four guards of an officer and fifteen men each; and a picket of a captain and thirty men, on the road over which the army had marched, two hundred and fifty yards in the rear of the second line; while, in front of the whole, three hundred yards in

[1] Report of the Committee of Cong.—[2] Adj.-Gen. Sargent's Diary, Oct. 26; Observations of Gen. St. Clair on the Report of the Committee; Atwater's Ohio, p. 137.

[3] Adj.-Gen. Sargent's Diary, Oct. 27; Testimony of Count de Malartie.—[4] Adj.-Gen. Sargent's Diary, Oct. 18, 28; Atwater's Ohio, p. 137; Marshall's Washington, v. p. 389.—[5] Adj.-Gen. Sargent's Diary, Oct. 31; Gen. St. Clair's Dispatch, Nov. 1, 1791; Gen. St. Clair's Narrative, pp. 19, 27.—[6] Adj.-Gen. Sargent's Diary, Oct. 31; Gen. St. Clair's Dispatch, Nov. 1, 1791; Gen. St. Clair's Narrative, pp. 27, 28.

[7] Adj.-Gen. Sargent's Diary, Nov. 3; His "Narrative of the Unfortunate Affair of Friday," &c., p. 30; Gen. St. Clair's Dispatch, Nov. 9.

[1] Burnett's Notes, p. 123.—[2] Adj.-Gen. Sargent's Diary, Nov. 3; Atwater's Ohio, p. 137; Adj.-Gen. Sargent's Narrative, p. 30.—[3] Adj.-Gen. Sargent's Narrative, p. 30, and the map therein. Gen. St. Clair (*Dispatch*, *Nov.* 9, 1791), says it was "about twelve yards wide."

advance of the stream, "across a piece of bottom land, and possessing a fine high flat and open wood, with proper pickets," were posted the militia under Lieutenant-colonel Oldham.[1]

On this spot it had been determined to construct a slight work for the safe keeping of the knapsacks, and "every thing else that was not of absolute necessity," by which means the troops would have been transformed into light troops, and rendered more efficient in the peculiar service in which they were engaged. With this intention, on the evening of the third, the general-in-chief had consulted with Major Ferguson and adopted a plan for the construction of the work; and it was designed to engage the entire force in that labor, until the First regiment, which had been sent after the deserters, should have reached the camp, with its convoy of flour.[2]

At a very early hour in the morning of the fourth of November, according to his usual practice, General St. Clair had paraded his troops;[3] and, about half an hour before sunrise, had dismissed them from parade,[4] when the enemy fell upon the advanced body of militia, under Lieutenant-colonel Oldham, without any warning and with great fury.[5] The first evidence of the enemy's presence was the discovery, by Ensign Pope, of a party of about thirty savages in pursuit of a pack-horseman, when the guard was advanced to cover the retreat of the fugitive.[1] At that moment a yell, as from three hundred Indians, arose "in the quarter where Captain Simmons was stationed;"[2] and, although but few of the enemy showed themselves—the policy of the Indians, during the entire action, having been to lay flat on the ground, and to deliver their fire from that position[3]—the militia were filled with alarm, and fled with great precipitation, without attempting to defend themselves.[4] Rushing over the stream, with the Indians following in pursuit, close on their heels, they broke through the first line, throwing the battalions of Pennsylvanians, under Majors Clarke and Butler, into considerable disorder, which was never wholly remedied.[5]

When the character of the attack on the militia, on the opposite side of the stream, and of its retreat, was fully understood, Major Ferguson prepared to cover the retreat of that body with his artillery;[6] and this, with a fire which was opened by the first line, served to check the advance of the enemy, and to throw him, in his turn, into some confusion.[7] Under the directions of "their leader, *on horseback, dressed in a red coat*," however, the savages soon

[1] Gen. St. Clair's Dispatch, Nov. 9, 1791; Adj.-Gen. Sargent's Narrative, pp. 30, 31, and the map therein.

[2] Gen. St. Clair's Dispatch, Nov. 9, 1791. See also Burnett's Notes, p. 123.—[3] Gen. St. Clair's Dispatch, Nov. 9, 1791; Marshall's Ky., i. p. 381; Adj.-Gen. Sargent's Narrative, p. 33.—[4] Gen. St. Clair's Dispatch, Nov. 9, 1791; Burnett's Notes, p. 123; Report. of Com. of Cong.; Atwater's Ohio, p. 138.—[5] Gen. St. Clair's Dispatch, Nov. 9, 1791; Report of Com. of Cong.; Adj.-Gen. Sargent's Narrative, p. 34.

[1] Testimony of Ensign Pope before the Com. of Cong.

[2] Ibid.—[3] Gen. St. Clair's Dispatch, Nov. 9, 1791.

[4] Burnett's Notes, p. 123; St. Clair's Narrative, p. 54; Report of Com. of Cong.; Atwater's Ohio, p. 138; Adj.-Gen. Sargent's Narrative, p. 34.—[5] Gen. St. Clair's Dispatch, Nov. 9, 1791; Burnett's Notes, p. 123; Gen. St. Clair's Narrative, p. 54; Report of Com. of Cong.; Adj.-Gen. Sargent's Narrative, p. 34.

[6] Testimony of Col. Semple.

[7] Gen. St. Clair's Dispatch, Nov. 9, 1791.

rallied,[1] and, attacking the centre of the line, where the artillery was posted, with great fury, they repeatedly drove the artillerists from their guns with great slaughter.[2]

With the celerity and secrecy of movement which characterize the warfare of the Indian tribes, the enemy quickly turned the left flank of the first line, and, with equal fury, assailed the second, directing his efforts in this, as in the other case, to the centre, where the artillery was posted.[3] A large body of savages, who had been directed to turn the right flank of the first line, was kept in check by Captain Faulkner's riflemen; but the peculiarity of the enemy's movements, and the weight of numbers, speedily overcame the gallant little band of sharp-shooters by whom he was opposed, and both flanks of the first line were turned.[4]

"Finding no great effect from his fire, and confusion beginning to spread, from the great number of men who were falling, in all quarters, it became necessary to try what could be done with the bayonet."[5] Accordingly, Lieutenant-colonel Darke was ordered to make a charge, with part of the second line, and turn the *left* flank of the enemy;[6] while the general, in person, "led up the troops which drove them back when they first entered the camp by the left flank," or, in other words, the charge which was made on the enemy's *right*.[1] These movements were made with great spirit, and as the troops approached the crouching and concealed savages, the latter instantly gave way and were driven back three or four hundred yards[2]—beyond the creek before referred to.[3] The advantage which had thus been gained could not be held, in consequence of the want of light troops to pursue the fugitives[4]—the small corps of riflemen, under Captain Faulkner, being the only light infantry in the army,[5] and the cavalry having been rendered useless by the want of provender for the horses[6]—and the enemy speedily rallied and compelled the troops to give way.[7]

Pressing forward towards the camp, the enemy forced the left of the line, when the Second regiment of United States troops, supported by Clarke's and Butler's battalions, made a second charge, and a second time drove him from the ground.[8] The same deficiency of light troops, which had destroyed the effect of the first charges, before referred to, also rendered this useless; and the enemy returned to the attack with greater fury. These movements—alternate charges by the troops, and successful renewals of the action by the enemy—continued for several hours,[9]

---

[1] Testimony of Col Semple.—[2] Gen. St. Clair's Dispatch, Nov. 9, 1791; Burnett's Notes, p. 124.—[3] Burnett's Notes, p. 124.—[4] Gen. St. Clair's "Observations on the Report of the Com. of Cong."—[5] Gen. St. Clair's Dispatch, Nov. 9, 1791. See also Atwater's Ohio, p. 138.

[6] Gen. St. Clair's Dispatch, Nov. 9, 1791; Gen. St. Clair's Narrative, p. 50. Adj.-Gen. Sargent (*Narrative*, p. 44) says this was "beyond *his* (*Darke's*) capacity"—evidently censuring his conduct.

[1] Gen St. Clair's Narrative, p. 50.—[2] Gen. St. Clair's Dispatch, Nov. 9, 1791.—[3] Burnett's Notes, p. 124.

[4] Gen. St. Clair's Dispatch, Nov. 9, 1791.—[5] Roster of the Army, in Adj.-Gen. Sargent's Diary.—[6] Gen. St. Clair's "Observations," &c.—[7] Gen. St. Clair's Dispatch, Nov. 9, 1791; Burnett's Notes, p. 124.—[8] Gen. St. Clair's Dispatch, Nov. 9, 1791; Adj.-Gen. Sargent's Narrative, p. 36.—[9] Gen. St. Clair's Dispatch, Nov. 9, 1791; Burnett's Notes, p. 124; Report of Com. of Cong.

by which time the greater part of the officers had been either killed or wounded, the artillery silenced, and the line of retreat cut off by the occupation of the road by the enemy;[1] and, at half-past nine o'clock[2]—four hours after the action commenced[3]—it was considered useless to attempt to hold the ground any longer. Accordingly, "the remains of the army were formed, as well as circumstances would admit, towards the right of the encampment, from which, by the way of the second line, another charge was made upon the enemy, as if with the design to turn his left flank, but, in fact, to gain the road."[4] Under the personal direction of General St. Clair,[5] "this was effected; and, as soon as it was open, the militia took along it, followed by the troops, Major Clarke, with his battalion, covering the rear."[6]

As may be supposed, the retreat was a precipitate one, especially while the pursuit, which continued four miles, was continued.[7] The militia, panic-stricken, not only hastened from the field of battle in the greatest confusion, but they actually threw away their arms and accoutrements, as they hastened through the woods,—even after the enemy had ceased to pursue them,—in order that their progress might not be impeded by what, in the time of their greatest need, they had found so little use for.[8]

[1] Gen. St. Clair's Dispatch, Nov. 9, 1791.—[2] Ibid.; Burnett's Notes, p. 125.—[3] Report of Com. of Cong.

[4] Gen. St. Clair's Dispatch, Nov. 9, 1791.—[5] Gen. St. Clair's Narrative, p. 50.—[6] Gen. St. Clair's Dispatch, Nov. 9, 1791; Burnett's Notes, p. 124.—[7] Gen. St. Clair's Dispatch, Nov. 9, 1791. Adj.-Gen. Sargent (*Narrative*, p. 38) says, "the enemy scarcely pursued beyond a mile and a half."—[8] Gen. St. Clair's Dispatch, Nov. 9, 1791; St. Clair's Narrative, p. 47.

The camp and the artillery were abandoned to the enemy—not a horse being left alive to draw them off, had it been otherwise practicable[1]—and the spoils of the victors were exceedingly valuable to them.[2]

During the entire day the shattered remains of the army pursued their weary way through the wilderness; and, a little after sunset, they reached Fort Jefferson, twenty-nine miles from the field of battle.[3] At this place the First regiment was met; but, as it would not add sufficient strength to the wreck of the army, it was determined to leave the wounded at Fort Jefferson, and continue the retreat to Fort Washington.[4]

In this disastrous action the loss of the Americans was very severe—thirty-eight officers, and five hundred and ninety-three non-commissioned officers and privates having been killed or missing; and twenty-one officers, and two hundred and forty-two non-commissioned officers and privates wounded, of whom many subsequently died.[5] Of the enemy's loss there is no reliable knowledge: and there is but little doubt that it was small when compared with that of the Americans.[6]

Of the relative strength of the two there is, also, no definite knowledge. While the American forces numbered about sixteen hundred men;[7] that of

[1] Gen. St. Clair's Dispatch, Nov. 9, 1791.—[2] John Brickell's Narrative, (*American Pioneer*), i. p. 50; Adj.-Gen. Sargent's Narrative, p. 43.—[3] Gen. St. Clair's Dispatch, Nov. 9, 1791.—[4] Marshall's Washington, v. p. 395; Burnett's Notes, pp. 126, 127.—[5] Marshall's Washington, v. p. 395.—[6] Ibid., p. 396.—[7] Report of Com. of Cong.; Marshall's Washington, v. p. 390; Adj.-Gen. Sargent's Narrative, p. 35.

the enemy is said to have been from five hundred to fifteen hundred;[1] and there is but little doubt that among the latter were many British subjects or disaffected Americans who were not less savage than their more swarthy associates. That a red-coated officer on horseback directed the enemy's movements has appeared in the evidence;[2] while there is no doubt expressed, by the writers of that day, that the British post at Detroit—one of the posts which had been retained, in violation of the treaty of 1783—supplied arms and ammunition for the purposes of the war.[3]

Of the causes of this disaster, there appears to be but little doubt. The commander-in-chief was one of the few general officers who had passed through the War of the Revolution with the entire confidence of General Washington. A veteran of the war with the French, he possessed a degree of professional skill which but few others enjoyed; while the honest sincerity of the man had rendered him, as similar traits of character had rendered some others, the object of ridicule and persecution by the cliques and cabals of that day, without impairing the confidence which his commander had reposed in him. He had assumed the command of the expedition in question, at the request of the President; but the inefficiency of the Department of War,[1] the favoritism or the speculation which attended the movements of the Quartermaster's Department,[2] the refuse of the Eastern population which was sent out as his troops,[3] the discontent or the heart-burnings which crept into the force from the improper selection of officers, and other causes,[4] not less influential, among the troops, had rendered his skill and his patriotism entirely unavailing. He asked for a court-martial, but the service did not furnish officers of a grade to form a court for his trial.[5] A committee of the House of Representatives, late in the season, inquired into the circumstances which led to the defeat, taking the testimony of both officers and civilians, and in its report it conceived "it but justice to the commander-in-chief to say, that, in its opinion, the failure of the late expedition can in no respect be imputed to his conduct, either at any time before or during the action; but that, as his conduct in all the preparatory arrangements was marked with peculiar ability and zeal, so his conduct during the action furnished strong testimonies of his coolness and intrepidity."[6] The claims of party, however, prevented the Con-

[1] Chief-justice Marshall supposes there were "from one thousand to fifteen hundred warriors" (*Life of Washington*, v. p. 396). The Com. of Cong. reported that the opinions of witnesses varied from five hundred to twelve hundred. Adj.-Gen. Sargent (*Narrative*, p. 35) estimates them at "upwards of a thousand."

[2] Testimony of Ensign Pope before the Com. of Cong.

[3] Adj.-Gen. Winthrop Sargent's Diary, Nov. 22, 1792.

[1] Burnett's Notes, p. 128; St. Clair's Narrative, pp. 10–13, 41–44; Report of Com. of Cong.; Adj.-Gen. Sargent's Diary, Oct. 10, 14.—[2] Burnett's Notes, p. 127; Gen. St. Clair's Narrative, pp. 20–22, 40, 41; Report of Com. of Cong.; Testimony of Gen. Harmar; Adj.-Gen. Sargent's Diary, Oct. 10, 14, 17.

[3] Gen. St. Clair's Narrative, pp. 14, 45, 266; Report of Com. of Cong.; Testimony of Col. Mentgetz, Inspector; Adj.-Gen. Sargent's Diary, Oct. 10 (pp. 9, 10).

[4] Gen. St. Clair's Narrative, pp. 36, 37.

[5] Marshall's Washington, v. p. 397; Atwater's Ohio, p. 142.

[6] Report of Committee of Congress.

gress from acting on this report;[1] and General St. Clair, like many other worthy men in more recent times, suffered the consequences of persecution—although he retained the confidence of General Washington—and he died the death of the needy, without a recognition of his merits on the part of that country for which he had suffered so severely.

DOCUMENT.

GENERAL ST. CLAIR TO THE SECRETARY OF WAR.

Fort Washington, *Nov.* 9, 1791.

Sir:—Yesterday afternoon the remains of the army under my command got back to this place, and I have now the painful task to give you an account of as warm and unfortunate an action as almost any that has been fought, in which every corps was engaged and worsted, except the First regiment—that had been detached upon a service I had the honor to inform you of in my last dispatch, and had not joined me.

On the 3d instant the army had reached a creek about twelve yards wide, running to the southward of west, which I believe to have been the River St. Mary, that empties itself into the Miami of the lake, at the Miami village, about four o'clock in the afternoon, having marched near nine miles, and were immediately encamped upon a very commanding piece of ground in two lines, having the above-mentioned creek in front. The right wing, composed of Butler's, Clarke's, and Patterson's battalions, commanded by Major-general Butler, formed the first line; and the left wing, consisting of Bedinger's and Gaither's battalions, and the Second regiment, commanded by Lieutenant-colonel Darke, formed the second line, with an interval between them of about seventy yards, which was all the ground would allow.

The right flank was pretty well secured by the creek, a steep bank, and Faulkner's corps; some of the cavalry and their pickets covered the left flank. The militia were thrown over the creek, and advanced about a quarter of a mile and encamped in the same order. There were a few Indians who appeared on the opposite side of the creek, but fled with the utmost precipitation on the advance of the militia. At this place, which I judged to be about fifteen miles from the Miami village, I had determined to throw up a slight work, the plan of which was concerted that evening with Major Ferguson, wherein to have deposited the men's knapsacks, and every thing else that was not of absolute necessity, and to have moved on to attack the enemy as soon as the First regiment had come up; but they did not permit me to execute either; for on the fourth, about half an hour before sunrise, and when the men had been just dismissed from the parade (for it was a constant practice to have them all under arms a considerable time before daylight), an attack was made upon the militia, those gave way in a very little time, and rushed into camp through Major Butler's battalion, which, together with part of Clarke's, threw them into considerable disorder, which, notwithstanding the exertions of both, and those officers, was never altogether remedied, the Indians following close at their heels. The fire, however, of the first line, checked them, but almost instantly a very heavy attack began upon that line, and in a few minutes it was extended to the second likewise. The great weight of it was directed against the centre of each, where the artillery was placed, and from which the men were repeatedly driven with great slaughter. Finding no great effect from our fire, and confusion beginning to spread from the great number of

[1] Burnett's Notes, pp. 128, 129.

men who were falling in all quarters, it became necessary to try what could be done by the bayonet. Lieutenant-colonel Darke was accordingly ordered to make a charge with part of the second line, and to turn the left flank of the enemy. This was executed with great spirit. The Indians instantly gave way, and were driven back three or four hundred yards; but for want of a sufficient number of riflemen to pursue this advantage, they soon returned, and the troops were obliged to give back in their turn. At this moment they had entered our camp by the left flank, having pushed back the troops that were posted there. Another charge was made here by the Second regiment, Butler's and Clarke's battalions, with equal effect, and it was repeated several times, and always with success. In all of them many men were lost, and particularly the officers, which, with so raw troops, was a loss altogether irremediable.

In that just spoken of, made by the Second regiment and Butler's battalion, Major Butler was dangerously wounded, and every officer of the Second regiment fell except three, one of whom, Mr. Greaton, was shot through the body. Our artillery being now silenced, and all the officers killed, except Captain Ford, who was very badly wounded, and more than half the army fallen, being cut off from the road, it became necessary to attempt the regaining it, and to make a retreat, if possible. To this purpose the remains of the army were formed, as well as circumstances would admit, towards the right of the encampment, from which, by the way of the second line, another charge was made upon the enemy, as if with the design to turn their right flank, but, in fact, to gain the road. This was effected; and as soon as it was open, the militia took along it, followed by the troops, Major Clarke, with his battalion, covering the rear. The retreat, in these circumstances, was, you may be sure, a very precipitate one—it was, in fact, a flight.

The camp and the artillery were abandoned; but that was unavoidable, for not a horse was left alive to have drawn it off, had it otherwise been practicable. But the most disgraceful part of the business is, that the greatest part of the men threw away their arms and accoutrements, even after the pursuit (which continued about four miles) had ceased. I found the road strewed with them for many miles, but was not able to remedy it; for, having had all my horses killed, and being mounted upon one that could not be pricked out of a walk, I could not get forward myself; and the orders I sent forward, either to halt the front, or to prevent the men from parting with their arms, were unattended to.

The rout continued quite to Fort Jefferson, twenty-nine miles, which was reached a little after sunsetting.

The action began about half an hour before sunrise, and the retreat was attempted at half an hour after nine o'clock.

I have not yet been able to get returns of the killed and wounded; but Major-general Butler, Lieutenant-colonel Oldham, of the militia, Major Ferguson, Major Heart, and Major Clarke, are among the former. Colonel Sargent, my Adjutant-general, Lieutenant-colonels Darke and Gibson, Major Butler, and the Viscount Malartie, who served me as an aide-de-camp, are among the latter; and a great number of captains and subalterns in both.

I have now, sir, finished my melancholy tale—a tale that will be felt sensibly by every one that has sympathy for private distress, or for public misfortune. I have nothing, sir, to lay to the charge of the troops but their want of discipline, which, from the short time they had been in service, it was impossible they should have acquired, and which rendered it very difficult, when they were thrown into confusion, to reduce them again to order, and is one reason why the loss has fallen so heavily upon the officers, who did every thing in their power to effect it; neither were my own exertions wanting; but, worn down with illness, and suffering under a painful disease, unable either to mount or dismount a horse without assistance, they were not so great as they otherwise would, or, perhaps, ought to have been. We were overpowered by numbers; but it is no more than justice to observe, that though composed of so many different species of troops, the utmost harmony prevailed through the whole army during the campaign.

* * * * * *

I have said, sir, in a former part of this letter, that we were overpowered by numbers; of that, however, I have no other evidence than the weight of the fire, which was always a most deadly one, and generally delivered from the ground, few of the enemy showing themselves on foot, except when they were charged; and that in a few minutes our whole camp, which extended above three hundred and fifty yards in length, was entirely surrounded and attacked on all sides.

* * * * * *

With every sentiment of respect and regard, I have the honor to be, sir,

Your most obedient servant,

Arthur St. Clair.

The Honorable Major-general Knox,
Secretary of War.

CHAPTER III.

November 6, 1792.

THE ACTION NEAR FORT St. CLAIR, OHIO.

The outrages committed by the savages, on the Western frontiers, continued without abatement; and the several expeditions which had moved against them, from time to time, had served rather to exasperate than to cripple them. The frontier settlements, therefore, as well as the troops which had been ordered to occupy the advanced posts of the army, were made the constant objects of the enemy's assaults; and many and severe were the losses which were imposed on the settlers and the troops.[1]

One of these advanced posts—Fort St. Clair, near the present site of Eaton, the county-seat of Preble County, Ohio[2]—during this "reign of terror," to which allusion has been made, became the scene of an animated conflict between the troops and the Indians, from which much encouragement was received.

It appears that a detachment of about one hundred Kentucky mounted infantry (volunteers) were encamped near Fort St. Clair, and that, at daybreak, on the morning of the sixth of November, 1792, it was suddenly attacked, with great fury, by a large body of hostile Indians.[1] No notice whatever of the approach of the enemy appears to have been given, from which it is to be inferred that no pickets or patrols had been thrown out to protect the camp, yet the troops appear to have resisted the assailants, even until the latter reached the line, and had engaged with the troops in a hand-to-hand conflict.[2]

Major John Adair, who commanded the detachment,[3] perceiving the desperate character of the assault, ordered his men to fall back to a stockade, which had been erected for the purpose of stables,—about eighty yards in the

---

[1] Burnett's Notes, p. 132; Marshall's Kentucky, ii. pp. 39-41.—[2] Burnett's Notes, pp. 133, 134.

[1] Maj. Adair's Dispatch, Nov. 6; Burnett's Notes, p. 134; Letter of Gen. Wilkinson, dated Nov. 6, 1792, copied into the "*Gazette of the United States*," No. 381, Phila., Dec. 22, 1792.—[2] Maj. Adair's Dispatch, Nov. 6.

[3] Ibid.; Gen. Wilkinson's Dispatch to the Secretary of War, Nov. 6, 1792.

rear of the line,—from which, it was properly supposed, a more advantageous defence could be made; and the movement was executed with skill and success—the savages following closely after them, through the camp of the detachment.[1]

From this point Major Adair ordered Lieutenant Madison to attempt to turn the enemy's right flank; while similar orders were sent to Lieutenant Hail to make a corresponding movement on the left. The latter having fallen before the order reached him, Major Adair led the attack on the left, in which he was accompanied by Ensigns Flinn and Buchanan. Both these parties "made a manly push;" and, although Lieutenant Madison was speedily wounded, and, with his party, retreated to the fort, the enemy fled, *carrying away with them, however, all, except five or six, of the volunteers' horses.*[2]

After pursuing the fugitives through the camp, at about six hundred yards beyond it the troops were again turned on by the Indians, and the battle was renewed with great warmth. Soon afterwards Major Adair discovered a party of sixty savages who were moving against his right flank, with the evident intention of turning it; and as it was impossible to extend his line so far as to prevent that purpose, he ordered his men to fall back, a second time, and take a position within the encampment. This retrograde movement—at all times

[1] Maj. Adair's Dispatch, Nov. 6.—[2] Ibid.; Burnett's Notes, p. 134.

a hazardous one, when made in the presence of an enemy—was again made with coolness, precision, and success, although the Indians followed closely after them, and renewed the action when the troops halted.[1]

From this, their first position, now re-occupied, that portion of the troops which remained on the field continued the conflict; and, soon afterwards, two hours after the action commenced, the enemy retired, without being pursued by the volunteers,[2] whose ammunition was nearly expended, although a fresh supply had been sent to them from the fort during the action.[3]

During this determined and complicated engagement the loss of the troops was, comparatively, small—six killed, five wounded, and four missing, being the reported loss. Of the enemy's loss, no definite account has been given.[4]

The result of this skirmish, which, in itself, amounted to but little, was very beneficial, and the country resounded with praises of Major Adair and his party. The organs of government conveyed the dispatches to the people, in all their minutia, and there is but little doubt that the *éclat* of this engagement was greatly beneficial in the preparations which were then in progress for the campaign under General Wayne, which, in the following year, crushed the power of the savages.

[1] Maj. Adair's Dispatch, Nov. 6; Burnett's Notes, p. 134.—[2] Ibid.; Gen. Wilkinson's letter, dated Nov. 6, in "*Gazette of United States.*" Mr. Butler (*Hist. Kentucky*, ii. p. 41) says the troops, "after a gallant resistance, *were compelled to retreat to the fort.*"—[3] Maj. Adair's Dispatch, Nov. 6.—[4] Ibid.; Burnett's Notes, p. 134.

DOCUMENT.

FORT ST. CLAIR, *November* 6, 1792.

SIR:—This morning, about the first appearance of day, the enemy attacked my camp within sight of this post. The attack was sudden, and the enemy came on with a degree of courage that bespoke them warriors indeed. Some of my men were hand-in-hand with them before we retreated, which however we did, about eighty yards, to a kind of stockade, intended for stables. We there made a stand. I then ordered Lieutenant Madison to take a party and gain their right flank, if possible. I called for Lieutenant Hail, to send to the left, but found he had been slain. I then led forward the men who stood near me, which, together with the Ensigns Buchanan and Flinn, amounted to about twenty-five, and pressed the left of their centre, thinking it absolutely necessary to assist Madison. We made a manly push, and the enemy retreated, taking all our horses, except five or six. We drove them about six hundred yards through our camp, where they again made a stand, and we fought them some time; two of my men were here shot dead.

At that moment I received information that the enemy was about to flank us on the right, and on turning that way, I saw about sixty of them running to that point. I had yet heard nothing of Madison. I then ordered my men to retreat, which they did with deliberation, heartily cursing the Indians, who pursued us close to our camp, where we again fought them until they gave way; and when they retreated our ammunition was nearly expended, although we had been supplied from the garrison in the course of the action. I did not think proper to follow them again, but ordered my men into the garrison to draw ammunition. I returned, however, in a few minutes, to a hill, to which we had first driven them, where I found two of my men scalped, who were brought in. Since I began to write this, a few of the enemy appeared in sight, and I pursued them, with a party, about a quarter of a mile, but could not overtake them, and did not think proper to go farther. Madison, whom I sent to the right, was, on his first attack, wounded, and obliged to retreat to the garrison, leaving a man or two dead.

To this misfortune I think the enemy are indebted for the horses they have got; had he gained their right flank, I once had possession of their left, and I think we should have routed them at that stage of the action, as we had them on the retreat. I have six killed and five wounded; four men are missing. I think they went off, early in the action, on horseback, and are, I suppose, by this at Fort Hamilton.

My officers and a number of men distinguished themselves greatly. Poor Hail died calling to his men to advance. Madison's bravery and conduct need no comment; they are well known. Flinn and Buchanan acted with a coolness and courage which does them much honor. Buchanan, after firing his gun, knocked down an Indian with the barrel. They have killed and taken a great number of the pack-horses. I intend following them this evening for some distance, to ascertain their route and strength, if possible. I can, with propriety, say that about fifty of my men fought with a bravery equal to any men in the world, and had not the garrison been so nigh, as a place of safety for the bashful, I think many more would have fought well.

The enemy have, no doubt, as many killed as myself; they left two dead on the ground, and I saw two carried off. The only advantage they have gained is our horses, which is a capital one, as it disables me from bringing the interview to a more serious and satisfactory decision.

I am sorry I cannot send you better news, and am, sir, your most obedient servant,

JOHN ADAIR,

Major Kentucky Mounted Infantry.

Brigadier-General WILKINSON.

CHAPTER IV.

August 20, 1794.

THE BATTLE ON THE MIAMIS.

The progress of events on the Western frontiers has been, already, alluded to in the preceding chapters of this book; and the depredations of the savages continued with the same severity as before. General Wayne, the hero of Stony Point, had accepted the command which President Washington had tendered to him, but in doing so had stipulated that he should not be required to march into the wilderness until his allotted force was completely filled up, and so far disciplined as to justify the movement.[1] Preparations for the ensuing campaign were immediately commenced; recruiting parties were sent out; and the organization of the army progressed as rapidly as possible.[2]

Desiring, if possible, to avoid the necessity of a hostile movement, while these preparations were in progress, the President attempted to reconcile the difficulties by negotiation, and for that purpose appointed General Benjamin Lincoln, Beverly Randolph, and Timothy Pickering, as Commissioners, to open negotiations with the Indians. In July, 1793, these Commissioners were met at Niagara by Joseph Brant, with Colonel Butler, the British Superintendent of Indian Affairs, and about

[1] Burnett's Notes, p. 133.—[2] Marshall's Washington, v. pp. 438, 439.

fifty Indians, and the negotiations were opened with every appearance of success. All parties thence proceeded to the mouth of the Detroit River, where the negotiations were continued several weeks, without success, and the Commissioners returned without having effected any thing.[1]

With the information of the failure of the negotiations referred to, preparations for hostilities were actively renewed; and, early in September, 1793, General Wayne and his troops rendezvoused on the bank of the Ohio, between Cincinnati and Mill Creek, to which the General gave the name of "*Hobson's Choice*," it being the only place, in that vicinity, which was suited for an encampment.[2] The troops, both those already with him and the recruits who came in, were constantly and laboriously engaged in such military exercises as would be found useful in the peculiar service in which they were to be engaged; and the General and his subordinate officers were actively engaged in perfecting the discipline and the appointments of the army.[3]

On the seventh of October, 1793, General Wayne moved the troops he

[1] Burnett's Notes, pp. 135–154; Marshall's Washington, v. pp. 535–537.—[2] Marshall's Washington, v. pp. 644, 645; Geo. Will to John S. Williams, May 25, 1842; Burnett's Notes, pp. 157, 158.—[3] Burnett's Notes, p. 158.

then had with him from "Hobson's Choice;"[1] and, on the thirteenth of the same month, having arrived at a fork of the southwest branch of Miami, now called "*Stillwater*," six miles in advance of Fort Jefferson, he halted to await the arrival of provisions.[2] Near this spot—a short distance from Greenville, Ohio—General Wayne decided to take up his winter quarters, from which he was enabled to hold the enemy in check, and, at the same time, be enabled to move with greater advantage on the opening of the spring.[3]

The encampment was called "*Greenville;*"[4] and the spacious log buildings of which it was composed, and the works by which it was defended, secured, at once, the comfort and the safety of the army. He also took possession of the field of General St. Clair's defeat, and erected thereon a strong work, to which he gave the name of "*Fort Recovery.*"[5] The army remained at these posts until the latter part of July, 1794, during which period it was subjected to a constant and systematic course of instruction, under the eye of the energetic and accomplished commander-in-chief.[6]

During the nine months which the army was thus occupied, the enemy was not unemployed. In June, 1794, assisted by the British at Detroit and the Rapids of the Maumee, preparations were secretly made to attack the advance post at Fort Recovery. On the morning of the twenty-ninth of June a provision-train had left Greenville for the fort, under an escort of ninety riflemen and fifty dragoons, who were commanded by Major McMahon; and, on the same evening, it had reached the fort in safety. On the next morning this detachment, as well as the fort itself, was attacked by a very large body of the allied enemy; and a severe conflict, extending through the greater part of the day, with varied success, ensued. The detachment and the garrison defended themselves with great courage; and the enemy was repulsed with very heavy loss. During the night, which was very dark and foggy, the enemy succeeded in removing the greater part of his dead and wounded; and, on the following morning,—Major McMahon's force having entered the fort,—the attack was renewed. Another day was spent in this second attempt to seize the fort, with the like result; and when the enemy, a second time was compelled to retire from the scene of his former triumph, he did so with a very heavy loss. The strength of the enemy has been estimated at from fifteen hundred to two thousand men; and many of the bravest of the chiefs and warriors perished in the enterprise. Among the Americans, Major McMahon, Captain Hartshorn, and Lieutenant Craig, and nineteen non-commissioned officers and privates were killed; and Captain Taylor and Lieutenant Drake, and twenty-eight men were wounded.[1]

[1] Burnett's Notes, p. 159.—[2] Atwater's Ohio, p. 147; Burnett's Notes, p. 159.—[3] Marshall's Washington, v. p. 645.—[4] Burnett's Notes, p. 160.—[5] Marshall's Washington, v. p. 645; Geo. Will to John S. Williams, May 25, 1842.—[6] Burnett's Notes, p. 168.

[1] Geo. Will to John S. Williams, May 25, 1842; Burnett's Notes, pp. 161–167.

A large body of mounted volunteers, from Kentucky, under General Scott, having joined the army,[1] on the twenty-eighth of July, 1794, General Wayne moved from Greenville, and advanced to Fort Recovery, on his way to the Indian settlements.[2] With a view of perplexing the enemy, before the army moved from Greenville, General Wayne took measures to deceive him concerning the line of march which would be taken—leading them to suppose that he would take either the Miami villages, on his left, or the foot of the Rapids, on his right, while his real design was to take neither of these, but a more central route, which was impracticable for an army, except in a very dry season.[3] Although the army halted at Girty's-town, at the crossing of the St. Mary's River, during the second and third of August, and erected a fort there,[4]—in which Lieutenant Underhill and a hundred men were left to protect it,[5]—it is said the enemy did not discover its progress until it had come almost within sight of Au Glaize, the great central post of the enemy, which it entered at half-past ten o'clock in the morning of the eighth of August.[6] It was afterwards discovered that the enemy had been entirely uninformed of the movement of General Wayne, until the preceding day, when a deserter from the army—a foreigner, named Newman—had given the information

[1] Burnett's Notes, p. 168.—[2] Lieut. Boyer's Daily Journal of Gen. Wayne's Campaign, July 28, 1794.

[3] Burnett's Notes, pp. 168, 169.—[4] Marshall's Washington, v. p. 648, *Note;* Lieut. Boyer's Daily Jour. of Gen. Wayne's Campaign, Aug. 2 and 3, 1794.—[5] Lieut. Boyer's Daily Jour., Aug. 4.—[6] Marshall's Washington, v. p. 648; Burnett's Notes, p. 169.

which enabled the inhabitants to escape.[1]

The beauty of this place, as well as the character and extent of the improvements around it, appear to have elicited the admiration of all who witnessed them. An eye-witness says, on this subject, "This place far excels in beauty any in the Western country, and is believed equalled by none in the Atlantic States. Here are vegetables of every kind in abundance, and we have marched four or five miles in cornfields down the Au Glaize, and there is not less than one thousand acres of corn around the town."[2]

After erecting a strong stockade fort, at this place, which he named *Fort Defiance*,[3] on the fifteenth of August, General Wayne resumed his march;[4] before doing which he dispatched a flag to the enemy, with an urgent appeal for peace.[5] This flag was returned—and met by the army, on the sixteenth—with an evasive answer;[6] and small bodies of the enemy commenced to show themselves to observe the movements or to check the progress of the army.[7]

On the nineteenth of August the army was engaged in throwing up works to secure the stores and baggage

[1] John Brickell's Narrative.—[2] Lieut. Boyer's Daily Journal, Aug. 8. See also Burnett's Notes, p. 169.

[3] Lieut. Boyer's Daily Jour., Aug. 9 to Aug. 14. A plan and description of this fort was published in the *American Pioneer*, ii. pp. 386, 387.

[4] Marshall's Washington, v. p. 649; Burnett's Notes, p. 172; Gen. Wayne to Sec. of War, Aug. 28.

[5] Marshall's Washington, v. p. 649; Atwater's Ohio, p. 147; Burnett's Notes, pp. 170–172.

[6] Lieut. Boyer's Daily Journal, Aug. 16; Burnett's Notes, p. 172.

[7] Lieut. Boyer's Daily Journal, Aug. 17, 18.

of the army;[1] and at eight o'clock, on the morning of the twentieth, it resumed its march against the enemy, who had taken a position about five miles in advance of the army, and there awaited its approach.[2]

The order of march was that which General Wayne had made in the opening of the campaign, and it was well adapted for the peculiarities of the service. The regulars, known as "*the Legion*," moved in a column on the right, its right being covered by the river; a brigade of mounted volunteers, under General Todd, moved in a parallel column on the left; a select battalion of mounted volunteers, under Major Price, moved so far in front of the Legion, that timely notice could be given in case of an attack; another advance guard, under Captain Cook, also preceded the column; and a brigade of mounted volunteers, under General Barber, protected the rear.[3]

After advancing about five miles, about eleven o'clock, Major Price's battalion was received with so severe a fire from the enemy—who had posted himself in three lines within supporting distance of each other; and was sheltered by the fallen timber which had been prostrated by a recent tornado[4]—that it was compelled to fall back in the utmost confusion, carrying with it the advance guard of the Legion, commanded

[1] Marshall's Washington, v. p. 649; Lieut. Boyer's Daily Jour., Aug. 19; Burnett's Notes, p. 172. This work was called "*Camp Deposite.*"—[2] Lieut. Boyer's Daily Jour., Aug. 20; Gen. Wayne to Sec. of War, Aug. 28.

[3] Marshall's Washington, v. p. 650; Atwater's Ohio, p. 148; Burnett's Notes, p. 172; Gen. Wayne to Sec. of War, Aug. 28.—[4] Marshall's Washington, v. p. 650; Burnett's Notes, p. 172.

by Captain Cook.[1] Following up the advantage which this sudden panic had produced, the enemy pressed forward and endeavored to turn the right flank of the army,—next to the river,—but those who had retreated rallied; and having been joined by part of Captain Springer's battalion of riflemen and by Captain Lewis's light-infantry, they drove back the assailants, with heavy loss.[2]

Meanwhile the Legion had formed in two lines, and had pressed forward, with orders to charge the savages and to drive them from their hiding-places, behind the logs and fallen trees, which at once had afforded shelter to them and prevented the cavalry from manœuvering.[3] The orders also directed that as soon as the enemy had fired and risen, a close and well-directed fire should be thrown on his back, followed by a brisk charge, in order to prevent him from reloading.[4] At the same time Captain Campbell, of the Legion cavalry, was commanded to turn the left flank of the enemy,—next to the river,—while Major-general Scott, with a large body of mounted men, by a circuitous route, was ordered to turn the right flank, which was extended nearly two miles from the river.[5]

These orders were obeyed with spirit and alacrity; but the weight and ex-

[1] Marshall's Washington, v. p. 650; Lieut. Boyer's Daily Jour., Aug. 20; Gen. Wayne to Sec. of War, Aug. 28.—[2] Lieut. Boyer's Daily Jour., Aug. 20.—[3] Marshall's Washington, v. p. 650; Atwater's Ohio, p. 148; Gen. Wayne to Sec. of War, Aug. 28.—[4] Marshall's Washington, v. p. 650; Atwater's Ohio, p. 148; Burnett's Notes, p. 173; Gen. Wayne to Sec. of War, Aug. 28.

[5] Marshall's Washington, v. p. 651; Burnett's Notes, p. 173; Gen. Wayne to Sec. of War, Aug. 28.

BATTLE OF MIAMI.

[illegible]

Johnson, Fry & C° Publishers, New York.

tent of the enemy's fire soon showed that he was in full force, and that his intention was to turn the left flank of the American line.[1] To prevent this the second line of the Legion was ordered to cover the left of the first line;[2] and both dashed forward with the greatest success.[3] Without appearing to offer much resistance, where resistance would have been useless, the allied enemy fled before the bayonets of the Legion with so much precipitation that, although every possible effort was made for that purpose, the mounted men could not reach their proper positions; and, within an hour from the first attack, the enemy was driven two miles, by a force less than one half his own.[4]

Without attempting to rally, the enemy abandoned the field, and fled in every direction, leaving the victors in quiet possession of the field.[5] The flight of the fugitives having been cut off from the river, by Captain Campbell, the prairie was the only course which had been left open to them. In this direction, therefore, they fled; and there the cavalry enjoyed a fine opportunity to display their activity and courage by pursuing them, and many were killed in that quarter.[6]

The number of the allies—one third of whom were British[7]—was estimated at from fifteen hundred to two thousand men;[1] while, as before stated, the Americans who were actually engaged did not exceed nine hundred.[2] The loss of the latter was, Captain Mis Campbell, Lieutenant Towles, three sergeants, and twenty-eight men, *killed;* and Captains Slough, Prior, Van Rensellaer, and Rawlins, Lieutenants Smith and McKenney, Ensign Duncan, four sergeants, three corporals, two musicians, and eighty-four men, *wounded.*[3]

The British had erected a very strong post immediately in the rear of the enemy's position, and occupied it in great force,[4] yet the enemy was completely routed, and his force broken down. An angry correspondence was carried on by General Wayne and the commander of this garrison, in which the unflinching courage of the former is remarkably prominent;[5] and there is but little doubt that the least interference on the part of the latter would have called into immediate requisition the skill and courage which were displayed, years before, at Stony Point.

The army remained in front of the battle-ground three days and nights, during which time all the villages and cornfields, for several miles, on both sides the river, were completely destroyed.[6] The houses and stores of

---

[1] Marshall's Washington, v. p. 651; Lieut. Boyer's Daily Journal, Aug. 20; Burnett's Notes, p. 173; Gen. Wayne to Sec. of War, Aug. 28.—[2] Marshall's Washington, v. p. 651; Atwater's Ohio, p. 148; Gen. Wayne to Sec. of War, Aug. 28.—[3] Marshall's Washington, v. p. 651.

[4] Ibid.; Burnett's Notes, p. 173; Gen. Wayne to Sec. of War, Aug. 28.—[5] Atwater's Ohio, p. 149; Gen. Wayne to Sec. of War, Aug. 28.—[6] Burnett's Notes, p. 174.

[7] Lieut. Boyer's Daily Journal, Aug. 20.

[1] Lieut. Boyer's Daily Jour., Aug. 20; Burnett's Notes, p. 174; Gen. Wayne to Sec. of War, Aug. 28.

[2] Gen. Wayne to Sec. of War, Aug. 28.—[3] Returns of Killed, &c., appended to Gen. Wayne's Dispatch, Aug. 28.

[4] Gen. Wayne to Sec. of War, Aug. 28.—[5] Lieut. Boyer's Daily Jour., Aug. 21. This correspondence, in full, will be found in Burnett's Notes, pp. 176–179.

[6] Marshall's Washington, v. p. 651; Lieut. Boyer's Daily Jour., Aug. 20 to 23; Burnett's Notes, p. 179; Gen. Wayne to Sec. of War, Aug. 28.

Colonel McKee, the British agent, and those of all other traders and Canadian settlers, in that vicinity, shared the same fate.[1]

On the twenty-third of August the army fell back to Camp Deposit, whence it marched on the morning of the battle;[2] and thence, on the next day, toward Fort Defiance, burning and destroying all the villages and cornfields which were near the line of march.[3] After reaching Fort Defiance and obtaining a supply of provisions, on the fourteenth of September the army proceeded to the Miami villages, which had been visited by General Harmar in 1790, and constructed a strong work, which was called *Fort Wayne*, and placed under the command of Colonel Hamtramck.[4] The volunteers were afterwards marched to Fort Washington (*Cincinnati*) and mustered out of service;[1] while the Legion returned to Greenville and entered into winter quarters.[2]

This victory, so unexpected and so complete, is said to have broken the power of the enemy, and to have saved the country from the evil of a general Indian War. In the South, as well as in the Northwest, the evidences of uneasiness which prevailed among the tribes indicated approaching trouble; while the machinations of the British agents, and the restless animosity, added to the great abilities and general influence of Joseph Brant, rendered the prospects of peace by no means flattering.[3] A general treaty of peace speedily followed, and, during several years, the quiet of the country was undisturbed.

[1] Marshall's Washington, v. p. 651; Gen. Wayne to Sec. of War, Aug. 28.—[2] Lieut. Boyer's Daily Jour., Aug. 23.—[3] Ibid., Aug. 24 to 27; Gen. Wayne to Sec. of War, Aug. 28.—[4] Lieut. Boyer's Daily Jour., Aug. 27 to Oct. 22; B. Van Cleve's Memoranda (with his plan of the fort), Oct. 27.

[1] Burnett's Notes, p. 181.—[2] Ibid., pp. 181, 182.

[3] Marshall's Washington, v. pp. 652, 653; Atwater's Ohio, p. 149.

DOCUMENT.

Head-quarters, Grand Glaize, *August* 28.

Sir:—It is with infinite pleasure that I now announce to you the brilliant success of the Federal army under my command in a general action with the combined force of the hostile Indians, and a considerable number of the volunteers and militia of Detroit, on the 20th inst., on the banks of the Miamis, in the vicinity of the British post and garrison at the foot of the Rapids.

The army advanced from this place on the 15th and arrived at Roche de Bout on the 18th, and the 19th we were employed in making a temporary post for the reception of our stores and baggage, and in reconnoitering the position of the enemy, who were encamped behind a thick bushy wood and the British fort.

At eight o'clock on the morning of the twentieth the army again advanced in column, agreeably to the standing order of march, the Legion on the right, its right flank covered by the Miamis, one brigade of mounted volunteers on the left, under Brigadier-general Todd, and the other in the rear, under Brigadier-general Barber. A selected battalion of mounted volunteers moved in front of the Legion, commanded by Major Price, who was directed to keep sufficiently advanced, was to give timely notice for the troops to form in case of action, it being yet undetermined whether the Indians would decide for peace or war.

After advancing about five miles, Major Price's corps received so severe a fire from the enemy, who were secreted in the woods and high grass, as to compel them to retreat.

The Legion was immediately formed in two lines, principally in a close, thick wood, which extended for miles on our left, and for a very considerable distance in front, the ground being covered with old fallen timber, probably occasioned by a tornado, which rendered it impracticable for the cavalry to act with effect, and afforded the enemy the most favorable covert for their mode of warfare. The savages were formed in three lines, within supporting distances of each other, and extending for near two miles at right angles with the river. I soon discovered, from the weight of their fire and extent of their lines, that the enemy were in full force in front, in possession of their favorite ground, and endeavoring to turn our left flank. I therefore gave orders for the second line to advance to support the first, and directed Major-general Scott to gain and turn the right flank of the savages, with the whole of the mounted volunteers, by a circuitous route; at the same time I ordered the front line to advance and charge with trailed arms, and rouse the Indians from their coverts, at the point of the bayonet, and when up to deliver a close and well-directed fire on their backs, followed by a brisk charge, so as not to give them time to load again.

I also ordered Captain Robert Mis Campbell, who commanded the Legionary Cavalry, to turn the left flank of the enemy next the river, and which afforded a favorable field for that corps to act in. All those orders were obeyed with spirit and promptitude, but such was the impetuosity of the charge, by the first line of infantry, that the Indians and Canadian militia and volunteers were drove from all their coverts in so short a time, that although every possible exertion was used by the officers of the second line of the Legion, and by Generals Scott, Todd, and Barbie, of the mounted volunteers, to gain their proper position, but part of each could get up in season to participate in the action, the enemy being drove, in the course of one hour, more than two miles, through the thick wood already mentioned, by less than one half their number.

From every account, the enemy amounted to two thousand combatants, the troops actually engaged against them were short of nine hundred. This horde of savages, with their allies, abandoned themselves to flight, and dispersed with terror and dismay, leaving our victorious army in full and quiet possession of the field of battle, which terminated under the influence of the guns of the British garrison, as you will observe by the inclosed correspondence between Major Campbell, the commandant, and myself, upon the occasion.

The bravery and conduct of every officer belonging to the army, from the Generals down to the Ensigns, merit my highest approbation.

There were some, however, whose rank and situation placed their conduct in a very conspicuous point of view, and which I observed with pleasure and the most lively gratitude; among whom I must beg leave to mention Brigadier-general Wilkinson and Colonel Hamtramck, the commandants of the right and left wings of the Legion, whose brave example inspired the troops. To these I must add the names of my faithful and gallant *aids-de-camp*, Captains de Butts and Thomas Lewis, and Lieutenant Harrison, who, with the Adjutant-general, Major Mills, rendered the most essential service, by communicating my orders in every direction, and by their conduct and bravery exciting the troops to press for victory.

Lieutenant Covington, upon whom the command of the cavalry now devolved, cut down two savages with his own hand; Lieutenant Webb one in turning the left flank.

The wounds received by Captains Slough and Prior, and Lieutenant Campbell Smith (an extra *aid-de-camp* to General Wilkinson of the Legionary Infantry), and Captain Van Rensselaer, of the dragoons; Captain Rawlins, Lieutenant McKenney, and Ensign Duncan, of the mounted volunteers, bear honorable testimony of their bravery and conduct.

Captains Howell, Lewis, and Brock, with their companies of light-infantry, had to sustain an unequal fire for some time, which they supported with fortitude; in fact, every officer and soldier who had an opportunity to come into action, displayed that true bravery which will always insure success. And here permit me to declare, that I never discovered more true spirit and anxiety for action, than appeared to pervade the whole of the mounted volunteers; and I am well persuaded that had the enemy maintained their favorite ground for one half hour longer they would have most severely felt the prowess of that corps.

But whilst I pay this just tribute to the living, I must not neglect the gallant dead, among whom we have to lament the early death of those worthy and brave officers, Captain Mis Campbell, of the dragoons, and Lieutenant Towles, of the light-infantry of the Legion, who fell in the first charge.

Inclosed is a particular return of the killed and wounded—the loss of the enemy was more than double that of the Federal army—the woods were strewed for a considerable distance with dead bodies of Indians and their white auxiliaries, the latter armed with British muskets and bayonets.

We remained three days and nights on the banks of the Miamis, in front of the field of battle; during which time all the houses and cornfields were consumed and destroyed for a considerable distance both above and below Fort Miamis, as well as within pistol-shot of that garrison, who were compelled to remain tacit spectators of this general devastation and conflagration, among which were the houses, stores, and property of Colonel McKee, the British Indian Agent, and principal stimulator of the war now existing between the United States and the savages.

The army returned to this place on the 27th, by easy marches, laying waste the villages and cornfields for about fifty miles on each side of the Miamis; there remain yet a number of villages and a great quantity of corn to be consumed or destroyed upon Au Glaize and the Miamis, above this place, which will be effected in the course of a few days.

In the interim we shall improve Fort Defiance; and as soon as the escort returns with the necessary supplies from Greenville and Fort Recovery the army will proceed to the Miamis villages, in order to accomplish the object of the campaign.

It is, however, not improbable that the enemy may make one desperate effort against the army, as it is said that a reinforcement was hourly expected at Fort Miamis from Niagara, as well as numerous tribes of Indians living on the margins and islands of the lakes.

This is a business rather to be wished for than dreaded, whilst the army remains in force; their numbers will only tend to confuse the savages, and the victory will be the more complete and decisive, and which may eventually insure a permanent and happy peace.

Under these impressions, I have the honor to be, your most obedient and very humble servant,

Anthony Wayne.

The Hon. Maj.-Gen. Knox,
Secretary of War.

Return of the killed, wounded, and missing of the Federal army, commanded by Maj.-Gen. Wayne, in the action of the 20th August, 1794.

* * * * * * *

Total.—*Killed.*—One captain, one lieutenant, three sergeants, twenty-eight privates.

Wounded.—Four captains, two lieutenants, one ensign, four sergeants, three corporals, two musicians, eighty-four privates.

* * * * * * *

John Mills,
Major of Infantry and Adj.-Gen.

CHAPTER V.

February 9, 1799.

THE CAPTURE OF L'INSURGENTE.

While the relations of France with the United States, during the War of the Revolution, had been productive of great benefit to both countries,—to the latter in the more speedy and effectual establishment of their independence, and to the former in the injury which the dismemberment of the British dominions had inflicted on the ancient enemy of France,—the progress of events, after the establishment of peace, had thrown jealousy and ill-will into the councils of both nations, and discord and animosity had gradually crept in and disturbed their peace.

The commerce of America was harassed by the cruisers of republican France; her vessels seized, carried into French ports, and condemned, on the plea that they contained property which belonged to British subjects—a nation with which France was at war; obsolete statutes were revived as pretexts under which the seizures could be sustained; and treaty stipulations, which should have governed the action of both governments, were disregarded by the French, in its misguided zeal, and in its malignant opposition to the monarchical enemies of the Republic.[1]

Within the boundaries of the United States, also, the agents of the French republic were also busily engaged in fostering a spirit of dissension and disunion; while the violent partisan feelings of both the great political parties into which the country had been divided,—the Federalists in opposition to, and the Republicans in extenuation of, the outrages of the authorities of republican France,—served rather to encourage than to check the insolence of the Directory, and the officers who bore its commissions.[1]

Alarmed by the unfriendly menaces of France, the Congress of the United States, in 1797, had organized a military force of eighty thousand men; taken steps for strengthening the defences of the harbors; ordered the equipment of three frigates; prohibited the exportation of arms and ammunition; and adopted other measures which a defensive policy demanded.[2] Soon afterwards General Washington was called to the command of the armies of the United States, and the country prepared for what appeared to be an inevitable war.[3]

Among the earlier of the ships which were constructed for the naval establishment of the United States, under the Act of Congress of March 27, 1794,

---

[1] Hildreth's United States, v. pp. 50, 51, 55.

[1] Hildreth, v. p. 57.—[2] Gibbs' Administration of Washington and Adams, ii. p. 41.—[3] Ibid., p. 59.

was the *Constellation*, a frigate of thirty-eight guns—twenty-eight eighteen-pounders on the main deck, and ten lighter pieces above.[1] At the period in question, this ship was commanded by Captain Thomas Truxtun; and, with the greater part of the naval force of the republic, was cruising in the West Indies to protect the commerce of the United States. About noon, on the ninth of February, having left the *Richmond* and *Norfolk* to convoy some merchant vessels from St. Christopher's to the United States, while cruising off Nevis, Captain Truxtun discovered a large ship to the southward.[2] As the *Constellation* was to the windward,[3] Captain Truxtun bore down towards the stranger, when she ran up the American colors; but being unable to answer the private signals, both American and British, which Captain Truxtun displayed, her character was suspected; and, by the usual challenge, of a gun fired to windward,[4] and by the display of French colors, the suspicions of her pursuer were soon afterwards confirmed.[5]

The chase continued three hours, and as "this was the first opportunity that had occurred, since the close of the Revolution, for an American vessel of war to get alongside of an enemy, of a force likely to make a combat certain, the officers and men of the *Constellation* displayed the greatest eagerness to engage."[1] Every sail on the *Constellation* was spread to the breeze, and preparation for action was made with the utmost alacrity.[2] About two o'clock the enemy's main-topmast went overboard; but she was quickly cleared of the wreck, and put before the wind.[3] At a quarter past three o'clock, Nevis bearing W. S. W., six leagues distant, the *Constellation* ranged alongside the chase, when the latter hailed the former, several times, but received no reply.[4] The *Constellation* ran under the enemy's lee, in order that her guns might be worked with greater facility;[5] and as soon as she had secured a position "for every shot to do execution," she opened a close and well-directed fire, which was returned with great spirit.[6] Captain Truxtun had previously ordered the lieutenants who commanded divisions of the crew, "to load with two round shot, and to fire directly into the enemy's hull,"[7] and the effects of this order, notwithstanding the skill and efficiency of the enemy, were soon visible. After raking her several times, and securing a position athwart the enemy's stern, which threatened very serious results,[8] at about half-past four o'clock,[9] the *Constellation* had so far

[1] Cooper's Naval Hist., i. pp. 266, 267.—[2] Capt. Truxtun to Sec. of Navy, Feb. 10, 1799.—[3] Cooper's Naval Hist., i. p. 297.—[4] Capt. Truxtun (*Letter to Sec. of Navy, Feb.* 10, 1799) says this gun was fired to "*leeward*," while all other authorities say it was to "*windward*."

[5] Capt. Truxtun's letter to Sec. of Navy, Feb. 10, 1799; Cooper's Naval History, i. p. 297.

[1] Cooper's Naval Hist., i. p. 297.—[2] A St. Christopher's paper, inclosed in Capt. Truxtun's letter to Sec. of Navy, Feb. 16, 1799.—[3] The St. Christopher's paper says it occurred at *half-past* 2 P. M.; Lieut. Rogers (*Letter to Maj. Stoddart, Feb.* 15, 1799) says, "at 2 P. M.;" and Lieut. Sterrett (*Letter to his brother*) says, "at 3 P. M."—[4] Capt. Truxtun to Sec. of Navy, Feb. 10, 1799; Lieut. Rogers to Maj. Stoddart, Feb. 15, 1799; St. Christopher's paper.

[5] Lieut. Rogers to Maj. Stoddart, Feb. 15, 1799.

[6] Capt. Truxtun's letter to Sec. of Navy, Feb. 10, 1799.

[7] Lieut. Rogers to Maj. Stoddart, Feb. 15, 1799.

[8] Ibid.—[9] Capt. Truxtun to Sec. of Navy, Feb. 10, 1799. Lieut. Rogers (*Letter to Maj. Stoddart*) says she struck "*at a quarter-past four* P. M."

gained the advantage, that the enemy struck her colors and surrendered.[1]

Lieutenant Rogers was ordered to take possession of the prize, and to send her captain and first lieutenant on board of the *Constellation;*[2] when it appeared that the prize was the French frigate *L'Insurgente*, one of the fastest vessels afloat, and the finest vessel in the French navy.[3] She mounted four thirty-six pounders, two twenty-four pounders, two eighteen-pounders, twenty-four twelve-pounders, eight six-pounders, and eight brass swivels—forty-eight pieces in all[4]—and was manned with four hundred and nine men,[5] of whom twenty-nine were killed, twenty-two badly wounded, and nineteen wounded.[6] The vessel was, also, badly cut up in her hull, masts, and rigging;[7] and it was with considerable difficulty that she was carried into port.[8]

The *Constellation* was considerably injured in her masts and rigging;[9] while of her crew only three—Midshipman McDonough, and John Andrews and Thomas Wilson, ordinary seamen—were wounded; Neal Harvey, another of her crew, having been run through by Lieutenant Sterrett, during the action, for cowardice.[10]

It is said[11] that M. Bureaut, the commander of the *Insurgente*, was imprisoned on a charge of cowardice, when he reached Guadaloupe; but there appears, from the record, that such a charge could not have been made on any just grounds. In the United States, "the result of this engagement produced great exultation, and it was deemed a proof of an aptitude to nautical service, that was very grateful to the national pride. Without pausing to examine details, the country claimed it as a victory of a thirty-eight over a forty; and the new marine was, at once, proclaimed to be equal to any in the world; a decision somewhat hazardous when made on a single experiment, and which was certainly formed without a full understanding of the whole subject. It is due to a gallant enemy, to say that Captain Bureaut, who defended his ship as long as there was a hope of success, was overcome by a superior force; and it is also due to Commodore Truxtun, and to those under his command, to add that they did their work with an expedition and effect every way proportioned to the disparity in their favor. There is scarcely an instance on record (we are not certain there is one) of a full-manned frigate, carrying twelves, prevailing in a contest with even a ship of eighteens; and, in this instance, we see that the *Insurgente* had twenty-fours to oppose. Victory was next to hopeless, under such circumstances, though, on the other hand, we are not to overlook the readiness with which a conflict with an unknown antagonist was sought, and the neatness and dispatch with which the battle was won."[1]

[1] Capt. Truxtun to Sec. of Navy, Feb. 10, 1799; St. Christopher's paper; Lieut. Rogers to Maj. Stoddart, Feb. 15, 1799; Lieut. Sterrett to his brother.—[2] Lieut. Rogers to Maj. Stoddart, Feb. 15, 1799.—[3] Capt. Truxtun to Sec. of Navy, Feb. 10, 1799.—[4] Ibid., Feb. 16, 1799.—[5] Ibid.

[6] Ibid., Feb. 14, 1799; Lieut. Sterrett to his brother.

[7] St. Christopher's paper.—[8] Capt. Truxton to Sec. of Navy, Feb. 10, 14, and 16, 1799.—[9] St. Christopher's paper; Capt. Truxtun to Sec. of Navy, Feb. 10.—[10] Lieut Sterrett to his brother.—[11] Advice from St. Johns, Antigua, in Claypole's American Daily Advertiser, No. 6955, Philadelphia, Friday, March 29, 1799.

[1] Cooper's Naval History, i. pp. 299, 300.

DOCUMENT.

EXTRACT FROM CAPTAIN THOMAS TRUXTUN'S DISPATCH TO THE SECRETARY OF THE NAVY.

ON BOARD THE U. S. SHIP CONSTELLATION, IN SIGHT OF THE ISLAND OF ST. CHRISTOPHER'S, *February* 10, 1799.

DEAR SIR:—I wrote to you the 4th inst., to which I must beg leave to refer, and soon after weighed from Basseterre road, St. Christopher's, and proceeded to sea, having made the necessary arrangements with the merchants and masters of vessels for a convoy, to sail this day for the United States, under charge of the *Norfolk* and *Richmond*, which vessels I directed to cruise, in the mean time, near St. Bartholomew's and St. Martin's, so as to be at hand to proceed with the convoy at the time appointed.

As soon as I left the road of Basseterre (which I did with the *Constellation*, solus) I stretched under Montserat and towards Guadaloupe, by the wind, and from thence under the lee of Antigua and Barbuda. In this route I only met two merchant vessels and a British frigate. I therefore thought it best to change my ground, which I did, and run down towards the island of Nevis, and on the ninth instant, at noon, that island bearing W. S. W., five leagues distance, discovered a large ship to southward, on which I bore down.

She hoisted American colors, and I made our private signals for the day, as well as that of the British, but finding she answered neither, I immediately suspected her to be an enemy, and, in a short time after, found that my suspicions were well founded, for she hoisted the French national colors, and fired a gun to leeward, which is the signal of an enemy. I continued bearing down on her, and at a quarter past three P. M., she hailed me several times; and as soon as I got in a position for every shot to do execution, I answered by commencing a close and successful engagement, which lasted until about half-past four P. M., when she struck her colors to the United States ship *Constellation*, and I immediately took possession of her. She proved to be the celebrated French national frigate *Insurgente*, of forty guns and four hundred and seven men, lately out from France, commanded by Monsieur Bureaut, and is esteemed one of the fastest sailing ships in the French navy. I have been much shattered in my rigging and sails, and my fore-topmast rendered, from wounds, useless; you may depend the enemy is not less so.

I intend to get into Basseterre road, St. Christopher's, if possible, with my prize; but the wind being adverse, and blowing hard, I much doubt, in the crippled state of both ships, whether I shall effect it, and if not, I must make a port to leeward. The high state of our discipline, with the gallant conduct of my officers and men, would have enabled me to have compelled a more formidable enemy to have yielded, had the fortune of war thrown one in my way. As it is, I hope the President and my country will, for the present, be content with a very fine frigate being added to our infant navy, and that too with the loss of only one man killed and two wounded, while the enemy had (the French surgeon reports) fifty-two or fifty-three killed and wounded. Several were found dead in the tops, &c., and thrown overboard, eighteen hours after we had possession.

I must not omit, in this hasty detail, to do justice to Monsieur Bureaut, for he defended his ship manfully, and from my raking him several times fore and aft, and being athwart his stern, ready, with every gun, to fire when he struck his colors, we may impute the conflict not being more bloody on our side, for had not these advantages been taken, the engagement would not have ended so soon, for the *Insurgente* was completely officered and manned.

*   *   *   *   *   *

CHAPTER VI.

February 2, 1800.

THE ACTION WITH LA VENGEANCE.

The troubles which had sprung up between the governments of the United States and Revolutionary France, have been briefly adverted to in the last chapter of this work. No accommodation of the difficulties having been effected, increased efforts were made to continue the operations which had been adopted, and, if necessary, to extend the operations beyond the limits of a strictly defensive policy. The navy had been considerably increased, and new vessels, of a larger size, had been ordered by Congress;[1] and the greater part of the force, as before, was kept in service in the West Indian waters, under the command of Commodore Talbot, in the *Constitution*, and of Commodore Truxtun, in the *Constellation*.[2]

At half-past seven in the morning of the first of February, 1800, while the latter was cruising off Guadaloupe—the road of Basseterre bearing East, five leagues distant—a strange sail was seen in the Southeast, standing to the Southwest. Supposing that she was an English ship from Martinico, of which he had some knowledge, and wishing to avoid a long chase to leeward, off his cruising ground, he endeavored, by showing British colors, to induce her to run down and speak him; but the signal was disregarded, and sail was made in chase of the stranger. The *Constellation* gained quite rapidly, and as she approached the chase, Commodore Truxtun examined her more minutely, and discovered that she was a heavy French frigate, mounting not less than fifty-four guns, when orders were given to haul down the British colors, the yards to be slung with chains, top-sail-sheets, &c., stoppered, the ship cleared, and every thing prepared for action. The chase continued until noon, when the wind became light, and the enemy having the advantage in sailing, she held away from the *Constellation* and gradually increased the distance between the two vessels.[1]

Notwithstanding the evident disparity of force, Commodore Truxtun showed no hesitation in continuing the pursuit, and every thread of canvas which the *Constellation* could carry was thrown to the breeze. In this manner the chase continued until one o'clock in the afternoon of the next day, (*Feb. 2d*), when the wind freshened, with an appearance of its continuance, and the *Constellation* again rapidly drew ahead, when the prospect of bringing the enemy to action began, again, to brighten.

---

[1] Cooper's Naval Hist., i. pp. 302, 303.—[2] Ibid., p. 303.

[1] Com. Truxtun's Journal, inclosed in his Dispatch to Sec. of Navy, Feb. 3, 1800.

At eight o'clock in the evening, having got within hailing distance of the enemy, Commodore Truxtun ordered the ensign to be hoisted, the battle-lanterns to be lighted, and the large trumpet placed in the lee gangway, ready to speak her, and demand her surrender, when, "at that instant," she opened a fire from her stern and quarter guns on the rigging and spars of the *Constellation*.[1]

No farther ceremony being necessary, Commodore Truxtun renewed the orders which he had previously given to the several officers who commanded divisions of the main battery—"not to throw away a single charge of powder, but to take good aim and fire directly into the hull of the enemy; to load, principally, with two round shot, and, now and then, with a round shot and a stand of grape; to encourage the men at their quarters; to cause or suffer no noise or confusion whatever; but to load and fire as fast as possible when it could be done with certain effect"—and, a few minutes afterwards, having gained an advantageous position on the enemy's weather-quarter, the *Constellation* opened her fire.[2]

Five hours the two vessels contended for the mastery, in the most desperate manner, during which time both appear to have been running free, side by side. None of the details of this obstinate conflict have come down to us; yet, from the condition of both vessels, at the close of the engagement, it is perfectly obvious that the crews of both did their duty manfully. At one o'clock in the morning (*Feb. 3d*), the stranger's fire had been silenced, and she attempted to sheer off.[1]

Considering the enemy as his legitimate prize, Commodore Truxtun gave immediate orders to trim his shattered sails, in the best possible manner, in order that he might get alongside again, as soon as possible, when it was found that the mainmast was entirely unsupported by rigging, every shroud having been shot away, and that even stoppers were useless, and could not be applied with effect. All hands were immediately ordered from the main deck to endeavor to secure this all-important spar, but every exertion was fruitless, and it went by the board within a few minutes after the enemy had sheared off.[2] Midshipman James Jarvis and all the topmen went over with the mast; and that gallant young officer—who had refused to abandon his post, although warned of the danger,—and all but one man were lost.[3]

Within an hour the *Constellation* was cleared from the wreck, but she was no longer in a fit condition to renew the chase or the action;[4] and she bore away for Jamaica for repairs, without knowing the name, and but little of the character of her gallant adversary.[5] The latter, also ignorant of the name and exact character of her opponent, bore away for Curaçoa—where she arrived on the sixth of February[6]—when it became known that she was the

[1] Com. Truxtun's Journal.—[2] Ibid.

[1] Com. Truxtun's Jour.—[2] Ibid.—[3] Report of Sec. of Navy to Cong., March 20, 1800; Com. Truxtun's Journal.
[4] Com. Truxtun's Jour.—[5] Com. Truxtun to Sec. of Navy, Feb. 12, 1800.—[6] Capt. Baker to Sec. of Navy, Curaçoa, Feb. 8, 1800.

French national ship *La Vengeance*, commanded by Captain D. M. Pitot, and armed with thirty-two long eighteen-pounders on the gun-deck, twelve thirty-six-pounder brass carronades and four long twelves on her quarter-deck, and six long twelve-pounders on her forecastle.[1] She was manned with four hundred men, including passengers[2]—among whom were the Governor of Guadaloupe and his family,[3] and two general officers returning to France[4]—and carried a full cargo of sugar and coffee,[5] with a very large amount of specie.[6] Fifty of her crew had been killed, and one hundred and ten wounded;[7] her bowsprit, fore and mizzen masts, were the only spars she had standing;[8] her fore and mizzen shrouds and ratlines had been so much cut up "that you could scarce see any

[1] Statement of Mr. James Howe, a prisoner, on board, at the time of the action.—[2] Ibid.—[3] Extract from *Daily Advertiser*, in Claypole's *Am. Daily Advertiser*, Phila., March 18, 1800.—[4] Capt. Baker to Sec. of Navy, Feb. 8, 1800.

[5] Letter from Curaçoa, Feb. 13, in Claypole's *Am. Daily Advertiser*, Phila., March 18, 1800.

[6] Capt. Baker to Sec. of Navy, Feb. 8, 1800. Mr. Howe (*Statement*, &c.) says, "upwards of a million dollars," while different statements from Curaçoa (where the *Vengeance* put in) say it amounted to *two millions* of dollars.

[7] Mr. Philips (Am. Consul at Curaçoa) to Sec. of State, Feb. 9, 1800.—[8] Capt. Baker to Sec. of Navy, Feb. 8, 1800; Letter from Curaçoa, in Claypole's *Am. Daily Advertiser*, Phila., March 18, 1800.

VOL. II.—5

of them for stoppers;"[1] she had received one hundred and eighty-six round shot in her hull;[2] and she had eight feet of water in her hold.[3]

The *Constellation*, since her action with *L'Insurgente*, had received a new armament of twenty-eight eighteen-pounders on her main-deck, and ten twenty-four pound carronades on her quarter-deck, and was manned with a crew of three hundred and ten men.[4] She lost Midshipman Jarvis and thirteen men, killed and missing, and seven officers and eighteen men, wounded.[5]

The Congress of the United States voted its thanks and a gold medal to Commodore Truxtun for his gallantry in this action; and by a solemn vote of the same body, the conduct of Midshipman Jarvis, "who gloriously preferred certain death to an abandonment of his post," was declared "deserving the highest praise, and that the loss of so promising an officer is a subject of national regret."[6]

[1] Capt. Baker to Secretary of Navy, Feb. 8, 1800.

[2] Statement of Mr. James Howe.

[3] Capt. Baker to Sec. of Navy, Feb. 8, 1800; Extract from *Daily Advertiser*, in Claypole's *Am. Daily Advertiser*, Phila., March 18, 1800.—[4] Cooper, i. p. 306.

[5] Returns, signed "*Isaac Henry, Surgeon*," appended to Com. Truxtun's Dispatch.

[6] Resolutions of Congress, approved March 29, 1800.

DOCUMENT.

UNITED STATES SHIP CONSTELLATION, AT SEA,
February 3, 1800.

SIR:—On the 30th ult. I left St. Christopher's, with the *Constellation*, in excellent trim, and stood to windward in order to gain the station for myself before the road of Guadaloupe; and at half-past seven in the morning of the day following, I discovered a sail to the southeast, to which I gave Chase, and for the further particulars of that chase, and the action after it, I must beg to refer to the extracts from my Journal, herewith, as being the best mode of exhibiting a just and candid account of all our transactions in the late business, which has ended in the almost entire dismantlement of the *Constellation*, though, I trust, to the high reputation of the American flag.

I have the honor to be, &c.,

THOS. TRUXTUN.

BENJAMIN STODDERT, Esq., Secretary of the Navy.

Occurrences on board the United States Ship Constellation, of thirty-eight guns, under my command, February 1, 1800.

Throughout these twenty-four hours very unsettled weather; kept on our tacks, beating up under Guadaloupe, and at half-past seven in the morning, the road of Basseterre bearing east, five leagues distance, saw a sail in the southeast standing to the southwest, which, from her situation, I at first took for a large ship from Martinico, and hoisted English colors on giving chase, by way of inducement for her to come down and speak me, which would have saved us a long chase to leeward off my intended cruising-ground; but finding she did not attempt to alter her course, I examined her more minutely, as we approached her, and discovered that she was a heavy French frigate, mounting at least fifty-four guns. I immediately gave orders for the yards to be slung with chains, topsail-sheets, &c., stoppered, and the ship cleared, and every thing prepared for action, and hauled down the English colors. At noon the wind became light, and I observed the chase that we had before been gaining fast on held way with us, but I was determined to continue the pursuit, though the running to leeward, I was convinced, would be attended with many serious disadvantages, especially if the object of my wishes were not gratified.

Passed two schooners standing to the northward, one of them showed American colors, and was a merchant vessel; and the other I supposed to be of the same description.

February second, at one P. M., the wind being somewhat fresher than at the noon preceding, and an appearance of its continuance, our prospect of bringing the enemy to action began to brighten, as I perceived we were coming up with the chase fast, and every inch of canvas being set that could be of service, except the bog-reefs which I kept in the topsails, in case of the chase, finding an escape from our thunder impracticable, should haul on a wind and give us fair battle. But this did not prove to be her commander's intention. I, however, got within hail of him at 8 P. M., hoisted our ensign, and had the candles in the battle-lanterns all lighted, and the large trumpet in the lee-gangway ready to speak him, and to demand the surrender of his ship to the United States of America; but he, at that instant, commenced a fire from his stern and quarter guns, directed at our rigging and spars. No parley being then necessary, I sent my principal aid-de-camp, Mr. Vandyke, to the different officers commanding divisions on the main battery, to repeat strictly my orders, before given, not to throw away a single charge of powder, but to take good aim and fire directly into the hull of the enemy, and load, principally, with two round-shot, and now and then with a round-shot and a stand of grape, &c.; to encourage the men at their quarters; to cause or suffer no noise or confusion whatever; but to load and fire as fast as possible when it could be done with certain effect. These orders being given, in a few moments I gained a position on his weather-quarter that enabled us to return, effectually, his salute; and thus a close and as sharp an action as ever was fought between two frigates, commenced and continued until within a few minutes of 1 A. M., when the enemy's fire was completely silenced, and he was again sheering off.

It was at this moment that I considered him as my prize, and was trimming, in the best manner I could, my much shattered sails; when I found the mainmast was totally unsupported by rigging, every shroud being shot away, and some of them in several places; that even stoppers were useless, and could not be applied with effect. I then gave orders for the officers to send the men up from the gun-deck to endeavor to secure it, in order that we might get alongside of the enemy again as soon as possible; but every effort was in vain, for the mainmast went over the side in a few minutes after, and carried with it the top-men, among whom was an amiable young gentleman, who commanded the main-top, Mr. James Jarvis, son of James Jarvis, Esq., of New York. It seems this young gentleman was apprised of the mast going in a few minutes by an old seaman, but he had already so much of the principle of an officer ingrafted on his mind, not to leave his quarters on any account, that he told the man, if the mast went they must go with it, which was the case, and only one of them was saved.

I regret much his loss, as a promising young officer and amiable young man, as well as on account of a long intimacy that has subsisted between his father and myself; but have great satisfaction in finding that I have lost no other, and only two or three slightly wounded, out of thirty-nine killed and wounded—fourteen of the former, and twenty-five of the latter.

As soon as the mainmast went, every effort was made to clear the wreck from the ship as soon as possible, which was effected in about an hour. It being impossible to pursue the enemy, and as her security was then the great object, I immediately bore away for Jamaica, for repairs, &c., finding it impossible to reach a friendly port in any of the islands to windward.

I should be wanting in common justice was I to omit here to journalize the steady attention to order, and the great exertion and bravery of all my officers, seamen, and marines, in this action, many of whom I had sufficiently tried before, on a similar occasion, and all their names are recorded in the muster-roll I sent to the Secretary of the Navy, dated the nineteenth of December last, signed by myself.

All hands employed at repairing the damages sustained in the action, so far as to get the ship into Jamaica as soon as possible.

THOMAS TRUXTUN.

CHAPTER VII.

August 1, 1801.

THE CAPTURE OF THE TRIPOLI.

THE Dey of Algiers, as early as July, 1785, having discovered that a new commercial nation had sprung into existence, began to prey on the commerce of the United States, and to seize such of their merchantmen as came within range of his piratical cruisers.[1] Gradually the spirit of plunder which had thus been let loose, extended to other of the Barbary states, notwithstanding the Federal government, in common with those of the maritime nations of Europe, had condescended to pay tribute, and to submit to other services of degradation which the rulers of these States imposed upon them.[1]

[1] Cooper's Naval Hist., i. p. 263.

[1] Cooper's Naval Hist., i. pp. 319–328.

At this time the foundation of the Federal navy was laid, by an Act of Congress, which authorized the construction or purchase of six frigates;[1] and, from time to time, in subsequent years, although the corsairs had been bribed to a nominal peace, this force was gradually increased.[2]

In April, 1799, the Bashaw of Tripoli pretended to have found cause for complaint against the United States, and commenced a series of outrages, both by sea and land,[3] which aroused the government, and called forth all its energies. A heavy squadron, under Commodore Dale, was sent into the Mediterranean, with instructions, however, to endeavor rather to maintain a peace, by presents and bribes, than to enforce it by a display and exercise of his power.[4]

About nine o'clock, on the first of August, 1801, one of the smaller vessels of this squadron,—the *Enterprize*, commanded by Lieutenant-commandant Sterrett, while running for Malta, to obtain a supply of water, fell in with a polacre-rigged ship, of fourteen six-pounders, and carrying the Tripolitan flag.[5] The *Enterprize*, at that time, bore British colors; and, suspecting the character and purposes of the stranger, she ran alongside and hailed her. Lieutenant Sterrett inquired the object of the cruise, and was informed by the captain of the corsair that "he came out to cruise after the Americans, and that he lamented that he had not come alongside of some of them."[1]

The intentions of the stranger having thus been openly declared, Lieutenant Sterrett immediately lowered the British and raised the American colors; giving the stranger, at the same time, a volley of musketry. She responded with a partial broadside, and a closely-contested action commenced. For three hours, with but little intermission, the battle continued to rage, within pistol-shot distance; during which time, three several attempts were made to board the *Enterprize*, which were as often repulsed with great loss. Three several times, also, the enemy struck her colors, and, as often, renewed the action, when the crew of the *Enterprize* had ceased to fire and exposed itself on the deck of the vessel. The last time this treacherous act occurred, Lieutenant Sterrett gave orders to sink the corsair, "on which a scene of furious combat ensued, until the enemy cried for mercy," throwing his colors into the ocean; bending his body, in the waist of his vessel, and supplicating for quarter.[2]

Listening to the dictates of humanity, Lieutenant Sterrett ordered a suspension of the fire, and directed the captain either to come on board the *Enterprize* or to send some of his officers; but the boats of the enemy having been destroyed the demand could not be complied with, and a boat was sent on

---

[1] Act of March 27, 1794.—[2] Cooper, i. pp. 278, 293, 295, 296, 303, 333, 334.—[3] Clark's Naval Hist., p. 102.

[4] Cooper, i. p. 344.—[5] Ibid., p. 345; Com. Dale's Dispatch, referred to in Poulson's *Am. Daily Advertiser*, Phila., Nov. 23, 1801; Badger's Naval Temple, p. 15; Hist. of War with Tripoli, p. 91.

[1] Com. Dale's Dispatch; Poulson's *Am. Daily Advertiser*, Phila., Nov. 19, 1801.—[2] Ibid.; Capt. Sterrett, in Poulson's *Am. Daily Advertiser*, Phila., Nov. 18, 1801; Badger's Naval Temple, pp. 15, 16; History of War with Tripoli, pp. 91, 92.

board, from the *Enterprize*, and the vessel taken possession of.[1]

The enemy proved to be the Tripolitan ship *Tripoli*, commanded by Mahomet Sous, armed with fourteen six-pounders, and manned with eighty men.[2] She had become a perfect wreck, having lost her mizzen-mast, and received eighty-one shot in her hull, between wind and water;[3] while of her crew, twenty had been killed and thirty wounded.[4]

The *Enterprize*, which carried twelve six-pounders and a crew of ninety men, received but little injury, either in her hull or rigging, and not a man of her crew was injured.[5]

As Lieutenant Sterrett's instructions did not allow him to carry the prize into port,[6] he ordered Lieutenant David Porter to dismantle her; and, after administering to the relief of the wounded, cutting down her masts, throwing her guns overboard, and raising a temporary spar, on which a tattered sail was hoisted, he dismissed the vessel and her piratical crew.[1]

It is said that, after a lengthy and dangerous trip, the *Tripoli* reached her port, when the sorry spectacle which she presented, and the terrible stories which her officers and crew related, excited the strongest feelings of shame and indignation in the government, and of alarm among the people. The unfortunate captain, notwithstanding his wounds, was sentenced to receive five hundred bastinadoes; and was mounted on a jackass and paraded through the streets of Tripoli as an object of public scorn and contempt. The cruisers which were then in port, however, suffered the immediate loss of their crews, who were thunderstruck at the result of this engagement, and, by desertion, sought their own safety.[2]

The effect of this action on the action of Tripoli generally, was also beneficial, inasmuch as but very few cruisers subsequently ventured out of port, or if they did so they confined their operations to the immediate vicinity of the shore.[3]

---

[1] Com. Dale's Dispatch; Poulson's *Am. Daily Advertiser*, Phila., Nov. 19, 1801; Capt. Sterrett, in Poulson's *Am. Daily Advertiser*, Phila., Nov. 18, 1801; Badger's Naval Temple, pp. 15, 16; Hist. of War in Tripoli, pp. 91, 92.

[2] Cooper, i. p. 345; Com. Dale's Dispatch; Letter from an officer on the *United States*, in Poulson's *Daily Advertiser*, Phila., Nov. 11, 1801; Com. Dale to the American Consul at Gibraltar, Aug. 19, 1801. Some accounts say she carried *eighty-five* men.

[3] Com. Dale's Dispatch. Some accounts state that only sixteen or eighteen balls were thus received.

[4] Com. Dale to the American Consul at Gibraltar, Aug. 19, 1801; Com. Dale's Dispatch.

[5] Ibid.; Hist. of War with Tripoli, p. 92; Badger's Naval Temple, p. 17.—[6] Cooper, i. p. 346; Clark, p. 103; Hist. of War with Tripoli, p. 92.

[1] Capt. Sterrett, in Poulson's *Am. Daily Advertiser*, Phila., Nov. 18, 1801; Com. Dale's Dispatch; History of War with Tripoli, p. 92.

[2] Com. Dale's Dispatch; Hist. of War with Tripoli, p. 92; Badger's Naval Temple, p. 17.

[3] Cooper, i. 346.

CHAPTER VIII.

August 3, 1804.

THE BOMBARDMENT OF TRIPOLI.

THE troubles with Tripoli having been unsettled, the American squadron, under Commodore Preble, had spent the earlier part of the year 1804 in a strict blockade of that port, in cruising in that vicinity, and in preparing for an attack on the town.[1]

For the latter purpose, among other measures, a loan of two bomb-ketches and six gunboats, with their equipments, had been asked and received from the King of Naples, and had sailed from Messina;[2] and, on the twenty-fifth of July, 1804, the squadron assembled before Tripoli,[3] when the Commodore found himself at the head of the *Constitution*, of forty-four guns; the *Argus*, commanded by Lieutenant Isaac Hull, mounting sixteen twenty-four pounders; the *Syren*, Lieutenant Charles Stewart, mounting sixteen twenty-four pounders; the *Scourge*, Lieutenant Dent, mounting fourteen eighteen-pounders; the *Vixen*, Lieutenant Smith, mounting twelve eighteen-pounders; the *Enterprize*, Lieutenant Stephen Decatur, mounting twelve six-pounders; the *Nautilus*, Lieutenant Somers, mounting twelve eighteen-pounders; the two Neapolitan bomb-ketches; and the six gunboats belonging to the same power.[1]

Opposed to this little force was a walled city, protected by heavy batteries, on which were mounted a hundred and fifteen guns; nineteen gunboats, each carrying a long brass eighteen or twenty-four pounder in the bow and two howitzers abaft; a brig of ten guns; two schooners, each mounting eight guns; and two galleys, each mounting four guns; the whole ot which were sheltered by a long range of rocks and shoals, extending more than two miles eastward from the town, and rendering it impossible for a vessel of the *Constitution's* draft of water to approach near enough to co-operate with the lighter vessels, and defended by a land force of about twenty-five thousand men.[2]

The weather was not favorable for anchoring until the twenty-eighth of July, when the squadron ran in, with the wind east-southeast; and, about three in the afternoon, anchored, by signal, about two miles and a half from the town. The squadron had no soon-

[1] Clark's Naval Hist., p. 109; Cooper, ii. pp. 37–40; Badger's Naval Temple, p. 28.—[2] Com. Preble to Sec. of Navy, Sept. 18; Cooper, ii. p. 38.—[3] Com. Preble to Sec. of Navy, Sept. 18. *The History of the War with Tripoli* (Salem, 1806, p. 110) says he "arrived on the *twenty-third.*" Mr. Clark (*Naval Hist.*, p. 109) says he "joined the vessels off Tripoli on the *twenty-first.*"

[1] Com. Preble to Sec. of Navy, Sept. 18; Cooper, ii. p. 40. Mr. Clark (*Naval Hist.*, p. 109) gives different armaments to most of the vessels.—[2] Com. Preble to Sec. of Navy, Sept. 18; Clark's Naval Hist., p. 109; Badger's Naval Temple, pp. 28, 29.

er anchored than a heavy gale arose, and continued until the first of August, during which the gunboats and bomb-vessels were in great danger, and were saved only by the most strenuous efforts of the officers and crew of the squadron.[1]

On the third of August, the weather being pleasant, the squadron ran in again, with an easterly breeze, and, about noon, had come within two or three miles from the batteries, on and around which the garrisons were displayed, either to intimidate the assailants or to invite an attack. Several of the enemy's gunboats and galleys[2] had left the harbor, and formed, in two divisions, outside the rocks and shoals, also with the intention of inviting an attack; and preparations were made for an immediate gratification of their wish. At half-past twelve the *Constitution* wore off shore, and signalled the smaller vessels to come within hailing distance; when Commodore Preble communicated to the several commandants his intention of attacking the enemy's shipping and batteries, with his orders for the disposition of their several crews. The gunboats and bomb-ketches were immediately manned and prepared to cast off, and within an hour from their receipt of the orders, the several com-

[1] Com. Preble to Sec. of Navy, Sept. 18; Cooper, ii. p. 41; Mackenzie's Decatur (*Sparks' Am. Biog.*, xxi.), p. 87.

[2] "Against *twenty-one* large gun and *several* smaller boats full of men."—*Letter of Com. Preble to Wm. Higgins*, Aug. 15, 1804, and cited in the *National Intelligencer*, Washington, D. C., Dec. 3, 1804. "The enemy had *seventeen* gunboats moored in a line in front of their batteries, also a brig of sixteen guns and a schooner of ten guns, moored to cover their boats."—*Letter from Lieut.-Com. Charles Stewart*, "*Off Tripoli, Aug.* 9, 1804," in the *National Intelligencer*, Washington, *Dec.* 5, 1804.

mandants were ready to perform their respective parts of the service to which they had been assigned.[1]

These small vessels were divided into two divisions of three gunboats and a ketch each. The first was commanded by Lieutenant Dent, in the ketch; by Lieutenant Somers, in gunboat *Number One;* by Lieutenant James Decatur, in gunboat *Number Two;* and by Lieutenant Blake, in gunboat *Number Three.* The second division was commanded by Lieutenant Robinson, in the ketch; by Lieutenant Stephen Decatur, in gunboat *Number Four;* by Lieutenant Joseph Bainbridge, in gunboat *Number Five;* and by Lieutenant Trippe, in gunboat *Number Six.*[2]

At half-past one o'clock, the arrangements having been, meanwhile, perfected, the squadron wore again, and stood towards the town. At two o'clock the gunboats—which had been towed by the several vessels—were cast off; at a quarter-past two the signal for them to advance and attack the enemy was displayed; at half-past two the general signal for battle was made; and, at a quarter before three, the action commenced by the ketches opening their fire on the town. The batteries and shipping immediately returned the fire with great spirit, and the American squadron responded, within grape-shot distance.[3]

In the mean time the two divisions

[1] Com. Preble to Sec. of Navy, Sept. 18; Mackenzie's Decatur, p. 88; Cooper, ii. p. 42.—[2] Com. Preble to Sec. of Navy, Sept. 18; Cooper, ii. p. 42; Clark, p. 110; Waldo's Life of Preble, p. 195.—[3] Com. Preble to Sec. of Navy, Sept. 18; Clark, p. 110; Waldo's Preble, pp. 197, 198.

of gunboats, covered by the brigs and schooners, advanced against the enemy's light vessels which had advanced from the harbor. In this, however, in consequence of the dull sailing qualities of the boats, the progress was not satisfactory to the ardent spirits by whom they were commanded; and their sweeps were thrown out, and worked with a will, to secure the positions which had been assigned to them by the Commodore.[1]

The first division was separated, and accomplished but little. *Number One*, commanded by Lieutenant Somers, bore down with great spirit, and attacked five of the gunboats, which formed, in part, the enemy's western division, defeating, and driving them within the rocks, in a shattered condition, and with the loss of a great number of men.[2] *Number Two*, under Lieutenant James Decatur, joined the second division, as will be seen hereafter, and lost his life through the treachery of his opponent.[3] *Number Three*, under Lieutenant Blake, was misled by an erroneous signal of recall, which was displayed by the Commodore, and accomplished nothing beyond opening a fire on the shipping within the harbor.[4]

The second division of gunboats was more successful, although the officers on this, too, were sadly annoyed by the bad sailing qualities of the vessels. *Number Four*, under Lieutenant Stephen Decatur, after pouring showers of grape and musket-balls on the enemy, as he approached, bore down on and attacked one of the largest of the enemy's squadron. Laying his boat alongside, Lieutenant Decatur boarded the enemy, followed by Lieutenant Thorne, Midshipman McDonough, and the American portion of his crew; and between them and the crew of the enemy—ranged on either side of a long, open hatchway, which divided the deck into two parts—a close contest, for the possession of the vessel, ensued. After a short struggle, at this distance, the Americans charged round each end of the hatchway, and either destroyed the crew or compelled it to surrender.[1] After securing his prize, Lieutenant Decatur took her in tow, and bore down to the next of the enemy's line.[2] Running his own vessel aboard, he boarded this as he had boarded the other, and was, immediately, engaged in a close and desperate struggle with the captain of the Tripolitan, whom Lieutenant Decatur attacked with a pike. The Turk was a large and exceedingly powerful man, and as his assailant approached he seized the pike, wrested it from his hand, and turned it against its owner. Parrying the thrust, Lieutenant Decatur drew his cutlass and attempted to cut off the head of the pike, but the weapon broke

[1] Com. Preble to Sec. of Navy, Sept. 18; Cooper, ii. p. 43.—[2] Com. Preble to Sec. of Navy, Sept. 18; Clark, pp. 110, 111; Mackenzie's Decatur, p. 89; Waldo's Preble, p. 202.—[3] Vide p. 42.—[4] Cooper, ii. 43.

[1] Com. Preble to Sec. of Navy, Sept. 18; Cooper, ii. p. 44; Mackenzie's Decatur, p. 90.

[2] Com. Preble to Sec. of Navy, Sept. 18; Clark, p. 111; Cooper, ii. pp. 44, 45; Hist. of War with Tripoli, p. 111. Lieut. Mackenzie (*Life of Decatur*, p. 91) says that "taking his prize in tow, Decatur was proceeding *out of the harbor*, when the boat, which had been commanded by his brother, came under his stern and informed him" of the murder of his brother, on *Number Two*, when *he returned to the enemy's line* and attacked this second boat. No other authority, which I have seen, refers to such a movement.

Painted by Chappel | Engraved by H.B. Hall

Stephen Decatur

From the original painting in the possession of the Publishers.

at the hilt, leaving the American, apparently, at the mercy of the Turk. A second thrust was parried with his arm, and Lieutenant Decatur sprang upon and grappled his opponent. The trial of strength which followed this resolute adventure speedily terminated in favor of the Turk, although, in falling, Lieutenant Decatur so far released himself that he laid, on the deck, side by side with his enemy. The latter immediately attempted to reach a small poniard which he carried in his sash, but Lieutenant Decatur, perceiving his object, grasped his hand, and at the same time drew from his own pocket a small pistol, which he passed around the body of the prostrate Turk, pointed inward, and fired. The ball passed entirely through the body of the Turk, killing him instantly, and Lieutenant Decatur, released from his grasp, sprang to his feet.[1] It was while the two commanders were thus struggling for the mastery, that the well-known act of Reuben James occurred. One of the crew of the Tripolitan, perceiving the desperate encounter in which his captain was engaged, ran to the rescue, and raised his sabre to cleave the skull of Lieutenant Decatur; when Reuben James, a quarter-gunner on the *Enterprize*, who had lost the use of both his arms by wounds, rushed in, and received, on the back of his head, without fatal effect, the blow which was intended for his gallant commander.[2]

[1] Cooper, ii. p. 45. Lieut. Mackenzie (*Life of Decatur*, pp. 91–93) and Mr. Clark (*Naval Hist.*, pp. 110, 111) give entirely different narratives of this adventure.—[2] Mackenzie's Decatur, pp. 92, 361–363. Mr. Cooper (*Naval Hist.*, ii. p. 45) supposes the blow was received on the young man's *arm*.

While this struggle was going on, the assailants were not idle; and the release of Lieutenant Decatur from the grasp of the Turk was speedily followed by the surrender of the vessel.[1] Gunboat *Number Five*, commanded by Lieutenant Bainbridge, had her lateen-sail shot away early in the action, which prevented her getting into the position which had been assigned to her; but she opened a steady and well-directed fire on the enemy, from musket-shot distance, which caused considerable trouble among the Tripolitans, and induced her to pursue a portion of the enemy until she grounded, under the batteries, and was saved only with considerable difficulty.[2] *Number Six*, commanded by Lieutenant Trippe, ran alongside one of the largest of the opposing squadron; and her commander, with Midshipman John Henley and nine men, immediately boarded her. *Number Six* falling off before any more of her men could get on board the enemy to assist those who were already on board, the struggle for the mastery was against great odds—eleven against thirty-six—and it was carried on with unusual desperation. After killing fourteen of the enemy, and wounding seven others, the Americans succeeded in capturing the vessel, with the loss of only four wounded—one of whom, Lieutenant Trippe, received eleven sabre wounds, some of which were very se-

[1] Com. Preble to Sec. of Navy, Sept. 18; Clark, pp. 110, 111; Cooper, ii. pp. 44–46; Hist. of War with Tripoli, p. 111; Mackenzie's Decatur, pp. 90–93.

[2] Com. Preble to Secretary of Navy, Sept. 18; Clark, p. 111; Mackenzie's Decatur, p. 90; Waldo's Preble, p. 202.

vere.[1] *Number Two*, to which allusion has already been made, was commanded by Lieutenant James Decatur—Stephen's brother—and joined the second division early in the action. Like his brother, the commander of this vessel ran alongside and engaged a large gunboat in the eastern division of the enemy's force, which he compelled to surrender, after a close and very severe contest. As he was about to take possession of his prize he was treacherously shot through the head by her commander,[2] who, taking advantage of this circumstance, and receiving the assistance of other boats of the enemy's squadron, secured his escape.[3] The bomb-ketches kept their stations, although covered with the spray of the sea, occasioned by the enemy's shot; and they kept up a constant and destructive fire on the town during the action between the gunboats.[4]

A division of the enemy's fleet, composed of five gunboats and two galleys, which had remained within the harbor, protected by the reefs before referred to, having been joined by those portions of the gunboats which had been driven into the harbor by the American squadron, two attempts were made to row out of the harbor for the purpose of surrounding the American gunboats and their prizes, but the fire which was opened on them by the brigs and schooners and by the *Constitution*, kept them in check, and prevented them from succeeding in this design.[1]

At half-past four, the wind inclining to the northward, signal was made for the bomb-ketches and gunboats to retire from action; which was followed, immediately afterwards, by another, for the brigs and schooners and their boats to tow off the gunboats and their prizes, which was done under a heavy covering fire from the *Constitution*. At a quarter before five o'clock the ketches were towed off, and the action closed.[2]

During the two hours in which the squadron was thus engaged, the grapeshot made great havoc among the enemy's forces, both those on board the vessels and those on shore; and the batteries were frequently silenced by the fire of the *Constitution*, although they were immediately re-occupied when the guns of that vessel could not be brought to bear on them. Three of the enemy's gunboats were sunk in the harbor, several had their decks cleared of men by the shot from the squadron,

[1] Com. Preble to Sec. of Navy, Sept. 18; Cooper, ii. pp. 46, 47; Clark, p. 111; Mackenzie's Decatur, pp. 94, 95; Waldo's Preble, p. 202; Lieut.-Com. Stewart's Letter, Aug. 9, 1804.—[2] Com. Preble to Sec. of Navy, Sept. 18; Clark, p. 112; Mackenzie, pp. 90, 91. Mr. Cooper (*Naval Hist.*, ii. p. 46), while he concurs in the general statement, appears to discredit the idea that the enemy *had surrendered* and afterwards renewed the action.

[3] Com. Preble to Sec. of Navy, Sept. 18; Cooper, ii. p. 46; Clark, p. 112. Lieut. Mackenzie (*Life of Decatur*, p. 91) says Lieut. Stephen Decatur—James' brother—pursued this boat, singled out the person who shot his brother, and after a desperate personal encounter, already referred to, killed him and captured the boat which he commanded. As Com. Preble says that, "with the assistance he received from other boats," "the poltroon" "was enabled *to escape*;" as Messrs. Clark and Cooper, after carefully examining the subject, concur in this statement; and as the latter gentleman has even disputed the statement that the boat had struck her colors,—which would remove all appearance, even, of treachery,—I have not felt warranted in differing from the official narrative.

[4] Com. Preble to Secretary of Navy, Sept. 18.

[1] Com. Preble to Sec. of Navy, Sept. 18; Clark, p. 112; Cooper, ii. p. 48.—[2] Com. Preble to Sec. of Navy, Sept. 18; Cooper, ii. p. 48; Mackenzie, pp. 95, 96.

and a very heavy loss of life and property has been said to have befallen the town from the explosion of the shells.[1]

The American squadron suffered but little damage. The *Constitution's* mainmast was wounded, and her main-royal yard and sail were shot away. Her sails and running rigging were also considerably cut; and one of her quarter-deck guns was damaged by a thirty-two pound shot. Gunboat *Number Five* lost her main-yard; and the brigs' and schooners' sails and rigging were considerably cut. The loss, among the crews, was confined to Lieutenant James Decatur, *killed;* Lieutenants Stephen Decatur and Trippe, and eleven men, *wounded*.[1]

The squadron anchored about two leagues from Tripoli to repair its damages, and to prepare for a renewal of the attack.[2]

The officers, seamen, and marines of the squadron are said to have behaved in the most gallant manner; and received the commendation of the commander in his dispatches to the government.[3]

1 Com. Preble to Sec. of Navy, Sept. 18; Cooper, ii. pp. 48, 49; Hist. of War in Tripoli, p. 111; Lieut. Stewart's letter, Aug. 9, 1804.

1 Com. Preble to Sec. of Navy, Sept. 18; Clark, pp. 112, 113.—2 Cooper, ii. p. 50.—3 Com. Preble to Sec. of Navy, Sept. 18.

DOCUMENT.

EXTRACT FROM COMMODORE PREBLE'S DISPATCH TO THE SECRETARY OF THE NAVY.

SIR:—

* * * * * * *

The weather was not favorable for anchoring until the twenty-eighth, when, with the wind E. S. E., the squadron stood in for the coast, and, at three in the afternoon, anchored, per signal, Tripoli bearing south, two and a half miles distant. At this moment the wind shifted suddenly from E. S. E. to N. N. W., and from thence to N. N. E. At five o'clock it blew strong, with a heavy sea, setting directly on shore. I made the signal to prepare to weigh. At six, the wind and sea having considerably increased, the signal was made for the squadron to weigh and gain an offing. The wind continued veering to the eastward, which favored our gaining sea-room, without being obliged to carry so great a press of sail as to lose any of our gunboats, although they were in great danger. The gale continued, varying from northeast to east-southeast, without increasing much, until the thirty-first, when it blew away our reefed foresail and close-reefed maintopsail. Fortunately the sea did not rise in proportion to the strength of the gale, or we must have lost all our boats.

August the first, the gale subsided, and we stood towards the coast; every preparation was made for an attack on the town and harbor.

August the third, pleasant weather, wind east, stood in with the squadron towards Tripoli; at noon we were between two and three miles from the batteries, which were all manned, and observing several of their gunboats and galleys had advanced in two divisions, without the rocks, I determined to take advantage of their temerity. At half-past twelve o'clock I wore off shore, and made the signal to come within hail, when I communicated to each of the commanders my intention of attacking the enemy's shipping and batteries. The gun and mortar boats were immediately manned and prepared to cast off; the gunboats, in two divisions of three each, the first division commanded by Captain Somers in No. 1, Lieutenant Decatur in No. 2, and Lieutenant Blake in No. 3. The second division commanded by Captain Decatur in No. 4, Lieutenant Bainbridge in No. 5, and Lieutenant Trippe in No. 6. The two bombards were commanded by Lieutenant-commandant Dent and Mr. Robinson, first lieutenant of this ship. At half-past one o'clock, having made the necessary arrangements for the attack, wore ship and stood towards the batteries; at two, signal made to cast off the boats; at a quarter-past two, signal for bombs and gunboats to advance and attack the enemy; at half-past two, general signal for battle; at three-quarters past two, the bombs commenced the action by throwing shells into the town. In an instant the enemy's shipping and batteries opened a tremendous fire, which was promptly returned by the whole squadron within grape-shot distance; while, at the same time, the second division, of three gunboats, led by the gallant Captain Decatur, was advancing, with sails and oars, to board the eastern division of the enemy, consisting of nine boats. Our boats gave the enemy showers of grape and musket balls as they advanced; they, however, soon closed, when the pistol, sabre, pike, and tomahawk, were made good use of by our brave tars. Captain Somers, being in a dull sailer, made the best use of his sweeps, but was not able to fetch far enough to windward to engage the same division of the enemy's boats which Captain Decatur fell in with. He, however, gallantly bore down with his single boat on five of the enemy's western division, and engaged within pistol-shot, defeated, and drove them within the rocks, in a shattered condition, and with the loss of a great number of men. Lieutenant Decatur, in No. 2, was closely engaged with one of the enemy's largest boats, of the eastern division, which struck to him, after having lost a large proportion of men; and at the instant that brave officer was boarding her, to take possession, he was treacherously shot through the head by the captain of the boat that had surrendered, which base conduct enabled the poltroon (with the assistance he received from other boats) to escape. The third boat of Captain Somers' division kept to windward, firing at the boats and shipping in the harbor. Had she gone down to his assistance, it is probable several of the enemy's boats would have been captured in that quarter. Captain Decatur, in No. 4, after having, with distinguished bravery, boarded and carried one of the enemy, of superior force, took his prize in tow and gallantly bore down to engage a second, which, after a severe and bloody conflict, he also took possession of. These two prizes had thirty-three officers and men killed, and twenty-seven made prisoners. Lieutenant Trippe of the Vixen, in No. 6, ran alongside of one of the enemy's large boats, which he boarded, with only Midshipman John Henley and nine men. His boat falling off before any more could get on board, thus was he left, compelled to conquer or perish, with the odds of thirty-six to eleven. The Turks could not withstand the ardor of this brave officer and his assistants; in a few minutes the decks were cleared, and her colors hauled down. On board of this boat fourteen of the enemy were killed and twenty-two made prisoners, seven of which were badly wounded, the rest of their boats retreated within the rocks. Lieutenant Trippe received eleven sabre wounds, some of which were severe; he speaks in the highest terms of Mr. Henley and those who followed him. Lieutenant Bainbridge, in No. 5, had his lateen-yard shot away early in the action, which prevented his getting alongside of the enemy's boats; but he galled them by a steady and well-directed fire within musket-shot, indeed, he pursued the enemy until his boat grounded under the batteries, but she was fortunately soon got off. The bomb-vessels kept their stations, although covered with the spray of the sea, occasioned by the enemy's shot, and were well conducted by Lieutenants Dent and Robinson, who kept up a constant fire from the mortars, and threw a great number of shells into the town. Five of the enemy's gunboats and two galleys, composing the centre division, and stationed within the rocks as a reserve, joined by the boats that had been driven in, and supplied by fresh men from the shore to replace those they had lost, twice attempted to row out to endeavor to surround our gunboats and their prizes; I as often made the signal to cover them, which was promptly attended to by the brigs and schooners, all of which were gallantly conducted, and annoyed the enemy exceedingly; but the fire from this ship kept their flotilla completely in check. Our grape-shot made great havoc among their men, not only on board their shipping, but on shore. We were several times within two cables' length of the rocks, and within three of their batteries; every one of which, in succession, were silenced so long as we could bring our broadsides to bear upon them. But the moment we passed a battery it was reanimated, and a constant heavy fire kept up, from all that we could not point our guns at. We suffered most when wearing or tacking; it was then I most sensibly felt the want of another frigate. At half-past four, the wind inclining to the northward, I made the signal for the bombs and gunboats to retire from action, and, immediately after, the signal to tow off the gunboats and prizes, which was handsomely executed by the brigs, schooners, and boats of the squadron, covered by a heavy fire from the *Constitution.* At three-quarters past four P. M., the light vessels, gunboats, and prizes, being out of reach of the enemy's shot, I hauled off to take the bomb-vessels in tow.

We were two hours under the fire of the enemy's batteries, and the only damage received on this ship is a twenty-four pound shot nearly through the centre of the mainmast, thirty feet from the deck; mainroyal yard and sail shot away; one of our quarter-deck guns damaged by a thirty-two pound shot, which at the same time shattered a marine's arm. Two lower shrouds and two back-stays were shot away, and our sails and running rigging considerably cut. We must impute our getting off thus well to our keeping so near that they overshot us, and to the annoyance our grape-shot gave them. They are, however, but wretched gunners. Gunboat No. 5 had the main-yard shot away, and the rigging and sails of the brigs and schooners were considerably cut.

Lieutenant Decatur was the only officer killed, but in him the service has lost a valuable officer. He was a young man who gave strong promise of being an ornament to his profession; his conduct in the action was highly honorable, and he *died nobly.*

The enemy must have suffered very much in killed and wounded, both among their shipping and on shore. Three of their gunboats were sunk in the harbor; several of them had their decks nearly cleared of men by our shot, and a number of shells burst in the town and batteries, which must have done great execution.

The officers, seamen, and marines of the squadron, behaved in the most gallant manner. The Neapolitans, in emulating the ardor of our seamen, answered my highest expectations. I cannot but notice the active exertions and officer-like conduct of Lieutenant Gordon, and the other lieutenants of the *Constitution.* Mr. Harriden, the master, gave me full satisfaction, as did all the officers and ship's company. I was much gratified by the conduct of Captain Hall and Lieutenant Greenleaf, and the marines belonging to his company, in the management of six long twenty-six pounders on the spar-deck, which I placed under his direction. Captain Decatur speaks in the highest terms of the conduct of Lieutenant Thorn and Midshipman McDonough of No. 4, as does Captain Somers of Midshipman Ridgely and Miller attached to No. 1. Annexed is a list of killed and wounded; and inclosed, a copy of my general orders on this occasion.

KILLED.—*Gunboat No.* 2, Lieutenant James Decatur.

WOUNDED.—*Constitution*, one marine.

Gunboat No. 4, Captain Decatur, slight, one sergeant of marines, and two seamen.

Gunboat No. 6, Lieutenant Trippe, severely, one boatswain's-mate, and two marines.

Gunboat No. 1, two seamen.

Gunboat No. 2, two seamen.

TOTAL.—One killed and thirteen wounded.

* * * * * *

I have the honor to be, &c.,

EDWARD PREBLE.

UNITED STATES SHIP CONSTITUTION,
MALTA HARBOR, *Sept.* 18, 1804.

CHAPTER IX.

August 7, 1804.

THE SECOND BOMBARDMENT OF TRIPOLI.

THE first attack on Tripoli, the capture of three of her gunboats, and the subsequent withdrawal of the fleet, for repairs, have been already alluded to in a former chapter of this work.[1] From the third to the eleventh of August all hands were busily employed in altering the rig of the three prizes, and in preparing for a second attack on the town.[2]

At nine in the morning of the seventh, signal was made to the light vessels of the squadron to weigh, and the gunboats and bomb-ketches to cast off, and stand in shore towards the western batteries of the town, in doing which both sails and oars were called into requisition. The breeze was a light one from the eastward, which, with a strong current which set in shore, rendered it prudent for the *Constitution* to remain at anchor; yet the squadron moved to the positions to which it had been assigned with great spirit.[3]

The bomb-ketches, under Lieutenants Dent and Robinson, and the several gunboats, formed into two divisions, under Lieutenants Somers and Decatur, were supported by the *Syren* and *Vixen;* while the *Constitution*, *Nautilus*, and *Enterprize*, stood to windward, ready to cut off any of the enemy's gunboats or galleys which might appear on the outside of the harbor.[1]

[1] Vide Chap. VIII.—[2] Preble's letter to Sec. of Navy, Sept. 18; Cooper's Naval Hist., ii. p. 50.

[3] Com. Preble to Secretary of Navy, Sept. 18.

At half-past two, the bomb-ketches and gunboats having gained their positions, the signal to begin the action was made by the Commodore, and the engagement commenced.[2] The fire opened at point-blank distance;[3] and, although the bombs which were thrown, with but one exception, were bad, and failed to explode,[4] the town and its defences suffered severely.[5]

At half-past three a hot shot struck *Number Nine*—one of the prizes which had been captured on the third of August, and placed under the command of Lieutenant James R. Caldwell of the *Syren*—and passed through her magazine; when that ill-fated vessel, with her crew, was blown up, with the loss of her commander, Midshipman John S. Dorsey, and eight men killed, and six men wounded. When the smoke had cleared away from the wreck, the only part above water was the forward part of the boat, on which were clustered

[1] Com. Preble to Sec. of Navy, Sept. 18.—[2] Ibid.; Clark's Naval History, p. 114; Cooper's Naval History, ii. p. 50. *The History of War with Tripoli*, p. 112, and Lieut. Charles Stewart (*Letter of Aug.* 9) say it was "*half-past twelve.*"—[3] Com. Preble to Sec. of Navy, Sept. 18; Letter from Lieut. Charles Stewart, Aug. 9, in the *National Intelligencer*, Washington, D. C., Dec. 5, 1804.

[4] Cooper's Naval History, ii. p. 53, *note.*

[5] Com. Preble to Secretary of Navy, Sept. 18.

Midshipman Robert T. Spence and eleven men, who were busily engaged in loading the long twenty-four-pounder, which had formed the armament of the boat. They completed their task, and as, with three hearty cheers, they discharged it at the enemy, the wreck sank from under their feet, and they were picked up by the boats which had been sent to their assistance from the other vessels of the squadron.[1]

While the action with the gunboats continued, the enemy's galleys and gunboats—fifteen in number—got in motion, with an evident intention of leaving the harbor to attack the Americans at closer quarters, but the *Constitution*, the *Nautilus*, and the *Enterprize*, were to windward, ready to cut them off from the harbor, if they made the attempt, and they "thought it most prudent to retire to their snug retreat behind the rocks, after firing a few shot."[1]

At half-past five o'clock the wind began to freshen from the north-northeast, when, on signal, the fire was suspended and the ketches and gunboats taken in tow; and at nine o'clock the entire squadron anchored about five miles southeast from Tripoli.[2]

In this affair the vessels suffered considerably. *Number Four* received a twenty-four pound shot through her hull; *Number Six* had her lateen-yard shot away; *Number Eight* also received a twenty-four pound shot through her hull and lost two of her crew; *Number Nine*, with her commander and nine of her crew, was lost, as before related, and some others were injured in their sails and rigging.[3] It is not known what injury was done to the town or the vessels of the enemy.

¹ Cooper's Naval Hist., ii. p. 51; Mackenzie's Decatur, p. 103; Clark's Naval Hist., p. 114. In the letter of Lieut. Stewart, Aug. 9, he says, "They had just time to load, and *were going to fire* their gun, when she sunk to the bottom;" and Com. Preble (*Letter to Sec. of Navy, Sept.* 18) says, "Mr. Spence was superintending the loading of the gun at this moment; and notwithstanding the boat was sinking, he and the brave fellows surviving, finished charging, gave three cheers as the boat went from under them, and swam to the nearest boats," &c., which appear to indicate that the gun was *not* discharged.

¹ Com. Preble to Sec. of Navy, Sept. 18.—² Ibid.—³ Ibid.

DOCUMENT.

EXTRACT FROM COMMODORE PREBLE'S DISPATCH.

* * * * * *

August 5th.—We were at anchor with the squadron, about two leagues north from the city of Tripoli; the *Argus* in chase of a small vessel to the westward, which she soon came up with, and brought within hail. She proved to be a French privateer of four guns, which put into Tripoli a few days since for water, and left it this morning. I prevailed on the captain, for a consideration, to return to Tripoli, for the purpose of landing fourteen very badly wounded Tripolitans, which I put on board his vessel with a letter to the prime minister, leaving it at the option of the Bashaw to reciprocate this generous mode of conducting the war. The sending these unfortunate men on shore, to be taken care of by their friends, was an act of humanity on our part, which I hope will make a proper impression on the minds of the Barbarians; but I doubt it.

All hands were busily employed altering the rig of the three prizes from lateen vessels to sloops, and preparing for a second attack. Observed one of the enemy's schooners and the brig (two corsairs) in the harbor to be dismasted; was informed by the French captain, that the damage these vessels received in the action of the third, had occasioned their masts being taken out.

The seventh, the French privateer came out and brought me a letter from the French consul, in which he observes, that our attack of the third instant had disposed the Bashaw to accept of reasonable terms; and invited me to send a boat to the rocks with a flag of truce, which was declined, as the white flag was not hoisted at the Bashaw's castle. At nine A. M., with a very light breeze from the eastward, and a strong current, which obliged the *Constitution* to remain at anchor, I made the signal for the light vessels to weigh, and the gun and bomb boats to cast off and stand in shore towards the western batteries—the prize boats having been completely fitted for service, and the command of them given to Lieutenants Crane of the *Vixen*, Thorn of the *Enterprize*, and Caldwell of the *Syren*—the whole advanced with sails and oars. The orders were for the bombs to take a position in a small bay to the westward of the city, where but few of the enemy's guns could be brought to bear on them, but from whence they could annoy the town with shells; the gunboats to silence a battery of seven heavy guns, which guarded the approach to that position; and the brigs and schooners to support them, in case the enemy's flotilla should venture out.

At half-past one P. M., with a breeze from N. N. E., I weighed with the *Constitution*, and stood in for the town; but the wind being on shore made it imprudent to engage the batteries with the ship, as in case of a mast being shot away, the loss of the vessel would probably ensue, unless a change of wind should favor our getting off.

At half-past two P. M., the bomb and gunboats having gained their stations, the signal was made for them to attack the town and batteries. Our bombs immediately commenced throwing shells, and the gunboats opened a sharp and well-directed fire on the town and batteries, within point-blank shot, which was warmly returned by the enemy. The seven-gun battery, in less than two hours, was silenced except one gun. I presume the others were dismounted by our shot, as the walls were almost totally destroyed.

At a quarter-past three P. M. a ship hove in sight to the northward, standing for the town. Made the *Argus* signal to chase.

At half-past three one of our prize gunboats was blown up by a hot-shot from the enemy, which passed through her magazine. She had on board twenty-eight officers, seamen, and marines; ten of whom were killed and six wounded. Among the killed were James R. Caldwell, first lieutenant of the *Syren*, and Midshipman John S. Dorsey, both excellent officers. Midshipman Spence and eleven men were taken up unhurt. Captain Decatur, whose division this boat belonged to, and who was near her at the time she blew up, reports to me that Mr. Spence was superintending the loading of the gun at that moment, and, notwithstanding the boat was sinking, he and the brave fellows surviving, finished charging, gave three cheers as the boat went from under them, and swam to the nearest boats, where they assisted during the remainder of the action.

The enemy's gunboats and galleys (fifteen in number) were all in motion close under the batteries, and appeared to meditate an attack on our boats. The *Constitution*, *Nautilus*, and *Enterprize* were to windward, ready at every hazard to cut them off from the harbor, if they should venture down; while the *Syren* and *Vixen* were near our boats, to support and cover any of them that might be disabled. The enemy thought it most prudent, however, to retire to their snug retreat behind the rocks, after firing a few shot.

Our boats, in two divisions, under Captains Somers and Decatur, were well conducted, as were our bomb-vessels by Lieutenants Dent and Robinson.

The town must have suffered much from this attack; and their batteries, particularly the seven-gun battery, must have lost many men.

At half-past five P. M., the wind beginning to freshen from the N. N. E., I made the signal for the gun and bomb boats to retire from action, and for the vessels to which they were attached to take them in tow.

The *Argus* made signal that the strange sail was a friend.

In this day's action No. 4 had a twenty-four pound shot through her hull; No. 6 had her lateen-yard shot away; No. 8 a twenty-four pound shot through her hull, which killed two men. Some of the other boats had their rigging and sails considerably cut. We threw forty-eight shells, and about five hundred twenty-four pound shot into the town and batteries. All the officers and men engaged in the action behaved with the utmost intrepidity.

At half-past six all the boats were in tow, and the squadron standing to the N. W.

At eight the *John Adams*, Captain Chauncey, from the United States, joined in company.

At nine the squadron anchored, Tripoli bearing S. E., five miles distant.

Gunboat No. 3 was this day commanded by Mr. Brooks, master of the *Argus;* and No. 6 by Lieutenant Wadsworth of the *Constitution.*

Annexed is a return of our loss in this attack.

KILLED.—*Gunboat No.* 9. One lieutenant, one midshipman, one boatswain's-mate, one quarter-gunner, one sergeant of marines, and five seamen.

Gunboat No. 8.—Two seamen.

WOUNDED.—*Gunboat No.* 9.—Six seamen, two of them mortally.

* * * * * *

I have the honor to be, &c.,

EDWARD PREBLE.

UNITED STATES SHIP CONSTITUTION,
MALTA HARBOR, *Sept.* 18, 1804.

CHAPTER X.

August 29, 1804.

THE FOURTH BOMBARDMENT OF TRIPOLI.

IN the night of the twenty-fourth of August a third attack had been made on the town, "but with what effect is uncertain;" and preparations were immediately made to renew it.[1]

At three in the afternoon of the twenty-eighth of August, the squadron weighed, and, with a pleasant breeze from the eastward, stood in for Tripoli; and at five the *Constitution* anchored about two miles, north by east, from Fort English, and two and a half from the Bashaw's castle—the gunboats keeping under weigh.[2]

Many of the officers and crew of the *Constitution* having been detailed to the bomb-ketches, gunboats, and boats of the ships, Captain Chauncey, of the *John Adams*, with several of his officers and about seventy of his men—seamen and marines—volunteered to take their places on the frigate; while the *John Adams*, the *Scourge*, the transports, and the bomb-ketches—which could not be brought into action—remained at anchor about seven miles north from the town. All the boats of the squadron were officered, manned, and attached to the several gunboats; and the crews were busily engaged, until eight in the evening, in making the preparations necessary for the attack.[1]

[1] Com. Preble to Sec. of Navy, Sept. 18, 1804; Cooper's Naval Hist., ii. p. 55.—[2] Com. Preble to Sec. of Navy, Sept. 18, 1804. Mr. Clark (*Naval Hist.*, p. 115), Mr. Badger (*Naval Temple*, p. 38), and Mr. Waldo (*Life of Preble*, p. 210), suppose the squadron moved on the *twenty-seventh.*

[1] Com. Preble to Sec. of Navy, Sept. 18, 1804; Cooper, ii. p. 55; Badger's Naval Temple, p. 38.

At half-past one in the morning of the twenty-ninth, the gunboats, in two divisions, led by Lieutenants Somers and Decatur, and accompanied by the *Syren*, Lieutenant Stewart; the *Argus*, Lieutenant Hull; the *Vixen*, Lieutenant Smith; the *Nautilus*, Lieutenant Reed; the *Enterprize*, Lieutenant Robinson, and the boats of the squadron, were ordered to advance and take their stations close to the rocks, at the entrance of the harbor, within grape-shot distance of the Bashaw's castle.[1]

At three o'clock the gunboats anchored, with springs on their cables, and opened a heavy fire on the town, shipping, and batteries, which was returned with equal spirit, but was not properly directed. The ships' boats remained near the gunboats to protect them from the attacks of the enemy, should he venture to leave the harbor; while the larger vessels kept under weigh, ready for the same service or any other duty which might be found necessary.[2]

The engagement continued until daylight, with unabated fury, when the *Constitution* weighed and stood in towards the harbor, under a heavy fire from Fort English, the Bashaw's castle, and the batteries. Supposing the gunboats had consumed the greater part of their ammunition, at half-past five, signal was made for them to withdraw from the action, and for the light vessels to take them in tow; while the *Constitution* covered the movement by a heavy fire of round and grape shot, at two cables' length, which proved exceeding destructive to the enemy. One of his gunboats was sunk, two others were run ashore to prevent them from sinking, and the ten which were least injured sought safety in an immediate retreat.[1]

Encouraged with this favorable opening, the Commodore continued to run in until the ship came within musket-shot of the batteries, when she was brought to, and opened a heavy fire on the town, batteries, and castle. Three-quarters of an hour afterwards, having silenced the castle and two of the batteries, sunk a Tunisian galliot in the mole, greatly damaged a Spanish ship in the harbor, and greatly cut up the enemy's galleys and gunboats—the American gunboats and smaller vessels having, meanwhile, retired beyond gun-shot distance from the town—the *Constitution* was hauled off, and, with the squadron, returned to the anchorage, about five miles from the town.[2]

In this attack upwards of seven hundred round-shot, besides grape and canister, were thrown into the town and batteries, with very good effect—the enemy having suffered more severely than in any of the attacks which preceded it.[3]

[1] Com. Preble to Sec. of Navy, Sept. 18, 1804; Cooper, ii. p. 56; Clark's Naval Hist., p. 115; Badger's Naval Temple, p. 38.

[2] Com. Preble to Sec. of Navy, Sept. 18, 1804; Cooper, ii. p, 56; Clark, p. 115; Mackenzie's Life of Decatur (*Sparks' Am. Biog.*, xxi.), p. 110.

[1] Com. Preble to Sec. of Navy, Sept. 18, 1804; Clark, pp. 115, 116; Mackenzie's Decatur, pp. 110, 111.

[2] Com. Preble to Sec. of Navy, Sept. 18, 1804; Cooper, ii. p. 56; Mackenzie's Decatur, p. 111; Badger's Naval Temple, p. 39.

[3] Com. Preble to Sec. of Navy, Sept. 18, 1804; Mackenzie's Decatur, p. 111.

The light vessels of the American squadron suffered considerably in their sails and rigging; the *Constitution* had three of her lower shrouds, two spring-stays, two topmast-backstays and the trusses, chains, and lifts of her main-yard shot away, and her sails and running rigging were also considerably cut. The gunboats were also considerably cut in their sails and rigging; and a boat belonging to the *John Adams* was sunk while in tow of the *Nautilus*, by a double-headed shot from one of the batteries.[1]

The details of the loss of the enemy, although it was heavy, are not known. The *Constitution* had not a man hurt, and no loss among the crews of the gunboats has been recorded. The only loss which is mentioned, is that of the crew of the boat belonging to the *John Adams*, already referred to, of whom three were killed, and one badly wounded.[2]

DOCUMENT.

EXTRACT FROM COMMODORE PREBLE'S DISPATCH TO THE SECRETARY OF THE NAVY.

SIR:—

* * * * * *

August 28.—We were favored with a pleasant breeze from the eastward. At three P. M. we weighed, and stood in for Tripoli. At five, anchored the *Constitution* two miles N. by E. from Fort English, and two and a half miles from the Bashaw's castle; the light vessels ordered to keep under weigh.

We were employed until eight P. M. in making arrangements for attacking the town. A number of the officers and many of the seamen of the *Constitution* being attached to the bomb, gun, and ship's boats, Captain Chauncey, with several of his officers, and about seventy of his seamen and marines, volunteered their services on board the *Constitution*. All the boats in the squadron were officered and manned, and attached to the several gunboats. The two bomb-vessels could not be brought into action, as one was leaky and the mortar-bed of the other had given way. The *John Adams*, *Scourge*, transports, and bombs, were anchored seven miles to the northward of the town. Lieutenant-commandant Dent, of the *Scourge*, came on board the *Constitution*, and took charge on the gun-deck. Lieutenant Izard, of the *Scourge*, also joined me. Lieutenant Gordon commands gunboat *No.* 2; and Lieutenant Lawrence, of the *Enterprize*, *No.* 5. These are the only changes.

At half-past one A. M. the gunboats, in two divisions, led by Captains Decatur and Somers, were ordered to advance, and take their stations close to the rocks, at the entrance of the harbor, within grape-shot distance of the Bashaw's castle. The *Syren*, *Argus*, *Vixen*, *Nautilus*, *Enterprize*, and boats of the squadron accompanied them. At three A. M. the boats anchored, with springs on, within pistol-shot of the rocks, and commenced a brisk fire on the shipping, town, batteries, and Bashaw's castle, which was warmly returned, but not as well directed. The ships' boats remained with the gunboats, to assist in boarding the enemy's flotilla, if it should venture out; while the brigs and schooners kept under weigh, ready for the same service, or for annoying the enemy, as occasion might present.

At daylight, presuming that the gunboats had nearly expended their ammunition, we

---

[1] Com. Preble to Sec. of Navy, Sept. 18, 1804; Cooper, ii. pp. 56, 57; Clark, p. 116.

[2] Com. Preble to Sec. of Navy, Sept. 18, 1804.

weighed with the *Constitution*, and stood in for the harbor. Fort English, the Bashaw's castle, Crown, and Mole batteries, kept up a heavy fire on us as we advanced. At half-past five I made the signal for the gunboats to retire from action; and for the brigs and schooners to take them in tow. We were then within two cables' length of the rocks, and commenced a heavy fire of round and grape on thirteen of the enemy's gunboats and galleys, which were in pretty close action with our boats. We sunk one of the enemy's boats; at the same time two more, disabled, ran on shore to avoid sinking; the remainder immediately retreated. We continued running in until we were within musket-shot of the Crown and Mole batteries, when we brought to, and fired upwards of three hundred round-shot, besides grape and canister, into the town, Bashaw's castle, and batteries. We silenced the castle and two of the batteries for some time.

At a quarter-past six, the gunboats being all out of shot and in tow, I hauled off, after having been three-quarters of an hour in close action.

The gunboats fired upwards of four hundred round-shot, besides grape and canister, with good effect. A large Tunisian galliot was sunk in the Mole; a Spanish ship, which had entered with an ambassador from the Grand Seignior, received considerable damage. The Tripolitan galleys and gunboats lost many men and were much cut. The Bashaw's castle and town have suffered very much; as have their Crown and Mole batteries.

Captains Decatur and Somers conducted their divisions of gunboats with their usual firmness and address; and were well supported by the officers and men attached to them. The brigs and schooners were also well conducted during the action, and fired a number of shot at the enemy; but their guns are too light to do much execution, They suffered considerably in their sails and rigging.

The officers and crew of the *Constitution* behaved well. I cannot, in justice to Captain Chauncey, omit noticing the very able assistance I received from him, on the quarter-deck of the *Constitution*, during the whole of the action. The damage which we have received is principally above the hull—three lower shrouds, two spring-stays, two topmast-back-stays, trusses, chains, and lifts of the main-yard shot away. Our sails had several cannon-shot through them, and were, besides, considerably cut by grape. Much of our running rigging cut to pieces; one of our anchor-stocks and our larboard cable shot away; and a number of grape-shot were sticking in different parts of the hull—but not a man hurt!

A boat belonging to the *John Adams*, with a master's-mate (Mr. Creighton) and eight men, was sunk by a double-headed shot from the batteries, while in tow of the *Nautilus*, which killed three men and badly wounded one, who, with Mr. Creighton, and the other four, were picked up by one of our boats. The only damage our gunboats sustained, was in their rigging and sails, which were considerably cut with the enemy's round and grape shot.

At eleven A. M. we anchored with the squadron, five miles N. E. by N. from Tripoli, and repaired the damage received in the action.

* * * * * *

I have the honor to be, &c.,

Edward Preble.

United States Ship Constitution,
Malta Harbor, *Sept.* 18, 1804.

CHAPTER XI.

September 3, 1804.

THE FIFTH BOMBARDMENT OF TRIPOLI.

AFTER the squadron had returned to its anchorage, the several vessels were repaired, and preparations for a final attack on the town were made.[1]

At four in the afternoon of the second of September, all things having been made ready, the squadron weighed anchor, and kept under sail all night.[2]

At half-past two in the afternoon of the third, the gunboats were ordered to cast off, and to advance and attack the enemy.[3]

It appears that the enemy had profited from his experience, and had now adopted a new system of operations. Instead of posting his galleys and gunboats behind the rocks, in positions to fire over them, or at the openings between them—bringing them to leeward of the American squadron—he had now put them in motion, and had worked them up to windward until they had gained the weather side of the harbor, directly under the fire of Fort English, and of a new battery which had been erected in that neighborhood.[4] This movement was an exceedingly judicious one, inasmuch as it prevented the American gunboats from attacking the town, without leaving the enemy's flotilla in their rear and directly to windward—an advantage in favor of the enemy which no prudent officer would allow.

This new plan of operations compelled a change in the plan which Commodore Preble had adopted; and therefore the bomb-ketches were sent to leeward to bombard the town; while, at the same time, the gunboats were kept to windward, to engage the enemy's galleys and boats.[1]

At half-past three in the afternoon, the bomb-ketches having gained the stations to which they had been ordered, the engagement commenced—the ketches, at one extremity of the harbor, throwing shells into the town; while the boats, on either side, and the American small vessels and the forts, at the other extremity, were also disputing for the mastery.[2]

The bomb-ketches were vigorously opposed by the garrisons of the Bashaw's, the Crown, the Mole, and several other batteries, and they were so much exposed that they were in great danger of being sunk. To cover these vessels, and to draw off the enemy's fire, the

---

1 Com. Preble to Sec. of Navy, Sept. 18, 1804; Cooper's Naval Hist., ii. p. 57.—2 Com. Preble to Sec. of Navy, Sept. 18, 1804.—3 Ibid.; Cooper, ii. p. 57; Mackenzie's Decatur (*Sparks' Am. Biog.*, xxi.), p. 112.—4 Com. Preble to Sec. of Navy, Sept. 18, 1804; Cooper, ii. pp. 57, 58.

1 Com. Preble to Sec. of Navy, Sept. 18, 1804; Cooper, ii. p. 58; Mackenzie's Decatur, p. 112.—2 Com. Preble to Sec. of Navy, Sept. 18, 1804; Badger's Naval Temple, p. 40; Clark's Naval History, p. 116.

Constitution ran down to the rocks, near which the ketches were stationed, and opened a heavy fire, at grape-shot distance. Eleven broadsides were poured in upon the castle, the town, and the batteries, by the frigate; while the ketches played upon the town with great effect.[1]

Meanwhile, the gunboats and small vessels, at the opposite extremity of the harbor, were also busily engaged. The gunboats, led by the commanders who had before led them to action—Captains Somers and Decatur—had advanced against the flotilla and driven it from its position; while the small vessels cannonaded Fort English.[2]

During an hour and a quarter this general contest continued; when, in consequence of the increase of the wind, which was also inclining to the northward, the Commodore considered it prudent to withdraw from the town.

Accordingly, signals were made for the small vessels to take the gunboats in tow, and soon afterwards the squadron withdrew.[1]

The sails and rigging of all the vessels suffered severely, and the *Argus* received a thirty-two pound shot in her hull, which cut off a bower cable as it entered, beyond which but little loss was experienced by the squadron.[2]

The damage to the town appeared to be considerable; but, as none of the particulars have come down to us, a more minute account cannot be given.[3]

With this engagement the naval "battles" connected with the Tripolitan troubles ended. Other exploits, requiring great courage and skill, were performed on shore, by those who represented the United States, in connection with a brother of the Bashaw, but a peace was soon afterwards effected, and the attention of the country was directed to another and more important opponent.

DOCUMENT.

EXTRACT FROM COMMODORE PREBLE'S DISPATCH TO THE SECRETARY OF THE NAVY.

Sir:—

* * * * * * *

29th and 30th (*August*) preparing the bomb-vessels for service; supplying the gunboats with ammunition, &c.

31st.—A vessel arrived from Malta with provisions and stores; brought no news of Commodore Barron, or the frigates. We discharged this vessel's cargo and ordered her to return.

September the 2d.—The bomb-vessels having been repaired and ready for service, Lieutenants Dent and Robinson resumed the command of them. Lieutenant Morris, of the *Argus*, took command of *No.* 3; and Lieutenant Trippe, having nearly recovered from his wounds, resumed the command of *No.* 6, which he so gallantly conducted the 3d ultimo. Captain Chaun-

[1] Com. Preble to Sec. of Navy, Sept. 18, 1804; Cooper, ii. p. 58; Badger's Naval Temple, p. 40; Mackenzie's Decatur, p. 113.—[2] Com. Preble to Sec. of Navy, Sept. 18, 1804; Cooper, ii. p. 59; Clark, p. 116; Mackenzie's Decatur, pp. 112, 113.

[1] Com. Preble to Sec. of Navy, Sept. 18, 1804; Badger's Naval Temple, pp. 40, 41; Mackenzie's Decatur, p. 113.

[2] Com. Preble to Sec. of Navy, Sept. 18, 1804; Cooper, ii. p. 59; Badger's Naval Temple, pp. 40, 41.

[3] Com. Preble to Sec. of Navy, Sept. 18, 1804.

cey, with several young gentlemen, and sixty men from the *John Adams*, volunteered on board the *Constitution.*

At four P. M. made the signal to weigh; kept under sail all night. At eleven P. M. a general signal to prepare for battle; a Spanish polacre, in ballast, came out of Tripoli, with an ambassador of the Grand Seignior on board, who had been sent from Constantinople to Tripoli to confirm the Bashaw in his title. This ceremony takes place in all the Barbary regencies every five years. The captain of this vessel informed us, that our shot and shells had made great havoc and destruction in the city and among the shipping; and that a vast number of people have been killed. He also informs us that three boats, which were sunk by our shot, in the actions of the 3d and 28th ult., had been got up, repaired, and fitted for service.

3d.—At 2 P. M. Tripoli bore S. S. W., two miles and a half distant, wind E. by N. At half-past two the signals were made for the gunboats to cast off, advance, and attack the enemy's gunboats and galleys, which were all under weigh in the eastern part of the harbor, whither they had, for some time past, been working up against the wind. This was certainly a judicious movement of theirs, as it precluded the possibility of our boats going down to attack the town, without leaving the enemy's flotilla in their rear, and directly to windward. I accordingly ordered the bomb-vessels to run down within proper distance of the town and bombard it, while our gunboats were to engage the enemy's galleys and boats to windward.

At half-past three P. M., our bombs having gained the station to which they were directed, anchored and commenced throwing shells into the city. At the same time our gunboats opened a brisk fire on the galleys, and within point-blank shot, which was warmly returned by them and Fort English, and by a new battery a little to the westward; but as soon as our boats arrived within good musket-shot of their galleys and boats, they gave way and retreated to the shore, within the rocks, and under cover of musketry from Fort English. They were followed by our boats, and by the *Syren*, *Argus*, *Vixen*, *Nautilus*, and *Enterprize*, as far as the reefs would permit them to go with prudence. The action was then divided. One division of our boats, with the brigs and schooners, attacked Fort English, while the other was engaged with the enemy's galleys and boats.

The Bashaw's castle, the Mole, Crown, and several other batteries, kept up a constant fire on our bomb-vessels, which were well conducted, and threw shells briskly into the town; but from their situation they were very much exposed, and in great danger of being sunk. I accordingly ran within them with the *Constitution*, to draw off the enemy's attention and amuse them while the bombardment was kept up. We brought to within reach of grape, and fired eleven broadsides into the Bashaw's castle, town, and batteries, in a situation where more than seventy guns could bear upon us. One of their batteries was silenced. The town, castle, and other batteries considerably damaged.

By this time it was half-past four o'clock. The wind was increasing and inclining rapidly to the northward. I made the signal for the boats to retire from action, and for the brigs and schooners to take them in tow, and soon after hauled off with the *Constitution* to repair damages. Our main-topsail was totally disabled by a shell from the batteries, which cut away the leech-rope and several cloths of the sail. Another shell went through the fore-topsail, and one through the jib. All our sails considerably cut, two top-mast back-stays shot away, main-mast, fore-tacks, lifts, braces, bowlines, and the running rigging generally very much cut, but no shot in our hull, excepting a few grape.

Our gunboats were an hour and fifteen minutes in action. They disabled several of the enemy's galleys and boats, and considerably damaged Fort English. Most of our boats received damage in their rigging and sails. The bomb-vessel *No.* 1, commanded by Lieutenant Robinson, was disabled, every shroud shot away, the bed of the mortar rendered useless, and the vessel near sinking. She was, however, towed off. About fifty shells were thrown into the town; and our boats fired four hundred round-shot, besides grape and canister. They were led into action by Captains Decatur and Somers, with their usual gallantry. The brigs and schooners were handsomely conducted, and fired many shot with effect at Fort English, which they were near enough to reach with their carronades. They suffered considerably in their rigging, and the *Argus* received a thirty-two pound shot in the hull forward, which cut off a bower-cable as it entered. We kept under weigh until eleven P. M., when we anchored, Tripoli bearing S. S. W. three leagues. I again, with pleasure, acknowledge the services of an able and active officer in Captain Chauncey, serving on the quarter-deck of the *Constitution*. At sunrise I made the signal for the squadron to prepare for action. The carpenters were sent on board the bombs to repair damages, and our boats employed in supplying the bombs and gunboats with ammunition, and to replace the expenditures.

* * * * * *

I have the honor to be, &c.,

EDWARD PREBLE.

UNITED STATES SHIP CONSTITUTION,
MALTA HARBOR, *Sept.* 18, 1804.

CHAPTER XII.

April 27, 1805.

THE CAPTURE OF DERNE.

THE services of Commodore Preble, before Tripoli, have been referred to in several preceding chapters of this work;[1] and the successive attacks which he made on that city have been fully described in the pages of those who have recorded the annals of the Navy of the Republic.[2] Soon afterwards he was superseded in the command of the squadron before Tripoli;[3] and Commodore Barron assumed the command of the station.[4]

It appears, however, that before the departure of Commodore Preble, and, probably with his approval, another and more singular course was adopted to chastise and cripple Tripoli. The reigning Bashaw of that country, some years before, had usurped the throne, and driven his brother, Hamet Caramelli, to whom it belonged, into exile. At the suggestion of Mr. Cathcart, the American Consul at Tripoli, and of Mr. Eaton, the American Consul at Tunis, it was resolved to take advantage of these difficulties; and, by uniting the forces and resources of America with those of the exiled Bashaw, to restore the latter to his throne, and to remove the author of the existing troubles beyond the power of doing mischief. The fugitive prince was immediately sought by Mr. Eaton, and the bold undertaking was not only proposed, but accepted, and arranged.[1]

The plan adopted provided for the movement of a body of troops, by land; while the American squadron, by water, should co-operate with it, against the usurper; and as it was known that the people were much discontented with the existing government, there appeared to

[1] Vide Chapters VIII., IX., X., XI.

[2] Cooper, ii. pp. 6–74; Clark, pp. 104–119; Naval Temple, pp. 20–43; Waldo's Preble, pp. 162–217; Hist. of War with Tripoli, pp. 107–114; Sabine's Life of Preble (*Sparks' Am. Biog.*, xxii.), pp. 79–104.

[3] Hist. of War with Tripoli, p. 114.—[4] Cooper, ii. p. 74.

[1] Felton's Life of Eaton (*Sparks' Am. Biog.*, ix.), pp. 257, 258; Noah's Travels, p. 346; Consul Eaton to Gen. S. Smith, "Tunis, Aug. 19, 1802."

be but little doubt of the successful termination of the enterprise.[1]

In consequence of this arrangement, and to be convenient of access to the commander of the squadron, the exiled Hamet repaired to Malta;[2] while the intelligence of his movements, which had reached Tripoli, had filled the government with alarm, and the people with joy. In fact, so great was the popular pleasure that it was considered a special interposition of Divine favor; and so imminent was the danger, that the chiefs of several of the principal villages were seized and confined to prevent an insurrection.[3]

Singular as it may appear, at that time the commanders of the American squadron—Commodore Morris, and Captains Barron, Bainbridge, and Murray — had disapproved the proposed junction of the American force with that of the exiled Bashaw; and, through their influence, the projected expedition had been defeated,[4] while Mr. Eaton returned to the United States.[5]

In June, 1804, Mr. Eaton returned to the Mediterranean, having learned that the exiled Bashaw, after the failure of the American squadron to co-operate with him, had returned to Derne—a provincial town in the regency of Tripoli, and, at the head of an armed force of Arabs, had boldly opened the campaign, with strong appearances of ultimate success. He had proposed such

[1] Consul Eaton to Mr. Madison, Sec. of State, "Tunis, Sept. 5, 1801;" Felton's Eaton, p. 258.—[2] Felton's Eaton, pp. 266, 274; Consul Eaton to Gen. S. Smith, Aug. 19, 1802.—[3] Consul Eaton to Mr. Madison, Aug. 5, 1802.

[4] Consul Eaton to Mr. Madison, June 8 and Aug. 9, 1802.

[5] Felton's Eaton, pp. 288, 289; Life of Gen. Eaton (*Ed. Brookfield*, 1813), p. 242.

terms to the government of the United States as had induced it to promise assistance; and Mr. Eaton, who had volunteered to lead the force against the enemy, was charged with authority to carry it into effect.[1]

On the twenty-fifth of November, 1804, Mr. Eaton reached Alexandria[2]—to which place the exiled Bashaw had retired[3]—when the negotiations were renewed and carried into effect, with the approval of the Viceroy of Egypt.[4] A series of difficulties now presented themselves, in which Mr. Eaton and his eighteen associates, in a strange country, were exposed to all the jealous animosities of Mussulmen, and endured great hardships.[5] At length the junction of the two parties was effected; a few Greek Christians were enlisted; and, on the sixth of March, 1805, at the head of nine Americans—Lieutenant O'Bannon, Mr. Peck, a non-commissioned officer, and six privates; a company of twenty-four cannoniers, under Selim Comb, and Lieutenants Connant and Rocco; a company of thirty-eight Greeks, under Captain Lucca Ulovix and Lieutenant Constantine; the Bashaw's suite of about ninety men; and a party of about two hundred mounted Arabs —less than four hundred in the aggregate[6]—with one hundred and five cam-

[1] Cooper, ii. p. 79; Noah's Travels, p. 348; Life of Eaton, p. 256.—[2] Gen. Eaton's Journal, Nov. 25.

[3] Hist. of War with Tripoli, p. 115; Consul Eaton to Secretary of Navy, Sept. 6, 1804.

[4] Felton's Eaton, p. 295; Hist. of War with Tripoli, pp. 116–118; Gen. Eaton's Journal, Dec. 17, 1804.

[5] Hist. of War with Tripoli, pp. 117–120; Gen. Eaton to Sec. of Navy, Dec. 13, 1804; Same to Com. Preble, Jan. 25, 1805; Same to Secretary of Navy, Feb. 13, 1805.

[6] Gen. Eaton's Journal, March 6, 1805; Felton's Eaton, pp. 300, 301.

els, laden with provisions and baggage, the army moved from the rendezvous, near Alexandria.[1] From that time to the seventeenth of April—forty-two days—the army, if an irregular and ungovernable horde of savage Arabs can be so called, was in the wilderness, slowly marching, like the Israelites of old, from Egypt to the "promised land." The marches were by irregular stages, and the army halted where water was to be procured, frequently suffering for the want of it. The only provisions it possessed were a handful of rice and two biscuits per day; while the wandering tribes of Arabs, by whom the party was constantly surrounded, were exceedingly troublesome. After enduring untold hardships—having for three days had no food whatever, except a little sorrel and the roots which were dug from the sands—the army, on the sixteenth of April, reached Bomba, and on the next day the *Argus* came into port and relieved its distress. The narrative of this journey, as related by General Eaton,[2] exhibits one of the most perilous marches on record; and it is said that, on the appearance of the *Argus*, "language was too poor to paint the joy and exultation which this messenger of life excited in every breast."

At two o'clock in the afternoon of the twenty-fifth of April, the motley army encamped on an eminence which overlooks Derne, reconnoitred the town and prepared for hostilities.[3]

[1] Gen. Eaton's Jour., March 6; Hist. of War with Tripoli, p. 121.—[2] Gen. Eaton's Jour., March 6 to April 16. See also Hist. of War with Tripoli, pp. 121–123; Felton's Eaton, pp. 301–319; Noah's Travels, pp. 349–351.

[3] Gen. Eaton's Journal, April 25.

Derne, the scene of the proposed operations, is the second port of consequence in the regency. It was the *Darnis* of the ancients, and is pleasantly situated, within view of the sea. Its port, in former times, possessed considerable importance; and at the time of the siege it contained, probably, five thousand inhabitants, who were governed by a Bey.[1]

The town had been strengthened with considerable good judgment by the commander of the garrison, who appeared to be prepared for a vigorous defence. A water-battery, on which eight nine-pounders had been mounted, protected the northeastern part of the town, and from thence to the southern extremity—where the walls of an old castle and some temporary breastworks had been occupied—the whole front of the city on the bay was occupied and defended by troops who had been stationed on the terraces and within the houses. The governor's palace had also been strengthened by the addition of a ten-inch howitzer, which had been mounted in battery on the terrace of his palace.[2]

In the evening several chicks, or chiefs, came out of the town, and assured the exiled Bashaw of their sympathy, and that of the inhabitants of two of the three departments of which the city was composed, although they appeared to have but little confidence in the success of the siege,[3] especially since a heavy force, which the reigning

[1] Rees' Cyclopædia, Art. "*Derne;*" Noah's Travels, p. 351.—[2] Gen. Eaton's Jour., April 25; Gen. Eaton to Com. Barron, April 29; Noah's Travels, p. 341.

[3] Gen. Eaton's Journal, April 25, 1805.

Bashaw had sent to the relief of the town, was within four days' march of the city, and was rapidly approaching.[1]

On the twenty-sixth, the *Nautilus* hove in sight, and exchanged signals; and on the next day the force was increased by the arrival of the *Hornet* and the *Argus*.[2] Preparations were made for an immediate assault, agreeably to the plan of operations which have been alluded to already—the Bey, or governor of the town, having returned a flag of truce, which had been sent to proffer terms of peace, with the emphatic answer, "My head or yours!"[3] Agreeably to the orders of General Eaton two field-pieces were landed from the *Argus*, one of which was hauled up the precipice, and the other returned to the ship, for want of time to raise it from the shore.[4]

A favorable breeze enabled the vessels to run in as near to the shore as they were required—the *Hornet*, with springs on her cables, anchoring within one hundred yards from the battery, on which it opened a well-directed fire; the *Nautilus*, half a mile distant; and the *Argus*, a short distance to the eastward from her—and at two in the afternoon they opened their fire on the town and batteries.[5] At the same time the main body of the army, led by Hamet, moved against the rear of the town; while a party of six American marines, with a company of twenty-four cannoniers with

[1] Gen. Eaton to Com. Barron, April 29, 1805.

[2] Gen. Eaton's Jour., April 26 and 27; Capt. Hull to Com. Barron, April 28, 1805.—[3] Gen. Eaton to Com. Barron, April 29, 1805.—[4] Ibid.; Capt. Hull to Com. Barron, April 28.—[5] Capt. Hull to Com. Barron, April 28; Cooper, ii. p. 81.

the field-piece, one of twenty-six Greeks, and a few Arabs, on foot, the whole under Lieutenant O'Bannon, took a position on an eminence and in a ravine on the southeast quarter of the town.[1]

At a little before two in the afternoon the action commenced, and was continued with great spirit and vigor by both parties[2] for about two hours and a half.[3]

After a fire had been kept on the water-battery for about three-quarters of an hour, its guns were silenced, and the greater part of the garrison retired, joining that portion of the garrison which was opposed to the party under Lieutenant O'Bannon—with whom also was General Eaton.[4] The undisciplined troops under the command of the latter, beginning to show signs of uneasiness from the annoying fire which had been kept up from the walls of the houses, the general resolved to put them *in motion*, and with this object ordered a charge, although it is said that his force was not more than one-tenth the strength of that which opposed him. Beyond his expectations, even, if we may judge from his remarks, the order was promptly obeyed and successfully accomplished. The enemy fled from their coverts in the greatest confusion, retreating from tree to tree and from wall to wall, offering

[1] Com. Eaton to Com. Barron, April 29, 1805.

[2] Noah's Travels, p. 339.—[3] Gen. Eaton to Com. Barron, April 29; Hist. of War with Tripoli, p. 123; Clark's Naval Hist., p. 119.—[4] Gen. Eaton to Com. Barron, April 29; Capt. Hull to Com. Barron, April 28; Felton's Eaton, pp. 320, 321. Mr. Cooper (*Naval Hist.*, ii. p. 81) supposes some marines had been landed from the vessels, forgetting that Gen. Eaton had brought *six* from Egypt.

a steady and spirited opposition to the progress of the assailants. At this moment General Eaton received a ball through his left wrist; but, notwithstanding this, the troops were led forward through a steady fire of musketry, seized the battery, lowered the Tripolitan colors and raised the flag of the United States, and turned the guns of the battery upon the fugitives, who fled with the greatest precipitation.[1]

In the mean time Hamet Bashaw and his troops had gained possession of the town from the rear, and the enemy was thus placed between two fires, although he occupied the houses and continued the defence, with great perseverance, until the guns of the shipping were opened on the town, when he fled with great precipitation.[2] The Bey's palace having been seized by Hamet,[3] the cavalry of the latter was sent out against the fugitives; and, falling on their flanks, handled them severely.[4] The Bey had taken refuge within a mosque, and afterwards, in the most sacred of all sanctuaries, in Mohammedan countries, the harem of one of his chiefs, where he was perfectly secure.[5]

At a little after four o'clock,—two hours and a half after the first attack,—the town was in the possession of General Eaton and Hamet Bashaw—the former occupying the water-battery, the latter the Bey's palace.[6]

[1] Felton's Eaton, p. 321; Cooper, ii. p. 81; Gen. Eaton to Com. Barron, April 29; Capt. Hull to Com. Barron, April 28.—[2] Gen. Eaton to Com. Barron, April 29; Capt. Hull to Com. Barron, April 28.—[3] Felton's Eaton, p. 321.

[4] Gen. Eaton to Com. Barron, April 29.—[5] Felton's Eaton, p. 322.—[6] Gen. Eaton to Com. Barron, April 29.

The inhabitants, rejoicing in the prospect of a relief from the oppression of their rulers, quickly declared their friendship for Hamet.[1]

In this assault the assailants are said to have numbered twelve hundred men, while that of the enemy, who defended the town, were not less than four thousand.[2] The loss of the latter is not known; that of the former was one marine, *killed;* and General Eaton, two marines, and nine Greek Christians, were *wounded*.[3]

Whether we consider the novelty of the enterprise, the hardships which were encountered, or the gallantry displayed in the charge on the garrison, this is one of the most remarkable in which the arms of the United States have been engaged.

The reigning Bashaw's troops attempted to retake the city, at different times, without success;[4] and the tyrant, in his alarm, took advantage of the anxiety for peace which the United States had shown, and hastened to secure it.[5] The city of Derne, and her inhabitants, without stipulation and without mercy, were abandoned to their fate by those whom they had received so cordially; and peace, once more, reigned within the borders of America.[6]

[1] History of War with Tripoli, p. 123.

[2] Cooper, ii. p. 81.

[3] Gen. Eaton to Com. Barron, April 29; Capt. Hull to Com. Barron, April 28.

[4] History of War with Tripoli, pp. 123, 124; Felton's Eaton, pp. 323–326; Clark's Naval History, p. 120.

[5] History of War with Tripoli, pp. 125, 126; Felton's Eaton, p. 327; *Salem* (Mass.) *Register*, Aug. 29, 1805.

[6] Felton's Eaton, pp. 331–334.

DOCUMENT.

GENERAL EATON'S DISPATCH TO COMMODORE BARRON.

DERNE, *April* 29, 1805.

SIR:—Owing to impediments, too tedious to detail, but chiefly to delinquency in our Quartermaster's Department, which I had confided to Richard Farquhar, I did not leave Alexandria till the third of last month. The host of Arabs, who accompanied the Bashaw from that place and joined him on the route, moving chiefly with their families and flocks, rendered our progress through the desert slow and painful. Add to this the ungovernable temper of this marauding militia, and the frequent fits of despondency, amounting sometimes to mutiny, occasioned by information, almost every day meeting us, of formidable reinforcements from the enemy for the defence of this place, and it will not seem unaccountable that it was not until the fifteenth instant we arrived at Bomba.

We had now been twenty-five days without meat, and fifteen without bread, subsisting on rice. Happily, the next morning discovered the *Argus*, to whom I made signals by smoke, which were discovered and answered. The *Hornet* soon afterwards appeared. Captain Hull sent off a boat. I went on board, and had the honor and inexpressible satisfaction of receiving your communications of 22d ult. The timely supplies which came forward in these vessels gave animation to our half-famished people; and no time was lost in moving forward.

On the morning of the twenty-fifth we took post on an eminence in the rear of Derne. Several chiefs came out to meet the Bashaw, with assurances of fealty and attachment. By them I learned that the city was divided into three departments; two of which were in the interest of the Bashaw, and one in opposition. This department, though fewest in numbers, was strongest in position and resources, being defended by a battery of eight guns, by the blind walls of the houses, which are provided in all directions with loopholes for musketry, and by temporary parapets, thrown up in several positions not covered by the battery. This department is the nearest the sea, and the residence of the Bey.

On the morning of the twenty-sixth, terms of amity were offered the Bey, on condition of allegiance and fidelity. The flag of truce was sent back to me with this laconic answer, "My head or yours!" At two P. M. discovered the *Nautilus*, and spoke her at six.

At six in the morning of the twenty-seventh the *Argus* and *Hornet* appeared and stood in. I immediately put the army in motion, and advanced towards the city. A favorable land-breeze enabled the *Nautilus* and *Hornet* to approach the shore, which is a steep and rugged declivity of rocks. With much difficulty we landed, and drew up the precipice one of the field-pieces. Both were sent in the boat for the purpose, but the apprehension of losing this favorable moment of attack induced me to leave one on board. We advanced to our positions. A fire commenced on the shipping. Lieutenant Evans stood in, and anchoring within one hundred yards of the battery, opened a well-directed fire; Lieutenant Dent dropped in and anchored in a position to bring his guns to bear on the battery and city; and Captain-commandant Hull brought the *Argus* to anchor a little south of the *Nautilus*,—so near as to throw her twenty-four pound shot quite into the town.

A detachment of six American marines, a company of twenty-four cannoniers, and another of twenty-six Greeks, including their proper officers, all under the immediate command of Lieutenant O'Bannon, together with a few Arabs on foot, had a position on an eminence opposite to a considerable party of the enemy, who had taken post behind their temporary parapets, and in a ravine at the S. E. quarter of the town. The Bashaw seized an old castle which overlooked the town on the s. s. w., disposing his cavalry upon the plains in the rear.

A little before two p. m. the fire became general in all quarters where Tripolitans and Americans were opposed to each other. In three-quarters of an hour the battery was silenced, but not abandoned; though most of the enemy withdrew precipitately from that quarter and joined the party opposed to the handful of Christians with me, which appeared our most vulnerable point. Unfortunately the fire of our field-piece was relaxed by the rammer being shot away. The fire of the enemy's musketry became too warm, and continually augmenting, our troops were thrown into confusion; and, undisciplined as they were, it was impossible to reduce them to order. I perceived a charge our *dernier* and only resort. We rushed forward against a host of savages, more than ten to our one. They fled from their coverts irregularly, firing in retreat from every palm-tree and partition-wall in their way. At this moment I received a ball through my left wrist which deprived me of the use of the hand, and, of course, of my rifle. Mr. O'Bannon, accompanied by Mr. Mann, of Annapolis, urged forward with his marines, Greeks, and such of the cannoniers as were not necessary to the management of the field-piece; passed through a shower of musketry from the walls of the houses; took possession of the battery; planted the American flag upon its ramparts; and turned its guns upon the enemy, who, being now driven from their outposts, fired only from their houses, from which they were soon dislodged by the whole fire of the vessels, which was suspended during the charge, being directed into them. The Bashaw soon got possession of the Bey's palace; his cavalry flanked the flying enemy; and a little after four o'clock we had complete possession of the town. The action lasted about two hours and a half. The Bey took refuge, first in the mosque, and then in a harem,—the most sacred of sanctuaries among the Turks,—and is still there; but we shall find means to draw him thence. As he is the third man in rank in the kingdom, he may, perhaps, be used in exchange for Captain Bainbridge.

I have fixed my post in the battery; raised parapets and mounted guns towards the country, to be prepared against all events; though I have no serious apprehension of a counter-revolution. The moment of gaining Derne has been peculiarly fortunate, as the camp, which long since left Tripoli for its defence, were within two days' (fourteen hours) march, the day of our attack; of which we had information in the morning, and from which circumstance it was with much difficulty I could prevail on the Bashaw's army to advance to the city, and to obey my dispositions. The camp will probably take up a retrograde march.

Of the few Christians who fought on shore, I lost fourteen killed and wounded; three of whom are marines, one dead and another dying; the rest chiefly Greeks, who in this little affair well supported their ancient character.

It would be going out of my sphere to comment on the conduct of naval commanders in the field; yet I should do violence to my own sense of duty and obligation, were I not to observe they could not have taken better positions for their vessels, nor managed their fire with more skill and advantage.

The detail I have given of Mr. O'Bannon's conduct needs no encomium; and it is believed the disposition our government have always discovered to encourage merit will be extended to this intrepid, judicious, and enterprising officer. Mr. Mann's conduct is equally meritorious. I am bound, also, by a sense of well-merited esteem, to mention to your particular patronage a young English gentleman, Mr. Farquhar, who has volunteered in our expedition through the desert, and has, in all cases of difficulty, exhibited a firmness and attachment well deserving my gratitude. If compatible with our establishments, I request you will insure him a lieutenancy in the marine corps.

I have the honor to be, with great respect and sincere attachment, sir, your very obedient servant, William Eaton.

Samuel Barron, Esq., Commander-in-chief.

CHAPTER XIII.

May 16, 1811.

THE ACTION WITH THE LITTLE BELT.

THE treaty of 1783, although, nominally, recognizing the independence of the confederated States, was, in reality, but little more than an armistice. The armies of the King had lingered within the infant republic,—unwilling to appear, even, to yield possession,[1]—and, on evacuating it, they had left the royal colors flying, to be struck by those who exercised no authority, from the King, to do so.[2] This refusal to surrender the sovereignty, by the formal act of striking the colors,—a part of a carefully-conceived and deliberately-executed plan of operations to retain for His Majesty the legitimate proprietorship of New York and the sovereignty of the country,—had been followed by the occupation of the Western Territory and the instigation of the savages to hostilities;[3] by the assumption of authority over such British-born subjects of the King as might have become citizens of either of the States, or have entered their service;[4] by the denial of the prerogatives of the flag of the Confederacy, in the denial that it protected the property of the persons over which it floated from seizure by the British authorities;[1] by the direct assertion that the King, notwithstanding the treaty, still remained the Sovereign of the country, with his rights, although dormant, still unextinguished;[2] and by other acts of similar character, and tending to a similar end. British cruisers hovered about our coasts and carefully guarded the entrances of our harbors[3]—as carefully, indeed, in some cases, as were the coasts of Great Britain guarded against the operations of the smugglers or the aggressions of her enemies. Our vessels were searched,[4] our seamen seized,[5] our vessels and their cargoes condemned and carried into British ports,[6] our frontiers devastated,[7] and the power and the influence, both of the Confederacy and the people, openly ridiculed and defied. Even the orders of a British vice-admiral had been enforced,[8] at the mouth of her

---

[1] Gen. Washington to Sir Guy Carleton, April 21, May 6, Nov. 6, Nov. 14, Nov. 22, 1783.—[2] Dunlap's New York, ii. pp. 232, 233; A letter from New York, in "*The Pennsylvania Packet,*" No. 1628, Phila., Dec. 2, 1783.

[3] Vide Chap. IV.; Drake's Life of Tecumseh, pp. 113, 121; Dallas' Exposition of Causes and Character of the War, p. 5.—[4] Auchinlech's Hist. of War, p. 8; Manifesto of the President, June 1, 1812.

[1] President's Manifesto, June 1, 1812; Report of Com. on Foreign Relations, June, 1812.—[2] This was done repeatedly in the earlier days of the Republic, as may be seen in the correspondence of Dr. Franklin.—[3] Pres. Madison's Message, Nov. 5, 1811 (Ed. Washington, 1811), p. 5; Dallas' Exposition, p. 25.—[4] Dallas' Exposition, p. 25.

[5] Ibid., pp. 7–14; President's Manifesto, June 1, 1812.

[6] Dallas' Exposition, p. 7.—[7] Vide Chapters I., II., III., and IV. of this Book; Ingersol's War of 1812, i. p. 46.

[8] "The captains and commanders of His Majesty's ships and vessels under my command, are, therefore, *hereby required and directed, in case of meeting with the American frigate,*

cannon, at sea, on one of the largest vessels in the Federal navy, commanded by one of its oldest and most respected officers; his crew mustered, before his own eyes, on his own deck, by a British officer; and a portion—such as the British lieutenant saw fit—removed from the ship and carried to the British ship, which laid not far distant.[1]

The consequences of this series of insults and aggressions may be readily conceived; and the government and the people, alike, had began to manifest great uneasiness and indignation. Negotiations between the diplomatists of the two nations had resulted in nothing but a reiteration of empty professions or of haughty assumptions; and the two nations were rapidly assuming the respective positions, before the world, which they had long occupied in fact—that of open and avowed enemies.

About this time—May, 1811—the United States frigate *President* was at Annapolis,[2] near which place, also, was Commodore John Rogers, one of the most respectable officers of the navy, with his family.[3] On the sixth of that month instructions were issued to that officer, from the Department of the Navy, to get the *President* ready for sea, and to sail as quickly as possible;[4] but the exact object of this order, or the causes which produced it, have not transpired.[1]

Four days from the date of this order, in Washington, the *President* sailed from Annapolis;[2] stopping on her way down the river, to take in a full supply of wads and shot;[3] and getting to sea on the fourteenth of May.[4] After cruising, off the Capes, until about noon of the sixteenth,[5] during which time Commodore Rogers supplied the wants of two vessels which were in distress,[6] at that time, Cape Henry bearing southwest, fourteen or fifteen leagues distant,[7] a sail was discovered from the mast-head, in the east, standing towards the *President* under a heavy press of sail.[8] Within an hour she was seen, from the decks, to be a man-of-war;[9] and, at that time, she displayed her signals.[10] At a quarter before two the *President* displayed her ensign and pendant;[11] when, finding her signals were not answered, but without showing her own

the Chesapeake, at sea, and without the limits of the United States, *to show to the captain of her this order, and to require to search his ship for the deserters from the before-mentioned ships, and to proceed and search for the same.*"—(*Orders by Admiral Berkeley, June* 1, 1807.)

[1] Mem. of Capt. Humphreys (*Naval Chronicle for* 1812, xxviii. p. 356); Com. Barron to Sec. of Navy, June 23, 1807.—[2] Com. Rogers to Sec. of Navy, May 23, 1811; Affidavit of Wm. Burket, Halifax, N. S., June 22, 1811.

[3] Affidavit of Wm. Burket.—[4] Com. Rogers to Sec. of Navy, May 23; Affidavit of Wm. Burket.

[1] The organs of the government did not inform the public what was the object of the cruise.

[2] Com. Rogers to Secretary of Navy, May 23.

[3] Affidavit of Wm. Burket, at Halifax.

[4] Com. Rogers to Secretary of Navy, May 23.

[5] Ibid.—[6] Ibid.—[7] Ibid.; Testimony of Capt. Ludlow before the Court of Inquiry, at N. Y., Aug. 31.

[8] Com. Rogers to Sec. of Navy, May 23.—[9] Testimony of Capt. Ludlow and Lieut. Creighton.—[10] Capt. Bingham to Adm'l Sawyer, May 21, 1811; Com. Rogers to Sec. of Navy, May 23; Testimony of Capt. Ludlow.

[11] Com. Rogers to Sec. of Navy, May 23; Testimony of Capt. Ludlow, Lieut. Creighton, and Lieut. Perry. Capt. Bingham (*Letter to Adm'l Sawyer, May* 21) says, that he "considered the *President* was an American frigate, *as she had a commodore's blue pendant flying at the main,*" *before* the *Little Belt* wore. This admission by the *Belt's* Captain is sustained by the testimony of her First Lieutenant (Moberly), Lieut. Lovell, Purser Hinshelwood, and Surgeon Turner, all of the *Little Belt*, before the Court of Inquiry at Halifax.

colors,[1] the stranger wore, set her studding and upper stay sails, and stood to the southward.[2]

At this time the ships were six miles apart, and the curiosity of Commodore Rogers—or, possibly, his orders from the Department—induced him to make chase, for the purpose of speaking the stranger, and of ascertaining who and what she was.[3] The *President*, therefore, edged away for her, but without making any more sail, until about half-past three, when she had so far gained on the stranger that the upper part of the latter began to show itself, above the horizon, from the deck of the

[1] "She appeared studiously to decline showing her colors."—(*Com. Rogers to Sec. of Navy, May* 23.) "At half-past seven P. M., *for the first time*, I saw colors flying on board the *Little Belt;* but I could not tell to what nation she belonged."—(*Testimony of Capt. Ludlow before the Court of Inquiry.*) "I did not observe any colors flying on the *Little Belt at any time during the chase.*"—(*Test. of Lieut. Creighton.*) This unequivocal testimony, on the principal point in dispute, is singularly sustained by that of the officers of the *Little Belt*. Capt. Bingham (*Letter to Adm'l Sawyer, May* 21, 1811), after saying, "he hoisted the colors," before wearing, and making off, says, "at half-past six o'clock—I imagined the most prudent method was to bring to, *and hoist the colors*, that no mistake might arise,"—which would not have been necessary had the colors been hoisted *at one o'clock*, as he had stated just before. Lieut. Lovell (*Test. before the Court of Inquiry at Halifax*) commits the same singular blunder of self-condemnation. Boatswain Franklin (*Test. before the same Court*) says, "About half-past seven, shortened sail and brought to; *hoisted the colors*," &c., without alluding to any display before that time; in which Purser Hinshelwood (*Test. before the same body*) fully sustains him. First-Lieut. Moberly (*Test.*, &c.) says the *Little Belt* "showed her colors" at half-past two P. M., and that when she hove to, at seven P. M., her colors were "*up*," in which he contradicts the testimony of his associates, and the official statement of his commandant.

[2] Test. of Lieut. Moberly, of the *Little Belt*, before the Court at Halifax, N. S.; Test. of Lieut. Lovell, at the same place; Capt. Bingham to Adm'l Sawyer, May 21; Test. of Capt. Ludlow, at N. Y.; Com. Rogers to Sec. of Navy, May 23.—[3] Com. Rogers to Sec. of Navy, May 23; Test. of Capt. Ludlow, at N. Y.; Capt. Bingham to Adm'l Sawyer, May 21; Test. of Lieut. Moberly, at Halifax.

VOL. II.—9

former;[1] but the wind, at that time, began, and continued, gradually, to decrease, preventing the *President* from approaching near enough, before sunset, to discover her force or, in the absence of her colors, even the nation to which she belonged,[2] notwithstanding the former also had hoisted her studding-sails, royals, and stay-sails.[3]

About a quarter-past seven, the *President* having come within gunshot of the stranger,[4]—who could clearly discern the stars in the Commodore's pendant,[5]—the latter "imagined the more prudent method was to bring to, *and hoist the colors*, that no mistake might arise, and that he (*Commodore Rogers*) might see what we (*the stranger*) were."[6] Accordingly she took in her studding-sails, hauled up her courses, hauled by the wind on the starboard-tack, and hoisted an ensign at the mizzen-peak,[7] but it was then too dark for the Commodore to distinguish what nation it represented.[8] Soon afterwards the extra canvas of the *President* was, also, taken in, and her foresail was hauled up;[9] while the ship slowly ran down for the stranger's weather-quarter, in

[1] Com. Rogers to Sec. of Navy, May 23.—[2] Ibid.; Test. of Capt. Ludlow, at N. Y.—[3] Test. of Capt. Ludlow, at N. Y.; Affidavit of Wm. Burket; Test. of Lieut. Moberly, Boatswain Franklin, and Surgeon Turner, at Halifax, N. S.—[4] Com. Rogers to Sec. of Navy, May 23; Test. of Capt. Ludlow, at N. Y.; Capt. Bingham (*Letter to Adm'l Sawyer, May* 21) says it was "*at half-past six;*" while Lieut. Moberly (*Test. at Halifax*) says it was "*at seven.*"

[5] "Clearly discerning the stars in his broad pendant."—(*Capt. Bingham to Adm'l Sawyer, May* 21.)—[6] Ibid. See also the Test. of Lieut. Moberly, at Halifax.—[7] Test. of Capt. Ludlow, in N. Y.; Com. Rogers to Sec. of Navy, May 23; Lieut. Lovell's Test., at Halifax.—[8] Com. Rogers to Sec. of Navy, May 23; Test. of Capt. Ludlow, at N. Y.; Affidavit of Wm. Burket, at Halifax, N. S.

[9] Testimony of Capt. Ludlow, at New York.

order to speak her.[1] This movement, however, appeared to annoy the stranger;[2] and she endeavored to prevent it by wearing three times,[3] but, by hauling by the wind, on different tacks, Captain Ludlow carried the *President* to the position which the Commodore had ordered to be taken,[4] and, at about half-past eight, rounded her to, on the stranger's weather-beam, within speaking-distance.[5]

At this time the ships were from seventy to one hundred yards distant;[6] the wind was very light;[7] and the darkness of the evening was not relieved by the light of the moon. The stranger, from having seen the stars in the Commodore's pendant,[8] and from other circumstances, *knew* the ship which was chasing her was an American, and supposed she was the frigate "*United States*."[9] She had also, during the afternoon, double-shotted her guns,[10] and "made every preparation, in case of a surprise"[11]—all of which indicated that her commander was not without expectations of an engagement, although *he* was not disposed to seek it, *when the force of his opponent had been ascertained.* On the other hand, Commodore Rogers and his officers had witnessed the sudden change in the course of the stranger, when her signals were not answered; and, from what appeared to have been the studied attempt, of her commander, to conceal her colors,[1] added to this sudden movement, they were entirely ignorant both of her nationality and her purposes.

Such were the peculiar circumstances which existed when, at about half-past eight, the *President* rounded to, under the stranger's weather-beam,[2] and the Commodore hailed, saying, "What ship is that?"[3] To this the answer was given—"What ship is that?"[4] although it appears that this answer was not heard by several who stood near the Commodore;[5] and, within a few moments, he repeated his former question —"What ship is that?"[6] which was answered with a shot,[7] which cut off one

---

[1] Test. of Capt. Ludlow, at N. Y.; Com. Rogers to Sec. of Navy, May 23; Test. of Lieut. Moberly, at Halifax.

[2] Com. Rogers to Sec. of Navy, May 23; Capt. Bingham to Adm'l Sawyer, May 21.—[3] Capt. Bingham to Adm'l Sawyer, May 21; Test. of Lieut. Moberly, at Halifax; Test. of Capt. Ludlow, at N. Y.—[4] Com. Rogers to Sec. of Navy, May 23; Test. of Capt. Ludlow, at N. Y.

[5] Test. of Capt. Ludlow, at N. Y.—[6] Com. Rogers to Sec. of Navy, May 23.—[7] Studding-sails had been used until within a few minutes.—[8] Capt. Bingham to Adm'l Sawyer, May 21; Test. of Lieut. Moberly, at Halifax, N. S.

[9] Testimony of Lieut. Moberly, at Halifax, N. S.

[10] Capt. Bingham to Adm'l Sawyer, May 21; Test. of Lieutenants Moberly and Lovell, at Halifax, N. S.

[11] Capt. Bingham to Adm'l Sawyer, May 21.

---

[1] Com. Rogers to Sec. of Navy, May 23.—[2] Test. of Capt. Ludlow, at N. Y.—[3] Com. Rogers to Sec. of Navy, May 23; Test. of Capt. Ludlow, Lieut. Creighton, Capt. Caldwell, Lieut. Perry, Lieut. Madison, Sailing-master Mull, Midshipman Jos. Smith, Chaplain Denison, Boatswain Roberts, Midshipmen Carson, Matthew C. Perry, Silas Duncan, and J. H. Clack, Lieuts. Gamble, Dallas, and Funk, at N.Y.; Affidavit of Wm. Burket, at Halifax, N. S.

[4] Com. Rogers to Sec. of Navy, May 23; Test. of Lieuts. Creighton, Gamble, and A. J. Dallas, Chaplain Denison, Midshipmen Carson, M. C. Perry, Silas Duncan, and J. H. Clack, at N. Y.—[5] Test. of Capt. Ludlow, Lieuts. H. J. Perry, L. B. Madison, Midshipman Smith, at New York.

[6] Com. Rogers to Sec. of Navy, May 23; Test. of Capt. Ludlow, Lieuts. Creighton, J. H. Perry, Madison, Gamble, Dallas, and Funk, Sailing-master Mull, Midshipmen Smith, Carson, M. C. Perry, Duncan, and Clack, Chaplain Denison and Boatswain Roberts, at N. Y.; Affidavit of Wm. Burket.—[7] Com. Rogers to Sec. of Navy, May 23; Test. of Capt. Ludlow, Lieuts. Creighton, H. J. Perry, Madison, Gamble, Dallas, and Funk, Capt. Caldwell, Sailing-master Mull, Midshipmen Smith, Carson, M. C. Perry, and Shubrick, and Carpenter Barns, at N. Y. This important fact was also substantiated by the testimony of the commander of each gun on the *President*, each of whom, as well as each of the officers, fully and unequivocally denied having fired a gun, until after the *Little Belt* had fired.

of the *President's* main-topmast breast-backstays, and lodged in her mainmast.[1] A single gun, from the *President's* gun-deck, responded to the stranger's fire,[2]—without the Commodore's order, but not contrary to his desire,[3]—which was, in turn, answered by three others from the stranger,[4] and, soon afterwards, by her musketry and broadside.[5]

Satisfied that the stranger's fire was intentional, and designed as an insult to the American flag,[6] the Commodore gave a general order to fire on her,[7] which was obeyed promptly and with great spirit.[8] Within five or six minutes afterwards the stranger suspended her fire;[9] when Commodore Rogers—believing her to be weaker than he had supposed, or that some unusually severe accident had befallen her[1]—gave orders to suspend the fire of the *President*, for the purpose of preventing any unnecessary sacrifice of life.[2] A few minutes afterwards, however, the stranger renewed her fire; and the Commodore was compelled, contrary to his wishes, to give orders for a renewal of the *President's* fire.[3] For about five minutes this cannonade continued, when, a second time, the stranger suspended her fire, and the fire of the *President* was also discontinued.[4]

After waiting a few seconds, to ascertain if the stranger was disposed to renew the action, and after satisfying himself that the damage which the former had received would probably induce him to keep silent, the Commodore hailed her again, "and learned, *for the first time*, that it was a ship of His Britannic Majesty," although, even at that time, he could not distinguish her name.[5] After having informed the stranger what vessel it was which she had attacked, the Commodore gave orders to wear, run under the stran-

[1] Com. Rogers to Sec. of Navy, May 23.—[2] Ibid.; Test. of Capt. Ludlow, Lieuts. Madison, Dallas, and Funk, Sailing-master Mull, Midshipmen Smith, Carson, M. C. Perry, and Clack. This gun was fired by Lieut. Alex. J. Dallas (since Com. Dallas), without orders from the Commodore.—[3] "At this instant, Capt. Caldwell, of the marines, who was standing very near me on the gangway, having observed, 'Sir, she has fired at us,' caused me to pause for a moment, *just as I was in the act of giving an order to fire a shot in return; and before I had time to resume the repetition of the intended order, a shot was actually fired from the second division of this ship.*"—(*Com. Rogers to Sec. of Navy, May* 23.) "As soon as I perceived the flash, and heard the reports from the *Little Belt*, I got in from the port, *and fired a gun from the second division, which I then commanded.*"—(*Test. of Lieut. A. J. Dallas, before the Court of Inquiry, in N. Y., Sept.* 7, 1811.—[4] Com. Rogers to Sec. of Navy, May 23; Test. of Capt. Ludlow, Capt. Caldwell, Lieut. Madison, and Midshipman Smith, at N. Y.—[5] Com. Rogers to Sec. of Navy, May 23, and the general testimony before both the Court at N. Y. and that at Halifax, N. S.—[6] Com. Rogers to Sec. of Navy, May 23.—[7] Ibid.; The testimony before the Court at N. Y.; Affidavit of Wm. Burket, at Halifax.

[8] Affidavit of Wm. Burket, at Halifax, N. S.; Test. of Surgeon Turner of *Little Belt*.

[9] On no portion of this complicated subject has there been more dispute than the *duration of the action*. Com. Rogers (*Letter to Sec. of Navy, May* 23) says, that after firing "*from four to six minutes*, as near as he could judge," he suspended the fire; that, "*in less than four minutes*," it was resumed; and that it "continued *from three to five minutes longer*"—making the entire duration from *eleven to fifteen minutes*. In this he is sustained by the sworn testimony of his officers, before the Court of Inquiry at N. Y. On the other hand, Capt. Bingham (*Letter to Adm'l Sawyer, May* 21) says, "The action became general, and continued so for *three-quarters of an hour*." Lieut. Moberly, of the *Little Belt* (*Test. before the Court of Inquiry, at Halifax*), says, "We continued firing *about an hour*;" in which Lieut. Lovell, Boatswain Franklin, and Purser Hinshelwood, concur. Surgeon Turner concurs with his captain in saying it lasted "forty-five minutes."

[1] Com. Rogers to Sec. of Navy, May 23; Test. of Capt. Ludlow, at N. Y.—[2] Com. Rogers to Sec. of Navy, May 23; Test of Capt. Ludlow, Lieut. Creighton, Capt. Caldwell, Lieuts. Perry, Madison, and Sailing-master Mull, in N. Y. See also note 9.—[3] Ibid.—[4] Ibid.

[5] Com. Rogers to Sec. of Navy, May 23; Test. of Capt. Ludlow, at N. Y.; Capt. Bingham to Adm'l Sawyer, May 21.

ger's lee, haul by the wind on the starboard-tack, and heave to under topsails, for the purpose of repairing the little injury which the *President* had received, and of rendering such assistance to the stranger as might be necessary.[1]

After lying to, on different tacks, with lights displayed, during the night, at daylight, on the seventeenth, the *President* was several miles to windward of the stranger, and orders were given to bear up and run down to her, under easy sail, for the purpose of sending a boat on board.[2] After hailing her, Lieutenant Creighton was sent with a boat "to ascertain the name of the ship and her commander; to express the Commodore's deep regret at what had taken place; to say he regretted the stranger had fired first; and that had he known her force he would even received a shot without returning it."[3] He also offered any assistance she stood in need of, and submitted to the commander that he had better put into one of the ports of the United States, for repairs, which was declined.[4] It then appeared that the stranger was the British sloop-of-war *Little Belt*, of eighteen guns, and commanded by Captain Arthur Batt Bingham; that the ship had suffered very severely from the *President's* fire; and that between twenty and thirty of her crew had been killed or wounded. Her captain declined receiving any assistance, and made sail for Halifax;[1] while the *President* bore away for New York.[2]

The *President* was one of the largest of the American frigates, rating forty-four guns, but mounting a greater number, and carrying a crew nearly double that of the *Little Belt*. Her main and mizzen masts suffered some injury from the fire of the *Little Belt*;[3] one of her fore-shrouds was cut off, and her running-rigging suffered slightly.[4] None of her crew was killed; and but one—a boy—was wounded.[5]

The *Little Belt* was a sloop-of-war, of eighteen guns, mounting thirty-two carronades,[6] and was one of the finest of her class in the navy. She was "almost a wreck"—her hull suffering very severely, besides having her bowsprit, foremast, mainmast, and mizzen-mast shot through; main-top, fore-top, fore-topgallant, and mizzen-topgallant masts shattered; main-topsail-yard, fore-topsail-yard, foreyard, the jolly-boat, and launch destroyed, and other of her spars very much injured.[7] One of her midshipmen and twelve of her crew were killed, and nineteen were wounded.[8]

The great disparity of force between the *President* and the *Little Belt* has never been questioned; and, in consequence, this engagement has called

[1] Com. Rogers to Secretary of Navy, May 23.

[2] Ibid.; Testimony of Capt. Ludlow, at New York; Capt. Bingham to Adm'l Sawyer, May 21.

[3] Com. Rogers to Secretary of Navy, May 23; Testimony of Lieut. Creighton, at New York, Sept. 2, 1811.

[4] Capt. Bingham to Adm'l Sawyer, May 21.

[1] Com. Rogers to Sec. of Navy, May 23.—[2] Affidavit of Wm. Burket, at Halifax.—[3] Com. Rogers to Sec. of Navy, May 23; Affidavit of Wm. Burket, at Halifax.

[4] Test. of Capt. Ludlow.—[5] Com. Rogers to Sec. of Navy, May 23.—[6] Letter from Naval Hospital, Halifax, May 29," in *Naval Chronicle*, xxvi. p. 37.

[7] Report of the state and condition of H. M. sloop *Little Belt*, signed, "Wm. Hughes, Master-shipwright, and J. Parryie, Foreman do., Halifax-yard, May 28, 1811."

[8] Return of officers, &c., killed and wounded, signed, "A. B. Bingham, Captain, and Wm. Turner, Surgeon."

forth none of the commendations which the commanders of other, and more equally matched vessels, have received. As the first action between the naval powers of Great Britain and the United States, however; as an instance of the summary punishment inflicted on a haughty and supercilious opponent; as productive of some of the most notable specimens of self-gratulation; and as an important element in the existing dispute with Great Britain, "the affair with the *Little Belt*" holds a prominent place in the annals of the United States. The partisans of that day—like the same class at the present day—condemned or approved the conduct of Commodore Rogers, according to the instructions of their leaders and the operations of their parties. The Republicans, of course, approved the action and lauded the Commodore, as a faithful defender of the honor of the flag; and the official organ of the government congratulated itself "that Commodore Rogers' conduct had been generally approved of by all parties;"[1] while the Federalists, of course, condemned both, and published elaborate articles[2]—which were reproduced in England[3]—to show that it was the duty of Commodore Rogers to answer the stranger's hail before receiving an answer to his own; that he was under "higher obligations than 'common politeness,' which should have disposed him to satisfy the ship he had chased, as soon as possible, that *he* was *a friend*."

In Great Britain and her colonies a violent storm of abuse was immediately let loose,[4] while the vanity of the people was flattered with the reports that the action was sustained a full hour, and that the colors—which were shot away—had not been struck to the American frigate.[5] Songs were sung in honor of the event, and in ridicule of Commodore Rogers;[6] and it became one of the events which was destined to be considered an epoch in the history of the world.

DOCUMENTS.

I.

COMMODORE ROGERS' DISPATCH TO SECRETARY OF NAVY.

U. S. FRIGATE PRESIDENT, OFF SANDY HOOK, *May* 23, 1811.

SIR:—I regret extremely being under the necessity of representing to you an event that occurred on the night of the 16th inst., between the ship under my command and His Britannic Majesty's ship of war the *Little Belt*, commanded by Captain Bingham; the result of which has given me much pain, as well on account of the injury she sustained, as that I should have been compelled to the measure that produced it, by a vessel of her inferior force. The circumstances are as follows: On the 16th instant, at twenty-five minutes past meridian, in seventeen-fathom water, Cape Henry bearing S. W.,

---

[1] National Intelligencer, Washington, D. C., June 1, 1811.

[2] N. Y. Evening Post, May 25, 1811; Boston Repertory, July 8, 1811.—[3] Naval Chronicle, xxvi. (London, 1811) pp. 33, 197, 198.—[4] Ibid., xxvii. (London, 1812) pp. 63, 64.—[5] Ibid., xxvi. (London, 1811) p. 35; Quebec Mercury, June 17, 1811.—[6] "Rogers and the *Little Belt*," in *Naval Chronicle*, xxvii. p. 151.

distant fourteen or fifteen leagues, a sail was discovered from our mast-head, in the east. standing towards us under a press of sail. At half-past one the symmetry of her upper sails (which were at this time distinguishable from our deck), and her making signals, showed her to be a man-of-war. At forty-five minutes past one P. M., hoisted our ensign and pendant; when, finding her signals not answered, she wore and stood to the southward. Being desirous of speaking her, and of ascertaining what she was, I now made sail in chase; and by half-past three P. M., found we were coming up with her, as by this time the upper part of her stern began to show itself above the horizon. The wind now began, and continued gradually to decrease, so as to prevent my being able to approach her sufficiently before sunset to discover her actual force (which the position she preserved during the chase was calculated to conceal), or to judge even to what nation she belonged, as she appeared studiously to decline showing her colors. At fifteen or twenty minutes past seven P. M., the chase took in her studding-sails, and soon after hauled up her courses, and hauled by the wind on the starboard-tack; she at the same time hoisted an ensign or flag at her mizzen-peak, but it was too dark for me to discover what nation it represented; now, for the first time, her broadside was presented to our view, but night had so far progressed, that although her appearance indicated she was a frigate, I was unable to determine her actual force.

At fifteen minutes before eight P. M., being about a mile and a half from her, the wind at the time very light, I directed Captain Ludlow to take a position to windward of her and on the same tack, within short speaking distance. This, however, the commander of the chase appeared, from his manœuvres, to be anxious to prevent, as he wore and hauled by the wind on different tacks four times, successively, between this period and the time of our arriving at the position which I had ordered to be taken. At fifteen or twenty minutes past eight, being a little forward of her weather-beam, and distant from seventy to a hundred yards, hailed, "What ship is that?" to this inquiry no answer was given, but I was hailed by her commander, and asked, "What ship is that?" Having asked the first question, I, of course, considered myself entitled, by the common rules of politeness, to the first answer. After a pause of fifteen or twenty seconds, I reiterated my first inquiry, of "What ship is that?" and before I had time to take the trumpet from my mouth, was answered by a shot, that cut off one of our main-top backstays and went into our mainmast. At this instant Captain Caldwell (of marines), who was standing very near me on the gangway, having observed, "Sir, she has fired at us," caused me to pause for a moment, just as I was in the act of giving an order to fire a shot in return; and before I had time to resume the repetition of the intended order, a shot was actually fired from the second division of this ship, and was scarcely out of the gun before it was answered from our assumed enemy by three others, in quick succession, and soon after the rest of his broadside and musketry. When the first shot was fired, being under an impression that it might possibly have proceeded from accident, and without the orders of the commander, I had determined at the moment to fire only a single shot in return; but the immediate repetition of the previous unprovoked outrage, induced me to believe that the insult was premeditated, and that from our adversary being, at that time, as ignorant of our real force as I was of his, he thought this, perhaps, a favorable opportunity of acquiring promotion, although at the expense of violating our neutrality, and insulting our flag. I accordingly, with that degree of repugnance incident to feeling equally determined neither to be the aggressor, or suffer the flag of my country to be insulted with impunity, gave a general order to fire; the effect of which, in from four to six minutes, as near as I can judge, having produced a partial silence of his guns, I gave orders to cease firing, discovering, by the feeble opposition, that it must be a ship of very inferior force to what I had supposed, or that some untoward accident had happened to her.

My orders in this instance, however (although they proceeded alone from motives of humanity, and a determination not to spill a drop of blood unnecessarily), I had, in less than four minutes, some reason to regret, as he renewed his fire, of which two thirty-two pound shot cut off one of our fore-shrouds and injured our foremast. It was now that I found myself under the painful necessity of giving orders for a repetition of our fire against a force which my forbearance alone had enabled to do us any injury of moment. Our fire was accordingly renewed, and continued from three to five minutes longer, when, perceiving our opponent's gaff and colors down, his maintop-sail yard upon the cap, and his fire silenced, although it was so dark that I could not discern any other particular injury we had done, or how far he was in a situation to do us farther harm, I nevertheless embraced the earliest moment to stop our fire and prevent the farther effusion of blood. Here a pause of half a minute or more took place, at the end of which, our adversary not showing a farther disposition to fire, I hailed again and asked, "What ship is that?" I learned, for the first time, that it was a ship of His Britannic Majesty; but, owing to its blowing rather fresher than it had done, I was unable to learn her name.

After having informed her commander of the name of this ship, I gave orders to wear, run under his lee, and haul by the wind on the starboard-tack, and heave to under topsails, and repair what little injury we had sustained in our rigging, which was accordingly executed; and we continued lying to, on different tacks, with a number of lights displayed, in order that our adversary might the better discern our position, and command our assistance, in case he found it necessary during the night. At daybreak on the 17th, she was discovered several miles to leeward, when I gave orders to bear up and run down to him under easy sail; after hailing him, I sent a boat on board with Lieutenant Creighton, to learn the names of the ship and her commander, with directions to ascertain the damage she had sustained, and to inform her commander how much I regretted the necessity on my part which had led to such an unhappy result; at the same time to offer all the assistance that the ship under my command afforded, in repairing the damages his had sustained. At nine A. M., Lieutenant Creighton returned, with information that it was His Britannic Majesty's ship *Little Belt*, Captain Bingham; who in a polite manner declined the acceptance of any assistance, saying, at the same time, that he had on board all the necessary requisites to repair the damages sufficiently to enable him to return to Halifax.

This, however, was not the most unpleasant part of Captain Bingham's communication to Lieutenant Creighton, as he informed him, that in addition to the injury his ship had sustained, between twenty and thirty of his crew had been killed and wounded.

The regret that this information caused me was much, you may be sure, as a man might expect to feel, whose greatest pride is to prove, without ostentation, by every public as well as private act, that he possesses a humane and generous heart; and with these sentiments, believe me, sir, that such a communication would cause me the most acute pain during the remainder of my life, had I not the consolation to know that there was no alternative left me between such a sacrifice and one which would have been still greater, namely, to have remained a passive spectator of insult to the flag of my country, while it was confided to my protection—and I would have you to be convinced, sir, that however much, individually, I may previously have had reason to feel incensed at the repeated outrages committed on our flag by British ships of war, neither my passions nor prejudices had any agency in this affair.

To my country, I am well convinced of the importance of the transaction which has imposed upon me the necessity of making you this communication; I must, therefore, from motives of delicacy, connected with personal considerations, solicit that you will be pleased to request the President to authorize a formal inquiry to be instituted into all the circumstances, as well as into every part of my conduct connected with the same.

The injury sustained by the ship under my command is very trifling, except to the fore and main masts, which I before mentioned. No person killed, and but one (a boy) wounded.

For farther particulars I refer you to Captain Caldwell, who is charged with the delivery of this communication.

I have the honor to be, with great respect, sir, your obedient servant,

John Rogers.

Hon. Paul Hamilton, Secretary of Navy.

II.

CAPTAIN BINGHAM'S DISPATCH TO ADMIRAL SAWYER.

His Majesty's Sloop Little Belt, *May* 21, 1811,
Lat. 36° 53′ N., Lon. 71° 49′ W., Cape
Charles bearing W. 48 Miles.

Sir:—I beg leave to acquaint you, that in pursuance of your orders to join His Majesty's ship *Guerriere*, and being on my return from the northward, not having fallen in with her—that about eleven A. M., May 16th, saw a strange sail, to which I immediately gave chase. At one P. M., discovered her to be a man-of-war, apparently a frigate, standing to the eastward, who when he made us out edged away for us, and set his royals. Made the signal 275, and finding it not answered, concluded she was an American frigate, as she had a commodore's blue pendant flying at the main. Hoisted the colors and made all sail south, the course I intended steering round Cape Hatteras; the stranger edging away, but not making any more sail. At half-past three he made sail in chase, when I made a private signal, which was not answered. At half-past six, finding he gained so considerably on us as not to be able to elude him during the night, being within gunshot, and clearly discerning the stars in his broad pendant, I imagined the most prudent method was to bring to, and hoist the colors, that no mistake might arise, and that he might see what we were. The ship was therefore brought to, her colors hoisted, her guns double-shotted, and every preparation made in case of a surprise. By his manner of steering down, he evidently wished to lay his ship in a position for raking, which I frustrated by wearing three times. At a quarter-past eight he came within hail. I hailed, and asked what ship it was? He again repeated my words, and fired a broadside, which I instantly returned. The action then became general, and continued so for three-quarters of an hour, when he ceased firing, and appeared to be on fire about the main hatchway. He then filled. I was obliged to desist from firing, as, the ship falling off, no gun would bear, and had no after-sail to keep her to. All the rigging and sails cut to pieces; not a brace nor a bowline left. He hailed, and asked what ship this was? I told him. He then asked me if I had struck my colors? My answer, no, and asked what ship it was? As plain as I could understand (he having shot some distance at this time) he answered, the *United States* frigate. He fired no more guns, but stood from us, giving no reason for his most extraordinary conduct.

At daylight in the morning saw a ship to windward, when having made out well what we were, bore up and passed within hail, fully prepared for action. About eight o'clock he hailed, and said if I pleased he would send a boat on board. I replied in the affirmative, and a boat accordingly came, with an officer and a message from Commodore Rogers of the *President*, of the United States, to say that he lamented much the unfortunate affair (as he termed it) that had happened, and that had he known our force was so much inferior he would not have fired at me. I asked his motives for firing at all? His reply was, that "we fired the first gun at him," which was positively not the case. I cautioned both the officers and men to be particularly careful and not suffer more than one man to be at a gun. Nor is it probable that a sloop-of-war, within pistol-shot of a large forty-four gun frigate, should commence hostilities. He offered me every assistance I stood in need of, and submitted to me that I had better put in to some port of the United States, which I immediately declined.

By the manner in which he apologized, it appeared evident to me that had he fallen in with a British frigate he would certainly have brought her to action. And what farther confirms me in that opinion is, that his guns were not only loaded with round and grape shot, but with every scrap of iron that could be collected.

I have to lament the loss of thirty-two men, killed and wounded, among whom is the master.

His Majesty's ship is much damaged in her masts, sails, rigging, and hull; and as there are many shot through between wind and water, and many shot still remain inside, and upper works all shot away, starboard pump also, I have thought it proper to proceed to Halifax, which will, I hope, meet with your approbation.

I cannot speak in too high terms of the officers and men I have the honor to command, for their steady and active conduct throughout the whole of this business, who had much to do, as a gale of wind came on the second night after the action. I have to request, sir, that you will be pleased to recommend to the notice of my Lords Commissioners of the Admiralty, my first-lieutenant, Mr. John Moberly, who is, in every respect, a most excellent officer, and afforded me very great assistance in stopping the leaks; himself, in the gale, securing the masts, and doing every thing in his power. It would be the greatest injustice, was I not also to speak most highly of Lieutenant Lovell, second-lieutenant, of Mr. M'Queen, master, who, as I have before stated, was wounded in the right arm, in nearly the middle of the action, and Mr. Wilson, master's-mate; indeed, the conduct of every officer and man was so good that it is impossible for me to discriminate.

I beg leave to inclose a list of thirty-two men killed and wounded, most of them mortally. I fear.

I hope, sir, in this affair I shall appear to have done my duty, and conducted myself as I ought to have done against so superior a force, and that the honor of the British colors was well supported.

I have the honor to be, &c.,
A. B. BINGHAM, *Capt.*

To HERBERT SAWYER, Esq.,
Rear-admiral of the Red.

CHAPTER XIV.

November 7, 1811.

THE BATTLE OF TIPPECANOE.

ONE of the most able of the many talented men who have appeared, from time to time, among the American Indians, was *Tecumthà* (*The Shooting Star*), a Shawanoe. His parents were both members of that tribe, and Tecumthà—their fourth child—was born on the bank of the Mad River, a few miles below Springfield, within the present limits of Clark County, Ohio.[1] He was engaged in the earlier wars between the Western Indians and the United States;[2] was present at the attack on Fort Recovery, in 1794,[3] and at the battle on the Miamis, in August of the same year;[4] declined attending the Council at Greenville, at which a general peace was agreed upon;[1] and gradually raised a party, of which he was the head, whose fundamental principle appears to have been to restore the Indians to their position as the sovereigns of the West.[2] He appears, however, to have lived in peace with the settlers, and to have secured their confidence to a remarkable degree.[3]

Soon afterwards a younger brother of Tecumthà—Laulewasikaw—assumed the office of *a Prophet*;[4] assembled large bodies of the Western Indians, of various tribes;[5] and gradually secured their adherence to the religious imposition of which he became the head and

[1] Drake's Life of Tecumseh (*Ed.* 1841), p. 66. Mr. Hinde (*Am. Pioneer*, i. p. 328) says he was born "near Xenia, on Mr. Saxon's lot, near a spring."—[2] Drake's Tecumseh, pp. 68–78; Perkins' History of Late War, p. 57.

[3] Drake's Tecumseh, p. 79.—[4] Ibid., p. 81.

[1] Drake's Tecumseh, p. 83.—[2] Ibid., pp. 83, 84; S. G. Drake's Biog. of Indians (*Ed.* 1832), pp. 329–331, 336; McAfee's War in Western Country, p. 9.

[3] Drake's Tecumseh, pp. 84, 85.

[4] McAfee, p. 10.—[5] Ibid.

leader.[1] He declaimed against witchcraft, and, like the pilgrims of Massachusetts, he condemned the witches. He denounced "fire-water," and, with remarkable success, he inculcated the practice of "total abstinence," threatening on those who disobeyed his injunction the severest punishment in a future state. He attributed the unhappiness of the Indians, in a great measure, to their intermarriages with the whites; declaimed against all innovations in the original dress and habits of the people; claimed for the Shawanoes a superiority over other tribes; insisted on a community of property; and proclaimed his power, received from "the Great Spirit," to cure all diseases, to confound his enemies, and to stay the arm of death, of sickness, or of the enemy in the field of battle.[2]

Tecumthà, taking advantage of this crusade, and of the radical sentiments which his brother inculcated, again commenced to agitate his peculiar sentiments on the sovereignty of the Indians; and considerable apprehension was entertained for the safety of the frontiers.[3] The provisions of the Treaty of Greenville, by which the lands, on which Tecumthà and his followers were, were ceded to the United States, were repudiated; the ownership of the lands claimed for the great body of the tribes instead of any one who might occupy them; and a general association of the Western and Southwestern tribes, for purposes of defence and mutual protection, was openly proclained and enforced.[1] Hostility to the United States was steadily disavowed[2] (notwithstanding it was known that the agents of the British government were active in keeping up the excitement),[3] and council after council had been held, with the hope of conciliating the Indians, without success.[4]

During this time the government of the Northwestern Territory had been vested in William H. Harrison, and the good judgment and great experience of that eminent man, found ample opportunity for exercise in guarding against the dangers which appeared to be gathering around that part of the country. While it is evident that he anticipated no hostile movement among the Indians, he carefully watched the progress of events, and was not inattentive to a provision of proper means of defence.

In the spring of 1808, Tecumthà and his brother removed to a tract of land on Tippecanoe, one of the tributaries of the Wabash;[5] and, much to the discontent of the Miamis and Delawares, a motley crowd of fanatics, from all the Western tribes, were brought thither through the influence of the Prophet.[6] While there was entertained among them a general love of their own people, rather than the whites—a love of country which is commendable, under all circumstances—there is no evidence that any other motive actuated this assemblage than a religious delusion,

[1] Perkins' Annals of the West (*Second Ed.*), p. 570.

[2] Drake's Tecumseh, pp. 87, 88; McAfee, p. 10.

[3] Drake's Tecumseh, pp. 92–97; Perkins' Annals of the West, pp. 570, 571.

[1] Perkins' Hist. of Late War, p. 57.—[2] Drake's Tecumseh, p. 93.—[3] Perkins' Annals of the West, pp. 577, 578.

[4] Drake's Tecumseh, p. 92.—[5] McAfee, p. 11; Drake's Tecumseh, p. 105; Marshall's Kentucky, p. 480.

[6] McAfee, p. 11; Drake's Tecumseh, p. 105.

compared with which other, and more recent, delusions, among the whites, are far more detrimental to the happiness of their votaries, and far less creditable to their intelligence. This singular combination of diverse elements, added to the mystery in which it was involved, filled the settlers with alarm, notwithstanding the disclaimers which the brothers had made; and it is probable this alarm hurried on the result which was so much dreaded.

During the years 1808 and 1809 there appears to have been no material change in the relations between the Indians at Tippecanoe, the settlers on the frontiers, and the United States. In 1809 Governor Harrison had made a treaty with the Miami, Eel River, Delaware, and Potawatomie tribes, at Fort Wayne, and had extinguished the Indian title to the lands east of the Wabash, adjoining those which had been ceded at the councils at Fort Wayne and Grousland.[1] This treaty conflicting with the great principle which both Tecumthà and the Prophet had maintained, early in 1810 a more hostile spirit appeared among the Indians at Tippecanoe. On the fifteenth of August, in that year, the memorable council at Vincennes revealed the fact that resistance would be offered to an extension of the boundary; that the British agents had participated in the movements at Tippecanoe; and that other tribes besides the Shawanoes had been drawn into the confederacy.[2]

From that time both parties—the confederated tribes of Indians and the United States—appear to have prepared for the inevitable struggle with the utmost coolness, and apparent unwillingness. The Indians were visited, at their distant homes, by the untiring Tecumthà,[1] and were gradually concentrating their forces at Tippecanoe:[2] the United States strengthened the Governor by sending the Fourth regiment of infantry and a company of riflemen to his support.[3]

While this singular spirit prevailed, Governor Harrison resolved to draw the dispute to a close; and early in October, 1811, he moved, with a large body of troops, to the vicinity of the Prophet's town on the Tippecanoe.[4] On the tenth of that month a sentinel was shot by the Indians;[5] and about the same time the Prophet—Tecumthà being absent—declared "that he had taken up the tomahawk, and would not lay it down but with his life, unless their wrongs were redressed," and endeavored to persuade the friendly Delawares to join his party.[6]

Under these circumstances, Governor Harrison was persuaded that forbearance had ceased to be a virtue; and on the fifth of November, 1811, at the head of about nine hundred effective troops, he encamped about eleven miles from the Prophet's town, on the Tippecanoe.[7] On the following day (*Nov.* 6) he moved forward, through a country

[1] Drake's Tecumseh, p. 112; McAfee, p. 11; Marshall's Ky., ii. p. 480.—[2] Drake's Tecumseh, pp. 124–130; Perkin's Annals of the West, p. 577.

[1] Drake's Tecumseh, pp. 141–145; McAfee, p. 12.

[2] Perkins' Annals of the West, p. 574.—[3] Drake's Tecumseh, p. 146; Marshall's Ky., ii. p. 489.

[4] McAfee, p. 18.—[5] Drake's Tecumseh, p. 147.

[6] Drake's Tecumseh, p. 147.—[7] Gen. Harrison's Dispatch, Nov. 18. McAfee (*Hist. of War in West*, p. 22) says, "*nine or ten miles.*"

composed of prairies, which were separated by small points of woods.[1] In his order of march he had adopted the same arrangement which General Wayne had employed—the infantry in two columns of files moving on either side of the road, while the cavalry and mounted riflemen moved in front, in the rear, and on the flanks of the columns.[2] Where the ground was not favorable for the action of the cavalry they were placed in the rear; but where it was otherwise they exchanged positions with one of the corps of mounted riflemen.[3] When he had come within four miles of the town, the troops were halted and formed in the order of battle. The regular troops in the centre, with two companies of militia infantry and one of mounted riflemen on each flank, formed the first line. The baggage and stores, drawn up as compactly as possible, moved next; while still farther in the rear was a reserve of three companies of militia. In the rear of these, three hundred yards from the first line, was the main body of the cavalry, forming the second line; while, three hundred yards in front of the column, a company of mounted riflemen moved as an advanced guard.[4]

To facilitate the march, the lines were broken into short columns of companies, in order that the order of battle might be formed as speedily as possible, in case of need, and the march was resumed.[5] At half-past two in the afternoon the army passed a small creek,

[1] McAfee, p. 22; Gen. Harrison's Dispatch, Nov. 18.
[2] Gen. Harrison's Dispatch, Nov. 18.—[3] McAfee, pp. 22, 23.—[4] Gen. Harrison's Dispatch, Nov. 18.—[5] Ibid.

about a mile and a half distant from the town; and, in an open wood, it was halted a second time, and drawn up in order of battle.[1] From this place Captain Dubois, of the Spies and Guides, was sent forward with a flag, at his own suggestion, to request a conference with the Prophet;[2] but the unfriendly manifestations of the Indians—parties of whom had been hovering around the army, during the whole of the day[3]—led the Governor to recall him, and to make preparations to encamp for the night where the army had halted.[4] While he was thus employed Major Joseph Davies—who commanded the dragoons—reported to him that the ground in front was very favorable, and that the Indians appeared to entertain the most inveterate hostility—treating every attempt to approach them with contempt and insolence.[5] At the same time the Governor was urged to move forward, both by the Major and by all the officers who were near him; while every man in the army appeared eager to meet the enemy at once.[6] Yielding to the general sentiment, the Governor ordered the army to advance;[7] but it had not moved more than a quarter of a mile when it was met by three Indians, who had been sent out by the Prophet, and had expressed a desire to speak with the Governor.[8] One of them, who appeared to be a man of consequence

[1] Drake's Tecumseh, p. 148; McAfee, p. 23.—[2] McAfee, p. 25; Gen. Harrison's Dispatch, Nov. 18.—[3] McAfee, pp. 24, 25.—[4] Gen. Harrison's Dispatch, Nov. 18.
[5] McAfee, p. 25.—[6] Gen. Harrison's Dispatch, Nov. 18.
[7] Drake's Tecumseh, p. 149; Gen. Harrison's Dispatch, Nov. 18.—[8] Drake's Tecumseh, p. 149; McAfee, pp. 25-27.

among them, informed the Governor that the chiefs were much surprised at the movement of the army against their village, from the fact that messengers had been sent to meet him with answers to his demands, on a former assurance that no movement would be made until those answers had been received. The Governor replied, that no attack would be made until the chiefs had received an opportunity to give their answers—which had not reached him—and that, for that purpose, he would encamp near the river until the next morning. Apparently satisfied with this explanation the delegation left, and the army moved forward and encamped for the night in the immediate vicinity of the village.[1]

The ground which was selected as the site of the encampment was reported, by Majors Taylor and Clarke, who had been dispatched to examine it, to be "excellent," although the Governor afterwards declared, it "was not altogether such as he could wish it—it was indeed admirably calculated for the encampment of regular troops that were opposed to regulars, but it afforded great facility to the approach of savages."[2] It was an elevated point of dry oak land, which ran out into a marshy prairie—terminating in an abrupt point about one hundred and fifty yards from the right flank of the encampment—in the rear of which, on the south side, at its foot, ran a small brook, which was skirted with willows and bushes. As the ground became wider as it receded from the point referred to, the site of the encampment was of a triangular form, the front, or north side of which —towards the village—was elevated about ten feet, and the rear, or south side, about twelve feet, from the marsh, into which it projected.[1] On this natural bank the troops encamped—the first line, fronting the village, on the north side of the bank, being composed of a battalion of regular troops, commanded by Major Floyd, flanked, on the right, by two companies of militia infantry, and, on the left, by one company of the same troops, under Colonel Joseph Bartholomew; the rear line, which was from eighty to one hundred and fifty yards distant from the front, was composed of another battalion of regulars, under Captain Baen, acting as Major, on the left, and Captains Snelling, Posey, Scott, and Wilson's companies of Indiana volunteers (*infantry*), on the right. The lines were flanked, on the left, by Geiger's and Robb's companies of mounted riflemen, under the general command of Major-general Wells, of Kentucky; and on the right by Captain Spencer's company of mounted riflemen—eighty in number. Two troops of dragoons,—about sixty men, in all,—under Major Joseph Davies, were encamped in the rear of the front line and left flank; and Captain Parker's troop of dragoons was also posted in the rear of the front line.[2] The order of encampment was the order of battle, and each man slept immediately

[1] McAfee, p. 26.—[2] Gen. Harrison's Dispatch, Nov. 18. See also McAfee, p. 27.

[1] Drake's Tecumseh, p. 150; McAfee, p. 27; Gen. Harrison's Dispatch, Nov. 18.—[2] McAfee, pp. 27, 28; Gen. Harrison's Dispatch, Nov. 18.

opposite to his post in the line.[1] Considering, properly, that a single line of troops, in Indian warfare, is nearly as good as two; that an extension of the lines is a matter of considerable importance; and that raw troops, such as the army was then composed of, were enabled to manœuvre with greater facility, when formed in single ranks, General Harrison formed his men in that manner; and, on the evening of the sixth of November, he had directed each corps, in case of an attack, to hold its ground, at any cost, until it could be relieved. At the same time the cavalry were directed, in that event, to parade dismounted, with their pistols in their belts, and to act as a reserve. Two "captains' guards," each composed of four non-commissioned officers and forty-two privates, and two "subalterns' guards," each composed of twenty men, protected the camp from surprise; and, with these precautions, the army sought rest, with but little apparent expectation of hostilities.[2]

The night passed quietly, and the weary soldiers enjoyed their guarded repose, without interruption, until a quarter-past four in the morning of the seventh, when a single gun, fired by a sentry who was stationed on the extreme left flank of the rear line, on the margin of the brook, gave warning of approaching danger.[3] The night had been dark and cloudy, with a drizzling rain;[4] and the savages, taking advantage of these circumstances, had crept

[1] Gen. Harrison's Dispatch, Nov. 18.—[2] McAfee, p. 28; Gen. Harrison's Dispatch, Nov. 18.—[3] Gen. Harrison's Dispatch, Nov. 18.—[4] Drake's Tecumseh, p. 150; McAfee, p. 28.

up to the line of sentries, with the evident intention of rushing on them before they could fire or give an alarm;[1] and, they intended, afterwards, to move against the encampment, and surprise the troops while they slept. One, more unfortunate or more audacious than his fellows, was discovered, and fired on by the guard;[2] and, although the latter immediately fled, without offering any farther resistance, the alarm had been sufficient to arouse the men, and, to some extent, to prepare them for the action.[3]

The affrighted guard, in his retreat, was followed closely by the Indians, who, with their usual yells and whoops, filled the air with the horrible din.[4] The first assault was made on the southeast angle of the encampment, where Captain Barton's company of regulars and Captain Geiger's company of mounted riflemen were posted; and it was sustained with great courage, although the enemy's fire was "excessively severe."[5] Indeed the orders which these companies had received, in common with the other corps of the army, on the preceding evening, were so faithfully obeyed, that "all the other companies were under arms and tolerably formed before they were fired on."[6] The camp-fires, which had afforded the enemy great facility in taking aim, were immediately extinguished;[7] the troops, with all the noiseless steadiness of veterans, formed and took their places, ready to receive and

[1] McAfee, p. 29.—[2] Ibid.; Gen. Harrison's Dispatch, Nov. 18.—[3] McAfee, p. 29.—[4] Ibid.—[5] Gen. Harrison's Dispatch, Nov. 18; McAfee, p. 29.—[6] Gen. Harrison's Dispatch, Nov. 18.—[7] Drake's Tecumseh, p. 151; McAfee, p. 28.

BATTLE OF TIPPECANOE.

From the original Painting by Chappel, in the possession of the Publishers.

execute any orders which might be received;[1] and the Governor—who was pulling on his boots when the attack was first made[2]—hastened to the scene of the attack.[3] Finding that both the gallant companies who had received the savages, had been very severely handled, the Governor ordered the companies of regulars under the command of Captain Cook and Lieutenant Peters, to advance from the centre of the rear line—where the ground was more defensible—and to form across the angle of the encampment, in the rear of the two companies who had sustained the attack, for their support.[4]

At this moment the enemy attacked the left of the front line,—the northeast angle of the encampment,—where had been stationed a small company of United States riflemen, and the companies of regulars under Captains Baen, Snelling, and Prescott. The reserve (Major Davies' dragoons) were immediately formed in the rear of these companies, for their support, and a heavy fire was thrown by both parties. Perceiving that the enemy's heaviest fire proceeded from a clump of trees which stood some fifteen or twenty yards distant from the front of the line, Major Davies obtained permission to charge with a part of his force, and attempt to dislodge them; but the greater numbers of the enemy enabled him to outflank the Major's command, and the latter was repulsed, with the loss of its gallant commander. Immediately afterwards the enemy was charged by Captain Snelling, with his company of regulars, and driven from the position, with heavy loss.[1]

While the engagement was thus raging along the left flank of the army, —the eastern front of the encampment, —the savages gradually extended along the entire front, the right flank, and a part of the rear of the position, and the army was nearly surrounded by the wily and savage enemy.[2] Upon the right of the rear line,—the southwest angle of the encampment,—where the mounted riflemen, under Captain Spencer, and the regulars, under Captain Warwick, were posted, the enemy appeared to concentrate his strength, and call forth his most desperate efforts. Every officer in the riflemen was killed, and Captain Warwick was mortally wounded, yet both companies maintained their ground with the utmost firmness.[3] At this moment Captain Robb's company, which had fallen back towards the centre of the encampment, from the left flank, fortunately attracted the attention of the Governor, and he moved it forward to the rear of Captains Spencer's and Warwick's position, for their support, at the same time detaching Captain Prescott's company of regulars to occupy the position, on the left flank, from which Captain Robb had fallen back.[4]

In this manner the contest continued, without abatement, until daybreak,[5] the

[1] Gen. Harrison's Dispatch, Nov. 18.—[2] Drake's Tecumseh, p. 151.—[3] Gen. Harrison's Dispatch, Nov. 18.
[4] McAfee, p. 29; Gen. Harrison's Dispatch, Nov. 18.

[1] McAfee, p. 30; Gen. Harrison's Dispatch, Nov. 18.
[2] Gen. Harrison's Dispatch, Nov. 18.—[3] McAfee, p. 30.
[4] Drake's Tecumseh, p. 30; Gen. Harrison's Dispatch, Nov. 18.—[5] McAfee, p. 31.

lines being kept entire, and the enemy prevented from breaking into the camp.[1]

At length the break of day relieved the Governor of the anxiety which he had before experienced, and he prepared to make a final charge on the enemy. For this purpose the companies commanded by Captains Snelling, Posey, and Scott, were withdrawn from the front line, and those commanded by Captain Wilson from the rear line, and posted on the left flank—the eastern front of the encampment; while the companies commanded by Captains Cook and Baen—the former from the rear, the latter from the front lines—were detached for the support of the right flank.[2] General Wells—acting as Major—took the command of the left flank, and with the co-operation of a body of cavalry, under Captain Parke, he made a gallant charge on the enemy; driving them before him, at the point of the bayonet, and forcing them to seek refuge in the marsh, whither the cavalry could not pursue them.[3] At the same time the left flank, strengthened by the reinforcement under Captain Cook and Lieutenant Larabee,—Captain Baen having fallen,—had also charged the enemy, and driven them before them, with heavy loss.[4]

With this success the engagement ended; and both parties appeared to have satisfied the expectations of their friends. The steady, undeviating courage of the American troops elicited great commendation;[5] while Governor

[1] Gen. Harrison's Dispatch, Nov. 18.—[2] McAfee, p. 31; Gen. Harrison's Dispatch, Nov. 18.—[3] McAfee, p. 31.

[4] Ibid.; Gen. Harrison's Dispatch, Nov. 18.

[5] McAfee, pp. 31, 32.

Harrison, speaking of his savage enemy, says, "The Indians manifested a ferocity uncommon even with them."[1] In this, however, they were inspirited by the religious fanaticism under which they acted[2]—the Prophet, during the action, being posted on a neighboring eminence, singing a war-song; and, in faint imitation of Moses in the wilderness, directing the movements of his people by the movement of his rod.[3]

The force of the Americans, exclusive of the dragoons,—who rendered but very little service,—was very little more than seven hundred;[4] that of the enemy was, probably, about the same number.[5] The loss of the former was Colonel Owens, one of Governor's aids, Captain Spencer, Lieutenants McMahan and Berry, one sergeant, two corporals, and thirty privates, *killed;* Major Davies, Captains Baen and Warwick, and twenty-two privates, *wounded and subsequently died;* and Lieutenant-colonels Bartholomew and Decker, Adjutant Hunter, Surgeon Scull, Captains Norris and Geiger, Lieutenants Peters and Gooding, Ensign Burchstead, nine sergeants, five corporals, one musician, and one hundred and two privates, *wounded.*[6] The loss of the enemy was supposed to have been greater than that of the Americans,[7] although the custom of removing the dead and wounded

[1] Gen. Harrison's Dispatch, Nov. 18.—[2] Drake's Tecumseh, p. 152.—[3] Ibid.; McAfee, p. 31.

[4] Gen. Harrison's Dispatch, Nov. 18; Marshall's Ky., ii. pp. 507, 508. McAfee (*Hist.*, p. 34) supposes it was "something more than *eight hundred.*"—[5] Gen. Harrison's Dispatch, Nov. 18. Mr. Drake (*Tecumseh*, p. 152) supposes they numbered "*between* 800 *and* 1000." McAfee agrees with him.—[6] Returns, appended to Gen. Harrison's Dispatch, Nov. 18.—[7] S. G. Drake's Indian Biog. (*Ed.* 1832), p. 337; Gen. Harrison's Dispatch, Nov. 18.

from the field, at the time of the retreat, prevents the collection of any certain account of it.[1]

It is said that the determination to attack the camp was not concluded until late on the preceding evening. The plan which had been formed, prior to that time, was to meet the Governor, in council, and appear to agree to his terms. At its close the chiefs were to retire to the warriors; while two Winnebagoes, who had volunteered for that service, were to assassinate the Governor, and give the signal for the uprising of the enemy. During the action he was under the direction of White Loon, Stone-eater, and Winnemac, a Potawatomie chief.[2]

The army remained in camp during the seventh and eighth of November to bury the dead, dress the wounds of the disabled, and prepare for its return.[1] On the ninth of November, after having burned the village, the line of march was taken up for its return.[2]

"The battle of Tippecanoe," like some other battles, has figured, prominently, in the partisan politics of the country; and with the same results. If the battle of Bunker's Hill, and all that relates to it, have suffered in a Gubernatorial election in a single State, how much more may not all that relates to Tippecanoe have suffered in the violent struggle for the ascendency in a Presidential campaign? It is not my desire to revive, in the least degree, the censures which have been cast on the Governor, — many of which are wholly without foundation in fact,— and I leave the subject to more able and willing hands.[3]

DOCUMENT.

GENERAL HARRISON'S DISPATCH TO SECRETARY OF WAR.

VINCENNES, *November* 18, 1811.

SIR:—In my letter of the 8th instant, I did myself the honor to communicate the result of an action between the troops under my command and the confederation of Indians under the control of the Shawanoe prophet. I had previously informed you, in a letter of the 2d instant, of my proceedings previously to my arrival at the Vermilion River, where I had erected a block-house for the protection of the boats which I was obliged to leave, and as a depository for our heavy baggage and such part of our provisions as we were unable to transport in wagons. On the morning of the 3d instant I commenced my march from the block-house. The Wabash, above this, turning considerably to the eastward, I was obliged, in order to avoid the broken and woody country which borders upon it, to change my course to the westward of north to gain the prairies which lie to the back of these woods. At the end of one day's march I was enabled to take the proper direction (N. E.), which brought me, on the evening of the 5th, to a small creek at about eleven miles from the Prophet's town. I had, on the preceding day, avoided the dangerous pass of Pine Creek by inclining a few miles to the left, where the troops and wagons were crossed with expe-

[1] McAfee, pp. 34, 35.—[2] S. G. Drake's Indian Biography, p. 337.

[1] McAfee, p. 36.—[2] Ibid., p. 36.—[3] Those who are interested in this subject may find counter-statements in Marshall's Kentucky, ii. pp. 491–521.

dition and safety. Our route on the 6th, for about six miles, lay through prairies, separated by small points of woods.

My order of march hitherto had been similar to that used by General Wayne; that is, the infantry were in two columns of files on either side of the road, and the mounted riflemen and cavalry in front, in the rear, and on the flanks. Where the ground was unfavorable for the action of cavalry they were placed in the rear, but where it was otherwise they were made to exchange positions with one of the mounted rifle corps. Understanding that the last four miles were open woods, and the probability being greater that we should be attacked in front than on either flank, I halted at that distance from the town and formed the army in order of battle. The United States infantry placed in the centre, two companies of infantry and one of mounted riflemen on each flank formed the front line. In the rear of this line was placed the baggage, drawn up as compact as possible, and immediately behind it a reserve of three companies of militia infantry. The cavalry formed a second line at the distance of three hundred yards in the rear of the front line, and a company of mounted riflemen the advanced guard at that distance in front. To facilitate the march, the whole were then broken off in short columns of companies, a situation the most favorable for forming in order of battle with facility and precision. Our march was slow and cautious, and much delayed by the examination of every place which seemed calculated for an ambuscade. Indeed, the ground was for some time so unfavorable that I was obliged to change the position of the several corps three times in the distance of a mile. At half-past two o'clock we passed a small creek at the distance of one mile and a half from the town, and entered an open wood, when the army was halted and again drawn up in order of battle. During the whole of the last day's march parties of Indians were constantly about us, and every effort was made by the interpreters to speak to them, but in vain. New attempts of the kind were now made, but proving equally ineffectual, a Captain Dubois, of the Spies and Guides, offered to go with a flag to the town. I dispatched him with an interpreter to request a conference with the Prophet. In a few moments a message was sent by Captain Dubois, to inform me that in his attempts to advance the Indians appeared in both his flanks, and although he had spoken to them in the most friendly manner, they refused to answer, but beckoned to him to go forward, and constantly endeavored to cut him off from the army. Upon this information I recalled the Captain, and determined to encamp for the night, and take some other measures for opening a conference with the Prophet. While I was engaged in tracing the lines for the encampment, Major Davies, who commanded the dragoons, came up to inform me that he had penetrated to the Indian fields, that the ground was entirely open and favorable, that the Indians in front had manifested nothing but hostility, and had answered every attempt to bring them to a parley with contempt and insolence. It was immediately advised by all the officers around me to move forward. A similar wish, indeed, pervaded all the army. It was drawn up in excellent order, and every man appeared eager to decide the contest immediately. Being informed that a good encampment might be had upon the Wabash, I yielded to what appeared the general wish, and directed the troops to advance, taking care, however, to place the interpreters in front, with directions to invite a conference with any Indians they might meet with. We had not advanced above four hundred yards, when I was informed that three Indians had approached the advanced guards and had expressed a wish to speak to me. I found, upon their arrival, that one of them was a man in great estimation with the Prophet. He informed me that the chiefs were much surprised at my advancing upon them so rapidly—that they were given to understand, by the Delawares and Miamis, whom I had sent to them a few days before, that I would not advance to their town until I had received an answer to my demands made through them; that this answer had been dispatched by the Potawatomie chief, Winemac, who had accompanied the Miamis and Delawares on their return; that they had left the Prophet's town two days before with a design to meet me, but unfortunately taken the road on the south side of the

Wabash. I answered, that I had no intention of attacking them until I discovered that they would not comply with the demands which I had made—that I would go on and encamp at the Wabash, and in the morning would have an interview with the Prophet and his chiefs, and explain to them the determination of the President — that in the mean time no hostilities should be committed. He seemed much pleased with this, and promised that it should be observed on their part. I then resumed my march, and struck the cultivated grounds about five hundred yards below the town, but as these extended to the bank of the Wabash, there was no possibility of getting an encampment which was provided with both wood and water. My guards and interpreters being still with the advanced guard, and taking the direction of the town, the army followed, and had advanced within about one hundred and fifty yards, when fifty or sixty Indians sallied out, and with loud exclamations, called to the cavalry and to the militia infantry, which were on our right flank, to halt. I immediately advanced to the front, caused the army to halt, and directed an interpreter to request some of the chiefs to come to me. In a few moments the man that had been with me before made his appearance. I informed him that my object for the present was to procure a good piece of ground to encamp on, where we could get wood and water. He informed me that there was a creek to the northwest, which he thought would suit our purpose. I immediately dispatched two officers to examine it, and they reported that the situation was excellent. I then took leave of the chief, and a mutual promise was again made for a suspension of hostilities until we could have an interview on the following day. I found the ground destined for the encampment not altogether such as I could wish it. It was, indeed, admirably calculated for the encampment of regular troops that were opposed to regulars, but it afforded great facility to the approach of savages. It was a piece of dry oak land, rising about ten feet above the level of the marshy prairie in front (towards the Indian town), and nearly twice that height above a similar prairie in the rear, through which and near to this bank ran a small stream clothed with willows and other brush wood. Towards the left flank this bench of high land widened considerably, but became gradually narrower in the opposite direction, and at the distance of one hundred and fifty yards from the right flank, terminated in the abrupt point. The two columns of infantry occupied the front and rear of this ground, at the distance of about one hundred and fifty yards from each other on the left, and something more than half that distance on the right flank. These flanks were filled up, the first by two companies of mounted riflemen amounting to about one hundred and twenty men, under the command of Major-general Wells of the Kentucky militia, who served as a major; the other by Spencer's company of mounted riflemen, which amounted to eighty men. The front line was composed of one battalion of United States infantry, under the command of Major Floyd, flanked on the right by two companies of militia, and on the left by one company. The rear line was composed of a battalion of United States troops under the command of Captain Baen, acting as major, and four companies of militia infantry under Lieutenant-colonel Decker. The regular troops of the line joined the mounted riflemen under General Wells on the left flank, and Colonel Decker's battalion formed an angle with Spencer's company on the left.

Two troops of dragoons, amounting in the aggregate to about sixty men, were encamped in the rear of the left flank, and Captain Parke's troop, which was larger than the other two, in the rear of the front line. Our order of encampment varied little from that above described, excepting when some peculiarity of the ground made it necessary. For a night attack the order of encampment was the order of battle, and each man slept immediately opposite to his post in the line. In the formation of my troops I used a single rank, or what is called Indian file, because in Indian warfare, where there is no shock to resist, one rank is nearly as good as two; and in that kind of warfare the extension of line is a matter of the first importance. Raw troops also manœuvre with much more facility in single than in double ranks. It was my constant custom to assemble all the field-officers at my tent every evening by signal, to give them the watch-word and their instructions for the night; those given for the night of the 6th were, that each corps which formed a part of the exterior line of the encampment should hold its own ground until relieved. The dragoons were directed to parade dismounted in case of a night attack, with their pistols in their belts, and to act as a *corps de reserve.* The camp was defended by two captains' guards, consisting each of four non-commissioned officers and forty-two privates—and two subalterns' guards of twenty non-commissioned officers and privates. The whole under the command of a field-officer of the day. The troops were regularly called up an hour before day, and made to continue under arms until it was quite light. On the morning of the 7th I had risen at a quarter after four o'clock, and the signal for calling out the men would have been given in two minutes, when the attack commenced. It began on our left flank. But a single gun was fired by the sentinels or by the guard in that direction, which made not the least resistance, but abandoned their officer and fled into the camp, and the first notice which the troops of that flank had of the danger, was from the yells of the savages within a short distance of the line; but even under those circumstances the men were not wanting to themselves or to the occasion. Such of them as were awake, or were easily awakened, seized their arms and took their stations; others, which were more tardy, had to contend with the enemy in the doors of their tents. The storm first fell upon Captain Barton's company of the Fourth United States regiment, and Captain Geiger's company of mounted riflemen, which formed the left angle of the rear line. The fire upon these was excessively severe, and they suffered considerably before relief could be brought to them; some few Indians passed into the encampment near the angle, and one or two penetrated to some distance before they were killed. I believe all the other companies were under arms, and tolerably formed before they were fired on. The morning was dark and cloudy. Our fires afforded a partial light, which, if it gave us some opportunity of taking our positions, was still more advantageous to the enemy, affording them the means of taking a surer aim; they were therefore extinguished as soon as possible. Under all these discouraging circumstances, the troops (nineteen-twentieths of whom had never been in action before) behaved in a manner that never can be too much applauded. They took their places without noise, and with less confusion than could have been expected from veterans placed in a similar situation. As soon as I could mount my horse I rode to the angle that was attacked; I found that Barton's company had suffered severely, and the left of Geiger's entirely broken. I immediately ordered Cook's company, and the late Captain Wentworth's, under Lieutenant Peters, to be brought up from the centre of the rear line, where the ground was much more defensible, and formed across the angle in support of Barton's and Geiger's. My attention was then engaged by a heavy firing upon the left of the front line, where were stationed the small company of United States riflemen (then, however, armed with muskets), and the companies of Baen, Snelling, and Prescott, of the Fourth regiment. I found Major Davies forming the dragoons in the rear of those companies; and understanding that the heaviest part of the enemy's fire proceeded from some trees about fifteen or twenty paces in front of these companies, I directed the Major to dislodge them with a part of the dragoons. Unfortunately, the Major's gallantry determined him to execute the order with a smaller force than was sufficient, which enabled the enemy to avoid him in front, and attack his flanks. The Major was mortally wounded, and his party driven back. The Indians were, however, immediately and gallantly dislodged from their advantageous position, by Captain Snelling, at the head of his company. In the course of a few minutes after the commencement of the attack, the fire extended along the left flank, the whole of the front, the right flank, and part of the rear line. Upon Spencer's mounted riflemen, and the right of Warwick's company, which was posted on the right of the rear line, it was excessively severe; Captain Spencer and his first and second lieutenants were killed, and Captain Warwick was mortally wounded; those companies, however, still bravely maintained their posts, but Spencer had suffered so severely, and having originally too much ground to occupy, I reinforced them with Robb's company of riflemen, which had been driven, or by mistake ordered, from their position on the left flank towards the centre of the camp, and filled the vacancy that had been occupied by Robb with Prescott's company of the Fourth United States regiment. My great object was to keep the lines entire to prevent the enemy from breaking into the camp until daylight, which would enable me to make a general and effectual charge. With this view I had reinforced every part of the line that had suffered much; and as soon as the approach of morning discovered itself, I withdrew from the front line Snelling's, Posey's (under Lieutenant Albright), and Scott's, and from the rear line, Wilson's companies, and drew them up upon the left flank, and at the same time I ordered Cook's and Baen's companies, the former from the rear and the latter from the front line, to reinforce the right flank, foreseeing that at these points the enemy would make their last efforts. Major Wells, who commanded on the left flank, not knowing my intentions precisely, had taken the command of these companies, and charged the enemy before I had formed the body of dragoons with which I meant to support the infantry; a small detachment of these were, however, ready, and proved amply sufficient for the purpose. The Indians were driven by the infantry at the point of the bayonet, and the dragoons pursued and forced them into a marsh, where they could not be followed. Captain Cook and Lieutenant Larabee had, agreeably to my order, marched their companies to the right flank, had formed them under the fire of the enemy, and being then joined by the riflemen of that flank, had charged the Indians, killed a number, and put the rest to a precipitate flight. A favorable opportunity was here offered to pursue the enemy with dragoons, but being engaged at that time on the other flank, I did not observe it until it was too late.

I have thus, sir, given you the particulars of an action, which was certainly maintained with the greatest obstinacy and perseverance by both parties. The Indians manifested a ferocity uncommon even with them. To their savage fury our troops opposed that cool and deliberate valor which is characteristic of the Christian soldier.

The most pleasing part of my duty (that of naming to you the corps and individuals who particularly distinguished themselves) is yet to be performed. There is, however, considerable difficulty in it; where merit was so common it is almost impossible to discriminate.

The whole of the infantry formed a small brigade under the immediate orders of Colonel Boyd. The Colonel, throughout the action, manifested equal zeal and bravery in carrying into execution my orders, in keeping the men to their posts, and exhorting them to fight with valor. His Brigade-major Clark, and his Aid-de-camp George Croghan, Esq., were also very serviceably employed. Colonel Joseph Bartholomew, a very valuable officer, commanded, under Colonel Boyd, the militia infantry. He was wounded early in the action, and his services lost to me. Major G. R. C. Floyd, the senior of the Fourth United States regiment, commanded immediately the battalion of that regiment, which was in the front line. His conduct, during the action, was entirely to my satisfaction. Lieutenant-colonel Decker, who commanded the battalion of militia on the right of the rear line, preserved his command in good order. He was, however, but partially attacked. I have before mentioned to you that Major-general Wells, of the Fourth division of Kentucky militia, acted under my command as a major at the head of two companies of mounted volunteers. The General maintained the fame which he had already acquired in almost every campaign, and in almost every battle which has been fought with the Indians since the settlement of Kentucky. Of the several corps, the Fourth United States regiment, and two small companies attached to it, were certainly the most conspicuous for undaunted valor. The companies commanded by Captains Cook, Snelling, and Barton, Lieutenants Larabee, Peters, and Hawkins, were placed in situations where they could render most service and encounter most danger, and those officers eminently distinguished themselves. Captains Prescott and Brown performed their duty also entirely to my satisfaction, as did Posey's company of the Seventh regiment, headed by Lieutenant Albright. In short, sir, they supported the fame of American regulars, and I have never heard that a single individual was found out of the line of his duty. Several of the militia companies were in nowise inferior to the regulars. Spencer's, Geiger's, and Warwick's maintained their posts amid a monstrous carnage, as indeed did Robb's, after it was posted on the left flank. Its loss of men (seventeen killed and wounded), and keeping its ground, is sufficient proof of its firmness. Wilson's and Scott's companies charged with the regular troops, and proved themselves worthy of doing so. Norris's companies also behaved well. Hargrove's and Wilkin's companies were placed in a situation where they had no opportunity of distinguishing themselves, or I am satisfied they would have done it. This was the case with the squadron of dragoons also. After Major Davies had received his wound, knowing it to be mortal, I promoted Captain Parker to the majority, than whom there is no better officer.

My two aids-de-camp, Majors Hurst and Taylor, with Lieutenant Adams of the Fourth regiment, the adjutant of the troops, afforded me the most essential aid, as well in the action as throughout the campaign.

The arrangements of Captain Pratt, in the quartermaster's department, were highly judicious; and his exertions on all occasions, particularly in bringing off the wounded, deserve my warmest thanks. But in giving merited praise to the living, let me not forget the gallant dead. Colonel Abraham Owen, commandant of the Eighteenth Kentucky regiment, joined me a few days before the action, as a private, in Captain Geiger's company; he accepted the appointment as a volunteer aid-de-camp to me; he fell early in the action. The representatives of his State will inform you that she possessed not a better citizen nor a braver man. Major J. H. Davies was known as an able lawyer and a great orator; he joined me as a private volunteer, and on the recommendation of the officers of that corps, was appointed to command the Third troop of dragoons. His conduct in that capacity justified their choice; never was there an officer possessed of more ardor and zeal to discharge his duty with propriety, and never one who would have encountered greater danger to purchase military fame. Captain Baen, of the Fourth United States regiment, was killed early in the action. He was unquestionably a good officer and valiant soldier. Captains Spencer and Warwick, and Lieutenants McMahan and Berry, were all my particular friends. I have ever had the utmost confidence in their valor, and I was not deceived. Spencer was wounded in the head. He exhorted his men to fight valiantly. He was shot through both thighs, and fell, still continuing to encourage them. He was raised up, and received a ball through his body, which put an immediate end to his existence! Warwick was shot immediately through the body. Being taken to the surgery to be dressed, as soon as it was over (being a man of great bodily vigor, and still able to walk), he insisted upon going back to head his company, although it was evident that he had but a few hours to live.

All these gentlemen, sir, Captain Baen excepted, have left wives, and five of them large families of children: this is the case, too, with many of the privates among the militia who fell in the action, or who have died since of their wounds. Will the bounty of their country be withheld from their helpless orphans, many of whom will be in the most destitute condition, and perhaps want even the necessaries of life? With respect to the number of Indians that were engaged against us, I am possessed of no data by which I can form a correct statement. It must, however, have been considerable, and perhaps not much inferior to our own; which, deducting the dragoons, who were unable to do us much service, was very little above seven hundred, non-commissioned officers and privates. I am convinced there were at least six hundred. The Prophet had, three weeks before, four hundred and fifty of his own proper followers. I am induced to believe that he was joined by a number of the lawless vagabonds who live on the Illinois River, as large trails were seen coming from that direction. Indeed, I shall not be surprised to find that some of those who professed the warmest friendship for us were arrayed against us; it is certain that one of this description came out from the town and spoke to me the night before the action. The Potawatomie chief, whom I mentioned to have been wounded and taken prisoner in my letter of the 8th instant, I left on the battle-ground, after having taken all the care of him in my power. I requested him to inform those of his own tribe who had joined the Prophet, and Kickapoos and Winnebagoes, that if they would immediately abandon the Prophet, and return to their own tribes, their past conduct would be forgiven, and that we would treat them as we formerly had done. He assured me that he would do so; and there was no doubt of their compliance. Indeed, he said he was certain that they would put the Prophet to death. I think, upon the whole, that there will be no farther hostilities; but of this I shall be enabled to give you some more certain information in a few days.

The troops left the battle-ground on the 9th instant. It took every wagon to transport the wounded. We managed, however, to bring off the public property, although almost all the private baggage of the officers was necessarily destroyed.

It may perhaps be imagined, sir, that some means might have been adopted to have made a more earlier discovery of the approach of the enemy to our camp the morning of the 7th instant; but if I had employed two-thirds of the army as outposts it would have been ineffectual; the Indians in such a night would have found means to have passed between them. Placed in the situation that we were, there is no other mode of avoiding a surprise, than by a chain of sentinels so close together that the enemy cannot pass between without discovery, and having the army in such readiness that they can get to their alarm-posts at a moment's warning. Our troops could not have been better prepared than they were, unless they had been kept under arms the whole night, as they lay with their accoutrements on, and their arms by their sides, and the moment they were up they were at their posts. If the sentinels and the guard had done their duty, even the troops on the left flank would have been prepared to have received the Indians.

I have the honor to inclose you a correct return of killed and wounded. The wounded suffered very much before their arrival here, but they are now comfortably fixed, and every attention has been, and shall continue to be, paid to them. Dr. Foster is not only possessed of great professional merit, but is, moreover, a man of feeling and honor.

I am convinced, sir, that the Indians lost many more men than we did; they left from thirty-six to forty on the field. They were seen to take off not only the wounded but the dead. An Indian that was killed and scalped, in the beginning of the action, by one of our men, was found in a house in the town; several others were also found in the houses, and many graves which were fresh dug; one of them was opened and found to contain three dead bodies.

Our infantry used principally cartridges containing twelve buck-shot, which were admirably calculated for a night action.

I have before informed you, sir, that Colonel Miller was prevented by illness from going on the expedition; he rendered essential service in the command of Fort Harrison; he is an officer of great merit.

There are so many circumstances which it is important for you to know, respecting the situation of this country, that I have thought it best to commit this dispatch to my aid-de-camp, Major Taylor, who will have the honor of delivering it to you, and who will be able to give you more satisfaction than I could do by writing. Major Taylor (who is also one of our supreme judges) is a man of integrity and honor, and you may rely upon any statements he may make.

With the highest respect, I have the honor to be, sir, your humble servant,

WILLIAM HENRY HARRISON.

P. S.—Not a man of ours was taken prisoner, and of three scalps which were taken two of them were recovered.

The Hon. W. EUSTIS, Sec. of War.

A general return of the killed and wounded of the army under the command of his Excellency William Henry Harrison, governor and commander-in-chief of the Indian Territory, in the action with the Indians, near Prophet's Town, November 7, 1811.

Killed.—One aid-de-camp, one captain, two subalterns, one sergeant, two corporals, thirty privates.

Wounded, since dead.—One major, two captains, twenty-two privates.

Wounded.—Two lieutenant-colonels, one adjutant, one surgeon's-mate, two captains, three subalterns, nine sergeants, five corporals, one musician, one hundred and two privates.

Total.—Killed and wounded, one hundred and eighty-eight.

Names of officers killed and wounded, as per general return.

General Staff.—Killed—Colonel Abraham Owen, aid-de-camp to the commander-in-chief.

Field and Staff. — *Wounded* — Lieutenant-colonel Joseph Bartholomew, commanding Indiana militia infantry; Lieutenant-colonel Luke Decker, of Indiana militia infantry; Major Joseph A. Davies, since dead, commanding a squadron of dragoons; Dr. Edward Scull, of the Indiana militia; Adjutant James Hunter, of mounted riflemen.

United States infantry, including the late Captain Whitney's rifle company. — *Wounded* —Captain W. C. Baen, acting major, since dead; Lieutenant George P. Peters; Lieutenant George Gooding; Ensign Henry Burchstead.

Colonel Decker's detachment of Indiana militia. — *Wounded* — Captain Jacob Warwick, since dead.

Major Redman's detachment of Indiana militia. — *Wounded* — Captain John Norris.

Major Wells' detachment of mounted riflemen. — *Wounded* — Captain Frederic Geiger.

Captain Spencer's company, including Lieutenant Berry's detachment of mounted riflemen. —*Killed*—Captain Spier Spencer; First-lieutenant Richard McMahan; Lieutenant Thomas Berry.

Nath'l. F. Adams,
Adj't. of the Army.

To his Excellency, the Commander-in-chief.

CHAPTER XV.

July 17, 1812.

THE SURPRISE OF MICHILIMACINAC.

The dispute with Great Britain, to which reference has heretofore been made, had resulted in a declaration of war by the Congress of the United States;[1] yet, notwithstanding an appeal to arms had been made by the infant republic, there appears to have been but little preparation made to carry it on. Not the least of the many subjects which appear to have been almost wholly neglected by the executive departments of the government, was the notification of the several military posts, on the frontiers, of the declaration—a neglect which was, subsequently, productive of great mischief to the country.

At the period in question, the United States occupied the Island of Michilimacinac (since called *Mackinac*) with a small garrison of regular troops, not more for the protection of the traders,[1] than for the purpose of holding a check over the Indians of the north-western part of the country.[2] This island is situated in the straits which lead from Lake Michigan to Lake Huron; is of a circular form, about seven miles in circumference, and from three to four

[1] "An Act declaring War," &c. Approved, June 18, 1812.

[1] Ingersoll's Hist. Sketch of the Second War, i. p. 80.

[2] The importance of the post, in this respect, is seen in the effects of its fall.

miles from the main. It is a rock of limestone, covered with a rough but fertile soil, on which is borne a heavy growth of timber. The fort occupied a high bank on the south-eastern side of the island, overlooking and commanding a fine harbor; and was, itself, commanded by the high ground in its rear, on which had been erected two block-houses, each of which was defended by a brass six-pounder. The main work was defended by two long nine-pounders, two howitzers, and a brass three-pounder;[1] and a company of fifty-seven men, officers included, commanded by Lieutenant Porter Hanks, of the United States artillery, formed the garrison.[2] About fifty miles north-east from this post, General Brock, in the spring of 1812, had erected a small work, called *Fort St. Joseph*, and had garrisoned it with a detachment of the Tenth Royal Veteran Battalion, forty-five in number, under Captain Charles Roberts.[3]

Intelligence of the declaration of war having been conveyed, by express, from New York to Queenstown and Montreal, at the expense of some British merchants residing at the former city, the enemy had been apprised of the measure at a much earlier date than that on which the American officers had received the information, and the latter, therefore, labored under great disadvantages. One of the most notable instances of this official neglect, which resulted in the most serious consequences to the country, was that of the neglect to notify the commanders of the northwestern posts, especially that of Michilimacinac, whose first information of the existence of war was received from the enemy, with a demand for his surrender.[1]

As before related, the enemy received early advice of the declaration of war from the British merchants residing in New York; and one of the first cares of Sir Isaac Brock was to notify Captain Roberts, at St. Joseph's, with orders to make an immediate attack on Michilimacinac, if practicable; or, in the event of an attack on his post, by the Americans, to defend it to the last extremity.[2] At a subsequent date the order was renewed, with directions to summon the neighboring Indians to his assistance, and to ask, for the same purpose, the co-operation of such of the employees of the British fur companies, who might happen to be near him;[3] and, still later, the Captain was left to his own discretion to adopt either offensive or defensive measures, as circumstances might warrant.[4] With a degree of promptitude which reflects honor on his professional character, Captain Roberts decided to act offensively; and he took immediate measures to insure a successful termination of his enterprise. He was far beyond the limits within which he could have command-

[1] Ingersoll, i. pp. 79, 80; Brock's Life of Sir Isaac Brock, p. 180.—[2] Lieut. Hanks to Gen. Hull, Aug. 4, 1812.

[3] Brock's Life of Sir Isaac Brock, p. 223.

[1] Lieut. Hanks to Gen. Hull, Aug. 4, 1812.

[2] Gen. Brock to Capt. Roberts, June 26, 1812; Brock's Life of Brock, p. 223.—[3] Gen. Brock to Capt. Roberts, Fort George, June 28, 1812; Brock's Life of Brock, p. 224; Christie's Mil. and Naval Operations in the Canadas, p. 64.—[4] Gen. Brock to Capt. Roberts, July 4, 1812; Brock's Life of Brock, p. 224.

ed the assistance of other portions of the Royal forces; and he fell back on the limited resources of his secluded position with remarkable good judgment and success. Calling to his quarters Mr. Pothier, an agent of the Southwest Company, who was then at St. Joseph's, he laid before that gentleman his proposed plan of operations, and solicited his assistance. Mr. Pothier, struck with the importance of the projected enterprise, and the feasibility of the plan of operations, immediately opened the stores of the Company, and placed every thing they contained, which might contribute to the success of the expedition, at the command of Captain Roberts; while, at the same time, he offered his own services, as a volunteer, with those of one hundred and eighty Canadian *voyageurs*—employees of the Company—one-half of whom he armed with muskets or fowling pieces.[1] Captain Roberts also invited the assistance of the neighboring Indians—both American and British—and about four hundred and twenty-five of the savages responded to his call.[2]

On the day after the receipt of the orders last referred to[1] (*July* 16), at ten o'clock in the morning, Captain Roberts embarked, with his entire force—regular, volunteer, and savage—and, two iron six-pounders, and under the convoy of the Northwest Company's brig *Caledonia*, which was laden with stores and provisions, he approached the Island of Michilimacinac.[2] At three o'clock in the morning of the seventeenth of July, the flotilla reached the place of rendezvous; and one of the two guns was immediately taken up the high ground in the rear of the fort, and placed in battery in a position which completely commanded the garrison.[3]

In the mean time, Lieutenant Hanks and his little command remained comparatively ignorant of their impending danger. It is true an Indian interpreter had told the Lieutenant, on the sixteenth, that the *Indians* at St. Joseph's intended to make an immediate attack on the post; and from the sudden coolness which some of the chiefs, in the vicinity of his post, had displayed, he appears to have been inclined to believe the interpreter's information. He immediately called a council, and invited "the American gentlemen at that time on the island" to participate in the deliberations; the result of which was the appointment of Captain Daurman, as a scout, to proceed to St. Joseph's to watch the motions of the *Indians*. The Captain embarked about sunset, and had proceeded only a short

[1] Christie's Operations in Canada, p. 64. Mr. C. says, "*One hundred and sixty voyageurs*" were thus secured; but Capt. Roberts (*Dispatch to Adj.-Gen., July* 17) and Mr. Brock (*Life and Corres. of Sir I. Brock*, p. 224) say there were "one hundred and *eighty*," and I have considered their authority the best. Some of the best authorities, British and American, speak also of a body of *two hundred Canadian militia*, under Mr. Crawford, but as they do not refer to the voyageurs, I have supposed the latter were the "Canadians" referred to.

[2] John Asken, jr., to Col. Claus, July 18, 1812. Mr. James (*Mil. Occurrences*, i. p. 56) says there were "393 Indians." J. L. Thomson (*Hist. Sketches*, p. 19) says "715 Indians."

[1] Capt. Roberts to Adj.-Gen., July 17, 1812; James' Mil. Occur., i. p. 56.—[2] Christie's Operations, &c., p. 65; Brock's Life of Brock, p. 224.

[3] Capt. Roberts to Adj.-Gen., July 17, 1812; James' Military Occurrences, i. p. 56.

distance before he met the enemy's flotilla, by whom he was captured, and returned with it to the island. At daybreak he was landed, with instructions to remove all the inhabitants of the little village to the west side of the island—where the enemy's flotilla then laid—in order that their persons and property might be protected; at the same time forbidding him from conveying any information to the garrison, and *threatening with extermination all those who might seek refuge with the garrison and offer any resistance.* The inhabitants of the village appear to have obeyed the order without any delay; and the intelligence of their exodus, which was carried to the fort by Doctor Day, who was passing that way, was the first intimation which Lieutenant Hanks had received of the presence of an enemy of any kind, nor did he then suspect that the intruders were subjects of his Britannic majesty, lawfully prosecuting a warfare which his own government had declared, nearly a month before that time. He lost no time, however, in ordering the blockhouses, on the high ground in his rear, to be occupied and supplied with ammunition and stores; and every gun in the main works was prepared for action.[1]

By this time, however, the enemy had gained the heights, and placed his gun in battery, as before referred to, while the Indians, in great numbers, showed themselves in the margin of the woods, nearer the fort.[2] At about eleven o'clock a flag was sent, requiring

[1] Lieut. Hanks to Gen. Hull. Aug. 4, 1812.—[2] Ibid.

the surrender of the fort and its garrison to his Britannic majesty's forces—the earliest notice which the garrison had received of the character of their enemy.[1] After consulting his officers and the American gentlemen who were present; and taking into consideration the strength and *disposition*[2] of the enemy, it was resolved to yield to the demand; and the fort and the island were, accordingly, surrendered to the arms of Great Britain.[3]

Of the great importance of this conquest, both parties were immediately fully sensible. Not only were the stores which were taken quite valuable, but seven hundred packages of furs were among the trophies of the victory. But not alone from the value of the spoils does the interest which has attached to this affair arise. General Hull has shown its effects in the most vivid colors when he said,[4] "*After the surrender of Michilimacinac*, almost every tribe and nation of Indians, excepting a part of the Miamis and Delawares, north from beyond Lake Supe-

[1] Lieut. Hanks to Gen. Hull, Aug. 4, 1812.

[2] "It was a fortunate circumstance, the fort capitulated without firing a single gun, for had they done so, *I firmly believe not a soul of them would have been saved.*"—*J. Askin, jr.*, *to Col. Claus, July* 18. As Mr. Askin was a *British* officer, and accompanied the Ottawas and Chippewas who were in the expedition, his statement is entitled to great weight. Mr. Thomson (*Hist. Sketches*, p. 20) says, "Capt. Roberts, of the British regulars, sent in a prisoner to inform the Commandant, that *if any resistance was made, the garrison and inhabitants would be indiscriminately put to the sword.*" Mr. Breckenridge (*Hist. of Late War*, p. 32), Lieut. Hanks, commander of the fort (*Dispatch to Gen. Hull, Aug.* 4, 1812), Dr. Peck (*Perkins' Annals of the West*, p. 600), and Mr. Lanman (*Hist. Michigan*, p. 190), bear the same testimony.

[3] John Askin, jr., to Col. W. Claus, July 18, 1812; Lieut. Hanks to Gen. Hull, Aug. 4, 1812.

[4] Letter to Secretary of War, Aug. 26, 1812.

rior, west from beyond the Mississippi, south from the Ohio and Wabash, and east from every part of Upper Canada, and from all the intermediate country, *joined in open hostility, under the British standard*, against the army I commanded, *contrary to the most solemn assurance of a large portion of them to remain neutral*." The same views were entertained by the enemy; and the standard British authorities[1] on the history of those times, have left on record their testimony to the same effect.

DOCUMENTS.

I.

LIEUTENANT HANK'S DISPATCH TO GENERAL HULL.

Detroit, *August* 4, 1812.

Sir:—I take the earliest opportunity to acquaint your Excellency of the surrender of the garrison of Michilimacinac, under my command, to His Britannic Majesty's forces under the command of Captain Charles Roberts, on the 17th ultimo, the particulars of which are as follows: On the 16th I was informed by the Indian interpreter, that he had discovered from an Indian, that the several nations of Indians then at St. Joseph (a British garrison, distant about forty miles), intended to make an immediate attack upon Michilimacinac. I was inclined, from the coolness I had discovered in some of the principal chiefs of the Ottawa and Chippewa nations, who had but a few days before professed the greatest friendship for the United States, to place confidence in this report. I immediately called a meeting of the American gentlemen at that time on the island, in which it was thought proper to dispatch a confidential person to St. Joseph, to watch the motions of the Indians. Captain Daurman of the militia was thought the most suitable for this service. He embarked about sunset, and met the British forces within ten or fifteen miles of the island, by whom he was made prisoner, and put upon his parole of honor. He was landed on the island at daybreak, with positive directions to give me no intelligence whatever. He was also instructed to take the inhabitants of the village, indiscriminately, to a place on the west side of the island, where their persons and property should be protected by a British guard; but should they go to the fort, they would be subject to a general massacre by the savages, which would be inevitable, if the garrison fired a gun. This information I received from Doctor Day, who was passing through the village, when every person was flying for refuge to the enemy. Immediately on being informed of the approach of the enemy, I placed ammunition, &c., in the blockhouses; ordered every gun charged, and made every preparation for action. About nine o'clock I could discover that the enemy were in possession of the heights that commanded the fort, and one piece of their artillery directed to the most defenceless part of the garrison. The Indians at this time were to be seen in great numbers in the edge of the woods. At half-past eleven o'clock the enemy sent in a flag of truce, demanding a surrender of the fort and island to His Britannic Majesty's forces. This, sir, was the first information I had of the declaration of war; I, however, had anticipated it, and

[1] Christie's Operations, &c., pp. 65, 66; Auchinleck's Hist. of the War, p. 51; Gov.-Gen. Prevost to Earl Bathurst, Col.-Sec., Aug. 26, 1812.

was as well prepared to meet such an event as I possibly could have been with the force under my command, amounting to fifty-seven men, including officers. Three American gentlemen, who were prisoners, were permitted to accompany the flag; from them I ascertained the strength of the enemy to be from nine hundred to one thousand strong, consisting of regular troops, Canadians, and savages; that they had two pieces of artillery, and were provided with ladders and ropes for the purpose of scaling the works, if necessary. After I had obtained this information, I consulted my officers, and also the American gentlemen present, who were very intelligent men; the result of which was, that it was impossible for the garrison to hold out against such a superior force. In this opinion I fully concurred, from the conviction that it was the only measure that could prevent a general massacre. The fort and garrison were accordingly surrendered.

The inclosed papers exhibit copies of the correspondence between the officer commanding the British forces and myself, and of the articles of capitulation. This subject involved questions of a peculiar nature; and I hope, sir, that my demands and protests will meet the approbation of my government. I cannot allow this opportunity to escape without expressing my obligation to Doctor Day for the service he rendered me in conducting this correspondence.

In consequence of this unfortunate affair, I beg leave, sir, to demand that a court of inquiry may be ordered to investigate all the facts connected with it; and I do further request, that the court may be specially directed to express their opinion on the merits of the case.

I have the honor to be, sir, &c.,

P. Hanks, *Lieut. of Artillery.*

His Excellency, Gen. Hull,
commanding N. W. Army.

II.

CAPTAIN ROBERTS' DISPATCH TO ADJUTANT-GENERAL OF THE ARMY.

Fort Michilimacinac, *July* 17, 1812.

Sir:—On the 15th instant I received letters by express, from Major-general Brock, with orders to adopt the most prudent measures, either for offence or defence, which circumstances might point out; and having received intelligence, from the best information, that large reinforcements were daily expected to be thrown into this garrison, with the thorough conviction that my situation at St. Joseph's was totally indefensible, I determined to lose no time in making the meditated attack on this fort.

On the 16th, at ten o'clock in the morning, I embarked my few men, with about one hundred and eighty Canadians, and two iron six-pounders. The boats arrived without the smallest accident at the place of rendezvous, at three o'clock the following morning; by the exertions of the Canadians, one of the guns was brought up a height commanding the garrison, and ready to act, about ten o'clock. A summons was then sent in; a copy of the capitulation which followed, I have the honor to inclose. At twelve o'clock the American colors were hauled down, and those of His Majesty were hoisted. A committee has been appointed to examine into the state of the public stores.

Inclosed, also, are the returns of the ordnance and military stores found in the fort, and the strength of the garrison. The greatest praise is due to every individual employed in the expedition; to my own officers I am indebted, in particular, for their active assistance in carrying all my orders into effect.

I have the honor to be, &c.,

Chas. Roberts, *Capt. Command'g.*

The Adjutant-general, &c., &c.

CHAPTER XVI.

July 19, 1812.

THE ATTACK ON SACKETTS' HARBOR, N. Y.

At an early period of the war, the command of the great northern lakes appears to have been made the object of great labor and expense, both by the Americans and the British. The former, notwithstanding all their care, appear to have been sadly deficient in their *naval* preparations; while the latter appear to have concentrated the greater part of their efforts on this branch of the service. This, for a time, gave to the enemy the control of Lake Ontario, and enabled him to exercise an undue influence over all the military movements in its immediate vicinity.

Among the posts on that lake which had been strengthened by the Americans was Sacketts' Harbor, a small village in New York, in which harbor was anchored the United States brig *Oneida*, of sixteen guns, under command of Lieutenant-commandant M. T. Woolsey.[1]

Against this post, in July, 1812, were dispatched five vessels from the Canada shore—the *Royal George* of twenty-four guns, the *Prince Regent* of twenty-two, the *Earl Moira* of twenty, the *Seneca* of eighteen, and one whose name and strength are unknown;[2] and about daylight on Sunday, the nineteenth of July, they approached the Harbor.[1] They were discovered by the look-out on the mast-head of the *Oneida;* and from the fact that the Americans had no *ships* on the lake, and as two of the strangers were ships, they were known, at once, to be British vessels.[2] The wind being dead ahead, they beat up for the Harbor; and, soon afterwards, they captured a boat belonging to the revenue department, which was returning from Cape Vincent.[3] When the squadron had nearly reached the Harbor, the captive custom-house officers were sent on shore, with a message to the commanders of the post, demanding the surrender of the *Oneida* and of the *Lord Nelson*—the latter a British schooner, which had been seized for a violation of the revenue laws—threatening, in case of a refusal, that the squadron would burn the village or lay the inhabitants under contribution.[4]

In the mean time expresses had been sent out to call in the neighboring detachments, and volunteers from the surrounding country; and a regiment under Colonel Bellinger, a company of artillery under Captain

---

[1] Cooper's Naval Hist. (*Ed.* 1839), ii. p. 326.—[2] The War, i. p. 32; Hough's Hist. of Jefferson Co., N. Y., p. 463.

[1] Letter from the Baltimore *Whig*, in "*The Aurora*," No. 6667, Phila., Tuesday, Aug. 4, 1812; The War, i. p. 32.—[2] Ibid.; Hough's Hist. Jefferson Co., N. Y., p. 463.

[3] The War, i. p. 32; Letter in Baltimore *Whig*.

[4] The War, i. p. 32; Hough's Jefferson Co., p. 463.

Camp, and a body of militia, in all upwards of three thousand men, responded to the summons during the day.[1] The *Oneida* was also prepared for action; and having received on board twenty-five volunteers, Captain Woolsey soon afterwards left the Harbor, and ran down to meet the enemy, hoping to induce the *Royal George*, the British commodore's ship, to engage in single combat.[2] Failing in this, the *Oneida* returned to the Harbor, and was moored, with springs on her cables, on a line with a three-gun battery which had been erected on the beach a few days previous. As she could employ only one half her armament, her starboard guns were landed, to be used on shore, if occasion required; and the vessel herself was so far warped around that her larboard broadside was brought to bear, with the best effect, on the entrance of the Harbor.[3]

About this time the two leading vessels of the enemy's squadron had come abreast of the three-gun battery on the beach; when Lieutenant-commandant Woolsey—perceiving the inefficiency of the fire therefrom, in consequence of the inexperience of its commander—left the *Oneida* in charge of a lieutenant, and took command of it himself, opening a fire on the enemy from the long thirty-two pounder which was

[1] The War, i. p. 32; Hough's Jefferson County, N. Y., p. 463.

[2] The War, i. p. 32; Letter in Baltimore *Whig*. Mr. Hough (*History of Jefferson County, N. Y.*, p. 463) says, 'The *Oneida* attempted to gain the lake, *but failed to do so*.''

[3] The War, i. p. 32; Letter in Baltimore *Whig;* Hough's Jefferson County, p. 463.

mounted thereon.[1] During this time the squadron stood off and on, and kept up a warm fire on the battery, the *Oneida*, and the village, without doing much damage to either.[2] The second shot, which Lieutenant Woolsey fired from the battery, struck the *Royal George* between her main and mizzen chains, and went through her sides. The third struck her between wind and water; when she hove in stays, and while putting about, the fourth struck her in her stern, and completely raked her—the splinters flying as high as her mizzen topsail-yard.[3]

About the same time the *Earl Moira* lost her fore topgallant-mast;[4] and one of the schooners was hulled in a serious manner.[5] After continuing this contest about two hours,[6] the squadron put about and stood out of the harbor, amidst the cheers of the citizens, the music at the post at the same time playing "*Yankee Doodle*."[7]

It is said that no injury was sustained, either by the *Oneida*, the village, or the people who had assembled to oppose the enemy.[8] This apparently singular result of the protracted action was occasioned by the enemy keeping beyond the range of the small pieces; the only guns which were employed, on either side, being those few which were of a heavier calibre.

[1] The War, i. p. 32; Letter in Balt. *Whig;* Cooper's Naval Hist. (*Ed.* 1839), ii. p. 327.—[2] The War, i. p. 32; Letter in Balt. *Whig;* Hough's Jefferson Co., p. 464.—[3] Letter in Balt. *Whig;* Hough's Jefferson Co., p. 464.—[4] Letter from the Balt. *Whig.*—[5] Ibid.—[6] The War, p. i. 32; Cooper, ii. p. 326.—[7] The War, i. p. 32; Hough's Jefferson County, p. 464.—[8] The War, i. p. 32.

CHAPTER XVII.

August 5, 1812.

THE DEFEAT OF MAJOR VAN HORN.

The American "Army of the North-west," under General Hull, had passed the Detroit River and invaded Upper Canada, when Colonel Proctor, of the Royal army, reached Malden, and adopted such measures as effectually cut off the communication between the army and the States; and, to a great extent, neutralized all the efforts of the former.[1] Early in August, 1812, the General had been advised of the march of one hundred and fifty men, under Captain Henry Brush, with a number of cattle, from Ohio;[2] and, after some persuasion, he had resolved to make an attempt to open the communication, in order that they might reach the camp with greater expedition and certainty.[3] For this purpose he detached Major Van Horn, of Colonel Findley's Ohio regiment of volunteers, with two hundred men;[4] and on the fourth of August they crossed the Detroit, and took up their line of march the same day.[5] After lying on their arms near the River De Corce, during the night of the fourth, on the next day they resumed their march, preceded by a small party of spies, under Captain McCullough.[6] His line of march appears to have been formed without any flanking parties—his "front guard of twenty-four men, divided into two columns, each preceded by three dragoons, and the main party in the same order, the mail, with an escort of horsemen, being placed in the centre"[1]—and the usual result of similar instances of neglect speedily befell the expedition.

After having passed the Maguaga village, Captain McCullough of the spies was shot and scalped before he could be saved by the detachment; and, soon afterwards, Major Van Horn was informed that a large body of the enemy was lying in ambush, near Brownstown, for the purpose of cutting off the party.[2] Supposing the report was one of the numerous false alarms which were constantly floating around the country, he disregarded it, and moved on without adopting the precautions which the character of his route, and that of the enemies among whom he was moving, would appear to have rendered necessary.[3]

It appears that the road on which Major Van Horn was marching, a short distance from Brownstown, "passes through a narrow prairie, skirted with thick woods, with a creek on the right. The woods on the creek come to a point, towards the town, through which point the road passes to the

[1] Perkins' Annals of the West, p. 598; Christie's Operations, &c., p. 69; Armstrong's Notices, i. p. 25.

[2] Gen. Hull to Sec. of War, Aug. 7, 1812; James' Mil. Occur., i. p. 61.—[3] McAfee (*Hist. of the War*, p. 73) says the General "seemed indifferent about the fate of Brush and his provisions."

[4] Perkins' Annals of the West, p. 599; Gen. Hull to Sec. of War, Aug. 7, 1812; McAfee's Hist. of War in West, p. 73.—[5] McAfee, p. 73.—[6] Ibid.

[1] McAfee, p. 74.—[2] Ibid.—[3] Armstrong's Notices, i. pp. 25, 26; Headley's Second War, i. p. 79.

ford. On the left of this road were several small cornfields and thickets of thorn-bushes;"[1] and as the detachment moved towards the town, with the creek on its right and the thickets and corn on its left, its ranks were formed into closer order than was usual in its line of march. In these thickets, on the left, and in the woods, on the opposite side of the stream, on the right of the line of march, a small party of Indians, under Tecumthà,[2] and, probably, a small detachment of the Forty-first regiment of the line, under Captain Tallon,[3] had formed an ambush; and when the column had entered the defile, they opened a fire on it from either side.[4] Ignorant of the character and strength of his hidden foe, Major Van Horn feared that he would be surrounded, and he immediately ordered a retreat.[1] The enemy immediately pursued; and a running fight was kept up between the parties for several miles—the detachment several times turning on its pursuers with great effect.[2]

By this engagement and defeat of Major Van Horn, the mail from the army passed into the hands of the enemy, from which the condition and sentiments of the troops were fully laid open to his inspection—a privilege which he was not tardy in taking advantage of, with great benefit to himself.[3] The detachment suffered the loss of Captains Gilchrist, Ullery, McCullough, and Bœrstler, Lieutenant Pentz, Ensigns Roby and Allison, and ten privates, *killed*, and nine *wounded*.[4] The loss of the enemy is not known.

DOCUMENT.

GENERAL HULL'S DISPATCH TO THE SECRETARY OF WAR.

SANDWICH, *August* 7, 1812.

SIR:—On the 4th inst. Major Van Horn, of Colonel Findley's regiment of Ohio volunteers, was detached from this army, with the command of two hundred men, principally riflemen, to proceed to the River Raisin, and farther, if necessary, to meet and reinforce Captain Brush, of the State of Ohio, commanding a company of volunteers, and escorting provisions for this army. At Brownstown, a large body of Indians had formed an ambuscade, and the Major's detachment received a heavy fire, at the distance of fifty yards from the enemy. The whole detachment retreated in disorder. Major Van Horn made every exertion to form, and prevent the retreat that was possible for a brave and gallant officer, but without success.

By the return of killed and wounded, it will be perceived that the loss of officers has been uncommonly great. Their efforts to rally their companies was the occasion of it.

I am, very respectfully, &c.,

WILLIAM HULL, *Brig.-Gen.*

HON. MR. EUSTIS, Secretary of War.

---

[1] McAfee, p. 74.—[2] James' Mil. Occur., i. p. 61; Brock's Life of Brock, p. 239; Auchinleck's Hist. of War, p. 52.

[3] Brock's Life of Brock, p. 239; Breckenridge's Hist. of War, p. 34; Christie's Operations, p. 69; Thomson's Sketches, p. 25. Mr. James (*Mil. Occur.*, i. pp. 61, 62) denies that any regulars were there.

[4] Gen. Hull to Sec. of War, Aug. 7; McAfee, p. 74.

[1] McAfee, p. 74.—[2] Gen. Hull to Sec. of War, Aug. 7.

[3] Christie's Operations, p. 69; Armstrong's Notices, i. p. 25; James' Mil. Occur., i. p. 61; Brock's Life of Brock, p. 239.—[4] Returns appended to Gen. Hull's Dispatch, Aug. 7; Breckenridge's Hist. of War, p. 34; Thomson's Sketches, p. 25; Sketches of the War, p. 21; McAfee, p. 74. Armstrong (*Notices*, i. p. 25) says Van Horn lost *sixty privates*, beside officers. Mr. Headley (*Second War*, i. p. 79) says, "Only about one half (*one hundred*) returned to the army." Davis (*Hist. of Late War*, p. 34) says, "7 officers and 19 privates were killed." Mr. Perkins (*Hist. of Late War*, p. 83) says *thirty* were wounded.

CHAPTER XVIII.

August 9, 1812.

THE ACTION AT MAGUAGA

THE defeat of the detachment under Major Van Horn, to which reference has been made in a former chapter,[1] had been followed by a still greater disaster—the sudden and mortifying retreat of the American army from Canada, and its reoccupation of the fort at Detroit[2]—when General Hull immediately determined to make a second attempt to open the communication with the River Raisin, and to escort the provision-train, which had been encamped there under Captain Henry Brush.[3]

For this purpose the Fourth regiment of regular troops; two small detachments from the First regiment, under Lieutenant Stansbury and Ensign McLabe; detachments from the Ohio and Michigan Volunteers; a corps of artillerists, with a six-pounder and a howitzer, under Lieutenant Eastman; and two small detachments of cavalry, under Captain Sloan of the Ohio Volunteers—the whole numbering six hundred men, under Lieutenant-colonel Miller of the Fourth regiment—were detached on the eighth of August; and, on the afternoon of that day, the party left Detroit.[4] Marching through the woods, in two parallel columns, with an advanced guard in front, the progress of the detachment was very slow;[1] and at four in the afternoon of the ninth, the detachment had proceeded no farther than Maguaga, an Indian village, about fourteen miles from Detroit.[2]

At this time Captain Snelling, of the Fourth regiment, being in command of the advance—the main body, in two columns, being half a mile in the rear—a heavy fire was opened on the former[3] by an unseen enemy, who had been awaiting the approach of the detachment for several hours;[4] and who had concealed himself in the bushes with so much success that his presence was not suspected until the fire was opened on the troops.[5]

It appears that early in the morning intelligence of the approach of the detachment had been taken, by the In-

---

[1] Vide Chap. XVI.—[2] Christie's Operations, &c., p. 70; Armstrong's Notices, i. p. 32; McAfee's War in West, p. 77.—[3] Sketches of the War, p. 21; Armstrong's Notices, i. p. 26; Davis' Hist. of War, p. 34; O'Connor's Hist. of War, p. 40.—[4] Gen. Hull to Sec. of War, Aug. 13.

[1] Gen. Hull to Sec. of War, Aug. 13. Maj. Richardson (*Narrative, cited by Mr. Auchinleck*) says the progress of the party was retarded by the difficulty in transporting the artillery.—[2] Gen. Hull to Sec. of War, Aug. 13; Perkin's Hist. of War, p. 83.—[3] Gen. Hull to Sec. of War, Aug. 13; Sketches of the War, p. 21; Armstrong's Notices, i. p. 27.

[4] Maj. Richardson's Narrative, cited by Mr. Auchinleck.

[5] Armstrong's Notices, i. p. 27; Headley's Second War, i. p. 80. Mr. Headley (*Hist. Second War*, i. p. 80), following the errors of many of his predecessors, and adding to them others of his own, gives a glowing account of *a breastwork*, and of an attack on it; but Maj. Richardson, and those who were present, as far as I have seen their statements, make no reference to any such work; and speak only of *laying on the ground*, for concealment.

dian scouts, to Brownstown, where was posted a large body of troops, which had been detached by Colonel Proctor, for the purpose of cutting off the communication between Detroit and the States. This party was composed of "about one hundred of the Forty-first, the same number of militia, and about two hundred and fifty Indians," under the command of Captain Muir, of the Forty-first regiment;[1] and, on receiving the information referred to, it moved out to meet the American detachment; took post about a quarter of a mile in front of Maguaga; and awaited the approach of its enemy.[2] While thus concealed, before the Americans came in sight, this party was strengthened by the arrival of Lieutenant Bullock, with twenty men from the grenadiers of the Forty-first, twenty men from the light-infantry, and twenty battalion-men, who had been sent from Amherstburg, for that purpose, by Colonel Proctor—making the enemy's force not less than five hundred and twenty-five men, including officers.[3] The Indians, under the leadership of Tecumthà, occupied the left, their white auxiliaries the right of the position;[4] and a single shot from the former, "followed by a heavy and desultory fire," first apprised the American detachment of the presence of their enemy.[5]

Captain Snelling and the advance received and returned the fire with great gallantry; maintaining their position, with the utmost firmness, until the main body had formed in order of battle and advanced to his support. Firing as he advanced, Lieutenant-colonel Miller gradually moved forward, until he had nearly reached the enemy, when a charge was ordered and vigorously executed.[1] At this time a body of Indians, who had been detached to the extreme right of the enemy's line, was driven from its position by the American troops; and, in its retreat, was mistaken, by its white auxiliaries, for a body of Americans. The consequence of this unfortunate mistake was the opening of a fire on it, by the regulars on its left; while, misled by this aggressive act of their friends, the Indians "returned the fire with equal spirit," and an internal contest, between the two arms of the Royal service, was for some time kept up.[2]

In the mean time the Americans pushed forward; and the regulars in the enemy's line—closely pressed in front by the American bayonets, while, as they falsely supposed, from their contest with their savage allies, their rear was also threatened—fell back, *in confusion*, and left the field to be contested by Tecumthà and his Indians.[3] Captain Muir succeeded, however, in rallying his troops on the brow of a hill, about a quarter of a mile distant from his first position; but, a few minutes afterwards, some firing was heard in the

[1] Auchinleck's Hist., p. 52.—[2] Maj. Richardson's Narrative.—[3] Ibid. Mr. Brock (*Life of Brock*, p. 240) falls into an error in saying the force was only 325 men in all; and Mr. James (*Mil. Occur.*, i. p. 65) has committed the same blunder.—[4] Gen. Hull to Sec. of War, Aug. 13.

[5] Maj. Richardson's Narrative.

[1] Gen. Hull to Sec. of War, Aug. 13; Perkins' Hist. War, p. 83; Breckenridge's Hist. of War, p. 36; Armstrong's Notices, i. p. 27.—[2] Maj. Richardson's Narrative.

[3] Ibid.; James' Military Occurrences, i. p. 65; Armstrong's Notices, p. 27.

woods on his left, when he fell back a second time "at the double quick," as one of his officers significantly remarks —leaving the Indians to fight the battle, or to run, as they thought best.[1]

The example which had been placed before the savages, by the regular troops, was not imitated; and the gallant chief and his warriors disdained to retreat while a hope remained. With the greatest obstinacy, therefore, they maintained the action, long after the regulars had retired; and when the antagonistic bayonets could no longer be resisted they retired with the greatest sullenness.[2]

When the enemy retreated he was pursued upwards of two miles, when the care of the wounded, the approach of night, and the danger of an ambuscade, induced Lieutenant-colonel Miller to order the troops to suspend the pursuit.[3]

The force of the two parties has been referred to already. Of the Americans, ten regulars and eight volunteers were *killed*, and forty-five regulars and twelve volunteers were *wounded*.[1] Of the enemy's force, the regulars—who were scarcely in action—lost twenty-four men, killed and wounded,[2] while the loss of the militia and the Indians has not been recorded. It is said, however, that about forty of the latter were found dead on the field; which indicates a very heavy aggregate loss.[3]

The communication having thus been opened, Lieutenant-colonel Miller sent a messenger to Detroit with a request for provisions and reinforcements to assist in removing the wounded. A second messenger carried the same request; but, instead of the provisions and relief, an order was received *directing the detachment to return to Detroit, leaving the route to the States entirely without protection*, and sacrificing, at a blow, the fruits of this hard-earned victory.[4]

[1] Maj. Richardson's Narrative; Armstrong's Notices, i. p. 27.—[2] Gen. Hull to Sec. of War, Aug. 13; Brock's Life of Brock, p. 240; Perkins' Hist. War, p. 83; Breckenridge's Hist. of War, p. 36; Armstrong's Notices, i. p. 28; Thomson's Sketches, p. 27.—[3] Gen. Hull to Sec. of War, Aug. 13; Perkins' Hist. War, p. 83.

[1] Gen. Hull to Sec. of War, Aug. 13, 1812; Perkins' Hist. War, p. 83.

[2] Maj. Richardson's Narrative.

[3] Gen. Hull to Secretary of War, Aug. 13, 1812.

[4] Armstrong's Notices, i. pp. 29, 30; McAfee, pp. 79, 80.

DOCUMENT.

GENERAL HULL'S DISPATCH TO THE SECRETARY OF WAR.

Detroit, *August* 13, 1812.

Sir:—The main body of the army having recrossed the river at Detroit, on the night and morning of the 8th inst., six hundred men were immediately detached, under the command of Lieutenant-colonel Miller, to open the communication to the River Raisin, and protect the provisions, which were under the escort of Captain Brush. This detachment consisted of the Fourth United States regiment and two small detachments, under the command of Lieutenant Stansbury and Ensign M'Labe, of the First regiment; detachments from the Ohio and Michigan Volunteers, a corps of artillerists, with one six-pounder and a howitzer, under the command of Lieutenant Eastman, and a part of Captains Smith and Sloan's cavalry, commanded by Captain Sloan, of the Ohio Volunteers. Lieutenant-colonel Miller marched from Detroit on the afternoon of the 8th instant, and on the 9th, about 4 o'clock P. M., the van-guard, commanded by Captain Snelling, of the Fourth United States regiment, was fired on by an extensive line of British troops and Indians at the lower part of Maguaga, about fourteen miles from Detroit. At this time the main body was marching in two columns, and Captain Snelling maintained his position in a most gallant manner, under a very heavy fire, until the line was formed and advanced to the ground he occupied, when the whole, excepting the rear-guard, was brought into action. The enemy were formed behind a temporary breastwork of logs, the Indians extending in a thick wood on their left. Lieutenant-colonel Miller ordered his whole line to advance, and when within a small distance of the enemy, made a general discharge, and proceeded with charged bayonets, when the whole British line and Indians commenced a retreat. They were pursued in a most vigorous manner about two miles, and the pursuit discontinued only on account of the fatigue of the troops, the approach of evening, and the necessity of returning to take care of the wounded. The judicious arrangements made by Lieutenant-colonel Miller, and the gallant manner in which they were executed, justly entitle him to the highest honor. From the moment the line commenced the fire, it continually moved on, and the enemy maintained their position until forced at the point of the bayonet. The Indians on the left, under the command of Tecumseh, fought with great obstinacy, but were continually forced and compelled to retreat. The victory was complete in every part of the line, and the success would have been more brilliant had the cavalry charged the enemy on the retreat, when a most favorable opportunity presented. Although orders were given for the purpose, unfortunately they were not executed. Majors Van Horn and Morrison, of the Ohio Volunteers, were associated with Lieutenant-colonel Miller, as field-officers in this command, and were highly distinguished by their exertions in forming the line, and the firm and intrepid manner they led their respective commands to action.

Captain Baker, of the First United States regiment, Captain Brevort, of the Second, and Captain Hull, of the Thirteenth, my aid-de-camp and Lieutenant Whistler, of the First, requested permission to join the detachment as volunteers. Lieutenant-colonel Miller assigned commands to Captain Baker and Lieutenant Whistler; and Captains Brevort and Hull, at his request, attended his person, and aided him in the general arrangements. Lieutenant-colonel Miller has mentioned the conduct of these officers in terms of high approbation. In addition to the captains who have been named, Lieutenant-colonel Miller has mentioned Captains Burton and Fuller, of the Fourth regiment, Captains Saunders and Brown, of the Ohio Volunteers, and Captain Delandre, of the Michigan Volunteers, who were attached to his command, and distinguished by their valor. It is impossible for me, in this communication, to do justice to the officers and soldiers who gained the victory which I have described. They have acquired high honor to themselves, and are justly entitled to the gratitude of their country.

Major Muir, of the Forty-first regiment, commanded the British in this action. The regulars and volunteers consisted of about four hundred, and a larger number of Indians. Major Muir and two subalterns were wounded, one of them since dead. About forty Indians were found dead on the field, and Tecumseh, their leader, was slightly wounded. The number of wounded Indians who escaped has not been ascertained. Four of Major Muir's detachment have been made prisoners, and fifteen of the Forty-first regiment killed and wounded. The militia and volunteers attached to his command were in the severest part of the action, and their loss must have been great—it has not yet been ascertained. I have the honor to be,

Your most obedient servant,

W. HULL, *Brig.-Gen.*

Commanding N. W. Army.

HON. W. EUSTIS, Secretary of War.

Return of killed and wounded in the action fought near Maguaga, August 9, 1812.

Fourth United States Regiment.—Ten non-commissioned officers and privates killed, and forty-five wounded; Captain Baker, of the First regiment of infantry; Lieutenant Larabee, of the Fourth; Lieutenant Peters, of the Fourth; Ensign Whistler, of the Seventeenth, doing duty in the Fourth; Lieutenant Silly, and an ensign, whose name has not been returned to me, were wounded.

In the Ohio and Michigan Volunteers, eight were killed and thirteen wounded.

W. Hull.

CHAPTER XIX.

August 13, 1812.

THE CAPTURE OF THE ALERT.

Soon after the declaration of war the frigate *Essex* sailed from New York, under command of Captain David Porter.[1] After cruising to the southward, for some weeks, she run up to the northward again, capturing several merchant ships during her cruise.[2]

On the thirteenth of August, while she was sailing under disguise,—having her gun-deck ports in, topgallant-masts housed, and sails trimmed slovenly,—she made a strange sail to windward.[3] The stranger made chase; and, probably, deceived by the disguise of the *Essex*, and by her apparent unwillingness to engage, the former ran down on her weather-quarter, set British colors, gave three cheers, and opened her fire.[4]

Without farther ceremony the *Essex* knocked out her ports, and returned the fire. The stranger threw in two or three broadsides; but the surprise with which her crew witnessed the effect of her rashness was such that it deserted her guns, and ran below for safety.[1] Within eight minutes after the action commenced the stranger struck her colors;[2] and Lieutenant Finch[3] having been sent on board, reported her to be His Britannic Majesty's ship *Alert*, of eighteen guns, commanded by Captain T. L. P. Laugharne; that she had seven feet water in her hold; and that she was in danger of sinking.[4]

The *Essex* mounted forty-six guns—forty thirty-two-pound carronades and six long twelves—and a complement of about three hundred and twenty-five men.[5] The *Alert*—which had been built for the coal trade, and purchased into the royal navy in 1804[6]—mounted twenty eighteen-pound carronades and six smaller guns, with a crew of one hundred and thirty men and boys.[7]

---

[1] Cooper's Naval Hist., ii. p. 53; Clark's Naval Hist., p. 137.—[2] Cooper, ii. p. 53.—[3] Ibid.

[4] Capt. Porter to Sec. of Navy, Aug. 17; Clark's Naval Hist., p. 137; Thomson's Hist. of War, p. 37; James' Naval Occurrences, p. 81; Cooper, ii. p. 53.

[1] Cooper, ii. p. 53.—[2] Capt. Porter to Sec. of Navy, Aug. 17; Clark, p. 137; Cooper, ii. p. 53; Sketches of the War, p. 105.—[3] Since Commodore Bolton.

[4] Capt. Porter to Sec. of Navy, Aug. 17; Cooper, ii. p. 53; Sketches of the War, p. 105; Perkins' Hist. of War, p. 122.—[5] James' Warden Refuted, Table I.

[6] James' Naval Occurrences, p. 82.—[7] Thomson's Hist. of War, p. 37; James' Warden Refuted, Table I. Mr. James (*Naval Occur.*, p. 81) contends that she had only *eighty-six* in her crew.

The latter had three men wounded; the former, both in the vessel and her crew, was uninjured.[1]

Although the great difference between the two ships, both in their armaments and crews, rendered this capture less interesting than it otherwise would have been; the fact that the *Alert* was the first national vessel of war which struck her colors since the declaration of war,[1] invests the affair with peculiar interest, and it has been noticed in this work for that reason.

DOCUMENT.

CAPTAIN PORTER TO SECRETARY OF THE NAVY.

At Sea, *August* 17, 1812.

Sir:—I have the honor to inform you that upon the thirteenth, His Britannic Majesty's sloop-of-war *Alert*, Captain T. L. P. Laugharne, ran down on our weather-quarter, gave three cheers, and commenced an action (if so trifling a skirmish deserves the name); and, after eight minutes firing struck her colors, with seven feet water in her hold, much cut to pieces, and three men wounded.

I need not inform you that the officers and crew of the *Essex* behaved as I trust all Americans will in such cases, and it is only to be regretted that so much zeal and activity could not have been displayed on an occasion that would have done them more honor. The *Essex* has not received the slightest injury.

The *Alert* was out for the purpose of taking the *Hornet*.

I have the honor, &c.,

D. Porter.

Hon. Paul Hamilton.

CHAPTER XX.

August 15, 1812.

THE MASSACRE AT CHICAGO.

When the war with Great Britain broke out in June, 1812, what has since become the large and enterprising city of Chicago, in Illinois, was but a small trading village, with a military post, which was known as Fort Dearborn. This outpost was garrisoned with fifty-four men, commanded by Captain Heald, Lieutenant Helm, and Ensign Ronan; beside whom were the wife of the commandant, a trader named John Kinzie, and his family, and a few Canadian voyageurs, and their wives and children.[2] They were surrounded by the Indian tribes of the West, and, although the neighboring savages were among those who had opposed Harmar,

---

1 Capt. Porter to Sec. of Navy, Aug. 17; Clark, p. 137; O'Connor's Hist. of War, p. 45; Breckenridge's Hist. of War, p. 48; Thomson's Hist. of War, p. 37; Cooper, ii. p. 53; Sketches of the War, p. 105.

1 Cooper, ii. p. 53.—2 Brown's Hist. of Illinois, pp. 304, 305; Perkins' Annals of the West, p. 601.

St. Clair, and Wayne, and had yielded to the influence of Tecumthà and the Prophet, they were, generally, on amicable terms with the garrison,[1] and became, ultimately, the means of securing the lives of the remnant which was saved.

On the afternoon of the ninth of August, 1812, Winnemeg (*The Catfish*), a friendly Potawatomie chief, arrived at the fort with intelligence of the loss of Michilimacinac, and with orders from General Hull "to evacuate the post, if practicable, and, in that event, to distribute the property belonging to the United States, in the fort, and in the factory or agency, to the Indians in the neighborhood."[2] This injudicious order was in keeping with much that General Hull had done since the declaration of war; and, in the absence of more positive proof to the contrary, it must be attributed to a constitutional incapacity in that officer. After delivering his message, Winnemeg sought Mr. Kinzie,—who had removed his family to the fort for safety,—and informed him that he was acquainted with the character of the message which he had brought; that it was dangerous to remove from the fort; and, as the garrison had plenty of ammunition, and provisions for six months, he urged Mr. Kinzie to use his influence with the commandant to remain at the post until reinforcements could be sent to his assistance. At the same time, he insisted, if Captain Heald would not listen to his advice, that the garrison should march *at once*, before the neighboring Indians were informed of the order; and that the fort be left as it then was, in order that time might be gained while the Indians would be engaged in pilfering and carrying off the stores.[1] Unfortunately this sensible advice was not followed—Captain Heald resolving to obey his orders, without regard to consequences, notwithstanding the earnest remonstrances of his officers, of Mr. Kinzie, of the faithful Winnemeg, and even of the privates of his command.[2] The Indians, also, were not without intelligence of the misfortunes which had befallen the American arms,—a message from Tecumthà having conveyed to them an account of the fall of Michilimacinac, the defeat of Major Van Horn, the retreat of General Hull from Canada, and the probable capture of his army,[3]—and they had shown greater signs of uneasiness than usual.[4]

With an infatuation which was equalled only by General Hull's indiscretion in issuing the order, Captain Heald disregarded these incontestable evidences of the animosity of the Indians, and resolved to hold a council with them preparatory to his withdrawal from the fort; and, on the thirteenth of August, the inhabitants of the neighboring villages met for that purpose.[5] Captain

---

[1] Brown's History of Illinois, p. 305.

[2] Capt. Heald's Dispatch, "Pittsburg, Oct. 23." Mrs. Kinzie (*Wau-bun*, p. 210) says it was received on the *seventh;* and Mr. Brown (*Hist. Illinois*, p. 306) concurs.

---

[1] Mrs. Kinzie's Wau-bun, p. 211; Brown's Illinois, p. 306. Capt. Heald (*Dispatch, Oct.* 23) says, "The neighboring Indians got the information *as early as I did*, and came from all quarters to receive the goods," &c.—[2] Mrs. Kinzie's Wau-bun, pp. 211–214; Brown's Illinois, pp. 306, 307.—[3] Brown's Illinois, p. 307, *note;* McAfee, p. 101.

[4] Mrs. Kinzie's Wau-bun, p. 215.—[5] As it is said to have been held on the day preceding the distribution, it must have been on the 13th. Capt. Heald makes no allusion to a Council in his dispatch; while Mrs. Kinzie, Mr Brown, and others, suppose it was held on the *twelfth*.

Heald had been informed, through his officers, that the young chiefs intended to kill him, while in council; and, from that reason, the latter refused to accompany him to the place of meeting. They adopted, however, a most effectual preventative against the intended treachery, by taking command of the two block-houses of the fort which overlooked the esplanade on which the council had assembled, by throwing open the ports, and by running out the guns of the fort so as to command every part of the ground; and the proceedings of the council were not interrupted by any act of bad faith.[1] Captain Heald informed the Indians that he intended to distribute the goods, stores, and ammunition, with which the garrison was well supplied, on the following day; that the garrison and white inhabitants would then evacuate the works; and that if they would furnish an escort to Fort Wayne they should be liberally rewarded when he arrived there, in addition to the presents which he was about to give them. With the most liberal professions of friendship and good-will, the Indians agreed to do as they had been requested, and the council broke up.[2]

After the Captain had returned to the fort Mr. Kinzie made another attempt to induce the commandant to reconsider his resolution; but the only modification he would make was to order the whiskey to be emptied into the creek, and the gunpowder to be thrown into the well; and on the next day

[1] Mrs. Kinzie's Wau-bun, p. 216; Brown's Illinois, p. 308.—[2] Mrs. Kinzie's Wau-bun, p. 216; Perkins' Annals of the West, p. 605.

(*Aug.* 14) the blankets, broadcloths, calicoes, paints, &c., were distributed in accordance with the agreement at the council.[1]

On the preceding day, after the promise for the distribution had been made, Captain Wells—the brother of Mrs. Heald—came to the fort with a party of friendly Indians,[2] to prevent, if possible, the evacuation of the fort, or, if that could not be done, to assist in securing the safety of the garrison and its neighbors.[3] This gentleman had lived among the Indians from his childhood; had become a chief among them, and was perfectly acquainted with their character and habits. While at Fort Wayne he had heard of the order which had been issued for the evacuation of the fort; and he had hurried across the country to prevent, if possible, what he knew would be a dangerous undertaking.[4] In the evening the whiskey was emptied into the creek; the gunpowder, flints, &c., were thrown into the well; and the spare arms, after having been broken, were also consigned to the same place.[5] It had been

[1] Capt. Heald's Dispatch, Oct. 23; McAfee's Hist. of War in West, p. 98. Mrs. Kinzie (*Wau-bun*, p. 218), Dr. Peck (*Perkins' Annals of the West*, p. 606), and Mr. Brown (*Hist. of Illinois*, p. 308), suppose this was done on the *thirteenth*.

[2] The number and character of this party have been disputed. Capt. Heald (*Dispatch, Oct.* 23) says it embraced "about *thirty Miamis.*" Mrs. Kinzie (*Wau-bun*, p. 218) says, "with *fifteen* friendly Miamis," with which Mr. Brown (*Hist. Illinois*, p. 309) and Dr. Peck (*Annals*, p. 606) concur. McAfee (*Hist.*, p. 98) says he brought "about *fifty* Miamis." Gen. Armstrong (*Notices of the War*, i. p. 39) says, "*a few Miamis*," in which Mr. James (*Mil. Occur.*, i. p. 67) and Mr. Thomson (*Sketches of the War*, p. 28) concur. Walter Jordan (*Letter to his wife, Oct.* 19) says he had "*one hundred Confute* Indians."—[3] Capt. Heald's Dispatch, Oct. 23.—[4] Mrs. Kinzie's Wau-bun, p. 219; Perkins' Annals, p. 606.—[5] Capt. Heald's Dispatch, Oct. 23.

designed that the Indians should be kept in ignorance of this breach of faith on the part of the garrison, but they were disappointed;[1] and at a second council, which was held on the fourteenth, the chiefs expressed great indignation, while it was with great difficulty that the braves were prevented from falling on the whites while they sat in the council, by the more influential of their number.[2]

The most incredulous could now see that the surrounding tribes had resolved on revenge; and Captain Heald, even, was not left without the most convincing evidence of that sad fact. On the evening of the fourteenth, the Black Partridge, one of the principal chiefs, asked to see the Captain, and entered his quarters, addressing him in these words: "Father, I come to deliver to you the medal I wear. It was given me by the Americans, and I have long worn it, in token of our mutual friendship. But our young men have resolved to stain their hands in the blood of the whites; and, as I cannot restrain them, I will not wear a token of peace while I am compelled to act as an enemy." After handing the medal to the Captain, the chief retired, and thenceforth the fate of the garrison was sealed.[3]

On the morning of the fifteenth—the day appointed for the evacuation of the fort—Mr. Kinzie placed his family, nurse, clerk, and two servants, with two Indians as their protectors, in a boat, in order that they might proceed to St. Joseph's by water—a precaution which he had adopted at the suggestion of To-pee-nee-bee, a friendly chief, who warned him of the intentions of the Indians; while, with his eldest son, he prepared to accompany the troops, in order, by his influence, to pacify the savages as much as possible. The boat was subsequently detained, however, by a message from the same chief, and Mr. Kinzie's family were compelled to witness many of the horrors of the massacre which followed.[1]

At nine o'clock on the fifteenth of August the garrison left the fort,[2] with colors flying, and the music playing *the Dead March*.[3] Captain Wells, *with his face painted black*,[4] moved out, with part of his friendly Indians, in advance; the little garrison, and the wagons—containing the women, children, and stores—following; and the remainder of the friendly Indians brought up the rear of the sad procession.[5] The countenances of all who were in it betrayed the sentiments which they entertained; and as the column moved down the bank of the creek and along the shore of the lake—the escort of Potawatomies moving with it, in front and on its flank—the knowledge of its impending fate appeared to be impressed on every movement and in every face.

When the column reached the point "where commenced a range of sand hills intervening between the prairie

[1] Mrs. Kinzie's Wau-bun, pp. 219, 220; Brown's Illinois, p. 308.—[2] Brown's Illinois, pp. 308-310; Perkins' Annals, p. 606.—[3] Mrs. Kinzie's Wau-bun, p. 420; Brown's Illinois, p. 310.

[1] Mrs. Kinzie's Wau-bun, pp. 422, 423; Mrs. Helm's Narrative.—[2] Capt. Heald's Dispatch, Oct. 23.

[3] Mrs. Kinzie's Wau-bun, p. 223.—[4] Brown's Illinois, p. 310; Perkins' Annals, p. 608.—[5] Capt. Heald's Dispatch, Oct. 23; Brown's Illinois, p. 310; McAfee, p. 99.

and the beach,"[1] the Indian escort kept on the prairie, while the column itself continued to move on the lake-shore beneath—the sand hills concealing the movements of the former from their intended victims below.[2] The column had marched about a mile and a half, in this manner,[3] when Captain Wells, who had been in advance, rode back, and shouted, "They are about to attack us; form instantly, and charge upon them." Almost at the same moment a volley was showered down from among the sand hills, without injuring any one.[4]

The troops were instantly formed into line, and charged up the bank, in doing which one man was killed;[5] while the friendly Indians instantly fled, notwithstanding the strenuous efforts which Captain Wells employed to induce them to stand their ground.[6] The contest, as is usual in such cases, was but a series of individual exploits—no concerted movement being possible under the circumstances. The fifty-four regulars and twelve civilians, who formed the party,[7] were engaged with four or five hundred savages,[8] and notwithstanding the little party fought with the utmost desperation, fifteen minutes closed the conflict.[9]

At this time the remnant of the whites had taken possession of a mound on the prairie, whither the Indians did not follow them. On the contrary, the latter also assembled on the top of the bank—between the troops and the wagons which had been left on the shore—and, after some consultation, they made signs to Captain Heald to approach them. He did so, alone, and was met by the Blackbird, one of the chiefs, who, after shaking hands, requested the Captain to surrender, and promised to spare the lives of the prisoners if he would do so. After reflecting a few minutes, Captain Heald agreed to do so—forgetting, however, or not appreciating, the necessity of a provision for the protection of *the wounded*.[1]

The prisoners were immediately conveyed to the camp near the fort;[2] and there appears to be no evidence that the capitulation was not faithfully adhered to by the victorious savages. While the negotiations were still pending,[3] one young warrior, whose zeal overcame his integrity, forgot the claims of humanity, and twelve helpless children, who occupied one of the wagons, fell a sacrifice to his murderous hatchet.[4] Captain Wells, who sat on his horse, near the scene of this terrible slaughter, injudiciously shouted, "If this be your game, I will kill too!" and, turning his horse, dashed towards the Indian camp, where the squaws and children had been left. Several of the most swift-footed of the savages immediately started in pursuit;

[1] Mrs. Kinzie's Wau-bun, p. 223.—[2] Capt. Heald's Dispatch, Oct. 23.—[3] Ibid.; Mrs. Kinzie's Wau-bun, p. 224; Brown's Illinois, p. 311. Walter Jordan says, "*half a mile.*"—[4] Mrs. Kinzie's Wau-bun, p. 224; McAfee, p. 99.

[5] Capt. Heald's Dispatch, Oct. 23; Brown's Illinois, p. 311.—[6] Mrs. Helm's Narrative, cited by Mrs. Kinzie; Brown's Illinois, p. 311.—[7] Capt. Heald's Dispatch, Oct. 23; McAfee, p. 99; James' Military Occur., i. p. 67.

[8] Capt. Heald's Dispatch, Oct. 23. McAfee (p. 99) says, "*five or six hundred.*" Walter Jordan says, "*six hundred.*"

[9] Capt. Heald's Dispatch, Oct. 23; Brown's Illinois, p. 311; McAfee, p. 99.

[1] Capt. Heald's Dispatch, Oct. 23; Mrs. Helm's Narrative; Brown's Illinois, p. 312; Breckenridge's Hist. of War, p. 37.—[2] Capt. Heald's Dispatch, Oct 23; McAfee, p. 100.—[3] Mrs. Helm's Narrative.

[4] Ibid.; Brown's Illinois, p. 312; Perkins' Annals, p. 610.

and the fire of numerous rifles, from all quarters, was sent after him. Laying himself flat on the neck of his horse, he had nearly passed beyond the range of the fire, when one ball, more truly aimed than the others, took effect, killing his horse and wounding himself. Two of his friends, Winnemeg and Wau-ban-see, endeavored to save him from the fury of his pursuers; and were supporting him, after having disengaged him from his horse, when another, Pee-so-tum, less friendly, stabbed him in the back.[1]

Other instances of individual courage are equally deserving notice, among whom are that of Mrs. Helm—the daughter of Mr. Kinzie, and wife of Lieutenant Helm—who engaged in a personal struggle with an Indian, and was rescued by the Black Partridge;[2] that of Mrs. Heald, who, when she was approached by an Indian, with uplifted tomahawk, looked him in the face with a smile, and said, "Surely, you will not kill a squaw?" saving her life, although during the action she received seven wounds;[3] that of Mrs. Corbin, a soldier's wife, who had resolved to die rather than be taken prisoner, and "literally suffered herself to be cut to pieces," while resisting the attempts which were made to take her;[4] that of Mrs. Holt, a sergeant's wife, who, after her husband had been wounded, took his sword, and so skilfully defended herself, on horseback, that she elicited the admiration of the Indians, as she dashed over the prairie amidst their shouts of "The brave woman! do not hurt her!"[1] and that of Ensign Ronan, who, after administering a bitter retort on his commander, fell under the blows of several enemies.[2]

The close of this tragedy, however, is the most grievous. The wounded having been excluded from the provisions of the agreement, *as the Indians understood it*, the unfortunate men who were wounded were immediately butchered and scalped;[3] while upon the remains of Captain Wells the most refined barbarities were exercised.[4]

Beside the twelve children, two women, all the civilians (except Mr. Kinzie and his son), Captain Wells, Ensign Ronan, Surgeon Van Voorhies, and twenty-six regulars, were killed.[5] Those who were taken prisoners were divided among the victors,[6] and, after suffering many hardships, generally returned to their homes.

In this terrible affair it is difficult to decide who was most culpable—General Hull or Captain Heald. The unwise order which was issued by the former, was, probably, the *original* cause of the massacre; but the obstinate perverseness of the latter, in persisting to move from the fort, while the destruction of his command was certain,—to say nothing of the bad faith which he displayed in destroying the ammunition, arms, and

[1] Mrs. Helm's Narrative; Brown's Illinois, pp. 312, 313.
[2] Letter of "*An Officer*," in Niles' Register, iv. p. 82; Mrs. Helm's Narrative; Brown's Illinois, pp. 311, 312.—[3] Mrs. Helm's Narrative; Brown's Illinois, pp. 315, 316; McAfee, p. 100.—[4] Mrs. Helm's Narrative; Brown's Illinois, p. 312.

[1] Mrs. Helm's Narrative.—[2] Ibid.; Brown's Illinois, p. 311.—[3] Mrs. Helm's Narrative; Perkins' Annals, p. 610.
[4] Walter Jordan's letter to his wife, Fort Wayne, Oct. 19; Communication of "*An Officer*," in Niles' Register, iv. p. 82; Mrs. Helm's Narrative; Brown's Illinois, p. 313; McAfee, p. 100.—[5] Capt. Heald's Dispatch, Oct. 23; Breckenridge's Hist. of War, p. 37.—[6] Brown's Illinois, p. 315.

whiskey,[1]—was, evidently, the *immediate* and moving cause.

Some of the survivors of this affair—Mrs. Heald among them—have, until recently, lingered among us—some of them may still survive; and the prairie and the beach, the creek and the broad lake, still mark the scene of this sad catastrophe. Not, however, in their original condition do any of these landmarks exist. A busy city, with its thousand souls, now occupies the sand hills and the lovely prairie; while the lofty and noble terminus of a net-work of railroads,—each carrying life, and light, and health throughout the country,—the busy wharves, and the ever-changing port-scenes of one of the emporiums of the mighty West, have taken the place of the winding creek and the sequestered margin of the lovely lake. How few there are, among the enterprising citizens of this beautiful young city, as they press forward after the phantoms of life, ever cast a thought on the dangers and privations of the generation who preceded them, in the great struggle between the aborigines and the settlers, between barbarism and civilization.

DOCUMENT.

EXTRACT FROM CAPTAIN HEALD'S DISPATCH.

PITTSBURG, *October* 23, 1812.

On the 9th of August I received orders from General Hull to evacuate the post, and proceed with my command to Detroit by land, leaving it at my discretion to dispose of the public property as I thought proper. The neighboring Indians got the information as early as I did, and came in from all quarters in order to receive the goods in the factory-store, which they understood were to be given them. On the 13th, Captain Wells, of Fort Wayne, arrived with about thirty Miamis, for the purpose of escorting us in, by the request of General Hull. On the 14th, I delivered the Indians all the goods in the factory-store and a considerable quantity of provisions which we could not take away with us. The surplus arms and ammunition I thought proper to destroy, fearing they would make bad use of it, if put in their possession. I also destroyed all the liquor on hand, soon after they began to collect. The collection was unusually large for that place, but they conducted with the strictest propriety till after I left the fort. On the 15th, at nine A. M., we commenced our march; a part of the Miamis were detached in front, the remainder in our rear as guards, under the direction of Captain Wells. The situation of the country rendered it necessary for us to take the beach, with the lake on our left, and a high sand bank on our right, at about one hundred yards' distance. We had proceeded about a mile and a half, when it was discovered the Indians were prepared to attack us from behind the bank. I immediately marched up with the company to the top of the bank, when the action commenced; after firing one round, we charged, and the Indians gave way in front and joined those on our flanks. In about fifteen minutes they got possession of all our horses, provision, and baggage of every description, and, finding the Miamis did not assist us, I drew off the few men I had left, and took possession of a small elevation in the open prairie, out of shot of the bank or any other cover. The Indians did not follow me, but assembled in a body on the top of the bank, and, after some consultation among themselves, made signs for me to approach them. I advanced towards them, alone, and

[1] It is said that Black Hawk stated that the troops would not have been attacked, but for this reason.

was met by one of the Potawatomie chiefs called the Black-bird, with an interpreter. After shaking hands, he requested me to surrender, promising to spare the lives of all the prisoners. On a few moments' consideration, I concluded it would be most prudent to comply with his request, although I did not put entire confidence in his promise. After delivering up our arms, we were taken back to their encampment near the fort, and distributed among the different tribes. The next morning they set fire to the fort, and left the place, taking the prisoners with them. Their number of warriors was between four and five hundred, mostly of Potawatomie nation; and their loss, from the best information I could get, was about fifteen. Our strength was fifty-four regulars and twelve militia, out of which twenty-six regulars and all the militia were killed in the action, with two women and twelve children. Ensign George Ronan and Doctor Isaac V. Van Voorhis, of my company, with Captain Wells, of Fort Wayne, are, to my great sorrow, numbered among the dead. Lieutenant Lina T. Helm, with twenty-five non-commissioned officers and privates, and eleven women and children, were prisoners, when we separated. Mrs. Heald and myself were taken to the mouth of the River St. Joseph, and being both badly wounded, were permitted to reside with Mr. Burnet, an Indian trader. In a few days after our arrival there, the Indians all went off to take Fort Wayne, and in their absence I engaged a Frenchman to take us to Michilimacinac by water, where I gave myself up as a prisoner of war, with one of my sergeants. The commanding officer, Captain Roberts, offered me every assistance in his power to render our situation comfortable while we remained there, and to enable us to proceed on our journey. To him I gave my parole of honor, and reported myself to Colonel Proctor, who gave us a passage to Buffalo; from that place I came by the way of Presque Isle, and arrived here yesterday.

CHAPTER XXI.

August 15 to 16, 1812.

THE SURRENDER OF DETROIT.

The invasion of Canada by the army of the Northwest, under General Hull, has been referred to in a preceding chapter of this work;[1] and the loss of Michilimacinac and its effect, on the operations of the army, have also received a passing notice.[2] At a subsequent day, from the liberation of the Indian tribes, who fell on his rear and flanks;[3] from the reinforcement of the enemy, in front;[4] and from the occupation, by the enemy, of all his lines of communication with the States,[1] General Hull had considered it prudent to withdraw from Canada, and fall back on Detroit; and on the seventh and eighth of August, the army crossed the river, and encamped at Detroit, leaving only a small garrison of three hundred men, on the opposite bank of the river, a few miles below.[2]

The occupation by the enemy of the only line of communication with the

[1] Vide pp. 94, 96.—[2] Vide Chap. XV.

[3] Sir Geo. Prevost to Earl Bathurst, Aug. 26; Gen. Hull to Sec. of War, Aug. 26.—[4] Gen. Hull to Sec. of War, Aug. 26; Col. Cass to Sec. of War, Sept. 10; Clark's Campaign of 1812, pp. 360, 361.

[1] Gen. Hull to Sec. of War, Aug. 26; Smith's Life of Cass, p. 42; Clark's Campaign of 1812, p. 364.

[2] Gen. Hull to Sec. of War, Aug. 26; Sheldon's History of Michigan, p. 396.

States, immediately arrested the attention of the Commander, and several efforts were made to remove him, without effect.[1] At length, on the thirteenth of August, General Sir Isaac Brock reached Malden, with a small party of three hundred regulars and militia;[2] and on the fifteenth he summoned General Hull to surrender the post and its garrison to the arms of Great Britain, which was refused.[3] On the receipt of General Hull's answer, General Brock opened a fire on the town, from the batteries which had been thrown up by Captain Dixon, on the opposite side of the river, which was continued until evening,[4] at which time the enemy's shipping moved up the river, towards the town, and anchored off Spring Wells, about three miles below the fort.[5]

Early on the morning of the sixteenth the cannonade was renewed,[6] while General Brock, with about seven hundred and thirty troops, and six hundred Indians, under Tecumthà,[7] crossed the river, at Spring Wells, under cover of the *Queen Charlotte* and *Hunter*.[8] Having effected a landing, without opposition,[9] the troops formed in column, upon the beach, and, at ten o'clock, it advanced towards the town, the river protecting its right flank and the Indians on its left.[1]

At that time the fort at Detroit was a regular rectangular work, composed of four curtains and four bastions, and was composed, in part, of earth. The parapet was eleven feet high, twenty-six feet wide at the base, and twelve at the top; the ditch was twelve feet wide at the bottom, and six feet deep, with a row of cedar pickets, twelve feet high, at the bottom; and the whole were in good repair. Twenty-eight pieces of artillery were mounted; an ample supply of small arms, ammunition, stores, &c., were in its magazines,[2] and ten hundred and sixty effective troops, exclusive of detachments, were assembled within the works.[3]

Against these, as has been said, seven hundred and thirty whites and six hundred Indians, with five pieces of artillery—three and six pounders—had moved; and as the column approached the town, a commanding eminence, strengthened with a picket and two twenty-four pounders, the whole commanded by Colonel Findley, by the General's order, were abandoned by the Americans, who retired to the fort.[4]

When the column had reached a point within a mile and a half from the town it was halted; the works were reconnoitred; and, in consequence of

---

1 Vide Chapters XVI., XVII.

2 James' Mil. Occur., i. p. 68; Brock's Life of Brock, pp. 241, 242; Clark's Camp. of 1812, p. 361; Gen. Brock to Sir G. Prevost, Aug. 17.—3 Gen. Brock to Gen. Hull, and the reply of the latter, Aug. 15.

4 James, i. p. 69; Christie, p. 71; Brock's Life of Brock, p. 247; Gen. Hull to Sec. of War, Aug. 16; Col. Cass to Sec. of War, Sept. 10.

5 Gen. Hull to Sec. of War, Aug. 16.—6 Sketches of the War, p. 46; Col. Cass to Sec. of War, Sept. 10.

7 James, i. p. 69; Brock's Life of Brock, p. 247; Christie, p. 71; Gen. Brock to Sir G. Prevost, Aug. 17; McAfee, p. 88.—8 Brock's Brock, p. 247; Christie, p. 71; Perkins, p. 86; Col. Cass to Sec. of War, Sept. 10.—9 Christie, p. 71; Perkins, p. 86; Lanman's Michigan, p. 197.

1 James, i. p. 69; O'Connor's Hist. of War, p. 38; Col. Cass to Sec. of War, Sept. 10; McAfee, p. 88.

2 Sketches of the War, p. 47; Headley, i. p. 84.

3 Col. Cass to Sec. of War, Sept. 10. Gen. Hull states the number at 800.—4 Brock's Life of Brock, p. 248; James, i. p. 70; Sketches of the War, p. 46; Col. Cass to Secretary of War, Sept. 10.

the weakness of the fort, on the land side, preparations were immediately made for an assault.[1] For this purpose the troops were immediately prepared; but, before the several columns could be formed, and before a single shot had been fired, a boat, with a flag, was dispatched from the fort to Sandwich; and another, borne by Captain Hull, approached the column, with proposals from General Hull for an immediate capitulation of the town.[2]

The surprise of the garrison at this sudden and unexplained surrender by the commanding general was shared by the enemy, and he took immediate steps to secure the honors which had fallen into his hands. Lieutenant-colonel McDouell of the militia, and Major Glegg of the Forty-ninth regiment, immediately accompanied the flag to the head-quarters of General Hull,[3] where, "*they, in a few minutes*, dictated the terms of capitulation,"[4] and the entire "Army of the Northwest"—including a detachment which had been sent out under Colonels McArthur and Cass—together with the Territory of Michigan,[5] "were surrendered to the British arms, without the effusion of a single drop of British blood."[1]

[1] Christie, p. 71; Brock's Life of Brock, p. 248; Gen. Brock to Sir G. Prevost, Aug. 17.

[2] Brock's Life of Brock, p. 248; McAfee, p. 89.

[3] Christie, p. 71; Brock's Life of Brock, p. 248; Gen. Brock to Sir G. Prevost, Aug. 17.—[4] Christie, p. 72; Articles of Capitulation, Aug. 16.—[5] James, i. p. 70; Gen. Brock to Sir G. Prevost, Aug. 17.

Thirty-three pieces of artillery—some of them a part of the train which was taken with General Burgoyne, at Saratoga, in 1777; the *Adams*, brig of war; an immense quantity of stores of all kinds; twenty-five hundred muskets; and a stand of colors, with about twenty-five hundred prisoners, were among the trophies of this victory.[2] It is not within the scope of this work to discuss the question of General Hull's surrender, farther than its effects on the country, that has been done by those whose duty it was, in other works; it is not improper to state, in the language of a well-informed British author, that "as there was a great deficiency of arms in the Upper Province, wherewith to equip the militia, the twenty-five hundred stand of American became a valuable acquisition. To this surrender," he continues, "the after preservation of Upper Canada, at least, may, in a great measure, be ascribed, as it caused a delay of nearly a whole year in the successful meditated invasion, and secured the support (*to the British*) of some of the Indian tribes, who were hesitating as to the side they should espouse."[3]

[1] Christie, p. 72.—[2] Brock's Life of Brock, p. 248; Gen. Brock to Sir G. Prevost, Aug. 17; Auchinleck's Hist. of War, p. 59.—[3] Brock's Life of Gen. Brock, p. 248.

DOCUMENTS.

I.

GENERAL HULL'S DISPATCH TO THE SECRETARY OF WAR.

MONTREAL, *September* 8, 1812.

SIR:—The inclosed dispatch was prepared on my arrival at Fort George, and it was my intention to have forwarded it from that place by Major Witherell, of the Michigan Volunteers. I made application to the commanding officer at that post and was refused, he stating that he was not authorized, and General Brock was then at York. We were immediately embarked for this place, and Major Witherell obtained liberty at Kingston to go home on parole.

This is the first opportunity I have had to forward the dispatches.

The Fourth United States regiment is destined for Quebec, with a part of the First. The whole consist of a little over three hundred.

Sir George Prevost, without any request on my part, has offered to take my parole and permit me to proceed to the States.

Lieutenant Anderson, of the Eighth regiment, is the bearer of my dispatches.

He was formerly a lieutenant in the artillery, and resigned his commission on account of being appointed Marshal of the Territory of Michigan.

During the campaign he has had a command in the artillery; and I recommend him to you as a valuable officer.

He is particularly acquainted with the state of things previous, and at the time when the capitulation took place. He will be able to give you correct information on any points about which you may think proper to inquire.

I am, very respectfully, &c.,

WILLIAM HULL.

FORT GEORGE, *August* 26, 1812.

SIR:—Inclosed are the articles of capitulation by which the Fort of Detroit has been surrendered to Major-general Brock, commanding His Britannic Majesty's forces in Upper Canada, and by which the troops have become prisoners of war. My situation at present forbids me from detailing the particular causes which have led to this unfortunate event. I will, however, generally observe, that after the surrender of Michilimacinac, almost every tribe and nation of Indians, excepting a part of the Miamis and Delawares, north from beyond Lake Superior, west from beyond the Mississippi, south from the Ohio and Wabash, and east from every part of Upper Canada, and from all the intermediate country, joined in open hostility, under the British standard, against the army I commanded, contrary to the most solemn assurances of a large portion of them, to remain neutral: even the Ottawa chiefs from Arbecrotch, who formed the delegation to Washington the last summer, in whose friendship I know you had great confidence, are among the hostile tribes, and several of them distinguished leaders. Among the vast number of chiefs who led the hostile bands, Tecumseh, Marpot, Logan, Walk-in-the-water, Split-log, &c., are considered the principals. This numerous assemblage of savages, under the entire influence and direction of the British commander, enabled him totally to obstruct the only communication which I had with my country. This communication had been opened from the settlements, in the State of Ohio, two hundred miles through a wilderness, by the fatigues of the army, which I marched to the frontiers on the River Detroit. The body of the lake being commanded by the British armed ships, and the shores and rivers by gun-boats, the army was totally deprived of all communication by water. On this extensive road it depended for transportation of provisions, military stores, medicine, clothing, and every other supply, on pack-horses. All its operations were successful until its arrival at Detroit; and in a few days it passed into the enemy's country, and all opposition seemed to fall before it. One month it remained in possession of this country, and was fed from its resources. In different directions, detachments penetrated sixty miles in the settled part of the province, and the inhabitants seemed satisfied with the change of situation, which appeared to be taking place. The militia from Amherstburg were daily deserting, and the whole country, then under the control of the army, was asking for protection. The Indians, generally, in the first instance, appeared to be neutralized, and determined to take no part in the contest. The Fort of Amherstburg was eighteen miles below my encampment. Not a single cannon or mortar was on wheels suitable to carry before that place. I consulted my officers, whether it was expedient to make an attempt on it with the bayonet alone, without cannon to make a break in the first instance. The council I called, was of the opinion it was not. The greatest industry was exerted in making preparation, and it was not until the 7th of August that two twenty-four pounders and three howitzers were prepared. It was then my intention to have proceeded on the enterprise. While the operations of the army were delayed by these preparations, the clouds of adversity had been for some time and seemed still thickly to be gathering around me. The surrender of Michilimacinac opened the northern hive of Indians, and they were swarming down in every direction. Reinforcements from Niagara had arrived at Amherstburg, under the command of Colonel Proctor. The desertion of the militia ceased. Besides the reinforcements that came by water, I received information of a very considerable force, under the command of Major Chambers, on the River Le French, with four field-pieces, and collecting the militia on his route, evidently destined for Amherstburg; and in addition to this combination, and increase of force, contrary to all my expectations, the Wyandots, Chippewas, Ottawas, Potawatomies, Munsees, Delawares, &c., with whom I had the most friendly intercourse, at once passed over to Amherstburg, and accepted the tomahawk and scalping-knife. There being now a vast number of Indians at the British post, they were sent to the River Huron, Brownstown, and Maguaga, to intercept my communication. To open this communication, I detached Major Van Horn, of the Ohio Volunteers, with two hundred men, to proceed as far as the River Raisin, under an expectation he would meet Captain Brush, with one hundred and fifty men, volunteers from the State of Ohio, and a quantity of provisions for the army. An ambuscade was formed at Brownstown, and Major Van Horn's detachment defeated, and returned to camp without effecting the object of the expedition.

In my letter of the 7th instant, you have the particulars of that transaction, with a return of the killed and wounded. Under this sudden and unexpected change of things, and having received an express from General Hall, commanding opposite the British shore, on the Niagara River, by which it appeared that there was no prospect of any co-operation from that quarter, and the two senior officers of the artillery having stated to me an opinion that it would be extremely difficult, if not impossible, to pass the Turkey River and River Aux Canard with the twenty-four-pounders, and that they could not be transported by water, as the Queen Charlotte, which carried eighteen twenty-four-pounders, lay in the River Detroit, above the mouth of the River Aux Canard; and as it appeared indispensably necessary to open the communication to the River Raisin and the Miami, I found myself compelled to suspend the operation against Amherstburg, and concentrate the main force of the army at Detroit. Fully intending at that time, after the communication was opened, to recross the river and pursue the object at Amherstburg, and strongly desirous of continuing protection to a very large number of the inhabitants of Upper Canada, who had voluntarily accepted it, under my proclamation, I established a fortress on the banks of the river, a little below Detroit, calculated for a garrison of three hundred men. On the evening of the 7th and morning of the 8th instant, the army, excepting the garrison of two hundred and fifty infantry, and a corps of artillerists, all under the command of Major Denny, of the Ohio Volunteers, recrossed the river, and encamped at Detroit. In pursuance of the object of opening the communication, on which I considered the existence of the army depending, a detachment of six hundred men, under the command of Lieutenant-colonel Miller, was immediately ordered. For a particular account of the proceedings of this detachment, and the memorable battle which was fought at Maguaga, which reflects the highest honor on the American arms, I refer you to my letter of the 13th instant, a duplicate of which is inclosed, marked G. Nothing, however, but honor was acquired by this victory; and it is a painful consideration that the blood of seventy-five gallant men could only open the communication as far as the points of their bayonets extended. The necessary care of the sick and wounded, and a very severe storm of rain, rendered their return to camp indispensably necessary for their own comfort. Captain Brush, with his small detachment, and the provisions, being still at the River Raisin, and in a situation to be destroyed by the savages, on the 13th instant, in the evening, I permitted Colonels McArthur and Cass to select from their regiment four hundred of their most effective men, and proceed an upper route through the woods, which I had sent an express to Captain Brush to take, and had directed the militia of the River Raisin to accompany him as a reinforcement. The force of the enemy continually increasing, and the necessity of opening the communication, and acting on the defensive, becoming more apparent, I had, previous to detaching Colonels McArthur and Cass, on the 11th instant, evacuated and destroyed the fort on the opposite bank. On the 13th, in the evening, General Brock arrived at Amherstburg, about the hour Colonels McArthur and Cass marched, of which, at that time, I had received no information. On the 15th I received a summons from him to surrender Fort Detroit, of which the paper marked A is a copy. My answer is marked B. At this time I had received no information from Colonels McArthur and Cass. An express was immediately sent, strongly escorted, with orders for them to return. On the 15th, as soon as General Brock received my letter, his batteries opened upon the town and fort, and continued until evening. In the evening all the British ships of war came nearly as far up the river as Sandwich, three miles below Detroit. At daylight, on the 16th (at which time I had received no information from Colonels McArthur and Cass, my expresses, sent the evening before, and in the night, having been prevented from passing, by numerous bodies of Indians), the cannonade recommenced, and in a short time I received information that the British army and Indians were landing below the Spring Wells, under the cover of their ships of war. At this time the whole effective force at my disposal, at Detroit, did not exceed eight hundred men Being new troops and unaccustomed to a camp-life; having performed a laborious march; having been engaged in a number of battles and skirmishes, in which many had fallen, and more had received wounds, in addition to which, a large number being sick and unprovided with medicine, and the comforts necessary for their situation; are the general causes by which the strength of the army was thus reduced. The fort at this time was filled with women, children, and the old and decrepit people of the town and country; they were unsafe in the town, as it was entirely open and exposed to the enemy's batteries. Back of the fort, above or below it, there was no safety for them on account of the Indians. In the first instance the enemy's fire was principally directed against our batteries; towards the close it was directed against the fort alone, and almost every shot and shell had their effect.

It now became necessary either to fight the enemy in the field; collect the whole force in the fort; or propose terms of capitulation. I could not have carried into the field more than six hundred men, and left any adequate force in the fort. There were landed at that time, of the enemy, a regular force of much more than that number, and twice the number of Indians. Considering this great inequality of force, I did not think it expedient to adopt the first measure. The second must have been attended with a great sacrifice of blood and no possible advantage, because the contest could not have been sustained more than a day for the want of powder, and but a very few days for the want of provisions. In addition to this, Colonels McArthur and Cass would have been in a most hazardous situation. I feared nothing but the last alternative. I have dared to adopt it. I well know the high responsibility of the measure, and I take the whole responsibility upon myself. It was dictated by a sense of duty, and a full conviction of its expediency. The bands of savages which had then joined the British force were numerous beyond any former example. Their numbers have since increased, and the history of the barbarians of the north of Europe does not furnish examples of more greedy violence than these savages have exhibited. A large portion of the brave and gallant officers and men I commanded, would cheerfully have contested until the last cartridge had been expended and the bayonets worn to the sockets. I could not consent to the useless sacrifice of such brave men, when I knew it was impossible for me to sustain my situation. It was impossible, in the nature of things, that an army could have been furnished with the necessary supplies of provisions, military stores, clothing, and comforts for the sick, on pack-horses, through a wilderness of two hundred miles, filled with hostile savages. It was impossible, sir, that this little army, worn down by fatigue, by sickness, by wounds and deaths, could have supported itself, not only against the collected force of all the northern nations of Indians, but against the united strength of Upper Canada, whose population consists of more than twenty times the number contained in the Territory of Michigan, aided by the principal part of the regular forces of the province, and the wealth and influence of the Northwest and other trading establishments among the Indians, which have in their employment, and under their entire control, more than two thousand white men. Before I close this dispatch, it is a duty I owe my respectable associates in command, Colonels McArthur, Findlay, Cass, and Lieutenant-colonel Miller, to express my obligations to them for the prompt and judicious manner they have performed their respective duties. If aught has taken place during the campaign which is honorable to the army, these officers are entitled to a large share of it. If the last act should be disapproved, no part of the censure belongs to them. I have likewise to express my obligation to General Taylor, who has performed the duty of quartermaster-general, for his great exertions in procuring every thing in his department which it was possible to furnish for the convenience of the army; likewise to Brigade-major Jessup, for the correct and punctual manner in which he has discharged his duty; and to the army, generally, for their exertions and the zeal they have manifested for the public interest. The death of Dr. Foster, soon after he arrived at Detroit, was a severe misfortune to the army; but it was increased by the capture of the Chachaga packet, by which the medicines and hospital stores were lost. He was commencing the best arrangements in the department of which he was the principal with the very small means he possessed. I was likewise deprived of the necessary services of Captain Partridge by sickness, the only officer of the corps of engineers attached to the army. All the officers and men have gone to their respective homes, excepting the Fourth United States regiment, and a small part of the First, and Captain Dyson's company of artillery. Captain Dyson's company was left at Amherstburg, and the others are with me, prisoners—they amount to about three hundred and forty. I have only to solicit an investigation of my conduct, as early as my situation and the state of things will admit; and to add the farther request, that the government will not be unmindful of my associates in captivity, and of the families of those brave men who have fallen in the contest.

I have the honor to be, very respectfully, your most obedient servant,

Wm. Hull, *Brig.-Gen.*
Commanding the N. W. Army, U. S.

Hon. W. Eustis, Sec. of the Depart. of War.

II.

SIR ISAAC BROCK'S DISPATCH TO THE COMMANDER-IN-CHIEF.

Head-quarters, Detroit, *August* 7.

Sir:—I have had the honor of informing your Excellency, that the enemy effected his passage across the Detroit River on the 12th ult., without opposition; and that, after establishing himself at Sandwich, he had ravaged the country as far as the Moravian town. Some skirmishes occurred between the troops under Lieutenant-colonel St. George and the enemy, upon the River Canard, which uniformly terminated in his being repulsed with loss. I had judged it proper to detach a force down the River Thames, capable of acting in conjunction with the garrison of Amherstburg offensively; but Captain Chambers, whom I had appointed to direct this detachment, experienced difficulties that frustrated my intentions. The intelligence received from that quarter admitting of no delay, Colonel Proctor was directed to assume the command, and his force was soon after increased with sixty rank and file of the Forty-first regiment.

In the mean time the most strenuous measures were adopted to counteract the machinations of the evil disposed, and I soon experienced the gratification of receiving voluntary offers of service from that portion of the embodied militia the most easily collected. In the attainment of this important point, gentlemen of the first character and influence showed an example highly creditable to them; and I cannot, on this occasion, avoid mentioning the essential service I derived from John McDonnell, Esq., His Majesty's Attorney-general, who, from the beginning of the war, has honored me with his services as my Provincial aid-de-camp. A sufficiency of boats being collected at Long Point for the conveyance of three hundred men, the embarkation took place on the 8th instant, and in five days arrived in safety in Amherstburg.

I found that the judicious arrangement which had been adopted immediately upon the arrival of Colonel Proctor had compelled the enemy to retreat, and take shelter under the guns of his fort; that officer commenced operations by sending strong detachments across the river, with a view of cutting off the enemy's communication with his reserve.

This produced two smart skirmishes, on the 5th and 9th instant, in both of which the enemy's loss was very considerable, while ours amounted to three killed and thirteen wounded, among the latter I have particularly to regret Captain Muir and Lieutenant Sutherland of the Forty-first regiment: the former an officer of great experience, and both ardent in His Majesty's service. Batteries had likewise been commenced opposite Fort Detroit, for one eighteen-pounder, two twelves, and two five-and-a-half inch mortars, all of which opened on the evening of the 15th (having previously summoned Brigadier-general Hull to surrender), and although opposed by a well-directed fire from seven twenty-four pounders, such was their construction, under the able direction of Captain Dixon, of the Royal Engineers, that no injury was sustained from its effect.

The force at my disposal being collected, in the course of the 5th, in the neighborhood of Sandwich, the embarkation took place a little after daylight on the following morning, and by the able arrangements of Lieutenant Dewar, of the quartermaster-general's department, the whole was in a short time landed, without the smallest confusion, at Spring Wells, a good position, three miles west of Detroit. The Indians, who had in the mean time effected their landing two miles below, moved forward, and occupied the woods about a mile and a half on our left.

The force which I instantly directed to march against the enemy consisted of thirty Royal artillery, two hundred and fifty Forty-first regiment, fifty Royal Newfoundland regiment, four hundred militia, and about six hundred Indians, to which were attached three six-pounders and two three-pounders. The services of Lieutenant Troughton, commanding the Royal artillery, an active and intelligent officer, being required in the field, the direction of the batteries was intrusted to Captain Hall, of the marine department, and I cannot withhold my entire approbation of their conduct on this occasion.

I crossed the river with an intention of waiting in a strong position the effect of our force upon the enemy's camp, and in hopes of compelling him to meet us in the field; but receiving information upon landing, that Colonel McArthur, an officer of high reputation, had left the garrison three days before with a detachment of five hundred men, and hearing soon afterwards that his cavalry had been seen that morning three miles in our rear, I decided on an immediate attack. Accordingly, the troops advanced to within one mile of the fort, and having ascertained that the enemy had taken little or no precaution towards the land side, I resolved on an assault, while the Indians penetrated his camp. Brigadier-general Hull, however, prevented this movement, by proposing a cessation of hostilities, for the purpose of preparing terms of capitulation. Lieutenant-colonel John McDonnell and Captain Glegg were accordingly deputed by me on this mission, and returned within an hour with the conditions, which I have the honor herewith to transmit. Certain considerations afterwards induced me to agree to the two supplementary articles.

The force thus surrendered to His Majesty's arms cannot be estimated at less than twenty-five hundred men. In this estimate, Colonel McArthur's detachment is included, as he surrendered agreeably to the terms of capitulation, in the course of the evening, with the exception of two hundred men, whom he left escorting a valuable convoy at some little distance in his rear; but there can be no doubt the officer commanding will consider himself equally bound by the capitulation.

The enemy's aggregate force was divided into two troops of cavalry; one company of artillery regulars; the Fourth United States regiment; detachments of the First and Third United States regiments, volunteers; three regiments of the Ohio militia; one regiment of the Michigan Territory.

Thirty-three pieces of brass and iron ordnance have already been secured.

When this contest commenced, many of the Indian nations were engaged in the active warfare with the United States, notwithstanding the constant endeavors of this government to dissuade them from it. Some of the principal chiefs happened to be at Amherstburg, trying to procure a supply of arms and ammunition, which for years had been withheld, agreeably to the instructions received from Sir James Craig, and since repeated by your Excellency.

From that moment they took a most active part, and appeared foremost on every occasion; they were led yesterday by Colonel Elliot and Captain M'Kee, and nothing could exceed their order and steadiness. A few prisoners were taken by them, during the advance, whom they treated with every humanity; and it affords me much pleasure in assuring your Excellency that such was their forbearance and attention to what was required of them, that the enemy sustained no other loss of men than what was occasioned by the fire of our batteries.

The high sense I entertain of the abilities and judgment of Lieutenant-colonel Myers induced me to appoint him to the important command at Niagara; it was with reluctance that I deprived myself of his assistance, but had no other expedient; his duties, as head of the quartermaster-general's department, were performed to my satisfaction by Lieutenant-colonel Nicholls, Quartermaster-general of the militia.

Captain Glegg, my aid-de-camp, will have the honor of delivering this dispatch to your Excellency; he is charged with the colors taken at the capture of Fort Detroit, and those of the Fourth United States regiment.

Captain Glegg is capable of giving your Excellency every information respecting the state of this province, and I shall esteem myself highly indebted to your Excellency to afford him that protection to which his merit and length of service give him a powerful claim.

I have the honor to be, &c.,

Isaac Brock, *Maj.-Gen.*

P. S.—I have the honor to inclose a copy of a proclamation which I issued immediately on taking possession of this country.

I should have mentioned in the body of my dispatch the capture of the *Adams;* she is a fine vessel, and recently repaired, but without arms.

CHAPTER XXII.

August 19, 1812.

THE CAPTURE OF THE GUERRIERE.

On the nineteenth of August, 1812, the *Constitution*, commanded by Captain Isaac Hull, was cruising in latitude 41° 42′ N., longitude 55° 48′ W.;[1] when, at two in the afternoon, a sail was made, bearing east-southeast, and to leeward, but her character could not be made out.[2]

All sail was instantly made, in chase; and so rapidly did the *Constitution* come up with her, that at three o'clock it was plainly seen that she was a ship on the starboard tack, under easy sail, close hauled;[3] and at half-past three she was seen to be a frigate, little doubt being entertained that she was an enemy.[4]

The *Constitution* continued on her course until she had come within three miles of the stranger,[5] when Captain Hull ordered the light sails to be taken in, the courses hauled up, and the ship prepared for action.[6] At the same time the stranger was made ready for action, and had laid her main-topsail aback, waiting for the *Constitution* to come down.[1] This unequivocal *challenge*, by the stranger, caused Captain Hull to prepare for action with the greater care.[2] He ordered her topgallant-sails to be furled, and stowed all her light stay-sails and her flying-jib.[3] Shortly afterwards she took a second reef in her top-sails, hauled up her courses, sent down her royal-yards, cleared for action, and beat to quarters, her crew receiving the order with three cheers.[4]

As soon as the *Constitution* was ready, she bore down with the intention to bring the enemy to close action, without the usual preliminary manœuvres;[5] but as she approached, at five o'clock, the latter hoisted three British ensigns, fired a broadside, filled away, and wore, firing a broadside on the other tack, without doing any damage.[6] Three-quarters of an hour were spent by the stranger in attempting to obtain a position in which she could rake the *Constitution*,[7] during which time the

---

1 Capt. Hull to Sec. of Navy, Aug. 30. Capt. Dacres states the position to have been Lat. 40° 20′ N., Lon. 55° W.

2 Capt. Hull to Sec. of Navy, Aug. 30; Particulars of the late action, &c., in "*The War*," i. p. 46.

3 Capt. Hull to Sec. of Navy, Aug. 30; Cooper's Naval Hist., ii. p. 55.—4 Capt. Hull to Sec. of Navy, Aug. 30; Particulars, &c.—5 Capt. Hull to Sec. of Navy, Aug. 30; Cooper, ii. p. 55.—6 Capt. Hull to Sec. of Navy, Aug. 30; Clark's Hist. Navy, p. 133.

---

1 Capt. Hull to Sec. of Navy, Aug. 30; Capt. Dacres to Adm'l Sawyer, Sept. 7; Particulars, &c.

2 Cooper, ii. p. 55.—3 Particulars, &c.; Cooper, ii. p. 55.

4 Particulars, &c.—5 Capt. Hull to Sec. of Navy, Aug. 30; Cooper, ii. p. 55.

6 Capt. Hull to Secretary of Navy, Aug. 30. Capt. Dacres (*to Adm'l Sawyer, Sept.* 7) says this was done at ten minutes past four.

7 Capt. Hull to Secretary of Navy, Aug. 30; Capt. Dacres to Adm'l Sawyer, Sept. 7; Particulars, &c.

latter had fired but few guns,[1] contenting herself with manœuvring in such a manner as defeated the attempts of the enemy to secure the weather-guage.[2]

At a few minutes before six o'clock the stranger bore up and ran off under her top-sails and jib, with the wind on her quarter;[3] and the *Constitution*, accepting the invitation which this manœuvre conveyed, immediately set her fore-sail and maintop-gallant-sail, and ran alongside.[4] At five minutes before six, the ships being alongside, within half pistol-shot, the fire became general and very heavy from the entire force of both ships.[5]

The *Constitution's* guns were double-shotted, with round and grape shot;[6] and so well were they managed, that, within fifteen minutes after the fire was opened, the stranger had lost her mizzen-mast, her main-yard was in the slings, and her hull, rigging, and sails were torn to pieces.[7] This disaster enabled the *Constitution* to run ahead of the stranger, and by luffing short round on her bows, to subject the latter to a destructive raking fire, as well as to a very destructive fire from the topmen of the former, in which both the officers and the men of the stranger suffered

[1] Particulars, &c.; Cooper, ii. p. 55.—[2] Capt. Hull to Sec. of Navy, Aug. 30; Cooper, ii. p. 55.

[3] Capt. Hull to Sec. of Navy, Aug. 30; Particulars, &c.

[4] Capt. Hull to Sec. of Navy, Aug. 30; Cooper, ii. p. 55.

[5] Capt. Hull's Dispatch, Aug. 30. Others state it was five minutes *after* six (*Particulars*, &c.), and Capt. Dacres (*Dispatch, Sept.* 7) that it was at *five* o'clock.

[6] Capt. Hull's Dispatch, Aug. 30; Clark's Naval Hist., p. 133.—[7] Capt. Hull's Dispatch, Aug. 30; Particulars, &c.; Cooper, ii. p. 55. Capt. Dacres says the mizzen-mast went over at twenty minutes past five.

very severely.[1] This manœuvre was facilitated by the operation of the wreck of her mizzen-mast on the movements of the stranger—the mast having gone over the weather-side the top acted as a complete back-water, and the head of the ship was brought up to the wind, in spite of every effort of the helmsman to prevent it.[2] At this time, also, from the effects of this manœuvre, the *Constitution* fell foul of the stranger—the bowsprit of the latter running into the larboard-quarter of the former—and both crews prepared to board.[3] The stranger turned up all hands from below, and mustered forward;[4] while Lieutenant Morris, of the *Constitution*, endeavored to lash both ships together.[5] The fire from the small-arms of both vessels was now exceedingly severe—Lieutenant Morris, Master Aylwin, and Lieutenant Brush of the marines, having received severe wounds—and both parties hesitated to move in the face of such a fire, with the heavy sea which was then on.[6]

About the same time the sails of the *Constitution* filled, and she shot ahead of the stranger;[7] when the foremast of the latter went over, carrying with it her mainmast, and leaving her a helpless wreck in the trough of the sea.[8]

Her enemy having thus been entirely

[1] Capt. Hull's Dispatch, Aug. 30; Capt. Dacres' Dispatch, Sept. 7.—[2] James' Naval Occurrences, p. 99.

[3] Capt. Hull's Dispatch, Aug. 30; Particulars, &c.; James' Naval Occur., pp. 99, 100.—[4] Capt. Dacres' Dispatch, Aug. 30; Cooper, ii. p. 55.—[5] Cooper, ii. p. 55. This officer was well known afterwards as Commodore Morris.—[6] Cooper, ii. p. 56; James' Naval Occur., pp. 99, 100.—[7] Particulars, &c.; Cooper, ii. p. 56.

[8] Capt. Hull's Dispatch, Aug. 30; Capt. Dacres' Dispatch, Sept. 7; Cooper, ii p. 56.

Engraved by James D. Smillie.

disabled, the *Constitution* hauled aboard her tacks, ran off a short distance, secured her masts, and rove new rigging.[1] At seven o'clock she wore round, and took a favorable position for raking, when a jack, which had been fastened on the stump of the stranger's mizzenmast, was lowered, a gun was fired to leeward, and she surrendered.[2]

Third-lieutenant George C. Read was sent on board the prize, and quickly returned with the information that she was the *Guerriere*, rating thirty-eight guns, and commanded by Captain J. A. Dacres.[3]

The *Constitution* remained near her prize all night, and at daylight the officer in charge hailed, to say the *Guerriere* had four feet water in the hold, and that there was danger of her sinking.[4] The prisoners, and some of the movables were immediately removed to the *Constitution;*[5] and that duty having been performed, at three in the afternoon the prize crew was withdrawn, after having set the wreck on fire, and within a few minutes afterwards she blew up.[6]

There is no subject connected with the history of our country which has been more fiercely contested than this; and almost every branch of it has been made the subject of violent discussion.

The relative force of the two ships has been misrepresented on either side. The *Constitution*, although rating *forty-four* guns, actually mounted thirty twenty-four pounders on the gun-deck, twenty-four thirty-two pound carronades, and two eighteen-pounders on the quarter-deck and forecastle—a total of fifty-six;[1] while the *Guerriere*, although rating *thirty-eight* guns, was pierced for *fifty-four*, and carried *forty-nine*, one of which was a light boat-carronade.[2] Her gun-deck metal was eighteen-pounders, while the remainder of her equipment was the same as that of the *Constitution*.[3]

The relative weight of their broadsides has also been disputed—British writers maintaining that the weight of the *Constitution's* broadside was seven hundred and sixty-eight pounds, while that of the *Guerriere* was only five hundred and seventeen.[4] On the other hand, it is said that the armament of the *Guerriere* was French—the vessel having been a prize to the *Blanche*, in 1806[5]—and that French eighteens carried nineteen and a half pounds shot; while the American twenty-fours seldom exceeded twenty-two pounds.[6]

The relative strength of the crews was greatly in favor of the *Constitution*, when mere numbers are considered; while in the efficiency and experience of her men, the *Guerriere* had the advantage. The experienced crew of the latter, then on duty, numbered two hundred and sixty-three, including ten Americans, who were generously excused from fighting against their coun-

1 Capt. Hull's Dispatch, Aug. 30; Capt. Dacres' Dispatch, Sept. 7.—2 Particulars, &c.; Cooper, ii. p. 56.

3 Capt. Hull's Dispatch, Aug. 30; Particulars, &c.; Cooper, ii. p. 56.—4 Particulars, &c.—5 Ibid.; Cooper, ii. p. 56.—6 Particulars, &c.; Clark, p. 134.

1 James' Naval Occurrences, p. 108; Cooper, i. p. 149.

2 Cooper, ii. pp. 57, 58. James (*Naval Occur.*, pp. 104, 105) says she mounted only *forty-seven*.

3 Cooper, ii. p. 58.—4 James' Warden Refuted, Table I.

5 Capt. Lavie to Lord Keith, July 26, 1806.

6 Cooper, ii. p. 58; Clark, p. 136.

trymen;[1] the crew of the *Constitution*, many of them raw hands, numbered four hundred and sixty-eight.[2]

The duration of the action, also, differs, according to the writers of the two nations—the British, after Captain Dacres, insisting that the vessels fought *two hours and twelve minutes;*[3] while the Americans, generally, maintain, with Captain Hull, that they fought but *thirty minutes*.[4]

The damage which the *Guerriere* received in her hull was very great, about thirty shot having taken effect on her larboard side, about five coppers down, and a large hole had been made under her starboard counter;[5] the *Constitution* also suffered severely—her lower masts having been severely wounded, and her rigging very much cut up.[6]

The loss of the *Constitution* was, Lieutenant Brush of the marines, and six men, *killed;* and Lieutenant Morris, Master Aylwin, four seamen, and one marine, *wounded:*[7] that of the *Guerriere* was, one officer and fourteen men, *killed;* Captain Dacres, three officers,

[1] James' Warden Refuted, Table I.; Cooper, ii. p. 58; James' Naval Occur., pp. 106, 107.—[2] James' Naval Occur., p. 109.—[3] James' Warden Refuted, Table I.; James' Naval Occur., pp. 100, 101; Auchinleck's Hist. of War, p. 68.—[4] Capt. Hull's Dispatch, Aug. 30; O'Connor's Hist. of War, p. 42; Perkins' Hist. of War, p. 121; Clark, p. 133.—[5] Capt. Dacres' defence before the Court-martial.—[6] Capt. Dacres' Dispatch, Sept. 7.—[7] "Returns," appended to Capt. Hull's Dispatch, Aug. 30.

and thirty-two men, *wounded severely;* two officers and sixteen men, *wounded slightly;*[1] and two officers and twenty-two men, *missing*.[2]

After the action the *Constitution* returned to Boston, carrying with her the intelligence of her triumph. At this distant day it is not easy to convey to the reader a correct idea of the deep impression which the capture of this frigate produced both in Europe and America. The constant success with which the naval flag of Great Britain had been accompanied, had filled the people of America with anxiety, and those of Great Britain with a degree of overbearing insolence which was unbecoming an enlightened nation. In fact, Captain Dacres himself had, a short time before, issued an insolent challenge to Commodore Rogers and the *President*, or any other ship of her class, little supposing that he would so soon receive the punishment which he merited. The Congress of the United States voted its thanks and fifty thousand dollars in lieu of prize-money; the Corporation of New York presented the freedom of the city to Captain Hull; and the heroes of the action were received with open arms wherever they went.

[1] "Returns," appended to Capt. Dacres' Dispatch, Sept. 7.—[2] "Returns," appended to Capt. Hull's Dispatch, Aug. 30.

DOCUMENTS.

I.

CAPTAIN HULL TO THE SECRETARY OF THE NAVY.

U. S. FRIGATE CONSTITUTION, OFF BOSTON LIGHT,
August 30, 1812.

SIR:—I have the honor to inform you, that on the 19th instant, at two P. M., being in latitude 41° 41′, longitude 55° 48′, with the *Constitution* under my command, a sail was discovered from the masthead, bearing E. by S. or E. S. E.; but at such a distance, we could not tell what she was. All sail was instantly made in chase, and soon found we came up with her. At three P. M., could plainly see she was a ship, on the starboard-tack, under easy sail, close on a wind. At half-past three P. M., made her out to be a frigate. Continued the chase until we were within about three miles, when I ordered the light sails taken in, the courses hauled up, and the ship cleared for action. At this time the chase had backed her maintop-sail, waiting for us to come down. As soon as the *Constitution* was ready for action, I bore down with an intention to bring her to close action immediately; but on our coming within gun-shot, she gave us a broadside and filled away and wore, giving us a broadside on the other tack, but without effect, her shot falling short. She continued wearing and manœuvring for about three-quarters of an hour, to get a raking position, but finding she could not, she bore up, and run under her topsails and jib, with the wind on the quarter. I immediately made sail, to bring the ship up with her, and five minutes before six P. M., being alongside, within half pistol-shot, we commenced a heavy fire from all our guns, double-shotted with round and grape, and so well directed were they, and so warmly kept up, that in sixteen minutes his mizzen-mast went by the board, and his main-yard in the slings, and the hull, rigging, and sails very much torn to pieces. The fire was kept up with equal warmth for fifteen minutes longer, when his mainmast and foremast went, taking with them every spar except the bowsprit. On seeing this, we ceased firing, so that in thirty minutes after we got fairly alongside the enemy she surrendered, and had not a spar standing, and her hull below and above water so shattered, that a few more broadsides must have carried her down.

After informing that so fine a ship as the *Guerriere*, commanded by an able and experienced officer, had been totally dismasted, and otherwise cut to pieces, so as to make her not worth towing into port, in the short space of thirty minutes, you can have no doubt of the gallantry and good conduct of the officers and ship's company I have the honor to command. It remains, therefore, for me to assure you that they all fought with great bravery; and it gives me great pleasure to say, that from the smallest boy in the ship to the oldest seaman, not a look of fear was seen. They all went into action, giving three cheers, and requesting to be laid close alongside the enemy.

Inclosed I have the honor to send you a list of killed and wounded on board the *Constitution*, and a report of the damages she has sustained; also, a list of the killed and wounded on board the enemy, with his quarter-bill, &c.

I have the honor to be, with very great respect, sir, your obedient servant,

ISAAC HULL.

The Hon. PAUL HAMILTON, &c.

Killed and wounded on board the United States frigate Constitution, Isaac Hull, Esq., Captain, in the action with His Britannic Majesty's frigate Guerriere, James R. Dacres, Esq., Captain, on the 20th August, 1812.

Killed.—W. S. Brush, Lieutenant of Marines, and six seamen.

Wounded.—Lieutenant C. Morris, Master J. C. Alwyn, four seamen, one marine.

Total killed and wounded, fourteen.

ISAAC HULL, *Captain.*
T. J. CHEW, *Purser.*

UNITED STATES FRIGATE CONSTITUTION,
August 21, 1812.

II.

CAPTAIN DACRE'S DISPATCH TO ADM'L SAWYER.

Boston, *September* 7, 1812.

Sir:—I am sorry to inform you of the capture of His Majesty's late ship *Guerriere*, by the American frigate *Constitution*, after a severe action, on the 19th of August, in latitude 40° 20′ N., and longitude 55° W. At two P. M., being by the wind on the starboard-tack, we saw a sail on our weather-beam, bearing down on us. At three, made her out to be a man-of-war; beat to quarters, and prepared for action. At four, she closing fast, wore to prevent her raking us. At ten minutes past four, hoisted our colors, and fired several shot at her; at twenty minutes past four, she hoisted her colors, and returned our fire; wore several times to avoid being raked, exchanging broadsides. At five, she closed on our starboard-beam, both keeping up a heavy fire and steering free, his intention being evidently to cross our bow. At twenty minutes past five, our mizzen-mast went over the starboard-quarter, and brought the ship up in the wind; the enemy then placed himself on our larboard-bow, raking us, a few only of our bow-guns bearing, and his grape and riflemen sweeping our deck. At forty minutes past five, the ship not answering her helm, he attempted to lay us on board; at this time Mr. Grant, who commanded the forecastle, was carried below badly wounded. I immediately ordered the marines and boarders from the main-deck; the master was at this time shot through the knee, and I received a severe wound in the back. Lieutenant Kent was leading on the boarders, when the ship coming to, we brought some of our bow-guns to bear on her, and had got clear of our opponent; when, at twenty minutes past six, our fore and main masts went over the side, leaving the ship a perfect unmanageable wreck. The frigate shooting ahead, I was in hopes to clear the wreck, and get the ship under command, to renew the action; but just as we had cleared the wreck, our spritsail-yard went, and the enemy having rove new braces, &c., wore round within pistol-shot to rake us, the ship lying in the trough of the sea, and rolling her main-deck guns under water, and all attempts to get her before the wind being fruitless; when, calling my few remaining officers together, they were all of opinion that any farther resistance would be only a needless waste of lives, I ordered, though reluctantly, the colors to be struck.

The loss of the ship is to be ascribed to the early fall of her mizzen-mast, which enabled our opponent to choose his position. I am sorry to say, we suffered severely in killed and wounded; and mostly while she lay on our bow, from her grape and musketry; in all, fifteen killed and sixty-three wounded, many of them severely. None of the wounded officers quitted the deck till the firing ceased.

The frigate proved to be the United States ship *Constitution*, of thirty twenty-four pounders on her main-deck, and twenty-four thirty-two pounders, and two eighteen-pounders on her upper deck, and four hundred and seventy-six men. Her loss in comparison with ours is trifling, about twenty; the first-lieutenant of marines and eight killed, and first-lieutenant, and master of the ship, and eleven men wounded; her lower masts badly wounded, and stern much shattered; and very much cut up about her rigging.

The *Guerriere* was so cut up that all attempts to get her in would have been useless. As soon as the wounded were got out of her, they set her on fire; and I feel it my duty to state, that the conduct of Captain Hull and his officers, to our men, has been that of a brave enemy; the greatest care being taken to prevent our men losing the smallest trifle, and the greatest attention being paid to the wounded; who, through the attention and skill of Mr. Irvine, surgeon, I hope will do well.

I hope, though success has not crowned our efforts, you will not think it presumptuous in me to say, the greatest credit is due to the officers and ship's company for their exertions, particularly when exposed to the heavy raking fire of the enemy. I feel particularly obliged for the exertions of Lieutenant Kent, who, though wounded early by a splinter, continued to assist me. In the second-lieutenant the service has suffered a severe loss. Mr. Scott, the master, though wounded, was particularly attentive, and used every exertion in clearing the wreck, as did the warrant officers. Lieutenant

Nicholl of the Royal marines, and his party supported the honorable character of their corps, and they suffered severely. I must recommend Mr. Snow, master's-mate, who commanded the foremost main-deck guns, in the absence of Lieutenant Pullman (and the whole after the fall of Lieutenant Reddy), to your protection, he having received a severe wound from a splinter. I must point out Mr. Garley, acting-purser, to your notice, who volunteered his services on deck, and commanded the after quarter-deck guns, and was particularly active, as well as Mr. Bannister, midshipman.

I hope, in considering the circumstances, you will consider the ship intrusted to my charge properly defended. The unfortunate loss of our masts; the absence of the third-lieutenant, second-lieutenant of marines, three midshipmen, and twenty-four men, considerably weakened our crew, and we only mustered at quarters two hundred and forty-four men and nineteen boys, on coming into action. The enemy had such an advantage from his marines and riflemen, when close, and his superior sailing enabled him to choose his distance.

I inclose herewith a list of killed and wounded on board the Guerriere; and have the honor to be, &c.,

JAS. R. DACRES.

List of officers, seamen, and marines, killed and wounded, on board His Majesty's ship Guerriere, &c. (of which the names are given, comprising)—

Killed.—The second-lieutenant, seven petty officers and able seamen, three ordinary seamen, one landsman, one sergeant, and two privates of marines—total, fifteen.

Wounded dangerously.—Seven petty officers and able seamen, five ordinary seamen, and five private marines—total, seventeen.

Wounded severely.—The captain, master, two master's-mates, five petty officers and able seamen, four ordinary seamen, one landsman, and five private marines—total, nineteen.

Wounded slightly.—The first-lieutenant, one midshipman, nine petty officers and able seamen, three landsmen, one boy, and three private marines—total, eighteen.

Fifteen killed, sixty-four wounded; total, seventy-eight.

JOHN R. DACRES,
JOHN IRVINE, *Surgeon.*

CHAPTER XXIII.

September 1 to 12, 1812.

THE SIEGE OF FORT WAYNE.

THE great energy, enlarged views, and patriotic designs of Tecumthà have been referred to in a former chapter of this work;[1] and the capture of Michilimacinac,[2] of Fort Dearborn (*Chicago*),[3] and of Detroit,[4] have also been made the subjects of especial notice. This series of disasters had confirmed the opposition of the Northwestern Indians, and very few remained friendly with the United States. The plans of Tecumthà, for the expulsion of the whites from the Northwest, appeared to be drawing to a close; and the few remaining posts served rather as monuments of the forbearance of the Indians, than as means of protection to the settlers.

Among these, and the most important of them, were Forts Wayne and Harrison; and against them simulta-

[1] Vide Chap. XIV.—[2] Vide Chap. XV.
[3] Vide Chap. XX.—[4] Vide Chap. XXI.

neous movements were planned by the energetic chief. The Winnebagoes and that part of the Miamis who had determined on hostility, were to attack Fort Harrison, and, if possible, to take it by surprise; while against Fort Wayne the Potawatomies and Ottawas, with a detachment of British regulars, under Major Muir, were the designated assailants. The first of September was the time which was appointed for the attack on the works, and the Indians were promptly on the spot; while the British auxiliaries, with a reinforcement of Indians, had left Malden on the eighteenth of August, and were rapidly approaching the fort.

In the mean time the government and the people had taken steps to relieve the forts and to oppose the progress of the enemy; and on the third of September a strong force, under General William H. Harrison, had reached Piqua, eighty miles from Cincinnati, on its march against the savages. On the same day the General detached a body of troops for the relief of the fort, beside which a regiment of volunteers from Ohio had advanced, with the same object, as far as Shane's Ferry, on the St. Mary's. The main body of the army moved on the sixth. Reinforcements, under Major Richard M. Johnson and others, joined the army as it progressed; and on the eighth of September the entire command numbered upwards of twenty-two hundred effective men. On the evening of the ninth it overtook the regiment of Ohio volunteers, before referred to; and the entire force moved cautiously and slowly forward towards the fort, encamping, on the evening of the eleventh of September, about twenty miles from it.

During the progress of the army, the garrison within the fort was harassed by the enemy. Until the day appointed for the assault (*Sept. 1st*), the savages in the neighborhood professed great friendship, probably with a hope of securing the fort by surprise, in which, however, they were disappointed. But they had closely invested it, notwithstanding this disappointment; and with all the ingenuity of which they were master they had prosecuted the siege.[1] To overcome the advantage which the artillery had given to the garrison, the Indians had bored out several large logs and had secured them with iron bands, as substitutes for a siege-train;[2] but it does not appear that this novel siege-train was employed by its ingenious possessors.

The party from Malden, after encountering many difficulties, approached the fort by way of the Miami, and had nearly reached it, when intelligence of the movements of General Harrison and his army was received through its scouts. Major Muir immediately halted his force and awaited farther intelligence, which was soon afterwards received; when he immediately retired by the route on which he had advanced, and returned to Malden.[3]

---

[1] Dr. Peck (*Annals of the West*, p. 619) says the fort was invested on the 28*th August*; Breckenridge (*Hist. of War*, p. 58), on the *sixth of September*; Thomson (*Hist. of War*, p. 56), on the *fifth of September*.

[2] Thomson's Sketches of War, p. 56.

[3] Narrative of Maj. Richardson, in Auchinleck's History of the War; Armstrong's Notices, i. p. 54.

At length, about two hours before sunset, on the twelfth of September, the army reached the fort, but the besiegers had disappeared; and nothing remained for it to do but to send small parties out on expeditions against a fugitive and more nimble enemy, with no other result than the destruction of the villages and cornfields of the neighboring Indians.[1]

The fort, around which the movements referred to took place, was on the spot where General Harmar met the savages in 1790. It was delightfully situated, on an eminence on the south bank of the Miami of the Lake, immediately below the junction of the St. Mary's and the St. Joseph's. It was well constructed of block-houses and picketing; and was well adapted to withstand any attack from a savage enemy, although a British force could not have been long resisted. At the time of the siege which is the subject of this chapter, it contained a full supply of stores and provisions, with a garrison of about seventy men, and four small field-pieces, the whole commanded by Captain Rhea.

It is not recorded that any damage was done to the fort, or that either party sustained any loss.

[NOTE.—The greater part of this short narrative has been taken from MCAFEE'S "*History of the War in the West*," published in Lexington, Kentucky, in 1816. Except where other works have been cited, therefore, that work has been my only authority.]

[1] Breckenridge, p. 58; Thomson, p. 57; Perkins' History of War, p. 97. Dr. Peck (*Perkins' Annals of the West*, p. 619) says the army reached the fort on the *sixteenth*.

CHAPTER XXIV.

September 4 to 6, 1812.

THE SIEGE OF FORT HARRISON.

THE plan of operations which Tecumthà had adopted, and the attack on Fort Wayne, in accordance with that plan, have been referred to in another chapter;[2] and it only remains, on that subject, to notice the attack on Fort Harrison, which formed part of the same plan of operations.

This frontier post was on the bank of the Wabash, a short distance above the present town of Terre Haute, Indiana.[1] It was garrisoned with a small party of the Seventh regiment of infantry, under the command of Captain Zachary Taylor, who, with his command, had suffered severely from sickness; and, at the time of the action now under consideration, only ten to fifteen effective men were within its lines.[2]

On Thursday evening, the third of September, two young men—settlers in

[2] Vide Chapter XXIII.

[1] Perkins' Annals of the West, p. 619.

[2] Capt. Taylor to Gov. Harrison, Sept. 10, 1812; Thomson's Sketches, p. 54.

that vicinity—were killed and scalped in the immediate neighborhood of the fort;[1] and late in the evening of the next day, some thirty or forty Indians, and about ten squaws, from the Prophet's town, came to the fort and desired admission.[2] They were generally chiefs of the several nations composing that band of fanatics, among whom was Joseph Lenar; they carried a white flag; and one of their number informed Captain Taylor that they desired an interview for the purpose of obtaining something to eat.[3]

As Captain Taylor had been warned of the approach of this party, and of its hostile intentions, by the neighboring Miamis, before it had reached the fort, the arms of the garrison were examined at retreat-beating, found to be in good order, and the supply of cartridges in the boxes increased to sixteen rounds per man.[4] Unusual precautions were also taken to prevent a surprise, as the weakness of the garrison prevented the detailing of more than six privates and two non-commissioned officers for guard duty; and when the guards were set they were enjoined to be vigilant in the discharge of their duties.[5]

At eleven o'clock the fire of the sentinels alarmed the commandant and the garrison, when it was discovered that a block-house, which formed a part of the exterior line of the works, had been set on fire by the Indians.[1] The lower part of the structure was occupied by the contractor as a store-house for the garrison's supplies, while the upper part was occupied by a corporal and ten men, as an alarm-post; and its destruction would not only deprive the garrison of provisions, and jeopardize the barracks which adjoined it, but, at the same time, would open a space of eighteen or twenty feet in the outer works of the fort.[2] Orders were, accordingly, given to get the buckets ready, and to extinguish the flames; but so slowly were these orders obeyed, that the fire had communicated with a barrel of whiskey, and the whole interior of the block-house was in flames, and beyond the control of the garrison, before any steps were taken to extinguish them.[3] In fact, the entire garrison appears to have been filled with the greatest alarm, and to have fallen into the utmost confusion; and this, with the yells of the savages,—who had been joined by several hundreds of others, who had, probably, been concealed in the immediate neighborhood,[4]—and with the cries of nine women and children, who had taken shelter in the fort, rendered the situation of the entire fort and garrison somewhat questionable.[5]

The gallant commandant, amid all this confusion, appears to have retained his presence of mind; and he imme-

[1] Capt. Taylor to Gov. Harrison, Sept. 10, 1812; Thomson's Sketches, p. 54. Mr. McAfee (*Hist. of War in the West*, p. 153) supposes this was done on the *second;* and other writers, following him, have fallen into the same error.—[2] McAfee, p. 153; Armstrong's Notices, i. p. 55; Perkins' Hist. of War, p. 94; Capt. Taylor to Gov. Harrison, Sept. 10.—[3] Perkins' Hist. of War, p. 94; Capt. Taylor to Gov. Harrison, Sept. 10; Breckenridge's Hist. of War, p. 66.—[4] Perkins, p. 94; Capt. Taylor to Gov. Harrison, Sept. 10.—[5] Ibid.; Breckenridge's Hist., p. 67.

[1] McAfee, p. 153; Thomson's Sketches, p. 54; Perkins, p. 94; Capt. Taylor to Gov. Harrison, Sept. 10.

[2] Capt. Taylor to Gov. Harrison, Sept. 10.

[3] Ibid.; Perkins, p. 94, Breckenridge's Hist., p. 67.

[4] McAfee, p. 153; Armstrong's Notices, i. p .55; Breckenridge's Hist., p. 67.—[5] Capt. Taylor to Gov. Harrison, Sept. 10; Breckenridge, p. 67.

diately ordered that portion of the roof of the barracks which was nearest the burning block-house to be thrown down, and the end of the barracks to be kept wet; quieting the fears of the men, at the same time, by endeavoring to convince them that by a prompt obedience to this order, the barracks might be saved and the enemy repulsed.[1] The success of this effort fully realized the expectations and desires of the commandant; and every man appeared to be inspired with new life. With a degree of deliberate courage, which more nearly approached desperation, the invalids and convalescents manned the two bastions and the remaining block-house, and by opening and keeping up a well-directed fire on the Indians, they held them in check, and protected that portion of the garrison which was engaged in checking the progress of the flames.[2] The men who were able to do so, with Doctor Clark at their head, mounted the roof of the barracks, and, in a few seconds, threw off that portion of the roof which was in jeopardy, with the loss of only one man killed and two wounded.[3] The end of the barracks, although it was several times in flames, was effectually preserved; and the space which the block-house had occupied was all which was exposed.[4] Notwithstanding the enemy kept up a constant and well-directed fire on every man who showed himself, for upwards of eight hours, the garrison had managed to raise a temporary breastwork, before

[1] Thomson's Sketches, p. 55; Capt. Taylor to Gov. Harrison, Sept. 10.—[2] Capt. Taylor to Gov. Harrison, Sept. 10.—[3] Ibid.; Thomson's Sketches, p. 55; Breckenridge's Hist., p. 67.—[4] Capt. Taylor to Gov. Harrison, Sept. 10.

daylight, and every effort of the wily enemy was frustrated.[1]

A constant fire was kept up by the savages until six o'clock on the morning of the fifth, when the garrison opened on them, "with some effect," and they immediately removed beyond the reach of the guns, and ceased to disturb the gallant captain and his little party.[2]

Not to be entirely disappointed, however, the assailants immediately collected the horses, cattle, and hogs of the neighboring farmers, shooting the hogs within sight of the garrison, and driving off the cattle. The horses they attempted to secure; but failing to accomplish this, to any considerable extent, they immediately shot them, also, within sight of the garrison.[3]

During the day (*Sept. 5th*) the garrison strengthened the temporary breastwork, which had been erected in the opening of the exterior line, which the destruction of the block-house had occasioned, by erecting a row of strong pickets within it, the timbers for which were obtained by tearing down the guard-house.[4] The savages, after hovering around the fort all the day and succeeding night, decamped on the morning of the sixth, without making any farther attempts on the fort.[5]

The little garrison, by this desperate and successful operation, saved the post and the lives of those who had sought

[1] Capt. Taylor to Gov. Harrison, Sept. 10; Breckenridge, p. 67.—[2] Thomson's Sketches, p. 55; Perkins, p. 94; Capt. Taylor to Gov. Harrison, Sept. 10.—[3] Capt. Taylor to Gov. Harrison, Sept. 10; Perkins, p. 95.

[4] McAfee, p. 153; Thomson's Sketches, p. 55; Perkins, p. 95.

[5] Capt. Taylor to Gov. Harrison, Sept. 10.

refuge within the lines; although the destruction of the block-house deprived it of the entire stock of provisions which had been provided for its use, and compelled it to subsist entirely on green corn, until a fresh supply could reach the post from Vincennes.[1]

The number of the entire garrison did not exceed fifty;[2] those who were effective, not more than "ten or fifteen" men.[3] That of the enemy comprised all the force they could raise in that part of the country, and they had assembled with a determination to take the fort either by stratagem or force.[4] The loss of the latter, of course, is not known; the garrison lost three men killed and three wounded[1]—all the former and one of the latter while disobeying or disregarding the orders of their commander.[2]

Captain Taylor and his party merited and received the thanks of the country for their gallant and successful defence of the post. The Captain received a brevet commission as Major—commencing, at this time, that series of brilliant exploits, which was continued until the close of his campaign in Mexico, when a grateful and admiring people rewarded him by bestowing the greatest of all human honors—their voluntary suffrages for the office of President of the Republic.

DOCUMENT.

LETTER FROM CAPTAIN Z. TAYLOR, COMMANDING FORT HARRISON, INDIANA TERRITORY, TO GENERAL HARRISON.

Fort Harrison, *September* 10.

Dear Sir:—On Thursday evening the 3d instant, after retreat-beating, four guns were heard to fire in the direction where two young men (citizens who resided here) were making hay, about four hundred yards' distance from the fort. I was immediately impressed with an idea that they were killed by the Indians, as the Miamis or Weas had that day informed me that the Prophet's party would soon be here for the purpose of commencing hostilities; and that they had been directed to leave this place, which we were about to do. I did not think it prudent to send out, at that late hour of the night, to see what had become of them; and their not coming in, convinced me that I was right in my conjecture. I waited until eight o'clock next morning, when I sent out a corporal, with a small party, to find them, if it could be done without running too much risk of being drawn into an ambuscade. He soon sent back to inform me that he had found them both killed, and wished to know my further orders; I sent the cart and oxen, had them brought in and buried; they had been shot with two balls, scalped, and cut in the most shocking manner. Late in the evening of the 4th instant old Joseph Lenar, and between thirty and forty Indians, arrived from the Prophet's town, with a white flag; among whom were about ten women, and the men were composed of chiefs of the different tribes that compose the Prophet's party. A Shawanoe man, that spoke good English, informed me that old Lenar intended to speak to me next morning, and try to get something to eat. At retreat-beating I examined the men's

[1] McAfee, p. 154; Thomson's Sketches, p. 55.
[2] McAfee, p. 154.—[3] Capt. Taylor to Gov. Harrison, Sept. 10.—[4] McAfee, p. 154; Capt. Taylor to Gov. Harrison, Sept. 10.

[1] Breckenridge's History, p. 67.—[2] Capt. Taylor to Gov. Harrison, Sept. 10.

arms, and found them all in good order, and completed their cartridges to sixteen rounds per man. As I had not been able to mount a guard of more than six privates and two non-commissioned officers, for some time past, and sometimes part of them every other day, from the unhealthiness of the company, I had not conceived my force adequate to the defence of this post, should it be vigorously attacked, for some time past. As I had just recovered from a very severe attack of the fever, I was not able to be up much through the night. After tattoo, I cautioned the guard to be vigilant, and ordered one of the non-commissioned officers, as the sentinels could not see every part of the garrison, to walk around on the inside during the whole night, to prevent the Indians taking any advantage of us, provided they had any intention of attacking us. About eleven o'clock I was awakened by the firing of one of the sentinels; I sprang up, ran out, and ordered the men to their posts; when my orderly-sergeant (who had charge of the upper block-house) called out that the Indians had fired the lower block-house (which contained the property of the contractor, which was deposited in the lower part, the upper having been assigned to a corporal and ten privates, as an alarm post). The guns had began to fire pretty smartly from both sides. I directed the buckets to be got ready and water brought from the well, and the fire extinguished immediately, as it was perceivable at that time; but from debility or some other cause, the men were very slow in executing my orders—the word fire appeared to throw the whole of them into confusion; and by the time they had got the water and broken open the door, the fire had unfortunately communicated to a quantity of whiskey (the stock having licked several holes through the lower part of the building, after the salt that was stored there, through which they had introduced the fire without being discovered, as the night was very dark), and in spite of every exertion we could make use of, in less than a moment it ascended to the roof and baffled every effort we could make to extinguish it. As that block-house adjoined the barracks that made part of the fortifications, most of the men immediately gave themselves up for lost, and I had the greatest difficulty in getting my orders executed; and, sir, what from the raging of the fire—the yelling and howling of several hundred Indians—the cries of nine women and children (a part soldiers' and a part citizens' wives, who had taken shelter in the fort)—and the desponding of so many of the men, which was worse than all—I can assure you that my feelings were very unpleasant—and, indeed, there were not more than ten or fifteen men able to do a great deal, the others being either sick or convalescent; and to add to our other misfortunes, two of the stoutest men in the fort, and that I had every confidence in, jumped the picket, and left us. But my presence of mind did not for a moment forsake me. I saw, by throwing off part of the roof that joined the block-house that was on fire, and keeping the end perfectly wet, the whole row of buildings might be saved, and leave only an entrance of eighteen or twenty feet for the Indians to enter after the house was consumed; and that a temporary breastwork might be erected to prevent their even entering there. I convinced the men that this could be accomplished, and it appeared to inspire them with new life, and never did men act with more firmness or desperation. Those that were able (while the others kept up a constant fire from the other block-house and the two bastions) mounted the roofs of the houses, with Dr. Clark at their head (who acted with the greatest firmness and presence of mind the whole time the attack lasted, which was seven hours), under a shower of bullets, and in less than a moment threw off as much of the roof as was necessary. This was done only with the loss of one man and two wounded, and I am in hopes neither of them dangerous; the man that was killed was a little deranged, and did not get off the house as soon as directed, or he would not have been hurt; and, although the barracks were several times in a blaze, and an immense quantity of fire against them, the men used such exertion that they kept it under, and before day raised a temporary breastwork as high as a man's head, although the Indians continued to pour in a heavy fire of ball and an innumerable quantity of arrows during the whole time the attack lasted, in every part of the parade. I had but one other man killed, nor any other wounded inside the fort, and he lost his life by being too anxious; he got into one of the gallies in the bastions, and fired over the pickets, and called out to his comrades that he had killed an Indian, and neglecting to stoop down, in an instant he was shot dead. One of the men that jumped the pickets, returned an hour before day, and running up towards the gate, begged for God's sake for it to be opened. I suspected it to be a stratagem of the Indians to get in, as I did not recollect the voice; I directed the men in the bastion, where I happened to be, to shoot him, let him be who he would; and one of them fired at him, but fortunately he ran up to the other bastion, where they knew his voice, and Dr. Clark directed him to lie down close to the pickets, behind an empty barrel that happened to be there, and at daylight I had him let in. His arm was broke in a most shocking manner, which he says was done by the Indians--which I suppose was the cause of his returning; I think it probable that he will not recover. The other, they caught about one hundred and thirty yards from the garrison, and cut him all to pieces. After keeping up a constant fire until about six o'clock the next morning, which we began to return with some effect after daylight, they removed out of the reach of our guns. A party of them drove up the horses that belonged to the citizens here, and as they could not catch them very readily, shot the whole of them in our sight, as well as a number of their hogs. They drove off the whole of the cattle, which amounted to sixty-five head, as well as the public oxen. I had the vacancy filled up before night (which was made by the burning of the block-house), with a strong row of pickets, which I got by pulling down the guard-house. We lost the whole of our provisions, but must make out to live upon green corn until we can get a supply, which I am in hopes will not be long. I believe the whole of the Miamis or Weas were among the Prophet's party, as one chief gave his orders in that language, which resembled Stone Eater's voice, and I believe Negro Legs was there likewise. A Frenchman here understands their different languages; and several of the Miamis or Weas, that have been frequently here, were recognized by the Frenchman and soldiers, next morning. The Indians suffered smartly, but were so numerous as to take off all that were shot. They continued with us until the next morning, but made no farther attempt on the fort, nor have we seen any thing more of them since. I have delayed informing you of my situation, as I did not like to weaken the garrison, and I looked for some person from Vincennes, and none of my men were acquainted with the woods, and therefore I would either have to take the road or river, which I was fearful was guarded by small parties of Indians that would not dare attack a company of rangers that was on a scout; but being disappointed, I have at length determined to send a couple of my men by water, and am in hopes they will arrive safe. I think it would be best to send the provisions under a pretty strong escort, as the Indians may attempt to prevent their coming. If you carry on an expedition against the Prophet this fall, you ought to be well provided with every thing, as you may calculate on having every inch of ground disputed, between this and there, that they can defend with advantage.

Wishing, &c., Z. Taylor.

His Excellency, Gov. Harrison.

CHAPTER XXV.

September 5 to 8, 1812.

THE ATTACK ON FORT MADISON.

At Bellevue, on the bank of the Mississippi River, a short distance from Saint Louis, at the time of which we write, was one of those outposts which are occasionally established for some temporary purpose among the Indians.[1] It was named "*Fort Madison*," and its garrison was a small party of the First regiment of light-infantry, under the command of Lieutenants Hamilton and Vasques.[2] The site of the "fort" was exceedingly ineligible, — on its south side the approach of an enemy was completely sheltered by a bank of the river; on its east "it was worse yet;" on its west a deep water-course afforded a similar shelter; and on the north was a hill which completely commanded the work,[3]—and it was entirely unfit for any purpose of defence whatever.

Late in the afternoon, on the fifth of September, 1812, it was suddenly attacked by a body of upwards of two hundred Winnebagoes.[4] They "sneaked" up to the fort, as was "their usual mode;" and one of the garrison, named John Cox, was shot and scalped within twenty-five paces of one of the sentinels, who fired on them as they approached.[1] From that time until dark the fire was kept up on both sides; yet the shelter which both enjoyed—the garrison from the fort, and the enemy from the banks already referred to—protected both from any loss.[2]

On the morning of the sixth the action was renewed; and, from every side, the enemy poured into the fort a constant shower of balls and buckshot, while, at the same time, another party was engaged in destroying all the live-stock in the neighborhood. At four in the afternoon the enemy appeared to concentrate his force under the bank of the river, for the purpose of an attack in that quarter, and upwards of four hundred shot were speedily thrown into the fort. One of these cut the flag-halyards, and the colors floated gently down to the ground, amid the shouts of triumph which the enemy sent up, under the impression that the garrison would now surrender.[3]

On the morning of the seventh the operations were commenced by a display, on sticks, of the head and heart of John Cox—the former painted after the fashion of the savages.[4] Immediately afterwards the fire was re-

---

[1] Sketches of the War, p. 77.—[2] Lieut. Hamilton's Dispatch, Sept. 10.—[3] Ibid.; Sketches of the War, p. 77; Niles' Register, iii. p. 142.

[4] Lieut. Hamilton's Dispatch, Sept. 10; Sketches of the War, p. 77.

[1] Lieut. Hamilton's Dispatch, Sept. 10; Niles' Register, iii. p. 142.—[2] Ibid.—[3] Lieut. Hamilton's Dispatch, Sept. 10.—[4] Ibid.

newed, and it was steadily continued during the entire day.[1] About seven o'clock a boat and her cargo, belonging to a Mr. Graham, were set on fire and destroyed;[2] and, soon afterwards, two boats belonging to the garrison, and a neighboring house and buildings, belonging to Mr. Juliean, were also destroyed.[3] During the day, perceiving that but little progress had been made in the reduction of the fort, by the means already employed, the enemy adopted the plan of attempting to do so by throwing firebrands on the roofs of the block-houses and barracks, and by discharging arrows, laden with combustibles, into the works.[4]

The moral effect of this expedient was very great, and the little garrison was thrown into a "little panic."[5] At this moment the ingenuity of the commander was taxed to the utmost, not only in devising means to prevent the destruction of the works, but in soothing the minds of his men, and in allaying their fears. He confesses "that at this moment *he* felt some little confusion," as well he might, but he immediately ordered eight old gun-barrels "*to be made into squirts*," and holes to be broken through the roofs of the buildings; when, by a skilful and constant use of his impromptu syringes, he was "able, in a few minutes, to make the roofs as wet as if there had fallen a shower of rain," and the arrangements of the enemy were again frustrated.[6]

[1] Lieut. Hamilton's Dispatch, Sept. 10; Sketches of War, p. 77.—[2] Niles' Register, iii. p. 142.—[3] Lieut. Hamilton's Dispatch, Sept. 10.—[4] Niles' Register, iii. p. 142; Sketches of the War, pp. 77, 78.—[5] Lieut. Hamilton's Dispatch, Sept. 10.—[6] Ibid.; Sketches of the War, p. 78; Niles' Register, iii, pp. 142, 143.

About sunset the house and buildings of Mr. McNabb, a neighboring settler, were set on fire, and the vigilant commander immediately understood that it was the intention of the enemy to destroy all the neighboring buildings in the same manner. A large store-house stood very near to the exterior line of the fort, and Lieutenant Hamilton feared that the enemy only waited a change of the wind—when the destruction of that building would jeopardize those within the fort—in their determined destruction of that also. As the wind had then fallen, and the building could *then* be burned, without any hazard, the Lieutenant determined to anticipate their movements by destroying it himself. For this purpose, after dark, he dispatched a man, with port-fire and other materials, and the building was burned to the ground without injuring the fort.[1]

During the same night (*Sept. 7th*) the enemy took possession of an old stable, near the works, and "fortified it;" and at nine o'clock in the morning of the eighth, he renewed his attack on the fort, by means of his small arms, arrows, burning brands, and prepared arrows.[2] Two cannon-shot, directed by Lieutenant Vasques, compelled the enemy to abandon the stable, with great precipitation;[3] while the gun-barrel syringes preserved the buildings from injury from the combustibles which were thrown by him.[4] The conflict

[1] Lieut. Hamilton's Dispatch, Sept. 10; Sketches of the War, p. 78.

[2] Lieut. Hamilton's Dispatch, Sept. 10; Niles' Register, iii. p. 143.

[3] Lieut. Hamilton's Dispatch, Sept. 10.

[4] Sketches of the War, p. 78.

was kept up with the greatest resolution until ten o'clock on the same night; when, probably, discouraged with the poor success which attended his efforts, the enemy disappeared.[1]

The loss of the enemy is not known; the only loss which the garrison sustained, beside the death of Cox, was the slight wound, in the nose, of one of the men.[1]

CHAPTER XXVI.

September 21, 1812.

THE EXPEDITION TO GANANOQUI.

IN all wars between adjoining countries, the most active of the combatants have ever been those who live on the borders; and the inhabitants of the Canadas and those on the border counties within the United States, during the last war with Great Britain, were not an exception to the general rule.

In the middle of September, 1812, Captain Benjamin Forsyth, of the New York Rifles, having learned that the King's store-house at Gananoqui, in Canada, was comparatively unprotected, he resolved to attack it. For this purpose he organized a party of one hundred and four men[2]—seventy of them being riflemen and thirty-four militia—and, on the evening of the twentieth of September, he embarked at Cape Vincent, in Jefferson County, New York, for that purpose.

Gananoqui then, as now, was a small, but flourishing village, in the town of Leeds, in Canada; and is situated on the northern bank of the St. Lawrence, at the mouth of the Gananoqui River, on the "Lake of the Thousand Isles."[2]

At an early hour in the morning of the twenty-first, the expedition landed at a short distance from the village, without opposition; although it was seen and fired on, shortly afterwards, by a party of regulars and about fifty Canadian militia, about a hundred and twenty-five in number.[3] After a short engagement the enemy fled in confusion, and were pursued by Captain Forsyth, until the former reached the village, where he rallied and renewed the engagement. After continuing it a short time, the enemy again fled,[4] leaving ten of his party dead on the field, besides the wounded; and eight regulars and several militia, prisoners, in the hands of the victors.[5]

After paroling the militia who had

[1] Lieut. Hamilton's Dispatch, Sept. 10. The author of the *Sketches* (p. 78) and the informant of Mr. Niles (iii. p. 143) suppose the enemy remained there, or in the vicinity, some days longer.—[2] Mr. Christie (*Military Operations in Canada*, p. 80) says it numbered *one hundred and fifty* men.

[1] Lieut. Hamilton's dispatch, Sept. 10.—[2] Smith's Canada, ii. p. 296.—[3] Mr. Christie (*Military Operations*, p. 80) says the militia were fifty in number, but makes no allusion to the regulars. As several regulars were among the prisoners, however, it is evident there were regulars in the party. Gen. Brown (*Dispatch to Gov. Tompkins*) says *one hundred and ten*.

[4] Christie's Military Operations in Canada, p. 80.

[5] Mr. Christie (*Military Operations*, p. 80) says "four men found in the hospital, and *a dragoon*, were made prisoners and carried away."

fallen into his hands, and setting fire to the store-house, which, with a quantity of flour and pork, was wholly consumed, Captain Forsyth and his party returned to New York, with his eight prisoners, sixty stand of arms, two barrels of fixed ammunition, a barrel of gunpowder, and one of gun-flints, and "some other articles of public property," as trophies of his prowess, only one man of his party having been killed, and one slightly wounded.

[Note.—This narrative has been taken from an account of the expedition which was printed in *Niles' Register*, iii. p. 93; in *Sketches of the War* (Rutland, Vt., 1815), p. 79; and in "*The War*" (N. Y., 1813), i. p. 71. Any other authority than this which has been employed, will be found referred to in the foot-notes.]

CHAPTER XXVII.

September 27, 1812.[1]

THE "NONSUCH, OF BALTIMORE."

Among the most active and successful of the private vessels of war, which were sent out during the last war with Great Britain, were the celebrated "Baltimore clippers."

One of these—the *Nonsuch*, commanded by Captain Levely, mounting twelve twelve-pound carronades, and manned with between eighty and ninety men[2]—was cruising near Martinique, on the twenty-seventh of September, 1812, when she fell in with a ship and schooner, showing British colors. The ship immediately opened a fire on the *Nonsuch*, when the latter bore down, showed her colors, and returned the fire.

The schooner immediately joined her consort, and during three hours and twenty minutes the *Nonsuch* sustained a close and determined action with both vessels—each of the three employing every means within her power to cripple her opponent—when the contestants separated without either of them striking her colors.

The details of the engagement have not been recorded; but the desperation with which it was conducted will be seen in the relative strength of the parties and in their respective losses.

The *Nonsuch*, after sustaining the action over three hours and a quarter, was unable to continue it, except with her small-arms, the bolts and breachings of every gun having been carried away. Her rigging, also, had suffered severely; her hull was considerably damaged; she leaked badly; and one officer and three of her crew had been *killed*, and one officer and six men *wounded*.

The ship—which mounted sixteen eighteen or twenty-four pound carronades, and carried two hundred men, in-

[1] Mr. Niles (*Register*, iii. p. 172) says it occurred on the *twenty-eighth*, and Capt. Coggeshall (*Hist. of Privateers*, p. 87) concurs with him. As the log-book of the *Nonsuch*, under date of "*Sept.* 27," gives the details of the engagement, I have followed it, in preference to what, otherwise, would be satisfactory authority.

[2] Niles' Register, iii. p. 172.

cluding soldiers—had received considerable damage, both in her hull and rigging, and lost twenty-three of her crew, killed and wounded.[1]

The schooner—which mounted six four-pounders, and carried sixty men—was also seriously damaged, but the details have not been given.

When the aggregate strength of the opposing vessels is considered, it will be seen that this engagement was exceedingly well conducted; and that the crew of the little clipper, as the captain expresses it on his log-book, "all fought like true Americans."

[NOTE.—Except where other authorities have been referred to, the Log-book of the *Nonsuch*, as quoted in "*The War*," i. 92, and in *Niles' Register*, iii. p. 172, have been my only authority.]

CHAPTER XXVIII.

October 4, 1812.

THE REPULSE AT OGDENSBURG, N. Y.

THE feeling which had been displayed by the inhabitants of the frontiers, both of Canada and the United States, has been alluded to in a preceding chapter; and an instance of the warlike spirit which prevailed has been given in that place.[2]

In retaliation of that expedition, it is probable, a counter-expedition was organized in Canada, without the concurrence of the commander of the district,[3] and Ogdensburg was the point against which it was determined to move. Accordingly, on Friday, the second of October, 1812, about forty boats were moved up the St. Lawrence; and, about sunset of that day, they reached Johnstown, under the escort of two gunboats.[4] Immediately afterwards a heavy fire was opened on the village of Ogdensburg, by the British batteries at Prescott, on the opposite side of the river;[1] under cover of which the flotilla moved up to Prescott, and reached that place in safety. The fire was harmless, and was promptly returned by the American batteries, under General Jacob Brown, of the New York militia.[2]

On the following morning (*Saturday, Oct. 3d*) the fire was renewed from the Canada shore, but as General Brown would not answer it, it was discontinued half an hour afterwards. The remainder of the day was spent, by the enemy, in preparing his boats for something more serious.[3]

At about ten o'clock on Sunday morning, the fourth of October, twenty-five boats, under convoy of two gunboats, mounting nine-pounders, moved up the St. Lawrence, from Prescott, about three-quarters of a mile, when

[1] Niles' Register, iii. p. 172.—[2] Vide Chap. XXVI.

[3] Christie's Military Operations, &c., p. 81.

[4] The Palladium, Ogdensburg, Tuesday Oct. 6, 1812; Hough's St. Lawrence County, p. 625.

[1] The Palladium, Ogdensburg, Tuesday, Oct. 6, 1812; Hough's St. Lawrence Co., p. 625; The War, i. p. 75; Niles' Register, iii. p. 126.—[2] The Palladium, Oct. 6; Hough's St. Lawrence Co., p. 625.—[3] Ibid.

they tacked and stood in for Ogdensburg.[1] They carried "a force of seven hundred and fifty men, regulars and militia,"[2] under Colonel Lethbridge, and, as soon as they tacked, the batteries at Prescott opened a heavy fire on the village, which was intended to cover the debarkation, and to facilitate the attack.[3]

When the flotilla had reached the middle of the river, until which time it had been silent, the battery at Ogdensburg opened its fire.[4] This battery was composed of a brass six-pounder under Adjutant Church, and an iron twelve-pounder, under a citizen named Joseph York; and the pieces were stationed "near the stone warehouse."[5] The company of riflemen, under Captain Benjamin Forsyth, who had commanded at Gananoqui,[6] had assembled with the militia;[7] and, under the command of General Jacob Brown, a heavy fire from their small-arms, also, was thrown upon the enemy as he approached the shore.[8] The fire was returned by the latter, both from his artillery and his small-arms; and, for about an hour, both parties contended for the victory.[1]

At that time, it is said,[2] two of the enemy's boats were so much injured that he was compelled to abandon them, and one, with its crew, was captured by the Americans; when he considered it expedient to withdraw from the contest and return to Prescott.

It is said, also, that "not a drop of blood was lost on the side of the Americans, but some little damage was done to property and buildings by the shot of the enemy."[3] Of the enemy, three were killed and four were wounded.[4]

It may appear remarkable to the reader, as it does to me, that so little damage was done, and with so little loss of life, while the conflict was so protracted. It can only be accounted for, from the fact that the troops on both sides were wholly inexperienced, and the practice with artillery was beyond the range of their abilities. In that case, at a quarter of a mile distant,—the range in this instance,—the contestants were comparatively safe; and the execution formed the exception rather than the rule.

---

[1] Christie, p. 81; The Palladium, Oct. 6; Hough's St. Lawrence Co., p. 625.—[2] Christie, p. 81.—[3] The Palladium, Oct. 6; Hough's St. Lawrence Co., p. 625.

[4] Christie, p. 81; The Palladium, Oct. 6; Hough's St. Lawrence Co., p. 625.—[5] Hough's St. Lawrence Co., p. 625.—[6] Vide Chap. XXVI.—[7] Hough's St. Lawrence Co., p. 625.—[8] Ibid.

[1] The Palladium, Oct. 6, 1812. Mr. Niles (*Register*, iii. p. 126) says, "*about two hours.*"—[2] Niles' Register, iii. p. 126. Neither Christie, Hough, or the Palladium allude to this loss; and I doubt the statement.

[3] Hough's St. Lawrence, p. 625; Niles' Register, iii. p. 126.—[4] Christie, p. 81.

CHAPTER XXIX.

October 9, 1812.

THE CAPTURE OF THE DETROIT AND CALEDONIA.

WITH the capture of Detroit, the United States brig of war *Adams* passed into the hands of the enemy; and the naval force of the Federal government, on Lake Erie, ceased to exist. The ascendency of the enemy's naval power, on all the upper lakes, gave him a great advantage in all those portions of the country which bordered on these waters; and the government of the United States took immediate measures to remedy the evil. For this purpose Lieutenant Jesse D. Elliott was sent to superintend the naval affairs in that quarter, with directions to purchase, or to provide material for building, a squadron, as circumstances might warrant.[1]

While thus employed, two British vessels dropped down the lake, and, on the morning of the eighth of October, cast their anchors off Fort Erie.[2] On the same day intelligence reached Lieutenant Elliott that a detachment of seamen was within a short march of the frontier; and they arrived at Buffalo on the same day.[3] As the seamen were almost entirely without arms, Lieutenant Elliott applied to General Smythe, the officer in command of the troops in that vicinity, for the necessary means; and that officer promptly complied, not only by issuing the necessary arms and ammunition, but also, by permitting fifty soldiers, under Captain Towson, to join the expedition as volunteers.[1]

By four o'clock in the afternoon all the necessary preparations had been made, and his party, embracing one hundred men,—sailors and soldiers,—had been stationed in two large boats, which had been provided for the purpose. At one o'clock in the morning of the ninth, accompanied by a boat-load or two of citizens, the expedition left the Buffalo Creek; and dropping down the river, in great silence, within two hours it was alongside the vessels without having been discovered.[2] Springing over the bulwarks of the strangers, the assailants overcame their crews, almost without a struggle; and in less than ten minutes the prisoners were all secured, the topsails all sheet-

---

[1] Cooper's Naval Hist., ii. p. 151.—[2] Lieut. Elliott's Dispatch, Oct. 9; Sir I. Brock to Sir G. Prevost, Oct. 11; Breckenridge's Hist., p. 70.—[3] Lieut. Elliott's Dispatch, Oct 9; Breckenridge, p. 71. Mr. Cooper (*Naval Hist.*, i. p. 152) says it was the *seventh* when they arrived.

[1] Lieut. Elliott's Dispatch, Oct. 9. Mr. Cooper (*Naval Hist.*, ii. p. 152) errs when he supposes Gen. Smythe was the commander, and had furnished this assistance on his own authority. Lieut. Elliott had applied to Gen. Van Rensselaer (*Letter to Gen. Hall, Sept.* 25), and *the latter had directed* the assistance to be afforded.

[2] Lieut. Elliott's Dispatch, Oct. 9; Brock's Life of Brock, p. 323; Sir I. Brock to Sir G. Prevost, Oct. 11; Breckenridge, p. 71; Maj. Richardson's Narrative, cited in *Auchinleck's History*, p. 92.

ed home, and the vessels under weigh.[1] The wind being too light to carry the vessels up the river, against the current, they were run down the stream, past the forts, and were exposed to a very heavy fire of round, grape, and canister, the larger of the two anchoring at a distance of about four hundred yards from the enemy's batteries; and the smaller running ashore near the American works at Black Rock.[2]

The enemy's fire continuing, the guns of the larger of the two vessels were all removed to one side, and the fire was returned "as long as the ammunition which was on board lasted, and circumstances permitted."[3] During all this time the most untiring efforts were made to tow the vessel to the American shore, beyond the reach of the enemy's guns, but the want of lines of sufficient length, and the strength of the current, prevented the accomplishment of this purpose.[4]

Finding that the enemy's fire was so heavy that the safety of the vessel was seriously endangered, Lieutenant Elliott determined to cut her cable and drift down the stream beyond the reach of the enemy's guns; but, at this moment, the discovery was made that the pilot had abandoned the brig, and, after drifting about ten minutes, she ran ashore on Squaw Island, near the American shore. The prisoners were immediately sent ashore; but the strength of the current

[1] Lieut. Elliott's Dispatch, Oct 9; Breckenridge, p. 71; Clark's Naval Hist., p. 160.—[2] Lieut. Elliott's Dispatch, Oct. 9; Brock's Life of Brock, p. 323; Sir I. Brock to Sir G. Prevost, Oct. 11; Breckenridge, p. 71.

[3] Lieut. Elliott's Dispatch, Oct. 9.—[4] Ibid.; Cooper, ii. p. 153; Clark's Naval History, p. 160.

prevented the return of the boats, with which it had been designed to remove some of the movable property from the vessel, and that project was abandoned.[1]

The vessel was immediately placed under the protection of Lieutenant-colonel Winfield Scott;[2] and, about the same time, she was boarded by a party of the Forty-ninth regiment, from Fort Erie.[3] A fire was immediately opened on the brig from the American shore; and, in their turn, her last possessors were driven from the vessel, with considerable loss.[4]

During the remainder of the day the troops on both sides of the river appeared to be determined to destroy the brig; and a very heavy fire was directed on her, rendering it impossible to remove her.[5] At an early hour in the evening General Sir Isaac Brock reached the spot, and made arrangements for a renewal of the attempt to recover the the vessel; but, before the preparations to do so had been completed, she was boarded by a party of the Fifth United States infantry, and in a few minutes was in flames.[6]

The larger of these two vessels was the *Detroit*, brig of war—the same which, under the name of *Adams*, had been taken from the Americans at Detroit.[7] She was commanded by Lieu-

[1] Sir I. Brock to Sir G. Prevost, Oct. 11; Lieut. Elliott's Dispatch, Oct. 9; Cooper, ii. p. 153.

[2] Lieut. Elliott's Dispatch, Oct. 9; Cooper, ii. p. 153.

[3] Sir I. Brock to Sir Geo. Prevost, Oct. 11, 1812.

[4] Sir I. Brock to Sir Geo. Prevost, Oct. 11; Cooper, ii. p. 153.—[5] Lieut. Elliott's Dispatch, Oct. 9; Cooper, ii. p. 153.—[6] Sir I. Brock to Sir G. Prevost, Oct. 11; Breckenridge, p. 71; Cooper, ii. p. 153; Clark's Hist., p. 161.

[7] Lieut. Elliott's Dispatch, Oct. 9; Brock's Life of Brock, p. 323; Cooper, ii. p. 151.

tenant Rolette,[1] mounted six six-pounders, and mustered fifty-six men; besides whom thirty American prisoners were on board.[2] The party who attacked her lost one man killed, and Midshipman Cummings was wounded.[3]

The smaller of the two was the Northwest Company's brig *Caledonia*[4]—that which performed a part in the capture of Michilimacinac.[5] She was commanded by Mr. Irvine,[6] mounted two small guns, and mustered twelve men, beside

¹ Sir I. Brock to Sir G. Prevost, Oct. 11.—² Lieut. Elliott's Dispatch, Oct. 9; Brock's Life of Brock, p. 323.

³ Lieut. Elliott's Dispatch, Oct. 9. Mr. Cooper supposes others were wounded on the *Detroit*.—⁴ Lieut. Elliott's Dispatch, Oct. 9; Brock's Life of Brock, p. 323.

⁵ Vide Chap. XV.—⁶ Maj. Richardson, cited in Auchinleck's History of War, p. 92.

whom ten prisoners were on board.[1] The party who had moved against her lost one man killed, and four others were mortally wounded.[2] On this vessel was a valuable cargo of furs and peltry[3]—probably a portion of that which had been received on board of this vessel at Michilimacinac.[4]

The conduct of Lieutenant Elliott was applauded throughout the country; and Congress voted him its thanks and a sword of honor.[5]

¹ Lieut. Elliott's Dispatch, Oct. 9; Brock's Life of Brock, p. 323.—² Lieut. Elliott's Dispatch, Oct. 9; Cooper, ii. p. 153.—³ Lieut. Elliott's Dispatch, Oct. 9; Perkins' Hist. of War, p. 105.—⁴ Vide Chap. XV.

⁵ Journal of Congress.

DOCUMENT.

LETTER FROM CAPTAIN ELLIOTT TO THE SECRETARY OF THE NAVY.

BLACK ROCK, *Oct.* 8.

SIR:—I have the honor to inform you, that on the morning of the 8th instant two British vessels, which I was informed were His Britannic Majesty's brigs *Detroit*, late the United States' brig *Adams*, and the brig *Hunter*, mounting fourteen guns, but which afterwards proved to be the brig *Caledonia*, both said to be well armed and manned, came down the lake and anchored under the protection of Fort Erie. Having been on the lines for some time, and in a measure inactively employed, I determined to make an attack, and if possible get possession of them. A strong inducement to this attempt arose from a conviction that with these two vessels, added to those which I have purchased and am fitting out, I should be able to meet the remainder of the British force on the upper lakes, and save an incalculable expense and labor to the government. On the morning of their arrival I heard that our seamen were but a short distance from this place, and immediately dispatched an express to the officers, directing them to use all possible dispatch in getting their men to this place, as I had important service to perform. On their arrival, which was about twelve o'clock, I discovered that they had only twenty pistols, and neither cutlasses or battle-axes. But on application to Generals Smith and Hall of the regulars and militia, I was supplied with a few arms, and General Smith was so good, on my request, as immediately to detach fifty men from the regulars armed with muskets.

By four o'clock in the afternoon I had my men selected and stationed in two boats, which I had previously prepared for the purpose. With these boats, fifty men in each, and under circumstances very disadvantageous, my men having scarcely had time to refresh themselves after a fatiguing march of five hundred miles, I put off from the mouth of Buffalo Creek, at one o'clock the following morning, and at three I was alongside the vessels. In the space of about ten minutes I had the prisoners all secured, the topsails sheeted home, and the vessels under way. Unfortunately the wind was not sufficiently strong to get up a rapid current into the lake, where I had understood another armed vessel lay at anchor, and I was obliged to run down the river by the forts, under a heavy fire of round, grape, and canister, from a number of pieces of heavy ordnance and several pieces of flying-artillery, was compelled to anchor at a distance of about four hundred yards from two of their batteries. After the discharge of the first gun, which was from the flying-artillery, I hailed the shore, and observed to the officer, that if another gun was fired I would bring the prisoners on deck and expose them to the same fate we should all share; but, notwithstanding, they disregarded the caution, and continued a constant and destructive fire. One single moment's reflection determined me not to commit an act that would subject me to the imputation of barbarity. The *Caledonia* had been beached in as safe a position as the circumstances would admit of, under one of our batteries at Black Rock. I now brought all the guns of the *Detroit* on one side, next the enemy, stationed the men at them, and directed a fire, which was continued as long as our ammunition lasted and circumstances permitted. During the contest I endeavored to get the *Detroit* on our side by sounding a line, there being no wind on shore, with all the line I could muster; but the current being so strong, the boat could not reach the shore. I then hailed our shore, and requested that warps would be made fast on land, and sent on board; the attempt to all which again proved useless. As the fire was such as would, in all probability, sink the vessel in a short time, I determined to drift down the river out of reach of the batteries, and make a stand against the flying-artillery. I accordingly cut the cable, made sail with very light airs, and at that instant discovered that the pilot had abandoned me. I dropped astern for about ten minutes, when I was brought up on our shore on Squaw Island; got the boarding-boat ready, had the prisoners put in and sent on shore, with directions for the officer to return for me and what property we could get from the brig. He did not return, owing to the difficulty in the boat's getting on shore. Discovering a skiff under the counter, I put the four remaining prisoners in a boat, and with my officers I went on shore to bring the boat off. I asked for protection to the brig of Lieutenant-colonel Scott, who readily gave it. At this moment I discovered a boat, with about forty soldiers from the British side, making for the brig. They got on board, but were soon compelled to abandon her, with the loss of nearly all their men. During the whole of this morning both sides of the river kept up alternately a continual fire on the brig, and so much injured her that it was impossible to have floated her. Before I left her she had several heavy shot of large size in her bends, her sails in ribbons, and rigging all cut to pieces.

To my officers and men I feel under great obligation. To Captain Towson and Lieutenant Roach, of the Second regiment of artillery, Ensign Prestman, of the infantry, Captain Chapin, Mr. John McComb, Messrs. John Town, Thomas Dain, Peter Overstocks, and James Sloan, resident gentlemen of Buffalo, for their soldier and sailor like conduct. In a word, sir, every man fought as if with their hearts animated only by the interest and honor of their country.

The prisoners I have turned over to the military. The *Detroit* mounted six six-pound long guns, commanding lieutenant marines, a boatswain and gunner, and fifty-six men; about thirty American prisoners on board, muskets, pistols, cutlasses, and battle-axes. In boarding her I lost one man, one officer wounded, Mr. John C. Cummings, acting midshipman, a bayonet through the leg: his conduct was correct, and deserves the notice of the department. The *Caledonia* mounted two small guns, blunderbusses, pistols, muskets, cutlasses, and boarding-pikes; twelve men, including officers, ten prisoners on board. The boat boarding her, commanded by Sailing-master George Watts, performed his duty in a masterly style. But one man killed, and four wounded badly, I am afraid mortally. I inclose you a list of the officers and men engaged in the enterprise, and also a view of the lake and river in the different situations of attack. In a day or two I shall forward the names of the prisoners. The *Caledonia* belongs to the Northwest Company, loaded with furs, worth, I understand, $200,000.

With sentiments of respect, I have the honor to be, &c., Jesse D. Elliot.

Hon. Paul Hamilton, Secretary of Navy.

CHAPTER XXX.

October 13, 1812.

THE BATTLE OF QUEENSTOWN.

THE campaign in the Northwest had been productive of nothing but disaster,—the invasion of, and the inglorious retreat from, Canada;[1] the loss of Michilimacinac,[2] the defeat of Major Van Horn,[3] the massacre at Chicago,[4] and the surrender of the entire army of the Northwest, at Detroit,[5] following each other in rapid succession,—and on the Northern and Western frontiers of New York had been thrown the entire strength of a victorious and haughty enemy.[6]

In the mean time, for the purpose of reducing "the pressure made upon General Hull, and to reinstate the ascendency he had lost on the Detroit,"[7] General Dearborn, to whom the command of "the army of the North" had been assigned, was ordered to threaten the enemy's posts on the Niagara frontier;[8] and he was directed, also, to hold himself in readiness to move against Kingston and Montreal, for the same purpose, should such a movement be considered necessary.[9] In the discharge of this duty, and by direction of the President, General Dearborn had made a requisition on Governor Tompkins, of New York, for a strong body of militia;[1] and these, too, had, by orders from the Secretary of War,[2] been concentrated in the immediate vicinity of Lewiston, on the Niagara River.[3] The command of this body of troops had been assigned, by the Governor, to General Stephen Van Rensselaer, of Albany,[4] the senior Major-general in New York, a gentleman whose purity of character had added lustre to a name already eminent in the annals of New York; and he had, diligently, employed all his energies in organizing his feeble and scattered forces, and in collecting the supplies which the general government had neglected to furnish for their use.[5] By the provisions of an armistice which General Dearborn had, fortunately, entered into with Sir George Prevost,[6] General Van Rensselaer was enabled

---

[1] McAfee's Hist. of War in Western Country, pp. 60–77.

[2] Capt. Roberts to Adj.-Gen., July 17, 1812; Lieut. Hanks to Gen. Hull, Aug. 14, 1812.—[3] McAfee, pp. 73–75.

[4] Dispatch of Capt. Heald, "Pittsburg, Oct. 23, 1812;" Annals of the West (*Second Ed.*), pp. 601–615; James' Military Occur., i. p. 67.—[5] Gen. Brock to Sir Geo. Prevost, Aug. 17; Gen. Hull to Sec. of War, Aug. 26, 1812.

[6] Wilkinson's Mem., i. p. 564.—[7] Armstrong's Notes, i. p. 97.—[8] Sec. of War to Gen. Dearborn, June 26, July 15, 20, 29, Aug. 1, 1812.—[9] Sec. of War to Gen. Dearborn, June 26 and Aug. 1, 1812.

[1] Van Rensselaer's Affair at Queenstown, p. 9; "The Battle of Queenstown," by Hon. Francis Baylies, in "*The Albany Argus*," Albany, Feb. 11, 1846.

[2] Sec. of War to Gen. Dearborn, July 29.

[3] Wilkinson's Mem., i. p. 566.—[4] Van Rensselaer's Queenstown, p. 9; Perkins' History of War, p. 104; Sketches of the War, p. 57.

[5] Van Rensselaer's Queenstown, pp. 9–13; Gen. Wilkinson's Memoirs, i. p. 566; Gen. Van Rensselaer to Gen. Dearborn, Oct. 8, 1812.

[6] Brock's Life and Correspondence of Sir Isaac Brock, pp. 293, 294; Van Rensselaer's Queenstown, p. 11.

to accomplish the latter,[1] although the troops which had been ordered to the frontier came in very slowly.[2]

Through the inefficiency of the Federal authorities,[3] and the weakness of the force already on the frontier, but little had been done; and the people and the army, alike, began to manifest considerable uneasiness on the subject.[4] In deference to the popular "clamor for active operations," General Van Rensselaer "resolved to gratify his own inclinations and those of the army, by commencing offensive operations;"[5] and he immediately prepared his plans, and, ineffectually, attempted to submit them for the consideration of his subordinates, in a council which he called for that purpose.[6] Through an oversight of the general, in his order, the proposed council was not assembled;[7] and General Van Rensselaer was constrained to issue his orders for the invasion of Canada, without having received any advice on the subject, from those who were associated with him in the command of the troops.[8] He had resolved to attack the village and heights of Queenstown, on the western bank of

[1] Col. Fenwick reached Four-mile Creek, with the cannon and stores, on the fourth of September.

[2] Van Rensselaer's Queenstown, pp. 10–18; Gen. Wilkinson's Mem., i. p. 567; Gen. Van Rensselaer to Gen. Dearborn, Oct. 8.—[3] Gov. Tompkins to Gen. Van Rensselaer, Sept. 9, 1812.—[4] Armstrong's Notices, i. p. 100; Thomson's Sketches of War, p. 68; Perkin's Hist. of War, p. 105.—[5] Van Rensselaer's Queenstown, pp. 18–20; Gen. Van Rensselaer to Gen. Dearborn, Oct. 14; Wilkinson's Mem., i. p. 572.—[6] Van Rensselaer's Queenstown, pp. 18–20; Gen. Van Rensselaer to Gen. Dearborn, Oct. 8, 1812.—[7] Gen. Van Rensselaer to Gen. Dearborn, Oct. 14, 1812; Wilkinson's Mem., i. pp. 566, 567; Van Rensselaer's Queenstown, p. 19.

[8] Gen. Van Rensselaer to Gen. Smyth, Sept. 30, 1812; Van Rensselaer's Queenstown, p. 20.

the Niagara[1]—a post which, at that time, more than at the present, possessed a great degree of importance, from the fact that it was the eastern terminus of the portage between Lake Ontario and the upper lakes;[2] and the occupation of that point would cut off the entire line of communication between the enemy's upper and lower posts.[3] He also desired to occupy the excellent barracks in that vicinity, as winter-quarters for his army, not only for the comfort of his troops, *per se*, but that he might be enabled to commence his operations at an early day in the ensuing spring.[4]

At the period in question General Smyth occupied a position at Black Rock, with sixteen hundred and fifty regulars; while distributed between the same post and Buffalo, were three hundred and eighty-six militia, under Lieutenant-colonels Swift and Hopkins. At the same time twenty-two hundred and seventy militia, under Generals Miller and Wadsworth, had been assembled in the immediate vicinity of headquarters at Lewiston; while a body of regulars, about five hundred and fifty in number, commanded by Lieutenant-colonel Fenwick, and about eight hundred regular troops, under Major Mullany, were in garrison at Fort Niagara.[5] On the other hand the strength of the

[1] Gen. Van Rensselaer to Gen. Dearborn, Oct. 8; Armstrong's Notices, i. p. 100; Sketches of the War, p. 62.

[2] Niles' Register, iii. p. 141.—[3] Gen. Van Rensselaer to Gen. Dearborn, Oct. 8.—[4] Ibid.

[5] Wilkinson's Mem., i. p. 580; James' Mil. Occur., i. p. 80; Auchinleck's Hist., p. 101. For other accounts of the disposition of the forces, see Thomson's Sketches, p. 68; Perkin's Hist. of War, p. 104; and other authors on the subject.

enemy, scattered along the same extent of the frontier as the American force, was about fifteen hundred men;[1] of which a small detachment of the Forty-first regiment, under Captain Bullock, and the flank companies of the Second regiment of Lincoln militia, under Captains Hamilton and Rous, were at Chippewa;[2] the flank companies of the Forty-ninth, under Captains Dennis and Williams, two companies of voltigeurs, and a small body of militia, were at Queenstown;[3] and, with the exception of a few small parties of militia scattered along the line, the remainder, under General Sheaffe, were at Fort George;[4] but in the person and abilities of General Sir Isaac Brock, the commander of this force, the enemy enjoyed an advantage which the mere strength of undisciplined and factious numbers could never overcome.

Queenstown, the contemplated point of attack, as has been said before, occupied the eastern terminus of the great portage between Lakes Erie and Ontario.[5] It stands on the western bank of the Niagara River, at the foot of the rapids, about seven miles below the falls; and occupies a plain at the foot of the heights, through which, at a right angle with them, the Niagara River has found a passage for the great body of waters from the upper lakes.[1] On these heights, south from the village, was a battery, on which an eighteen-pounder had been mounted;[2] while at Vromont's Point—about a mile below, on the bank of the river—was another work, on which was mounted a twenty-four pound carronade.[3]

The tardiness of the troops, from whom so much had been expected, had arrested the attention of the press and the people; and the disaffection among the latter had begun to show itself in the ranks of the army itself, from which it speedily became apparent that a movement against the enemy was absolutely necessary.[4] Whether or not it was borne in mind that the commanding general had steadily opposed the war from the beginning; and that, from thence, it had been supposed that the delay was caused by him, for political or personal purposes, does not certainly appear; yet there are circumstances connected with this disaffection, with the subsequent movements, and with the resignation of the command, soon afterwards, by General Van Rensselaer, which can only be explained by such an hypothesis.

At length "the calls to be led to battle became more and more urgent and imperious, and the general found himself, at last, obliged either to dismiss the troops, or to gratify their

---

[1] Brock's Life of Sir Isaac Brock, p. 322. Mr. Auchinleck (*Hist. of War*, p. 100) and Mr. James (*Mil. Occur.*, p. 80) say the enemy "could not muster 1200 men." Mr. Perkins (*Hist. Late War*, p. 104) says it numbered 2400 men and 400 Indians; while the *Sketches of War*, p. 62, makes it 2800.—[2] Auchinleck's Hist. of War, p. 101.

[3] Wilkinson's Mem., i. pp. 571, 574; Van Rensselaer's Queenstown, p. 29; Brock's Life of Brock, p. 462, *note*.

[4] Auchinleck's Hist. of War, p. 101.—[5] Niles' Register, iii. p. 141; Thomson's Sketches, p. 69.

[1] Thomson's Sketches, p. 69; James' Military Occurrences, i. p. 84; Smith's Canada, ii. p. 197.

[2] Christie's Military and Naval Operations in the Canadas, p. 83; Brock's Life of Gen. Brock, p. 329.

[3] Brock's Life of Gen. Brock, p. 329; Map in Auchinleck's History of War, p. 98.—[4] Gen. Van Rensselaer's Dispatch, Oct. 14, 1812; Perkins' History of War, p. 105.

wishes."[1] The several posts which the enemy occupied had been carefully examined by different officers, who had visited them on official business; and the character of the defences, as well as the strength of their garrisons, had been carefully noted, and was known to the general.[2] At an early hour, on the tenth of October, thirteen large boats, capable of transporting three hundred and forty men, with their equipments, were brought, on wagons, from Gill's Creek, two miles above the falls, and launched at Lewiston;[3] and experienced boatmen were obtained, and held in readiness to take them across the river at the time appointed.[4] Lieutenant-colonel Fenwick's flying-artillery, and a detachment of the regular troops, had been ordered from Fort Niagara;[5] and General Smyth, with as large a detachment from his command as existing circumstances might warrant, had been ordered from Buffalo[6]—both of them for the purpose of supporting the expedition, and of rescuing it should it be unsuccessful. Three o'clock in the morning of the eleventh of October had been appointed as the hour when the movement should be made;[7] and Lieutenant-colonel Solomon Van Rensselaer, the commanding general's aid, had been placed in command

[1] Van Rensselaer's Queenstown, p. 20. See also Wilkinson's Mem., i. p. 572; Baylies' Battle of Queenstown; Breckenridge's War, p. 71.—[2] Van Rensselaer's Queenstown, pp. 20, 21.—[3] Ibid., p. 21; Perkins' Hist. of War, p. 106.—[4] Gen. Van Rensselaer to Gen. Dearborn, Oct. 14.

[5] Van Rensselaer's Queenstown, p. 21; Perkins' Hist. of War, p. 106; Thomson's Sketches, p. 69.

[6] Van Rensselaer's Queenstown, p. 21; Gen. Van Rensselaer to Gen. Dearborn, Oct. 14.—[7] Van Rensselaer's Queenstown, p. 21; James' Military Occurrences, i. p. 85; Perkins' History of War, p. 106.

of the proposed expedition[1]—an arrangement which, at this time, appears unaccountable, when it is remembered that some of the officers of the regular troops, who had been ordered to join the expedition, ranked Lieutenant-colonel Van Rensselaer, whose commission was only in the militia of New York, while they were in the service of the United States.[2] At the appointed hour the troops were at the rendezvous, ready for embarkation, but there were no boats to receive them; and after standing on the bank of the river, exposed to the pelting of an unusually severe northeast storm, until the next morning, the expedition was postponed.[3]

It appeared, afterwards, that Lieutenant Sims—to whom, as "the man of the greatest skill for this service," the management of the boats had been intrusted—had carried them up the river, far beyond the appointed place of rendezvous; that he had then ran his boat ashore; and that, after securing it, he had "abandoned the detachment."[4] The cotemporary historians of the affair have not recorded the motive which influenced Lieutenant Sims to adopt so remarkable a course; yet, subsequent events would appear to indicate the

[1] Gen. Van Rensselaer to Gen. Dearborn, Oct. 14; Baylies' Battle of Queenstown; Perkins' History, p. 106.

[2] "Lieut.-Col. N. Y. militia volunteers: commanded in assault on Queenstown Heights, U. C., Oct. 13, 1812."—*Gardner's Dict. of Am. Army*, p. 461. Lieut.-Col. Fenwick took rank from Dec. 2, 1811; Lieut.-Col. Chrystie, from March 12, 1812; and Lieut.-Col. Scott, from July 6, 1812.

[3] Gen. Van Rensselaer to Gen. Dearborn, Oct. 14; Thomson's Sketches, p. 70; Brock's Life Gen. Brock, p. 329; Breckenridge's History of the War, p. 70.

[4] Gen. Van Rensselaer to Gen. Dearborn, Oct. 14; O'Connor's History of War, p. 46; Thomson's Sketches, p. 69; Davis' History of War, p. 36.

fact that the selection, for the command of the expedition, of the General's aid—an officer of the *militia;* one who had steadily reprobated the war, and opposed the government; and an inferior in rank to some of the officers of the regular troops who had been ordered to take part in the movement under his command—had produced dissatisfaction among the officers and distrust in the ranks; and it is not improbable that Lieutenant Sims had found, in this novel step, an effectual means of ridding himself and his brethren of a service which was mortifying to their honor, as soldiers and officers.[1]

It appears that General Van Rensselaer, instead of taking advantage of the enthusiasm which prevailed among the troops, "had hoped that their patience would have continued until he could submit his plan" (of operations to his officers, to which allusion has been made), "that he might act under, and in conformity to, the opinion which might be then expressed."[2] But, to use his own words, "his hope was idle; the previously excited ardor seemed to have gained new heat from the late miscarriage;" and, "such was the pressure upon him, from all quarters, that he became satisfied that his refusal to act might involve him in suspicion and the service in disgrace,"[1] and preparations were made for a second attempt to storm Queenstown.[2]

Unfortunately the commanding general appears either to have misunderstood the true state of affairs, or to have resolved on braving the troubles which were destroying the efficiency of his force. His cousin, Lieutenant-colonel Solomon Van Rensselaer, was continued in the command, notwithstanding Lieutenant-colonels Scott, Fenwick, and Chrystie, who were expected to cooperate, in some degree, were his superiors in rank;[3] and notwithstanding it was known to the militia that he was opposed to the war.[4] It was even reported that Lieutenant-colonels Scott and Fenwick had declined to move under the command of Lieutenant-colonel Van Rensselaer; and that Lieutenant-colonel Chrystie—who had reached Four-mile Creek with three hundred and fifty newly-enlisted regular troops, part of the Thirteenth regiment of infantry, under Captains Wool, Ogilvie, Malcolm, Lawrence, and Armstrong—on the evening of the tenth of October, had been induced to do so, virtually, under some private arrangement for

[1] "Through the neglect or cowardice of the officer intrusted with preparing and conducting the boats to the place of embarkation, the attack miscarried" (*Christie's Mil. and Naval Operations*, p. 82)—"it was frustrated either by the ignorance, the cowardice, or the treachery of a boatman, who had been selected," &c. (*Stone's Life of Brant*, ii. p. 503)—"through some mismanagement in conducting the boats," &c. (*Brock's Life of Brock*, p. 329)—"he played his countrymen a trick and ran away" (*James' Military Occurrences*, i. p. 86).

[2] Gen. Van Rensselaer to Gen. Dearborn, Oct. 14.

[1] Gen. Van Rensselaer to Gen. Dearborn, Oct. 14; Baylies' Battle of Queenstown; Wilkinson's Mem., p. 572.

[2] Thomson's Sketches, p. 70; Baylie's Battle of Queenstown.—[3] Vide p. 146, note 2. Lieut.-Col. Van Rensselaer (*Queenstown*, p. 81) refers to this subject in such a manner as to confirm the rumor. Mr. Stone (*Life of Brant*, ii. p. 504) says Lieut.-Cols. Chrystie and Fenwick *had waived their rank;* while Lieut.-Col. Scott did not do so. The former of these officers (*Letter to Adj.-Gen., Feb.* 22, 1813) says that when conversed with on this subject, he had told Lieut.-Col. Van Rensselaer that "*it was impossible,*" although he agreed to act with him.

[4] Lieut.-Col. Solomon Van Rensselaer, although Adjutant-general of the State of New York, was known as a decided Federalist.

the distribution of the laurels which, it was hoped, the expedition would secure.[1]

The display of the boats on the bank of the river, at Lewiston, while a large body of troops were posted at a considerable distance below, was well calculated to deceive the enemy respecting the exact point of the intended attack;[2] and the active mind of Sir Isaac Brock found ample employment in preparing his several posts to receive the Americans at whatever point they might appear.[3] It appears, however, that Queenstown was not the point at which Sir Isaac expected to receive his enemy;[4] and the troops at that place were, in consequence, less numerous than would, otherwise, have been provided for its protection.

Agreeably to the arrangements, at an early hour in the evening of the twelfth of October, Lieutenant-colonel Chrystie moved, by the rear road, from the Four-mile Creek to Lewiston, with three hundred men;[5] while, about the same time, the regiments of militia, under Lieutenant-colonels Stranahan, Mead, and Bloom, moved from Niagara Falls,[6] and reached Lewiston "in good season."[7]

It was designed that Lieutenant-colonel Chrystie, with three hundred men, and Lieutenant-colonel Van Rensselaer with a similar number of militia, should first cross the river, "before day," for the purpose of carrying the battery on the heights of Queenstown; and that the remainder of the troops should "pass over together, as soon as the heights should be carried."[1] The boats had been intrusted to the management of Mr. Cook, a respectable citizen of Lewiston, who had engaged to provide proper men to manage them; while to Mr. Lovett, of Troy, had been intrusted the management of the battery on the heights of Lewiston, with instructions to cover the landing of the detachment on the Canadian shore.[2]

All the necessary preliminaries having been arranged, a little after three o'clock on the morning of the thirteenth of October,[3] a cold and stormy morning,[4] the detachments—regulars and militia—moved to the bank of the river, where they were halted until the lieutenant-colonel commanding, "with Major Lush and Lieutenant Gansevoort, who acted as his aids, descended to see the boats arranged, and formed in two divisions, one for the regulars and the other for the militia," that both might

[1] "We conversed about my waiving rank with him, *which I told him was impossible;* but . . . . I consented to take a part without interfering with his arrangements for it."—*Lieut.-Col. Chrystie to the Adj.-Gen., Feb.* 22, 1813.

[2] Van Rensselaer's Queenstown, pp. 22–33.

[3] Brock's Life of Brock, p. 330; Christie's Mil. and Naval Operations in the Canadas, p. 82.

[4] The greater part of his force was at Fort George, where he was at that time.—[5] Baylies' Battle of Queenstown; Van Rensselaer's Queenstown, p. 24; Thomson's Sketches, p. 70; Lieut.-Col. Chrystie to Adj.-Gen., Feb. 22, 1813.—[6] Van Rensselaer to Gen. Dearborn, Oct. 14.

[7] Ibid. See also Thomson's Sketches, p. 70.

[1] Wilkinson's Memoirs, i. p. 572; Van Rensselaer's Queenstown, p. 24; Armstrong's Notices, i. p. 101; James' Military Occurrences, i. p. 86.

[2] Van Rensselaer's Queenstown, p. 23.

[3] Baylies' Battle of Queenstown; Memoir of Gen. Wool, in the *Democratic Review*, Nov., 1851; Lieut.-Col. Chrystie to Adj.-Gen., Feb. 22. 1812; Lieut. Fink's MS. Jour. Gen. Wilkinson (*Memoirs*, i. p. 572) says, "the embarkation was to have taken place on the *morning of the twelfth;*" and Mr. James (*Military Occurrences*, i. p. 86) concurs with him in this error.

[4] Auchinleck's Hist. of the War, p. 104. "At 4 o'clock A. M. we arrived at the ferry in *a heavy shower of hail.*"—*Lieut. Fink's MS. Diary, Oct.* 13, 1812.

embark simultaneously.[1] The thirteen boats which had been provided were sufficient to transport but one half the force;[2] and the regular troops, pressing forward more promptly than the militia, were among the first to take their places.[3] The consequence was, that instead of one-half of each — regulars and militia — three companies of the Thirteenth regiment of infantry, commanded by Captains Wool, Malcolm, and Armstrong;[4] with forty picked men from Captain Leonard's old company of artillery, at Fort Niagara, under Lieutenants Gansevoort and Rathbone,[5] and about sixty militia,[6] took their places in the boats; and Lieutenant-colonel Van Rensselaer, finding all things in readiness, ordered the regulars to push off, after which "he leaped" into another boat and followed, with the artillery and militia[7]—Major Morrison having been ordered to follow, in the return boats, with the remainder of the detachment.[8]

The boats having been properly manned, within ten minutes from the time when they pushed off, the greater part of them struck the Canadian shore "at the identical spot aimed at;" and the regulars landed a short distance below (on the right of) the landing-place of the militia.[9] Three only, of

[1] Wilkinson's Mem., i. p. 573. See also Van Rensselaer's Queenstown, p. 25; James' Mil. Occur., i. p. 86.

[2] Wilkinson's Memoirs, i. p. 572; Baylies' Battle of Queenstown.—[3] Wilkinson's Mem., i. p. 573; Van Rensselaer's Queenstown, p. 25; James' Mil. Occur., i. p. 86.

[4] Baylies' Battle of Queenstown.—[5] Ibid.—[6] Ibid.

[7] Van Rensselaer's Queenstown, p. 25; Baylies' Battle of Queenstown.—[8] Wilkinson's Memoirs, i. p. 573.

[9] Van Rensselaer's Queenstown, p. 25; James' Military Occurrences, i. p. 87.

the thirteen boats, missed their way;[1] and the ten, having landed the troops, immediately returned to the American shore.[2]

In the mean time Captain Dennis, of the Forty-ninth regiment of the line, who commanded at Queenstown, had been apprised of the movement in the American camp;[3] and rallying sixty men from his company (the grenadiers of the Forty-ninth) and Captain Hatt's company of voltigeurs,[4] with a three-pound field-piece,[5] he moved down to resist the debarkation.[6] This was done with considerable spirit; Lieutenant Rathbone having been mortally wounded before he could effect a landing, and some other loss was sustained by the detachment.[7] As Lieutenant-colonel Chrystie *had not crossed the river*, the command of the regular troops devolved on Captain John E. Wool, the senior officer present;[8] and, under his com-

[1] Auchinleck's Hist. of the War, p. 104; Nile's Register, iii. p. 141; Brock's Life of Brock, p. 329; James' Mil. Occur., i. p. 87. These were commanded by Lieut.-Col. Chrystie, Capt. Lawrence, and a subaltern—all of the Thirteenth regiment. The first was driven back to the New York shore, after sustaining some loss; the second returned *by orders from Lieut.-Col. Chrystie;* the third was, probably, captured by the enemy.

[2] Van Rensselaer's Queenstown, p. 25.—[3] Auchinleck, p. 104; Wilkinson's Mem., i. p. 574; Capt. Ogilvie, in Niles' Register, iii. p. 141. It has been said (*Thomson's Sketches*, p. 70) that Capt. Dennis had "been *surreptitiously apprised* of the contemplated movement of the American troops."—[4] Auchinleck, p. 104; Brock's Life of Brock, p. 329; James' Mil. Occur., i. pp. 87, 88.—[5] Brock's Life of Brock, p. 329; James' Military Occurrences, i. p. 88.

[6] Auchinleck, p. 104; Brock's Life of Brock, p. 329; James' Mil. Occur., i. p. 88.—[7] Niles' Register, iii. pp. 140, 141; Christie, p. 82; Smith's Canada, ii. p. 154.

[8] Wilkinson's Memoirs, i. p. 574; Baylies' Battle of Queenstown; Mem. of Gen. Wool; James' Mil. Occur., i. p. 89; Perkins' Hist. of War, p. 106; Stone's Life of Brant, ii. p. 506; Gen. Van Rensselaer to Capt. Wool, Dec. 24; Lieut.-Col. Chrystie to Capt. Wool, Dec. 21, 1812.

mand, the three companies ascended the bank from the water, and formed on the plateau near the foot of the heights, above the village.[1] Soon afterwards Judge-advocate Lush, the commander's aid, conveyed orders to Captain Wool to "prepare for storming the heights," and was informed, in reply, that the command was *then* ready.[2] A few minutes afterwards orders were given for it to march; but before it began to ascend the heights the order was countermanded, and the three companies halted for further orders.[3]

While the Americans were thus employed, the little party under Captain Dennis had been strengthened by the arrival, on the heights, of Captain Williams, with the light-infantry of the Forty-ninth regiment, and Captain Chisholm, with his company of voltigeurs;[4] and while, with his original force, embracing two full companies and a field-piece, the enemy fell on the right flank of Captain Wool's line, a fire was opened at the same time on his front, from the brow of the heights, by Captains Williams and Chisholm.[5] Without waiting for orders from Lieutenant-colonel Van Rensselaer, Captain Wool wheeled his command to the right, fronting on that portion of the enemy's force which was on the plain;[6] and, with his small-arms against the enemy's artillery, he

[1] Brock's Life of Brock, p. 329; Baylies' Battle of Queenstown; Mem. of Gen. Wool.—[2] Baylies' Battle of Queenstown.—[3] Ibid.; Mem. of Gen. Wool; Armstrong's Notices, i. p. 102.—[4] Brock's Life of Brock, p. 330; Armstrong's Notices, i. p. 102; James' Mil. Occur., i. p. 88.

[5] Brock's Life of Brock, p. 330; Baylies' Battle of Queenstown; Memoir of Gen. Wool; James' Military Occurrences, i. p. 88.—[6] Baylies' Battle of Queenstown; Memoir of Gen. Wool.

commenced his military career by throwing a well-directed fire into the ranks of the grenadiers and voltigeurs.[1] A short, but severe engagement took place in this position;[2] and the enemy soon afterwards was compelled to retire, falling back on the village of Queenstown in his rear.[3] In this short, but decisive action, the detachment from the Thirteenth regiment, under Captain Wool, suffered very severely—of the ten officers who were present, two (Lieutenants Valleau and Morris) were killed; and four (Captains Wool, Malcolm, and Armstrong, and Lieutenant Lent) were severely wounded;[4] while the militia, under Lieutenant-colonel Van Rensselaer, who occupied the left of the line, suffered but very little.[5] The only officer on that wing who suffered was Lieutenant-colonel Van Rensselaer, who was very severely wounded, and rendered unable to continue in command of the expedition.[6]

Notwithstanding the repulse of Captains Dennis and Hatt, on the plains, the troops under Captains Williams and Chisholm, on the heights, continued to throw down a desultory fire on the left flank of Captain Wool's command;[7] and Lieutenant-colonel Van Rensselaer, "much crippled now, by a number of wounds and with the loss of blood, un-

[1] Baylies' Battle of Queenstown.—[2] Van Rensselaer's Queenstown, p. 25; Baylies' Battle of Queenstown; Mem. of Gen. Wool; James' Mil. Occur., i. p. 89.—[3] Van Rensselaer's Queenstown, p. 25; Baylies' Battle of Queenstown; Mem. of Gen. Wool.—[4] Baylies' Battle of Queenstown; Mem. of Gen. Wool.—[5] Baylies' Battle of Queenstown.—[6] Wilkinson, i. p. 574; Van Rensselaer's Queenstown, p. 26; Mem. of Gen. Wool; James' Mil. Occur., i. p. 88.—[7] Van Rensselaer's Queenstown, p. 26; Baylies' Battle of Queenstown; James' Military Occurrences, i. p. 88; Armstrong's Notices, i. p. 103.

able to proceed any farther"[1]—in the absence of Lieutenant-colonel Chrystie, who had not landed in Canada[2]—directed the detachment from the Thirteenth regiment to fall back from the position it then occupied, near the foot of the heights; to form on the beach, out of the range of the enemy's fire.[3]

Agreeably to these orders the troops fell back to the margin of the river, but they were still exposed—one man having been killed and several wounded.[4] While in this position the detachment was joined by a fourth company of the Thirteenth regiment, under Captain Ogilvie;[5] when Captain Wool—still the senior officer in the detachment—sought the commander of the expedition, who had fallen from loss of blood, and asked for orders by which his command might be relieved from its unpleasant and discouraging position.[6] He was told that the capture of the heights—*the great object for which the expedition was organized*—was the only remedy;[7] when, notwithstanding his wounds and his inexperience, and the inexperience of his troops, he promptly *volunteered* to make the attempt,[8] and he received orders to do so;[9] while Judge-advocate Lush—the commander's aid—at the same time received orders to follow the column, and to shoot every man who faltered in the discharge of his duty.[1]

Returning to his command, on the bank of the river, Captain Wool ordered the fresh troops, under Captain Ogilvie, to take the right of the column;[2] and, immediately afterwards, he moved to execute his perilous but important undertaking.[3] Sheltering his column under a precipice, which also concealed the movement from the enemy's troops

---

Van Rensselaer's Queenstown, p. 26. See also Baylies' Battle of Queenstown.—[2] Baylies' Battle of Queenstown; Mem. of Gen. Wool; O'Connor's Hist. of War, p. 48; Van Rensselaer's Queenstown, pp. 25, 26.—[3] Van Rensselaer's Queenstown, p. 26; Brock's Life of Brock, p. 329; Baylie's Battle of Queenstown; James' Mil. Ocur., i. p. 88.

[4] Baylies' Battle of Queenstown.—[5] Ibid.—[6] Letter in *National Intelligencer*, Washington, Nov. 7, 1812; Baylies' Battle of Queenstown.—[7] Ibid.—[8] Baylies' Battle of Queenstown; Memoir of Gen. Wool.—[9] Wilkinson's Memoirs i. p. 574; Baylies' Battle of Queenstown.

[1] Wilkinson's Memoirs, i. p. 574; Van Rensselaer's Queenstown, p. 26; Baylies' Battle of Queenstown.

[2] Baylies' Battle of Queenstown. Many writers, from the fact that Capt. Ogilvie led the column, have supposed that he was in command of the troops which captured the battery. Mr. Davis (*Hist. of Late War*, pp. 37, 38), Mr. Breckenridge (*Hist. of War*, p. 72), Mr. Thomson (*Sketches of the War*, p .72), and Mr. O'Connor (*Hist. of War*, p. 48), have fallen into this error; but, on the other hand, Gen. Wilkinson (*Mem.*, i. p. 574) says Lieut.-Col. Van Rensselaer "ordered *Capt. Wool, the senior officer capable of doing duty*, to ascend the mountain and carry the battery." Mr. Stone (*Life of Brant*, i. p. 506) uses the same words, adding, "this enterprise was gallantly executed *by Capt. Wool.*" Mr. Perkins (*Hist. of War*, p. 106) says, "The men were rallied, and one hundred and sixty, *under the command of Capt. Wool*, mounted the rocks on the right of the batteries, and took them." The author of "*Sketches of the War*" (Rutland, Vt., 1815) uses the same words, adding to Capt. Wool's name, *and following it*, the names of six other officers. Mr. Mansfield (*Life of Scott*, p. 39), speaking of Lieut.-Col. Van Rensselaer's order to storm the heights, says, "This order was promptly obeyed *by Capt.* (now General) *Wool.*" Mr. Brock (*Life and Corres. of Sir Isaac Brock*, London, 1847) says, "a strong detachment of American regulars, *under Capt. Wool*, had succeeded in gaining the crest of the heights," &c. Mr. James (*Mil. Occur.*, London, 1818, i. p. 89) says, "Sixty American regulars, *led by Capt. Wool*, and accompanied by Maj. Lush, a volunteer, &c., ascended a fisherman's path." Gen. Van Rensselaer (*Letter to Capt. Wool*, Dec. 24, 1812) says, "The manner in which *you* met and repulsed the troops under Gen. Brock, when he fell, *with the troops under your command*, merits the notice of Government," &c.; while Lieut.-Col. Chrystie. in a letter to Capt. Wool (*New York, Dec.* 21, 1812), gives the entire honor of the day to that officer. For these reasons I have not hesitated to assign to Capt. Wool the command of the forces which stormed, carried, and occupied the Heights of Queenstown, on the thirteenth of October, 1812.

[3] Capt. Wool to Col. Van Rensselaer, Oct. 23; Baylies' Battle of Queenstown; James' Mil. Occur., i. p. 89.

on the heights,[1] under the guidance of Lieutenants Gansevoort and Randolph,[2] the young Captain commenced his silent ascent of the heights. In many places the pathway was so steep that the soldiers were compelled to support themselves by their muskets, or to pull themselves up by the bushes which were growing there;[3] but the example of their commander, the severity of whose wounds—a ball having passed through both his thighs—had not kept him back, cheered them onward and silenced every rising discontent, until, when near the summit of the heights, he struck a fisherman's path[4]—which was seldom used and but little known,[5] and which, in consequence of a report that it was impassable, had been left unguarded.[6]

In the mean time General Sir Isaac Brock, then at Fort George, had heard the cannonade, awoke Major Glegg, and called for his horse *Alfred*.[7] As has been stated before,[8] he was not satisfied, in his own mind, where or when the attack would be made; and he had taken every conceivable precaution which his great genius considered necessary to check the progress of the invaders, wherever or whenever they might cross the river.[9] He considered, however, that the alarm at Queenstown was but a feint to draw the garrison

[1] Gen. Wool to the Author, Nov. 11, 1859.

[2] Wilkinson's Memoirs, i. p. 574; Van Rensselaer's Queenstown, p. 26.—[3] Baylies' Battle of Queenstown.

[4] Brock's Life of Brock, p. 330; James' Mil. Occur., i. p. 89.—[5] Gen. Wool to the Author, Nov. 11, 1859.

[6] Auchinleck's Hist., p. 104; Brock's Life of Brock, p. 330; James' Mil. Occur., i. p. 89.—[7] Brock's Life of Brock, p. 330; Baylies' Battle of Queenstown.

[8] Vide p. 148.—[9] Christie's Military and Naval Operations, p. 82; Brock's Life of Brock, p. 330.

from Fort George, while a stronger force might be concealed behind Fort Niagara, in readiness to cross the river and seize the fort as soon as the *ruse* had succeeded.[1] With commendable caution, however, he determined to ascertain, by personal inspection, the exact character of the attack before he withdrew the garrison; and, for that purpose, with his two aids,—Lieutenant-colonel McDonell and Major Glegg,—he galloped up to Queenstown, and thence up to the battery on the heights,[2] where they dismounted, "and took a view of passing events, which at that moment appeared highly favorable"[3]—little aware of the great change which was so near at hand.

While he still occupied that position,[4] watching the operations of Captains Williams and Chisholm, and of the Americans below, a discharge of musketry in his rear arrested his attention.[5] The same measure of success which had crowned the labors of the youthful Wolfe, at Quebec, had been vouchsafed to the young commander of the detachment from the Thirteenth, at Queenstown—the heights had been scaled without the loss of a man,[6] and Captain Wool and his command were rapidly approaching the spot where he stood.[7]

[1] Brock's Life of Brock, p. 330.—[2] Gen. Sheaffe to Sir G. Prevost, Oct. 13, 1812; Brock's Life of Brock, p. 330.

[3] Brock's Life of Brock, p. 330.—[4] Ibid.; James' Mil. Occur., i. pp. 88, 89. It has, generally, been supposed that Sir Isaac was ascending the heights, for the first time that morning, when he fell. The great care with which this biography of that officer has been written, to say nothing of Mr. James' work, leads me to place great confidence in its statements, especially since it has been prepared by a member of his family.

[5] Brock's Life of Brock, p. 330.—[6] Gen. Wool to the Author, Nov. 11, 1859.—[7] Brock's Life of Brock, p. 330; James' Military Occurrences, i. p. 89.

Without having time to remount, Sir Isaac and his aids "were obliged to retire precipitately,"[1] with the small force which occupied the battery, while the Americans pressed forward and occupied the works[2]—the American colors, floating at the flag-staff and greeting the rising sun, proclaiming at once the triumph of the Thirteenth regiment, and the success of the expedition.

Passing rapidly down the slope, leading his horse,[3] Sir Isaac Brock dispatched orders to General Sheaffe to hasten forward with the troops from Fort George[4] and to open a fire on Fort Niagara, on the American shore.[5] Having done this, he placed himself at the head of Captain Williams' detachment,[6] which had occupied the heights during the entire morning, and moved up the slope towards the battery—in the rear of which Captain Wool had formed his command, fronting the village[7]—and, soon afterwards, he was strengthened by Captain Dennis and the troops from below the hill.[8] Sir Isaac led his little force with an apparent design of turning Captain Wool's left flank;[9] when the latter detached fifty men to hold him in check, and to take possession of the heights above the battery.[1] This little party was unable to cope with the superior force under Sir Isaac; and, even when reinforced with a detachment, which Captain Wool afterwards sent forward,[2] it was not strong enough to accomplish that object.[3] Elated with this temporary success, the enemy pressed forward; and the Americans fell back, in some confusion, to the edge of the precipitous bank of the river.[4] In this critical position—with the enemy, led by the ablest general in America, in front, and the chasm of the Niagara River in their rear—some hearts faltered;[5] and one (*Captain Ogilvie*),[6] more timid than the rest, raised a white handkerchief on a bayonet, as a token of submission.[7] With his own hands Captain Wool tore down this emblem of defeat;[8] and in a few brief sentences he reanimated his troops,[9] at the same time directing his officers to continue their fire while their stock of ammuni-

[1] Brock's Life of Brock, p. 330.—[2] Van Rensselaer's Queenstown, p. 26; Capt. Wool to Col. Van Rensselaer, Oct. 23; Letter in *National Intelligencer;* Baylies' Battle of Queenstown; James' Military Occurrences, i. p. 89.

[3] "Sir Isaac and his aid-de-camp *had not even time to remount*, but were obliged to retire *precipitately*," &c.—*Brock's Life of Brock*, p. 330.—[4] Brock's Life of Brock, p. 331.—[5] Gen. Sheaffe to Sir Geo. Prevost, Oct. 13, 1812; Brock's Life of Brock, p. 331.—[6] "Capt. Williams' detachment, *personally directed by the General*, advanced to meet them," &c.—*Brock's Life of Brock*, p. 331. "Capt. Williams and his detachment were now recalled; and Gen. Brock, *putting himself at the head of this force*, advanced to meet," &c.—*James' Military Occurrences*, i. p. 89.

[7] Capt. Wool to Col. Van Rensselaer, Oct. 23.

[8] Baylies' Battle of Queenstown.—[9] Capt. Wool to Col. Van Rensselaer, Oct. 23.

[1] Capt. Wool to Col. Van Rensselaer, Oct. 23; James' Mil. Occur., i. pp. 90, 91. Gen. Wilkinson (*Mem.*, i. p. 576) and all who have followed him have erred in stating that *one hundred and fifty* were so detached. A copy of this letter, *corrected by its distinguished author*, is now before me, in which it is said that only *fifty* were detached.

[2] Capt. Wool to Col. Van Rensselaer, Oct. 23.

[3] Ibid.; Brock's Life of Brock, p. 331; Letter in *National Intelligencer*, Nov. 7, 1812; James' Mil. Occur., i. p. 90.—[4] Auchinleck, p. 112; Letter in *National Intelligencer*, Nov. 7, 1812; Baylies' Battle of Queenstown.

[5] Letter in *National Intelligencer;* Baylies' Battle of Queenstown.—[6] Gen. Wool to the Author, Nov. 11, 1859.

[7] Brock's Life of Brock, p. 331; Letter in *National Intelligencer;* Baylies' Battle of Queenstown; Perkins' Hist. of War, p. 107; Sketches of War, p. 63.

[8] Brock's Life of Brock, p. 331; Letter in *National Intelligencer*, Nov. 7, 1812; Baylies' Battle of Queenstown; Perkins' History of War, p. 107.—[9] Baylies' Battle of Queenstown; Memoir of Gen. Wool.

tion lasted, and then to resort to the bayonet.[1] Cheered by the words of their commander, and inspirited with his example, the Americans renewed the contest with great vigor;[2] while equally zealous were the efforts of Sir Isaac Brock, and equally determined were the spirits of his troops.[3] In the brief engagement which ensued, the Americans fought bravely until their ammunition was nearly exhausted,[4] when preparations were made to charge the enemy; and with Captain Ogilvie's command on the right of the line, and Captain Armstrong's company, under Lieutenant John L. Fink,—formerly a butcher in Bear Market, New York,—on the extreme left,[5] with such vigor was the movement executed that the enemy fell back, down the slope, morally, if not entirely, defeated.[6]

The gallant and respected commander of the opposing force—Sir Isaac Brock—witnessed the defeat of his troops with the greatest concern;[7] and he hastened to rally the grenadiers of the Forty-ninth regiment (Captain Dennis' command), which was his favorite corps, to check the progress of the Americans.[8] At the same time Lieutenant-colonel McDonell, his aid, brought the two flank companies of the York volunteers,[1] under Captains Cameron and Heward,[2]—which had just arrived from Brown's Point, three miles distant,[3]—on the field of action; and hastened to support the grenadiers which Sir Isaac was attempting to rally. At that moment,[4] with the order, "*Push on the York volunteers*" on his lips,[5] the gallant hero of Detroit, the pride of the Colonial army, fell, mortally wounded, the ball having entered his right breast and passed through his left side.[6] He lived only long enough to request that the information of his fall might not be communicated to the troops, and that some token of remembrance might be conveyed to his sister;[7] and he died, as he had lived, without a personal enemy even among those who were the enemies of his country—both they and his companions in arms, a few days afterwards, forgetting, for a time, the grievances of their respective countries, uniting in a common testimonial of respect to the memory of the departed chief.[8]

---

[1] Capt. Wool to Col. Van Rensselaer, Oct. 23, 1852.

[2] Brock's Life of Brock, p. 331; Baylies' Battle of Queenstown.—[3] Baylies' Battle of Queenstown.

[4] Lieut. Fink's MS. Jour.—[5] Ibid.—[6] Letter in *National Intelligencer*, Nov. 7, 1812; Capt. Wool to Lieut.-Col. Van Rensselaer, Oct. 23, 1812; Stone's Brant, ii. p. 507; Perkins' Hist. of War, p. 107; Sketches of War, p. 63.

[7] "The British general, like the American captain, well knew the language which warriors could understand when pressed with dangers; in tones that rose above the din of the fight, he rallied his troops anew to the conflict. 'This is the first time,' said he, 'that I have seen the 49th turn their backs,'" &c.—*Baylies' Battle of Queenstown.*

[8] Capt. Wool to Col. Van Rensselaer, Oct. 23; Christie's Operations, p. 83.

[1] James' Mil. Occur., i. p. 90.—[2] Auchinleck, p. 105.

[3] James' Mil. Occur., i. p. 90.

[4] Auchinleck, p. 105; Sir Geo. Prevost to the Government. It is said (*Capt. Ogilvie, in Niles' Register*, iii. p. 141) that Sir Isaac's *horse* had been shot, previously, by an Orange County man, named *Wilklow;* but it is not mentioned who shot the General. Mr. Christie (*Mil. and Naval Operations*, p. 83) says that Sir Isaac, after receiving the ball, "*fell from his horse*," which would appear to indicate that his horse had not *then* been shot; while Mr. James (*Mil. Occur.*, i. p. 91) says that Capt. Dennis, after the death of McDonell, "*mounted the General's horse*, rode up, and tried to rally the troops." All which are inconsistent with the loss of that animal.

[5] Christie's Operations, p. 83; Brock's Life of Brock, p. 331.—[6] Brock's Life of Brock, p. 331.—[7] Ibid.

[8] "Such was the esteem in which Sir Isaac was held by the enemies of his country, for he had or could have no private enemies, that Maj.-Gen. Van Rensselaer, in a let-

The loss of the general could not be long concealed from the troops whom he was leading; and a cry of "*Revenge the General!*" was raised by the Forty-ninth, as the enemy struggled to remount the heights.[1] But the enthusiasm of the occasion, the momentary desire for "revenge," and the noble exertions of Lieutenant-colonel McDonell, who assumed the command on the fall of Sir Isaac,[2] were alike unavailing, the steady, determined opposition of Captain Wool and his little party compelling the enemy to retire with considerable loss[3]—Lieutenant-colonel McDonell being mortally wounded,[4] and Captains Dennis and Williams among the wounded[5]—and Queenstown Heights and their vicinity remained in possession of Captain Wool and his command,[6] ten men of the Forty-ninth and an Indian chief remaining prisoners in the hands of the victors.[7]

When it is borne in mind that the troops who had met and repulsed the enemy, three times in succession, killing the most able general in British America; and, without artillery, scaling the heights and capturing the battery—were, generally, recruits who had never before seen service;[1] and when, still farther, it is remembered that they were led by a young man, scarce twenty-three years of age, who, but a few weeks before, had been taken from the walks of civil life;[2] and who was, that day, for the first time engaged with an enemy, while he was still suffering from two severe wounds, it must be admitted that this was, "indeed, a display of intrepidity rarely exhibited, in which the conduct and the execution were equally conspicuous."[3]

Having thus been left the undisputed master of the field, at about ten o'clock, Captain Wool formed his men on the heights, fronting the village; directed Lieutenants Gansevoort and Randolph to take possession of the battery, to drill out the eighteen-pounder—which had been spiked by Lieutenant Gansevoort—and to bring it to bear on the enemy below; and ordered scouts to be sent out, to watch the progress and movements of the enemy; while flanking parties were also detached, for the protection of the main body.[4] About the same time reinforcements, under Captains McChesney of the Sixth regiment, and Lawrence of the Thirteenth, with a party of New York State rifle-

ter of condolence, informed Maj.-Gen. Sheaffe that immediately after the funeral solemnities were over, on the British side, a compliment of minute-guns would be paid to the hero's memory on theirs!!! Accordingly, the cannon of Fort Niagara were fired, 'as a mark of respect due to a brave enemy.'"—*Brock's Life of Brock*, p. 342. See also Ingersoll, i. p. 94.

[1] Auchinleck, p. 105; Christie, p. 83; James' Mil. Occur., i. p. 90.—[2] Auchinleck, p. 105; Brock's Life of Brock, p. 332; James' Military Occurrences, i. p. 90.

[3] Auchinleck, p. 105; Brock's Life of Brock, p. 332; Letter in *National Intelligencer*, Nov. 7, 1812; James' Mil. Occur., i. p. 90.—[4] Christie, p. 84; Brock's Life of Brock, p. 332; Baylies' Battle of Queenstown; James' Mil. Occur., i. p. 90.—[5] Brock's Life of Brock, p. 332; Baylies' Battle of Queenstown; James' Mil. Occur., i. p. 90.—[6] Christie, p. 84; Brock's Life of Brock, p. 332; Letter in *National Intelligencer*, Nov. 7, 1812; Baylies' Battle of Queenstown.—[7] Baylie's Battle of Queenstown; Gen. Wool to the Author, Nov. 11, 1859.

[1] Baylies' Battle of Queenstown; Wilkinson's Mem. i. p. 578.—[2] Van Rensselaer's Queenstown, p. 26; Baylies' Battle of Queenstown; Gen. Wool to the Author, Nov. 11, 1859. At the time of Capt. Wool's appointment (April 13, 1812) he was engaged in studying law in an office which still stands within sight from his windows, in the city of Troy, N. Y.—[3] Wilkinson's Memoirs, i. p. 577.

[4] Capt. Wool to Col. Van Rensselaer, Oct. 23; Letter in *National Intelligencer*, Nov. 7, 1812; Baylies' Battle of Queenstown; Memoir of Gen. Wool.

men under Lieutenant Smith, came on the heights;[1]—the latter of whom gallantly rescued Lieutenant-colonel Fenwick, Major Mullany, and another officer, who had been taken prisoners by the enemy while they were crossing the river,—and, soon afterwards, General Wadsworth and Lieutenant-colonels Winfield Scott and Chrystie joined the detachment.[2] The former, waiving his rank, gave the command to Lieutenant-colonel Scott;[3] and the latter, a few hours afterwards, also commenced his brilliant career, by meeting an enemy, *the first time*, on the heights of Queenstown.[4] At the same time Lieutenant-colonel Chrystie assumed the command of the detachment from the Thirteenth regiment;[5] and Captain Wool obtained leave to withdraw from the heights—the scene of his hard-earned, but undisputed victory—for the purpose of having his wounds dressed, and of enjoying that repose which his loss of blood rendered necessary.[6]

With the reinforcements which had reached the heights, after the close of the last engagement, Lieutenant-colonel Scott found himself at the head of about three hundred and fifty regulars, and two hundred and fifty militia; and this force he formed in such a position that the enemy, if he returned to the attack, could be properly received, while, at the same time, the passage of the militia across the river—which was momentarily expected—could be effectually covered.[1] At this time "a cloud of Indians"[2] approached the detachment;[3] and, about two o'clock, during a momentary absence of Lieutenant-colonel Scott from the field, they dashed forward, tomahawk in hand, on the American line.[4] When the Lieutenant-colonel reached the spot he found the troops were filled with alarm and on the eve of an ignoble flight; but, by an instantaneous change of front, the enemy was foiled and the detachment enabled to recover its presence of mind.[5] Under the leadership of John Brant and Captain Jacobs,[6] the Mohawks gallantly sustained the action;[7] and, even when they were driven from the field, they were not overcome. With a degree of spirit and activity which was worthy of his name, the youthful chief (John Brant) continued to harass the

---

[1] Baylies' Battle of Queenstown; Gen. Wool to the Author, Nov. 11, 1859.—[2] Mansfield's Life of Scott, p. 40; Capt. Wool to Col. Van Rensselaer, Oct. 23; Letter in *National Intelligencer*, Nov. 7, 1812; Baylies' Battle of Queenstown.—[3] Mansfield's Life of Scott, p. 40.

[4] Ingersoll's War of 1812, i. p. 93. It is a singular coincidence that the present distinguished General-in-chief of the armies of the United States (Lieut.-Gen. Scott), and the distinguished commander of the Eastern Division of the United States (Maj.-Gen. Wool) both met the enemy, for the first time, on the Heights of Queenstown; and that one succeeded the other in the command of the troops who were engaged on that field.

[5] Capt. Wool to Col. Van Rensselaer, Oct. 23; Baylies' Battle of Queenstown.—[6] Capt. Wool to Col. Van Rensselaer, Oct. 23; Letter in *National Intelligencer*, Nov. 7, 1812; Baylies' Battle of Queenstown.

[1] Mansfield's Scott, pp. 40, 41.—[2] Stone's Life of Brant, ii. p. 508. See also Perkins' History of War, p. 107.

[3] Mansfield's Scott, p. 41; Stone's Brant, ii. p. 508.

[4] Mansfield's Scott, pp. 41, 42; O'Connor's History of War, pp. 49, 50; Brock's Life of Brock, p. 334; Letter in *National Intelligencer*, Nov. 7, 1812; Stone's Brant, ii. p. 508.—[5] Mansfield's Scott, p. 42; Christie, p. 84; Brock's Life of Brock, p. 334; Letter in *National Intelligencer*, Nov. 7, 1812; James' Military Occurrences, i. p. 94.

[6] Stone's Life of Brant, ii. p. 509. Mr. Auchinleck (*Hist. of War*, p. 105) says this chief was *Norton;* and Gen. Sheaffe (*Dispatch*, Oct. 13), Mr. James (*Mil. Occur*, i. p. 94) agree with him.

[7] Auchinleck, p. 105; Stone's Brant, ii. pp. 508, 509.

Americans, without affording them an opportunity to inflict any serious loss;[1] until, later in the day, when Lieutenant-colonel Scott, in person, led his men against the savages and drove them from the heights.[2]

About this time a strong body of British troops, under the command of General Sheaffe, was seen approaching from Fort George;[3] and General Van Rensselaer, who had crossed the river, returned to Lewiston to expedite the passage of the militia.[4] Small parties of the militia had crossed the river, from time to time, during the entire day, and had sustained their part of the several engagements with the most commendable spirit and fidelity;[5] yet, at this time, not one of those who were still in New York could be induced to cross the river.[6] General Van Rensselaer rode through their ranks and entreated them to move to the relief of their associates in arms, but in vain, all resolutely refusing to move beyond the boundaries of the United States.[7] It has not been shown what cause produced this unhappy result. By the commander of the expedition it has been said, that the return of the three boats which failed to reach the Canadian shore, *when the first detachment left the United States*, had intimidated them;[1] but more than twelve hours had elapsed since that occurred, and there had been no evidence that this great change of sentiment was then produced. It appears to be far more probable that the fact had become known to them, that all the boats which had been provided for the passage of the troops, except one small scow, *had been allowed to float away with the current, or to be captured by the enemy*, for the want of proper officers to take charge of them, *as was, truly, the case.*

Intelligence of this disaster was immediately conveyed to Lieutenant-colonel Scott;[2] yet, severe as was the shock, that gallant officer and his command, although worn down by the fatigues of the day, "resolved to abide the shock, and to think of surrender only when battle was impossible."[3]

Meanwhile the reinforcements from Fort George were approaching the heights by a circuitous route.[4] Not, however, with that "pomp and circumstance" which became the pretensions of British troops did they approach; but, with an unusual degree of circumspection and caution, as a cotemporary remarks,[5] he "manœuvred from right to left, and from left to right, countermarching nearly the whole length of the American line twice, as if determined to count every man in the ranks,

[1] Mansfield's Scott, p. 42.—[2] Stone's Brant, ii. p. 509; Armstrong's Notices, i. p. 105.

[3] Ingersoll's Historical Sketches, i. p. 92; Stone's Brant, ii. p. 509; Gen. Van Rensselaer to Gen. Dearborn, Oct. 14, 1812.

[4] Van Rensselaer's Queenstown, p. 37; Ingersoll's War, i. p. 93.—[5] Mansfield's Scott, p. 42.—[6] Auchinleck, p. 106; Mansfield's Scott, p. 42; Van Rensselaer's Queenstown, p. 37; Brock's Life of Brock, p. 332; Letter in *National Intelligencer*, Nov. 7, 1812; Baylies' battle of Queenstown; Ingersoll, i. p. 93.

[7] Baylies' Battle of Queenstown; Ingersoll, i. p. 93.

[1] Van Rensselaer's Queenstown, p. 37. See also Wilkinson's Mem., i. p. 573.—[2] Stone's Brant, ii. p. 510; Armstrong's Notices, i. p. 106.

[3] Mansfield's Scott, p. 43.—[4] Brock's Life of Brock, p. 332; James' Military Occurrences, i. p. 94.

[5] Armstrong's Notices, i. p. 106. See also Baylies' Battle of Queenstown; Mansfield's Scott, p. 43.

and to make himself familiar with every foot of the position before he hazarded an attack." While the enemy was thus, unintentionally, rendering homage to the bravery of the troops and the skill of their commanders, Lieutenant-colonel Scott mounted a log and addressed his command, encouraging the men, appealing to their patriotism and their pride, and asking, "Who dare to stand?"[1] The unanimous response of the men proved that, with them, the spirit which they had displayed in the morning still lingered in the ranks; and the regulars and the volunteers vied with each other in the determination with which they prepared to renew the struggle.

The fragments of the force which Sir Isaac Brock and Lieutenant-colonel McDonell had led up the heights, after its repulse, having been driven from a more advanced position by the artillery on the heights of Lewiston,[2] had formed in the vicinity of Vromont's battery, and there awaited the approach of General Sheaffe and the reinforcements under his command.[3] These consisted of three hundred and eighty rank and file of the Forty-first regiment of the line, under Captain Derenzy;[4] the flank companies of the First regiment of Lincoln militia, under Captains James Crooks and McEwen; the flank companies of the Fourth regiment of Lincoln militia, under Captains Nellis and W. Crooks; Captains Hall's, Durand's, and Applegarth's companies of

[1] Mansfield's Scott, p. 43; Stone's Life of Brant, ii. p. 511.—[2] Brock's Life of Brock, p. 332; Auchinleck, p. 105.
[3] Auchinleck, p. 105; James' Military Occurrences, i. p. 91.—[4] Gen. Sheaffe to Sir Geo. Prevost, Oct 13.

the Fifth regiment of Lincoln militia; Major Merrit's yeomanry corps, and a body of Swayzee's militia artillery, under Captains Powell and Cameron; and, a short time afterwards, Colonel Clark arrived from Chippewa with Captain Bullock's company of grenadiers of the Forty-first regiment; the flank companies of the Second Lincoln regiment, under Captains Hamilton and Row; and the Volunteer Sedentary militia.[1] The Indians, under John Brant and Captain Jacobs;[2] and two three-pounders, under Lieutenant Crowther of the Forty-first regiment,[3] also accompanied them.

With this overpowering force, General Sheaffe moved forward with great caution;[4] and, at four in the afternoon,[5] the action commenced on the left of the enemy's line, by the advance of the light company of the Forty-first, under Lieutenant McIntyre, supported by a body of militia and Indians, and a company of colored men, under Captain Runchey.[6] After firing a single volley, the enemy charged, and the right of the American line, against which it was directed, being overpowered by the enemy, was compelled to give way.[7] Perceiving the success which attended this movement, General Sheaffe supported it by ordering his entire line to charge, when—having received orders to that effect from General Van Rensselaer, who promised to provide boats

[1] Auchinleck, p. 105.—[2] Vide p. 156, col. 2, note 6.
[3] Gen. Sheaffe to Sir Geo. Prevost, Oct. 13; Auchinleck, p. 105; James' Military Occurrences, i. p. 94.
[4] Vide p. 156, col. 2, note 5.—[5] Van Rensselaer's Queenstown, p. 35; Breckenridge, p. 74.—[6] Auchinleck, p. 105; James' Military Occurrences, i. pp. 94, 95.—[7] Auchinleck, p. 105; James' Military Occurrences, i. p. 95.

for their passage across the river[1]—the Americans retreated by their right flank,[2] over the first ridge of heights, to the road leading from Queenstown to the falls.[3] Some few dropped down, with the help of the bushes and their muskets, to the margin of the river, and escaped;[4] but the greater part of the force, after some difficulty in passing a flag through the bands of Indians which watched the roads,[5] surrendered to the enemy, prisoners of war[6]—General Van Rensselaer having no boats with which to withdraw them.

Of the American forces which were in the series of engagements at Queenstown, it is difficult to obtain an exact account. The entire party which first passed from Lewiston to Queenstown—ten boats full—did not exceed two hundred and twenty-five in number;[7] and with the regulars from this force—one hundred and seventy in number[8]—on the American side, the first action was fought by Captain Wool, at the heights. The militia who had

[1] Letter in *National Intelligencer*, Nov. 7, 1812; Thomson's Sketches, p. 75; Christie's Mil. Operations, p. 85.

[2] Brock's Life of Brock, p. 334; James' Mil. Occur., i. p. 95.—[3] Auchinleck, p. 105; Brock's Life of Brock, p. 334; James' Mil. Occur., i. p. 95.—[4] Auchinleck, p. 106; Mansfield's Scott, p. 44; Brock's Life of Brock, p. 334; Letter in *National Intelligencer*, Nov. 7, 1812; James' Mil. Occur., i. p. 95.—[5] Mansfield's Scott, p. 44; James' Mil. Occur., i. p. 95; Stone's Brant, ii. pp. 512, 513.

[6] Mansfield's Scott, p. 44; Letter in *National Intelligencer*, Nov. 7, 1812; Ingersoll, i. p. 93; Gen. Van Rensselaer to Gen. Dearborn, Oct. 14.—[7] Van Rensselaer's Queenstown, p. 27; Wilkinson's Mem., i. p. 578; Brock's Life of Brock, p. 329.—[8] From the fact that the three boats which missed the landing on the British shore contained regulars only,—Lieut.-Col. Chrystie, Capt. Lawrence, and Lieut. Fink commanding,—it is evident the whole of the militia, sixty in number, landed in Canada. This would leave but about 170 regulars, yet I have thought some few others might have accompanied Capt. Wool.

crossed in the first detachment—sixty in number—do not appear to have, generally, ascended the heights, until after the battery had been taken by Captain Wool;[1] and the two engagements on the heights which preceded the death of Sir Isaac Brock, must have been sustained, therefore, by a party of not exceeding two hundred and forty men.[2] After that time, while Captain Wool still retained the command, several small parties crossed the river and joined his detachment,[3] making, with the militia who had first crossed, and subsequently ascended the heights, a force, when Lieutenant-colonel Scott took the command, of six hundred men.[4] With this number the attack of the Mohawks was sustained; but, when General Sheaffe was seen on his way to attack the party, it was reduced by desertion[5]—many concealing themselves among the rocks and bushes[6]—so that but little more than three hundred sustained the final attack of General Sheaffe.[7]

Nor is it less difficult to ascertain the strength of the enemy, during the different periods of the action. Captain

[1] Capt. Ogilvie, who led the advance (*Niles' Register*, iii. p. 141), says *ten militiamen* only were with him.

[2] Baylies' Battle of Queenstown. This will be seen in the fact that to Capt. Wool's first party—one hundred and seventy men—was added, subsequently, Capt. Ogilvie's company, and that, with this addition, including ten militiamen, the heights were stormed.

[3] Maj. Mullany to Gen. Van Rensselaer, Jan. 5, 1813; Van Rensselaer's Queenstown, pp. 36, 37; Capt. Ogilvie, in *Niles' Register*, iii. p. 141; Christie's Operations, p. 83; Brock's Life of Brock, p. 332; Lieut.-Col. Chrystie to Adj.-Gen., Feb. 22, 1813.—[4] Mansfield's Scott, p. 40.

[5] Lieut.-Col. Chrystie to Adj.-Gen., Feb. 22, 1813.

[6] Mansfield's Scott, p. 45; Christie's Military Operations, p. 84.—[7] Mansfield's Scott, p. 43; Armstrong's Notices, i. p. 106.

Dennis's party, which first attacked Captain Wool, at the foot of the heights, numbered sixty regulars and about as many militia;[1] the party on the heights, under Captain Williams, embraced two full companies—not less than one hundred and fifty men[2]—and with this number he sustained the first action with Captain Wool on the heights. Sir Isaac Brock consolidated these two parties, to which were added two flank companies of the York volunteers, a body of militia, and some Indians, and the second attack on Captain Wool, on the heights, in which Sir Isaac lost his life, must, therefore, have been made with not less than four hundred and fifty men. Of the Mohawks who attacked Lieutenant-colonel Scott, it is said there were five hundred warriors.[3] The reinforcement which General Sheaffe brought on the ground numbered about eight hundred and fifty men;[4] which, added to the remnants of those companies which Sir Isaac had rallied, made a force of not less than thirteen hundred and fifty men, exclusive of Indians.[5]

It will thus be seen that, with the possible exception of Captain Wool's first action on the heights, the enemy in each engagement was much the stronger of the two; while in all the elements which, ordinarily, contribute to success—experience, discipline, and supplies—the latter was, also, greatly superior.

[1] James' Mil. Occur., i. p. 87; Brock's Life of Brock, p. 329.—[2] James' Mil. Occur., i. p. 88.—[3] Mansfield's Scott, p. 41. Mr. Auchinleck (*Hist.*, p. 111) denies that they amounted to *one hundred;* Mr. James (*Mil. Occur.*, i. p. 94) says they numbered "*about fifty.*"

[4] Mansfield's Scott, p. 42; Armstrong's Notices, i. p. 106. Capt. Ogilvie, in *Niles' Register*, iii. p. 141, says it numbered *eleven hundred* men. Mr. Christie (*Mil. and Naval Operations*, p. 84) says it numbered *five hundred and fifty* men, exclusive of Indians.

[5] Mansfield's Scott, p. 43. Mr. Brock (*Life of Brock*, p. 333) says, "The whole force thus assembled rather exceeded 1000 men of all grades, of whom nearly 600 were regulars."

The loss of the Americans, in this diversified affair, was very serious. About ninety, including Lieutenants Valleau and Rathbone, and Ensign Morris, were *killed;*[1] about one hundred, including Lieutenant-colonels Fenwick, Chrystie, and Van Rensselaer, Captains Wool, Malcolm, and Armstrong, and Lieutenant Lent, were *wounded;*[2] and about nine hundred and eighty,[3] of whom *only one hundred and thirty-nine regulars and one hundred and fifty-four militia had been in action,*[4] were *taken prisoners.* The loss of the enemy was about one hundred and fifty men killed and wounded,[5] exclusive of Indians.

Thus terminated the "Battle of Queenstown"—a series of engagements in which were blended the most perfect plans of operations and the most incomplete arrangements for their execution, the most undaunted courage and the most flagrant cowardice, the most triumphant success and the most disastrous defeat; an affair which, from its results, was second in importance to

[1] Brock's Life of Brock, p. 334; Thomson's Sketches, p. 76.—[2] Brock's Life of Brock, p. 334.—[3] Auchinleck, p. 106; Brock's Life of Brock, p. 334.

[4] Mansfield's Scott, p. 44. "To his (*Scott's*) intense chagrin and mortification the number of prisoners was soon swelled by several hundreds of militia, who had crossed to the Canada shore, and, in the confusion of the moment, had concealed themselves under the rocks higher up the river, and were not in the slightest degree engaged in the action of the day."—*Mansfield's Scott*, p. 45.

[5] Auchinleck, p. 106. Mr. James (*Mil. Occur.*, i. p. 97) and Mr. Christie (*Mil. and Naval Operations*, p. 86) says the total loss was only about *eighty men*, including Indians.

no other which took place on the Northern frontier. When it is borne in mind, also, that, on the one side, it was maintained by militia, or by regulars who possessed but little more experience than militia; that they were led—in the preliminary engagement, in the assault on the heights, in the maintenance of that position, and in the final engagement, alike—by a captain and a lieutenant-colonel who were fresh from civil life and had never been in action before; and that they were unsupported by their countrymen, who were in force to do so; while, on the other, they were opposed by veteran troops, led by one of the most accomplished soldiers of the age, it will be seen that "*the Battle of Queenstown*" is one of the most remarkable, in every respect, which appears on the battle-roll of America.[1]

There are two singular facts, in this connection, which deserve notice. While the commanding general (Van Rensselaer), in his dispatches, studiously concealed the *true* causes of the disastrous termination of the expedition,—*the imperfect arrangements for the passage of the river*,—he exerts all his energies to make the militia the scapegoat of his inefficiency, and justifies the want of confidence which the latter had manifested; and, at the same time, for political or other causes, known only to himself, while the names of officers, who, with one exception, *had not been engaged in action*, were honorably mentioned in his dispatches, the commanders of the troops who *had met the enemy*, carried and occupied the heights, and gallantly defended them afterwards,—Captain Wool and Lieutenant-colonel Scott, of the United States army,—were not even referred to, by name, in any portion of the report. The enemy, more generous than he, not only commemorated the gallantry of the fallen leader of the opposing force, by a monument, erected near the spot where he fell; but, joining with the impartial historians of our own country, and with General Van Rensselaer himself, in his *private* correspondence, his annalists—James, Auchinleck, and Brock,—have not forgotten to award the meed of praise *where it properly belongs*.

---

[1] Much of the error which prevails respecting the commandant of the regulars on this eventful day, may be attributed to the fact that Mr. Niles copied into the *Register* (vol. iii., p. 141) an account of the battle which *Captain Ogilvie had given to an Albany paper;* and subsequent writers, following *Niles*, have only perpetuated Capt. Ogilvie's version. As Capt. Wool was Capt. Ogilvie's superior officer,—the rank of the officers having been determined by lot, a short time before,—it will be seen, at once, that Capt. Wool commanded the party, and *captured and retained possession of the heights of Queenstown*, until the arrival of Lieut.-Col. Scott relieved him of the command.

DOCUMENTS.

I.

LETTER FROM MAJOR-GENERAL VAN RENSSELAER TO MAJOR-GENERAL HENRY DEARBORN.

HEAD-QUARTERS, LEWISTOWN, *Oct.* 14, 1812.

SIR:—As the movements of this army under my command, since I had last the honor to address you on the 8th instant, have been of a very important character, producing consequences serious to many individuals; establishing facts actually connected with the interest of the service and the safety of the army; and as I stand prominently responsible for some of these consequences, I beg leave to explain to you, sir, and through you to my country, the situation and circumstances in which I have had to act, and the reasons and motives which governed me; and if the result is not all that might have been wished, it is such that when the whole ground shall be viewed, I shall cheerfully submit myself to the judgment of my country.

In my letter of the 8th instant I apprised you that a crisis in this campaign was rapidly advancing; and that (to repeat the same words), "the blow must be soon struck, or all the toil and expense of the campaign go for nothing, for the whole will be tinged with dishonor."

Under such impressions I had, on the 5th instant, written to Brigadier-general Smyth, of the United States' forces, requesting an interview with him, Major-general Hall, and the commandants of the United States' regiments, for the purpose of conferring upon the subject of future operations. I wrote Major-general Hall to the same purport. On the 11th I had received no answer from General Smyth; but in a note to me of the 10th, General Hall mentioned that General Smyth had not yet then agreed upon any day for the consultation.

In the mean time the partial success of Lieutenant Elliott, at Black Rock (of which, however, I have received no official information), began to excite a strong disposition in the troops to act. This was expressed to me through various channels, in the shape of an alternative; that they must have orders to act—or, at all hazards, they would go home. I forbear here commenting upon the obvious consequences to me, personally, of longer withholding my orders under such circumstances.

I had a conference with ———, as to the possibility of getting some person to pass over to Canada and obtain correct information. On the morning of the 4th he wrote to me that he had procured the man, who bore his letter to go over. Instructions were given him; he passed over—obtained such information as warranted an immediate attack. This was confidentially communicated to several of my first officers, and produced great zeal to act; more especially as it might have a controlling effect upon the movements at Detroit, where it was supposed that General Brock had gone, with all the force he dared to spare from the Niagara frontier. The best preparations in my power were, therefore, made to dislodge the enemy from the heights of Queenstown, and possess ourselves of the village, where the troops might be sheltered from the distressing inclemency of the weather.

Lieutenant-colonel Fenwick's flying-artillery, and a detachment of regular troops, under his command, were ordered to be up in season from Fort Niagara. Orders were also sent General Smyth, to send down from Buffalo such detachment of his brigade as existing circumstances in that vicinity might warrant. The attack was to have been made at three o'clock on the morning of the 11th, by crossing over in boats from the Old Ferry opposite the heights. To avoid any embarrassment in crossing the river (which is here a sheet of violent eddies), experienced boatmen were procured to take the boats from the landing below to the place of embarkation. Lieutenant Sim was considered the man of the greatest skill for this service; he went ahead, and in the extreme darkness passed the intended place far up the river; and there, in a most extraordinary manner, fastened his boat to the shore, and abandoned the detachment. In this front boat he had carried nearly every oar which was prepared for all the boats. In this agonizing dilemma stood officers and men, whose ardor had not been cooled by exposure through the night to one of the most tremendous north-east storms, which continued, unabated, for twenty-eight hours, and deluged the whole camp. The approach of daylight extinguished every prospect of success, and the detachment returned to camp. Colonel Van Rensselaer was to have commanded the detachment.

After this result, I had hoped the patience of the troops would have continued until I could submit the plan suggested in my letter of the 8th, that I might act under, and in conformity to, the opinion which might be then expressed. But my hope was idle: the previously excited ardor seemed to have gained new heat from the late miscarriage—the brave were mortified to stop short of their object, and the timid thought laurels half won by the attempt.

On the morning of the 12th, such was the pressure upon me from all quarters, that I became satisfied that my refusal to act might involve me in suspicion and the service in disgrace.

Viewing affairs at Buffalo as yet unsettled, I had immediately countermanded the march of General Smyth's brigade, upon the failure of the first expedition; but having now determined to attack Queenstown, I sent new orders to General Smyth to march; not with the view of his aid in the attack, for I considered the force detached sufficient, but to support the detachment should the conflict be obstinate and long continued.

Lieutenant-colonel Chrystie, who had just arrived at the Four Mile Creek, had, late in the night of the first contemplated attack, gallantly offered me his own and his men's services; but he got my permission too late. He now again came forward, had a conference with Colonel Van Rensselaer, and begged that he might have the honor of a command in the expedition. The arrangement was made. Colonel Van Rensselaer was to command one column of three hundred militia, and Lieutenant-colonel Chrystie a column of the same number of regular troops.

Every precaution was now adopted as to boats, and the most confidential and experienced men to manage them. At an early hour in the night, Lieutenant-colonel Chrystie marched his detachment, by the rear road, from Niagara to camp. At seven in the evening Lieutenant-colonel Stranahan's regiment moved from Niagara Falls; at eight o'clock, Mead's; and at nine, Lieutenant-colonel Blan's regiment marched from the same place. All were in camp in good season. Agreeably to my orders issued upon this occasion, the two columns were to pass over together. As soon as the heights should be carried, Lieutenant-colonel Fenwick's flying-artillery was to pass over; then Major Mullany's detachment of regulars; and the other troops to follow in order.

At dawn of day the boats were in readiness, and the troops commenced embarking, under the cover of a commanding battery mounting two eighteen-pounders and two sixes. The movement was soon discovered, and a brisk fire of musketry was poured from the whole line of the Canada shore. Our battery then opened to sweep the shore; but it was, for some minutes, too dark to direct much fire with safety. A brisk cannonade was now opened upon the boats from three different batteries. Our battery returned the fire, and occasionally threw grape upon the shore, and was itself served with shells from a small mortar of the enemy's. Colonel Scott, of the artillery, by hastening his march from Niagara Falls in the night, arrived in season to return the enemy's fire with two six-pounders.

The boats were somewhat embarrassed with the eddies, as well as with a shower of shot; but Colonel Van Rensselaer, with about one hundred men, soon effected his landing, amid a tremendous fire directed upon him from every point; but to the astonishment of all who witnessed the scene, this van of the column advanced slowly against the fire. It was a serious misfortune to the van, and indeed to the whole expedition, that in a few minutes after landing, Colonel Van Rensselaer received four wounds—a ball passed through his right thigh, entering just below the hip-bone; another shot passed through the same thigh, a little below; the third through the calf of his left leg; and a fourth cartused his heel. This was quite a crisis in the expedition. Under so severe a fire it was difficult to form raw troops. By some mismanagement of the boatmen, Lieutenant-colonel Chrystie did not arrive till some time after this, and was wounded in the hand in passing the river. Colonel Van Rensselaer was still able to stand; and with great presence of mind ordered his officers to proceed with rapidity and storm the fort. This service was gallantly performed, and the enemy driven down the hill in every direction. Soon after this both parties were considerably reinforced, and the conflict was renewed in various places; many of the enemy took shelter behind a stone guard-house, where a piece of ordnance was now briskly served. I ordered the fire of our battery directed upon the guard-house; and it was so effectually done, that with eight or ten shot the fire was silenced. The enemy then retreated behind a large stone-house; but in a short time the rout became general, and the enemy's fire was silenced, except from a one-gun battery, so far down the river as to be out of the reach of our heavy ordnance, and our light pieces could not silence it. A number of boats now passed over unannoyed, except from the one unsilenced gun. For some time after I had passed over, the victory appeared complete; but in the expectation of farther attacks, I was taking measures for fortifying my camp immediately: the direction of this service I committed to Lieutenant Totten, of the engineers. But very soon the enemy were reinforced by a detachment of several hundred Indians from Chippewa. They commenced a furious attack, but were promptly met and routed by the rifle and bayonet. By this time I perceived my troops were embarking very slowly. I passed immediately over to accelerate their movements; but to my utter astonishment, I found that at the very moment when complete victory was in our hands, the ardor of the unengaged troops had entirely subsided. I rode in all directions; urged the men by every consideration to pass over, but in vain. Lieutenant-colonel Bloom, who had been wounded in action, returned, mounted his horse, and rode through the camp; as did also Judge Peck, who happened to be here, exhorting the companies to proceed, but all in vain.

At this time a large reinforcement from Fort George were discovered coming up the river. As the battery on the hill was considered an important check against their ascending the heights, measures were immediately taken to send them a fresh supply of ammunition, as I had learned there were left only twenty shot for the eighteen-pounders. The reinforcements, however, obliqued to the right from the road and formed a junction with the Indians in the rear of the heights. Finding, to my infinite mortification, that no reinforcement would pass over; seeing that another severe conflict must soon commence; and knowing that the brave men of the heights were quite exhausted and nearly out of ammunition, all I could do was to send them a fresh supply of cartridges. At this critical moment I dispatched a note to General Wadsworth, acquainting him with our situation,—leaving the course to be pursued much to his own judgment,—with assurance that if he thought best to retreat, I would endeavor to send as many boats as I could command, and cover his retreat by every fire I could safely make. But the boats were dispersed,—many of the boatmen had fled, panic-struck,—and but few got off. But my note could but little more than have reached General Wadsworth, about four o'clock, when a most severe and obstinate conflict commenced and continued about half an hour, with a tremendous fire of cannon, flying-artillery, and musketry. The enemy succeeded in repossessing their battery; and gaining advantage on every side, the brave men who had gained the victory, exhausted of strength and ammunition, and grieved at the unpardonable neglect of their fellow-soldiers, gave up the conflict.

I can only add that the victory was really won, but lost for the want of a reinforcement. One third part of the idle men might have saved all.

I have been so pressed with the various duties of burying the dead, providing for the wounded, collecting the public property, negotiating an exchange of prisoners, and all the concerns consequent of such a battle, that I have not been able to forward this dispatch at as early an hour as I could have wished. I shall soon forward you another dispatch, in which I shall endeavor to point out to you the conduct of some most gallant and deserving officers. But I cannot in justice close this without expressing the very great obligation I am under to Brigadier-general Wadsworth, Colonel Van Rensselaer, Colonel Scott, Lieutenant-colonels Chrystie and Fenwick, and Captain Gibson. Many others have also behaved gallantly. As I have reason to believe that many of our troops fled to the woods, with the hope of crossing the river, I have not been able to learn the probable number of killed, wounded, or prisoners. The slaughter of our troops must have been very considerable; and the enemy have suffered severely.

General Brock is among their slain, and his aid-de-camp mortally wounded.

I have the honor to be, sir, with great respect and consideration, your most obedient servant,

STEPHEN VAN RENSSELAER,
Major-general.

MAJOR-GENERAL DEARBORN.

II.

CAPTAIN WOOL'S REPORT.

BUFFALO, *October* 23, 1812.

DEAR SIR:—I have the honor to communicate to you the circumstances attending the storming of Queenstown battery on the 13th instant; with those which happened previously, you are already well acquainted.

In pursuance of your order we proceeded round the point, and ascended the rocks, which brought us partly in rear of the battery. We took it without much resistance. I immediately formed the troops in the rear of the battery, and fronting the village, when I observed General Brock with his troops formed, consisting of four companies of the Forty-ninth regiment and a few militia, marching for our left flank. I immediately detached a party of fifty men, to take possession of the heights above Queenstown battery and to hold General Brock in check, but in consequence of his superior force they retreated. I sent a reinforcement, notwithstanding which, the enemy drove us to the edge of the bank, when with the greatest exertion we brought the troops to a stand, and ordered the officers to bring their men to a charge as soon as the ammunition was expended, which was executed with some confusion, and in a few minutes the enemy retreated. We pursued them to the edge of the heights, when Colonel McDonald had his horse shot from under him, and himself mortally wounded. In the mean time General Brock, in attempting to rally his forces, was killed, when the enemy dispersed in every direction. As soon as it was practicable, I formed the troops in a line on the heights fronting the village, and immediately detached flanking parties, which consisted of Captain M'Chesney of the Sixth regiment, Lieutenant Smith and Ensign Grosvenor with a small detachment of riflemen which had that moment arrived; at the same time I ordered Lieutenant Gansevoort and Lieutenant Randolph, with a detachment of artillery, to drill out an eighteen-pounder which had been previously spiked, and if possible to bring it to bear upon the village. The wounded and prisoners I ordered to be collected and sent to the guard-house. About this time, which was between three and four o'clock in the afternoon, Lieutenant-colonel Chrystie arrived and took the command. He ordered me across the river to get my wounds dressed. I remained a short time. Our flanking parties had been driven in by the Indians, but General Wadsworth and other officers arriving, we had a short skirmish with them and they retreated, and I crossed the river.

The officers engaged in storming the battery, were Captains Wool and Ogilvie; Lieutenants Kearney, Hugonin, Carr, and Sammons of the Thirteenth; Lieutenants Gansevoort and Randolph of the light artillery, and Major Lush of the militia. I recommend to your particular notice Lieutenants Randolph, Carr, and Kearney, for their brave conduct, exhibited during the whole of the action.

I have the honor to be your most obedient, humble servant,

JOHN E. WOOL,
Capt. 13th Regt. Infantry.

Col. SOLOMON VAN RENSSELAER.

[NOTE.—This copy of the Report, which differs in one particular from those which have heretofore appeared, has been printed from a corrected copy which I received from the distinguished author—General Wool. The error into which he fell, in stating that "*four* companies of the 49th regiment" opposed him, instead of *two, with two of voltigeurs*, was caused by the error of the prisoners whom he captured, from whom he received the information respecting the number and character of the enemy's force.—H. B. D.]

III.

GENERAL SHEAFFE'S DISPATCH TO SIR GEORGE PREVOST.

Fort George, *October* 13, 1812.

Sir:—I have the honor of informing your Excellency that the enemy made an attack with a considerable force this morning before daylight, on the position of Queenstown. On receiving intelligence of it, Major-general Brock immediately proceeded to that post, and I am excessively grieved in having to add, that he fell while gallantly cheering his troops to an exertion for maintaining it. With him, the position was lost; but the enemy was not allowed to retain it long. Reinforcements having been sent up from this post, composed of regular troops, militia, and Indians, a movement was made to turn his left, while some artillery, under the able direction of Captain Holcroft, supported by a body of infantry, engaged his attention in front. This operation was aided too by the judicious position which Norton, and the Indians with him, had taken on the woody brow of the high ground above Queenstown. A communication being thus opened with Chippewa, a junction was formed with succors that had been ordered from that post. The enemy was then attacked, and, after a short, but spirited conflict, was completely defeated. I had the satisfaction of receiving the sword of their commander, Brigadier-general Wadsworth, on the field of battle; and many officers, with upwards of nine hundred men, were made prisoners, and more may yet be expected. A stand of colors and one six-pounder were also taken. The action did not terminate till near three o'clock in the afternoon, and their loss in killed and wounded must have been considerable. Ours I believe to have been comparatively small in numbers. No officer was killed besides Major-general Brock, one of the most gallant and zealous officers in His Majesty's service, whose loss cannot be too much deplored, and Lieutenant-colonel McDonell, Provincial Aid-de-camp, whose gallantry and merit rendered him worthy of his chief. Captains Dennis and Williams, commanding the flank companies of the Forty-ninth regiment, which were stationed at Queenstown, were wounded, bravely contending, at the head of their men, against superior numbers; but I am glad to have it in my power to add, that Captain Dennis fortunately was able to keep the field, though with pain and difficulty; and Captain Williams' wound is not likely to deprive me long of his services. I am particularly indebted to Captain Holcroft, of the Royal Artillery, for his judicious and skilful co-operation with the guns and howitzers under his immediate superintendence, the well-directed fire from which contributed materially to the fortunate result of the day. Captain Derenzy, of the Forty-first regiment, brought up the reinforcement of that corps from Fort George; and Captain Bullock led that of the same regiment from Chippewa; and under their command these detachments acquitted themselves in such a manner as to sustain the reputation which the Forty-first regiment had already acquired in the vicinity of Detroit. Major-general Brock, soon after his arrival at Queenstown, had sent down orders for battering the American Fort Niagara. Brigade-major Evans, who was left in charge of Fort George, directed the operations against it with so much effect as to silence its fire, and to force the troops to abandon it, and by his prudent precautions he prevented mischief of a most serious nature, which otherwise might have been effected, the enemy having used heated shot in firing at Fort George. In these services he was most effectually aided by Colonel Claus (who remained in the fort at my desire) and by Captain Vigoreux, of the royal engineers; Brigade-major Evans also mentions the conduct of Captains Powell and Cameron, of the militia artillery, in terms of commendation. Lieutenant Crowther, of the Forty-first regiment, had charge of two three-pounders that had accompanied the movement of our little corps, and they were employed with very good effect. Captain Glegg, of the Forty-ninth regiment, Aid-de-camp to our lamented friend and General, afforded me most essential assistance; and I found the services of Lieutenant Fowler, of the

Forty-first regiment, Assistant Deputy Quartermaster-general, very useful. I derived much aid, too, from the activity and intelligence of Lieutenant Kerr, of the Glengary fencibles, whom I employed in communications with the Indians and other flanking parties. I was unfortunately deprived of the aid of the experience and ability of Lieutenant-colonel Myers, Deputy Quartermaster-general, who had been sent up to Fort Erie a few days before, on duty which detained him there. Lieutenant-colonels Butler and Clarke, of the militia, and Captains Hatt, Durand, Rowe, Applegarth, James Crooks, Cooper, Robert Hamilton, McEwen, and Duncan Cameron, and Lieutenants Richardson and Thomas Butler, commanding flank companies of the Lincoln and York militia, led their men into action with great spirit. Major Merritt, commanding the Niagara dragoons, accompanied me, and gave me much assistance with part of his corps. Captain A. Hamilton, belonging to it, was disabled from riding, and attached himself to the guns under Captain Holcroft, who speaks highly of his activity and usefulness. I beg leave to add, that volunteers Shaw, Thomson, and Jarvis, attached to the flank companies of the Forty-ninth regiment, conducted themselves with great spirit; the first was wounded, the last taken prisoner: I beg leave to recommend these young men to your Excellency's notice. Norton is wounded, but not badly: he and the Indians particularly distinguished themselves, and I have very great satisfaction in assuring your Excellency that the spirit and good conduct of His Majesty's troops, of the militia, and of the other provincial corps, were eminently conspicuous on this occasion. I have not been able to ascertain yet the number of our troops, or of those of the enemy engaged. Ours, I believe, did not exceed the number of the prisoners we have taken; and their advance, which effected a landing, probably amounted to thirteen or fourteen hundred. I shall do myself the honor of transmitting to your Excellency farther details when I shall have received the several reports of the occurrences which did not pass under my own observation, with the return of the casualties, and those of the killed and wounded, and of the ordnance taken.

I have the honor to be, &c.,

R. H. SHEAFFE, *Major-general.*

To His Excellency Sir GEORGE PREVOST, Bart., &c.

CHAPTER XXXI.

October 18, 1812.

THE CAPTURE OF THE FROLIC.

Among the vessels which had been added to the navy immediately after the close of the Tripolitan war, was the *Wasp*, a fine ship, mounting sixteen thirty-two-pound carronades and two long-twelves.[1] At the opening of the war with Great Britain she was in Europe, and returned home shortly afterwards, when she was refitted; and after a short run of three weeks, and making one capture, she returned to the Delaware.[2]

On the thirteenth of October, 1812, she sailed a second time,[3] steering an east by southerly course, in order to clear the coast and to get into the track of vessels steering to the northward.[4] On the sixteenth she was overtaken by a heavy gale, and lost her jib-boom, with two of her crew, who were on it at the time.[5] On the seventeenth, the storm having abated, she continued on her course; and at half-past eleven o'clock in the night of that day, being then in latitude 37° N., and longitude 65° W., she made several sail, two of them appearing to be large vessels.[6] Not considering it prudent to run too near the strangers, while their character was unknown, the *Wasp* stood from them for some time; when, having reached what was considered a safe distance, she shortened sail and steered, during the remainder of the night, on the same course which the strangers had taken, with the intention of making their acquaintance in the morning, if it could be done prudently.[1]

At daylight (*Sunday, October* 18) the strangers were discovered ahead and to leeward, and the *Wasp* gave chase.[2] She soon discovered that she was closing with a convoy of six sail of armed merchantmen, protected by a sloop of war;[3] and that the evident intention of the latter was to receive the *Wasp* and engage her, while the convoy would have an opportunity to escape.[4]

The stranger was under very little sail,[5]—her mainyard being on her deck, where it was undergoing some repairs,[6]—and as she appeared desirous to cover her convoy, but little manœuvring was necessary to bring the vessels alongside

---

[1] Cooper's Naval Hist., ii. p. 63; James' Naval Occur., p. 149.—[2] Cooper, ii. p. 63; Analectic Magazine, ii. p. 79.

[3] Capt. Jones to Sec. of Navy, Nov. 24, 1812; Analectic Magazine, ii. p. 79; Clark's Naval History, p. 139.

[4] Cooper, ii. p. 63.—[5] Capt. Jones to Sec. of Navy, Nov. 24, 1812; Cooper, ii. p. 63.—[6] Capt. Jones to Sec. of Navy, Nov. 24, 1812; Clark, p. 139. Capt. Whinyates (*Dispatch*, Oct. 23) says 36° N. lat., and 64° W. long.

[1] Capt. Jones to Sec. of Navy, Nov. 24; Cooper, ii. p. 63; Breckenridge's Hist. of War, p. 50.—[2] Capt. Jones to Sec. of Navy, Nov. 24; Clark, p. 140.—[3] Capt. Jones to Sec. of Navy, Nov. 24; James' Naval Occur., p. 140; Cooper, ii. p. 63.—[4] Capt. Whinyates' Dispatch, Oct. 23; James' Naval Occur., p. 140; Perkins' Hist. of War, p. 123.—[5] Cooper, ii. p. 63.

[6] Capt. Whinyates' Dispatch, Oct. 23.

of each other.[1] The *Wasp*, therefore, sent down her top-gallant yards, close-reefed her topsails, and slowly came up with her opponent, under short, fighting canvas.[2]

At half-past eleven o'clock, when the *Wasp* had come within fifty or sixty yards of the enemy, the latter opened her fire.[3] Slowly and steadily she ranged close up on the starboard side of the stranger;[4] and slowly, but surely, she returned her fire.[5] So much more rapidly, indeed, did the enemy fire than the crew of the *Wasp*, that it is said the former fired three guns to two of the latter;[6] yet as the sea was rolling heavily, and the enemy fired while on the crest of the waves, the tops of the *Wasp* suffered more than her hull; while the stranger received the fire of the *Wasp* from the trough of the sea, and her hull, more than her tops, suffered in consequence.[7]

The action had continued only five or six minutes when the main-topmast of the *Wasp* was shot away;[8] and as the wreck fell across the larboard fore and fore-topsail braces, her head-yards were rendered unmanageable during the remainder of the action.[9] In two or three minutes more the gaff and mizzen-topgallant-mast of the *Wasp* were also shot away;[1] and within ten or twelve minutes more every brace and nearly all her rigging were cut to pieces.[2] Thus crippled, by the loss of her main-topsails, her mizzen-topgallant-sails, and her gaff, and by the immovable condition of her head-yards, the *Wasp* slowly closed on her enemy until her bends rubbed against the stranger's bows.[3] Immediately afterwards the former was so far warped across the bows of the latter, that the stranger's bowsprit entered between the main and mizzen masts of the *Wasp*, forcing the bows of the latter up into the wind, and enabling her to throw in a close and raking fire.[4]

Perceiving the advantage which this unexpected good fortune had thrown into his hands, Captain Jones determined to defer boarding until he had thrown in another raking broadside.[5] So near were the ships, at this time, that the crew of the *Wasp* struck the side of the stranger with their rammers while they were engaged in loading their guns;[6] and the havoc which was made in the crew of the latter was terrible in the extreme.[7] Fortunately, for the cause of humanity, the crew of the *Wasp* thirsted for victory and prize-

---

1 Cooper, ii. p. 64; Headley's Hist. of War, i. p. 156.

2 Cooper, ii. p. 64; Analectic Mag., ii. p. 80; Clark, p. 140.—3 Capt. Jones' Dispatch, Nov. 24. Capt. Whinyates (*Dispatch, Oct.* 23) says the action began "*about ten o'clock.*" Mr. Cooper (*Naval Hist.*, ii. p. 64) says it began "at 32 minutes past 11 A. M.;" in which the editor of the *Analectic Magazine* (ii. p. 80) concurs.

4 Capt. Jones' Dispatch, Nov. 24; Cooper, ii. p. 64.

5 Cooper, ii. p. 64; Sketches of the War, p. 107.

6 Cooper, ii. p. 64; Clark, p. 140.—7 Analectic Mag., ii. p. 80; Breckenridge, p. 51.—8 Capt. Jones' Dispatch, Nov. 24. Capt. Whinyates (*Dispatch, Oct.* 23) says it was the *fore topmast.*—9 Capt. Jones' Dispatch, Nov. 24; Cooper, ii. p. 64; Analectic Magazine, ii. p. 80; Clark, p. 140.

1 Capt. Jones' Dispatch, Nov. 24; Clark, p. 140.

2 Capt. Jones' Dispatch, Nov. 24; Clark, pp. 140, 141.

3 Cooper, ii. p. 64; Clark, p. 141; Davis' Hist. of War, p. 263; Sketches of the War, p. 107.—4 Capt. Whinyate's Dispatch, Oct. 23, 1812; James' Naval Occur., p. 141; Cooper, ii. p. 64; Analectic Mag., ii. p. 80; Clark, p. 141.

5 Cooper, ii. p. 64; Analectic Mag., ii. p. 80; Clark, p. 140.—6 Capt. Jones' Dispatch, Nov. 24, 1812; Analectic Mag., ii. p. 80.—7 Cooper, ii. p. 64; Analectic Mag., ii. p. 81; Clark, p. 141.

money more than for blood; and, at this moment, casting off some portion of the restraint which is so characteristic of the sailor,[1] they sprang on board the stranger,[2]—which was, morally, a prize already,—and were *followed* by Lieutenants Biddle and G. Rodgers, as quickly as possible.[3] *There was no enemy to oppose them, however*,[4] the man at the wheel and two or three wounded officers, on the quarter-deck, alone appearing.[5] The decks were covered with the dead and wounded; and every man who was able to do so, with the exception of the old seaman at the wheel, had ran below, to escape from the terrible raking fire of the *Wasp*.[6]

The officers having thrown down their swords, in token of submission, and no person, belonging to the enemy, being able to do so, Lieutenant Biddle struck the colors of the stranger with his own hands;[7] and the prize passed into the hands of the victors, after an action of forty-three minutes.[8] She proved to be His Britannic Majesty's brig *Frolic*, Captain T. Whinyates, commander;[9] mounting sixteen thirty-two-pound carronades, four long-twelves, and two twelve-pound carronades on

[1] Cooper, ii. p. 64; Clark, p. 141; Davis' Hist. of War, p. 263; Sketches of the War, p. 107.—[2] Capt. Whinyates' Dispatch, Oct. 23, 1812; Cooper, ii. p. 64.

[3] Cooper, ii. p. 64; Clark, p. 141; Headley's History of War, i. pp. 157, 158.—[4] James' Naval Occur., p. 141; Cooper, ii. p. 64; Clark, p. 141; Perkins, p. 123.

[5] Cooper, ii. p. 64; Analectic Mag., ii. p 81; Breckenridge, p. 51; Clark, p. 141; Perkins, p. 123; Auchinleck's History of War, p. 71.

[6] Cooper, ii. p. 64; Clark, p. 141; Perkins, p 123.

[7] James' Naval Occurrences, p. 141; Cooper, ii. p. 64; Breckenridge, p. 51; Perkins, p. 123.

[8] Capt. Jones' Dispatch, Nov. 24; Cooper, ii. p. 64; Breckenridge, p. 51.

[9] Capt. Whinyates' Dispatch, Oct. 23, 1812.

her forecastle;[1] and manned with a crew of one hundred and ten men and boys.[2] She was convoying the Honduras fleet, and by her disinterested course secured the escape of her convoy, although at the loss of herself and her crew.[3]

The *Wasp* was severely wounded in her masts and rigging, as has been already stated;[4] and she lost five of her crew, *killed*, and five *wounded*.[5] The *Frolic* had scarcely passed into the hands of the victors before both her masts went over;[6] while her hull had been so completely riddled that she was a complete wreck.[7] The loss of men which she sustained was very great, although the exact number was never ascertained.[8] As Captain Whinyates reported to his government that "every individual officer was wounded, and the greater part of his men either killed or wounded, there not being twenty persons remaining unhurt,"[9] the aggregate loss could not have been less than a hundred.[10]

[1] Capt. Jones to Sec. of Navy, Nov. 24, 1812; Analectic Mag., ii. p. 82. Lieut. Biddle (*Letter to his father, Oct.* 21) says she mounted "eighteen thirty-two-pound carronades and two long-nines;" while Mr. James (*Naval Occur.*, p. 148) says her "real force was sixteen thirty-two-pound carronades, two long-sixes, and a twelve-pound boat-carronade."—[2] James' Naval Occurrences, p. 149.

[3] Capt. Whinyates' Dispatch, Oct. 23, 1812; James' Naval Occurrences, p. 140.—[4] Vide p. 169, notes 8, 1, 2, 3.

[5] Capt. Jones' Dispatch, Nov. 24, 1812; Breckenridge, p. 52.—[6] James' Naval Occur., i. p. 147; Clark, p. 142.

[7] Cooper, ii. p. 65.—[8] Capt. Jones' Dispatch, Nov. 24; O'Connor's History of War, p. 62.

[9] Capt. Whinyates' Dispatch, Oct. 23, 1812. Mr. James (*Naval Occur.*, p. 147) very adroitly attempts to evade the force of this sentence by saying, "Not above twenty men remained *on the Frolic's deck unhurt;* the remainder were below, attending the wounded and performing other duties there."—[10] If the crew was no greater than 110 the loss would have been *ninety*. See also Headley, i. p. 158.

The victory had scarcely been secured when a large ship was seen standing towards the *Wasp* and her prize, neither of which were in a condition either to renew an action or to escape, and it soon appeared that she, too, was an enemy.[1] A shot from His Britannic Majesty's ship *Poictiers*, of seventy-four guns, was the earnest of disaster; and, as she ranged alongside the little *Wasp*, within two hours of the capture of the *Frolic*, her gallant captain surrendered, with his prize, without attempting an opposition.[2]

The intelligence of this victory, between vessels so nearly equal in force, was received with the greatest satisfaction in America; while in Europe the subject was not lost sight of, even in those times of blood and contention. The Congress of the United States voted twenty-five thousand dollars as a compensation to the crew for its loss of prize-money;[1] Captain Jones was promoted to the command of the *Macedonian*—a prize which had been taken while he had been a prisoner;[2] and Lieutenant Biddle was also promoted, as a mark of the respect which the country entertained for his gallantry.[3]

DOCUMENTS.

I.

CAPTAIN JONES' DISPATCH TO THE SECRETARY OF THE NAVY.

NEW YORK, *November* 24, 1812.

SIR:—I here avail myself of the first opportunity of informing you of the occurrences of our cruise, which terminated in the capture of the *Wasp*, on the 18th of October, by the *Poictiers*, of seventy-four guns, while a wreck, from damages received in an engagement with the British sloop of war *Frolic*, of twenty-two guns, sixteen of them thirty-two-pound carronades, and four twelve-pounders on the main-deck, and two twelve-pounders, carronades, on the top-gallant-forecastle, making her superior in force to us by four twelve-pounders. The *Frolic* had struck to us, and was taken possession of about two hours before our surrendering to the *Poictiers*.

We had left the Delaware on the 13th; the 16th, had a heavy gale, in which we lost our jib-boom and two men. Half-past eleven, on the night of the seventeenth, in latitude 37° N., and longitude 65° W., we saw several sail, two of them apparently very large. We stood from them some time, then shortened sail, and steered the remainder of the night the course we had perceived them on. At daylight, on Sunday the 18th, we saw them ahead; gave chase, and soon discovered them to be a convoy of six sail, under the protection of a sloop of war; four of them large ships, mounting from sixteen to eighteen guns. At thirty-two minutes past eleven A. M., we engaged the sloop of war, having first received her fire, at the distance of fifty or sixty yards, which space we gradually lessened, until we laid her on board, after a well-supported fire of forty-three minutes; and although so near, while loading the last broadside, that our rammers were shoved against the sides of the enemy, our men exhibited the same alacrity which they had done during the whole of the action. They immediately surrendered, upon our gaining the forecastle, so that no loss was sustained on either side, after the boarding.

Our main-topmast was shot away between

[1] Cooper, ii. p. 65; Clark, p. 142.

[2] Capt. Jones' Dispatch, Nov. 24, 1812; Capt. Whinyates' Dispatch, Oct. 23, 1812; Lieut. Biddle to his father, Oct. 21, 1812.

[1] Journals of Congress.—[2] Cooper, ii. p. 67; Clark, p. 144.—[3] Ibid.

four and five minutes from the commencement of the firing, and falling, together with the main-topsail yard, across the larboard fore and fore-topsail braces, rendered our head-yards unmanageable the remainder of the action. At eight minutes the gaff and mizzen-topgallant-mast came down, and at twenty minutes from the beginning of the action, every brace and most of the rigging was shot away. A few minutes after separating from the *Frolic*, both her masts fell upon deck; the mainmast going close by the deck, and the foremast twelve or fifteen feet above it.

The courage and exertion of the officers and crew fully answered my expectations and wishes. Lieutenant Biddle's active conduct contributed much to our success, by the exact attention paid to every department during the engagement, and the animating example he afforded the crew by his intrepidity. Lieutenants Rodgers, Booth, and Mr. Rapp, showed, by the incessant fire from their divisions, that they were not to be surpassed in resolution or skill. Mr. Knight, and every other officer, acted with a courage and promptitude highly honorable, and, I trust, have given assurance that they may be relied on whenever their services may be required.

I could not ascertain the exact loss of the enemy, as many of the dead lay buried under the masts and spars that had fallen upon deck, which two hours' exertion had not sufficiently removed. Mr. Biddle, who had charge of the *Frolic*, states, that from what he heard said, and from information from the officers, the number killed must have been about thirty, and that of the wounded about forty and fifty. Of the killed is her first lieutenant and sailing-master; of the wounded, Captain Whinyates and the second lieutenant.

We had five killed and five wounded, as per list. The wounded are recovering. Lieutenant Claxton, who was confined by sickness, left his bed a little previous to the engagement, and though too indisposed to be at his division, remained upon deck, and showed by his composed manner of noticing its incidents, that we had lost, by his illness, the services of a brave officer.

I am, respectfully, yours, &c.,

Jacob Jones.

Hon. Paul Hamilton, Secretary of the Navy.

II.

CAPTAIN WHINYATES' DISPATCH TO ADMIRAL WARREN.

H. M. Ship Poictiers, at Sea,
October 23, 1812.

Sir:—It is with the most bitter sorrow and distress, I have to report to your Excellency the capture of His Majesty's brig *Frolic* by the ship *Wasp*, belonging to the United States of America, on the 18th instant.

Having under convoy the homeward-bound trade from the Bay of Honduras, and being in latitude 36° N., and 64° W., on the night of the 17th, we were overtaken by a most violent gale of wind, in which the *Frolic* carried away her main-yard, lost her topsails, and sprung the main-topmast. On the morning of the 18th, as we were repairing the damages sustained in the storm, and reassembling the scattered ships, a suspicious ship came in sight, and gave chase to the convoy.

The merchant ships continued their voyage before the wind, under all sail. The *Frolic* dropped astern, and hoisted Spanish colors, in order to decoy the stranger under her guns, and to give time for the convoy to escape. About ten o'clock, both vessels being within hail, we hauled to the wind, and the battle began. The superior fire of our guns gave every reason to expect its speedy termination in our favor; but the gaff-head braces being shot away, and there being no sail on the mainmast, the brig became unmanageable, and the enemy succeeded in taking a position to rake her, while she was unable to bring a gun to bear.

After lying sometime exposed to a most destructive fire, she fell with her bowsprit between the enemy's main and mizzen rigging, still unable to return his fire.

At length the enemy boarded, and made himself master of the brig, every individual officer being wounded, and the greater part of the men either killed or wounded, there not being twenty persons remaining unhurt.

Although I shall ever deplore the unhappy issue of this contest, it would be great injustice to the merits of the officers and crew if I failed to report that their bravery and coolness are deserving of every praise; and I am convinced, if the *Frolic* had not been crippled in the gale, I should have had to make a very different report to your Excellency. The *Wasp* was taken, and the *Frolic* recaptured the same evening by His Majesty's ship the *Poictiers*. Being separated from them, I cannot transmit, at present, a list of killed and wounded. Mr. Charles McKay, the first-lieutenant, and Mr. Stephens, the master, have died of their wounds.

I have the honor to be, &c.,

T. WHINYATES.

To the Right Hon. Sir J. B. WARREN, Bart., &c.

CHAPTER XXXII.

October 23, 1812.[1]

THE AFFAIR AT ST. REGIS.

"ON a beautiful and elevated point which juts into the St. Lawrence, where that river is crossed by the forty-fifth parallel of latitude, and between the mouths of the St. Regis and Racquette rivers, stands a dilapidated and antique-looking village, whose massive and venerable church, with tin-covered spire, whose narrow and filthy streets, and the general appearance of indolence and poverty of its inhabitants, and especially the accents of an unaccustomed language, almost convey to the casual visitor an impression that he is in a foreign land."[2]

Such is the Indian village of *Ak-wis-sas-ne*, or St. Regis—the home of one branch of the Caughnawaga Indians—in the extreme northeastern extremity of the State of New York, and, to some extent, in the neighboring province of Canada East. The peculiar position of the inhabitants induced the belligerent nations, at the opening of the war between the United States and Great Britain, in 1812, to agree with each other that this should be neutral ground, and that the inhabitants should not be employed by either party in the approaching contest.[1] Early in the fall of that year, however, in violation of the provisions of this agreement, Captain McDonnell,[2] with a company of Canadian voyageurs, occupied the village;[3] and attempted to induce the inhabitants to join the British standard.[4] At the same time a detachment of New York militia, mostly from the village of Troy, commanded by Major Guilford D. Young, of that place, was occupying French Mills, on the St. Regis River;[5] and when the movement of

[1] The date of this transaction has been variously stated. I have followed Maj. Young's Dispatch, preferring that to the statements of Messrs. Davis, James, and Auchinleck, who assign to it the *twenty-first;* or to those of Messrs. O'Connor, Ingersoll, and the editor of "*The War*," who say it occurred on the *twenty-second*.

[2] Hough's History of St. Lawrence Co., p. 110.

[1] Hough, p. 156.—[2] Adj.-Gen. Baynes' instructions to Capt. McDonnell, "*Montreal, Oct.* 16, 1812;" James' Mil. Occur., i. p. 106; Auchinleck's Hist. of War, i. p. 117. Mr. Hough (*Hist. St. Lawrence*, p. 156) supposes *Capt. Montigny* commanded the voyageurs.—[3] Christie's Mil. and Naval Operations, p. 88; James' Mil. Occur., i. p. 106; Hough's St. Lawrence Co., p. 156.—[4] Thomson's Sketches of the War, p. 78; Adj.-Gen. Baynes to Capt. McDonnell, Oct. 16, 1812.—[5] Davis' History of the War, p. 47; Thomson, p. 78; O'Connor's History of the War, p. 59.

the enemy on St. Regis became known to him he resolved to attack him.[1]

With this object, early in October, Major Young had marched through the woods, under the guidance of William Gray, the interpreter of the Caughnawagas, but when he reached the bank of the river, opposite St. Regis, he found no means for crossing, and was compelled to return.[2]

After remaining at French Mills a few days, in order that the alarm which his former visit had excited might subside, and causing the enemy's position to be reconnoitred by "several confidential friends," he prepared to renew the attempt. For this purpose, at eleven o'clock in the evening of the twenty-second of October, 1812, he moved, with his command, crossing the river in a boat and a canoe, and on a raft of lumber, at Gray's Mills (*Hogansburg, St. Lawrence County, N. Y.*), and reached the outskirts of the village, without attracting the notice of the enemy, at five o'clock the next morning.[3]

Being concealed from the enemy by a small "rise of ground," Major Young halted his troops for the purpose of reconnoitring, of taking refreshments, and of making dispositions for the attack. The enemy was quartered in two houses—one belonging to Captain Montigny, the British agent, the other to a Mr. Donnelly—and against these Major Young moved with considerable caution and skill. Captain Lyon (editor

[1] Davis, p. 47; "*The War*," i. p. 90.—[2] Hough's St. Lawrence Co., pp. 156, 157.—[3] Maj. Young's Dispatch, Oct. 24; Davis, p. 47; O'Connor, pp. 59, 60; "*The War*," i. p. 90.

of the Troy "*Northern Budget*") and his company were detached from the right, with orders to march by the road on the bank of the St. Regis River and gain the rear of Captain Montigny's house; while Captain Tilden, with his company, were detached from the left, with orders to move along the bank of the St. Lawrence River, to gain the rear of Mr. Donnelly's house, to secure the enemy's boats, and to cut off his retreat. At the appointed time, Major Young, with Captain Higbie's and McNeil's companies, moved against the front of the enemy's position; and when he had arrived within a hundred and fifty yards of Captain Montigny's house, the fire of Captain Lyon's company, in its rear, indicated that the latter had reached his position and engaged the enemy. At that instant an ensign of the enemy, in attempting to escape from the house, in front, attracted the fire of Captain Higbie's first platoon; when the enemy, finding himself surrounded, surrendered without offering any resistance.[1]

The fruit of this well-conducted little affair was forty prisoners, with their arms, a stand of colors, two batteaux, a quantity of baggage and stores,[2] among which were eight hundred blankets, which had been sent by Sir George Prevost as subsidies to the Indians.[3] Of the Americans, not a man was hurt;[4]

[1] Maj. Young's Dispatch, Oct. 24; Thomson's Sketches, p. 78; O'Connor, p. 60; "*The War*," i. p. 90; Hough, p. 157.—[2] Maj. Young's Dispatch, Oct. 24; Niles' Register, iii. p. 171; Thomson's Sketches, p. 78; O'Connor, p. 60; James' Mil. Occur., i. p. 106; Ingersoll's Hist. of War, i. p. 98.—[3] Niles' Register, iii. p. 171.

[4] Maj. Young's Dispatch, Oct. 24; O'Connor, p. 60; "*The War*," i. p. 90; Hough, p. 157.

of the enemy, Lieutenant Rottotte, Sergeant McGillivray, and six men were killed.[1]

The Americans, after securing the trophies of their victory, recrossed the St. Regis River at the village; and, with their prisoners and spoils, reached the camp at eleven o'clock the same morning.[2]

It is an interesting fact—on which much of the interest which attaches to this affair depends—that the flag which was captured at St. Regis, on this occasion, was the *first flag which had been taken*, by the land-forces of the United States, during the war;[1] and that the captor of that interesting trophy was Lieutenant William L. Marcy, then a young man, residing in Troy, afterwards one of the most accomplished statesmen of his time, and head of the Department of War during the war with Mexico.[2]

[NOTE.—The Dispatch of Maj. Young to Gen. Bloomfield, which had been provided for the illustration of this chapter, has been omitted by the Publishers for want of room.]

CHAPTER XXXIII.

October 25, 1812.

THE CAPTURE OF THE MACEDONIAN.

HAVING refitted his squadron, on the eighth of October, 1812, Commodore Rodgers sailed from Boston, with the *President*, bearing his own flag; the *United States*, commanded by Captain Stephen Decatur; the *Congress*, commanded by Captain Smith; and the *Argus*, Lieutenant-commandant Sinclair.[3] On the twelfth, after cruising without meeting any thing, the *United States* and the *Argus* parted company with the Commodore, and each was left alone to follow her fortunes.[4]

Captain Decatur resolved to cruise on the track of the British East Indiamen; and, with that object, he stood to the southward and eastward,[3] until, on Sunday, the twenty-fifth of October, he neared the island of Madeira.[4] On the same day, while cruising in latitude 29° N., longitude 29° 30′ W.,[5] Captain Decatur made a large sail to windward—the former running towards the latter, who was standing to the northwest, under a heavy press of sail.[6]

Having come within a league, the stranger hauled up, and passed to wind-

[1] Christie, p. 88. Maj. Young supposes that *five*, only, fell; but Mr. Christie being a Canadian authority, I have followed him.—[2] Maj. Young's Dispatch, Oct. 24; Thomson's Sketches, p. 78; Hough, p. 157.

[3] McKenzie's Life of Decatur (*Sparks' American Biog.*, xxi.), p. 170; Cooper's Naval Hist., (*Ed.* 1856), ii. p. 60.

[4] McKenzie, p. 170; Sketches of the War, p. 113.

[1] Christie, p. 88; O'Connor, p. 60; James' Mil. Occur., i. p. 107; Ingersoll's War, i. p. 98; Auchinleck, p. 117.

[2] Ingersoll, i. p. 98; Hough, p. 157.

[3] Cooper, ii. p. 61; McKenzie, p. 170.—[4] McKenzie, p. 170.—[5] Capt. Decatur to Sec. of Navy, Oct. 30; Capt. Carden to the Admiralty, Oct. 28; Cooper, ii. p. 61; Naval Chronicle, xxviii. p. 507.—[6] Capt. Decatur to Sec. of Navy, Oct. 30, 1812; Capt. Carden to the Admiralty, Oct. 28, 1812; Cooper, ii. p. 61.

ward; but, immediately afterwards, she wore, and came round on the same tack with the *United States*, hauled up on an easy bowline, with her mizzen-topsail aback; and, at the distance of about a mile, soon after nine o'clock, she opened her fire.[1] Captain Decatur, perceiving her design, delivered his larboard broadside, wore round, and came up to the wind on the other tack, heading northerly.[2] As he passed the stranger he delivered his starboard broadside, and wore a second time, bringing the *United States* on the same tack as the stranger; when both vessels, with their mizzen-topsails aback, steered the same course and continued the action.[3]

The fire of the *United States* told fearfully on the stranger; while that of the latter did but little injury on the former; until half an hour after the commencement of the action, when the mizzen-topmast and gaff were shot away, and the stranger bore up for closer action.[4] But then, even more than before, the splendid gunnery of the American crew was fully displayed; and it was not long before the mizzen-mast of the stranger came over her lee-quarter.[5] Soon afterwards her fore and main topmasts went over her side, her mainyard was cut away in the slings, her foremast was tottering, and her bowsprit and mainmast were badly wounded; while the *United States* was, comparatively, uninjured.[6] Perceiving that the stranger was no longer capable of an effectual resistance, Captain Decatur

[1] Capt. Carden to the Admiralty, Oct. 28; Cooper, ii. p. 61; McKenzie, p. 172.—[2] Cooper, ii. p. 61.—[3] Ibid.
[4] McKenzie, p. 173; New London "*Gazette*," Dec. 5, 1812.
[5] Cooper, ii. p 61; McKenzie, p. 173.—[6] Ibid.

now filled his mizzen-topsail, gathered fresh way, and tacked.[1]

It is said the stranger supposed the *United States* was preparing to run away when she filled her mizzen-topsail; and that her crew saluted the supposed fugitive with three cheers: but when they witnessed the manœuvre which was intended by Captain Decatur, and knew that the object was to close with them, for more effectual action, they struck their colors and surrendered,[2] an hour and a half after the opening of the engagement.[3]

As the *United States* crossed the stern of the stranger, she hailed and demanded the name of her opponent, when it appeared that she was His Britannic Majesty's frigate *Macedonian*, of thirty-eight guns, commanded by Captain John S. Carden, and that she had struck her colors.[4] She was found to have suffered very severely—in Captain Carden's own words,[5] "the mizzen-mast having been shot away by the board; topmasts shot away by the caps; main-yard shot in pieces; a small proportion only of the foresail left on the foreyard; all the guns on the quarter-deck and forecastle disabled but two, and filled with wreck; two guns on the main-deck disabled; several shot between wind and water; and a very great proportion of the crew killed and wounded."

In this well-conducted engagement

[1] Cooper, ii. p. 61.—[2] Ibid.; Headley's History of War, i. p. 153.—[3] Capt. Decatur to Secretary of Navy, Oct. 30. Capt. Carden says they fought *two hours and ten minutes*.
[4] Cooper, ii. p. 61.—[5] Capt. Carden to the Admiralty. See also Capt. Decatur to Secretary of Navy, Oct. 30; Auchinleck's History of War, p. 71; Clark's Naval History, p. 157.

Painted by Chappel. Engraved by Duthie.

BATTLE BETWEEN THE UNITED STATES AND THE MACEDONIAN.

From the original Picture in the possession of the Publishers.

the strength of the opposing ships was nearly equal—the *United States* mounting thirty long twenty-fours on her main-deck, and twenty-two forty-two pound carronades and two long twenty-fours on her quarter-deck and forecastle;[1] and was manned with a crew of four hundred and seventy-eight men:[2] while the *Macedonian* mounted twenty-eight long eighteen-pounders on her gun-deck, and eighteen thirty-two-pound carronades, one twelve-pound carronade, and two brass nine-pounders on her quarter-deck and forecastle;[3] while her crew numbered three hundred souls.[4] She was a new ship, of the first class, and had, only a short time before, left the dock-yard, where she had been put in complete order.[5]

The loss of the *United States* was five men *killed*, and Lieutenant John M. Funk and six men *wounded*, of whom Lieutenant Funk and one man died soon afterwards.[6] The loss of the *Macedonian* was her master's-mate, schoolmaster, boatswain, and twenty-five seamen, and one sergeant, and seven marines, *killed;* Lieutenant Hope, one midshipman, twenty-nine seamen, and five marines, *severely wounded*—of whom

[1] McKenzie, p. 171.—[2] James' Naval Occurrences, pp. 160, 161.—[3] Ibid., p. 158; Capt. Decatur to Sec. of Navy, Oct. 30; Clark, p. 157.—[4] James' Naval Occurrences, p. 159.—[5] Capt. Decatur to Secretary of Navy, Oct. 30; Memoir of Decatur, in *Analectic Magazine*, i. p. 463; McKenzie, p. 170.—[6] Capt. Decatur to Secretary of Navy, Oct. 30; Cooper, ii. p. 62.

the greater portion subsequently died; and Lieutenant Bulford, one master's-mate, twenty-six seamen, and four marines, were *wounded*—making a total loss of one hundred and four men in the crew of the *Macedonian*.[1]

Having carried his prize into Newport, and the *United States* into New London,[2] Captain Decatur received the highest honors from every part of the country. Congress voted its thanks and a gold medal; the States of Virginia and Pennsylvania their thanks and swords of honor; the States of Massachusetts, New York, and Maryland, their thanks; the city of Philadelphia a sword of honor; the city of New York its freedom;[3] while the people, from one extreme of the confederacy to the other, from that time to the present, have not ceased to honor him. On the other side, the people of Great Britain were deeply agitated on the subject; and, especially among the officers of the navy, were the causes and remedies of these repeated misfortunes made the subject of an extended, anxious, and protracted discussion.[4]

[1] Capt. Carden to the Admiralty, Oct. 28; Cooper, ii. p. 62; Naval Chronicle, xxviii. p. 507.

[2] Cooper, ii. p. 62; "*The War*," i. p. 107.

[3] Clark, pp. 158, 159.

[4] Vide letters signed, "*Æolus*," "*An Iron Gun of a large Calibre*," "*Albion*," "*An Englishman*," "*Faber*," "*Noah*," "*Arion*," "*J. C.*," "*Albion*," "*William Henry Tremlett*, Capt. R. N.," "*Naval Patriot*," "*M.*," "*Impartial*," "*An half-pay Officer*," &c., in the *Naval Chronicle*, vol. xxix., beside others in the succeeding volumes of that work.

DOCUMENTS.

I.

COMMODORE DECATUR'S DISPATCH TO THE SECRETARY OF THE NAVY.

U. S. SHIP UNITED STATES, AT SEA,
October 30, 1812.

SIR:—I have the honor to inform you, that on the 25th instant, being in the latitude 29° N., longitude 29° 30′ W., we fell in with, and after an action of an hour and a half, captured His Britannic Majesty's ship *Macedonian*, commanded by Captain John Carden, and mounting forty-nine carriage-guns (the odd gun shifting). She is a frigate of the largest class, two years old, four months out of dock, and reputed one of the best sailers in the British service. The enemy being to windward, had the advantage of engaging us at his own distance, which was so great, that for the first half hour we did not use our carronades, and at no moment was he within the complete effect of our musketry or grape—to this circumstance, and a heavy swell, which was on at the time, I ascribe the unusual length of the action.

The enthusiasm of every officer, seaman, and marine on board this ship, on discovering the enemy—their steady conduct in battle, and precision of their fire, could not be surpassed. Where all met my fullest expectations, it would be unjust for me to discriminate. Permit me, however, to recommend to your particular notice my first-lieutenant, William H. Allen. He has served with me upwards of five years, and to his unremitted exertions in disciplining the crew, is to be imputed the obvious superiority of our gunnery, exhibited in the result of this contest.

Subjoined is a list of the killed and wounded on both sides. Our loss, compared with that of the enemy, will appear small. Among our wounded you will observe the name of Lieutenant Funk, who died in a few hours after the action. He was an officer of great gallantry and promise, and the service has sustained a severe loss in his death.

The *Macedonian* lost her mizzen-mast, fore and main topmasts, and mainyard, and was much cut up in her hull. The damage sustained by this ship was not such as to render her return into port necessary, and had I not deemed it important that we should see our prize in, should have continued our cruise.

With the highest consideration,

I am yours, &c.,

STEPHEN DECATUR.

The Hon. PAUL HAMILTON.

II.

CAPTAIN CARDEN'S DISPATCH TO THE ADMIRALTY.

U. S. SHIP UNITED STATES, AT SEA,
October 28, 1812.

SIR:—It is with the deepest regret I have to acquaint you, for the information of my Lords Commissioners of the Admiralty, that His Majesty's late ship *Macedonian* was captured on the 25th instant, by the United States ship *United States*, Commodore Decatur commander. The detail is as follows:

A short time after daylight, steering N. W. by W., with the wind from the southward, in latitude 29° N., and longitude 29° 30′ W., in the execution of their lordships' orders, a sail was seen on the lee-beam, which I immediately stood for, and made her out to be a large frigate, under American colors. At nine o'clock I closed with her, and she commenced the action, which we returned; but, from the enemy keeping two points off the wind, I was not enabled to get as close to her as I could have wished. After an hour's action the enemy backed, and came to the wind, and I was then enabled to bring her to close battle. In this situation I soon found the enemy's force too superior to expect success, unless some very fortunate chance occurred in our favor, and with this hope I continued the battle to two hours and ten minutes; when, having the mizzen-mast shot away by the board, topmasts shot away by the caps, main-yard shot in pieces, lower masts badly wounded, lowering rigging all cut to pieces, a small proportion only of the foresail left to the fore-yard, all the guns on the quarter-deck and forecastle disabled, but two, and filled with wreck, two also on the main-deck disabled, and several shot between wind and water, a very great proportion of the crew killed and wounded, and the enemy comparatively in good order, who had now shot ahead, and was about to place himself in a raking position, without our being enabled to return the fire; being a perfect wreck, and unmanageable log, I deemed it prudent, though a painful extremity, to surrender His Majesty's ship; nor was this dreadful alternative resorted to, till every hope of success was removed, even beyond the reach of chance, nor till, I trust their lordships will be aware, every effort had been made against the enemy by myself, my brave officers, and men; nor should she have been surrendered while a man lived on board, had she been manageable. I am sorry to say our loss is very severe; I find, by this day's muster, thirty-six killed, three of whom lingered a short time after the battle; thirty-six severely wounded, many of whom cannot recover; and thirty-two slightly wounded, who may all do well: total, one hundred and four.

The truly noble and animating conduct of my officers, and the steady bravery of my crew to the last moment of the battle, must ever render them dear to their country.

My first-lieutenant, David Hope, was severely wounded in the head, towards the close of the battle, and taken below, but was soon again on deck, displaying that greatness of mind and exertion, which, though it may be equalled, can never be excelled. The third-lieutenant, John Balford, was also wounded, but not obliged to quit his quarters; Second-lieutenant Samuel Mottley, and he, deserve my highest acknowledgments. The cool and steady conduct of Mr. Walker, the master, was very great during the battle; as also that of Lieutenants Wilson and Magill of the Marines. On being taken on board the enemy's ship, I ceased to wonder at the result of the battle. The *United States* is built with the scantling of a seventy-four-gun ship, mounting thirty long twenty-four-pounders (English ship-guns) on her main-deck, and twenty-two forty-two-pound carronades, with two long twenty-four-pounders on her quarter-deck and forecastle, howitzer-guns in her tops, and a travelling carronade on her upper deck, with a complement of four hundred and seventy-eight picked men.

The enemy has suffered much in masts, rigging, and hull, above and below water. Her loss in killed and wounded I am not aware of, but I know a lieutenant and six men have been thrown overboard.

Inclosed you will be pleased to receive the names of the killed and wounded on board of the *Macedonian;* and,

I have the honor to be, &c.,

J. S. CARDEN.

JOHN WILLIAM CROKER, Esq.

List of officers and men killed and wounded on board His Majesty's ship Macedonian, &c. (of which the names are given, comprising):

Killed.—One master's-mate, the schoolmaster, boatswain, twenty-three petty officers and seamen, two boys, one sergeant, and seven privates of marines—total, thirty-six.

Wounded dangerously.—Seven petty officers and seamen (two since dead). *Severely.*—One lieutenant, one midshipman, eighteen petty officers and seamen, four boys, and five private marines—total, dangerously and severely, thirty-six.

Wounded slightly.—One lieutenant, one master's-mate, twenty-six petty officers and seamen, and four private marines—total, thirty-two.

J. S. CARDEN, *Captain.*

CHAPTER XXXIV.

November 25 to December 18, 1812.[1]

THE EXPEDITION AGAINST THE MISSISSINNEWAY TOWNS.

Reference has been made in several preceding chapters of this volume to the disaffection of the Miamis, whose defeat by General Wayne, in 1794, had not been either forgotten or forgiven. The enmity of this tribe had been marked with the most relentless cruelty; their professions of a desire for peace, made when a body of troops, near their villages, threatened their destruction, had been disregarded when the producing cause was removed; and there appeared no hope of a peaceful conclusion of the troubles.

For these reasons, among others, General Harrison, who commanded in the northwest, detached Colonel Simrall's regiment of dragoons, Major Ball's squadron of cavalry, Captain Elliott's company of the Nineteenth United States infantry, Colonel Alexander's regiment of mounted riflemen, and "The Pittsburg Blues," under Captain Butler—all mounted—about six hundred in all, under the command of Lieutenant-colonel Campbell of the Nineteenth infantry, to visit the villages of this tribe on the Mississinneway, and to punish their inhabitants.[2] The detachment marched from Franklinton on the twenty-fifth of November, by way of Dayton, to Greenville; and on the fourteenth of December, each man carrying ten days' rations, it left the latter place, taking up its line of march for the Indian towns, about eighty miles distant.[1]

The weather was exceedingly cold, and the ground, hard frozen, was covered with snow. On the evening of the third day of the march, when about twenty miles from the villages, a council was called, to determine on a plan of operations; when it was determined to march all night, and to assault the villages early next day. Accordingly the troops formed in order of battle—Colonel Simrall's regiment forming the left column, the infantry the centre, and Major Ball's cavalry the right—and, with proper caution, they approached the villages. An intervening swamp, of which the guides were ignorant, delayed their progress a short time; but it was quickly turned, and the line of march was again renewed.[2]

When within a short distance of the villages a scout of four Indians, mounted, was seen in front—the first evidence of the presence of an enemy—and they were pursued without success. The approach of the column having been dis-

---

[1] From a misprint of the date of Lieut.-Col. Campbell's dispatch, Mr. O'Connor has supposed there were *two* expeditions, and Mr. Breckenridge and Mr. Davis have fallen into the same error.—[2] McAfee's War in the Western Country, p. 178; Perkins' Western Annals, p. 625.

[1] McAfee, p. 178.—[2] Ibid.

covered, it became necessary to hasten the attack, in order to prevent the escape of the savages; and at eight o'clock the detachment charged at full speed, surrounding the nearest village within a few minutes after the disappearance of the scout. The greater part of the villagers, however, had escaped by crossing the river; while of those who had not been able to secure their flight, after a slight resistance, the greater part—embracing forty-two men, women, and children—surrendered. In the attack, seven warriors and two of the assailants were slain.[1]

Having secured the prisoners and burned the village, the dragoons proceeded down the river, three miles, to the village of Silver Heels, which, with two others, was plundered and burned; after which the detachment encamped for repose.[2] The spot selected for the encampment was on the bank of the Mississinneway, on which, forming a square of about two hundred yards front, the troops pitched their tents. The infantry and riflemen occupied the bank of the river; Colonel Simrall's dragoons formed the left and half the rear line; and Major Ball's squadron formed the right and the remainder of the rear. Strong guards were thrown out, with small redoubts at each angle of the encampment, at the distance of sixty yards from it; and beyond these, at the same distance, were placed the line of sentinels.[3]

Every thing remained quiet during the day; and, with the exception of an occasional glimpse of a prowling Indian, the greater part of the succeeding night, also, passed without disturbance. The watchful commander of the expedition did not appear to rest easily under the movements of the savages; and when, at an early hour, a signal fire appeared down the river, the detachment was quietly aroused, and prepared to receive an enemy. The result showed that his caution was well-timed; and when the reveille beat,—two hours before daylight,—and the officers were summoned to a council, at head-quarters, it betokened something serious.[1] Yet all remained quiet until half an hour before day, when a large body of savages suddenly attacked the angle of the encampment where the rear of the right column rested.[2] In a moment the lines were formed, and the assault was repelled with great spirit. Captain Pierce, who commanded the redoubt which covered the point of attack, bravely maintained his ground until he was shot and tomahawked; and, soon afterwards, his command was overpowered and compelled to give way. Captains Garrard and Hopkins, who commanded the companies which were directly attacked, resisted the savages with great firmness; and within a few minutes the entire right column and part of the rear—Major Ball's command—were engaged. The spies and the "Pittsburg Blues" moved promptly to the support of the defence,—taking post on the left of Captain Hopkins,—

[1] Lieut.-Col. John B. Campbell to Gen. W. H. Harrison, Dec. 18, 1812; McAfee, pp. 178, 179; Perkins' Hist. of War, p. 98.—[2] Lieut.-Col. Campbell's Dispatch; McAfee, p. 179; Sketches of the War, p. 158.—[3] McAfee, p. 179.

[1] McAfee, pp. 179, 180.—[2] Lieut.-Col. Campbell's Dispatch; McAfee, p. 180.

and, for nearly an hour, the conflict was continued with great spirit.[1]

At length, soon after daybreak, Captain Trotter, with his troop, moved against the enemy's right flank; while, at the same time, Captain Johnston made a similar movement on his left, the design being to take the Indians in their flanks and rear. This combined movement was beyond the understanding of the enemy; and, notwithstanding the savages strugged manfully, for the victory, a short time, they, at length, yielded and fled in every direction, leaving fifteen of their dead behind them—an evidence, in itself, of the completeness of their rout.

The loss of the detachment was eight killed and forty-eight wounded, several of whom subsequently died.[2]

After dressing the wounds and providing litters for the removal of the wounded, the detachment commenced its return; and as Colonel Campbell learned that Tecumthà, with six hundred warriors, was not far distant, the

[1] McAfee, p. 180; Sketches of the War, p. 158; Breckenridge's History of War, p. 68.

[2] Lieut.-Col. Campbell's Dispatch; McAfee, p. 180; Perkins' History of War, p. 99.

march was conducted with all possible speed. Many of the troops were frost-bitten, however; and this, with the care of the wounded, rendered the progress a slow one, and much distress was experienced. Intrenchments were thrown up every night, and, at the same time, one-third of the detachment was placed on guard—steps which were made necessary by the vigilance of the enemy. With the utmost firmness and gallantry, however, the detachment pushed forward, and when, some days afterwards, it reached Greenville, three hundred of its number were rendered "unfit for duty by frost, sickness, and wounds."[1]

Of the good effects of this expedition the entire West were soon the witnesses. The Delawares and other tribes who had been inclined towards peace, without accepting it, separated from Tecumthà and his party; and the moral strength of the Western alliance was completely broken.[2]

[1] McAfee, p. 181; Perkins' Western Annals, p. 625; Sketches of the War, p. 158.—[2] McAfee, p. 182.

[Note.—Lieut.-Col. Campbell's Dispatch, which was provided for the illustration of this chapter, has been omitted by the Publishers for want of room.]

Painted by Chappel. Engraved by W. Wellstood.

W. Bainbridge

From the original in the possession of the Publishers

Johnson Fry & Co. Publishers, New York.

CHAPTER XXXV.

December 29, 1812.

THE CAPTURE OF THE JAVA.

THE *Constitution*, after her engagement with the *Guerriere*, had been placed under the command of Captain William Bainbridge;[1] and, after having been refitted, she sailed from Boston, in company with the *Hornet*, on the twenty-sixth of October, 1812. After looking into the port of San Salvador, and leaving the *Hornet* before that harbor, to watch a British cruiser which laid at anchor there, Commodore Bainbridge stood to the southward, along the coast of Brazil.[2]

At nine in the morning of the twenty-ninth of December, when in latitude 13° 6′ S., and longitude 38° W., thirty miles from the coast, two strange sails were made.[3] They were inshore and to windward;[4] and as one of them altered her course, with an apparent desire to meet the *Constitution*, the latter, also, tacked to close with her.[5]

It was a pleasant day, the wind being light, from E. N. E., with but little sea;[6] and at eleven o'clock, being satisfied the stranger was an enemy, Commodore Bainbridge tacked again, making to the southward and eastward, for the purpose of drawing her off the land.[1] At a quarter-past twelve both vessels showed their colors, and threw out their signals.[2] At twenty-six minutes past one o'clock, having drawn the stranger a sufficient distance from the shore, the *Constitution* took in her mainsails and royals, tacked, and stood for her;[3] while the stranger, twenty-five minutes afterwards, bore down with an intention of raking, which was prevented by wearing.[4] The stranger having, meanwhile, lowered his ensign, at two o'clock, the Commodore ordered a single gun to be fired ahead of him, to draw it out again, which was successful;[5] when a broadside was delivered from the larboard guns, which was returned from the stranger's starboard guns, and the action commenced with round and grape shot, but at a greater distance than was desirable.[6] At thirty minutes past two the wheel of the *Constitution* was shot away,[7] and as the stranger was

---

[1] Cooper's Naval History, ii. p. 59.—[2] Ibid., p. 67.

[3] Com. Bainbridge's Dispatch, Jan. 3, 1813; Com. Bainbridge's Jour., Dec. 29; Details of the Action, presented by Lieut. Chads to the Court of Inquiry; Clark, p. 162.

[4] Cooper, ii. p. 68.—[5] Com. Bainbridge's Journal, Dec. 29; Lieut. Chads' Dispatch, Dec. 31.

[6] Cooper, ii. p. 68.

[1] Com. Bainbridge's Journal; Lieut. Chads' Dispatch, Dec. 31; Details of the Action.—[2] Com. Bainbridge's Jour.; Details of the Action, &c.; Cooper, ii. p. 68.

[3] Com. Bainbridge's Journal; Lieut. Chads' Dispatch, Dec. 31; Cooper, ii. p. 68.—[4] Com. Bainbridge's Jour.; Cooper, ii. p. 69.—[5] Ibid.; Thomson's Sketches, p. 96; Clark, ii. p. 163.—[6] Com. Bainbridge's Journal; Lieut. Chads' Dispatch, Dec. 31; Details of the Action, &c.

[7] Com. Bainbridge's Journal; Cooper, ii. p. 69; Thomson's Sketches, p. 96.

making an effort to secure a position for raking, the former wore again, and the stranger following, the heads of both vessels were again brought to the eastward.[1] Soon afterwards the same attempt was repeated with the same result, during which the *Constitution* succeeded in throwing in an efficient raking fire into her opponent.[2] Both vessels now ran free, with the wind on their quarter, the stranger being to windward; and the latter, at five minutes before three, attempted to close by running down on the *Constitution's* quarter.[3] Running her jib-boom into the mizzen-rigging of the *Constitution*, the stranger suffered severely without acquiring any advantage;[4] and at three o'clock her jib-boom and the head of her bowsprit were shot away.[5] About the same time a heavy raking broadside was thrown into her stern;[6] and, a few minutes afterwards, her foremast went overboard.[7]

The same complicated movements, to secure an opportunity for raking and to prevent it, continued some time longer; when, at five minutes past four, having shot away the stranger's main-topmast and the mizzen-mast, and wounded his fore and main masts, the *Constitution* hauled aboard her tacks, luffed athwart the stranger's bow, and passed out of the combat to windward, with her topsails, courses, spanker, and jib set, and

[1] Com Bainbridge's Journal; Details of the Action, &c.

[2] Com. Bainbridge's Journal; Cooper, ii. p. 69.

[3] Com. Bainbridge's Journal; Details of the Action, &c.

[4] Com. Bainbridge's Journal; Cooper, ii. p. 69.

[5] Com. Bainbridge's Journal; Lieut. Chads' Dispatch, Dec. 31; Cooper, ii. p. 69.

[6] Details of the Action, &c.

[7] Com. Bainbridge's Journal; Cooper, ii. p. 69.

spent an hour in repairing her damages and securing her masts.[1]

Having done so the *Constitution* bore up to the wreck[2]—for the stranger was but a wreck, having lost her mainmast, also, while the *Constitution* was repairing[3]—but the commander of the former had fallen,[4] and her second in command wisely considered his condition and determined to continue the contest no longer.[5] Her colors were accordingly struck, and Lieutenant Parker took possession of her at six o'clock;[6] reporting her as His Britannic Majesty's frigate *Java*, of thirty-eight guns, Captain Henry Lambert commanding.[7]

In this very spirited affair, which reflected equal credit both on the victor and the vanquished, the *Java* was entirely dismasted; six of her quarter-deck guns, four forecastle guns, and many of those on the main-deck were disabled; her hull was "knocked to pieces;" the foremast, in falling, had gone through the forecastle and main decks; the ship was leaking badly, with one of her pumps disabled;[8] and of her crew, three mates, two midshipmen, three petty officers, and fourteen men, were *killed;* Captain Lambert, Lieutenant Chads, her master, boatswain, four midshipmen, and fifty-nine seamen; Lieutenant Davies of the Royal ma-

[1] Com. Bainbridge's Journal; Lieut. Chads' Dispatch, Dec. 31.—[2] Com. Bainbridge's Jour.; Cooper, ii. pp. 69, 70.—[3] Com. Bainbridge's Jour.; Lieut. Chads' Dispatch, Dec. 31.—[4] Lieut. Chads' Dispatch, Dec. 31; Details of the Action, &c.; Communication of Dr. T. C. Jones, in *Naval Chronicle,* xxix. p. 416.—[5] Lieut. Chads' Dispatch, Dec. 31; Lieut. Chads' defence before the Court of Inquiry.—[6] Com. Bainbridge's Jour.; Details of the Action, &c.; Cooper, ii. p. 70.—[7] Com. Bainbridge's Jour.; Cooper, ii. p. 70.—[8] Lieut. Chads' Dispatch, Dec. 31; Details of the Action, &c.

rines, and twenty-one petty officers and privates (marines), and thirteen passengers, *wounded*.[1] The *Constitution* did not lose a spar.[2] An eighteen-pound shot passed through her mizzen-mast, her foremast was wounded, and her main-topmast was slightly injured; her sails and running-rigging were considerably cut up; her hull had received several round shot;[3] and of her crew nine were *killed*, and Commodore Bainbridge, Lieutenant Aylwin, and twenty-three men were wounded.[4]

The *Java* was one of the finest vessels in the service; mounted twenty-eight long eighteen-pounders, eighteen thirty-two pound carronades, a twenty-four-pounder, and two long nines;[5] and was bound to the East Indies, having on board, as passengers, Lieutenant-general Hislop and his staff, Captain Marshall and Lieutenant Saunders, of the Royal Navy, and upwards of a hundred other officers and men, who were destined for the service in the East;[1] the *Constitution* mounted thirty-two long twenty-four-pounders, twenty-two thirty-two-pound carronades, and one eighteen-pound carronade.

After examining his prize, Captain Bainbridge determined to destroy her, in consequence of her severe injuries, the distance she was from the United States, and the difficulty in obtaining masts in that vicinity; and after lying by her two days, and removing the wounded, she was blown up,[2] the *Constitution* returning to San Salvador, and thence to Boston, where she arrived on the eighth of February.[3]

[1] Com. Bainbridge's Dispatch, Jan. 3.—[2] Ibid.; Lieut. Chads' defence before the Court of Inquiry.

[3] Niles' Register, iii. p. 412.

DOCUMENTS.

I.

CAPTAIN BAINBRIDGE'S DISPATCH TO THE SECRETARY OF THE NAVY.

U. S. FRIGATE CONSTITUTION, ST. SALVADOR, *January* 3, 1813.

SIR:—I have to inform you, that on the 29th ultimo, at two P. M., in south latitude 13° 6′, and west longitude 38°, ten leagues distance from the coast of Brazil, I fell in with and captured His Britannic Majesty's frigate *Java*, of forty-nine guns, and upwards of four hundred men, commanded by Captain Lambert, a very distinguished officer. The action lasted one hour and fifty-five minutes, in which time the enemy was completely dismasted, not having a spar of any kind standing. The loss on board the *Constitution* was nine killed and twenty-five wounded, as per inclosed list. The enemy had sixty killed and one hundred and one wounded, certainly (among the latter, Captain Lambert, mortally); but, by the inclosed letter, written on board the ship (by one of the officers of the *Java*), and accidentally found, it is evident that the enemy's wounded must have been much greater than as above stated, and who must have died of their wounds previously to their being removed. The letter states sixty killed

[1] Report of loss, &c., appended to Lieut. Chads' Dispatch, Dec. 31, 1812. It is said to have been much more by some writers.—[2] Cooper, ii. p. 70.

[3] Com. Bainbridge's Jour.; Niles' Register, iii. p. 412.

[4] List of killed, &c., appended to Com. Bainbridge's Dispatch, Jan. 3, 1813. It has been said the loss was greater, but I have found no authority to sustain the assertion.—[5] Niles' Register, iii. p. 412; Com. Bainbridge's Dispatch, Jan. 3, 1813. Lieut. Chads (*Dispatch, Dec.* 31) says she mounted *forty-six*.

and one hundred and seventy wounded. For further details of the action, I beg leave to refer you to the inclosed extracts from my journal. The *Java* had, in addition to her crew, upwards of one hundred supernumerary officers and seamen, to join the British ships of war in the East Indies: also, Lieutenant-general Hislop, appointed to the command of Bombay, Major Walker and Captain Wood, of his staff, and Captain Marshall, master and commander in the British navy, going to the East Indies to take command of a sloop of war there.

Should I attempt to do justice, by representation, to the brave and good conduct of all my officers and crew, during the action, I should fail in the attempt; therefore, suffice it to say, that the whole of their conduct was such as to merit my highest encomiums. I beg leave to recommend the officers particularly to the notice of government, as also the unfortunate seamen who were wounded, and the families of those brave men who fell in the action.

The great distance from our own coast, and the perfect wreck we made of the enemy's frigate, forbad every idea of taking her to the United States; and, not considering it prudent to trust her into a port of Brazil, particularly St. Salvador, as you will perceive by the inclosed letters, numbers one, two, and three, I had no alternative but burning her, which I did on the 31st ultimo, after receiving all the prisoners and their baggage, which was very tedious work, only having one boat left (out of eight), and not one left on board the *Java*. On blowing up the frigate *Java*, I proceeded to this place, where I have landed all the prisoners on their parole, to return to England, and there remain until regularly exchanged, and not to serve in their professional capacities in any place or in any manner whatever against the United States of America, until the exchange shall be effected.

I have the honor to be, &c.,

WILLIAM BAINBRIDGE.

To the Secretary of the Navy.

[Inclosure.]

EXTRACT FROM COM. WM. BAINBRIDGE'S JOURNAL.

TUESDAY, *December* 29, 1812.

At nine o'clock A. M. discovered two strange sails on the weather-bow. At ten discovered the strange sails to be ships; one of them stood in for the land, and the other stood off shore, in a direction towards us. At three-quarters past ten A. M., we tacked ship to the northward and westward, and stood for the sail standing towards us, and at eleven A. M. tacked to the southward and eastward, hauled up the mainsail and took in the royals. At half-past eleven, made the private signal for the day, which was not answered, and then set the mainsail and royals, to draw the strange sail off from the neutral coast, and separate her from the sail in company.

WEDNESDAY, *December* 30, 1812.

In latitude 13° 19′ S., longitude 38° W., ten leagues from the coast of Brazil, commences with clear weather and moderate breezes from E. N. E., hoisted our ensign and pendant. At fifteen minutes past meridian, the ship hoisted her colors—an English ensign, having a signal flying at her main—red, yellow, red.

At twenty-six minutes past one P. M., being sufficiently from the land and finding the ship to be an English frigate, took in the mainsail and royals, tacked ship and stood for the enemy. At half-past one P. M. the enemy bore down with an intention of raking us, which we avoided by wearing. At two P. M., the enemy being within half a mile of us, and to windward, and having hauled down his colors, except the Union Jack at the mizzen-masthead, induced me to give orders to the officers of the Third division to fire one gun ahead of the enemy, to make him show his colors, which being done, brought on a fire from us of the whole broadside, on which the enemy hoisted his colors, and immediately returned our fire. A general action with round and grape then commenced; the enemy keeping at a much greater distance than I wished; but could not bring him to close action without exposing ourselves to several rakes. Considerable manœuvres were made by both vessels to rake and avoid being raked.

The following minutes were taken during the action:

At 2:10 P. M., commenced the action within good grape and canister distance, the enemy to windward, but much farther than I wished.

2:30, our wheel was shot entirely away.

2:40, determined to close with the enemy,

notwithstanding his raking. Set the fore and main sails, and luffed up to him.

2 : 50, the enemy's jib-boom got foul of our mizzen-rigging.

3 : 00, the head of the enemy's bowsprit and jib-boom shot away by us.

3 : 5, shot away his foremast by the board.

3 : 15, shot away his main-topmast just above the cap.

3 : 40, shot away the gaff and spanker-boom.

3 : 55, shot away his mizzen-mast nearly by the board.

4 : 5, having silenced the fire of the enemy completely, and his colors in the main-rigging being down, supposed he had struck; then hauled aboard the courses to shoot ahead to repair our rigging, which was extremely cut; leaving the enemy a complete wreck; soon after discovered that the enemy's flag was still flying. Hove to, to repair some of our damage.

4 : 20, the enemy's mainmast went nearly by the board.

4 : 50, wore ship and stood for the enemy.

5 : 25, got close to the enemy, in a very effectual raking position, athwart his bows, and was at the very instant of raking him, when he most prudently struck his flag; for had he suffered the broadside to have raked him, his additional loss must have been extremely great—as he laid an unmanageable wreck upon the water. After the enemy had struck, wore ship and reefed the topsails—then hoisted out one of the only two remaining boats we had left out of eight, and sent Lieutenant Parker, first of the *Constitution*, to take possession of the enemy, which proved to be His Britannic Majesty's frigate *Java*, rated thirty-eight, but carried forty-nine guns, and manned with upwards of four hundred men, commanded by Captain Lambert, a very distinguished officer, who was mortally wounded. The action continued, from the commencement to the end of the fire, one hour and fifty-five minutes. The *Constitution* had nine killed and twenty-five wounded. The enemy had sixty killed and one hundred and one certainly wounded; but, by a letter written on board the *Constitution* by one of the officers of the *Java*, and accidentally found, it is evident the enemy's wounded must have been considerably greater than as above stated, and must have died of their wounds previously to their being removed. The letter states sixty killed and one hundred and seventy wounded. The *Java* had her own complement of men complete, and upwards of one hundred supernumeraries, going to join the British ships of war in the East Indies—also several officers, passengers, going out on promotion. The force of the enemy, in number of men at the commencement of the action was, no doubt, considerably greater than we have been able to ascertain, which is upwards of four hundred men. The officers were extremely cautious in discovering the number. By her quarter-bill, she had one man more stationed at each gun than we had.

The *Constitution* was very much cut in her sails and rigging, and many of her spars injured.

At 7 P. M., the boat returned with Lieutenant Chads, the first-lieutenant of the enemy's frigate, and Lieutenant-general Hislop (appointed governor of Bombay), Major Walker, and Captain Wood, belonging to his staff.

Captain Lambert, of the *Java*, was too dangerously wounded to be removed immediately.

The cutter returned on board the prize for the prisoners, and brought Captain Marshall, master and commander in the British navy, who was a passenger on board, also several other naval officers, destined for ships in the East Indies.

The *Java* was an important ship, fitted out in the completest manner, to carry Lieutenant-general Hislop and staff to Bombay.

II.

CAPTAIN CHADS' DISPATCH.

U. S. FRIGATE CONSTITUTION, OFF ST. SALVADOR, *December* 31, 1812.

SIR:—It is with deep regret that I write to you, for the information of the Lords Commissioners of the Admiralty, that His Majesty's ship *Java* is no more, after sustaining an action on the 29th instant, for several hours, with the American frigate *Constitution*, which resulted in the capture and ultimate destruction of His Majesty's ship. Captain Lambert being dangerously wounded in the height of the action, the melancholy task of writing the detail devolves on me.

On the morning of the 29th instant, at eight

A. M., off St. Salvador (coast of Brazil), the wind at N. E., we perceived a strange sail; made all sail in chase, and soon made her out to be a large frigate. At noon, prepared for action, the chase not answering our private signals, and tacking towards us under easy sail. When about four miles distant she made a signal, and immediately tacked and made all sail away upon the wind. We soon found we had the advantage of her in sailing, and came up with her fast, when she hoisted American colors. She then bore about three points on our lee bow. At fifty minutes past one P. M. the enemy shortened sail, upon which we bore down upon her. At ten minutes past two, when about half a mile distant, she opened her fire, giving us her larboard broadside, which was not returned until we were close on her weather-bow. Both ships now manœuvred to obtain advantageous positions, our opponent evidently avoiding close action, and firing high to disable our masts; in which he succeeded too well, having shot away the head of our bowsprit, with the jib-boom, and our running rigging so much cut as to prevent our preserving the weather-gage.

At five minutes past three, finding the enemy's raking fire extremely heavy, Captain Lambert ordered the ship to be laid on board, in which we would have succeeded had not our foremast been shot away at this moment, the remains of our bowsprit passing over his taffrail; shortly after this the main-topmast went, leaving the ship totally unmanageable, with most of our starboard guns rendered useless from the wreck lying over them.

At half-past three our gallant Captain received a dangerous wound in the breast, and was carried below. From this time we could not fire more than two or three guns until a quarter-past four, when our mizzen-mast was shot away. The ship then fell off a little, and brought many of our starboard-guns to bear. The enemy's rigging was so much cut that he could not avoid shooting ahead, which brought us fairly broadside to broadside. Our main-yard now went in the slings; both ships continued engaged in this manner till thirty-five minutes past four, we frequently on fire in consequence of the wreck lying on the side engaged. Our opponent now made sail ahead, out of gun-shot, where he remained an hour, repairing his damages, leaving us an unmanageable wreck, with only the mainmast left, and that tottering. Every exertion was made by us, during this interval, to place the ship in a state to renew the action. We succeeded in clearing the wreck of our masts from our guns; a sail was set on the stumps of the foremast and bowsprit; the weather-half of the main-yard remaining aloft, the main-tack was got forward, in the hope of getting the ship before the wind, our helm being still perfect. The effort, unfortunately, proved ineffectual, from the mainmast falling over the side, and from the heavy rolling of the ship, which nearly covered the whole of our starboard-guns. We still waited the attack of the enemy, he now standing towards us for the purpose. On his coming nearly within hail of us, and from his manœuvres perceiving he intended a position ahead, when he could rake us without the possibility of our returning a shot; I then consulted the officers, who agreed with myself, that our having a great part of our crew killed and wounded, our bowsprit and three masts gone, several guns useless, we should not be justified in wasting the lives of more of those remaining; who, I hope their lordships and the country will think have bravely defended His Majesty's ship. Under these circumstances, however, reluctantly, at fifty minutes past five, our colors were lowered from the stump of the mizzen-mast, and we were taken possession of a little after six by the American frigate *Constitution*, commanded by Commodore Bainbridge, who, immediately after ascertaining the state of the ship, resolved on burning her, which we had the satisfaction of seeing done as soon as the wounded were removed. Annexed I send you a return of the killed and wounded; and it is with pain I perceive it is numerous; also a statement of the comparative force of the two ships, when I hope their lordships will not think the British flag tarnished, although success has not attended us. It would be presumptuous in me to speak of Captain Lambert's merits, who, though still in danger from his wound, we still entertain the greatest hopes of his being restored to the service and his country.

It is most gratifying to my feelings to notice

the gallantry of every officer, seaman, and marine on board. In justice to the officers, I beg leave to mention them individually. I can never speak too highly of the able exertions of Lieutenants Hevingham and Buchanan, and also Mr. Robinson, master, who was severely wounded, and Lieutenants Mercer and Davis, of the royal marines, the latter of whom also was severely wounded. To Captain John Marshall, Royal Navy, who was a passenger, I am particularly obliged for his exertions and advice throughout the action. To Lieutenant Alpin, who was on the main-deck, and Lieutenant Saunders, who commanded the forecastle, I also return my thanks. I cannot but notice the good conduct of the mates and midshipmen, many of whom are killed, and the greater part wounded. To Mr. T. C. Jones, surgeon, and his assistants, every praise is due for their unwearied assiduity in the care of the wounded. Lieutenant-general Hislop, Major Walker, and Captain Wood, of his staff, the latter of whom was severely wounded, were solicitous to assist and remain on the quarter-deck.

I cannot conclude this letter without expressing my grateful acknowledgments, thus publicly, for the generous treatment Captain Lambert and his officers have experienced from our gallant enemy, Commodore Bainbridge and his officers. I have the honor to be, &c.,

HENRY D. CHADS,

First-Lieut. of His Majesty's late ship Java.

P. S.—The *Constitution* has also suffered severely, both in her rigging and men; having her fore and mizzen masts, main-topmasts, main-topsail-yards, spanker-boom, gaff, and trysail-mast, badly shot; and the greatest part of the standing-rigging very much damaged; with ten men killed, the commander, fifth-lieutenant, and forty-six men wounded, four of whom are since dead.

CHAPTER XXXVI.

January 14, 1813.

THE PRIVATEER COMET, OF BALTIMORE.

THE privateers which sailed from the ports of the United States, during the war with Great Britain, as before stated, were exceedingly active and successful. One of these, the *Comet*, of Baltimore, commanded by Captain Boyle, sailed from that port in the latter part of December, 1812; and, taking advantage of a dark, stormy night, succeeded in passing through the enemy's blockading squadron, at the mouth of the Chesapeake, without being discovered. Shaping his course for the coast of Brazil, he reached the offing of the harbor of Pernambuco on the ninth of January, 1813, and was informed by a coaster that some English vessels which were in the harbor were to sail within a few days.

At one o'clock in the afternoon of the fourteenth, four sail of vessels were seen standing out of the harbor; when the *Comet* laid to for the purpose of giving them an opportunity to get off shore, and, afterwards, of cutting them off. Two hours afterwards, the strangers standing before the wind, six leagues from the shore, the *Comet* bore up, and made all sail in chase. The superior sailing qualities of the clipper enabling her to outsail the heavily-laden strangers, she quickly overhauled them; and at seven o'clock she hoisted her colors, and sheered close up to the largest of the four,—a large man-of-war brig,—which had hoisted Portuguese colors. The captain of the latter hailed the clipper, and sent his boat on board the latter, from the commander of which Captain Boyle learned that the brig was a Portuguese brig of war, mounting twenty thirty-two-pounders, and manned with one hundred and sixty-five men; that the three others were English vessels, laden with wheat,—a ship mounting fourteen guns, and two brigs, each mounting ten guns,—bound for Europe, under his protection; and that *the Comet must not molest them.* After Captain Boyle had informed the officer of the character of the *Comet;* that she had been authorized to seize British vessels; that she would do so, in this instance, if she could; and that he (the Portuguese) had no right to interfere with her, the boat returned whence it came, promising to return, but not doing so.

After waiting some time for the return of the boat, Captain Boyle inquired if she was coming back; but the captain of the brig equivocated, and Captain Boyle "told him again of his determination, very distinctly, so that he might not be misunderstood." At the same time he made sail on the clipper, which shot ahead and quickly came up with the ship—although the three vessels were close together—when he hailed her and ordered her to back her main-topsail. Being under full headway, the *Comet* shot past the strangers in a very short time; yet Captain Boyle hailed again, telling them he would be alongside within a few minutes, and if his orders were not obeyed he would then give them a broadside. A few minutes afterwards—the Portuguese brig, meanwhile, pursuing the *Comet* as rapidly as possible—the latter tacked; and, at half-past eight in the evening, she ranged alongside the ship, and opened her broadside on that vessel and on one of the brigs which had closed in with the ship. All the vessels were running before the wind, under a crowd of canvas, and the clipper was frequently compelled to tack, in order to check her progress and keep within range of the strangers. These manœuvres enabled the clipper to bestow her fire, in turn, on *all* the vessels, as she nimbly sped between them; while the convoy, suffering very severely in the contest, was compelled to open, from time to time, in order that the Portuguese brig might throw in her fire in return.

Thus tiring out the entire squadron, while she remained comparatively uninjured, the *Comet* continued the contest until one o'clock the next morning (*Jan.* 15, 1813), when the ship surrendered, "being cut to pieces, and rendered unmanageable." Immediately afterwards the brig *Bowes* surrendered, and was taken possession of; when the Portuguese brig sheered off, followed by the *Comet*, which continued the action. A short time afterwards the third vessel struck her colors; but the Portuguese continuing the action, Captain Boyle was unable to take possession of the brig which last surrendered, or of the ship, both of which were very much cut, and were kept afloat only with great difficulty. About two o'clock the moon went down, and the night becoming very dark and squally, it was considered prudent to suspend the action until morning. At that time the Portuguese stood for the clipper, with an evident desire to renew the action; and, at the same time, the latter tacked and stood for the ship and brig which had not been taken possession of. For some reasons, which have not been recorded, it appears that they were not boarded; and that the Portuguese, joining them, made for Pernambuco; while the *Comet* and her prize—the *Bowes*—also went their way without farther obstruction.

It appeared afterwards that the vessels which escaped were the ship *George*, of Liverpool, and the brig *Gambia*, of Hull; that they were carried into port with the greatest difficulty, with damaged cargoes; that the Portuguese lost her first-lieutenant and five men killed, and a number, including the Captain, were wounded; and that she, also, was a very severe sufferer.

When it is considered that the clipper mounted only two long-nines and ten twelve-pounders, with a crew of one hundred and twenty men; and that, with these, she gallantly engaged four vessels, mounting fifty-four guns, compelling three of them to strike their colors, the character of the contest will need no farther elucidation.

[NOTE.—The extract from the *Comet's* log-book, in Capt. Coggeshall's "*History of American Privateers*," has been my sole authority for this chapter.]

CHAPTER XXXVII.

January 18, 1813.

THE BATTLE OF FRENCHTOWN.

AT the close of the year 1812 the left wing of the army of the West, commanded by General Winchester, was marching towards the Miami Rapids;[1] and Leslie Combs, of Kentucky,—well known to many, at the present day, as a devoted friend to the late Henry Clay,—had been sent through the woods, *on foot*, a distance of more than a hundred miles, to inform General Harrison of the movement.[2] While the detachment was still on its march, a dispatch, from the commander-in-chief, had reached General Winchester *recommending* him to abandon the intended movement, in consequence of the reported strength of the Indians on the Wabash; but General Winchester did not notice it, and on the tenth of January he reached the Rapids, occupied a position on the north bank of the river, and fortified his camp.[1]

On the evening of the thirteenth of January two messengers, from the settlements on the River Raisin, reached the camp, informing the General that the Indians were uniting their forces

[1] Armstrong's Notices of the War of 1812, i. p. 66.

[2] McAfee's Hist. of the War in the West, p. 201. In consequence of an immense fall of snow, and the absence of any appearance even of a pathway through the unbroken forest, this was an undertaking as perilous as it was important, and the youthful Combs, and his guide,—A. Ruddle,—deserved great credit for the perseverence and courage which they displayed in this undertaking.

[1] McAfee, pp. 201, 202; Western Annals, p. 625.

with those of the British at Malden; that they had threatened to revenge themselves at the expense of the settlements; and that the protection of the troops would alone secure these outposts of civilization from the fury of the savages. On the fourteenth a second messenger arrived; and, on the sixteenth, two others, all from the Raisin River, imploring protection for the exposed settlements.[1]

With that ardor which characterized the men of the West, at that early day, the entire detachment was aroused to the greatest degree; and when a council of officers met to consult with the General, on the subject, and advised the detachment of a strong force to cover the settlements, it only reflected the general sentiment of the army, from the field-officers to the privates.[2] Accordingly, on the morning of the seventeenth, five hundred and fifty men, under Colonel Lewis, left the camp; and, a few hours afterwards, an additional force of one hundred and ten men, under Colonel Allen, of Kentucky, followed to support him.[3] These two parties united at Presque Isle (Erie, Penn.), where they passed the night; and thence, on the morning of the eighteenth, an express was dispatched to General Winchester, with intelligence of the strength of the Indians at the Raisin River, and of the approach of a strong British force, from Malden, with the intention of resisting, in connection with the Indians, the progress of the army towards Detroit.[1] Not, in the least, intimidated with the information which they had received from the Raisin, and forwarded to General Winchester, Colonels Lewis and Allen called forth the greater energies to overcome the enemy before the allied savages and British could unite their respective forces; and for this purpose, with the desire of reaching the Raisin as speedily as possible, the detachments were moved from Presque Isle at a very early hour in the morning (*January* 18, 1813); and taking the frozen surface of Lake Erie and the Miami Bay, it pressed forward as rapidly as possible.[2]

When yet six miles from its destination, the progress of the detachment was discovered by a party of Indians, who hastened to alarm the main body of the enemy; and, soon afterwards, while it was still on the margin of the lake, it halted to take refreshments. Before reaching the Raisin the detachment was formed in order of battle—the right column, composed of Captains McCracken's, Bledsoe's, and Matson's companies, being commanded by Colonel Allen; the left column, composed of Captains Hamilton's, Williams', and Kelly's companies, commanded by Major Graves; and the centre, composed of Captains Hightower's, Collier's, and Sebree's companies, under Major Madison; while the companies under Captains Hickman, Claver, and James, commanded by Captain Ballard, acted

[1] McAfee, p. 204; James' Mil. Occur., i. p. 184; Hall's Life of Gen. Harrison, p. 207; Darnell's Jour., Jan. 13, 15, 16.—[2] McAfee, p. 204; Hall's Life of Gen. Harrison, p. 207.—[3] McAfee, p. 205; James' Military Occurrences, i. p. 184; Darnell's Journal, Jan. 17.

[1] McAfee, p. 205; Hall's Life of Gen. Harrison, p. 207; Darnell's Journal, Jan. 17; Col. Lewis to Gen. Winchester, Jan. 20.—[2] McAfee, p. 205; Darnell's Journal, Jan. 18; Col. Lewis to Gen. Winchester, Jan. 20.

as an advanced guard—and in this order it approached Frenchtown.[1]

When within a quarter of a mile of the village, Colonel Lewis formed his lines in order to receive the enemy, whose movements appeared to indicate a projected attack; but it soon became evident that an engagement in the open field was not the plan of operations which had been adopted, and a corresponding change of the order of the Americans became necessary. The lines were broken into columns by the right of companies, and in this order the detachment moved forward, under a heavy fire from the enemy, until it reached the south bank of the river, when the lines were again formed, and preparations were made to attack the enemy.[2]

The village of Frenchtown, in which the enemy was posted, among the houses and behind the pickets of the gardens, is situate on the north bank of the River Raisin; and the line of the detachment was formed, as before stated, on the opposite bank of the river, under a heavy fire of musketry and a howitzer, with which the enemy's position was defended.[3] Although the ice on the river, in many places, was exceedingly slippery; and notwithstanding the troops were, generally, engaged for the first time, the passage of the river was successfully accomplished; and when the detachment reached the northern bank, the "long roll" of the

[1] McAfee, pp. 205, 206; Hall's Harrison, p. 208; Thomson's Sketches, p. 101; Col. Lewis to Gen. Winchester, Jan. 20.—[2] McAfee, p. 206; Darnell's Jour., Jan. 18; Thomson's Sketches, p. 101; Col. Lewis to Gen. Winchester, Jan. 20.—[3] McAfee, p. 206; Darnell's Journal, Jan. 18; Armstrong's Notices, i. p. 70; Col. Lewis to Gen. Winchester, Jan. 20.

drum summoned it to a general charge on the position of the enemy.[1] Majors Graves and Madison moved against it in front; while Colonel Allen, by a detour, moved against the enemy's left flank—both pressing forward, with the greatest gallantry, under a heavy fire, and both being alike successful in dislodging the enemy from his well-chosen position.[2] After retreating about half a mile, to a piece of woods, he rallied his troops, and made a stand with his howitzer, under cover of some houses and a range of fences, having a thick wood, filled with fallen timber, on his rear; and in this position he renewed the action with great vigor.[3]

Against this new position the American troops moved with great resolution—Majors Graves and Madison, by a detour, occupying the wood on the left, and falling on the enemy's right flank; while Colonel Allen moved against him in front, as soon as the fire on the left indicated the engagement of the flanking parties under Majors Graves and Madison.[4] Thus simultaneously attacked in front and on his right flank, the enemy again fell back, slowly, into the woods; while, at the same time, he gradually concentrated his forces on his left, with the intention of forcing the right of Colonel Allen's line. In this, however, he was not successful; and he

[1] McAfee, p. 206; Darnell's Jour., Jan. 18; Thomson's Sketches, p. 101; Breckenridge's History of War, p. 97; Col. Lewis to Gen. Winchester, Jan. 20.—[2] McAfee, p. 206; Hall's Harrison, p. 208; Darnell's Jour., Jan. 18; Thomson's Sketches, p. 101.—[3] McAfee, p. 206; Hall's Harrison, p. 208; Darnell's Jour., Jan. 18; Col. Lewis to Gen. Winchester, Jan. 20.—[4] McAfee, p. 206; Thomson's Sketches, p. 102; Armstrong's Notices, i. p. 70; Col. Lewis to Gen. Winchester, Jan. 20.

was kept slowly retreating, contesting every foot of the ground, until dark, when the detachment returned to the village, in good order, and encamped.[1]

In this spirited and carefully conducted engagement, "every officer and soldier did his duty. There was not a solitary instance of delinquency;"[2] while the arrangement of the forces, both on the march and in the action, reflected great credit on the skill of Colonel Lewis, the commanding officer.

The enemy's force was composed of about one hundred British soldiers, under Major Reynolds,[3] and about four hundred Indians,[4] under Round-head and Walk-in-the-water,[5] with a piece of artillery; while the Americans, as already stated, numbered about six hundred and sixty men, armed only with small-arms.[6]

The loss of the Americans was twelve killed and fifty-five wounded, among the latter of whom were Captains Hickman, Matson, and Ballard;[1] the loss of the enemy, although not certainly known, must have been great, as fifteen were left dead on the ground where the first engagement took place.[2]

On the same evening a messenger was sent to General Winchester, with intelligence of the victory;[3] and the troops were permitted to enjoy a temporary repose before entering, a few days afterwards, on another and more disastrous field.

[Note.—The Dispatches of the commanders of both forces, to their respective governments, which had been provided for the illustration of this chapter, have been omitted by the Publishers for want of room.]

¹ McAfee, p. 207; James' Mil. Occur., i. p. 185; Hall's Harrison, p. 209; Darnell's Jour., Jan. 18; Armstrong's Notices, i. p. 71; Col. Lewis to Gen. Winchester, Jan. 20.

² McAfee, p. 207; Thomson's Sketches, p. 102.

³ McAfee, p. 207; Col. Lewis to Gen. Winchester, Jan. 20. Mr. James (*Mil. Occur.*, i. p. 185) says it was only "*thirty of the Essex militia;*" and Mr. Auchinleck (*Hist. of the War*, p. 125) sustains him.—⁴ McAfee, p. 207; Col. Lewis to Gen. Winchester, Jan. 20. Mr. James (*Mil. Occur.*, i. p. 185) says it was "a band of *two hundred* Indians (Potawatomies)," &c.—⁵ Drake's Book of the Indians, book v. pp. 129, 130.—⁶ Vide p. 192, col. 1, note 3.

¹ Col. Lewis to Gen. Winchester, Jan. 20; Breckenridge, p. 98; McAfee, p. 207. Darnell (*Jour.*, *Jan.* 18) says it was "*eleven* killed and *fifty* wounded;" Gen. Harrison (*Dispatch to Gov. Meigs*, *Jan.* 20) says, "Our loss is *ten* killed—two captains and twenty privates wounded;" The "*Sketches of the War*" (Rutland, Vt., 1815), p. 159, say *fifty-two* were wounded.—² McAfee, p. 207. It was reported (*Darnell's Jour.*, *Jan.* 18) that the enemy lost 54 killed and 140 wounded.—³ McAfee, p. 208.—⁴ Chap. XXXVII.

⁵ McAfee, p. 208; Ingersoll's Hist. of War, i. p. 133.

CHAPTER XXXVIII.

January 22, 1813.

THE BATTLE AND MASSACRE AT THE RIVER RAISIN.

The advance of Colonel Lewis, with a detachment from the left wing of the army of the Northwest; his successful occupation of Frenchtown; and the dispatch of a messenger to the head-quarters of General Winchester, with intelligence of his victory, have been already alluded to in the preceding chapter of this book.[4]

The intelligence of Colonel Lewis' success created "a complete ferment" in General Winchester's camp;[5] and as

Frenchtown, where the former was encamped, was only eighteen miles from Malden, the principal post of the British, in the Northwest, the situation of the detachment was considered a critical one, and an immediate movement was made to relieve it.[1] Leaving Captain Morris's command, as a rear-guard,—with whom was also left the baggage,[2]—General Winchester and Colonel Wells moved with about two hundred and fifty men, on the afternoon of the nineteenth of January, 1813, and reached Frenchtown at three o'clock in the afternoon of the next day.[3] Colonel Lewis was encamped in the gardens of the village,—where the pickets afforded shelter to his troops against the small-arms of any enemy who might appear,[4]—and when Colonel Wells came on the ground he encamped below, and on the right of the detachment, about a hundred yards from it.[5] There was but little order in the encampment, and another and more eligible position was selected and surveyed; preparations being made to occupy and fortify it the next day.[6] That event, however, was never to be seen by the unfortunate party; and the sun of another day witnessed a sadder spectacle than the opening of newer and stronger defences for its protection.

Late in the evening of the twenty-first, a Frenchman, from the neighborhood of Malden, came to General Winchester's quarters and informed him that a large body of British and Indians—not far from three thousand in number — was about to march from that place when he left it;[1] but both officers and men appeared to discredit it, and not the smallest preparation was made for the protection of the troops.[2] Indeed so wholly secure did the troops appear to consider themselves, that many of them wandered around the town—singly or in small parties, as their humors dictated—until late at night, notwithstanding Colonel Lewis and Major Madison cautioned them to be prepared for a visit from the enemy, at any moment.[3] The usual sentries were placed; but, on the plea of the severity of the weather, no pickets were sent out on the roads which approached the village.[4]

On the next morning (*Jan.* 22, 1813) the reveille commenced to beat at the usual time, and the troops were arousing themselves for the discharge of their morning duties, when three mus-

[1] McAfee, p. 208.—[2] Mem. of conversation of Gen. Winchester with Sec. of War; Maj. Madison's Narrative. Gen. Harrison (*Letter to Gov. Meigs, Jan.* 24, 1813) and Mr. Darnell (*Jour., Jan.* 21) say "*two hundred and thirty* men."

[3] Mem. of conversation, &c.; Maj. McClanehan to Gen. Harrison, Jan. 26, 1813.—[4] Mem. of conversation, &c.; McAfee, p. 208.—[5] Mem. of conversation, &c.; Maj. McClanehan to Gen. Harrison, Jan. 26, 1813. Mr. Ingersoll (*Hist. of War*, i. p. 135) says Col. Lewis urged the General to post Col. Wells *within the pickets*, where, on his left, there was room unoccupied; that as Col. Wells belonged to the regular army, and ranked Col. Lewis, he would not take position on the *left* of the latter; that, in order to form on *the right*, he went into an open field, in that direction; and hence the trouble.—[6] Darnell's Jour., Jan. 21; Maj. McClanehan to Gen. Harrison, Jan. 26, 1813.

[1] Darnell's Jour., Jan. 21; Armstrong's Notices, i. p. 73; Mem. of conversation, &c.; Maj. McClanehan to Gen. Harrison, Jan. 26, 1813.—[2] Mem. of conversation, &c.; Maj. McClanehan to Gen. Harrison, Jan. 26, 1813; McAfee, p. 212. Mr. Darnell (*Journal, Jan.* 21) denies that the *men* were indifferent to the Frenchman's story, although he admits that by "some of the leading men, who were regaling themselves with whiskey and loaf-sugar," it "was not believed."—[3] McAfee, p. 212; Armstrong's Notices, i. p. 72.—[4] Armstrong's Notices, i. p. 72; Mem. of conversation, &c.; McAfee, p. 212.

ket-shots, in quick succession, from the line of sentries, indicated the immediate presence of a stranger, and, possibly, of an enemy.[1] It was still dark, and the surrounding gloom, in which the camp was enveloped, gave no indication of the character or strength of the intruders; yet the troops instantly formed in order of battle, and prepared for the worst.[2]

Suddenly a heavy fire, from *several pieces of artillery*, on the front of the encampment, followed by volleys of musketry on its flanks, mingled with the yells and war-whoops of the Indians, told too plainly the character and strength of the assailants, and the folly of the commanding officers in disregarding, with such fatal recklessness, the information which the Frenchman had brought to the camp.[3]

It appears that when intelligence of Colonel Lewis's occupation of Frenchtown reached Malden, Colonel Proctor, who commanded there, prepared to march for its relief. With this object he marched from Brownstown, on the 21st, at the head of detachments from the Forty-first regiment of the line, the Royal Newfoundland regiment, the Tenth veteran battalion, some militia and sailors, and a party of the Royal artillery with three three-pounders and a five-and-a-half-inch howitzer.[4] These

[1] Gen. Harrison to Gov. Meigs, Jan. 24; Darnell's Jour., Jan. 22; Armstrong's Notices, i. p. 72; Mem. of conversation, &c.; McAfee, p. 212.—[2] Darnell's Jour., Jan. 22; Maj. McClanehan to Gen. Harrison, Jan. 26; McAfee, p. 212.

[3] Darnell's Jour., Jan. 22; Hall's Life of Harrison, p. 210; Armstrong's Notices, i. p. 72; Mem. of conversation, &c.; Gen. Winchester to Sec. of War, Feb. 11, 1813.

[4] Montreal Courant, Feb. 6, 1813, cited by Mr. Niles; Letter from "Fort George, Jan. 30," in the same work; Gen. Proctor to Gen. Sheaffe, Jan. 26, 1813; James' Military Occurrences, i. p. 186.

troops—said to have numbered five hundred men[1]—were accompanied by six hundred Indians, under Round-head and Walk-in-the-water;[2] and, favored by the recklessness of General Winchester, at an early hour the party approached the camp, put its artillery in battery, and occupied its several positions around the encampment, without disturbing its occupants, as before related.[3]

As soon as the enemy approached the front of the position which had been occupied by Colonel Lewis since the close of the action on the eighteenth, a steady and well-directed fire was opened on him with great success, and his shattered forces fell back in considerable disorder.[4]

On the right of the position, where were posted the troops which had come forward with General Winchester and Colonel Wells, the enemy was more successful—the Americans, after maintaining their ground for some time, with considerable firmness, being compelled to give way before a greatly superior force—and when General Winchester came on the field of action he found them retreating, and opening the right of Colonel Lewis's line to the as-

[1] Christie's Naval and Military Operations, p. 100. The Montreal *Courant*, Feb. 6, says it embraced "300 regulars, 150 militia, and some Indians." The Montreal *Herald*, Feb. 6, 1813, says, "300 troops of the line and sailors."

[2] Montreal Herald, Feb. 6, 1813; Christie, p. 100; Mr. Thomson (*Sketches of War*, p. 103) makes the enemy *two thousand one hundred* strong, with *Tecumthà* at the head of the Indians; Mr. Perkins (*History of War*, p. 100) says the Indians numbered *one thousand;* and Mr. Drake (*Book of the Indians*, book v. p. 129) sustains the assertion.

[3] Armstrong, i. p. 72; McAfee, p. 212.

[4] Darnell's Journal, p. 22; Hall's Harrison, p. 210; Armstrong, i. p. 73; Gen. Winchester to Secretary of War, Feb. 11, 1813; McAfee, p. 212.

saults of the enemy.[1] To prevent the mischief which this retrograde movement would inevitably produce, the General ordered the fugitives to rally behind a fence and the second bank of the river, and to incline towards the centre, where shelter could be obtained behind the pickets of the gardens, which were in that vicinity.[2] At the same time a reinforcement of a hundred men was sent by Colonel Lewis to support this part of the army;[3] but all this availed nothing, and while the British continued to press forward in front, a large body of Indians fell on the right flank, and the whole of that wing retreated, in disorder, over the river, sweeping away with it the reinforcement which Colonel Lewis had sent to its assistance.[4] Duly appreciating the consequences which would ensue unless this misfortune could be overcome, Colonels Lewis and Allen had both followed the fugitives and attempted to rally them; leaving their own commands under the control of Majors Graves and Madison.[5] After they had passed the river the most desperate efforts to rally them, behind the houses and garden-fences, were again made by General Winchester, Colonels Lewis and Allen, and their own officers; but here, too, the same want of success attended their efforts; and, immediately afterwards, the left and rear of the line, as well as the right and front of it, were possessed by the Indians.[1] In their confusion the fugitives sought safety in flight, by way of the road which leads from the village towards the rapids, but the Indians lined the fences on either side, and shot them down in every direction.[2] Others turned to their right, and plunged into the pathless forest, hoping to find safety in its deep recesses; but here, too, the savages surrounded and massacred them, without distinction—nearly one hundred men falling under the tomahawks within the distance of a hundred yards.[3] A small party of fifteen or twenty men, under Lieutenant Garrett, after retreating about a mile and a half, were compelled to surrender, and all, except the Lieutenant, were immediately tomahawked and scalped.[4] A similar party of about forty men, after securing a retreat nearly three miles, was overtaken, and more than one-half its number was massacred in cold blood.[5] Colonel Allen, although wounded, gallantly attempted, in vain, to rally the men; and, when all hope had vanished, had escaped about two miles, when from exhaustion he sat down on a log, determined to meet, without resistance, any fate which might befall him. An Indian chief observing him, and knowing his rank, approached and demanded his surrender, promising protection if he would do so without resistance. At the same moment two other savages

[1] Darnell's Journal, Jan. 22; Hall's Harrison, p. 210; Armstrong, i. p. 73; McAfee, pp. 212, 213.—[2] Darnell's Journal, Jan. 22; Memorandum of conversation, &c.; Maj. McClanehan to Gen. Harrison, Jan. 26, 1812.

[3] Armstrong, i. p. 73; Mem. of conversation, &c.; Breckenridge, p. 98; Perkins' Western Annals, p. 627; Niles' Register, iv. p. 11; Perkins' Hist. War, p. 101.

[4] Hall's Harrison, p. 211; Niles' Register, iv. p. 11; McAfee, p. 213.—[5] Hall's Harrison, p. 211; Mem. of conversation, &c.; McAfee, p. 213.

[1] Niles' Register, iv. p. 12; McAfee, p. 213.

[2] McAfee, p. 213.—[3] Ibid.—[4] Hall's Harrison, p. 211.

[5] Statement of Lieut. Baker, its commandant, in the "*Albany Argus;*" Hall's Harrison, p. 211.

approached, from other directions, and showed signs of hostility. One of these was killed, as he approached, by a single stroke of the Colonel's sword; the other, raising his rifle, shot the prisoner.[1] Colonel Lewis and General Winchester were taken prisoners by Roundhead, the Indian chief, stripped of their cloaks, coats, vests, and hats, and carried back to the British lines, where Colonel Proctor rescued them from the hands of their captors, after considerable trouble.[2]

In the mean time the party of troops on the left, which Colonels Lewis and Allen had left behind the pickets of the gardens, defended itself in the most obstinate manner, notwithstanding every effort which the enemy made to overcome it;[3] and, at ten o'clock, finding that his loss was becoming very serious, Colonel Proctor withdrew his forces, with the intention of abandoning the attempt, or of awaiting the return of his savage allies, who had not yet completed their bloody work with the unfortunate men who had formed the right wing of the American force.[4]

Unfortunately, about this time the commanding-general was brought into Colonel Proctor's lines, a prisoner in the hands of the Indians; and the latter officer, with that cowardice which always characterizes such as he, determined to avail himself of the anxiety of the General, in his unhappy situation, to secure what his own prowess could not accomplish by force of arms. Accordingly, "he represented to the General that nothing but an immediate surrender would save the Americans from an indiscriminate massacre by the Indians;" and General Winchester, ignorant of the position and success of his left wing, yielded to the wiles of the dishonorable enemy.[1] A flag of truce was sent by Major Overton, one of the aids of General Winchester, with *orders* from that officer for the surrender of the gallant party behind the garden pickets; while Colonel Proctor, in person, accompanied it to receive the submission, through diplomacy, which he had failed to secure by force.[2]

Whether the General, a prisoner in the hands of an enemy, could legally exercise any authority over those who were still at their post of duty, under the flag of their country, is exceedingly questionable; and Major Madison, with great propriety, so far disregarded the "*order*" of the General, that he refused to "agree to any capitulation which General Winchester might direct, unless the safety and protection of his men were stipulated."[3] Colonel Proctor, with the haughtiness which is so general among men of little minds, imperiously inquired if the Major meant "to dictate to *him?*" and when he had been informed that the Major "meant

[1] Hall's Harrison, p. 211; McAfee, pp. 213, 214.

[2] Darnell's Journal, Jan. 22; Hall's Harrison, p. 211; Christie, p. 100; Gen. Proctor to Gen. Sheaffe, Jan. 26, 1813; Drake's Book of Indians, book v. p. 129; James' Mil. Occur., i. pp. 188, 189.—[3] Darnell's Jour., Jan. 22; Hall's Life of Harrison, p. 212; Christie, p. 100; Gen. Proctor to Gen. Sheaffe, Jan. 26, 1813; Gen. Winchester to Secretary of War, Jan. 23, 1813.

[4] Darnell's Journal, Jan. 22; Hall's Life of Harrison, p. 212; McAfee, pp. 214, 215.

[1] Darnell's Jour., p. 54, *note;* Hall's Harrison, p. 212; Christie, p. 100; Armstrong, i. pp. 74–76; Mem. of conversation, &c.; Gen. Winchester to Sec. of War, Jan. 23, 1813.—[2] Hall's Harrison, p. 212; Christie, p. 100; Gen. Winchester to Sec. of War, Jan. 23, 1813; McAfee, p. 215.

[3] Darnell's Journal, Jan. 22; Hall's Harrison, pp. 212, 213; McAfee, p. 215.

to dictate *for himself;*" and that he and his party preferred "to sell their lives as dearly as possible, rather than be massacred in cold blood," he reconciled himself to his fate, and agreed to receive a surrender on the condition "that all private property should be respected; that sleds should be procured for the removal of the wounded, on the following day, to Amherstburg; that, meanwhile, the disabled should be protected by a guard; and that the side-arms of the officers should be returned when the prisoners reached Malden.[1] *On these conditions*, after consulting with his officers, Major Madison surrendered, with his entire party, as prisoners of war.[2]

The Indians *immediately* began to plunder the baggage of the prisoners, but Major Madison ordered them to oppose the intruders, even to the extent of a charge of bayonets;[3] and, so far as this portion of the detachment was concerned, the practice ceased.

About twelve o'clock, on the twenty-second, the British took up their line of march for Malden, taking with them all the prisoners who could march;[4] and leaving behind them, as guards of the wounded, under the provisions of the surrender, only Major Reynolds—the commander of the force which had been defeated at Frenchtown, four days before—and a few interpreters.[5] The wounded appear to have been collected and taken into several houses in the village, where they were properly attended to by Doctors Todd and Bowers, of the Kentucky volunteers;[1] while the greater part of the savages accompanied the British as far as Stoney Creek, six miles from Malden, where "a frolic" had been provided for them by their civilized allies.[2]

The night was passed, both by the wounded prisoners and by Major Reynolds, in the most intense anxiety, the fact being apparent to all, that the savages intended to return to Frenchtown, and that the nominal "guard" which Colonel Proctor had left was wholly inadequate to insure the safety of the prisoners.[3]

At an early hour the next morning (*Jan.* 23, 1813), about two hundred Indians, painted black and red, entered the village from Malden.[4] A council was immediately held, in which it was resolved to kill all the prisoners who could not march with them, as a sacrifice to appease the spirits of those of their companions who had fallen in the battle; and a series of the most frightful antics were immediately commenced, as an earnest of their cruelties.[5] Thence they proceeded to plunder the houses of the inhabitants; and, afterwards, those in which the wounded were laid were entered, the sufferers robbed of their clothing and blankets, and then tomahawked without mercy.[6] Captain Hickman was dragged to the door of one of the houses, tomahawked, and thrown back into the house; and this

---

[1] Darnell's Jour., Jan. 22; Christie, p. 100; McAfee, pp. 215, 216.—[2] Darnell's Jour., Jan. 22; McAfee, p. 216.
[3] McAfee, p. 216.—[4] Darnell's Jour., Jan. 22; Armstrong, i. p. 77.—[5] Darnell's Jour., Jan. 22; McAfee, p. 216.

[1] Darnell's Journal, Jan. 22; Narrative of John Davenport.—[2] McAfee, p. 217.—[3] Darnell's Journal, Jan. 22; McAfee, p. 217.—[4] Darnell's Journal, Jan. 23.
[5] McAfee, p. 217.—[6] Darnell's Journal, Jan. 23; Dr. Bower to J. Bledsoe, April 24, 1813.

appeared to be the signal for the consummation of the outrages.[1] The houses of Jean B. Jereaume and Gabriel Godfrey, into which the greater part of the prisoners had been taken, were set on fire; and, as many of the wounded were able to drag themselves to the doors and windows, hoping to save themselves from the flames, they were met by the savages, tomahawked, and thrown back into the burning buildings, amidst the triumphant yells of the Indians.[2] Others, who were not in those houses, were tomahawked and thrown into the flames;[3] while others, similarly mutilated, were left in the streets and highways, to be devoured by the dogs or hogs which rambled around.[4] A few, stronger than their fellows, were marched off towards Malden, and, as often as their strength failed, they were tomahawked, scalped, and left by the side of the road.[5]

The details of this tragedy, as narrated by the writers of that day, are too horrible to be repeated.[6] Suffice it to say that the vilest passions of which man is capable, appear, in this case, to have been allowed to run wild. Even Wyoming was less terrible; and the the darkest of all the chaplets which had been woven in America for the brow of Britannia, was that which was sent from the banks of the Raisin River.

Of the American forces only thirty-three escaped—three hundred and ninety-seven having been killed or missing, and five hundred and thirty-seven taken prisoners.[1] The enemy (British) is said to have lost twenty-four killed, and one hundred and fifty-eight wounded;[2] his allies (the Indians) had many killed and wounded, but the number is not known.

For his cowardly inhumanity,—to use no stronger term,—Colonel Proctor was promoted to the command of a Brigadier-general; and the government affirmed the appointment.[3]

The severity of this blow was felt throughout the entire Confederacy, but in Kentucky, above all other States, it was felt most keenly. Nearly every prominent family was thrown into mourning; and on every hand the most poignant grief was manifested. But then, more than ever before, did the people of that gallant State rally around the banners of their country; and under the leadership of the veteran Shelby, Johnson, and other well-known officers, they visited the same Proctor, and his savage allies, some months afterwards, with a terrible retribution.

[Note.—The Dispatches of Gen. Winchester to the Secretary of War, and those of Col. Proctor to Gen. Sheaffe, which had been provided for the illustration of this chapter, have been omitted by the Publishers for want of room.]

[1] McAfee, p. 218.—[2] Darnell's Journal, Jan. 23; Armstrong, i. p. 78.—[3] McAfee, p. 218.—[4] Ensign Baker to Gen. Winchester, Feb. 25, 1813.—[5] Darnell's Jour., Jan. 23; Mallary's Narrative; McAfee, p. 218.—[6] Those who feel desirous of more elaborate details of the massacre can find them in Darnell's *Journal*; McAfee's *History of War in Western Country*; Mallary's *Narrative*; Davenport's *Narrative*; Armstrong's *Notices of the War*; Thomson's *Sketches*; Niles' *Register*, iv.; Perkins' *Annals of the West*, &c.

[1] Returns, signed "James Garrard, jr., *Brig.-Insp.*," appended to Gen. Winchester's Dispatch to Secretary of War, Feb. 11, 1813.—[2] Montreal Courant, Feb. 6; Christie, p. 100; Auchinleck's History of War, p. 125; British "General Orders," signed "Ed. Baynes, *Adj.-Gen. N. A.*"

[3] Christie, p. 101; Auchinleck, p. 126.

CHAPTER XXXIX.

February 7, 1813.[1]

THE EXPEDITION TO ELIZABETHTOWN, U. C.

THE troubles between Great Britain and the United States, during the last war between the two countries, produced the most intense excitement along the borders of Canada and the northern States; and the respective countries found few more zealous advocates than among those who lived in the immediate vicinity of the boundary between the two nations. In many cases, indeed, the zeal which was there displayed was not tempered with prudence or propriety; and gradually, but surely, a most bitter state of animosity was produced on either side. Among other instances of this zealous interference with the policy of the enemy, were the inducements which were offered to the discontented among his troops to encourage desertion, and the faithful protection of those who thus abandoned the service of the King. As a legitimate consequence of this system of operations, the King's officers made frequent inroads into the border counties of the United States—especially into St. Lawrence County, New York—and seized such of the deserters as they could lay their hands on; in the course of which, it is probable, they extended their operations, where they could do so with safety, by harassing the inhabitants, by seizing their property, and by carrying off their persons.[1]

In the beginning of 1813, several of these persons, prisoners and deserters, were confined in the common jail at Elizabethtown, in Upper Canada;[2] and a knowledge of that fact was speedily productive of a determination to rescue them—a desire to retaliate, probably, influencing the people, in this respect, as much as sympathy with the prisoners. With this avowed object, on the evening of the sixth of February, Major Benjamin Forsyth, of the United States Rifles,[3] who was then stationed at Ogdensburg, assembled detachments from his own command, and from Captain Lydle's company of volunteers, together with a party of citizens,[4]—the whole numbering about two hundred men,[5]—

[1] Mr. Auchinleck (*Hist of the War*, p. 130) and some other writers say this affair occurred on the *sixth* of February.

[1] Breckenridge's Hist. of War, p. 116; Letter from Ogdensburg, Feb. 7, in Niles' Register, iii. pp. 408, 409; Hough's Hist. of St. Lawrence Co., p. 625; Thomson's Sketches, p. 118.—[2] Letter in Niles' Register; Hough's History of St. Lawrence Co., p. 625.

[3] This officer has been styled "*Captain* Forsyth" by Messrs. Hough, Niles, Thomson, and other writers; but as his commission as *Major* was issued Jan. 20, 1813, there is no reason why he should be so styled. He was an officer of long-standing and of great gallantry, and his subsequent services have not received that notice which they justly merit.

[4] "*The War*," i. p. 147; Breckenridge, p. 116; Letter in Niles' Register.—[5] "*The War*," i. p. 147; Letter in Niles' Register; Hough's History of St. Lawrence Co., pp. 625, 626; Thomson's Sketches, p. 118.

and proceeded, at about nine o'clock, in sleighs, along the southern bank of the river to Morristown.[1] At this place they halted a short time, and procured a guide,—one Arnold Smith, a tavern-keeper of that place,[2]—after which the party prepared to cross the river, the icy surface of which afforded every facility for that purpose.

Dividing his party into two divisions, with proper flanking parties,—the Major leading one division, in person; while Colonel Benedict, of the New York militia, led the other; Lieutenants Wells and Johnson commanding the flanking parties,[3]—at three o'clock the expedition commenced to move across the river.[4] As the ice was not strong, the columns moved in open order; and, as they approached the opposite shore, the flanking parties were detached, on either side of the village, to cut off the retreat, and to hold in check any reinforcements which might approach to strengthen the place.[5]

Elizabethtown,—now well known to all Northern tourists as *Brockville*,—Upper Canada, is pleasantly situated on the northern bank of the St. Lawrence River, about eleven miles above Ogdensburg. It is built on a succession of ridges, rising gradually, one above another, from the water's edge, and running parallel with the river; on the upper one of which—the highest part of the village—then, as now, were the court-house and jail, an elegant brick building, occupying one side of a public square.[1] Passing through the village the expedition moved towards the jail,—where had been confined the deserters and prisoners who had been the objects of the excursion,—and, after detaching small parties to secure the different streets in the village, Major Forsyth, with a small party, entered the building, demanded the keys from the jailer, and released those of the prisoners—sixteen in number—who had been taken from the United States—leaving a murderer, the only felon in the prison, as the solitary occupant of the cells, notwithstanding his urgent appeal for a participation in the freedom which had been extended to his fellow-prisoners.[2]

After securing Major Carley, three captains, two lieutenants,—all belonging to the militia, and, probably, not on duty,—with forty-six other prisoners; one hundred and twenty muskets, twenty rifles, two casks of fixed ammunition, and some other public stores, the expedition returned to Morristown, and, thence, to Ogdensburg, where it arrived before daylight, without the loss of a man.[3]

This gallant exploit elicited considerable applause throughout the country; and Major Forsyth was rewarded with a brevet rank as Lieutenant-colonel in the army, dating from the sixth of February, as a memorial of the event.[4]

---

[1] "*The War*," i. p. 147; Hough's St. Lawrence Co., p. 626.—[2] Hough's St. Lawrence Co., p. 626.—[3] Ibid.

[4] "*The War*," i. p. 147; Thomson's Sketches, p. 118.

[5] Hough's St. Lawrence Co., p. 626.

[1] Smith's Canada, ii. p. 303.—[2] Hough's St. Lawrence Co., p. 626; Letter in Niles' Register; James' Military Occurrences, i. p. 134.

[3] Breckenridge, p. 116; Hough's St. Lawrence Co., p. 626, in which *the names of the prisoners* appear; Letter in Niles' Register; Thomson's Sketches, p. 116; "*The War*," i. p. 147; James' Military Occurrences, i. p. 134.

[4] Gardner's Dictionary of the Army, p. 177.

CHAPTER XL.

February 22, 1813.

THE ATTACK ON OGDENSBURG, N. Y.

THE expedition against Elizabethtown, under Major Forsyth, which has been made the subject of a chapter in this work, excited the enemy to retaliation; and for this purpose an expedition against Ogdensburg was prepared, under the direction of Lieutenant-colonel McDonnell. Information of these designs had been communicated to Major Forsyth, and he had applied, in vain, to General Dearborn for assistance; although permission was given to evacuate the place whenever the Major might desire to do so.[1]

The militia having returned home, Major Forsyth's command alone remained in the garrison; and, on receipt of the General's letter, having taken council of his officers, that officer resolved to defend the village to the last extremity. With this object, an iron twelve-pounder—a trophy of Saratoga—was placed in battery near the corner of Ford and Euphamia (now State) streets, under the command of Captain Kellog, of the Albany Volunteers; in Ford-street, between State and Isabella streets, was placed a brass six-pounder, mounted on wheels, under the command of Joseph York, sheriff of the county; at a short distance north from the northeast corner of Mr. Parish's store, was a rude wooden breastwork, on which had been mounted an iron twelve-pounder,—a trophy of Saratoga,—which was commanded by Joshua Conkey, of the town of Canton; on the point where now stands the light-house had been mounted a brass six-pounder, mounted on a sled, and commanded by a Sergeant of the Albany Volunteers; behind "the old stone garrison," below the village, were two old-fashioned iron six-pounders, on sleds, under the command of Daniel W. Church and Lieutenant Baird, of the Rifles; and in front of the same buildings were two other six-pounders, one brass and one iron, also on sleds. On the bank of the river, dismounted, were several pieces of cannon, which had been thrown ashore from gunboats which had been dismantled there.[1]

On the morning of the twenty-second of February, a strong body of the enemy—regulars and militia—crossed the river and approached the village. His force moved in two divisions[2]—the right composed of a detachment from the Glengary Light-infantry Fencibles, and a body of militia, commanded by Captain Jenkins, of the former, moved against the left of the American posi-

[1] Hough's History of St. Lawrence County, p. 627.

[1] Hough's St. Lawrence Co., pp. 627, 628.—[2] Lieut.-Col. McDonnell to Sir G. Prevost, Feb. 23, 1813; Hough's St. Lawrence Co., p. 629; Thomson's Sketches, p. 119.

tion, above "the stone garrison," to hold that portion of the garrison in check, and to cut off its retreat; the left, composed of detachments from the King's regiment and the Royal Newfoundland Corps, and of a large body of local militia, commanded by Lieutenant-colonel McDonnell, moved against the village.[1]

As the right division approached "the stone garrison," where were stationed Major Forsyth and his small command, that officer formed his men in the rear of that building and prepared to defend his position. The brass six-pounders, under Lieutenant Baird, occupied the right of the line; while Adjutant Church, with the iron six-pounder, was about two-thirds of the way down the line; and, as the enemy approached the position, Major Forsyth walked down the front of the line, encouraged his men, and directed them to reserve their fire until the word of command was given. When the enemy reached the edge of the bank he opened his fire, but without effect; soon after which Major Forsyth gave orders to open his fire, when eight men of the enemy fell at the first discharge.[2] It is said that the enemy afterwards attempted to charge on the American line; but, the militia failing to support the light-infantry, the effort failed, with the loss of a number of prisoners, together with several killed and wounded, and he was compelled to withdraw.[3]

[1] Lieut.-Col. McDonnell to Sir G. Prevost, Feb. 23, 1813; Hough's St. Lawrence Co., p. 629; James' Mil. Occur., i. p. 137.—[2] Hough's St. Lawrence Co., p. 629; Deposition of Adj. Church, Feb. 24, 1814.

[3] Lieut.-Col. McDonnell to Sir G. Prevost, Feb. 23, 1813; Deposition of Adj. Church, Feb. 24, 1814.

In the mean time, Lieutenant-colonel McDonnell had entered the village, notwithstanding the fire of the pieces under Sheriff York and Captain Kellog[1]—the former maintaining his post until two of his men had fallen, and he and his entire party had been taken prisoners; the latter until his gun had been disabled, when he retired, with his command, and joined Major Forsyth.[2] Captain Conkey surrendered, with his men and gun, without resistance;[3] and, the few men who had been posted therein having retired, the village was entirely in the hands of the enemy. About this time the enemy's right wing had retreated, and "the stone garrison" became the next object of the enemy's attention; but "he procured time" for his men "to recover their breath,"[4] by sending a flag to the garrison with a summons to surrender,[5] accompanied with a threat that if they did not, "every man should be put to the bayonet."[6] Major Forsyth replied, "there must be more fighting done first;" and, at the earliest opportunity after the return of the flag, he discharged two of his field-pieces into the ranks of the enemy, with good effect. Fearing a renewal of the fire, the enemy took shelter behind the neighboring buildings, and began to pick off the men who had assembled around the pieces near "the stone garrison;" while another party appeared to be preparing for an assault on the work. The strength of the as-

[1] Lieut.-Col. McDonnell to Sir G. Prevost, Feb. 23, 1813; Hough's St. Lawrence Co., p. 629.—[2] Hough's St. Lawrence Co., p. 629.—[3] Ibid.; Deposition of Adj. Church, Feb. 24, 1814.—[4] Lieut.-Col. McDonnell to Sir G. Prevost, Feb. 23, 1813.—[5] Ibid.—[6] Hough's St. Lawrence Co., p. 629; Deposition of Adj. Church, Feb. 24, 1814.

sailants—nearly four to one, it is said—being so great, Major Forsyth considered all farther resistance useless, and he evacuated "the garrison" and the village.[1]

Thus left in undisputed possession of the village, the enemy immediately commenced to remove the public property to Canada; while the Indians[2] and camp-followers,—among whom were a number of women, or "furies," as a contemporary print calls them,—amused themselves by abusing the inhabitants and plundering the houses.[3]

In this affair the enemy numbered not less than eight hundred men;[4] while the garrison embraced only one company of riflemen, a small number of volunteers from Albany, and the inhabitants of the village.[5] The loss of the Americans, besides the prisoners,

[1] Hough's History of St. Lawrence Co., p. 630; Lieut.-Col. McDonnell to Sir G. Prevost, Feb. 23, 1813.

[2] No writer alludes to the presence of any Indians, but the village paper, published at the time, after the incursion, says, positively, there *were* Indians present, and I have followed its statement.

[3] Ogdensburg *Palladium*, Feb. 25; Hough's St. Lawrence Co., p. 631; Letter from Mrs. Yorke, "Ogdensburg, Feb. 26," in Niles' *Register*, cited by Dr. Hough.

[4] Deposition of Adj. Church, Feb. 24, 1814. Mr. Thomson (*Sketches of the War*, p. 118) says it numbered *twelve hundred* men; Lieut.-Col. McDonnell (*Dispatch, Feb.* 23), "about *four hundred and eighty* regulars and militia;" and Mr. James (*Military Occurrences*, i. p. 137) agrees with him. Gen. Macomb (*Dispatch, Feb.* 23) and Mr. Breckenridge (*Hist. of War*, p. 116) say it was *twelve hundred* men.

[5] Hough's St. Lawrence Co., p. 628.

was five killed, eighteen wounded, and a few prisoners;[1] that of the enemy was one sergeant and six men, *killed;* and Lieutenant-colonel McDonnell, Captains Jenkins and McDonnell, Lieutenants McKay, Empey, McLean, and McDermott, and forty-one men, *wounded.*[2] But the loss of the Americans was still greater. Two armed schooners and two gun-boats were burned;[3] fourteen hundred stand of arms, with accoutrements, complete; twelve pieces of artillery; "a vast quantity of ammunition; two stands of colors; three hundred tents; and a large quantity of camp equipage, together with a very considerable quantity of beef, pork, flour, &c.,"[4] were taken, and considerable damage was done to private property in the village.

[NOTE.—The dispatches of Maj. Forsyth and Lieut.-Col. McDonnell, which had been provided for the illustration of this chapter, have been omitted by the Publishers for want of room.]

[1] Hough's St. Lawrence Co., p. 630.

[2] Returns appended to "General Orders," signed "E. BAYNE, *Adj.-Gen.*" Mr. Auchinleck (*History of War*, p. 131) says the loss was *eight* killed and *fifty-two* wounded.

[3] "General Orders," signed "JOHN HARVEY, *Dep. Adj.-Gen.;*" James' Military Occurrences, i. p. 139.

[4] Ogdensburg *Palladium*, March 3, 1813; Lieut.-Col. McDonnell to Sir G. Prevost, Feb. 23; Auchinleck's History of War, p. 131; James' Military Occurrences, i. p. 139. Col. McComb (*Dispatch to Gen. Dearborn, Feb.* 23, 1813) says, "there were no stores of any consequence there;" and Mr. Thomson (*Sketches of the War*, p. 119) agrees with him.

CHAPTER XLI.

February 24, 1813.

THE CAPTURE OF THE PEACOCK.

In a former chapter of this work, the blockade of San Salvador, by the United States ship *Hornet*, Captain James Lawrence, was briefly referred to.[1] Eighteen days after the departure of the *Constitution* from that port,—the *Hornet*, meanwhile, holding the *Bonne Citoyenne* in close quarters,—His Britannic Majesty's ship *Montague*, of seventy-four guns, drove the *Hornet* into the harbor, from which, taking advantage of a dark night, she soon afterwards escaped.[2]

After cruising along the coast until the twenty-fourth of February, at which time she was off the mouth of Demarara River, at half-past three o'clock of that day, the *Hornet* suddenly made two strange sails—one, which was evidently an English brig of war, at anchor without the bar; the other, whose character was not ascertained, was on her weather-quarter, edging down for the *Hornet*. At twenty minutes past four the second, which also appeared to be a brig of war, showed British colors; when the *Hornet* beat to quarters, cleared for action, and kept close to the wind, in order to gain the weather-gage. Fifty minutes afterwards, finding that she could weather the strangers, the *Hornet* showed her colors and tacked; and five minutes afterwards—both vessels being close by the wind, and standing towards each other—they exchanged broadsides, at half pistol-shot distance, as they passed, each employing her larboard battery. Immediately afterwards the stranger put her helm hard up, with the intention of wearing short around, to get an opportunity to rake the *Hornet;* but her design was understood, and by wearing, and receiving her larboard broadside, the *Hornet* was enabled to run her close on board on the starboard-quarter; and after continuing, from that favorable position, a steady and well-directed fire, for about fifteen minutes, she compelled her to surrender.[1]

Immediately after striking her colors, the stranger raised a signal of distress; and, immediately afterwards, her mainmast went over the side.[2] Lieutenant Shubrick having been dispatched to take possession of her, he soon afterwards reported her to be His Britannic Majesty's brig of war *Peacock*, of eighteen guns, Captain William Peake; that her captain had been killed late in the

---

[1] Vide Chap. XXXV, p. 183.—[2] Capt. Lawrence to Sec. of Navy, March 19, 1813; Cooper's Naval Hist., ii. p. 72; Clark's Naval Hist., p. 171; Auchinleck's Hist., p. 78, *note*.

[1] Capt. Lawrence to Secretary of Navy, March 19, 1813; Cooper, ii. pp. 72, 73; Clark, p 172; Sketches of the War, p. 290.

[2] Capt. Lawrence to Secretary of Navy, March 19, 1813; James' Naval Occurrences, p. 200.

action; that a large proportion of her crew had fallen; and that she was fast sinking.[1]

Orders were immediately issued for the removal of the wounded; and both vessels were brought to an anchor, to facilitate the removal. The guns of the prize were also thrown overboard; her shot-holes were plugged; and her pumps were rigged, with the same object; and every exertion was called into requisition to save the ship, until the wounded could be removed; yet all these were unsuccessful—the *Peacock* suddenly settling down and sinking, carrying with her thirteen of her crew, of whom four were saved by the *Hornet's* boats, and three men belonging to the *Hornet*, who had been sent to render assistance to her wounded prisoners. Several others, including Lieutenant Connor, of the *Hornet*, narrowly escaped the same fate.[2]

The relative force of the ships favored the *Hornet*—the *Peacock* mounting sixteen twenty-four-pound carronades, two long-nines, one twelve-pound carronade on her forecastle, one four or six pounder, and two swivels,[1] manned with one hundred and thirty men;[2] while that of the *Hornet* was eighteen thirty-two-pound carronades and two long-twelves,[3] manned with one hundred and thirty-five efficient men.[4]

The loss of the *Hornet* was inconsiderable—although her sails and rigging were much cut, her hull was scarcely touched; and, with the exception of slight wounds in her mainmast and bowsprit, her spars were uninjured; while of her crew, only one was killed and two slightly wounded, in addition to two who were burned by the explosion of a cartridge.[5] That of the *Peacock* is not known, with any degree of certainty. Captain Peake and four men were found *killed;* four officers and twenty-nine men were found *wounded;* and nine were drowned, as before related.[6]

[1] Capt. Lawrence to Sec. of Navy, March 19, 1813; Cooper, ii. pp. 73, 74.—[2] Capt. Lawrence to Sec. of Navy, March 19, 1813; Clark, pp. 172, 173; Auchinleck, p. 135.

[1] Capt. Lawrence to Sec. of Navy, March 19, 1813; Clark, p. 174. Mr. Cooper (*Hist.*, ii. p. 74) says nothing of her *swivels*. Mr. James (*Naval Occur.*, p. 202) admits the *swivels*, but denies "the four or six pounders."

[2] Capt. Lawrence to Sec. of Navy, March 19, 1813; Cooper, ii. p. 74. Mr. James (*Naval Occur.*, p. 202) says she had only *one hundred and twenty-two* men and boys.

[3] Cooper, ii. p. 74. Mr. James (*Naval Occur.*, p. 203, and *Warden Refuted*, Table I.) makes her nine-pounders *twelves*.—[4] Cooper, ii. p. 74; Lieut. Conner to *N. Y. Commercial Advertiser*. Mr. James (*Naval Occur.*, pp. 203, 204, and *Warden Refuted*, Table I.) makes her crew *one hundred and sixty-five* men.—[5] Capt. Lawrence to Secretary of Navy, March 19, 1813; Clark, p. 173.—[6] Capt. Lawrence to Secretary of Navy, March 19, 1813.

DOCUMENT.

CAPTAIN LAWRENCE'S DISPATCH TO THE SECRETARY OF THE NAVY.

U. S. SHIP HORNET, HOLMES' HOLE,
March 29, 1813.

SIR:—I have the honor to inform you of the arrival at this port of the United States ship *Hornet*, under my command, from a cruise of one hundred and forty-five days, and to state to you, that after Commodore Bainbridge left the coast of Brazil (January 6th), I continued off the harbor of St. Salvador, blockading the *Bonne Citoyenne*, until the 24th, when the *Montague*, seventy-four, hove in sight, and chased me into the harbor, but night coming on I wore, and stood out to the southward. Knowing that she left Rio Janeiro for the express purpose of relieving the *Bonne Citoyenne*, and the packet (which I had also blockaded for fourteen days, and obliged her to send her mail to Rio in a Portuguese smack), I judged it most prudent to shift my cruising-ground, and hauled by the wind to the westward, with the view of cruising off Pernambuco; and, on the 14th of February, captured the English brig *Resolution*, of ten guns, from Rio Janeiro, bound to Maranham, with coffee, &c., and about twenty-five thousand dollars in specie. I took out the money and set her on fire; I then ran down the coast for Maranham, and cruised there a short time; from thence ran off Surinam. After cruising off that coast, from the 5th until the 22d of February, without meeting a vessel, I stood for Demerara, with an intention, should I not be fortunate on that station, to run through the West Indies on my way to the United States. But on the morning of the 24th I discovered a brig to leeward, to which I gave chase; ran into quarter less four, and not having a pilot, was obliged to haul off—the fort at the entrance of Demerara River at this time bearing southwest, distance two and a half leagues. Previously to giving up the chase, I discovered a vessel at anchor outside the bar, with English colors flying, apparently a brig of war. In beating round Corobano bank, in order to get at her, at half-past three P. M., I discovered another sail on my weather-quarter, edging down for us. At twenty minutes past four she hoisted English colors, at which time we discovered her to be a large man-of-war brig;—beat to quarters, and cleared ship for action, kept close by the wind, in order, if possible, to get the weather-gage. At ten minutes past five, finding I could weather the enemy, I hoisted American colors, and tacked. At twenty minutes past five, in passing each other, exchanged broadsides within half-pistol shot. Observing the enemy in the act of wearing, I bore up, received his starboard broadside, ran him close on board on the starboard quarter, and kept up such a heavy and well-directed fire, that in less than fifteen minutes he surrendered, being literally cut to pieces, and hoisted an ensign, union down, from his fore-rigging, as a signal of distress. Shortly after, his mainmast went by the board;—dispatched Lieutenant Shubrick on board, who soon returned with her first-lieutenant, who reported her to be His Britannic Majesty's late brig *Peacock*, commanded by Captain William Peake, who fell in the latter part of the action,—that a number of her crew were killed and wounded, and that she was sinking fast, having then six feet of water in the hold;—dispatched the boats immediately for the wounded, and brought both vessels to anchor. Such shot-holes as could be got at, were then plugged; her guns thrown overboard; and every possible exertion used to keep her afloat, until the prisoners could be removed, by pumping and bailing, but without effect, and she unfortunately sunk in five and a half fathoms water, carrying down thirteen of her crew, and three of my brave fellows, viz.: John Hart, Joseph Williams, and Hannibal Boyd. Lieutenant Connor, Midshipman Cooper, and the remainder of the *Hornet's* crew employed in removing the prisoners, with difficulty saved themselves by jumping into a boat that was lying at her bows, as she went down. Four men of the thirteen mentioned, were so fortunate as to gain the foretop, and were afterwards taken off by the boats. Previous to her going down, four of her men took to her stern-boat, which had been much damaged during the action, which I hope reached the shore in safety; but from the heavy sea running at the time, the shattered state of the boat, and the difficulty of landing on the coast, I fear they were lost. I have not been able to ascertain from her officers the exact number killed. Captain Peake and four men were found dead on board. The master, one midshipman, carpenter, and captain's clerk, and twenty-nine seamen, were wounded, most of them very severely, three of whom died of their wounds after being removed, and nine drowned. Our loss was trifling in comparison:—John Place, killed; Samuel Coulson and Joseph Dalrymple, slightly wounded; George Coffin and Lewis Todd, severely burnt by the explosion of a cartridge. Todd survived only a few days. Our rigging and sails were much cut. One shot through the foremast, and the bowsprit slightly injured. Our hull received little or no damage. At the time the *Peacock* was brought to action, the

L'Espiegle (the brig mentioned above as being at anchor), mounting sixteen thirty-two-pound carronades and two long nines, lay about six miles in shore, and could plainly see the whole of the action. Apprehensive she would beat out to the assistance of her consort, such exertions were used by my officers and crew, in repairing damages, &c., that by nine o'clock our boats were stowed, a new set of sails bent, and the ship completely ready for action. At two o'clock A. M., got under weigh, and stood by the wind to the northward and westward, under easy sail.

On mustering next morning, found we had two hundred and seventy-seven souls on board, including the crew of the American brig *Hunter*, of Portland, taken a few days before by the *Peacock*. And, as we had been on two-thirds allowance of provisions for some time, and had but three thousand four hundred gallons of water on board, I reduced the allowance to three pints a man, and determined to make the best of my way to the United States.

The *Peacock* was deservedly styled one of the finest of her class in the British navy, probably about the tonnage of the *Hornet*. Her beam was greater by five inches; but her extreme length not so great by four feet. She mounted sixteen twenty-four-pound carronades, two long nines, one twelve-pound carronade on her topgallant-forecastle, as a shifting-gun, and one four or six pounder and two swivels mounted aft. I find by her quarter-bill, that her crew consisted of one hundred and thirty-four men; four of whom were absent in a prize.

The cool and determined conduct of my officers and crew during the action, and their almost unexampled exertions afterwards, entitle them to my warmest acknowledgments; and I beg leave most earnestly to recommend them to the notice of government.

By the indisposition of Lieutenant Stewart I was deprived of the services of an excellent officer; had he been able to stand the deck, I am confident his exertions would not have been surpassed by any one on board. I should be doing injustice to the merits of Lieutenant Shubrick, and acting Lieutenants Connor and Newton, were I not to recommend them particularly to your notice.

Lieutenant Shubrick was in the action with the *Guerriere* and *Java*. Captain Hull and Commodore Bainbridge can bear testimony to his coolness and good conduct on both occasions.

With the greatest respect, I remain, &c.,

JAMES LAWRENCE.

Hon. WILLIAM JONES, Secretary of Navy.

P. S.—At the commencement of the action, my sailing-master and seven men were absent in a prize, and Lieutenant Stewart and six men on the sick list.

CHAPTER XLII.

March 11, 1813.

THE PRIVATEER GENERAL ARMSTRONG, OF NEW YORK.

THE enterprise of Baltimore, in the equipment of vessels for the privateer service, has been referred to in a former chapter of this work;[1] and the services of the merchants of the city of New York—by whom a greater number of privateers were sent out, during the war, than by those of any other port in the United States—deserve especial notice and commendation. As in the early days of the War of the Revolution, the merchants of the city of New York *were the leaders of the people in every other colony;* and as *they* struck the earliest and heaviest blow on that occasion, so in the "War of 1812,"

[1] Vide Chapter XXVII.

among the earliest, most active, and most consistent of the leaders of the people of the United States, were the merchants of the emporium of America. Within four months after the declaration of war twenty-six fast-sailing vessels, bearing eighteen long guns, one hundred and ninety-four pieces of artillery, and two thousand, two hundred and thirty-three men had sailed from New York; while seventeen from Baltimore, carrying twenty-two long guns, and one hundred and twenty-seven guns,[1] nobly seconded the enterprise and gallantry of their neighbors; and all, alike, vindicated the freedom of the seas and the rights of man.

One of these, the *General Armstrong*, of New York—a fine schooner of two hundred and forty-six tons, mounting a "long tom" (a forty-two-pounder) and six long nines,[2] and owned by Rensselaer Havens, Thomas Farmer, Thomas Jenkins, and other merchants of that city[3]—early in March, was cruising on the coast of South America; and on the morning of the eleventh of March, was off the mouth of the Surinam River. At seven o'clock in the morning of that day she made a vessel, bearing S. S. E.; at eight, the stranger, which had been at anchor under the land, got under way; and at half-past eight she stood to the northward, firing three guns at the privateer, and hoisting British colors. The latter immediately gave chase; and at ten minutes past nine she fired her "long tom," and hoisted American colors.

Both vessels being still on the same course, at five minutes before ten, the stranger tacked and stood as near the schooner as the wind would permit, keeping up a brisk fire on the latter from her main battery, with but little effect. About twenty minutes later, the schooner still standing to the northward, the crew of the latter, under the supposition that the stranger was a British letter-of-marque, "unanimously agreed" to bear down and board her; and with this intention, a few minutes afterwards, the schooner put her helm up, and bore down with the intention to give the stranger her starboard broadside; to wear ship, run alongside, and give her larboard broadside; and then to board her. This bold design, except the boarding, was fully carried out, in the course of which it was discovered that she was a sloop-of-war, mounting fourteen guns on her main-deck, six on her quarter-deck, and four on her forecastle; and that instead of being a private ship she was one of the Royal navy.

This important discovery would have justified an immediate retreat, had such a course, at that time, been included in the plan of operations. Such, however, was not the case; but keeping up the fire, with the utmost coolness, within pistol-shot of her opponent, the *General Armstrong* contended gallantly for the mastery. Three-quarters of an hour this contest continued—the officers and crews using their pistols, and the topsmen of the stranger employing their

[1] Coggeshall's Hist. of American Privateers, pp. 4, 5.

[2] Capt. Coggeshall (*Hist. of Am. Privateers*, p. 4) says she mounted *eighteen* guns and a "long-tom;" but a reference to the "*Protest*" of her Captain, in the hands of the representatives of her owners, enables me to correct his error, as above.—[3] The original records and accounts are still in possession of the family of Mr. Havens.

muskets as opportunity offered. At that time the captain of the schooner (*Guy R. Champlin*) was wounded by a musket-ball, fired from the stranger's maintop,—the ball passing through his left shoulder,—and went below to have his wound dressed.

Influenced by this disaster, and, probably, seeing that it was a hopeless contest, the crew appear to have suggested, at this time, the propriety of surrendering; and information of the proposal was conveyed to the captain, then in the hands of the surgeon, below. Fired with resentment at such a proposal, although faint from the loss of blood, he seized a loaded pistol, and directed the surgeon to go on deck, and "tell the officers and men, that if any one of them dare to strike the colors, he would immediately fire into the magazine, and blow them all up together."[1] This message had the desired effect; and as the alternative of running or sinking was offered, the former was preferred. Accordingly the schooner luffed to windward, and forereached on the stranger; when, with the assistance of the schooner's jib and topgallant-sail, and by a vigorous use of her sweeps, she soon secured her escape, notwithstanding the stranger opened a heavy fire on her as she left her.

In this desperate encounter the *Armstrong* had all the halyards of her head sails shot away; her foremast and bowsprit were badly wounded; all her shrouds, except one, were shot away; both her mainstays and her running-rigging were cut to pieces; her sails had been severely cut; several shot, between wind and water, had caused her to leak badly; and six of her crew were killed and sixteen wounded.

It appeared, subsequently, that the stranger was His Britannic Majesty's sloop-of-war *Coquette*, mounting eighteen thirty-two pound carronades upon the main-deck, six eighteen-pound carronades and a twelve-pound launch-carronade on the quarter-deck, and two long sixes on the forecastle; and manned with one hundred and twenty-one men and boys;[1] and when the relative strength of the two vessels are considered, it will be seen that this was one of the most daring exploits of the war.

Captain Champlin recovered; the schooner ran into Charleston, where she arrived on the fourth of April;[2] the owners of the vessel, in session at Tammany Hall, on the fourteenth of April, 1813, voted the thanks of the meeting to the officers and crew, "for their gallant defence;" and "a sword, at the expense of the stockholders," by a vote at the same meeting, was presented to Captain Champlin "for his gallant conduct in the *rencontre* above mentioned."[3]

[NOTE.—The extract from the schooner's log-book, cited by Mr. Niles, in the *Weekly Register*, Saturday, April 24, 1813, has been the basis of this narrative; and, where no other work has been cited, this is the *only* authority. Several other accounts have been examined, but as they have all been based on the log-book I have not cited them.—H. B. D.]

[1] Coggeshall's American Privateers, p. 108.

[1] James' Naval Occurrences, pp. 484, 485.—[2] Thomson's Sketches of the War, p. 203.—[3] Proceedings of the meeting, published in Niles' *Register*, iv. p. 133.

CHAPTER XLIII.

March 13, 1813.[1]

THE SCHOONER ADELINE AND THE BRITISH GUNBOATS.

EARLY in February, 1813, a strong naval force from the British fleet entered the Chesapeake. After anchoring in Lynnhaven Bay, with the *San Domingo* and the *Dragon*, of seventy-four guns each, the *Belvidera*, *Acaster*, *Maidstone*, and two other frigates, and several smaller vessels, the bay was declared to be in a state of blockade, and considerable depredation was done, both on the adjacent shores and among the shipping which entered the harbor. The smaller vessels, in addition to their duties as tenders, acted as *decoys* to entice such American vessels, as were ignorant of the blockade, within reach of the guns of the enemy's ships within the bay; and several vessels were thus treacherously led to destruction.[2]

On the thirteenth of March, 1813, three of these small vessels appeared off the anchorage-ground of a flotilla of United States gunboats, which was stationed a short distance above; and appeared desirous of drawing the latter from their moorings.[3] One of these small vessels was the *Lottery*, of Baltimore, a clipper-schooner, mounting six guns, which had been captured, after a desperate action, a short time previously, by the boats of the enemy's squadron; and Commander Arthur Sinclair, who commanded the flotilla, immediately hoisted sail on the schooner *Adeline*, mounting two or three guns, and, in company with three gunboats, he got under weigh. Notwithstanding the superiority of their force the enemy fled before him; and night coming on, at midnight Commander Sinclair anchored off Gwynn's Island, with two of the gunboats—the third not being able to fetch in, having entered the Rappahannock.[1]

Soon afterwards the *Adeline* was hailed by one of the schooners, and having answered, giving her name and character, Commander Sinclair repeated the question, without receiving a reply.[2] He was ordered, however, by the stranger, in the most peremptory manner, to send a boat on board the stranger, which he declined to do, and fired a musket ahead of the latter. It was immediately answered with a broadside of round and grape shot, and with a discharge of small-arms from the stranger; when, in his turn, he gave her a broadside, and a severe engagement ensued.[3] After continuing the action twenty minutes the stranger was silenced; but the extreme darkness of the night prevent-

---

[1] Commander Sinclair's letter, March 13, 1813. Mr. Clark (*Naval Hist.*, p. 166) says it occurred on the *tenth*.

[2] "*The War*," i. pp. 147, 148.—[3] Com. Sinclair to his friend, March 13, 1813.

[1] Clark's Naval Hist., p. 166; Thomson's Sketches of the War, p. 203.—[2] Com. Sinclair to his friend, March 13; Thomson's Sketches, p. 203.—[3] Clark, pp. 166, 167.

ed Commander Sinclair from seeing if she had surrendered, and, for the purpose of ascertaining her condition, he directed one of his gunboats which laid near her, to hail and make the inquiry. Instead of answering, however, the stranger renewed the fire; and Commander Sinclair, notwithstanding he feared she was one of his "imprudent, headstrong countrymen,"[1] was constrained to open a general fire from all the vessels under his command. Twenty minutes more the action was continued—the uncertainty of the character and strength of his opponent adding to the interest which an engagement in the night naturally produces—and as the flashes of her guns broke, for a moment, the darkness of the night, the crowds of men on her deck indicated the general character of the stranger. A second time her fire was suspended, and a second time Commander Sinclair, still uncertain of her nationality, ordered his command to discontinue the action. In the most treacherous manner, however, no sooner had the American fire ceased than the stranger renewed the action; and, a third time, the broadside of the *Adeline*, seconded by the gunboats, poured their fire into her, in return. This third engagement continued half an hour, when, a third time, the stranger suspended her fire. Still anxious to avoid an unnecessary effusion of blood, although the bad faith of the stranger would have warranted a more severe course, Lieutenant Sinclair, a third time, ordered a discontinuance of the action; and an officer was immediately sent to take possession of her.[1] After a thorough search, he returned *without finding her*,[2] and the mystery which surrounded the entire affair was increased by the uncertainty which prevailed respecting the fate of the stranger and her crew. When daylight dispelled the gloom the floating fragments of the wreck—some of them ten or twelve feet long, torn from the hull of the vessel by the *Adeline's* shot—appeared to give weight to the supposition that she had gone down, with all her crew; while an anchor, weighing about eight hundred pounds, and a large cable, which was secured, indicated a vessel of not less than two hundred tons burden.[3]

It appeared, subsequently, that the unknown opponent of the *Adeline* was the clipper *Lottery*, before referred to; that, taking advantage of the night, she slipped away from the scene of her protracted struggle; that her injuries were so great that the most determined efforts of her crew to save her were unavailing; and that she sank before morning, before she could reach the anchorage of the fleet near New Point Comfort.[4]

In this desperate conflict the *Adeline* and her consorts suffered but little injury; and of the crews, only one man was wounded.[5]

---

[1] Com. Sinclair to his friend, March 13.

[1] Clark, p. 167; Thomson's Sketches, p. 203.—[2] Mr. Clark (*Hist. of War*, p. 167) says she was pursued and fired on, but I find no evidence of such a course. On the contrary, Com. Sinclair expressed great anxiety concerning her fate; and he could not have done so, consistently, had he known she escaped.—[3] Com. Sinclair to his friend, March 13, 1813.

[4] Clark, p. 167.—[5] Ibid.; Thomson's Sketches, p. 203.

CHAPTER XLIV.

April 27, 1813.

THE CAPTURE OF YORK.

The operations of the army of the North, on the Canadian frontiers, in the spring of 1813, appear to have been dilatory and fruitless; and in this result the indecision of the Federal government, in its organization of a plan of operations, was not less instrumental than the inactivity of the commanders.[1]

At length, on the twenty-fifth of April, 1813, General Dearborn embarked at Sackett's Harbor; and, on the twenty-fifth, with about seventeen hundred troops,[2] and the squadron, composed of the *Madison*, *Oneida*, *Fair American*, *Hamilton*, *Governor Tompkins*, *Conquest*, *Asp*, *Pert*, *Julia*, *Growler*, *Ontario*, *Scourge*, *Lady of the Lake*, and *Raven*, under Commodore Chauncey,[3] he moved against York, the capital of Upper Canada.[4] After a tedious passage of two days,[5] on the twenty-seventh the expedition entered the harbor; and at eight o'clock commenced to land the troops.[6] It had been designed to land near the site of the old French fort, *Toronto*, about two miles and a half to the westward from the village; but, in consequence of the prevalence of a strong easterly wind and a heavy sea, the boats were driven farther to the westward; and, half a mile from the intended point of debarkation, the troops landed.[1] The ill effects of this change in the plan of operations, were increased by the inability of the shipping to cover the landing of the troops as effectually as had been intended;[2] and when Major Forsyth and his riflemen, who led the column,[3] approached the shore, they were severely harassed by a party of Indians under Major Givens,[4] and by a company of the Glengarry Fencibles, which had been sent forward to support them, both of which had taken a position in a thick wood within rifle-shot of the place of landing.[5]

As speedily as possible Major Forsyth was supported by Major King and a battalion of infantry—not, however,

[1] Armstrong's Notices, i. pp. 127–129.—[2] Com. Chauncey's Dispatch to Sec. of Navy, April 28, 1813; Cooper's Naval History, ii. p. 161; Thomson's Sketches, p. 120; Whiting's Biog. of Pike (*Sparks' Am. Biog.*, xv.), p. 298; Christie's Military and Naval Operations, p. 103. Gen. Sheaffe supposed there were from 1890 to 3000 men.

[3] Cooper, ii. p. 161.—[4] Armstrong's Notices, i. p. 129; Com. Chauncey's Dispatch, April 28, 1813; Thomson's Sketches, p. 120.—[5] "After a tedious passage of some days, by adverse winds, we arrived," &c.—*Gen. Dearborn's Dispatch, April* 28, 1813.—[6] Gen. Dearborn's Dispatch, April 28; Com. Chauncey's Dispatch, April 28; James' Military Occurrences, i. p. 141.

[1] Gen. Dearborn's Dispatch, April 28; Com. Chauncey's Dispatch, April 28; Cooper, ii. p. 161; Auchinleck's Hist., p. 151; Christie, p. 103.—[2] Gen. Dearborn's Dispatch, April 28.—[3] Ibid.; James' Mil. Occur., i. p. 143; Auchinleck's Hist., p. 151.—[4] Gen. Dearborn's Dispatch, April 28; Com. Chauncey's Dispatch, April 28; Gen. Sheaffe's Dispatch, May 5, 1813; James' Mil. Occur., i. p. 143; Auchinleck, p. 151.—[5] Gen. Dearborn's Dispatch, April 28; Gen. Sheaffe's Dispatch, April 28; James' Mil. Occur., i. p. 143; Capt. Moore to his brother, May 5, 1813; Auchinleck, p. 152.

until he had "lost some men, but no credit;"[1] and soon afterwards, Brigadier-general Pike and the main body of the land force also landed.[2] In the mean time, while the skirmishers continued to harass the respective forces, the enemy had been strengthened by the arrival of two companies of the Eighth (*or King's*) regiment of the line —"two hundred strong"[3]—by a company of the Royal Newfoundland regiment, and by a large body of militia;[4] and as the American troops, immediately after landing, had formed and pressed forward,[5] they soon encountered this strong force, in a thick wood, in which it had taken a position.[6] The column was composed of the Sixth, Fifteenth, Sixteenth, and Twenty-first regiments of infantry, and detachments of light and heavy artillery; with Major Forsyth's riflemen and Lieutenant-colonel McClure's volunteers as flanking parties; and when it entered the wood, the artillery was unable to move without great difficulty.[7] The enemy, taking advantage of this difficulty, fell on the flanks with a six-pounder and two howitzers; but, after a sharp contest, in which both suffered severely,[8] the enemy slowly retired to his works, followed by the Americans,[1] under the immediate command of General Pike.[2]

[1] Armstrong's Notices, i. p. 130. See also Whiting's Biog. of Pike, pp. 299–302.—[2] Gen. Dearborn's Dispatch, April 28; Thomson's Sketches, p. 121.—[3] Auchinleck, p. 152.—[4] Gen. Sheaffe's Dispatch, May 5; James' Military Occurrences, i. p. 143.—[5] Thomson's Sketches, p. 122; Whiting's Biography of Pike, p. 303; Christie, p. 104.

[6] Gen. Sheaffe's Dispatch, May 5; Letter from a field-officer, in "*The War*," i. p. 204; Whiting's Biography of Pike, p. 304.—[7] Letter from a field-officer, in "*The War*," i. p. 204; Thomson's Sketches, i. p. 122.

[8] Com. Chauncey's Dispatch, April 28; James' Military Occurrences, i. p. 144; Thomson's Sketches, p. 122; Breckenridge's History of War, pp. 118, 119.

At the time of this action, York was a small village, finely situated on the northern shore of an excellent harbor;[3] and was defended by several batteries, manned by a force of about six hundred men, besides Indians and militia, under the command of Major-general Sheaffe, the successor of the gallant Brock.[4] It was the seat of government of the Province, and the depository of large quantities of naval stores and provisions; and, at the time in question, a fine ship of war, nearly finished, was on the stocks,[5] and the *Duke of Gloucester*, a brig of war, was at anchor in the harbor, awaiting repairs.[6]

The American column pressed forward towards the village; and as it approached the first and second redoubts, the enemy who were posted therein spiked the guns and retired without offering any opposition.[7] As the troops were somewhat fatigued, the column was immediately halted; and a party of observation, under Lieutenant Riddle, was sent forward to reconnoitre the main, or, as it was called, "*The Western Battery*."[8] During this brief period of repose, the men had thrown themselves on the grass, and were watching the effect of the artillery with that anxiety

[1] Gen. Sheaffe's Dispatch, April 28; Auchinleck, p. 152; Breckenridge's History of War, pp. 118, 119.

[2] Gen. Dearborn's Dispatch, April 28; Com. Chauncey's Dispatch, April 28; Whiting's Biography of Pike, p. 303.

[3] Map in Auchinleck's Hist. of War; Smith's Canada, ii. p. 1.—[4] Gen. Sheaffe's Dispatch, May 5; James' Mil. Occur., i. p. 143.—[5] Gen. Dearborn to Sec. of War, May 3.

[6] Christie, p. 104.—[7] Gen. Dearborn's Dispatch, April 28; Letter from field-officer, in "*The War*," i. p. 204; Thomson's Sketches, p. 123.—[8] James' Military Occurrences, i. p. 145; Whiting's Biography of Pike, p. 304.

which the circumstances would naturally elicit;[1] while General Pike, seated on a stump, and surrounded by his staff, occupied his time in an examination of a wounded sergeant who had fallen into the hands of his troops.[2] At this moment a magazine, in which had been stored large quantities of military stores, exploded, and spread its ruins far and wide around.[3]

When the smoke and the excitement of the moment had cleared away, the terrible effects of the explosion were seen on every hand. Within a circle of three or four hundred yards from the site of the magazine, the heavy fragments of stone and timbers had scattered destruction and death; and fifty-two of the American column laid dead, while one hundred and eighty others, wounded, increased the melancholy spectacle.[4] But, chief among the lost, and most generally lamented, was General Pike, on whose back a heavy mass of stones had fallen, and who, with

[1] Whiting's Biog. of Pike, p. 304.—[2] James' Mil. Occur., i. p. 145; Biog. of Pike, in *Analectic Mag.*, iv. p. 394.

[3] Gen. Dearborn's Dispatch, April 28; Com. Chauncey's Dispatch, April 28; Gen. Sheaffe's Dispatch, April 28; Letter from field-officer; Capt. Moore to his brother, May 5; Auchinleck, pp. 152, 153; Thomson's Sketches, pp. 123, 124. Com. Chauncey says, "a train" had been laid previously, and many authors, following him, have entertained the idea that the explosion was intentional. Without denying that a train *might* have been laid, inasmuch as the industrious James and Auchinleck (British authorities) also *state that such was the case*, I am much inclined to believe that Gen. Sheaffe was correct when he states that it was accidental. Nor could I condemn the enemy, even if a train had been laid. It is a perfectly legitimate mode of defence, as every student of history knows; and why should we censure the garrison for thus employing an acknowledged means of defence, to check the progress of an invader?

[4] "*The War*," i. p. 204. Mr. Rogers (*History of Canada*, i. p. 212) says one hundred of the enemy also were killed.

two of his aids and the wounded sergeant, laid struggling with death.[1]

As quickly as order could be restored among the terrified troops, the column was again formed; and, under the command of Colonel Pierce, it gave three cheers, and resumed its march towards the village.[2]

While the land force had been thus employed on shore, Commodore Chauncey had not been a disinterested spectator. As soon as the troops had debarked, the light vessels were directed to take positions near the main works of the enemy, and to open a fire, which was handsomely performed, against a head wind, under the direction of Lieutenant Elliott.[3]

While the column under Colonel Pierce was approaching the village, the enemy's troops were withdrawn from the works;[4] and after General Sheaffe had directed the magistrates and officers of the militia to treat for a capitulation, he retired, with the greater part of his command, over the River Don, and marched towards Kingston.[5]

The offer of a capitulation, which was tendered to Colonel Pierce, deceived that officer; and he was amused with the project until General Sheaffe had secured his retreat, and burned large quantities of stores and the ship on the

[1] Gen. Dearborn's Dispatch; Com. Chauncey's Dispatch; Capt. Moore to his brother, May 5; Whiting's Biography of Pike, p. 305.—[2] Com. Chauncey's Dispatch, April 28; Letter from a field-officer, in "*The War*," i. p. 204; Thomson's Sketches, p. 124; Whiting's Biography of Pike, p. 306.—[3] Biography of Com. Elliott, pp. 24, 25; Gen. Dearborn's Dispatch, April 28; James' Military Occurrences, i. p. 144.—[4] Gen. Sheaffe's Dispatch, May 5.

[5] Gen. Dearborn's Dispatch, April 28; Gen. Sheaffe's Dispatch, May 5; James' Military Occurrences, i. p. 146; Whiting's Biography of Pike, p. 307.

stocks,[1] after which the unoccupied capital of Upper Canada passed into the hands of the victors, with those portions of the stores which still remained.[2]

The loss of the Americans, in this affair, amounted to fourteen killed and twenty-three wounded in action; and fifty-two killed and one hundred and eighty wounded by the explosion of the magazine;[3] beside whom seventeen were killed and wounded in the navy:[4] that of the enemy's regular force amounted to Captain McNeal and sixty-one non-commissioned officers and privates, *killed;* Captains Loring and Jarvis, Lieutenant Koven, Ensign Robins, and eighty-five men, *wounded;*[5] and, exclusive of militia, about two hundred and ninety *prisoners;*[6] while that of the militia is not recorded. Large quantities of stores were removed by the squadron or destroyed;[1] and, by some unexplained means, the public buildings were entirely destroyed.[2]

Having accomplished the first objects of the expedition, the troops re-embarked on the first of May; and on the eighth the squadron left the harbor.[3]

Before closing the narrative of the capture of York, it will be proper to notice the termination of the honorable career of General Pike. As soon as he was discovered among the wreck, and the extent of his wounds was ascertained, he was removed to the schooner *Pert*, and, soon afterwards, to the *Madison*, where he lingered several hours, and was gratified with the reception of the colors of the captured capital before he died.[4]

1 Com. Chauncey's Dispatch, April 28; James' Mil. Occur., i. p. 146; Thomson's Sketches, p. 124.

2 Com. Chauncey's Dispatch, April 28; Gen. Dearborn's Dispatch, April 28; Capitulation, appended to Gen. Sheaffe's, Gen. Dearborn's, and Com. Chauncey's Dispatches.—3 "*The War*," i. p. 204. Mr. Thomson (*Sketches*, p. 127) says, "14 were killed and 32 wounded *in battle*, and 38 were killed and 222 wounded *in the explosion*."

4 Cooper, ii. p. 161.—5 Returns appended to Gen. Sheaffe's Dispatch. Mr. Thomson (*Sketches*, p. 128) says his entire loss was *two hundred men*, killed and wounded.

6 Articles of Capitulation.

1 James' Mil. Occur., i. p. 148; Armstrong's Notices, i. p. 132.—2 James' Mil. Occur., i. p. 148; "*The War*," i. p. 206.—3 Cooper, ii. p. 162; "*The War*," i. p. 206; Thomson's Sketches, p. 129.—4 Thomson's Sketches, p. 125.

DOCUMENTS.

I.

GENERAL DEARBORN'S DISPATCH TO THE SECRETARY OF WAR.

HEAD-QUARTERS, YORK, CAPITAL OF UPPER CANADA, *April* 28, 1813.

SIR:—After a detention of some days by adverse winds, we arrived at this place yesterday morning, and at eight o'clock commenced landing the troops about three miles westward from the town, and one and a half from the enemy's works. The wind was high and in unfavorable direction for the boats, which prevented the landing of the troops at a clear field, the site of the ancient French fort Toronto. It prevented, also, many of the armed vessels from taking positions, which would have most effectually covered our landing, but every thing that could be done was effected.

The riflemen under Major Forsyth first landed, under a heavy fire from the Indians and other troops. General Sheaffe commanded in person. He had collected his whole force in the woods near the point where the wind compelled our troops to land. His force consisted of seven hundred regulars and militia, and one hundred Indians. Major Forsyth was supported as promptly as possible; but the contest was sharp and severe for nearly half an hour, and the enemy were repulsed by a number far inferior to theirs. As soon as General Pike landed with seven or eight hundred men, and the remainder of the troops were pushing for the shore, the enemy retreated to their works. Our troops were now formed on the ground originally intended for their landing, advanced through a thick wood, and after carrying one battery by assault, were moving in columns towards the main work; when within sixty rods of this, a tremendous explosion took place from a magazine previously prepared, and which threw out such immense quantities of stone as most seriously to injure our troops. I have not yet been able to collect the returns of the killed and wounded, but our loss will, I fear, exceed one hundred; and among those I have to lament the loss of that brave and excellent officer Brigadier-general Pike, who received a contusion from a large stone, which terminated his valuable life within a few hours. His loss will be severely felt.

Previously to this explosion the enemy had retired into the town, excepting a party of regulars, to the number of forty, who did not escape the effects of the shock, and were destroyed.

General Sheaffe moved off with the regular troops, and left the commanding officer of the militia to make the best terms he could. In the mean time all farther resistance on the part of the enemy ceased, and the outlines of a capitulation were agreed on.

As soon as I heard that General Pike had been wounded, I went on shore. To the General I had been induced to confide the immediate attack, from a knowledge that it was his wish, and that he would have felt mortified had it not been given to him.

Every movement was under my view. The troops behaved with great firmness and deserve much applause, particularly those first engaged, and under circumstances which would have tried the steadiness of veterans.

Our loss in the morning and in carrying the first battery was not great, perhaps forty or fifty killed and wounded, and of them a full proportion of officers.

Notwithstanding the enemy's advantage in position and numbers in the commencement of the action, their loss was greater than ours, especially in officers. It was with great exertion the small vessels of the fleet could work into the harbor against a gale of wind, but as soon as they got into a proper position, a tremendous cannonade opened upon the enemy's batteries, and was kept up against them until they were carried or blown up, and had, no doubt, a powerful effect upon the enemy.

I am under the greatest obligations to Commodore Chauncey for his able and indefatigable exertions, in every possible manner, which could give facility and effect to the expedition. He is equally estimable for sound judgment, bravery, and industry. The government could not have made a more fortunate selection.

Unfortunately the enemy's armed ship *Prince Regent*, left this place for Kingston a few days before we arrived. A large ship on the stocks and nearly planked up, and much naval stores, were set fire to by the enemy soon after the explosion of the magazine. A considerable quantity of military stores and provisions remain, but no vessels fit for use.

We had not the means of transporting the prisoners, and must of course leave them on parole. I hope we shall so far complete what is necessary to be done here, as to be able to sail to-morrow for Niagara, whither I send this by a small vessel, with notice to General Lewis of our approach.

I have the honor to be, sir, &c.,

Henry Dearborn.

To Gen. Armstrong, Secretary of War.

II.

COMMODORE CHAUNCEY'S DISPATCH TO THE SECRETARY OF THE NAVY.

U. S. ship Madison, at anchor off York,
April 28, 1813.

Sir:—Agreeably to your instructions and arrangements made with Major-general Dearborn, I took on board of the squadron under my command the General and suite, and about seventeen hundred troops, and left Sackett's Harbor on the 25th instant for this place. We arrived here yesterday morning, and took a position about one mile to the south and westward of the enemy's principal fort, and as near the shore as we could with safety to the vessels. The place fixed upon by the Major-general and myself for landing the troops, was the site of the old French fort Toronto.

The debarkation commenced about eight o'clock A. M., and was completed about ten. The wind blowing heavy from the eastward, the boats fell to leeward of the position fixed upon, and were in consequence exposed to a galling fire from the enemy, who had taken a position in a thick wood near where the first troops landed; however, the cool intrepidity of the officers and men overcame every obstacle. Their attack upon the enemy was so vigorous that he fled in every direction, leaving a great many of his killed and wounded upon the field.

As soon as the troops were landed, I directed the schooners to take a position near the forts, in order that the attack upon them by the army and navy might be simultaneous. The schooners were obliged to beat up to their position, which they did in very handsome order, under a very heavy fire from the enemy's batteries, and took a position within about six hundred yards of their principal fort, and opened a heavy cannonade upon the enemy, which did great execution, and very much contributed to their final destruction. The troops, as soon as landed, were formed under the immediate orders of Brigadier-general Pike, who led, in a most gallant manner, the attack upon the forts; and, after having carried two redoubts, in their approach to the principal work the enemy (having previously laid a train) blew up his magazine, which, in its effects upon our troops, was dreadful, having killed and wounded a great many, and among the former the ever-to-be-lamented Brigadier-general Pike, who fell at the head of this column, by a contusion received by a heavy stone from the magazine. His death at this time is much to be regretted, as he had the perfect confidence of the Major-general; and his known activity, zeal, and experience, make his loss a national one.

In consequence of the fall of General Pike, the command of the troops devolved for a time upon Colonel Pierce, who soon after took possession of the town. At about two P. M. the American flag was substituted for the British, and at about four our troops were in quiet possession of the town. As soon as General Dearborn learned the situation of General Pike, he landed and assumed the command. I have the honor of inclosing a copy of the capitulation which was entered into and approved by General Dearborn and myself.

The enemy set fire to some of his principal stores, containing large quantities of naval and military stores, as well as a large ship upon the stocks, nearly finished. The only vessel found here is the *Duke of Gloucester*, undergoing repairs. The *Prince Regent* left here on the 24th for Kingston. We have not yet had a return made of the naval and military stores, consequently can form no correct idea of the quantity, but have made arrangements to have all taken on board that we can receive, the rest will be destroyed.

I have to regret the death of Midshipmen Thompson and Hatfield, and several seamen, killed—the exact number I do not know, as the returns from the different vessels have not yet been received.

From the judicious arrangements made by General Dearborn, I presume that the public stores will be disposed of so that the troops will be ready to re-embark to-morrow, and proceed to execute other objects of the expedition the first fair wind.

I cannot speak in too much praise of the cool intrepidity of the officers and men, generally, under my command; and I feel myself particularly obliged to the officers commanding vessels for their zeal in seconding all my views.

I have the honor to be, very respectfully, sir, your most obedient servant,

ISAAC CHAUNCEY.

Hon. WM. JONES, Secretary of Navy.

III.

GENERAL SHEAFFE'S DISPATCH TO SIR GEORGE PREVOST.

KINGSTON, *May* 5, 1813.

SIR:—I did myself the honor of writing to your Excellency, on my route from York, to communicate the mortifying intelligence that the enemy had obtained possession of that place on the 27th of April. I shall now give your Excellency a farther detail of that event.

In the evening of the 26th, information was received that many vessels had been seen to the eastward. Very early the next morning they were discovered lying to, not far from the harbor. After some time had elapsed they made sail, and to the number of sixteen, of various descriptions, anchored off the shore, some distance to the westward. Boats full of troops were immediately seen assembling near their Commodore's ship, under cover of whose fire, and that of other vessels, and aided by the wind, they soon effected a landing, in spite of a spirited opposition from Major Givens and about forty Indians. A company of Glengarry light-infantry, which had been ordered to support them, was, by some mistake (not in the smallest degree imputable to its commander), led in another direction, and came late into action. The other troops, consisting of two companies of the Eighth or King's regiment, and about a company of the royal Newfoundland regiment, with some militia, encountered the enemy in a thick wood. Captain McNeal, of the King's regiment, was killed while gallantly leading his company, which suffered severely. The troops at length fell back; they rallied several times, but could not maintain the contest against the greatly superior and increasing numbers of the enemy. They retired under cover of our batteries, which were engaged with some of the enemy's vessels that had moved nigher to the harbor. By some unfortunate accident the magazine at the western battery blew up, and killed and wounded a considerable number of men, and crippled the battery.

It became too evident that our numbers and means of defence were inadequate to the task of maintaining possession of York against the vast superiority of force brought against it. The troops were withdrawn towards the town, and were finally ordered to retreat on the road to Kingston; the powder-magazine was blown up, and the new ship and the naval stores destroyed. Lieutenant-colonel Chervet and Major Allen, of the militia, residents in the town, were instructed to treat with the American commanders for terms: a statement of those agreed on with Major-general Dearborn and Commodore Chauncey is transmitted to your Excellency, with returns of killed and wounded, &c. The accounts of the number of the enemy vary from one thousand eight hundred and ninety to three thousand. We had about six hundred, including militia and dock-yard men. The quality of these troops was of so superior a description, and their general disposition so good, that under less unfavorable circumstances, I should have felt confident of success, in spite of the disparity of numbers. As it was, the contest, which commenced between six and seven o'clock, was maintained nearly eight hours.

When we had proceeded some miles from York we met the light company of the King's regiment, on its route for Fort George: it retired with us, and covered the retreat, which was effected without molestation from the enemy.

I have the honor to be, &c.,

R. H. Sheaffe, *Maj.-Gen.*

His Excellency, Sir George Prevost, &c.

CHAPTER XLV.

April 28 to May 9, 1813.

THE SIEGE OF FORT MEIGS.

When the defeat and massacre of the left wing of the army, at the River Raisin, had spread terror throughout the western frontiers, and grief among the inhabitants of the older settlements,[1] General Harrison established his advanced post at the foot of the rapids of the Miami, and gave to it the name of *Fort Meigs*.[2] The situation of this post was considered among the most eligible in the West—combining, as it did, facilities for keeping open a communication with Kentucky and Ohio; and, at the same time, for protecting the borders of Lake Erie, for operating against Detroit, and for aggressive measures, generally, against the enemy's territory.[3]

This movement was exceedingly annoying to the enemy; and, as soon as the breaking up of the ice permitted, General Proctor—the notorious hero of the River Raisin—moved from Malden, with all his available force, for the purpose of attacking it.[4] He embarked from Amherstburg, on the twenty-third of April,[5] with five hundred and twenty-two regulars, four hundred and sixty-one militia,[1] and about twelve hundred Indians,[2] "accompanied by two gunboats and some artillery;"[3] and, on the twenty-eighth, he landed on the north side of the river, about two miles below the fort.[4] The incessant rains, and the consequent bad state of the roads, however, so much retarded his progress that it was not until the morning of the first of May that the fire from his batteries was opened on the fort.[5]

At the period in question Fort Meigs embraced an area of about eight acres, on the high bank of the Miami; and besides its inclosure of pickets, it was defended with several block-houses and a good supply of field-pieces; although the supply of balls for the latter was somewhat limited.[6]

When it was known that the enemy was approaching the fort, Captain Oliver, with one white, and one Indian, was sent with letters to the Governors of Ohio and Kentucky, and to General

[1] Vide Chap. XXXVIII.—[2] Perkins' Hist. of the War, p. 217; McAfee's Hist. of War in Western Country, pp. 243-245.—[3] Ingersoll's Hist. of the War, i. p. 145; Christie's Mil. and Naval Operations, p. 110; Perkins' Hist. of War, pp. 217, 218.—[4] Gen. Proctor to Sir G. Prevost, May 14, 1813.—[5] Auchinleck's History of War, p. 142; James' Military Occurrences, i. p. 195.

[1] Returns inclosed in his Dispatch of May 14, 1813.

[2] Gen. Proctor to Sir G. Prevost, May 14, 1813. Mr. Auchinleck (*Hist. of War*, p. 142), a Canadian author of merit, says he had *fifteen hundred Indians*.

[3] Auchinleck, p. 142.—[4] Gen. Harrison to Sec. of War, April 28, 1813; McAfee, p. 258; Breckenridge's Hist. of War, p. 109; Perkins' Annals of the West, p. 631.

[5] Gen. Proctor to Sir G. Prevost, May 14, 1813; Gen. Harrison to Sec. of War, May 5, 1813. Gen. Armstrong (*Notices of War*, i. p. 123) says the fire opened on the *30th of April*.—[6] Gen. Proctor to Sir G. Prevost, May 14, 1813; McAfee, pp. 243, 244; Hall's Memoir of Harrison, pp. 220, 221; James' Military Occurrences, i. p. 196.

Clay, of the latter State, who was then on his way to the fort, requesting the immediate dispatch of reinforcements;[1] and, soon afterwards, the enemy's gun-boats approached old Fort Miami, on the opposite bank of the river, to cover the debarkation of his troops, and the passage of the Indians, under Tecumthà, who were designed to invest the rear and flanks of the fort.[2] With great labor, while the enemy was thus employed, the garrison, also, was strengthening its position; and when, as before stated, one of the enemy's batteries was opened on the works, a heavy traverse, twelve feet high and twenty feet thick, had been completed, and effectually sheltered the garrison.[3] A heavy fire was opened on the fort, without any serious effect, on the morning of the first of May,[4] from a battery mounting two twenty-four-pounders, above the fort, and from a mortar-battery, mounting one eight-inch and two five and a half-inch howitzers, below it;[5] on the morning of the second, a second battery, mounting three twelve-pounders, also above the fort, added its fire;[6] and in the night of the third, a detachment, from the besieging force, crossed the river and opened another three-gun and one mortar battery on the American flank, from a position which was within two hundred and fifty yards from the lines—the latter of which, however, was speedily driven to a more respectful distance.[1]

During the three days since the enemy opened his fire, an incessant fire was thrown into the fort from the enemy's works; the fourth it was less vehement;[2] and the fifth was occupied with other and more exciting services. About midnight, on the fourth of May, Major David Trimble, accompanied by Captain Oliver and fifteen men, having rowed down the river, entered the fort, and conveyed to the garrison the information that General Clay was within eighteen miles of the fort, with eleven hundred men; and that he would probably join the garrison about daylight.[3] It appeared, however, that his pilot feared to run down the river in the dark; and not until daylight did he leave the head of the rapids: in consequence of which Captain Hamilton, and a subaltern who had been sent up the river to meet him, with a message from General Harrison, directing his movements, did not meet him as early as he expected.[4]

The orders which Captain Hamilton delivered were in these words, a reference to which will show, to some extent, the General's proposed plan of operations: "You must detach about

[1] McAfee, pp. 258, 259.—[2] Ibid., p. 259; Sketches of War, p. 163; Hall's Harrison, pp. 226, 227.

[3] McAfee, pp. 260–262; Hall's Harrison, p. 227; Perkins' Western Annals, p. 631.—[4] Vide note 5, col. 2, p. 221.

[5] James' Mil. Occur., i. p. 196. Mr. Thomson (*Sketches of War*, p. 110) and Mr. Breckenridge (*Hist. of War*, p. 109) suppose the armament was 1 24-pounder, 1 12-pounder, 1 6-pounder, and 1 howitzer.—[6] Gen. Harrison to Sec. of War, May 5; James' Military Occurrences, i. p. 197.

[1] Gen. Harrison to Sec. of War, May 5; McAfee, p. 263; Breckenridge, pp. 109, 110; Perkins' Hist. of War, p. 218. Mr. James (*Mil. Occur.*, i. p. 197) says it mounted *two* 6-pounders and one 5½-inch mortar.—[2] Gen. Harrison to Sec. of War, May 5; James' Mil. Occur., i. p. 197; McAfee, pp. 262–264; Sketches of War, pp. 163, 164; Thomson's Sketches, p. 111; Auchinleck, p. 142.

[3] Gen. Harrison to Sec. of War, May 5; McAfee, p 264; Armstrong's Notices, i. p. 123; Hall's Harrison, pp. 228, 229.—[4] McAfee, p. 264; Perkins' History of War, p. 219.

eight hundred men from your brigade, and land them at a point I will show you, about a mile, or a mile and a half above Camp Meigs. I will then conduct the detachment to the British batteries, on the left (*or eastern*) bank of the river. The batteries must be taken, the cannon spiked, and carriages cut down; and the troops must then return to their boats and cross over to the fort. The balance of your men must land on the fort side of the river, opposite the first landing, and fight their way into the fort through the Indians. The route they must take will be pointed out by a subaltern officer now with me, who will land the canoe on the right bank of the river, to point out the landing for the boats."[1] It was the intention of General Harrison, when General Clay arrived, to make a general sally from the fort, for the destruction of the batteries last erected; and it was expected that the general cooperation of the two forces would secure the defeat of the enemy.[2]

The order in which General Clay descended the river was in solid column, each officer taking position according to his rank—Colonel Dudley, the senior field-officer, leading the van, with twelve boats;[3] and when the orders from General Harrison were received, orders were issued to that officer to move forward with his detachment, and execute the orders of the General, on the eastern bank of the river; while General Clay, in person, would direct the movements against the Indians, on the western bank.[1]

In the discharge of the duties which had been assigned to Colonel Dudley, that officer effected a landing in tolerably good order; and, under the direction of Captain Hamilton, he moved rapidly through the woods towards the batteries. Before the enemy was aware of his presence, the batteries were surrounded; and, raising the Indian yell, the assailants rushed forward and carried them, before the affrighted artillerists knew by whom they had been assailed. But, with the indiscretion which generally prevails among undisciplined troops, the detachment was not satisfied with the complete success of its part of the work; and, after loitering around the batteries, notwithstanding the signals which were thrown out from Fort Meigs, the greater portion of the detachment was drawn into a disorderly pursuit of a party of Indians, and of the entire detachment all, save about one hundred and fifty men, were cut off, and either captured or killed by the British, who had come up from their camp, or by the Indians, before they could reach their boats and cross the river.[2]

Meanwhile, on the opposite bank, the movements of the troops under General Clay, although diversified, had been more fortunate. The violence of the

[1] McAfee, p. 265; Gen. Clay to Gen. Harrison, May 13.
[2] Perkins' Hist. of War, p. 219; Auchinleck, p. 142; Ingersoll, i. p. 146; Thomson's Sketches, p. 111; Armstrong, i. p. 123.—[3] Perkins' Hist. of War, p. 219; McAfee, pp. 265, 266; Gen. Clay to Gen. Harrison, May 13.

[1] Perkins' History of War, p. 219; Gen. Clay to Gen. Harrison, May 13.—[2] Gen. Proctor to Sir G. Prevost, May 14, 1813; James' Mil. Occur., i. pp. 197–199; Gen. Harrison to Sec. of War, May 5, 1813; McAfee, pp. 269–271; Sketches of War, pp. 164, 165; Christie, p. 111; Armstrong's Notices, i. p. 124; Gen. Clay to Gen. Harrison, May 13; Gen. Harrison to Gov. Shelby, May 18, 1813.

current had separated the boat in which were the General and fifty men from the other boats of his command, and they had landed half a mile in his rear; yet, after some difficulty from the Indians, and some loss from their fire, both parties reached the fort.[1]

While the reinforcements, on either bank of the river, were thus struggling, with varied fortune, against the effects of their own indiscretion, the promised sortie of the garrison against the three-gun and mortar battery, on the right bank of the river, was successfully executed. For the performance of this important duty, the commands of Captains Langham, Croghan, Bradford, Nearing, and Elliott, and Lieutenants Gwynne and Campbell, of the Federal troops; Major Alexander's volunteers; and Captain Sebree's company of Kentucky militia, numbering in the aggregate three hundred and fifty men, were detached, under the command of Colonel Miller; and, after gallantly charging on the enemy, and driving him from his works, they spiked his guns, and retired with but little loss, taking with them forty-three prisoners, and reached the fort in safety.[2]

In the mean time, on the opposite side of the fort, another contest was going on with the Indians, in which the troops which had just reached the fort, under General Clay, and a detachment from the garrison were the assailants. The latter, embracing General Clay's troops on the right, Major Alexander's Virginia troops in the centre, and Major Johnson's Kentuckians on the left, marched out against a large body of Indians who occupied the flank of the fort, and drove them into the woods, a distance of half a mile, at the point of the bayonet. In this, as in all the movements before referred to, the greatest ardor was displayed by the troops; and the greatest difficulty was experienced in controlling the Kentuckians in the impetuosity of their pursuit. The wily and experienced Tecumthà was not slow in seeing and availing himself of this indiscretion on the part of his enemy; and, while the latter was rushing forward, without order, and almost without discipline, the former moved a strong body of Indians and a small British force, by a file movement, to fall on the left and rear of General Clay's troops, and to cut off the retreat of the column. In this, however, the skill of the chief found more than a match in the watchful care of General Harrison, who had taken a position on one of the batteries; and had seen the movement, understood the purpose, and—although with much difficulty—secured the retreat of the detachment, with but little loss.[1]

Throughout the entire operations of the day, complicated and severely contested as they were, there were no complaints to be made against the American troops, beyond those which arose

[1] Gen. Harrison to Sec. of War, May 5; James' Mil. Occur., i. p. 200; McAfee, pp. 266, 267; Sketches of War, p. 165; Armstrong's Notices, i. pp. 124, 125; Gen. Clay to Gen. Harrison, May 13.—[2] Gen. Proctor to Sir G. Prevost, May 14, 1813; James' Mil. Occur., i. pp. 197, 199, 200; Gen. Harrison to Sec. of War, May 5 and 9, 1813; McAfee, pp. 267-269; Armstrong's Notices, i. p. 125; Gen. Clay to Gen. Harrison, May 13.

[1] Gen. Harrison to Sec. of War, May 9, 1813; McAfee, p. 267.

from their indiscreet zeal and uncontrollable impetuosity. Both the great contending parties fought gallantly for the success of their respective flags; both were directed with the greatest skill—so far as the commanders could direct them; and, when the closing day had terminated the contest, both retired to their respective quarters, with the consolation of having, generally, done their duty to their respective countries.

In all this, however, there must be made an exception against the honor of the infamous Proctor, the commander of the allied forces of the enemy. When the prisoners who had been taken from Colonel Dudley's command were taken to the British camp, below the fort, they were put into old Fort Miami, near by, and, in the language of an eye-witness, "the Indians were permitted to garnish the surrounding rampart, and to amuse themselves by loading and firing at the crowd, or at any particular individual. Those who preferred to inflict a still more cruel and savage death, selected their victims, led them to the gateway, and there, under the eye of General Proctor, and in the presence of the whole British army, tomahawked and scalped them."[1] "This work of destruction," it is said by another officer,[2] "continued near two hours, during which time upwards of twenty prisoners, defenceless and confined, were massacred in the presence of the magnanimous Britons to whom they had surrendered, and by the allies, too, with whom those Britons had voluntarily associated themselves, knowing and encouraging their mode of warfare. The chiefs, at the same time," he continues, "were holding a council on the fate of the prisoners; in which the Potawatomies, who were painted black, were for killing the whole; and by *their* warriors the murders were perpetrated. The Miamis and Wyandots were on the side of humanity, and opposed the wishes of the others. The dispute between them had become serious, when Colonel Elliott and Tecumthà came down from the batteries to the scene of carnage. As soon as Tecumthà beheld it, he flourished his hatchet (burying it in the head of a chief who was engaged in the massacre),[1] and, in a loud voice, ordered them—'For shame, to desist. It is a disgrace,' he said, 'to kill a defenceless prisoner.' His orders were obeyed, to the great joy of the prisoners, who had, by this time, lost all hope of being preserved. In this single act," as he truly observes, "Tecumthà displayed more humanity, magnanimity, and civilization than Proctor, with all his British associates in command, displayed through the whole war on the Northwestern frontiers."

With the actions referred to, the siege virtually closed, notwithstanding the enemy remained before it four days longer, and, on the fifth of May, gravely summoned the fort to surrender, an in-

---

[1] Capt. Wood, of the Engineers, cited by Mr. McAfee. See also Maj. Richardson's statement, in Auchinleck's *History of War*, pp. 143, 144.

[2] McAfee, pp. 271, 272. See also Auchinleck, pp. 143, 144; Perkins' History of War, pp. 220, 221; "*The War*," i. p. 213.

[1] James' Military Occurrences, i. p. 201.

sult which was properly resented.[1] Intelligence of the loss of Fort George had reached his camp; and the Indians, dissatisfied and dispirited, had begun to return to their homes. General Proctor, foreseeing the effects of the disasters on the Niagara frontier, and of the arrival of the reinforcements which were hastening to the relief of Fort Meigs,—the impossibility of any reinforcement reaching him, and the certainty of his own destruction if he remained in his present position,—he immediately took steps to retire;[2] and having shipped his artillery and baggage, on board his sloop and gunboats, on the night of the eighth of May, at an early hour on the ninth he moved off, leaving behind him a part of his stores.[3]

The loss of the Americans, during the siege, and in the several actions on the fifth of May, was about eighty-one *killed*, two hundred and sixty-nine *wounded* (including about fifty who were massacred by the Indians), and four hundred and sixty-seven *prisoners*;[1] that of the British was said to have been fourteen *killed*, Captain Bandy, Lieutenant Bullock, and forty-five *wounded*, and Lieutenants Hales and McIntire, and forty-one men *prisoners*. There is little doubt, however, that it was much greater.[2]

[Note.—The Dispatches of Gen. Harrison, May 5, 9, and 13; that of Gen. Green Clay, May 13, 1813; and that of Gen. Proctor, May 14, 1813, which had been prepared for the illustration of this chapter, have been omitted by the Publishers for want of room.]

CHAPTER XLVI.

May 3, 1813.

THE CONFLAGRATION OF HAVRE DE GRACE.

The blockade of the Chesapeake, by the enemy's fleet, has been already referred to in a preceding chapter of this work;[4] and considerable alarm was excited along the shores of the bay, in consequence of the rumors of invasion which were circulated in the vicinity. Occasionally the boats of the fleet had landed, and scouting parties had driven off the cattle from the nearest farm—not in all cases, however, without leaving an ample remuneration behind them—for the supply of the fleet; and the small vessels, which coasted along the shores, had been uniformly captured, plundered, and burned, yet no cause had been given for so general and sweeping a desolation as that which had been threatened.

Among the villages which were then exposed to the ravages of the enemy

[1] McAfee, p. 273; Thomson's Sketches, p. 116; Hall's Harrison, p. 235; Armstrong's Notices, i. p. 126.

[2] James' Mil. Occur., i. p. 201; McAfee, pp. 273, 274; Perkins' Annals of the West, p. 632.—[3] Gen. Harrison to Sec. of War, May 9; James' Mil. Occur., i. p. 201; McAfee, p. 274.—[4] Vide Chap. XLIII.

[1] Returns appended to Gen. Harrison's Dispatch, May 13.—[2] Returns appended to Gen. Proctor's Dispatch, May 14. The author of "*Sketches of the War*" (p. 165), says his loss was equal to that of the Americans. Capt. McAfee (p. 274) says, "It was undoubtedly very severe."

was Havre de Grace—a commercial village, in Harford County, Maryland, which is beautifully situated on the western bank of the Susquehanna, a short distance above its confluence with the Chesapeake, and sixty-four miles northeast from Annapolis.[1] At the period under consideration, in consequence of an obstruction at the mouth of the river, the trade of the village was rather on the decline; although the herring-fishery, which was carried on quite extensively, was a source of considerable profit to its inhabitants.

On the 28th of April, a brig and two or three schooners came to an anchor near the village; and, on the next morning, another brig and schooner joined them—the whole casting anchor on the precise spot where the fleet, under the command of Lord Howe, cast anchor in 1777, a short time before the battle of Brandywine.

During the day, without doing any damage near Havre de Grace, these vessels weighed, turned Turkey Point, and sailed up the Elk River—burning two vessels, and landing and destroying one or two warehouses, without injuring any other property, at Frenchtown; and returned to their anchorage, near Havre, on the 30th.

During this exciting period, the inhabitants of Havre de Grace made some preparations for the defence of the village; and several companies of militia were sent to assist them in that undertaking. A battery, mounting one eighteen-pounder and two nines, was erected at Point Comfort, a short distance below the village; and it had been manned by a company of volunteers, composed of men who had seen some service and who were considered as "exempts." Patrols were stationed along the river and bay, and every appearance indicated a determination to defend the place to the last extremity.

It is probable that this spirited conduct insured the very result which the inhabitants sought to avoid. Finding the inhabitants disposed to contest his advance, the enemy appears to have hesitated before making the attempt; and after some three weeks spirited service, without an enemy to oppose, and, apparently, without even a reason for supposing that he designed to approach Havre, the military ardor of the garrison and the people began to flag, and insubordination gradually crept into the ranks—some returning home, others performing but little duty, and some of the officers absenting themselves without leave.

It was at this time, when, by a masterly course of inactivity, the enemy had accomplished a greater triumph than the opposite course would have secured, he prepared to attack the village on the night of the first of May. A few hours before the time appointed for the descent, however, a deserter from the enemy entered the village, and gave intelligence of the projected expedition; and it spread with great rapidity over the entire neighborhood. The women and children were removed to places of safety; the militia who remained—some two hundred and fifty in number—were at their posts; the patrols guarded the shores of the river

[1] McCulloch's Gazetteer, i. p. 1077.

and bay; the "exempts" returned to the battery on Point Comfort; and, in every direction, the people appeared to be disposed to contest the possession of every inch of ground.

But, with great skill, after the loss of the deserter had become known to the enemy, although every preparation had been perfected, he postponed the attack; and the morning sun arose on a people who were, more than ever before, disposed to consider that there was no danger, and that the enemy entertained no hostile intentions against them. The next day, therefore (*May* 2, 1813), was occupied in still greater scenes of insubordination among the troops, and in acts of still greater indiscretion on the part of the inhabitants; and when, at daybreak, on the morning of the third, the guns on Point Comfort and the drums in the village sounded an alarm, the people, aroused by the stern reality from their imaginary security, displayed the greatest consternation.

Twenty barges, filled with the enemy's troops, rapidly approached the village, under a fire from the battery at Point Comfort,[1] and as the streets were thronged by the *half-dressed* and terrified villagers, each hastening to some distant place of safety,[2] and the militia, scarcely less terrified, were running to and fro, without a commander and without discipline, a discharge of Congreve rockets, from the enemy's boats, completed the confusion, and removed all obstacles to his landing.

Before a landing had been effected the village was in flames—the rockets and shells which had been discharged among the fugitives having communicated with some of the buildings. Immediately after the debarkation a party was dispatched to take possession of the battery, which was abandoned as the enemy approached, and the three guns which were mounted there were turned on the village, increasing the confusion, and scattering, still farther, the destruction to which the village had been doomed. The main body of the enemy, however, moved up into the village; and when it reached the public square, in its centre, it was divided into parties of thirty or forty men each, and sent, in different directions, to plunder, systematically, the houses which were not already in flames. But very little attention was paid to the villagers or the retreating militia; and the rapacity of the enemy, and his savage ferocity, have been thus graphically described by an eye-witness, in terms which no language of mine can equal: "Their manner was, on entering a house, to plunder it of such articles as could be of any service to them, and easily transported, and convey them to their barges. Every man had a hatchet at his girdle, and when wardrobes and bureaus happened to be locked, they were made to yield to the force of this instrument. This was not a work of much time, and as soon as it was accomplished, they set fire to the house, and entered another for the same purpose." * * *

"The conduct of the sailors, while on shore, was exceedingly rude and wanton.[1] The officers gave such of the in-

[1] Niles' Register, iv. p. 164.—[2] Letter from a lady near Havre de Grace, May 7, in *Niles' Register*, iv. p. 196.

[1] See also Niles' Register, iv. p. 195.

habitants as remained behind, liberty to carry out such articles of furniture as they chose, while the sailors were plundering the houses; but the sailors, not content with pillaging and burning, broke and defaced these also, as they were standing in the streets. Elegant looking-glasses were dashed in pieces, and beds were ripped open for the sport of scattering the feathers in the wind.[1] These outrages, to be sure, were not commanded by the officers, but they were not restrained by them. Little can be said, indeed, in favor of the officers' conduct in this particular. They selected tables and bureaus for their private use, and after writing their names on them, sent them on board the barges. The *Admiral* himself was pleased with *an elegant coach*, which fell in his way, and commanded it to be put on board a boat, which belonged to the proprietor of the ferry, and taken to his ship. This order was executed, although he was told it belonged to a poor coachmaker, whose family must suffer by its loss.

"The firing of cannon had ceased," he continues, "and no other noise was heard, than the roaring of the flames, the crash of falling timbers, and the occasional lamentations and entreaties of a few of the inhabitants, who had braved every danger with the hope of preserving from destruction their only means of subsistence."

In this manner (officers and men alike entering, with zest, on the work of destruction) the property of the villagers was scattered and consumed; until, when one-half the town had been destroyed, the Admiral (*Cockburn*)[1] came on shore; and was approached by two or three ladies, who had courageously remained near their houses. Appealing to his sympathy, with all the eloquence of actual distress, his humble memorialists urged their cause with the most earnest perseverance, even after their prayer had been frequently and sternly rejected; and pointed out to him "the misery he was causing, and the smoking ruins, under which was buried all that could keep their proprietors from want and wretchedness." Against such an appeal as this, even the relentless sailor was not long able to hold out; and, after gradually yielding to their entreaties, he at length countermanded his orders, and those houses which had not been reached, escaped.

While this terrible act of destruction was being enacted in the village, two barges ascended the Susquehanna to a warehouse,[2] about five miles above, and burned it; but a number of vessels which had been anchored there, by being sunk, escaped without material damage.

After remaining at Havre de Grace about four hours, the enemy embarked, and descended the river. The work of destruction, however, was not yet complete; and, during the day, the enemy visited the extensive iron works of Colonel Hughes, at Princippi,[3] eight miles north of Havre de Grace, where large numbers of cannons were in progress

[1] See also letter from Havre de Grace, in *Niles' Register*, iv. p. 165; and another in the same volume, p. 196.

[1] *National Intelligencer*, May 6, 1813.

[2] The warehouse was known as "*Stump's Warehouse.*"—*Nat. Intelligencer, May* 6, 1813; Niles' Register, iv. p. 164.

[3] National Intelligencer, Washington, May 6, 1813.

of manufacture. The entire establishment, with its extensive and valuable machinery, was also entirely destroyed; and at sunset, wearied with his wantonness, the enemy retired to his shipping.

After the enemy had retired, at the close of the day, slowly and sadly the villagers returned from their hiding-places, only to witness the utter destruction of all they possessed, and to reflect on the misery and want which awaited them. Some of the heads of families, to add to the sorrows of the people, had been carried off, as prisoners, by the enemy; and their families, more disconsolate even than those of their neighbors, rendered still more severe the gloom which surrounded the scene.

Of the sixty dwellings of which the village was composed, more than forty were burned;[1] while others were plundered and much injured, and scarcely one remained which had not been more or less injured by the shot or shells which the enemy had thrown among them.

The force of the enemy was said to have been six hundred men, of whom four hundred landed at Havre de Grace, and the loss of each—the villagers and the enemy—was about equal, each having lost three or four men.[1]

As there were no stores in the village, and as none of its inhabitants had aided in prosecuting the war, it appears that the caprice of the Admiral was the only cause which led to this terrible visitation on a defenceless village; and, from that reason, there appears to be no excuse for the deed.[2]

[Note.—This narrative has been taken from a description of the scene by my friend, Jared Sparks, LL. D., who was present, and witnessed the outrages he has described. It may be found in the *North American Review*, July, 1817, and I am indebted to his attention for the privilege of using it. Where no other work has been referred to, this has been my sole authority.—H. B. D.]

[1] The *National Intelligencer* (Washington, May 6, 1813) says, "They burnt *twenty-four* of the best houses in the town, and *plundered* all the rest."

[1] National Intelligencer, Washington, May 6, 1813. *The Baltimore American*, published on the Thursday after the destruction of Havre de Grace, says the enemy lost three killed and two wounded; the Americans only the one who was killed by the rocket.

[2] Other accounts of this affair can be found in Niles' Register, iv. pp. 164, 182, 195, 196; Perkins' History of Late War, pp. 161, 162; The *National Intelligencer*, Washington, D. C., May 8; "*The War*," i. pp. 199, 200; Thomson's Sketches of the War, pp. 209–211; Breckenridge's History of War, pp. 148–150; Sketches of the War, p. 325; Ingersoll's History of War, pp. 197, 198; Auchinleck's History of War, pp. 266–269; Adm'l Cockburn's Dispatch to Adm'l Warren, May 3, 1813; and Naval Chronicle, xxx. pp. 164–166.

CHAPTER XLVII.

May 27, 1813.

THE CAPTURE OF FORT GEORGE.

The capture of York, the capital of Upper Canada, by the combined land and naval forces, under General Dearborn and Commodore Chauncey, has been already noticed; and the embarkation of the troops, on the first of May, and their subsequent detention in that harbor, by adverse winds, until the 8th of that month, have also been alluded to.[1]

As soon as the weather permitted, the squadron sailed from the harbor of York; and, on the eighth, the troops debarked about four miles eastward from Fort Niagara—at which point an encampment had been laid out; when the Commodore returned to Sackett's Harbor for the purpose of landing the sick and wounded, of obtaining supplies, and of receiving reinforcements.[2] On the 25th he returned;[3] when the *Fair American* and the *Pert* were ordered down the lake to watch the movements of the enemy's force at Kingston,[4] and preparations were made for an attack on Fort George, as soon as the weather permitted.[5] On the twenty-sixth the Commodore reconnoitred the enemy's position; and, during the early part of the night, he sounded the shore in person, and placed buoys for the direction of the movements of his vessels during the projected attack.[1]

At three in the morning, of the twenty-seventh, the signal was given to weigh; and, soon after four, Generals Dearborn and Lewis, with their suites, went on board the *Madison*, and the squadron stood for the Canadian shore. There being but little wind the vessels used their sweeps, and one after another the covering vessels gracefully fell into the positions to which they had been assigned. The *Julia* and the *Growler* took a position in the mouth of the Niagara River, in order to hold in check, or silence, a battery which stood near the light-house, and which, from its position, commanded that part of the shore where the troops had been ordered to land. The *Ontario* took a position north from the light-house, so near the shore that she could enfilade the same battery and cross the fire of the *Julia* and *Growler*. The *Conquest* and the *Governor Tompkins* were directed to positions from whence they could check the operations of a battery which had been erected near the Two mile Creek; while, at the same time,

---

[1] Vide Chap. XLIV.—[2] Cooper's Naval Hist., ii. p. 162.
[3] Com. Chauncey to Sec. of Navy, May 28, 1813; Christie's Military and Naval Operations, p. 105; Thomson's Sketches, p. 129.—[4] Com. Chauncey to Sec. of Navy, May 28, 1813; Cooper's Naval Hist., ii. p. 162.—[5] Com. Chauncey to Sec. of Navy, May 28; Thomson's Sketches, p. 129.

[1] Com. Chauncey to Sec. of Navy, May 28; Cooper, ii. p. 162; James' Mil. Occur., i. p. 150.

the *Hamilton*, the *Asp*, and the *Scourge*, were directed to anchor close in shore, and to cover the landing of the forces. The gallant Oliver Hazard Perry, who, like the war-horse of Job, had "smelled the battle from afar off," had hastened from Lake Erie, where he commanded the naval force, and, as a volunteer, was rendering "great assistance" "in arranging and superintending the debarkation of the troops," being personally "present at every point where he could be useful, under showers of musketry," without suffering injury.[1]

The boats advanced in six divisions (three brigades); in the advance of which, leading the column, were Colonel Winfield Scott and Major Forsyth of the rifles. Following these, and supporting them, was Colonel Moses Porter of the light-artillery, with his train; who, in his turn, was supported by the commands of Generals Boyd, Winder, and Chandler; and, closing the column, as a reserve, were the marines of the squadron and Colonel Alexander Macomb's regiment of artillery.[2] The flotilla had been preceded by the small vessels of the squadron; and the *Governor Tompkins* and the *Conquest*, in the most graceful style, as before described, had taken their assigned positions near the mouth of the Two-mile Creek—the place appointed for the debarkation of the troops—and had opened their fire on the battery which commanded the shore in that vicinity. At

[1] Com. Chauncey to Sec. of Navy, May 28; James' Mil. Occur., i. pp. 153, 154; Thomson's Sketches, pp. 130, 131.

[2] Gen. Dearborn to Sec. of War, May 27; Thomson's Sketches, p. 131; Perkins' Hist. of War, p. 251; Richard's Mem. of Macomb, p. 59; Mansfield's Scott, p. 79.

musket-shot distance, only, the fire was well-directed and exceedingly efficient; and, before it had continued ten minutes, the batteries "were completely silenced and abandoned;"[1] when, under the personal direction of Captain Oliver H. Perry, the boats dashed in, and the troops effected a landing.[2]

While the army and the squadron were thus employed, other circumstances were transpiring, which rendered great service in securing the objects of the expedition. While some boats were descending the river, on the day preceding the movement referred to, a fire had been opened on them from Fort George; and as it was returned from Fort Niagara, on the east bank of the river, a heavy cannonade ensued.[3] It is said, by British authorities,[4] that the supply of powder in Fort George was limited, and that in consequence the fire could not be returned with proper spirit; but, whether or not this statement is correct, we have no official evidence concerning it. It is true, however, that while Fort Niagara suffered no injury, the block-houses and wooden buildings within Fort George, as well as the fort itself, were "considerably injured."[5]

When the boats approached the shore, as before mentioned, the advance of the enemy's force—consisting of detachments from the Glengarry and

[1] Com. Chauncey to Sec. of Navy, May 28; Breckenridge, p. 127; Cooper, ii. p. 163.—[2] Mansfield's Scott, p. 79; Cooper, ii. p. 163.—[3] Auchinleck's Hist., p. 157; James' Mil. Occur., i. pp. 151, 152; Thomson's Sketches, p. 130; Breckenridge, p. 127.—[4] Auchinleck, p. 157; James' Military Occurrences, i. p. 152.—[5] James' Military Occurrences, i. p. 152; Thomson's Sketches, p. 130; Christie, p. 106; Breckenridge, p. 127.

Newfoundland regiments, about two hundred in number, under Captain Winter; and forty Indians under Norton—which occupied a point of wood and a ravine, near the point of debarkation—opened a fire, and opposed the landing.[1] With considerable spirit the ground was disputed by this handful of men, and the column was greatly annoyed as it advanced; yet the fire from the vessels soon compelled it to fall back on the enemy's left column, half a mile in the rear, and the landing was secured.[2] The left column of the enemy's force, which had been posted in another ravine, a quarter of a mile in the rear of the advance, was composed of three hundred and twenty men from the Eighth regiment, one hundred and fifty militia, and a detachment of the Royal artillery, with two or three field-pieces; commanded by Colonel Myers, the Deputy Quartermaster-general of the army; and, when the advance gave way, it was moved forward to support it, and to oppose the progress of the Americans.[3] Against these combined forces, numbering not less than eight hundred men,[4] well posted on the summit of a precipitous bank, the American advance was compelled to move; and, as it climbed up the bank, three several times it was compelled to fall back before it reached the summit.[5] At length,

[1] Breckenridge, p. 128; Thomson's Sketches, p. 131; Gen. Vincent to Sir G. Prevost, May 28; James' Mil. Occur., i. p. 154.—[2] Gen. Vincent to Sir G. Prevost, May 28; James' Mil. Occur., i. pp. 154, 155.—[3] Gen. Vincent to Sir G. Prevost, May 28; James' Mil. Occur., i. p. 156.

[4] Mr. James (*Mil. Occur.*, i. p. 156) says it numbered "*about six hundred men;*" but a simple addition of his own figures will show his error.—[5] Mansfield's Scott, p. 80; Roger's Rise of Canada, i. p. 213; Christie, p. 106; James' Mil. Occur., i. pp. 156, 157; Auchinleck, p. 157.

supported by Colonel Porter's light-artillery and part of General Boyd's brigade, Colonel Scott secured the bank, after a most desperate conflict[1]—the brave commander (Myers) and one hundred and fourteen of the advance, six officers and one hundred and ninety-eight men of the Eighth regiment, and five officers and eighty men of the militia, killed or wounded, bearing testimony, not less to the gallantry of the attack, than to the obstinacy of the defence.[2]

Colonel Scott immediately pursued the enemy as far as the village of Newark (*or Niagara*),[3] from whence the riflemen and light-troops were detached, and sent forward to cut off the retreat of the enemy towards Burlington Heights;[4] while another detachment, led by Colonel Scott, advanced towards Fort George, in which a small party of fifty men from the Forty-ninth, and eighty militia, had been left in the morning.[5]

The day had been contested and lost; and Brigadier-general Vincent—the commander of the post—justly considered that any farther opposition would not only be useless, but "the height of rashness."[6] He resolved, therefore, to concentrate his forces at the Beaver-dams; and, for this purpose, he ordered Lieutenant Bisshopp to evacuate Fort Erie, Major Ormsby to abandon Chippewa, and the little

[1] Gen. Dearborn to Sec. of War, May 27; Armstrong's Notices, i. p. 134; Mansfield's Scott, p. 80; Christie, p. 106; Perkins' War, p. 251.—[2] James' Mil. Occur., i. p. 157.—[3] Mansfield's Scott, p. 80.—[4] James' Mil. Occur., i. p. 158.—[5] Mansfield's Scott, p. 80; James' Mil. Occur., i. p. 158.—[6] Auchinleck, p. 157; Christie, p. 106; Armstrong's Notices, i. p. 134.

party within the fort, after setting fire to its magazine, to join the main body;[1] while, without molestation, he marched thither with the remnants of his command.

In the mean time Colonel Scott approached the fort; and when the head of the column had approached within "some eighty paces" the magazine exploded. A heavy piece of timber struck him, throwing him from his horse, and severely bruising him; yet he summoned sufficient strength to remount, and, after forcing open the gate of the fort, was the first to enter it,[2] and, with his own hands, he struck the enemy's colors and hoisted those of his own country.[3]

As the fort had been rendered untenable by the fire from Fort Niagara, its capture was the work of but a very few minutes; and the detachment which occupied it surrendered itself prisoners of war.[4]

Having thus secured the fort, the Colonel thirsted for still greater honors; and, disregarding the orders of General Lewis, he pressed forward in pursuit of the retreating enemy. Two aids-de-camp—Lieutenant William Jenkins Worth (since the lamented Major-general Worth) and Major Vandeventer—were sent after him, with positive orders for his return, and yet he pressed forward, with the main body of the enemy full in sight, and with every prospect of a most triumphant success. At this moment General Boyd, in person, overtook him, and, no longer disregarding the positive orders of a superior, *on the field*, he countermarched and unwillingly returned to the main body.[1]

The strength of the enemy has been noticed already: that of the Americans was about six thousand men,[2] although not more than one-fifth of the land forces were employed in this action—the advance, Colonel Porter's light-artillery, and part of General Boyd's brigade, having been alone engaged.[3] The loss of the enemy, also, has been referred to:[4] that of the Americans was seventeen killed, and forty-five wounded.[5] Among the trophies of this important victory were three hundred and sixty-six regulars and five hundred and seven militia, prisoners of war.[6]

[Note.—The Dispatches of Gen. Dearborn to Sec. of War; of Com. Chauncey to Sec. of Navy; and of Gen. Vincent to Sir Geo. Prevost, which had been provided for the illustration of this chapter, have been omitted by the Publishers for want of room.]

---

[1] Auchinleck, p. 157; James' Mil. Occur., i. p. 158.

[2] Mansfield's Scott, p. 81; Thomson's Sketches, p. 132.

[3] Mansfield's Scott, p. 81. Mr. Thomson (*Sketches*, p. 132) says, "*Capt. Hindman* succeeded in taking the flag which the enemy left flying," &c.; but I have preferred the statement of Mansfield.

[4] James' Military Occurrences, i. p. 158.

[1] Mansfield's Scott, p. 81; Armstrong's Notices, i. p. 134.—[2] Armstrong's Notices, i. p. 133; James' Military Occurrences, i. p. 153; Ingersoll's War, i. p. 280.

[3] Vide p. 233.—[4] Ibid.

[5] Gen. Dearborn to Secretary of War, May 27.

[6] Thomson's Sketches, p. 133.

CAPTURE OF FORT GEORGE.

(COL. WINFIELD SCOTT LEADING THE ATTACK)

From the original Painting by Chappel in the possession of the Publishers.

CHAPTER XLVIII.

May 29, 1813.

THE ATTACK ON SACKETT'S HARBOR, N. Y.

The expedition against Fort George and other posts in possession of the enemy, on the Niagara frontier, already referred to,[1] having rendered necessary the withdrawal of the forces from Sackett's Harbor, the commanders of the enemy's land and naval forces,—Sir George Prevost and Sir James L. Yeo,—who were then at Kingston, organized an expedition against that place.[2] A plan which was better arranged, or which promised more success, has been seldom seen; and it is a remarkable fact, that while, by a characteristic blunder, on the part of General Dearborn, the village was left, with all its stores, with but a nominal guard, by a similarly characteristic blunder, on the part of the enemy, the advantage which was thus opened to him, was unproductive of any success. It was pre-eminently an age of blunders, and the northern frontiers were the most productive of all the fields of operations—the commanders of either nation, and the governments by whom they were respectively employed, being alike inefficient and improvident.

Commodore Yeo had recently arrived at Kingston, with a strong party of seamen and officers for the squadron on Lake Ontario;[1] and Sir George Prevost, who had accompanied Sir James from Montreal,[2] had consented to join him, with a strong body of the land-forces, in the projected expedition. Accordingly, on the 27th of May, the troops embarked, with Sir George Prevost at their head;[3] and early the next day the squadron weighed anchor, reaching Sackett's Harbor about noon on the same day.[4] The land-forces which were thus employed embraced the grenadier company of the One Hundredth regiment, a section of the Royal Scots, two companies of the Eighth regiment, four companies of the One Hundredth and Fourth regiment, one company of the Glengarry's, two companies of the Canadian Voltigeurs, a detachment of the Newfoundland regiment, and one from the Royal Artillery, with two six-pounders,[5] numbering, in the aggregate, about a thousand men.[6] There appears to have been present, also, a strong party of Indians, notwithstanding the enemy's historians have carefully excluded all reference to them in their

1 Vide Chap. XLVII.—2 Auchinleck's Hist. of War, p. 161; Christie's Military and Naval Operations, p. 107; Cooper's Naval History, ii. p. 165; James' Military Occurrences, i. pp. 164, 165.

1 Auchinleck, p. 161; James, i. p. 164; Christie, p. 107.
2 Christie, p. 107; Auchinleck, p. 161; Rogers' Canada, i. p. 215.—3 Christie, p. 107.—4 Ibid.; Auchinleck, p. 162.
5 "General Orders," signed, "Edward Baynes, *Adj.-Gen.*;" James' Mil. Occur., i. p. 165; Auchinleck, p. 162.
6 Gen. Brown to Gov. Tompkins, May 29; Ingersoll's History of War, i. p. 280.

enumeration of his forces.[1] The squadron embraced the *General Wolfe*, of twenty-four guns; the *Royal George*, of twenty-four guns; the *Earl of Moira*, of eighteen guns; and four schooners, mounting from ten to twelve guns each, with two gunboats and a sufficient number of batteaux for landing the troops.[2]

The village of Sackett's Harbor is situated on the south side of Black-river Bay, near the foot of Lake Ontario—being a post village in the town of Houndsfield, Jefferson County, New York. The harbor, which is well sheltered, is small; and from its northwest extremity a low point of land, called Navy Point, extends into the lake.[3] Two forts, known as Fort Pike and Fort Tompkins, defended the village and the harbor; and, at the time of the descent under consideration, it was garrisoned with detachments from the First regiment of light-dragoons, from the light-artillery, and from the Ninth, Twenty-first, and Twenty-third infantry, a subaltern and eight men from the "heavy-artillery," and a party of volunteers from Albany, the whole numbering, exclusive of the volunteers, seven hundred and eighty-seven men, including officers, commanded by Lieutenant-colonel Backus of the light-dragoons.[4] General Dearborn and Colonel Macomb, before the departure of the forces on the expeditions to York and Fort George, had requested Brigadier-general Jacob Brown, of the New York militia, who resided near by, to assume the command in case of an attack by the enemy;[1] and to his good judgment, not less than to the bravery of the regular troops, was the country indebted for the success which subsequently attended the American arms before this village.

The weather was remarkably fine, and after the enemy's squadron had stood off the Harbor a sufficient time to enable the enemy to make the necessary reconnoissance, the troops were embarked in the batteaux and boats of the squadron and every thing was put in readiness to land, whenever the signal to do so should be displayed by the commander-in-chief. Notwithstanding the promise of success which the surprise of the little garrison appeared to insure, after the troops had occupied the boats about half an hour, orders were issued for their return to the shipping; and, with similarly remarkable affright, the squadron, immediately afterwards, wore and stood for Kingston.[2]

While thus engaged in a most ignominious flight, a squadron of boats was seen near the shore, in the distance; and, as they appeared to be heading towards Sackett's Harbor, it was properly supposed that they were carrying a reinforcement to the garrison. Among those who were "dissatisfied at being called back without effecting any thing,"

[1] James, i. p. 165. Lieut. Davis (*Hist. of War*, p. 68) says there were *three hundred* Indians present.

[2] James, i. p. 165; Breckenridge's Hist. of War, p. 135; Rogers' Canada, i. p. 215.—[3] McCulloch's Geog. Dict., ii. p. 736.—[4] Report, signed "Thomas Aspinwall, *Maj. 9th regiment*," in *Wilkinson's Memoirs*, i. p. 582.

[1] Gen. Brown to Sec. of War, June 1; Wilkinson's Memoirs, i. p. 581; Richards' Memoir of Macomb, p. 58.

[2] James, i. p. 165. It is proper to remark that no other author alludes to this retreat; yet the character of Mr. James, as a faithful and industrious author, leads me to respect his statements.

"particularly as their unsophisticated minds could devise no reason for abandoning the enterprise," were the Indian allies of His Britannic Majesty, already referred to; and no sooner had *they* seen the squadron of boats than they "fearlessly paddled back to attack them."[1] Whether the zeal of the allies shamed Sir George and his command does not certainly appear; yet it is certain that the boats were sent out, again, from the squadron, and co-operated with the Indians in *their* enterprise against the American boats, and assisted in driving ashore, and capturing twelve of them, with about seventy dragoons, who formed part of the force which had been on board of them[2]—seven boats only, of the squadron, escaping into Sackett's Harbor.[3]

Encouraged by this unexpected success Sir George Prevost appears to have reconsidered his determination to retire—in which he had been opposed, from the beginning, by Sir James Yeo and the officers of the army—and the squadron stood back towards the Harbor. A change of the wind, however, prevented it from coming within six miles of the point which it had reached in the forenoon, and nothing was done during the remainder of the day.[4]

In the mean time an alarm had been raised; and five hundred militia from the neighboring towns had reached the village,[5] and were posted behind a sharp ridge of sand and gravel, which had been thrown up some distance west from the village; the volunteers, before referred to, being formed on their right, with a six-pounder on their left.[1] This position was selected, from the fact that a landing would be more probable at this place than any other; and the result proved that the supposition was well founded.[2] At the same time the regular troops, under Lieutenant-colonel Backus, were formed in front of their camp,[3] a mile distant from the militia, between whom and the former was a thick wood.[4]

At an early hour in the morning the enemy debarked his troops;[5] and, before day, the boats approached the shore under cover of two gunboats, commanded by Captain Mulcaster of the Royal navy.[6] As they approached the spot where the militia and volunteers were concealed, the latter rose, and threw into the boats a scattering fire,[7] which was returned by the gunboats, under Captain Mulcaster;[8] while the enemy's boats pulled around to the other side of Horse Island, and there landed, with but little loss, although it was executed in the face of the militia, who were posted on the other side of the cove.[9] Forming his party as quick-

[1] James, i. p. 166.—[2] Wilkinson's Memoirs, i. p. 582; Cooper, ii. p. 165; James, i. p. 166; Christie, p. 108; Breckenridge, p. 136.—[3] James, i. p. 166; Thomson's Sketches. p 141.—[4] James, i. p 166.—[5] Gen. Brown to Sec. of War, June 1; Wilkinson's Mem., i. p. 582; Perkins' Hist. of War, p. 250; Armstrong's Notices, i. p. 144.

[1] Col. Baynes to Sir G. Prevost, May 30: Gen. Brown to Sec. of War, June 1; Wilkinson's Memoirs, i. p. 583; Christie, p. 108.—[2] Gen. Brown to Sec. of War, June 1; Perkins, p. 249.—[3] Gen. Brown to Sec. of War, June 1; Wilkinson, i. p. 583.—[4] Wilkinson, i. p. 583; Col. Baynes to Sir G. Prevost, May 30.—[5] Col. Baynes to Sir G. Prevost, May 30; James, i. p. 169.—[6] Col. Baynes to Sir G. Prevost, May 30; Gen. Brown to Gov. Tompkins, May 29.
[7] Col. Baynes to Sir G. Prevost, May 30; Christie, p. 108.—[8] "The gunboats *which had covered our landing,*" &c.—*Col. Baynes' Dispatch.* Rogers' Canada, i. p. 216.—[9] Col. Baynes to Sir G. Prevost, May 30; Wilkinson, i. p. 583.

ly as possible, with the grenadiers of the One Hundredth in front, Colonel Baynes—who commanded the descent—moved over the narrow causeway which connects Horse Island with the mainland; and, with the greatest gallantry, they advanced against the American troops.[1] As they approached, the militia rose, fired a scattering volley, and, without farther resistance, fled, by a bridle-path, into the woods, leaving behind them the six-pounder which covered their left flank.[2] At the urgent solicitation of General Brown, about eighty of the militia, under Captain McKnitt, took post behind a large fallen tree, in the rear of a small open field, and gave the enemy three or four volleys; but, being pressed by superior numbers, they were compelled to retire, *with the General*, after their companions.[3]

While, on the left, the militia were thus disgracing themselves, by their shameful desertion of their colors, the Albany Volunteers, on the right of the line, manfully stood their ground until they were overpowered by numbers;[4] when they slowly retired by way of a wagon-road on the bank of the lake, skirmishing with the advance of the enemy, as they retreated.[5] In this they were supported by small parties of regulars who were sent out by Lieutenant-colonel Backus, for that purpose;[1] and the enemy suffered severely, notwithstanding the gunboats and light vessels of his squadron scoured the woods through which the volunteers were retiring.[2]

When the assailants had passed the wood they displayed, and moved forward against the regular troops, which awaited their approach, and against the volunteers, who had already so faithfully resisted them, and afterwards fallen into the line on the left of the regulars. The right of the line was occupied by the dismounted light-dragoons; the left by the volunteers, already referred to; and the centre by the infantry and artillery; while the guns on Fort Tompkins were brought to bear on the advancing columns of the enemy. Encouraged by the successful termination of their attack on the militia, the enemy pressed forward against the extreme of this line—probably with the hope of turning the flank of the American line—but he was hurled back by the gallant dragoons, with considerable loss. Like the waves of the ocean on a lee shore, again and again the enemy's column dashed against the American lines, but Lieutenant-colonel Backus and his command stood firm, and every movement of the veteran assailants was successfully opposed.[3]

At length, after an hour's conflict, the superiority of numbers in the enemy's column had begun to oppress the

[1] Col. Baynes to Sir G. Prevost, May 30; James, i. p. 168; Christie, p. 108.—[2] Gen. Brown to Sec. of War, June 1; Col. Baynes to Sir G. Prevost, May 30; Wilkinson, i. p. 583; Perkins, i. p. 250; James, i. p. 168.

[3] Gen. Brown to Sec. of War, June 1; Wilkinson, i. p. 583; Perkins, p. 250; James, i. p. 169; Christie, p. 108. As this is the last of Gen. Brown's services, *during the action*, it is difficult to conceive why *he* was considered the hero of the day; and especially since Lieut.-Col. Backus and Lieut.-Col. Mills commanded the only troops who stood their ground.

[4] Col. Baynes to Sir G. Prevost, May 30; Wilkinson, i. p. 584.—[5] Wilkinson, i. p. 584; James, i. p. 170.

[1] Wilkinson, i. p. 584.—[2] Col. Baynes to Sir G. Prevost, May 30.—[3] Wilkinson, i. p. 584.

Americans, and a successful termination of his efforts began to be looked for. A portion of the Americans had fallen back into a log-barracks near by;[1] and Lieutenant Chauncey, influenced by erroneous information, had set on fire the new ship *General Pike*, which was nearly ready to be launched; while orders had been sent to set on fire, also, the store-houses, the barracks, and the schooner *Duke of Gloucester*, which had been captured at York, a few days before.[2] At this moment Sir George Prevost, who was in the rear, appears to have been suddenly impressed with the knowledge that there was "no object within his reach, to attain, that could compensate for the loss he was momentarily sustaining from the heavy fire of the American cannon,"[3] and a retrograde movement was ordered;[4] and soon afterwards the troops, "leisurely, and in perfect order," returned to their boats and the squadron;[5] leaving behind them, however, their dead and wounded.[6]

As quickly as possible, after the retreat of the enemy, the flames which had been set to the shipping and other property were extinguished, but not until large quantities of stores—principally those which had been captured at York—had been consumed. The *General Pike*, owing to the unseasoned wood of which she was constructed, was but little injured.[1]

Soon afterwards Sir George Prevost sent a flag to the village demanding its surrender; but, as might have been reasonably expected, the demand was peremptorily refused; and the squadron returned to Kingston.[2]

In this remarkable action the enemy lost Captain Gray, Acting Deputy Quartermaster-general, and forty-seven men, *killed;* Majors Evans, Drummond, and Moody, Captains Blackmore, Tythe, Leonard, Shore, and McPherson, Lieutenants Nutal, Lowry, Rainford, Moore, and Delancy, Ensigns Greig and Matthewson, and one hundred and ninety-four men, *wounded:*[3] that of the Americans was twenty regulars, one volunteer, and Colonel Mills, and about twenty-five militia, *killed;* Lieutenant-colonel Backus, three lieutenants, one ensign, and seventy-nine men, *wounded:* and thirty-six *missing.*[4]

On the conduct of Sir George Prevost British authors have been strongly and properly severe;[5] while, on the same subject, a careful writer of those times, on the American side, has used

1 Wilkinson, i. p. 584; James, i. p. 170.

2 Col. Baynes to Sir G. Prevost, May 30; Letter from an officer, in "*The War*," i. p. 212; Perkins, p. 250; Cooper, ii. p. 166; James, i. p. 170; Davis, p. 69; Armstrong, i. p. 147.

3 Col. Baynes to Sir G. Prevost, May 30; Christie, p. 109. It has been stated that Sir George considered an immediate retreat necessary, from the fact that Gen. Brown was returning, with the militia, through the bridle-path, to cut off his retreat. As this would have been a plausible excuse, *which was not employed*, for the retreat; as *a different cause was assigned* by Col. Baynes; and as Gen. Brown does not allude to any such movement, I have discredited the statement.

4 Col. Baynes to Sir G. Prevost, May 30.—5 Ibid.

6 James, i. p. 173; Ingersoll, i. p. 281; Armstrong, i. p. 147; Thomson's Sketches, p. 145.

1 James, i. p. 172.—2 Letter from an officer, in "*The War*," ii. p. 212; Breckenridge, p. 138; Thomson's Sketches, p. 146. Gen. Brown (*Letter to Gov. Tompkins, May* 29) speaks of a flag, bearing a message concerning the killed and wounded; but he does not allude to the summons.—3 Returns appended to Col. Baynes' report to Sir G. Prevost, May 30.—4 Returns appended to Gen. Brown's report to the Secretary of War, June 1.

5 James, i. pp. 173–177; Auchinleck, pp. 161–168; Christie, p. 110; Rogers' Canada, i. pp. 216, 217.

the following just and very appropriate language:[1]

"Had the result of the expedition against Sackett's Harbor been of that character of unparalleled brilliancy which would have entitled it to the encomiums of its commander, and to the warmest admiration of the British nation, its effects would have been long and deplorably felt by the American government. Immense quantities of naval and military stores, which had been from time to time collected at that depot; the frames and timbers which had been prepared for the construction of vessels of war, and the rigging and armaments which had been forwarded thither for their final equipment; as well as all the army clothing, camp equipage, provisions, ammunition, and implements of war, which had been previously captured from the enemy, would have fallen into his hands. The destruction of the batteries, the ship then on the stocks, the extensive cantonments, and the public arsenal, would have retarded the building of another naval force, and that which was already on the lake, in separate detachments, could have been intercepted in its attempt to return, and might have been captured in detail. The prize vessel, which was then lying in the harbor, and which had been taken by the Americans, and the two United States' schooners, would have been certainly recaptured, and the whole energies of the American government, added to their most vigorous and unwearied struggles, might never again have attained any prospect of an ascendency on the lake. As it proved, however, all these impending evils were averted, and the wisdom of the commanding officer, and the invincible firmness of those of his troops who withstood the brunt of the action, converted that event into a splendid victory, which would otherwise have been an irretrievable disaster."

[Note.—The Dispatches of Gen. Brown to the Sec. of War, and Col. Baynes to Sir Geo. Prevost, which had been supplied for the illustration of this chapter, have been omitted by the Publishers for want of room.]

CHAPTER XLIX

June 1, 1813.

THE LOSS OF THE CHESAPEAKE.

The frigate *Chesapeake* having returned to Boston from a long but unsuccessful cruise, and thereby established her character as an "unlucky ship,"[2] she was refitted, and, late in May, 1813, was again ready for sea.[1] At this time the harbor of Boston was blockaded by a squadron of the enemy's vessels; and when it was understood that the *Chesapeake* was ready, one of that squadron, the *Shannon*, of

[1] Thomson's Sketches, pp. 147, 148.

[2] Washington Irving's Memoir of Capt. Lawrence (*Analectic Mag.*, ii. p. 136); Cooper's Naval History, ii. p. 101.

[1] Auchinleck's History of War, p. 137; Perkins' History of War, p. 176; Cooper's Naval History, ii. p. 102.

thirty-eight guns, commanded by Captain Philip Bowes Vere Broke, appeared in the offing and courted an engagement.[1] To insure such a result, on the first of June Captain Broke addressed a letter to "the Commander of the United States frigate *Chesapeake*," inviting him to a single combat, "ship to ship, to try the fortune of their respective flags;"[2] and, after clearing his ship for action, laid to, off the Boston Light-house, and awaited the answer.[3]

At the period in question the *Chesapeake* mounted twenty-eight long-eighteens on the main-deck, sixteen thirty-two-pound carronades on the quarter-deck, and four of the latter and a long eighteen-pounder on the forecastle—forty-nine guns in all.[4] Her crew had been recently enlisted, a considerable number were considerably disaffected from some supposed irregularity concerning prize-money; and all had been on board so short a time, that the officers had not acquired any of that influence over them which a more extended term of service has never failed to insure.[5] Captain James Lawrence, her commander, had taken the command of her with great reluctance;[6] her first-lieutenant (O. A. Page) was on shore, sick; her third and fourth lieutenancies were filled with midshipmen; and a greater proportion than usual were landsmen.[1] The *Shannon*, on the contrary, was manned with a a picked and experienced crew, whose confidence in its officers had been produced by long service under their command; and every conceivable preparation which could be devised had been made to insure success in an action, in which the honor of the flag and that of the individual were the controlling motives.[2]

When Captain Lawrence saw the movements of the *Shannon* he understood their import, and decided to accept the proffered meeting.[3] In this rash determination he was earnestly opposed by many experienced officers, who knew and properly appreciated the disadvantages under which the *Chesapeake* would meet the *Shannon*, in such an encounter;[4] but, influenced by an irresistible, if not an intemperate zeal, he disregarded their arguments and their entreaties, and rushed madly to the destruction which stared him in the face.

With this intent, after temporizing with his disaffected crew, by giving checks for its demands, he addressed it in a short speech;[5] and endeavored to enlist its sympathies by raising three ensigns, on different parts of his rigging,[6] and the white burgee, on which

[1] Mem. of Sir P. B. V. Broke, in the *Naval Chronicle*, xxxiii. pp. 15, 16; Irving's Mem. of Capt. Lawrence (*Analectic Mag.*, ii. p. 136); Cooper, ii. p. 102; Com. Bainbridge to Secretary of Navy, June 2, 1813.

[2] This "challenge" was landed at Salem, and mailed, thence, to Boston, arriving at that place *after the action.* It may be found in the *Naval Chronicle*, xxx. pp. 413, 414 (*London*, 1813), and in James' Naval Occurrences, Appendix, No. 36.—[3] Mem. of P. B. V. Broke; James' Naval Occur., p. 213.—[4] James' Naval Occurrences, p. 231.

[5] Irving's Mem. of Capt. Lawrence (*Analectic Mag.*, ii. pp. 36, 37); Cooper, ii. pp. 102, 103.—[6] Irving's Mem. of Capt. Lawrence (*Analectic Mag.*, ii. p. 136); Sketches of the War, p. 298; Capt. Lawrence to Capt. Biddle, May 27, 1813.

[1] Irving's Mem. of Capt. Lawrence (*Analectic Mag.*, ii. p. 137); Perkins, p. 176; The Boston *Palladium*, cited in "*The War*," i. p. 214.—[2] Irving's Mem. of Capt. Lawrence (*Analectic Mag.*, ii. p. 136).—[3] Ibid.; Sketches of the War, p. 298; Thomson's Sketches, p. 197.—[4] Irving's Mem. of Capt. Lawrence (*Analectic Mag.*, ii. pp. 137, 233).

[5] Ibid., p. 138; Sketches of the War, p. 293.

[6] Capt. Broke's Dispatch, June 6.

was inscribed the motto, "*Free trade and sailors' rights;*"[1] but in this, also, he was quite unsuccessful. He had not received Captain Broke's letter of challenge;[2] but understanding the purpose of his movements, at noon, on the first of June, Captain Lawrence weighed anchor and stood down the bay, with a pleasant breeze from the southwest.[3] As the *Chesapeake* approached the *Shannon*, the latter stood off, under easy sail;[4] and thus, until half-past four in the afternoon, the two ships moved farther from the shore. At that time Captain Lawrence fired a gun, and the *Shannon* hove to, with her head to the southeastward.[5] The breeze having freshened, at five o'clock the *Chesapeake* took in her royals and topgallant sails;[6] and at half-past five she hauled up her courses.[7] At this time the two ships were about thirty miles from the light-house;[8] the *Shannon* under single-reefed topsails and jib, and the *Chesapeake*, under her topsails and jib, coming down fast.[9]

Captain Lawrence, as the *Chesapeake* approached the *Shannon*, decided to lay the enemy alongside, yard-arm to yard-arm; and for this purpose he luffed and ranged up abeam, on the *Shannon's* starboard quarter.[1] As the guns of the latter ship were brought to bear, commencing with her cabin guns, she threw in a fire; but the *Chesapeake* did not return it until her entire broadside bore on the enemy, when she commenced the action with great effect.[2] While passing the enemy's broadside the *Chesapeake* had her fore-topsail tie and her jib-sheet shot away; and, at the same time, her spanker-brails were loosened, and the sail blew out.[3] The effect of this slight damage was speedily apparent; and, after the action had continued a few minutes, the ship was brought up into the wind, got sternway, and fell aboard the *Shannon*—her mizzen-rigging locking in with the enemy's fore-chains.[4]

In this unfortunate position the *Chesapeake* was raked by the *Shannon*;[5] and her crew (not yet acquainted with their officers and with each other, and not stimulated with that *esprit de corps* which alone could sustain men in such a situation), began to flinch from their guns.[6] Captain Lawrence had, mean-

---

[1] Irving's Mem. of Capt. Lawrence (*Analectic Mag.*, ii. p. 137); Auchinleck, p. 138; Sketches of the War, p. 293; James' Naval Occur., p. 215.—[2] Irving's Mem. of Capt. Lawrence (*Analectic Mag.*, ii. p. 137); Auchinleck, p. 138; Cooper, ii. p. 102; Breckenridge's History of War, p. 164.

[3] Lieut. Budd to Secretary of Navy, June 15; Testimony of Lieut. Budd in Court-martial on Lieut. Cox, April 16, 1814; Cooper, ii. p. 103; Com. Bainbridge to Secretary of Navy, June 2.

[4] Auchinleck, p. 138; Cooper, ii. p. 103; Perkins, p. 176; Sketches of the War, p. 293; James' Naval Occur., p. 214.—[5] Lieut. Budd to Sec. of Navy, June 15; Auchinleck, p. 138; Cooper, ii. p. 103; Thomson's Sketches, p. 197.—[6] Lieut. Budd to Sec. of Navy, June 15; Auchinleck, p. 138; Cooper, ii. p. 103; Capt. Broke's Dispatch, June 6.—[7] Lieut. Budd to Sec. of Navy, June 15; Cooper, ii. p. 103.—[8] Cooper, ii. p. 103. James (*Naval Occurrences*, p. 214) says they were *six leagues* from the light-house.

[9] Cooper, ii. p. 103.

[1] Testimony of Lieut. Budd on Cox's trial; Cooper, ii. p. 103; Capt. Broke's Dispatch, June 6, 1813; James' Naval Occurrences, p. 215.

[2] Irving's Mem. of Capt. Lawrence (*Analectic Mag.*, ii. p. 138); Cooper, ii. p. 103; James' Naval Occur., pp. 215, 216; Letter from Halifax, June 9, in "*The War*," ii. p. 4.

[3] Thomson's Sketches, p. 198; James' Naval Occur., p. 216; Perkins, p. 177; Cooper, ii. p. 103.

[4] Thomson's Sketches, p. 198; James' Naval Occur., p. 216; Perkins, p. 177; Capt. Broke's Dispatch, June 6; Cooper, ii. p. 103; Lieut. Budd's Dispatch, June 15.

[5] James' Naval Occur., p. 216; Sketches of the War, p. 293; Cooper, ii. p. 103.—[6] Capt. Broke's Dispatch, June 6; James' Naval Occur., p. 217; Cooper, ii. p. 104.

while, received a very severe wound in the leg and a mortal wound in the body; Mr. Broom, the officer of marines, had received a mortal wound, as, also, had First-lieutenant Ludlow, Mr. Ballard, the acting fourth-lieutenant, and Mr. Adams, the boatswain; and Mr. White, the master, had been killed.[1] The watchful eye of Captain Broke instantly detected the weakness of his adversary[2]—with no officer above the rank of a midshipman on deck[3]—and he ordered his boarders forward; when, putting himself at the head of twenty of them, he dashed over the bulwarks and led them to the quarter-deck of the *Chesapeake*.[4] He met with but little resistance[5]—the American boarders, through the terror of the bugler who had been ordered to call them,[6] having received but imperfect *verbal* orders, had not come on deck[7]—and as the leader of the malcontents had removed the gratings of the berth-deck,[8] the enemy speedily secured the control of the ship, and Lieutenant Watts, of the *Shannon*, hauled down her colors.[1]

It was during the action, while he was being carried below, after receiving his second and mortal wound, that Captain Lawrence uttered his last words, which, slightly paraphrased, have since become a battle-cry for the navy, and a proverb among the people.[2] "*Don't give up the ship*," floated at the mast-head of Commodore Perry's flag-ship, on Lake Erie; and the same laconic motto has given new life and energy to the wearied and the weak-handed, from that day to the present.

The loss of the *Chesapeake*, in this short but sanguinary conflict, was Captain Lawrence, Lieutenants Ludlow, Ballard, and Broom, Master White, Boatswain Adams, three midshipmen, twenty-seven seamen, and eleven marines, *killed;* and ninety-eight, officers and men, *wounded:*[3] that of the *Shannon* was, First-lieutenant Watt, Purser Aldham, and twenty-two men, *killed;* and Captain Broke, a midshipman, and fifty-six men, *wounded*.[4]

The strength of the *Chesapeake* has been already noted; the *Shannon* "mounted twenty-four guns on her broadside, and one light boat-gun; eighteen-pounders on her main-deck, and thirty-two-pound carronades on

---

[1] Sketches of the War, p. 293; Perkins, p. 177; Cooper, ii. pp. 103, 104; Irving's Mem. of Capt. Lawrence (*Analectic Mag.*, ii. p. 139).

[2] Capt. Broke's Dispatch, June 6; James' Naval Occurrences, p. 217; Sketches of the War, p. 294; Cooper, ii. p. 104.

[3] Perkins, p. 177; Cooper, ii. p. 104; Irving's Mem. of Capt. Lawrence (*Analectic Mag.*, ii. pp. 139, 140).

[4] Letter from Halifax, June 9, in "*The War*," ii. p. 4; Thomson's Sketches, p. 198; James' Naval Occur., p. 217; Perkins, p. 177; Capt. Broke's Dispatch, June 6.

[5] James' Naval Occur., pp. 217, 218; Perkins, p. 177; Capt. Broke's Dispatch, June 6; Testimony of Lieut. Budd in trial of Lieut. Cox, April 16, 1814; Cooper, ii. p. 104.—[6] Sketches of the War, p. 294; Perkins, p. 177; Cooper, ii. p. 104; Decision of the Court of Inquiry on the loss of the ship.

[7] Testimony of Lieut. Budd and Midshipman Curtiss in trial of Lieut. Cox, April 16, 1814; Cooper, ii. p. 104; Lieut. Budd's Dispatch, June 15.

[8] This man was the boatswain's mate. Thomson's Sketches, p. 198; Perkins, p. 178; Cooper, ii. p. 104.

---

[1] Thomson's Sketches, p. 198; James' Naval Occurrences, p. 219; Capt. Broke's Dispatch, June 6.

[2] Sketches of the War, p. 294; Perkins, p. 178. Dr. John Dix, a surgeon's-mate on the *Chesapeake* (*Trial of Lieut. Cox, April* 18, 1814), testified that Capt. Lawrence "ordered *me* to go on the deck and TELL THE MEN TO FIRE FASTER, AND NOT GIVE UP THE SHIP, which I attempted to do," &c.—[3] Returns appended to Lieut. Budd's Dispatch, June 15.—[4] Returns appended to Capt. Broke's Dispatch, June 6.

her quarter-deck and forecastle; and was manned with a complement of three hundred men and boys, besides thirty seamen, &c., who were taken out of recaptured vessels."[1]

Thus terminated one of the most interesting actions connected with the navy of the United States. Short, desperate, and bloody—it has never failed to excite, both among Americans and Britons, the liveliest sensations of pride and gratification—the former referring to the gallant and noble-hearted Lawrence as one of their brightest jewels; the latter, although they may have been surcharged with naval honors of a deeper, bloodier hue, yielding, to this and to the victor, the homage which older and better soldiers had struggled for and failed to secure. The former, gathering the remains of their fallen ones, conveyed them to the city of New York—the centre of that commerce which they had fallen to protect—and there they were interred, amidst the people whom they loved; the latter pouring honors of unusual splendor on the conqueror, sent down to the latest generation the story of his prowess and of their gratitude.

[Note.—The Dispatches of Lieut. Budd to the Sec. of Navy, and Capt. Broke's to the Admiral of N. A. Station, which had been prepared for the illustration of this chapter, have been omitted by the Publishers for want of room.]

CHAPTER L.

June 6, 1813.

THE ACTION AT STONY CREEK.

The capture of Fort George; the retreat of General Vincent, who commanded the enemy's forces; the concentration of all his troops near the Beaver-dams, have been noticed in a preceding chapter of this work.[2] Within a few days after he had reached this point General Vincent was strengthened by the arrival of two companies of the Eighth, or King's, regiment of the line, and a small party of seamen under Captain Barclay, of the Royal navy, who was then on his way to Lake Erie.[3] General Dearborn, misled by information which the enemy had placed in his way, frittered away several days in an "unsuccessful and mortifying" pursuit; and a subsequent difference of opinion between that officer and Commodore Chauncey, and the subsequent withdrawal of the squadron, cut off the little remaining hope of a successful termination of the campaign, which the General had entertained.[1]

Preferring, in that emergency, to attack the enemy in the mountain-passes, with diminished hopes of success, to a season of inactivity, in the prosecution of a purely defensive policy, on the

---

[1] Capt. Broke's challenge, June 1, 1813.

[2] Vide Chap. XLVII.—[3] Auchinleck's History of the War, p. 160; Armstrong's Notes, i. p. 134.

[1] Armstrong, i. pp. 135, 136.

first of June he detached General Winder, with a small brigade of less than eight hundred men, to attack the enemy and drive him from his position.[1] It was not long, however, before the strength of the enemy was discovered; and General Winder properly decided to halt at Forty-mile Creek, until the arrival of reinforcements warranted him in advancing.[2]

On the morning of the fifth of June Brigadier-general John Chandler joined General Winder with a second, but weak brigade;[3] and as General Winder's troops were under marching orders, after a short halt the entire force marched for Stony Creek, reaching that place between five and six in the afternoon, and driving before them a small picket which the enemy had posted there.[4] With considerable risk the advance-guard—consisting of the light-infantry under Captains Hindman, Biddle, and Nicholas, a part of the rifle corps under Captain Lytle, and detachments from the Second dragoons under Captain Selden—was allowed to pursue the fugitives until a second picket was fallen in with;[1] and after a slight resistance that also was defeated—the advance continuing the pursuit even longer than the General "could have wished."[2]

The troops having taken the Lake road, the Thirteenth and Fourteenth regiments, and Captain Samuel B. Archer's company of artillery, were ordered to take a position, for the night, near the mouth of the creek, to cover the boats which were expected there;[3] while the remainder of the division, about one thousand in number, was encamped where it had halted. The troops were ordered to lay on their arms; flank-guards and a rear-guard were posted; and a picket was thrown out from a half to three-quarters of a mile in front, with express orders to keep a patrol constantly in motion. As the commanding general (*Chandler*) appears to have been impressed with the idea that an attack would be made before morning, he had provided for the emergency by every means in his power. He had directed where and how the line should be formed, in case of attack; and he had directed that the harness should not be taken from off the horses which belonged to the artillery.[4]

---

[1] Armstrong, i. p. 136; Mansfield's Scott, p. 85. Mr. Thomson (*Sketches of the War*, p. 135) says this party embraced, in addition to Gen. Winder's brigade, a regiment from Gen. Chandler's brigade.—[2] Armstrong, i. p. 136.

[3] Gen. Chandler to Gen. Dearborn, June 18. Mr. Armstrong (*Notes*, i. p. 136) says he "brought up a second brigade on the *third* of June." Col. Burn, on whom the command devolved after the engagement, reported the strength of Gen. Chandler's brigade at 500 men—making 1300 in all. Respecting the strength of these two brigades, there has been the usual amount of controversy. Gen. Vincent (*Dispatches, June* 6, 1813) reports it at 3750 men; Mr. James (*Mil. Occur.*, i. p. 205), at 3500 men; Mr. Christie (*Mil. and Naval Occur.*, p. 112) and Mr. Rogers (*Hist. of Canada*, i. p. 214), at 3250 men; while, on the American side, Mr. Ingersoll (*Hist. of War*, i. p. 285) says they amounted to 1300 men, in which, as we have seen, Col. Burn sustains him. Mr. Perkins (*Hist. of War*, p. 252) and Gen. Armstrong (*Notices*, i. p. 136) also concur in this statement.

[4] Gen. Chandler's Dispatch, June 18; Armstrong, i. p. 137; Auchinleck, p. 168.

[1] Col. Burn to Gen. Dearborn; Gen. Chandler's Dispatch, June 18; Gen. Lewis to Sec. of War, June 14.

[2] Gen. Chandler to Gen. Dearborn, June 18.

[3] As this detachment was three miles from the camp, and took no part in the engagement, this portion of the expedition must be excluded in all estimates of the relative strength of the contestants.—[4] Gen. Chandler to Gen. Dearborn, June 18; Armstrong's Notices, i. p. 137.

The night was an exceedingly dark one, and as the broken pickets reached General Vincent's encampment, it was apparent to all that his situation was exceedingly critical.[1] Desiring, however, to know the strength and position of the American forces, he immediately detached Lieutenant-colonel John Harvey, Deputy Adjutant-general of the army, with the light companies of the Eighth and Forty-ninth regiments, to reconnoitre and take an accurate view of the position of the American encampment. That distinguished officer quickly reported, "that the enemy's camp-guards were *few and negligent;* that his line of encampment was *long and broken;* that his artillery was *feebly supported;* and that several of the corps were placed too far in the rear to aid in repelling a blow which might be rapidly and vigorously struck at the front;" and he advised, therefore, that a night attack should be hazarded, notwithstanding the scarcity of ammunition in the encampment.[2]

In accordance with this advice, at a little before midnight on the fifth of June, General Vincent, at the head of five companies of the Eighth, or King's, regiment, and the whole of the Forty-ninth—seven hundred and four privates, in all—marched out of camp;[3] and, after having united with the scout which Lieutenant-colonel Harvey had taken out of the camp,[1] two hours afterwards, with fixed bayonets, he dashed into the centre of the American camp[2]—the sentries having been bayoneted without raising any alarm.[3]

The Forty-ninth, led by Major Plenderleath, was in the advance, and pushed forward to the artillery, bayoneting one of the American artillerists, who was in the act of discharging his piece, and capturing two six-pounders. It was gallantly supported, in this charge, by one-half the detachment from the Eighth, the remainder of the latter party, under Major Ogilvie, charging the left wing of the American encampment, and, eventually, throwing it into the greatest confusion.[4]

The left wing of the American forces was composed of the Fifth, Sixteenth, and Twenty-third regiments of the line, and some riflemen, under General Winder,[5]—the cavalry, under Colonel Burn, being in the rear,[6]—and when the enemy's fire was opened, it was immediately

[1] Gen. Vincent's Dispatch, June 6; Auchinleck, p. 168; Armstrong's Notices, i. p. 138.—[2] Gen. Vincent's Dispatch, June 6; Auchinleck, p. 168; Ingersoll, i. p. 285; James' Mil. Occur., i. p. 204; Armstrong's Notices, i. p. 138; Christie, p. 112. This gentleman has since become better known to us as Sir John Harvey, Lieutenant-governor of New Brunswick during the troubles concerning the Northeastern boundary question.

[3] Gen. Vincent's Dispatch, June 6. Mr. James (*Mil. Occur.*, i. pp. 205–210), and Messrs. Armstrong, Christie, Rogers, and Ingersoll, suppose Lieut.-Col. Harvey was sent out *with this party; which is not true.* That gallant officer was already in the field, with *all the light troops;* had "*sent back* to propose to *me* a night attack on the camp" (*Gen. Vincent's Dispatch*); "*I* moved forward" with the line companies of the 8th and 49th regiments, "amounting to *seven hundred and four firelocks*" (*Ibid.*),—eight hundred men who could fight,—and joined the scout under Harvey, and made the attack. The number of the assailants, therefore, may be safely estimated at *a thousand men,* including officers, and excluding the Indians who accompanied them.

[1] As Lieut.-Col. Harvey did not return, but "*sent back*" to report and advise the attack, it is evident the parties joined before the attack.—[2] Gen. Lewis to Sec. of War, June 14; Perkins, p. 252; James, i. pp. 205, 206; Mansfield's Scott, p. 85; Armstrong, i. p. 138.

[3] Letter, signed "A Forty-ninth Man," in *Auchinleck's Hist.*, p. 179.—[4] Gen. Vincent's Dispatch, June 6; James, i. p. 206.—[5] Col. Burn's Report.

[6] Gen. Lewis to Secretary of War, June 14.

answered, with good effect, from the greater part of the line, and from the Twenty-fifth, which was near the centre of the position.[1] Immediately afterwards, however, a fire was opened in the rear, by some detached parties from the enemy's forces, when Colonel Milton, with the Fifth regiment, was ordered to form in that direction, near the woods, to protect that part of the encampment; while, at the same time, the Twenty-third was ordered to form so far to the right, that its right might cover the artillery.[2] At this moment a fire was opened on the *right* flank of the American position; and thither General Chandler hastened, in the darkness, to prevent the enemy from turning his flank, in that direction. Unfortunately his horse stumbled and fell, injuring the General very severely, but he succeeded in reaching the flank, and in providing for its safety.[3] While returning to the centre, however, he heard a confusion near the artillery, where he had ordered the Twenty-third to form; and, supposing it to be that regiment, he hastened to the spot, and "hobbled in among them, began to rally them, and directed them to form." Much to his surprise, however, he found himself among the enemy,—the Forty-ninth regiment already referred to,—and he was disarmed and taken to the rear, a prisoner of war.[4]

About the same time, by a similar mistake, General Winder and Major Vandeventer were also captured;[1] and the most extreme confusion, on both sides, ensued.[2] In this confusion, some singular scenes were enacted. General Vincent, the commander of the enemy's force, having been thrown from his horse, was unable either to regain his seat or find his command; and, after wandering through the woods, without his hat or sword, and almost famished, he was discovered by some of his own party, the following day, at the distance of four miles from the scene of the action — his horse and accoutrements, meanwhile, having fallen into the hands of the Americans.[3] Colonel Burn, who commanded the dragoons, having cut his way through the Forty-ninth regiment (*British*), continued his course until he had also cut a passage through the centre of the Sixteenth (*American*), which had rallied and was forming on its colors, under Captain Steele.[4] The different companies of the last-named regiment, disconcerted by the movement of the cavalry, opened a fire at random, and answered each other in the darkness, each supposing the others were enemies;[5] and the most intense excitement prevailed. Nor were the Americans the only party which suffered from this cause. The British, also, were thrown into the greatest confusion, especially when Captain Towson of the artillery moved forward his pieces, and, taking advantage of the light which the American camp-fires

[1] Letter from "A FORTY-NINTH MAN;" Col. Burn's Report; Gen. Chandler to Gen. Dearborn, June 18; James, i. p. 206.—[2] Gen. Chandler to Gen. Dearborn, June 18; Armstrong, i. pp. 138, 139.—[3] Gen. Chandler to Gen. Dearborn, June 18.—[4] Ibid.; Perkins, p. 252; James, i. p. 206; Breckenridge, p. 133.

[1] Gen. Chandler to Gen. Dearborn, June 18; Perkins, p. 252; James, i. p. 206; Breckenridge, p. 133.

[2] James, i. p. 207.—[3] Gen. Lewis to Secretary of War, June 14; Armstrong, i. p. 139; Ingersoll, i. p. 286.

[4] Thomson's Sketches, p. 136.

[5] Ibid.

supplied, opened a fire on the assailants.[1]

As soon as Lieutenant-colonel Harvey could collect his scattered forces he hastened back to the encampment at Burlington Heights, leaving behind him two of the six-pounders which he had taken, his general, and part of his men; having fully accomplished the object of the expedition, and earned for himself the credit of possessing great skill in the practice of his profession.[2]

The strength of the contestants has been already noticed. The loss of the Americans was seventeen men *killed*, thirty-eight *wounded*, and ninety-nine *missing*;[3] nine horses, eight sets of harness, one limber and one tumbril, an iron six-pounder and a brass five-and-a-half-inch howitzer:[1] that of the enemy was Lieutenant Hooper, three sergeants, and nineteen privates, *killed;* Majors Plenderleath, Taylor, Clark, Dennis, and Ogilvie, Captains Munday, Goldrick, and Manners, Lieutenants Wayland and Boyd, Ensign Davy, an adjutant, nine sergeants, two drummers, and one hundred and thirteen men, *wounded;* three sergeants and fifty-two men *missing*.[2]

[Note.—An extract from Gen. Lewis's Dispatch, with the inclosure; Gen. Chandler's Dispatch to the Secretary of War; and Gen. Vincent's Dispatch to Sir Geo. Prevost, which had been provided for the illustration of this chapter, have been omitted by the Publishers for want of room.]

[1] Col. Burn's Report.—[2] Armstrong's Notices, i. p. 139.

[3] Report appended to Gen. Lewis's Dispatch. A return appended to Gen. Vincent's Dispatch states that the prisoners taken by the British, besides the two Generals, were a major, 5 captains, 1 lieutenant, and 116 men.

[1] Return appended to Gen. Vincent's Dispatch, signed "Wm. Holcroft, *Major commanding Royal Artillery*."

[2] Return appended to Gen. Vincent's Dispatch, signed "Edward Baynes, *Adj.-Gen.*"

CHAPTER LI.

June 14, 1813.

THE DEFENCE OF THE ASP.

The occupation of Chesapeake Bay by the enemy's shipping, and his incursions along its shores, have been already noticed; and one of many similar gallant acts, in which the naval officers and seamen of the United States opposed these predatory expeditions, is the subject of this chapter.

For the purpose of defending the tributary streams and harbors which are scattered along the shores of the bay from these marauders, the Federal government had fitted out several small vessels, and given the command of them to the younger officers of the navy—generally to midshipmen—furnishing to them not only the best possible means of acquiring a practical knowledge of their profession, but, at the same time, inciting them to acts of daring which, when under the control of older officers, they would not have been permitted to attempt.

On the fourteenth of June, two of these little vessels, the *Scorpion* and the

Asp—the latter carrying three small guns and twenty-one men, commanded by Midshipman Sigourney—got under way and stood out of the Yeocomico—a small stream which flows into the Chesapeake—and at ten o'clock they discovered a considerable number of the light vessels of the enemy's fleet, which immediately gave chase. The greatly superior force of the enemy rendering any attempt at defence not only inexpedient but hopeless, the commander of the *Scorpion*, who was the senior officer, signalled to the *Asp* to act at discretion, and stood up the Chesapeake. In consequence of a strong head wind and the bad sailing qualities of the *Asp*, the latter was not able to secure her escape by following her consort; and Mr. Sigourney determined to return to the Yeocomico, the shallowness of whose waters, he hoped, would prevent the enemy from pursuing him. Two brigs were detached to follow her, while the remainder of the squadron stood up the bay; and when the former reached the bar which obstructed the mouth of the Yeocomico they cast anchor, manned their boats, and continued the pursuit. The *Asp* having anchored before the brigs had thus showed their designs, Mr. Sigourney resolved to run farther up the creek; and with this object he cut his cable, and stood up the stream. While thus engaged he was overtaken by three boats, well manned and armed, and a spirited engagement ensued, resulting in the complete repulse of the assailants, and their retreat to the brigs.

About an hour afterwards five boats, with a heavy and well-armed force, proceeded up the creek and renewed the attack, the gallant little crew manfully defending itself against a force three times more numerous than itself, until—overpowered by the assailants, with its commander and *one-half its number* killed or disabled, and with fifty of the enemy occupying its deck and *refusing quarters to the powerless handful of men who remained*—it was "compelled to leave the vessel, as the enemy had possession."

After setting the vessel on fire the boats returned to the brigs; but Midshipman McClintock, the second officer of the *Asp*, immediately returned to her, and with much difficulty extinguished the flames.

As already stated, the loss of the *Asp*, out of a crew of twenty-one men, was her gallant young commander and ten men—an evidence, in itself, of the severity of the attack and of the desperate obstinacy of the defence.[1]

[NOTE.—The Dispatch of Midshipman McClintock, which had been provided for the illustration of this chapter, has been omitted by the Publishers for want of room.]

---

[1] Those curious in a farther examination of this affair are referred to Midshipman H. M. McClintock's Dispatch to the Secretary of Navy, July 13, 1813; Cooper's Naval History, ii. p. 118; Sketches of the War, p. 326.

CHAPTER LII.

June 20, 1813.

THE ATTACK ON THE JUNON.[1]

In the prosecution of the enemy's predatory designs in the Chesapeake, to which reference has been made in other parts of this volume, on the seventeenth of June, three frigates anchored in Hampton Roads—one of them nearly as far up as the Quarantine-ground—and sent their boats up the James River to destroy some small vessels which were there, and to plunder the neighboring planters.[2]

While the enemy was thus employed Captain Joseph Tarbell, of the *Constellation*, organized an expedition to attack the frigate which laid nearest the town; and, with this object, at eleven o'clock in the evening of Saturday, the nineteenth of June, with fifteen gunboats, he descended the harbor. The flotilla was formed into two divisions—one under Lieutenant John M. Gardner, the other under Lieutenant Robert Henley; and, besides their own crews, the gunboats had been strengthened with fifty musketeers, who had been ordered from Craney Island for that purpose.[3]

[1] Auchinleck's Hist. of War, p. 272; Perkins' Hist. of War, p. 163; James' Mil. Occur., ii. p. 54.

[2] James' Mil. Occur., ii. p. 54; Cooper, ii. p. 116. Mr. Thomson (*Sketches*, p. 214) supposes this affair transpired in *May*.

[3] Com. Cassin to Secretary of Navy, June 21, 1813; James' Mil. Occur., ii. pp. 54, 55; "*The War*," ii. p. 7; Cooper, ii. p. 116; Sketches of the War, p. 325; Thomson's Sketches, p. 214.

A steady head-wind prevented the flotilla from reaching its designated anchorage until four in the morning of the following day[1] (*Sunday, June* 20), when, under cover of the darkness and of a fog which prevailed,[2] at three-quarters of a mile distant, it opened "a heavy galling fire" on the frigate. It is said that she was taken completely by surprise; that she returned the fire with but little spirit and only after a considerable delay; and that strong hopes were entertained that she would be compelled to surrender. The wind being very light, she could neither close with her tiny assailants or haul off to her consorts; while the sweeps with which the gunboats were provided enabled their crews to place them in any desired position.[3]

Half an hour this singular engagement was sustained, every moment rendering the prospect of a final success more apparent;[4] when, suddenly, a fresh breeze sprung up from the east-northeast, and the two frigates which had been anchored below, made sail

[1] Com. Cassin to Sec. of Navy, June 21. Mr. Thomson (*Sketches*, p. 214) supposes they approached in *the afternoon;* and Mr. James (*Military Occurrences*, ii. p. 54) agrees with him.

[2] Cooper's Naval History, ii. pp. 116, 117.

[3] Ibid., p. 117; "*The War*," ii. p. 7; Thomson's Sketches, p. 214.—[4] "*The War*," ii. p. 7; Sketches of the War, p. 325.

and joined the one above, opening their fire on the gunboats as they came up.[1]

Without manifesting any undue fear, the gunboats hauled off, as the ships came up; while, at the same time, they continued their fire for nearly an hour longer, after which they retired.[2]

The damage which the *Junon*—the uppermost frigate—sustained in this action, is said to have been very severe, requiring a deep careen and extensive temporary repairs before she could regain the position occupied by the fleet:[3] that of the gunboats was very trifling—*Number One hundred and fifty-four* having received a shot between wind and water; *Number Sixty-seven* losing her franklin; and several others sustaining slight injuries. Master's-mate Allison was killed, and two seamen were slightly wounded, which were the only losses sustained by the crews.[1]

This apparently insignificant affair led to the retaliatory visits by the enemy to Craney Island and to Hampton; and on this account it possesses an importance which it would not otherwise have secured.

[NOTE.—The Dispatch of Com. Cassin, to the Secretary of the Navy, has been omitted by the Publishers for want of room.]

[1] Com. Cassin to Sec. of Navy, June 21; "*The War*," ii. p. 7; Cooper, ii. p. 117; Sketches of the War, p. 325; James, ii. p. 55. These ships are said (*James' Mil. Occur.*, ii. p. 55) to have been the *Barrosa*, of 42, and the *Laurestinus*, of 28 guns.—[2] Com. Cassin to Sec. of Navy, June 21; Cooper, ii. p. 117; Thomson's Sketches, p. 214.

[3] Com. Cassin to Sec. of Navy, June 21; Thomson's Sketches, p. 214. Mr. James (*Mil. Occur.*, ii. pp. 55, 56) denies all this.—[4] Vide Chap. LII.

[1] Cooper, ii. p. 117.—[2] Com. Cassin to Secretary of Navy, June 21; "*The War*," ii. p. 7; Cooper, ii. p. 117.

CHAPTER LIII.

June 22, 1813.

THE DEFENCE OF CRANEY ISLAND.

THE assault on the enemy's frigate by the American gunboats, already referred to,[4] appears to have aroused him, and led to more active operations against the defences of the Americans in the vicinity of Norfolk.

With this object in view, the gunboats had no sooner retired, on the morning of the twentieth of June, than the enemy began to prepare for retaliatory measures; and with the next tide fourteen sail of vessels entered the Roads, ascended to the mouth of the James River, and prepared to send out their boats.[2]

At the same time Captain Tarbell, who commanded the naval force in that vicinity, sent Lieutenants Neale, Shubrick, and Sanders, of the *Constellation*, with one hundred seamen, and Lieutenant Breckenridge with fifty marines, to take charge of the principal battery on the northwest point of Craney Island, and to strengthen the garrison of militia—five hundred and eighty-seven in number—under Lieutenant-colonel Beatty, which was already on the island.[1]

At an early hour on the morning of the twenty-second of June the enemy commenced the debarkation of a large body of troops, some two thousand five hundred in number, and commanded by Admiral Cockburn,[2] near the point of the Nansemond River, with the evident intention of approaching Craney Island by land, on the west side of the island, between which and the mainland infantry could readily pass at low water.[3] At eight o'clock the boats from the squadron—some forty-five or fifty in number, on board of which were about twenty-five hundred men, under Admiral Warren—moved from the squadron, and, passing around to the north side of the island, beyond the reach of the gunboats' fire, they approached the spot where Lieutenant Neale and his party of seamen and marines were posted.[4]

The attack began with a discharge of Congreve rockets, but without producing any other effect than alarming a body of the militia, among whom the first was thrown.[5] The gunners from the *Constellation*, however, were differently constituted, and they directed their fire

[1] "*The War*," ii. p. 7; Gen. Taylor to Sec. of War, July 4; Ingersoll, i. p. 200.

[2] Letter from an officer of the *Constellation*, June 28, in "*The War*," ii. p. 10; Col. Beatty's Dispatch, June 25; Naval Chronicle, xxx. p. 182. The strength of this party, as usual, has been the subject of great dispute—varying from 800 by the British partisan writers, to 4000 by the Americans. I have adopted the number which appears to be best sustained by the testimony of all parties.—[3] Letter from an officer, &c.; Col. Beatty's Dispatch, June 25.

[4] Ibid.; Cooper, ii. pp. 117, 118. The same trouble exists concerning the number of these troops that prevails concerning those heretofore referred to; and I have adopted the number which appears to have been best sustained by the evidence.—[5] Letter from an officer, &c.

with so much certainty that one of the enemy's rocket-vessels was speedily sunk;[1] and when his barges had come within grape-shot distance they poured in so severe a fire that, after four or five of the boats had been sunk, the remainder were withdrawn by Admiral Warren.[2]

While the seamen were thus engaged with the enemy's barges, the troops who had been debarked on the mainland also opened a fire on the island, from a field-piece and a howitzer, which they had placed in battery under cover of a neighboring thicket.[3] Their fire was returned by two twenty-four-pounders and four six-pounders, under Major Faulkner; and when the retreat of the boats had relieved the seamen of their enemy on the water, they turned their guns on Admiral Cockburn and the force on shore, and with similar success.[4] After continuing the action for some time, and suffering severely, perceiving, at the same time, that the boats had withdrawn from the assault, this body of the assailants also retired, and the contest ended.[5]

In this engagement the Americans suffered no loss; the assailants, besides the loss of their boats, had three *killed;* Captain Hanchett of the *Diadem*—an illegitimate son of George III.[6]—and fifteen men *wounded;* and sixty-two *missing* (prisoners).[7]

[1] Letter from an officer, &c.; Letter from an English officer, in the *Naval Chronicle*, xxx. p. 183.

[2] "*The War*," ii. p. 7; Letter from an officer; Col. Beatty's Dispatch, June 25; Adm'l Warren's Dispatch, June 24; Cooper, ii. p. 118.—[3] Letter from an officer; Col. Beatty's Dispatch, June 25.—[4] Ibid.—[5] Letter from an officer; James, ii. p. 57.—[6] Ingersoll, i. p. 201.

[7] Reports appended to Adm'l Warren's Dispatch.

Thus terminated the operations of an expedition which, both in its organization and its execution reflected no credit on the professional skill of the British officers, and which has not ceased to receive the hearty condemnation of their historical students and military and naval authorities from that time to the present.

[NOTE.—The Dispatch of Gen. Taylor to the War Department, with the inclosure; that of Com. Cassin to the Naval Department; and that of Adm'l Warren to the Admiralty, have been omitted by the Publishers for want of room.]

CHAPTER LIV.

June 24, 1813.

THE BATTLE AT THE BEAVER-DAMS.

AFTER the affair at Stony Creek, of which notice has been already taken, the enemy was reinforced with a detachment of troops from Sir James L. Yeo's squadron on Lake Ontario, and assumed aggressive measures;[1] while the Americans fell back and concentrated their forces, even beyond the limits of propriety or self-respect—the enemy, meanwhile, occupying the positions from which the former had retired.[2]

The enemy's advance had been placed under the command of Lieutenant-colonel Bisshopp; and about the twenty-second of June that officer sent detachments forward and occupied the cross-roads at the Ten-mile Creek and the strong position at the Beaver-dams—the latter, consisting of thirty men from the One hundred and fourth, occupying a stone house near that place.[3]

Against this party, which appears to have been smaller than had been reported, General Dearborn, then at Fort George, planned a formidable expedition; and, in the evening of the twenty-third, Lieutenant-colonel Boerstler, of the Fourteenth infantry, moved from that post with five hundred and seventy men, with orders to attack and disperse it.[1] This detachment had nearly reached the Beaver-dams, and was moving through the woods, when its rear—where were posted twenty light-dragoons[2]—was suddenly attacked by a body of four hundred and fifty Mohawks,[3] led by John Brant and Captain William Johnson Kerr,[4] who had laid in ambush near the road on which the troops were advancing.[5] With great coolness, Lieutenant-colonel Boerstler immediately formed his troops, and charged on his hidden foe; but, with

[1] James' Mil. Occur., i. pp. 213, 214.—[2] Ibid., p. 214; Perkins' Hist. of War, p. 252.—[3] James, i. p. 215; Auchinleck, p. 174.

[1] Gen. Dearborn to Secretary of War, June 25.

[2] Maj. C. Chapin, in Buffalo *Gazette*, July 20, 1813.

[3] Stone's Life of Brant, ii. p. 516. Mr. Auchinleck (*Hist.*, p. 174) says there were but *two hundred* Indians, in which Mr. James (*Mil. Occur.*, i. p. 215) concurs. Mr. Ingersoll (i. p. 287) says they numbered "*five or six hundred.*"—[4] This gentleman was grandson of Sir Wm. Johnson, and the husband of Elizabeth, the youngest daughter of the chief, Joseph Brant.—[5] Gen. Dearborn's Dispatch, June 25; Letter from Fort George, June 28; Maj. C. Chapin's statement; Auchinleck, p. 174; Stone's Brant, ii. p. 516; James' Mil. Occur., i. p. 215.

characteristic agility, the Indians eluded him, and opened a fire from other and not more exposed positions. Thus singularly engaged,—the enemy never showing his strength, but, from the thickets, steadily harassing the Americans on every side,—the uneven contest was maintained nearly three hours, with unusual spirit on both sides, the Indians, meanwhile, gradually falling back before their opponents' bayonets.[1] At length, Lieutenant-colonel Boerstler determined to retire; and, while thus moving off, he was encountered in the woods by a small party of militia, under Lieutenant-colonel Clark, when he considered it necessary to halt, and, subsequently, to occupy an open field which was near by, until he could inform General Dearborn of his situation and receive reinforcements.[2]

About the same time another small party of forty-seven men, belonging to the Forty-ninth (British) regiment, led by Lieutenant Fitzgibbon — who had been warned of Lieutenant-colonel Boerstler's advance by Mrs. Secord of Queenstown, who had travelled from her home on foot for that purpose—also approached, and reconnoitred the position occupied by Lieutenant-colonel Boerstler.[3] While thus engaged, probably perceiving the confusion which prevailed in the American ranks, Lieutenant Fitzgibbon conceived the idea of demanding the surrender of the expedition; and with this design he displayed the greater part of his little party in such a manner as to convey the impression that it was only the advance of a much larger force. Acting on these principles, the surrender of the Americans was immediately demanded in the name Major De Haren—the commandant of the district[1]—and Lieutenant-colonel Boerstler was informed, "on the honor of a British soldier," that Lieutenant-colonel Bisshopp, with fifteen hundred British troops and seven hundred Indians, were in his rear, advancing to support him.[2]

Trusting to the "word of honor" of the British officer, Lieutenant-colonel Boerstler very properly supposed that a retreat would be impossible, in view of the fact that no supporting party had followed him; and he resolved to surrender—providing that the militia and volunteers of his party should return to the United States on their paroles.[3] At that moment Major De Haren —who had been sent for by Lieutenant Fitzgibbon—with upwards of two hundred men, came up, and received the submission of the Americans[4]—five hundred and forty-two of whom, with one twelve-pounder, one six-pounder, and a stand of colors, graced the victory.[5]

It is said, by an eye-witness,[6] that "the articles of capitulation were no

[1] Maj. Chapin's statement; Auchinleck, p. 174; Stone's Brant, ii. 516; James' Military Occurrences, i. p. 215.

[2] Maj. Chapin's statement; Auchinleck, p. 174; James' Military Occurrences, i. p. 216; Perkins, p. 254.

[3] "General Orders," "Kingston, June 28," signed "E. Baynes, *Adj.-Gen.;*" Col. Fitzgibbon's statement; Ingersoll, i. p. 287; Stone's Brant, ii. p. 516; James, i. p. 217; Lieut. Fitzgibbon to Maj. De Haren, June 24.

[1] "General Orders," &c.; Stone's Brant, ii. p. 517; James' Mil. Occur., i. p. 217; Lieut. Fitzgibbon to Maj. De Haren, June 24.—[2] Maj. Chapin's statement; Stone's Brant, ii. p. 517; Roger's Canada, i. p. 214; Christie, p. 115.—[3] Maj. Chapin's statement; Roger's Canada, i. p. 214.

[4] Auchinleck, p. 175; James' Mil. Occur., i. p. 217; Articles of Capitulation, &c.—[5] Return of Prisoners, signed "E. Baynes, *Adj.-Gen.*"—[6] Maj. Chapin's statement.

sooner signed than they were violated. The Indians immediately commenced their depredations, and plundered the officers of their side-arms. The soldiers, too, were stripped of every article of clothing to which the savages took a fancy, such as hats, coats, shoes, &c." The commander also violated the articles by refusing to allow the militia and volunteers to be paroled—a violation which was reciprocated by many of them rising on their guards and escaping, carrying their guards with them to the United States.[1]

The result of this disaster serving, as it did, as a climax to the series of mistakes and disasters in the North, filled the entire country with indignation and excitement; and Congress, an index of the popular sentiment, informally desired the President to remove General Dearborn from the command—a measure which was adopted soon afterwards.[1]

[NOTE.—The Dispatches of Lieut. Fitzgibbon and of Lieut.-Col. Boerstler have been omitted by the Publishers for want of room.]

¹ Maj. Chapin to Gen. Dearborn, June 13; Buffalo *Gazette*, July 20; James' Mil. Occur., i. p. 218.

¹ Ingersoll, i. pp. 287, 288.

CHAPTER LV.

June 25, 1813.

THE DESCENT ON HAMPTON, VA.

THE attack on Craney Island by the combined land and naval forces of the enemy, under the command of Admirals Warren and Cockburn; its gallant defence by a small party of seamen and marines, under Lieutenant Neale, and of militia under Lieutenant-colonel Beatty; and the repulse of the assailants by the garrison, have been briefly noted in a preceding chapter of this work;[2] and a retaliatory movement, which was undertaken against Hampton—a flourishing village, the county-seat of Elizabeth City County, Virginia, and situated on the western bank of the Hampton River, one mile above its entrance into Hampton Roads—is the subject of this.[3]

With this object, during the night of the twenty-fourth of June,[2] the enemy's land force, numbering about twenty-five hundred men,[3] under Major-general Sir Sydney Beckwith, were transferred from the shipping into light sailing-vessels and boats; and, under the personal direction of Admiral Cockburn, it moved against the village. Before daybreak the advance, led by Lieutenant-colonel Napier, and consisting of the One hundred and second regiment, two companies of Canadian chasseurs, three com-

² Vide Chap. LIII.—³ McCulloch's Gazetteer, ii. p. 1058.

² The Dispatch of Sir Sydney Beckwith, published in the *Naval Chronicle*, xxx. p. 245, says this was done on the night of the 25*th;* but it is inconsistent with every other part of the dispatch, and with the statement of every other officer, and I have not followed it.—³ Maj. Crutchfield to Gov. Barbour, June 28, 1813; Sketches of War, p. 325. It will be seen that this agrees with the report of Sir Sydney's strength at Craney Island.

panies of marines, and two six-pounders, was landed two miles west from the village; and soon afterwards the main body, under Lieutenant-colonel Williams, was also landed, without any opposition, under cover of the *Mohawk* sloop-of-war.[1]

At the period in question, at English's plantation, southwest from the village, and only separated from it by a small creek, were three hundred and forty-nine infantry and riflemen, sixty-two artillery, and twenty-five cavalry—all Virginia militia — under Major Sta. Crutchfield; while four six-pounders had been mounted, and covered the water-front of the encampment and the village.[2]

The plan of operations which the enemy had adopted was well adapted to secure the object of the expedition; especially when it was considered that an undisciplined force of militia, greatly inferior in numbers to his own, was the only force in the village or its vicinity. It was designed, with this force, to move against the rear of the village and the encampment; and, while Admiral Cockburn, by a feint, amused the Americans on their front, to fall on the rear of their position.[3] Accordingly the forces under General Beckwith moved silently and rapidly, by way of the great road, towards the rear of the village;[4] while the armed launches and boats—thirty or forty in number—approached the mouth of the Hampton River, by way of Newport's Noose.[1]

As the boats approached the shore they were discovered by the patrols near Mill Creek, and the camp was alarmed. Orders were immediately issued for the formation of the troops, and with the greatest alacrity the orders were obeyed. In a very short time afterwards, however, Celey's patrol reported the approach of the party under General Beckwith, in the rear; and, threatened both in front and rear at the same time, the little party prepared to defend the position it occupied with the greatest coolness.[2]

As the boats approached Blackbeard's Point they opened a fire of round-shot on the encampment, which was immediately returned from the four-gun battery on shore; and, with so much success, that the flotilla fled under cover of the Point, and contented itself with occasionally throwing a shot or a rocket into the American camp.[3]

In the mean time a company of riflemen, under Captain Servant, had been detached, with orders to conceal themselves in the woods, near the road on which General Beckwith was advancing, and to check his progress. This had been done with great success; and as it was now apparent that an attack on the rear was intended, while the

[1] Sir Sydney Beckwith's Dispatch, June 28; Adm'l Warren's Dispatch, June 27; James' Military Occurrences, ii. pp. 64, 65; Auchinleck, p. 275.—[2] Maj. Crutchfield's Dispatch, June 28; Ingersoll, i. p. 201; Thomson's Sketches, p. 218.—[3] Sir Sydney Beckwith's Dispatch, June 28; Adm'l Warren's Dispatch, June 27; Maj. Crutchfield's Dispatch, June 28; Armstrong's Notices, ii. p. 47.—[4] Sir Sydney Beckwith's Dispatch, June 28; Maj. Crutchfield's Dispatch, June 28; Perkins, p. 164.

[1] Sir Sydney Beckwith's Dispatch, June 28; Maj. Crutchfield's Dispatch, June 28; Ingersoll, i. p. 201; Perkins, p. 164.—[2] Maj. Crutchfield's Dispatch, June 28.
[3] Ibid.; Perkins, p. 164; Breckenridge, p. 154; Thomson's Sketches, p. 218.

movement in front was merely a diversion, the officers in command of the Americans appear to have turned their attention chiefly in that direction. Accordingly Major Crutchfield, with the infantry, moved to the support of the riflemen, marching in column of platoons through a lane and an open cornfield which led to "the great" and Celey's roads, for that purpose; when he was fired on by a body of the enemy which had gained a piece of woods which bordered the road. Orders were immediately issued to wheel to the left into line, and to charge the enemy. This order was also obeyed with a precision which would have honored veteran troops; but the line had not moved more than fifty yards when a fire was opened from the enemy's six-pounders, loaded with grape and canister, while a number of small Congreve rockets also added to the severity of the fire.[1]

During this time the enemy's right flank had been severely harassed by Captain Servant's riflemen, and his left by a troop of dragoons, under Captain Cooper — both of which officers, and their men, rendered great service, both in covering the movements of the infantry, under Major Crutchfield, and in harassing the enemy.[2]

After having faced this unexpected fire a short time, Major Crutchfield broke his line into column again and retired under a heavy fire, when part of his command fled in confusion—the remainder, under Captains Shield, Herndon, Ashby, Brown, Miller, Cary, and Goodall, rallying on the flanks of Captain Servant's riflemen, and renewing the action with great spirit.[1]

Finding the opposition stronger than he had anticipated, General Beckwith detached a strong party towards the flanks of the Americans, for the purpose of cutting off their retreat, on seeing which Major Crutchfield considered it his duty to withdraw his men, and discontinue the engagement. The enemy pursued him, in his retreat, nearly two miles; but the activity of the American light troops protected the fugitives from serious loss.[2]

While the contest was being thus carried on in the rear, the flotilla and the battery in front amused themselves with an occasional shot. Captain Pryor, who had been left in command, maintained his position even after the retreat of the main body; and only when the enemy had approached within sixty or seventy yards did he spike the guns, break through the ranks of the assailants, and, by swimming a creek, make good a retreat, carrying his firelocks with him, and without losing a man.[3]

There is little doubt that, as the land force employed was the same which had been led by Sir Sydney against Craney Island, the flotilla was also manned in a similar manner, in which case the enemy's force was not less

---

[1] Maj. Crutchfield's Dispatch, June 28; Sir Sydney Beckwith's Dispatch, June 28; Ingersoll, i. p. 201; Breckenridge, p. 154; Thomson's Sketches, p. 218.

[2] Maj. Crutchfield's Dispatch, June 28; Ingersoll, i. p. 201; Thomson's Sketches, p. 219.

[1] Maj. Crutchfield's Dispatch, June 28; Ingersoll, i. p. 201; Thomson's Sketches, pp. 219, 220.

[2] Maj. Crutchfield's Dispatch, June 28; Breckenridge, p. 154.

[3] Ibid.; Ingersoll, i. pp. 201, 202; Thomson's Sketches, pp. 219, 220.

than four thousand men:[1] that of the Americans, as before stated, was six hundred and thirty-six men.[2]

The enemy's reported loss was five *killed*, thirty-three *wounded*, and ten *missing*:[3] that of the Americans, seven *killed*, twelve *wounded*, one taken *prisoner*, and eleven *missing*—the latter of whom were supposed to have fled to their homes.[4] Seven pieces of artillery and two stands of colors, also—those of the Sixty-eighth regiment (*James' City Light-infantry*) and of the Eighty-fifth regiment—were among the enemy's trophies.[5]

Having thus secured the possession of the village, the enemy gave it up to pillage and outrage; and every excess which a brutal and outlawed soldiery could invent was freely employed. Not only were the houses of the citizens robbed of their contents; their negroes carried away and sent to Bermuda and the West Indies; and the aged and decrepit made the objects of abuse and injury; but the females were outraged in the most brutal manner. A respectable lady (*Mrs. Turnbull*), after having been seized and stripped naked by five or six ruffians, escaped, and fled to the river for safety; but she was pursued, dragged on shore, and outraged by each of her brutal persecutors. Another, with her infant child in her arms, and two young women, were subjected to the same fate, all in open day, and in the presence of many others, whose inability or depravity prevented them from interfering; while, to add to the horrors of the scenes, the negroes were encouraged and urged to violate their own mistresses.[1] So great, indeed, were the excesses of every kind, that even the most violent partisan writers in England and the colonies were filled with shame, and denounced them;[2] and General Beckwith and Admiral Cockburn, acknowledging the justice with which the ministers of "the higher law" had condemned their conduct, removed from the service the renegadoes—the sweepings of the British prisons—with which it had been disgraced, and Hampton desolated.[3]

[Note.—The Dispatch of Maj. Crutchfield to Gov. Barbour; that of Sir Sydney Beckwith to Adm'l Warren; and that of Adm'l Warren to the Admiralty, which had been provided for the illustration of this chapter, have been omitted by the Publishers for want of room.]

---

[1] Including both parties—that with Adm'l Cockburn and that under Sir Sydney Beckwith.

[2] Vide p. 255, col. 2, note 2.—[3] Sir Sydney Beckwith's Dispatch, June 28. Other writers, on the report of British officers, make the loss much greater.

[4] Maj. Crutchfield's Dispatch, June 28. The "official report," published in "*The War*," ii. p. 28, shows *sixteen* wounded—five "*slightly*."

[5] Sir Sydney Beckwith's Dispatch, June 28.

[1] Letter from an officer, at "*Armistead's, near Hampton, July* 10;" Maj. Crutchfield's Dispatch, June 28; Wilkinson's Mem., i. p. 733; Ingersoll, i. pp. 202–204; Armstrong, ii. p. 47; Perkins, pp. 164, 165; Sketches of War, p. 325; Breckenridge, pp. 154–157; Thomson's Sketches, pp. 220, 221.—[2] James' Military Occurrences, ii. pp. 66–69; Auchinleck, p. 277.—[3] James, i. p. 69.

CHAPTER LVI.

July 11, 1813.

THE ATTACK ON BLACK ROCK, N. Y.

THE predatory excursions which generally characterize a border warfare were, as we have seen, peculiarly successful on the Northern frontier, and led to their frequent organization in the armies of both nations.

In July, 1813, one of these was organized by Lieutenant-colonel Bisshopp, formerly commander of the British post of Fort Erie, against the village of Black Rock, on the eastern bank of the Niagara River, where were a dock-yard, storehouses, &c.[1] For this purpose, at two in the morning of the eleventh of July, 1813, a detachment of Royal artillery, under Lieutenant Armstrong; forty men from the Eighth or King's regiment, under Lieutenant Barstow; one hundred men from the Forty-first, under Captain Saunders; forty men from the Forty-ninth, under Lieutenant Fitzgibbon; and forty from the Second and Third Lincoln militia, were embarked on the Canada shore; and at half an hour before daylight it landed near Black Rock, without having been discovered, and, after a slight resistance from the garrison and the troops who were stationed there, it succeeded in capturing the post.[2]

¹ Ingersoll, i. p. 289; Rogers' Canada, i. p. 214.

² Lieut.-Col. Clark to Adj.-Gen. Harvey, July 12, 1813; Rogers' Canada, i. p. 214; James' Mil. Occur., i. p. 228; Buffalo *Gazette*, July 16, 1813.

After setting fire to the block-houses, the seamen's barracks, the navy-yard, and a large schooner which laid there, and carrying off as many of the stores as he could secure, the enemy retired to his boats and moved off.[1]

While the enemy was engaged in removing the stores he was attacked by a body of regulars, volunteers, and militia from Buffalo, and a small party of Indians, the whole under General Peter B. Porter; and a brisk engagement ensued, resulting, within twenty minutes, in a hasty retreat of the enemy,[2] leaving behind him Captain Saunders and nine men, killed and wounded, and fifteen prisoners.[3] After he had reached his boats the fire was more effective than before, and the commander of the expedition, Lieutenant-colonel Bisshopp, together with many of his men, were added to the list of his losses.[4]

The loss of the Americans was a sergeant and two men *killed*, and three men and two Indians *wounded*;[5] that

¹ Lieut.-Col. Clark to Adj.-Gen. Harvey, July 12; Ingersoll, i. p. 289; Rogers' Canada, i. p. 214; James' Mil. Occur., i. p. 228; Buffalo *Gazette*, July 16, 1813.

² Lieut.-Col. Clark to Adj.-Gen. Harvey, July 12; Auchinleck, p. 176; Ingersoll, i. p. 289; James' Mil. Occur., i. p. 229; Buffalo *Gazette*, July 16, 1813.

³ Rogers' Canada, i. p. 215; Buffalo *Gazette*, July 16, 1813.

⁴ Lieut.-Col. Clark to Adj.-Gen. Harvey, July 12; Rogers' Canada, i. p. 215; Buffalo *Gazette*, July 16, 1813.

⁵ James' Mil. Occur., i. p. 229; Buffalo *Gaz.*, July 16, 1813.

of the enemy is not fully known—the militia and the Forty-ninth having made no reports.[1] As the other detachments lost thirteen *killed*, three officers and twenty-one men *wounded*, and six *missing*,[2] the enemy's aggregate loss could not have been less than seventy men.

Four guns, one hundred and seventy-seven muskets, and other stores were taken by the enemy; and two twelves and two nines—all iron—were spiked and abandoned.[3]

Much as the loss of the stores was felt by the Americans, the loss which the enemy experienced in the death of Lieutenant-colonel Bisshopp—one of the most energetic and promising of the British officers of that day—was immeasurably greater. Young, and indefatigable in the discharge of his duties, his superiors in office missed the benefit of his co-operations in the subsequent movements on the frontier; and his country no longer secured the fruits ot his dashing, well-arranged, and successful enterprises.

[Note.—The Dispatches of Gen. Peter B. Porter to Gov. D. D. Tompkins, and of Lieut.-Col. Clark to Adj.-Gen. Harvey, which had been provided for the illustration of this chapter, have been omitted by the Publishers for want of room.]

CHAPTER LVII.

August 1 and 2, 1813.

THE DEFENCE OF FORT STEPHENSON, OHIO.

The defeat of the allied forces before Fort Meigs, in May, 1813, did not appear to satisfy the ambition of the notorious Proctor, or the desires of his swarthy companions;[4] and in July they began a second time to infest the country in that vicinity.[5] Tecumthà and his warriors, and Dixon,—a Scotch ruffian,—with his band of Indian desperadoes, numbering, in the aggregate, about three thousand five hundred braves, had assembled in that vicinity;[6] and the intelligence of their movements reached General Harrison while that officer was at Lower Sandusky, the site of a stockade-fort known as *Fort Stephenson*.[1] Leaving that post in command of Major George Croghan, he moved up to Seneca Town, with one hundred and forty men, and there established his head-quarters; where he was joined, soon afterwards, by Colonels Paul and Ball, with four hundred and fifty regulars, and by Generals McArthur and Cass.[2]

---

[1] Lieut.-Col. Clark to Adj.-Gen. Harvey, July 12.

[2] Ibid.—[3] Returns, signed "R. S. Armstrong, *Lieut.-Col. R. A.*," and "Thos. Clark, *Lieut.-Col. 2d Lincoln militia.*"

[4] Auchinleck, p. 184; McAfee's War in the West, p. 317.

[5] Ingersoll, i. p. 146; Perkins' Annals of the West, p. 633; McAfee, pp. 316, 317.—[6] Perkins' Annals of the West, p. 633; Breckenridge's Hist. of War, pp. 159, 160; Christie's Naval and Mil. Operations, p. 117. The prisoners told Gen. Harrison that they numbered *twenty-five hundred;* Mr. James (*Mil. Occur.*, i. p. 264) says they were *twenty-two hundred;* Gen. Armstrong (*Notices*, i. p. 164) says *four thousand;* and Capt. McAfee (*War in West*, p. 321) says *five thousand*.

[1] McAfee, p. 319.—[2] Ibid.

Soon afterwards the allied enemies abandoned Fort Meigs and moved against Fort Stephenson—the savages marching across the country, and guarding the approaches to the fort, to prevent both the movement of reinforcements and the escape of the garrison; the British, at the same time, sailing around into Sandusky Bay, and approaching the fort by water.[1]

At the period in question Fort Stephenson was an oblong stockade-fort, about one hundred yards long and fifty yards wide, protected with pickets about twelve feet high, and fraized *with bayonets*.[2] It was surrounded with a ditch eight feet wide and eight feet deep; and at each angle it was strengthened with a block-house.[3] It was defended by one hundred and sixty men,[4] with a single six-pounder, and Major George Croghan, a young man of twenty-one years, was its commandant.[5]

It had been pronounced untenable by General Harrison and his officers;[6] and orders were issued to the Major to abandon it, set it on fire, and, with the

[1] Gen. Harrison to Sec. of War, Aug. 1 and 4, 1813; Letter from Chilicothe, Aug. 12, in "*The War*," ii. p. 47; McAfee, p. 321; Sketches of War, p. 166.

[2] Auchinleck, p. 185; James' Mil. Occur., i. pp. 263, 264; Letter from Chilicothe, Aug. 12. Mr. Perkins (*Hist. of War*, p. 223) says the pickets were *eighteen feet* high; the author of *Sketches of War* (p. 167) says they were *ten* feet high.—[3] Letter from Chilicothe, Aug. 12. Mr. Auchinleck (*Hist.*, p. 185) and Mr. James (*Mil. Occur.*, i. p. 264) says it was *twelve* feet wide and *seven* feet deep; Mr. Perkins (*Hist. of War*, p. 223), "*six feet wide and deep;*" Mr. Breckenridge (*Hist. of War*, p. 175), *six* feet wide and *nine* feet deep.—[4] McAfee, p. 319; James' Mil. Occur., i. p. 264; Breckenridge, p. 175. Mr. Perkins (*Annals of West*, p. 633) and Gen. Armstrong (*Notices of War*, i. p. 165) say it was only *one hundred and fifty* men; and the author of *Sketches of the War* (p. 166) says of these only *one hundred and thirty-three* were effective.

[5] Gen. Harrison to Secretary of War, Aug. 4.

[6] McAfee, p. 321; Hall's Harrison, p. 246.

garrison, to repair to head-quarters;[1] but the messengers having lost their way, the order did not reach the fort until the Indians had surrounded it, and a retreat was utterly impossible.[2] He resolved, therefore, "to maintain the place," and sent information of his design to head-quarters;[3] but the General relieved him of his command until he had given an explanation, in person, at head-quarters, of the causes which induced him to disobey his orders.[4]

It will very easily be seen that this incident was not lost sight of in the subsequent defence of the post; and the rebuke which the Major received for his disobedience of orders served rather to increase his determination "to maintain the post" at all hazards, than to discourage it.

Early in the evening of the first of August,[5] General Proctor, with the Forty-first regiment and seven or eight hundred Indians, under Dixon, appeared before the fort, and after having landed his forces and disposed them agreeably to his wishes, he sent Colonel Elliott and Major Chambers, with a flag, to demand the surrender of the post.[6] The latter, in accordance with the custom of the allies, informed Ensign Shipp, who represented Major Croghan, that General Proctor possessed "a number of cannon, a large

[1] Gen. Harrison to Maj. Croghan, July 29, 1813.

[2] McAfee, pp. 322, 323; Hall's Harrison, p. 247.

[3] Maj. Croghan to Gen. Harrison, July 30.

[4] A. B. Holmes, Assistant Adj.-Gen., to Maj. Croghan July 30; Letter from Chilicothe, Aug. 12.

[5] Maj. Croghan to Gen. Harrison, Aug. 5; Letter from Chilicothe, Aug. 12; Auchinleck, p. 185; Perkins' Hist. of War, p. 223; James' Mil. Occur., i. p. 264; McAfee, p. 324.—[6] Maj. Croghan to Gen. Harrison, Aug. 5, 1813. Capt. McAfee (*Hist.*, p. 324) supposes the flag was borne by Maj. Chambers and *Dixon*.

body of regular troops, and so many Indians, whom it was impossible to control, that if the fort was taken, as it must be, the whole of the garrison *would be massacred*," unless it surrendered without opposition. To this threat the Ensign replied that "it was the determination of Major Croghan, his officers, and men, to defend the garrison or be buried in it; and that they might do their best."[1]

Immediately after the return of the flag the enemy opened his fire from the gunboats and from a five-and-a-half-inch howitzer which he had taken ashore;[2] and it was continued, with but little intermission, during the entire night.[3] While it was yet dark the enemy mounted three six-pounders in battery, within two hundred and fifty yards of the pickets; and, at an early hour on the second, their fire, also, was thrown into the fort, with little effect.[4]

Continuing this inefficient fire until four P. M.,[5] the enemy at that time appeared to change his plan of operations, and concentrated his fire on the northwestern angle of the fort;[6] and Major Croghan properly considered that his object was to make a breach, preparatory to storming the works at that point. He immediately ordered his command to strengthen that angle; and by means of sand-bags, sacks of flour, &c., he was so far successful that no injury was sustained by the fort or its garrison.[1]

It does not appear from *the Major's dispatch* that this fire was returned, except with small arms[2]—the six-pounder which was in the fort having been secretly placed in the block-house, which commanded the ditch near the northwest angle, *and was masked*,[3] in order that the assailants might not abandon or change the details of what was his evident design on that part of the fort.

Every man of the garrison was at his post and fully aware of the responsibility which was rapidly devolving upon him;[4] and when, after sunset, darkness had begun to gather around the fort and its defenders, the enemy opened a more furious and concentrated fire on the devoted northwest angle, and it was apparent to every one that the trying moment had come.[5] Taking advantage of the darkness—rendered still more effective by the volumes of dense smoke which hung over the scene[6]—the enemy, in three columns, approached the

[1] Gen. Harrison to Sec. of War, Aug. 4, 1813; Maj. Croghan to Gen. Harrison, Aug. 5; "*The War*," ii. p. 49; Ingersoll, i. p. 148; Perkins' Annals of West, p. 633; McAfee, p. 325.—[2] Maj. Croghan to Gen. Harrison, Aug. 5; Letter from Chilicothe, Aug. 12; McAfee, p. 325; Armstrong's Notices, i. p. 165.—[3] Maj. Croghan to Gen. Harrison, Aug. 5; Perkins' Hist. of War, p. 223; McAfee, p. 325; Armstrong's Notices, i. p. 165.

[4] Maj. Croghan to Gen. Harrison, Aug. 5; Auchinleck, p. 185; Perkins' Hist. of War, p. 223; Sketches of War, p. 167; James' Mil. Occur., i. p. 265.—[5] Maj. Croghan to Gen. Harrison, Aug. 5. Mr. Auchinleck (*Hist. of War*, p. 185) says until *three* in the afternoon.—[6] Maj. Croghan to Gen. Harrison, Aug. 5; Letter from Chilicothe, Aug. 12; Perkins' Annals, pp. 633, 634; McAfee, p. 326.

[1] Maj. Croghan to Gen. Harrison, Aug. 5; Perkins' Annals, p. 634; Sketches of War, p. 167.

[2] I am aware that the report of the Major's six-pounder has added to the "effect" in many narratives, which have been written by those who were not in the fort. Had these been true I see no use for the efforts to *conceal it*; nor can I understand why *the enemy* did not prepare for it.

[3] Letter from Chilicothe, Aug. 12; Perkins' Annals, p. 634; Perkins' War, p. 224; James' Mil. Occur., i. p. 266.

[4] Maj. Croghan to Gen. Harrison, Aug. 5.

[5] Ibid.; Letter from Chilicothe, Aug. 12; McAfee, p. 326.—[6] Maj. Croghan to Gen. Harrison, Aug. 5; Perkins' Annals, p. 634; Perkins' Hist. of War, p. 224; Sketches of War, p. 167; McAfee, p. 326.

works with every appearance of an intention to storm the lines.[1] Two of these, however, headed by the grenadiers under Lieutenant-colonel Warburton, passed around the western side of the fort in order to make a feint on its southern front, where Captain Hunter of the Seventh regiment, the second in command, had been stationed with his company.[2] As it was necessary to make a circuit through the woods, this column did not reach its appointed scene of operations until after the principal attack had been made on the northwestern angle of the fort; and after making two demonstrations—producing nearly all which had been designed, in keeping a portion of the little garrison on the *qui vive* at a distance from the real point of attack—they were withdrawn, and returned to their camp with but little loss.[3]

In the mean time the other column—with which had been intrusted the duty of storming the fort—had been led against the northwest angle by Lieutenant-colonel Short.[4] Approaching the point of attack under cover of the smoke which had been raised by the artillery,[5] the column had come within eighteen or twenty yards before it was discovered;[6] when every musket and rifle on that part of the lines was directed against it.[1] As the greater part of these were handled by Kentuckians of "the olden time," the effect of this fire can be better conceived than described. It did not check the advance of the column, however; and with some difficulty Lieutenant-colonel Short succeeded in getting over the outer line of pickets, and gained the ditch which surrounded the fort.[2] Followed closely by his command—until the dry ditch had become well filled with the assailants[3]—the Lieutenant-colonel ordered his men to follow him, telling them to "scale the pickets, and show the damned Yankee rascals no quarters,"[4] and moved towards the devoted northwest angle.[5] At that instant the port was opened, and the masked six-pounder, which, under the direction of private Brown of the Petersburg volunteers,[6] had been loaded with half a charge of powder and a double charge of small slugs,[7] was run out and fired on the head of the column, at that time not more than ten yards distant,[8] completely raking the ditch, and sweeping down the greater part of the assailants.[9] A

[1] Maj. Croghan to Gen. Harrison, Aug. 5; Maj. Richardson, in *Auchinleck's Hist.*, p. 185. Gen. Harrison (*Dispatch, Aug.* 4, 1813), and many others, following him, speak of but *two* columns.—[2] Maj. Croghan to Gen. Harrison, Aug. 5; James' Mil. Occur., i. p. 265.—[3] James' Mil. Occur., i. p. 265.—[4] Auchinleck, p. 185; Ingersoll, i. p. 148; James' Mil. Occur., i. p. 265; Christie, p. 118.—[5] Maj. Croghan to Gen. Harrison, Aug. 5; Sketches of the War, p. 167; McAfee, p. 326; Armstrong, i. p. 166.

[6] Maj. Croghan to Gen. Harrison, Aug. 5; Perkins' Annals, p. 634; Sketches of War, p. 167; Christie, p. 118.

[1] Maj. Croghan to Gen. Harrison, Aug. 5; Auchinleck, p. 185; Perkins' Hist. of War, p. 224; McAfee, pp. 326, 327; Armstrong, i. p. 166.—[2] Maj. Croghan to Gen. Harrison, Aug. 5; Auchinleck, p. 185; McAfee, p. 327; Armstrong, i. p. 166.—[3] Letter from Chilicothe, Aug. 12; Perkins' Annals, p. 634; Sketches of the War, p. 167; McAfee, p. 327; Breckenridge, p. 176.—[4] Letter from Chilicothe, Aug. 12; Ingersoll, i. p. 148; Perkins' Hist. of War, p. 224; Sketches of War, p. 167; Breckenridge, p. 176.—[5] James' Mil. Occur., i. p. 266.—[6] Gen. Harrison to Sec. of War, Aug. 4.—[7] Auchinleck, p. 185; Sketches of the War, p. 167; James' Mil. Occur., i. p. 266; Thomson's Sketches, p. 163.—[8] Perkins' Annals, p. 634; James' Mil. Occur., i. p. 266; McAfee, p. 327; Thomson's Sketches, p. 163.—[9] Maj. Croghan to Gen. Harrison, Aug. 5; Perkins' Hist. of War, p. 224; Sketches of the War, p. 167; James' Mil. Occur., i. p. 266; McAfee, p. 327; Armstrong, i. p. 166.

volley of rifle-balls finished the work which the six-pounder had begun;[1] and but few remained, of those who had entered the ditch, to carry back the intelligence of the disaster.

Still others of the column remained who had not yet scaled the pickets, and approached the northwest angle; and another officer, emulous of glory, called for their co-operation, and tried the experiment. A second time the slugs and rifle-balls were called into requisition, and a second time the ditch was cleared; after which the attempt was not renewed.[2]

In the course of the night the enemy gathered his killed and wounded, so far as he was able to do so, and embarked on his vessels;[1] and at eight o'clock on the morning of the third he sailed down the river, leaving behind him a boat containing a considerable quantity of clothing and military stores.[2]

The loss of the garrison was one man *killed* and seven *wounded*;[3] the enemy acknowledged the loss of Lieutenant-colonel Short and twenty-six men *killed*, and seventy *wounded*[4]—although it is supposed, from the number of those who were left behind, that it was much greater.[5] The loss of the Indian allies, according to custom, was not recorded.

[Note.—The Report of Maj. Croghan to Gen. Harrison, and the "General Orders" issued by Sir Geo. Prevost, which had been provided for the illustration of this chapter, have been omitted by the Publishers for want of room.]

[1] Sketches of the War, p. 167; James' Mil. Occur., i. p. 266; Breckenridge, p. 176.—[2] Sketches of the War, p. 167; James' Mil. Occur., i. p. 266; Thomson's Sketches, p. 163.—[3] Capt. Dent to Secretary of Navy, Aug. 21; Royal Naval Chronicle, xxx. p. 348; Coggeshall's Hist. of Privateers, p. 172. Mr. Breckenridge (*Hist. of War*, p. 172) says it occurred on the 15*th*.

[4] Vide Chapters XXVII., XXXVI., XLII.

CHAPTER LVIII.

August 5, 1813.[5]

THE CAPTURE OF THE DOMINICA.

The enterprise and gallantry of the privateers which sailed from the several ports of the United States have been referred to in former chapters of this work;[4] and the subject of this is a continuation of that series of exploits.

Among the vessels which were thus equipped and authorized to cruise against the enemy was the schooner *Decatur*, of Charleston, South Carolina, carrying six twelve-pound carronades, one long-eighteen, on a pivot, and one hundred and three men, Captain Dominique Diron, commanding.[6] She had been cruising in the track of the West In-

[1] Letter from Chilicothe, Aug. 12; Auchinleck, p. 185; McAfee, p. 328.—[2] Maj. Croghan to Gen. Harrison, Aug. 12; Auchinleck, p. 185; McAfee, p. 328.

[3] Letter from Chilicothe, Aug. 12; McAfee, p. 327.

[4] Return, appended to "*General Orders*," Sept. 3, 1813, signed "E. Bayne, *Adj.-Gen.*"—[5] Maj. Croghan to Gen. Harrison, Aug. 5; Letter from Lower Sandusky, Aug. 12, in "*The War*," ii. p. 43.

[6] Breckenridge, p. 172; Capt. Dent to Secretary of Navy, Aug. 21; Coggeshall, p. 172. Mr. Auchinleck (*Hist.*, p. 199), while he *diminishes* the strength of the *Dominica*, coolly makes that of the *Decatur twelve* guns and *one hundred and twenty* men; and Mr. James (*Naval Occur.*, p. 259) says a court-martial said she carried "*one hundred and forty* men," although *he* afterwards (p. 260) considers *one hundred and twenty-two* enough.

dia traders;[1] and, on the fifth of August, she was in latitude 23° 4′ N., longitude, about 67° W., steering to the northward, under easy sail. At half-past ten in the morning two sail were discovered from the masthead; and the schooner, tacking to the southward, immediately made chase. Half an hour afterwards they were made out to be a ship and schooner, standing to the northward; and at half-past twelve the *Decatur* came abreast of the schooner, which showed British colors. At one o'clock the *Decatur* wore round, still keeping to windward of the schooner; and half an hour afterwards the latter opened a fire, which inflicted no injury.[2]

The *Decatur's* crew were called to quarters; the guns and small-arms were loaded; the grapplings, swords, pikes, and other arms were got in readiness for boarding; the necessary ammunition, water, &c., were taken on deck; the hatches were fastened down; and every preparation was made for an engagement. The plan of operations was to bear down on her opponent, to throw in a fire from all her guns and small-arms, and, taking advantage of the smoke, to board.[3]

With this design, at two o'clock, the *Decatur* wore, in order to pass under the schooner's stern, and give her a raking fire; but this object was thwarted, by the enemy luffing, and throwing in a full broadside, as the former came up, without doing any damage. A cannonade, with the *Decatur's* long gun, followed; and, the latter having hoisted American colors, at half-past two, the schooner appeared desirous of shaking off her antagonist. To prevent this the *Decatur* hauled upon the larboard-tack, with the hope of bringing her bowsprit over the schooner's stern; but this was prevented, and another broadside, which injured the *Decatur's* sails and rigging, was given by the former, and answered with the long gun of the latter.[1]

Thus the contest continued—the one attempting to run into and board her antagonist, the latter skilfully avoiding her, and keeping up a warm fire—until half-past three o'clock, when the bowsprit of the *Decatur* was run over the schooner's stern,—her jib-boom piercing the mainsail of the latter,—and under "a terrible fire" from her guns and small-arms, the boarders, led by the first prize-master (*Vincent Safith*) and the quarter-master (*Thomas Wasborn*), rushed to the schooner's quarter-deck. The crew of the schooner being unable to separate the vessels, a terrible scene of slaughter ensued on the schooner's quarter-deck; and the vessels, meanwhile, gradually worked alongside of each other. While thus situated Captain Diron ordered *his entire crew* to board; and, having abandoned their guns, the order was "executed with the promptness of lightning." The contest now became a close hand-to-hand engagement, and it was carried on with the most desperate energy. Pistols, cutlasses, boarding-pikes, cold-shot hurled by hand, and every other

[1] Coggeshall's Hist. Privateers, p. 172.—[2] Sketches of War, p. 331; Log-book of the *Decatur*, published in "*The War*," ii. p. 49.

[3] Log-book of the *Decatur*; Coggeshall, p. 173.

[1] Log-book of the *Decatur*; Sketches of the War, pp. 331, 332.

conceivable means of offence and defence were resorted to by both the crews; and one of the bloodiest and most desperately contested engagements on record was carried on on the schooner's deck.[1]

At length, the deck having been covered with the dead and wounded, the Captain and all the principal officers of the schooner having fallen, and the *Decatur's* crew having overpowered their opponents, the colors of the schooner were struck *by the victors*, and the engagement ended.[2]

The force of the *Decatur* has been already noticed;[3] that of the schooner—which proved to be His Britannic Majesty's schooner *Dominica*—was twelve twelve-pound carronades, two long-sixes, a thirty-two-pound carronade on a pivot, and a brass four-pound swivel,[1] with a crew of seventy-seven men.[2] The loss of the former was three *killed* and fifteen *wounded;*[3] that of the latter was Captain Barrette, her commander, Master Sackett, Purser Brown, Midshipmen Archer and Parry, and eight men, *killed;* Midshipman Nichols and forty-six men, *wounded*—leaving the surgeon, Midshipman Lindo, and fifteen of her crew, alone, without having suffered injury.[4]

It was said, by a contemporary writer, that "This engagement has been the most bloody, and the loss of the killed and wounded, on the part of the enemy, in proportion to the number engaged, perhaps the greatest of any action to be found in the records of naval warfare."

CHAPTER LIX.

August 14, 1813.

THE LOSS OF THE ARGUS.

The government of the United States having been unrepresented at the French Court, in the middle of June, 1813, William Henry Crawford was appointed to that important station; and, shortly afterwards, he sailed from New York, in the brig of war *Argus*, of which Lieutenant William H. Allen, of Rhode Island, was the commander. After a passage of twenty-three days he arrived at L'Orient in safety; and,

---

[1] Log-book of the *Decatur;* Breckenridge, p. 172; Coggeshall, pp. 173, 174.

[2] Log-book of the *Decatur;* Coggeshall, pp. 174, 175.

[3] Vide p. 264.

[1] James' Naval Occur., p. 259; James' Warden Refuted, Table II., p. 25; Breckenridge, p. 177; Coggeshall, p. 172. Mr. Auchinleck (*Hist.*, p. 199) says she carried "*twelve* guns."—[2] James' Naval Occur., p. 259. Capt. Coggeshall (*Hist. of Privateers*, p. 172) supposes she had *eighty-eight* men; but as it is admitted that all her crew, except 17, were killed or wounded, *I* cannot understand where more than an aggregate of *seventy-seven* is found. Mr. Auchinleck (*Hist.*, p. 199) says she had only "*fifty-seven men and nine boys*," which is *less* than the number of men who were killed and wounded.—[3] Log-book of the *Decatur;* Auchinleck's History, p. 199; Capt. Dent to Secretary of Navy, Aug. 21.—[4] Log-book of the *Decatur;* Auchinleck's History, p. 199; Naval Chronicle, xxx. p. 348.

three days afterwards, the *Argus* left that port on a cruise.[1]

From that time, until the middle of August, the *Argus* cruised in the chops of the English Channel and in the Irish Channel, carrying, as Paul Jones had carried before him,—but with more honor and integrity than the former had possessed,—the greatest dismay into the counting-rooms of mercantile England. Twenty sail of valuable merchantmen, taken and destroyed within sight of the firesides of England, had so far alarmed the underwriters in London that insurance on merchant vessels was obtained only with the greatest difficulty, and then only at the most extraordinary rates.[2]

On the fourteenth of August she fell in with a vessel from Oporto, laden with wine; and, it is said, that through *this means* the misfortunes which soon after befell her, were principally produced. "A good deal of the liquor," the rumor says, "was brought on the brig clandestinely, as the boats passed to and fro, and many of the people, who had been overworked and kept from their rest, partook of the refreshment it afforded too freely."[3] After setting the prize on fire, early the next morning, the *Argus* left her, under easy sail[4]—her situation being latitude 52° 15′ N., longitude 5° 50′ W.[5]

In the mean time the British authorities had aroused themselves for the removal of the daring enemy who was thus carrying destruction to the entrances of their harbors;[1] and among other vessels which had been sent out in quest of the *Argus* was the brig of war *Pelican*,[2] mounting sixteen thirty-two-pound carronades, four long-sixes, and a twelve-pound carronade, and commanded by Commander J. F. Maples.[3] The light of the burning wine-ship told the story of the situation of the *Argus*, although it was yet scarcely daybreak;[4] and the *Pelican* stood for the scene, with every stitch of her canvas set.[5] Her approach was not discovered by the *Argus* until she had come too near to allow any manœuvres; and Captain Allen shortened sail, in order that she might have an opportunity to close.[6]

At six o'clock, the *Argus* having hoisted her colors, she wore, and gave her larboard broadside, at grape-shot distance; and the action commenced, the two brigs still approaching each other.[7] Within four minutes after the opening of the fire a round-shot carried away Lieutenant Allen's left leg; and about the same time the main-braces, mainspring-stay, gaff, and trysail-mast of the *Argus* were shot away. Eight minutes later, Lieutenant Watson, the

[1] Lieut. Watson to Sec. of Navy, March 2, 1815; Cooper, ii. p. 113; Perkins' Hist., p. 179.—[2] James' Naval Occur., p. 269; Auchinleck, p. 199; Cooper, ii. p. 113; Perkins, pp. 179, 180; Thomson's Sketches, p. 235.

[3] Cooper, ii. p. 113.—[4] Extract from a Plymouth, Eng., paper, in "*The War*," ii. p. 71; Cooper, ii. p. 113.

[5] Lieut. Watson's Dispatch; Sketches of the War, p. 313.

[1] Cooper, ii. p. 113; Perkins, p. 130.—[2] Capt. Maples to Adm'l Thornborough, Aug. 14; James' Naval Occur., p. 269; Auchinleck, p. 199.—[3] James' Warden Refuted, Table IV., p. 33; Cooper, ii. p. 114; Sketches of the War, p. 314.—[4] Capt. Maples' Dispatch; James' Naval Occur., p. 270; Extract from a Plymouth paper; Auchinleck, p. 199; Breckenridge, p. 167.—[5] Lieut. Watson's Dispatch, Capt. Maples' Dispatch; Extract from a Plymouth paper; Auchinleck, p. 199.—[6] Lieut. Watson's Dispatch; James' Naval Occur., p. 270; Extract from a Plymouth paper; Auchinleck, p. 199; Cooper, ii. p. 113.

[7] The time when the action commenced has been singularly mistated by Mr. Breckenridge as "at *five* P. M."

second in command, was wounded by a grape-shot, and was carried below, the command of the deck devolving upon Lieutenant William H. Allen, jr.,[1] by whom "nothing which the most gallant exertions could effect was left undone" for the defence of the brig and the honor of the flag. At a quarter-past six, the enemy being on her weather-quarter, he edged off for the purpose of getting under the stern of the *Argus*, for the purpose of raking her; but Lieutenant Allen beautifully frustrated his purpose by luffing close to, with main-topsail aback; and, at the same time, he threw in a raking broadside into the *Pelican*. A few minutes afterwards, her rigging having been severely cut, and the use of her after-sails having been lost, the *Argus* fell off before the wind, and the *Pelican* succeeded in crossing her stern and raking her. At twenty-five minutes past six, the wheel-ropes and running-rigging of the *Argus* having been shot away, she became unmanageable, and the enemy selected that position which best answered his purpose, occasionally changing his position for the more effectual accomplishment of his object.[2]

Notwithstanding the severe injuries which the *Argus* had received, and the hopelessness of her condition, her officers and crew battled manfully, and attempted to board the *Pelican*; but, as might have been expected, in all their efforts they were alike unsuccessful. At length, having suffered severely in her hull and rigging, her guns being much disabled, without being able to oppose but little more than musketry to the broadside of the enemy, Lieutenant Allen, jr. considered farther resistance improper, and surrendered, after an obstinate engagement of forty-seven minutes' duration.[1]

The force of the *Pelican* has been noticed already;[2] that of the *Argus* was eighteen twenty-four-pound carronades and two long-twelves.[3] The loss of the former was Master's-mate Young and one seaman, *killed;* and five men, *wounded;*[4] that of the latter was Midshipmen Delphy and Edwards, and four men, *killed;* and Lieutenant-commandant Allen, Lieutenant Watson, Boatswain McLeod, Carpenter White, and thirteen men, *wounded.*[5]

Concerning this action, one who was peculiarly competent to form a correct opinion,[6] says: "The enemy was so much heavier, that it may be doubted if the *Argus* could have captured her antagonist under any ordinary circumstances; but it has been usual, in the service, to impute this defeat to the want of officers and to the fact that the people of the *Argus* were not in a fit condition to go into action. The Ameri-

[1] This officer, although bearing the same name, was not, in any way, related to his commander.

[2] Capt. Maples' Dispatch; Lieut. Watson's Dispatch; Extract from a Plymouth, Eng., paper; James' Naval Occur., pp. 270–273; Cooper, ii. pp. 113–115; Perkins, p. 180; Sketches of the War, pp. 313, 314; Breckenridge, pp. 167, 168; Thomson's Sketches, pp. 236, 237.

[1] Capt. Maples' Dispatch; Lieut. Watson's Dispatch; Extract from a Plymouth, Eng., paper; James' Naval Occur., pp. 270–273; Cooper, ii. pp. 113–115; Perkins, p. 180; Sketches of the War, pp. 313, 314; Breckenridge, pp. 167, 168; Thomson's Sketches, pp. 236, 237.

[2] Vide p. 267. With singular dishonesty the Royal Naval Chronicle (xxx. p. 160) gives her force as "*sixteen thirty-two-pound carronades*" only.—[3] Sketches of the War, p. 314; Cooper, ii. p. 114.—[4] Capt. Maples' Dispatch.

[5] Lieut. Watson's Dispatch; Report of Dr. Inderwick to the Sec. of Navy, Sept. 5, 1814.—[6] Cooper, ii. p. 114.

can vessel was *particularly well-officered*, so far as quality was concerned, though her batteries were necessarily left without a proper supervision after Lieutenant Watson was wounded. It is not easy to believe that Captain Allen would have engaged with his people under a very obvious influence from a free use of wine, but nothing is more probable than that the crew of the *Argus* should have been overworked, in the peculiar situation in which they were placed; and they *may have been exposed* to the peculiar influence mentioned, without the circumstance having come to the knowledge of the superior officers. They have, indeed, been described as 'nodding at their guns,' from excessive fatigue. One thing would appear to be certain, that while the brig was beautifully handled, so long as she was at all manageable, the fire of no other American cruiser, in this war, was as little destructive as that of the *Argus*. This has been attributed to the fatigue of the crew, and it is reasonable to suppose that the circumstance of the two lieutenants having been so early taken from the batteries, did not contribute to the accuracy of the fire."

The wounded commandant of the *Argus* lived to reach England, and, on the eighteenth of August, he died in the hospital of Mill Prison, at the early age of thirty years.[1]

[NOTE.—The Dispatches of Lieut. Watson to the Sec. of Navy, and of Capt. Maples to the Admiral, which had been provided for the illustration of this chapter, have been omitted by the Publishers for want of room.]

CHAPTER LX.

August 30, 1813.

THE MASSACRE AT FORT MIMMS.

THE influence of Tecumthà, in his opposition to the Americans, was not confined to the Indians of the Northwest; but the Creeks, also, had been tampered with, and gradually embittered against the people among whom they lived.[1] From time to time this hostile feeling was manifested by outrages committed on the neighboring settlers; and, at length, several families were murdered in different parts of the Southwestern country, notwithstanding every effort which the Indian agents could employ to restore good feelings.[2]

In the prosecution of their hostile designs, the first point which was designated for attack was Fort Mimms, in the Tensaw settlement,[3]—a stockade on the Alabama River, in the State of Alabama,[4]—and one of a line of similar posts, which had been erected for the defence of the frontiers, and as places of refuge for the settlers in times of

¹ Report of Dr. Inderwick to the Sec. of Navy, Sept. 5, 1814.

¹ Claiborne's Notes on the War in the South, pp. 17–19; Eaton's Life of Jackson, p. 31; Ingersoll, i. pp. 323–326.—² Eaton, p. 31; Ingersoll, i. p. 324; Perkins, p. 198; McAfee, p. 460.—³ Eaton, p. 33; Goodwin's Jackson, p. 44.—⁴ Ingersoll, i. p. 325.

danger.[1] At the period in question it was manned with a garrison of about one hundred and fifty men, under the command of Major Daniel Beasley, of the Mississippi Volunteers;[2] and twenty-four families—embracing about one hundred and sixty whites, seven Indians, and one hundred negroes—had also entered it for protection.[3] It had, originally, been a square stockade, surrounding a large dwelling-house and the usual offices; but it had, recently, been extended, about fifty feet, on two sides, the old pickets dividing the area of the inclosure into two unequal parts. "The back gate" had also been partially inclosed with a bastion, and in one corner of the fort a block-house appears to have been erected.[4]

Notwithstanding the alarm which the congregation of the settlers within the forts would appear to indicate, a strange idea appears to have prevailed that the danger was not *immediate;* and the warnings which were conveyed to the fort were entirely disregarded. The Choctaws had sent word that an attack was intended; negroes, who had been sent out, had also reported, at different times, the approach of the savages, and some of them had been whipped for their watchfulness—the garrison and the assembled settlers, meanwhile, remaining almost wholly unmindful of the duties which devolved upon them.[5]

[1] Judge Toulmin's Letter, Sept. 7, 1813; McAfee, p. 461.
[2] Eaton, p. 33; Ingersoll, i. p. 328; Perkins, p. 198; Davis' Jackson, p. 65.—[3] Ingersoll, i. p. 330; McAfee, p. 461.—[4] Claiborne, p. 21; Gen. Claiborne to Gen. Flourney, Sept. 3, 1813; Ingersoll, i. pp. 328, 329; McAfee, pp. 461, 462.—[5] Judge Toulmin's Letter, Sept. 7, 1813; Ingersoll, i. pp. 328, 329; McAfee, p. 461.

At length, on the thirtieth of August, a party of Creeks—six or seven hundred in number,[1] and led by Weatherford, one of their principal chiefs[2]—approached the fort. The gate was open, and every thing indicated a most perfect feeling of security; the sentries allowing the savages to cross an open field in front of the fort, one hundred and fifty yards in width, and to come within thirty yards of the gate before they noticed their approach. The alarm of the sentries and the yell of the savages, as each rushed for the open gate, conveyed at the same moment the dreadful intelligence to the occupants of the fort; and, before the barrier could be closed, the torrent rushed in and decided the fate of all within it. Major Beasley appears to have attempted to rally the occupants, and was shot in the body while he was near the gate; directing his men, as he fell, to take care of the ammunition and to retreat to the dwelling-house.[3]

Notwithstanding the advantage which the savages had gained in the beginning, the garrison and the settlers appear to have fought nobly in defence of their lives and their families; and the enemy was, evidently, confined to the outer area of the work. Taking possession of the port-holes with which the

[1] Eaton, p. 33; Perkins, p. 198. The number of the assailants is variously stated, by different authors, ranging from 400 to 1500. I have thought, after a careful examination of the subject, that this was as near as could be ascertained.—[2] Claiborne, p. 21; Eaton, p. 33.
[3] Claiborne, p. 21; Judge Toulmin's Letter, Sept. 7; Letter from Fort St. Stephens, Sept. 4, in "*The War*," ii. p. 66; Gen. Claiborne to Gen. Flourney, Sept. 3; Ingersoll, i. p. 329; Perkins, p. 198; McAfee, p. 462; Goodwin's Jackson, pp. 44, 45; Breckenridge, pp. 216, 217.

MASSACRE AT FORT MIMMS.

From an original Painting by Chappel in the possession of the Publishers.

old line of pickets was pierced, the savages fired through into the inner area of the fort, inflicting severe loss upon those who occupied it; and, at the same time, another party attempted to cut open "the back gate" of the fort with the settlers' axes, which had been carelessly left outside the lines by those who had been working on the bastion with which the gate was sheltered. At the same time another party of Indians had scaled the pickets and effected a lodgment on the block-house; from whence they fired down upon the people within the works, and inflicted some injury. After a short time, however, they were dislodged, but not before they had set fire to a house which was near the pickets, and from which it was communicated to the kitchen, and, finally, to the main dwelling.[1]

In this manner the garrison and the settlers struggled, for some time, against every effort which the savages put forth to enter the inner area of the fort; and they were entirely successful. At length, however, the number of those who had fallen, the continued occupation of the outer area by the Indians, and the progress of the flames, which nothing had succeeded in checking, discouraged the garrison; and while a few — not more than twenty-five or thirty, in all—succeeded in effecting their escape, the greater part yielded to the terrible fate which awaited them.[2]

[1] Claiborne, p. 21; Judge Toulmin's Letter, Sept. 7; Letter from Fort St. Stephens, Sept. 4, in "*The War*," ii. p. 66; Gen. Claiborne to Gen. Flourney, Sept. 3; Ingersoll, i. p. 329; Perkins, p. 198; McAfee, p. 462; Goodwin's Jackson, pp. 44, 45; Breckenridge, pp. 216, 217.

[2] Ibid.

It was now late in the afternoon,—the engagement having continued several hours,—and the old men, women, and children, for safety, had fled to the upper story of the dwelling, the lower part of which was in flames, while the men had, generally, fallen before the merciless tomahawks of the enemy. With the most diabolical pleasure, the enemy danced around the burning buildings, filling the air with their yells and shouts of derision; and they witnessed the melancholy spectacle with every conceivable manifestation of fiendish satisfaction. The bodies of all whom they could reach were mutilated with scrupulous and studied insult; and old age and childhood, the hardy settler and the careworn matron, without discrimination and without mercy, were hurled to a common and untimely end.[1]

In this terrible catastrophe, the savages destroyed upwards of three hundred lives;[2] yet the victory was dearly bought, upwards of two hundred Indians having been *killed*, and double that number *wounded*,[3] in the severe and prolonged engagement at the inner gate.

[NOTE.—An extract of a letter from Gen. Ferdinand L. Claiborne to Gen. Flourney, which had been provided for the illustration of this chapter, has been omitted by the Publishers for want of room.]

[1] Claiborne, p. 21; Judge Toulmin's Letter, Sept. 7; Letter from Fort St. Stephens, Sept. 4, in "*The War*," ii. p. 66; Gen. Claiborne to Gen. Flourney, Sept. 3; Ingersoll, i. p. 329; Perkins, p. 198; McAfee, p. 462; Goodwin's Jackson, pp. 44, 45; Breckenridge, pp. 216, 217.

[2] Letter from Fort St. Stephens, Sept. 4; Ingersoll, i. p. 330; Perkins, p. 199; McAfee, p. 463. Several weeks afterwards a body of troops were sent out, under Capt. J. P. Kennedy, to collect and bury the remains of those who were killed at Fort Mimms, and, at that time, found and buried 247 bodies.—*Capt. Kennedy's Report, Sept.* 26.

[3] Letter from Fort St. Stephens, Sept. 4; McAfee, p. 463.

CHAPTER LXI.

September 5, 1813.

THE CAPTURE OF THE BOXER.

One of the most "lucky vessels"—as the sailors understand that term—which the American navy ever possessed was the little brig "*Enterprize*,"[1] the captor of the Tripolitan ship *Tripoli*, during the war with that power.[2] In the summer of 1813 she was commanded by Lieutenant William Burrows, and was employed in watching the enemy's cruisers between Cape Ann and the Bay of Fundy.[3]

She sailed from Portsmouth, New Hampshire, on the first of September; and, steering to the eastward, on the morning of the third, when off Wood Island, she made a schooner and chased her into Portland.[4] While there Lieutenant Burrows received information that several of the enemy's cruisers were off Manhagan; and, on the morning of the fourth, he weighed anchor, swept out of the harbor, and stood to the eastward, with the intention of examining the neighborhood in which the enemy was said to have frequented. On the morning of the fifth he looked into a bay near Penwin Point, and discovered a brig which was then getting under weigh; and, as she appeared to be a cruiser, the *Enterprize* immediately gave chase.[5]

[1] Cooper, ii. p. 108.—[2] Vide Chap. VII.—[3] Cooper, ii. p. 108.—[4] Lieut. McCall to Com. Hull, Sept. 7, 1813.—[5] Portland *Argus*, Sept. 8, 1813; Lieut. McCall to Com. Hull, Sept. 7, 1813; Cooper, ii. p. 108; Thomson's Sketches, p. 238.

The stranger witnessed this movement, and after having fired several guns, for the purpose of recalling one of her boats, which had gone to the shore,[1] she hoisted four ensigns and made sail to close with the *Enterprize*—the latter, meanwhile, having reconnoitred the stranger, hauled upon a wind and stood out of the bay, in order to clear the land.[2]

At three in the afternoon, having completed his preparations, and being at a sufficient distance from the shore, Lieutenant Burrows shortened sail, tacked and ran down to meet the stranger and to bring her to close action. As they neared each other, at twenty minutes past three o'clock, they kept away together; and immediately afterwards, at half pistol-shot distance, the action began—the *Enterprize* opening with her larboard, and the stranger with her starboard, guns. At half-past three the *Enterprize* ranged ahead of the enemy, when her helm was put a-starboard, and, as she sheered across the stranger's

[1] Cooper, ii. pp. 108, 109. It appears from James' *Naval Occur.*, p. 262, that this boat, with the surgeon and two midshipmen, who were "pigeon-shooting" on shore, did not reach the *Boxer*. Mr. Perkins (*Hist.*, p. 180) supposes these guns indicated a challenge, but in this he appears to have been mistaken.—[2] Portland *Argus*, Sept. 8, 1813; Lieut. McCall to Com. Hull, Sept. 7, 1813; Cooper, ii. p. 109; Thomson's Sketches, p. 238; Perkins, p. 181; Auchinleck, p. 200; W. Irving's Mem. of Lieut. Burrows, in the *Analectic Magazine*, ii.

bows she fired her stern-chaser with great effect, rounding to on her starboard tack, immediately afterwards, and throwing in a raking fire from her starboard broadside. Five minutes afterwards the stranger's maintop-mast and topsail yard came down, when the *Enterprize* took a position on her starboard bow, and continued to rake her until about four o'clock, when she surrendered. As her colors were nailed to the mast, her commander could not strike them; and he surrendered by hailing, explaining his difficulty, and asking a suspension of the fire from the *Enterprize's* guns.[1]

The stranger proved to be His Britannic Majesty's brig *Boxer*, of fourteen guns,—twelve eighteen-pound carronades and two long-sixes,[2]—and was commanded by Commander Samuel Blyth, one of the most promising of the younger officers of the navy,[3] who had been killed by a cannon-shot from the first broadside fired on the *Enterprize*.[4]

By a singular coincidence, about the same time that Commander Blyth fell, on the *Boxer's* deck, Lieutenant Burrows fell, on the deck of the *Enterprize*, from a canister or musket-shot wound;[5]

[1] Portland *Argus*, Sept. 8, 1813; Lieut. McCall to Com. Hull, Sept. 7, 1813; James, pp. 262, 263; Thomson's Sketches, p. 238; Sketches of the War, pp. 303, 304; Auchinleck, p. 200; W. Irving's Memoir of Lieut. Burrows.

[2] James' Naval Occurrences, p. 263. The *Naval Chronicle* (xxx. p. 348) errs when it states that she mounted only *ten* eighteens.—[3] Memoir of Samuel Blyth, Esq., in the *Naval Chronicle*, xxxii. pp. 441–473.

[4] Lieut. McCall to Com. Hull, Sept. 7, 1813; James, p. 262.—[5] Lieut. McCall to Com. Hull, Sept. 7, 1813; Cooper, ii. p. 110, *note*.

and after lingering eight hours, he, also, passed away.[1]

The *Boxer* was very much cut up, both in her hull and rigging; and besides her commander, she lost several men *killed*, and seventeen *wounded* were taken prisoners.[2] The *Enterprize* suffered but very slightly, and lost, besides her commander, one *killed*, and Midshipman Waters and eleven *wounded*.[3]

The ships were taken into Portland by Lieutenant Edward R. McCall; and the two commanders, no longer antagonists, were borne to their resting-places with every honor which the rank and bravery of the deceased, while living, had entitled them to receive.[4] They were buried side by side, with all the honors of war; and Congress and the country bestowed upon the memory of Burrows, and upon Lieutenant McCall and the crew of the *Enterprize*, the reward, both of fame and of prize-money, which they had so gallantly fought for.

[NOTE.—The Dispatch of Lieut. McCall to Com. Hull, which had been provided for the illustration of this chapter, has been omitted by the Publishers for want of room]

[1] Lieut. McCall to Com. Hull, Sept. 7, 1813.

[2] Com. Hull to Com. Bainbridge, Sept. 10, 1813. Her loss, *killed*, has been the subject of a prolonged and angry discussion. The British authorities claim that only *three* were killed, besides Captain Blyth; while Com. Hull, after a careful examination, declared that it exceeded *thirty*. "*Boxer*" (in the *Naval Chronicle*, xxxii. p. 471) says her total loss was 21 men. Mr. Thomson (*Sketches*, p. 239) says *twenty-five of her crew were killed*, in which Mr. Perkins (*Hist.*, p. 181) concurs. After carefully examining the original evidence, I prefer the statements of the British authors, and suppose her *killed* did not exceed *four*.

[3] Report appended to Lieut. McCall's Dispatch; Com. Hull to Com. Bainbridge, Sept. 10, 1813.

[4] "*The War*," ii. p. 55.

CHAPTER LXII.

September 10, 1813.

THE BATTLE OF LAKE ERIE.

The command of the upper lakes, as has been seen in former chapters of this volume, was a subject which received the early attention of both Great Britain and the United States; and it was important in facilitating the military movements of the party who held it, on every part of the extended shores of these immense inland seas.

With the fall of Michilimacinac the *Caledonia* passed into the hands of the British;[1] and when the *Adams*, with Detroit and the Northwestern army, was surrendered by General Hull,[2] the naval power of the United States was entirely broken, and the enemy commanded, not only the waters of Lake Erie, but the shores of Michigan, Ohio, and western New York.[3] To restore, in some measure, this command of the western waters, steps were taken by the Federal government at an early date. Sailing-master Dobbins was employed in the preliminary preparations;[4] and, in the summer of 1812, Lieutenant Jesse D. Elliott was ordered to Lake Erie for the purpose of consulting with General Van Rensselaer "as to the best position to build, repair, and fit for service, such vessels or boats as might be required to retain the command of Lake Erie;" and to "purchase any merchant vessels or boats that could be converted into vessels of war or gunboats, and to commence their equipment immediately."[1] At the same time thirty *carpenters* were sent from New York;[2] on the twenty-first of September eighty more followed; and on the twenty-fourth the force was increased by the addition of one hundred and forty more, all from the same city[3]—all of whom were employed in equipping some small vessels which Lieutenant Elliott had purchased,[4] or in preparing to lay the timbers for two larger vessels at Presque Isle.[5] About the same time Lieutenant

[1] Vide Chap. XV.—[2] Vide Chap. XXI.

[3] Dr. Parsons' Battle of Lake Erie, pp. 3, 4; Perkins' Hist. of War, p. 226.—[4] Cooper's Nav. Hist., ii. p. 186.

[1] Com. Chauncey to Lieut. Elliott, New York, Sept. 7, 1812; Com. Elliott's speech at Hagerstown, p. 3.

[2] Com. Chauncey to Lieut. Elliott, Sept. 7, 1812.

[3] Ibid., Sept. 24, 1812.—[4] Cooper's Nav. Hist., ii. pp. 153, 186; Parsons, p. 4; Mackenzie's Perry, i. pp. 147, 148.

[5] Parsons, p. 4; Mackenzie's Decatur, i. p. 131. In passing, it may not be amiss to remark that Mr. Burgess (*Battle of Lake Erie*, p. xv.) says that "Com. Perry was a native of Rhode Island; and that he carried with him, *from that State* up to the lake, those men, who, *under his direction*, with the aid of a few others, *built and equipped the fleet*, which, under his command, subdued the enemy on those waters;" and from this he considers "it is not too much to regard *this distinguished enterprise* as a part of the maritime affairs of *Rhode Island*." As *Commander* Perry did not reach Lake Erie until *the 24th of March*, 1813, and then only as the commander of *seamen;* and as the *carpenters* went from *the city of New York*, and were directed by Noah Brown, *of that city*, under the general supervision of the celebrated ship-builder Henry Eckford, *of the same city*, who personally directed the work at Black Rock, I am disposed to claim shares of the honor which attaches to the *building* of this fleet for the mechanics of New York, and for those of some other places besides Newport and Providence.

Elliott gallantly recaptured the *Adams* and the *Caledonia*—destroying the former, and restoring the latter to the American navy.[1] Soon afterwards part of the crew of the *John Adams*, which had been laid up at New York, was sent to Buffalo, under Lieutenant Samuel Angus, when Lieutenant Elliott returned to Lake Ontario, leaving the former officer in command on Lake Erie.[2]

On the seventeenth of February, 1813, Commander Oliver H. Perry, then commanding the flotilla of gunboats in Narragansett Bay, was ordered "to the Lakes;" and on the twenty-third of March he reached Buffalo; and Erie (*Presque Isle*) on the twenty-seventh.[3] Contending with the multitude of difficulties which his peculiar situation—remote from all the means for constructing, equipping, arming, and manning a squadron, except *green timber standing in the woods*, and a small force of seamen and carpenters—all the ingenuity, perseverance, and self-denial, which formed such prominent parts of his character, were constantly called into requisition.[4]

The capture of Fort George, and the subsequent evacuation of the Niagara frontier, relieved the five small vessels which Lieutenant Elliott had purchased;[1] and, after great labor in towing them into the lake, the entire naval force on Lake Erie assembled at Presque Isle on the eighteenth of June.[2] The two brigs which had been laid down in the winter, at that place, had been launched;[3] and, although they were not yet ready to leave the port, the concentration of the entire force in one harbor facilitated the completion of the whole.

In the mean while the enemy, under the direction of Commander Finnis, had not been idle; and he also had built or equipped a squadron;[4] which soon afterwards left port on a cruise, under the command of Commander Barclay, who had been detached for that purpose.[5] After occasionally looking into the harbor where the American squadron lay, finished, but without crews, without venturing an attack, he as often returned to Malden;[6] and on the fourth of August, but for a party, at which Commander Barclay was a guest, he might have been a witness, and a disa-

[1] Vide Chap. XXIX.—[2] Cooper's Nav. Hist., ii. pp. 153, 186.—[3] Mackenzie's Perry, i. pp. 129, 130; Calvert's Oration on the Battle of Lake Erie, pp. 5, 6; Cooper's Naval History, ii. p. 186.

[4] While the difficulties with which Com. Perry had to contend were of the most vexatious and perplexing character, they were *not* exactly such as Mr. Burgess has described in pp. 19–24 of his "Lecture" on this subject, before the R. I. Hist. Society. "His hardy Rhode Island *mariners*" were *not* "required to change the oaks, and the green pines, and the *hemlocks*, then standing on those shores, into a fleet of ships and vessels, and fit them out," &c. That work was given to the appropriate *mechanics;* and the principal trouble of Perry consisted in delays which these mechanics experienced in their passage from New York and Philadelphia; in procuring the necessary iron-work, cordage, duck, and other stores; and in obtaining crews for his vessels, after they had been finished and made ready for sea.

[1] Mackenzie's Perry, i. p. 147; Calvert, pp. 6, 7; Parsons, p. 5; Cooper's Naval History, ii. p. 186.

[2] Mackenzie's Perry, i. pp. 149, 150; Calvert, p. 7; Parsons, p. 5.—[3] "They were launched on the 24th of May."—*Mackenzie's Perry*, i. p. 136. See also Cooper's Nav. Hist., ii. p. 187.—[4] Mackenzie's Perry, i. p. 149; Cooper's Nav. Hist., ii. p. 187.—[5] Mackenzie's Perry, i. pp. 156–158; Cooper's Nav. Hist., ii. p. 187; Christie's Mil. and Nav. Operations, p. 131; Perkins, p. 227.—[6] Mackenzie's Perry, i. pp. 157, 158, 160; Calvert, p. 7; Parsons, p. 5; Cooper's Nav. Hist., ii. p. 187; Christie, p. 131; Com. Perry to Com. Chauncey, July 23, 1813.

greeable one, of the passage of the squadron over the bar at Erie.[1]

At this time Commander Barclay commanded the ship *Detroit*, mounting nineteen guns; the ship *Queen Charlotte*, mounting seventeen guns; the schooner *Lady Prevost*, mounting thirteen guns; the brig *Hunter*, of ten guns; the sloop *Little Belt*, of three guns; and the schooner *Chippewa*, of one gun:[2] while Commander Perry commanded the brig *Lawrence*, of twenty guns; the brig *Niagara*, Lieutenant Turner, of twenty guns; the brig *Caledonia*, of three guns, under Purser Magrath; the *Ariel*, of four guns, under Lieutenant Packett; the schooner *Somers*, of two guns, under Sailing-master Almy; the schooner *Porcupine*, of one gun, under Midshipman Senat; the schooner *Tigress*, of one gun, under Master's-mate McDonald; the schooner *Scorpion*, of two guns, under Sailing-master Champlin; the sloop *Trippe*, of one gun, under Lieutenant Smith; and the schooner *Ohio*, of one gun, under Sailing-master Dobbin.[3]

After having received reinforcements of soldiers, volunteers, and sailors, at different times[4]—the whole leaving the vessels still insufficiently manned—the squadron ran across the lake several times without meeting the enemy, or being able to draw him from Malden;[1] and on the ninth of September it returned to Put-in-Bay,[2] a harbor off Ottawa County, Ohio, near the western extremity of the lake,[3] which had been selected as its rendezvous, anchored, and prepared for the action which was now seen to be not far distant.[4] The several commanders were summoned on board the *Lawrence*, and received the final instructions of their young commander; and as they left the brig they were told that in case of an engagement "they could not be out of their proper places, if they laid their enemy close alongside."[5]

At sunrise on the morning of the tenth of September, while the squadron was at anchor in Put-in-Bay, the lookout at the masthead of the *Lawrence* discovered the enemy standing in towards that place, with an evident desire to draw the former into an engagement;[6] and Commander Perry immediately ordered the several vessels to get under weigh.[7] Within an hour the squadron was beating out of the bay against a light southwesterly breeze,

[1] Com. Perry to Sec. of Navy, "Aug. 4, 1812; 9 P. M.;" Parsons, pp. 6, 7; Cooper's Nav. Hist., ii. pp. 188, 189; Mackenzie, i. pp. 174–178. Mr. Calvert (*Oration*, p. 7) and Gen. Armstrong (*Notices*, i. p. 167) say the vessels crossed on the *second*.—[2] James' Warden Refuted, Table I.; Parsons, p. 6; Mackenzie's Perry, i. p. 149; Cooper's Nav. Hist., ii. p. 187.—[3] Parsons, p. 6; Cooper's Nav. Hist., ii. p. 188.—[4] Mackenzie's Perry, i. pp. 148, 159, 163, 166, 184; Biog. of Elliott, p. 26; Cooper's Nav. Hist., ii. p. 188; Calvert's Oration, pp. 7, 8; Parsons, pp. 7, 8. Thirty-six of these were volunteers from Gen. Harrison's army.

[1] Mackenzie's Perry, i. pp. 180, 181, 198–202, 206, 207; Cooper's Nav. Hist., ii. pp. 188, 189; Calvert, pp. 7, 8; Parsons, pp. 7, 8.—[2] Mackenzie's Perry, i. p. 221; Cooper's Nav. Hist., ii. p. 189; Parsons, p. 8.—[3] Howe's Hist. Coll. of Ohio, p. 394; Parsons, p. 7.—[4] Mackenzie's Perry, i. pp. 221, 222; Cooper's Nav. Hist., ii. p. 189.

[5] Mackenzie's Perry, i. p. 222; Calvert's Oration, p. 8; Sailing-master Taylor's Affidavit.

[6] Com. Perry to Sec. of Navy, Sept. 13; Testimony of Lieut. Webster, April 24, 1815; Sailing-master Taylor's and Capt. Brevoort's Affidavits; Lieut. Montgomery to Capt. Elliott, Feb. 11, 1821; Mackenzie's Perry, i. p. 223; Cooper's Nav. Hist., ii. p. 189; Parsons, p. 8.

[7] Com. Perry to Sec. of Navy, Sept. 13; Test. of Lieut. Webster; Sailing-master Taylor's Affid.; Letter of Lieut. Forrest, Jan. 29, 1821; Lieut. Montgomery to Capt. Elliott, Feb. 11, 1821; Mackenzie's Perry, i. p. 224; Cooper's Nav. Hist., ii. p. 189; Parsons, p. 8.

with the boats assisting by towing;[1] but the enemy appeared to have secured the weather-gage, and it was only by beating around some of the small islands which cluster around the entrance of the bay that it could be taken from him.[2] The length of time that such a movement would have required, as well as the uncertainty of the result, induced Commander Perry to yield the advantage which the weather-gage would have given him, and he determined to pass to the leeward of the islands, and to press forward and compel the enemy to engage, notwithstanding the advantage which the long guns of the latter would possess over the carronades of the American squadron, while the latter would be to leeward.[3] Providentially, at this moment, the wind suddenly shifted to the southeast;[4] and, without turning the islands, the squadron was enabled to approach the enemy, and to gain the desired weather-gage.[5]

When the enemy perceived the American squadron was clearing the bay, he attempted, in a series of unsuccessful manœuvres, to gain the wind;[1] and having failed in all his attempts, at ten in the morning *he hove to*, and formed his line of battle with the heads of his vessels to the southward and westward.[2] At this time the wind was very light, from the southeast;[3] and, at the rate of about three miles an hour, the American squadron,—formed in the order of battle which had been determined on the day before,—was approaching that of the enemy,[4] which was about nine miles distant,[5] and still lying with its topsails aback, awaiting its adversary. A light shower had fallen in the morning; but with the change of the wind the clouds had been scattered, and one of the loveliest days of our early autumn was lending its enchantment to the scene. In the distance the newly-painted vessels of the enemy's line, in close order, and with all their canvas and their colors set, presented a novel spectacle to the greater part of the American crews;[6] and the contrast between the appearance of the rival squadrons is said to have been greatly in favor of the enemy.

Nothing occurred to disturb the solemn stillness of the scene until the American line had approached within three miles of the enemy,[7]

---

[1] Test. of Lieut. Webster; Sailing-master Taylor's and Capt. Brevoort's Affidavits; Lieut. Forrest's Letter, Jan. 29, 1821; Lieut. Montgomery to Capt. Elliott, Feb. 11, 1821; Boatswain's Berry's Affidavit, May 14, 1821; Com. Barclay to Sir James Yeo, Sept. 12, 1812; Mackenzie's Perry, i. p. 224; Cooper's Nav. Hist., ii. p. 189.

[2] Sailing-master Taylor's Affid.; Mackenzie's Perry, i. p. 224; James' Nav. Occur., p. 287; Cooper's Nav. Hist., ii. p. 189.—[3] Sailing-master Taylor's Affid.; Mackenzie's Perry, i. p. 225; Cooper's Nav. Hist., ii. p. 189.

[4] Com. Perry's Dispatch, Sept. 13; Lieut. Forrest's Letter, Jan. 29, 1821; Sailing-master Taylor's Affid.; Lieut. Montgomery to Capt. Elliott, Feb. 11, 1821; Cooper's Nav. Hist., ii. p. 189; Mackenzie's Perry, i. p. 225.

[5] Com. Perry's Dispatch, Sept. 13; Test. of Lieuts. Webster and Yarnall, 1815; Lieut. Forrest's Letter, Jan. 29, 1821; Sailing-master Taylor's Affid.; Cooper's Nav. Hist., ii. p. 189; Mackenzie's Perry, i. p. 225.

[1] Burgess' Lecture, p. 32; Mackenzie's Perry, i. p. 226.

[2] Sailing-master Taylor's Affid.; Mackenzie's Perry, i. p. 227; Burgess' Lecture, p. 32; Cooper's Nav. Hist., ii. p. 189.—[3] Sailing-master Taylor's Affid.; Mackenzie's Perry, i. p. 227; Cooper's Nav. Hist., ii. p. 189.

[4] Mackenzie's Perry, i. p. 227; Burgess' Lecture, p. 34.

[5] Sailing-master Taylor's Affid.; Burgess' Lecture, pp. 32, 34; Cooper's Nav. Hist., ii. p. 189. Mr. Mackenzie (*Biog. of Perry*, i. 228) says it was only *six* miles distant; Mr. Calvert (*Oration*, p. 9), "*six or seven;*" and Dr. Parsons (*Battle of Lake Erie*, p. 8), "*four or five.*"—[6] Mackenzie's Perry, i. pp. 227, 228; Parsons, p. 8.

[7] Capt. Champlin to the Author, Jan. 31, 1860; Mac-

when Commander Perry signalled the *Niagara*, which was ahead of the *Lawrence*, and came within hailing distance. He then inquired from Captain Brevoort, the marine officer on the former brig, whose family lived in Detroit, the name and force of each ship in the enemy's line;[1] when, perceiving that a change had been made in the expected order of battle,[2] he also determined to change, to conform with the new order of his opponent.[3] Accordingly the *Scorpion* Sailing-master Champlin, was ordered to the van, to oppose the *Chippewa*, which was in the enemy's van, and the *Ariel*, Lieutenant Packett, next to her, on the weather-bow of the *Lawrence;* while, with the latter, Commander Perry followed next, with the intention of engaging the *Detroit*, which was the enemy's flag-ship. The *Caledonia*, Lieutenant Turner, was next in order, with directions to engage the *Hunter;* then the *Niagara*, Commander Elliott, which was ordered against the *Queen Charlotte;* and the *Somers*, Sailing-master Almy, the *Porcupine*, Midshipman Senat, the *Tigress*, Lieutenant Conklin, and the *Trippe*, Lieutenant Holdup, followed in the order named, to engage the *Lady Prevost* and the *Little Belt*.[4]

Gradually the line of battle was closed, and all, except the small vessels astern of the *Niagara*, having taken their positions, half a cable's length apart—all, at the same time, "preserving their stations in the line," in conformity with the orders which they had received from Commander Perry[1]—in this order they slowly approached the enemy.

About this time[2] the signal for action—a blue burgee, with the inscription "Don't give up the ship," at the *Lawrence's* mainroyal-masthead—was displayed, amidst the hearty cheers of the several crews.[3] With this flag at the *Lawrence's* masthead, in the appointed order, the squadron slowly approached the enemy;[4] during which time the bread-bags were freely resorted to, the noonday-grog was distributed, and all the precautionary individual arrangements, which men about to engage in deadly combat may reasonably be expected to enter into, were discussed and perfected.[5]

At a few minutes before twelve o'clock a bugle sounded on the deck of the enemy's flag-ship, the *Detroit;* and as its clear notes, the signal for com-

kenzie's Perry, i. p. 227; Cooper's Nav. Hist., ii. p. 189; Parsons, pp. 8, 9. Capt. Elliott (*Speech*, p. 6) says it was "when approaching the enemy, *nearly within gunshot;*" Lieut. Webster (*Testimony*) says this change was made "*after the Commodore's battle-flag was raised*, I think;" and Lieut. Forrest, in his testimony, agrees with him.

[1] Capt. Brevoort's Affidavit; Com. Elliott's Speech, p. 6.

[2] Lieut. Webster's Test.; Com. Elliott's Speech, p. 6; Burgess' Lecture, p. 28; Cooper's Nav. Hist., ii. p. 189; Mackenzie's Perry, i. pp. 227, 228.

[3] Lieuts. Webster and Forrest's Test.; Capt. Brevoort's Affidavit; Burgess' Lecture, p. 28; Cooper's Nav. Hist., ii. p. 189; Mackenzie's Perry, i. pp. 227, 228.

[4] Lieut. Smith to Gen. Stansbury, Oct. 16; Officers of the *Niagara* to Sec. of Navy, Oct. 13; Mackenzie's Perry, i. pp. 227, 228; Elliott's Speech, p. 6; Parsons, pp. 8, 9; Cooper's Nav. Hist., ii. pp. 189, 190.—[1] Com. Perry's Charges against Com. Elliott, Charge IV. Mr. Burgess (*Lecture*, p. 35) singularly supposes the "*half a cable's length*" referred to the distance between the *two lines of battle*, instead of that between *the several vessels in the same* (American) *line*.—[2] Lieut. Webster's Test.; Parsons, pp. 8, 9; Calvert, p. 10; Mackenzie's Perry, i. p. 228; Letter from the *Hunter*, Sept. 24, 1813. Lieuts. Yarnell and Forrest (*Test.*) suppose they were "about *three miles from the enemy*."—[3] Parsons, p. 9; Calvert, p. 10; Mackenzie's Perry, i. pp. 222, 228.—[4] The wind was not heavier than a *a two or three knot* breeze.—(Vide p. 277, col. 2, note 3.)

[5] Parsons, p. 9; Mackenzie's Perry, i. p. 229.

mencing the action, reached the other vessels of the squadron, it was answered with the hearty cheers which seamen of all nations know so well how to give.[1] Immediately afterwards a twenty-four-pound shot from the *Detroit* carried the message towards the *Lawrence*[2]—at that time on the weather-quarter of the former vessel, and about a mile and a half distant[3]—without reaching her;[4] when Commander Perry renewed the order to the vessels astern, to close the line of battle;[5] and directed the *Scorpion*, ahead and a little on the weather-bow of the *Lawrence*, to answer the *Detroit*—an order which was promptly obeyed by Sailing-master Champlin.[6]

At this moment the American line was slowly approaching that of the enemy—the two forming two sides of an acute angle, with the small vessels of each receding from each other[7]—and as the enemy's long guns gave him the advantage over the American carronades, at this distance, the former properly appeared anxious to maintain the action *without closing*, while Commander Perry, as properly, desired to take those positions where the armaments of his vessels could be handled with the greatest advantage.[1] Accordingly signals were made for each vessel to engage her opponent in the line, as designated in previous orders;[2] and at about five minutes before twelve o'clock the action began.[3] As there appears to have been no signal made for breaking the line, or for changing the relative positions of the several vessels, the *Caledonia* and the *Niagara* "preserved their stations in the line," *agreeably to their orders*,[4] and opened and continued their fire in the best possible manner;[5]

[1] Mackenzie's Perry, i. p. 231; Calvert, p. 11; Letter from the *Hunter*, Sept. 24.—[2] Lieut. Yarnall's Testimony; Lieut. Turner's, Chaplain Breeze's, Sailing-master Taylor's, and Capt. Brevoort's Affidavits; Mackenzie's Perry, i. p. 231; Burgess' Lecture, p. 35; Cooper's Nav. Hist., ii. p. 190.—[3] Lieuts. Webster and Yarnall's Test.; Lieut. Montgomery to Capt. Elliott, Feb. 11, 1821; Mackenzie's Perry, i. p. 231; Officers of the *Niagara* to Sec. of Navy, Oct. 13; Cooper's Nav. Hist., ii. p. 190. Many of the officers have testified that the *Lawrence* and *Detroit* were not more than *a mile* apart; while Mr. Calvert says the lines were *at an average distance of one mile* apart.

[4] Mackenzie's Perry, i. p. 231; Calvert, p. 11.

[5] Sailing-master Taylor's Affid.; Mackenzie's Perry, i. p. 233; Cooper's Nav. Hist., ii. p. 190; Letter from the *Hunter*, Sept. 24.—[6] Lieut. Yarnall's Test.; Mackenzie's Perry, i. p. 232; Cooper's Nav. Hist., ii. p. 190.

[7] Cooper's Nav. Hist., ii. p. 190; Diagram in Navy Department.

[1] Com. Perry's Dispatch, Sept. 13; Lieut. Webster's Test.; Mackenzie's Perry, i. p. 233; Cooper's Naval History, ii. p. 190.—[2] Lieut. Forrest's Test.; Lieuts. Turner and Stevens', Sailing-master Champlin's, Master's-mate Brownell's, and Sailing-master Taylor's Affidavits; Mackenzie's Perry, i. p. 231; Burgess' Lecture, p. 35; Cooper's Nav. Hist., ii. p. 190.

[3] Com. Perry's Dispatch, Sept. 13; Mackenzie's Perry, i. 232; Cooper's Nav. Hist., ii. p. 190; Calvert, p. 11.

[4] With all proper respect to those who have participated in the angry and prolonged controversy respecting the part taken by Commander Elliott and the *Niagara*, I submit that this fact, *per se*, would have relieved that officer from just blame, *in any event*. It is very evident that it is *not* the duty of a subordinate to question the propriety of, or to disregard, at his own pleasure, the *orders* which he may receive from his superior in command; nor can it be done without throwing the service into anarchy, and reducing all authority to the dictates of individual will. In "preserving his station in the line," even *after Com. Elliott desired to pass him*, to go to the relief of the *Lawrence*, Lieut. Turner enforced my views by his example; and his subsequent condemnation of the former officer, *for acting just as* HE *acted*, with the *Caledonia*, was at once unwise and inconsistent. Whether the *Niagara* and her commander, while "preserving their station in the line," did their duty, is not a question to be discussed in this note; but simply whether they could *change the order of battle and the positive orders of their senior officer in command*, without exposing themselves to the condemnation of those who now condemn them for an opposite line of action.

[5] Lieut. Conklin, of the *Tigress*; Lieut. Montgomery to Capt. Elliott, Feb. 11, 1821; Lieut. Adams', Dr. Barton's, and Boatswain Berry's Affidavits; Officers of the *Niagara*

although, from their distance, with but little effect;[1] while the *Lawrence*, under the immediate orders of Commander Perry, appears to have left the line; and, after furling his topgallant-sail, hauling up his foresail, and rounding to,[2] he closed with the enemy "within canister-shot distance,"[3] receiving during that time, a period of not less than half an hour, a heavy and destructive fire from the long guns of the enemy.[4] The *Ariel* and the *Scorpion* were also engaged during this time with their long guns, and rendered great assistance to the *Lawrence;*[5] while the vessels which remained in the line gradually worked down towards the enemy, receiving his fire with but little damage, and returning it with skill and effect.[6]

to Sec. of Navy, Oct. 13; Cooper's Nav. Hist., ii. p. 190; Lieut. Smith to Gen. Stansbury, Oct. 16; Letter from the *Hunter*, Sept. 24; Lieut. Webster's Test.

[1] Officers of the *Niagara* to Sect. of Navy, Oct. 13.

[2] Lieut. Yarnall's Testimony.

[3] The *real* distance here referred to has caused considerable discussion, and exemplifies the improper spirit with which this question has been examined. While Com. Perry (*Dispatch, Sept.* 13, 1813) says he sustained the fire of his opponents at "*within canister-shot distance*" (1320 yards), in which he is sustained by Sailing-master Taylor (*Affid.*); and Mr. Cooper (*Nav. Hist.*, ii. p. 190), Lieut. Forrest (*Test.*), and the Letter from the *Hunter, Sept.* 24, make it carronade "*point-blank*" (450 yards); Lieut. Forrest (*Letter, Jan.* 29, 1821), Lieuts. Stevens and Turner, Sailing-master Champlin, Chaplain Breeze, and Master's-mate Brownell, in their *Affidavits*, and Mr. Mackenzie (*Biog. of Perry*, i. p. 234), at "*close action*" (say 350 yards); Lieut. Yarnall, in his *Testimony, April*, 1815, and Mr. Burgess (*Lecture*, p. 36), calls it *half-musket shot* (50 yards).

[4] As the action began at 12 M., the *Lawrence* "sustaining the action, in close order, upwards of *two hours;*" and Com. Perry leaving her at *half-past two*, it is obvious that she was half an hour reaching her position off the *Detroit.*—[5] Com. Perry's Dispatch, Sept. 13; Mackenzie's Perry, i. pp. 234, 236; Cooper's Nav. Hist., ii. pp. 190, 191; Calvert, p. 11.

[6] Com. Perry's Dispatch, Sept. 13.

The *Lawrence* having thus broken the standing orders and the line of battle, leaving her consorts, who were astern; and, with the support of the *Ariel* and the *Scorpion* only, having attacked the head of the enemy's line, where his strength chiefly laid, without enabling the commanders of those vessels, which have been referred to, to move independently to his support, by relieving them from their obligation to obey his previous orders, "to keep within half a cable's length *of each other*, and enjoining upon the commanders to preserve their stations in the line, and to keep as near the *Lawrence* as possible," Commander Perry assumed the grave responsibility of conducting the engagement single-handed, and without any prospect of immediate assistance. At this distance of time, and with the limited amount of evidence at our command, the motives of the Commander, in his preliminaries to the action, are indistinct and incomprehensible. His change in the first order of battle[1]—at all times, on sea or land, when in front of an enemy, a dangerous experiment, especially, as in this case, when inexperienced troops are thus transferred—was, evidently, productive of some confusion; and his alteration of his own prescribed order of battle, without releasing his subordinates from their obligations to it; and the hazardous abandonment of his associates to attack the enemy's line single-handed, without giving authority for any of his subordinates to leave "their stations in the line," and move to his support, have

[1] Vide pp. 277, 278.

received no explanation from those who have testified on this complicated and controverted subject.

Having thus opened his fire on the *Detroit*, it was evidently continued with spirit, until the enemy, perceiving the failure of the American line to come to closer action in support of the *Lawrence* —which the want of orders from Commander Perry, and the absence of authority, in his subordinates, to break the prescribed order and line of battle before referred to, appear to have prevented—the *Hunter*, the *Queen Charlotte*, and the *Chippewa* concentrated their fire, with that of the *Detroit*, and endeavored to cripple and overpower the *Lawrence;*[1] evidently hoping thereby to overcome the divided forces of their antagonist before they could be concentrated in a new line of battle. In this unequal contest, for upwards of two hours,[2] the *Lawrence* struggled desperately and suffered severely. Her rigging is said to "have been much shot away, and was hanging down or towing overboard; her sails were torn to pieces; her spars wounded and falling to the deck; her braces and bowlines cut, so as to render it impossible to trim the yards or keep the vessel under control." "On deck the destruction was even more terrible. One by one her guns had been dismounted, until only one remained that could be fired; the bulwarks had been entirely beaten in; and the enemy's round-shot passed completely through the vessel. The slaughter among her crew was beyond any recorded in the history of naval warfare. Of one hundred efficient men who had gone into action, twenty-two had been killed and sixty-one wounded." In short, she was an unmanageable wreck—an unimpeachable witness of the desperation of the attack, as well as the dogged obstinacy of the defence.[1]

In the mean time, during the two hours and a half since the *Lawrence* had left the line, the *Caledonia* and all the vessels astern of her had "kept within half a cable's length of each other, preserved their stations in the line, and kept as near the *Lawrence* as possible;" while, at the same time, as far as the exceeding light summer breeze allowed, each had "engaged her opponent, as designated in previous orders."[2] With the exception of the *Porcupine*, *Tigress*, and *Trippe*, they had gradually come into close action, and were taking part in the engagement with spirit and effect. The *Caledonia* appears to have been a dull sailer, and it is said, that in order to "preserve his station in the line" without running into her stern, Commander Elliott, more than once, had been obliged to back his topsail and brail his jib.[3] At about

[1] Lieut. Yarnall's Test.; Burgess' Lecture, p. 39; Mackenzie's Perry, i. pp. 234, 236; Cooper's Nav. Hist., ii. p. 190; Calvert, pp. 11, 12; W. Foster to S. Grosvenor, Erie, Sept. 19, 1813.—[2] Com. Perry's Dispatch, Sept. 13; Mackenzie's Perry, i. p. 237.

[1] Mackenzie's Perry, i. pp. 237, 238; Calvert, p. 11.

[2] Lieut. Webster's and Midship. Montgomery's Test.; Midship. Nichols to Capt. Elliott, Jan. 22, 1821; Lieut. Conklin, of the *Tigress;* Lieut. Montgomery to Capt. Elliott, Feb. 11, 1813; Com. Elliott's Speech, pp. 6, 7.

[3] Lieut. Webster's Test., April 24, 1815; Purser Magrath to the Erie *Sentinel;* Mr. Cooper, in Graham's *Magazine*, May, 1843. Lieuts. Yarnall and Turner, Mr. Mackenzie, and many others, who were not present, have intimated that this was done to keep the *Niagara* out of action.

two o'clock, however, a breeze suddenly struck the foremost vessels in the American line, and enabled them to bear down on the enemy, and to relieve the *Lawrence*, by "engaging their opponents, as designated in previous orders."[1] At the same time the *Queen Charlotte* felt the breeze, and leaving her place in the enemy's line, she bore down and brought her entire battery, long guns and carronades, to bear on the *Lawrence*.[2] Perceiving this movement of the *Queen Charlotte*, and considering the existing state of affairs as a sufficient justification for assuming the authority to do so, Commander Elliott hailed the *Caledonia*, and ordered Lieutenant Turner to bear up and let the *Niagara* pass her to the assistance of the *Lawrence*.[3] "Without stopping to inquire whether Commander Elliott, a subordinate like himself, had a right to give an order involving a change in the order of battle,"[4] although it is evident that he had doubts on the subject, Lieutenant Turner put up his helm and made room for the *Niagara*,[5] which passed to windward of the *Caledonia*, and bore down for *the head of the enemy's line*,[1] the latter vessel at the same time bearing down and closing with the *Hunter*.[2]

This sudden and temporary breeze, trivial as it may appear to many, completely changed the current of passing events; and from that moment the scene changed. Both squadrons taking the breeze at the same time, and both drawing slowly ahead,[3] the *Lawrence* entirely unmanageable, as has been shown, gradually dropped astern, and the battle as steadily passed ahead of her.[4] From this cause, while the *Caledonia* passed to her leeward, while bearing down to close with the *fourth* vessel in the enemy's line, the *Niagara* was obliged, in bearing down on the *head* of that line, to pass to the windward of the *Lawrence*, at a few yards' distance,[5] receiving and returning, as she bore

---

[1] Midship. Nichols to Capt. Elliott, Jan. 22, 1821; Boatswain Berry's Affidavit, May 14, 1821; Midship. Montgomery's Test., April 25, 1815.—[2] Lieut. Montgomery to Capt. Elliott, Feb. 11, 1821; Boatswain Berry's Affidavit, May 14, 1821; Lieut. Smith to Gen. Stansbury, Oct. 16; Cooper's Nav. Hist., ii. p. 191. Mr. Calvert (*Oration*, p. 11) supposes this was done at *half-past twelve;* and Mr. Burgess (p. 40) and Mr. Mackenzie (*Biog. of Perry*, i. p. 236) appear to sustain him. As the *enemy's* accounts of the battle agree with those of the authorities cited, I have preferred their statements.—[3] Lieut. Webster's, Midshipmen Montgomery and Cummings', and Capt. Brevoort's Test.; Lieut. Montgomery to Capt. Elliott, Feb. 11, 1821; Boatswain Berry's Affidavit, May 14, 1821; Officers of the *Niagara* to Sec. of Navy, Oct. 13, 1813; Purser Magrath to Erie *Sentinel;* Com. Elliott's Speech, p. 7; Cooper's Nav. Hist., ii. p. 191; Mackenzie's Perry, i. p. 235.—[4] Mackenzie's Perry, i. p. 235.

[5] Lieut. Webster's Test.; Lieut. Montgomery to Capt. Elliott, Feb. 11, 1821; Officers of the *Niagara* to Sec. of Navy, Oct. 13; Com. Elliott's Speech, p. 7.

[1] Lieut. Webster's and Midshipmen Montgomery and Adams' Test.; Midship. Nichols to Capt. Elliott, Jan. 22, 1821; Boatswain Berry's Affidavit, May 14, 1821; Parsons, p. 11; McAfee, p. 357; Elliott's Speech, p. 7; Cooper's Nav. Hist., ii. p. 191. Com. Perry (*Dispatch, Sept.* 13, 1813) says he "was enabled to bring his vessel, the *Niagara*, gallantly into close action."

[2] Com. Perry's Dispatch, Sept. 13; Parsons, p. 11; Cooper's Nav. Hist., ii. p. 191.—[3] Cooper's Nav. Hist., ii. p. 191.—[4] Lieut. Webster's Test.; Calvert, p. 13; Burgess, p. 45; Officers of the *Niagara* to Sec. of Navy, Oct. 13; Purser Magrath to Erie *Sentinel;* James' Nav. Occur., p. 288; Cooper's Nav. Hist., ii. p. 191; Lieut. Smith to Gen. Stansbury, Oct. 16.

[5] Lieut. Webster (*Test., April* 25, 1815) says "*it did not exceed thirty yards;*" Midship. Montgomery (*Test.*), "*at about twenty-five yards' distance;*" Master's-mate Tatem (*Test.*), at "very little more than room enough to pass to windward;" Capt. Brevoort (*Affidavit, Nov.* 7, 1818) says, "coming *near the Lawrence*, a boat was discovered," &c.; Boatswain Berry (*Affidavit, May* 14, 1821) says, "*within twenty or thirty yards;*" Com. Elliott (*Speech*, p. 7) says, "*within twenty yards of the Lawrence.*"

Painted by W. H. Powell.

Engraved by T. Phillibrown.

BATTLE OF LAKE ERIE

down, a heavy fire from the *Detroit*, the *Chippewa*, the *Lady Prevost*, and the *Queen Charlotte*.[1]

It was at this moment, while the *Niagara* was passing the *Lawrence*, that the well-known transfer of the flag from the latter to the former brig took place. Commander Perry, perceiving that his own ship had become entirely useless, and no longer able to keep up with the current of the action, as it was gradually moving towards the southward and westward, determined to leave the *Lawrence* and go on board the *Niagara*, which was then passing towards the head of the enemy's line.[2] Accordingly he lowered his battle-flag—the blue burgee already referred to—and taking it,[3] with his young brother, Midshipman J. Alexander Perry,[4] he passed over the weather-gangway of the *Lawrence*, entered his cutter, and directed his course towards the *Niagara*. During the time which was occupied in this celebrated trip, the *Niagara* was steadily and "gallantly"[5] bearing down on the enemy; and the boat's-crew was compelled to pursue her, all the time exposed to the fire of the heaviest ships in the enemy's line.[1] The zealous young Commander, actuated by the most commendable motives, thirsting for that honest renown which he so quickly secured, and disregarding the danger with which he was threatened, had determined "*if a victory was to be gained, to gain it*,"[2] and standing erect in his boat,[3] he urged his crew to give way cheerily.[4] With the rising breeze the headway of the *Niagara* increased, and for fifteen minutes the oarsmen labored steadily in the pursuit.[5] At length, passing under the stern of the *Niagara*, he came alongside, and went on board by her weather-gangway.[6]

It is said that Commander Perry, when he reached the deck of the *Niagara*, expressed some fears concerning the final result of the action, and great dissatisfaction with the failure of the small vessels to come into action.[7] For the purpose of restoring the fortunes of the day, if possible, Commander Elliott immediately volunteered to take the cutter in which Commander Perry had just passed from the *Lawrence*, to pass up the line, and bring the small vessels forward,[8] declaring, at the same time,

---

1 Midship. Montgomery's and Lieut. Webster's Test.; Lieut. Montgomery to Capt. Elliott, Feb. 11, 1821; Lieut. Cummings' Affidavit, Nov. 25, 1818; Dr. R. Barton's Affidavit, April 24, 1821; Officers of the *Niagara* to Sec. of Navy, Oct. 13; Lieut. Smith to Gen. Stansbury, Oct. 16.

2 Lieuts. Webster, Yarnall, and Forrest's, Midshipmen Montgomery, Adams, and Cummings' Test.; Lieut. Forrest to M. C. Perry, Jan. 29, 1821; Lieut. Brownell's, Sailing-master Taylor's, Capt. Brevoort's, and Lieuts. Adams and Cummings' Affidavits; Calvert, p. 12; Parsons p 11; Burgess, pp. 43, 44; Mackenzie's Perry, i. pp. 243–246; Elliott's Speech, p. 7; James Webster to *Evening Post*, March 11, 1843; Cooper's Nav. Hist., ii. p. 191.

3 Burgess, p. 43; Armstrong's Notices, i. p. 169; Christie, p. 132; McAfee, p. 357; Irving's Perry; Letter from the *Hunter*, Sept. 24.—4 Mr. Cooper, in Graham's *Magazine*, May, 1843.—5 Com. Perry's Dispatch, Sept. 13.

---

1 Sailing-master Taylor's Affidavit; Mackenzie's Perry, i. p. 245; Burgess, p. 44.—2 Lieut. Forrest to M. C. Perry, Jan. 29, 1821.—3 Sailing-master Taylor's Affidavit; Mackenzie's Perry, i. p. 245; Burgess, p. 44; Calvert, p. 12.

4 Mackenzie's Perry, i. p. 245.—5 Ibid., i. pp. 245, 246.

6 Midship. Montgomery's Testimony.

7 Capt. Brevoort's Affidavit, Nov. 7, 1818; Lieuts. Adams and Cummings' Affidavits, Nov. 25, 1818; Boatswain Berry's Affidavit, May 14, 1821; Biog. of Elliott, p. 34; Officers of the *Niagara* to Sec. of Navy, Oct. 13; Capt. Brevoort to Maj. Swearingen, Nov. 1, 1813; Lieut. Cummings to Capt. Elliott, Nov. 22, 1818.

8 Com. Perry's Dispatch, Sept. 13; Capt. Brevoort's Affidavit, Nov. 7, 1818; Midship. Nichols to Capt. Elliott, Jan. 22, 1821; Lieuts. Adams and Cummings' Affi-

that the case was not as hopeless as the latter had supposed.[1] In this proposal Commander Elliott "anticipated the wish" of Commander Perry;[2] and, leaving the *Niagara* in charge of Commander Perry, he entered the cutter, "passed along the line of small vessels, hailed each as he passed, ordered them to cease firing, to get out their sweeps, to close with and fire upon the *large* ships of the enemy; and then, returning along the line of small vessels, he went on board the *Somers*, and bore up with all possible dispatch."[3]

As the *Niagara* was bearing down upon *the head of the enemy's line* when Commander Perry took the command of her, it does not appear that he changed her course, or issued any order farther than was necessary to take her more to leeward, in order that, instead of running to the *head of the line*, she might be taken *alongside the Detroit and the Queen Charlotte*, in which case the *Chippewa* and *Lady Prevost*, which were at some distance ahead of the former, would necessarily be separated from their consorts and left to windward of the *Niagara*. With the greatest gallantry, therefore, Commander Perry directed the *Niagara*, under foresail, topsails, and topgallant-sails, into the midst of the enemy's line, dividing it, and throwing her fire on either hand as she went.[1] The *Chippewa* and the *Lady Prevost*, as before stated, were separated from the main body of the enemy, and received the larboard broadside of the *Niagara*, at half-pistol-shot distance; while the *Detroit* and the *Queen Charlotte*—which in attempting to wear had got foul of each other—and the *Hunter*, at the same time and at the same distance, were favored with her starboard guns.[2] Having passed under the bows of the enemy's flag-ship (*the Detroit*), the *Niagara* appears to have come to the wind on the starboard tack, with her head to the northward and eastward;[3] and with her starboard guns she opened a terribly effective raking fire on the two ships which lay foul of each other;[4] while with her stern chasers she threw in an occasional shot on the *Lady Prevost* and the *Chippewa*, which she had cut off from their line.[5]

At the same time the *Caledonia*, which had closed with the *Hunter*,[6] and the small vessels which had come up, under the orders which they had received through Commander Elliott,[7] were pouring a cross-fire into the enemy's line, while the *Ariel* and the *Scorpion* continued to throw in an equally

davits, Nov. 25, 1818; Boatswain Berry's Affidavit, May 14, 1821; Biog. of Elliott, p. 34; Officers of the *Niagara* to Sec. of Navy, Oct. 13.

[1] Lieuts. Adams and Cummings' Affidavits, Nov. 25, 1818.—[2] Com. Perry's Dispatch, Sept. 13.

[3] Biog. of Elliott, p. 34. See also Lieuts. Webster and Yarnall's, and Midship. Montgomery's Test., April, 1815; Midship. Nichols to Capt. Elliott, Jan. 22, 1821; Lieut. Conklin's Affid.; McAfee, p. 358; Lieut. Page to Capt. Elliott, May 20, 1821; Lieut. Adams' Affidavit, Nov. 25, 1818; Cooper's Nav. Hist., ii. p. 191; Com. Perry's Dispatch, Sept. 13, 1813; Elliott's Speech, pp. 7, 8.

[1] Lieut. Yarnall's Test.; Sailing-master Taylor's Affid.; Cooper's Nav. Hist., ii. p. 192.—[2] Com. Perry's Dispatch, Sept. 13; Capt. Elliott's Speech, p. 8; McAfee, p. 358; Calvert, p. 13; Cooper's Nav. Hist., ii. p. 192.

[3] Burgess, p. 46; Diagram No. 3 of the action, in Graham's *Magazine*, May, 1843; Cooper's Nav. Hist., ii. p. 192; Irving's Biography of Perry.—[4] Burgess, p. 46; Cooper's Nav. Hist., ii. p. 192; Mackenzie's Perry, i. p. 252.—[5] Cooper's Nav. Hist., ii. p. 192; Mackenzie's Perry, i. p. 252.—[6] Vide p. 282, col. 2, note 2.

[7] Vide p. 284, col. 1, note 3.

effective cross-fire on the *Chippewa*, the *Lady Prevost*, and the *Detroit*, from the extreme left of the American line.

While the current of the engagement was thus setting in favor of the Americans, the shattered hulk of the *Lawrence*—glorious in its helplessness—was falling to leeward, like a veteran who has performed his part of the service and been relieved from active duty. The remnant of her gallant crew, not a dozen in number,[1] had witnessed the departure of their commander, and had anxiously watched his passage to the *Niagara*:[2] one by one her guns had been deprived of their crews and rendered unfit for further service:[3] her berth-deck, exposed to the enemy's fire, was crowded with the shattered forms of more than sixty of her crew; and her youthful surgeon's-mate, on whom the heavy responsibility of their treatment had fallen, was busy relieving their immediate necessities, amidst the occasional intrusion of a round-shot from one of the enemy's vessels;[4] and her carefully sanded decks, now slippery with the gore of the fallen ones, no longer afforded a secure foothold to those who trod them:[5] yet, battle-scathed as she was, her colors still floated at her peak, and, like a regenerated conscience, held in check the rising distrust of her officers and crew. But the steady fire of the enemy on the defenceless and unopposing brig forced the feeble band, unwillingly, to take counsel of each other, and to entertain an idea of surrendering. Under the discretionary powers with which Commander Perry had vested Lieutenant Yarnall when he stepped into the cutter,[1] therefore, a brief consultation was held on the quarter-deck; and in order to prevent an unnecessary sacrifice of life, the surviving officers resolved to strike their colors.[2] In the midst of the most enthusiastic cheers of the enemy's crews, therefore, the colors of the flag-ship were lowered;[3] and the important part which the *Lawrence* performed in this interesting drama closed.

In the mean time the action continued between the *Niagara*, the *Caledonia*, and the smaller American vessels, on the one side, and the entire strength of the enemy, on the other; and within half an hour after Commander Perry took the command of the *Niagara*,[4] an officer appeared on the taffrail of the *Queen Charlotte* to signify that she had surrendered; and, within a few minutes, all the enemy's line, except the *Little Belt* and *Chippewa*, on the extremes of the line, followed her example.[5] These, making sail, attempted to escape to leeward; but, after a chase of an hour, they were overtaken by the *Scorpion* and the *Trippe*, and brought back to their proper places among the trophies of the victor.[6]

The *Lawrence*, floating helplessly on

[1] Of her crew, only ten remained who were not killed or wounded.—[2] Mackenzie's Perry, i. p. 247.

[3] Ibid., p. 237.—[4] Parsons, pp. 11, 13; Mackenzie's Perry, i. p. 238.—[5] Mackenzie's Perry, i. pp. 226, 254; Parsons, p. 14.

[1] Lieut. Yarnall's Test.; Mackenzie's Perry, i. p. 247.

[2] Mackenzie's Perry, i. p. 247; Cooper's Nav. Hist., ii. p. 191.—[3] Parsons, p. 11; Cooper's Nav. Hist., ii. p. 191; Irving's Perry; Mackenzie's Perry, i. p. 248.

[4] Lieuts. Webster and Yarnall's Test.—[5] Cooper's Nav. Hist., ii. p. 192; Mackenzie's Perry, i. p. 253.

[6] Com. Perry's Dispatch, Sept. 13, 1813; McAfee, p. 358; Burgess, p. 46; Mackenzie's Perry, i. pp. 253, 254.

the waters, by this result was relieved from the unpleasant position into which, as a prize to the enemy, she had fallen; and, with the fall of the enemy's colors, her own—on which her surrender had imposed no stain or taint of dishonor—again floated at her masthead.[1]

Immediately afterwards the victors began the discharge of their final duty—that of taking possession of their prizes and of receiving the formal surrender of their commanders. The former, satisfactory as it must have been, was not unalloyed, when the severe loss which the enemy had sustained was seen; the latter was a fitting finale of the events which have been referred to; and it consummated the glory which clusters around the quarter-deck of the *Lawrence*, on which, with delicate propriety, the young conqueror received the swords of his gallant opponents.[2]

In this engagement—the first in which an American squadron had been a party since Benedict Arnold, on Lake Champlain, opposed the progress of General Carleton in 1776[3]—the relative strength of the opposing forces has been already noticed.[4] Of the enemy, Commander Finnis of the *Queen Charlotte*, Lieutenant Gordon of the marine force, and Lieutenant Garland of the *Detroit*, and thirty-eight men were *killed;* and Commander Barclay, the senior officer of the squadron, First-lieutenant Stokoe and Midshipman Foster of the *Queen Charlotte*, Lieutenant-commandant Buchan and First-lieutenant Roulette of the *Lady Prevost*, Lieutenant-commandant Bignall and Master's-mate Gateshill of the *Hunter*, Master's-mate Campbell, commanding the *Chippewa*, Purser Hoffmeister of the *Detroit*, and eighty-five men were *wounded:*[1] while in the American vessels, Lieutenant Brooks, Midshipmen Laub and Clark, Quartermaster Mayhew, Boatswain's-mate White and twenty-two men were *killed;* and Lieutenants Yarnall, Forrest, and Edwards, Sailing-master Taylor, Purser Hambleton, Midshipmen Claxton, Swartwout, and Cummings, Carpenter Stone, and eighty-seven men *wounded;* of whom eighty-three were on the *Lawrence*, twenty-seven on the *Niagara*, three on the *Caledonia*, two on the *Somers*, four on the *Ariel*, two on the *Trippe*, and two on the *Scorpion.*[2]

As the intelligence of this victory was carried through the country, the most extravagant expressions of delight were everywhere displayed; and Commander Perry was hailed as the savior of the Northwest. Salutes, and illuminations, and public meetings gave evidence of the popular sentiment; and it is said "the general joy was unequalled since the surrender of Cornwallis at Yorktown."[3]

But not alone from its effects on the affairs of the nation was this action memorable. In the language of one of the most eminent of our cotemporaries,[4] "were any thing wanting to perpetuate

[1] Parsons, p. 13; Cooper's Nav. Hist., ii. p. 192; Mackenzie's Perry, i. p. 253.—[2] Mackenzie's Perry, i. pp. 254, 263, 264; Calvert, p. 15; Parsons, p. 14.
[3] Vide Book I., Chap. XIII.—[4] Vide p. 276.

[1] Reports appended to Com. Barclay's Dispatches.
[2] Reports appended to Com. Perry's Dispatches.
[3] Mackenzie's Perry, ii. p. 11.
[4] Washington Irving.

the fame of this victory, it would be sufficiently memorable from the scene where it was fought. The war had been distinguished by new and peculiar characteristics. Naval warfare had been carried into the interior of a continent; and navies, as if by magic, launched from among the depths of the forest. The bosoms of peaceful lakes which, but a short time before, were scarcely navigated by man, except to be skimmed by the light canoe of the savage, had all at once been ploughed by hostile ships. The vast silence, that had reigned for ages on those mighty waters, was broken by the thunder of artillery; and the affrighted savage stared with amazement from his covert at the sudden apparition of a sea-fight amid the solitudes of the wilderness."

Time and the angry disputes—unworthy of the subject—to which this event has given rise, have failed in their usual effects, and at the present day, not less than in the fall of 1813, the names of Perry and the *Lawrence* are on every tongue. The historian of that day spake not more enthusiastically of the glory of the achievement than is *our* privilege; and, with him, we can say, with honest pride, that "in future times, when the shores of Lake Erie shall hum with busy population; when towns and cities shall brighten where now extend the dark and tangled forest; when ports shall spread their arms, and lofty barks shall ride where now the canoe is fastened to the stake; when the present age shall have grown into venerable antiquity, and the mists of fable begin to gather around its history; then will the inhabitants of the mighty West look back to this battle, which we have recorded, as one of the romantic achievements of the days of yore. It will stand first on the page of their local legends, and in the marvellous tales of the borders. The fisherman, as he loiters along the beach, will point to some half-buried cannon, half corroded with the rust of time, and will speak of ocean warriors who came from the shores of the Atlantic; while the boatman, as he trims his sail to the breeze, will chant, in rude ditties, the name of Perry, the early hero of Lake Erie."

DOCUMENTS.

I.

COMMODORE PERRY'S DISPATCH TO THE SECRETARY OF THE NAVY.

U. S. SCHOONER ARIEL, PUT-IN-BAY,
September 13, 1813.

SIR:—In my last I informed you that we had captured the enemy's fleet on this lake. I have now the honor to give you the most important particulars of the action. On the morning of the tenth instant, at sunrise, they were discovered from Put-in-Bay, where I lay at anchor with the squadron under my command. We got under weigh, the wind light at southwest, and stood for them. At ten A. M. the wind hauled to southeast, and brought us to windward; formed the line and bore up. At fifteen minutes before twelve the enemy commenced firing; at five minutes before twelve the action commenced on our part. Finding their fire very destructive, owing to their long guns, and it being mostly directed at the *Lawrence*, I made sail and directed the other vessels to follow, for the purpose of closing with the enemy. Every brace and bowline being soon shot away, she became unmanageable, notwithstanding the great exertions of the sailing-master. In this situation she sustained the action upwards of two hours within canister-distance, until every gun was rendered useless, and the greater part of her crew either killed or wounded. Finding she could no longer annoy the enemy, I left her in charge of Lieutenant Yarnall, who, I was convinced, from the bravery already displayed by him, would do what would comport with the honor of the flag. At half-past two, the wind springing up, Captain Elliott was enabled to bring his vessel, the *Niagara*, gallantly into close action. I immediately went on board of her, when he anticipated my wish by volunteering to bring the schooners, which had been kept astern by the lightness of the wind, into close action. It was with unspeakable pain that I saw, soon after I got on board the *Niagara*, the flag of the *Lawrence* come down, although I was perfectly sensible she had been defended to the last, and that to have continued to make a show of resistance would have been a wanton sacrifice of the remains of her brave crew. But the enemy was not able to take possession of her, and circumstances soon permitted her flag again to be hoisted. At forty-five minutes past two the signal was made for close action. The *Niagara* being very little injured, I determined to pass through the enemy's line; bore up, and passed ahead of their two ships and a brig, giving a raking fire to them from the starboard guns, and to a large schooner and sloop from the larboard side, at half pistol-shot distance. The smaller vessels, at this time having got within grape and canister distance, under the direction of Captain Elliott, and keeping up a well-directed fire, the two ships, a brig, and a schooner surrendered, a schooner and sloop making a vain attempt to escape.

Those officers and men who were immediately under my observation evinced the greatest gallantry, and I have no doubt that all others conducted themselves as became American officers and seamen. Lieutenant Yarnall, first of the *Lawrence*, although several times wounded, refused to quit the deck. Midshipman Forrest (doing duty as a lieutenant) and Sailing-master Taylor were of great assistance to me. I have great pain in stating to you the death of Lieutenant Brooks of the marines, and Midshipman Laub, both of the *Lawrence*, and Midshipman John Clark of the *Scorpion*: they were valuable and promising officers. Mr. Hambleton, purser, who volunteered his services on deck, was severely wounded late in the action. Midshipmen Claxton and Swartwout of the *Lawrence*, were severely wounded. On board the *Niagara*, Lieutenants Smith and Edwards, and Midshipman Webster (doing duty as sailing-master), behaved in a very handsome manner. Captain Brevoort of the army, who acted as a volunteer, in the capacity of a marine officer, on board that vessel, is an excellent and brave officer, and with his musketry did great execution. Lieutenant Turner, commanding the *Caledonia*, brought that vessel into action in the most able manner, and is an officer that in all situations may be relied on. The *Ariel*, Lieutenant Parker, and *Scorpion*, Sailing-master Champlin, were enabled to get early into action, and were of great service. Captain Elliott speaks in the highest terms of Mr. Magrath, purser, who had been dispatched in a boat on service, previous to my getting on board the *Niagara*; and being a seaman, since the action has rendered essential service, in taking charge of one of the prizes. Of Captain Elliott, already so well known to the government, it would be almost superfluous to speak. In this action he evinced his characteristic bravery and judgment; and since the close of the action has given me the most able and essential assistance.

I have the honor to inclose you a return of the killed and wounded, together with a statement of the relative force of the squadrons. The captain and first-lieutenant of the *Queen Charlotte*, and first-lieutenant of the *Detroit*, were killed. Captain Barclay, senior officer, and the commander of the *Lady Prevost*, severely wounded. The commanders of the *Hunter* and *Chippewa* slightly wounded. Their loss in killed and wounded I have not yet been able to ascertain; it must, however, have been very great.

Very respectfully,

O. H. Perry.

Hon. Wm. Jones, Secretary of the Navy.

II.

COMMANDER BARCLAY TO SIR JAMES L. YEO.

H. M. late Ship Detroit, Put-in-Bay,
Lake Erie, *Sept.* 12, 1813.

Sir:—The last letter I had the honor of writing to you, dated the sixth instant, I informed you, that unless certain intimation was received of more seamen being on their way to Amherstburg, I should be obliged to sail with the squadron, deplorably manned as it was, to fight the enemy (who blockaded the port), to enable us to get supplies of provisions and stores of every description. So perfectly destitute of provisions was the post, that there was not a day's flour in store, and the crews of the squadron under my command were on half allowance of many things, and when that was done there was no more. Such were the motives which induced Major-general Proctor (whom, by your instructions, I was directed to consult, and whose wishes I was enjoined to execute, as far as related to the good of the country) to concur in the necessity of a battle being risked, under the many disadvantages which I labored; and it now remains to me, the most melancholy task, to relate to you the unfortunate issue of the battle, as well as the many untoward circumstances that led to that event.

No intelligence of seamen having arrived, I sailed on the ninth instant, fully expecting to meet the enemy next morning, as they had been seen among the islands; nor was I mistaken. Soon after daylight, they were seen in motion in Put-in-Bay, the wind then southwest, and light, giving us the weather-gage. I bore up for them, in hopes of bringing them to action among the islands; but that intention was soon frustrated by the wind suddenly shifting to the southeast, which brought the enemy directly to windward.

The line was formed according to a given plan, so that each ship might be supported against the superior force of the two brigs opposed to them. About ten, the enemy cleared the islands, and immediately bore up, under sail, in a line abreast, each brig being also supported by the small vessels. At a quarter-before twelve, I commenced the action, by firing a few long guns; about quarter-past, the American Commodore, also supported by two schooners, one carrying four long twelve-pounders, the other a long thirty-two and twenty-four pounder, came to close action with the *Detroit;* the other brig of the enemy, apparently destined to engage the *Queen Charlotte*, supported in like manner by two schooners, kept so far to windward as to render the *Queen Charlotte's* twenty-four-pound carronades useless, while she was, with the *Lady Prevost*, exposed to the heavy and destructive fire of the *Caledonia*, and four other schooners, armed with long and heavy guns like those I have already described.

Too soon, alas! was I deprived of the service of the noble and intrepid Captain Finnis, who, soon after the commencement of the action, fell; and with him fell my greatest support. Soon after, Lieutenant Stokes, of the *Queen Charlotte*, was struck senseless by a splinter, which deprived the country of his services at this very critical period. As I perceived the *Detroit* had enough to contend with, without the prospect of a fresh brig: Provincial-lieutenant Irvine, who then had charge of the *Queen Charlotte*, behaved with great courage; but his experience was much too limited to supply the place of such an officer as Captain Finnis, hence she proved of far less assistance than I expected.

The action continued with great fury until half-past two, when I perceived my opponent drop astern, and a boat passing from him to the *Niagara* (which vessel, at this time, was perfectly fresh); the American Commodore, seeing that as yet that the day was against him (his vessel having struck soon after he left her), and also the very defenceless state of the *Detroit*, which ship was now a perfect wreck, principally from the raking fire of the gunboats, and also that the *Queen Charlotte* was in such a situation that I could receive very little assistance from her, and the *Lady Prevost* being at this time too far to leeward, from her rudder being injured, made a noble, and, alas! too successful an effort to regain it, for he bore up, and, supported by his small vessels, passed within pistol-shot, and took a raking position on our bow; nor could I prevent it, as the unfortunate situation of the *Queen Charlotte* prevented us from wearing. In attempting, we fell on board her. My gallant First-lieutenant Garland was now mortally wounded, and myself severely, that I was obliged to quit the deck. Manned as the squadron was, with not more than fifty British seamen, the rest a mixed crew of Canadians and soldiers, and who were totally unacquainted with such service, rendered the loss of officers more sensibly felt, and never, in any action, was the loss more severe, every officer commanding vessels, and their seconds, were either killed or wounded so severely as to be unable to keep the deck.

Lieutenant Buchan, in the *Lady Prevost*, behaved most nobly, and did every thing that a brave and experienced officer could do, in a vessel armed with twelve-pound carronades, against vessels carrying long guns. I regret to state that he was severely wounded. Lieutenant Bignall, of the *Dover*, commanding the *Hunter*, displayed the greatest intrepidity; but his guns being small (two, four, and six pounders), he could be of much less service than he wished.

Every officer in the *Detroit* behaved in the most exemplary manner. Lieutenant Inglis showed such calm intrepidity, that I was fully convinced that, on leaving deck, I left the ship in excellent hands; and for an account of the battle after that, I refer you to his letter which he wrote to me for your information.

Mr. Hoffmeister, purser of the *Detroit*, nobly volunteered his services on deck, and behaved in a manner that reflects the highest honor on him. I regret to add, that he is very severely wounded in the knee.

Provincial-lieutenant Purvis, and the military officers, Lieutenants Gordon of the Royal Newfoundland Rangers, and O'Keefe of the Forty-first regiment, behaved in a manner that excited my warmest admiration. The few British seamen I had, behaved with their usual intrepidity; and, as long as I was on deck, the troops behaved with a calmness and courage worthy of a more fortunate issue to their exertions.

The weather-gage gave the enemy a prodigious advantage, as it enabled them to not only choose their position, but their distance also, which they did in such a manner as to prevent the carronades of the *Queen Charlotte* and *Lady Prevost* from having much effect, while their long guns did great execution, particularly against the *Queen Charlotte*.

Captain Perry has behaved in a most humane and attentive manner, not only to myself and officers, but to all the wounded.

I trust that, although unsuccessful, you will approve of the motives that induced me to sail under so many disadvantages, and that it may be hereafter proved that, under such circumstances, the honor of His Majesty's flag has not been tarnished.

I inclose the list of killed and wounded.

I have the honor to be, &c.,

R. H. Barclay,

Commander and late senior officer.

Sir James Lucas Yeo, &c., &c.

III.

LIEUTENANT INGLIS TO COMMANDER BARCLAY.

H. M. late Ship Detroit, *Sept.* 10, 1813.

Sir:—I have the honor to transmit to you an account of the termination of the late unfortunate battle with the enemy's squadron.

On coming on the quarter-deck, after your being wounded, the enemy's second brig, at that time on our weather-beam, shortly afterwards took a position on our weather-bow, to rake us; to prevent which, in attempting to wear, to get our starboard broadside to bear upon her, a number of the guns of the larboard broadside being at this time disabled, fell on board the *Queen Charlotte*, at this time running up to leeward of us. In this situation the two ships remained for some time.

As soon as we got clear of her, I ordered the *Queen Charlotte* to shoot ahead of us, if possible, and attempted to back our fore-topsail, to get astern, but the ship lying completely unmanageable, every brace cut away, the mizzen-topmast and gaff down, all the other masts badly wounded, not a stay left forward, hull shattered very much, a number of the guns disabled, and the enemy's squadron raking both ships, ahead and astern, none of our own in a situation to support us, I was under the painful necessity of hailing the enemy, to say we had struck, the *Queen Charlotte* having previously done so.

I have the honor to be, &c.,

George Inglis.

To Captain Barclay.

CHAPTER LXIII.

October 5, 1813.

THE BATTLE OF THE THAMES.

THE victory on Lake Erie, to which reference has been made,[1] had secured to the Americans the command of that lake; and the occupation of Canada and the recovery of the territory of Michigan were the next steps which were proposed by the commander of the Northwestern army. For this purpose the most ample preparations were made by General Harrison.

In the prosecution of this design, the small vessels of the squadron[2]—the smaller prizes as well as the American vessels—were employed in transporting the troops, under General Harrison, to Put-in-Bay;[3] thence, on the twenty-first, to a small island,—known as the "Eastern Sister," distant four leagues from Malden,—on the Canadian shore;[4] and thence, on the afternoon of the twenty-seventh of September, to the mainland, at a point about three miles below Amherstburg, where it landed at three o'clock;[5] from which place, on the same day, it marched to Malden, and occupied it without opposition.[1]

General Proctor, with the troops under his command, before the arrival of the Americans, had destroyed the fort, navy-yard, barracks, and extensive public store-houses, and had fled to Sandwich, taking with him upward of one thousand horses, of which the Americans were entirely destitute.[2] The force under General Proctor, on the morning of the battle, embraced four hundred and eight men of the Forty-first regiment; six field-pieces, with thirty men of the Royal Artillery, and thirty-eight provincial dragoons; besides which, an officer and one hundred and forty-three men of the Forty-first, and thirty men from the Royal Veteran Battalion, were with the batteaux; one hundred and one invalids in the hospital, with sixty-three attendants, all from the Forty-first regiment, were at the Moravian village; and a large body of Indians, under the command of Tecumthà, also accompanied him in his retreat.[3]

Leaving Colonel Smith at Amherstburg to occupy that position with a

---

[1] Vide Chap. LXII.—[2] The *Lawrence* had been sent to Erie with the wounded; and the *Detroit* and *Queen Charlotte*, dismasted, were moored in Put-in-Bay.—Vide *Com. Perry to Sec. of Navy, Sept.* 13, 1813.—[3] Com. Perry to Sec. of Navy, Sept. 20, 1813.—[4] Ibid., Sept. 24, 1813; James' Military Occurrences, i. p. 272.

[5] Gen. Harrison to Sec. of War, Sept. 27, 1813. There appears to be considerable confusion respecting the date of this movement—Christie, Rogers, and several others, supposing it occurred on the *twenty-third*, and in some instances Gen. Harrison's dispatch of the 27th has been dated "*Sept.* 23, 1813."

[1] Com. Perry to Sec. of Navy, Sept. 27, 1813; James' Mil. Occur., i. p. 274.—[2] Gen. Harrison to Sec. of War, Sept. 23; Gen. McArthur to Sec. of War, Oct. 6; Ingersoll, i. p. 175.—[3] James' Mil. Occur., i. p. 278. The number of these Indians is variously stated at from 800 to 1500.

regiment of riflemen, on the twenty-eighth, General Harrison moved to Sandwich,[1] although he appears to have had but little hope of overtaking his adversary;[2] and, after leaving General Cass's brigade and Lieutenant-colonel Ball's regiment at Sandwich,[3] and General McArthur, with his brigade,—seven hundred effective men,—to occupy Detroit,[4] on the second of October he continued the pursuit in the direction of the River Thames,[5] where it was supposed General Proctor intended to establish himself.[6] From various causes, after the delay at Sandwich, General Harrison was able to take with him "only about one hundred and forty of the regular troops, Colonel Richard M. Johnson's mounted regiment, and such of Governor Shelby's volunteers (*Kentuckians*) as were fit for a rapid march, the whole amounting to about three thousand five hundred men."[7]

While General Harrison was thus detained at Sandwich, General Proctor halted at Dalston's, on the right bank of the Thames, fifty-six miles from Detroit;[8] and, notwithstanding the small force which he commanded, he appears to have taken no steps to retard the progress of the American army, either by breaking down the bridges, obstructing the roads, or skirmishing with his Indians and light troops. On the contrary, as will be seen hereafter, the destruction of the bridges over impassable streams does not appear to have been thought of until after General Harrison had moved from Sandwich; and even at that late day the work was either unaccomplished or but imperfectly performed.

As before stated, on the second of October, General Harrison renewed the pursuit,—General Lewis Cass and Commander Perry accompanying him as volunteer aids,—and marched twenty-five miles, halting at the *Riscum*, one of the four streams which crossed his route, and emptied into the Thames. The bridge over this stream had not been broken; and as all these "rivers" were deep, muddy, and unfordable for a considerable distance up the country, it appears very remarkable that this fine opportunity to harass the progress of General Harrison should have been overlooked.[1]

On the morning of the third, fearing that General Proctor might perceive the singular neglect of duty, to which reference has been made, General Harrison pushed forward with Colonel Johnson's regiment of mounted Kentuckians,—a thousand strong,[2]—"to save, if possible, the other bridges." When the detachment reached the second bridge, a lieutenant and eleven dragoons were found there, and captured. They had been sent to destroy that pass; but had not fully accom-

[1] James' Mil. Occur., i. p. 274; Thomson's Sketches, p. 170; McAfee, pp. 373, 374.—[2] Gen. Harrison to Sec. of War, Sept. 27, 1813. Mr. Smith (*Life and Times of Gen. Cass*, p. 74) strangely maintains that Gen. Harrison entertained "no such opinion or fear."—[3] Gen. Harrison to Sec. of War, Oct. 9; James, i. p. 275; McAfee, p. 382.

[4] Gen. McArthur to Sec. of War, Oct. 6; James, i. p. 275; McAfee, p. 381.—[5] Gen. Harrison to Sec. of War, Oct. 9; Sketches of War, p. 172; James, i. p. 275.

[6] Gen. Harrison to Secretary of War, Sept. 27, 1813.

[7] Ibid., Oct. 9.—[8] Ibid.; Perkins' History of War, p. 236; James, i. p. 275.

[1] Gen. Harrison to Sec. of War, Oct. 9; Thomson's Sketches, p. 170; McAfee, pp. 382, 383.

[2] Col. R. M. Johnson to Gen. Armstrong, Dec. 22, 1834.

plished it when they fell into the hands of the Kentuckians. The bridge, however, had been partially destroyed; but when the army came to it, it was speedily repaired, and after crossing the stream the army continued the pursuit, and encamped at Drake's farm, four miles from Dalston's, where Proctor had taken a position.[1]

The American army, in its pursuit, had been accompanied as far as Dalston's by a flotilla of batteaux and the small vessels of the squadron,—the line of march having been along the banks of the Thames, a fine stream, which was navigable for vessels of considerable burden,—but the character of the country on its banks having changed, above Dalston's, the vessels were left at that place, under a guard of one hundred and fifty men; and thenceforth the General "determined to trust to fortune and the bravery of his troops to effect the passage of the river."[2]

On the morning of the fourth the pursuit was continued; and General Proctor retired as rapidly as possible. When the American army had marched four miles,—having reached Chatham,—it came to the third of the impassable streams which have been referred to, over which was a partially-destroyed bridge, protected by a strong body of Indians, which had been stationed not only on the opposite bank of the stream, but also on that of the Thames. Supposing that these were but the advance-guard of the enemy, and that his main body was close at hand, the American army was halted and formed in order of battle; while Major Wood, with the two six-pounders, with which the army had been accompanied, were moved forward to cover the operations of the party who had been ordered to repair the bridge. A few shot from these field-pieces drove off the Indians, and two hours afterwards, the bridge having, meanwhile, been repaired, the pursuit was renewed.[1]

At McGregor's Mills, a mile beyond the last, was another bridge, which, like the former, had been removed and guarded by a strong force of Indians. To secure this pass before it could be wholly destroyed, Colonel Johnson and the mounted Kentuckians pushed forward; and, under a galling fire from the savages, they occupied and repaired it, with the loss of two men killed and three or four wounded. The army immediately crossed the stream and seized a house, near by, in which had been stored a considerable number of muskets. The enemy, when it became impossible to prevent the progress of the army, had set fire to this house, as well as to three vessels laden with arms and military stores, and to a distillery which had been filled with similar property. The house was preserved, but the vessels and the distillery, with a considerable portion of their contents, were destroyed.[2]

At an early hour on the fifth, the

---

[1] Gen. Harrison to Sec. of War, Oct. 9; Thomson's Sketches, pp. 170, 171; McAfee, pp. 383, 384; James, i. p. 276; Sketches of the War, p. 173.—[2] Gen. Harrison to Sec. of War, Oct. 9; James, i. p. 276; Sketches of the War, p. 173.

[1] Gen. Harrison to Sec. of War, Oct. 9; Thomson's Sketches, p. 171; Breckenridge, p. 182; McAfee, pp. 384–386.—[2] Gen. Harrison to Sec. of War, Oct. 9; McAfee, pp. 385, 386; Sketches of War, p. 173.

pursuit was renewed; in the course of which two gunboats and several batteaux, laden with provisions and ammunition, fell into the hands of the Americans. At an early hour in the afternoon the site of the encampment of the enemy's rear-guard, on the preceding night, was reached; when a detachment from Colonel Johnson's regiment was sent forward to obtain intelligence. The officer in command quickly sent information to the General that the enemy had formed across the line of march, a short distance in advance; and a wagoner, who was captured about the same time, not only confirmed the intelligence, but gave such farther information as enabled the General to form his order of battle in accordance with the requirements of the enemy's position.[1]

The route which the two armies had taken was on the banks of the Thames River (*Rivière La Tranche*); and at about two and a half miles from the Moravian Town, in the township of Orford, Canada West, General Proctor had formed his troops, and awaited the approach of the Americans who were pursuing him.[2] About two miles along the right bank of the Thames, parallel with it, and not more than two or three hundred yards distant from it, is a narrow swamp, the road, at the period in question, passing over this intervening strip of ground, through a beech-wood, which was incumbered with but little underbrush. Across this strip of high ground, at right angles with the road, with its right near the swamp, and its left on the river, the British line had been drawn up.[1] The detachment from the Forty-first regiment was on the left of the line, flanked by the river, while its right was in air, unless the Indians can be said to have formed the right wing. The Indians, under Tecumthà, were posted on the right of the regulars, forming an obtuse angle with the line, by which means they hoped to be better able to turn the flank of the assailants. A six-pounder enfiladed the road by which the Americans were advancing; and, as a reserve, the provincial dragoons were posted a little in the rear of the regulars.[2] Against this force the American army, numbering "something above three thousand" men, moved, in order of battle.[3] The front line embraced General Calmes' brigade of five hundred men, under Colonel Trotter, and extended from the road, on the right, to the swamp, on the left. One hundred and fifty yards in the rear of the first line, and flanked, also, by the road and the swamp, was General King's brigade; while still farther in the rear, flanked in the same manner, General Chiles' brigade formed a reserve. These three brigades were under the command of General Henry; while two other brigades, under General Deshaw, were formed, *en potence*, upon the left of the front line, to hold the Indians in check,

[1] Gen. Harrison to Sec. of War, Oct. 9; McAfee, pp. 386-388.—[2] Gen. Harrison to Sec. of War, Oct. 9; Smith's Canada, i. p. 29.

[1] Gen. Harrison to Sec. of War, Oct. 9; McAfee, p. 388; Sketches of War, p. 174; James, i. p. 279; Perkins, p. 238; Col. R. M. Johnson to Gen. Armstrong, Dec. 22, 1834.

[2] McAfee, p. 388; James, i. p. 279; Armstrong's Notices, i. pp. 171, 172; Rogers' Rise of Canada, i. p. 232; Col. R. M. Johnson to Gen. Armstrong, Dec. 22, 1834.

[3] Gen. Harrison to Sec. of War, Oct. 9.

and to prevent them from falling on the left of the line. In front of all these, the mounted riflemen under Colonel Richard M. Johnson, who had been in the advance, were formed in two columns, with its right at the distance of fifty yards from the road, and its left on the swamp; while on the right of the column, between the road and the river, were about one hundred and twenty men from the Twenty-seventh regiment, who, under Colonel Paul, had been formed into column of sections of four, with its right on the river.[1] At the head of the columns of mounted men were their Colonel, Richard M. Johnson, and his brother James, the Lieutenant-colonel of the regiment; at the *crotchet* formed by General Desha's command and the front column, at the head of his troops, the venerable Governor of Kentucky (*Shelby*), then sixty-six years of age, took his position; while at the head of the regulars, between the road and the river, surrounded by his aids, the Acting-assistant-adjutant-general Butler, Commander Perry, the hero of Lake Erie, and General Lewis Cass, sat General Harrison.[2] In this order the armies were formed—the British and their dusky allies awaiting the attack; the Americans moving forward to the assault with coolness and decision.

When the head of the right column of Colonel Johnson's regiment came within musket-shot of the enemy's line, a heavy fire was thrown into it, and the horses in the front line recoiled.

[1] Gen. Harrison to Sec. of War, Oct. 9; McAfee, pp. 389, 390; Armstrong, i. p. 172; James, i. p. 280.

[2] Gen. Harrison to Sec. of War, Oct. 9; McAfee, p. 390.

A second fire soon followed, but the gallant Kentuckians having got in motion, the column immediately dashed through the line, and within a minute the action, *in front*, was ended. The first line of the enemy, unacquainted with the novel mode of conducting an engagement which had been brought against them, was thrown into the greatest disorder. The second line, about thirty yards in the rear of the former, after giving a scattering fire, also gave way, and on every part of the line the utmost confusion prevailed. In the mean time, while this disorder prevailed, the column of horsemen had gained the rear of the line, when it wheeled to the right and left, threw a destructive fire into the rear of the broken ranks of the enemy, and produced that perfect terror which no authority could overcome. The entire force, paralyzed with fear, threw down its arms, and, on the right, the battle was ended before Colonel Trotter's troops, in the first line, could join in the conflict.[1]

While this great measure of success attended the first battalion of Kentuckians, under Lieutenant-colonel James Johnson and Major Payne, in its opposition to the *British* line, the second battalion, led by Colonel Richard M. Johnson and Major Thompson, which had been opposed to the *Indians*, in front of Governor Shelby's division, was opposed with greater vigor and determination. Under the command of

[1] Gen. Harrison to Sec. of War, Oct. 9; McAfee, p. 391; Rogers' Canada, i. p. 232; Armstrong, i. pp. 173, 174; Col. R. M. Johnson to Gen. Armstrong, Dec. 22, 1834; Christie, p. 135; Perkins' Annals of the West, p. 636; James, i. pp. 281, 282; Sketches of the War, p. 175.

Tecumthà, the Indians coolly reserved their fire until the head of the column had come within a few paces of their position, when it was opened with very great effect. Nearly the entire advanced guard was cut down by it, and Colonel Johnson, the commander of the regiment, was very severely wounded. The ground which the Kentuckians occupied being unfavorable for operations on horseback, the Colonel immediately ordered his men to dismount; and, for a period of seven or eight minutes, the rifles of Kentucky and those of the savages were tested with equal skill. Governor Shelby, perceiving the severity of the contest, was not an inactive or disinterested spectator of the scene. Having ordered Lieutenant-colonel John Donaldson's regiment of the Kentucky volunteers to advance to support Colonel Johnson, he next moved General King's brigade to the front line; but, before the latter could occupy the new position which it had been assigned, the enemy had begun to retire, and Major Thompson was pushing after them with great spirit.[1]

The action was continued no longer—the British troops, on the left of the enemy's line, having yielded almost without a blow; the Indians, on the right, as has been seen, continuing the engagement, with the utmost gallantry, long after General Proctor, in his precipitate flight, had passed beyond the sound of the strife.

[1] Gen. Harrison to Sec. of War, Oct. 9; McAfee, pp. 391–393; Rogers' Canada, i. p. 232; Armstrong, i. p. 174; Col. R. M. Johnson to Gen. Armstrong, Dec. 22, 1834; Christie, pp. 135, 136; Perkins' Hist. of War, p. 240; Sketches of the War, pp. 175, 176; Auchinleck, pp. 217–220.

The strength of both parties has been noticed in another part of this chapter. The loss of the Americans was seven *killed* and twenty-two *wounded*;[1] that of the British was twelve *killed*, twenty-two *wounded*, and six hundred and one *prisoners*;[2] that of the Indians was thirty-three *killed* on the field, besides those who fell in the retreat.[3] Among these was Tecumthà, the chief of the Indians, whose powerful intellect had made him one of those whom the United States most dreaded; whose place neither Britain or his own people have ever been able to fill.[4]

General Proctor, with a small escort of horsemen, hurried away from the field of action, and so severely was he pressed that his sword and his private papers fell into the hands of his pur-

[1] Gen. Harrison to Sec. of War, Oct. 9; Christie, p. 136; Perkins, p. 240. Mr. McAfee (p. 394) says the loss was greater; and the author of *Sketches* (p. 176) concurs with him.—[2] Gen. Harrison to Sec. of War, Oct. 9; Christie, p. 136; James, i. p. 282. Mr. McAfee (p. 394) says the enemy had 18 *killed* and 26 *wounded*.

[3] Gen. Harrison to Sec. of War, Oct. 9; McAfee, p. 394; Christie, p. 136.

[4] Letter from Maj. Rowland, Oct. 9; McAfee, p. 394; Rogers' Canada, i. pp. 232, 233; Armstrong, i. p. 174; James, i. p. 287. The question whether or not Col. R. M. Johnson or some other person killed the chief, has been discussed with great bitterness of feeling, from that day to the present. Capt. McAfee (*War in West*, p. 394), Mr. Rogers (*Rise of Canada*, i. p. 232), Mr. Perkins (*Hist. of War*, p. 240), Mr. James (*Mil. Occur.*, i. p. 287), the author of the *Sketches of the War* (pp. 175, 176), Maj. Richardson, who was with Tecumthà (*Auchinleck's Hist. of the War*, p. 220), Mr. Breckenridge (*Hist. of War*, p. 184), Mr. Thomson (*Sketches*, p. 174), Mr. Hall (*Mem. of Gen. Harrison*, p. 279), Mr. O'Connor (*Hist. of War*, p. 128), all maintain that Tecumthà was killed by *Col. Johnson;* while Mr. Drake (*Book of the Indians*, Bk. v., p. 124) says, "that story must no longer be believed." Col. Johnson, in my hearing, related the circumstances, *without either claiming or disclaiming the honor* which has attached to this act.

suers.[1] He found safety from the pursuit of his enemies; but he did not escape from the indignation of his country. He was arrested, and tried by a general court-martial, and sentenced to be publicly reprimanded and suspended from duty and emoluments during the space of six months, for his criminal neglect of duty in this retreat—a sentence which, in its confirmation by the Prince Regent, in a "General Order," received additional force in the severity of the language employed, and in the means employed for its dissemination.[1]

[NOTE.—The Dispatch of Gen. Harrison to the Sec. of the Army, and General Orders, signed "E. BAYNE, *Adj.-Gen.*," which had been provided for the illustration of this chapter, have been omitted by the Publishers for want of room.]

CHAPTER LXIV.

October 26, 1813.

THE ACTION AT CHETEAUGUA.

THE command of the Northern army having been vested in General Wilkinson,[2] that officer reached Sackett's Harbor on the twentieth of August, and proceeded to complete the arrangements for a descent on Canada.[3] The force under his command was scattered along the entire northern frontier of New York—the right being at Plattsburg, under General Hampton; the centre at Sackett's Harbor, under the commander-in-chief; and the left, at Fort George, under General Boyd.[4] It numbered, in the aggregate, fourteen thousand three hundred and fifty-six men;[5] and was opposed to about eight thousand British troops, the left of whose line was at Montreal, the centre at Kingston, and the right on the Niagara frontier.[6]

The most elaborate preparations were made, and in the most showy style, for the service in which these troops were to be engaged; council succeeded council, and orders reiterated former orders; while, as if to add especial dignity to the army and its purposes, the government itself *left Washington and established the Department of War at Sackett's Harbor.*[2] The Secretary of War had been an officer in the army of the Revolutionary War; and the commander-in-chief and General Hampton had seen service in the same war; and, after due consultation, it was determined to make a descent on Kingston, and, afterwards, on Montreal, the great centres of the enemy's power.[3] For this purpose the troops from the left and

[1] Gen. Harrison to Sec. of War, Oct. 9; McAfee, p. 393; James, i. p. 284.—[2] Ingersoll, i. p. 288.

[3] Gen. Wilkinson to Sec. of War, Aug. 21.—[4] The entire correspondence between the War Department and Gen. Wilkinson.—[5] Ingersoll, i. p. 293.—[6] Perkins, p. 255.

[1] General Orders, "*Horse Guards, Sept.* 9, 1815," signed "H. CALVERT, *Adj.-Gen;*" Auchinleck, pp. 223–241.

[2] Gen. Armstrong to Gen. Wilkinson, "War Department, Sept. 6, 1813, Sackett's Harbor."

[3] Plan of Operations, approved July 23; Gen. Wilkinson to Sec. of War, Aug. 6.

centre of the army were concentrated on Grenadier Island and at French Creek,—the former in Lake Ontario, eighteen miles below Sackett's Harbor; the latter on the bank of the St. Lawrence, about eighteen miles still farther down,—with a design of moving against Kingston;[1] and, about the same time, the right wing was ordered to hold itself in readiness, in case of a descent of the St. Lawrence, to move towards "the mouth of the Cheteaugua, or other point which would favor the junction of the forces, and hold the enemy in check."[2]

A division in the councils of the army, amounting almost to open rupture, and the positive orders of the Secretary of War, in opposition to the remonstrances of the commander-in-chief, soon after led to an abandonment of the intended movement against Kingston;[3] and, in accordance with his instructions, General Hampton prepared to join the main body of the army, on its way down the St. Lawrence. With this design, on the nineteenth of September, the army moved from Cumberland Head towards Canada—the infantry in batteaux, and the artillery and dragoons by land.[4] At an early hour on the twentieth, with the intention of moving by way of Champlain and Caughnewaga, the advance under Majors Wool, Snelling, and McNeil had crossed into Canada and reached Odletown, when, in consequence of the drought, the entire body countermarched and proceeded towards the St. Lawrence by way of Cheteaugua.[1] On the twenty-sixth of September it had proceeded as far as Cheteaugua Four Corners,—about thirty miles from Plattsburg, and about forty-five from the point of junction on the St. Lawrence,—where, by direction of the Secretary of War,[2] it remained in camp until the main body was ready to move down the St. Lawrence, when it was ordered to "approach the mouth of the Cheteaugua or other point which shall better favor the junction with the grand army, and hold the enemy in check;"[3] and, on the twenty-first of October, it commenced its movement, as directed.[4]

In front, the proposed line of march passed through an extensive wood, in which the enemy had posted bodies of Indians and light troops, and by cutting down trees and forming abatis, the passage was seriously obstructed. To overcome these, General Izard was detached with the light troops and a regiment of the line to turn the enemy's flank and seize the open country in the rear of the impediments; while, by a detour in the opposite direction, the army, preceded by strong working parties, advanced by a more circuitous but practicable route for a road. This manœuvre was entirely successful; and, on the following day (*Oct.* 22), the main body

[1] James, i. p. 301; Thomson's Sketches, p. 179.

[2] Sec. of War to Gen. Hampton, Oct. 16.—[3] Sec. of War to Gen. Wilkinson, Oct. 19 and 20; Gen. Wilkinson to Sec. of War, Oct. 19.—[4] Gen. Hampton to Sec. of War, Sept. 22; Report, signed "W. King, *Adj.-Gen.;*" Armstrong, ii. p. 2; Palmer's Lake Champlain, p. 170.

[1] Gen. Hampton to Secretary of War, Sept. 22; Report, signed "W. King, *Adj.-Gen;*" Col. Purdy's Report to Gen. Wilkinson.—[2] Sec. of War to Gen. Hampton, Sept. 19 and 25.—[3] Ibid., Oct. 16.—[4] Gen. Hampton to Sec. of War, Nov. 1; Letter from Plattsburg, Nov. 13, 1813; Sir Geo. Prevost to Earl Bathurst, Oct. 30.

occupied the advanced position, at Spears', and two days afterwards the stores and artillery came up.[1]

Seven miles of open country, which was immediately in front of the army, afforded no defensible point for the enemy; but, beyond it, another wood, which was completely defended with abatis, and breastworks of timber defended with artillery, obstructed the progress of the army. The guides assured the General that the stream along which was the line of march was fordable, opposite the lower flank of the enemy's defences, and he determined to attempt to force a passage. Accordingly, at an early hour in the evening of the twenty-fifth, he detached Colonel Robert Purdy, of the Fourth infantry, with the light troops and the First brigade of infantry of the line, ordering him to gain the ford and fall on the rear of the enemy's works, at an early hour in the following morning; at which time, on hearing the fire in the rear, the General, with the main body, would attack the enemy in front; and it was confidently expected that the pass would be carried before the distant troops of the enemy could be moved forward for his support.[2]

The detachment under Colonel Purdy crossed the stream, as it was ordered, and took up its line of march; but, from the darkness of the night, or the ignorance of the guides, it wandered in the woods, and failed in its attempts to find the ford, as it also did, soon afterwards, in finding the main body from which it had been detached. In fact, the story of the adventures of this party, in its eccentric wandering through the hemlock swamp,—the head of the column sometimes coming in contact with its rear, and filling both with alarm,—as narrated by a veteran, who was an eye-witness of the scene, has furnished amusement to the listeners, and conveyed a lesson which cannot, very soon, be forgotten.[1]

The position against which these movements were made was near the confluence of the Cheteaugua and Outarde rivers; and it had been very carefully strengthened with breastworks and abatis, and a garrison of about a thousand men, including Indians, under the command of Lieutenant-colonel De Salaberry.[2]

At about two in the afternoon of the twenty-sixth, General Izard, with the Second brigade, moved against the

---

[1] Gen. Hampton to Sec. of War, Nov. 1; Sir Geo. Prevost to Earl Bathurst, Oct. 30; James, i. p. 306; Armstrong, ii. p. 3.—[2] Gen. Hampton to Sec. of War, Nov. 1; Auchinleck, p. 247; Letter from Plattsburg, Nov. 13; Christie, pp. 144, 145; Col. Purdy's Report; Report, signed "W. KING, *Adj.-Gen.*"

[1] Gen. Hampton to Sec. of War, Nov. 1; Letter from Plattsburg, Nov. 13; Auchinleck, p. 247; Col. Purdy's Report. Col. Purdy says the detachment was intrusted by Gen. Hampton "to the guidance of men, each of whom repeatedly assured him that *they were not acquainted with the country*, and were not competent to direct such an expedition;" while, "at the same time he had a man who *had* a perfect knowledge of the country, whom he promised to send, but which he neglected to do. The defeat of the expedition," he adds, "was the consequence of this neglect."

[2] Gen. Hampton to Sec. of War, Oct. 12; James, i. p. 307; Auchinleck, p. 247; General Orders, signed "E. BAYNE, *Adj.-Gen.;*" Christie, pp. 142, 143. Mr. James (*Mil. Occur.*, i. pp. 306, 307) says it embraced two flank companies of fencibles, four of voltigeurs, six of embodied militia and chasseurs, and 172 Indians, forming an aggregate of about 1000 men. The Report to the Sec. of War, by "W. KING, *Adj.-Gen.*," says, "the enemy's entire force on this line *three hundred and fifty combatants* altogether, Canadian and Indian."

front of the works, driving in the enemy's pickets as he advanced. Lieutenant-colonel De Salaberry promptly advanced to meet him, with Captain Ferguson's light company of Canadian fencibles, and two companies of voltigeurs, under Captains Chevalier and L. J. Duchesnay. The first of these he posted, in open order, in front of the abatis, with its right on the woods in which he had posted a body of Abenaqui Indians; on the left of this he posted Captain Chevalier Duchesnay's company of voltigeurs, with its left extending to the Cheteaugua; and Captain L. J. Duchesnay's company, with thirty-five militia, were thrown, *en potence*, along the margin of the river, to protect the flank of his line. A most gallant defence was here presented, but the Americans gradually gained ground, and finally compelled the enemy to fall back on his main body.[1] At the same time the detachment under Colonel Purdy encountered a company of Cheteaugua chasseurs, under Captain Bruyers, supported by the light company of the Third battalion of embodied militia, under Captain Daly; and, here, also, a spirited, but profitless, engagement took place;[2] and the report of the musketry in this part of the action, added to the sound of a few bugles, which the enemy had scattered, for that purpose, through the swamp,[3] appears to have terrified Gen. Hampton and he withdrew from the field of action without success and without honor.[1]

[1] Christie, pp. 145, 146; Gen. Hampton to Sec. of War, Nov. 1; General Orders, &c.; Letter from Plattsburg, Nov. 13; "*The War*," ii. p. 92; Sir G. Prevost to Earl Bathurst, Oct. 30.—[2] Col. Purdy's Report; Christie, pp. 146, 147; James, i. p. 310.—[3] Christie, p. 146; Ingersoll, i. p. 299; James, i. p. 310; Armstrong, i. p. 4.

While it is probably true that only the advance of both armies were actually engaged, it is equally true that the entire affair reflected no credit on General Hampton; while the enemy, with the plausible pretence of having repulsed four thousand effective troops with less than a quarter the number,—of which less than one half was in action,—could fairly boast of having gained a decided victory.

Nor was this claim diminished by subsequent events, which principally resulted from this action. Immediately afterwards the entire army fell back on Cheteaugua Four Corners;[2] and when it was ordered, some weeks afterwards, to join General Wilkinson on the St. Lawrence, and move against Montreal, it was found impossible to do so,[3] and the latter officer, in consequence of that failure, *it is said*, was compelled to abandon the enterprise, which was never renewed.[4]

The loss of the Americans was about fifteen *killed*, and twenty to twenty-five *wounded;* that of the enemy was five men *killed*, two officers and fourteen men *wounded*, and four men *missing*.

[Note.—The Dispatches of Gen. Hampton to Sec. of War, Gen. Sir Geo. Prevost to Earl Bathurst, and Col. Purdy's Report to the Commander-in-chief, which had been provided for the illustration of this chapter, have been omitted by the Publishers for want of room.]

[1] Col. Purdy's Report; Gen. Hampton to Sec. of War, Nov. 1; Christie, p. 146.—[2] Christie, p. 148; Col. Purdy's Report; Gen. Hampton to Sec. of War, Nov. 1.—[3] Gen. Wilkinson to Gen. Hampton, Nov. 6, and Gen. Hampton's reply, Nov. 8; Gen. Hampton to Sec. of War, Nov. 12 and 15; Gen. Wilkinson to Sec. of War, Nov. 16.—[4] Gen. Wilkinson to Gen. Hampton, Nov. 12; Same to Sec. of War, Nov. 16, 17.

CHAPTER LXV.

November 3, 1813.

THE BATTLE AT TALLUSHATCHES.

THE rising animosities of the Creeks, and their massacre of the garrison of Fort Mimms, to which reference has been made in a former chapter of this work, aroused the entire communities of the Southern and Southwestern States, and nothing was thought or spoken of but retaliatory vengeance.[1] In Tennessee, especially, this feeling prevailed; and the Legislature of that State, which convened a short time after the reception of the intelligence, authorized the Governor to send a body of troops against the savages, and voted three hundred thousand dollars to defray the necessary expenses. Accordingly Generals Jackson and Coffee were ordered to assemble a force of two thousand five hundred men for the protection of the frontiers; and early in October they took the field.[2]

In the mean time the war-party of the Creeks—for there were two parties among them, one who had yielded to, and the other who had resisted, the arguments of Tecumthà—had been equally active; and a large body of them had taken post at Tallushatches, on the south side of the Coosa, a northern branch of the Alabama.[3]

On the second of November General Jackson issued orders to General John Coffee, directing him to detail a part of his brigade of cavalry and mounted riflemen, and to destroy the settlement; and, in accordance with that order, at an early hour on the morning of the third, he marched in person, at the head of nine hundred men, crossed the Coosa at Fish-dam Ford, and approached the village. When he had come within a mile and a half of the enemy, the General formed his troops into two columns—the cavalry, under Colonel Allcorn, on the right, with orders to cross a large creek which laid in front, and to encircle one-half of the village; the mounted riflemen, under Colonel Cannon, on the left, with orders to encircle the left side of the village, and to unite with the head of the right column beyond it.[1]

The General marched with Colonel Cannon; and when the heads of the diverging columns had come within half a mile of the village, "the drums of the enemy began to beat, mingled with their savage yells, preparing for action." It was, at that time, an hour after sunrise; and, as an assault on the village was not considered expedient, the companies under Captain Hammond and

[1] Eaton's Jackson, p. 33; Perkins' Hist. of War, p. 200.
[2] Eaton's Jackson, pp. 33–40; Davis's Jackson, p. 67.
[3] Drake's Book of Indians, Book iv., p. 55.

[1] Gen. Coffee to Gen. Jackson, Nov. 4; Gen. Jackson to Gov. Blount, Nov. 4.

Lieutenant Patterson were ordered to move against it, in front, for the purpose of drawing the enemy from the buildings. The detachment moved according to orders, and formed in front of the village, throwing in a few shots, which the enemy returned; when, with singular fatality, he made a vigorous charge and attempted to overpower the two companies who had assailed him, before they could reach the main body. Without awaiting to receive the shock, the detachment retreated, leading its pursuers towards the right wing; and as soon as the fugitives had led the excited savages within gunshot of the main body a general fire was opened on them, and they retreated, falling back on the village, and firing as they retreated.[1]

At this moment the two columns which encircled the settlement closed their ranks, and gradually strengthened their grasp by reducing the extent of the fatal circle; during which time the enemy defended himself with the most terrible determination. Taking their places at the doors of their dwellings, in the midst of their families, surrounded by their little ones, and assisted by their squaws,[2] the warriors fought "for their altars and their fires" with a devotion and a bravery which in any other people, and in any other age, would have been considered the very sum of patriotic virtue;[3] and which, even in this case, entitles the devoted Creeks, who thus sacrificed themselves on the altar of *their* country, to a place beside the greatest and most patriotic of any age, or nation. It is indeed true, that the cruelties which these people had practised at Fort Mimms had ostracized them from the sympathies of the whites; but it is not less true that they were *thus* contending, *in their own established manner*, for their homes and their rights; and their stern devotion in that cause entitles them to our sympathy and respect.

As has been said, these warriors fought desperately. Even General Coffee, in the excitement of the moment, has been compelled to bear testimony to their bravery in terms such as have not been exceeded in any narrative of a similar character since the time when Herodotus recited the deeds of Leonidas. "The enemy fought," he says,[1] "with savage fury, and met death, with all its horrors, *without shrinking or complaining.* NOT ONE *asked to be spared, but fought so long as they could* STAND OR SIT;" and, as if to impress the great truth still more indelibly on the minds of their enemies, they fought with bows and arrows as well as rifles; and the bodies of two Tennesseans, killed with the primitive weapons of the aborigines,[2] conveyed to the firesides of Tennessee, the solemn truth that the homes and the rights of the aborigines had been faithfully defended by aboriginal instrumentalities.

The Tennesseans carried the conflict

---

[1] Gen. Coffee to Gen. Jackson, Nov. 4; Goodwin's Jackson, p. 48; Drake's Book of Indians, Book iv., p. 56.

[2] Drake's Book of Indians, Book iv., p. 56; Eaton's Jackson, p. 55.—[3] Gen. Coffee to Gen. Jackson, Nov. 4; Perkins, pp. 200, 201; Eaton's Jackson, pp. 53–55.

[1] Gen. Coffee to Gen. Jackson, Nov. 4. See also Ingersoll, i. p. 335, and Eaton's Jackson, p. 54.—[2] Gen. Coffee to Gen. Jackson, Nov. 4; Ingersoll, i. p. 335.

even "to the doors of the houses" in which the wives, and the children, and the aged relatives of these savages had sought shelter; yet even then the undaunted fathers, and brothers, and sons, neither faltered, or complained, or sought mercy. "THEY FOUGHT AS LONG AS ONE EXISTED," General Coffee says; and when the *last of the devoted band*, still struggling for the mastery, had fallen beneath the hatchets and hunting-knives of his enemies, one hundred and eighty-six warriors were stretched, lifeless, in the fine open woodland in which their village was situated.[1]

Of the Americans, five men were *killed;* and eight officers, and thirty-three non-commissioned officers and privates were *wounded;* and eighty-four prisoners, squaws and children, many of them wounded, were the trophies of the victory.[2]

[NOTE.—The Report of Gen. Coffee to Gen. Jackson, which had been provided for the illustration of this chapter, has been omitted by the Publishers for want of room.]

CHAPTER LXVI.

November 9, 1813.

THE BATTLE OF TALLADEGA.

WHILE General Jackson remained at the Ten Islands, on the evening of the seventh of November, a runner came into his camp from Fort Talladega,—a fortified post occupied by the friendly Indians, about thirty miles distant from the camp,—with information that the enemy, in great numbers, had encamped in front of it, and that it would be inevitably destroyed, unless immediate relief could be afforded. Urged by the danger of these friendly Indians, as well as by a strong desire, on his own part, to meet the main body of the enemy, as soon as possible, he prepared to move forward without delay; and, on the same night, with twelve hundred infantry and eight hundred cavalry and mounted riflemen, he crossed the Coosa, encamping on the following afternoon within six miles of the enemy.[1]

Between three and four o'clock the army took up the line of march again; and at sunrise it had come within half a mile of the enemy, when the line of battle was formed, and preparations made for action. The infantry was formed in three lines,—the militia on the left and the volunteers on the right,—while the cavalry, on either flank, were thrown forward, *en potence*, with their lines formed in a *curve*, for the purpose of inclosing the enemy, as had been done at Tallushatches.[3] At the same time an advance party, composed of the companies commanded by Captains Dederick, Caperton, and Bledsoe, under the command of Colonel William Carroll, was sent forward to open the engagement and draw the

[1] Gen. Jackson to Gov. Blount, Nov. 11; Letter from Nashville, Nov. 17; Eaton's Jackson, pp. 56–58; Claiborne's Notes, p. 30.

[1] Gen. Coffee to Gen. Jackson, Nov. 4; Eaton's Jackson, pp. 54, 55; Claiborne's Notes on the War in the South, p. 29.—[2] Gen. Coffee to Gen. Jackson, Nov. 4; Gen. Jackson to Gov. Blount, Nov. 4.—[3] Gen. Jackson to Gov. Blount, Nov. 11; Eaton, pp. 59, 60.

Indians from their encampment;[1] while a body of cavalry, composed of troops under Captains Smith, Morton, Axune, Edwards, and Hammond, under Lieutenant-colonel Dyer, was held in reserve.[2]

With great gallantry the advance moved within rifle-shot, and threw in four or five destructive rounds; when, in accordance with its orders, it fell back on the main body, for the purpose of decoying the enemy within reach of the rifles of that body, and to facilitate the operations of the cavalry in uniting their columns in the rear. As the enemy, in the eagerness of his pursuit, approached the main body, the first line of infantry was ordered to advance and meet him; but, either from the severity of the shock, or from some other cause,—concerning which the General has not seen fit to give us any information,—the militia, which formed the left of this line, "commenced a retreat; and the army was thrown into temporary disorder." The quick eye and prompt determination of the General, however, saw and remedied this misfortune at the same moment; and the reserve, *dismounted*, immediately occupied the position which the militia had deserted, and the battle went on.[3]

The fire immediately became general, and after a close and very severe action of half an hour, the enemy fell back and retreated. Notwithstanding the obstinacy of the engagement, the enemy did not, in this instance, exhibit the same devotion which was shown by the warriors at Tallushatches, but turned and fled to the mountains, closely pursued by the right wing, in which he suffered severely.[1] The enemy was enabled to secure his retreat from the disaffection of the militia, the disobedience of Colonel Bradley, of the Volunteers—who refused to bring his regiment into the line, and the too extended *detour* of Colonel Allcorn, all of which, combined, produced a vacancy in the line, through which the enemy escaped.[2]

The loss of the enemy in this action was very severe—two hundred and ninety-nine braves having been left dead on the field, besides those who were carried off, in accordance with the custom of the Indians;[3] while that of the Americans, of whom fifteen were killed and eighty wounded, proved the spirit with which the savages sustained the contest.[4] A stand of colors, bearing the Spanish arms, was taken from the enemy[5]—a circumstance which indicated, very clearly, the part which the Spanish authorities of Florida had taken in the troubles; and, to some extent, justified the decisive steps which were subsequently taken by General Jackson against that colony.[6]

[Note.—The Dispatch of Gen. Jackson to Gov. Blount, which had been provided for the illustration of this chapter, has been omitted by the Publishers for want of room.]

[1] Col. Wm. Carroll to his brother in Nashville; Gen. Jackson to Gov. Blount, Nov. 11 and 15; Letter from Nashville, Nov. 17.—[2] Gen. Jackson to Gov. Blount, Nov. 11 and 15; Eaton, p. 60.

[3] Gen. Jackson to Gov. Blount, Nov. 11. Mr. Eaton (*Life of Gen. Jackson*, p. 60) says they "were alarmed by the number and yells" of the enemy.

[1] Gen. Jackson to Gov. Blount, Nov. 11; Letter from Nashville, Nov. 17.—[2] Eaton's Jackson, p. 61.—[3] Gen. Jackson to Gov. Blount, Nov. 15; Col. Carroll to his brother.

[4] Report appended to Gen. Jackson's Dispatch, Nov. 15, signed "J. W. Sittler, *Adj.-Gen.*"—[5] "Mr. Thomas H. Fletcher, of this town, has just arrived from Gen. Jackson's army. . . . He was the bearer of a stand of colors, taken from the enemy, bearing the Spanish cross."—*Letter from Nashville, Nov.* 17.—[6] Eaton, pp. 238–257.

CHAPTER LXVII.

November 11, 1813.

THE BATTLE AT CHRYSTLER'S FARM.

THE projected expedition against Montreal by the American "Army of the North," under General Wilkinson, has heretofore received a passing notice in this volume; and the defeat of its right wing, at Cheteaugua, has been made the subject of a chapter.[1]

By a singular freak of judgment, the American squadron had attempted to block the British, for the purpose of enabling the flotilla to proceed from Grenadier Island and French Creek without obstruction, and to prevent the concentration of the scattered forces of the enemy at Kingston; but General De Rottonburg, who commanded in the upper province, and Commodore Sir James Yeo, who commanded the squadron, taking advantage of a fair wind, eluded the blockade, and strengthened Kingston so much that the commanders considered it imprudent to attack that place, and Montreal was determined as the point against which the expedition should move.[2]

Accordingly, the right wing was ordered to move from Lake Champlain to the St. Lawrence, for the purpose of effecting a union with the main body;[3] General Brown was placed in command

[1] Vide Chap. LXIV.—[2] Gen. Wilkinson to Sec. of War, Sept. 27, 6 A. M., Oct. 2 and 19; Christie, p. 149; Sec. of War's Diary, Oct. 4, 1813.—[3] Sec. of War to Gen. Hampton, Oct. 16.

of the advance of the main army at French Creek, which, on the first and second of November, was attacked by the British squadron without success;[1] and, all preparations having been made, on the fifth the entire body of the left and centre moved down the river in a grand flotilla of three hundred boats, extending a distance of five miles.[2] For the purpose of avoiding the works at Prescott, which commanded the passage of the river, on the sixth the military stores and the greater part of the troops were debarked and conveyed by land; while the boats passed the works by night without material injury, and received the men and ammunition on board again, when they had come to the Red Mill, a safe distance below the fort.[3]

But although Prescott had been passed, other points on the river had been strengthened in order to obstruct the progress of the flotilla; and on the seventh, Colonel Alexander Macomb, "with the *élite*" of the army—twelve hundred in number—was ordered to

[1] Gen. Wilkinson to Sec. of War, Nov. 1; Gen. Wilkinson's Diary, Oct. 25 to Nov. 2.

[2] Gen. Wilkinson's Diary, Nov. 5; James' Mil. Occur., i. p. 317. Mr. Christie (*Mil. and Nav. Operations*, p. 149) says it entered the river on the *third.*

[3] Gen. Wilkinson's Diary, Nov. 6; Richards' Macomb, pp. 64, 65; James, i. pp. 317, 318; Rogers' Canada, i. p. 239; Auchinleck, p. 243.

cross the river and "remove" them.[1] On the same day he was followed by Lieutenant-colonel Forsyth and his riflemen[2]—whose gallant exploits on the Northern frontier have been noticed in other chapters of this work—and on the eighth the cavalry and General Brown's brigade also passed over the river.[3] From that time the progress of the flotilla was considerably retarded by the opposition which the enemy presented, both to the troops on shore and to the flotilla; while the strong parties which hovered around the rear of the columns, constantly threatening them, called forth the constant care of the general officers.[4]

In the mean time General De Rottonburg, who had arrived from Queenstown, and strengthened the garrison at Kingston, with eight companies of the Forty-ninth regiment of the line, on the morning of the seventh, detached them, with nine companies of the Eighty-ninth, two six-pounders, and a small body of artillerists, the whole under Lieutenant-colonel Morrison, with the schooners *Beresford* and *Sir Sidney Smith*, seven gunboats, and a number of batteaux, under Captain Mulcaster of the Royal navy, to follow the American forces and to harass their rear. With strange and unaccountable neglect this detachment was allowed to pass from the harbor, without injury from the American squadron under Commodore Chauncey,—notwithstanding the assurances which the latter had given, that no such interruption should be allowed to leave Kingston,—and it proceeded down the St. Lawrence in pursuit of the American expedition. On the next day (*Nov. 7th*) it reached Prescott, and was strengthened with the two flank companies of the Forty-ninth, and with detachments from the Canadian Fencibles, the Voltigeurs, and the Provincial dragoons, with another six-pounder and its company, the whole under Lieutenant-colonel Pearson.[1] It is very evident that a body of Indians also accompanied this "corps of observation," yet the authorities studiously keep them out of sight.

On the ninth, after passing down the river as far as Point Iroquois, this "corps of observation" debarked; and thenceforth the enemy's land and naval forces acted in concert, but each on its proper element. The rear and flanks of the American army were harassed with great spirit; and, not only in rear but in front also, the flotilla under General Wilkinson was energetically opposed.[2]

On the morning of the eleventh of November, while the flotilla was preparing to enter the Longue Sault, for which orders had been given, the enemy appeared in force, and the gunboats which covered the rear opened a fire on him. Orders were given to General Boyd, who commanded in the rear, to attack the assailants;[3] while the flotilla

---

[1] Gen. Wilkinson's Diary, Nov. 7; Richards' Macomb, p. 65; Christie, p. 150; Rogers, i. p. 240; Perkins, p. 257.

[2] Gen. Wilkinson's Diary, Nov. 7; Ingersoll, i. p. 304.

[3] Gen. Wilkinson's Diary, Nov. 8; Richards' Macomb, p. 66; Christie, p. 150; James, i. p. 320.

[4] Gen. Wilkinson's Diary, Nov. 9; Rogers, i. p. 240.

[1] Christie, p. 150; James, i. pp. 323, 324; Rogers, i. p. 239.—[2] James, i. pp. 324, 325.

[3] Gen. Wilkinson's Diary, Nov. 11. In confirmation of this, Gen. Boyd "*ordered Gen. Swartwout to dislodge the ene-*

was ordered to remain where it then laid. Accordingly General Swartwout, with the Fourth brigade, was detached with orders to dislodge them; and General Covington, with the Third brigade, was ordered to move back within supporting distance of General Swartwout. The latter officer "dashed into the woods," and the Twenty-first regiment of infantry, under Colonel E. W. Ripley, which he led, drove the assailants who had first shown themselves back upon the enemy's main body, which was in the rear.[1]

At this time the enemy had formed in order of battle on the open fields of "Chrystler's Farm," near the village of Williamsburg—three companies of the Eighty-ninth, on the extreme right, resting on the river, formed *en échelon*, with a six-pounder, were commanded by Captain Barnes; on their left, and somewhat in the rear, were the flank companies of the Forty-ninth and the detachment of Fencibles, with another six-pounder, under Lieutenant-colonel Pearson; still farther to the left and rear were the battalion companies of the Forty-ninth and Eighty-ninth regiments, with the third six-pounder, under Lieutenant-colonel Morrison, their left resting on a pine wood; while in front of all, as tirailleurs, covering the left flank, were the Voltigeurs, under Major Herriot, and the Indians under Lieutenant Anderson.[2] The position was favorable for defence, in consequence of several deep ravines by which the ground was intersected; and which rendered it difficult of access, and to some extent unapproachable with artillery;[1] while a heavy rail-fence, behind which the enemy took shelter, effectually protected him from the effects of the American fire.[2]

As before stated, the enemy's light troops fell back on this position, as Colonel Ripley and the Twenty-first regiment pressed forward in their charge; and soon afterwards the entire Fourth brigade (*General Swartwout's*) attacked the left of the British line, in which he was supported by Colonel Coles, with part of the First brigade; while the right was, simultaneously, attacked by the Third brigade, under General Covington.[3] Under the most promising circumstances the action was conducted for some time,—although the enemy's artillery gave him great advantages, while the American field-pieces were unable to pass the ravines and come on the field,—and it was only after the failure of the supply of ammunition, on the right, and the fall of General Covington, who received a mortal wound while at the head of his brigade, on the left, that the fortunes of the day were changed.[4] Having exhausted its supply of ammunition, the Fourth brigade was compelled to fall back; and Colonel Coles, with his command, was, in consequence, compelled also to retire;

my," yet on Gen. Wilkinson's trial he testified that his orders were—"Should the enemy advance upon us, *beat them back*"—a purely *defensive* policy. The cause of this contradiction has not been explained.

[1] Gen. Boyd to Gen. Wilkinson, Nov. 12.

[2] Lieut.-Col. Morrison to Gen. De Rottonburg, Nov. 12; James, i. pp. 328, 329; Rogers, i. p. 240.

[1] Gen. Boyd to Gen. Wilkinson, Nov. 12; Perkins, p. 258.—[2] Richards' Macomb, p. 67.—[3] Gen. Boyd to Gen. Wilkinson, Nov. 12; James, i. p. 330; Lieut.-Col. Morrison to Gen. De Rottonburg, Nov. 12.—[4] Gen. Wilkinson to Sec. of War, Nov. 16; Breckenridge, p. 196.

and, soon afterwards, discouraged by the fall of General Covington,—or rather, failing to fall into the hands of an officer of equal spirit and ability,—the Third brigade also fell back in some disorder.[1]

Thus relieved of their assailants, on the left, the Forty-ninth and Eighty-ninth British regiments, on that part of the enemy's line, advanced,—"firing occasionally by platoons,"—and took a position, *en échelon*, in support of the companies on the right, which were still engaged with the Third (*General Covington's*) brigade; and this, from the cause already referred to, and from the effect of this increase in the opposing force, was, soon afterwards, also compelled to retire.[2]

An attempt was then made, by the enemy's right, to seize the American artillery, which was gallantly frustrated by a charge of American cavalry under Adjutant-general Walbach.[3] Soon afterwards, however, in consequence of the confusion resulting from the death of Lieutenant Smith, who commanded it, and the greater part of his men, one piece was lost.[4]

During about two hours, with great skill on both sides, the advantage thus fluctuated; and victory rested, alternately, on the banners of both armies.[5] At length, considering that "the contest had become somewhat dubious," General Wilkinson ordered up a reserve of six hundred men, under Lieutenant-colonel Upham; by whom they were led into the field, and checked the disorder into which some portions of the line had fallen.[1] Falling back to the edge of the wood from which the enemy's light troops had been driven in the early part of the day, the American army formed there, and awaited the enemy;[2] but, having not only retained the ground which he first occupied, but driven the assailants, in confusion, from it, with the loss of one of their field-pieces, he appears to have been content, and did not pursue. *Both* parties claim that the approach of night, *alone* prevented them from continuing the engagement; and while the enemy occupied the field of battle during the night, the Americans retired to their boats without interruption.[3]

The relative numbers of the contestants has, as is usual, been the subject of grave dispute. The enemy, from the best evidence, appears to have numbered not exceeding eight hundred men, exclusive of Indians;[4] while the Americans, from like reliable testimony, appear to have numbered not less than seventeen hundred.[5] The superior discipline of the enemy,[6] added to the fatigue of the Americans,—who "had

[1] Gen. Boyd to Gen. Wilkinson, Nov. 12; James, i. p. 330; Breckenridge, p. 196.—[2] Lieut.-Col. Morrison to Gen. De Rottonburg, Nov. 12; James, i. p. 330.

[3] Lieut.-Col. Morrison to Gen. De Rottonburg, Nov. 12; James, ii. pp. 330, 331.—[4] Gen. Boyd to Gen. Wilkinson, Nov. 12; Lieut.-Col. Morrison to Gen. De Rottonburg, Nov. 12; Gen. Wilkinson to Sec. of War, Nov. 16.

[5] Gen. Wilkinson to Sec. of War, Nov. 16; Gen. Wilkinson's Diary, Nov. 11; Christie, p. 153.

[1] Gen. Wilkinson to Sec. of War, Nov. 18.

[2] Gen. Boyd to Gen. Wilkinson, Nov. 12.

[3] Gen Wilkinson to Sec. of War, Nov. 16; Gen. Wilkinson's Diary, Nov. 11; James, i. p. 331.

[4] Lieut.-Col. Morrison to Gen. De Rottonburg, Nov. 12; James, i. pp. 325, 326; Christie, p. 150; Rogers' Canada, i. p. 240. Other writers disagree respecting the number of this detachment, rating it at from 1500 (*Dict. of the Army*, p. 568) to 2170 (*Gen. Wilkinson to Sec. of War, Nov.* 18).

[5] Gen. Wilkinson to Sec. of War, Nov. 16; Thomson's Sketches, p. 185. Other authors give various numbers, from 1600 (*Gardner*, p. 568) to 4000 (*Rogers' Canada*, p. 240).

[6] James, i. p. 332.

been in arms all the preceding night, during an incessant rain, and who had to march to the attack over ploughed ground, almost knee-deep in mud,"[1]—and the advantages of a position in which, among others, the advance of the American artillery was prevented,[2] while his own were very effectively employed,[3] more than made up the deficiency of his force; and there is but little doubt, notwithstanding he pursued the expedition no farther, that the advantage remained, legitimately, with the enemy.

Among those who especially distinguished themselves in this engagement, besides those already mentioned, were Colonel Edmund P. Gaines, Lieutenant-colonel Aspinwall, and Lieutenant (since well known to his country as Major-general) William J. Worth.[4]

The loss of the Americans in this well-fought field was Lieutenants Smith, Hunter, and Olmstead, and ninety-nine non-commissioned officers and privates, *killed;* and General Covington, Colonel Preston, Majors Chambers, Cummings, and Noon, Captains Foster, Townsend, Myers, Campbell, and Murdoch, Lieutenants Heaton, Williams, Lynch, Pelham, Brown, and Crary, and two hundred and twenty-one non-commissioned officers and privates, *wounded.*[1] That of the enemy was Captain Nairne and twenty-one men, *killed;* Captain Brown, Lieutenants Jones, Bartley, Claus, Morton, Richmond, Holland, and De Lorimiere, Ensigns Leaden and Armstrong, one hundred and forty men and one warrior, *wounded;* and twelve men and three warriors, *missing.*[2]

[NOTE.—The Dispatch of Gen. Boyd to Gen. Wilkinson, and that of Lieut.-Col. Morrison to Gen. De Rottonburg, which had been provided for the illustration of this chapter, have been omitted by the Publishers for want of room.]

James, i. p. 332.—[2] Richards' Macomb, p. 67.

[3] Rogers' Canada, i. p. 241.—[4] Gen. Boyd to Gen. Wilkinson, Nov. 12.—[5] Vide Chapters LXV., LXVI.

[1] Returns appended to Gen. Wilkinson's Report, Nov. 16.

[2] Returns appended to Lieut.-Col. Morrison's Report, Nov. 12.

CHAPTER LXVIII.

November 18, 1813.

THE MASSACRE AT THE HILLIBEE TOWNS.

WHILE the West Tennessean troops, under Generals Jackson and Coffee, were actively engaged in the midst of the enemy's country, as has been already related in other parts of this volume,[5] those from Eastern Tennessee, under Generals Cocke and White, were not idle. It is true that these officers objected to a consolidation of the two bodies of troops, and that General Jackson was by no means satisfied with their conduct; yet it did not follow that the former were inactive, or desired to avoid the responsibilities which devolved upon their official station.

Among the principal sufferers at Talladega had been the Indians from the Hillibee Towns, on the Tallapoosa, and they had determined to ask for peace at the hands of the victors. Accordingly they had dispatched messengers to General Jackson's camp, declaring their willingness to receive his friendship on such terms as he might be pleased to dictate; and, on the morning of the eighteenth of November, his answer had been returned, extending to them the terms on which they could be reconciled to the United States.[1] Unfortunately, while these negotiations were pending, General Cocke, in his independent capacity, detached General White with a large body of cavalry, mounted infantry, and three hundred friendly Cherokees,—about fourteen hundred in all,—against the enemy; and, after destroying several villages, on the evening of the seventeenth of November he approached the Hillibees.[2]

The plan of operations which General White had adopted, was similar to those which had been employed by Generals Coffee and Jackson; and the unsuspecting and terror-stricken villagers were surrounded and attacked before they knew of the existence of an enemy in the vicinity of their position. Relying on the sincerity of their own professions, and on the faith of all nations—even the savages—during a truce, and especially while negotiations are pending, the warriors had not only taken no means for their defence, but the ordinary precautionary measures to prevent surprise had not been employed;[1] and "the dangers and the glories of the field," about which General Cocke had been so sensitive a short time before,[2] were alike empty and valueless.

The village was surrounded, and the warriors and their families—glorious in their integrity to their own honor, plighted through their messengers to General Jackson—received the blows of their assailants without complaint and *without resistance*, until the arm of the spoiler became weary of the slaughter. The bodies of sixty warriors killed on the spot, and two hundred and fifty-six prisoners, of all classes, in the hands of the victors, bore testimony to the vigor of the assault and the animus of the assailants; the General's report—"We lost not one drop of blood in accomplishing this enterprise"[3]—bears testimony, equally strong, of the unwavering honor of the savages, in declining to engage in hostilities, even in self-defence, while their application for reconciliation was still pending.

[Note.—The Dispatch of Gen. White to Gen. Cocke, which had been provided for the illustration of this chapter, has been omitted by the Publishers for want of room.]

[1] Eaton, pp. 63, 64; Perkins' War of 1812, pp. 202, 203; Drake's Book of Indians, Book iv., p. 57.

[2] Gen. White to Gen. Cocke, Nov. 24; Letter from Knoxville, Nov. 29.

[1] Gen. White to Gen. Cocke, Nov. 24.

[2] This had been the principal cause which Gen. Cocke had assigned for declining to recognize the authority of Gen. Jackson over the Eastern Tennessee troops.

[3] Gen. White to Gen. Cocke, Nov. 14; Letter from Knoxville, Nov. 29.

CHAPTER LXIX.

November 29, 1813.

THE BATTLE OF AUTOSSEE.

While the Tennesseans were engaged on the northern sections of the Creek country, a large body of troops from Georgia, under General John Floyd, entered it from the east, and commenced active operations against the common enemy.[1]

In the course of his operations, the General received information that a large number of Indians had assembled at Autossee, on the southern bank of the Talapoosa, about twenty miles above its junction with the Coosa. This town, which occupied a portion of their "holy ground," on which they supposed that no pale face could set his foot and live, appeared to have been regarded with great veneration by the Indians; and a strong body of warriors, from all the neighboring villages, appears to have congregated for its defence.[2]

On the evening of the twenty-eighth of November General Floyd encamped, within a few miles of the town, with nine hundred and fifty Georgia militia; while between three hundred and four hundred friendly Indians, under William McIntosh and the Mad-dog's son, accompanied the expedition; and about one o'clock in the morning of the twenty-ninth he advanced against the village. At half-past six, having approached within a short distance of the town, the General formed his troops in order of battle—Colonel Booth's command forming the right column, Colonel Watson's the left, Captains Adams' and Meriweather's rifle companies on either flank, and Captain Thomas's artillery in front of the right column.[1]

When daylight revealed the true position of the enemy, it was discovered that *two* villages, a short distance apart, instead of one, were before the columns; and that new and entirely different arrangements were necessary. Instead of the favorite expedient of *surrounding* the village, which had been first intended, it became necessary, therefore, under the real state of affairs, to detach three companies of infantry, Captain Meriweather's riflemen, and two troops of light dragoons, by the left, against the lower town; while the residue of the force, apparently in line, approached the upper one; and within a few minutes the action became general—"the Indians presenting themselves at every point," as General Floyd says, "and fighting with the desperate bravery of real fanatics."[2]

---

[1] Perkins' Late War, p. 203.—[2] Gen. Floyd to Gen. Pinckney, Dec. 4; Breckenridge, p. 219; Ingersoll, i. p. 336.

[1] Gen. Floyd to Gen. Pinckney, Dec. 4; Drake's Book of Indians, Book iv., pp. 51, 56.—[2] Gen. Floyd to Gen. Pinckney, Dec. 4; Claiborne's Notes, p. 36.

The overpowering numbers of the Georgian troops, however, and the field-pieces with which they were provided, accomplished more than the most active and determined "fanaticism" of the savages could overcome; and, after a few minutes' contest, the Indians were compelled to abandon their homes and "take refuge in the out-houses, thickets, and copses in the rear of the town."[1] The "fanaticism" which induced these Indians to fight for their humble homes,—some of which were "of a superior order for the dwellings of savages, and filled with valuable articles,"—appeared despicable to those against whom they defended their firesides; yet, at this distance of time, it appears somewhat excusable, in the fact, which is evident in every line of General Floyd's report, that not one of the assailants would have done otherwise had the situation of the parties been reversed.

After the Indians had ceased to resist, it appears they were hunted by the Georgians and their Indian allies, and butchered without mercy, until the bodies of the victims of their worse than Indian barbarity, were piled up in heaps on the banks of the Talapoosa, "by their surviving friends;"[1] while of their houses, the number which were burned was "supposed to be four hundred." The loss which the Georgians sustained from these "fanatics," in their gallant defence of their village, was eleven *killed* and fifty-four *wounded;* that which fell on the friendly Indians has not been recorded;[2] while that which the savages sustained was estimated at two hundred.[3]

[Note.—The Dispatch of Gen. Floyd to Gen. Pinckney, which had been provided for the illustration of this chapter, has been omitted by the Publishers for want of room.]

CHAPTER LXX.

December 18 to 30, 1813.

THE INVASION OF NEW YORK.

The departure of General Wilkinson and the regular troops from the Niagara frontier, imposed upon General McClure and the New York militia, whom he commanded, the responsibility of defending that portion of the lines against the strong force of the enemy who still remained in that vicinity; and when, on the sixteenth of November, General Harrison left Fort George for Sackett's Harbor, nearly the last American regular left that important frontier.[4] The indiscretion of this abandonment of the frontier posts, while the terms of service for which the militia had been ordered out expired on the ninth of December, was soon apparent; and on the tenth of December General

[1] Gen. Floyd to Gen. Pinckney, Dec. 4; Perkins, p. 203.

[1] Gen. Floyd to Gen. Pinckney, Dec. 4; Drake's Book of Indians, Book iv., pp. 51, 58.

[2] Gen. Floyd to Gen. Pinckney, Dec. 4; Perkins, p. 204.

[3] Gen. Floyd to Gen. Pinckney, Dec. 4.

[4] Gen. McClure's Address "To the Public;" James' Military Occurrences, ii. p. 6; Perkins, pp. 265–267.

McClure found himself at Fort George with no more than sixty effective men, belonging to the Twenty-fourth United States infantry, with a much more powerful enemy in front, and with no prospect of the arrival of reinforcements.[1]

About the same time, in consequence of the unsuccessful termination of General Wilkinson's projected attack on Montreal, the enemy's forces on the Niagara had been strengthened by the arrival of reinforcements from below, under Lieutenant-general Drummond;[2] and when that officer pushed forward his *élite*,—about four hundred effective troops, besides seventy Indians,—under Colonel Murray, General McClure called a council, and, with its advice, determined to evacuate the post.[3] Accordingly, on the same day, after removing the greater part of the public stores to Fort Niagara, the fort was evacuated; and, at the same time, with a laudable desire to deprive the enemy of shelter,—yet with an inexcusable and terrible severity on the defenceless inhabitants,—the entire village of Newark, except one house, was committed to the flames;[4] and orders were soon after given to open a fire, with hot-shot, on Queenstown, for the same purpose.[5]

The extreme severity of this visitation of the miseries of war on the non-combatants residing in Newark and Queenstown, was productive of the most disastrous results, both in Canada and New York. In the midst of an unusually severe Canadian winter, the inhabitants were summoned to abandon their homes, at very short notice; and then, without shelter or provisions, even for their sick, to witness the entire destruction of all their property.[1] There is no evidence that any personal outrage was offered to any of the sufferers; but the indiscriminate desolation of a flourishing village, and the expulsion of its inhabitants, without shelter and without supplies, into the depths of a Canadian forest, in a Canadian winter, was an instance of barbarity, compared with which the horrors of legitimate warfare are tender mercies.

As has been stated, General McClure did not wholly succeed in his intended removal of his stores—tents for fifteen hundred men, several pieces of artillery, and a large quantity of shot, with ten of his men, falling into the hands of Colonel Murray and his detachment;[2] and the enemy once more occupied his own territory, without opposition.

The feelings of resentment, which the destruction of Newark had aroused, speedily directed the attention of the enemy to the opposite shore of the Niagara; and preparations were made for a retaliatory descent on the American posts and the neighboring villages in the State of New York.[3] Accordingly, on the evening of the eighteenth of

[1] Gen. McClure's Address.—[2] Rogers' Rise of Canada, i. p. 243. These reinforcements consisted of the Royal Scots, the 49th and 100th regiments of the line, with a small provincial corps, and 200 Indians.—*Armstrong's Notices*, ii. p. 19.—[3] Gen. McClure to Sec. of War, Dec. 10, 1813; Gen. McClure's Address; Col. Murray to Gen. Vincent, Dec. 12; James, ii. pp. 7, 8.

[4] Gen. McClure to Sec. of War, Dec. 10, 1813; "*The War*," ii. p. 116; Gen. McClure's Address; Col. Murray to Gen. Vincent, Dec. 12.—[5] Gen. McClure to Sec. of War, Dec. 25, 1813; Armstrong's Notices, ii. p. 20

[1] Gen. McClure to Sec. of War, Dec. 25, 1813; James, ii. pp. 8, 9.—[2] James, ii. p. 11.—[3] Ibid., p. 13; Thomson's Sketches, p. 189.

December, Colonel Murray, with a detachment of Royal Artillery, the grenadiers of the Royal Scots, the flank companies of the Forty-first regiment, and the One hundredth regiment,[1] in all, about five hundred and fifty men,[2] crossed the river, and landed at Five-mile Meadows, about three miles above Fort Niagara;[3] and, at four the next morning, he commenced his march for the fort.[4]

His advance succeeded in capturing two of the pickets which had been thrown out from the fort; and the intelligence of his approach having thus been withheld, the garrison slept soundly. The sentries on the glacis and at the *open* gate of the fort, by sudden and expert movements of the enemy's advance, were also seized and silenced; and from them *the countersign was obtained*.[5] The enemy's forces had been arranged for a systematic assault, on the several bastions of the fort; and a supply of scaling-ladders, &c., were carried to facilitate his operations. The main gate of the fort, *standing wide open*, however, without a soul to present any opposition to his entrance, rendered all these preparations unnecessary; and, with his entire party, Colonel Murray entered the fort. The guard, who occupied the southeast block-house, when the enemy presented himself, rushed out of its quarters and fired a volley; and the invalids, who occupied the "red barracks," also offered a slight resistance; but the greater part of the garrison—without an officer to command it[1]—was too fast asleep to realize its danger until it was too late to offer any opposition.[2]

Smarting under the grievances which the destruction of Newark had imposed, and closing his eyes and ears to every plea of humanity, Colonel Murray's bayonets not only "overpowered all resistance,"[3] but, at the same time, destroyed his character, both as a man and a soldier.[4] Sixty-five men—two-thirds of whom were hospital patients[5]—were bayoneted as they laid in their beds, besides fifteen others who were bayoneted in the cellars of the houses; fourteen others were wounded; and a captain, nine lieutenants, two ensigns, two staff-officers, and three hundred and thirty men were taken prisoners. Twenty, only, of the entire garrison, escaped;[6] and twenty-seven pieces of artillery, three thousand stands of arms, with immense quantities of ordnance and commissariat stores, clothing and camp-equipage, were also among the trophies of the victory.[7] Of the enemy, Lieutenant Nowlan and five men were

[1] "*General Orders*," signed "J. Harvey, *Lieut.-Col.*, *D. A. G.*," Dec. 19, 1813; Col. Murray to Gen. Drummond, Dec. 19; Rogers, i. p. 243.—[2] James, ii. p. 13; Armstrong, ii. p. 22. Robert Lee's Narrative, in the Buffalo *Gazette*, says about *four hundred*; Mr. Perkins (*Hist.*, p. 269), *twelve hundred*.—[3] Gen. McClure to Sec. of War, Dec. 22, 1813; Col. Murray to Gen. Drummond, Dec. 19.

[4] Robert Lee's Narrative; James, ii. p. 14.

[5] Col. Murray to Gen. Drummond, Dec. 19; James, ii. p. 14; Armstrong, ii. p. 22; Rogers, i. p. 244.

[1] It is said that Capt. Leonard, the commander of the fort, was with his family, on that night; while Gen. McClure was at Buffalo.—[2] Gov. D. D. Tompkins to Sec. of War, Dec. 24; Gen. McClure to Sec. of War, Dec. 22, 1813; Robert Lee's Narrative; James, ii. p. 14; Perkins, p. 269; Thomson's Sketches, p. 189; Rogers, i. p. 243.

[3] "*General Orders*," signed "J. Harvey, *Lieut.-Col.*, *D. A. G.*," Dec. 19; James, ii. p. 14.—[4] Armstrong, ii. p. 22.

[5] Ibid.—[6] Gen. McClure to Sec. of War, Dec. 22, 1813; "*General Orders*," signed "J. Harvey, *Lieut.-Col.*, *D. A. G.*," Dec. 19; Robert Lee's Narrative.

[7] "*General Orders*," signed "Edw. Bayne, *Adj.-Gen.*," Dec. 27, 1813; Col. Murray to Gen. Drummond, Dec. 19.

killed, and Colonel Murray, a surgeon, and three men were *wounded*.[1]

On the same morning on which the fort was captured, General Rial, at the head of detachments from the Royal Scots, under Lieutenant-Colonel Gordon, and from the Forty-first regiment, with upwards of five hundred Indians,[2] crossed the river from Queenstown to Lewiston,[3] and after a slight opposition from a small party of Americans, under Major Bennett, took possession of the village, and two guns which had been abandoned by the Americans.[4] The village was no sooner occupied than it was given up to plunder and destruction; and the Indians pillaged and burned it with the most aggravated enormities.[5] The villages of Youngstown, Manchester, Fort Schlosser, and the Indian village at Tuscarora, and the neighboring farms, immediately afterwards shared the same fate;[6] and the entire frontier, for several miles back from the river, presented one scene of universal desolation, while the inhabitants were either butchered, in cold blood, by the savages, or were flying before their pursuers, terror-stricken and without hope.[7]

After desolating the country as far as Tonewanta Creek, and leaving no signs of civilization, the enemy's progress was checked, by the destruction of the bridge which crossed that stream, and he returned to the site of Lewiston and recrossed to Queenstown.

Meanwhile the frontier above the falls had not been visited, and General Hall, of the New York militia, on the twenty-sixth of December, reached Buffalo, at which place he found "a considerable body of irregular troops, of various descriptions," who had previously assembled there for the purpose of checking the progress of the enemy. The troops, however, were "disorganized and confused; every thing wore the appearance of consternation and dismay;" and the entire force numbered only seventeen hundred and eleven men. Another regiment, numbering three hundred men, joined him on the twenty-ninth; but the entire force was poorly supplied with arms or ammunition, and the cartridges of one regiment were made and distributed after it was paraded on the morning of the battle.[1]

While these troops were thus collecting at Buffalo, Lieutenant-general Drummond moved to Chippewa; and, on the twenty-eighth of December, having reconnoitred the American camp, he determined to attack it.[2] Accordingly, in the evening of the next day (*December 29th*), General Rial was dispatched with a detachment from the Royal Scots, four companies of the Eighth regiment, two hundred and fifty men from the Forty-first, the flank com-

[1] "*General Orders*," signed "J. HARVEY, *Lieut.-Col.*, *D. A. G.*," Dec. 19; Returns appended to Col. Murray's Dispatch, Dec. 19.—[2] "*General Orders*," signed "J. HARVEY, *Lieut.-Col.*, *D. A. G.*," Dec. 19; James, ii. p. 18.

[3] Gen. Hopkins to Gov. Tompkins, Dec. 20; James, ii. p. 18.—[4] Gen. McClure's Address; Gen. McClure to Sec. of War, Dec. 22, 1813; James, ii. p. 19.—[5] Gen. Hopkins to Gov. Tompkins, Dec. 20; Gen. McClure to Sec. of War, Dec. 22, 1813; James, ii. p. 19.—[6] Gen. Hopkins to Gov. Tompkins, Dec. 20; Gen. McClure to Sec. of War, Dec. 22, 1813.—[7] Letter from Le Roy, Jan. 6; Appeal to the Benevolent, Canandaigua, Jan. 8, 1814; Rogers, i. p. 245.

[1] Gen. Hall to Gov. Tompkins, Jan. 6, 1814.

[2] James, ii. p. 20; Rogers, i. p. 245.

panies of the Eighty-ninth and the One hundredth, a body of Canadian militia, and one of Indians;[1] and having crossed the river, landed about two miles below Black Rock,[2] without opposition, and, apparently, without the knowledge of the Americans. The light company of the Eighty-ninth, as an advance-guard, having pushed forward to Canjokaties Creek, after a slight resistance from a horse patrol under Lieutenant Boughton, took possession of the "Sailor's Battery" and the bridge at that place;[3] and having secured the pass, and moved the grenadiers and the detachment from the Forty-first to sustain the light-troops, the enemy halted there until morning.[4]

Supposing this movement to have been intended as a feint, General Hall continued to occupy the village of Buffalo with his main body, while Colonels Warren and Churchill were ordered to drive the enemy from the Canjokaties back to his boats; which, although attempted, was, of course, entirely unsuccessful—the men not only dispersing before the enemy's fire, but they also *deserted.* A larger body,—some four hundred and fifty strong,—under Lieutenant-colonel Chapin and Major Adams, were equally unsuccessful and unfaithful.[5]

At daybreak the Royal Scots, eight hundred strong, also crossed the river,

[1] "*General Orders,*" signed "Edw. Bayne, *Adj,-Gen.,*" Jan. 8, 1814; Gen. Rial to Gen. Drummond, Jan. 1, 1814; James, ii. p. 20.—[2] Gen. Rial to Gen. Drummond, Jan. 1, 1814; "*The War,*" ii. p. 123; James, ii. p. 20.

[3] Gen. Hall to Gov. Tompkins, Jan. 6, 1814; Gen. Rial to Gen. Drummond, Jan. 1; James, ii. pp. 20, 21.

[4] Gen. Rial to Gen. Drummond, Jan. 1; James, ii. p. 21.

[5] Gen. Hall to Gov. Tompkins, Jan. 6; Perkins, p. 270.

and landed between Black Rock and Buffalo, under cover of a five-gun battery on the Canadian shore, yet not without meeting some considerable loss.[1] Having landed and displayed his force, enabling General Hall to understand his intended order of battle, the latter ordered Lieutenant-colonel Granger, with eighty-three Indians, and Major Mallory, with ninety-seven, "Canadian Volunteers," to attack the enemy's left wing, while Lieutenant-colonel Blakeslie, with four hundred and thirty-three Ontario county militia and exempts, was opposed to his right, and Colonel McMahan, with three hundred Chatauque militia, was posted at the Battery as a reserve, "to act as emergencies should require."[2]

The action was commenced soon afterwards, by the artillery of both parties, and by the regiment under Lieutenant-colonel Blakeslie; and, with the coolness of veterans, the latter disputed every inch of ground. As the enemy advanced, however, the Indians and Canadians fell back, apparently without a struggle, and the right flank of the left wing of the American line was exposed to the overpowering numbers of the enemy's left wing. To prevent such a catastrophe, General Hall immediately ordered the reserve, under Colonel McMahan, to move forward and take the right of the line; but, as in the case of its predecessors, "terror had dissipated the corps, and but few of the men could be rallied by their officers and brought to the attack."[3]

[1] Gen. Hall to Gov. Tompkins, Jan. 6; Gen. Rial to Gen. Drummond, Jan. 1.—[2] Gen. Hall to Gov. Tompkins, Jan. 6.—[3] Ibid.; James, ii. p. 22.

Thus deserted by the greater part of his force, and with the Ontario militia alone to oppose the progress of the enemy, General Hall was compelled to fall back, and every subsequent attempt to rally the troops was ineffectual;[1] while to the enemy were abandoned the villages of Black Rock and Buffalo, which shared the fate of Lewiston, Youngstown, and that portion of the frontier which were first visited.[2] In fact, so completely was the work of desolation carried on, that in Buffalo the only buildings which remained standing were the jail (a stone building), and a frame dwelling, owned by a widow St. John, "who had the address to appease the ferocity of the enemy so far as to remain in her house uninjured;" while in Black Rock, all except one—a log-house, in which some women and children had taken refuge—were either burned or blown up.[3] At the same time, the *Ariel*, *Little Belt*, *Chippewa*, and *Trippe*,—the prizes and their victors,—also fell into the enemy's hands, and shared the common fate.[1]

During this invasion the most refined barbarities were practised on the inhabitants, both by the soldiery and the Indians;[2] and no mercy, except to the widow St. John, and the occupants of the log-house at Black Rock, appears to have been shown to any one.[3] The loss of the Americans, in the defence of Buffalo and Black Rock, is not known, but over fifty dead were afterwards picked up and buried;[4] that of the enemy was reported to have been thirty-one men *killed;* Lieutenant-colonel Ogilvie, Captains Fawcett and Scroos, Lieutenant Young, and sixty-eight men *wounded;* and nine men *missing.*[5]

[NOTE.—Gen. McClure's Report to the Sec. of War, and Lieut.-Col. Murray's to Gen. Drummond, concerning Forts George and Niagara, and the destruction of the lower villages; and Gen. Hall's Report to Gov. Tompkins, and Gen. Rial's to Gen. Drummond, concerning the action at Black Rock and the destruction of the upper villages, have been omitted by the Publishers for want of room.]

CHAPTER LXXI.

December 23, 1813.

THE BATTLE AT ECCANACHACA.

WHILE the Creeks of the Coosa and Tallapoosa were encountering the arms of Tennessee and Georgia, under Generals Jackson and Floyd, those of the Southwest, under General Ferdinand L. Claiborne, approached the enemy's country which laid in the vicinity of

[1] "*The War,*" ii. p. 130; "*General Orders,*" signed "EDW. BAYNE, *Adj.-Gen.*," Jan. 8, 1814; Gen. Hall to Gov. Tompkins, Jan. 6; Gen. Rial to Gen. Drummond, Jan. 1.—[2] Gen. Hall to Gov. Tompkins, Jan. 6; Gen. Rial to Gen. Drummond, Jan. 1; "*The War,*" ii. p. 130; James, ii. p. 22.—[3] "*The War,*" ii. p. 130; "*General Orders,*" signed "EDW. BAYNE, *Adj.-Gen.*," Jan. 8, 1814; Anthony Lamb to Gov. Tompkins, Jan. 20.

[1] "*The War,*" ii. p. 130; "*General Orders,*" signed "EDW. BAYNE, *Adj.-Gen.*," Jan. 8, 1814; Anthony Lamb to Gov. Tompkins, Jan. 20. Mr. James (*Mil. Occur.*, ii. p. 22) alludes *only* to the three vessels last named.

[2] "*The War,*" ii. p. 123; The *Argus*, Albany, Jan. 21, 1814; Anthony Lamb to Gov. Tompkins, Jan. 20.

[3] Gen. McClure to Sec. of War, Dec. 22, 1813; Letter from Le Roy, Jan. 6; Appeal to the Benevolent, Jan. 8, 1814.—[4] Gen. Hall to Gov. Tompkins, Jan. 13.

[5] Returns appended to Gen. Rial's Dispatch.

the Alabama, where Weatherford—the commander of those who carried Fort Mimms and massacred its garrison—had taken up a position at Eccanachaca, or the Holy Ground, on the bank of that river.[1]

After a perilous march through an almost unbroken forest of upwards of a hundred miles in extent, on the morning of the twenty-third of December the expedition approached the town, and a disposition was made for the attack. The troops were disposed in three columns, with Lester's guards and Wells' troop of dragoons to act as a reserve. The right column was composed of twelve-months' volunteers, under Colonel Joseph Carson; the centre, of a detachment from the Third regiment of United States infantry and of mounted militia riflemen, under Lieutenant-colonel Russell; and the left, of militia and a party of Choctaws, under Major Smoot.[2]

The position which the enemy occupied was nearly surrounded by swamps and deep ravines, which rendered the approach of the troops very difficult; and at the same time they facilitated the escape of those by whom the position was occupied. Large quantities of provisions, and property of great value

[1] Claiborne's Notes, p. 36; Goodwin's Jackson, p. 68.
[2] Gen. Claiborne to Sec. of War, Jan. 1, 1814.

had been collected there; and the idea of the sacred character of the ground, with which this spot, like Autossee, was supposed to have been invested, and the consequent inability of the pale-faces to take possession of it, caused its defenders to resist the assailants with great energy and determination.[1]

With the utmost coolness the three columns took up their line of march; and at about noon that on the right came within sight of the enemy, by whom it was attacked with great resolution. The volunteers sustained the attack with so much spirit, that before the centre and left could, generally, unite in the charge, the power of the enemy had been broken, and he had sought refuge in a precipitate flight.[2]

The town, embracing two hundred houses, and the property which it contained, were committed to the flames; and on the following day another village, not far distant, shared the same fate.[3]

In this engagement thirty Indians were *killed;* while of the assailants one was *killed*, and six were *wounded.*[4]

[Note.—The Dispatch of Gen. Claiborne to the Secretary of War has been omitted by the Publishers for want of room.]

[1] Gen. Claiborne to Sec. of War, Jan. 1, 1814; Goodwin's Jackson, p. 68; Perkins, p. 206.—[2] Gen. Claiborne to Sec. of War, Jan. 1.—[3] Ibid.; Goodwin's Jackson, p. 68.—[4] Gen. Claiborne to Sec. of War, Jan. 1; Breckenridge, p. 220.

CHAPTER LXXII.

January 22, 1814.

THE BATTLES OF EMUCKFAU.

THE Tennessean volunteers commanded by General Jackson, having claimed their discharge and abandoned the service;[1] and another body, to take the places of the former, having gradually assembled at head-quarters, preparations were made to renew the operations against the enemy.[2]

Accordingly, on the fifteenth of January, 1814, the mounted troops commenced their march from Fort Strother into the enemy's country; and on the following day the remainder of the force followed—the whole numbering nine hundred and thirty effective men.[3] The bad effects of keeping the troops without employment, added to a threatened attack on Fort Armstrong, by the Indians, led the General to delay his march as little as possible; and on the eighteenth he encamped at Talladega, where he was joined by a party of friendly Indians—two or three hundred in number—under Jim Fife.[4] Pressing forward as rapidly as possible towards the Tallapoosa—on which, near the mouth of the Emuckfau Creek, the enemy had assembled in great numbers—on the evening of the twentieth he encamped at Enotochopco, about twelve miles from Emuckfau; marching from thence, on the following morning, towards the latter place; and towards evening, having struck a large trail, he encamped for the night and proceeded to reconnoitre.[1] Posting his troops in a hollow square, he sent out his pickets and spies, doubled his sentinels, and made every preparation for a proper reception of the enemy in case of an attack, which, from the reports of his spies, appeared to be intended; and in this order he awaited the attack and the approach of day.[2]

At six o'clock on the morning of the twenty-second, the enemy suddenly, and with great fury, fell on the left flank of the encampment, where Colonel Higgins was posted; and, as the troops who were stationed there, maintained their position with great resolution, under the direction of General Coffee, and Colonels Sittler and Carroll, the assailants made but little progress. For half an hour they were amused and held in check by the Tennesseans, but when daylight afforded an opportunity to pursue them advantageously, the left

[1] Perkins' Hist. of War, pp. 206–208; Eaton's Jackson, pp. 78–124.—[2] Eaton, pp. 124–132; McAfee, p. 473.

[3] Gen. Jackson's Dispatch to Gen. Pinckney, Jan. 29, 1814; McAfee, p. 473.—[4] Gen. Jackson to Gen Pinckney, Jan. 29; Eaton, p. 132; Drake's Book of Indians, Bk. iv., p. 58.

[1] Gen. Jackson to Gen. Pinckney, Jan. 29; Perkins. p. 208; McAfee, pp. 473, 474.—[2] Gen. Jackson to Gen. Pinckney, Jan. 29; Eaton, p. 134; Drake, Bk. iv., p. 59.

wing was strengthened with Captain Ferrill's company of infantry, and, under the direction of General Coffee, it charged and repulsed them on every side; and the friendly Indians joining in the pursuit, they were chased about two miles, suffering severely as they fled.[1]

Immediately afterwards General Coffee, with the friendly Indians and four hundred men, was sent to destroy the enemy's encampment on the Emuckfau; but it was found to be too strong, and he returned to the camp for the purpose of guarding the artillery on its march to his assistance. While he was still there, however, a strong body of savages fell on the right of the encampment; and he solicited and obtained permission to move to the support of that portion of the lines with two hundred men, and with them to fall on the enemy's left flank, while the friendly Indians should, simultaneously, fall on his right. In consequence of some mistake, however, he took with him only fifty-four men; and with these he gallantly attacked the enemy, and kept him in check, while General Jackson, whose good judgment led him to suppose this attack was but a feint to divert his attention from another and heavier assault, wisely ordered the remainder of his troops to remain at their respective posts ready for instantaneous action.[2]

The prudence of this step was soon apparent; as, simultaneously with General Coffee's attack on the savages on the right of the encampment, the main body of the enemy, with great vigor, renewed its attack on the left flank, from whence, a short time before, he had been driven. With the discharge of the first gun in that quarter, however, General Jackson led in person, to the support of the troops—who were already fatigued by their participation in the action in the morning—the same company (*Captain Ferrill's*) which had before supported them, and participated with them in their first triumph; and thus united with their former associates and under the eye of their commanding general, they again moved to meet their enemy. After two or three volleys, they resorted again to the bayonet; and dashed forward against their assailants with spirit and success. In the language of the General, "the effect was immediate and inevitable." The assailants fled with precipitation, and was pursued to a considerable distance by the left flank; while the friendly Indians, forsaking their post on the right flank, fell in the pursuit and harassed the fugitives with a galling and destructive fire.[1]

In the mean time General Coffee was gallantly struggling, with the fifty-four men of his command, against the assailants on the right of the encampment; and since the friendly Indians, who had been ordered to co-operate with him, had preferred the more exciting scenes of the chase, on the opposite flank, and had forsaken him, his situation was at once critical and important. Accordingly Jim Fife, with one hundred of

[1] Gen. Jackson to Gen. Pinckney, Jan. 29, 1814; Eaton, pp. 134, 135; Claiborne's Notes, p. 38.—[2] Gen. Jackson to Gen. Pinckney, Jan. 29, 1814; Eaton, pp. 135, 136; Perkins, p. 209; McAfee, p. 474.

[1] Gen. Jackson to Gen. Pinckney, Jan. 29, 1814; Eaton, pp. 136, 137; Perkins, pp. 209, 210; Drake, Bk. iv., p. 59.

his warriors, when he had returned from the pursuit, was ordered a second time to fall on the enemy's right flank, which was promptly and gallantly executed; and at the same time General Coffee, with his little party, charged on the left flank with equal spirit and effect. Dispirited by the retreat of his main body, and unable to continue the contest against the simultaneous attacks on both his flanks, the enemy at length gave way, and retreated precipitately in every direction, suffering, from the same hands as before, another heavy loss. It was not, however, without cost that this victory was gained, as General Coffee was severely wounded, and Colonel A. Donaldson, his aid, was killed.[1]

Without renewing his attempt to destroy the enemy's encampment at Emuckfau, General Jackson found it "necessary" to fall back on Fort Strother on the following day;[2] and the enemy, with good reason, considered this a victory for *his* cause, hanging on his rear, and harassing his retreat.[3]

[NOTE.—An extract from the Dispatch of Gen. Jackson to Gen. Pinckney has been omitted by the Publishers for want of room.]

CHAPTER LXXIII.

January 24, 1814.

THE BATTLE OF ENOTOCHOPCO.

THE repulse of the Indians at Emuckfau, and the subsequent retrograde movement of the troops under General Jackson, have been referred to in the last chapter of this work; and the belief that he had been defeated, which the enemy reasonably entertained, has also been noticed.

At half-past ten in the morning of the twenty-third, the expedition commenced its "return march" from the scene of its engagement on the preceding day; and the General congratulated his superior officer that he was allowed to reach Enotochopco before night, without interruption from the enemy. Having fortified his camp, he passed the night in safety; and fearing an attack at a defile, near which he crossed a large creek, while advancing into the country, he resolved to seek some other and less dangerous crossing-place for his passage on his return.[4]

Accordingly, in the morning of the twenty-fourth, he broke up his encampment and moved off in regular order, leading down a handsome ridge to the Enotochopco Creek, at a point where it was clear of reed, except immediately on its margin. A general order had been issued, in which the order of battle was designated; the officers had been particularly cautioned to halt and form, the instant the word should be given; and every possible preparation had been made to guard not only against a surprise, but against any hostile movement which the enemy might undertake.[5]

[1] Gen. Jackson to Gen. Pinckney, Jan. 29; Eaton, pp. 137, 138; Drake, Bk. iv., p. 59.—[2] Gen. Jackson to Gen. Pinckney, Jan. 29; McAfee, p. 476.—[3] Perkins, pp. 210, 211; Drake, Bk. iv., p. 59.—[4] Gen. Jackson to Gen. Pinckney, Jan. 29; Drake, Bk. iv., p. 59.—[5] Gen. Jackson to Gen. Pinckney, Jan. 29; Claiborne, p. 38; Eaton, pp, 140, 141.

In this order the expedition approached the creek and commenced its passage; but the advance-guard and part of the flank columns, with the wounded, had only crossed, and the artillery was entering the stream, when an alarm-gun was heard in the rear, and the approach of the enemy was made known. Having the most perfect confidence in his troops, General Jackson heard the signal without any surprise or uneasiness; and he turned back to direct the operations. Colonel Carroll commanded the centre column of the rear-guard, Colonel Perkins that on the right, and Colonel Stump that on the left; and the design was to wheel the flanking columns, which had passed the creek, on their pivots; to recross the creek above and below the enemy; and to fall on his flanks and rear, while the rear-guard would engage him in front. The plan thus formed appeared to guarantee success, and Colonel Carroll ordered the centre to halt and form in order of battle, in accordance with this order. But to the surprise of every one, and so far as is now known, without any cause, the right and left columns of the rear-guard suddenly broke and fled in the greatest confusion. Thus deprived of all support, with its flanks exposed to the assaults of the enemy, the greater part of the centre, also, gave way, and not more than twenty-five men rallied around Colonel Carroll to oppose the enemy. The company of artillery, under Lieutenant Robert Armstrong,[1] and the company of spies, under Captain William Russell, soon afterwards moved to their support; and, with great labor, and under a heavy fire, having dragged a six-pounder up the slope from the creek, they opened a well-directed and destructive fire on the enemy, which threw him into confusion; when they charged and repulsed him.[1]

It was during this part of the engagement that the gallant conduct of Constantine Perkins and Craven Jackson, two privates in the artillery, acting as gunners, was signally displayed, and secured the victory. "In the hurry of the moment, in separating the gun from the limber, the rammer and picker of the cannon were left tied to the limber. No sooner was this discovered, than Jackson, amidst the galling fire of the enemy, pulled out the ramrod of his musket, and used it as a picker; primed with a cartridge, and fired the cannon. Perkins having pulled off his bayonet, using his musket as a rammer, drove down the cartridge; and Jackson, using his former plan, again discharged her."[2]

The loss of the enemy in this engagement was very heavy, twenty-six of his warriors having been picked up—a fraction only of those who fell.[3] The loss of the Americans has not been recorded.

The expedition then continued on its march, and reached Fort Strother without farther interruption.[4]

[Note.—An extract from the Dispatch of Gen. Jackson to Gen. Pinckney has been omitted by the Publishers for want of room.]

---

[1] Since the well-known Consul of the United States at Liverpool.

[1] Gen. Jackson to Gen. Pinckney, Jan. 29; Claiborne, pp. 38, 39; Drake, Bk. iv., p. 59; Eaton, pp. 141-144.

[2] Gen. Jackson to Gen. Pinckney, Jan. 29; Claiborne, p. 39.—[3] Gen. Jackson to Gen. Pinckney, Jan. 29. Mr. Drake (*Book of Indians*, Bk. iv., p. 60) has erroneously stated that the Indians lost, "*in this battle*," 189 warriors. This was the number which fell "in these several engagements,"—those at Emuckfau as well as this,—and not in this alone.—[4] Claiborne, p. 39.

CHAPTER LXXIV.

January 27, 1814.[1]

THE BATTLE AT CHALIBBEE.[2]

WHILE General Jackson, with the Tennesseans, was actively engaged with the Indians in one part of the enemy's country, General Floyd, with the Georgians, continued to harass him on the Chatahoochie.

In the prosecution of his designs, in the latter part of January, 1814, he encamped about fifty miles west from the Chatahoochie; where the enemy made all necessary preparations to attack him. Accordingly at twenty minutes past five, in the morning of the twenty-seventh of January, 1814, a very large body of Indians stole upon the camp, shot the sentinels, and with great fury rushed upon the lines—attacking, simultaneously, the front and both flanks, and pressing on them with the most resolute determination. In front, the artillery under Captain Jett Thomas, the riflemen under Captain William E. Adams, and a picket under Captain Robert Broadnax, with great gallantry and severe loss, stemmed the current of the enemy, notwithstanding he rushed within thirty yards of the artillery; and, on either flank, the battle also raged furiously, while the darkness of the morning, rendered still more dark by the forest of heavy pines in which the camp was situated,[1] added terror to the hideous yells with which the assailants filled the air.[2]

When daylight relieved the scene of the greater part of its terrors, by revealing the situation and movements of the enemy, the right wing of the forces, embracing the battalions commanded by Majors Booth and Cleveland, supported by those commanded by Majors Watson and Freeman, and a troop of cavalry under Captain Duke Hamilton, was ordered to charge on the enemy. This order was promptly obeyed; and, with but very little resistance, the enemy fled in every direction before the bayonets of the infantry. At this moment the cavalry was directed to join in the pursuit; and the friendly Indians, with Meriweather's and Ford's companies of riflemen, accompanying the troopers, a heavy loss was inflicted on the fugitives, thirty-seven of whom were left dead on the field, besides those who were carried away.[3]

The loss of the Georgians was seven-

---

[1] Mr. Perkins (*Hist. of War*, p. 204) supposes this action was fought on the *second* of January.

[2] This is sometimes known as "The Attack on Camp Defiance." I have adopted the name given in the official documents.

[1] White's Historical Collections of Georgia, p. 291.

[2] Gen. Floyd to Gen. Pinckney, Jan. 27, 1814; Claiborne's Notes, pp. 36, 37; Perkins' History of War, pp. 204, 205.

[3] Gen. Floyd to Gen. Pinckney, Jan. 27; Claiborne's Notes, pp. 36, 37.

teen *killed* and one hundred and thirty-two *wounded;* that of the friendly Indians was five *killed* and fifteen *wounded.*[1]

Within a few days after this action, the term for which the troops had been raised expired, and the several companies were honorably discharged;[1] and no expedition was afterwards organized in Georgia against the Creeks.[2]

[Note.—The Dispatch of Gen. Floyd to Gen. Pinckney has been omitted by the Publishers for want of room.]

CHAPTER LXXV.

March 4, 1814.

THE ACTION AT LONGWOOD, U. C.

During the winter of 1813–14, no movement of importance was organized in the Northwest; and each of the great contending parties contented itself with an occasional minor operation against some outpost of its opponent.[2]

One of these was planned in February, 1814, by Lieutenant-colonel Butler, who commanded at Detroit, in the absence of General Lewis Cass; and he intrusted its execution to Captain Holmes of the Twenty-fourth regiment. Its object was to attack Fort Talbot, a British outpost about one hundred miles down Lake Erie; and for this purpose a small party of artillerists, with two six-pounders, small detachments from the Twenty-fourth and Twenty-eighth regiments of infantry, a company of Rangers under Captain McCormick, and a troop of militia dragoons, in all about one hundred and sixty men, were detached, and left Detroit on the twenty-first of February.[3]

Unexpected difficulties on his line of march preventing the passage of his field-pieces, Captain Holmes determined to change his course, for the purpose of breaking up a British outpost which had been erected at Delaware on the River Thames; and, on the 3d of March, while still approaching that place, he learned that its garrison was ascending the river and would, probably, meet him within an hour. His force being much smaller than that which his opponent was reported to have under his command, Captain Holmes resolved to leave Captain Gill, with twenty Rangers, to cover his rear, and, with his main body, to fall back to Twenty-mile Creek, five miles in his rear, on the western bank of which was a good position for defence. Accordingly he retrograded; and, as the enemy pursued him, the night of the third was spent, by both parties, on the banks of that stream—the Americans on the western and the British on its eastern margin.[3]

---

[1] Returns appended to Gen. Floyd's Report, signed "Charles Williamson, *Hospital-surgeon.*"—[2] McAfee, pp. 410, 411; James' Mil. Occur., ii. p. 75.—[3] Lieut.-Col. Butler to Gen. Harrison, March 7; James, ii. p. 76; Breckenridge, p. 235; Armstrong's Notices, ii. p. 67.

[1] White's Hist. Coll. of Georgia, p. 292.—[2] Claiborne's Notes, p. 37.—[3] Capt. Holmes to Lieut.-Col. Butler, March 10, 1814; James, ii. p. 76; Breckenridge, p. 235; McAfee, p. 412.

At this place the Twenty-mile Creek runs a southerly course, through a deep and wide ravine; and, of course, it became necessary, before the enemy could attack the position which Captain Holmes occupied, that he should descend into the ravine and then ascend the western bank—an operation which would involve much danger in the experiment.[1]

After passing the night without any interruption, at sunrise on the fourth, Captain Holmes discovered a very small party of the enemy, on the opposite bank; and, soon afterwards, after firing several times, it disappeared. After waiting some time for its reappearance, Lieutenant Knox, of the Rangers, was sent to reconnoitre; and, on his return, reported that the enemy had retreated, apparently, with the utmost precipitation; that his baggage, &c., were scattered along his route, where it had been thrown in his haste to escape; and that, from his fires and his trail, he did not appear to have had more than seventy men. Mortified with the reflection that he had retreated before so weak an enemy, and without even thinking that this might be a stratagem, by means of which he could be drawn from his position, and be placed on ground which was more assailable, Captain Holmes "instantly commenced the pursuit, with the design of attacking Delaware before the opening of another day." He had not proceeded more than five miles, however, before Captain Lee, who commanded his advance, discovered the enemy arranging himself for battle; and the secret, at once, flashed across his mind, that he had committed a rash and, probably, a fatal error. As rapidly as possible, however, the Captain retrograded, and assumed his former position on the western bank of the creek; strengthening it, as much as possible, with a breastwork of logs, faced with brush. Taking into consideration the character of his troops, and desiring to "prevent the necessity of evolutions which he knew all his men were incompetent to perform in action," Captain Holmes adopted the order of the hollow square—the detachments from the Twenty-fourth and Twenty-eighth occupying the brow of the heights, fronting the east; that from the garrison of Detroit (Captain Gill's command), on the north front; the Rangers, on the west; the militia, on the south; and the horses and baggage, in the centre.[1]

When the enemy perceived that his pursuers had returned to the position from which they had just been drawn, he, in his turn, became the pursuer, and prepared to cross the creek and attack the Americans within their lines. For this purpose he threw his militia and Indians across the creek, above the encampment; and with them he invested its northern, western, and southern fronts; while, at the same time, his regular troops pushed over the bridge, and charged up the heights in front of the American lines, in the face of a ter-

[1] Capt. Holmes to Lieut.-Col. Butler, March 10; James, ii. p. 76.

[1] Capt. Holmes to Lieut.-Col. Butler, March 10; Auchinleck, p. 278; Breckenridge, pp. 235, 236; Armstrong, ii. pp. 69, 70.

ribly destructive fire. Notwithstanding the American regulars—who occupied the eastern front, and opposed those of the enemy—were entirely uncovered, through the good management of their commander (in ordering them to kneel for the purpose of concealing the greater part of their bodies) they suffered but little loss from the enemy; while their fire was exceedingly severe, cutting down the whole of his front section, and greatly thinning those which followed. At length, dispirited with his loss, and scarcely hoping for success, the enemy's regular troops abandoned their position on the eastern front of the American lines; and, in open order, they took cover in the adjacent woods, and continued a desultory fire with considerable spirit until late in the afternoon.[1]

In the mean time, sheltered behind their log breastworks, the Americans on the northern, western, and southern fronts sustained the fire of their assailants without confusion, and returned it with spirit and effect. Their muskets and rifles, aimed at leisure, generally sent the balls with unerring aim; and on these fronts, as on the eastern, victory perched on the banners of the Americans, notwithstanding the activity which characterized the assailants on those fronts.[2]

At length, about sunset, after an engagement of over an hour, the several bodies of the enemy, apparently "in concert, and favored by the shades of twilight, commenced a general retreat," in which, from proper considerations, he received no interruption.[1]

The effective force of the Americans in this severe engagement was one hundred and fifty, of whom seventy were militia;[2] that of the enemy embraced the two flank companies of the Royal Scots, the light-company of the Eighty-ninth regiment, and detachments from the Rangers and the Kent militia, with a large body of Indians, being, in the aggregate, not less than three hundred men, of whom from one hundred and fifty to one hundred and eighty were regulars.[3] The loss of the Americans, killed and wounded, was a sergeant and six privates;[4] that of the enemy, including his killed, wounded, and prisoners, was about seventy,[5] exclusive of that of his Indian allies.

[Note.—The Dispatch of Capt. Holmes to Lieut.-Col. Butler, and General Orders from British Adj.-Gen.'s office, have been omitted by the Publishers for want of room.]

---

[1] Capt. Holmes to Lieut.-Col. Butler, March 10; James, ii. pp. 76, 77; Breckenridge, p. 236; Armstrong, ii. pp. 70, 71; McAfee, p. 413; Thomson's Sketches, pp. 271, 272.

[2] Capt. Holmes to Lieut.-Col. Butler, March 10; James, ii. p. 77; Breckenridge, p. 236; McAfee, pp. 413, 414.

[1] Capt. Holmes to Lieut.-Col. Butler, March 10; James, ii. p. 77; "General Orders, Quebec, March 18," signed "E. Bayne, *Adj.-Gen.*"—[2] Capt. Holmes to Lieut.-Col. Butler, March 10; Lieut.-Col. Butler to Gen. Harrison, March 7; Thomson's Sketches, p. 272.—[3] Capt. Holmes to Lieut.-Col. Butler, March 10; McAfee, p. 412; "General Orders, Quebec, March 18," signed "E. Bayne, *Adj.-Gen.*"—[4] Capt. Holmes to Lieut.-Col. Butler, March 10.

[5] The *National Intelligencer*, cited by Mr. Niles (*Register*, vi. p. 69), says it was "upwards of 70;" the Returns, appended to the "General Orders," March 18, "at *sixty-seven*, killed, wounded, and missing;" Lieut.-Col. Butler (*Letter to Gen. Harrison, March* 7) says it was "about 80;" Capt. Holmes (*Report to Lieut.-Col. Butler*), "between 80 and 90;" Mr. Christie (*Mil. and Nav. Operations*, p. 179) says *seventy-two* were killed and wounded.

CHAPTER LXXVI.

March 27, 1814.

THE BATTLE OF TOHOPAKA, OR THE HORSE-SHOE BEND.

The expedition to the Tallapoosa, under General Jackson, the actions at Emuckfau and at Enotochopco, and the return of the General and his command to the Coosa, under strong appearances of defeat, have been noticed in preceding chapters of this volume;[1] and, with the stern severity of his character, he determined *to exterminate the savages* with whom he had been engaged. Brooding over this bloody determination, during the succeeding two months he received large reinforcements, and in the middle of March he found himself in a condition to carry it into execution.[2]

Accordingly, on the fourteenth of March he moved from head-quarters; and seven days afterwards he reached the mouth of Cedar Creek, where he established a post, calling it Fort Williams.[3] On the twenty-fourth, taking with him eight days' provisions, he left that post for the Tallapoosa, with a force of about three thousand effective men, besides a body of Indians;[4] and, at ten o'clock in the morning of the twenty-seventh, he reached the Indian village of Tohopaka, near Emuckfau, at the Great, or Horse-shoe Bend of the Tallapoosa—about three miles from the battle-field of Emuckfau.[1]

Fully apprised of the approach of the expedition, and of the exterminating intentions of its commander, the savages had assembled in great numbers from the neighboring villages, and had strengthened their naturally strong position with great skill and labor. They had taken post within a horse-shoe-shaped bend of the river, which at this place was upwards of one hundred yards wide, and unfordable; and, entirely across its neck, they had thrown up a very strong breastwork of logs, from five to eight feet high, extending in such a direction that an attacking force approaching it would be exposed to a double or cross fire, while its defenders would lie in perfect security behind it; and a cannon, placed at one extremity, could not have raked it with any advantage. For the purpose of defending themselves efficiently and securely, two rows of port-holes had been opened in the logs; and, while its defenders could throw an effective fire on any who approached the position, it was not necessary that he should, in the least, be exposed.[2] From this forti-

[1] Chaps. LXVI., LXXII., LXXIII.—[2] McAfee, p. 479; Eaton, p. 157.—[3] Gen. Jackson to Gov. Blount, March 31; Perkins, p. 211.—[4] Gen. Jackson to Gov. Blount, March 31; Col. Morgan to same, April 1; Eaton, p. 158.

[1] Gen. Jackson to Gen. Pinckney, March 28; Same to Gov. Blount, March 31; Eaton, p. 158.

[2] Gen. Jackson to Gen. Pinckney, March 28; Same to Gov. Blount, March 31; Col. Morgan to same, April 1.

fied neck of land, running back, along the middle of the Bend, and descending, on either hand, and at its extremity, to the river, is a ridge of high ground, from which, at that time, nearly all the timber had been cleared; while the heavy forest along its slopes, and on the margin of the river, had been felled in such a manner that the fallen trees formed a breastwork and abatis, which not only protected the flanks and rear of the position, but afforded shelter to such as might, necessarily, be required for their defence.[1]

Thus strengthened with all the art of which the Creeks were masters, the Bend was prepared for the great struggle which should decide if at that time, or at some future day, the nation should cease to exist; and, apparently, imbued with the awful responsibility which had devolved upon them, the warriors from Oakfuskee, Oakchaga, New Yaucan, the Hillibees, the Fish Pond, and Eufaula,—about eight or nine hundred in number,—assembled to contend for their lives and their nationality.[2] The result of the engagement will show the sense which these Indians entertained of the character of the approaching contest; and while the love of country prompts us, at all times, to rejoice when victory crowns the services of the army with laurels, the tear of sympathy should not be withheld, or the record of their virtues be left imperfect, when, *as in this case*, a united people resists, with energy and singleness of purpose, the determination to exterminate them, by which an enemy may be actuated.

"*Determining to exterminate them*,"[1] before the expedition came before the enemy, his situation and numbers were known to General Jackson; and, early in the morning, for the purpose of surrounding the Bend, and of cutting off the retreat of the savages, he detached General Coffee, with the mounted men and nearly all the friendly Indians, ordering him to cross the river about three miles below the Bend;[2] while, against the front of the enemy's works, the General marched in person, with the remainder of his force.[3] The former officer had nearly surrounded the Bend when the fire was opened on the breastwork, in front, by the main body; and several Indians, who attempted to escape at that time, by crossing the river, fell at his hands. Soon afterwards some of the friendly Indians, impatient to join in the fray, swam over the river and carried off the canoes from the village, with which upwards of two hundred men were rowed across, and attacked the works in the rear, setting the village on fire, and moving against the rear of the breastwork.[4]

In the mean time, having planted his field-pieces—a six and a three pounder—on an eminence, within two hundred

---

[1] Col. Morgan to Gov. Blount, April 1; McAfee, pp. 479, 480.—[2] Gen. Jackson to Gen. Pinckney, March 28; Same to Gov. Blount, March 31. Gen. Jackson says it was reported that 1000 men were present; but the returns of the killed show the error, when added to the number of those who escaped.

[1] Gen. Jackson to Gen. Pinckney, March 28; Ingersoll, i. p. 346.—[2] Gen. Jackson to Gen. Pinckney, March 28; Same to Gov. Blount, March 31; Gen. Coffee to Gen. Jackson, April 1; Col. Morgan to Gov. Blount, April 1.

[3] Gen. Jackson to Gen. Pinckney, March 28; Same to Gov. Blount, March 31.—[4] Gen. Jackson to Gov. Blount, March 31; Gen. Coffee to Gen. Jackson, April 1; Col. Morgan to Gov. Blount, April 1.

yards of the breastwork, to cover his advance, General Jackson moved "slowly and in order," along the ridge which led to the Bend, "playing upon the enemy with the muskets and rifles whenever they showed themselves beyond the works." After continuing this mode of attack for a period of two hours, the rising volume of smoke in the rear of the breastwork indicated the successful occupation of the village, at the extremity of the Bend, by the troops under General Coffee, who had crossed the river in canoes for that purpose, as before stated; and, relying on the co-operation of that officer, in the enemy's rear, General Jackson determined to storm the breastwork.[1]

Accordingly, with the Thirty-ninth regiment of United States infantry, under Colonel John Williams, in the van, supported by the Tennessee Volunteers, under General James Doherty, he moved against the breastwork, in the face of a most tremendous fire from the Indians who defended it.[2] When the assailants had reached the face of the breastwork a hand-to-hand fight took place through the port-holes; and so bitterly was it conducted that "many balls of the enemy were welded to the bayonets of our muskets."[3] After this desperate conflict had continued several minutes, the breastwork was mounted, and the Indians were driven from the lines at the point of the bayonet;[4]

[1] Gen. Jackson to Gen. Pinckney, March 28; Same to Gov. Blount, March 31; Col. Morgan to same, April 1.

[2] Gen. Jackson to Gen. Pinckney, March 28; Same to Gov. Blount, March 31.—[3] Gen. Jackson to Gov. Blount, March 31.—[4] Gen. Jackson to Gen. Pinckney, March 28; Eaton, p. 160.

when, true to the purpose of the commanding General, the work of extermination commenced.

Although many of the Indians defended themselves with that bravery which desperation inspires, the greatly superior force of the Americans gave them great advantages, and it was not long before the Bend became the scene of one of the most dreadful acts of butchery on record. Although the sheltered position of the enemy had protected him from any serious injury, while the action was pending, the whites, with their Indian allies, were nearly, if not fully, four times as numerous as the Creeks; and the slaughter—the predetermined act of "extermination"—was both rapid and effective. The women and children who occupied the village appear to have been spared;[1] but all others were pursued and butchered with the most relentless fury.[2] Crouching for concealment among the bushes or in the reeds on the bank of the river, they were hunted out and slaughtered with the ferocity of tigers by their merciless conquerors, until evening drew her sable curtain between the victors and the vanquished, and extended that temporary reprieve which no earthly power could

[1] Gen. Jackson to Gen. Pinckney, March 28; Same to Gov. Blount, March 31.

[2] It is surprising, after the express declaration of Gen. Jackson himself, to the contrary, that Mr. Eaton (*Life of Gen. Jackson*, pp. 161, 162) should have ventured to publish such a tissue of *assertion*, to establish the merciful intentions of Gen. Jackson, in this engagement, and to throw upon the terror-stricken and concealed savages the responsibility of the massacre. If the truth of our country's history is to be bartered for political effect, it should be made known, that the value of such works may be understood.

have secured.[1] On the following morning, sixteen warriors, who had succeeded in concealing themselves during the reign of terror on the preceding day, were discovered; and, as neither the slaughter of their brethren, or the temporary cessation of the butchery, during the night, had satiated the thirst for blood which their victors had exhibited, they, too, with the most perfectly diabolical spirit, were added to the victims of the hero of the Horse-shoe Bend.[2]

In this inglorious field, twenty-six Americans, eighteen Cherokees, and five friendly Creeks were *killed*, and one hundred and six Americans, thirty-six Cherokees, and eleven friendly Creeks were *wounded;*[3] while of the hostile Creeks, five hundred and fifty-seven dead bodies were picked up within the works,[4] from two hundred and fifty to three hundred were killed while, unresisting, they were attempting to escape across the Tallapoosa,[5] and "it was believed that no more than ten had escaped."[1] Indeed, so completely predominant was General Jackson's iron will, in his predetermined extinction of the nation, that General Coffee says, "*Not one, even, escaped; very few even reached the bank, and that few was killed the instant it landed.*"[2] Over three hundred widowed women and fatherless children were taken prisoners;[3] and, besides these friendless ones and the bloody laurels, there appears to have been no trophies to grace the triumph of the conqueror.

After sinking his own killed in the river to prevent the enemy from scalping them,[4] General Jackson returned to Fort Williams on the day after the battle;[5] and as the power of the Creeks had been broken, and their principal chiefs soon afterwards gave themselves up, with peculiar marks of submission,[6] the war with the Creeks virtually closed.[7]

[Note.—The Dispatch of Gen. Jackson to Gov. Blount, and that of Gen. Coffee to Gen. Jackson, have been omitted by the Publishers for want of room.]

CHAPTER LXXVII.

March 28, 1814.

THE LOSS OF THE ESSEX.

One of the most remarkable cruises on record is that of the frigate *Essex*, commanded by Captain David Porter. Intended as a consort of the *Constitution* and *Hornet*, under the general command of Commodore Bainbridge—whose cruise and good fortune, as well as that of the *Hornet*, has been already

[1] Gen. Jackson to Gen. Pinckney, March 28; McAfee, p. 483.—[2] Gen. Jackson to Gen. Pinckney, March 28; Same to Gov. Blount, March 31; Col. Morgan to Gov. Blount, April 1.—[3] Gen. Jackson to Gen. Pinckney, March 28; Same to Gov. Blount, March 31; McAfee, p. 484.

[4] Gen. Jackson to Gen. Pinckney, March 28; Same to Gov. Blount, March 31; Col. Morgan to same, April 1.

[5] Gen. Coffee to Gen. Jackson, March 31.

[1] Gen. Jackson to Gen. Pinckney, March 28.

[2] Gen. Coffee to Gen. Jackson, April 1.—[3] Gen. Jackson to Gov. Blount, March 31.—[4] Eaton, p. 166.

[5] Gen. Jackson to Gen. Pinckney, March 28; Ingersoll, i. p. 347.—[6] Gen. Jackson to Gen. Pinckney, March 28; Niles' *Register*, vi. p. 194.—[7] Claiborne's Notes, p. 39.

alluded to[1]—she sailed from the Delaware on the twenty-eighth of October, 1812, and ran to Port Praya (*St. Jago*), the appointed place of rendezvous. In consequence of her heavy supply of stores, and her consequent dull sailing, she did not reach the rendezvous until after the Commodore had left; and the same misfortune befell him while he was approaching the Island Fernando de Norouha, which had been appointed the second place of rendezvous.[2]

Thus thrown upon his own resources, Captain Porter determined to turn Cape Horn and cruise in the Pacific Ocean, where a heavy British commerce was almost wholly unprotected; and from which, it was hoped, the most desirable success might be obtained. On her progress thither the most provoking want of success was experienced; but between the fifth of March, 1813, when she anchored off the Island of Mocha, and the time of her capture, fortune favored her crew; and one of the most successful, if not the most romantic, cruises on record fell to her lot.

The enemy's letters of marque, which had been sent out to harass the American whalers, were checked and overpowered; the enemy's commerce was completely cut up and destroyed; the single ship which entered the Pacific, without a consort, and but poorly supplied with many of the necessaries for a cruise, by manning her prizes and by levying on the enemy's commerce, had become the flag-ship of a victorious squadron, whose progress from port to port, and from harbor to harbor, was only a series of triumphs; whose adventures assumed a character kindred to those of the marvellous navigators of earlier and darker days; whose exploits spread terror wherever it found the British flag, and even along the wharves, in the counting-rooms, and around the firesides of Britain herself.[1]

One of our own writers, a favorite son of New York, speaking of the *Essex*, at this time, says it "was sufficiently remarkable to merit a brief notice. She had been the first American to carry the pennant of a man-of-war round the Cape of Good Hope, and now she had been the first to bring it into this distant ocean. More than ten thousand miles from home, without colonies, stations, or even a really friendly port to repair to, short of stores, without a consort, and otherwise in possession of none of the required means of subsistence and efficiency, she had boldly steered into this distant region, where she had found all that she required, through her own activity; and having swept the seas of her enemies, she had now retired to the little-frequented Marquesas to refit, with all the security of a ship at home."[2]

After having thoroughly overhauled and refitted the *Essex*, at the Marquesas, on the twelfth of December, 1813, in company with one of her prizes which had been armed with twenty guns, and called the *Essex, Junior*, the *Essex* sailed from Madison Island; and

[1] Vide Chaps. XXXV., XLI.—[2] Com. Porter to Sec. of Navy, July 3, 1814; Cooper, ii. pp. 75–77.

[1] The particulars of this interesting and important cruise can be found in the "*Journal of a Cruise, &c.*," by Com. Porter, in two volumes, New York, 1822.

[2] Cooper's Naval History, ii. p. 87.

on the third of February, 1814, she anchored in the bay of Valparaiso. Four days afterwards, two British vessels of war—the frigate *Phœbe*, Captain Hillyer, of thirty-six guns, and the sloop-of-war *Cherub*, Captain Tucker, of twenty-eight guns—also entered the bay; and the former ranged up alongside the *Essex*, between that vessel and the *Essex, Junior*. Being nearer to the former than "prudence or a strict neutrality would justify Commodore Porter in permitting," the old acquaintance which had existed between the two captains was renewed by the latter giving orders to his crew to board the *Phœbe* in case the two vessels fouled; and by the hasty withdrawal of the latter to a safer and more respectful position; and thenceforth the neutrality of the port was respected until the morning of the engagement which this chapter is intended to describe.[1]

During the succeeding forty-three days the four vessels were in the bay, restrained by the neutrality of the port; and the officers and crews of all became acquainted with each other and extended acts of courtesy to their enemies, or relieved the monotony of their employment by singing good-natured songs of defiance—many of them impromptu productions—to the tunes of "*Yankee Doodle*," or "*The sweet little* CHERUB *that sits up aloft;*"[2] while, at the same time, the officers bantered each other by the display of motto flags—that lettered "FREE TRADE AND SAILORS' RIGHTS," which had floated triumphantly at the mast-head of the *Essex* during so many months, having excited the animosity of the enemy, the *Phœbe* hoisted one lettered "GOD AND COUNTRY; BRITISH SAILORS' BEST RIGHTS; TRAITORS OFFEND BOTH;" when the *Essex* immediately retorted with one lettered, "GOD, OUR COUNTRY, AND LIBERTY—TYRANTS OFFEND THEM."[1] An occasional test of the sailing qualities of the several vessels added interest to the blockade; and it was vigilantly enforced, notwithstanding every effort which was made to detach the *Cherub*, and allow the *Essex* to test her qualities with those of the *Phœbe*.[2]

At length, having grown weary of the blockade, and understanding that the enemy's force would be increased at an early day, Commodore Porter determined to leave the port, and rely on the speed of his vessels and his skill in sailing them as the means of escape. Accordingly, on the twenty-eighth of March, with a fresh breeze from the southward, the *Essex* stood out to sea; but before she cleared the harbor a squall struck her, carrying away her main-topmast, after which, failing in her attempt to regain the common anchorage, she ran into a small bay on the east side of the harbor, about three-quarters of a mile from the battery, and cast anchor, within pistol-shot from the shore, with the intention of repairing her damage at that place.[3]

---

[1] Com. Porter to Sec. of Navy, July 3; Porter's Journal, ii. pp. 143–147; James' Naval Occurrences, pp. 306, 307.

[2] Porter's Journal, ii. p. 148; Niles' *Register*, vi. p. 420; Ingersoll, ii. p. 20.

[1] Porter's Jour., ii. pp. 146, 147; Certif. of Lieut. Downes and other officers; Ingersoll, ii. p. 20.—[2] Porter's Jour., ii. pp. 153, 154; James, pp. 307, 308; Cooper, ii. p. 91.

[3] Com. Porter to Sec. of Navy, July 3; James, p. 308; Capt. Hillyer to the Admiralty, March 30; Cooper, ii. p. 91; Letter in *Weekly Messenger*, ii. p. 250.

In the mean time the *Phœbe* and *Cherub* had pursued the *Essex;* and when the latter, disabled, anchored within the limits of the harbor, and under the protection of its neutrality, it was properly supposed the enemy, also, would respect the rights which Commodore Porter had, previously, recognized in him. The approach of the two vessels, decked with their battle-flags, jacks, pennants, and ensigns, speedily dispelled that illusion, however; and the crippled *Essex* separated from her "*Junior*," which had been left in the harbor, was warned, therefrom, of the hostility of his intentions, and prepared for his reception. At fifty-four minutes past three in the afternoon, the *Phœbe*—having come within range of her *long guns* while yet the *carronades* of the *Essex* were still useless—opened a fire on the *stern* of the latter, at long-shot distance; while, at the same time, the *Cherub*, on her starboard bow, also opened an effective fire. The bow-guns of the *Essex*, however, soon rendered the situation of the latter vessel an uncomfortable one; and she bore up and ran under the stern of the *Essex*, joining with the *Phœbe* in a hot, raking fire. Having ran three long twelves out from the stern-ports of the *Essex*, her crew was enabled to return the compliments of the combined enemy; and, with so much skill and effect was it done, that, within half an hour from the opening of the engagement, both vessels were compelled to haul off and repair damages.[1]

During this brief engagement the *Essex* and her crew suffered considerably, and her ensign at the gaff, and the battle-flag at her mizzen-masthead had been shot away; but when, "a few minutes" afterwards, the enemy returned to the contest, the original "FREE TRADE AND SAILORS' RIGHTS," at her main-masthead, sent forth the defiance which the crew on her decks so gallantly ratified a few minutes afterwards.[1]

Having repaired his damages, the enemy returned to the action; and both his vessels, having taken their position on the starboard-quarter of the *Essex*, out of the reach of her carronades, and where her stern-guns could not be brought to bear, they opened a destructive fire on the devoted, and, comparatively, helpless, vessel. Under these circumstances, Commodore Porter was compelled to choose between a tame surrender, and running down and becoming the assailant. His topsail-sheets and halyards, as well as his jib and foretop-mast-staysail-halyards, having been shot away, leaving only his flying-jib-halyards, he hoisted the latter sail, cut his cable, and ran down on both ships, with an intention of laying the *Phœbe* on board. During the time which this manœuvre occupied, the fire, on both sides, was very severe—that of the *Essex* with the hope of disabling her opponent and preventing her escape; that of the enemy to disable, still more, his opponent, and prevent her progress in the desperate mission on which she had ventured.[2]

[1] Com. Porter to Sec. of Navy, July 3; Capt. Hillyer's Dispatch, March 30; Letter in *Weekly Messenger;* Letter from officer of the *Essex*, in the same work, ii. pp. 251, 252.

[1] Com. Porter to Sec. of Navy, July 3; Cooper, ii. pp. 92, 93.—[2] Com. Porter to Sec. of Navy, July 3; Letter in *Weekly Messenger;* Letter from officer of *Essex*, in same work.

The *Cherub*, distrusting her abilities for a successful defence, at close action, immediately hauled off, and thenceforth continued to perform her part of the drama at a distance, with her long guns only. The *Phœbe*, also, preferring to fight at a distance, edged off as the *Essex* neared her; and, with characteristic prudence, selected that position which best suited her long guns, continuing her fire with terrible effect, while that of the *Essex* was, from her position and her helplessness, of but little use. At that time, as already stated, the running rigging of the *Essex* was almost wholly shot away; and, as her sails could not be handled, she was almost entirely unmanageable. Many of her guns had been rendered useless by the enemy's shot, and many of them had their entire crews destroyed—some of them had, indeed, been remanned twice, and one of them three times.[1]

Perceiving that the enemy had it in his power to choose his distance, and to keep off rather than to come to close action, Commodore Porter determined to run the *Essex* on shore, land his crew, and set fire to his ship. The wind favored the design, and every thing appeared to favor it, until the ship had moved to within musket-shot of the shore, when the wind suddenly shifted, and, blowing *from* the shore, the head of the *Essex* instantly payed down on the *Phœbe*, and exposed the decks of the devoted ship to another severe, raking fire—an advantage which was not lost sight of by the enemy.[2]

[1] Com. Porter to Sec. of Navy, July 3; Cooper, ii. p. 93; Perkins, p. 186.—[2] Com. Porter to Sec. of Navy, July 3; Cooper, ii. p. 93; Sketches of the War, p. 435.

At this moment Lieutenant Downes, who commanded the *Essex, Junior*, came on board the *Essex* to receive the final orders of Commodore Porter respecting the disposition of the former vessel, under the impression that his commander would soon become a prisoner. After receiving orders to prepare for defending and destroying his ship, in case she should be attacked, the Lieutenant left the *Essex*, taking with him some of the wounded crew and leaving three of his boat's-crew, and returned to his own ship—a trip which, when the heavy fire which the *Phœbe* and *Cherub* were then throwing into the *Essex* is considered, possesses unusual interest.[1]

The fire on the *Essex*, meantime, continued with unabated fury, although the unmanageable ship was unable to bring a single gun to bear on the enemy. In this dilemma Commodore Porter ordered a hawser to be bent to the sheet-anchor, and the anchor to be cut down from the bows; when her head was brought round, and the broadside again bore on the enemy. Soon afterwards the hawser parted, and the ship took fire; when, by Commodore Porter's directions, some of the crew attempted to swim ashore, while those who remained turned their attention to a suppression of the flames, in which, after a severe struggle, they were finally successful.[2]

By this time the crew had become so weary, and so many had fallen, that farther resistance was considered not

[1] Com. Porter to Sec. of Navy, July 3; Cooper, ii. p. 94; Perkins, p. 187.—[2] Com. Porter to Sec. of Navy, July 3; Cooper, ii. p. 94; Sketches of the War, p. 436.

only useless but criminal; and, after consultation with his only remaining officer, Lieutenant Stephen D. McKnight, the colors were lowered and the action terminated.[1]

At this time the situation of the ship and her crew was truly lamentable. In the words of her commander, "the cockpit, the steerage, the ward-room, and the berth-deck, could contain no more wounded; the latter were killed while the surgeons were dressing them; and it was evident that unless something was speedily done to prevent it, the ship would soon sink from the number of shot-holes in her bottom. The carpenter reported that his crew had been killed or wounded; and that he had been once over the side to stop the leaks, when his slings had been shot away, and it was with difficulty he was saved from drowning."[2] There were, therefore, no hopes of saving the ship, or of preventing her from falling into the enemy's hands, and a farther sacrifice of life would have been unjustifiable.

The strength of the *Essex*, in this engagement, was forty thirty-two-pound carronades and six long-twelves, with a crew of two hundred and fifty-five men:[3] that of the enemy was thirty long-eighteens and sixteen thirty-two-pound carronades, with a howitzer and six three-pounders in her tops, on the *Phœbe*;[4] and eighteen thirty-two-pound and eight twenty-four-pound carronades and two long-nines on the *Cherub*[1]—the former having a crew of three hundred and twenty and the latter one of one hundred and eighty men and boys. The peculiarity of the movements, however, were such that, with but a slight exception, the ships fought at long gunshot distance; and the fighting strength therefore was thirty long eighteen-pounders and two long-nines, on the part of the enemy, against six long-twelves on the *Essex*—a disparity which will explain, at a glance, the disastrous termination of the engagement. The loss of the enemy, from the same cause, was much less than that of the *Essex*—the *Phœbe* losing four *killed* and seven *wounded*; the *Cherub*, one *killed* and three *wounded*;[2] and the *Essex*, fifty-eight *killed*, sixty-six *wounded*, and thirty-one *missing*.[3]

The action, as before stated, was fought within the bounds of a neutral port; and the Chilian authorities, while they offered to *request* the enemy to cease his fire, *if the Essex would return to her former anchorage*, took no steps to enforce their neutrality; and the matter resulted in the withdrawal of Mr. Poinsett, and the suspension of intercourse between that country and the United States.

[Note.—The Dispatch of Capt. Hillyer to the Admiralty, and extracts from Com. Porter's to Secretary of the Navy, have been omitted by the Publishers for want of room.]

---

[1] Com. Porter to Sec. of Navy, July 3; Capt. Hillyer's Dispatch, March 30.—[2] Com. Porter to Sec. of Navy, July 3.

[3] Ibid. Mr. James (*Nav. Occur.*, pp. 310, 311) has labored hard to disprove the statements of Com. Porter, but I have seen no reason sufficiently strong to lead me to distrust them.—[4] Com. Porter to Sec. of Navy, July 3. Mr. James (*Nav. Occur.*, p. 312) says she mounted *twenty-six* long-18's, *fourteen* 32-pound carronades, 4 long-nines, an 18-pound and a 12-pound carronade, besides *four* small pieces in her tops; with a complement of *two hundred and ninety-five* men and boys.

[1] Com. Porter to Sec. of Navy, July 3. Mr. James (*Nav. Occur.*, p. 312) says she carried *eighteen* 32, *six* 18, and *one* 12 pound carronades, with 2 long-*sixes*; and a complement of 121 men and boys.—[2] James, pp. 310, 311; Returns appended to Capt. Hillyer's Dispatch.

[3] Com. Porter to Sec. of Navy, July 3.

CHAPTER LXXVIII.

March 30, 1814.

THE ACTION AT THE MILL ON LA COLLE RIVER, L. C.

THE want of success which attended the movements of the army of the North, and its subsequent settlement in winter-quarters at the French Mills, have been noticed in a preceding chapter of this work;[2] and it remained in that position until the thirteenth of February, when the cantonment was broken up, and General Wilkinson and the main body of the army moved to Plattsburg, while General Brown and his division, at the same time, moved to Sackett's Harbor.[3]

In the latter part of March the forces under General Wilkinson were concentrated at Champlain, with the design of moving into Canada, on another of those Quixotic expeditions—the fourth—which had rendered the arms of the United States so contemptible on the northern frontiers during the last war with Britain; and on the thirtieth of that month the army marched from that place, in the prosecution of the projected campaign.[4]

At the period in question the strength of the army was "three thousand nine hundred and ninety-nine combatants, including one hundred cavalry, and three hundred and four artillerists with eleven pieces of artillery;"[5] while opposed to it, scattered over a wide extent of country, in small detachments, were about a thousand British regulars and four hundred and thirty organized militia.[1] There is no mention, in the American accounts, of any irregular force, and the presumption is that but a small one was engaged.

Having reached Odletown, five miles from Champlain, the column halted for refreshments;[2] and, soon afterwards, it encountered one of the enemy's pickets, which, having been reinforced, opened an effective fire on the head of the column, and inflicted some loss, although it was subsequently driven in.[3]

At an early hour in the afternoon the army reached the grist-mill at La Colle River—a military station, at which were posted about seventy of the marine corps, a corporal, and three artillerists, one company of the Thirteenth regiment of the line, and a detachment of Canadian militia, the whole embracing about two hundred men, under Major Handcock, of the Thirteenth.[4] This mill was a substantial stone edifice, two stories high, with a shingle roof, standing on the southern bank of La Colle River, about three-quarters of a mile above its junction with the Riche-

[1] Mr. Christie (*Mil. and Nav. Operations*, p. 174) supposes it occurred on the *thirteenth*.—[2] Vide Chapter LXVII.

[3] Perkins, pp. 363, 364.—[4] Gen. Wilkinson to Sec. of War, March 31, 1814; Letter from an officer, in Albany *Register*, April 8, 1814; James' Mil. Occur., ii. p. 82.

[5] Minutes of a Council of War, Champlain, March 29, 1814; Ingersoll, iv. p. 83.

[1] James' Mil. Occur., ii. pp. 82, 83; Richards' Macomb, p. 72.—[2] Letter from an officer, in Albany *Register*.

[3] Gen. Wilkinson to Sec. of War, March 31, 1814; British "*General Orders*," March 31; Lieut.-Col. Williams to Sir G. Prevost, March 31; James, ii. p. 85; Perkins, p. 365; Ingersoll, iv. p. 83.—[4] Gen. Wilkinson to Sec. of War, March 31, 1814; James, ii. p. 83; Christie, pp. 174, 175.

lieu. Its heavy walls, eighteen inches thick, were well adapted for defence; and its windows had been barricaded with logs, between which loop-holes for musketry had been opened. Communicating with the mill by a bridge, on the opposite bank of the river, stood a small house, which had been converted into a block-house, and surrounded with a breastwork; and in the rear of this house was a barn. Southward from the mill was an open space of about two hundred yards, and on the north of it was one of half the width; beyond which, and on either hand, the primitive forest, in its original majesty, hemmed in the scene.[1]

The advance of the column was commanded by Colonel Isaac Clarke and Major Forsyth; Captain McPherson, with four pieces of artillery, followed; Generals Smith and Bissel, with their brigades, covered the guns; and General Alexander Macomb commanded the reserve.[2] Colonel Miller, with six hundred men, invested the rear of the works, for the purpose of cutting off the retreat of the garrison, and of holding in check any reinforcements which might approach for its support;[3] while, three hundred yards in front (from the edge of the wood), the artillery opened a steady and incessant fire on the mill, from a twelve and a six pounder, and a five-and-a-half-inch howitzer.[4]

[1] James, ii. pp. 83, 84; Auchinleck, pp. 281, 282.

[2] Gen. Wilkinson to Sec. of War, March 31, 1814; American "*General Orders*," March 31; Letter from an officer, in Albany *Register;* Ingersoll, iv. p. 83.—[3] Gen. Wilkinson to Sec. of War, March 31; James, ii. p. 85; Ingersoll, iv. p. 83; Armstrong, ii. p. 67.—[4] British "*General Orders*," March 31; Letter from an officer, in Albany *Register;* Lieut.-Col. Williams to Sir G. Prevost, March 31; James, ii. p. 86; Ingersoll, iv. pp. 83, 84; Armstrong, ii. p. 67.

Soon after the attack commenced the garrison was strengthened by the arrival of two flank companies of the Thirteenth regiment, under Captains Ellard and Holgate, from the Isle aux Noix, seven miles distant; and they inaugurated their services by a most gallant sortie, in which the artillerists suffered very severely, and the guns were saved only by a vigorous movement of the infantry. After a desperate struggle of a few minutes, they retired across the bridge and occupied the block-house.[1]

About the same time the grenadiers of the Canadian Fencibles and a company of Voltigeurs arrived from Burtonville, two miles from the mill; and having joined the flank companies in the block-house, under the directions of Captain Ellard, who volunteered for the occasion, a second charge on the artillery — more desperate even than the first—took place; and, like the former, was repulsed, only after a severe struggle, by the covering brigades.[2]

During upwards of two hours this cannonade continued, without inflicting any injury on the peaceful mill, whose dusty walls—as if in perfect contempt of this modern antitype of the well-known knight of old, in an almost parallel attempt on a somewhat similar edifice—defied the best efforts of General Wilkinson, and, like his prototype, the General and his army *retired*.[3]

[1] Gen. Wilkinson to Sec. of War, March 31, 1814; British "*General Orders*," March 31; Letter from an officer, in Albany *Register;* Lieut.-Col. Williams to Sir G. Prevost, March 31; James, ii. p. 86; Ingersoll, iv. p. 84.

[2] Gen. Wilkinson to Sec. of War, March 31, 1814; British "*General Orders*," March 31; Letter from an officer, in Albany *Register;* Lieut.-Col. Williams to Sir G. Prevost, March 31; James, ii. pp. 86, 87.

[3] Gen. Wilkinson to Sec. of War, March 31, 1814; Brit-

The relative strength of the besiegers and the besieged has been noticed already: and the loss inflicted on the former—thirteen *killed*, one hundred and twenty-eight *wounded*, and thirteen *missing*[1]—sufficiently attest the gallantry of the latter in their chivalrous defence of their post. Of the garrison, eleven were *killed;* two officers and forty-four men were *wounded;* and four men were *missing*.[2]

This inglorious affair closed the military career of General Wilkinson; and, borne down with the torrent of obloquy with which the disasters of his campaigns had surrounded him, he soon afterwards relinquished the command of the army; was tried and acquitted by a court-martial; and, at the peace, was "dropped" from the army lists.[1]

[Note.—The Dispatch of Gen. Wilkinson to the Secretary of War, and that of Lieut.-Col. Williams to Sir Geo. Prevost, have been omitted by the Publishers for want of room.]

CHAPTER LXXIX.

April 29, 1814.

THE CAPTURE OF L'EPERVIER.

In March, 1814, the United States sloop of war *Peacock*, commanded by Master-commandant Warrington, went to sea; and proceeded to the southward on a cruise.[3] On the twenty-ninth of April, while in latitude 27° 47′ N., longitude 89° 9′ W., three sail were made to windward, under the convoy of a large brig of war; and soon afterwards the brig edged away for the *Peacock*, and invited an engagement.[4]

The stranger's first broadside inflicted considerable injury on the *Peacock*, disabling her fore-yard, depriving her of the use of her fore and foretop sails during the action, and compelling her officers to fight running large, without manœuvring, and to depend on their skill in gunnery for the success which they coveted.[2] It is said, also, by the historians of Great Britain, that the armament of the stranger was not in order, and that she, too, fought at great disadvantage.[3] Be this as it may, within forty-two minutes of steady fire, during which time there appears to have been no manœuvring whatever, the stranger struck her colors, and became the prize of the *Peacock* and her crew.[4]

The stranger proved to be His Britannic Majesty's brig *L'Epervier*, Captain Wales, mounting eighteen thirty-two-pound carronades,[5] and manned with a crew of one hundred and twenty-eight men, of whom eight were killed and fifteen wounded. Her main-boom

ish "*General Orders*," March 31; Letter from an officer, &c.; James, ii. pp. 89, 90; Ingersoll, iv. p. 84; Christie, pp. 174, 175.—[1] James, ii. p. 90; Rogers, i. p. 267.

[2] British "*General Orders*," March 31; Lieut.-Col. Williams to Sir G. Prevost, March 31.

[3] Cooper, ii. p. 131.—[4] Ibid.; James' Nav. Occur., p. 342.

[1] Ingersoll, iv. p. 84; Christie, p. 176.—[2] Capt. Warrington to Sec. of Navy, April 29; Cooper, ii. p. 131.

[3] James, pp. 342–344.—[4] Capt. Warrington to Sec. of Navy, April 29; Cooper, ii. p. 131.

[5] Mr. James (*Naval Occurrences*, p. 345) says she carried *sixteen* 32's and two 18's, with a complement of 101 men and 16 boys.

and her main-topmast had been shot away, her foremast had been cut through and was tottering, her fore-rigging and stays had been shot away, her bowsprit was badly wounded, forty-five round-shot holes were in her hull—twenty of which were within a foot of her water-line, and she had five feet of water in her hold.[1]

The armament of the *Peacock* was twenty thirty-two-pound carronades and two long-nines,[2] with a crew of one hundred and sixty men,[3] of whom two only were slightly wounded.[4] Not a shot had struck her hull, and, with the exception already named, her masts and spars were as sound as ever; and in fifteen minutes after the *L'Epervier* struck her colors, her victor "was ready for another action."[1]

Besides the value of the brig, which was sold for fifty-five thousand dollars,[2] one hundred and eighteen thousand dollars in specie, which was found on board,[3] became prize-money, and was distributed among the officers and crew of the *Peacock*.

[NOTE.—The Dispatch of Master-com. Warrington to the Secretary of the Navy has been omitted by the Publishers for want of room.]

[1] Capt. Warrington to Sec. of Navy, April 29; Lieut. Nicholson to same, May 1; James, p. 344; Cooper, ii. p. 131.—[2] Cooper, ii. p. 112; James, p. 349.—[3] The Naval Temple, p. 134. Mr. James (*Nav. Occur.*, p. 345) says she had a crew of *one hundred and eighty-five* men.—[4] Capt. Warrington to Sec. of Navy, April 29; Cooper, ii. p. 131.

[1] Capt. Warrington to Sec. of Navy, April 29; Lieut. Nicholson to same, May 1.—[2] Niles' *Register*, vi. p. 447.

[3] Capt. Warrington to Sec. of Navy, April 29; Lieut. Nicholson to same, May 1; James, p. 342.

CHAPTER LXXX.

May 5 to 7, 1814.

THE ATTACK ON OSWEGO, N. Y.

THE victory which had been gained by Commander Perry on Lake Erie, and the superior strength of the American squadron on Lake Ontario, appear to have led the British government to make desperate efforts to regain the supremacy on all the lakes before the opening of the campaign of 1814; and at the same time the American government as strenuously opposed it. In consequence of this struggle, in May of that year, besides gunboats and small vessels in both squadrons, the Americans had built and launched eight vessels, mounting two hundred and seven guns, and the British a like number, mounting two hundred and twenty-two guns; while each had a ship on the stocks—that of the former being pierced for one hundred and twenty guns; and that of the latter for one hundred guns.[4]

For the equipment and supply of the American squadron large quantities of stores and provisions had been collected at Oswego Falls, on the Seneca River, about thirteen miles above the village and fort of the same name—now the well-known port of Oswego, Oswego County, N. Y.,[5] and for their defence

[4] Perkins, pp. 365, 366; James' Nav. Occur., p. 394; Breckenridge, p. 230.—[5] Lieut.-Col. Mitchell's Report to Gen. Brown; James' Mil. Occur., ii. pp. 98, 99; James' Nav. Occur., p. 396.

Lieutenant-colonel George E. Mitchell, with the companies commanded by Captains Boyle, Romagne, McIntire, and Pierce, of the Third artillery, in all less than three hundred men,[1] had been detached from Sackett's Harbor, reaching Fort Oswego on the thirtieth of April, repairing, as far as he was able to do so, its ruined defences; and putting its armament—"five old guns, three of which had lost their trunnions"—into fit condition for use in case of necessity.[2]

Against this post, with the intention of destroying the stores referred to, the British authorities at Kingston determined to move their forces; and on the third of May six companies of De Watteville's regiment, the light company of Glengarrys, the entire second battalion of marines, a detachment from the Royal Artillery, with two field-pieces, and detachments of rocketeers, sappers, and miners, numbering, in the aggregate, it is said, about ten hundred and eighty men, exclusive of officers,[3] embarked on the squadron at Kingston;[4] and, on the following day, Lieutenant-general Drummond having taken the command of the troops, it weighed anchor and set sail.[5] The squadron, on which these troops had embarked, embraced the ship *Prince Regent*, mounting fifty-eight heavy guns; the ship *Princess Charlotte*, mounting forty-two heavy guns; the ship *Montreal*, mounting twenty-one guns; the ship *Niagara*, mounting twenty-three guns; the schooner *Charwell*, of fourteen guns; the schooner *Magnet*, of twelve guns; the brig *Star*, of fourteen guns, and several small vessels; and was commanded by Sir James L. Yeo.[1]

At reveille, on the morning of the fifth, the distant fleet was first seen from the fort; and information was sent to Commander Woolsey, of the *Growler*, which laid in the harbor, and to the neighboring militia; and, as far as possible, the necessary preparations were made for the contest which, it was now apparent, was speedily to take place.[2] As the small force which Lieutenant-colonel Mitchell commanded could not be divided,—while the fort, standing on one side of the river, and the village on the other, appeared to require such a division, for the protection of both,—the happy thought occurred to him that by *pitching the tents which were in store*, in front of the village, while, with the force which he commanded, he occupied the barracks, on the opposite side of the river, the enemy would be deceived concerning his strength; and would not venture to land where the stronger party appeared to be posted, while a weaker one, on the opposite bank, offered an easier conquest.[3] This well-formed plan was perfectly successful; and early in the

[1] "General Orders" of Gen. Brown, May 19; James' Mil. Occur., ii. p. 100.—[2] Lieut.-Col. Mitchell's Report; James' Mil. Occur., ii. p. 100.—[3] Gen. Drummond to Sir Geo. Prevost, May 7; James' Mil. Occur., ii. p. 100; James' Nav. Occur., p. 396. Gen. Scott, in *General Orders*, stated the force at 1800; and this has, generally, been supposed to be the number of those who served in the expedition.—[4] "General Orders," signed "E. Bayne, *Adj.-Gen. N. A.*;" Gen. Drummond to Sir G. Prevost, May 7; James' Mil. Occur., ii. p. 100.—[5] Gen. Drummond to Sir G. Prevost, May 7; James' Mil. Occur., ii. p. 100.

[1] Cooper's Nav. Hist., ii. p. 202.—[2] Lieut.-Col. Mitchell's Report; James' Mil. Occur., ii. p. 101; Letter from an officer, May 7.—[3] Lieut.-Col. Mitchell's Report; James' Mil. Occur., ii. p. 101; Thomson's Sketches, p. 262.

afternoon, without troubling the defenceless village, fifteen large boats, crowded with troops, and covered by the gunboats and small vessels, moved simultaneously and slowly towards the shore; while the ships, the brig, and the schooners opened a heavy fire on the old fort.[1]

In the mean time, Captain Boyle and Lieutenant Legate had been sent down to the shore with one of the old guns; and, as soon as the enemy's boats came within range of their fire, they opened on them, injuring their boats,—some of which were abandoned,—and compelled him to retire to his shipping.[2] A heavy breeze, which happened to blow at that time, furnished an excuse to the enemy for his retreat; and, soon afterwards, the entire squadron were compelled to stand off and gain an offing.[3] After posting picket-guards, at all exposed points, the little garrison laid on its arms until morning.[4]

On the following morning (*May 6th*), the squadron having returned to the attack, the *Princess Charlotte*, the *Montreal*, and the *Niagara*, opened a heavy fire on the fort; while the *Magnet* took her station in front of the town, and the *Star* and the *Charwell* were towed in,

[1] Com. Chauncey to Sec. of Navy, May 7; Lieut.-Col. Mitchell's Report; Gen. Drummond to Sir G. Prevost, May 7; James' Military Occurrences, ii. p. 101.

[2] Com. Chauncey to Sec. of Navy, May 7; Gen. Brown to Sec. of War, May 7; Lieut.-Col. Mitchell's Report; Letter from an officer, May 7. Gen. Drummond states that this was intended merely to induce the Americans to show their fire, in order that the number and position of their guns might be ascertained; and that it was not then intended to seek a landing.—[3] British "*General Orders*," signed "E. BAYNE, *Adj.-Gen. N. A.*;" Gen. Drummond to Sir G. Prevost, May 7; James' Mil. Occur., ii. p. 102; Auchinleck, p. 285; Letter from an officer, May 7.

[4] Lieut.-Col. Mitchell's Report; Thomson, p. 262.

and covered, with the boats, the place selected for the landing of the troops.[1] "Every thing being ready," the flank companies of De Watteville's regiment, under Captain De Bersey; the light company of the Glengarry's, under Captain McMillan; the battalion of marines, under Lieutenant-colonel Malcolm; and two hundred seamen, armed with pikes, under Captain Mulcaster, of the *Princess Charlotte*, the whole under Lieutenant-colonel Fischer, embarked in the boats, leaving the remainder of the troops, as a reserve, on board the vessels;[2] and, after lying aground for some time, at half-past one in the afternoon they effected a landing, under a heavy fire from the American troops, and from a small body of militia who had responded to the call for assistance which Lieutenant-colonel Mitchell had issued, but left when the enemy approached.[3]

Finding that the enemy had secured a landing, Lieutenant-colonel Mitchell withdrew his little party from the fort, and formed in the rear of it; when, with the companies commanded by Captains Romeyn and Melvin, he moved against the front, while the remainder of his force attacked the flanks of the enemy's column.[4] The *Growler* having been sunk in the harbor, part of her

[1] Letter from Onondaga, May 12, in the Baltimore *Patriot;* Lieut.-Col. Mitchell's Report; British "*General Orders;*" Gen. Drummond to Sir G. Prevost, May 7; Sir James L. Yeo to the Admiralty; James' Military Occurrences, ii. p. 103.—[2] British "*General Orders;*" Gen. Drummond to Sir G. Prevost, May 7; James' Mil. Occur., ii. p. 103; Letter from an officer, May 7.—[3] British "*General Orders;*" Gen. Drummond to Sir G. Prevost, May 7; Letter from an officer, May 7; James' Nav. Occur., p. 396; Christie, p. 180.—[4] Letter from Onondaga, May 12; Lieut.-Col. Mitchell's Report; Gen. Drummond to Sir G. Prevost, May 7; Letter from an officer, May 7.

crew, under Lieutenant Pearce, joined the troops, and assisted in holding him in check, with their characteristic gallantry;[1] and the progress of the assailants was opposed with spirit and determination.

After contesting the possession of the ground for half an hour,[2] the enemy, meanwhile, having taken possession of the fort, and the works and stores in its vicinity, without attempting to advance into the country, Lieutenant-colonel Mitchell fell back on a position from which he could protect the stores at the falls;[3] and at five o'clock in the morning of the seventh, having embarked the guns and stores which he found in Oswego, burned the barracks, and dismantled the fort, as far as was practicable, the enemy returned to his shipping, and immediately left the harbor.[4]

The loss of the Americans, in this gallant defence of their works, against a vastly superior force, was six *killed*, thirty-eight *wounded*, and twenty-five *missing*;[1] that of the enemy was Captain Holloway, fifteen soldiers, and three seamen *killed*, Captain Lendergrew and Lieutenant May, of the army, Captain Mulcaster, of the *Princess Charlotte*, Captain Popham, of the *Montreal*, Lieutenant Griffin, Master Richardson, two sergeants, sixty soldiers, and seven seamen *wounded*.[2] The *Growler* and two boats, which had been sunk, were raised and carried away; besides which and their cargoes, with some of the villagers, who had relied on his honor and remained at home, the enemy took but few trophies; while of glory, the amount was very inconsiderable.[3]

[Note.—The Dispatches of Gen. Brown to the Sec. of War, Sir James L. Yeo to the Admiralty, and Gen. Drummond to Sir G. Prevost, have been omitted by the Publishers for want of room.]

¹ Lieut.-Col. Mitchell's Report; Thomson's Sketches, p. 262.—² Lieut.-Col. Mitchell's Report; Letter from an officer, May 7.

³ Letter from an officer, May 7; James' Military Occurrences, ii. p. 104.

⁴ Letter from Onondaga, May 14; British "*General Orders*;" Gen. Drummond to Sir Geo. Prevost, May 7; Sketches of the War, p. 339; Rogers, i. p. 269.

¹ Letter from Onondaga, May 14; Lieut.-Col. Mitchell's Report.—² British "*General Orders*;" Gen. Drummond to Sir G. Prevost, May 7.

³ Letter from an officer, May 7.

CHAPTER LXXXI.

May 30, 1814.

THE ACTION AT SANDY CREEK, N. Y.

Although the enemy had been repulsed, and the greater part of the cannon and stores which had been collected at or near Oswego, for the equipment and supply of the squadron on Lake Ontario, had been saved; the transportation of these indispensable articles, from the Seneca River to Sackett's Harbor, was a work of considerable danger; and, at the same time, the state of the roads and the distance rendered their carriage by land too costly and laborious.[4] Under the direction of

⁴ Com. Chauncey to Sec. of Navy, June 2; Cooper's Naval History, ii. p. 204.

Captain Woolsey of the navy, whose energy and gallantry had won for him a most enviable reputation, the task of removing these guns and supplies by water commenced; while, in order to deceive the enemy, who still watched the neighborhood with great vigilance, reports were circulated that they were to be transported by way of Oneida Lake.[1]

In the prosecution of his orders Captain Woolsey ran the guns over the falls; and at sunset of the twenty-eighth of May, he reached Oswego with nineteen boats, on which were twenty-one long thirty-two-pounders, ten twenty-fours, three forty-two-pound carronades, and ten cables; intending to pass down the lake as far as Sandy Creek, and from that place, to avoid the blockade which the enemy maintained, to transport them by land to Sackett's Harbor.[2]

The coast being clear, the flotilla,[3] accompanied by one hundred and twenty riflemen under Major Appling, left Oswego at early dusk; and after rowing all night, all, except one boat, reached the Big Salmon River in safety, at sunrise on the twenty-ninth.[4] At that place a small body of Oneida Indians joined the expedition;[5] and thence it proceeded in safety until, at noon on the twenty-ninth, it reached Sandy Creek—eight miles from the Harbor—

[1] Capt. Woolsey to Com. Chauncey, June 1; Cooper, ii. p. 204; Ingersoll, iv. p. 82.—[2] Com. Chauncey to Sec. of Navy, June 2; Capt. Woolsey to Com. Chauncey, June 1.

[3] The reconnoissance of the coast was made by Mr. Dixon in Capt. Woolsey's gig.—[4] Gen. Gaines to Sec. of War, May 30; Capt. Woolsey to Com. Chauncey, June 1.

[5] Com. Chauncey to Secretary of Navy, June 2; Capt. Woolsey to Com. Chauncey, June 1; Cooper, ii. p. 204.

the boat already alluded to being still unaccounted for.[1]

In the mean time the boat which had left the flotilla, from some unexplained cause, had pushed on and sought Sackett's Harbor, near which place Sir James Yeo had anchored with the British squadron, and had fallen—whether purposely or otherwise is not known—into the hands of the enemy; and its crew had informed Sir James of the approach and destination of the flotilla.[2] Immediate steps were taken to intercept the boats before they reached Sandy Creek, or to capture them after they entered it; and for this purpose Captain Popham of the *Montreal* was detached with a gunboat, and Captain Spilsbury, also of the navy, with another, three cutters and a gig being also in their company.[3] After cruising all day, separately, without seeing the flotilla, the two parties united; and, on the morning of the thirtieth, they entered the creek in pursuit of it.[4]

Having received intelligence of the approach of the enemy, Major Appling ambuscaded his riflemen and Indians at about half a mile below the place where the flotilla laid, and awaited the approach of the enemy;[5] while a squad-

[1] Gen. Gaines to Sec. of War, May 30 and 31; Letter from Sackett's Harbor, May 31, in Albany *Argus, Extra*, June 4; Com. Chauncey to Sec. of Navy, June 2; Capt. Woolsey to Com. Chauncey, June 2; "*The War*," ii. p. 205.

[2] Letter from Sackett's Harbor, May 31; Auchinleck, p. 292; Rogers, i. p. 269; Sir G. Prevost to Earl Bathurst, June 8.—[3] Auchinleck, p. 292; Cooper, ii. p. 204; Rogers, i. pp. 269, 270.—[4] Armstrong's Notices, ii. pp. 73, 74; James' Nav. Occur., p. 398; Rogers, i. p. 270; Capt. Popham to Sir James L. Yeo, June 1.

[5] Letter from Sackett's Harbor, May 31; Gen. Gaines' "*General Orders*," June 1; Com. Chauncey to Sec. of Navy, June 2; Capt. Woolsey to Com. Chauncey, June 1; "*The War*," ii. p. 205.

ron of dragoons under Captain Harris, and a company of light artillery under Captain Melvin, with two six-pound field-pieces, which had been sent from Sackett's Harbor to strengthen the escort, halted near the boats, to act as circumstances required.[1] At about eight in the morning of the thirtieth, the enemy having come within long gun-shot distance, he opened his fire on the flotilla; and at ten he landed part of his troops, for the purpose of flanking the gunboats, pushing forward up the creek, and throwing grape and canister into the bushes, as he went, to secure himself from surprise.[2]

With the utmost gayety, and cheering as he went, evidently supposing the victory had been gained without a blow,[3] the enemy pressed forward until he had come within range of the fatal rifles of Major Appling's concealed party, when a deadly fire was opened on his flank and rear;[4] while from the front the two field-pieces threw in an occasionally effective shot,[5] although there does not appear to have been any material opposition either from the artillery or the dragoons, and the Indians

[1] Letter from Sackett's Harbor, May 31; Com. Chauncey to Secretary of Navy, June 2; Capt. Woolsey to Com. Chauncey, June 1.

[2] Com. Chauncey to Sec. of Navy, June 2; Capt. Woolsey to Com. Chauncey, June 1; Capt. Popham to Sir James L. Yeo, June 1.

[3] Gen. Gaines' "*General Orders*," June 1; Perkins, p. 368.

[4] Letter from Sackett's Harbor, May 31; Com. Chauncey to Secretary of Navy, June 2; Capt. Woolsey to Com. Chauncey, June 1.

[5] Letter from Sackett's Harbor, May 31.

are said to have been so situated that they took no part in the affair until after the enemy had surrendered.[1] Against this unseen foe, on his flanks and rear, and against the feeble opposition on his front, the enemy battled manfully about ten minutes; when, having suffered severely, he surrendered[2]—a victim of his own rashness.

In this affair, the only loss sustained by the Americans was one rifleman and a warrior wounded;[3] while of the enemy, Midshipman Hoare and seventeen men were *killed*, and fifty men dangerously *wounded*.[4] One of the boats which was captured mounted a sixty-eight-pound carronade, one a long thirty-two-pounder, one a long twenty-four-pounder, one two long twelve-pounders, and another two small brass howitzers;[5] besides which, Captains Popham and Spilsbury, Lieutenants Cox and Knight of the marines, besides the killed and wounded, of which no record has been made, and one hundred and sixty-one marines and seamen were taken prisoners.[6]

[Note.—The Dispatches of Maj. Appling to Gen. Gaines, Capt. Woolsey to Com. Chauncey, and Capt. Popham to Sir James L. Yeo, have been omitted by the Publishers for want of room.]

[1] The Indians had been dispersed, early in the day, by the enemy's artillery, and returned only when the action had terminated.—*Capt. Popham to Sir James L. Yeo, June* 1.

[2] Gen. Gaines to Sec. of War, May 31; Gen. Gaines' "*General Orders*," June 1; Com. Chauncey to Sec. of Navy, June 2.—[3] Gen. Gaines' "*General Orders*," June 1.

[4] Capt. Popham to Sir James L. Yeo, June 1.

[5] Letter from Sackett's Harbor, May 31; Com. Chauncey to Secretary of Navy, June 2; "*The War*," ii. p. 205; Rogers, i. p. 270.—[6] Maj. Appling to Gen. Gaines, May 30; Gen. Gaines' "*General Orders*," June 1.

CHAPTER LXXXII.

June 28, 1814.

THE CAPTURE OF THE REINDEER.

The sloop of war *Wasp*, commanded by Captain Johnson Blakely, sailed from Portsmouth, New Hampshire, on the afternoon of the first of May, 1814;[1] and, after a very successful cruise in the chops of the English Channel—rivalling the celebrated cruise of the *Argus* in the same vicinity—at an early hour in the morning of the twenty-eighth of June, while in latitude 48° 36′ N., and longitude 11° 15′ W., she made a strange sail on her weather-beam, and immediately made chase.[2]

At ten o'clock the stranger hoisted an English ensign and pendant; yet, notwithstanding every effort was made for that purpose, it was not until seventeen minutes past three in the afternoon that the action commenced. At that time, the stranger being on the weather-quarter of the *Wasp*, sixty yards distant, the former opened her fire from her shifting gun—a twelve-pound carronade—mounted on her topgallant-forecastle, loaded with round and grape shot; and four times the fire was repeated before the guns of the latter could be brought to bear. At length, finding the stranger did not get sufficiently on the beam to enable him to bring his guns to bear, Captain Blakely put his helm a-lee; and at twenty-six minutes past three the *Wasp* opened her fire with her after carronade, on the starboard side, and fired her guns in succession as they bore. At thirty-four minutes past three Captain Blakely hauled up his mainsail; and as the two ships were now very near, and every shot told, the action became very severe.[1]

The fire of the *Wasp* having proved too heavy for the stranger, and that from her tops having scattered destruction on her decks, she ran aboard the *Wasp*, and several attempts to retrieve her fortune by boarding, led by her commander in person, were made and repelled. At length, at forty-four minutes past three, the boarders of the *Wasp* were called; and, after a vigorous resistance of only a minute's duration, her crew was overpowered, and her colors were struck.[2]

The prize proved to be His Britannic Majesty's sloop of war *Reindeer*, Captain William Manners commanding; mounting sixteen twenty-four-pound carronades, two long guns, and a shifting twelve-pounder, and manned with a crew of one hundred and eighteen men.[3] She was "literally cut to pieces in a line with her ports, and her upper-works, boats, and spare spars were one complete wreck;" and soon afterwards her foremast went overboard.[4] Her gallant commander, Purser Barton, and twenty-three of her crew had been *killed;* and her First-lieutenant (Chambers), Master Jones, and forty of her crew had been *wounded;*[5] and when

[1] Capt. Blakely to Sec. of Navy, May 1.—[2] Minutes of the Action, &c., inclosed in Capt. Blakely's Dispatch.

[1] Minutes, &c.—[2] Ibid.; "London Paper," in Niles' *Register*, vii. p. 12; Weekly Messenger, ii. p. 344.

[3] Capt. Blakely to Sec. of Navy, July 8; Cooper, ii. p. 126.—[4] Capt. Blakely to Sec. of Navy, July 8.

[5] Returns appended to Capt. Blakely's Dispatch.

her flag was lowered the captain's-clerk was the senior officer, and performed the sad ceremony of surrendering the ship.[1]

The *Wasp* was a new ship, on her first cruise,[2] mounting twenty thirty-two-pound carronades and two long guns,[3] with a crew of one hundred and seventy-three men.[4] Six round-shot had struck her hull; her foremast had been wounded with a twenty-four-pound shot; and her rigging and sails had been considerably injured.[1] Five of her crew had been *killed*, and two midshipmen and nineteen of her crew had been *wounded*.[2]

In this short, but sanguinary conflict, the conduct of both crews entitled them to the highest honor; and in no engagement during the war were there displayed any finer specimens of seamanship, discipline, or courage, than in this.

CHAPTER LXXXIII.

July 3 to August 21, 1814.

THE EXPEDITION AGAINST MICHILIMACINAC.

The loss of Michilimacinac, at an early period of the war, and the evils which resulted from it, have been frequently referred to in preceding chapters of this work; and both the British and the American governments naturally desired its possession. It was the key to the Indian nations of the Northwest, and of the valuable fur-trade which flowed therefrom; and while one power prepared to strengthen and defend the post, the other as steadily provided means for its capture.

In this struggle for suprémacy, in April, 1814, the enemy sent forward a strong party of men, under Lieutenant-colonel McDouall;[5] and, soon afterwards (*July* 17, 1814), the American post at Prairie-du-Chien was surrendered to a detachment from the garrison, led by Lieutenant-colonel McKay.[6] In the mean time, in April, 1814, Commander Arthur St. Clair, of the navy, had been placed in command of the upper lakes, with the *Niagara*, *St. Lawrence*, *Caledonia*, *Scorpion*, and *Tigress*,—all known to the reader as connected with Commander Perry's victory on Lake Erie,—and, on the third of July, he was joined by Lieutenant-colonel Croghan, with five hundred regular troops and two hundred and fifty militia.[3] On the twelfth, Colonel William Cotgreave, with a regiment of Ohio Volunteers, joined the expedition;[4] and after a tedious trip,—rendered still more tedious by what appears to have been a strong desire to increase the prize-money by securing the enemy's furs,[5]—on the twenty-sixth of July, it reached its destination.[6]

A serious difference of opinion ap-

[1] James' Nav. Occur., pp. 355, 356.—[2] Cooper, ii. p. 125; "*The War*," iii. p. 49.—[3] Cooper, ii. p. 112.

[4] Naval Temple, p. 136; James' Naval Occurrences, pp. 357, 358.—[5] Christie, p. 195; James, ii. pp. 186, 187.

[6] Lieut. Col. McKay to Lieut.-Col. McDouall, July 27; Christie, p. 196; James, ii. pp. 187–190.

[1] Capt. Blakely to Sec. of Navy, July 8.—[2] Returns appended to Capt. Blakely's Dispatch.—[3] Ingersoll, iv. p. 75; James, ii. pp. 190, 191; Armstrong, ii. p. 74.

[4] Ingersoll, iv. pp. 75, 76.—[5] Ibid., p. 76.

[6] Lieut.-Col. Croghan to Sec. of War, Aug. 9, 1814; James, ii. p. 193.

pears to have existed between the military and the naval chiefs, concerning the propriety of an immediate attack on the post,—the naval, it is said, refusing to risk his vessels in an attack on a post on which he could not bring his guns to bear, from its height above the water,[1]—and it was not until the fourth of August the forces landed, which was done, without obstruction from the enemy, at Dowsman's farm, on "the back part of the island."[2] After the landing had been effected the troops appear to have been formed into column, with the militia in front, and moved towards the enemy's works; but they had not proceeded far when their progress was obstructed by the garrison, under Lieutenant-colonel McDouall, which had been withdrawn from the works and posted in "an excellent position"—the ground being commanding; in front as clear as the Lieutenant-colonel could wish, and on both his flanks and rear was a thick wood." A strong Indian force, posted in the woods, covered his flanks; "a natural breastwork protected his men from every shot," in front; and two field-pieces, commanding the open ground, rendered his position truly an "excellent" one.[3]

After having reconnoitred the enemy's position, Lieutenant-colonel Croghan determined to change his order; and having moved Major Holmes' battalion of regulars to the right of the militia, with the intention of turning the enemy's left flank, he advanced against the enemy. In this, however, the Lieutenant-colonel appears to have overlooked, or not known of, the Indians who were posted on the enemy's flanks; and as the line moved forward, the regulars, on the American right, were met with a severe volley from the rifles of the savages, in which Major Holmes and Captain Desha fell,—the former killed, the latter wounded,—and the men were thrown into "confusion, from which the best exertions of the officers were not able to recover them."[1] From this cause, and from the thickness of the woods, Lieutenant-colonel Croghan found it impossible to gain the enemy's left; and he immediately resolved to charge the front of his position. In this, while he was more successful than on the right of the line, and while the enemy was driven from his breastwork into the wood on his rear, the Lieutenant-colonel was not able to accomplish much, or to dislodge the enemy from the thicket; and, soon afterwards, he withdrew from the contest, and retired to the shipping.[2]

In this attempt the forces of the respective belligerents is not certainly known—the marines and seamen from the squadron serving with the American soldiers on shore;[3] and the Indians, who never faltered in the discharge of their duties, having scarcely been referred to in the report, and, as usual, not alluded to in the returns.[4]

The loss of the Americans was Major

[1] Ingersoll, iv. p. 76. It is proper to remark that I find no other reference to this diversity of opinion.

[2] Lieut.-Col. Croghan to Sec. of War, Aug. 9, 1814; Ingersoll, iv. p. 76; Christie, p. 197; James, ii. p. 193.

[3] Lieut.-Col. McDouall to Sir G. Prevost, Aug. 14; Ingersoll, iv. pp. 76, 77; Armstrong, ii. p. 75.

[1] Lieut.-Col. Croghan to Sec. of War, Aug. 9; Ingersoll, iv. p. 77.

[2] Lieut.-Col. Croghan to Sec. of War, Aug. 9; Lieut.-Col. McDouall to Sir G. Prevost, Aug. 14; Christie, p. 197; James, ii. pp. 194, 195.

[3] This is evident, from the returns of the killed and wounded, which include men of these branches of the service.

[4] Lieut.-Col. McDouall to Sir G. Prevost, Aug. 14.

Holmes and twelve men *killed*, Captains Vanhorn and Desha, Lieutenant Jackson, and fifty-two men *wounded*, and two men *missing*;[1] that of the enemy, if any, has not been recorded.[2]

After leaving Michilimacinac the squadron sailed to the mouth of the Nautauwasaga, and destroyed the works and a schooner which laid there; and, on the twenty-first of August, the expedition reached the mouth of the St. Clair River on its return.[1]

CHAPTER LXXXIV.

July 5, 1814.

THE BATTLE OF CHIPPEWA.

The officers who had conducted the operations on the Niagara frontier, in 1812 and 1813, having given place to other and younger officers, the greatest anxiety was manifested throughout the country concerning the probable result of the change; and while, on the one hand, the people recollected only the *disasters* of the past, and regarded the future with despair rather than with hope; on the other hand the old officers, and those who sympathized with them, fostered this distrust, and maintained that "those who succeeded them were incapable of doing any thing which would reflect the least honor to themselves or their country."[3]

Major-general Jacob Brown, assisted by Brigadier-generals Winfield Scott and Eleazar W. Ripley, commanded on that frontier;[4] and having been instructed "to cross the river, capture Fort Erie, march on Chippewa, risk a combat, menace Fort George, and, if assured of the ascendency and co-operation of the fleet, to seize and fortify Burlington Heights," preparations were made for that purpose.[2] In accordance with these instructions orders were issued, on the second of July, for the troops to pass the river;[3] and while it was yet dark, on the morning of the third,[4] the landing was effected by the Ninth, Eleventh, part of the Twenty-second, and the Twenty-fifth regiments, under General Scott, below Fort Erie;[5] and, at a later hour, the Seventeenth, Nineteenth, Twenty-first, and Twenty-third regiments, under General Ripley, also landed above the fort.[6] The enemy's pickets were immediately driven in by the Indians and light troops, which were sent against them; and, soon afterwards, with only a slight show of resistance, Fort Erie, with its small garrison,—embracing one hundred and seventy men, under Major Buck,[7]—surren-

[1] Returns, signed "N. H Moore, *A. A. A. G.*," appended to Lieut.-Col. Croghan's Report.—[2] The loss of the Indians was seldom noticed in the British reports of loss; and their numbers, and their presence even, were seldom referred to.—[3] Reminiscences of the Campaign of 1814, on the Niagara Frontier, by Maj. David B. Douglass, of the Engineers, in manuscript.—[4] Perkins, p. 369.

[1] Lieut.-Col. Croghan to Gen. McArthur, Aug. 23; James, ii. pp. 195, 196.—[2] Armstrong, ii. p. 83.

[3] Gen. Brown to Sec. of War, July 7.—[4] Maj. Douglass's Reminis.; Armstrong, ii. p. 83.—[5] Maj. Douglass's Reminis.; Mansfield's Scott, pp. 102, 103; Buffalo *Gazette*, July 5, 1814.—[6] Mansfield's Scott, p. 103; Buffalo *Gazette*, July 5, 1814. Gen. Armstrong (*Notices*, ii. pp. 83, 219) says Gen. Ripley was not satisfied with the arrangements, and crossed reluctantly.—[7] James' Mil. Occur., ii. p. 116; Utica *Gazette*, July 9, 1814; Buffalo *Gazette*, July 5. The returns of the prisoners, appended to Gen. Brown's Report, show that only 137 passed into the hands of the victors.

dered;[1] the garrison losing one man,[2] and the Americans four.[3]

On the morning of the fourth, General Scott, with his brigade, and the corps of artillery, under Captain Towson, moved down the Niagara, and took a position behind Street's Creek — a small stream which enters the Niagara about a mile and a half above Chippewa.[4] On his march, General Scott had encountered, and driven before him, the British advance, embracing the light companies of the Royal Scots and of the One hundredth regiments, and a detachment from the Nineteenth dragoons, the whole commanded by Lieutenant-colonel Pearson;[5] and, after a warm, skirmishing fire, he encamped with his front protected by the creek, his right, supported by the artillery, resting on the Niagara River, and his left "in air."[6] On the same evening, the main body, embracing the Second brigade, the field and battery train, and Major Hindman's corps of artillery, also advanced, and encamped in the rear of General Scott; and, on the morning of the fifth, General Peter B. Porter, with part of the New York and Pennsylvania Volunteers, and a small party of friendly Indians, followed, and encamped still farther in the rear.[7]

At this time, General Rial, with a large force of the *élite* of the British army, was posted behind a heavy line of intrenchments below the Chippewa Creek;[1] and he was strengthened by the arrival, on the morning of the fifth of July, of the Eighth regiment of the line, from York.[2] In his front, extending up to Street's Creek, where the Americans were encamped, — a mile and a half distant,—was a level plain, about a mile wide, bounded, on the east by the Niagara, and on the west by a heavy wood, with occasional patches of low ground.[3]

During the early part of the fifth the pickets and scouts of both armies amused themselves with an active fire; and about noon the woods on the American left were occupied by strong bodies of the enemy's light troops and Indians, which considerably annoyed the American pickets.[4] To disperse these, and if possible to intercept them, at four in the afternoon General Porter was detached with his brigade and the Indians, and ordered to move through the woods still farther to the left; but his advance having met some of the enemy's scouts, the latter was informed of the movement, and fell back on his main body at Chippewa. The enemy was immediately strengthened, however; and, in his turn, General Porter and his command were driven back on the American lines, notwithstanding the troops were animated by the presence of the commander-in-chief.[5]

While these skirmishes were adding to the interest of the scene on the left and front of the American line, other

[1] Maj. Douglass's Reminis.; Gen. Brown to Sec. of War, July 7; Christie. p. 183.—[2] James, ii. p. 116; Buffalo *Gazette*. July 5.—[3] Gen. Brown to Secretary of War, July 7; Buffalo *Gazette*, July 5.—[4] Gen. Brown to Sec. of War, July 7; James, ii. p. 118.—[5] Gen. Rial to Gen. Drummond, July 6; James, ii. p. 118; Gen. Scott's Report, July 15. Mr. Mansfield (*Life of Gen. Scott*, p. 103) says the 100th regiment, under the Marquis of Tweesdale, composed this advance; but he appears to be in error.

[6] Maj. Douglass's Reminiscences; Armstrong, ii. p. 84.

[7] Gen. Brown to the Secretary of War, July 7; Armstrong, ii. p. 85.

[1] Maj. Douglass's Reminis.—[2] Gen. Rial to Gen. Drummond, July 6.—[3] Maj. Douglass's Reminis.; Mansfield's Scott, pp. 103, 104.—[4] Gen. Brown to Sec. of War, July 7; Mansfield, p. 104; Armstrong, ii. p 85.—[5] Gen. Brown to Sec. of War, July 7; American "*General Orders*," July, 1814; James, ii. p. 121; Armstrong, ii. p. 85; Christie, p. 184.

and more important movements were being provided for. On the one side, General Scott, ignorant of any movement of the enemy's main body, was moving his brigade over the bridge which spanned Street's Creek, with the design of drilling on the plain;[1] while, on the other hand, at the same time, the main body of the enemy, under General Rial, was entering the plain, on its northern border, for the purpose of attacking the American encampment.[2] Fortunately General Brown, while on the left, with General Porter's brigade, had seen the cloud of dust and the head of the enemy's column;[3] and the attempt to surprise the encampment, which the latter had intended, was not successful; while the dress-parade and drill with which General Scott proposed to relieve his brigade, and to improve its discipline, became a scene of sterner and more important duties.

With his troops disposed in three columns—the light companies of the Royal Scots and of the One hundredth regiment, with the Second regiment of Lincoln militia, forming his advance-guard; and three hundred Indians on his extreme right—General Rial moved towards the Americans; and soon afterwards he displayed his force on the plain, near the southern extremity of

[1] Mansfield's Scott, p. 105; Armstrong, ii. p. 86.

[2] Gen. Brown to Sec. of War, July 7; British "*General Orders*," Kingston, July 9, 1814; James, ii. pp. 120, 121; Christie, p. 184; Rogers, i. p. 271. Gen. Armstrong (*Notices*, ii. p. 86) appears to suppose the enemy was drawn from his lines by Gen. Porter's operations, for the purpose of sustaining his outposts, and of checking an anticipated movement of the Americans. As Gen. Rial appears to have been prompted by the *arrival of reinforcements*, and left his lines after having "made his dispositions for *attack*," I have not considered he was on the *defensive*, but an *assailant*.—[3] Gen. Brown to Sec. of War, July 7; Mansfield's Scott, p. 105.

it, with the Eighth (*King's*) regiment on his right, the First (*Royal Scots*) and the One hundredth in front, and his artillery, with two twenty-four-pounders and a five-and-a-half-inch howitzer on his extreme left.[1] While the enemy, with all the grandeur and mechanical precision which mark the movements of soldiers such as these were, was thus moving forward and deploying into line, with equal grandeur and precision the First brigade, under General Scott—instead of a parade and drill—was also breaking its columns and displaying, in line, to confront the enemy and to check his progress—the Ninth and part of the Twenty-second regiments, commanded by Major Leavenworth, covered by Towson's artillery, forming on the extreme right, the Eleventh, commanded by Major McNeil, in the centre, and the Twenty-fifth, commanded by Major Jesup, on the extreme left.[2]

While the several regiments composing the First brigade were thus moving into their appointed places in the line, the Volunteers and Indians, composing General Porter's brigade, who occupied the wood on the extreme left of the American position, suddenly broke and fled in every direction, leaving the left flank of the line entirely exposed to the right of the enemy's line;[3] when Major Jesup, with the Twenty-fifth regiment, by an oblique movement extended the left of the line and remedied the defection, before the Twenty-first regiment and General Rip-

[1] Gen. Rial to Gen. Drummond, July 6. Mr. Christie (*Mil. and Nav. Occur.*, p. 184) says the Eighth regiment was placed on the *left*, but I prefer Gen. Rial's statement.

[2] Gen. Brown to Sec. of War, July 7; Mansfield, p. 106; Armstrong, ii. pp. 86, 87.—[3] Gen. Brown to Sec. of War, July 7; James, ii. p. 121.

ley, which General Brown had ordered to the spot, could reach the position.[1]

The instant the line was formed it engaged the enemy; and from its entire extent a terrible fire was opened, by word of command, and with deliberate aim, inflicting a heavy loss on the several parts of the opposing force.[2] As each regiment was, to some extent at least, acting independently, the success with which they checked the progress of the several opposing regiments differed; and, with singular negligence, the line of the enemy was broken, and in some cases its several parts were widely separated.[3] His extreme right, for instance, was held in check, by the Twenty-fifth much earlier and much more effectually than were his centre and left; while his centre, also, had not been permitted to advance as far as his left had gone. In this manner he offered as many exposed flanks as he had regiments on the field; and the advantage which he thus offered was not allowed to pass unnoticed. General Scott having thrown forward the left of some of the regiments, the exposed flanks of their opposing forces were sometimes severely handled;[4] and in one instance—that in which Captains Weeks and Bliss, on the right of the Eleventh regiment, flanked and severely cut up the corps on the enemy's extreme left[5]—the effect was at once marked and decisive.

The destructive effect of the American fire on every part of his line speedily awakened the enemy to a sense of the danger of his position; and he ordered his troops "to charge in front, for which they advanced with the greatest gallantry, under a most destructive fire. In this attempt, however, they suffered so severely that General Rial was obliged to withdraw them, finding their further efforts would be unavailing;"[1] and immediately afterwards the compliment was reciprocated with a charge by the whole of the American line,[2] "with admirable coolness and promptitude, and with an effect which, considering the nature of the troops opposed, it was hardly possible to realize. The columns which had been in full march upon us but a few moments before, were now, in another brief minute, routed and flying in uncontrollable disorder towards the Chippewa."[3]

In this decisive action the strength of the parties engaged has, as usual, been the subject of great controversy. As the only force employed by the Americans was the First (*General Scott's*) brigade, and Captain Towson's artillery,—the brigade of Volunteers, under General Porter, having ran away before the battle opened; and General Ripley's brigade having failed in its efforts to come up before the enemy had been repulsed,[4]—the strength of the regiments which were in the battle could not have been greater than fourteen hundred men;[5] while the First (*Royal Scots*), the Eighth (*King's*), and the One hundredth regiments, the Second Lincoln militia, the detachment from the Royal Artillery, and the Indians on

[1] Mansfield, p. 110; Gen. Brown to Sec. of War, July 7; James, ii. p. 123.—[2] Maj. Douglass's Reminis.; Gen. Rial to Gen. Drummond, July 6; Christie, p. 184.

[3] Mansfield's Scott, p. 106; J. H. Bliss to Rev. M. Douglass, Aug. 18, 1853; Gen. Scott to Gen. Brown, July 15.—[4] Mansfield's Scott, pp. 106, 107; J. H. Bliss to Rev. M. Douglass, Aug. 18, 1853; Armstrong, ii. p. 87.

[5] J. H. Bliss to Rev. M. Douglass, Aug. 18, 1853.

[1] Gen. Rial to Gen. Drummond, July 6; James, ii. pp. 123, 124.—[2] Maj. Douglass's Reminis.; Mansfield, p. 107.

[3] Ibid.; Christie, p. 184; Gen. Scott's Report, July 15.

[4] Gen. Brown to Secretary of War, July 7.—[5] Mansfield's Scott, p. 112. Gen. Wilkinson (*Mem.*, i. p. 654) says it "consisted of barely 1100 men and a company of artillery."

the right, amounted to not less than two thousand four hundred men.[1]

The loss of the Americans, in the skirmish preceding the battle, was three Volunteers and nine Indians *killed*, two Volunteers and eight Indians *wounded*, and three officers and four non-commissioned officers of the Volunteers and ten Indians *missing;* and in the battle which ensued, it was forty-eight men *killed*, Colonel Campbell, Captains King, Read, and Harrison, Lieutenants Palmer, Barron, De Witt, Patchin, and Burnhall, and two hundred and thirty-six *wounded*, and two men *missing;*[2] that of the enemy was Captains Bailey, Rowe, and Tomey, Lieutenants Gibson and McDonnell, Ensign Rea, one hundred and thirty-three regulars, ten of the Lincoln militia, and eighty-seven Indians *killed*, Lieutenant-colonel Gordon, of the Royal Scots, Lieutenant-colonel the Marquis of Tweesdale, of the One hundredth, Captains Holland, Bird, Wilson, Sherrard, and Sleigh, Lieutenants Jack, W. Campbell, Fox, Jackson, Hendrick, McDonald, A. Campbell, Connell, Boyd, Williams, Lyon, and Valentine, Ensigns Clarke and Johnson, Adjutant Kingston, and two hundred and eighty-three regulars, with four officers and twelve men of the Lincoln militia *wounded*, and Lieutenant Fortune, thirty regulars, and fifteen militia *missing*.[1]

¹ Report appended to Gen. Rial's Dispatch, July 6.

² Armstrong, ii. p. 88; Map in Maj. Douglass's MS. Reminiscences.

CHAPTER LXXXV.

July 25, 1814.

THE BATTLE OF LUNDY'S LANE.[3]

The enemy having returned, discomfited, to his encampment at Chippewa, as related in the last chapter of this work, the rash desire of General Brown to continue his victorious march northward was checked, for the moment, by the timely remonstrances of his aid, Captain Austin, those of Major Wood, of the engineer corps, and by those of General Scott.[4] On the following day (*July* 6), however, the country was reconnoitred; and an old, disused road having been discovered at some distance from the enemy's right,—"leading from Street's Creek to the junction of Lyon's Creek with the Chippewa," and crossing the latter at that place,—on the seventh, a small fatigue party cleared it and made it passable.[2]

It appears that General Ripley—who had, at the beginning of the campaign, protested against the proposed movements, under existing circumstances—again interposed, with the objections, which his good judgment had raised against the proposed plan of operations; and when, on the eighth, in accordance with the indiscreet designs of the com-

¹ Gen. Rial says (*Dispatch, July* 6) that he had "about 1500 regular troops," and "not above 300 Indians," to which the Second Lincoln militia must be added, and I have supposed these will form, in the aggregate, a force of 2500 men; and in this opinion I am sustained by Mr. Rogers, an intelligent Canadian writer (*Rise of Canada*, i. p. 271.)—² Report appended to Gen. Brown's Dispatch, July 6.—³ This has been known variously as "*The Battle of Bridgewater*," "*The Battle of Niagara*," and "*The Battle of Lundy's Lane*." I have adopted that generally used, although there are authorities for both the others.

⁴ Gen. Brown to Secretary of War, July 7.

¹ Report appended to Gen. Rial's Dispatch, July 6.

² Armstrong, ii. p. 88; Map in Maj. Douglass's MS. Reminiscences.

mander-in-chief, he was ordered to march, with his own brigade, that of General Porter, and two companies of artillery, by the road on the extreme left of the position, to cross the Chippewa, and to fall on the enemy's right flank, while General Scott would hold the left of that enemy in check, he hesitated, and General Brown hastened forward, and, in person, "took on himself the direction of the movement."[1]

The enemy appears to have discovered the arrangements which had been made to cut off his force, however; and while General Brown was thus engaged in "directing the movement" of the expedition which General Ripley had objected to lead, General Rial broke up his encampment at Chippewa, and fell back on Queenstown; and, soon afterwards, having thrown part of his force into Forts George and Mississaga, with the remainder, and with the former garrisons of the forts, he took post on Twenty-mile Creek.[2] The route of the American army having thus been cleared, General Brown moved forward, and, on the tenth, encamped at Queenstown.[3]

While General Brown had been thus pursuing a phantom of his own imagination, General Rial had not been idle or inattentive to his duties. After abandoning the line of the Niagara, he withdrew the garrisons of the forts and substituted older and better soldiers; and with nearly fifteen hundred men he moved towards Burlington Heights, where he expected to join the One hundred and third regiment and the flank companies of the One hundred and fourth; but having effected a junction before he reached the Heights, he returned and took post at the Fifteen-mile Creek, about thirteen miles from the American camp at Queenstown.[1]

Information of this movement of General Rial, but without an allusion to the reinforcement, having reached the American camp at Queenstown, a council was held to determine the course to be pursued; and while Major Hindman, commandant of the artillery, declined to express an opinion, and Generals Ripley and Porter, and Colonels McRee and Wood, of the Engineers, advised an attack on General Rial *during the ensuing night, before the reinforcements could reach him*, Adjutant-general Gardner and General Scott advised the investment of Fort George.[2] Notwithstanding there was no siege train in the army, and although no provision had been made for the conveyance of stores from Buffalo, the advice of the minority prevailed; and after having solicited the co-operation of the squadron on Lake Ontario, promising great achievements with its aid,[3] on the morning of the twentieth of July, General Brown advanced from Queenstown, and at mid-day the army was in position about a mile from the fort.[4]

In this remarkable excursion—remarkable only from the small foundation on which it was based, which was composed of his own opinion, that, with a *fleet* to carry the necessary supplies, he was able "to meet the enemy in the field, and to march *in any direction over his country;*"[5] of his professed expectation of meeting Commodore Chauncey at the head of the lake, while he had,

[1] Gen. Jesup's MS. Memoir of the Campaign, cited by Gen. Armstrong.—[2] Armstrong, ii. p. 88; James' Mil. Occur., ii. pp. 128-132; Maj. Douglass's MS. Reminis.
[3] Maj. Douglass's MS. Reminiscences.

[1] James, ii. p. 132.—[2] Wilkinson's Mem., i. p 669.
[3] Gen. Brown to Com. Chauncey.—[4] Maj. Douglass's MS. Reminis.—[5] Gen. Brown to Com. Chauncey, July 13, 1814—the day before the Council was convened.

before that time, been informed that the fleet would not come there unless that of the enemy led it there, and then only to seek an action rather than to become depots for the stores of the army;[1] and of the danger of leaving an active and disciplined army in a position to harass his flank and, with impunity, to cut off his supplies, if not, indeed, to cut off his retreat, should one become necessary,[2] — General Brown soon discovered the imperfections of his plan, and hastened to correct them. After spending two days on the shore of the lake,—long enough to protect his own dignity, but *not* long enough to secure the co-operation of even a wind-bound fleet, much less of one which was blockaded in a distant port,—on the twenty-second of July, General Brown commenced a retrograde movement; and on the twenty-fourth he had retreated as far as Chippewa, where he encamped on the south side of the river, with the village in front.[3]

Intelligence of the retreat of the American army, and of its arrival at Chippewa, reached General Rial, in his encampment at the Fifteen-mile Creek, on the same afternoon,—an evidence of the animosity of the people against the Americans; and at eleven o'clock in the evening the advance of the British army,—embracing the regiment of Glengarry militia, commanded by Lieutenant-colonel Battersby; the incorporated and sedentary militia, under Lieutenant-colonels Robinson and Parry; detachments from the One hundred and fourth, under Lieutenant-colonel Drummond, and from the Royal Artillery—the latter with two twenty-four-pounders, three six-pounders, and a howitzer; and a troop of the Nineteenth light-dragoons,—left the Twelve-mile Creek, where it had been posted; and, under Lieutenant-colonel Pearson, at seven the next morning, it took a position near Lundy's Lane, — a road which enters the main road below the Falls of Niagara,—at a distance of two and three-quarter miles from the American camp.[1]

This movement appears to have been made without the knowledge of General Brown; and although the commander of the American outpost (*Captain A. W. Odell*, of the Twenty-third infantry) reported the presence of the enemy in his front, at nine in the morning, the General "ridiculed the idea that the enemy was in force near the falls,"[2] and it was not until *late in the afternoon* that any movement was made to counteract the enemy's efforts or to dislodge him from his position.[3] It is true, that a report which the General had received from below—occasioned, probably, by the arrival at Fort Niagara of Sir Gordon Drummond, with the reinforcements hereafter referred to[4]—had led him to suppose that the enemy had crossed the Niagara and moved up the eastern bank;[5] but, at this distance of time, and in the absence of any testimony on the subject, it appears unac-

[1] "A conversation we held on this subject at Sackett's Harbor, previous to your departure for Niagara," referred to in *Com. Chauncey's letter to Gen. Brown, Aug.* 10, 1814.

[2] Gen. Rial's position was but little farther from Queenstown Heights than that occupied by Gen. Brown.

[3] Maj. Douglass's MS. Reminiscences; James, ii. p. 138; Letter from an officer, Fort Erie, July 28.

[1] James, ii. pp. 138, 139.—[2] Maj. Leavenworth's Letter, Jan. 15, 1815; Report of Capt. A. W. Odell, 23d infantry.

[3] It was "between five and six o'clock" when Gen. Scott left the camp.—*Report of Capt. Odell.*

[4] See p. 356, col. 2, and p. 362, col. 1, note 3.

[5] This report was probably founded on the fact that Lieut.-Col. Tucker, with detachments of the 41st and Royal Scots, and a party of Indians, had crossed to Lewiston to disperse a body of militia, whom Gen. Drummond could not, prudently, have left on his flank and rear—a notable contrast with the rashness of Gen. Brown.

countable that a strong body of the enemy should occupy an open position within three miles of the American camp, from early morning until late in the afternoon of a fine July day, without the knowledge of the American commander; and more strange than that does it appear that no reconnoissance was made, on either bank of the river, although it was *supposed* that the enemy, in force, had crossed to New York, and was advancing on the right flank of the army, and might cut off its supplies; while, at the same time, it was *known* that a patrol, at least, was in front, and that, "frequently, throughout the day, in different directions, small parties of the enemy were observable from the picket" which Captain Odell commanded, "about a quarter of a mile from the encampment."[1]

While in this state of blissful ignorance concerning the strength, position, and purposes of his enemy, late in the afternoon, General Brown conceived that, *if* the enemy had crossed into New York, "the most effectual method of recalling him from that object, was to put *himself* in motion towards Queenstown"[2] — never supposing, it would appear, that, possibly, the enemy might *not* have crossed into New York, and that he *might* be ready to oppose the progress of the American army on its march to Queenstown. Rashly, and without those precautionary steps which should precede every movement into an enemy's country, therefore, General Brown ordered the First brigade, Captain Towson's artillery, and all the cavalry and mounted men, under General Winfield Scott, to

[1] Capt. Odell's Report.—[2] Gen. Brown to Sec. of War (no date); Maj. Leavenworth's Letter, Jan. 15, 1815; Col. Miller's Letter, Sept. 4, 1814.

move towards Queenstown, "with orders to report *if* the enemy appeared, and to call for assistance, *if* that was necessary;"[1] and "between five and six o'clock"[2] in the afternoon the column moved from the encampment, and proceeded down the road towards the Falls of Niagara.[3]

At that time an old dwelling-house, occupied by a widow named Wilson, stood on the eastern side of the road, opposite Table Rock; and as the head of the American column, turning a point of woods, came in sight of the house, a number of cavalry-horses, in charge of a dragoon or two, were seen in the widow's yard. At the same instant, eight or ten British officers stepped hastily from the house and rode away; while three or four of the party, with their glasses, surveyed the moving column,—one of them, more carefully than the others,—and, after exchanging salutes, followed their associates. Colonel Wood and Lieutenant Douglass, of the Engineers,[4] who were a little in advance, hastened forward; and "with well-affected concern," the widow met them at her door, with her well-feigned regret that they had not come earlier and "caught" her former guests. General Scott and his staff soon came up, and with artful manner and poisoned words the widow informed him her visitors were General Rial and his staff, and

[1] Gen. Brown to Secretary of War (no date).

[2] Maj. Douglass's MS. Reminis.; James, ii. p. 139; Capt. Odell's Report.—[3] Maj. Douglass's MS. Reminis.; Gen. Brown to Sec. of War (no date); James, ii. p. 139.

[4] Since favorably known to the world as Major David B. Douglass, of the Engineers, Professor of Engineering in the Military Academy at West Point, President of Kenyon College, Ohio, and Professor of Mathematics at Geneva, N. Y. He died Oct. 21, 1849, leaving, in manuscript, his "*Reminiscences of the Campaign of* 1814 *on the Niagara Frontier*," which, through the kindness of his sons, have been placed before me to assist me in following the thread of this complicated subject.

that eight hundred regulars, three hundred militia, and two pieces of artillery were in advance. Lieutenant Douglass was immediately sent back to the encampment with the intelligence of the enemy's supposed strength, and of General Scott's intention to "engage it in battle;" and the latter, with his detachment, moved forward, so far as now appears, also without reconnoitring, and without intelligence beyond that which the widow had imparted.[1]

The column had not advanced far, however,—not even beyond the open ground in which the widow's dwelling stood,—when it was halted, and Colonel Leavenworth and the Ninth regiment of infantry were thrown out, on the west side of the road, as a flanking party. Again the column moved forward, with Captain Harris's troop of cavalry and Captain Pentland's company of infantry in the advance, until it reached the fork of the roads, where was a narrow piece of woods, in which a small party of the enemy had been posted, when the flanking party was *called in*, and the Twenty-fifth regiment, under Colonel Jesup, was detached to the right, to seek and attack the left of the line, which the *unseen* enemy was *supposed* to have formed in that direction. Having thus disposed of his force,—the Twenty-fifth regiment moving off to the right of the main body, and the Ninth, Twenty-second, and Eleventh, in column, continuing their march down the main road, towards Queenstown,—General Scott ordered the advance—Captains Harris and Pentland's commands—to halt and fall in the rear of the column; and in this order the divided column entered the narrow strip of woods, behind which the enemy was calmly awaiting its approach.[1]

With the anxious, but determined, step of veterans, in quick time,[2]—as if pursuing an enemy, rather than entering an engagement with a superior force,—the column passed the wood and debouched into an open space,—evidently a farm clearing,—in the rear of which, not more than six hundred yards distant, and commanding every inch of the ground,[3] was an elevated hill, on which frowned seven pieces of artillery, in battery; while supporting it, on either hand, was the entire strength of General Rial's command, together with a heavy reinforcement, with which Lieutenant-general Drummond had just come up from Queenstown.[4]

The effect of this rash movement—or rather the beginning of it—was, at once, apparent. A handful of men, not more than thirteen hundred in all,[5] and they divided into two parties,—with two field-pieces only,—had been pushed, without their knowledge, within canister-shot distance[6] of an overwhelming force, which, with its wings thrown forward from its artillery in the centre, appeared to be ready to infold and crush in its embraces those whom the murderous fire of the battery might spare from its slaughter. On their right—east of the Queenstown road, and thrown forward from the hill on which the battery was planted[7]—was the extreme

[1] Maj. Douglass's MS. Reminis.; Mansfield's Scott, p. 124. Other writers have differed from me in this part of the narrative, but I have preferred the testimony of the gallant messenger to the suppositions of other parties.

[1] Maj. Leavenworth's Letter, Jan. 15, 1815.—[2] Ibid.
[3] MS. Map in Maj. Douglass's Reminis.; Col. Miller's Letter, Sept. 4, 1814.—[4] Gen. Drummond to Sir G. Prevost, July 27; James, ii. pp. 142, 143.—[5] Mansfield's Life of Scott, p. 123.—[6] Maj. Leavenworth's Letter, July 15, 1815.—[7] Gen. Drummond to Sir G. Prevost, July 27.

left of the enemy's line, consisting of three companies of the Eighth (*or King's*) regiment of the line,[1] five hundred *rank and file* of the "incorporated militia," under Lieutenant-colonel Robinson,[2] and three hundred of the "sedentary militia," under Lieutenant-colonel Parry,[3] supported by Major Lisle's troop of light-dragoons;[4] in the centre, fronting General Scott's command,—with their left on the Queenstown road,[5] and the battery thrown forward in front,—were the Eighty-ninth regiment of the line;[6] a battalion of Royal Scots, numbering four hundred men;[7] and the light company of the Forty-first regiment;[8] and in the woods, on the extreme right of the line, also formed *en potence*, was that gallant and untiring body, known as the Glengarry regiment of provincials.[9]

Into the midst of this force, posted and prepared for battle, as before stated, General Scott led the skeletons of three regiments, without preparation and without warning; while the fourth—the Twenty-fifth—had been thrown off to the right, away from its fellows, and left to combat, unaided, the extreme left of the enemy's position. It was now near sunset, and the appearance of the little column, as it deployed, by an *echelon* movement, into line, on the left of the road, was the signal for "a brisk fire" both from the battery in front, and from the "heavy line of infantry posted to the right, and obliquely in front of the artillery"[1]—scattering death and destruction on every hand. Captain Towson, with his puny park of artillery, moved up and formed on the right of the line, "and, by its frequent and incessant discharges, highly animated the spirits of the troops," a very desirable result, in itself, although the enemy suffered but little from it.[2]

While General Scott and the main body of his detachment were thus engaged, in front of the enemy, and gallantly maintained their ground, notwithstanding the strength of the opposing force, Major Jesup, with the Twenty-fifth, on the extreme right, was not idle. He was opposed, as will be remembered, by upwards of a thousand of the enemy's troops;[3] yet, in the language of General Drummond, *the enemy's commander*, "after repeated attacks, the troops on the (*British*) left were *partially forced back*, and the enemy (*the Americans*) gained a momentary *possession of the road*."[4] He consoled himself, however, for this defeat—as the left wing of the enemy was posted on the *east side of the road*, Major Jesup could not have gained even "a momentary possession of the road" until he had driven that entire wing *across* the road—with the reflection that "it gave the Americans no material advantage, as the troops which had been forced back (*the entire left wing*) formed in the rear

[1] Gen. Drummond to Sir G. Prevost, July 27; James, ii. p. 143.—[2] Gen. Drummond to Sir G. Prevost, July 27. The strength of this body of militia may be seen by comparing James, ii. p. 132, with Gen. Rial's Dispatch to Sir G. Prevost, July 7, in which it is stated that he had not over 300 Indians with him.—[3] This militia was withdrawn from the forts, and then (*July* 9) numbered 300 men.—*James' Mil. Occur.*, ii. p. 131.—[4] Gen. Drummond to Sir G. Prevost, July 27; James, ii. p. 143.—[5] Gen. Drummond to Sir G. Prevost, July 27.—[6] James, ii. p. 143.

[7] Gen. Drummond to Sir G. Prevost, July 27. There were 320 *rank and file*, exclusive of officers.—*James*, ii. p. 143.—[8] Gen. Drummond to Sir G. Prevost, July 27; James, ii. p. 143.—[9] Gen. Drummond to Sir G. Prevost, July 27.

[1] Maj. Leavenworth's Letter, July 15, 1815.

[2] The pieces could not be sufficiently elevated to prove effective.—[3] Vide p. 357, col. 1.—[4] Gen. Drummond to Sir G. Prevost, July 27. See also James, ii. p. 143; Maj. Douglass's MS. Reminiscences.

of the Eighty-ninth regiment (*the left of the centre*), fronting the road, and secured the flank"[1] (*of the entire line*); and he does not even pretend that the left wing ever recovered the position from which it had been driven by the handful of men composing the Twenty-fifth. But more than this, even,—glorious as was such an achievement,—was the capture of Major-general Rial and his staff, and the aid of General Drummond, which added still more lustre to the achievements of the regiment, and still greater loss to the enemy.[2]

In the mean time, Lieutenant Douglass, at the top of his speed, dashed into the encampment; and, at the same moment, "the distant sound of the first firing"—probably that at the fork of the roads—conveyed to the entire army the intelligence of which the young lieutenant had, before, been the sole possessor. The privates,—many of them "older, if not better soldiers" than their General,—as well as the officers, were instantly aroused; and the messenger and his foaming steed became, at once, the objects of universal and anxious attention. The message was delivered to General Brown, in his marquee; and, after consulting Colonel McRee, of the Engineers, he ordered General Ripley, with the Second brigade, and General Porter, with the Volunteers, to "advance and support General Scott."[1] With the great good judgment which generally characterized the professional actions of General Ripley, he had anticipated the order by directing his brigade to form at the moment he heard the first fire, already alluded to; and before the reports of the artillery, which soon afterwards reached the camp, were distinguished,—if not before the receipt of the General's orders,—the brigade was in readiness, and anxious for the fray.[2] Soon afterwards an aid, with the expected order, rode up to the anxious column, and it was put in motion.

The shades of evening were gathering around the encampment when the order was given; and before the skeletons of the First, Twenty-first, and Twenty-third regiments—composing General Ripley's command—had reached the fork of the road, below Mrs. Wilson's, it had become quite dark.[3] Having dispatched an aid to report his approach to General Brown,—who had preceded him,—and solicited orders for the disposition of his men, General Ripley, in accordance with the orders which he received, commenced the formation of a line *on the right of the First brigade*, on the *east* side of the Queenstown road.

[1] Gen. Drummond to Sir G. Prevost, July 27; Gen. Brown to Secretary of War.

[2] Gen. Drummond to Sir G. Prevost, June 17; Gen. Brown to Sec. of War (no date); James, ii. pp. 146, 147. Maj. Douglass, in his MS. *Reminiscences*, relates the particulars of the capture of Gen. Rial in these words: "Gen. Rial was captured by one of Maj. Jesup's flanking parties, under Capt. Ketchum. It is said that an aid of Gen. Rial, mistaking the company for British soldiery, and observing that they obstructed the way, called out, 'Make room there, men, for Gen. Rial.' At which Capt. Ketchum, seeing a party following the officer at the distance of a few horse-lengths, promptly responded, 'Ay, ay, sir,' and suffered the aid to ride quietly on. As the General, with his staff, approached, they found the passage intercepted by an armed force, which closed instantly upon them with fixed bayonets, their bridles seized, and they were politely requested to dismount. 'What does all this mean?' said the astonished General. 'You are prisoners, sir,' was the answer. 'But I am General Rial,' he said. 'There is no doubt on that point,' replied the Captain; 'and I, sir, am Captain Ketchum, of the United States Army.' The General, seeing that resistance was useless, quietly surrendered. remarking, in a kind of half soliloquy, 'Captain Ketchum! *Ketch*um! *Ketch*um! Well, you have caught us, sure enough!'"

[1] Maj. Douglass's MS. Reminis.; Gen. Brown to Sec. of War.—[2] Capt. McDonald's Testimony on Gen. Ripley's trial, Troy, March, 1815.—[3] Maj. Douglass's MS. Reminis.; Capt. McDonald's Testimony.

He had not completed this movement, however, when he perceived that such a position would serve no useful purpose; and he assumed the responsibility of violating the order, by moving farther to the left, whence he could cover the First brigade, and render more efficient service.[1] While thus engaged, the fire of the battery on the hill, in the enemy's centre,—in front of which the remnants of the First brigade were still standing,—arrested his special attention; and remarking to Colonel Miller and Captain McDonald that "unless that battery was carried it would destroy the whole force, or compel it to fall back," he prepared to carry it.[2] In accordance with *his* orders, the Twenty-first regiment (*Colonel Miller's*), by a flank movement, ascended the hill in front; while, simultaneously, General Ripley led the Twenty-third, under Major McFarland, in column, against its left flank.[3] An eye-witness has described the movement of the gallant Twenty-first in such expressive terms that I am happy in having an opportunity to transfer them to my page, rather than to employ less-meaning words of my own. "The Twenty-first was moved forward, silently and cautiously," he says, "but in perfect order, to a fence on the slope of the hill, about forty or fifty yards from the battery, behind which it drew up in line, and after pouring one well-directed volley into the battery, the men pushed the fence flat before them, and rushed forward with the bayonet. The whole was the work of an instant; the hill was completely cleared of the enemy in almost as little time as I have occupied in narrating it, and the battery was ours."[1]

In the mean time, as appears from the statements of those who were present, the First brigade (*General Scott's*) had neither advanced or fallen back from the position into which it had been first led; but it remained, with dogged obstinacy, receiving and returning the fire which the enemy, on the heights in front, and on its left flank, continued, without cessation, to hurl down upon it. The Eleventh regiment, having lost its commandant (*Major McNeil*) and all its captains, and all its ammunition having been expended, "had retired from the field;" and the gallant spirits who remained, true to their country, but without leaders, rallied around the standards of the Twenty-second and the Ninth; and as volunteers, continued the engagement—rendering "very able and essential services" to those with whom they had thus connected themselves. It was not long, however, before Colonel Hugh Brady, of the Twenty-second, was severely wounded, and that regiment, too, exhausted its supply of ammunition; when

1 Capt. McDonald's Test.—2 Ibid.; Col. Miller's Letter, Sept. 4, 1814. The originator of this movement, as well as the particular officer who issued the order to Col. Miller, has been the subject of protracted discussions. The popular idea of Col. Miller's "I'll try, sir," connects it with an order from *Gen. Brown;* and Maj. Douglass asserts, of his own knowledge, that Col. McRee, of the Engineers, introduced the subject to Gen. Brown's attention. While I have no doubt the Colonel's experienced eye had noticed the importance of the position and the necessity of its capture,—as would that of any other experienced soldier,—I am constrained to believe, on the testimony of Col. Miller himself, as well as that of Capt. McDonald, that the idea, *on which was based the assault*, was Gen. Ripley's; that *he* ordered its execution; and that the troops had moved to execute it before Gen. Brown knew any thing about the matter.

3 Capt. McDonald's Test.; Col. Miller's Letter, Sept. 4, 1814. Maj. Douglass supposes all, except the 21st regiment, "filed along the road, and halted as a right wing to Gen. Scott."

1 Maj. Douglass's MS. Reminis. See also James, ii. p. 144; Capt. McDonald's Test.; Col. Miller's Letter, Sept. 4, 1814.

the remnants of that, also, as those of the Eleventh had done before, broke their ranks, and rallied, as volunteers, around the officers of the Ninth,—the only remaining regiment in the line,—"and fought the enemy with a spirit and bravery bordering upon desperation." While the consolidated regiments were thus battling the enemy, single-handed, General Scott ordered them, through Lieutenant Worth, his aid, "to advance upon the enemy, with a view to charge him;" and with a degree of resolution and bravery which few, besides "the gallant six hundred" at Balaklava, have ever exhibited, they "ceased firing, and advanced, with supported arms," towards the very jaws of death, until the order was countermanded; when, without moving farther, they occupied their places, in line, until the capture of the battery, as before related, relieved them from immediate danger, and changed the current of the battle.[1]

It was now not far from half-past ten o'clock,[2] and not a ray of light, except the occasional flashes of the artillery or muskets of the combatants, relieved the monotony of the gloomy evening. The fragments of the unwavering First brigade,—led by the officers of the Ninth, but rallying around the tattered and dusty colors of the Eleventh,[3]—under General Scott, still occupied the position at the foot of the slope, on which it had so long struggled for an existence; the Twenty-fifth, under Major Jesup, reposing on its laurels, remained in the undisputed possession of the ground on the eastern side of the Queenstown road, from which it had so gallantly driven the enemy's left wing; the Second brigade, under General Ripley, on the crown of the heights, held the enemy's lines and his battery—the scene and the trophies of its recent victory; and the enemy,—right, centre, and left,—truly and entirely discomfited, had fallen back, dispirited and broken, with his second in command, his lines, and all his artillery, in the hands of the assailants.

As may have been reasonably expected, the enemy rallied in the rear of his former position; and, during the succeeding two hours, he made a series of most desperate efforts to regain his battery and the position which he had lost; while the Second brigade, under General Ripley, as obstinately resisted.[1] In these conflicts, the din of the invisible battle, intermingled with the report of small-arms and the clash of the opposing bayonets,—in which the antagonists were guided through the darkness by the flash of the musketry or the sound of the voices,—added to the horrors which are incident to all battle-fields; and which, in this case, were greatly increased by the almost impenetrable darkness which, everywhere, covered the field. Speaking of the first of these attempts to recover the heights, an eye-witness says: "The bayonet is a potent weapon on the side of high discipline and strong nerves; and, especially, when united with the characteristic determination of the British soldier. The charge of the bayonet is not often used, except as a last resort, and then seldom goes beyond the mere crossing of the weapons—one or other party then breaks or retires.

[1] Maj. Leavenworth's Letter, July 15, 1815.
[2] Maj. Douglass's MS. Reminiscences.—[3] Maj. Leavenworth's Letter, July 15, 1815.

[1] Maj. Douglass's MS. Reminis.; Gen. Drummond to Sir G. Prevost, July 27; James, ii. p. 146; Capt. McDonald's Test.; Col. Miller's Letter, Sept. 4, 1814; Gen. Brown to Secretary of War.

LUNDY'S LANE.

From the original Painting by Chappel, in the possession of the Publishers.

Johnson, Fry & Co Publishers, New York.

But it was not so in this instance. It was maintained, on both sides, with an obstinacy of which the history of war furnishes few examples, and finally resulted in the *second* repulse of the enemy. A succession of similar charges—sometimes repelled by counter-attacks upon the flanks of the assailing party, and sometimes by the fire of musketry in front, in volleys perfectly deafening—were continued in rapid succession for nearly an hour, with the same result; until the enemy, having suffered very severely, and wearied with the obstinacy of the combat, and hopeless of success, abstained from farther attacks, and left us in undisputed possession of the field."[1]

During these several attacks on the Second brigade, and the position it occupied, both parties had been strengthened with fresh troops. General Ripley's three skeleton regiments had, indeed, driven the combined forces of the enemy's left and centre from the centre of his position, and had captured his battery, while his right had fallen back, of course, to preserve itself; and the same small party had maintained that proud position, and held the battery, notwithstanding the subsequent effort of the enemy to regain them. Part of the brigade of Volunteers, under General Porter, had, however, moved forward and formed on the left of General Ripley;[2] while Captain Towson, with his field-pieces, Major Jesup, with the Twenty-fifth, and General Scott, with the fragments of his gallant brigade, had moved forward and covered his right;[1] and, at the same time, Colonel Scott, with the One hundred and third regiment of the line, "the head-quarter divisions" of the Royal Scots and of the Eighth (*or King's*) regiment, the flank companies of the One hundred and fourth, and upwards of three hundred rank and file of the sedentary militia, under Lieutenant-colonel Hamilton,—upwards of fifteen hundred men in all,—with two six-pounders, came up to the assistance of the enemy.[2] Of course, when the enemy had been thus strengthened with fresh troops, the most desperate efforts were necessary to secure the captured position and the battery which rested there.

Soon afterwards the command devolved on General Ripley,—Generals Brown and Scott having been wounded,[3]—and, after holding undisputed possession of the field "for about an hour,"[4] in accordance with orders received from General Brown,[5] "he retired, without the slightest molestation, to the encampment at Chippewa."[6] Unfortunately, the advice of General Ripley, at an earlier hour, had been disregarded;[7] and when the retreat was ordered there were no means left by which the train of artillery, which the Second brigade had captured, could be withdrawn from the heights; and, in consequence, they returned into the hands of their former owners.[8] The troops reached

[1] Maj. Douglass's MS. Reminis. See also Gen. Drummond to Sir G. Prevost, July 27; Capt. McDonald's Test.; Col. Miller's Letter, Sept. 4, 1814; Gen. Brown to Sec. of War (no date).—[2] Maj. Douglass's MS. Reminis.; Capt. McDonald's Test.; Col. Miller's Letter, Sept. 4, 1814.

[1] Maj. Leavenworth's Letter, July 15, 1815; Capt. McDonald's Test.; Col. Miller's Letter, Sept. 4, 1814.

[2] James, ii. p. 141.—[3] Adj. Livingston's Letter, March 6, 1815.—[4] Maj. Douglass's MS. Reminis. Gen. Porter and Col. Miller (*Letter to Gen. Brown, July* 29, 1815) say "more than an hour."—[5] Gen. Brown to Sec. of War (no date); Maj. Leavenworth's Letter, July 15, 1815; Capt. McDonald's Test.—[6] Maj. Douglass's MS. Reminis.; James, ii. p. 146; Gen. Drummond to Sir G. Prevost, July 17; Gen Porter and Col. Miller to Gen. Brown, July 29, 1815; Capt. McDonald's Test.—[7] Capt. McDonald's Test.

[8] Maj. Douglass's MS. Reminis.; Capt. McDonald's Test.; Maj. Hindman's Statement; James, ii. p. 146.

the encampment between one and two o'clock.[1]

In this sanguinary engagement the strength of the original occupants of the height near Lundy's Lane, under General Rial, numbered upwards of seventeen hundred and fifty men,[2] to which were added, before the engagement began, the reinforcement, under Lieutenant-general Drummond, numbering not less than fifteen hundred and twenty men,[3] exclusive of three hundred Indians.[4] Against these troops, *in a strong position*, selected by themselves, General Scott led his brigade, numbering not more than thirteen hundred men.[5] When Generals Ripley and Porter had added their commands to General Scott, not more than thirteen hundred fresh troops were brought on the field;[6] while the strength of Lieutenant-colonel Scott's command afterwards added more than fifteen hundred fresh combatants to the enemy's strength.[7] Thus it will be seen that while the enemy numbered, in the aggregate, not less than four thousand five hundred men,[1] the Americans were not more than two thousand six hundred in number.[2]

The loss of the Americans was, in the *dragoons*, one killed and two wounded; in the *artillery*, one captain and nine men killed, three officers and thirty-two men wounded, and one missing; in the First brigade (*General Scott's*),—Major Leavenworth commanding the Ninth, Maj. McNiel commanding the Eleventh, Colonel Brady commanding the Twenty-second,—six officers and one hundred and two men killed, twenty-five officers and three hundred and twenty-one men wounded, and five officers and forty-five men missing; in the Second brigade (*General Ripley's*),—Major McFarland commanding the Twenty-third,—one officer and thirty-four men killed, fifteen officers and one hundred and twenty-seven men wounded, and forty-eight men missing; and in General Porter's brigade of Volunteers, two officers and fourteen men killed, five officers and thirty-five men wounded, and three officers and eight men missing—a total of one hundred and seventy-one *killed*, five hundred and seventy-one *wounded*, and one hundred and ten *missing;*[3] while that of the enemy was five officers and seventy-nine men *killed*, Generals Drummond and Rial, thirty-seven officers, and five hundred and eighteen men *wounded*, six officers and one hundred and eighty-seven men *missing*, and forty-two *prisoners*.[4]

1 Maj. Douglass's MS. Reminis.; Maj. Leavenworth's Letter, July 15, 1815; Capt. McDonald's Test.

2 Incorporated militia, "500;" troop of Dragoons, 60; regiment of Glengarry's, 800; detachment from 104th and artillery, 100; sedentary militia, "300"=1760 men. Notwithstanding Mr. James had before stated the number of the militia as above, in his *Mil. Occur.*, ii. p. 139, he says this force numbered only "*about nine hundred and fifty rank and file.*"

3 Eighty-ninth regiment, 800; 2d battalion of Royal Scots, "400 strong;" light company of 41st, 80; three companies of the 8th regiment, 240=1520 men. Mr. James (*Military Occurrences*, ii. p. 142) says it numbered 815 rank and file.

4 There were *Indians* present, on the enemy's side, of which no account is made in the British accounts of the action.—5 Mansfield's Scott, p. 123.—6 Maj. Douglass's MS. Reminiscences.

7 The 103d regiment, 800; flank companies of the 104th, 160; sedentary militia, "300;" two companies each of Royal Scots and 8th, 320=1580 men. Mr. James (*Military Occurrences*, ii. p. 144) says, "it numbered 1230 *rank and file.*"

1 Letter from an officer, Fort Erie, July 28; Sketches of War, p. 358.—2 Some others have estimated it as high as 2800 men.—3 Reports appended to Gen. Brown's Dispatch.—4 Reports appended to Gen. Drummond's Dispatch.

CHAPTER LXXXVI.

August 3 to September 21, 1814.

THE SIEGE OF FORT ERIE.

THE victory on the heights at Lundy's Lane, had been followed, through orders from General Brown,[1] by a retreat to the camp at Chippewa,[2] and by the dissipation of the glory which belonged, legitimately, to the American army; and on the twenty-sixth of July the army retreated still farther, by falling back on Fort Erie.[3] In this, however, it was not, in the remotest degree, compulsory—the enemy remaining quietly in his camp near Lundy's Lane, without sending out even a light party to harass the march, until after he had received reinforcements, four days after the battle;[4] while the American army moved deliberately, and occupied its assigned position without the least excitement or appearance of alarm.[5] "In other words," to use the language of an officer who was present,[6] "the motive of the retreat was *strategical*—having regard to the general scheme of operations; not *tactical* or *evolutionary*—having regard to the strength of a certain position or the relative force of the two armies."

As has been said, the American army fell back on Fort Erie on the twenty-sixth of July; and it immediately began to intrench itself, with the old fort as one of its strong points, but extending the new works more than half a mile from it, along the shore of the lake, with numerous other redoubts and batteries, and embracing an area sufficient for the accommodation of two or three thousand men. Diligently, and under experienced officers, the troops labored to strengthen the new position, until the third of August,—when the enemy first showed himself,—at which time the works assumed an appearance of strength and perfection, in some degree, commensurate with the purposes for which they had been erected.[1]

On the extreme right of the American line, at this time,—between the old fort and the shore of the lake, about nine feet above the surface of the latter, and as much below the level of the former,—was a small two-gun battery, with its armament mounted on top of the parapet, or *en barbette*, named "*The Douglass Battery*," which had been built, was then occupied, and, afterwards, defended by the Sappers and Miners under Lieutenant David B. Douglass, of the Engineer corps. The space between this battery and the water was not defended by any work; but a six-pounder was so posted that the approach was entirely commanded. The epaulement, or earthen breastwork,

[1] Testimony of Capt. McDonald on Gen. Ripley's trial, Troy, March 15, 1815; Col. Leavenworth's Letter, Delhi, Jan. 15, 1815; Gen. Miller's Letter, Sept. 4, 1814; Gen. Brown to Sec. of War (no date); Letter of Adj. J. P. Livingston, March, 1815; Maj. Hindman's Statement. Many writers have stated that Gen. Ripley retreated *without orders*, and I have considered it proper to give the principal authorities for a contrary statement.

[2] Maj. Douglass's MS. Reminiscences; Gen. Brown to Sec. of War (no date); Armstrong, ii. p. 94.

[3] Rogers, i. p. 274; Perkins, p. 377; Armstrong, ii. p. 95.—[4] Gens. Porter and Miller to Gen. Brown, July 29, 1815.—[5] Maj. Douglass's MS. Reminiscences; Thomson's Sketches, p. 302.—[6] Maj. Douglass's MS. Reminiscences.

[1] Maj. Douglass's Reminiscences; James, ii. p. 161; Armstrong, ii. pp. 95, 96.

which extended up the slope from the left of the Douglass Battery towards the right of the old fort, was eighteen feet thick and about seven feet high, with a ditch in front, and was occupied by the First brigade of infantry (*General Scott's*). From the left of this epaulement to the line of the old fort was only a slight abatis. The old fort was but a small and imperfect affair; and the additions which had been projected and commenced—in consequence of the attention which had been paid to the flanks—were far from complete. From the left of the old fort, in a line which was parallel with the lake shore, or nearly so, was a breastwork with banquettes and a ditch; but, as it had been hastily thrown up, the breastwork was not uniform in thickness, or the ditch in depth or width—the former varying from five to sixteen feet thick, and from six to seven feet high; the latter from six to ten feet wide, and about three or four feet deep. At the termination of this breastwork was a battery known as "*Towson's Battery*," on which were mounted five guns, under the command of Captain Nathan Towson, of the artillery; and, from the left of Towson's Battery to the shore of the lake, the position was defended by an abatis.[1]

Although the enemy had not yet completed any regular battery, he opened his fire from two or three twenty-four-pounders, posted among some sycamore bushes, on the day of his arrival (*Aug.* 3),[2] and from that time until the seventh, he was busily employed, under cover of the neighboring woods, in throwing up works, amusing himself, during the interval, with an occasional shot, which was returned with spirit and effect from "The Douglass Battery."[1]

At sunrise of the seventh of August, the enemy's first battery was unmasked; and, from five pieces, he poured a volley upon the American lines. The chopping had been heard during the night and understood; and the troops had been paraded within the lines, "as for a grand field-day," to receive, with becoming ceremony, the first formal fire of the enemy. "The national standard was displayed at every flagstaff; and as soon as the expected volley was received, the regimental bands of the entire army commenced playing the most animating national airs, and, in the midst of it, a salvo of artillery was fired from every piece which could be brought to bear upon the hostile position."[2] Such is "the pomp and circumstance of glorious war;" and of such as these are the bright spots of that which, otherwise, would be but a continued series of misery and woe.

From this time the siege was prosecuted with great vigor; and the garrison conducted the defence with equal vigilance and determination. The fire, on both sides, was unremitting, severe, and marked with all the evidences of the most skilful gunnery; the fatigue parties of both armies were constantly and steadily increasing and strengthening their respective lines of operations; and the enemy, by the arrival of De Watteville's regiment, and the Forty-first regiment of the line, had received

[1] Maj. Douglass's MS. Description (Aug., 1814), sent to his father-in-law, Andrew Ellicott, the celebrated engineer, who surveyed the line between Spanish America and the United States.—[2] Maj. Douglass's MS. Reminis.; Breckenridge, pp. 275, 276.

[1] Maj. Douglass's MS. Reminiscences; Thomson's Sketches, p. 305.—[2] Maj. Douglass's MS. Reminiscences.

valuable and powerful reinforcements.[1] Under the impression that the enemy would resort to an assault, the garrison was constantly on the ground, ready for duty at a moment's notice. "In anticipation of this (*expected*) attack," Major Douglass remarks, "the men were distributed for night-service in three watches; one to be on duty under arms, and the other two to lie down in their accoutrements, with arms at hand, so as to be ready for action at a moment's notice. In the batteries the guns were carefully charged afresh every evening with round-shot, grape, or canister, either, or all together, as the case might require; dark lanterns burning; with linstocks and other instruments in their places, ready for use. In my own battery," the Major continues, "in addition to other missiles, bags of musket-balls had been quilted up in the fragments of an old tent, adapted to the calibre of the different pieces, and made ready for use."[2]

At length, as if by mutual consent,—the experienced eyes of the American engineers judging, from causes, of effects in the future,—the night of the fourteenth of August was selected for the important movement; and both parties appear to have prepared for the event with the most interesting minuteness.[3] In the garrison, General Gaines—who had taken the command of the fort at an early day—visited every part of the works in person, and admonished the officers and the men to "be watchful and vigilant, in the certain expectation of an assault;" the Chief-engineer, Colonel McRee, followed, with a word of counsel or instructions on the more

[1] Maj. Douglass's MS. Reminis.; Perkins, p. 379; James, ii. pp. 161, 164.—[2] Maj. Douglass's MS. Reminis.—[3] Armstrong, ii. pp. 98, 99.

practical part of the expected duty; and, everywhere, throughout the intrenchments, the most careful, but subdued, vigilance was manifested;[1] while in the enemy's camp the gun-flints were withdrawn from the muskets,[2] the scaling-ladders were collected and placed in readiness, and the several columns of attack were formed in accordance with the "Secret General Order" which Lieutenant-General Drummond had issued on the evening before;[3] while the still more secret "Instructions" which had been communicated to Colonel Scott and Lieutenant-colonels Fischer and Drummond,[4] were directing the attention of the commanders of the columns to the minutiæ of their respective lines of duty.

Until two o'clock in the morning of the fifteenth, an unusual quietness prevailed; and the weary ones, in the garrison, tired and doubtful, began to give way to the demands of nature, and lost themselves, occasionally, in broken and uneasy naps. The time rolled heavily along, and still the same quiet prevailed around the intrenchments and in the enemy's lines; and the officers and men on duty "began to be doubtful whether their apprehensions had not been ex-

[1] Maj. Douglass's MS. Reminiscences.

[2] Letter from an officer, in "*The War*," iii. p. 47.

[3] I have before me an original copy of this "*Secret Order*," which was taken from the pocket of one of the officers who fell in the attack, and is stained with his blood. The original possessor of the paper appears to have fallen by a *bayonet-wound;* and, by a singular coincidence, the weapon passed through that part of the paper which states, "The Lieut.-Gen. most strongly recommends *a free use of the bayonet.*" This interesting paper belongs to Samuel Jaudon, Esq., of New York, and will, by his kindness, pass from my hands to the library of the New York Historical Society.

[4] "Lieut.-Col. Fischer, commanding the right column, will follow *the instructions which he has received;* copies of which are communicated to Col. Scott and Lieut.-Col. Drummond for their guidance."—*Gen. Drummond's Secret General Order.*

cited upon insufficient grounds."[1] Within the enemy's lines, however, all was activity, yet all the movements were made in silence and with the utmost secrecy, notwithstanding the darkness with which the troops were surrounded.

At length, about two o'clock, the picket in front of the extreme left of the intrenchment gave an alarm;[2] and, a few minutes afterwards, the enemy's right column—the Eighth (*or King's*) regiment of the line, a strong detachment from De Watteville's regiment, the flank companies of the Eighty-ninth and One hundredth regiments, a strong detachment from the Royal Artillery, with rockets, and Captain Eustace's picket of cavalry, the whole numbering from fifteen hundred to two thousand men, under Lieutenant-colonel Fischer[3]—dashed through the darkness, and charged on the abatis and Towson's battery, which protected the camp in that quarter.[4] In conformity with the spirit of the "Secret General Order," it is said that the flints had been withdrawn from the muskets of the assailants, probably for the purpose of making "a free use of the bayonet;"[5] but the Twenty-first regiment of infantry (*Colonel Miller's*), under Major Wood, of the Engineers, behind the abatis, Captain Towson's artillerists, within the battery, and the Twenty-third regiment on the right of Towson's battery, were fully prepared to receive them.[6] Within a few seconds after the enemy had made his appearance the position of the Twenty-first, behind the abatis, "was marked by an illumination of exquisite brilliancy, shining far up in the dark, cloudy atmosphere which hung over the encampment; while the battery on its right, elevated some twenty feet above the level, was lighted up with a blaze of artillery fires, which gained for it, after that night, the appellation of 'Towson's Light-house.' To the ear the reports of musketry and artillery were blended together in one continuous roar, somewhat like the close double-drag of a drum on a grand scale."[1] When the heavy column of the enemy had come within ten feet of this line of fire it faltered; but recovering itself, immediately afterwards, it charged boldly up to the lines with the greatest spirit and determination, and attempted to force the abatis or scale the battery, but after a short, but desperate, struggle, bayonet to bayonet, it was overcome, and fell back.[2] Four times more the assault was renewed, and as often it was defeated, with very heavy loss, and, at length, it was abandoned.[3] In one of these charges the enemy lost his way, and becoming entangled in the rocks on the shore of the lake, the guns of the battery were directed against him; and before he could recover from the disorder into which he was thrown a considerable number of his men were taken prisoners.[4]

Soon after the action had opened on the extreme left of the American lines,

[1] Maj. Douglass's MS. Reminis.—[2] Ibid.; James, ii. p. 169.—[3] Gen. Drummond's Secret General Order, Aug. 14; Gen. Drummond to Sir G. Prevost, Aug. 15; Christie, p. 193.—[4] Gen. Gaines' Dispatch, Aug. —, 1814; Buffalo *Gazette*, Aug. 16, 1814; Thomson's Sketches, pp. 309, 310.—[5] Gen. Drummond's Secret General Order, Aug. 14; Letter from an officer, in "*The War*," iii. p. 47; Gen. Ripley's Report, Aug. 17.—[6] Gen. Gaines' Dispatch, Aug. —, 1814; Maj. Douglass's MS. Reminis.; James, ii. p. 169; Perkins, p. 380.

[1] Maj. Douglass's MS. Reminis.; Gen. Gaines' Dispatch, Aug. —, 1814.—[2] Gen. Gaines' Dispatch, Aug. —, 1814; James, ii. p. 170; Armstrong, ii. p. 99.—[3] Gen. Drummond to Sir G. Prevost, Aug. 15; Lieut.-Col. Fischer's Report, Aug. 15; James, ii. p. 170; Armstrong, ii. p. 99.

[4] Gen. Gaines' Dispatch, Aug., 1814; Lieut.-Col. Fischer's Report, Aug. 15; James, ii. p. 170.

and while the Twenty-first and Twenty-third regiments, and Captain Towson, were gallantly and successfully contending with more than double their own number of the enemy, on that flank, a volley of musketry, closely followed by a running fire of small-arms and artillery, from the epaulements and redoubts, which extended from Towson's battery, on the left, to and including the old fort, on the right—what may be called the centre of the American lines.[1] In this part of the intrenchments the brigade of New York and Pennsylvania Volunteers, under General Peter B. Porter, and the rifle corps (*First and Fourth regiments*), were posted, with detachments of artillery under Major Hindman, while the redoubts on the left were commanded by Captains Fanning and Biddle, and the old fort by Captain Williams;[2] and against them were brought the flank companies of the Forty-first and One hundred and fourth regiments, a detachment of fifty Royal marines, one of ninety seamen, and a small one from the Royal Artillery, with rockets, the whole numbering about five hundred men, and led by Lieutenant-colonel Drummond.[3] The assailants appear to have directed their efforts, principally, against the old fort; and approaching every assailable part of the work at the same time, they dashed forward, with their scaling-ladders, and gained the parapet. The garrison, led by Captain Williams and Lieutenants McDonough and Watmough, met them with equal spirit, however, and they were hurled back from the salient bastion, with considerable loss;

[1] Maj. Douglass's MS. Reminis.; James, ii. pp. 170, 171.
[2] Gen. Gaines' Dispatch, Aug., 1814.—[3] Gen. Drummond's Secret General Order, Aug. 14; Gen. Drummond to Sir G. Prevost, Aug. 15; James, ii. 171.

and the garrison was immediately strengthened by General Ripley's brigade of regulars, on the extreme right, and from General Porter's Volunteers, in the centre of the lines. A second and a third time the scaling-ladders were planted, and the assailants mounted the parapets of the salient bastion, to meet, in hand-to-hand conflict, and be driven back by Captain Williams and his command.[1] Soon afterwards, "taking advantage of the darkness of the morning, and of the heavy columns of smoke, which concealed all objects from the view of the garrison, Lieutenant-colonel Drummond moved his troops silently round the ditch, repeated his charge, and reascended his ladders with such celerity as to gain footing on the parapet before any effectual opposition could be made. Being in the very midst of his men, he directed them to charge vigorously with their pikes and bayonets, and *to show no mercy to the garrison*. This order was executed with the utmost rapidity, and the most obstinate previous parts of the engagement formed no kind of parallel to the violence and desperation of the conflict at this time."[2] The Captain and both Lieutenants fell—the former mortally wounded; and notwithstanding every effort which could be made, the enemy retained possession of the bastion. Charge followed charge, in rapid succession, until daybreak; and, from both armies, reinforcements were sent, both to the garrison and the successful assailants.[3]

In the mean time, the extreme right

[1] Gen. Gaines' Dispatch, Aug., 1814; Maj. Douglass's MS. Reminis.; Perkins, pp. 380, 381.—[2] Thomson's Sketches, pp. 311, 312; Perkins, pp. 380, 381; Breckenridge, p. 279.—[3] Gen. Gaines' Dispatch, Aug., 1814; Gen. Drummond to Sir G. Prevost, Aug. 15; James, ii. pp. 176, 177

of the intrenchments—extending from the old fort, down the slope, to the shore of the lake—had also been the scene of a vigorous assault. The epaulement, between the old fort and the Douglass Battery, was defended by the remnants of the First brigade (*General Scott's*), under the command of Lieutenant-colonel Aspinwall; the corps of bombardiers, under Lieutenant Douglass, occupied "The Douglass Battery;" and the open space between the latter and the lake was occupied by Colonel McRee, the chief-engineer, with a six-pound field-piece; by two companies of New York Volunteers, under Captains Claudius V. Boughton and Micajah Harding.[1] Against these, simultaneously with the attack on the old fort, by the enemy's centre,[2] the left wing of the opposing force—embracing the entire One hundred and third regiment of the line, under Lieutenant-colonel Scott[3]—moved along the shore of the lake. The darkness of the night prevented the garrison, in this, as in other parts of the works, from witnessing the precise effect of its fire, yet being well acquainted with the ground in its front, no difficulty was experienced in giving the proper elevation and direction to the guns. As Major Douglass subsequently remarked, "The cannon were loaded habitually for short quarters. They were filled with round-shot, grape, canister, and bags of musket-balls, at discretion, until the last wad could be touched with the hand in the muzzle of the pieces."[4] There is no wonder, with such opposition as this to contend with, that the *flintless* muskets of the enemy reached but few victims, or that the assailants—much more numerous than the garrison—were generally repulsed. In this quarter, as on the extreme left, the enemy dashed forward, and slowly retired as the garrison beat him back,—alternately repeating the attempt, and as often retiring,—for upwards of an hour; and it was not until the day began to dawn, that, dispirited and completely overcome, with its commander fallen on the field, the One hundred and third finally fell back and joined the reserve of the enemy near the edge of the woods.[1]

In the mean time, the conflict continued within the salient bastion of the old fort, with its wonted fury; and thither, after the day broke, the attention of both armies began to centre, since the action, on either wing, had virtually ceased.[2] The enemy's reserve appeared to be preparing to move forward to support the successful occupants; and, to prevent such an accession of strength, the guns on every commanding face of the works were brought to bear on the glacis of the bastion, in order to enfilade the expected column.[3] At this instant, and without any premonitory warning, in the words of an eye-witness, already known to the reader, "every sound was hushed by the sense of an unnatural tremor beneath our feet, like the first heave of an earthquake. Almost at the same instant the centre of the bastion burst up with a terrific explosion; and a jet of flame, mingled with fragments of timber, earth, stone, and bodies of men, rose to the height of one or two hundred feet

[1] Gen. Gaines' Dispatch, Aug., 1814; Maj. Douglass's MS. Reminis.—[2] Maj. Douglass's MS. Reminis.; Gen. Drummond to Sir G. Prevost, Aug. 15.—[3] Gen. Drummond's Secret General Order, Aug. 14; Gen. Drummond to Sir G. Prevost, Aug. 15.—[4] Maj. Douglass's MS. Reminiscences.

[1] Maj. Douglass's MS. Reminis.—[2] Gen. Gaines' Dispatch, Aug., 1814; Maj. Douglass's MS. Reminiscences.
[3] Gen. Gaines' Dispatch, Aug., 1814.

in the air, and fell in a shower of ruins to a great distance all around."[1] The enemy's reserve immediately fell back; and soon afterwards the conflict ended in the entire defeat of the enemy, whose shattered columns—two of them without their commanders—returned dispirited to his encampment,[2] leaving behind him, on the field, two hundred and twenty-two dead, one hundred and seventy-four wounded, and one hundred and eighty-six prisoners, besides those who were carried off by their comrades.[3]

The American army immediately repaired the ruined bastion;[4] and during the succeeding thirty-three days it was busily employed in strengthening the works which had been opposed to the enemy, and in adding new ones;[5] while the enemy, at the same time, increased his works and strengthened those which he had previously occupied.[6] General Gaines, having been wounded by a bomb-shell, which fell into his quarters, had left the encampment and returned to Buffalo;[7] while General Brown, who had recovered from his wound, received at Lundy's Lane, had resumed the command of the army.[8] Both armies had received reinforcements during the interval;[9] and the siege was prosecuted, and the defence sustained, with all the spirit and skill which might, reasonably, have been expected from such opponents.

At length, for the purpose of checking the progress of the enemy, and of harassing the troops, a sortie was planned, and the morning of the seventeenth of September was selected as the time for its execution.[1] With this object a road had been *marked*[2] through the woods from the extreme left of the encampment to a point within pistol-shot of the enemy's right wing; yet with so much secrecy had it been accomplished that the enemy had not been alarmed;[3] and on the appointed morning a heavy fog, accompanied with occasional showers, was well calculated to conceal the operations, and to increase the confusion of the enemy.[4] The assailants were organized into two divisions—the one to move from the extreme left of the encampment, by way of the marked route, against the enemy's right flank; the other, from the right, by way of a ravine in front, was to assault the centre of his line—while General Ripley, with the Twenty-first regiment, as a reserve, was posted between the new bastions of Fort Erie, out of sight from the enemy's works.[5]

The left division, under General Peter B. Porter,—including his brigade of New York and Pennsylvania Volunteers, detachments from the First and Fourth rifle regiments, under Colonel

[1] Maj. Douglass's MS. Reminis.; Gen. Drummond to Sir G. Prevost, Aug. 15.—[2] Gen. Drummond to Sir G. Prevost, Aug. 15; Rogers, i. pp. 275, 276; Brackenridge, p. 280.—[3] Report, signed "N. N. HALL, *A. Inspec.-Gen.*," appended to Gen. Gaines' Dispatch, Aug., 1814. It is proper to state that the enemy's official report gives a different statement—58 *killed*, 309 *wounded*, and 539 *missing*.

[4] Maj. Douglass's MS. Reminis.; James, ii. p. 228.

[5] Maj. Douglass's MS. Reminis.; Same to A. E. Ellicott, Sept. 9, 1814; James, ii. p. 228.—[6] Maj. Douglass's MS. Reminis.; James, ii. p. 230; Perkins, p. 384; Armstrong, ii. p. 100.—[7] Maj. Douglass's MS. Reminis.; Brackenridge, p. 280.—[8] Maj. Douglass's MS. Reminis.; James, ii. p. 228; Armstrong, ii. pp. 100, 101.

[9] James, ii. p. 229; Rogers, i. p. 276; Christie, p. 195; Brackenridge, pp. 280, 281.

[1] Gen. Brown's Dispatch, Sept. 29.—[2] Although Gens. Brown and Porter, in their Reports, both state this road was "*opened*," I have not considered that word in its literal sense; as that appears to be inconsistent with the *secrecy* of the movement. This, also, appears to have been Maj. Douglass's version.—[3] Gen. Porter's Report, Sept. 22; James, ii. pp. 231, 232; Thomson's Sketches, p. 325.

[4] Rev. M. Douglass's Notes on Maj. Douglass's MS. Reminis.; Gen. De Watteville to Gen. Drummond, Sept. 19; James, ii. p. 231; Christie, p. 209.—[5] Gen. Brown's Dispatch, Sept. 29.

Gibson; from the First and Twenty-third infantry, under Major Wood, of the Engineers; and one of dismounted cavalry,[1]—moved from the encampment at noon, and proceeded through the woods, following the marked trees, as before stated; and at about a quarter before three,[2] without the enemy having suspected such a visit, it rushed upon the right of his lines, and carried them by assault.[3] Two batteries, known as *Numbers Three* and *Four*, were first taken;[4] and, soon afterwards, a block-house in the rear of the former battery (*No. Three*) also fell into the hands of the assailants, and its garrison was made prisoners. Three twenty-four pounders and their carriages were destroyed, and the magazine of battery *Number Three* was exploded.[5]

Simultaneously with this movement, on the left, General Miller, with the right division,—embracing the fragments of the Ninth, Eleventh, and Nineteenth regiments of infantry,—moved against and attacked the centre of the enemy's line, between batteries *Numbers Two* and *Three;* and, after a sharp contest, carried the former and another block-house, which the enemy had erected in the rear of them; while from battery *Number One* the enemy retired with precipitation, before the assailants reached it.[6] In all these works, also, the guns were rendered unserviceable; and the works themselves, to some extent, were demolished.[1]

Within an hour the objects of the sortie had been fully accomplished—the batteries of the enemy had been captured, and, with their armaments, had been destroyed; his forces had been greatly reduced by capture, disability, or death; and his stores had been diminished; and the assaulting columns were recalled.[2]

In this gallant and successful achievement the Americans suffered severely—Major-general Davis, of the New York militia, commanding the Volunteers, Lieutenant-colonel Wood, commanding the column of regulars, Colonel Gibson, commanding the riflemen, in the left division, seven officers, and seventy men having been *killed;* Generals Porter and Ripley, Lieutenant-colonel Aspinwall, twenty-two officers, and one hundred and ninety men *wounded;* and ten officers and two hundred and sixteen men *missing:*[3] while the enemy's loss was equally severe—his own reports indicating a loss of three officers and one hundred and twelve men *killed;* seventeen officers and one hundred and sixty-one men *wounded;* and thirteen officers and three hundred and three men *missing.*[4]

After collecting his scattered forces, in the night of the twenty-first of September, General Drummond broke up his encampment, and retired to his former position, behind the Chippewa; leaving behind him, before Fort Erie, part of his stores, and destroying others, at the Frenchman's Creek, while on his way.[5]

---

[1] Gen. Brown's Dispatch, Sept. 29; Gen. Porter's Report, Sept. 22; Armstrong, ii. p. 101.

[2] Gen. Brown's Dispatch, Sept. 29; Gen. Porter's Report, Sept. 22.

[3] Gen. De Watteville to Gen. Drummond, Sept. 19; James, ii. p. 232.

[4] Gen. Brown's Dispatch, Sept. 29; Gen. Porter's Report, Sept. 22; Gen. De Watteville to Gen. Drummond, Sept. 19; James, ii. pp. 233, 234.

[5] Gen. De Watteville to Gen. Drummond, Sept. 19; Armstrong, ii. p. 102.—[6] Gen. Brown's Dispatches, Sept. 29 and Oct. 1; Gen. De Watteville to Gen. Drummond, Sept. 19.

[1] Gen. Brown's Dispatches, Sept 29 and Oct. 1; Gen. Varnum's Letter, Buffalo, Sept. 18; James, ii. p. 232.

[2] Gen. Brown's Dispatch, Sept. 29; Brackenridge, p. 283.—[3] Report appended to Gen. Brown's Dispatch, Sept. 29.—[4] Report appended to Gen. Drummond's Dispatch.

[5] Gen. Brown's Dispatch, Sept. 29; James, ii. pp. 236, 237; Perkins, p. 384; Christie, p. 210.

CHAPTER LXXXVII.

August 19 to 25, 1814.

THE CAPTURE OF WASHINGTON.

The federal government, notwithstanding the warning which the enemy had given, by his devastations, in that vicinity, in the preceding year, and notwithstanding the more positive information, respecting his designs, during the current year, which was subsequently received,[1] appears to have taken no measures to protect the capital of the confederacy beyond a merely *theoretical* organization of an imaginary force of two thousand regular troops, besides militia, and an appointment to the command of the imaginary army, of General William H. Winder.[2] It is true, the District of Columbia and the adjacent counties of Maryland and Virginia, were formed into a distinct "military district"[3] (*the Tenth*); that an accomplished and popular officer had been placed in command of it;[4] that the President had ordered to be held in readiness, for the defence of the District, a force of fifteen thousand militia, besides the regulars who might be stationed there;[5] and that the veteran Commodore Barney, with a flotilla of gunboats, had been assigned to the command of the naval defences;[1] yet it is not less true, that when the enemy entered the Chesapeake, on the twelfth and fourteenth of July,[2] there were only six hundred and twelve regulars within the District, of whom two hundred and eighty-two were on garrison duty in Forts McHenry, Severn, and Washington;[3] that the organization of the militia was left to the State authorities, after the necessity for their services should have arisen;[4] and that, beyond this, nothing had been done.

In this perfectly defenceless condition, therefore, the city of Washington stood when the enemy approached; and he was, apparently, *invited, by its helplessness*, to move forward and take possession of it.[5] It is evident that the commanding General had exerted himself to collect a force sufficiently strong to protect his District; yet the unfortunate character of the requisitions for the militia, and an apparent want of harmony, if not of confidence, between himself and the Secretary of War (*Gen-*

---

[1] It appears that the enemy's squadron was employed, as early as March, 1814, in making soundings and in placing buoys (*National Intelligencer*, March 22, 1814), besides which, every week, the same paper conveyed to the government, whose organ it was, intelligence of the number and destination of the enemy's troops. Even as late as July 1, 1814, the arrival of "a fleet of transports" at Bermuda, and its probable destination "for the Potomac," was announced in the same paper.

[2] General Orders, July 2, 1814; Williams' History of the Invasion, pp. 63, 76–80; Sketches of the War, p. 414.

[3] General Orders, July 2, 1814; Williams, p. 62.

[4] Ingraham's Sketch of Events, pp. 37, 38; National Intelligencer, Aug. 22, 1814.

[5] By the orders of the Sec. of War, July 12 and 17, the "quotas" from Maryland (6000 men), besides 2000 from Virginia, 5000 from Pennsylvania, and 2000 from the District of Columbia, were assigned to this duty.

[1] Sec. of War to Gen. Winder, July 17, 1814; James' Mil. Occur., ii. pp. 240–262; Brackenridge, p. 291.

[2] National Intelligencer, July 16 and 18; Gleig, p. 83.

[3] Ingraham, p. 9, *note;* Williams, p. 82; Gen. Winder to Committee of Investigation, Sept. 14, 1814.

[4] Ingraham, pp. 9–13; Williams, pp. 88, 89.

[5] Whether or not the original design of the expedition was to capture Washington, or whether it was the result of circumstances which occurred during the march, has been the subject of considerable discussion. Adm'l Cochrane (*Dispatch to the Admiralty, Sept.* 2) says that the position of Com. Barney's flotilla "*afforded a pretext* for ascending the river, to attack him, *while the ultimate destination of the combined force was Washington*, should it be found that the attempt might be made with any prospect of success."

eral John Armstrong), not less than between the Secretary and the President, appears to have paralyzed his efforts;[1] and when, on the nineteenth of August, the enemy landed at Benedict, on the western bank of the Pawtuxet, about forty miles southeast from Washington, the District was not better prepared for defence than it had been six weeks before—three hundred and thirty infantry and two troops of cavalry, one hundred and twenty-five men, constituting the entire defending force.[2] The evident purposes of the expedition, however, aroused the government; and the War Department called on the Maryland militia for support, a call which was responded to by the movement of General Stansbury's brigade,—thirteen hundred and fifty-three men,—from Baltimore, on the twentieth, to which Lieutenant-colonel Steret's command—eight hundred men, also from Baltimore—was added on the twenty-third;[3] while Colonel Beale's regiment of Maryland militia reached the ground a few minutes before the action began; and Colonel Minor's regiment of Virginia militia, in consequence of delays in their supply of flints, did not come on the ground at all.[4]

In the mean time, the enemy had sailed up the Pawtuxet, as far as Benedict; and on the morning of the nineteenth of August, 1814, under cover of a single gun-brig, he commenced the debarkation of his troops, completing it by three in the afternoon, *without any opposition*—indeed, "not only was there no opposition to the landing, but, apparently, no enemy within many miles of the place."[1] The invading force embraced the Fourth, Twenty-first, Forty-fourth, and Eighty-fifth regiments of the line, a battalion of marines, "a party of disciplined negroes," and a detachment of artillerists and drivers,—numbering, in the aggregate, four thousand two hundred and twenty men, exclusive of officers,—with one six and two three pounders, which were dragged by seamen sent for the purpose.[2] Without throwing up the least defence, the men laid at Benedict until four in the afternoon of the twentieth, when the enemy moved leisurely forward, less than six miles, towards Nottingham;[3] at which place he arrived on the evening of the twenty-first, without any opposition—the village having been evacuated on his approach.[4] On the following morning (*Aug.* 22) he advanced ten miles farther, to Upper Marlborough, where he remained until after noon of the next day (*Aug.* 23), also *without molestation*.[5] At two in the afternoon of the twenty-third, he moved from Marlborough towards Washington, after having been joined by a body of marines and seamen from the squadron; and soon afterwards he encountered a small body of troops, under Major Peters, which had been detached by General Winder, for the purpose of reconnoitring and annoying him. After "a sharp contest," Major Peters was forced to fall back, and the enemy ad-

[1] Gen. Winder to Sec. of War, June 30, July 9, 16, 23, 25, 27, and Aug. 13; Ingraham's Sketch, entire; Williams' Hist. of the Invasion, entire; Brackenridge, p. 292.
[2] Ingraham, pp. 9, 23.—[3] Ibid., pp. 23, 24; Williams, pp. 136, 137.—[4] Ingraham, pp. 25, 30.

[1] Gen. Ross to Earl Bathurst, Aug. 30, 1814; Adm'l Cochrane to the Admiralty, Sept. 2; Gleig's Narrative (*Octavo, London*, 1826), pp. 89-91; Williams, p. 127; Ingersoll, iv. p. 158.—[2] Gleig, pp. 92, 93; Ingraham, p. 14; Ingersoll, iv. p. 159.—[3] Gen. Ross to Earl Bathurst, Aug. 30; Gleig, pp. 96-98.—[4] Gen. Ross to Earl Bathurst, Aug. 30; Adm'l Cochrane to the Admiralty, Sept. 2; Gleig, pp. 103, 104.—[5] Gen. Ross to Earl Bathurst, Aug. 30; Adm'l Cochrane to the Admiralty, Sept. 2; Williams, p. 174; James' Nav. Occur., p. 376; Gleig, pp. 105-107.

vanced to the junction of the roads which led, respectively, to Alexandria and Washington, where a still stronger body—the advance of the American army, it has been called—was posted; and this party, too, fell back in disorder, with scarcely a sign of opposition, as soon as the enemy had sent a small detachment against it.[1] That night the enemy bivouacked near the Long Old Field, "with nothing to disturb his repose or self-complacency;"[2] and the American troops, who had been out as far as that place during the day, returned to Washington.[3]

On the morning of the twenty-fourth of August, therefore, the enemy was within a few miles of Washington, and, apparently, on his route for that place; while all the forces of the United States, belonging to that District, were within the city of Washington, or encamped near Bladensburg.[4] The force of the enemy, including the reinforcement received from the fleet, was not less than five thousand men,[5] commanded by competent officers, and in a fine state of discipline; while that of the Americans, including the regulars, the flotilla men, under Commodore Barney, the militia from Baltimore and the District of Columbia, and the volunteer cavalry, was not more than five thousand one hundred men[6]—"a mass suddenly assembled, without organization or discipline," with a nominal commander, whose duties were interfered

[1] Gen. Ross to Earl Bathurst, Aug. 30; Adm'l Cockburn to Adm'l Cochrane, Aug. 27; Gleig, pp. 107, 108.

[2] Williams, pp. 182, 202; Gleig, p. 109.

[3] Com. Barney to Sec. of Navy, Aug. 29; Perkins, pp. 310, 311; Brackenridge, p. 295.—[4] Com. Barney to Sec. of Navy, Aug. 29; Perkins, pp. 311, 312.

[5] The seamen from the squadron who joined the expedition at Marlborough, numbered about 500 men.

[6] Gen. Winder to Sec. of War, Aug. 27; Ingraham, p. 25.

with, directly, as their caprices dictated, by the Secretary of War, the Secretary of State (*James Monroe*), the Secretary of the Treasury (*Richard Rush*), and the President of the United States (*James Madison*).[1]

On the morning of the twenty-fourth, the enemy moved early; and after proceeding a short distance on the road towards Washington, he suddenly turned to the right and advanced towards Bladensburg—ten miles distant.[2] Information concerning this movement of the enemy reached General Winder, in Washington, at about ten o'clock, and the troops then in that city were immediately sent to Bladensburg; while Commodore Barney and the flotilla men were also directed to assemble at that place, without delay.[3]

The village of Bladensburg, towards which place both the armies—if such bodies of men as General Winder commanded, can be called an army—were approaching, to contend for the possession of the capital, is about six miles northeast from Washington, on the eastern branch of the Potomac River, over which there is a bridge of ninety feet in length.[4] On the western bank of this stream, in a very strong position which commanded the bridge, the American forces were formed; and the order, as well as the position, appears to have been all that could have been desired for purposes of defence.[5] While the eastern bank of the river—from which the enemy was approaching—was low,

[1] Perkins, p. 309; Brackenridge, p. 295; Williams, pp. 184–204; Ingersoll, iv. pp. 173, 174; Gen. Winder to Com. of Investigation, Sept. 26, 1814.

[2] Adm'l Cockburn to Adm'l Cochrane, Aug. 27; Gleig, pp. 110–115; Williams, p. 202.—[3] Com. Barney to Sec. of Navy, Aug. 29; Williams, p. 203.—[4] Williams, p. 205; Ingersoll, iv. p. 174.—[5] Gen. Ross to Earl Bathurst, Aug. 30; Gleig, p. 115; Ingersoll, iv. p. 174.

without shrubbery, and completely exposed, the opposite bank, in front of the lines, was covered with a narrow strip of willows and larches, in which was thrown a party of riflemen, to cover the front and right of the lines, and to harass the enemy in his advance. In the rear of these riflemen the ground ascended gradually from the river, and was either cleared or occupied by an orchard. On this slope, about three hundred yards from the river, had been thrown up an earthen breastwork, on which had been mounted, *en barbette*, six six-pounders, under Captains Myers and Magruder, of Baltimore. Two companies of Baltimore Volunteers, under Captains Ducker and Gorsuch, were posted on the left and rear of the battery, under cover of a barn, to cover the battery and defend the Georgetown road, which passed in that vicinity; while, on its right and front, were posted Major Pinkney's riflemen.[1] In the rear of the battery, parallel with it, and about five hundred yards farther up the slope, Mr. Monroe had taken the responsibility of forming the Fifth regiment of Baltimore Volunteers (*Lieutenant-colonel Steret's*) and the two regiments of Maryland militia, commanded by Lieutenant-colonels Ragan and Schutz, *after they had been formed on the right of the battery by General Stansbury*,[2] and leaving the latter, entirely without support, except from its small flanking parties of riflemen and militia, to contend, single-handed, with the enemy. Before General Winder could restore this line to its former position, or do any thing to support the first line of artillery, except to order two or three

[1] Gleig, pp. 115–117; Williams, pp. 205, 206; Gen. Winder to Com. of Investigation, Sept. 26; Gen. Stansbury to same, Nov. 15.—[2] Williams, pp. 207–209.

pieces to the left of the second line, with a rifle company to support them, the enemy came within range of the front battery, and its fire was opened with spirit and good effect.[1] Soon afterwards two pieces of artillery were ordered to the right of the second line.[2] On the extreme left, and a little in the rear of this line, were congregated the cavalry — a useless appendage, from which no benefit was derived at any time.[3] In front of both these lines—the artillery and the infantry—were strong rail-fences, and the position was capable of a vigorous defence.[4]

On the summit of the hill, about a mile from the bridge, the third line was formed, embracing a regiment of Maryland militia, under Colonel Beale,—which had just come on the ground,—on the extreme right; Commodore Barney's flotilla men and marines in the centre; and Colonel Magruder's regiment of District militia, and the detachment of regular troops, under Lieutenant-colonel Scott, on the left, with Major Peters' battery,—six six-pounders,—Davidson's light-infantry, and Stull's riflemen in front.[5]

At about half-past twelve, the enemy entered Bladensburg, and came within range of the first line of American artillery; when, as before stated, a vigorous and well-directed fire was thrown, which compelled him to seek the shelter of the houses in the village. Soon afterwards the enemy advanced to the bridge, in double-quick time; and as soon as it was covered with men, the

[1] Adm'l Cockburn to Adm'l Cochrane, Aug. 27; Ingraham, p. 30; Gen. Winder to Com. of Investigation, Sept. 26.—[2] Williams, p. 212.—[3] Ingraham, p. 34; Williams, pp. 212, 213.—[4] Gleig, pp. 115, 116; Gen. Stansbury to Com. of Investigation, Nov. 15.—[5] Ingraham, pp. 30, 31; Williams, pp. 213, 214; Gen. Winder to Com. of Investigation, Sept. 26.

entire force of artillery in the first and second lines opened on it "with tremendous effect," nearly an entire company having been swept down at the first fire, while the riflemen also poured in a very destructive fire. Those who succeeded in passing the bridge immediately deployed into line, and advanced on the first line and compelled it to fall back on the second, farther up the hill, leaving two guns in the hands of the enemy.[1]

Flushed with this success, and thirsting for still more renown, the assailants threw off their knapsacks and haversacks and extended their ranks so as to show a front equal in extent to that of the second line; when they pushed forward to attack that also, before the Second brigade of his own troops could come to his support. But the practised eye of General Winder, who was at the head of the Fifth Baltimore regiment, detected the error; and with a gallantry, which was nobly seconded by the raw troops which formed the second line, he "first checked the ardor of the assailants by a heavy fire, and then, in his turn, advanced to recover the ground which had been lost," at the point of the bayonet. "Against this charge the extended order of the assailants would not permit them to offer an effectual resistance, and they were accordingly borne back to the very thicket upon the river's brink, where they maintained themselves with determined obstinacy," until the Second brigade could come to their rescue.[2]

When the latter had crossed the bridge, the Forty-fourth regiment moved to the right, and turned the left flank of the American line;[1] and, at the same time, some rockets, which were thrown among the companies in that vicinity,[2] completed the confusion, and they immediately fled.[3] Not so, however, with the Fifth regiment, which gallantly maintained its ground until both its flanks had been gained by the enemy, when General Winder ordered it to retire,[4] which was effected, while "clouds of riflemen covered their retreat."[5]

The enemy then moved forward and attacked the third line, which, with the exception of the seamen, appears to have offered but little resistance. The latter, under the veteran Commodore Barney, won the admiration even of the enemy; and the damage which they inflicted was very severe.[6]

In this contest, the loss of the Americans was twenty-six *killed* and fifty-one *wounded;*[7] that of the enemy "was severe, since, out of two-thirds of the army, which were engaged, upwards of five hundred men were killed and wounded; and what rendered it doubly severe was, that among these were numbered several officers of rank and distinction."[8]

Without attempting to pursue the Americans the First and Second bri-

[1] Gen. Ross to Earl Bathurst, Aug. 30; Adm'l Cockburn to Adm'l Cochrane, Aug. 27; Ingraham, pp. 30–32; Gleig, pp. 116–119; Maj. Pinkney, cited by Williams, pp. 221, 222; Gen. Stansbury, in the same work, pp. 227, 228; Gen. Winder to Com. of Investigation, Sept. 26.

[2] Gleig, pp. 119, 120; Ingraham, p. 32; Maj. Pinkney and Gen. Stansbury, in Williams; Gen. Winder to Com. of Investigation, Sept. 26.

[1] Gleig, p. 120.—[2] Ingraham, p. 32; Gleig, p. 122; Gen. Winder to Com. of Investigation, Sept. 26.

[3] Adm'l Cockburn to Adm'l Cochrane, Aug. 27; Gen. Ross to Earl Bathurst, Aug. 30; Ingraham, p. 32.

[4] Ingraham, p. 32; Gleig, p. 120; Gen. Winder to Com. of Investigation, Sept. 26.—[5] Gleig, p. 120.

[6] Com. Barney to Sec. of Navy, Aug. 29; Ingraham, pp. 32–34; Gleig, pp. 120–122; Gen. Winder to Com. of Investigation, Sept. 26.—[7] Williams, p. 238.

[8] Gleig, pp. 120, 121. It is proper to remark that the official account is much less; while the account by the Americans is much greater.

gades were left on the field "to recover their order," while the Third, which had not been engaged, moved to the front, and pushed on to Washington, meeting no farther opposition, and witnessing nothing more distressing than the terror of the inhabitants among which it moved.[1]

"As it was not the intention of the British government to attempt permanent conquests in this part of America; as the General was aware, that, with a handful of men, he could not pretend to establish himself, for any length of time, in an enemy's capital;"[2] and, probably, for the purpose, if possible, of increasing the prize-money to which he would, individually, be entitled,[3] General Ross offered to spare the city, it is said, for a pecuniary consideration, and halted his troops in its immediate vicinity, to await the return of his flag which conveyed the offer.[4] He failed in this attempt, however;[5] and "judging it of consequence to complete the destruction of the public buildings with the least possible delay, so that the army might retire without loss of time,"[6] the troops were moved into the city, and, "without a moment's delay, burned and destroyed every thing in the most distant degree connected with the government."[7] In the general devastation, the Capitol, the President's house, the Arsenal, the store-houses, with great quantities of stores, the War-office, the Treasury, barracks for two or three thousand men, the Navy-yard, a new frigate, nearly ready to be launched, the bridge across the Potomac, the private rope-walks belonging to Heath & Co., Tench Ringgold, and John Chalmers, the sloop of war *Argus*, the library of Congress, the material, type, and presses of the *National Intelligencer*, besides other private property, to a large amount, were destroyed.[1]

"The object of the expedition being accomplished," in the vandalism just referred to, the enemy sneaked away from the scene of destruction, and hastened back to his shipping,—occupying three days in his retreat to Benedict,[2]—in which he met with, comparatively, no opposition.[3]

In this celebrated foray neither party gained the least credit. The Americans, from causes already referred to, and from partisan causes, which it is not the province of this work to discuss, were as effectually without leaders as if there had been no General in the field. The dispositions which General Winder ordered were disregarded, with perfect impunity, by General Stansbury, under the implied, if not expressed, authority of the President; what General Stansbury ordered was countermanded by the Secretary of State; the apparent rivalry of two members of the Cabinet for the succession to the Presidency, induced others to countermand or disregard what the Secretary had ordered; and in the midst of the rivalry and confusion the commander of the troops was not heard, or, if heard, not regarded. In fact, it ap-

[1] Gleig, p. 124. A graphic description of this alarm may be found in "*Memoirs of Rev. Dr. Cone,*"—who was in the battle,—pp. 111–114.—[2] Gleig, p. 124.

[3] "It is true, that if they chose to reject his terms, he and his army *would be deprived of their booty.*"—*Gleig*, pp. 124, 125.—[4] Gleig, pp. 124, 125; Armstrong, ii. p. 131.

[5] Gleig, p. 125; Armstrong, ii. p. 131, *note.*

[6] Gen. Ross to Earl Bathurst, Aug. 30.—[7] Ibid.; Armstrong, ii. p. 131.

[1] Gen. Ross to Earl Bathurst, Aug. 30; Adm'l Cockburn to Adm'l Cochrane, Aug. 27; Gleig, pp. 125–132; Ingraham, p. 36; Williams, pp. 254–271; Armstrong, ii. p. 131.—[2] Gen. Ross to Earl Bathurst, Aug. 30; Adm'l Cockburn to Adm'l Cochrane, Aug. 27; Gleig, pp. 138–145.—[3] Gleig, p. 145; Ingraham, p. 15.

pears to have been considered his duty to "approve" what the amateurs had done for him, rather than to act as the acknowledged and responsible Commander of the Tenth District. On the part of the enemy the expedition produced nothing either to compensate the expense or to add to his renown. In Europe, as in America, the voice of condemnation was general, and expressive of the utmost indignation; while the loss among his troops was not calculated to soothe his feelings, beyond the consolation which his prize-money, for plundered tobacco warehouses, could impart.

CHAPTER LXXXVIII.

September 1, 1814.

THE CAPTURE OF THE AVON.

THE engagement between the *Wasp* and the *Reindeer*, and the capture of the latter, have been already noticed in a preceding chapter of this volume;[1] and the arrival of the victor at L'Orient was also alluded to.

The *Wasp* remained in that port until the twenty-seventh of August, when she sailed on another cruise, in in which she succeeded in capturing several vessels—one of them under circumstances of peculiar daring.[2] In the evening of the same day, while running free, in latitude 47° 30′ N., and longitude 11° W., she made four sail, nearly at the same time—two on the larboard and two on the starboard bow.[3] Hauling up for the most weatherly of them, at seven o'clock she was prepared for action; and, twenty-six minutes afterwards, she hoisted her colors. At thirty-eight minutes past eight the stranger fired one of her stern-chasers; and at twenty minutes past nine she hailed the *Wasp*, being on her weather-quarter. Captain Blakely, without answering, hailed in reply, and ordered her to heave to. As she did not comply, at twenty-six minutes past nine, the *Wasp* fired her twelve-pound carronade to compel her to do so; when the latter opened the action from her larboard-guns, which was responded to by the *Wasp* three minutes afterwards.[1]

As the night appears to have been dark, there were no incidents in the action which are worthy of notice, beyond the fact that it was close and very severe; and at twelve minutes past ten, when the *Wasp's* fire was suspended, and the stranger was hailed, she answered that she had surrendered.[2]

A boat was immediately lowered to take possession of the prize, when another sail—a brig—was discovered close on board of the *Wasp*, and orders were given to clear the ship for another action. Just as she was ready to open her fire on her fresh antagonist, at twenty-six minutes past ten, a third

---

1 Vide Chap. LXXXII.—2 Capt. Blakely to Secretary of Navy, Sept. 11, 1814; Niles' *Register*, vii. p. 174; Cooper, ii. p. 128.—3 Capt. Blakely to Sec. of Navy, Sept. 11, 1814; Cooper, ii. p. 128.

1 Capt. Blakely to Sec. of Navy, Sept. 11, 1814; Niles' *Register*, vii. p. 174; Minutes of the Action, &c.

2 Capt. Blakely to Sec. of Navy, Sept. 11; Cooper, ii. p. 128; Minutes of the Action, &c.

and fourth appeared,—the one astern, the other on the lee-quarter of the *Wasp*,—and the latter determined "to stand from the strange sails." Accordingly her helm was put up, and she ran off dead before the wind, in order to reeve new braces; while the second of the four vessels made chase and opened a fire on her, at pistol-shot distance, cutting away one of her lower main-crosstrees, and doing other damage. At this moment, the *Wasp's* first opponent and prize commenced firing signals of distress, when the chase was abandoned; and, without securing her prize, the *Wasp* continued on her course.[1]

The armament of the *Wasp* has been noticed in a former chapter; her loss was two men *killed* and one *wounded* by a wad. She had many grape in her, had been hulled four times, and much cut up aloft.[1] It appeared, subsequently, that her antagonist was His Britannic Majesty's brig *Avon*,[2] mounting eighteen thirty-two-pound carronades, besides bow and stern guns,[3] with a crew of one hundred and twenty men;[4] that her loss was forty-one killed and wounded;[5] that she sank immediately after the action had terminated;[6] and that the second vessel which came up was the brig of war *Castilian*, of eighteen guns.[7]

After capturing several other vessels, and sending one into Savannah, the *Wasp* and her crew were never heard from. Whether she foundered at sea, or was blown up, or sunk by an enemy, are questions which will never be determined with any degree of certainty.[8]

CHAPTER LXXXIX.

September 1 to 12, 1814.

THE SECOND INVASION OF NEW YORK.[2]

During the spring and summer of 1814, the contention between Great Britain and the United States, for the command of the lakes, was extended to Champlain, and both powers were vigorously employed in building, manning, and equipping a squadron for the accomplishment of this purpose.[3] At the same time the land-forces of the respective belligerents were assembled in considerable numbers, in that vicinity; and, although the latter were comparatively idle, it was evident that more important events were in the future.[9] In fact, the British had already thrown out intimations of their intention to "change

---

[1] Capt. Blakely to Sec. of Navy, Sept. 11; Niles' *Register*, vii. p. 174; James' Nav. Occur., p. 362; Minutes of the Action, &c.—[2] I have employed the term which was used by Sir George Prevost, in his "*Proclamation* to the People of New York," on entering the State, and by Gen. Macomb, in his "*General Orders*," Sept. 14, 1814, rather than the usual terms of "*The Battle of Plattsburg*," and "*The Battle of Lake Champlain*."

[3] Cooper's Naval History, ii. pp. 211, 212; James's Naval Occurrences, p. 404.

[1] Capt. Blakely to Sec. of Navy, Sept. 11; Naval Temple, p. 137; Cooper, ii. p. 128.—[2] Naval Chronicle, xxxii. p. 243; James' Nav. Occur., p. 362.—[3] Niles' *Register*, vii. p. 208; Cooper, ii. p. 129. Mr. James (*Nav. Occur.*, p. 363) says 16 32-pound carronades and 2 long-6's.

[4] Cooper, ii. p. 129. Mr. James (*Nav. Occur.*, p. 364) says 104 men and 13 boys.—[5] Naval Chronicle, xxxii. p. 243; Mr. James (*Nav. Occur.*, p. 363) says *forty-two*.

[6] James' Nav. Occur., p. 362; Cooper, ii. p. 129.

[7] Naval Chronicle, xxxii. p. 243; James' Nav. Occur., p. 362.—[8] Cooper, ii. pp. 129, 130.—[9] Gen. Izard occupied Champlain with 7000 men, and Gen. De Rottonburg was near La Prairie with a large British force.

the boundary" of New York,[1] — that portion of the Confederacy, which was, peculiarly, the King's property, and in which his sovereignty, although dormant, had never been extinguished,— and to cut off, from that State, and from the people of the United States, their rights on the St. Lawrence and the great lakes;[2] and it was evident that one of the first movements towards that result would be made in the occupation of the coveted territory and of Lake Champlain.

Accordingly, when, in July and August, some sixteen thousand men, from the Duke of Wellington's triumphant armies on the Garonne, reached Montreal,[3] one brigade only was sent to the Westward;[4] while, with the remainder, "Sir George Prevost determined to invade the State of New York, by way of Lake Champlain;"[5] and the most extraordinary measures were taken to complete the squadron, at the Isle-aux-Noix, in order that both arms of the service might act in concert, and more effectually accomplish the purposes of the expedition.[6] In the prosecution of these designs, the troops encamped between La Prairie and Chambly, under the command of General De Rottonburg, to await the completion of the squadron;[7] while, to expedite the latter,— Sir James L. Yeo appearing to share but little of the anxiety which Sir George Prevost displayed on the subject,[1]—strong detachments of seamen were sent from the *Ajax* and *Warspite*, then at Quebec, by Admiral Otway and Captain Lord James O'Brien.[2]

While the enemy was thus concentrating his forces on the Northeastern frontiers of New York, the Secretary of War suddenly ordered, from Plattsburg to the Niagara frontiers, the greater part of the force, under General Izard, which had been posted near the former place, for the purpose of holding the enemy in check;[3] and, immediately afterwards, taking advantage of this diversion of the main body of the American forces, from that vicinity, and of the invitation which had thus, virtually, been extended to him, Sir George put his command in motion, without waiting for the co-operation of the squadron;[4] and, on the first of September, he entered New York and occupied Odelltown.[5] On the third he moved to Champlain, the small American force, under General Alexander Macomb, retiring from its intrenched camp, near that place, as he approached; and, on the following day (*Sept.* 4), he advanced to Chazy, without meeting any opposition.[6] On the fifth, he continued his march, in the course of which he met serious obstructions from the trees which had been felled in the roads, and from the removal of the bridges on his route,

[1] Letter from Commissioners at Ghent, Aug. 12. See also Gen. Macomb's General Orders, Sept. 14, 1814; Brackenridge, p. 322.—[2] Gen. Macomb's Dispatch, Sept. 15.—[3] Sir G. Prevost to Earl Bathurst, Sept. 11; James' Mil. Occur., ii. p. 205; Rogers, i. p. 285; Christie, p. 200; Perkins, p. 389.—[4] Ingersoll, iv. p. 123; James' Mil. Occur., ii. p. 205; Christie, p. 201; Rogers, i. p. 286.

[5] Rogers, i. p. 286. See also Christie, p. 200.

[6] James' Nav. Occur., pp. 404–406; Christie, p. 200; Rogers, i. p. 286.—[7] Sir G. Prevost to Earl Bathurst, Sept. 11; Rogers, i. p. 286; Christie, p. 201; Ingersoll, iv. pp. 123, 124.

[1] Auchinleck, p. 385; Christie, pp. 200, 201, 216–220.

[2] James' Nav. Occur., pp. 404, 405; Letter from Midship. Lea, to his brother, Sept. 21, 1814, in Naval Chronicle, xxxii. p. 475; Christie, p. 200; Rogers, i. p. 286.

[3] Sec. of War to Gen. Izard, July 27 and Aug. 12; Rogers, i. p. 286; Christie, p. 201; Armstrong, ii. p. 102.

[4] Ingersoll, iv. p. 124; Christie, p. 201; Perkins, p. 389.

[5] Gen. Macomb's Dispatch, Sept. 15; Ingersoll, iv. p. 124; Palmer's Hist. of Lake Champlain, p. 188.

[6] Sir G. Prevost to Earl Bathurst, Sept. 11; James' Military Occurrences, ii. p. 207; Ingersoll, iv. p. 124; Palmer, pp. 188, 189.

—a duty which had been efficiently performed by Majors Appling and Sproul, with their commands, who had been detached by General Macomb[1] for that purpose,—and he halted near Sampson's, within eight miles of Plattsburg, and remained until morning.[2]

While the enemy was thus moving, cautiously, but in apparent triumph, towards Plattsburg, impressing the teams of the farmers into his service, as he advanced, for the conveyance of his heavy baggage and stores,[3] the fragments of the American army, under General Macomb,—numbering "not more than fifteen hundred effective men for duty,"[4]—fell back on Plattsburg, and completed the defences which had been commenced on the southern bank of the Saranac—a small stream which enters the lake at that place.[5] The general course of this stream, until it comes within about half a mile of the lake, is eastward; but, at that place, it turns, and pursues a northeasterly course about a mile, when it enters Plattsburg Bay. Within this triangular space, with its front and right flank covered by the Saranac and the lake, and its left by a ravine, which extended from the bend of the stream nearly to the lake, the American army—if so small a party could be called an army—took its position, within the works which had been commenced or designed by General Izard. About a quarter of a mile below the bend of the Saranac, near the centre of the village, is a bridge, which, now as then, is known as "*The Lower Bridge;*" while, about a mile above, by way of the stream, is another bridge, on the road leading to Salmon River, which is called "*The Upper Bridge.*" About a mile and a half above the "upper bridge," near the spot where General Pike encamped, is a ford; while at each bridge, and at a point midway between them, the stream is also fordable.[1]

Within the triangular area formed by the Saranac, the lake, and the ravine, therefore, the main body of the army laid; and the utmost exertions were made to render the position defensible while the enemy was on his march.[2] About midway between the bend of the Saranac and the lake-shore, north from the ravine, was a redoubt, named Fort Moreau; another, named Fort Brown, stood on the bank of the Saranac, near the bend, and about two hundred and seventy-five yards west from Fort Moreau; and a third, named Fort Scott, occupied the bank of the lake, also on the north side of the ravine, east from Fort Moreau. In front of this line, at the point formed by the mouth of the Saranac and the lake, were a block-house and battery; while south of the ravine, midway between the river and the lake, stood another block-house.[3] Fort Moreau was garrisoned with "the old Sixth and the Twenty-ninth regiments," under Colonel Melancton Smith; Fort Brown, with parties from the Thirtieth and Thirty-first regiments, under Lieutenant-colonel Storrs; Fort Scott, with the Thirty-third and Thirty-fourth infantry,

[1] Gen. Wool to the Author, March 28, 1860.—[2] Sir G. Prevost to Earl Bathurst, Sept. 11.—[3] Gen. Macomb's Dispatch, Sept. 15; Brackenridge, p. 322.—[4] Gen. Macomb's Dispatch, Sept. 15; Ingersoll, iv. p. 124; Cooper, ii. p. 212; James' Mil. Occur., ii. p. 207.—[5] Gen. Macomb's Dispatch, Sept. 15; James' Mil. Occur., ii. p. 207; Perkins, p. 391.

[1] Palmer's Lake Champlain, p. 189.—[2] Gen. Macomb's Dispatch, Sept. 15; Thomson's Sketches, p. 317; Perkins, p. 391.—[3] Palmer's Lake Champlain, p. 190; Gen. Macomb's Dispatch, Sept. 15; Rogers, i. pp. 286, 287; Sir G. Prevost to Earl Bathurst, Sept. 11.

BATTLE OF PLATTSBURG.

From the original Painting by Chappel in the possession of the Publishers.

under Major Vinson; the block-house on the point, by Lieutenant Fowler, of the Artillery, with his command; and the block-house south from the ravine, with parties from the First Rifles and Fourth Infantry, under Captain Smith, of the Rifles.[1]

Against this post, with its little garrison, were moving four troops of the Nineteenth light-dragoons, four companies of Royal Artillery, "a brigade" (*twenty-five men*) of Rocketeers, and one (*seventy-five men*) of Royal Sappers and Miners, the light brigade—embracing Muron's Swiss regiment, a regiment of Canadian Chasseurs, one of Voltigeurs, and a detachment of Frontier Light-infantry; and the Third (*Buffs*), Fifth, and Sixth, the Second battalion of the Eighth (*King's*), the Thirteenth, the First and Third battalions of the Twenty-seventh, the Thirty-ninth, Forty-ninth, and Fifty-eighth, the Third battalion of the Seventy-sixth and the Eighty-eighth regiments of the line—in the aggregate, not less than fourteen thousand of the most highly disciplined troops,[2] with Lieutenant-general De Rottonburg, as second in command; Major-generals Robertson, Powers, and Brisbane, as commandants of brigades; and Major-general Baynes as Adjutant-general.[3]

As has been stated, Sir George halted near Sampson's, on the evening of the fifth of September,[4] his progress having been obstructed by detachments from the Thirteenth regiment, under Captain Sproul, and of riflemen, under Lieutenant-colonel Appling;[1] and during the same evening, intelligence reached the American lines that at an early hour, on the following morning (*Sept.* 6), the enemy would move, in two columns, on both the roads which led to Plattsburg; and measures were taken to check his progress.[2] On the upper, or Beekmantown, road, as stated before, General Mooers and seven hundred militia had been posted, near the stone meeting-house in Beekmantown;[3] and Major John E. Wool, of the Twenty-ninth regiment,[4] having volunteered his services, he was ordered to march early the next morning, with two hundred and fifty regular troops and two pieces of artillery, on the Beekmantown road, "to support the militia, and set them an example of firmness;"[5] while to Lieutenant-colonel Appling and Captain Sproul was intrusted the defence of the lower or lake-shore road.[6]

Agreeably to the enemy's arrangements, at an early hour on the sixth, his right column—led by the Third battalion of the Twenty-seventh regiment, eight hundred men; the Thirty-ninth regiment, nine hundred men; the Third battalion of the Seventy-sixth regiment, nine hundred men; and the Eighty-eighth regiment, one thousand men, under General Powers, and *supported by* four companies of light-infantry, and a demi-brigade under Captain Robertson[7]—moved over to the

[1] Gen. Macomb's General Orders, Sept. 5, 1814.

[2] Ibid., Sept 14, 1814; Schedule "*No.* 2," appended to Gen. Macomb's Dispatch, Sept. 15; Geo. M. Beckwith's Address, Sept. 11, 1858.

[3] Schedule "*No.* 2," appended to Gen. Macomb's Dispatch, Sept. 15; Palmer's Lake Champlain, p. 188.

[4] Palmer's Lake Champlain, pp. 189, 191.

[1] Gen. Macomb's Dispatch, Sept. 15; Thomson's Sketches, p. 317; Brackenridge, p. 323.

[2] Gen. Macomb's Dispatch, Sept. 15; Palmer's Lake Champlain, p. 191.

[3] Gen. Macomb's Dispatch, Sept. 15; Palmer's Lake Champlain, p. 191.—[4] Now Major-general John E. Wool, commanding the Eastern Division of the Army of the United States.—[5] Gen. Macomb's Dispatch, Sept. 15; Gen. Wool to Philip B. Roberts, Jan. 6, 1859.—[6] Gen. Macomb's Dispatch, Sept. 15; James' Mil. Occur., ii. p. 207.

[7] Sir G. Prevost to Earl Bathurst, Sept. 11.

Beekmantown road;[1] and descending more rapidly than the left column, when near the residence of Ira Howe, in Beekmantown, he met Major Wool, with his infantry, and thirty volunteers from Plattsburg[2]—Captain Leonard, with the field-pieces, having refused to join the detachment.[3] The Major opened a brisk fire on the head of the enemy's column, as it approached, severely wounding Lieutenant West, of the Buffs, and several privates.[4] The pressure of the greatly superior force which constituted the enemy's column, however, compelled Major Wool to retire; yet, although "the militia could not be prevailed on to stand, notwithstanding the exertions of their general and staff officers," he "disputed the ground with great obstinacy," skirmishing, as he retreated, with great coolness.[5] When he reached Culver's Hill, four and a half miles from Plattsburg, he made a stand, and compelled the enemy's advance to fall back on his main body, with the loss of Lieutenant-colonel Willington and Ensign Chapman, of the Buffs.[6] The dense masses of the enemy's column still pressing forward, however, the detachment under Major Wool was

[1] Palmer's Lake Champlain, p. 191; James' Military Occurrences, ii. p. 208.

[2] Gen. Macomb's Dispatch, Sept. 15; Gen. Wool to Philip B. Roberts, Jan. 6, 1859; Palmer's Lake Champlain, pp. 191, 192. The volunteers referred to were principally lads under 18 years of age, who were known as "*Aiken's Volunteers*," and rendered good service. After the war had closed, Congress ordered a rifle to be presented to each of these youthful defenders, as a testimonial of the gratitude of their country. Azariah C. Flagg, Esq., late Controller of the city of New York, was one of this little party, and received one of the rifles referred to.

[3] Gen. Macomb's Dispatch, Sept. 15; Gen. Wool to P. B. Roberts, Jan. 6, 1859.—[4] Gen. Macomb's Dispatch, Sept. 15; Palmer's Lake Champlain, p. 192; G. M. Beckwith's Address, Sept. 11, 1858.—[5] Gen. Macomb's Dispatch, Sept. 15; James' Mil. Occur., ii. p. 208; Sketches of the War, p. 405; Perkins, p. 390.—[6] Gen. Wool to P. B. Roberts, Jan. 6, 1859; Palmer's Lake Champlain, p. 192; Williams' Life of Te-ho-ra-gwa-ne-gen, p. 78.

again compelled to fall back, tearing up a bridge on the way, and making another stand, at about eight o'clock, near "Halsey's Corners," about a mile and a half from the bridge in Plattsburg.[1] He was joined, at this place, by Captain Leonard, with his field-pieces; and that officer having placed his guns in battery, he inflicted considerable loss on the advancing columns of the enemy.[2] After having been driven from that post, also, he again fell back, making short stands, opposite the residence of Judge Bayly, and at Gallows Hill, in the village of Plattsburg;[3] and, finally, with Lieutenant-colonel Appling's and Captain Sproul's commands, he crossed the Saranac and joined the main body, tearing up, on his way, "the lower bridge," under a severe fire from the head of the enemy's column.[4]

While General Powers' command was thus opposed on the Beekmantown road, the left column, on the lower road, was also greatly annoyed by the exertions of Lieutenant-colonel Appling and Captain Sproul, as well as by a detachment of gunboats, which Commander Macdonough had ordered to the head of the bay.[5] After a successful retreat from their position at Dead Creek Bridge, the Lieutenant-colonel and Captain joined Major Wool, and with him kept up a brisk fire until they got under cover of the works.[6]

[1] Gen. Wool to P. B. Roberts, Jan. 6, 1859; Palmer's Lake Champlain, p. 192; G. M. Beckwith's Address, Sept. 11, 1858.—[2] Gen. Macomb's Dispatch, Sept. 15, 1814; Gen. Wool to P. B. Roberts, Jan. 6, 1859; Sketches of War, p. 405; Palmer's Lake Champlain, p. 192.

[3] Gen. Wool to P. B. Roberts, Jan. 6, 1859.

[4] Gen. Macomb's Dispatch, Sept. 15, 1814; Gen. Wool to P. B. Roberts, Jan. 6, 1859; James' Mil. Occur., ii. p. 209; Palmer's Lake Champlain, p. 193.—[5] Gen. Macomb's Dispatch, Sept. 15, 1814; Palmer's Lake Champlain, p. 193; Thomson's Sketches, p. 318; Cooper, ii. p. 212.

[6] Gen. Macomb's Dispatch, Sept. 15, 1814; Sketches of War, p. 405; Palmer's Lake Champlain, p. 193.

As soon as the American skirmishers had passed and destroyed "the lower bridge," they threw the plank which had formed it into a temporary breastwork, to hold the enemy in check, should he attempt the passage of the stream; while the latter contented himself with the occupation of the storehouses and dwellings on the northern bank, and with opening and continuing a brisk fire on his opponents on the other side of the Saranac. Soon afterwards, these annoyances were removed by a volley of hot-shot, which was thrown in on them by Captain Brooks, of the foot-artillery; and having *burned him out* from his coverts,—one building having been set on fire,—the enemy appears to have reconciled himself to the limits which had thus been set to his operations, without any other efforts to extend them than an occasional shot from his light troops.[1]

While one party of the enemy was thus held in check, at "the lower bridge," another pressed forward towards the upper one; and the militia, under General Mooers, like the regulars at "the lower," retired before him, tore up the planks and made a breastwork of them, and, by a vigorous resistance, kept the assailants in check, notwithstanding his efforts to cross the river.[2]

The ridge and high ground north from the village was selected as the site for the enemy's encampment;[3] and, after having thus disposed of his troops, he employed himself until the eleventh "in getting on his battering train, and erecting his batteries and approaches"[4]

¹ Gen. Macomb's Dispatch, Sept. 15, 1814; Gen. Wool to the Author, March 28, 1860; Palmer's Lake Champlain, p. 194; Ingersoll, iv. p. 125.—² Gen. Macomb's Dispatch, Sept. 15, 1814.—³ Palmer's Lake Champlain, p. 194.

⁴ Gen. Macomb's Dispatch, Sept. 15, 1814.

—a battery on the lake-shore, north from the mouth of the Saranac; another on the bank above the mill-pond; a third near the burial-ground; a fourth, for rockets, on the hill opposite Fort Brown; and four block-houses, smaller than the forts, at other points within range of the American works.[1]

During this time the American squadron, under Commander Thomas Macdonough, laid at anchor in the bay, off Plattsburg.[2] It embraced the following vessels: the *Saratoga*, mounting eight long twenty-four-pounders, six forty-two-pound and twelve thirty-two-pound carronades; the *Eagle*, Commander John D. Henley, mounting twelve thirty-two-pound carronades and eight long-eighteen's; the *Ticonderoga*, Lieutenant Stephen Cassin, mounting eight long twelve-pound, four long eighteen-pound, and five thirty-two-pound carronades; and the *Preble*, Lieutenant Charles Budd, mounting seven long-nine's; together with the galleys *Allen*, *Burrows*, *Borer*, *Nettle*, *Viper*, and *Centipede*, each mounting one long twenty-four-pound and an eighteen-pound Columbiad; and the galleys *Ludlow*, *Wilmer*, *Alwyn*, and *Ballard*, each mounting a long twelve-pounder;[3] and it was held in readiness to meet the enemy's squadron, whenever the latter might appear and afford an opportunity to do so.[4] The enemy's vessels, meanwhile, rendezvoused at the Isle la Motte, under Captain George Downie, of the Royal Navy; and, at that place, completed, as far as their

¹ Palmer's Lake Champlain, p. 194.—² Gen. Macomb's Dispatch, Sept. 15, 1814; Com. Macdonough to Sec. of Navy, Sept. 13; Cooper, ii. p. 213.

³ "Statement of American force," &c., appended to Com. Macdonough's Dispatch, Sept. 13, 1814.

⁴ Com. Macdonough's Dispatch, Sept. 13, 1814.

crews could do so, their preparations for action.[1]

Sir George Prevost having, before, "earnestly solicited," from Captain Downie, "the co-operation of the naval force to attack that of the Americans, which was placed for the support of their works at Plattsburg, which, it was proposed, should be stormed by the troops at the same moment that the naval action should commence in the bay"[2]—"on the morning of the eleventh of September, the squadron was seen over the isthmus which joins Cumberland Head with the mainland, steering for Plattsburg Bay;"[3] and Sir George ordered the advance of the army, under General Robertson, to "force the fords of the Saranac, and to advance, with ladders, to escalade the American works upon the heights," on the southern bank of that stream;[4] while his batteries were directed to open their fire "the instant the ships engaged,"[5] and, at the same time, it is said, ordered the main body to *cook its dinner*.[6]

Having thus manifested his intention of throwing upon the squadrons the duty of contending for the possession of Plattsburg and Lake Champlain, while, with the land-forces, he would "co-operate" so far as to take advantage of the result, whatever it might be, Sir George Prevost and the main body of the army continued their culinary occupations, while the light infantry (*two thousand eight hundred men*), the First and Third battalions of the Twenty-seventh regiment (*seventeen hundred men*), the Third battalion of the Seventy-sixth regiment (*nine hundred men*), the Third, or Buffs (*nine hundred men*), the Fifth (*one thousand men*), and the Fifty-eighth regiment (*nine hundred men*),—an aggregate of eight thousand two hundred veteran troops,[1]—provided with immense quantities of scaling-ladders,[2] attempted to pass the Saranac, with a view of assaulting the works;[3] while, at the same time, the batteries opened their fire, with bomb-shells, shrapnells, balls, and Congreve-rockets.[4] At both bridges, and at the ford above, attempts were made, simultaneously, to cross the stream; and in each case, with indifferent success. At "the upper bridge" a body of riflemen, under Captain Grovener and Lieutenants Hamilton and Riley, supported by the pickets in that vicinity, contested the passage and repulsed him; while, at "the lower bridge," the ordinary guards, supported by the fire of the redoubts and block-houses, were equally successful.[5] At the fords, above the village, where the enemy was opposed only by the volunteers and militia, he was driven back, after repeated attempts, with heavy loss.[6] In one of these attempts he succeeded in forcing the passage, and a heavy body of regulars was thrown across the stream. Rallying, under their own officers, however, the yeomanry hastened to expel the invaders; and after a se-

[1] Capt. Pring to Sir J. L. Yeo, Sept. 12, 1814; Cooper, ii. pp. 214, 215.—[2] Sir G. Prevost to Earl Bathurst, Sept. 11, 1814; Capt. Pring to Sir J. L. Yeo, Sept. 12, 1814.

[3] Sir G. Prevost to Earl Bathurst, Sept. 11; Gen. Macomb's Dispatch, Sept. 15; Cooper, ii. p. 215.

[4] Sir G. Prevost to Earl Bathurst, Sept. 11; Perkins, p. 392.—[5] Sir G. Prevost to Earl Bathurst, Sept. 11; Gen. Macomb's Dispatch, Sept. 15.—[6] "*Veritas*," cited by Mr. James (*Military Occurrences*, ii. p. 214).

[1] Vide p. 381.—[2] Gen. Macomb's Dispatch, Sept. 15, 1814; Sir G. Prevost to Earl Bathurst, Sept. 11, 1814.

[3] Sir G. Prevost to Earl Bathurst, Sept. 11, 1814; Palmer's Lake Champlain, p. 204.—[4] Gen. Macomb's General Orders, Sept. 14; His Dispatch, Sept. 15, 1814; Sir G. Prevost to Earl Bathurst, Sept. 11, 1814.

[5] Gen. Macomb's General Orders, Sept. 14; Palmer's Lake Champlain, p. 204.—[6] Gen. Macomb's General Orders, Sept. 14; His Dispatch, Sept. 15.

vere struggle, in which he was a severe loser, the enemy was hurled back to the northern bank, and retired, in shame, to his camp on the heights north of the village.[1]

In the mean time, the squadrons in the bay were struggling for the mastery. As already stated, the enemy's squadron left the Isle la Motte on the morning of the eleventh;[2] and with a good working-breeze from the north-east, it ran up the lake[3]—the sloop *Finch*, Lieutenant Hicks, mounting six eighteen-pound carronades, one eighteen-pound Columbiad, and four long-six's, leading the column. Close astern of her, in the order named, were the ship *Confiance*, Captain Downie, mounting thirty-one long-twenty-four's and six heavy carronades; the brig *Linnet*, Captain Pring, mounting sixteen long-twelve's; and the sloop *Chubb*, Lieutenant McGhee, mounting ten eighteen-pound carronades and one long-six; while close in shore, without regard to order, were twelve gunboats, eight of which mounted two guns each, and four one each.[4]

At this time the American squadron lay in Plattsburg Bay, in a line parallel with the shore, and distant from it about two miles.[5] At the head of the line were anchored two galleys, next to them the *Eagle;* one or two galleys lay next, and then the *Saratoga;* after which another detachment of the galleys, and the *Ticonderoga;* still more galleys, and, closing the line, the *Preble.*[6] This line had also been formed with all the skill which characterized Commander Macdonough's professional career, in which the greatest advantage had been taken of the peculiarities of the bay. A shoal and a small island (*Crab Island*), on which had been erected a single-gun battery, covered its southern extremity, and prevented the enemy from doubling it; there was not room for him to anchor beyond the range of the American carronades; and, coming to an engagement, he was compelled to approach the American line with his bows on. He had also anchored with springs on his cables; and, as an additional safeguard, he had laid a kedge broad off on each bow of the *Saratoga*, and brought their hawsers in, upon the two quarters, letting them hang in bights, under water.[1]

As the enemy came around Cumberland Head,—the northern point of the entrance to Plattsburg Bay,—he hauled up to the wind in a line abreast, lying to until his galleys could come up; and as soon as the latter joined him they passed to leeward, and formed in the same manner as the larger vessels. As soon as this had been done, and the officers had received their orders, the enemy filled, with his starboard-tacks aboard, and headed in, towards the American line, in a line abreast—the *Chubb* being to windward, moving against the head of the opposing line, and the *Finch* to leeward, heading towards the *Preble;* while the galleys were mostly to leeward of the *Finch.*[2] As the enemy approached the American line, the *Chubb* looked well to windward of the *Eagle*, and the *Linnet* laid

[1] Gen. Macomb's General Orders, Sept. 14; *National Advocate*, in Niles' *Register*, vii. p. 45.—[2] Vide p. 384.
[3] Cooper, ii. p. 215.—[4] "Statement of enemy's force," &c., appended to Com. Macdonough's Dispatch, Sept. 13.
[5] Cooper, ii. p. 213; Perkins, p. 391; Palmer's Lake Champlain, p. 197.—[6] Capt. Pring to Sir J. L. Yeo, Sept. 12, 1814; Cooper, ii. pp. 213, 214; Palmer's Lake Champlain, p. 197.

[1] Cooper, ii, pp. 215, 216; Palmer's Lake Champlain, p. 197.—[2] Capt. Pring to Sir J. L. Yeo, Sept. 12, 1814; Cooper, ii. p. 216.

her course for the bows of the same vessel; the *Confiance* tried to fetch far enough ahead of the *Saratoga* to lay that ship athwart hawse; and the *Finch* and the gunboats stood for the *Ticonderoga* and *Preble*.[1]

As the enemy filled, the American vessels sprung their broadsides to bear;[2] and, while the former approached, but was yet beyond the range of the carronades of the latter,—that most solemn and interesting period, when a moment may change a scene of most perfect quietude to one of the most boisterous strife,—it is said, the young Commander, Macdonough, united with such of his crew as would join him in public prayer to the Supreme Disposer of events for his blessing on the approaching contest.[3] Suddenly, and without orders, the *Eagle* opened her fire, without any effect;[4] and, about the same time, a young cock, which, with others, had been liberated from his coop in the preparations of the *Saratoga* for battle, startled by the report of the *Eagle's* guns, flew upon a gun-slide, clapped his wings, and crowed lustily, much to the amusement and encouragement of the sailors, who responded to his note of defiance with three hearty cheers.[5]

As the *Eagle* continued to throw her fire away, she was closely watched; and, as soon as it told, the *Saratoga*, and, after her, the other vessels, opened with their long guns; in the midst of which, without returning it, the enemy stood in steadily, and gallantly prepared for the contest.[1] Because the fire which she met was more severe than was expected, and at the same time, the wind baffling her,[2] the *Confiance* suddenly anchored, while yet a quarter of a mile distant from the *Saratoga*, and "not so advantageously as had been intended;"[3] while the *Linnet*, *Chubb*, and *Finch* were still standing in.[4] Soon afterwards the *Linnet* anchored in a very favorable position, forward of the *Eagle's* beam, throwing into the *Saratoga*, as her guns bore, a well-directed broadside.[5] The *Chubb* kept on her course, intending to take a position from which she could rake the American line; in the course of which—within fifteen minutes after the battle commenced—she received a broadside from the *Eagle*, which carried away her cables, bowsprit, and boom, and inflicted other injury; and she drifted down between the two opposing lines, until, after having received a shot from the *Saratoga*, she surrendered, and was towed in-shore by one of the *Saratoga's* boats, commanded by Midshipman Platt.[6] The *Finch*, with the gunboats, stood for the *Ticonderoga;* and, against that vessel and the *Preble*, extraordinary efforts were made during the action.[7]

In the mean time, the *Confiance* had been properly secured; *but not until then* had she opened her fire, which fell on the *Saratoga* with terrible effect—her first broadside having killed or dis-

---

[1] Com. Macdonough to Sec. of Navy, Sept. 13; Capt. Pring to Sir J. L. Yeo, Sept. 12, 1814; Perkins, p. 392.

[2] Cooper, p. 216.—[3] Letter from Burlington, Sept. 15, in Niles' *Register*, vii. p. 43; Letter from Rev. H. P. Bogue to the Author, March 7, 1860.—[4] Cooper, ii. p. 216; Palmer's Lake Champlain, p. 199.—[5] Niles' *Register*, vii. p. 43; Letter from Burlington, Sept. 15; Cooper, ii. p. 216; Letter from Com. La Valette to the Author, Feb., 1860; Letter from Rev. H. P. Bogue to the Author, March 7, 1860.

[1] Cooper, ii. p. 216; Palmer's Lake Champlain, p. 199.

[2] Capt. Pring to Sir J. L. Yeo, Sept. 12, 1814; Cooper, ii. pp. 216, 217.—[3] Capt. Pring to Sir J. L. Yeo, Sept. 12, 1814; Com. Macdonough to Sec. of Navy, Sept. 13; James' Nav. Occur., p. 409.—[4] Capt. Pring to Sir J. L. Yeo, Sept. 12, 1814; Cooper, ii. p. 217.—[5] Cooper, ii. p. 217.

[6] Capt. Pring to Sir J. L. Yeo, Sept. 12, 1814; James' Naval Occurrences, p. 409.—[7] Com. Macdonough to Secretary of Navy, Sept. 13; Cooper, ii. p. 217.

abled about forty of the crew of the latter vessel.[1] Thenceforth the cannonade continued,—steadily and gradually decreasing, as the guns became disabled, —without any, or but few, manœuvres, for upwards of an hour,[2] when the *Finch* was driven, badly disabled, from her position by the *Ticonderoga;* and, having drifted on Crab Island, she was captured by the invalids from the hospital at that place.[3] Soon afterwards the *Preble* was driven from her position in the American line by the enemy's gunboats,—or by that portion of them which remained in the action,—and fell back, in-shore, beyond the range of the enemy's guns;[4] but every effort which was made against the *Ticonderoga* was unsuccessful.[5]

The contest, at this moment, as will be seen, had narrowed down to the *Confiance* and the *Linnet*, on the right of the line, against the *Eagle*, the *Saratoga*, and the American galleys; and the British gunboats against the *Ticonderoga* on the left—the *Preble*, on the one side, having fallen back, and the *Chubb* and the *Finch*, on the other, having surrendered. The *Linnet*, at the head of the enemy's line, had secured an admirable position, and was gallantly sustaining the honor of her flag against the fire of the *Eagle;*[6] the *Confiance*, also, with great spirit, but diminished effect, was pouring in her heavy fire on the *Eagle* and the *Saratoga;*[7] while the British gunboats, with a gallantry bordering on desperation, as before stated, struggled with the *Ticonderoga* for the command of the southern extremity of the line. The *Eagle*, soon afterwards lost her springs, and was prevented from bringing her guns to bear; when Commander Henley cut his cable, sheeted home his topsails, cast the brig, and, running down, behind the *Saratoga*, anchored by the stern, between the latter vessel and the *Ticonderoga*, a little in-shore of both, where, from his larboard guns, he opened afresh, and with much better effect, on the *Confiance* and *Linnet*[1]—the latter, at the same time, springing her broadside, so that she was enabled to rake the *Saratoga* on her bows.[2]

The *Saratoga* continued this uneven contest, until, gradually, her entire starboard-battery had become disabled by the enemy's shot, or by hard usage, and she was left in the midst of her opponents without a single available gun. At this moment the admirable seamanship of Commander Macdonough was displayed in all its brilliancy, in his determination to wind the ship, and to bring around her fresh, uninjured larboard-battery to bear on the enemy. With the assistance of Philip Brum, the able Sailing-master of the ship, this was accomplished with the most satisfactory success, notwithstanding the heavy raking fire which was thrown in by the *Linnet;* and Lieutenant La Vallette, who took the command of the guns, opened a fresh and exceedingly effective fire on the *Confiance*—commencing with the aftermost gun, and continuing it as fast

[1] Capt. Pring to Sir J. L. Yeo, Sept. 12, 1814; Cooper, ii. p. 217.—[2] Cooper, ii. p. 218.—[3] Com. Macdonough to Sec. of Navy, Sept. 13; Capt. Pring to Sir J. L. Yeo, Sept. 12, 1814; James' Nav. Occur., p. 409.—[4] Cooper, ii. p. 218; Palmer's Lake Champlain, p. 200.—[5] Com. Macdonough to Sec. of Navy, Sept. 13; Cooper, ii. p. 218.

[6] James' Naval Occurrences, p. 411.

[7] Cooper, ii. pp. 218, 219.

[1] Com. Macdonough to Secretary of Navy, Sept. 13; Capt. Pring to Sir J. L. Yeo, Sept. 12; James' Naval Occurrences, p. 411.

[2] Com. Macdonough to Secretary of Navy, Sept. 13; Capt. Pring to Sir J. L. Yeo, Sept. 12; Cooper, ii. p. 218; Palmer's Lake Champlain, p. 200.

as the battery could be brought to bear.[1]

In the mean time, the *Confiance*, perceiving the advantage which would accrue to her opponent by the use of a fresh battery, against one which had been severely wounded, attempted to imitate the manœuvre of the latter, and to wind around in the same manner.[2] In this, however, she failed; and having struggled manfully against the superior skill and more efficient fire of the American flag-ship, with scarcely a single gun to oppose to the fresh broadside of the latter, she struck her colors, after a contest of about two hours and a quarter.[3]

Immediately afterwards the *Saratoga's* broadside was swung to bear on the *Linnet*, and within fifteen minutes after the surrender of the *Confiance*, she, too, struck her colors, after a most gallant opposition;[4] but the gunboats, which had been opposed to the *Ticonderoga*, pulled off and escaped.[5]

The triumph was complete, unequivocal, undeniable.[6] Lieutenant La Vallette had taken possession of the *Confiance;* and the former commanders of the prizes were approaching the *Saratoga*, to make a formal surrender of their swords to the victorious chief. In the words of an eye-witness: "They were very fine-appearing fellows, and their reception by Macdonough—considering the time, place, circumstances, manner, and sentiments expressed—was one of the most beautiful exhibitions of moral sublimity ever witnessed. They came under convoy-guard, directly from the flag-ship *Confiance*, and as they stepped upon the deck of the *Saratoga* they met Commodore Macdonough, who kindly bowed to them, while they, holding their caps in their left hands, and their swords, by the blades, in their right, advanced towards him, and, bowing, presented the weapons. The Commodore bowed and said, 'Gentlemen, return your swords into your scabbards, and wear them; you are worthy of them;' and having obeyed the order, arm-in-arm, with their swords by their sides, they walked the deck of their conqueror." Lieutenant La Vallette was ordered to "prepare the prisoners for Crab Island as fast as possible;" to "treat them kindly," and to "speak to them encouragingly," and the cup of Macdonough's glory was full.[1]

---

[1] Com. Macdonough to Sec. of Navy, Sept. 13; Letter from Burlington, Sept. 15, 1814; Capt. Pring to Sir J. L. Yeo, Sept. 12; Cooper, ii. pp. 218, 219; Perkins, p. 392; Commodores Paulding and La Vallette's Letters to the Author, Feb., 1860.—[2] Letter from Burlington, Sept. 15, 1814; Capt. Pring to Sir J. L. Yeo, Sept. 12, 1814; Cooper, ii. p. 219; Perkins, p. 392.—[3] Letter from Burlington, Sept. 15, 1814; Capt. Pring to Sir J. L. Yeo, Sept. 12, 1814; Cooper, ii. p. 219.—[4] Com. Macdonough to Sec. of Navy, Sept. 13; Capt. Pring to Sir J. L. Yeo, Sept. 12, 1814; James' Nav. Occur., p. 411; Cooper, ii. p. 220.

[5] Com. Macdonough to Sec. of Navy, Sept. 13; Letter from Burlington, Sept. 15; Gen. Macomb's General Order, Sept. 14, 1814; Perkins, p. 392. Mr. Cooper (*Nav. Hist.*, ii. p. 220) says, "As soon as they found that the large vessels had submitted, they ceased the combat, and *lowered their colors.*" Mr. Palmer (*History of Lake Champlain*, p. 201) says both are right—they struck, but afterwards escaped.

[6] The severity of the engagement has been frankly admitted by the enemy. In a letter from Midshipman Lea, of the *Confiance*, to his brother, published in the *Nav. Chron.*, xxxii. p. 475 (London, Dec., 1814), says, "At forty minutes after nine we ran down alongside the Yankee Commodore's ship, and came to anchor; when the action commenced by a vigorous cannonade of all the Yankee fleet on our ship, which we immediately returned; a little before ten o'clock the action was general, and kept up with the greatest spirit until twenty-five minutes after noon, when our spring and rudder were shot away, and all our masts, yards, and sails so shattered, that one looked like so many bunches of matches, and the other like a bundle of old rags. . . . The havoc on both sides is dreadful. I don't think there are more than five of our men, out of three hundred, but are killed and wounded. Never was a shower of hail so thick as the shot whistling about our ears. There is one of our marines who was in the Trafalgar action with Lord Nelson, who says it was a mere flea-bite in comparison with this."

[1] Rev. H. P. Bogue to the Author, March 7, 1860. See also Capt. Pring's Dispatch, Sept. 12, 1814. The strange story told by Mr. James (*Nav. Occur.*, p. 411) concerning the Commodore's address to the officers is here put to rest.

With the capture of the squadron all the troops were withdrawn from before the American lines by Sir George Prevost;[1] and, although the cannonade was continued until sunset,[2] it was done more for the purpose of concealing his projected retreat than for offensive purposes. Having been "deprived of the co-operation of the fleet, without which the farther prosecution of the service had become impracticable," he not only "did not hesitate to arrest the course of the troops advancing to the attack" of the American works,[3] but, as soon as the sun had gone down, and the shades of evening had afforded the means of concealment, he dismantled his several batteries and sent off his artillery and stores;[4] and, during the night, with the utmost secrecy, with his entire army, he followed,[5] leaving behind him his sick and wounded,[6] together with immense quantities of stores, provisions, camp equipage, &c., as evidences of his utter and undeniable discomfiture.[7]

In this remarkable expedition the enemy's force, on shore, as already stated, was not less than fourteen thousand veteran troops;[8] and on the lake it was one thousand and fifty men, with ninety-five guns:[1] while that of the Americans, on shore, did not exceed fifteen hundred effective regular troops,[2] and two thousand five hundred militia and volunteers;[3] and, on the lake, eight hundred and twenty men, with eighty-six guns.[4] The loss of the former, on shore, was Lieutenant-colonel Willington, Captain Purchase, Ensign Chapman, thirty-four men, and "*one horse*," *killed;* Captains Crosse and Westropp, Lieutenants Kingsbury, West, Benson, Howe, Brokier, and Lewis, one hundred and forty-two men, and "*two horses*," *wounded;* and Lieutenants Hutch, Ogilvie, Marchington, and Vigneau, fifty-one men, and "*six horses*," *missing;*[5] while, on the lake, it was Captain Downie, four officers, and fifty-two men *killed*, and three officers and sixty-nine men *wounded*.[6] The loss of the Americans, on land, was Lieutenant Runk and thirty-six men, *killed;* Lieutenants Harrison and Taylor, and sixty men, *wounded;* and twenty men, *missing:*[7] on the lake, Lieutenants Gamble and Stansbury, Master's-mate Vandermere, Sailing-master Carter, and forty-eight men, *killed;* and Lieutenants Smith and Spencer, Midshipman Baldwin, Master's-mate Breeze, and fifty-four men, *wounded*.[8]

[1] Sir G. Prevost to Earl Bathurst, Sept. 11, 1814.
[2] Gen. Macomb to Sec. of War, Sept. 12, 1814.
[3] Sir G. Prevost to Earl Bathurst, Sept. 11.
[4] Gen. Macomb's General Orders, Sept. 14, 1814; His Dispatch, Sept. 15; Sir G. Prevost to Earl Bathurst, Sept. 11, 1814; Perkins, p. 394.
[5] Gen. Macomb to Sec. of War, Sept. 12 and 15, 1814; Letter from Burlington, Sept. 15; Gen. Macomb's General Orders, Sept. 14, 1814.—[6] Gen. Macomb to Sec. of War, Sept. 12, 1814, and his General Orders, Sept. 14, 1814; Niles' *Register*, vii. p. 45.—[7] Gen. Macomb to Sec. of War, Sept. 12 and 15, 1814; Niles' *Register*, vii. p. 45.
[8] Vide p. 381.

[1] Burlington (Vt.) *Sentinel*, Sept. 16, 1814, on authority of Com. Macdonough.—[2] Vide p. 380.—[3] Niles' *Register*, vii. p. 55. "*Veritas*" (*James' Mil. Occur.*, pp. 216, 217), says, "perhaps *three thousand* militia."—[4] Burlington *Sentinel*, Sept. 16, 1814, on authority of Com. Macdonough.
[5] Report appended to Dispatch.
[6] Report appended to Capt. Pring's Dispatch. The Burlington *Sentinel*, Sept. 16, 1814, on authority of Com. Macdonough, stated it at 84 *killed* and 110 *wounded*.
[7] Report appended to Gen. Macomb's Dispatch, Sept. 15, 1814.—[8] Report appended to Com. Macdonough's Dispatch, Sept. 13, 1814.

CHAPTER XC.

September 12 to 14, 1814.

THE EXPEDITION AGAINST BALTIMORE.

THE unexpected success of the enemy, in his expedition against Washington, appears to have encouraged him to make still farther attempts of the same character; and Baltimore was the point selected as the scene of his next exploit. Indeed, it is said that "General Ross boasted that he would make that city his winter-quarters," and that, "with his command, he could march where he pleased in Maryland;"[1] and he certainly acted, as did his entire army, in a spirit which indicated these as his well-formed opinions.

On the ninth of September, the enemy's fleet, after hovering on the shores of the Chesapeake several days, in order to distract the attention of the Americans, suddenly put about and headed towards the Patapsco; and on the eleventh, it made North Point, where, on the following day, under cover of the small vessels, but without opposition, the enemy landed a heavy force, under General Ross.[2] Three days' provisions had been cooked; and these, with eighty rounds of ammunition per man, were given to the soldiers, while every thing which could be spared, was left on shipboard, to render their baggage as light as possible.[3]

In the mean time, the inhabitants of Baltimore and its vicinity had been busily employed in preparing to defend the city; and under General Samuel Smith, of the Maryland militia,—the hero of Fort Mifflin,[1]—and General William H. Winder, of the United States army, and General Stricker, of the militia, about nine thousand men men turned out to oppose the invaders.[2] Vessels were sunk at the entrance of the harbor, near Fort McHenry;[3] extended lines of defence were thrown up, on the route which the enemy had taken;[4] the treasury of the city was thrown open and exhausted, for defensive purposes;[5] and individuals and the banks freely advanced the means required for completing the works.[6] The point selected for the defence of the city was the heights three miles in advance of it, towards the mouth of the Patapsco; and there the entire force of the citizens, and of the volunteers from the surrounding country, together with the regular troops belonging to that district, had assembled.[7]

Anticipating the debarkation of the enemy, before referred to, General Smith had detached General Stricker, on the evening of the eleventh, with a

---

[1] Niles' *Register*, vii. p. 23.—[2] Gen. Smith to Sec. of War, Sept. 19, 1814; Gen. Stricker to Gen. Smith, Sept. 15, 1814; Col. Brook to Earl Bathurst, Sept. 17, 1814; Gleig's Narrative (*Octavo edition*), pp. 163–170.—[3] Gleig, p. 166.

[1] Vide Vol. I., pp. 360–367.—[2] The number behind the works is said to have been 4000; to these add the garrisons, upwards of 1000, and Gen. Stricker's command, and the result will be as stated. Mr. Perkins (*Hist. of War*, p. 338) says they numbered *fifteen thousand* men.

[3] Col. Brook to Earl Bathurst, Sept. 15, 1814; Adm'l Cochrane to the Admiralty, Sept. 17; Griffith's Annals of Baltimore, p. 211.—[4] Col. Brook to Earl Bathurst, Sept. 15; Adm'l Cochrane to the Admiralty, Sept. 17; James' Mil. Occur., ii. p. 311; Niles' *Register*, vii. p. 13.

[5] Griffith's Annals of Baltimore, p. 213.

[6] The loans enabled the Committee of Citizens to expend $79,000 on public account, for defensive purposes.—*Griffith's Annals of Baltimore*, p. 213.—[7] Perkins, p. 338; Griffith's Annals, pp. 210, 211.

portion of his brigade, to observe the enemy's movements on the road leading to North Point;[1] while, at the same time, Major Randal, of the Maryland militia, with a light corps from General Stansbury's brigade and the Pennsylvania Volunteers, was detached to the mouth of Bear Creek, with orders to co-operate with General Stricker, and to check the debarkation, should any be attempted in that vicinity.[2] On the twelfth of September, General Stricker moved down to the meeting-house at the head of Bear Creek, near the junction of the two roads leading from Baltimore to the Point; and at that place prepared to check the advance of the enemy — his right being covered by Bear Creek and his left by a marsh on the margin of a branch of Back River.[3] A detachment of one hundred and forty cavalry, under Lieutenant-colonel Biays, was sent down to Gorsuch's farm, three miles in advance; one hundred and fifty riflemen, under Captain Dyer, were posted at a blacksmith's shop, one mile in the rear of the cavalry; the Fifth regiment (five hundred and fifty men), under Lieutenant-colonel Steret, was posted near the head of Long-log Lane, with its right resting on a branch of Bear Creek, and its left on the main road to the Point; the Twenty-seventh regiment (five hundred men), under Lieutenant-colonel Long, was posted on the left of the Fifth, extending from the road, before alluded to, to the Back River; the "Union Artillery," of Baltimore, seventy-five men, with six four-pounders, under Captain Montgomery, occupied the road, in the centre of the first line. The Thirty-ninth regiment (four hundred and fifty men), under Lieutenant-colonel Fowler, was posted in a line which was parallel with, and three hundred yards in the rear of, the Twenty-seventh; the Fifty-first regiment (seven hundred men), under Lieutenant-colonel Amey, occupied a position on the right of the Thirty-ninth, and three hundred yards in the rear of the Fifth. The Sixth regiment (six hundred and twenty men), under Lieutenant-colonel McDonald, as a reserve, was thrown back to Cook's Tavern, about half a mile in the rear of the second line; and in this position the approach of the enemy was awaited.[1]

The enemy having landed, as before stated, the same arrangements which had been so successfully employed in the former expedition were repeated in this; and with the light companies of the Fourth, Twenty-first, and Forty-fourth regiments, the entire Eighty-fifth regiment, a battalion of "disciplined negroes," and a company of marines (in all about eleven hundred men), commanded by Major Jones, of the Forty-first regiment, in advance; followed by the artillery,—six field-pieces and two howitzers,—drawn by horses; the Second brigade—the Fourth and Forty-fourth regiments (about fourteen hundred and fifty men), under Colonel Brook; a body of upwards of one thousand sailors, under Captain Crofton; and by the Third brigade—the Twenty-first regiment and a battalion of marines (about fourteen hundred and fifty men), under Colonel Patterson, he moved gayly forward on his bootless errand[2]—

[1] Gen. Smith to Sec. of War, Sept. 19, 1814; Gen. Stricker to Gen. Smith, Sept. 15, 1814; Thomson's Sketches, p. 340.—[2] Gen. Smith to Sec. of War, Sept. 19.

[3] Gen. Stricker to Gen. Smith, Sept. 15, 1814; Col. Brook to Earl Bathurst, Sept. 17; Gen. Smith to Sec. of War, Sept. 19.

[1] Gen. Stricker to Gen. Smith, Sept. 15.—[2] Gleig, pp. 92, 164, 170, 171; James' Mil. Occur., ii. pp. 313, 314.

the frigates, sloops, and bomb-ships, meanwhile, having moved forward to force their way through every obstacle, to obtain possession of the navigation of the river, and to co-operate with the army by bombarding the place from the water.[1]

After advancing an hour,[2] the troops halted "that the rear might be well up, and the men fresh and ready for action;" and they "rested," in that position, "for the space of an hour,"[3] although it does not appear how their *fatigue* could have required that delay after so short a march. The light parties of the Americans were soon afterwards encountered; and they appear to have skirmished with his advance, with great spirit,[4] one of the victims of their gallantry being General Ross, the commander of the expedition, who was shot in the side by a rifleman, and died before his bearers could reach the boats at North Point.[5] Under the command of Colonel Brook, of the Forty-fourth regiment, the expedition continued to advance;[6] and the American light parties fell back on the main body—the riflemen and part of the cavalry being ordered to cover the right flank of the first line[7] (*the right of the Fifth regiment*).

Soon after noon, the enemy approached "the well-chosen" position occupied by the American troops;[8] and as the several brigades came up, they filed off to the right and left, and formed, in order of battle, "just within cannon-shot," while the Rocketeers and Artillery opened a brisk fire on the American lines.[1] The First, or Light Brigade, in line, supported by the Forty-fourth, the seamen, and the marines, threatened the entire front of the American position; while the Twenty-first remained in column, as a reserve; and the Fourth, by a detour, moved off to the right, for the purpose of turning the left of the American line; against which, also, the enemy's artillery played vigorously.[2]

Perceiving the purposes of the enemy, General Strickland moved the Thirty-ninth regiment from the rear to the left of the front line, with two field-pieces to cover its left flank; while, as additional security, the Fifty-first was ordered to form, in line, at right angles with the first line, and with its right resting near the left of the Thirty-ninth. Some confusion was created by the execution of the last order; but through the exertions of some of the General's staff, it was overcome, and the order was executed.[3]

During two hours the fire was continued on both sides with spirit and effect.[4] Volley succeeded volley, and shout responded to shout, during that time;[5] and yet, as the enemy himself has admitted, the Americans, inexperienced and undisciplined as they may have been, "maintained themselves with great determination, and stood to receive the fire of the enemy until scarcely twenty yards divided them."[6] At length the

[1] Gleig, p. 166; Adm'l Cockburn to Adm'l Cochrane, Sept. 15, 1814.—[2] Gleig, p. 171.—[3] Ibid., p. 172.

[4] Gen. Smith to Sec. of War, Sept. 19; Gen. Stricker to Gen. Smith, Sept. 15; Col. Brook to Earl Bathurst, Sept. 17; Adm'l Cockburn to Adm'l Cochrane, Sept. 15; Gleig, pp. 172, 173, 175, 176.—[5] Col. Brook to Earl Bathurst, Sept. 17; Adm'l Cochrane to the Admiralty, Sept. 17; Thomson, p. 341; Gleig, pp. 171–175.

[6] Col. Brook to Earl Bathurst, Sept. 17; Adm'l Cochrane to the Admiralty, Sept. 17; James' Mil. Occur., ii. p. 317; Gleig, p. 175.—[7] Gen. Stricker to Gen. Smith, Sept 15; Col. Brook to Earl Bathurst, Sept. 17.

[8] Gen. Smith to Sec. of War, Sept. 19; Gleig, pp. 175, 176.

[1] Gleig, p. 177; Niles' *Register*, vii. p. 23.—[2] Col. Brook to Earl Bathurst, Sept. 17; Gleig, p. 177.—[3] Gen. Stricker to Gen. Smith, Sept. 15; Thomson, p. 341.

[4] Gen. Stricker to Gen. Smith, Sept. 15, 1814; Gleig, pp. 180, 181. Col. Brook calls it a "*short* but brilliant affair," and intimates it lasted only *fifteen minutes*.

[5] Gleig, p. 179.—[6] Ibid., pp. 179, 180.

Fourth (*British*) regiment "began to show itself upon the brink of the water which covered the left flank" of the American line, and made an effort to cross over, when the Fifty-first (*American*) regiment, which had been thrown back at right angles with the first line, for the protection of that flank, suddenly and disgracefully gave way, and in such perfect disorder did it fall back, that no efforts of the officers could rally it.[1] This unaccountable and disastrous defection not only exposed the left of the Thirty-ninth to the assault of the enemy, but it dispirited many of the troops belonging to the latter regiment, and a few gave way;[2] yet the greater part stood firm, and gallantly resisted every effort of the enemy to drive them from their position.[3]

At length, after continuing the action until a quarter before four o'clock, and finding that the greatly superior force of the enemy could no longer be kept in check, General Stricker ordered the line to fall back on the reserve; and, with few exceptions, the order was obeyed with coolness and in good order.[4] Soon afterwards the entire detachment fell back to Worthington's mill;[5] and on the next day (*Tuesday*, *Sept.* 13), the retreat was continued to the main body.[6]

Without continuing the pursuit, with any spirit, beyond the battle-ground, the enemy was, "*of necessity*, content with the success which he had obtained; and having collected the stragglers, and called in the pursuers, it was resolved to pass the night in this situation." The night was a wet and dreary one; and, without any covering, the men bivouacked on the field until morning, when the line of march was resumed; and, soon afterwards, came in sight of the works.[1]

In the mean time, the squadron of frigates, small vessels, and bomb-ketches, under Admiral Cochrane,[2] had moved up the Patapsco, and at nine o'clock in the morning of the twelfth of September, they anchored off Fort McHenry, but beyond the range of its guns—the bomb and rocket vessels anchoring in a position from which they could act on the lines which covered the army, as well as on the fort; while the frigates took their stations outside of all.[3]

At this time Fort McHenry was garrisoned with one company of the Second regiment of United States Artillery, under Captain Evans; two companies of Sea Fencibles, under Captains Bunbury and Addison; the "Washington Artillery," of Baltimore, Captain John Berry; "The Baltimore Independent Artillerists," Captain Charles Pennington; "The Baltimore Fencibles," Captain Josh. H. Nicholson; a detachment of flotilla-men, under Lieutenant Rodman; and detachments from the Twelfth, Fourteenth, Thirty-sixth, and Thirty-eighth regiments of regular troops, under Lieutenant-colonel Stuart and Major Lane—the whole numbering about one thousand effective men, commanded by Lieutenant-colonel Armistead, of the United States Artillery.

---

1 Gen. Stricker to Gen. Smith, Sept. 15, 1814; Gen. Smith to Sec. of War, Sept. 19; Gleig, p. 180; Thomson, pp. 341, 342.—2 Gen. Stricker to Gen. Smith, Sept. 15; Gen. Smith to Sec. of War, Sept. 19; Thomson, p. 342.

3 Gen. Smith to Sec. of War, Sept. 19; Thomson, p. 342.

4 Gen. Stricker to Gen. Smith, Sept. 15; Gen. Smith to Sec. of War, Sept. 19; Niles' *Register*, vii. p. 24.

5 Gen. Stricker to Gen. Smith, Sept. 15; Perkins, p. 339.

6 Gen. Smith to Sec. of War, Sept. 19; Thomson, p. 342.

1 Col. Brook to Earl Bathurst, Sept. 15; Adm'l Cockburn to Adm'l Cochrane, Sept. 15; Gleig, pp. 182, 185–187.—2 Adm'l Cochrane to the Admiralty, Sept. 17.

3 Gen. Smith to Sec. of War, Sept. 19; Lieut.-Col. Armistead to same, Sept. 24, 1814; James' Mil. Occur., ii. p. 322; Niles' *Register*, vii. pp. 23, 24.

Fort Covington was manned with a party of sailors, under Lieutenant Newcomb, of the Navy; and the six-gun battery was manned with flotilla-men, under Lieutenant Webster, of that service.[1]

At an early hour on the thirteenth, a heavy fire was opened on Fort McHenry, the Star-fort, and the water-batteries, which was promptly and steadily returned, notwithstanding the range of the enemy's guns was still greater than those on the works, and prevented the latter from being as effective as they would otherwise have been.[2] At about three in the afternoon, tired of the useless employment on which they had been engaged, Admiral Cochrane ordered the bomb and rocket vessels to weigh anchor and stand in nearer to the fort; when an opportunity was afforded to the garrison to prove its character and abilities, as well as its bravery.[3] The result of the temerity of these vessels was soon apparent in their precipitate return to their former anchorage, half an hour afterwards;[4] while the *Erebus*, rocket-ship, was so much injured that the Admiral was obliged to send a division of boats to tow her beyond the range of the fire of the Fort.[5] After resuming their former stations, the vessels bombarded the works more vigorously than ever, until the morning of the fourteenth, when they retired, with the army with which it had been intended they should co-operate.[6]

While the squadron was thus busily employed in bombarding the works at the entrance of the harbor, the enemy moved cautiously and slowly forward until he came within sight of the American lines, when he halted to reconnoitre.[1] He appears, *then*, for the first time, to have entertained doubts of his ability to accomplish what he had undertaken; and he wisely sought the counsel of the Admiral, who, as has been seen, had learned, before the works at the entrance of the harbor, that it was "impracticable to afford any essential cooperation to the army by sea."[2] The latter, as the result of his observation, informed Colonel Brook—who had become the commander of the land-forces, by the death of General Ross—that he "considered that an attack on the enemy's (*American's*) strong position by the army only, with such disparity of force, *though confident of success*, might risk a greater loss than *the possession of the town would compensate for*, while holding in view the ulterior operations of this force in the contemplation of His Majesty's government," and he advised, and Colonel Brook approved, with the advice of a council of officers,[3] an immediate withdrawal of the united forces from before the works, and their return to the fleet.[4]

"Accordingly," in the words of an English officer, who was present, "about three hours after midnight, the troops were formed upon the road, and began

[1] Lieut.-Col. Armistead to Sec. of War, Sept. 24; Thomson's Sketches, p. 339.—[2] Gen. Smith to Sec. of War, Sept. 19; Adm'l Cochrane to the Admiralty, Sept. 17; Lieut.-Col. Armistead to Sec. of War, Sept. 24; James' Mil. Occur., ii. p. 322.—[3] Gen. Smith to Sec. of War, Sept. 19; Lieut.-Col. Armistead to same, Sept. 24; James' Mil. Occur., ii. pp. 322, 323; Perkins, p. 340.—[4] Gen. Smith to Sec. of War, Sept. 19; Lieut.-Col. Armistead to same, Sept. 24; James' Mil. Occur., ii. p. 323.—[5] James' Mil. Occur., ii. p. 323.

[6] Gen. Smith to Sec. of War, Sept. 19; Lieut.-Col. Armistead to same, Sept. 24; James' Military Occurrences, ii. pp. 323, 324.

[1] Gen. Smith to Sec. of War, Sept. 19; Col. Brook to Earl Bathurst, Sept. 15; Adm'l Cockburn to Adm'l Cochrane, Sept. 15; Gleig, pp. 186–188.—[2] Col. Brook to Earl Bathurst, Sept. 17; Adm'l Cochrane to the Admiralty, Sept. 17; James' Mil. Occur, ii. pp. 325, 326.

[3] Gleig, p. 192.—[4] Col. Brook to Earl Bathurst, Sept. 17; Adm'l Cochrane to the Admiralty, Sept. 17; James' Military Occurrences, ii. p. 326.

their retreat, leaving the pickets to *deceive the enemy* (*Americans*), and to follow as a rear-guard;"[1] and in this important movement—although it does not appear why this great caution was necessary, if the Admiral's opinion of the relative strength of the two armies was correct—the enemy appears to have been exceedingly successful, as "he was so favored by the extreme darkness and a continued rain, that the Americans did not discover the movement *until* daylight,"[2] when all attempts at pursuit were unavailing, and he gained his shipping during the same day and the succeeding morning.[3]

In the action at the Long-log Lane,—or, as it is sometimes called, at North Point,—General Stricker's original force was three thousand one hundred and eighty-five men;[4] but as the Fifty-first regiment (*seven hundred men*), and part of the Second battalion of the Thirty-ninth regiment, had run away, and the reserve—the Sixth regiment (*six hundred and twenty men*), with three companies from the Fifth regiment (*Captains Levering's, Howard's, and Sadtler's*), and Captain Aisquith's company of riflemen, which had been sent forward to check the enemy, and had

[1] Gleig, p. 193. See also Thomson, p. 343; Perkins, p. 339.—[2] Gen. Smith to Sec. of War, Sept. 19; Thomson, p. 343; Armstrong, ii. p. 136.

[3] Gen. Smith to Sec. of War, Sept. 19; James' Military Occurrences, ii. p. 326; Gleig, pp. 195, 196.

[4] Gen. Stricker to Gen. Smith, Sept. 15; Niles' *Register*, vii. p. 23.

fallen into the rear of the lines, for temporary repose, as they came up—had not been brought into the action, the force actually engaged, on the American lines, was only about fourteen hundred men;[1] while that of the enemy was not less than "five thousand fighting men,"[2] exclusive of officers, artillery drivers, and others of a similar character. The loss of the former was twenty-four *killed*, one hundred and thirty-nine *wounded*, and fifty *prisoners*, with two field-pieces;[3] that of the latter was was General Ross, Lieutenant Gracie, and thirty-seven men *killed*, and eleven officers and two hundred and forty men *wounded*.[4]

In the attack on the forts by the squadron, the relative strength of the assailants and the garrisons—although the former was much greater, numerically, than the latter—is not known. The loss of the former was Lieutenant Claggett and three men *killed*, and twenty-four men *wounded*;[5] while the enemy reports no loss, either of life or limb.

[1] Gen. Stricker to Gen. Smith, Sept. 15.

[2] Gleig, p. 164. That the statement of Lieut. Gleig is not far from the truth may be seen from the statements of the strength of the enemy during his attack on the troops at Bladensburg:—First brigade, 1100 men; Second brigade, 1460 men; Third brigade, 1460 men; artillerists and drivers, 200 men = 4220 men. To these add 1000 seamen, under Capt. Edward Crofton, and deduct those disabled at Bladensburg,—64 *killed* and 185 *wounded*,—the result will show "*about five thousand fighting men.*"

[3] Report, signed "L. FRAILEY, *late Brigade-major*."

[4] Report, signed "HENRY DEBBEIG, *Major*," appended to Col. Brook's Dispatch.

[5] Lieut.-Col. Armistead to Sec. of War, Sept. 24.

CHAPTER XCI.

September 26 and 27, 1814.

THE LOSS OF THE PRIVATEER GENERAL ARMSTRONG.

Reference has been made, in former chapters of this work, to the enterprise and gallantry of the privateer service; and the exploits of the brig *General Armstrong*, of New York, have been made the subject of a chapter.[1]

After several successful cruises, the *General Armstrong*, commanded, at that time, by Captain Samuel C. Reid, left New York early in September, 1814; and on the twenty-sixth of the same month she anchored in the harbor of Fayal, one of the Azores or Western Islands, belonging to the King of Portugal. In the evening of the same day, a squadron of British vessels of war—the *Plantagenet*, of seventy-four guns; the *Rota*, of forty-four guns; and the *Carnation*, of eighteen guns—anchored in the same port; and it appears that hostile intentions were manifested, as Captain Reid entertained doubts of his safety, and, after having cleared for action, he determined to haul in nearer the shore.[2]

When the design of Captain Reid was noticed the *Carnation* cut her cable, made sail, and dispatched four boats in pursuit of the *Armstrong;* when the latter anchored, with springs on her cables, and prepared to receive them. The moon shone brightly; and as the boats approached, they were hailed, but gave no answer; and, as they dashed forward with greater speed, they were soon "cleverly alongside" the little brig. At that moment the guns of the *Armstrong* opened their fire, which was immediately returned, and a short conflict ensued, which resulted in the repulse of the assailants, with a heavy loss—the brig, at the same time, losing one man (*Burton Loyd*) *killed*, and her first-lieutenant (*Frederick A. Worth*) *wounded*.[1]

The boats having returned to the ships, the *Armstrong* immediately hauled in close to the beach, and moored head and stern within half pistol-shot from the castle; and again prepared for action. At nine o'clock, the same evening, the *Carnation* weighed, and stood in towards the privateer, towing the boats of the squadron; and after some time spent in manœuvring, at about midnight, the latter moved to the attack in one direct line, in close order—twelve boats being distinctly visible. As soon as they had come within proper distance, the *Armstrong* opened her fire, a second time, which was promptly returned by the enemy, both with his small-arms and his carronades. Although the privateer's long gun appeared to stagger them, the assailants moved forward with great gallantry, cheering as they advanced; and they soon reached the bows and starboard quarter of the brig, when orders were given to "board." From that moment the conflict became close and desperate. Relying, altogether, on their small-arms,

[1] Vide Chap. XLII.—[2] Capt. Reid's Letter, Oct. 4, 1814; Memorial of Jenkins and Havens, presented to the Senate, Jan. 23, 1817; Consul Dabney to Sec. of State, Oct. 5, 1814.

[1] Capt. Reid's Letter, Oct. 4, 1814; Jenkins and Haven's Memorial; Protest of the *General Armstrong's* officers, Sept. 27, 1814.

pikes, and cutlasses, the crew met the assailants wherever they showed themselves; and, with the greatest resolution, the latter were kept from the deck of the brig. At length, after sustaining a conflict of about forty minutes, and suffering a very heavy loss, both of boats and men, the enemy again retired, leaving two of the *Rota's* boats in the hands of the privateer's crew. In this second attack the *Armstrong* suffered considerably, several of her carriages being broken, her "long Tom" dismounted, and some of her crew having left the vessel. No time was lost, however, in preparing the brig for still farther resistance, should any be offered; and, although the second-lieutenant (*Alexander O. Williams*) had been killed, and the third-lieutenant (*Robert Johnson*) wounded, in the last attack, there appeared to be no hesitation among the crew in its devotion to the vessel.[1]

During the night Captain Reid received a letter from J. B. Dabney, Esq., consul of the United States at Fayal, informing him that although the Portuguese authorities had remonstrated against a repetition of the assault, the enemy had sent for answer that he was determined to seize the privateer at every hazard; and, considering the safety of the brig as no longer certain, the Captain returned and ordered the wounded and dead, together with the effects of the crew, to be taken ashore, without farther delay. While thus engaged, at about daylight, the *Carnation* stood close in, and opened her fire on the devoted brig; yet the crew of the latter, with a degree of courage which contrasts finely with the timidity displayed by the enemy, returned it with spirit and steadiness—cutting up the rigging of the *Carnation*, wounding her fore-topmast, hulling her, and finally, compelling her to withdraw for repairs.[1]

Soon afterwards the enemy returned, and anchored close to the privateer, with the evident intention of attempting to crush the latter by mere weight of metal; and Captain Reid, considering farther resistance useless, scuttled her, and with his crew, went ashore. The enemy immediately sent his boats on board of the sinking vessel and set her on fire; and, by the combined efforts of the enemy, the flames, and the waters of the harbor, the *General Armstrong* soon afterwards ceased to exist.[2]

As the reader will recollect, the privateer was a brig of two hundred and forty-six tons, mounting seven guns, with a crew of ninety men.[3] Her loss was one officer and one man *killed*, and three officers and four men *wounded*.[4] The strength of the enemy has been already noticed; his loss was said to have been one hundred and twenty killed, and one hundred and thirty wounded, besides the boats which were lost.[5]

---

1 Capt. Reid's Letter, Oct. 4, 1814; Jenkins and Haven's Memorial; Consul Dabney to Secretary of State, Oct. 5, 1814.

1 Capt. Reid's Letter, Oct. 4, 1814; Jenkins and Haven's Memorial; Letter to Wm. Cobbett, signed H. R. F., Fayal, Oct. 15, 1814.—2 Capt. Reid's Letter, Oct. 4, 1814; Jenkins and Haven's Memorial; Consul Dabney's Letter, Oct. 5, 1814.—3 Report of Naval Committee of House of Representatives, March 4, 1818.—4 Capt. Reid's Letter, Oct. 4, 1814; Consul Dabney to Secretary of State, Oct. 5, 1814; Protest of officers, &c., Sept. 27, 1814.

5 Capt. Reid's Letter, Oct. 4, 1814; Jenkins and Haven's Memorial; Naval Committee's Report, March 4, 1818; Consul Dabney's Letter, Oct. 5, 1814.

CHAPTER XCII.

October 19, 1814.

THE ACTION AT LYONS' CREEK, U. C.

THE movement of General Izard, with the right division of the army, from Plattsburg to the Niagara frontier, has been noticed in a preceding chapter of this work;[1] and, on his arrival at that part of the frontiers, he superseded General Brown in the command of the army.[2]

Soon after his arrival at Fort Erie, information was received that a heavy supply of stores had been collected near Cook's Mills, on a branch of the Chippewa named Lyons' Creek; and, on the eighteenth of October, he detached General Bissell, with nine hundred men from his brigade, a company of riflemen under Captain Irvine, and a party of dragoons, under Lieutenant Anspaugh,[3] with orders to seize and destroy them.[4]

The detachment encountered many obstructions on its march, and reached the Mill only in season to encamp for the night, after having driven a picket of regular troops and one of militia from the post, the latter with the loss of its commander. To insure his own safety, General Bissell threw out a picket of two select companies, under Captain Dorman and Lieutenant Horrel, and the riflemen under Captain Irvine, on the opposite side of the creek; while still more advanced, on the Chippewa road, Lieutenant Gassaway was posted with a small party.

During the night, this picket was attacked by a detachment of Glengarry Light Infantry, which was repulsed with the loss of one man only; and, on the following morning (*Oct.* 19, 1814), the attack was renewed by Colonel Murray,[1] with a select body of troops, embracing detachments from the Eighty-second, Eighty-seventh, One Hundredth, and One Hundred and fourth regiments of the line, and the Glengarry Light Infantry, a small party of dragoons, one of rocketeers, and one field-piece.[2] The picket gallantly maintained its ground against this overwhelming force, without faltering, upwards of fifteen minutes; when the main body, which had formed, and been brought to its support, joined in the engagement.

The detachment from the Fifth regiment, under Colonel Pinckney, by a detour, moved against the enemy's right flank, and threatened his field-piece; while the Fourteenth, under Major Bernard, moved against his front, and supported the light troops; and the Fifteenth and Sixteenth were held in reserve in the rear. When the Fifth

---

[1] Vide Chap. LXXXIX.—[2] Thomson's Sketches, p. 328.

[3] The language of Gen. Bissell has been strangely perverted by many authors, in speaking of the strength of the detachment. The greater part consider 900 men embraced the *entire detachment*, while the General expressly refers to the dragoons and riflemen, in addition to that number of infantry. On the other hand, Mr. Ingersoll (*Hist. of War*, iv. p. 154) supposes the 5th, 14th, 15th, and 16th regiments, together with the riflemen and the dragoons, were *in addition to the nine hundred;* instead of being the parties which, united, formed that aggregate.

[4] General Orders, Oct. 23, 1814.

[1] James' Mil. Occur., ii. p. 239; Auchinleck, p. 339. Gen. Bissell, in his Report, and others, after him, have supposed the Marquis of Tweedale commanded; but it appears he was still an invalid at Kingston.

[2] Mr. James (*Mil. Occur.*, ii. p. 238), by implication, denies that the 87th and 104th, the dragoons, rocketeers, or field-piece, was present.

had turned his flank, the light companies and riflemen poured in a deadly fire, which was followed up with a charge by the Fourteenth, when the enemy fell back in great confusion, leaving behind him his killed, many of his wounded, and some prisoners.

The Americans pursued the fugitives some distance; and the latter continued their flight to Chippewa, while the former destroyed some two hundred bushels of wheat which were found at the Mill—a sorry reward for so severe a struggle.

The loss of the Americans was twelve men *killed*, five officers and forty-nine men *wounded*, and one man taken:[1] the enemy reports his loss at nineteen *killed* and *wounded*,[2] while the Americans claim that he lost near two hundred killed, wounded, and prisoners.[3]

[Note.—This chapter has been based on General Bishop's Report to General Izard, October 22, 1814, and on General Izard's "General Orders," October 23, 1814; and where no other reference is given, these have been my only authorities.]

CHAPTER XCIII.

December 10, 1814, to January 18, 1815.

THE INVASION OF LOUISIANA.

The plan of the campaign of 1814 (as displayed by the enemy in his official communication with the Secretary of State,[1] in his systematic plunder of farm-houses and sacking of villages,[2] in his robbery of tobacco-warehouses,[3] and in his carrying off, to a West India market, of the slaves of the planters[4]) was extended as the winter approached; and the conquest of the queen city of the Southwest, the value of her well-filled warehouses,—groaning under the weight of three unsold annual crops,[5]—and the agreeable climate which it offered, during the winter season, appeared to invite him to that quarter as a proper scene for his next adventure.

In the prosecution of this plan the enemy had endeavored to foment another Indian war in the Southwest; and, by his emissaries, had made Pensacola the centre of his operations—hoping thereby to divert the attention of the Georgians, the Mississippians, the Tennesseeans, and the Kentuckians, whose rifles he so much dreaded.[4] He had also sent a heavy force against Fort Bowyer, near the entrance to the harbor of Mobile;[5] and he had opened negotiations with Lafitte, the head of a gang of smugglers, who had infested the Gulf of Mexico, for the services of his band of outlaws as guides and auxiliaries.[6] The first of these designs, by

[1] Returns appended to Gen. Bissell's Dispatch, Oct. 22, 1804.—[2] James' Military Occurrences, ii. p. 239; Auchinleck, p. 339.—[3] Sketches of the War, p. 385.

[1] Adm'l Cochrane to Mr. Madison, Aug. 18, 1814.
[2] Vide Chaps. XLVI., LV., LXX., LXXXVII.
[3] The robbery of tobacco-warehouses was the principal source of the enemy's gain in prize-money.—[4] Niles' *Register*, vii. p. 54.—[5] James' Mil. Occur., ii. p. 340; Latour's War in Florida and Louisiana, p. 9; Auchinleck, p. 387.

[4] Proclamation of Lieut.-Col Nicholls, Pensacola, Aug. 29, 1814; Gen. Jackson to Gov. Claiborne, July 20, 1814; Armstrong's Notices, ii. pp. 156, 159–162; Latour, p. 11.
[5] Armstrong's Notices, ii. pp. 157, 158; Auchinleck, pp. 387, 388; Sketches of War, p. 451.—[6] Lieut.-Col. Nicholls and Capt. Percy, R. N., to Mr. Lafitte, Aug. 31, 1814, and his subsequent correspondence with them; James' Mil. Occur., ii. p. 341; Latour, pp. 11-25.

the prompt, but illegal, movement of General Jackson, had been frustrated, and Pensacola itself was garrisoned with American troops.[1] The second design, by the gallantry of the little garrison who occupied the fort, had also failed; and discomfited, and with the loss of one of his ships, he had retired from before it.[2] The third resulted even more disastrously than the others, as the smugglers not only did not fulfil their engagements with the invader, but his entire plan of operations, and all his correspondence with them, were regularly and promptly submitted to the authorities of Louisiana, and the latter were thereby enabled to act with greater certainty for his overthrow.[3]

At length, on the second of December, 1814, General Jackson reached New Orleans, and measures were immediately taken for its defence. The military companies were reviewed and inspected; a committee of the Legislature appointed to provide for the safety of the State, but wholly inactive before his arrival, now showed signs of life and vigor; disputes between different factions were quieted; the works of defence were examined and repaired, and others were erected where they were found necessary; and in the minds of the people despondency gave way to confidence, and determination succeeded despair.[4]

At daybreak, on the tenth of December, the enemy's fleet was discovered at

[1] James' Mil. Occur., ii. pp. 345, 346; Latour, pp. 44–51; Sketches of the War, pp. 452–454; Claiborne's Notes, pp. 52, 53.—[2] James' Mil. Occur., ii. pp. 342–345; Latour, pp. 30–44; Armstrong, ii. pp. 157, 158; Auchinleck, p. 388; Claiborne's Notes, pp. 50, 51.—[3] Mr. Lafitte to Mr. Blanque, Sept. 4 and 7; Same to Gov. Claiborne (no date); Latour, pp. 11–25; James' Mil. Occur., ii. p. 341.

[4] Latour, pp. 52–57; Perkins, pp. 409, 410; Eaton's Jackson, pp. 260–275.

anchor in the channel between Cat and Ship Islands, near the entrance to Lake Borgne; and its strength gradually increased until the thirteenth, when it numbered not less than sixty sail.[1] The approach of this force had been communicated, anonymously, from Pensacola, to Commander Patterson, the naval commandant on that station, a few days previous to its arrival;[2] and he had dispatched five gunboats, a tender, and a dispatch-boat, under Lieutenant Thomas Ap Catesby Jones, to the Mariana and Christiana passes, with instructions to observe the enemy's movements; to advise him (*the Commander*), as frequently as possible, of the progress and purposes of the enemy; and, if necessary, to fall back and to check his advance as much as possible.[3]

On the twelfth of December the enemy's strength, off Ship Island, had been increased so much that it was no longer safe or prudent for the gunboats to continue in that part of the lake; and, in the afternoon of the thirteenth, Lieutenant Jones fell back to a position near the Malheureux Islands, where he awaited the pleasure of the enemy—the schooner *Seahorse*, and a quantity of stores which had been collected in the Bay of St. Louis, having been destroyed, to prevent the enemy from seizing them.[4]

In the mean time, on the morning of the thirteenth, a flotilla of forty-two heavy launches and gun-barges, and three gigs, mounting forty-three heavy guns, and manned with twelve hundred

[1] Thomson's Sketches, p. 347; Capt. Cooke's Narrative (London, 1835), p. 178; Niles' *Register*, vii. p. 279.

[2] "N****" to Com. Patterson, Pensacola, Dec. 5, 1814; James' Mil. Occur., ii. p. 347.—[3] Latour, pp. 57, 58; Ingersoll, iii. p. 112.—[4] Lieut. Jones to Com. Patterson, March 12, 1815; Latour, p. 59.

men,[1] under Captain Lockyer, of the *Sophia*, left the enemy's fleet, and, by way of the Christiana Pass, entered the lake in pursuit of the gunboats. On his way the enemy pursued and captured the *Alligator*, the tender before referred to; and at about ten in the morning of the fourteenth, he came to a grapnel, and took his breakfast. Immediately afterwards, in three columns, commanded by Captains Lockyer, Montresor, of the *Manley*, and Roberts, of the *Meteor*, he weighed, and again started in the pursuit.[2]

As there was but little wind, and a strong ebb-tide setting through the pass, it was not possible for Lieutenant Jones to retire through the channel; and he determined to put himself in the most advantageous position, and to give the enemy as warm a reception as possible. The commanders of the several boats were ordered on board *Number One hundred and fifty-six*, the flag-boat of the squadron, to receive their orders; and the whole were anchored, by their sterns, in a close line, abreast, across the channel and in front of the passage, a low marsh covered with reeds, flanking the line on either hand. The flag-boat, *Number One hundred and fifty-six*, mounting five guns, with forty-one men, was in the centre; and *Number Five*, Sailing-master Ferris, mounting five guns, with thirty-five men, *Number Twenty-three*, Lieutenant McKeever, mounting five guns, with thirty-nine men, *Number One hundred and sixty-two*, Lieutenant Spedden, mounting five guns, with thirty-five men, and *Number One hundred and sixty-three*, Sailing-master Ulrick, mounting three guns, with thirty-one men, were formed on either hand; while the dispatch-boat laid astern.[1]

At half-past ten, as before stated, the enemy weighed, and rowed towards the American line, from which a heavy and destructive fire was opened as he approached. At ten minutes before eleven Captain Lockyer, in the *Seahorse's* barge, aided by her first barge and by the boats of the *Tonnant*, attacked the flag-boat (*Number One hundred and fifty-six*), while the greater part of the enemy's flotilla appears to have concentrated its efforts on *Numbers One hundred and sixty-two* and *One hundred and sixty-three.* The crew of the flag-boat fought manfully, and succeeded in repulsing their assailants with heavy loss; while their associates, under Lieutenant Spedden and Master Ulrick, resisted the enemy with great determination. Immediately afterwards, the enemy's flag-officer returned to the attack on *Number One hundred and fifty-six* with a reinforcement; and Lieutenant Jones, badly wounded, was driven from the deck. Master's-mate Parker having assumed the command, the defence was continued with great gallantry until he, too, was wounded, and compelled to retire; and soon afterwards, at ten minutes past twelve o'clock, the enemy, by force of numbers, gained the deck and overpowered the crew, turning the guns of the prize on her consorts, who were still battling with the enemy. *Numbers One hundred and sixty-two* and *One hundred and sixty-three* were the next

[1] Statement of the British forces, appended to Lieut. Jones' Dispatch, March 12, 1815; Ingersoll, iii. p. 113.

[2] Lieut. Jones to Com. Patterson, March 12, 1815; Capt. Lockyer to Adm'l Cochrane, Dec. 18, 1814; Latour, pp. 60, 61; Naval Chronicle, xxxiii. p. 485.

[1] Lieut. Jones to Com. Patterson, March 12, 1815; Map IV., in Latour's Atlas. Capt. Lockyer, in his Report, makes the American flotilla much stronger, both in guns and men.

to surrender, but only after a most desperate struggle; and the fire of the three prizes, in support of the enemy's flotilla, was then turned on *Numbers Five* and *Twenty-three*, which were still engaged. The overwhelming force of the enemy, aided by the captured gunboats, could not be effectually resisted, any length of time, and at about half-past twelve the flag of *Number Twenty-three*—the last of the squadron—was lowered.[1]

The strength of the opposing flotilla has been already noticed; the loss of the Americans was six *killed* and thirty-five *wounded*;[2] that of the enemy has been variously stated at from ninety-four killed and wounded[3] to four hundred;[4] the probability being that it was about three hundred.

The conduct of the young commandant, and his officers and crews, in this gallant opposition, has been hailed as a triumph throughout the entire country; and, in the service, even a participation in this *defeat* has always secured as much credit as that of a signal victory.

The intelligence of this affair, and of the approach of the enemy, soon reached General Jackson; and he immediately detached the battalion of free "men of color," commanded by Major Lacoste, and the Feliciana dragoons, with two field-pieces, to the confluence of the Bayou Sauvage and the river of Chef-Menteur, with orders to throw up a close redoubt, surrounded with a fosse, to cover the road to the city on that side, and to watch the movements of the enemy.[1]

As it was not known what the enemy intended to do, it became necessary to protect every assailable point; and the General and the people acted with promptitude and perseverance in the emergency which had arisen. Captain Newman, who commanded the fort of Petites Coquilles, at the entrance of Lake Pontchartrain, was positively ordered to defend his post to the last extremity, and, if compelled to do so, to spike his guns, blow up his magazine, and fall back on the Chef-Menteur, where Major Lacoste had been posted:[2] Captain P. Jugeaut was authorized to organize the Choctaw Indians for actual service: General Coffee, with his Tennessee riflemen, then near Baton Rouge, General Carroll, also from Tennessee, with his command, and General Thomas, with the Kentucky Volunteers, then on their way towards New Orleans, were advised of the loss of the gunboats, and urged to hasten forward:[3] General Winchester, commanding at Mobile, was directed to exercise every precaution in the defence of that place:[4] the Federal authorities were urged to send forward arms and supplies, which had been ordered months before:[5] a second battalion of free men of color was organized, under Major Daquin:[6] the armed vessels, then in the Mississippi, were got ready for service, and an embargo for three days was laid by the Legislature, in order that crews might be obtained for them:[7] all kinds of stock, provisions, horses, &c., were removed from the plan-

---

[1] Lieut. Jones to Com. Patterson, March 12, 1815; Capt. Lockyer to Adm'l Cochrane, Dec. 18, 1814; Latour, p. 61; Cooper, ii. pp. 143, 144; James' Naval Occurrences, p 388.—[2] Latour, pp. 60, 61.

[3] Returns appended to Capt. Lockyer's Dispatch, Dec. 18, 1814.—[4] Niles' *Register*, vii. p. 280.

[1] Latour, p. 64; Brackenridge, pp. 339.—[2] Latour, pp. 64, 65; Eaton's Jackson, pp. 284, 285.—[3] Ingersoll, iii. p. 114; Latour, p. 65.—[4] Latour, p. 65; Eaton's Jackson, pp. 282, 283.—[5] Latour, p. 65.—[6] Ibid., pp. 66, 67; Brackenridge, p. 339.—[7] Ingersoll, iii. p. 119.

Painted by Chappel. Engraved by Phillibrown.

Andrew Jackson

tations in front of the city:[1] the outposts were strengthened:[2] the public prisoners, in many instances, were liberated from confinement, on the promise to assist in the defence of the city:[3] and, finally, on the fifteenth of December, martial-law was proclaimed by the commanding General.[4] With this event, new life was imparted to the operations; and the entire people moved and acted as with one mind. The guard of the city was intrusted to the corps of veterans and the firemen;[5] the smugglers of Barataria, under Captain Lafitte, were received into the service of the government, and their offences forgiven—part of them under Captains Dominique and Beluche, serving in the lines, as will, hereafter, be noticed; and others, under Captains Songis, Lagaud, and Colson, serving with equal honor in the Forts Petites Coquilles, and St. Philip, and at the Bayou St. John.[6]

The situation of affairs, within the city, at this time, has been very graphically described by a distinguished officer who was present; and the reader will learn from him, more readily than from me, the character and sentiments of those among whom the enemy was seeking to thrust himself: "All classes of society," he says, "were now animated with the most ardent zeal. The young, the old, men, women, and children, all breathed defiance to the enemy, firmly resolved to oppose, to the utmost, the threatened invasion. General Jackson had electrified all hearts; all were sensible of the approaching danger; but they waited its presence undismayed. They knew that, in a few days, they must come to action with the enemy, yet, calm and unalarmed, they pursued their usual occupations, interrupted only when they tranquilly left their homes to perform military duty at the posts assigned to them. It was known that the enemy was on our coast, within a few hours' sail of the city, with a presumed force of between nine and ten thousand men; while all the forces we had to oppose him amounted to no more than one thousand regulars, and from four to five thousand militia.

"These circumstances were publicly known, nor could any one disguise to himself, or to others, the dangers with which we were then threatened. Yet, such was the universal confidence, inspired by the activity and decision of the commander-in-chief, added to the detestation in which the enemy was held, and the desire to punish his audacity, should he presume to land, that not a single warehouse or shop was shut, nor were any goods or valuable effects removed from the city. At that period New Orleans presented a very affecting picture to the eyes of the patriot, and of all those whose bosoms glow with the feelings of national honor, which raise the mind far above the vulgar apprehension of personal danger. The citizens were preparing for battle as cheerfully as if it had been a party of pleasure, each in his vernacular tongue singing songs of victory. The streets resounded with *Yankee Doodle*, the *Marseilles Hymn*, the *Chant du Départ*, and other martial airs, while those who had been long unaccustomed to military duty, were furbishing their arms and accoutrements. Beauty applauded valor, and promised, with her

[1] General Order, Dec. 18.—[2] Ingersoll, iii. p. 114; Latour, p. 69.—[3] Latour, pp. 69, 70; Brackenridge, p. 339.
[4] General Orders, Dec. 16, 1814; Claiborne's Notes, p. 55; Latour, pp 70, 71.—[5] Ingersoll, iii p. 124; Latour, p. 71.—[6] Ingersoll, iii. pp. 121, 124; Latour, pp. 71, 72.

smiles, to reward the toils of the brave. Though inhabiting an open town, not above ten leagues from the enemy, and never, until now, exposed to war's alarms, the fair sex of New Orleans were animated with the ardor of their defenders, and with cheerful serenity, at the sound of the drum, presented themselves at the windows and balconies, to applaud the troops going through their evolutions, and to encourage their husbands, sons, fathers, and brothers, to protect them from the insults of our ferocious enemies, and prevent a repetition of the horrors of Hampton."[1]

Among other means of defence which were adopted by General Jackson, was the obstruction of the many bayous and canals which furnished facilities for approaching the city from Lakes Borgne and Pontchartrain;[2] yet, strange as it may appear, one of the most important of these, the Bayou Bienvenu, and its principal branch, the Bayou Mazant, were left unobstructed;[3] and, by an equally strange coincidence, a picket, which had been posted near the mouth of the former, was surprised by the enemy when he moved against the city.[4] When it is considered that as early as the eighteenth of December, the enemy had reconnoitred this passage, and satisfied himself that, by water-carriage, through these bayous, and the canals on Laronde's, Lacoste's, and Villère's plantations, which communicated with them, a perfect line of communication could be obtained to the Mississippi, in front of the city;[5] that a settlement of Spanish fishermen, near the mouth of the Bienvenu, had furnished him with a body of most competent guides;[1] and that the loss of the gunboats had secured the approach of the enemy, without hazard of discovery, the mystery of the oversight through which this passage was left open to the enemy will be perceived and understood.

At length, on the morning of the twenty-second of December, the First, and part of the Second, division of the enemy's force were transferred to boats and small vessels, and moved towards the city.[2] The light brigade—embracing the Fourth, Eighty-fifth, and Ninety-fifth regiments of infantry, a detachment of rocketeers, and two three-pounders, about eighteen hundred rank and file[3]—was the division which thus led the column; and after a most uncomfortable trip from the Isle of Peas,—where the enemy's land-forces had rendezvoused,[4]—the American outpost, which had been stationed at the mouth of the Bayou Bienvenu, was surprised while *sleeping in a fisherman's hut*, and the landing was effected.[5] The scene, at this unfrequented spot, surrounded by marshes, and without a sign of life, was new to the half-frozen soldiers who had been left at the landing; yet it was well adapted to the secret service on which the brigade had been detached; and the urgency of the deserters who had accompanied the brigade, their as-

[1] Latour, pp. 72, 73.—[2] Eaton's Jackson, pp. 295, 306; Latour, pp. 77, 78.—[3] Eaton's Jackson, p. 306; McAfee, p. 509.—[4] Latour, pp. 77, 78, 82–85; Ingersoll, iii. pp. 131, 132; Capt. Cooke's Narrative, p. 183; Gleig's Narrative, pp. 273, 274.—[5] Gen. Keane to Gen. Packenham, Dec. 26, 1814; James' Mil. Occur., ii. p. 358.

[1] Latour, pp. 82, 83; Ingersoll, iii. p. 132.

[2] Adm'l Cochrane to the Admiralty, Jan. 18, 1815; Naval Chronicle (*London*, 1815), xxxiii. p. 485.

[3] Gen. Keane to Gen. Packenham, Dec. 26, 1814; Adm'l Cochrane to the Admiralty, Jan. 18, 1815; Latour, p. 86; James' Mil. Occur., ii. p. 355.—[4] Gen. Keane to Gen. Packenham, Dec. 26, 1814; Letter from an officer, Jan. 30, 1815, in *Naval Chronicle*, xxxiii. p. 386.

[5] Gen. Jackson to Sec. of War, Dec. 27; Adm'l Cochrane to the Admiralty, Jan. 18, 1815; Latour, pp. 84, 85; Gleig, pp. 273, 274.

surance of the weakness of the city and of the disaffection of the masses of the people, and their statements of the want of preparation for defence, induced Colonel Thornton, who commanded the brigade, and General Keane, who accompanied it, to advance through the swamps towards the city.[1] Under the guidance of these deserters, or of the recreant fishermen, therefore, on the morning of the twenty-fourth, the enemy moved forward, and occupied a position, on the plantations of MM. Villère, Lacoste, and Jumonville, on the eastern bank of the Mississippi,[2] capturing a company of militia which had been posted there.[3]

Not a soul was to be seen in any direction, and it appeared that the deserters had spoken truly, when they said the country offered no adequate means of defence. After obtaining as good a position as the level country afforded, however, the enemy halted, and awaited the arrival of the remainder of the forces.[4] It was about noon when the weary advance threw itself on the grass, near the levee; or wandered through the neighboring plantations, in quest of "hams, fowls, and wines of various descriptions," with which to satiate its hunger; or refreshed itself by bathing in the waters of the noble river which flowed steadily past its bivouac.[5] A scout from the city, about three o'clock, had excited a momentary alarm; but it had disappeared;[6] and the insolent soldiery, fresh from the fields of Bladensburg and Long-log Lane, returned to their former occupations, "remarking that as the Americans had never yet dared *to attack*, there was no great probability of their doing so on the present occasion."[1] The fires blazed brightly, the evening meal had been taken, and the troops had been preparing for their night's repose, when, at half-past seven o'clock, a large vessel dropped quietly down the river, let go her anchor opposite the enemy's bivouac, and furled her sails. She was hailed, but she returned no answer; and the impression that she was a British cruiser, which had come to cover the movement, began to prevail. Muskets were fired at her, but she still preserved the secret of her mission; and her sails were furled with perfect coolness, and her broadside swung around on the bivouac, in the presence of hundreds of anxious, but confident, spectators. Suddenly a voice on her deck was heard ordering her crew to "*Give them this for the honor of America;*"[2] and "the words were instantly followed by the flashes of her guns, and a deadly shower of grape swept down numbers in the camp."[3] It was the schooner *Carolina*, which had been detached for this purpose by Commander Patterson; and against the fire of her nine guns, loaded with grape and canister, the enemy's three-pounders could offer no resistance; while her distance prevented his musketry from reaching her with any effect, and his rockets deviated so far from

[1] Gen. Keane to Gen. Packenham, Dec. 26, 1814; Gleig, pp. 274–276; Ingersoll, iii. p. 133.—[2] Gen. Keane to Gen. Packenham, Dec. 26, 1814; Com. Patterson to Sec. of Navy, Dec. 28; Gen. Jackson to Sec. of War, Dec. 27; Gleig, pp. 275–278; Latour, p. 88; Map VI., in Latour's Atlas.—[3] Gen. Jackson to Sec. of War, Dec. 27; Latour, p. 87; Gleig, p. 277; Capt. Cooke's Narrative, p. 185.

[4] Gen. Keane to Gen. Packenham, Dec. 26, 1814.

[5] Gleig, pp. 282, 283.—[6] Latour, p. 88; Cooke, pp. 188, 189.

[1] Gleig, pp. 283, 284. See also a Letter from an officer, Jan. 30, 1815; Claiborne's Notes, p. 59.—[2] Gen. Keane to Gen. Packenham, Dec. 26, 1814; Com. Patterson to Sec. of Navy, Dec. 28; Latour, p. 95; Gleig, p. 284; Cooke, pp. 190, 191.—[3] Gleig, p. 284. See also Gen. Keane to Gen. Packenham, Dec. 26, 1814; Cooper's Naval History, ii. p. 145.

their object that they became the subjects of contempt and ridicule. Huddled together behind the levee, or in the negro-huts on M. Lacoste's plantation, or behind any object which offered the least shelter, the astonished and mortified soldiery was held in check by the gallant schooner; and the camp-fires were suffered to go out, or were hastily smothered, with the hope of securing, in the more intense darkness of the night, the safety which the flickering of the former tended, somewhat, to exclude from the bivouac.[1]

While the shivering invaders were thus learning that the Americans could attack, as well as defend, a position; and were seeking a shelter from the grape-shot which penetrated every part of their position,—"unable to move from his ground, or to offer any opposition to those who kept him there," as one of his own officers describes his situation,[2]—a straggling fire of musketry, among his picket-guards, betokened the approach of new and unknown dangers. It was true, every tree might be mistaken for an American by the half-terrified sentries; and the exposure of the troops to the fire of the schooner, unnecessarily, might be productive of a heavy and uncalled-for loss of life. It was not many minutes, however, before "the heavens were illuminated, on all sides, by a semicircular blaze of musketry; and that no alternative remained, but to surrender at discretion, or to beat back the assailants," by whom they were surrounded.[3]

It appears, in explanation of the mystery which surrounded the movements of the Americans, that when the enemy surprised the company of militia on the plantation of M. Villère, his son, Major Villère, escaped, crossed the river, and hastened to the city with intelligence of the enemy's movements.[1] Commander Patterson immediately determined to employ the naval force, which he commanded, against the invaders; and, for this purpose, he ordered the *Louisiana*, Lieutenant-commander Thompson, and the schooner *Carolina*, Commander John D. Henley,—one of Captain Macdonough's gallant associates, in the victory off Plattsburg,[2]—to drop down with the current, to anchor off the enemy's position, and to open a fire on his flank; while the army, moving against him in front, was expected to co-operate, by taking advantage of his confusion. The former of these vessels did not reach her position until the next morning; while Commander Henley, taking advantage of his sweeps, moved into his designated position, and, with the coolness which had been displayed by his distinguished chief in Lake Champlain, he opened his fire on the astonished invaders, as already related, with terrible effect.[3]

At the same time, General Jackson received the intelligence, and the drums were beat to arms throughout the city. Leaving General Carrol's Tennesseeans and the New Orleans militia on the Gentilly road, to guard the approach to the city, in that direction,[4] at five o'clock in the afternoon of the twenty-third, he moved down to attack the enemy in his bivouac. His force embraced the Mississippi dragoons, under Major Hind;

[1] Gen. Keane to Gen. Packenham, Dec. 26, 1814; Com. Patterson to Sec. of Navy, Dec. 28; Adm'l Cochrane to the Admiralty, Jan. 18; Latour, p. 95; Gleig, pp. 284, 285; Cooke, pp. 191, 192.—[2] Gleig, p. 285.—[3] Ibid., p. 286.

[1] Latour, p. 87.—[2] Vide p. 383.—[3] Com. Patterson to Secretary of Navy, Dec. 28.

[4] Gen. Jackson to Secretary of War, Dec. 27; McAfee, p. 510; Eaton's Jackson, p. 309.

General Coffee's brigade of mounted Tennessee riflemen; parts of the Seventh and Forty-fourth regiments of the line; the uniformed companies of New Orleans militia, under Major Planché;[1] the Second battalion of free men of color, under Major Daquin; and a detachment of artillery, with two six-pounders, under Lieutenant-colonel McRee[2]—the whole numbering about fifteen hundred men;[3] and at about seven o'clock he reached the vicinity of the enemy's lines. General Coffee, with his mounted riflemen, Captain Beale's company of "*Orleans Riflemen*," and part of the Mississippi dragoons,—seven hundred and thirty-two men in all,[4]—was ordered to turn the enemy's right, and for this purpose, with Colonel de la Ronde as a guide, he moved to the edge of the marsh, dismounted, and left his horses in charge of a detachment of his brigade;[5] while, at the same time, General Jackson, in person, with the remainder of the forces, moved against the front of the enemy's position.[6] In this order, both wings of the land forces awaited the movement of the *Carolina*—whose first gun was the appointed signal for the engagement. As has been seen, that signal was not long withheld; and with its earliest echo both wings were in motion, eager for the fray.

The first movement was made by a company of the Seventh regiment, under Lieutenant McClelland, which advanced from the gate of La Ronde's plantation, down the main road, to the boundary of Lacoste's plantation, where one of the enemy's outposts was stationed, drove it in, and occupied the position. A heavy reinforcement was moved to the support of the picket; and, at the same time, the entire Seventh regiment, by heads of companies, moved to the support of Lieutenant McClelland,—both parties joining in a very close and spirited fire. Immediately afterwards the Forty-fourth regiment came up and supported the Seventh, forming on its left,—while the artillery, also, was put in battery on the road, on the right of the Seventh; and the marines, on the right of the artillery, prevented the enemy from turning the right of the line, below the levee. Along the entire extreme right of the line, therefore, the fire was close and well directed; while the enemy, in the midst of the darkness, rallied as he was best able, to repel the assailants. The Eighty-fifth and Ninety-fifth regiments had been moved to support the pickets, while the Fourth, "stealing to the rear, formed close column, and remained as a reserve." It was soon found, however, that the enemy's right outflanked the left of the American Forty-fourth regiment, and supposing he had got the victory within his grasp, he pushed forward to secure it. Unfortunately for him, however, while he was "advancing silently in the dark," with this intention, he suddenly and unexpectedly fell within pistol-shot of Major Daquin's battalion of free colored men, which was on the left of the American right wing, and was received with a close and destructive fire. On hearing the alarm on its left, where the colored battalion was engaged, the bat-

1 Latour says the following companies composed this battalion:—The Carbiniers, Capt. Roche, 86 men; Dragoons, Maj. St. Genie, 78 men; Louisiana Blues, Capt. White, 31 men; Le Francs, Capt. Hudry, 33 men; and the Chasseurs, Capt. Guibert, 59 men.

2 Gen. Jackson to Sec. of War, Dec. 27; Latour, p. 89; Ingersoll, iii. pp. 138, 139.—3 Gen. Jackson to Sec. of War, Dec. 27. Maj. Latour (p. 105) says it numbered 2131 men.—4 Latour, pp. 91, 105.—5 Ibid., pp. 97, 98; McAfee, p. 511.—6 Gen. Jackson to Sec. of War, Dec. 27; McAfee, p. 511; Eaton's Jackson, p. 311.

talion of uniformed companies, under Major Planché, which was on the left of the centre, also moved forward; and along the entire line—forming a curve from the Mississippi River, near the boundary between the plantations of MM. La Ronde and Lacoste, to the mansion of the former—the fire was as warm, and the action as animated, as the darkness and uncertainty with which every thing was surrounded would admit.[1]

In the mean time, while the action was thus going on, on the right of the line, General Coffee and his command, in open order, were moving silently but certainly against the extreme right of the enemy's position. Having dismounted his Tennesseans, and ordered them to "fire at will," *taking aim with their utmost skill*, it was not long before the unerring rifles sent to the enemy the most unwelcome intelligence. "Long practice had enabled these men to keep up a very brisk fire, the more destructive, as not a man discharged his piece without doing execution." As the division advanced, the enemy fell back, until the circuit was made, when it confronted the Eighty-fifth in front of Lacoste's plantation, and gave it a most destructive fire. Unused to such opponents, the veteran regulars did not wait for a repetition of the fire, but fell back, in confusion, at once, behind the old levee, towards their own bivouac. The negro-quarters on M. Lacoste's plantation were next cleared; and, soon afterwards, the division took a position in front of the old levee, near M. La Ronde's boundary, and assisted the right wing in consummating the victory in that quarter.[1]

The action had now raged nearly two hours; the darkness was intense, and the flashes of the fire-arms were the principal guides for the movements of the troops. In the American lines there was more order, from the fact that there was less effort made to preserve it. The individuality of the soldier was more completely preserved, although the necessity for concert of action was fully understood and recognized. In the enemy's ranks, as one of his officers has said, "all order, all discipline were lost. Each officer, as he was able to collect twenty or thirty men around him, advanced into the middle of the enemy (*Americans*), when they fought hand to hand, bayonet to bayonet, and sword to sword, with all the tumult and ferocity of one of Homer's combats." "Attacked unexpectedly, and in the dark," he continues, "surrounded by enemies before any arrangements could be made to oppose them, it is not conceivable that order, or the rules of disciplined war, could be preserved. We (*the British*) were mingled with the Americans, frequently before we could tell whether they were friends or foes, because, speaking the same language with ourselves, there was no mark by which to distinguish them, at least none whose influence extended beyond the distance of a few paces. The consequence was, that more feats of individual gallantry were performed in the course of that night, than many campaigns might have afforded an opportunity of performing; while viewing

[1] Gen. Jackson to Secretary of War, Dec. 27; Gen. Keane to Gen. Packenham, Dec. 26; Latour, pp. 95–97; Claiborne's Notes, p. 59; Eaton's Jackson, pp. 315–317.

[1] Gen. Jackson to Secretary of War, Dec. 27; Gen. Keane to Gen. Packenham, Dec. 26; Latour, pp. 97–100; Eaton's Jackson, pp. 312–315.

the affair as a regular action, none can be imagined more full of blunders and confusion. No man could tell what was going forward in any quarter, except where he himself chanced immediately to stand; no one part of the line could bring assistance to another, because, in truth, no line existed. It was, in one word, *a perfect tumult*, resembling, except in its fatal consequences, those scenes which the night of an Irish fair usually exhibits, much more than an engagement between two civilized armies."[1]

While the action was still pending, a strong detachment from the First and Second (*British*) brigades came up from the fleet and engaged the Americans[2]—increasing the number of combatants and the confusion which prevailed on the field of battle; yet even this accession did not secure the victory or maintain the position. After driving the enemy back to General Villère's plantation, General Jackson fell back on that of M. La Ronde, where he remained until four o'clock the next morning, when he retired to the left bank of Rodriguez's canal, about two miles behind the field of battle.[3]

The number of combatants engaged in this action has been well ascertained. The advance of the enemy—which first engaged—numbered about nineteen hundred and fifty men;[4] while of the reinforcements, there were not less than four hundred men.[5] The strength of the Americans, in the aggregate, was two thousand one hundred and thirty-one men,[1] but two companies of Tennesseans and the Mississippi dragoons were not brought into action,[2] and the actual force engaged, therefore, did not exceed fifteen hundred men.[3] The *reported* loss of the former was five officers and forty-one men *killed*, twelve officers and one hundred and fifty-five men *wounded*, and three officers and sixty-one men *missing*.[4] An intelligent officer who was present, observes, however, "Our loss was enormous. Not less than five hundred men had fallen, many of whom were our finest soldiers and best officers, and yet we could not but consider ourselves fortunate in escaping from the toils, even at the expense of so great a sacrifice."[5] The loss of the Americans was twenty-four *killed*, one hundred and fifteen *wounded*, and seventy-four *missing*.[6]

As already stated, the Americans fell back on Rodriguez's canal, where, at "Camp Jackson," they commenced to intrench, in order to check the enemy's movement against the city. On the other hand, the enemy continued to press forward his forces through the Bienvenu, and before dark, on the twenty-fourth of December, the whole army was in position on the bank of the Mississippi[7]—the advance-guard below M. La Ronde's plantation, while the main body occupied the field of battle.[8] Still, notwithstanding his strength, the schooner *Carolina* and the ship *Louisiana*, which had also reached the scene,

[1] Gleig, pp. 286, 287, 291, 292.—[2] Latour, p. 100; James' Mil. Occur., ii. pp. 361, 362.—[3] Latour, p. 113.

[4] Mr. James (*Mil. Occur.*, ii. p. 355) says it numbered 1688 *rank and file*. The 4th regiment numbered 800 men, the 85th numbered 350 men, the six companies of the 95th numbered 600 men, the sappers and miners, &c., 100, and rocketeers and artillerists, 100.

[5] James' Military Occurrences, ii. p. 362.

[1] Latour, p. 105; Ingersoll, iii. p. 183.—[2] Latour, pp. 105, 106.—[3] Although the greater number of writers consider the force was stronger, I have not felt at liberty to dispute Gen. Jackson's positive statement.

[4] Returns appended to Gen. Keane's Dispatch, Dec. 26, 1814.—[5] Gleig, p. 292.—[6] Returns of loss, appended to Gen. Jackson's Dispatch, Dec. 27, 1814.—[7] Gleig, p. 299.

[8] Map V., in Latour's Atlas.

kept him in check; and no attempt was made either to extricate himself or to drive the vessels from their positions, until, on the evening of the twenty-fifth, when Sir Edward Packenham and General Gibbs, two experienced officers, unexpectedly reached the camp, and assumed the command of the army.[1] They had been dispatched from Europe, on receipt of the intelligence of the death of General Ross, and after a very short trip, with strong reinforcements, they had reached the scene of strife.

After examining the position of the schooners, Sir Edward ordered a detachment of heavy pieces to be transported from the mouth of the Bayou Bienvenu; and working parties were ordered out to erect a battery, from which, at daybreak on the morning of the twenty-seventh, a heavy fire of red-hot shot was poured on her. The second ball is said to have set her on fire; and, in little more than an hour she blew up; while the *Louisiana*, with the assistance of her boats, was carried beyond the range of his fire, and escaped without injury.[2]

The remainder of the day (*Dec.* 27) was spent by the enemy in bringing up stores and heavy guns from his shipping;[3] and he appears to have been greatly harassed by small parties of riflemen, who were sent down by General Jackson, and through whose vigilance the enemy's outposts and sentries were kept in constant alarm, while the main body was prevented from obtaining any sound or refreshing sleep. "Scarcely had the troops lain down," one of the enemy's officers observes, "when they were roused up by a sharp firing at the outposts, which lasted only till they were in order, and then ceased; but as soon as they had dispersed, and had once more addressed themselves to repose, the same cause of alarm returned, and they were again called to their ranks. Thus was the entire night spent in watching, or, at best, in broken and disturbed slumbers, than which nothing is more trying, both to the health and spirits of an army."[1]

[1] Gleig, p. 301.—[2] Capt. Henley to Capt. Patterson, Dec. 28; Gen. Jackson to Secretary of War, Dec. 29.
[3] Adm'l Cochrane to the Admiralty, Jan. 18, 1815; Gleig, p. 305.

While the enemy was thus harassed by the riflemen, and "kept stationary," by a little schooner, on the twenty-fifth of December, General Morgan, who occupied a position on the "English Turn" of the river (*Détour des Anglais*), was ordered to leave a small corps of observation at that point; to remove the artillery to Fort St. Leon; and to occupy a position on the west bank of the river, opposite Camp Jackson, and covering its right flank; and in accordance with these orders Flood's plantation was occupied, and works were thrown up.[2]

Having removed the schooner which had so long kept his force in a state of siege,[3] on the afternoon of the same day (*Dec.* 27), the enemy prepared to move against the American lines; and in the evening his light troops drove in the American outposts which had occupied the plantation of M. La Ronde.[4] At daybreak, on the morning of the twenty-eighth, his pickets were called in, and the several regiments which composed his army were formed in order of attack. His right wing, commanded by General Gibbs, embraced the Fourth, Twenty-first, and Forty-fourth regi-

[1] Gleig, pp. 305, 306.—[2] Latour, p. 117.—[3] Capt. Cooke, pp. 199, 207.—[4] Latour, p. 119.

ments of the line, and a regiment of negroes, and took post near the edge of the marsh which flanked the position occupied by both the armies; while the left wing, with which moved the artillery, under General Keane, embraced the Eighty-fifth, Ninety-third, and Ninety-fifth regiments of the line, and another of negroes, and was formed with its left on the bank of the Mississippi—a line of riflemen, in open order, uniting the two wings, and covering their flanks. As these columns advanced, the American light troops fell back; and the *Louisiana*, at anchor in the river, received the attention of his artillery—an attention which, in due time, was fully and terribly reciprocated.[1]

The ignorance of the army concerning the character of the service in which it was moving has been graphically described by Lieutenant Gleig; and it appears that as the American light troops fell back without offering much opposition, the future was not "a matter of much anxiety. Their spirits, in spite of the troubles of the night, already referred to, were good, and their expectations of success were high; consequently, many rude jests were bandied about, and many careless words spoken."[2] But they did not yet know what adversary they had to contend with; and the flanking fire which, soon afterwards, was thrown into his left by the *Louisiana*, conveyed the first tidings of the preparations which had been made to receive him. His own artillery was quickly silenced; and when a cross-fire was thrown in, on his front, from the breastwork behind the canal Rodriguez, his loss was exceedingly severe.[1] "That the Americans are excellent shots, as well with artillery as with rifles," says Lieutenant Gleig, "we have had frequent cause to acknowledge; but, perhaps, on no occasion did they assert their claim to the title of good artillerymen more effectually than on the present. Scarce a bullet passed over, or fell short of its mark, but all striking full into the midst of our ranks, occasioned terrible havoc. The shrieks of the wounded, therefore, the crash of firelocks, and the fall of such as were killed, caused, at first, some little confusion; and what added to the panic, was that from the houses beside which we stood, bright flames suddenly burst forth." "The scene was altogether very sublime," he continues. "A tremendous cannonade mowed down our ranks and deafened us with its roar; while two large chateaux and their outbuildings almost scorched us with the flames, and blinded us with the smoke which they emitted."[2]

With an indiscreet, if not a foolhardy, rashness,—as if for the purpose of intimidating the Americans with a display of the close columns of his veteran troops,—Sir Edward Packenham moved his columns to the very edge of the canal, and exposed them to the deadly fire which Lieutenant Gleig has described, without affording the least means of crossing, or the smallest amount of shelter.[3] The victims of this ignorant self-conceit—it can be called nothing less than that—stood on the outer brink of the canal and received

[1] Capt. Patterson to Sec. of Navy, Dec. 29, 1814; James' Mil. Occur., ii. p. 368; Latour, pp. 119, 120; Cooke's Narrative, pp. 207, 208; Gleig, pp. 307, 308.

[2] Gleig, pp. 307, 308. See also Latour, p. 120; Eaton's Jackson, pp. 339, 340.

[1] Latour, pp. 120, 121; Cooke's Narrative, p. 208; Eaton's Jackson, pp. 340, 341.—[2] Gleig, pp. 309, 310. See also Cooke's Narrative, p. 208; Eaton's Jackson, p. 341.—[3] Cooke's Narrative, p. 208; Gleig, p. 310.

the murderous fire, or crouching, sought to avoid it, until Sir Edward discovered that his Peninsular experience had not prevented him from making mistakes; when a retreat was ordered, and other, and not less difficult, troubles were presented. To remove the troops, in the face of such a fire, was a task which required more skill for its execution than that which had placed them in their present position; while the dismounted guns—the effects of the *Louisiana's* fire—could not be left on the field, without tarnishing, too greatly, the escutcheon of the army.

At length a party of *sailors* were sent for; and these, "running forward to the spot where the guns laid, lifted them up, in spite of the whole of the enemy's (*American*) fire, and bore them off in triumph."[1] As soon as this had been done, "regiment after regiment *stole away*—not in a body, but one by one, under the same discharge which saluted their approach;"[2] and, about two miles below, wiser, if not better men, they halted.

In this rash adventure, the enemy *reported* a loss of one officer and fifteen men *killed*, three officers and thirty-five men *wounded*, and two men *missing*.[3] The loss of the Americans, on the *Louisiana*, was one man *wounded*;[4] and in the lines, Colonel Henderson and eight men *killed*, and two officers and six men *wounded*.[5]

During the twenty-ninth, thirtieth, and thirty-first of December, the enemy was busily employed in bringing up from the fleet his heavy guns and the stores necessary for their use, and in erecting batteries on which to employ them[1]—in which latter work the hogsheads of sugar on the neighboring plantations were pressed into the service.[2] At the same time the Americans were busily employed in completing the lines at Camp Jackson and on Flood's plantation,—Camp Journeay,—on the opposite side of the Mississippi.[3] Commander Patterson, of the navy, also erected a battery on the west side of the river, which he manned with sailors; and with it he commanded the left flank of the enemy's camp, compelling him to fall back from his advanced position;[4] the First regiment of Louisiana militia, under Colonel Dejau, was ordered to take a position in a wood near the canal which connected M. Pierna's plantation—in the rear of Camp Jackson—with the Bayou Bienvenu, through which, it was feared, the enemy might ascend with schooners, and attack the city;[5] new lines were also thrown up—similar to that at Camp Jackson—on the plantations of MM. Dupré and Montreuil, also in the rear of Camp Jackson, behind which the troops might rally, in case they were driven from the latter defences;[6] and outposts and pickets were posted wherever it was thought possible an enemy might force a passage.[7]

At length, having completed his arrangements, at an early hour on the first of January, 1815, the enemy renewed his attack on the line at Camp Jackson, by a heavy fire from his bat-

[1] Gleig, p. 311.—[2] Ibid.—[3] Returns of casualties, signed "Fred. Stovin, *Lieut.-Col. Dep.-Adj.-Gen.*"

[4] Capt Patterson to Secretary of Navy, Dec. 29.

[5] Returns appended to Adj.-Gen. Butler's letter to Gen. Parker, Jan. 16, 1815.

[1] Journal of A. Q. M. G. Forrest; Gleig, p. 313; Eaton's Jackson, p. 352.—[2] Gleig, p. 315; Ingersoll, iii. pp. 184, 185.—[3] Latour, pp. 126, 127; Jour. of A. Q. M. G. Forrest.

[4] Latour, p. 126; Cooke's Narrative, p 210.

[5] Latour, p. 129.—[6] Map V., in Latour's Atlas.

[7] Latour, pp. 126–131.

teries, accompanied with a cloud of Congreve rockets.[1] One battery, near the road, mounting two twelve-pounders; another, farther to the right, containing eight eighteen's and twenty-four-pound carronades; a third, towards the edge of the marsh, also mounting eight pieces of artillery; and three others, mounting twelve guns, in other parts of the field, simultaneously opened their fire—the two former being directed mainly against the American head-quarters, compelled General Jackson to seek shelter in some less-exposed place.[2] The fire was furious and well-directed,—the enemy evidently intending to breach the line,—which was returned, both from the batteries within the lines and from those on the west side of the river, with precision and steadiness.[3] As the enemy's guns, either by being dismounted or from a lack of ammunition, began to drop their fire, that of the Americans was redoubled—the guns from the vessels in the river being landed for that purpose;[4] and "they soon convinced the enemy," Lieutenant Gleig says, "that all endeavors to surpass them, in this mode of fighting, would be useless."[5] The enemy, therefore, retired again from the American lines, covered with defeat, mortification, and disgrace, and leaving his heavy guns to their fate—a circumstance of which General Jackson appears, unaccountably, to have taken no advantage, notwithstanding many of his men left the lines to look at them;[6] and working parties were afterwards sent, under cover of the

[1] Latour, pp. 132, 133; Gleig, p. 316; Ingersoll, iii. p. 184.—[2] Latour, p. 132; Eaton's Jackson, p. 353.

[3] A. Q. M. G. Forrest's Journal; Gleig, p. 317; Claiborne's Notes, pp. 67, 68; Ingersoll, iii. p. 185.

[4] Gleig, p. 317.—[5] Ibid.

[6] Latour, pp. 135, 136, 138; Gleig, p. 317; Armstrong, ii. p. 169.

darkness of night to recover and remove them to the enemy's camp.[1]

In this affair the Americans lost eleven *killed* and twenty-three *wounded*;[2] that of the enemy was reported at three officers and twenty-nine men *killed*, four officers and forty men *wounded*, and two men *missing*.[3]

While the enemy was thus engaged, General Thomas, commanding the Second division of Louisiana militia, came down from Baton Rouge, and encamped within the Dupré line; and two days later, twenty-two hundred and fifty Kentuckians, many of whom were *without rifles*, also joined the army;[4] while on the sixth, the enemy was strengthened by the arrival of two splendid regiments from Europe.[5] Both armies, during the succeeding week, were also actively engaged in preparing for another struggle—the enemy under the experienced eyes of Generals Packenham, Gibbs, Keane, and Lambert; the Americans under "Andrew Jackson, Esquire,"—as an English writer, attempting to be witty, has styled him,[6]—and Generals Coffee, Carroll, Thomas, Adair, Humbert, and Morgan. The former added a square redoubt to his offensive works, near the American lines, besides reconstructing those batteries which had been destroyed on the first of January; and, having determined to attack the lines on the west bank of the river, in order to enfilade Camp Jackson, he had extended the Canal Villère to the Mississippi, in order that his boats might be employed in that important under-

[1] Gleig, p. 317; A. Q. M. G. Forrest's Journal; Cooke's Narrative, p. 211.—[2] Returns appended to Adj.-Gen. Butler's letter to Gen. Parker, Jan. 16, 1815.

[3] "Return of casualties," &c., signed "FRED. STOVIN, *Lieut.-Col. Dep.-Adj.-Gen.*"—[4] Latour, pp. 136, 141; Eaton's Jackson, p. 360.—[5] Adm'l Cochrane to the Admiralty, Jan. 18.—[6] Cooke's Narrative, p. 188.

taking:[1] the latter had strengthened their several works, and reinforced the parties which defended them, throughout his entire works.[2]

At this time (*Jan.* 8) the works and forces of both armies may be said to have been completely organized. Camp Jackson, the principal defence of the Americans, as has been stated, was on the northern side of Rodriguez's canal, and extended from the Mississippi on the right to the marsh on the left—a distance of about one thousand yards, and thence into the marsh about a third of a mile, making the entire length about a mile. By great exertions an earthen breastwork had been thrown up—the neighboring fences being employed to line the parapet and to prevent the light alluvial soil from sliding into the canal; and along the extended but almost perfectly straight line, scarce five feet high and of various thickness, the lines afforded shelter, not only from the enemy's musketry, but also from his cannon. On the extreme left, the line was extended into the wood and marsh upwards of a third of a mile, and there the defences were composed of logs and earth, perfectly musket-proof.[3] On the right of the line, seventy feet from the Mississippi, two brass twelve-pounders and a six-inch howitzer were in battery —the former manned by a detachment of United States Artillery, the latter by the volunteer dragoons under Major St. Geme—the whole commanded by Captain Humphreys, of the former; ninety yards east from the last (*Number One*) was *Battery Number Two*, mounting one twenty-four-pounder, under Lieutenant Norris of the navy, and manned with part of the crew of the late schooner *Carolina;* fifty yards east from the latter, also in the line, was *Battery Number Three*, mounting two twenty-four-pounders, manned with Baratarian smugglers, under their captains, Dominique and Bluche; twenty yards east from the latter was *Battery Number Four*, mounting one thirty-two-pounder, manned by part of the crew of the late schooner *Carolina*, under Lieutenant Crawley of the navy; one hundred and ninety yards east from the last, also in the line, was *Battery Number Five*, mounting two six-pounders, under Colonel Perry; thirty-six yards from the last, was *Battery Number Six*, a brass twelve-pounder, manned by a detachment from the volunteer company of "Francs," under General Flaujeac and Lieutenant Bertel; one hundred and ninety yards east from the last, also in the line, was *Battery Number Seven*, a long eighteen and a six-pounder, manned with regular artillerists under Lieutenants Spotts and Cheauveau; and sixty yards from the last was *Battery Number Eight*, a small carronade, manned with a detachment of militia, under a corporal whose name is not given.[1] The "New Orleans Rifles," a volunteer company, about thirty in number, occupied the extreme right, between the river and *Battery Number One;* the Seventh regiment of militia, four hundred and thirty in number, under Major Peire, occupied the lines between *Number One* and *Number Three;* the New Orleans uniformed companies, two hundred and eighty-nine in number, under Major Planché, and the First battalion of free men of color, two hun-

[1] Gen. Jackson to Sec. of War, Jan. 9, 1815; Latour, p. 144; Gleig, p. 320; Eaton's Jackson, p. 362.

[2] Latour, p. 144.—[3] Ibid., pp. 145–147; Map V., in Latour's Atlas.

[1] Latour, pp. 147, 148.

dred and eighty in number, under Major Lacoste, occupied the interval between *Number Three* and *Number Four;* the Second battalion of free men of color, one hundred and fifty men, under Major Daquin, and the Forty-fourth regiment, two hundred and forty men, under Captain Baker, manned the lines between *Number Four* and *Number Six;* the space between *Number Six* and the edge of the swamp was defended by General Carroll's Tennesseeans, supported by General Adair's Kentuckians—both corps numbering about sixteen hundred; while the remainder of the line was manned by General Coffee's Tennesseeans, about five hundred in number[1]—the entire force *on duty, on the line*, therefore, being not more than thirty-two hundred men.[2]

On the western bank of the Mississippi, the quota of Louisiana—two hundred and sixty men—under General Morgan, was posted on Raguet's old canal—having fallen back from Flood's plantation—and formed the extreme right of the line; on its left, forming the centre of the line, was the Second regiment Louisiana militia—one hundred and seventy-six men—under Colonel Cavelier; and still farther to the left, forming the extreme left of the line, on the bank of the river, was the First regiment of Louisiana militia—one hundred and ten men—the whole being commanded by General Morgan, and on the evening of the seventh a detachment of five hundred Kentuckians was sent over, under Colonel Davis, to strengthen the garrison. Works of defence had been thrown up, along the bank of the canal, about two hundred yards in length, leaving eighteen hundred yards extent, on the right of the position, entirely unprotected.[1]

[1] Latour, pp. 150, 151.—[2] Ibid., p. 152.

Against these works the enemy had assembled the Fourth (*eight hundred men*), Seventh (*eight hundred and fifty men*), Twenty-first (*eight hundred men*), Forty-third (*eight hundred and fifty men*), Forty-fourth (*four hundred and twenty-seven men*), Eighty-fifth (*three hundred and fifty men*), Ninety-third (*nine hundred men*), Ninety-fifth (*six hundred men*) regiments of infantry, the Fourteenth regiment light-dragoons (*two hundred and ninety-five men*), the First and Second West India regiments of negroes (*each eight hundred men*), a detachment of Royal Artillery (*five hundred and seventy men*), a corps of sappers and miners (*ninety-eight men*), general staff (*fifty-seven men*), and a body of twelve hundred seamen and marines—in all about nine thousand four hundred men, exclusive of officers.[2]

As already stated, an effort had been made, by the enemy, to extend the Villère canal to the Mississippi, in order that the boats designed for the transportation of the troops to the opposite bank of the river might be brought through from the Bayou Bienvenu. In this work, however, although a very large party of troops was employed, he was not entirely successful; and the boats ran aground, detaining the expedition beyond its appointed time, and throwing the entire proposed operations into confusion.[3]

It had been designed to attack the Americans on the western bank of the

[1] Latour, pp. 165, 166.—[2] James' Mil. Occur., ii. p. 373. It is proper to remark, however, that the *strength* of these several regiments, as given in the list, although taken from the statements of *British* officers who were in the battle, are not in agreement with those given by Mr. James.—[3] Gen. Lambert to Earl Bathurst, Jan. 10; James' Mil. Occur., ii. p. 374; Gleig, p. 321; Cooke, p. 243.

river at an early hour; and while the fire from these works would be diverted, and while the attention of the troops in Camp Jackson, also, to some extent, at least, would be directed towards that flank, the main body of the enemy was to move forward and assault the lines.[1] This bold, but well-arranged, plan of operations,—worthy of the school in which Sir Edward Packenham had studied the art of war,—intrusted, for its execution, to a body of the finest troops ever seen in America, there need be little wonder that the expectations of the assailants ran very high, even while the more experienced eye of their commander detected causes which led him to forebode a disastrous result.[2]

Measures had been taken to transport fourteen hundred troops to the opposite side of the river,—the Eighty-fifth regiment, the marines, and a detachment of sailors being designated for that service,—and they were to form and push forward, "so as to carry all the batteries, and point the guns (*on the flank of Camp Jackson*) before daylight"—a rocket thrown up by this party, when they were ready to strike the first blow, being also the signal for the attack, by the main body, on the front of the lines at the canal Rodriguez.[3] Unfortunately for the plan and its designers, however, the canal was not dug deep enough, and the boats grounded; so that, even after great personal exertions by the detachment, only boats sufficient to convey three hundred and fifty men were dragged through, and brought into the Mississippi;[1] and with this small force, just before dawn of day, several hours behind the appointed time, Colonel Thornton pushed off. But even then the troubles of the expedition did not forsake it. Without considering the strength of the current, the boats headed for the desired landing-place; but, on striking the opposite shore, it was found that they had been borne a considerable distance down the stream, and were four miles below the lines at the canal Raguet. After debarking his little force, without oppositon, Colonel Thornton moved rapidly up the road towards the city, driving before him a party of observation, under Major Arnaud, who had been sent down to oppose his landing. When the enemy reached Mayhew's canal, a mile in advance from the line at Raguet's, he was met by Colonel Davis, with the five hundred Kentuckians, to whom reference has been made; yet, strange as it may appear, although the two parties under Colonel Davis and Major Arnaud, combined, greatly exceeded in number the enemy's force, they fled after delivering two or three volleys, and formed on the right of General Morgan, in the open space between the latter and the marsh. Pursuing the fugitives as rapidly as possible, along the main road, the enemy pressed forward, while the American artillery played vigorously on him as he approached, and, as he came within range, the small-arms, also, opened on the head of his column. He was not long, however, in perceiving the weakness of the American right; and, wisely turning from the front, he moved to his left, and attacked that part of the

[1] Gen. Lambert to Earl Bathurst, Jan. 10; Gleig, p. 319.

[2] "Sir E. Packenham augured an ominous result, and every officer and soldier in the bivouac heard these opinions, which were given in no measured terms. *The happy moment had passed,* but was not irretrievably lost."—*Cooke's Narrative,* p. 203.—[3] Gleig, pp. 321, 322; Cooke's Narrative, pp. 243, 244; Ingersoll, iii. 207.

[1] Gen. Lambert to Earl Bathurst, Jan. 10; Gleig, pp. 321, 322; Cooke, p. 243.

line. Having quickly turned the right flank of the American line, the victory had been won, the Kentuckians falling back in great confusion; and, soon afterwards, after spiking their guns, both General Morgan and Commander Patterson, with their respective commands, also retired—the latter to the *Louisiana*, the former along the road towards New Orleans.[1]

In the mean time the main body had met the Americans and been defeated. The several regiments had been formed under cover of the darkness and the fog—the Forty-fourth, under Lieutenant-colonel Mullens, having been intrusted with the fascines and the scaling-ladders—and in the stillness of early dawn awaited for the signal-rocket on the west side of the river.[2] From causes which have been already noticed, that signal was not thrown up at the appointed time; nor was the main body itself, at that time, properly formed or prepared for the assault. The engineers had not attended to their duties properly; and the Forty-fourth had passed the redoubt where the fascines and ladders had been deposited, without finding any one ready to attend to their delivery;[3] the different advance-guards, or forlorn-hopes, were without their proper columns of support, and many of them without any orders to regulate their movements; and every preparation had been made without judgment and without order. In this condition, shivering in the cold fog which surrounded them, the troops stood awaiting the expected rocket, but no rocket ascended until Sir Edward, out of patience, and without knowing his own want of preparation, threw one up himself.[1]

At this moment the column on the right—moving against the left of the American line—was headed by the Forty-fourth regiment, to whose care the fascines and ladders had been intrusted, and it marched forward *without its allotted burdens*,[2] to the very edge of the canal, without appreciating the serious character of its error. The consequence of this mishap was a perfect repetition, on the left, of the scene which was exhibited on the twenty-eighth of December; and without being able to cross the ditch, the enemy's troops were mowed down, on every hand, in the most destructive manner.[3] In the midst of the confusion which this error had occasioned, Sir Edward Packenham galloped forward, and meeting Lieutenant-colonel Mullens, he ordered the Forty-fourth to return for the ladders and fascines[4]—the remainder of the right column, in the mean time, without understanding the cause of the halt, and perplexed by the want of orders, being exposed to the rifles in front and to the cross-fires from the several batteries on either flank.[5] At length the Forty-fourth—assisted on the left by the regiment of negroes[6]—came staggering un-

[1] Col. Thornton to Gen. Packenham, Jan. 8, 1815; Adm'l Cochrane to the Admiralty, Jan. 18; Gen. Jackson to Sec. of War, Jan. 9, 1815; Capt. Patterson to Sec. of Navy, Jan. 13, 1815; Latour, pp. 165–175; Ingersoll, iii. pp. 207, 212.—[2] Gleig, p. 324; Cooke's Narrative, pp. 225–229.—[3] Cooke's Narrative, p. 247.

[1] Gen. Lambert to Earl Bathurst, Jan. 10; Latour, p. 154; Cooke's Narrative, p. 229.

[2] It has been seen that the Engineer Department was not ready to deliver the fascines and ladders when the 44th took its position, although it had halted nearly a quarter of an hour for the officer in charge. It then moved forward, and had been in position, at the head of the line *three hours*, when it was called back as related. Whether the regiment was "ahead of time" over three hours, or the Engineers that space "behind time," does not appear.—*Cooke's Narrative*, pp. 247, 248.

[3] Gen. Lambert to Earl Bathurst, Jan. 10; Gleig, p. 324.

[4] Gleig, p. 324.—[5] Gen. Lambert to Earl Bathurst, Jan. 10.—[6] Cooke's Narrative, pp. 231–233, 252.

der the heavy loads of *green sugar-cane* fascines, and of rough fence-rails formed into scaling-ladders; and as they reeled under the weight of their burdens, or threw them down from their inability to carry them, or fell under the fire which was concentrated on them, Sir Edward saw that unless prompt measures were adopted his well-laid plans would all be frustrated. To prevent this, if possible—although it does not appear to have engaged his attention how the canal should be crossed or the parapet be scaled—Sir Edward ordered the right column *to advance*, and throwing himself at its head they rushed forward. The Twenty-first and Fourth regiments having been "almost cut to pieces, and thrown into some confusion,"[1] the Ninety-third pushed on and took the lead, but halted on the brink of the canal, "to scale the parapet without ladders being impossible." "Some few," an eye-witness says, "by mounting one upon another's shoulders, succeeded in entering the works, but these were instantly overpowered, most of them killed, and the rest taken; while as many as stood without were exposed to a sweeping fire, which cut them down by whole companies. It was in vain that the most obstinate courage was displayed. They fell by the hands of men whom they absolutely did not see; for the Americans, without so much as lifting their faces above the rampart, swung their firelocks by one arm over the wall, and discharged them directly upon their heads. The whole of the guns, likewise, from the opposite bank, kept up a well-directed and deadly cannonade upon their flank; and thus were they destroyed without an opportunity being given of displaying their valor, or obtaining so much as revenge."[1] Anxious to check this carnage by enabling the column to cross the canal, and desiring to hurry forward the fascines and ladders, Sir Edward Packenham rode up to the Forty-fourth, which was returning to the front, and was urging it forward, when a musket-ball hit his knee and killed his horse. He immediately mounted another, and was cheering on the weary regiment, when a second ball struck him in the body and he fell, lifeless, into the arms of Major McDougall, his aid-de-camp.[2]

In the mean time three light companies from the Seventh, Forty-third, and Ninety-third regiments, which led the attack on the left, gallantly rushed forward and entered a battery which had been erected on the extreme right of the line; but here, as elsewhere, the advantage was not maintained in the face of so terrible a fire. In fact, although the fire on the left, already described by an eye-witness in the opposite wing, was terribly severe, that on the right was equally overpowering. On every hand was the most complete confusion—"the misty field of action," says Captain Cooke of the Forty-third (British) regiment, "was now *inundated* with wounded officers and soldiers, who were going to the rear from the right, left, and centre; in fact, little more than one thousand soldiers were left unscathed out of the three thousand that attacked the American lines, and they fell like the very blades of grass beneath the scythe of the mower.

[1] Gleig, p. 325.

[1] Gleig, pp. 325, 326. See also Gen. Lambert to Earl Bathurst, Jan. 10.—[2] Gen. Lambert to Earl Bathurst, Jan. 10; Test. of Maj. McDougall on trial of Lieut.-Col. Mullens; Cooke's Narrative, pp. 231, 232, 252; Gleig, p. 326.

Packenham was killed; Gibbs was mortally wounded, and his brigade was dispersed like the dust before the whirlwind."[1] The command of the troops necessarily devolved on General Lambert, who commanded the reserve,—all who were on the field having fallen.[2] All being now confusion and dismay, "without leaders, ignorant of what was to be done, the troops first halted, and then began to retire; till, finally, the retreat was changed into a flight, and they quitted the ground in the utmost disorder,"[3] covered by the reserve under General Lambert.

A flag was sent to the American lines, on the morning of the ninth, and a truce was asked, and granted, for the purpose of picking up the wounded and of burying the dead; and the scene which the field presented was truly a melancholy one.[4] It is said by one who saw it, as he had seen other battle-fields,[5] "of all sights I ever witnessed, that which met me there was, beyond comparison, the most shocking and the most humiliating. Within the small compass of a few hundred yards, were gathered together nearly *a thousand bodies, all of them arrayed in British uniforms.* Not a single American was among them; all were English; and they were thrown by dozens into shallow holes, scarcely deep enough to furnish them with a slight covering of earth. Nor was this all. An American officer stood by, smoking a cigar, and apparently counting the slain with a look of savage exultation; and repeating over and over, to each individual

[1] Cooke's Narrative, pp. 236, 237. See also Gen. Lambert to Earl Bathurst, Jan. 10.—[2] Gen. Lambert to Earl Bathurst, Jan. 10; Gleig, p. 334.—[3] Gleig, p. 327. See also Gen. Lambert to Earl Bathurst, Jan. 10; Cooke's Narrative, p. 235.—[4] Cooke's Narrative, pp. 262, 263.

[5] Gleig, pp. 332, 333.

that approached him, that their loss amounted only to eight killed and fourteen wounded. I confess," he adds, "that when I beheld this scene, I hung down my head, half in sorrow, half in anger."

As has been intimated in Lieutenant Gleig's remarks, the loss on the part of the great contending parties was very unequal, the Americans reporting theirs at thirteen *killed*, three officers and thirty-six men *wounded*, and nineteen men *missing*, of which only seven were *killed* and six *wounded*, *in the action* before the lines.[1] The enemy *reported* General Packenham, Lieutenant-colonels Dale and Renny, Majors King and Whitaker, Captains Wilkinson, Henry, Hickins, and Mairhead; Lieutenants McDonald and Davies, Ensigns Crowe and McLoskey, and two hundred and seventy-eight men *killed;* Generals Gibbs and Keane; Lieutenant-colonels Brooke, Patterson, and Thornton; two majors, eighteen captains, thirty-eight lieutenants, nine ensigns, one staff, and one thousand one hundred and eighty-nine men *wounded;* and fifteen officers and four hundred and sixty-nine men *missing*[2]—although it is well known that it was not far from two thousand five hundred in the aggregate.

In the mean time, on the ninth of January, a detachment from the fleet had approached Fort St. Philip, at Plaquemine, a work which commanded the passage of the river, a few miles below the city; and, on the same day, it commenced to bombard the fort. At that time the garrison numbered three hundred and sixty-six men, under Major Overton, while gunboat *Number Sixty-*

[1] Returns appended to Gen. R. Butler, Adj.-Gen., to Gen. Parker, Jan. 16, 1815.—[2] Returns, &c., signed "FRED. STOVEN, *Lieut.-Col., Dep.-Adj.-Gen.*"

five, which had warped into a neighboring bayou, and rendered good service in covering the rear of the works, had a crew of fifty men. The enemy's force embraced a sloop of war, a gun-brig, a schooner, and two bomb-vessels; and they opened a fire at three thousand nine hundred and sixty yards distant.

During the succeeding nine days the bombardment was continued, with but little cessation, and inflicting but little damage, when, on the eighteenth of January, he retired. The loss inflicted on the garrison was two *killed* and seven *wounded*.[1]

After remaining on the bank of the Mississippi until the evening of the eighteenth, the enemy retired, under cover of the darkness, to his shipping, leaving his wounded to the care of the Americans.

CHAPTER XCIV.

January 16, 1815.

THE LOSS OF THE PRESIDENT.

On the fourteenth of January, 1815, the *President*, under command of Captain Stephen Decatur, dropped down to Sandy Hook; and during the night she attempted to cross the bar and put to sea.[1] From some unexplained cause the pilots missed the channel, and ran the ship on one of the shoals which obstruct the entrance of the harbor of New York; and she was detained five hours by that unexpected misfortune.[2] As a squadron of the enemy's ships had been blockading the harbor several weeks, and had been blown off by a gale which had prevailed on the previous day, the opportunity to run the frigate out had been embraced by Captain Decatur, and the mishap referred to, for this reason, was peculiarly unfortunate, resulting, as it probably did, in the loss to the country of the fine ship which he commanded.[3]

At five in the morning of the next day (*January* 15, 1815), while steering southeast by east, three strange sail were made, within gun-shot of the *President*, and directly ahead; when she was hauled up, and passed to the northward of them, two miles distant. At daylight, however, four ships were seen in chase,—two of them astern, and one on each quarter,—the leading ship being about three miles distant. As the *President* was deeply laden with stores for a long cruise, Captain Decatur ordered all hands to lighten the ship; and for that purpose water-casks were started, anchors were cut away, provisions, cables, spare spars, boats, and every article that could be got at were thrown overboard, and the sails were kept wet, from the royals down. The wind was light and baffling; and the *President's* pursuers, lightly laden, and favored with stronger breezes, gained

---

[1] Capt. Decatur to Sec. of Navy, Jan. 18, 1815; Cooper, ii. p. 285; Mackenzie's Decatur, in Sparks' American Biography, xxi. pp. 210, 211.—[2] Capt. Decatur to Sec. of Navy, Jan. 18, 1815; Niles' *Register*, viii. pp. 44, 45; James' Nav. Occur., p. 427; Mackenzie, p. 211.

[3] Naval Chronicle, xxxiii. p. 157; Capt. Hayes to Adm'l Hotham, Jan. 17, 1815; Niles' *Register*, viii. pp. 44, 45; Com. Murray, President of Court of Inquiry, to Secretary of Navy, April 17, 1815.—[1] Gen. Jackson to Sec. of War, Feb. 17; Latour, pp. 187–197.

rapidly on her—the nearest, at three o'clock in the afternoon, opening her fire from her bow-guns; and, at five, obtaining a position on her starboard-quarter, within half point-blank-shot distance, on which neither her stern or quarter guns could be brought to bear.[1]

After occupying this position half an hour,—the enemy's fire, meanwhile, having become quite troublesome, as every shot carried away some of the *President's* rigging,—and after endeavoring to prevail on the stranger to range alongside, which was declined, Captain Decatur determined to exchange ships with her, if possible; and his crew cheerfully received the information, and joined in the measures adopted for its execution.[2] With this object, at half-past five o'clock, while it was yet light, the *President's* helm was put up, and the course of the ship laid to the southward, with the intention of closing with her opponent.[3] The stranger, however, appeared to understand the purpose of Captain Decatur; and she, too, at the same time, kept off—the ships soon afterwards coming abeam of each other, and each delivering her broadside.[4] During the succeeding two hours and a half the two ships appear to have run off dead before the wind, about a quarter of a mile apart; and every attempt to close, which was made by the *President*, was frustrated by the simultaneous sheering off of the stranger.[1] The action, therefore, was altogether with heavy guns; and the efforts of both appear to have been mainly directed against the spars and rigging of her opponent, until eight o'clock, when the stranger having been dismantled,—"her sails being cut from her yards,"[2]—she dropped astern, and the *President* pursued her *former* course, repairing her damages, and seeking to shake off the three strangers, which, with a brig, which had also joined in the pursuit, still continued the chase, and were also rapidly gaining on her.[3]

The chase continued in this order until eleven o'clock, when the four fresh vessels had come within gun-shot of the *President*—one of them (the *Pomone*) opening her fire on her larboard-bow, within musket-shot distance; another (the *Tenedos*), within two cables' length of her quarter; and the remainder (the *Majestic* and the *Despatch*), within gun-shot astern. Thus surrounded by a force greatly superior to his own, with his ship badly crippled, and one-fifth of her crew killed or wounded, and with no chance to escape from his fresh pursuers, Captain Decatur considered it his duty to surrender, and he hoisted a light as an indication of that purpose.[4]

The force of the *President* was thirty-two long twenty-four-pounders, one

---

[1] Capt. Decatur to Sec. of Navy, Jan. 18, 1815; Letter from an officer of the *Pomone*, Jan. 29, in the Naval Chronicle, xxxiii. p. 370; Capt. Hayes to Adm'l Hotham, Jan. 17.—[2] Cooper, ii. p. 237; Mackenzie, p. 214. It is proper to state that Com. Decatur makes no allusion to this subject.—[3] Capt. Decatur to Sec. of Navy, Jan. 18, 1815; Naval Chronicle, xxxiii. p. 157; Letter from an officer of the *Pomone*, Jan. 29, 1815.

[4] Capt. Decatur to Secretary of Navy, Jan. 15, 1815; Cooper, ii. p. 237; Log-book of the *Endymion*; Mackenzie, p. 216.

[1] Capt. Decatur to Secretary of Navy, Jan. 18, 1815; Letter from officer of the *Pomone*, Jan. 29, 1815; Capt. Hayes to Adm'l Hotham, Jan. 17.

[2] Naval Chronicle, xxxiii. p. 157; Capt. Hayes to Adm'l Hotham, Jan. 17.—[3] Capt. Decatur to Secretary of Navy, Jan. 18, 1815; Letter from officer of the *Pomone*, Jan. 29; Capt. Decatur's Testimony, at Bermuda, Jan. 15; Mackenzie, pp. 219, 220.

[4] Capt. Decatur to Secretary of Navy, Jan. 18, 1815; Naval Chronicle, xxxiii. p. 157; Letter from officer of the *Pomone*, Jan. 29, 1815; Capt. Decatur's Testimony; Capt. Hayes to Adm'l Hotham, Jan. 17.

twenty-four-pound howitzer, twenty forty-two-pound carronades, and five small pieces in her tops;[1] the *Endymion*—with which the conflict opened—was *rated* a *forty*-gun ship, but *mounted* twenty-six long twenty-four-pound, twenty-two thirty-two-pound, and one twelve-pound carronades, and one long-eighteen;[1] while of the *Majestic*, razee, rated fifty-six guns, the *Tenedos* rated thirty-eight guns, the *Pomone* rated thirty-eight guns, and the *Despatch*, the real strength is not known. The loss on the *President* was twenty-four *killed* and fifty-six *wounded*;[2] that of the *Endymion* was eleven *killed* and fourteen *wounded*.[3]

CHAPTER XCV.

February 20, 1815.

THE CAPTURE OF THE CYANE AND LEVANT.

On the seventeenth of December, 1814, the frigate *Constitution*, commanded by Captain Charles Stewart, sailed from Boston on a cruise; and after looking into Bermuda, she ran over to Madeira and the Bay of Biscay, making two prizes on her way, one of which was destroyed, the other sent in.[2]

At one o'clock in the afternoon of the twentieth of February, the Island of Madeira bearing west-southwest, sixty miles distant, a strange sail was made on the larboard-bow, when the *Constitution* hauled up two or three points, and made sail in chase. Three-quarters of an hour afterwards a second sail was made, ahead; and both were soon ascertained to be ships, standing close hauled, with their starboard-tacks on board.[3]

The strangers were not long in ascertaining the character of the *Constitution*, although her *strength* was not, at first, discovered;[4] and at four o'clock the weathermost ship made signals to her consort, and bore up for her—the *Constitution*, meanwhile, bearing up after her, setting all her canvas, and carrying away her mainroyal-mast in the chase. At five she opened her fire with her larboard bow-guns, but without effect; and perceiving that a junction of the two strangers could not be prevented, at half-past five she cleared for action, being then four miles astern of them. A few minutes afterwards the strangers passed within hail of each other, and hauled by the wind on the starboard-tack, hauled up their courses, and prepared for action. A series of manœuvres, by the consorts, for the purpose of gaining the position, occupied their attention until near six o'clock, without securing any benefit to them; and they then shortened sail, and at half cable length distance from

---

[1] Letter from officer of the *Pomone*, Jan. 29; James' Nav. Occur, pp. 445, 446. The Naval Chronicle gives her two guns more. Mr. Mackenzie (p. 209) makes no allusion to the howitzer or small top-guns.

[2] Lieut. Ballard to Secretary of Navy, May 2, 1814; Cooper, ii. p. 229.

[3] Capt. Stewart to Secretary of Navy, May, 1815, and the Minutes inclosed therein.

[1] James' Naval Occurrences, p. 444. The Naval Chronicle gives her two guns less.

[2] Cooper, ii. p. 238.

[3] Capt. Hope to Capt. Hayes, Jan. 15.—[4] Niles' *Register*, viii. p. 289.

each other, they awaited the approach of the *Constitution*.[1]

At five minutes past six the frigate ranged up on the starboard side of the sternmost ship, about three hundred yards distant; and opened her fire by broadsides, both her opponents answering her with spirit and effect. During a quarter of an hour the cannonade continued, when the fire of the consorts slackened; and the frigate also held her fire to allow the smoke to clear away, and that the position of her opponents might be ascertained. Immediately afterwards the *Constitution* found that she was abreast the headmost ship, while her consort was luffing up for the frigate's larboard-quarter; when the latter gave the former a broadside, and braced aback her main mizzen-topsails, backing astern, under cover of the smoke, abreast of the latter, and continued the action. During the succeeding quarter of an hour the cannonade continued, when the enemy's fire again slackened, and the headmost ship was seen, through the smoke, bearing up, with the intention of crossing the frigate's fore-foot; when the *Constitution* filled her topsails, shot ahead, and gave her two raking broadsides over the stern. It was then discovered that the sternmost ship was also wearing, when Captain Stewart immediately wore ship after her, and gave her a raking broadside; while she luffed, too, on the frigate's starboard broadside, and threw in her larboard broadside with great spirit and determination. On receiving this fire the *Constitution* ranged up on the stranger's larboard-quarter, within hail, and was about to give her starboard fire, when the latter fired a gun to leeward, and, at a quarter before seven, she surrendered. Lieutenant Hoffman was immediately sent to take possession of the prize, and reported her to be His British Majesty's frigate *Cyane*, Captain Falcon, mounting thirty-six guns, with a crew of one hundred and eighty men.[1]

About an hour afterwards the *Constitution* filled away after the ship which had been driven out of the action, but was still visible through the dim moonlight which relieved the darkness of the night. At half-past eight the two ships met—the stranger gallantly coming up to meet the frigate, with her starboard-tacks close hauled, her topgallant-sails set, and her colors flying. Ten minutes later the *Constitution* ranged close alongside to windward of her, on an opposite tack; and the two ships exchanged broadsides. The frigate having thrown in her fire, immediately wore under the stranger's stern, and raked her; when she made sail and endeavored to escape. The frigate immediately made sail in chase; and at half-past nine she opened a fire on the fugitive from her starboard bow-guns, which cut her spars and rigging very severely. At ten o'clock, finding she could not escape, the stranger fired a gun to leeward, and she, too, surrendered—proving to be the sloop of war *Levant*, Captain Douglass, mounting twenty-one guns, with a crew of one hundred and fifty-six men.[2]

The armament of the *Constitution*, at this time, was fifty-two guns,[3] and her

1 Capt. Stewart's Dispatch and Minutes; Naval Chronicle, xxxiii. p. 466; James' Naval Occurrences, p. 458.

1 Capt. Stewart's Dispatch and Minutes; Naval Chronicle, xxxiii. pp. 466, 467; Cooper, ii. p. 230.

2 Capt. Stewart's Dispatch and Minutes; Naval Chronicle, xxxiii. p. 467; James' Naval Occurrences, pp. 460, 461.—3 Cooper, ii. p. 231.

loss, during this action, was three *killed*, and twelve *wounded*;[1] the strength of the enemy has been already noticed, and his loss, as near as can be ascertained, was, on the *Cyane*, twelve *killed* and twenty-six *wounded*; and on the *Levant*, twenty-three *killed* and sixteen *wounded*.[1]

CHAPTER XCVI.

March 23, 1815.

THE CAPTURE OF THE PENGUIN.

The capture of the *President*, already referred to, in a preceding chapter of this work, being unknown to the commanders of the other vessels composing the squadron, they followed her to sea on the twenty-second of January, 1815; and made the best of their way to the Island of Tristan d'Acunha, the place of rendezvous appointed by Captain Decatur. The *Peacock* and *Tom Bowline* reached that place about the middle of March; and on the morning of the twenty-third of the same month the *Hornet*, also, arrived at the same place.[2] She had not cast anchor, however, when the men aloft discovered a sail to windward, standing westward; when Captain Biddle immediately sheeted home his topsails again, and making a stretch to windward, made chase. Soon afterwards the stranger was seen running down before the wind; and, as her character was apparent, the *Hornet* hove to and waited for her to come down.[3]

At forty minutes past one in the afternoon, the stranger having come within musket-shot, she set English colors and fired a gun; when the *Hornet* luffed up, displayed her colors, and answered with a broadside.[2] During the succeeding fifteen minutes the fire of both vessels was warm and effective, the enemy, meanwhile, gradually drifting nearer to the *Hornet*; and, soon afterwards, she put her helm hard up and ran down on the starboard broadside of the *Hornet*, to lay her aboard; and she succeeded in passing her bowsprit through the starboard-quarter of the latter.[3] At that instant the stranger's foremast and bowsprit went by the board, the former falling directly on her larboard guns; and her crew, probably in consequence of this mishap, made no attempt whatever to take advantage of her situation, but allowed the vessels to separate.[4] An attempt was made to bring the brig around, in order to use her starboard battery, but in this, also, the crew was unsuccessful, and the *Hornet* succeeded in raking her.[5] Perceiving that any further resistance was useless, the

1 Returns appended to Capt. Stewart's Dispatch.

2 Cooper, ii. p. 239.—3 Capt. Biddle to Capt. Decatur, March 25, 1815; Cooper, ii. p. 239; Letter from an officer of the *Peacock*, April 10, 1815.

1 Returns appended to Capt. Stewart's Dispatch. The *Naval Chronicle* (xxxiii. p. 467) says the *Cyane* lost 4 *killed* and 13 *wounded*, and the *Levant* 6 *killed* and 16 *wounded*.

2 Capt. Biddle to Capt. Decatur, March 25, 1815; Lieut. McDonald's Letter, April 6, 1815; Letter of an officer, &c., April 10, 1815.

3 Capt. Biddle to Capt. Decatur, March 25; Lieut. McDonald's Letter, April 6, 1815; Cooper, ii. p. 239.

4 Lieut. McDonald's Letter, April 6, 1815; James' Naval Occurrences, p. 488.—5 Lieut. McDonald's Letter, April 6, 1815; Cooper, ii. p. 240.

enemy hailed the *Hornet*, and surrendered.[1]

An unfortunate circumstance occurred immediately afterwards, which for a time threatened serious consequences. Two marines, on the enemy's deck, seeing Captain Biddle standing on the *Hornet's* taffrail, raised their pieces and fired, inflicting a severe, but not a dangerous wound. Aroused with indignation at this instance of supposed treachery—although it is probable it was rather the result of the confusion which necessarily attended the action—the *Hornet's* crew was restrained from sinking the brig only with the greatest difficulty.[2]

The prize proved to be His Britannic Majesty's brig *Penguin*, Captain Dickinson, mounting nineteen guns, besides guns in her tops; and she was manned with a crew of one hundred and thirty-two hands.[3] The loss of the *Hornet* was one man *killed*, and Captain Biddle, Lieutenant Conner, and eight men *wounded*;[1] that of the *Penguin* was Captain Dickinson, her boatswain, and twelve men *killed*, the second-lieutenant, two midshipmen, purser, and twenty-four men *wounded*.[2] The former suffered little injury, except in her sails and rigging; the latter was completely riddled, her foremast and bowsprit were carried away, and her mainmast was so much injured that it could not be secured.[3]

It has been said of this—the last "battle" of the war with Britain—that "it was one of the most creditable to the character of the American marine that occurred in the course of the war. The vessels were very fairly matched, and when it is remembered that an English flag-officer had sent the *Penguin* on especial service against a ship believed to be materially heavier than the vessel she actually encountered, it is fair to presume she was thought to be, in every respect, an efficient cruiser."[4]

---

[1] Capt. Biddle to Capt. Decatur, March 25, 1815; Lieut. McDonald's Letter, April 6, 1815.

[2] Capt. Biddle to Capt. Decatur, March 25, 1815; James' Naval Occurrences, p. 488; Niles' *Register*, viii. p. 336.

[3] Capt. Biddle to Capt. Decatur, March 25, 1815; Cooper, ii. p. 240.

[1] Cooper, ii. p. 241; Niles' *Register*, viii. pp. 335, 336.

[2] Capt. Biddle to Capt. Decatur, March 25, 1815. The enemy reports his *killed* much less than this number.

[3] Capt. Biddle to Capt. Decatur, March 25; Cooper, ii. p. 241. Mr. James (*Naval Occurrences*, pp. 490, 491) says the *Hornet's* hull was severely injured.

[4] Cooper, ii. p. 241.

CHAPTER XCVII.

May 14 to August 2, 1832.

THE BLACK HAWK WAR.

The acquisition of territory has always been a fruitful source of trouble. In ancient, as well as in modern times, the stronger has generally overpowered the weaker nations, appropriated to their own use the territory of the latter, and resorted to arms in defence of their enlarged dominions. In this no more fitting example can be found than that which is afforded by the United States in its intercourse with the aboriginal tribes whose hunting-grounds and burial-places were within its boundaries; and when the victims have mustered courage and numbers sufficient to assert their rights, and endeavored to maintain them, the entire strength of the Confederacy, as well as those of the border States, have generally been brought into requisition, and the "*audacity*" of the savages has been visited with the severest penalties.

Among those tribes with whom the Federal Government has been in trouble, are the Sauks and Foxes—powerful nations, whose homes were then on the banks of the Mississippi, in the present States of Wisconsin and Illinois—with some portions of whom, on the third of November, 1804, a treaty was signed at St. Louis, ceding to the United States a large district of their territory.[1] These negotiators had not visited St. Louis for such a purpose, however, and the act of cession was promptly repudiated by the greater part of both nations.[2] For many years a series of troubles, based on the rival claims of the parties, occurred between the government and the nations; and these troubles increased with the influx of settlers into that portion of the mighty West, at a later date.[1] Taking advantage of this disaffection, Tecumthà and the agents of the British government, at an early day, prompted them to move, with other nations of the West, for the redress of the grievances under which they lived;[2] and a series of "wars" occurred, of which the reader has been informed in preceding chapters of this volume.

The troubles which this state of affairs produced grew more and more serious until 1831, when, in accordance with subsequent treaty stipulations, all, including Black Hawk, removed from Illinois and settled on the western bank of the Mississippi.[3] During that year, however, with his band of warriors and his family, he appears to have returned to his former home; and caused much annoyance to the settlers, although he showed no disposition to resort to hostilities.[4] After a display of the military forces of the State, under General Duncan, and of the United States, under General Gaines, the troubles were settled by another treaty;

[1] Boss' History of Ogle County, Illinois, p. 19; Smith's History of Wisconsin, iii. p. 113.

[2] Autobiography of Black Hawk, edited by J. B. Patterson, pp. 27, 28; Smith's Wisconsin, i. p. 258; iii. pp. 113–117.

[1] Autobiog. of Black Hawk, pp. 28–31; Smith's Wisconsin, i. pp. 258, 259; iii. pp. 112, 113; Coll. of Wis. Hist. Soc., ii. pp. 91, 92.—[2] Autobiog. of Black Hawk, p. 31.—[3] Ibid., p. 36; Drake's Book of Indians, Bk. v., pp. 145, 146.

[4] Autobiography of Black Hawk, pp. 98–101; Recollections of Wisconsin since 1820, by Col. Ebenezer Childs; Mr. Burnett, Indian Agent, to Gen. Clark, June 13, 1831. The Indians appear to have injured no one beyond that produced by their reoccupation, quietly, of their former homes. They ordered the inhabitants to vacate the property; put their furniture out of doors; and sought, by *peaceable* means, to repossess themselves of their former homes. Black Hawk also appealed to the Indian Agent for redress—by no means a *hostile* step; and there appears to have been no movement whatever, except those of a peaceful character.—*Ford's Illinois*, p. 111; *Smith's Wisconsin*, i. p. 252; *Autobiography of Black Hawk*, pp. 98–101.

and Black Hawk and his party returned to their new homes, west of the Mississippi.[1]

Notwithstanding the apparent settlement of the troubles, in 1831, the emissaries of the British government in Canada appear to have continued the agitation of the treaty question among the Indians;[2] and in the spring of 1832, encouraged by their promises, Black Hawk prepared for another visit to his former home in Illinois. Still he assumed no warlike attitude; but with his band of warriors on horseback, and their families and property in canoes, they crossed the Mississippi at the Yellow Bank, on the sixth of April, and moved slowly towards Rock River.[3] It is difficult to conceive how such a cavalcade could have been considered *an Indian invasion*, especially since the squaws and children never accompanied war-parties on their excursions; yet the people of Illinois considered it in that light, and treated their visitors as *enemies*. The Governor called for Volunteers to repel the *invaders;*[4] General Atkinson, then on his way up the river with six companies of the Sixth infantry, to demand some murderers from the Sauks, joined in the crusade;[5] three companies of the First infantry were ordered from Fort Crawford;[6] the militia of North-western Illinois and of Michigan were ordered to be held in readiness for active duty;[7] the co-operation of the Dahkotas and Menomonees—hereditary enemies of the Sauks—was solicited by the Federal authorities;[8] and stores and supplies were ordered from St. Louis, to be in readiness for the campaign.[1] In the mean time, the Indians pursued their way *quietly*, but steadily; interfering with no one; and without inflicting any injury on the settlers. To the messengers who were sent after them, they replied, "they would not go back, as they were acting peaceably;" and when the messages became more urgent,—threatening to *drive* them back,—they were informed, if General Atkinson "wished to *fight*," he could "come on," as they were determined never to be driven, and equally so, "*not to make the first attack*."[2]

While the cavalcade, under Black Hawk, was thus pursuing its way up the Rock River, Governor Reynolds and General Whitesides, with about eighteen hundred Volunteers, were mustered into the service of the United States,[3] when General Atkinson detached them in pursuit of the Indians; while, with his regulars and the stores, he followed, in boats, in the rear, but at too great a distance to afford any support to the former.[4] On the twelfth of May this detachment, eager for action, reached Dixon's Ferry, where it was joined by Major Stillman, with two hundred and seventy-five men from the northern counties.[5] The Major, considering his command an independent one, declined to join General Whitesides' brigade; and, on the next day, he solicited from the Governor, as commander-in-chief, an order to go out on a scout. In accordance with that request, with Major Bailey, he received orders to march to the

---

[1] Autobiog. of Black Hawk, pp. 101–106; Smith's Wisconsin, i. pp. 253, 254; Ford's Illinois, p. 112; Drake, Bk. v., pp. 146, 147.—[2] Autobiog. of Black Hawk, pp. 108–111; Smith's Wisconsin, i. pp. 255, 259.

[3] Autobiog. of Black Hawk, pp. 112, 113; Gen. Atkinson to Gov. Reynolds, April 13, 1832; Smith's Wisconsin, i. p. 260.

[4] Child's Recollections; Smith's Wisconsin, i. p. 260; Wakefield's History of the War, pp. 7, 10.

[5] Autobiog. of Black Hawk, pp. 113, 114; Smith's Wisconsin, i. p. 260; Drake, Bk. v., p. 147; Col. Backus's Paper on this subject, read before the Mich. Hist. Soc., March 1, 1860.

[6] Col. Backus's Paper.—[7] Ibid.

[8] Gen. Atkinson to Gen. Street, Indian Agent, May 23, 1832; Gen. Street to T. P. Burnett, May 30, 1832; T. P. Burnett's Report to Gen. Street, July, 1832.

[1] Col. Backus's Paper.

[2] Autobiography of Black Hawk, pp. 114, 115. See also Smith's Wisconsin, i. p. 260; Drake, Bk. v., p. 148; Wakefield, p. 12.—[3] Wakefield, pp. 13, 14; Smith's Wisconsin, i. p. 260; Boss's Ogle County, pp. 37, 38; Col. Backus's Paper.

[4] Smith's Wisconsin, i. p. 261; Drake, Bk. v., p. 148. Col. Backus says Gen. Atkinson, in consequence of the impatience of the volunteers, "*consented*" to this movement "*with great reluctance*."

[5] Wakefield, pp. 16, 17; Boss's Ogle County, p. 38.

Old Man's Creek,[1] and to ascertain, if possible, the movements of the Indians;[2] and the two battalions, after wading through unusually muddy roads, encamped in company, but independent of each other, some eight or ten miles from the ferry. On the following morning (*May* 14), the two battalions were temporarily placed in command of Major Stillman, and, under his orders, they continued the pursuit until sunset, when they encamped *in front* of a small creek, known as the Kish-wau-kêe (since then known as "*Stillman's Run*"), in the vicinity of Sycamore Creek, and about thirty miles above Dixon.[3]

In the mean time Black Hawk had learned that the promised assistance of the British would not be available, and he began to relent.[4] At the same time intelligence of the approach of the two battalions under Majors Stillman and Bailey reached him; and he "immediately started three young men, with a flag," to meet them and conduct them to his camp, that a council might be held, and that he might descend Rock River again, probably with the design of returning to the western bank of the Mississippi.[5] Five others were, soon afterwards, detached after the former messengers, as a party of observation.[6] The first party, it is said, reached Major Stillman's encampment in safety and were taken prisoners, notwithstanding their flag;[7] and when the second party came in sight, also with a flag—with their guns held horizontally over their heads, and knocking the priming out, as a signal of peace[8]—they were pursued, and two of them were killed.[1] On the arrival, at Black Hawk's camp, of the three messengers who had escaped, all ideas of flags and truces ended. Blood had been shed by the whites while the victims were extending assurances of peace; and those who, before, had merely travelled over the soil of Illinois without committing any offence, were instantly changed into active and determined enemies.

At this time Black Hawk had only about forty men with him, the greater part of his party being ten miles distant, and with this small force he started back to meet the assailants.[2] There is no evidence whatever that the chief had either desired to engage in hostilities, or expected the whites would do so; and it is equally clear that in this "invasion" the first act of aggression was committed by those among whom the Indians moved.[3] What wonder, then, need there be, when his flag had been disregarded and its bearers seized as prisoners, when his messengers of peace, subsequently dispatched, had been shot down or pursued with that intent, that Black Hawk, with the forty who were with him, should turn on his pursuers, sound the war-whoop, and sell their lives as dearly as possible? He did so, and he did that only which any one, unless the veriest poltroon, would have done under the same circumstances.

Rushing upon the cowardly pursuers of the peaceful embassy, with his handful of

1 "Now '*Stillman's Run*,' a small stream, which rises in White Rock Grove, in Ogle Co., and empties into Rock River, near Byron."—*Boss's Ogle County*, p. 38.

2 Smith's Wisconsin, i. p. 261; Drake, Bk. v., p. 148; Wakefield, p. 17.

3 Child's Recollections; Smith's Wisconsin, i. p. 261; Wakefield, p. 18.

4 Autobiography of Black Hawk, pp. 116–118.

5 Ibid., p. 118; Smith's Wisconsin, i. p. 261; Drake, Bk. v., p. 148.—6 Autobiography of Black Hawk, p. 118; Smith's Wisconsin, i. p. 261.

7 Autobiography of Black Hawk, pp. 118-121: Smith's Wisconsin, i. p. 261; Drake, Bk. v., p. 148.

8 Col. Backus's Paper.

1 Col. Backus's Paper; Drake, Bk. v., pp. 148, 149; Autobiog. of Black Hawk, p. 118; Smith's Wisconsin, i. pp. 261, 262. Mr. Boss (*Ogle Co.*, p. 38) says *three* were killed, and Mr. Wakefield (p. 18) agrees with him.

2 Autobiog. of Black Hawk, p. 118; Drake, Bk. v., p. 149; Smith's Wisconsin, i. p. 262. Mr. Boss (*Ogle Co.*, p. 38) says the chief rallied with *seven hundred* men; evidently following Mr. Wakefield (p. 19), who considered them as "*six or eight* hundred." Maj. P. Parkison, jr. (*Strictures on Gov. Ford's Hist.*), says he was "most shamefully defeated *by a force much inferior to his own*;" and J. W. Biddle (Pittsburg *Chronicle*, *Nov.* 12, 1856) uses the same language.

3 See also Drake's Book of the Indians, Bk. v., p. 149; Smith's Wisconsin, i. pp. 262, 263; Col. Whittlesey's Recollections of a Tour through Wisconsin in 1832.

braves, and sending the shrill war-whoop into their ranks in advance of his rifle-balls or tomahawks, the indignant Black Hawk accomplished, in a few minutes, what had been considered the work of a host—he scattered them in every direction, and filled their minds with the greatest alarm. A few minutes afterwards the main body of Major Stillman's command also came in sight—having followed in pursuit of the fugitive embassy—when the chief concealed his forty braves among "some bushes," and, in concealment, awaited its approach, shrewdly "intending to have *the first fire*"—knowing its effect on militia—"when it approached close enough." As Major Stillman halted on the prairie before he came within gunshot distance of the ambuscade, it is probable he had discovered the Indians; but the latter did not wait for a development of his plans or for his fire. Giving another of their terrible yells, the chief and his little party rushed from their hiding-places, and charged on the irregular mass of mounted men, and that also—unnerved by the injustice of the cause in which it was engaged, and magnifying every Indian warrior tenfold—also *turned and fled* in the greatest confusion.[1] The Indians, of course, pursued them; but, although twenty-five of his braves continued it, the chief "found it useless to follow, as they rode so fast;" and, after returning to his encampment, he "lighted his pipe, and sat down to thank the Great Spirit for what he had done."[2]

On the following day, incited by the terrible stories of the fugitives, as they reached Dixon, after a flight of fifty miles, Governor Reynolds issued a proclamation calling for an additional force of two thousand mounted Volunteers;[3] and throughout the entire West the exaggerated stories of Major Stillman and his followers—enlarged in the "Proclamation" of Governor Reynolds, and increased, in horrible incidents, in every subsequent version—were creating the greatest alarm.[1]

On the day after the battle, after burying the two Indians, belonging to the second party, who had been shot, and one of the first party, who had shared the same fate, Black Hawk visited the deserted camp of Major Stillman's party, and found "arms, ammunition, and provisions, all of which, especially the latter, he was in want of"—the *empty* whiskey kegs which he found there, creating the greatest surprise, as he "had understood that all the pale-faces belonged to the *temperance societies*."[2]

In this action—"*the battle at Stillman's Run*," *May fourteenth*, 1832—and in the pursuit which followed it, the Indians lost none; the Volunteers lost Major Perkins, Captain Adams, and nine men, and perhaps twenty horses killed, and five men were wounded.[3] On the morning of the fifteenth, General Whitesides, with his brigade of Volunteers—fifteen hundred in number—moved forward to the battle-ground on Stillman's Run, and buried the dead; when he, too, without venturing beyond the bounds of *acknowledged* safety, returned to Dixon—the troops, in the mean time, having become "dissatisfied, and wished to be discharged from the service."[4] On the seventeenth General Atkinson reached Dixon's Ferry, with his regulars and a supply of provisions; and on the nineteenth, with the entire army—two thousand four hundred in number—he also advanced up the Rock River towards the scene of the late battle.[5] The disaffection of the Volunteers continued, how-

[1] Smith's Wisconsin, i. p. 262; iii. p. 172; Ford's Illinois, p. 172; Col. Backus's Paper; Autobiog. of Black Hawk, pp. 119–123; Wakefield, pp. 19, 20; Drake, Bk. v., p. 149.

[2] Autobiography of Black Hawk, p. 119.

[3] Proclamation, Dixon's Ferry, May 15, 1832.

[1] Col. Parkison's Pioneer Life in Wisconsin; Smith's Wisconsin, i. pp. 263, 264; Wakefield, p. 21.

[2] Autobiog. of Black Hawk, p. 122; Smith's Wisconsin, iii. p. 172; Col. Backus's Paper.—[3] Smith's Wisconsin, iii. p. 172; Col. Backus's Paper; Wakefield, p. 20; Drake, Bk. v., p. 149.—[4] Smith's Wisconsin, iii. p. 173; Col. Backus's Paper; Wakefield, pp. 22, 24.

[5] Col. Backus's Paper; Wakefield, p. 24.

ever, and on the twenty-seventh and twenty-eighth of May they were disbanded and discharged at Ottawa, by Governor Reynolds,[1] leaving the defence of the frontiers with the regular troops, and with a small body of citizens who volunteered, temporarily, for that purpose.[2]

In the mean time the Indians were waging the war in accordance with their usages. The settlements were visited and destroyed; the settlers and their families were butchered or carried away captive; and, as has been said elsewhere, "the Indians had now shown themselves to be a courageous, active, and enterprising enemy. They had scattered their war-parties over all the north, from Chicago to Galena, and from the Illinois River into the Territory of Wisconsin; they occupied every grove, waylaid every road, hung around every settlement, and attacked every party of white men that attempted to penetrate the country."[3]

Among those who temporarily volunteered to defend the frontiers, on the discharge of the troops at Ottawa, was Adam M. Snyder, to whom was assigned the command of a company. In the night of the seventeenth of June, while he was encamped near Burr Oak Grove, thirty-five miles east from Galena,[4] he was fired on by the Indians; and, on the following morning (*June* 18), he went in pursuit of them. After a spirited chase he overtook them—*four in number*—and after a warm engagement and a vigorous charge, he succeeded in killing all of them, with the loss of one of his own command.[5] It appears, however, that later in the day, while Captain Snyder's company was returning to its encampment, the action was renewed by a larger body of Indians—seventy or eighty, it is said—two "gentlemen" of Captain Snyder's command being killed, and one wounded, at the first fire. The suddenness of the attack and the loss which the company experienced filled it with alarm, and many of the men, terror-stricken, commenced a retreat. The captain, with great presence of mind, halted, "and endeavored to form them for action;" but so completely were they overcome with fear, that it was only after General Whitesides—who was acting as a *private* in the company—had threatened to shoot the first man who attempted to run away, that any thing like order could be restored.[1] At length they formed, and taking to the trees, as the Indians had done before them, the action was carried on with great warmth, until the fall of the leader of the Indians dispirited them and they retired. Besides the loss referred to—one killed—the Indians appear to have sustained no loss in this affair; while the whites, besides the two "gentlemen" who were killed, are said to have had one wounded.[2] Captain Snyder immediately marched to head-quarters (*Fort Willbourne*), and as the new levy, under Governor Reynolds' "Proclamation," had assembled and was ready for duty, the temporary force of Volunteers, of which Captain Snyder's company was part, was disbanded.[3]

While these proceedings of the temporary volunteer force, in the vicinity of Kellogg's Grove, were adding to the interest of the struggle—on the fourteenth of June—a party of men were attacked in a cornfield near the mouth of Spafford's Creek, and five were killed. Information of the affair was immediately conveyed to Fort Defiance, when Captain Hoard dispatched an express to Colonel Henry Dodge, at Dodgeville, with the intelligence; while, at the same time, Lieutenant Charles Bracken, the second officer of the garrison, was dispatched to the scene of

1 Smith's Wisconsin, iii. p. 173; Col. Backus's Paper; Wakefield, p. 25. It does not appear by what authority the troops, which had been mustered into the *Federal* service, were discharged by the *State* authorities.

2 Smith's Wisconsin, iii. p. 175; Wakefield, p. 25.

3 Ford's Illinois, p. 128. See also Autobiog. of Black Hawk, pp. 125, 126; Drake, Bk. v., pp. 150, 151.

4 Smith's Wisconsin, iii. p. 176; Wakefield, p. 28.

5 Ibid.; Drake, Bk. v., p. 152.

1 Wakefield, p. 29; Smith's Wisconsin, iii. p. 176.

2 Wakefield, pp. 29, 30; Boss's Ogle County, p. 40.

3 Wakefield, p. 30.

the massacre with eleven men—all for whom horses could be obtained. Stopping all night at Fort Hamilton (*Wiola, Wis.*), on the following morning he was joined by nine men, and with his entire command of about twenty men, the lieutenant proceeded to Spafford's cornfield. After burying the victims, the expedition returned to Fort Hamilton, where it found Captain Gentry with a few men; and on the next day (*June* 16, 1832) Colonel Dodge came in and assumed the command.[1]

As the Colonel, with two friends, approached Fort Hamilton, they met a German named Apple—a settler in that vicinity—who was returning to his log-cabin to prepare for active service; and, immediately afterwards, he was shot by an enemy concealed in the bushes. As soon as the Colonel reached the fort, therefore, he sallied out again, at the head of the party which Lieutenant Bracken had commanded and of Captain Gentry's party—twenty-eight men in all; and taking their trail he pursued the Indians, overtaking them on the bank of the Pecatonica, behind which they had concealed themselves under a sand-bank and in the bushes. Having "told off" in sections of seven, the fourth, or central man of each section, remained on horseback and took charge of the horses of the other six, while four others were sent on the neighboring heights as look-outs, and the remainder dismounted and prepared for the attack by renewing their flints, repriming their guns, unbuttoning their shirt collars, and tightening their belts. When all were ready, Colonel Dodge addressed them in a few homely sentences, and the party, in line, waded the stream and entered the thicket. As soon as the position of the enemy was seen—he occupied the bed of a pond, in front of which was a natural breastwork three feet in height—the order was given to "*Charge 'em, boys, charge 'em.*" Mounting the embankment, after having received the enemy's fire, the whites engaged with the Indians in a hand-to-hand conflict, before the latter could reload their pieces; and with such spirit was the attack conducted, that in a few minutes, with the loss of three men, the enemy was completely overpowered — eleven having been killed on the spot, while two others, wounded, were tracked up the bank of the stream, and were scalped; and four others crept beneath the surrounding brushwood or into the long grass on the neighboring prairie, and died of their wounds—not one of the seventeen assailants escaping to tell the story of the *Battle of the Pecatonica.*[1]

While Colonel Dodge was thus engaged with the enemy at Pecatonica, Captain James W. Stephenson, with the Galena company of Volunteers, was on the look-out for Indians near the head of Yellow Creek, when he discovered a party of them, and pursued them into the bushes. The Indians having secured the advantage of position, immediately stood on their defence; and, having lost three of his men, Captain Stephenson, after a spirited attack, was obliged to order a retreat. He appears to have changed his mind after he had withdrawn from the action, however, and returned to the thicket, charging, a second and a third time, on the hiding-places of the enemy, with greater determination than success; until, having received a severe wound, he was compelled to retire. It is not known what was the strength of the enemy or his loss; and although the assault was spirited and well contested, the loss of the Volunteers indicated a spirited and gallant defence.[2]

---

[1] Drake, Bk. v., p. 151; Col. Dodge to Capt. Hoard, June 16, 1832.

[1] Descriptions of this action can be found in Smith's Wisconsin, i. pp. 274–276; Gen. Dodge's Report to Gen. Atkinson, June 18, 1832; Charles Bracken's Letter to Gen. W. R. Smith, Oct. 3, 1852; Edward Beauchard's Narrative; Col. H. Dodge to Capt. Shearman, June 16, 1832; Col. Parkison's Pioneer Life; "The Pecatonica Controversy," between Gen. Bracken and Maj. Parkison; and in various other parts of the Collections of the Wis. Hist. Soc.—[2] Autobiog. of Black Hawk, pp. 128, 129; Col. D. M. Parkison's Pioneer Life in Wisconsin; Wakefield, pp. 37, 38; Drake, Bk. v., p. 152.

On the twenty-fourth of June, Black Hawk, with one hundred and fifty Indians, made an attack on Apple River Fort, near the present village of Elizabeth, Illinois, and twelve miles from Galena. This work was a square stockade of logs driven into the ground, and strengthened with a block-house at each angle. It was garrisoned with twenty-five men, under Captain Stone, and was designed as a place of refuge, during the night, for the miners and their families, although, during the day, they attended to their affairs outside the walls, as they had done before the war. In the afternoon of the day in question, an express of three men, on its way from Galena to Dixon's Ferry, passed the fort; and had not proceeded more than three hundred and fifty yards before it was fired on by the Indians, who were concealed in the bushes. One of the three was wounded; and, although all were intoxicated, his comrades covered his retreat to the fort, affording an opportunity, at the same time, for the miners and their families to secure their safety in the same manner. As the express entered the fort, the enemy dismounted, hitched his horses, and opened a heavy fire on it for upwards of an hour, without inflicting any injury beyond killing one man and wounding another. At length the Indians entered the log-houses which stood near the fort, and having knocked holes in the walls, for port-holes, they continued the fire without exposing themselves to that of the garrison. Finding that his rifles were useless in such an attack, and fearing to set fire to the fort or the houses, lest the light or the smoke should discover their position, and direct the army or the people in their pursuit, Black Hawk "thought it more prudent to be content with what flour, provisions, cattle, and horses he could find," and to retire. Before doing this, however, it is said, the Indians plundered the houses, "chopping, splitting, and tearing up a quantity of fine furniture." It is said by by an eye-witness, that "there was scarcely a man or woman that was left with a second suit of clothing. They went into my father's house," he continues; "there was a large bureau full of fine clothes, and they took six fine cloth coats and a number of fine ruffle-shirts. With their tomahawks they split the drawers, and took the contents. They ripped open the bedticks, emptied the feathers, took all the bed-clothing, and broke all the delf in the cupboards. Some of the outhouses were kept for the purpose of storing away provisions; they got into those houses where a number of flour-barrels were stowed away; they would lie down on their faces and roll a barrel after them, until they would get into a ravine, where they were out of danger, they then would empty the barrels of flour; after they had destroyed this necessary article, and when they found they could not succeed in taking the fort as they expected, they commenced a warfare upon the stock. They killed all the cattle that were near the fort, and took a number of fine horses, to the number of about twenty, which were never got again by their owners." At length, having remained before the fort fifteen hours, and done all the damage they could, the Indians retired, with the loss of several of their number.[1]

In the mean time the volunteers which Governor Reynolds had called for, had assembled at Fort Wilbourn, been organized into three brigades, mustered into the service of the United States, and ordered to rendezvous at Dixon's Ferry.[2] The battalion of spies commanded by Major John Dement, and attached to the First brigade, was ordered to move forward, as an advance-guard; and it had reached Kellogg's Grove, when, on the morning of the twenty-fifth of June, an express reached that place reporting the existence of a heavy trail on the north side of the grove. At daylight the Major went out with twenty-five men to re-

[1] Letter of Capt. Flack to Mr. Wakefield; Drake, Bk. v., p. 152; Autobiography of Black Hawk, pp. 126, 127.

[2] Wakefield, p. 38.

connoitre; at the same time directing the remainder of his battalion to saddle their horses and hold themselves in readiness to act as circumstances might warrant. He had not proceeded far from his encampment before he discovered a small party of Indians, when part of his men, disregarding his orders, pursued it, and were drawn into an ambuscade. The Major immediately formed those who remained with him, together with a few who had followed from the encampment, into a covering party, and with them he gallantly endeavored to rescue those who had been led into danger. The yells of the enemy, as he rushed from his coverts, intimidated the greater part of those who were with him, and they fled, leaving the Major to contend with the enemy, with but few supporters. With these he gallantly resisted the Indians, while, at the same time, he fell back on the main body, and occupied a line of log-houses, from which he was enabled to hold them in check, until, an hour afterwards, they retired with the loss of nine of their number. Although the strength of the whites was much greater than that of the Indians—the latter being the same party, under Black Hawk, who had attacked the Apple River Fort, on the preceding day—and although the personal gallantry of the Major called forth the admiration of the chief who opposed him, and afforded an example to his men which they did not imitate, this affair has, properly, been considered a defeat of the whites, of whom five were killed and three wounded. Upwards of sixty horses belonging to the battalion were also killed.[1]

While Major Dement was thus engaged, one of his men was sent back to General Posey for assistance, and met him on the road; but, notwithstanding his march was quickened, the Indians had retired in the direction of Lake Koshkonong before he could reach the field of battle.[1]

During the succeeding three or four weeks the several divisions of the forces appear to have succeeded in none of their undertakings. At one time they concentrated their strength in the vicinity of Koshkonong Lake—probably for the purpose of inclosing the enemy who was supposed to have been there;[2] and at another, finding that Black Hawk had slipped away from them and scattered his forces, they too separated, and went in different directions in pursuit of the fragments of their enemy's party.[3] At one time the several divisions, in full pursuit, promised a speedy termination of the conflict; at another, a few days afterwards, they were brought to a sudden halt for the want of supplies,[4] or, the victims of Indian shrewdness—the deception of an enemy can be called nothing more than this—in leading them into quagmires and over streams which, without bridges, were impassable.[5]

At the same time the Indians were not in a condition to take complete advantage of these delays and mistakes. Originally entering Illinois without a hostile intent, and accompanied with their women and children, and all their worldly effects—a people returning to the homes of their fathers, as the Israelites returned from Egypt—they had been forced into a war, without preparation or the opportunity to disencumber themselves of their families; and they were not only checked in their movements from this cause, but they were also suffering for the means of subsistence. A gallant officer of the army, then with the troops, has recently alluded to the position of the Indians on the

[1] Autobiography of Black Hawk, pp. 127, 128; Ford's Illinois, p. 129; Smith's Wisconsin, i. pp. 270, 271; Col. Backus's Paper; Col. Parkison's Pioneer Life in Wisconsin; Boss's Ogle County, p. 41.

[1] Smith's Wisconsin, i. p. 270; Col. Backus's Paper.

[2] Smith's Wisconsin, i. p. 277; iii. p. 218; Col. Parkison's Pioneer Life in Wisconsin; Drake, Bk. v., p. 153.

[3] Col. Backus's Paper; Col. Parkison's Pioneer Life in Wisconsin; Drake, Bk. v., p. 153.—[4] Col. Backus's Paper; Gen. Bracken's Further Strictures on "*Ford's Hist. of Illinois;*" Wakefield, p. 74; Drake, Bk. v., p. 153.

[5] Smith's Wisconsin, i. p. 278; iii. pp. 218, 219; Col. Backus's Paper; Col. Parkison's Pioneer Life in Wisconsin.

White Water and Rock Rivers, and said that "here they found some game, roots, and vegetable substances, on which they had subsisted, *or existed.* But our delays, our marches and countermarches, had misled and deceived them, and had prevented them from separating to hunt or fish; hence their supplies were exhausted, and they were actually in a state of starvation. Our masterly inactivity, occasioned by treacherous advice and want of stores, had already conquered them; but we were not yet aware of this fact."[1] The brave, but unfortunate, Black Hawk, also bears testimony to the same sad truths. "During our encampment at the Four Lakes," he says, "we were hard put to, to obtain enough to eat to support nature. Situate in a swampy, marshy country (which had been selected in consequence of the great difficulty required to gain access thereto), there was but little game of any sort to be found, and fish were equally scarce. The great distance to any settlement, and the impossibility of bringing supplies therefrom, if any could have been obtained, deterred our young men from making farther attempts. We were forced to dig roots and bark trees, to obtain something to satisfy hunger and keep us alive. Several of our old people became so much reduced as actually to die with hunger."[2]

The singular spectacle was thus seen of two contending forces severally held in check by the want of the means of support, and of each being ignorant of the position or condition of the other. For the purpose of relieving the wants of the whites, Generals Henry and Alexander, and Colonel Dodge, with their commands, were detached to Fort Winnebago for a supply of provisions for twelve days;[3] while for the relief of the Indians, soon afterwards, Black Hawk "concluded to remove his women and children

[1] Col. Backus, U. S. A., who, at that time, was an Aid-de-camp of Gen. Brady.—[2] Autobiog. of Black Hawk, p. 130. Every writer, on this subject, confirms this statement.—[3] Col. Backus's Paper; Drake, Bk. v., p. 153.

across the Mississippi, that *they* might return to the Sauk nation again;"[1] while, it is probable, he, with his braves, intended to continue the contest.

It appears that General Alexander returned to the camp with the stores, while General Henry and Colonel Dodge, with their commands, moved towards the Rock River Rapids in search of the enemy. Without knowing that the escort had not included the entire detachment, Black Hawk immediately moved towards the Wisconsin River, with the purpose of descending that stream to the Mississippi; and was hastening in that direction when General Alexander and Colonel Dodge struck his trail, and started in pursuit of him.[2] It is said that "evidences of the poverty and sufferings of the Indians were seen upon every mile of their trail. The bones of horses which had been killed to prevent the starvation of the women and children, were hourly passed, and eventually a few stragglers in their rear were discovered" in the vicinity of the Wisconsin.[3]

At this moment the force of the whites, under General Henry and Colonel Dodge, embraced a thousand men, besides a battalion of volunteers from Michigan and Galena, and was well supplied with stores and anxious for the engagement;[4] while that under Black Hawk numbered less than three hundred half-starved and dispirited warriors.[5] A rear-guard of twenty men, under Ne-a-pope, had been thrown back, to give notice of the approach of the whites; and the remainder of the party was busily employed in transporting the women and children, the aged and the infirm, to an island

[1] Autobiog. of Black Hawk, p. 130.—[2] Col. Backus's Paper; Wakefield, p. 61; Tenney's Early Times in Wisconsin.—[3] Col. Backus's Paper.

[4] Col. Backus says the brigades of Posey and Alexander "consisted of about 1000 men," and that "Gen. Dodge, with a battalion of Michigan and Galena Volunteers, arrived on the opposite bank of Lake Koshkonong."

[5] Drake, Bk. v., p. 154. It is exceedingly doubtful if Black Hawk had more than 300 at any time.

in the river, when, suddenly—the outpost having been avoided—the head of the American column came in sight. Black Hawk was thus compelled to fight, or to sacrifice his women and children and the helpless of his party; and he appears to have acted promptly and honorably in the emergency. Leaving the greater part of his party to continue the removal of their families, with fifty braves he went out to meet General Henry and dispute his progress. He was well mounted, and after addressing his warriors in a few well-timed remarks, he moved forward and endeavored to secure a position on a high ground, near by, "that he might have some advantage over the whites."[1]

In the mean time General Henry had formed his troops, and was ready for action. His first line was formed with Major Ewing's "Spy Battalion" in the centre, the companies under Captains Gentry and Clark on the right, and those under Captains Camp and Parkinson on the left. His second line was composed of Colonel Collins' regiment in the centre, with that under Colonel Jones on his left, and that under Colonel Fry on his right. His men were all dismounted, and his horses were left in the rear—the central man of each section of seven having been detailed for that purpose; and he had formed his men on foot, in the order referred to, and had prepared for action.[2]

Against this force Black Hawk and his fifty braves moved, without wavering or manifesting the least fear—"raising the war-whoop, screaming, and yelling hideously, and rushing forward, meeting it with a heavy charge."[3] The superior force of the whites, however, insured the safety of their position; and "with a tremendous volley of musketry, accompanied with the most terrific yells that ever came from the head of mortals, except from the savages themselves,"[1] they succeeded in occupying the high ground which Black Hawk aimed to secure, and in driving the fifty Indians into a deep ravine, notwithstanding the determined attempt of the latter to turn, first, the left of the American line, and then its right. With the utmost determination the fifty "savages" withstood the three regiments and two battalions of whites—but little less "savage" than the former, in their habits and mode of warfare; and much more so in the spirit which actuated them—until sunset,[2] when "finding that the whites would not come near enough to receive his fire, in the dusk of the evening, and *knowing that the women and children had had sufficient time to reach the island in the* Wisconsin," Black Hawk ordered his warriors to disperse, in different directions, and to "meet him at the Wisconsin," and, strange as it may appear, *the victors "were not disposed to pursue them.*"[3]

The loss of the whites, in this action, was one killed and eight wounded;[4] and, although the army supposed that of the Indians to have been "about sixty killed and a great number wounded," there is no reason to disbelieve Black Hawk when he says, "I defended my passage over the Wisconsin with a loss of only six men, though opposed by a host of mounted militia."[5]

In recording the result of this engagement —"*the Battle of Wisconsin Heights, July twenty-first,* 1832"—it is difficult to determine which to admire most, the self-sacrificing spirit of the chief and his fifty braves, or the skill and determination with which

[1] Autobiography of Black Hawk, p. 131.

[2] Wakefield, pp. 65, 66, 68; Lieut. Bracken's Narrative.

[3] Parkison's Strictures on Ford's History of Illinois; Wakefield, p. 68.

[1] Wakefield, p. 68. Considering this is the testimony of an officer in Col. Ewing's battalion, it may be supposed that he spoke from his own knowledge, and that it was not exaggerated.—[2] Wakefield, pp. 68, 69; Autobiog. of Black Hawk, p. 131; Smith's Wisconsin, iii. p. 184; Lieut. Bracken's Narrative.

[3] Autobiog. of Black Hawk, pp. 131, 132. See also Smith's Wisconsin, iii. p. 184.

[4] Wakefield, p. 68; Smith's Wisconsin, iii. p. 184; Capt. Este's Statement.—[5] Autobiog. of Black Hawk, p. 132. The writers of that day say the Indian loss was much greater.

they accomplished their purposes; and Black Hawk, in referring to it, was excusable in indulging in a little self-gratulation, when he remarked, "whatever may be the sentiments of the white people, in relation to this battle, my nation, though fallen, will award to me the reputation of a great brave, in conducting it."[1]

During the succeeding day the troops remained on the field of battle;[2] and early on the morning of the twenty-third, they were terrified by the sound of something on a neighboring hill-top, which, in their fright, they supposed was an Indian chief, giving orders to his men.[3] In the mean time, while part of the Indians descended the Wisconsin, with the hope of reaching the Mississippi more speedily,[4] Black Hawk and his band started over the rugged country for the same purpose. His progress was necessarily slow; and, having no means of support, several of his old men and little children perished from hunger on the way.[5] Soon afterwards General Atkinson, with the main body of the army, joined in the pursuit of the famishing "invaders" of Illinois; and following their trail over the "rugged country" of which the chief speaks, as will be seen, he came up with them near the mouth of the Bad Axe.

While the Indians and their pursuers were thus traversing the wilderness towards the Upper Mississippi, intelligence of the action at the Wisconsin Heights was conveyed to Prairie du Chien by express, and Colonel Loomis, the commander of that post, immediately employed a steamboat to cruise on the river, and to cut off the retreat of the miserable fugitives. This vessel (the *Enterprise*) soon gave place to a faster one (the *Warrior*); and, on the first of August, she discovered the Indians on the bank of the river, near the mouth of the Bad Axe, making preparations to cross the river. The chief was acquainted with the captain of the vessel, and ordered his warriors not to fire, "as he intended to go on board of her, so that he might save their women and children;" and with this purpose he displayed a white flag, "and called to the captain of the boat, telling him to send his little canoe ashore, and let him come on board." He was hailed from the boat with the inquiry, if they were Sauks or Winnebagoes; and when he answered they were Sauks, a fire was opened on him and his party, with a six-pounder, by Lieutenant Kingsbury and a detachment of regular troops, who occupied the forward deck of the boat.[1] As Lieutenant Kingsbury, and Captain Throckmorton of the *Warrior*, have stated that they saw the flag,[2] this fire appears to have been a wilful violation of every rule which governs the actions of military men; and when Black Hawk's party returned the fire with their small-arms they were justified by every law, both military and civil.

After the first discharge of the six-pounder, the Indians took to the trees and returned the fire, keeping it up until the "*Warrior*" found it necessary to return to Prairie du Chien for another supply of fuel.[3]

It is said that twenty-three warriors were killed in this disgraceful affair; while of the crew of the *Warrior*, and the troops on board of her, only one was wounded.[4]

On the following morning (*Aug.* 2), General Atkinson and his force approached the Mississippi; and at an early hour the spies came in sight of the Indian outposts. The latter immediately attempted to surrender by exhibiting a white flag, "but the whites

---

[1] Autobiog. of Black Hawk, p. 132.—[2] Wakefield, p. 69; Drake, Bk. v., pp. 154, 155.—[3] Wakefield, pp. 71, 72.

[4] Autobiog. of Black Hawk, p. 132. It is said the greater part of these were destroyed by a party of troops which had been sent to intercept them.

[5] Autobiography of Black Hawk, p. 133.

[1] Neil's Hist. of Minnesota, pp. 412, 413; Boss's Ogle Co., p. 47; Smith's Wisconsin, i. p. 282; Autobiog. of Black Hawk, pp. 133, 134.—[2] Capt. Throckmorton's Letter, Prairie du Chien, Aug. 2, 1832; Lieut. Kingsbury's Report, cited in Drake, Bk. v., p. 156.—[3] Neil's Minnesota, p. 413; Capt. Este's Narrative; Smith's Wisconsin, i. p. 283; Autobiog. of Black Hawk, p. 134.—[4] Capt. Throckmorton's Letter; Boss's Ogle Co., p. 47.

paid no attention to their entreaties, and commenced slaughtering them;" when, forced to resist or to submit to the sacrifice, they resolved to sell their lives dearly, and returned the fire. The main body hastening forward to support its light troops, the Indians slowly retired, firing as they retreated, and fell back on their main body, which was on the bottom, busily employed in transporting the women and children, and the aged and infirm over the Mississippi.[1]

At this moment the scene was a touching one. In front were a people who had been led, by influences which controlled their action, to seek the recovery of the homes of their fathers which been fraudulently taken from them by the whites; and who, in the course of their journey, without provocation on their part, and without any overt act of hostility, had been forced to resort to arms in defence of their lives and the lives of their families who accompanied them. Without friends to counsel them, without aid to strengthen their force, without food to sustain the demands of nature, without sympathy, and denounced as "monsters" of the most hideous character, they had been hunted from one point to another with all the power of the Federal government, with all the voluntary strength of Illinois, Michigan, and Wisconsin, and with all the energy of individual cupidity. Seeking shelter in the swamps, they had sought *existence* among the roots which they could dig up, or the young grass which they boiled for their little ones, or the bark which they peeled from the trees for those who required more delicate nourishment;[2] or flying, anxiously, towards the Mississippi, the boundary of their new homes, they had killed their horses for their families' nourishment, leaving nothing but the bones and the hair of the animals to tell the story of their sufferings.[3]

[1] Galena paper of Aug. 6, 1832, cited by Drake, Bk. v., p. 156; Lieut. Bracken's Narrative; Autobiog. of Black Hawk, p. 135.—[2] Col. Whittlesey's Recollections of a Tour in Wisconsin in 1832.—[3] Eye-witnesses of the trail have left this statement on record.

Those who, from any cause, had fallen into the hands of their pursuers, had been "left behind," as it was heartlessly called, notwithstanding their "pleas for quarters;"[1] and when they had begged for peace and shelter, and had urged the acknowledgment of the sacred character of a white flag, a Federal cannon, and Federal grape and canister, had communicated the answer of the Federal government to their appeal for mercy, and the indorsement of the Federal government of the acts of their spoilers. They were now busily engaged in removing their families to their acknowledged homes. With canoes and temporary rafts, on horseback or being towed over by their faithful steeds, and even by swimming, bearing their little ones on their backs as they went, the women were eagerly pressing forward to a place of supposed safety,[2] while their husbands, and fathers, and brothers—as Black Hawk had done at the Wisconsin—covered the retreat by preparing for battle.

Behind these, five times more numerous than they, were the Federal troops and the Volunteers—the latter not less savage, in every respect, than the Indians—who were the instruments of their spoliation or the supporters of the wrong. The former, under their experienced and gallant officers, were but the instruments of an unjust policy of the government under whose orders they acted; while the latter, moving in their own cause, were regardless of discipline or order, relentless in their animosities against an unresisting or an overpowered enemy, unreliable, if not cowardly, before a determined opponent, and anxious for the slaughter rather than the battle. The latter had been formed in order of battle—Generals Posey and Alexander, with their brigades, being moved to the extreme right, up the river, to prevent the escape of the Indians in that direction; Colonels Jones and Collins, and Major Ewings, with their regiments, under

[1] Wakefield, p. 81.—[2] Col. Backus's Paper.

General Henry, in line, moving down against the Indians; General Dodge with his Volunteers, and Colonel Zachary Taylor with the regular troops, on the right, being engaged with the outposts of the Indians; and Colonel Fry, with his regiment, covering the rear. After a short contest General Dodge and Colonel Taylor, with their commands, moved to the left, and joined the line in its attack on the main body of the Indians; and with such resolution did the latter defend themselves and cover the retreat of their families that, soon afterwards, the companies commanded by Captains Gentry, Gruer, and Richardson, and the regiment of Colonel Fry—the former from Generals Dodge and Alexander on the extreme right; the latter from the rear—were found necessary to support and strengthen the line of attack. The action on the river bottom continued but little longer, when the Indians, overpowered, either fell before the rifles of their pursuers, or fled to one of the islands with which the Mississippi, at this place, abounds—vainly hoping that they would not be pursued.

Unfortunately for the luckless fugitives, at this moment (ten in the morning) the steamboat *Warrior* returned to the scene of her exploit on the preceding evening, and opened a fire, with her cannon, on the fugitives—men, women, and children—who were huddled together on the islands referred to; and, at the same time, she sent her two boats to transport the regular troops, under Colonel Taylor, to the islands to complete the work of destruction. As may be readily supposed, the scene no longer deserves the name of a battle, as it possessed none of the characteristics of one. It was, in truth, a massacre of unresisting Indians, of every age and sex, and of the entire party *only one escaped.*[1]

[1] Drake, Bk. v., p. 157; Col. Backus's Paper; Neil's Minnesota, pp. 413, 414; Boss's Ogle County, pp. 47, 48; Smith's Wisconsin, i. p. 283; ii. p. 186; Lieut. Bracken's and Capt. Este's Statements; Gen. Bracken's Further Strictures on Ford's History of Illinois, &c.

In this important engagement—"*The Battle of the Bad Axe, August second,* 1832"—the whites lost twenty-seven killed and wounded; while of the Indians, it is supposed that one hundred and fifty were killed.[1] It is said by an eye-witness, that "when the Indians were driven to the bank of the Mississippi, some hundreds of men, women, and children, plunged into the river, and hoped by diving to escape the bullets of our guns. Very few, however, escaped our sharp-shooters;"[2] and those who did escape to the western bank of the Mississippi were butchered in cold blood by a party of Dahkotahs—their hereditary enemies—who had been brought there, for that purpose, by the Federal officers.[3]

This was the finishing stroke of the war. The vengeance of the government, like the mutterings from Moloch in the valley of Tophet, having been appeased by the sacrifice of the squaws and their children, if not by that of the braves who had fallen by hunger or the rifle-ball, no longer asked for blood; while the settlers in Illinois and Wisconsin, no longer annoyed by "the monsters" who had dared to ask a restoration of the homes and the graves of their fathers, turned back to enjoy the plunder of which their cruelties had confirmed the possession. Soon afterwards the gallant chief—worthy a better fate—surrendered himself into the hands of the Federal authorities; and, like many a patriot in ancient times, he was chained to the car of the victor, and gave eclat to the triumphal march of the conqueror through the country.[4]

[1] Drake's Book of Indians, Bk. v., p. 157.

[2] Letter in Galena paper, Aug. 6, cited by Mr. Drake.

[3] Neil's Minnesota, p. 414; Boss's Ogle County, p. 48; Smith's Wisconsin, i. p. 284; Gen. Atkinson to Gen. Macomb, Aug. 5, 1832.

[4] Smith's Wisconsin, i. pp. 284, 285; iii. p. 186; Autobiography of Black Hawk, pp. 136–152.

CHAPTER XCVIII.

December 7, 1835, to April 19, 1842.

THE FLORIDA WAR.

In the South, as well as in the West, the struggle between the Indians and the whites for the possession of the soil, was protracted, and conducted with great bitterness of feeling. In the former, as well as in the latter, the law of "might maketh right" prevailed; and as early as 1821, when Florida passed into the hands of the United States, the acts of aggression, on the part of the whites, commenced. The villages and cultivated grounds of the Indians—generally among the most lovely and desirable spots in the territory—were seized by speculators or settlers; the owners of these homes "were considered as undeserving of liberty and kindness;" and the most unjust means were employed by the government, and the most oppressive by the white settlers, to get rid of the race "for which was entertained but little sympathy or charity." Treaty after treaty, and negotiation after negotiation followed, without any beneficial result, for upwards of fourteen years, until December seventh, 1835, when the first blow appears to have been struck, and the antagonistic forces were brought in contact.

From that time, led by their several chiefs, the Indians struggled against the whites, led by the most distinguished officers of the army, with great resolution and bravery, until the nineteenth of April, 1842, when they, too, were compelled to give way and seek in new and distant countries a home for their wives and little ones. At the Allachua Savannah (*Dec.* 19, 1835), at Micanopy (*Dec.* 20, 1835), on Dade's Battle-ground (*Dec.* 28, 1835), at the Ford of the Withlacoochie River (*Dec.* 31, 1835), at Dunlawtown (*Jan.* 18, 1836), at the Fords of the Withlacoochie (*Feb.* 27, 28, *and* 29, *and March* 5, 1836), at Oloklikaha (*March* 31, 1836), at Cooper's Post (*April* 5 *to* 17, 1836), at Thlonotosassa Creek (*April* 27, 1836), at Micanopy (*June* 9, 1836), at Welika Pond (*July* 9, 1836), at Ridgely's Mill (*July* 27, 1836), at Fort Drane (*Aug.* 12, 1836), near the Withlacoochie (*Nov.* 14 *and* 18, 1836), at the Wahoo Swamp (*Nov.* 21, 1836), at the Hatcheeluskie Creek (*Jan.* 27, 1837), at Camp Monroe (*Feb.* 8, 1837), at Clear River (*Feb.* 9, 1837), near the Musquito Inlet (*Sept.* 10, 1837), at Okeechobee Lake (*Dec.* 25, 1837), at the Waccassassa River (*Dec.* 25, 1837), at Jupiter Creek (*Jan.* 15, 1838), at the Jupiter Inlet (*Jan.* 24, 1838), at Newmansville (*June* 17, 1838), at Carloosahatchee (*July* 23, 1839), near Fort King (*April* 28, 1840), at Leoy's Prairie (*May* 19, 1840), at Waccahoota (*Sept.* 6, 1840), in the Everglades, with Lieutenant-colonel Harney and his command (*Dec.* 3 *to* 24, 1840), near Micanopy (*Dec.* 28, 1840), at Fort Brooks (*March* 2, 1841), with Captain Wade's expedition (*Nov.* 6, 1841), at Hawe Creek (*Jan.* 25, 1842), at Pilaklikaha (*April* 19, 1842), and at other places, the Indians met the whites, and, after their own manner, fought the battles of their own country.

The record of these engagements is full and complete; and many of the participants are still among us, to impart more minute information, to correct the errors which may have crept into current accounts of the engagements, to justify their own actions, or to defend the memory of those—their companions in arms—who no longer remain on duty. Justice to all concerned—the Indians, the gallant officers and soldiers who were engaged in the prolonged struggle, the friends of those who no longer survive, and the writer of these pages—should the same plan be adopted in this, as in other parts of the work—would require a greater amount of space than can be allotted to it, and the subject is reluctantly passed with a few general remarks.

While Spain occupied the territory of Florida, the Indians who inhabited it were treated with consideration and respect; and, in return, they sustained a lucrative trade with the Spaniards among whom they dwelt. This state of affairs terminated, however, when the United States entered into the possession of Florida, and the Indians quickly understood that they were no longer considered as important, either politically or in a business light, as they had been by their former neighbors. The villages which had dotted the country from St. Augustine to the Appalachicola, and the little clearings which surrounded the palmetto cabins of the Seminoles, quickly became the objects of envy among the land speculators who had wandered over the country; and the Federal government, the instrument of politicians, speedily endeavored to secure them, "peaceably if it could, forcibly if it must." Agents were appointed to negotiate, and "as the Indians resisted the efforts to assemble for the purpose of making a treaty, innumerable difficulties accumulated from day to day, which pressed heavily upon them;" while, at the same time, the arguments, and persuasions, and representations of professed friends—the purchased tools of the operators—gradually overcame their determined opposition, and they reluctantly entered into a "negotiation," of the nature and the effects of which they were both ignorant and unwilling to learn. A "treaty" followed, which was subsequently modified by a supplemental article; and, as has been said by a faithful historian of the event, "a net-work was thrown around the Florida Indians, from which there was no escape. Their destiny, their happiness, and prosperity were now in the hands of *the people*." What wonder, then, need there be, that a change so disastrous to the Indians should produce dissatisfaction and enmity? What wonder need there be that the action of a government which is "actuated more by the disposition to gratify the populace than to vindicate the rights of the savages," should result in war and desolation?

In 1824 the limits of the Indian country were curtailed; and many of the Indians were required to abandon their homes, and find new ones where proper new ones could not be obtained; the promised rations, for their supply of food while preparing their new homes for occupation, were partially withheld, and great sufferings were experienced by the tribes—sixteen hundred persons, instead of sixteen hundred rations, as promised, receiving only one thousand; the imaginary lines which bounded their new homes, being unsurveyed, were innocently crossed by the savage hunters, at the expense of personal chastisement or the loss of their rifles; the written passes of the Indian agent were disregarded, and their holders shot and robbed of their peltry and their guns; and the tribes were *driven* into hostilities in defence of the dearest rights of mankind. Troops were ordered out to punish "the Indian outrages," as they were styled, and a general Indian war appeared inevitable. Fortunately, better councils prevailed—a peace was immediately *purchased* by the whites, and the Indians resumed a friendly intercourse. Well might it be said by a Federal officer, in view of the facts, "any man who reads the history of this inglorious *war* and its effects, will learn and see much which, as an *American*, a member of a nation calling itself *Christian*, he must blush at."

From that time forward the Indians suffered great hardships, and were made the victims of a series of impositions and misrepresentations. The agents of the government and the commissioners appointed to treat with them, appear to have made the expulsion of the Indians, at any cost, and under any circumstances, the sole end of their appointment; while justice, and fair-dealing, and humanity, were not considered, and Christianity would have blushed to have seen the misery which was produced.

A delegation which had visited Arkansas for the purpose of examining the country to which it had been proposed the Indians should emigrate, although it condemned it, was intrapped into an approval of it in a cunningly-devised "treaty," of which the delegates could not read or understand a syllable; and when it was afterwards charged with having "touched the quill," in approval of the emigration, the delegation vehemently denied it, declared its dissatisfaction with the Western country, and held itself in readiness to oppose the fulfilment of the provisions of the instrument which bore *the marks* of their approval. Micanopy, Arpeika (*Sam Jones*), Halpatter-Tustenuggee (*Alligator*), Jumper, Black Dirt, and Os-se-se-he-ho-la (*Oseola*, or *Powell*), were the great leaders of the Indians; and William P. Duvall, James Gadsden, and Bernard Segui, as Commissioners in 1823, Colonel Brooke, as the *unwilling* military officer in 1828, Thomas L. McKenney, as Superintendent of Indian Affairs, Major John Phagan,—a tool of the speculators,—as Seminole Agent, from March, 1830 to 1834, Montfort Stokes, Henry L. Ellsworth, and John F. Schermerhorn, Commissioners in 1833, and General Wiley Thompson, Seminole Agent in 1834, were among the instrumentalities which were employed in intrapping the savages, in defrauding them of their property, and in effecting their removal.

The farce of "ratifying the treaty of Payne's Landing," and the "additional treaty" of satisfaction with the Western country, which had been secured from the delegation at Fort Gibson, Arkansas, was completed in April, 1834, when General Clinch was ordered to Florida to remove the victims; and a force sufficiently strong to overcome the more obstinate of them, as was supposed, was placed under his authority. At the first council which followed this measure the Indians boldly and plainly declared their determination to offer resistance—Ossesehehola, who, although not a chief, was the ruling spirit, drawing his knife and striking it into the table, with the declaration—"The only treaty I will execute is *with this;*" and all receiving the information that the government would use force in executing the treaty with groans, violent gestures, and terms of abuse, and telling the Agent that "it was a white man's treaty, which they did not understand, as the interpretation of the negotiation was false."

In February, 1835, ten companies were added to General Clinch's command; transports were prepared at Tampa Bay to convey the Indians to New Orleans; steamboat passages up the Mississippi had been arranged; and wagons, for their transportation from the mouth of the Arkansas to Fort Gibson, had also been procured; while, on the other hand, the Indians as resolutely determined to remain in Florida.

In April, 1835, another council was held, with the same result; and the agent, General Thompson, assumed the authority of *deposing from power, as chiefs*, Micanopy, Jumper, Alligator, Sam Jones, and Black Dirt, the leading chiefs of the nation. This new aggression, in attempting to interfere with the hereditary rights of the chiefs, added fuel to the flame, and the most submissive of the warriors were aroused, and demanded vengeance. Even the Secretary of War and the President felt the force of the blow, in its rebound on the whites; and, in order to soothe the feelings of the nation, the time for the removal was postponed. With a degree of forethought, which reflected great credit on the minds who originated it, this respite was employed in procuring and storing away a full supply of powder and lead, even after the agent had forbidden the sale of any of these articles to them; and the chiefs and Ossesehehola were not backward in defying the power of the government and the skill of its officers. On one of these occasions the latter was seized by General Thompson, the agent, put in irons, and confined in Fort King; but after remaining there six days, he *professed* to have become satisfied with the treaty, and was set at liberty—a more uncompromising enemy of the whites, a more unflinching opponent of their policy, a more resolute supporter of Indian rights and of Indian property than ever.

The time fixed for removal (*Jan.* 1, 1836) at length arrived, but the deliberate assassination of Charley-E-Mathlar (a friendly chief, who had been led, by bribes, to favor emigration), by Ossesehehola, a few days before that time, clearly indicated that the knife of the latter was, truly, his sole negotiator.

The charm of peace having been broken, on the twenty-eighth of December, 1835, General Thompson — the obnoxious agent who had placed Ossesehehola in irons at Fort King, and whose sole purpose appeared to tend to the spoliation of the nation—and Lieutenant Smith, his companion, were shot and scalped near Fort King; and immediately afterwards Mr. Rogers,—the sutler at the fort,—and four others, shared the same fate, and the dwelling and store of the former were burned to the ground, also within sight of the same post.

The "Florida War" had fairly commenced; and the question was yet unanswered whether the *might* of the government, or the *right* of the Indians should prevail. Black Hawk and the Sauks, not less gallant or less patriotic than the Florida braves, had succumbed a short time before, and the brave old chief had been carried around the country, in his bonds, as a gazing-stock for the people; Micanopy and the Seminoles, victims of a similar fraud, although still the occupants of the soil, were not a whit less patriotic than the former, not a particle less devoted to their homes and their families, nor surrounded by a population which was more friendly or less avaricious; and, like their Northwestern brethren,—as New York had done at Golden Hill in 1770, as New England had done at Bunker's Hill, and Virginia at the Great Bridge in 1775, and as North Carolina had done at Moore's Creek Bridge in 1776,—they resolved to *fight for their homes, their property, their families, and their rights.*

In accordance with that determination, on the twenty-eighth of December, 1835, Micanopy, Jumper, and Alligator, intercepted two companies of Federal troops, commanded by Major Dade, and killed eight officers and one hundred men, only two men, wounded, escaping to tell the terrible tale. In the dance which followed this success, "the more humorous of the company addressed speeches to the scalp of General Thompson, imitating his gestures and manner of talking to them in council."

On the thirty-first of December, two hundred and fifty warriors, under Ossesehehola and Alligator, attacked General Clinch and two hundred and twenty-seven men, near the ford of the Withlacoochie, killed four and wounded forty of his men, and compelled him to return to Fort Drane, with a loss, to themselves, of three killed, and Ossesehehola and four wounded.

At this time other chiefs and braves began to appear, and the older chiefs gradually fell back. Among the former were Ta-ho-loochee (*The Little Cloud*), Ho-lar-too-chee, Co-a-coo-chee (*Wild Cat*), Thlock-lo Tustenuggee (*Tiger-tail*), Nethlock-Mathlar, Chekika, and Octiarche; and the utmost activity prevailed throughout all the villages on the peninsula; while General Clinch, who was authorized to call on the States of South Carolina, Georgia, and Alabama, for any amount of force which he might consider necessary to enforce the provisions of the treaty and secure the removal of the Indians, was gradually strengthening himself and preparing for the struggle.

During the succeeding month (*Jan.*, 1836), sixteen plantations were destroyed in East Florida, while the planters fled for their lives without provision or property; and the greatest consternation prevailed among the people. At the same time General Gaines prepared to strengthen the force which was already in Florida; and, on the eighth of February, he left New Orleans with eleven hundred men, reaching Fort Brooke on the tenth, and taking the field on the thirteenth. As he carried with him only ten days' provisions, it would appear that the gallant General expected a speedy triumph; but he was destined to feel his own insufficiency. After a tedious march to Fort King, in search of provisions, he was obliged to return to Fort Brooke without them; and, on his way, was intercepted at the fords of the Withlacoochie, by Ossesehehola and a strong body of warriors, and was held in check at that place from the twenty-seventh of February to the sixth of March—when the General was glad to postpone the destruction of his army by offering that he would not interfere with the Indians if the latter would not trouble the inhabitants, a proposition which was promptly rejected by Ossesehehola; and after having been joined by General Clinch and his command, which secured the *retreat* of the army, he wisely left Florida without adding a single leaf to his laurels, and General Clinch retreated, with the entire body, to Fort Drane, on the following day.

On the twenty-first of January, 1836, General Scott was ordered to Florida with ample authority and unlimited means at his control; and he, too, expected to settle the difficulties in a few days. After calling for large forces from South Carolina, Georgia, and Alabama, he took the field on the twenty-second of February, and continued in it until the thirtieth of May, when, having accomplished *nothing*, he too left the seat of war; and, like General Gaines before him, found more agreeable duties elsewhere.

Of the several engagements which ensued, as before stated, no details can be given in this work, in consequence of the small space which has been allotted to this chapter, and with the mere mention of their usual titles and the dates on which they were fought, that part of the subject must be reluctantly passed. Suffice it to say, therefore, that from General Scott the command of the army passed to Governor Call; that soon afterwards General Jesup was ordered thither; and that, on the fifteenth of May, 1838, General Taylor received the command. On the twentieth of May, 1839, General Macomb, General-in-chief of the army, arrived at Fort King and "terminated the war," but scarcely two months elapsed before hostilities were renewed. General Taylor again assumed the command; but, on the twenty-first of April, 1840, he was relieved, at his own request, by General Armistead, and on the thirty-first of May, 1841, the latter officer gave place to Colonel William J. Worth, of the Eighth infantry, through whose energy and abilities the struggle terminated on the fourteenth of August, 1842.

"Peace was at last granted to suffering Florida, which for seven years had been the scene of rapine and murder. The inhabitants had been driven from their homes, and many had seen their families massacred by the light of their burning dwellings. Industry and enterprise had forsaken the land, and *the savage roamed triumphant* in the midst of devastation, poverty, and sorrow."

[The reader will find in the very excellent work "*The origin, progress, and conclusion of the Florida War. By Major John T. Sprague,*" every information on the subject of this war which a general inquirer may desire. A little work entitled "*The War in Florida. By a late Staff-officer,*" Baltimore, 1836; one entitled "*Sketch of the Seminole War. By a Lieutenant of the Left-wing,*" Charleston, 1836; the files of *Niles' Register;* and the various *Congressional Documents,* will give farther information where any may be required.]

THE MEXICAN WAR.

CHAPTER XCIX.

April 25, 1846.

THE RECONNOISSANCE BY CAPTAIN THORNTON.

During a long series of years, ending with 1845, the Mexican government and that of the United States were gradually becoming more and more at variance. It was claimed, on the one hand, and admitted on the other, that wrongs had been inflicted by the former on the citizens of the latter; and treaty had followed treaty—all alike disregarded—for the adjustment of the difficulties and for the redress of grievances. This series of misunderstandings was increased by the annexation of Texas to the United States, and by the renewed claim by the Mexican government that the Nueces is the boundary of that republic; and the latter had even threatened to occupy the territory between the Rio Grande and the Nueces by force, should it be necessary. To protect the frontiers, therefore, an armed force had occupied Corpus Christi; and, in March, 1846, in accordance with the orders of the government, that force, under General Zachary Taylor, had moved westward, and occupied the eastern bank of the Rio Grande opposite Matamoras; strengthened its position by the erection of the necessary field-works; and established a depot of supplies at Point Isabel, about thirty miles in its rear, and near the coast.[1]

On the twenty-fourth of April, 1846, General Arista, the general-in-chief of the Mexican army of the North, commanding at Matamoras, informed General Taylor, on the opposite side of the Rio Grande, "that he considered hostilities commenced, and should prosecute them;"[1] and in accordance with that determination, he sent General Torrejon, with the Light regiment of cavalry of Mexico, the Eighth regiment of cavalry, the battalion of Sappers, and two companies of the Second light-infantry,[2] the whole embracing a force of two thousand five hundred men, over the river, at La Palangana, some miles above the position of General Taylor. It was not long before General Taylor heard of the movement; and, feeling desirous of gaining correct information concerning the reported invasion of Texas, on the same day (*April* 24) he dispatched Captain Seth B. Thornton,[3] of the Second dragoons, with sixty-three men,[4] on a reconnoissance.

During that afternoon the detachment moved fifteen miles, when it encamped for the night; and on the following morning the march was renewed. Every inquiry "tended to the conviction that the enemy had crossed in strength;" and after proceeding thirteen miles farther, the guides refused to proceed, compelling the Captain to go on without them. Two or three miles farther, on the line of march, the party discovered a large plantation, on the bank of the river, and inclosed with a high chaparral fence; while, near the *upper* extremity of it, were some Mexicans and the usual buildings. As there appeared to be no entrance near the buildings, Captain Thornton and his party

[1] President Polk's Annual Message, Dec. 8, 1846; Secretary of War's Report, Dec. 5, 1846.

[1] Gen. Taylor to Adj.-Gen., April 26 and May 3, 1846.

[2] This statement is made on the authority of Gen. Arista.

[3] The official report of this engagement, published by order of Congress, is printed "*T.* B. Thornton."

[4] Gen. Taylor to Adj.-Gen., April 26, 1846.

Zachary Taylor

AT THE PERIOD OF HIS COMMANDING IN MEXICO.

From the original Picture in the possession of the Publishers.

passed around the inclosure to the *lower* extremity—two hundred yards from the house,—when the Captain halted the advance-guard, let down a pair of bars, and, unattended, entered the inclosure to speak to the Mexicans. The latter immediately fled, and the Captain turned and beckoned to the advance-guard to follow him, probably for the purpose of pursuing them, when the main body, which had come up, supposing the order extended to it, also filed into the inclosure, through the bars, without leaving a sentinel there, and without taking any precautions to prevent a surprise. The men immediately scattered, without order, in every direction, while the Captain, having found an old man, entered into conversation.[1]

The entire party was thus inclosed in the field by a high chaparral fence, with no means of egress except the open bars through which it had entered, and without a sentinel to give warning of approaching danger, or a thought that such danger really existed. At this moment the bars were occupied by a detachment of the enemy's force, while other portions of it silently but completely surrounded the inclosure; and before the Americans were aware of the presence of the Mexicans their retreat was wholly cut off. The Captain immediately ordered the command to charge, leading the column himself, but it was too late. The overpowering strength of the enemy gave no hope of success; and, with his infantry within the field and his cavalry outside, his fire was opened on the entrapped Americans from every side. The troops, led by Captain Thornton, then turned to the right and dashed around the inclosure, learning, too surely, that their case was a hopeless one. They attempted to tear down the fence, but the Mexicans were behind it; they attempted to swim the river, but their horses were mired in its boggy margin at every effort. The Captain's horse soon afterwards fell, with his rider under him, and the latter, disabled, was taken prisoner—Captain Hardee assuming the command of the detachment.[1]

Soon afterwards, perceiving that all efforts to escape would be fruitless, the commandant surrendered, with his men, prisoners of war, and were taken to Matamoras—Lieutenant Mason and sixteen men having been killed or severely wounded.[2]

This was the first action (if action that may be called) in the war with Mexico; and, for that reason, it possesses more interest than it would otherwise command.

[1] Capt. Hardee's Report, April 26, and Capt. Thornton's Report, April 27, 1846; Ripley, i. pp. 107, 108.

[1] Captains Thornton and Hardee's Reports.

[2] Capt. Hardee's Report, April 26, 1846.

CHAPTER C.

May 8, 1846.

THE ACTION AT PALO ALTO.

THE establishment of a depot of supplies for the American army at Point Isabel (or the Fort Santa Isabel), has been referred to in the last chapter; and the importance of the post will be readily perceived. At the same time, in consequence of the misfortune which had befallen the command of Captain Thornton, as well as a similar one which had befallen an outpost between the camp and Point Isabel. General Taylor "was kept ignorant, in a great degree," of the movements of the enemy; and, while he feared the latter entertained designs against the depot, the works in front of Matamoras were not in a position to warrant a movement of the troops.[1]

In the mean time General Arista had seen the peculiar position of General Taylor's affairs, and he had resolved to take advantage of them. By cutting off the communication between the General and his depot of supplies, he wisely considered the Americans would be drawn from before Matamoras for the purpose of reopening it, or of securing the retreat of the army; and that for this purpose a general engagement would ensue, in the result of which he felt great confidence. This sensible opinion, in view of General Taylor's numerical weakness, evinces the ability of the Mexican general-in-chief; and had he been seconded by officers as able as himself, or had his appointments been as perfect as his plans, the result might have been very different from that which ensued. With this object in view, General Torrejon, with his command, was moved by a circuitous and secret march around the rear of the American camp; and from *above* it, following the course of the river, he suddenly appeared *below* it, in the vicinity of Trasquila; at the same time General Arista, leaving General Mejía at Matamoras, with a small force, moved secretly down the west bank of the river, with twelve pieces of artillery and the greater part of the garrison, to the rancho Longoreño, fifteen miles below Matamoras, with the intention of crossing the river at that place, under cover of General Torrejon's detachment; and after having effected a junction of the two commands he designed to occupy the line of communication between the American camp and its depot of supplies, and act as circumstances might warrant. Unfortunately those to whom had been intrusted the care of providing boats for the transportation of the army over the river, had entirely failed, or neglected, to perform their duty, and only two boats were provided for that. With these, however, the movement was commenced, and within twenty-four hours the army had crossed the stream and united with that under General Torrejon.[1]

In the mean time General Taylor had hastened the operations on the field-work opposite Matamoras; and, leaving Major Brown, with the Seventh regiment, Captain Lowd's and Lieutenant Bragg's companies of artillery and the invalids of the army, to man the work, at half-past three in the afternoon of the first of May, 1846, he moved towards Point Isabel with the main body of his force.[2] He appears to have been ignorant of the presence of Torrejon, in the vicinity of his bivouac—ten miles from the Point—and he reached the depot at noon, on the next day, "without discovering any signs whatever of the enemy."[3]

While General Taylor was preparing to move from before Matamoras, on the afternoon of the first of May, General Arista appears to have entertained some doubts concerning his destination—knowing that while he might have determined to "*retreat*," he also *might* have determined to *advance*—an operation which might prove disastrous in the then weak condition of the garrison. He therefore ordered the battalion of Morelia to move back on the town, and to strengthen the garrison if it should be found necessary.

It was not long, however, that the movement of General Taylor was enshrouded in mystery; and General Arista learned with regret, it is said, that "availing himself suddenly of the delay in the troops crossing the river, General Taylor had marched for Point Isabel." At length the Mexican army had secured a passage across the river, and General Arista and his combined forces awaited the return of the Americans, at Palo Alto.

[1] Gen. Taylor's Dispatch, No. 32, May 3, 1846.

[1] Notes for the History of the War, &c., from the Mexican, pp. 43, 44.—[2] Gen. Taylor's Dispatch, No. 32, May 3, 1846; Ripley, pp. 109, 110.

[3] Gen. Taylor's Dispatch, No. 32, May 3, 1846.

He is said to have become impatient, after two days' delay, and "to the end that General Taylor might *immediately* return, he determined to make more critical the position of the Americans abandoned in the fortification, and against this, therefore, he opened his fires on the third to menace the place." As the garrison of Matamoras, at this time, was too weak to attempt to assault the fort; and as the Mexicans had nothing to gain by the delay, while in the reinforcements which General Taylor might possibly meet at the Point they might have much to lose, it appears highly probable that in the absence of opposition to General Taylor's downward march, and in the opening of the fire by the small garrison of Matamoras, we have the first fruits of the inefficiency of the Mexican staff, and the laudable attempt of an intelligent officer to remedy the evil. On the fourth of May General Arista fell back on the Tanques del Raminero for a supply of water; while General Ampudia, with a detachment, was sent to operate in front of the fort.[1]

At five o'clock in the afternoon of the third the garrison of Matamoras opened a fire on the detachment which had been left in the fort by General Taylor; and the report of the artillery was heard, distinctly, at Point Isabel, creating a very natural interest in the success of the defence. Although General Taylor especially disclaims any such emotion, he very naturally sent out a detachment to communicate with the fort; and on its return he, as naturally, dispatched the answer of Major Brown, conveying intelligence of his welfare to the adjutant-general of the army at Washington.[1]

At length, General Taylor having completed the defences necessary to secure the Point Isabel, and leaving a sufficient force of recruits for its defence, on the afternoon of the seventh of May he commenced his return march to the encampment opposite Matamoras. His force was no greater, numerically, than when he went down; but he had two eighteen-pounders mounted, in addition to his former strength of artillery; and three hundred wagons laden with subsistence and ammunition followed in his train. His progress appears to have been uninterrupted until near noon on the following day, when his advance-guard, then near Palo Alto, discovered the enemy, and preparations were made for immediate action.[2]

It appears that the movement of General Taylor had been reported to General Arista at an early hour, and that after recalling General Ampudia, with his detachment, from before the camp, opposite to Matamoras, he had prepared for action on the plain of Palo Alto. His right, resting on a slight elevation, was a squadron of the Light regiment of Mexico (*cavalry*), on the left of which was a single piece of artillery, and still farther to the left, in a straight line, in the order named, were the battalion of Sappers, the Second regiment of Light-cavalry, the fine battalion of the Guarda Costa of Tampico, a battery of eight pieces of artillery, and the First, Sixth, and Tenth regiments of the line (*infantry*). These constituted the right and centre of his line, and were commanded by Generals De la Vega and Garcia. Four hundred yards distant from the left of the centre—which space was occupied by two pieces of artillery—were the Seventh and Eighth

[1] Maj. Ripley has stated (*The War with Mexico*, i. p. 111) that the "Fanques del Raminero" are within a thousand yards from Fort Brown; and, starting with that misconception, he supposes (p. 119) Gen. Arista, in person, conducted the operations in front of the fort, and that, on the morning of the 8th, he "left Ampudia, for a time," to continue the blockade. A Mexican map of the vicinity of Matamoras, now before me, shows that this place was about eight miles northeast from that town, on the route between Longoreño and Palo Alto; while the Proclamation or General Orders, issued by Gen. Parrode to his command, stating that the action of Palo Alto had been fought *in* or *near that place*, proves that it could not have been within half-gunshot of Fort Brown. Maj. Ripley's authority for this statement, if I understand him correctly, does not sustain his construction of its meaning.

[1] Gen. Taylor's Dispatch, No. 33, May 5, 1846, inclosing Maj. Brown's Report, May 4.—[2] Gen. Taylor's Dispatches. Nos. 34 and 35, May 7 and 9, 1846.

regiments of cavalry, two squadrons of the Light regiment of cavalry, and the Presidial Companies, forming, together, what may be called the left wing of the army, under General Torrejon,[1] a force which numbered, in the aggregate, about six thousand men.[2]

When the advance of General Taylor's army discovered this imposing line, stretching across the plain, with all the pomp and circumstance of *untried* war, the intelligence was conveyed to the General, and the column halted. After a short rest the several regiments were formed in order of battle, the wagon-train being left in the rear under guard of Captain Ker's squadron of dragoons. On the extreme right of his line, General Taylor posted the Fifth regiment, under Lieutenant-colonel McIntosh; and on its left, in the order named, were posted Ringgold's light-artillery, the Third infantry, under Captain Morris, Lieutenant Churchill's eighteen-pound battery, and the Fourth infantry, under Lieutenant-colonel Garland—the whole forming the right wing, under Colonel Twiggs. The left wing, under Lieutenant-colonel Belknap, embraced a battalion of artillery, serving as infantry, Captain Duncan's light-artillery, and the Eighth infantry, under Lieutenant-colonel Belknap.[3]

At about two in the afternoon the line advanced by heads of regiments, and when it had approached within six or seven hundred yards, the Mexican batteries opened their fire, and General Ampudia, with the Fourth regiment of the line, a company of Sappers, and two hundred men from the "Auxiliary troops," were thrown in front to act as skirmishers and to "draw on the engagement."[4] Perceiving the order of the enemy's position and his plan of operations, General Taylor immediately halted, advanced his artillery, and answered the enemy's fire, driving in his light troops,—the Fourth regiment falling in on the left of the Tenth regiment, and the Sappers and the "Auxiliaries," with their respective corps,—and producing "a destructive and deadly" effect. It is said that the Mexican troops withstood this fire with the sternest bravery; and that during upwards of an hour this terrible cannonade continued with unremitted severity.[1]

At length General Arista, urged forward by his officers and men,—who had become tired of the cannonade in which they were exposed, without an opportunity to defend themselves or injure their opponents,—determined to pursue a new and more active course. Accordingly, he ordered General Torrejon, with the left wing, the central battery of two guns, and a covering party of infantry, to turn the American right flank. Perceiving the movement, and understanding the purposes of the enemy, Major Ringgold and Lieutenant Churchill opened their fire on this moving column, inflicting a heavy loss, and driving it into the chaparral, but without checking its progress; and General Taylor was obliged to move the Fifth regiment from his extreme right still farther to the right, for the purpose of meeting and checking it. The Fifth moved to its designated position with great alacrity, and formed in hollow square on the edge of the thicket, immediately behind a narrow lagoon; and, soon afterwards, a portion of General Torrejon's cavalry, having turned the lagoon, came up on its right and rear, unslung its escopetas, and opened a noisy but harmless fire at short musket-range. A single well-directed volley from one front of the square into which the Fifth had been formed, sufficed in this part of the field, and with upwards of twenty men killed or wounded, this portion of General Torrejon's cavalry fled into the thicket, and were seen no more in that direction. At the same time, however, another portion of the Mexican left wing, which General Torrejon had moved against

[1] Notes for the History, &c., pp. 45, 46.—[2] Gen. Taylor's Dispatch, No. 35, May 9, 1846; Sec. Marcy's Report, Dec. 5, 1846.—[3] Ripley, i. p. 117.—[4] Notes for the History, &c., pp. 46, 47.

[1] Ripley, i. p. 118; Thorpe's Rio Grande, p. 82.

the American right flank, was moving through the chaparral still farther towards the rear of that flank, threatening the wagons which were in the extreme rear of the American position, when Colonel Twiggs moved the Third regiment of infantry from the centre of the American right wing to meet and check it—an operation which was eminently successful; as also was a similar movement of two of Major Ringgold's guns, under Lieutenant Ridgely, which were thrown forward, at a gallop, to check the movements of the two guns which General Torrejon had carried with him.[1]

During this demonstration on the American right by General Torrejon and his command, the main bodies of both armies had remained in line, and continued the cannonade which had so long and so terribly cut up the Mexican ranks. The long wiry grass, rendered more combustible by the discharges of the cannon, had taken fire from the burning wads or the flashes of the pieces; and as the sheet of flame skimmed along the surface of the plain and sent its clouds of smoke into the faces of the Mexicans, it added to the sadness of the spectacle, while it embarrassed the operations of both the contending armies. A temporary cessation of hostilities, therefore, ensued; and, as if by mutual agreement, the work of destruction was stayed about an hour. During this time both armies reformed their lines; and both, alike, appeared to look forward to a renewal of the conflict with determination.[2]

General Arista drew back his left wing, which had suffered so severely in its attempts to turn the American right;[3] and with his extreme right still occupying the position, near the rising ground, which it originally occupied, he formed his new line on the margin of the thicket. General Taylor, perceiving this change in the enemy's position, immediately advanced the right of his line, and preserved, as nearly as possible, the relative positions originally occupied by the two armies.[1]

At length the artillery, pushed forward in advance of the American line, renewed its terrible work, and the battle was continued. The Mexican troops, with a cool and deliberate bravery which justly excited the admiration of their enemies, steadily maintained a position, from which, considering their own personal inactivity, they might reasonably have retired without dishonor; while every moment the batteries of Ringgold, and Duncan, and Churchill, swept through the lines, and scattered confusion and death on every hand.[2] Soon afterwards some of the battalions, becoming impatient by the loss which they suffered, fell into disorder, demanding to advance against their enemy or to fall back "from so exposed a position;" and General Arista so far yielded to their requirements that he ordered a second movement against the American line. Accordingly the battalion of the Guarda Costa, the Second Light regiment, and the fragment of the Seventh regiment of cavalry —the latter of which, after its repulse on the American right, under General Torrejon, had reformed on the right and rear of the main body—the whole supported by the battalion of Sappers, and commanded by Colonel Montero, moved from the right wing, under cover of a concentrated fire from all the Mexican batteries; and, enveloped in the smoke which the burning grass and the artillery produced, they pressed forward against the American left; while, at the same time, the remainder of General Torrejon's command—embracing the Eighth

[1] Notes for the History, &c., pp. 47, 48; Ripley, i. pp. 118, 119; Gen. Arista's Dispatch, May 8, 1846.

[2] Ripley, i. p. 120; Thorpe's Rio Grande, pp. 79, 80.

[3] Ripley, i. p. 120. The *Notes for the History*, &c., the work of a company of Mexican scholars,—and the part relating to this action, said to have been written under the direction of Gen. Arista,—says the Mexican *right were thrown forward*. While this movement would have formed a line *parallel* with the real line, it would have been much in advance of the position he really occupied—the incorrectness of which will be apparent to every one who examines the subject.

[1] Maps of the action in Ripley, &c.—[2] Ripley, i. p. 120.

regiment of cavalry, two squadrons of the Light regiment of cavalry, and the Presidiales—which had formed, after its repulse, on the left and rear of the main line, moved forward and threatened a renewal of the attack on the American right.[1]

The former of these parties had no sooner got in motion than Captain Duncan discovered it; and having reported the fact to Lieutenant-colonel Belknap, who commanded the American left wing, with his battery at a gallop, he dashed forward to the left, to check the enemy's progress. Turning a point of blazing grass which had concealed his movement, he suddenly showed himself in front of Colonel Montero; and with one section of his battery he opened a fire on the cavalry in his front; while, with the other, a second corps, which was showing itself in the chaparral, was also engaged. Comparatively isolated from the main body, and entirely without support, the gallant Duncan plied his batteries on the moving masses of the Mexican right wing, with the greatest spirit and determination; while the latter, filled with astonishment at the ubiquity of the artillerists, whose presence was so completely unexpected, pulled up with amazement and chagrin, and received his fire with sullenness and unaccountable inactivity. Soon afterwards the Eighth regiment of infantry and Captain Ker's squadron of dragoons came up, to support Captain Duncan, and, after a short struggle, the Mexicans fell back in disorder.[2]

In the mean time the party which had returned to the attack on the American right, came in contact with Lieutenant Churchill's eighteen-pound battery, and with the Third artillery, under Lieutenant-colonel Childs, which had been moved up to support that wing; and, after sustaining the fire a short time, it also fell back in disorder, and gave up the contest.[1]

With the exception of here and there a straggling fire the battle of Palo Alto ended with these repulses; and as it was then quite dark, both parties willingly suspended their operations until another day. The Americans, reposing on the battle-field with their arms by their side, were ready for service at a moment's warning;[2] the Mexicans, by a detour, occupied the high ground on the extreme right of their original position;[3] and both, alike weary after the desperate struggle through which they had passed, remained quiet until morning.

The strength of the Americans in the action of Palo Alto "did not exceed, all told, two thousand three hundred men;[4] while their loss was comparatively trifling—four men killed, Major Ringgold, Captain Page, and Lieutenant Luther, and thirty-nine men wounded."[5] The strength of the Mexicans was "four thousand men, exclusive of the *numerous* auxiliary troops,"[6] probably about six thousand men in all;[7] while "two hundred and fifty-two men dispersed, wounded, and killed," were reported as his loss.[8]

The result of this action, while it reflected credit on the Mexican character, greatly dispirited the troops; and, without apparent reason, charges of treason were publicly made against one of the general officers present. General Arista appears to have acted coolly and with consideration; and, while the subsequent death of Major Ringgold spread sadness over the United States, the fame of General Taylor's gallantry was heralded by every tongue.

---

[1] Notes for the History, p. 49; Ripley, i. pp. 120, 121; Gen. Arista's Dispatch, May 8, 1846.—[2] Ripley, i. p. 121.

[1] Ripley, i. p. 122.—[2] Thorpe, pp. 83, 84.—[3] Notes for the History, p. 49.—[4] Sec. Marcy, in his Annual Report, Dec. 6, 1846, says it numbered 2288.—[5] Gen. Taylor's Dispatch, No. 35, May 9, 1846.—[6] Gen. Arista to Minister of War (no date).—[7] Sec. Marcy's Report, Dec. 6, 1846; Gen. Taylor's Dispatch, No. 35, May 9, 1846.
[8] Gen. Arista's Dispatch, May 8, 1846.

CHAPTER CI.

May 9, 1846.

THE BATTLE OF RESACA DE LA PALMA.

As has been stated in the last chapter, the Mexican army retired from its position near Palo Alto, at an early hour on the morning of the ninth of May; and at ten o'clock it reached a spot which was known as Resaca de Guerrero,[1] near the Resaca de la Palma, where General Arista had determined to await the movements of General Taylor.

The position referred to was in the midst of a dense wood or chaparral; and the ravine, which formed its strength—in shape, an irregular curve, of which the convexity is towards the south—was crossed, at nearly right angles, by the road along which the American army would necessarily move; while at either extremity of it were pools of standing water.[2] Within the northern margin of this ravine—towards which the Americans were approaching—and protected to their breasts by its bank, were posted, on the right of the road, the Sixth and Tenth regiments of Mexican infantry, the regiment of Sappers, the Second regiment of light-infantry, and the First regiment of infantry; on the left of the road, but in the rear of the ravine, were posted the Guarda Costa and company of Tampico, supported, on either flank, by the Second and Fourth regiments of the line; the regiment of Canales covered the extreme left of the line, in the rear of the ravine; and, still farther in the rear, were formed, in line, the Presidiales, the Light-cavalry, and the Seventh and Eighth regiments of cavalry. The companies of sharp-shooters displayed in front of the position, and three batteries—one of three guns, on the northern margin of the ravine; and two, of two guns each, on either side of the road, south of the ravine—defended the pass with both a direct and cross fires.[1]

In the mean time, a council of war had been called in the American camp, and a large majority of its members had advised the adoption of a defensive course—some preferring to intrench on the spot, while others advised a retrograde movement to Point Isabel. Lieutenant-colonel Belknap and Captain Duncan, however, urged the propriety of an advance; and General Taylor, adopting the views of the latter, immediately ordered the necessary preparations for the march. The wounded were sent back to the Point under an escort of cavalry, commanded by Lieutenant Steele; and the train was parked on the field, and the First brigade of artillery, under Lieutenant-colonel Childs, and the Eighth regiment of infantry, with two twelve-pounders, were assigned for its protection.[2]

At about two o'clock the army moved from its position, on its route towards Matamoras, preceded by Captain Walker's troop of Texan Rangers, a small party of the Second dragoons, under Lieutenant Pleasanton, and one hundred and twenty picked skirmishers, under Captains McCall and Smith, as an advance-guard; and when the head of the column had come within sight of the ravine, it was brought to a halt by a shot from the Mexican battery which was posted there. Orders were immediately issued to Captain McCall to bring on the action; and, with his own and Captain Smith's commands, he pressed forward, on both sides of the road, driving the Mexican sharp-shooters, and harassing those regiments—the Sixth and

---

[1] It is said, in the "*Notes for the History*," &c., that the site of the battle was *not the Resaca de la Palma*, but the *Resaca de Guerrero*, while the former was the site of the American bivouac after the battle.—[2] Notes, &c., p. 51; Ripley, i. pp. 125, 126; Thorpe's Rio Grande, p. 93.

[1] Notes, &c., p. 51.—[2] Ripley, i. pp. 123, 124.

Tenth infantry—whose left flanks covered the passage of the ravine. At the same time Lieutenant Ridgely's four-gun battery was ordered forward, and the Third, Fourth, and Fifth regiments of infantry, as skirmishers, were also ordered to cover the battery and engage the enemy, as circumstances might require. The artillery occupied a position within three hundred yards of the Mexican battery, and opened and received a lively fire, but the obstruction, by the intervening chaparral, prevented the artillerists from taking their accustomed aim, and the fire on both sides was not as effective as usual.[1]

In the mean time, the Fifth and the left wing of the Fourth infantry had moved forward on the left of Lieutenant Ridgely's battery, and the Third, with the right wing of the Fourth infantry on the right of it, both having deployed as skirmishers and supported the advance-guard. Throughout the entire field the most unceasing confusion prevailed; and every officer appeared to exercise an independent command, so dense was the chaparral among which they moved against the enemy. In their unceasing and vigorous opposition to the enemy's light troops, however, as well as in their steady fire against the dense masses of his infantry, these several detached and apparently confused commands, acted with harmony and effect; and while Lieutenant Ridgely, with his battery, was repeating the lesson taught the enemy on the preceding day, the infantry, scattered among the briers and bushes along the margin of the ravine, was enforcing it with their small-arms, and throwing them into confusion.[2]

While the action was thus raging in all its peculiar fury, the Eighth infantry and Duncan's battery were ordered up from the intrenchment at Palo Alto, and joined in the fray; yet the admirable position which the enemy occupied, prevented the Americans from exercising their powers to the full extent, and protected the Mexican troops, even under the disadvantages of a partial defeat.[1]

A desperate case, such as this was, requires a desperate remedy, and General Taylor did not hesitate in adopting one after having seen the character of the conflict in which his men were engaged. Ordering forward Captain Charles A. May of the Second dragoons, with his squadron, he sent him to charge the foremost of the Mexican batteries, and to take it sword in hand. Moving down as far as the position occupied by Lieutenant Ridgely, he halted until that officer had drawn the fire of the coveted battery, when he dashed forward, at a gallop, on his desperate mission—the observed of all observers.[2] Of this charge it has been said, truly, that "it was a soul-stirring sight to witness it." "The dragoons were stripped of every unnecessary incumbrance," continues the same author, "and they brandished their weapons with their naked arms that displayed the well-filled muscle glittering like the bright steel they wielded. Captain May, far in the advance, seemed to be a living messenger of death that Ridgely had sent from his battery at its last discharge. His long hair and beard streamed beneath his gold-tasselled cap, like the rays of a comet; and upon his sabre the tropical sun glistened with burning effulgence. There followed in his lead the long dark line of his squadron; and, as his charger rose upon the enemy's batteries, the rider turned to wave on his men, when he found at his heels the gallant Inge, who answered the challenge with a shout. That instant the enemy poured a terrible fire of grape and canister from the upper batteries, which swept over the squadron a cloud of winged messengers of death. Eighteen horses and seven brave men came in bloody, mangled masses to the earth. Lieutenant Sackett whirled from his killed horse, sword in hand, among the ene-

[1] Gen. Taylor's Dispatch, No. 36, 10 P. M., May 9; Notes, &c., p. 52; Ripley, i. p. 126.—[2] Gen. Taylor's Dispatch, No. 36, May 9; Ripley, i. pp. 126, 127.

[1] Ripley, i. p. 128.—[2] Notes, &c., p. 52; Ripley, i. pp. 127, 128.

my; and, beyond the battery, the gallant Lieutenant Inge, mortally wounded by a cannon-shot in his throat, wavered for a moment, and then, with his steed, fell headlong down. But there was no checking those who lived. On they rushed with Lieutenant Stevens, carrying every thing before them, while Captain Graham, Lieutenants Winship and Pleasanton, with their command, swept to the left of the road, and leaped over the battery there situated. The Mexicans were completely driven from their guns, and their fire silenced. But the men about these pieces, though repulsed, were not beaten. Back they rushed to them, and with their bayonet points determined to retain them or die. Captain May and his squadron having accomplished their work, checked and scattered themselves among a host of enemies who were pouring on them a galling fire of musketry, or having rushed back to the guns, commenced ramming home the fatal grape, to again scatter it among our ranks. Gathering five or six men Captain May charged back to our own lines. As his tall form rose and fell on the gigantic leaps of his charger, the Mexicans shrank from his powerfully dealt sword, as if they had been assailed by lightning. One Mexican kept his ground, and vainly tried to rally his men; despairing of success, with his own hand he seized a match, when Captain May ordered him to surrender. Discovering the command came from an officer, the Mexican touched his breast and said, 'General La Vega is a prisoner,' at the same time handing his sword to Captain May. Under a galling fire from the enemy's infantry, General La Vega was carried to our lines in charge of Lieutenant Stevens and a non-commissioned officer, and by them conducted in safety to our rear. Shortly afterwards Captain May presented the distinguished captive's sword to the commanding general."[1]

This daring feat, as triumphant as it was brilliant, was followed up both by Lieutenant Ridgely, with his battery, and by the skirmishers; and soon afterwards the Eighth infantry, from Palo Alto, joined in the contest for the possession of the battery. With a determination worthy of a better fate the Mexicans struggled manfully for the possession of their guns; and step by step the possession of the enemy's position was contested by the great contending forces.[1] In their progress down the road, in column, the Fifth and Eighth regiments were met, face to face, by the justly celebrated Guarda Costa of Tampico, and in a hand-to-hand contest of great obstinacy contended for the mastery and gained it, with the standard of the battalion; and over the entire field the action raged with equal violence.

At length the enemy gave way, sullenly and slowly retiring from his position, and leaving in the hands of the victors his artillery and its equipments, three standards, his camp and five hundred pack-mules, and his personal baggage, including that of General Arista.[2] Soon afterwards, although the pursuit was trifling, the dispersion of the Mexican forces became general. "The soldiers sought the river in all directions, not believing themselves safe while they were on the other side." The general-in-chief, with the cavalry, passed at the Villa de Ampudia, while every place which afforded a means of passage was crowded to excess;[3] and many were drowned in their attempts to ford or swim the stream.[4]

In this engagement the loss of the enemy has not been reported, that of the Americans was Lieutenants Inge, Cochrane, and Chadbourne, and thirty-six men *killed;* and Lieutenant-colonels Payne and McIntosh, Captains Hooe and Montgomery, Lieutenants Dobbins, Fowler, Gates, Selden, Maclay, Burbank, Morris, and Jordan, and seventy men *wounded.*[5]

---

1 Col. Thorpe's Our Army on the Rio Grande, pp. 97, 98.

1 Notes, &c., pp. 52, 53; Ripley, i. p. 128.—2 Gen. Taylor's Dispatch, No. 36, May 9; Ripley, i. p. 129.

3 Notes, &c., p. 55.—4 Ibid., p. 56; Thorpe's Rio Grande, p. 127.—5 Gen. Taylor's Dispatches, No. 36, May 9, and No. 72, Aug. 3.

CHAPTER CII.

June 6, 1846, to January 10, 1847.

THE CONQUEST OF NEW MEXICO AND CALIFORNIA.

Immediately after the opening of hostilities in the valley of the Rio Grande, of which notice has been taken in preceding chapters of this work, among the expeditions which were organized by the Federal authorities, was one to move against, and take possession of, California and New Mexico, two provinces, in the northern part of the enemy's country.[1] The command of this expedition had been vested in General Stephen W. Kearney, and the force under his command—embracing the First regiment of Missouri Mounted Volunteers, under Colonel Alexander W. Doniphan; two companies of light-artillery (*Captains Weightman's and Fischer's*), from St. Louis; five troops of the First regiment United States dragoons; "The Saclede Rangers," a volunteer troop, from St. Louis, and two companies of infantry (*volunteers*), from Cole and Platte counties, Missouri, under Captains Augney and Murphy[2]—sixteen hundred and fifty-eight men in all, with twelve six-pounders and four twelve-pound howitzers, had rendezvoused at Fort Leavenworth; and the most energetic measures had been adopted to insure its early departure and its ultimate success.[3]

Having completed all his arrangements, on the twenty-sixth of June the main body of this expedition had moved from the fort; and after a rapid, but interesting, march of eight hundred and seventy-three miles, on the eighteenth of August it entered and took possession of Santa Fé, the capital of New Mexico—the Mexican forces, four thousand in number, which had been collected to defend the town, having dispersed, without offering the least opposition, as it approached.[1]

While these operations, in New Mexico and on the western frontier of the United States, were transpiring, Brevet-captain John C. Fremont, who had been engaged in explorations on the western slope of the Rocky Mountains, had also revolutionized the province of California; and, to some extent, at least, had anticipated the movements of the expedition commanded by General Kearney. The character of his mission being scientific and peaceful, rather than warlike, he had not had an officer or soldier of the regular army in his company; and his whole force had consisted of sixty-two men, employed by himself for security against the Indians, and for procuring subsistence in the wilderness and desert country through which he had passed. For the purpose of obtaining game for his men, and grass for his horses, in an uninhabited part of California, during the winter of 1845–46 he had solicited, and obtained, permission from the Mexican authorities to winter in the valley of San Joaquin; but he had scarcely established himself before he received advices that the Mexican commander was preparing to attack him, under the pretext that under the cover of a scientific mission he was exciting the American settlers, in that vicinity, to revolt. In view of this threatened attack, and for the purpose of repelling it, Lieutenant Fremont immediately occupied a mountain which overlooked Monterey, although it was thirty miles from that city; and having intrenched it, and raised the flag of the

---

[1] Secretary of War to Gen. Kearney (*Confidential*), June 3, 1846.

[2] Hughes' Doniphan's Expedition, pp. 27, 36; Secretary Marcy's Annual Report, Dec. 5, 1846.

[3] Cutts' Conquest of California and New Mexico, p. 36.

[1] Secretary Marcy's Annual Report, Dec. 5, 1846; Gen. Kearney to Adjutant-general, Aug. 24, 1846; Maj. Emory's Notes of a Reconnoissance (*N. Y. Ed.*), p. 40.

United States, he awaited the approach of the enemy. After remaining there until the tenth of March, 1846, he retired to the northward, intending to march, by way of Oregon, to the United States; but, about the middle of May, after he had quietly passed into Oregon, he received information, through Samuel Neal and Levi Sigler, two hunters who had been sent after him from Lassen's rancho, that the Mexican governor of California was pursuing him, while the Indians, by whom he was surrounded, instigated by the enemy, had, soon afterwards, shown signs of hostility, and killed or wounded five of his men.[1]

Under these circumstances, on the sixth of June, 1846, Lieutenant Fremont had resolved to turn on his pursuers, with the little party under his command, and to seek safety not merely in the overthrow of his pursuers, but in that of the entire government of Mexico in the province of California.[2] Accordingly, on the eleventh of June, Lieutenant Fremont, assisted by Captain Merritt and fourteen of the settlers, had attacked and captured an escort of horses destined for General Castro's troops—Lieutenant Arce, fourteen men, and two hundred horses remaining in his hands as the trophies of his victory.[3] On the fifteenth the military post of Sonoma was surprised, and General Vallejo, Captain Vallejo, Colonel Greuxdon, and several other officers, nine pieces of brass cannon, two hundred and fifty stand of muskets, and other stores and arms were taken;[4] and, on the twenty-fifth, the military commandant of the province, who had moved towards the post, with a heavy force, to retake it, was attacked by Lieutenant Fremont and twenty men, and completely routed.[1] Having thus cleared the province, north of the Bay of San Francisco, of the enemy, it is said, that on the fifth of July Captain Fremont had assembled the American settlers, at Sonoma, addressed them upon the dangers of their situation, and recommended a declaration of independence, and war on Mexico, as the only remedy; and that the hardy frontiersmen promptly accepted the proposal, and raised the flag of independent California[2]—a bear and a star, on a red ground.

While these revolutionary movements were destroying the power of Mexico in the interior of the province of California, and the expedition under General Kearney—ignorant of the fact that the work had been done already—was approaching its eastern borders, for the same purpose; the naval force of the United States in the Pacific, under Commodore Sloat, had been assisting in the work of conquest. Having heard of the opening of hostilities on the Rio Grande,[3] the Commodore—then at Mazatlan—hastened, with the *Savannah*, to Monterey, in California, where he arrived on the second of July, and on the seventh he took possession of the town, without opposition, the custom-house was seized, the American flag raised, and California declared to be "henceforward a part of the United States."[4]

Within a few days intelligence of the

[1] T. O. Larkin, U. S. Consul, to Sec. of State, March 27 and April 2; Capt. Fremont to his wife, "On the Sacramento River, April 1, 1846;" Maj. Gillespie's "American Military Operations in California, No. 1," in the San Francisco *Golden Age*, Sept. 30, 1855.

[2] Capt. Fremont to T. H. Benton, "Mission of Carmel, July 25, 1846;" Sec. Marcy's Annual Report, Dec. 5, 1846.—[3] Capt. Fremont to T. H. Benton, July 25, 1846; Sec. Marcy's Annual Report, Dec. 5, 1846; Maj. Gillespie's "Am. Mil. Operations, No. 1;" Ripley, i. p. 291.

[4] Capt. Fremont to T. H. Benton, July 25, 1846; Sec. Marcy's Annual Report, Dec. 5, 1846; Ripley, i. p. 291. Maj. Gillespie says Capt. Fremont had nothing to do with the capture of Sonoma.

[1] Capt. Fremont to T. H. Benton, July 25, 1846; Sec. Marcy's Annual Report, Dec. 5, 1846; Ripley, i. p. 291.

[2] Capt. Fremont to T. H. Benton, July 25, 1846; Sec. Marcy's Annual Report, Dec. 5, 1846; Ripley, i. pp. 291, 292. Maj. Gillespie says that the flag of Independence was raised by one Ide; and that Fremont had nothing to do with the movement or the meeting; and Mr. Hughes (*Doniphan's Expedition*, p. 232) agrees with him.

[3] Maj. Gillespie supposes Com. Sloat was influenced by the receipt of intelligence of *the internal movements among the settlers*; but the Commodore (*Dispatch, July* 31, 1846) assigns a different reason, as stated in the text.

[4] Com. Sloat's Proclamation at Monterey; Same to Secretary of Navy, July 31, 1846; Ripley, i. p. 293.

action of Commodore Sloat was received by the revolutionary leaders at Sonoma; and a battalion of mounted riflemen which had been organized among them, was immediately moved to Monterey,[1] the flag of the United States was substituted for the bear and star,[2] and the authority of the Commodore was immediately recognized.[3] The battalion of mounted riflemen referred to, on its arrival at Monterey (*July* 23, 1846), was mustered into the service of the United States by Commodore Stockton, who had succeeded Commodore Sloat in command of the squadron—Captain Fremont being appointed its commandant, and Lieutenant A. H. Gillespie of the marines, its second officer[4]—and it was immediately dispatched, on the sloop of war *Cyane*, to San Diego, for the purpose of cutting off the retreat of General Castro of the Mexican service, who had encamped, and fortified his position, near Ciudad de los Angeles,[5] while the Commodore, with his sailors—who landed from the *Congress* at San Pedro—moved against him in front.[6] The expedition was eminently successful, as the Mexicans, on the approach of the Commodore, immediately evacuated their camp, and fled in the greatest confusion—although most of the principal officers were subsequently captured—and, on the thirteenth of August, the Ciudad de los Angeles (*City of the Angels*) was occupied, also without opposition, by the American troops and seamen, and the conquest of California was apparently completed.[7]

A short time afterwards Commodore Stockton appointed Captain Fremont governor of the Territory into which, by the proclamation of Commodore Sloat, the province had been transformed; while Captain Gillespie was left, with nineteen men, in possession of Los Angeles; Lieutenant Talbot, of the Topographical Engineers, with nine men, was left at Santa Barbara; and, with his squadron, Commodore Stockton proceeded to San Francisco; while Governor Fremont, on the eighth of September, also moved to Monterey.[1]

The main body had no sooner left Los Angeles, than the Californians—who before the departure of the Commodore and the Governor had held secret meetings for the purpose—rose in arms for the expulsion of the invaders of their country. Indeed an attempt appears to have been intended before the Governor left the city; but, by timely precautions, it had been prevented; although the purpose and determination still continued, and were called into requisition at a more convenient season. The necessary preparations having been made for that purpose, under the directions of José Antonio Carrillo, a professed conspirator, of that vicinity, at an early hour in the morning of the twenty-third of September, the quarters of Captain Gillespie were attacked by Cerbulo Varela,—a metamorphosed captain, under Governor Fremont,—at the head of sixty-five men, under cover of a thick fog. The morning was auspicious for such purposes, yet the Captain was not surprised; and the twenty-one rifles which he controlled were quickly brought to bear on the assailants, who retired, soon afterwards, with three of their number killed and several wounded; and, at daylight, the remainder were driven from the town, with the loss of several taken prisoners, by a few men, under Lieutenant Hensley, and Doctor Gilchrist, of the navy.[2]

The insurgents who were thus expelled from the city, formed a nucleus, around

1 Capt. Fremont to T. H. Benton, July 25, 1846; Sec. Mason's Annual Report, Dec. 5, 1846; Com. Sloat to Sec. of Navy, July 31, 1846.—2 Sec. Marcy's Annual Report, Dec. 5, 1846.—3 Com. Stockton to Sec. of Navy, Aug. 28, 1846; Capt. Fremont to T. H. Benton, July 25, 1846.

4 Com. Stockton to Sec. of Navy, Aug. 28, 1846; Maj. Gillespie's Am. Mil. Operations, No. 2.—5 Com. Stockton to Capt. Fremont, July 23, 1846; Maj. Gillespie's Am. Mil. Operations, No. 2.—6 Com. Stockton to Sec. of Navy, Aug. 28, 1846; Hughes, p. 235.—7 Com. Stockton to Sec. of Navy, Aug. 28; Com. Stockton's Proclamation, Aug. 17, 1846; Cutts' Conquest of California, p. 155.

1 Maj. Gillespie's Am. Mil. Operations, No. 3; Lieut. Talbot's Letter, Jan. 15, 1847; Ripley, i. pp. 470, 471.

2 Maj. Gillespie's American Military Operations, No. 3.

which the disaffected gathered; and as the party gained strength, day by day, it harassed the little garrison, and killed one of its number. There was but little concert of action in its ranks, however; and as the rival aspirants to power struggled for authority, while the numbers rapidly increased, the efficiency of the insurgents was but slightly increased. At length, in a spirit of compromise, Captain Antonio Flores was urged to take the command of the party, and reluctantly accepted it; and he soon found himself at the head of six hundred men, armed with lances, escopetas, and a brass six-pounder, light and well mounted.[1]

In the mean time, the little garrison had found an old honey-combed iron six-pounder, and had drilled out the spike, cleaned, and mounted it, and, by melting the lead pipes of a distillery, had provided—unknown to the insurgents—thirty rounds of ball and grape for it. Two other pieces having been added to this, on the following day, the little garrison and its gallant commander resolved to die rather than surrender, notwithstanding the extreme efforts which had been made to strengthen its position, and the great fatigue which was incident thereto. To render his little party still more secure, however, on the twenty-seventh of September Captain Gillespie withdrew his command from his quarters in the city, and occupied a height which commanded it, when he strengthened his position and prepared for an obstinate defence.[2]

No sooner had this movement been effected, than Captain Flores sent Don Eulogeo Celis to inquire on *what terms Captain Gillespie would surrender the city;* and that officer, after consulting with his subordinates, answered that *if the enemy would propose* that he should march out of the city with the honors of war, colors flying, and drums beating; that he should take *every thing* with him; that he should be furnished with means for transporting his baggage and provisions, at his own expense; and that the enemy should not come within a league of his party, while on its line of march to San Pedro, he would accept it, while no other terms would be accepted, and that Captain Flores would be held responsible for any damage which might ensue, in case they were rejected. After some negotiation these terms were offered by Captain Flores and accepted by Captain Gillespie; and, on the twenty-ninth of September, the garrison commenced its march; reached San Pedro on the same evening; and, on the fourth of October embarked on the *Vandalia*, after spiking its three old guns—an exploit which, when the circumstances under which Captain Gillespie occupied Los Angeles, the smallness of his force, the strength of his opponent, and the temper of the people among whom he moved are taken into consideration, may well be ranked as one of the most brilliant feats of that remarkable campaign.[1]

While these difficulties were surrounding Captain Gillespie at Los Angeles, Lieutenant Talbot, at Santa Barbara, with his nine men, was not less dangerously situated; and when the former had made terms with the insurgents, Manuel Garpio with two hundred men moved against Lieutenant Talbot, surrounded the town, and demanded his surrender, offering two hours for his deliberation. As the men had resolved that they would not give up their arms, and as the barracks were untenable, with so small a force, the Lieutenant resolved to abandon the town and push for the hills; and, strange to say, he marshalled his men and marched out of the town, *without opposition*—"those who lay on the road retreated to the main force which was on the lower side of the town." Having reached the hills he encamped, and remained there eight days, when the Californians endeavored "to rout him out," but were repulsed with the loss of

[1] Maj. Gillespie's Am. Mil. Operations, No. 3.—[2] Ibid.

[1] Maj. Gillespie's American Military Operations, No. 3.

a horse. The insurgents then offered him his arms and freedom if he would engage to remain neutral in the anticipated hostilities, but "he sent word back that he preferred to fight." They next built fires around him, *and burned him out;* but in doing so they did not capture or injure him, and he pushed through the mountains for Monterey; and after a month's travel, in which he endured unheard of hardships and suffering, he reached that place in safety.[1]

Intelligence of the insurrection having reached Commodore Stockton at San Francisco, and Lieutenant-colonel Fremont at Sacramento, both took immediate steps to check its progress and to punish the offenders. In conformity with the Commodore's orders Lieutenant-colonel Fremont hastened to San Francisco, whence he embarked, with one hundred and sixty men, on the ship *Sterling*, for Santa Barbara,[2] to which port the frigate *Savannah*, Captain Mervine, had previously been ordered;[3] while, on the same day, the Commodore, in person, sailed for the same port in the *Congress*.[4]

The latter vessel reached San Pedro on the sixth of October, and, at sunrise on the seventh, Captain Mervine landed with his seamen and marines; and, after having been joined by Captain Gillespie and his brave-hearted little party, he found himself at the head of three hundred and ten men, "as brave and valiant as ever were led to battle upon any field." At eight o'clock the party commenced its march towards Los Angeles,—Captain Gillespie being in advance,—and when the column reached the hills of Paloverde, the insurgents showed themselves and opened a fire with their escopetas. The march was rapid; and the jolly tars, unused to such extended journeys, appear to have suffered from its effects; in consequence of which, although the enemy gradually fell back before the advancing column, between one and two o'clock, when near the Rancho de los Domingos, fourteen miles from San Pedro, it became necessary to halt and encamp for the night.[1]

As may have been expected, the sailors and marines were *ashore*, and the strict discipline which *the deck* had inculcated appears to have been left on board the frigate. As a necessary consequence the camp displayed but little of the order which such a locality should have insured; and many and marvellous were the adventures of that night; while, on the other hand, the enemy profited by the delay, in the moral effect of the disorder with which the march had been conducted, and of the entire absence of any artillery.[2]

On the following morning, at daylight, the column was again put in motion; and, with Captain Gillespie's men in front, in still greater disorder than on the preceding day, it moved towards Los Angeles, twelve miles distant. It had marched only three miles, when, posted behind a small stream which intersects the line of march, the advance of the insurgents — seventy-six men, with a small field-piece, under José Antonio Carrillo—was discovered in front; and as the column approached a fire was opened on it, which was answered with a characteristic shout. The Volunteers—Captain Gillespie's command—pressed forward; and, by taking advantage of the neighboring shelter, they drove the enemy, and compelled him to abandon his field-piece; but, before it could be reached and taken possession of, Captain Mervine gave orders *to withdraw*. With great indignation, therefore, the Volunteers discontinued the action; and after having picked up his killed and wounded,—harassed by the enemy, who pressed after the column, and covered by the Volunteers and sixteen marines, under Captain Gillespie,—Captain Mervine slowly and sadly fell back

---

1 Lieut. Talbot's Letter, Jan. 15, 1847.—2 Maj. Gillespie's Am. Mil. Operations, No. 4; Com. Stockton's Report, Feb. 18, 1848; Lieut. Talbot's Letter, Jan. 15, 1847.

3 Maj. Gillespie's Am. Mil. Operations, No. 3; Com. Stockton's Report, Feb. 18, 1848.—4 Com. Stockton's Report, Feb. 18, 1848; Ripley, i. p. 472.

1 Maj. Gillespie's Am. Mil. Operations, No. 4; Notes for the History, p. 409.—2 Ibid.

to San Pedro, where he arrived about dark on the same day. "Thirteen noble tars were buried on the island in front of San Pedro," the victims of this badly managed expedition.[1]

On the twenty-third of October the Commodore reached San Pedro — Lieutenant-colonel Fremont, meanwhile, having returned to Monterey;[2] and on the thirty-first he sailed for San Diego, which had been invested by the insurgents, and needed assistance.[3] He reached that port a few days afterwards; and, with the assistance of Captain Gillespie's command, the besiegers were repulsed, and a fort was erected to protect the town from similar troubles in future.[4] Strenous efforts were made to obtain horses, for the use of the troops, with some degree of success; and Commodore Stockton sailed towards San Pedro again. During this temporary absence of the Commodore the insurgents appear, on the eighteenth of November, 1846, to have moved against San Diego a second time, and were again driven back by Captain Gillespie and the Volunteers and marines under his command;[5] and on the third of December a messenger came into the town bearing a letter from General Kearney, apprising the Commodore of his approach, and expressing a wish that a communication might be opened with him, and that he might be informed of the state of affairs in California.[6]

It appeared that after the General had taken Santa Fé, as before related, on the first of October, he had moved from that city with the regular cavalry, which he had brought there — Colonel Doniphan's regiment, and Major Clarke's and Captain Angney's battalions being left at that place; the former and Captain Weightman's company of artillery having orders to report to General Wool, at Chihuahua; the company of artillery under Captain Fischer and Captain Angney's battalion of infantry with orders to remain in Santa Fé. Soon afterwards (*Oct.* 7) he had reduced his force to one hundred men—sending the remainder back to Santa Fé—and after an interesting march, overland,[1] on the third of December, 1846, he had reached Warner's rancheria, the outpost of civilization in California. From thence a letter had been dispatched to San Diego, as before related, by Mr. Stokes, an Englishman who lived in a neighboring rancheria; and on the fourth the command had moved fifteen miles nearer to the city.[2]

On the receipt of General Kearney's letter, Commodore Stockton dispatched Captain Gillespie to meet him, with a letter of welcome. The Captain was accompanied by Lieutenant Beale, Midshipman Duncan, ten seamen, Captain Gibson's company of riflemen (*twenty-five men*), and a field-piece; and on the fifth he reached the General's camp; when, having learned on his way that the insurgents were encamped at San Pasqual, nine miles from the camp, Lieutenant Hammond was sent out by General Kearney to reconnoitre the enemy's position.

At a very early hour on the sixth, the troops were put in motion, Captain Johnston, with twelve dragoons, forming the advance-guard; the main body of the General's party, under Captain Moore, following next; after which moved Captain Gillespie, with Captain Gibson and his small company;[3] and Lieutenant Davidson, with the General's

---

[1] Maj. Gillespie's Am. Mil. Operations, No. 4; Notes for the History, p. 409; Ripley, i. pp. 472, 473.

[2] Ripley, i. p. 472.—[3] Maj. Gillespie's Am. Mil. Operations, No. 4; Com. Stockton's Report, Feb. 18, 1848.

[4] Com. Stockton's Report, Feb. 18, 1848; Ripley, i. p. 474.—[5] Maj. Gillespie's Am. Mil. Operations, No. 5.

[6] Ibid.; Com. Stockton's Report, Feb. 18, 1848.

[1] The details of this march have been graphically described, with great care, by my esteemed friend, Col. William H. Emory, of the Topographical Engineers, in his "*Notes of a Military Reconnoissance from Fort Leavenworth, Missouri, to San Diego, California,*" presented to Congress by the Secretary of War, Dec. 15, 1847.

[2] Emory's Notes, pp. 188–140; Gen. Kearney to Adj.-Gen., Dec. 12, 1846; "Rough Notes" of Capt. Johnston, Dec. 4.—[3] Maj. Gillespie (*Am. Mil. Operations*, No. 5) says Lieut. Davidson moved in his front, and that he (*Capt. Gillespie*) was in the rear, while Gen. Kearney (*Letter to Adj.-Gen., Dec.* 13) gives the order which I have adopted in the text.

howitzers, brought up the rear. When the column had reached a hill which overlooked the valley of the San Pasqual, the insurgents' encampment, it was halted, and the General gave the final orders to his command—"One thrust of the sabre is worth a dozen cuts; and to depend upon them more than upon the carbines and rifles." Without farther delay the column advanced down the hill; and as soon as Captain Johnston had struck the plain, with the advance, with his twelve dragoons, having mistaken the purport of an order from the General, he uttered a yell, and, without waiting for the support of the main body, dashed on the heavy ranks of the enemy, falling a victim of his own indiscretion. The main body hastened, by a flank movement, down the hill, to support the charge of the advance, and received the enemy's fire from an Indian village on its right flank; but the enemy waited to do no further mischief, and fled from the charge of the advance, before the line could be formed. Perceiving the defection of the enemy, Captain Moore, with a portion of his command, pursued the fugitives down the right of the valley; while Captain Gillespie, with his volunteers, did the same on the left side—the latter taking Pablo Beja, the insurgents' second officer, prisoner. In this pursuit, however, the ranks of the Americans were greatly broken; and, as the Mexicans greatly outnumbered them, the latter soon afterwards made a stand, using their lances with good effect. Captain Moore fell, pierced in the breast by nine lances; the General was severely wounded, and his life was saved, from an attack on his rear, by a ball from Lieutenant Emory; Captain Gillespie was attacked by seven Californians, received three wounds, and saved himself with great difficulty; Captain Gibson received two wounds; Lieutenant Hammond received nine lance wounds in the breast; and many others were severely injured. For five minutes the enemy held the ground; when, the main body of the Americans having come up, he again turned and fled.[1]

In this spirited affair about eighty Americans were engaged;[2] while of the Californians there is said to have been one hundred and sixty, under Andreas Pico.[3] Of the former, Captains Moore and Johnston, Lieutenant Hammond, and sixteen men were *killed;* and General Kearney, Captains Gillespie and Gibson, Lieutenant Warner, and eleven men were *wounded;*[4] while of the latter, it is said, twenty-eight were killed and wounded.[5]

The dead were buried as soon as night closed in; the wounded were properly attended to by the single surgeon who was with the party; and ambulances were prepared for their conveyance to San Diego, thirty-nine miles distant; and on the morning of the seventh the order to march was given—the column taking the right-hand road over the hills, and leaving the River San Barnardo to the left—the enemy retiring as it advanced. A proper regard for the comfort of the wounded compelled the column to move slowly; and it was after noon before it reached the San Barnardo rancheria (*Mr. Snooks'*). After a short halt at that place the column moved down into the valley; and, immediately afterwards, the hills on the rear of the column (around the rancheria) were covered with Californian horsemen, a portion of whom dashed at full speed past the Americans, to occupy a hill which commanded the route of the latter, while the remainder of the party threatened the rear of the column. Thirty or forty of the enemy quickly occupied the hill referred to; and as the column came up six or eight

[1] Gen. Kearney to Adj.-Gen., Dec. 13, 1846; Maj. Gillespie's Am. Mil. Operations, No. 5; Emory's Notes, p. 142; Com. Stockton's Report, Feb. 18, 1848.

[2] Maj. Gillespie says there were less than *fifty;* but his own statement appears to contradict his conclusion, in this respect.—[3] Gen. Kearney to Adj.-Gen., Dec. 13, 1846. Maj. Gillespie says they numbered "*seventy-eight strong.*"

[4] Gen. Kearney to Adj.-Gen., Dec. 13, 1846. Maj. Gillespie says *sixteen* men, besides the officers, were wounded.

[5] Maj. Gillespie's Am. Mil. Operations, No. 5.

Americans filed off to the left, and, under Lieutenant Emory, charged up the hill, when the Californians delivered their fire and fled, five of their number having been killed or wounded by the rifles of the assailants.[1]

The wounded having been removed with great difficulty, the cattle having been lost, and the danger of losing the sick and the packs being great, the General determined to halt at that place, and await the arrival of reinforcements, for which messengers had been sent to San Diego, on the morning of the sixth. Accordingly the Americans occupied the high ground on which the action had been fought, bored holes for water, killed their fattest mules for meat, and awaited the arrival of their friends until the morning of the eleventh, when they were joined by one hundred seamen and eighty marines,[2] under Lieutenant Gray, who had been sent out to meet them by Commodore Stockton; and, on the afternoon of the twelfth, the combined parties entered the town in safety.[3]

At this time commenced that memorable conflict between the two commanders—General Kearney and Commodore Stockton—respecting the chief command, which subsequently created so much trouble in the American ranks and throughout the country. Commodore Stockton appears, however, to have retained the authority; and, having organized a force sufficiently strong to warrant the undertaking, and General Kearney having accepted an invitation to accompany the expedition, on the twenty-ninth of December, he marched from San Diego with two officers and fifty-five privates—dragoons, two officers and forty-five seamen acting as artillery, eighteen officers and three hundred and seventy-nine seamen and marines acting as infantry, six officers and fifty-four privates—Volunteers, and six pieces of artillery, against the main body of the insurgents, near Los Angeles. The command appears to have been given, at his own request, to General Kearney; and, as the wagon-train was heavily laden, the progress of the column was very slow,—the expedition reaching the Rio San Gabriel on the eighth of January, 1847,—although the enemy had offered no opposition to its progress, even in passes where a small force could have effectively kept it back. At this place, however, he had made a stand to dispute the passage of the river; and here the second action was fought between the Americans and the Californians.[1]

The Rio San Gabriel, at the spot where this action was fought, is about one hundred yards wide, the current about knee-deep, flowing over a quicksand bottom. The left bank, by which the Americans approached, is level; that on the right is also level for a short distance back, but, beyond this narrow plain, a bank, fifty feet in height, commands the ford and the intervening flat, while both banks were fringed with a thick undergrowth. On this bank, directly in front of the ford, four pieces of artillery were posted, supported on either flank by strong bodies of cavalry, while on the slope of the hill and the flat in front were posted the sharp-shooters.[2]

Against this position the American column moved—the Second division in front, with the First and Third divisions on the right and left flanks; the cattle and the wagon-train moved next; the volunteer riflemen and the Fourth division brought up the rear. As the head of the column approached the bank of the river the enemy's sharp-shooters opened a scattering fire; and the

[1] Maj. Gillespie's Am. Mil. Operations, No. 6; Gen. Kearney to Adj.-Gen., Dec. 13, 1846; Emory's Notes, pp. 144, 145; Ripley, i. pp. 478, 479.

[2] Lieut. Emory's Notes, p. 147. Maj. Gillespie (*Am. Mil. Operations*, No. 6) says it was composed of "*two hundred and fifty* sailors and marines;" Com. Stockton (*Report, Feb.* 18, 1848) says, "*two hundred and fifteen* men."

[3] Maj. Gillespie's Am. Mil. Operations, No. 6; Gen. Kearney to Adj.-Gen., Dec. 13, 1846; Emory's Notes, pp. 145–149.

[1] Emory's Notes, pp. 149–157; Com. Stockton's Report, Feb. 18, 1848.

[2] Emory's Notes, p. 157; Ripley, i. p. 483.

Second division was ordered to deploy as skirmishers, cross the river, and drive the former from the thicket; while the First and Third divisions covered the flanks of the train, and, with it, followed in the rear. When this line of skirmishers had reached the middle of the stream and was pressing forward towards the opposite bank, the enemy brought his artillery to bear, "and made the water fly with grape and round shot;" and the American field-pieces were immediately dragged across the river, and placed in counter-battery on the right bank, in opposition to those of the enemy. The fire of the Americans appears to have caused some considerable confusion in the ranks of the insurgents; and under its cover the wagon-train and cattle, with their guard, passed the river, during which time the enemy attacked its rear and was repulsed.[1]

Having safely crossed the river, the American column appears to have deployed under cover of the high ground—the Californian grape and round shot rattling over the heads of the men—and the enemy immediately charged on both its flanks, simultaneously, dashing down the slope with great spirit. With great coolness the Second division was thrown into squares, and, after a round or two, drove off the enemy from the left flank; the First division received a similar order, but as the assailants on the right hesitated, and did not come down as far as their associates on the opposite flank, the order was countermanded, and the division was ordered to charge up the hill, where the enemy's main body was supposed to be posted. With great coolness this movement was executed and the heights were gained, *but there was no enemy*—he had abandoned his position; and although he pitched his camp on the hills, in view of the Americans, when morning came he had moved still farther back.[2]

[1] Emory's Notes, pp. 157, 158; Ripley, i. pp. 483, 484; Com. Stockton's Report, Feb. 18, 1848.

[2] Emory's Notes, p. 158; Gen. Kearney to Adj.-Gen., Jan. 12, 1847; Notes for the History, p. 413.

The strength of the Americans in this action—*the action of the Rio San Gabriel*—has been shown already; that of the Californians was about six hundred, with four pieces of artillery. The loss of the former was one man *killed* and nine men *wounded;* that of the enemy is not known.[1]

On the following morning (*Jan.* 9, 1847) the American column resumed its march over the Mesa,—a wide plain, which extends from the Rio San Gabriel to the Rio San Fernando, — surrounded by reconnoitring parties from the enemy; and when about four miles from Los Angeles the enemy was discovered on the right of the line of march, awaiting its approach. When the column had come abreast of the enemy's position he opened a fire from his artillery on its right flank, and, soon afterwards, he deployed his force, making a horse-shoe in front of the American column, and opening two pieces of artillery on its front, while two nine-pounders continued their fire on its right flank.[2]

After stopping about fifteen minutes to silence the enemy's nine-pounders, the column again moved forward; when, by a movement similar to that employed on the Rio San Gabriel, the day before, two charges were made simultaneously on its left flank and its right and rear. Contrary to the positive injunctions of the officers, in the former of these charges, the enemy was met with a fire at long distance; yet, although he had not come within a hundred yards of the column, several of his men were knocked out of their saddles, and a round of grape, which was immediately sent after him, completely scattered his right wing. The charge on the right and rear of the column fared but little better; and the entire force of the insurgents was withdrawn.[3]

The strength of both parties was probably

[1] Gen. Kearney to Adjutant-General, Jan. 12, 1847.

[2] Emory's Notes, p. 159; Ripley, i. p. 484; Gen. Kearney to Adjutant-general, Jan. 12, 1847.

[3] Emory's Notes, p. 159; Notes for the History, p. 413.

Painted by Chappel. Engraved by Phillibrown.

W. J. Worth

From the original Painting in the possession of [illegible]

[illegible]

the same as on the preceding day, at the Rio San Gabriel; the loss of the Californians is not known; that of the Americans was Captain Gillespie, Lieutenant Rowan, and three men *wounded*.[1]

The troops encamped near the field of battle; and, on the following morning (*Jan.* 10, 1847), the enemy surrendered, when the city of Los Angeles was occupied by the Americans without farther opposition.[2]

"This was the last exertion made by the sons of California for the liberty and independence of their country," say the Mexican historians, "and its defence will always do them honor; since, without supplies, without means or instructions, they rushed into an unequal contest, in which they more than once taught the invaders what a people can do who fight in defence of their rights. The city of Los Angeles was occupied by the American forces on the tenth of January, *and the loss of that rich, vast, and precious part of the Mexican territory was consummated*."[1]

CHAPTER CIII.

September 19 to 24, 1846.

THE SIEGE OF MONTEREY.

THE defeat of the Mexican forces at Palo Alto and Resaca de la Palma was followed by their retreat across the Rio Grande to Matamoras,[3] and thence, on the eighteenth of May, to Monterey, the capital of the State of Nueva Leon;[4] while, following up his advantages, General Taylor had advanced over the Rio Grande,[5] taken possession of Matamoras,[6] and thence gradually advanced into the country. First Reynosa was occupied,[7] then Carmargo;[8] and on the nineteenth of August, General Worth, with the First brigade of regulars, advanced from the latter place for Cerralvo, seventy miles farther in advance.[9] On the twenty-fifth, the Second brigade followed on the same line;[10] and on the fifteenth and sixteenth of September, Generals Twiggs and Worth encamped on the banks of the San Juan, three miles from Marin, and twenty-four from Monterey.[2] Three days afterwards the army continued its march from the San Juan; and on the nineteenth it encamped before Monterey.[3]

While the Americans were thus leisurely moving from the coast into the interior of Mexico, General Ampudia, by a revolution at the capital, had succeeded General Arista in the command of the Mexican army; and, aided by the wealthy inhabitants, he had strengthened the works of Monterey with great skill and expense.[4] A garrison of more than ten thousand men, seven thousand of whom were regular troops, had also been assembled within its lines;[5] immense stores of provisions and ammunition had been collected for their use;[6] and Generals Mejía, Ortega, Garcia Conde, Raquena, Ro-

---

1 Returns appended to Gen. Kearney's Dispatch, Jan. 12, 1847.—2 Emory, i. pp. 160, 161; Ripley, i. p. 485.

3 Notes for the History, pp. 55, 56.—4 Ripley, i. p. 131; Gen. Taylor's Dispatch, No. 40, May 18, 1846.

5 Gen. Taylor's Dispatch, No. 40, May 18, 1846.

6 Ibid.; MS. Diary of the Campaign, May 18.

7 Gen. Taylor's Dispatch, No. 52, June 17, 1846; MS. Diary, June 10.—8 Gen. Taylor's Dispatch, No. 49, June 3; No. 60, July 11; No. 63, July 22, 1846.

9 Gen. Taylor's Dispatch, No. 76, Aug. 19, 1846; General orders, No. 99, Aug. 17.—10 Gen. Taylor's Dispatch, No. 78, Aug. 25, 1846; General Orders, No. 105, Aug. 24, 1846.

1 Notes for the History, pp. 413, 414.—2 Gen. Taylor's Dispatch, No. 88, Sept. 17, 1846.—3 Gen. Taylor's Dispatch, No. 89, Sept. 22, 1846.—4 Notes for the History, pp. 66, 67.—5 Ripley, i. pp. 198, 199; Campaign in Northern Mexico, p. 155.—6 Ripley, i. p. 199.

mero, and Torrejon, under General Ampudia's orders, directed the movements of the masses who were to resist the progress of the Americans.[1]

Monterey, the scene of the impending struggle, is a city of about ten thousand inhabitants, the capital of a State, and the centre of considerable wealth. It is nearly surrounded by mountains, and the little valley in which it nestles makes up by its great fertility what it lacks in extent. Immediately on its western bounds, the city is overlooked by the Obispado, a steep and bare hill, on which was the Bishop's Palace; and, still farther to the westward, by the towering heights of the Sierra Madre; on its southern front flows a small stream,—the San Juan de Monterey,—which separates the city from a branch of the Sierra, on one spur of which had been thrown up two works of defence; and the Saddle Mountain closes the scene farther to the east. On the northern front, commanded by the citadel, the city was bounded by a small branch of the San Juan, beyond which a range of highly cultivated fields and gardens, intersected by lofty hedge-rows, by rows of fruit-trees, and by cuts for the irrigation of the soil. From the north the great road from Marin, Cerralvo, and the Rio Grande, enters the city; from the east, that from Guadaloupe; and from the west, through a narrow pass, that from Saltillo. On its northern front, on which the American army appeared, and about a thousand yards from the city, the strong work known as "*The Citadel*," within which was an unfinished cathedral, commanded every approach from that direction; while the hedge-rows, which furnished shelter for light troops; the small branch of the San Juan, with its substantial stone bridge of the Purísima and its *tête-de-pont;* and the barricades, which protected the several streets, at the small stream where they terminated, rendered the approach a work of difficulty and danger. Nor were the other fronts less carefully guarded. By a curve of the river, the eastern front of the town, as well as the southern, was covered by the San Juan, yet a line of strong works rendered it still more secure. On the northern bank of the smaller stream, near its junction with the San Juan, and flanking the citadel, was the strong redoubt, "*El Teneria*," mounting four guns; connected with which, farther up the river, was another, mounting three guns, called "*El Diablo;*" and still farther, a third, mounting four guns, named "*Libertad.*" From the latter a strong line of barricades extended along the bank of the San Juan, covering the entire eastern and southeastern fronts of the city. On the southern front, crowning the spur of the Sierra, heretofore referred to, *Forts Federacion* and *Soldado* commanded the valley on either hand, while they presented an almost inaccessible front to the city and the American camp. Westward from the city, as before related, frowned the Obispado, midway up which was the *Bishop's Palace*, and above it, on the crest of the hill, was *Fort Independencia*—both strong and well-appointed defences. In addition to these complicated exterior defences, commanding every approach, there was a vast number of interior street fortifications. Every street was defended with barricades, many of them from ten to twelve feet thick, with embrasures for guns; the bridge of the Purísima was defended with a *tête-de-pont;* the "*Campo Santo*," a strong stone inclosure in the Plaza de la Capilla, was prepared for defence; and the flat roofs of the substantial stone houses, in many instances, had been carefully surrounded with parapets of sand-bags, with loop-holes for musketry.[1]

Against this town, thus fortified and garrisoned, as already related, General Taylor

[1] Notes for the Hist., pp. 63, 66, 79.

[1] Campaign in Northern Mexico, pp. 141, 142, 152–155; Ripley, i. pp. 194–199; Notes for the History, p. 65; Furber's Journal of a Private in the Tennessee Regiment, pp. 96–98.

led his army on the nineteenth of September.[1] Flushed with his own success, or thinking too lightly of the character and resources of his enemy,—possibly from both causes combined,—General Taylor affected to despise his antagonist and to underrate his strength;[2] and, with none of the caution which he had displayed on the banks of the Rio Grande, he hastened to attack the town, with a mere handful of men, and entirely without a siege-train or heavy guns of any kind.[3] Of his four brigades of regular troops, one was commanded by a colonel, two by lieutenant-colonels, and one by a major! while his regiments were, necessarily, commanded by majors or, in four instances, by captains—a fact which proves, incontestably, that the triumph was owing more to the unflinching courage and general intelligence of the subordinate officers and of the men they commanded, than to the professional abilities of their commanding general or the policy of the government.

On the part of the enemy the very reverse of all this was true. Tried and skilful officers commanded the troops—whose bravery cannot be impeached or be treated with disrespect; the town had been carefully protected, and was well supplied with artillery and the means of offensive operations; the lines had been very closely masked; and without the least display or parade, husbanding his strength, the enemy laid quietly within his lines, vigilantly watching his antagonist.[4]

During the afternoon of the nineteenth, a close reconnoissance, on both flanks of the town, was made by the officers of engineers and topographical engineers, under the directions of Major Mansfield; when it was discovered that the western side of the city was its most important point; and as the Saltillo road, in that direction, afforded the only means of access to the city from the interior of Mexico, it was determined to occupy that road,—thereby cutting off the possibility of receiving supplies or reinforcements, as well as the means of retreat, from the garrison,—and, if practicable, to carry the several fortifications in that direction.[1]

"Deeming this to be an operation of essential importance," as it was, General Taylor assigned the command of the movement to General Worth, whose pre-eminent qualifications peculiarly fitted him for it; and with his division—composed of Brevet-lieutenant-colonel Duncan's battery, the battalion of artillery, serving as infantry, under Brevet-lieutenant-colonel Childs, and the Eighth infantry, under Captain Screvin, the whole under Brevet-lieutenant-colonel Staniford, acting as Brigadier-general; and of Lieutenant Mackall's battery, the Fifth infantry, under Major Scott, the Seventh infantry, under Captain Niles, and a company of Louisiana Volunteers, Captain Blanchard, the whole under Colonel Persifer F. Smith, acting as Brigadier-general—and Colonel Hays' regiment of Texan Rangers, he moved from the camp at two o'clock in the afternoon of the twentieth, for the purpose of executing it. He was ordered to move, by a detour to the right, around the northern and western fronts of the city; but the obstacles which he experienced so much retarded the movement of his artillery that he marched only six miles, and was abreast of the Obispado, within gunshot of the Fort Independencia, when he halted for the night; and, subsequently, he extended his reconnoissance under cover of the Rangers.[2]

Notwithstanding the secrecy of this movement, the Mexicans were soon advised of it; and judging what its purpose was, General Ampudia immediately detached a heavy body of cavalry to the junction of the Topo and Saltillo roads, and one of infantry to reinforce the Bishop's Palace; while, at the

[1] MS. Diary of the Campaign.—[2] Gen. Taylor's Dispatch, No. 88, Sept. 17, 1846; Ripley, i. p. 200.—[3] Campaign in Northern Mexico, p. 155.—[4] Ibid., pp. 142, 143.

[1] Gen. Taylor's Dispatches, No. 89, Sept. 22; No. 94, Oct. 9, 1846.—[2] Gen. Taylor's Dispatch, No. 94, Oct. 9; Gen. Worth's Report, Sept. 28, 1846; Ripley, i. pp. 201, 202.

same time, the First division, under General Twiggs, and the division of Volunteers, under General Butler, displayed in front of the city, until evening, for the purpose of diverting the enemy and of holding him in check.[1]

Thus the two armies spent the night of the twentieth—the Mexican, with its western front strengthened, and its cavalry, under Generals Torrejon and Romero, occupying the Saltillo road;[2] the main body of the American within its camp at El Bosque de Santa Domingo;[3] the Fourth regiment of infantry in front of the city, covering a mortar-battery, which had been erected during the night;[4] and General Worth's command, six miles distant, on the right of the camp, ready to spring forward, at the earliest moment, on its important mission.[5]

At six o'clock on the morning of the twenty-first, led by the Texan Rangers and the light companies of the First brigade, under Captain C. F. Smith,—both in open order, sweeping the entire width of the valley,—the Second division, under General Worth, resumed its march; but it had proceeded only a short distance, when, at an abrupt turn in the valley, near the hacienda called San Jeromino, it was met by General Torrejon, and the cavalry under his command. Without any ceremony the heavy column of Lancers dashed forward at a charge, but were met by the Texan Rangers with their unerring rifles and their usual gallantry, and by the light companies, with a well-directed fire, while Lieutenant-colonel Duncan's light battery, *within one minute after the first attack*, was in action, delivering its fire over the heads of the Texans and light companies, in its front, and scattering destruction throughout the solid columns of the Mexicans beyond. A section of Mackall's battery promptly opened its fire, also, in the same gallant style; and the First brigade, under Brevet-lieutenant-colonel Staniford, hastening forward, soon afterwards formed to the front, on the right and left, and also delivered its fire. A movement so prompt and, at the same time, so efficient, could not be long resisted; and, after continuing the action about fifteen minutes, the enemy fled in great confusion, with heavy loss—the brigade of cavalry under General Romero having been "cut to pieces" in the encounter. The fugitives flying before the victors as far as the Saltillo road, and, turning *up* the gorge, were excluded from the city by the occupation of the pass by the Americans; and thenceforth all communication between the devoted city and the other parts of Mexico was completely cut off.[1]

Having secured this important pass and accomplished the principal, or more positive, part of his orders, General Worth halted his division for farther observation and reconnoissance. In doing so the General soon discovered that the occupation of the heights which envelop the city on its western and southern faces was indispensably necessary, both for the restoration of his line of communication with the main body of the army—which had been abandoned in order to secure the gorges of the Saltillo road—and for the purpose of insuring the success of the movement of the main body against the city itself; and he took the necessary steps for securing that object. He had written a note to General Taylor on the preceding evening, in which he had suggested a strong diversion against the centre and left of the town, to favor his movements; and, as will presently be seen, it had been done; while, at the same time, the Second dragoons, under Lieutenant-colonel May, and the Texan Mounted Volunteers, under Colonel Wood, the whole under General Henderson, were

[1] Notes for the History, p. 71; Ripley, i. pp. 203, 204.
[2] Notes for the History, p. 71.—[3] Campaign in Northern Mexico, p. 147; Furber, p. 99.—[4] Gen. Taylor's Dispatch, No. 94, Oct. 9, 1846; Furber, p. 99.—[5] Gen. Worth's Report, Sept. 28, 1846; Ripley, i. pp. 203, 204.

[1] Gen. Worth's Report, Sept. 28; Furber, p. 100; Notes for the History, pp. 71–73; Campaign in Northern Mexico, p. 161; Thorpe's Monterey, pp. 63–65; Ripley, i. pp. 216–218.

thrown to the right, to support General Worth, if necessary, and to make an impression, if practicable, upon the upper part of the city. At length, at noon, companies K of the Second artillery, B of the Third artillery, and G and H of the Fourth artillery, and Captains Green's, McGowans', R. A. Gillespie's, Chandlis's, Ballowes', and McCulloch's companies of Texan riflemen, about three hundred in all, under Captain C. F. Smith, were detached, with orders to storm the battery on the crest of the nearest hill (*Fort Federacion*), and, after taking that, to carry that on the ridge of the same height (*Fort Soldado*). As these two works commanded the slopes and roads of either valley, and, consequently, the approaches to the city from the west, their importance to both armies will be readily perceived. The progress of this storming party, therefore, as it approached the foot of the heights, was promptly noticed by the commandant of the troops on its summit; and, besides sending out numerous light troops, who posted themselves at favorable points on the slope, to oppose the ascent, he opened a fire from both the forts with the same purpose. When it had become apparent that the enemy intended to interpose a vigorous resistance to the movement, General Worth detached the Seventh regiment of infantry, under Captain Miles, to support the storming party; and the enemy gradually retired up the rugged slope of the hill, while the Americans pressed forward with equal steadiness in pursuit. It soon became apparent to the General, however, that the enemy intended to renew the contest, with greater energy, on the summit of the hill; and that, for that purpose, he was concentrating heavy reinforcements around the forts. "The cardinal importance of the operation," however, precluded the idea that even this opposition must not be overcome, at any cost; and General Worth immediately ordered General Smith, with Captain Blanchard's company of Louisiana Volunteers and the Fifth regiment of infantry, to advance and render still farther support to the storming party. When he had reached the advance party, General Smith discovered that, by the formation of the ground, he could advantageously make simultaneous movements against the Fort Federacion and the Fort Soldado, and by that means divide and overcome the opposition which, otherwise, would be concentrated on one point; and he very judiciously directed the original storming party, under Captain Smith, against Fort Federacion, while, with the two covering parties, he made a simultaneous movement to the right against Fort Soldado. Both columns moved forward with great gallantry, in the face of a heavy fire, against their respective objects of attack; but it was for Captain Smith, with his little party, to gain the first laurels, in the triumphant occupation of Fort Federacion, in training the gun which was mounted there—a nine-pounder—on Fort Soldado, and in detaching Colonel John Hays—who had hastened, from special service, to mix in the fray—with fifty of his riflemen to assist in securing Fort Soldado on the heights above him. Soon afterwards the upper work also fell into the hands of the Americans—Lieutenant Pitcher and the color-bearer of the Fifth infantry, being the first to enter it.[1]

Having gained an important advantage over the enemy, although but half the work had been completed, the troops might have reasonably sought repose; but they and their General alike thirsted for the glory which was before them, and they sought new fields of adventure, and fresh honors. The guns of the two batteries which had just been taken, therefore, were brought to bear on the works on the Obispado, on the opposite side of the valley; and a heavy fire was opened on them. A violent storm soon

[1] Gen. Worth's Report, Sept. 28, 1846; Ripley, i. pp. 219–222; Furber, p. 105; Thorpe's Monterey, pp. 65–69; Campaign in Northern Mexico, pp. 190–192; Notes for the History, p. 73.

came up, however; and this, with the approach of night, and the fatigue of the troops—who had been thirty-six hours without food and constantly taxed, during that time, to the utmost physical exertions—induced the General to postpone all farther movements until the next day. Those of them who could be permitted to do so, therefore, slept on their arms; while their less fortunate comrades mounted guard—both alike being exposed to the unbroken pelting of a pitiless storm during the greater part of the night.[1]

While General Worth and the Second division were thus gallantly leading their associates in the race for honor, the main body of the army, also, was actively engaged on the northern and eastern fronts of the city.

It has been already noticed that General Worth, on the evening of the twentieth, had suggested, what General Taylor had previously intended, a strong diversion on the front and right of the enemy's lines, in order that his movements, on the left and rear, might be favored.[2] Leaving behind them, therefore, one company from each regiment as a camp-guard, at an early hour, the remainder of the troops moved towards the city—the First and Third infantry, the battalion of Baltimore and Washington Volunteers, and Captain Bragg's battery, the whole under Lieutenant-colonel Garland, being first in motion, designed to operate against the lower, or eastern, part of the city, "to make a strong demonstration, and to carry one of the enemy's advanced works, if it could be done without too heavy loss;" while the Fourth infantry covered the mortar-battery; and the Second dragoons, under Lieutenant-colonel May, and the Texan mounted Volunteers, under Colonel Wood, the whole under General Henderson, were detached to the right to support General Worth, as before related, and to make an impression, if possible, on the upper part of the city.[1]

The latter party had proceeded as far as "the gorge of the mountain," when it was ordered to countermarch and join the few troops under the immediate orders of General Taylor, near the lower part of the city; but it did not reach there until after the troops under Lieutenant-colonel Garland had carried the point against which it had moved; and it did not, therefore, share in the dangers or participate in the glory of the day.[2]

The former of these—the command of Lieutenant-colonel Garland—moved forward, on the road, towards the town, until it had nearly reached the mortar-battery, when it inclined to the left (*the eastward*), and occupied a position which was covered by some low shrubbery. Captain Field, of the Third, with two companies, was thence detached to cover the engineers, who, with Colonel Kinney for a guide, were in front, making a reconnoissance; while the remainder of the party appears to have remained quietly in its position until Major Mansfield and his associate engineers could determine, by an examination of the enemy's position, which would be the most advantageous line of approach.[3] It was designed, as has been stated, that this movement should be concealed; and the chaparral, and the high corn which grew there, were well calculated to secure such a result. At that moment, however, the victorious troops under General Worth, moving over the heights near Fort Federacion, arrested the attention of the men as they stood in their places; and some zealous, but indiscreet, individual, unable to enjoy the sight without proclaiming his satisfaction, called for "*Three cheers for General Worth; he has carried the heights;*" and the men, in their enthusiasm, being not more

[1] Gen. Worth's Report, Sept. 28, 1846; Ripley, i. p. 222; Thorpe's Monterey, p. 69.—[2] Gen. Taylor's Dispatch, No. 94, Oct. 9, 1846.

[1] Gen. Taylor's Dispatch, No. 94, Sept. 9, 1846; MS. Diary of a participant.—[2] Gen. Henderson's Report, Oct. 1, 1846; Gen. Taylor's Dispatch, No. 94, Oct. 9, 1846.

[3] Lieut.-Col. Garland's Report, Sept. 29, 1846; MS. Diary, &c.

prudent than their leader, the demand was responded to with alacrity, and *revealed their position to the enemy*, who prepared for their reception.[1] Immediately afterwards, at the request of Major Mansfield, of the engineers, the column moved from its place of concealment into the open plain, for the purpose of supporting the covering party; and, at about three-quarters of a mile distant from the city, at the request of the same officer, the line was formed—the Third infantry, under Major William W. Lear, being on the right; the First infantry, under Brevet-major Abercrombie, in the centre; and the Baltimore and Washington Volunteers, under Lieutenant-colonel Watson, on the left. The detachment moved forward in line, at quick time, but had proceeded scarcely a hundred paces when a fire was opened on it, in front, from Fort El Teneria and from the citadel on its right flank, from which the line experienced some loss. Immediately afterwards the covering party which accompanied the engineers, in front, came in contact with the enemy's skirmishers, when Major Mansfield sent back a request that the main body should "change its point of direction more to the right"—a movement which is always hazardous, but especially so when under the enemy's fire, with inexperienced and imperfectly drilled troops. The object of this change was to direct the detachment into the city, *behind* the line of batteries and the exterior defences on its eastern and northeastern fronts, instead of leading them to the *front* of these works; but while the First and Third infantry moved steadily forward, under the change to which allusion has been made, the left of the line—the Baltimore and Washington Volunteers—first faltered, and then broke into fragments—a very few, without order, and on their individual merits, seconding the efforts of the regulars in their assault on the city, and entering the city with them; while by far the greater part concealed themselves in the neighboring quarries, or sneaked back to the camp at El Bosque de Santa Domingo.[1] Thus deserted by their volunteer associates,—nearly one-half the entire strength of the detachment,[2] — the First and Third moved steadily forward, by the right flank,—running over an unfinished battery on their line of march,—and entered the city, by one of the streets which extended north and south, from the plain to the Rio San Juan. Soon afterwards a ditch obstructed their progress; and, thenceforth, each regiment—or, rather, each officer, with such men as he could collect—appeared to fight on its own account, without especial regard to the movements of its comrades, all, as with the mind of one man, however, pressing forward on the enemy, although in different directions.[3]

The Third regiment crossed the ditch on a log or narrow foot-bridge, and formed in line on the street near by, without effecting much; while the First—or rather the main body of that regiment, as Captain Miller had been sent to escort Captain Bragg's battery, and Captain J. N. Scott had been detached in front as a skirmisher, leaving only the two companies commanded by Captains Backus and Lamotte, *eighty-eight men in all*—halted on the northern bank of the ditch; and, after facing to the front (*the eastward*), it moved against a party of Mexicans, which had opened a fire from the adjacent shrubbery, drove the latter from its position, and occupied the ground itself. In this movement Major Abercrombie, the commandant of the regiment, was wounded, and the command devolved on Captain Electus Backus, by whom the little party was led forward about a hundred yards; and, at that place, it also crossed the ditch

[1] MS. "Sketch of the Battle of Monterey," by a participant.

[1] MS. Diary, &c.; MS. "Sketch of the Battle," &c.; Campaign in Northern Mexico, p. 165.

[2] The 1st infantry numbered 187 men; the 3d infantry, 296; the Baltimore and Washington Volunteers, 334. Total, 817.—*MS. "Sketch," &c.*—[3] Lieut.-Col. Garland's Report, Sept. 29, 1846; MS. "Sketch," &c.; MS. Diary; MS. Map of "Eastern end of Monterey, Sept. 21, 1846."

on a log, and formed on the same street on which the Third still stood in line, more to the westward.[1]

At this moment, as will be seen, the First and Third infantry occupied positions *within the limits of the city;* while of the Baltimore battalion only some fragments were on the field, with their associates. The Third regiment, in its original position, in line, in the street, was exposed to a heavy fire, both from the trenches west of Fort Diablo, in its front, and from the street defences and the roofs of the houses, on its flanks; and it suffered very severely—Brevet-major Philip N. Barbour falling at that place, soon after he had crossed the ditch—until it was withdrawn by Lieutenant-colonel Garland, as will be seen hereafter. The First regiment, meanwhile, from its crossing place, moved towards the east, under Captain Backus, towards Fort El Teneria; but it was suddenly brought to a stand by a tremendous fire which was opened on it by a party of Mexicans which occupied a tannery on the north side of the street. Taking shelter as well as they could, the Americans returned this fire, and quickly compelled the enemy to seek quarters; but a subsequent act of treachery on the part of the garrison of this outpost led the victors to shoot down all except eight, who were taken prisoners[2]—*the first prisoners captured within the lines of the city.* Taking possession of this position, Captain Backus quickly mounted the flat roof from which he had driven the Mexicans;[3] when, for the first time, the defences of the city, in that direction, were fairly before him. On his right, about two hundred yards distant, and partially concealed by shrubbery, was Fort Diablo, with its three guns and its curtains on either hand: directly in front, and about one hundred and twenty yards distant, was a large and strong stone building, which had been used as a distillery and tannery, on the flat roof of which, fully exposed to his fire, were a large body of Mexicans, protected *on the opposite face* of the building—whence alone any opposition was expected—by a parapet of sandbags: and, on his left and front—directly north from the distillery—and one hundred and eighteen yards distant from his position on the tannery, was the Fort El Teneria—a lunette, the gorge of which opened towards the tannery, and exposed one half its area to the fire of those who occupied the roof of the latter building.[1]

It was now between nine and ten o'clock, and the little party under Captain Backus had been joined by Captain J. M. Scott with about ten of his men; and the whole immediately occupied the roof of the tannery, lying flat on its surface, and opening, over the low parapet on its eastern face, a careful and destructive fire on the Mexicans who occupied the roof of the distillery. Within five minutes the roof was cleared of the enemy; and by ten o'clock the building was evacuated—the troops, as well as a body of women and children who had sought shelter within it, retiring in disorder across the small branch of the Rio San Juan, heretofore referred to, to Fort Diablo.[2] From this moment—about ten in the morning—both the tannery and the distillery were in possession of the First infantry; and as the latter commanded the Fort El Teneria—the key to the eastern front of the city—one of the most important acts of the great drama had been performed by Captain Backus and the gallant ninety whom he commanded.

---

[1] MS. "Sketch," &c.; MS. Diary.—[2] "We ceased firing, but before we could secure the prisoners, *they again fired on us*, and compelled us to shoot down all except eight."—*MS. "Sketch," &c.*

[3] MS. "Sketch," &c.; MS. Diary; MS. "Details of the Controversy between the Regulars and Volunteers," &c.; MS. Letter from Maj. Henry (*Commander of 3d regiment*) to the Editor of the *Courier and Enquirer*, "*Camp near Monterey, Dec* 21, 1846;" Col. Kinney to Capt. Backus, "*Tampico, March* 6, 1847;" Gen. Taylor's Dispatch, No. 94, Oct. 9, 1846.

[1] MS. Map of "Eastern end of Monterey, Sept. 21, 1846;" MS. Diary.—[2] MS. "Sketch," &c.; MS. "Details of Controversy," &c.; MS. Diary; Maj. Henry to *The Spirit of the Times.*

The way being somewhat clear since the enemy had been driven from the distillery, Majors Mansfield and Lear successively attempted to reconnoitre; and both retired with an opinion that the positions of the brigade—both that occupied by Captain Backus, with the First, and that by Major Lear, with the Third regiment—could not be maintained; and this opinion was reported, by the former, to the commandant of the brigade.[1] Accordingly orders were given to the greater part of the troops who had entered the city to "Retire in good order, slowly;"[2] and, soon afterwards, *all those who had received the orders* "*through an officer*," fell back amidst the *vivas* of the enemy; and the bells of the cathedral rang a merry peal, in evidence of the general joy.[3] In the midst of this exciting scene an attempt of the enemy to harass Lieutenant-colonel Garland's rear was frustrated by a few men belonging to the First infantry, led by Captain Backus, who sallied from the tannery, charged on the pursuers, and routed them;[4] after which, having received no orders to retire, and feeling confident of his ability to hold his position, if not to do more than that, with his men, the Captain returned to his stronghold in the tannery, and did not leave it again, unless to pursue the enemy in his retreat from El Teneria, until the conquest of the eastern front of the city had been completed.[5]

While the Third brigade (*Lieutenant-colonel Garland's*) was thus engaged, General Taylor ordered the Fourth infantry to its support;[6] but it did not come on the ground until after the former had retired.[7] Three small companies of this regiment, under Major Allen, were considerably in advance of their associates, and came, suddenly, and without support, in front of the Fort El Teneria, when a most murderous fire was opened on them, in which "almost in one moment, one-third of the officers and men were struck down, and rendered it necessary for them to retire and effect a junction with the two other companies then advancing,"[1] when the entire regiment joined Lieutenant-colonel Garland's command, and, with it, engaged the enemy again in the latter part of the day.[2]

It was now nearly twelve o'clock, and the garrison of El Teneria, elated with its double success, if such it could be called, appears to have turned its attention to Captain Backus and the First regiment, who still occupied the roof and yard of the tannery, and commanded the evacuated distillery. Opening the gorge of the work the Mexicans brought a piece of artillery to bear on the intruders; while the latter, in their turn, brought their muskets to bear on the men and mules with which the fort was crowded. Before the piece had been discharged three times, the gunners had been shot down by the occupants of the tannery; and the fire of the latter was turned on the general occupants of the fort, by which considerable loss was inflicted on them.[3] At the same time, in the distance, but not yet within range of their fire, the Tennessee and Mississippi regiments of Volunteers, commanded by General Quitman, were seen from the Fort El Teneria as they approached the front of the work; when, without farther resistance, the greater part of the garrison abandoned its post, leaving the wounded behind it; and rushing through the gorge, retreated towards the Fort Diablo,[4] with Captain Backus and his

[1] MS. Diary; MS. "Sketch," &c.; Lieut.-Col. Garland's Report, Sept. 29, 1846.—[2] MS. "Sketch," &c.; MS. Diary; Maj. Henry to *Spirit of Times*.—[3] MS. "Sketch," &c.

[4] Ibid.—[5] Ibid.; MS. Diary; Maj. Henry to *Courier and Enquirer*, Dec. 21, 1846; Same to *Spirit of Times*; Col. Kinney to Capt. Backus, March 6, 1847; Lieut.-Col. Garland's Report, Sept. 29, 1846; Thorpe, pp. 53, 54.

[6] Gen. Taylor's Dispatch, No. 94, Oct. 9, 1846.

[7] MS. "Sketch," &c.; Maj. Henry to *Spirit of Times*.

[1] Lieut.-Col. Garland's Report, Sept. 29, 1846. See also MS. "Sketch," &c.; Maj. Henry to *Spirit of Times;* Thorpe, p. 54; Ripley, i. p. 210.—[2] Lieut.-Col. Garland's Report, Sept. 29, 1846.—[3] MS. "Sketch," &c.; MS. Diary; Maj. Henry to *Spirit of Times;* Thorpe, p. 54.—[4] MS. Diary; MS. "Sketch," &c.; Col. McClung, of Mississippi Rifles, cited in MS. "Details of Controversy," &c.; Col. Whiting, Q. M. G., cited in same; Col. Kinney to Capt. Backus, March 6, 1847; Maj. Henry to *Spirit of Times;* Thorpe, p. 54.

party on its rear.[1] While the former was pushing over the small branch of the Rio San Juan, before referred to, the Captain came up with it, and captured some twenty men—the second success of that kind, within the lines of the city, by the same command—and as he was returning to his post in the tannery, or to the fort, he discovered, *for the first time*, the approach of the Volunteers.[2] The latter, in their haste, rushed into the deserted fort, *finding no opponents*, and, except the dead and wounded, and a very few who had remained, without making any resistance, no occupants;[3] while, with vociferous cheers, proclaiming their bloodless victory in their assault on an *abandoned* battery, they immediately dashed forward, and were restrained with great difficulty from firing on the command of Captain Backus, as the latter, with its prisoners, was quietly moving back to the scene of its gallantry and of its glorious success. In the midst of the confusion which this reckless conduct produced, some sixteen of the prisoners escaped, and four only were retained as trophies of the victory.[4] The command of Captain Backus and the Volunteers returned to the lines; the former, after filling his cartridge-boxes from those of the killed and wounded, joined his brigade in the subsequent operations of the day, while the latter continued to occupy these works—the fort, the distillery, and the tannery—amusing themselves, meanwhile, with firing on the Fort El Diablo and on the trenches in its vicinity, but as no apparent benefit resulted from the fire, it is reasonable to suppose that but little damage was done.[5]

Soon after the successful issue of the movements against the Fort El Teneria, and its two outworks, General Butler led the Ohio regiment of Volunteers against the front of the city, at a point northwest from the bridge "Purisima," and nearly in a line between it and the citadel; but it was withdrawn by General Taylor, at the suggestion of Major Mansfield, of the engineers. Immediately afterwards he moved towards the city again, but farther to the eastward—"striking at a point in the enemy's line between the *tête-de-pont* of the Purisima and Fort Diablo," and in a line between the the latter work and citadel. With great gallantry the regiment moved in the face of a heavy fire to a point "within, say, one hundred yards of the enemy's second fort, El Diablo, when it encountered an overwhelming cross-fire from the *tête-de-pont* of the Purisima; while from every house-top in the vicinity the murderous fire was also poured down." In this dilemma, sudden and overpowering, the Volunteers behaved nobly. "There was no hesitation or wavering," says an eye-witness; "no turning or even looking to the right or the left." General Butler, Colonel Mitchell, and Adjutant Armstrong fell under the fire; and soon afterwards the regiment was withdrawn by direction of General Hamer. It had no sooner reached the border of the plain, however, than it was attacked by the Third and Seventh regiments of Lancers, under General Garcia Conde; but it fortunately found shelter behind one of the hedges which abound in that vicinity, and succeeded in repulsing its assailants, with considerable loss.[1]

Soon afterwards, between one and two o'clock, the scattered fragments of his brigade were collected by Lieutenant-colonel Garland; and, under orders from General Taylor, another attempt was made to enter the city from its front. Captain Miller, of the First infantry, with his company, escorted Captain Bragg's battery, and Captain Backus, of the same regiment, with three skeleton companies,—the heroes of El Tene-

[1] MS. "Sketch," &c.; MS. Diary.—[2] Ibid.
[3] MS. "Sketch," &c.; Maj. Henry to *Spirit of Times;* Thorpe, p. 54.—[4] MS. Diary; MS. "Sketch," &c.
[5] MS. "Sketch," &c.

[1] Campaign in Northern Mexico, pp. 166–183; Gen. Taylor's Dispatch, No. 94, Oct. 9, 1846; Gen. Butler's Report, Sept. 30, 1846; Notes for the History, pp. 74, 75; Ripley, i., pp. 211, 212.

ria,—escorted Ridgely's battery; while the Third and Fourth regiments, and Colonel Watson, of the Baltimore battalion, with a fragment of his command, moved into the city for the purpose, if possible, of carrying the Fort El Diablo at the point of the bayonet. "In attempting the execution of this order, with not more than one-half my original force," Lieutenant-colonel Garland says, "I passed several barricaded streets, raked both by artillery and infantry, until I believed the command sufficiently advanced into the town to enable me to enter the rear of the redoubt. I then directed Captain Morris, who headed the Third infantry, to enter the back of a garden to his left, and press forward to the street nearest the rivulet; Brevet-major Graham, with the remnant of the Third infantry, followed. These two commands, although few in number, sustained themselves in the most admirable manner, under the heaviest fire of the day; for, instead of the second redoubt (*El Diablo*), of which we were in search, we unluckily ran foul of a *tête-de-pont*, the strongest defence of the city, and, from the opposite side of the bridge, two pieces of artillery were brought to bear upon us at a little more than a hundred yards' distance. Here the brave Morris fell, and his friend, Lieutenant Hazlett, who had just placed him in a house. Captain Henry, who succeeded to the command of the Third infantry, Captain Bainbridge having been wounded and retired, and Brevet-major Graham, the senior officer at this point, with the Fourth, in their exposed situation, maintained their position against fearful odds, until their ammunition began to fail, when hearing nothing of the battery for which two staff-officers had, at different times, been dispatched, I reluctantly ordered the truly Spartan band to retire, and I am proud to say, under all their afflictions, it was accomplished in good order."[1]

[1] Lieut.-Col. Garland's Report, Sept. 29, 1846; MS. Diary; MS. Sketch of the Battle, &c.; Gen. Taylor's Dispatch, No. 94, Oct. 9, 1846; Gen. Twiggs' Report, Sept. 29, 1846.

With the exception of a "demonstration" by the enemy's cavalry, in the direction of the citadel, the operations of both armies ceased with the withdrawal of the First brigade from the city; and, soon afterwards, with that great, good judgment which generally marked General Taylor's orders, he proved, by his disposition of the troops, for the night, the extent of his confidence in the respective corps of his army. "At the approach of evening, all the troops that had been engaged were ordered back to camp, except Captain Ridgely's battery and the regular infantry of the First division, who were detailed as a guard for the works during the night, under the command of Lieutenant-colonel Garland. One battalion of the First Kentucky regiment was ordered to reinforce this command."[1] There can be no doubt of the prudence of this course, notwithstanding the vanity of some, and the interest of others, may have led them to maintain that the *Volunteers* were the only *successful* combatants in the desperate struggle through which the army had passed; and those troops which had been first in the action, and had continued, without intermission, to oppose the enemy, were now significantly and appropriately left to occupy the position and to guard the trophies of which they had been the victors.

The night of the twenty-first, therefore, was passed in significant silence. General Worth and the Second division, as has been seen, spent it entirely exposed to the peltings of a severe storm, on the heights around the Forts Federacion and Soldado—the scenes of their gallantry and perseverance; the remains of the First, Third, and Fourth infantry, under Lieutenant-colonel Garland, occupied the Fort El Teneria and the outposts around it—the scenes of their bravery and their triumph—while the First Kentucky regiment covered them, and assisted, under direction of the engineers, in render-

[1] Gen. Taylor's Dispatch, No. 94, Oct. 9, 1846. See also MS. Diary; Gen. Twiggs' Report, Sept. 29, 1846.

ing still more secure the fruits of their hard-earned victory.[1] The remainder of the troops, in the distant camp, at El Bosque de Santa Domingo, sought the repose, in safety, which it so much needed.

The next day (*Sept.* 22) no movements were made, on either side, on the lower, or eastern, part of the city; and at noon the guard which had occupied it during the night, except Captain Ridgely's battery, was relieved and returned to the camp.[2]

On the western, or upper front, however, General Worth and the Second division completed what they had commenced on the preceding day. At three in the morning the troops were aroused to carry the works on the opposite side of the valley; and the storming party—embracing companies J and G of the Third artillery, A of the Fourth artillery, A, B, and D of the Eighth infantry, under Captain Screvin, and two hundred Texan riflemen, under Lieutenant-colonel Walker and Colonel Hays, the whole under Lieutenant-colonel Childs—moved from its bivouac for that purpose, under the guidance of Lieutenant Meade and Captain Sanders of the Engineers. "At the base of the hill the force was divided into two parties, and silently commenced to climb the dark slopes. It required all the strength of the men to overcome the difficulties which nature had, at places, thrown in their way. Perpendicular ledges of rock and projecting crags were to be scaled, and thickets of stunted chaparral to be crept under. But those invincible men slowly and cautiously pressed up towards the lofty apex, then clothed with a thick mantle of mist. It was night's last, still, and dark hour, always the most favorable for such enterprises." At daybreak the storming party had reached a point, within one hundred yards of the crest, where, among the clefts of the rocks, an outpost of the enemy had been posted in apparent anticipation of the attack. A rapid fire was immediately opened on the assailants, which was but the prelude of a more general fire from the heights above. With great coolness, however, the storming party pressed onward, without noticing the opposition even with a shout; and it was only when the Texans had come within a few yards of the top that the unerring fire of the latter, thrown into the disordered ranks of the Mexicans who opposed them, prepared the way for the bayonets of the regular troops, and, with the latter, gave the victory to the Americans.[1] Dashing forward, therefore, the storming party was not long in dispersing the enemy, and in taking possession of the summit of the hill, and of Fort Independencia, which occupied that height; but as the enemy had *dismantled it*, before this result had been accomplished, the value of the acquisition was not as great as had been expected; and the fugitives retired down the slope towards the Bishop's Castle, without annoyance, except from the rifles and muskets of the victors.[2]

It was soon discovered that the solid walls of the Bishop's Castle, which was the next point of attack, opposed too serious an opposition to the unsupported small-arms of the assailants; and as the enemy had withdrawn the artillery from Fort Independencia, it became necessary to replace it with other pieces from the camp. Accordingly Lieutenant Roland, of "Duncan's battery," was ordered forward from the main camp with a twelve-pound howitzer; and within two hours, that officer, with fifty men under Captain Sanders of the Engineers, had come up with his gun and ascended the rugged and almost perpendicular steep, between seven and eight hundred feet in height, and was gallantly pouring a rapid and effective

[1] Gen. Taylor's Dispatch, No. 94, Oct. 9, 1846; Thorpe, p. 61.—[2] Gen. Taylor's Dispatch, No. 94, Oct. 9, 1846; MS. Diary; MS. Sketch; Ripley, i. p. 223.

[1] It is stated, by the Mexican authorities, that this height was occupied by only 70 men of the 4th Light-infantry—Gen. Garcia Conde insisting that it was inaccessible.—[2] Gen. Worth's Report, Sept. 28, 1846; Gen. Taylor's Dispatch, No. 94, Oct. 9, 1846; Campaign in Northern Mexico, pp. 192–194; Thorpe, pp. 70, 71.

fire upon the rear of the astonished and terror-stricken Mexicans. At the same time the Fifth infantry under Major Scott, and Captain Blanchard's company of Louisiana Volunteers, which had been ordered forward from the opposite side of the valley, reached the heights of the Obispado in time to participate in the operations against the Bishop's Castle.[1]

Supposing the enemy would endeavor to regain the position, on the crest of the hill, which he had lost—especially since several feints and many sallies of light troops had already been made—Lieutenant-colonel Childs had advanced two companies of light troops, commanded by Lieutenants Bradford and Ayres, the whole under Captain Vinton; with Colonel Hays' Texans to cover their right, and Lieutenant-colonel Walker's Texans their left. It was not long before the Mexican Lancers, under General Torrejon, supported by a heavy body of infantry, made their appearance; and pressing forward, at a brisk pace, they appeared determined to attempt the expulsion of Lieutenant-colonel Child's command from the commanding position which it occupied. As it approached the spot where Captain Vinton's command lay in ambush, the latter arose and poured in its fire; while the Lancers, with their usual lack of courage, turned and fled, carrying confusion into the ranks of the infantry which supported them, and giving the victory to the Americans. The latter pressed after them, in pursuit; while the confused mass rushed down the hill into the city, "spreading terror," or turning into the sally-port, *in company with their pursuers*, dashed pell-mell into the castle, a mixed, incongruous mass; and after a brief struggle within the walls,—the constituent parts of the mass resolving themselves into their original elements,—the stars and stripes, on the flag-staff, proclaimed to the anxious citizens of Monterey, and to the invading army beyond its walls, the story of the result.[1]

General Worth, not less anxious than any other of the witnesses of this gallant exploit, immediately dispatched Lieutenant-colonel Duncan and Lieutenant Mackall, with their batteries, to the scene; and they came up at a gallop and joined the victors of the castle in pouring upon the rear of the retiring and confused masses of Mexicans, as they fled down the hill-side into the city, a prompt and terribly destructive fire. Soon afterwards, leaving a small force to occupy the the heights on the opposite side of the valley,—Forts Soldado and Federacion,—and another to hold Fort Independencia, General Worth concentrated his division around the Bishop's Palace, on the Obispada, "and preparation was made to assault the city on the following day, or sooner, should the general-in-chief either so direct, or, before communication be had, renew the assault from the opposite quarter. In the mean time, attention was directed to every provision the circumstances permitted, to alleviate the condition of the wounded soldiers and officers, and to the decent interment of the dead—not omitting, in either respect, all that was due to those of the enemy.[2]

Thus passed the night of the twenty-second—General Worth in possession of the works which commanded the western front of the city; General Quitman occupying the Fort El Teneria, the tannery, and distillery, on its eastern front; and the main body in repose at the camp at El Bosque de Santa Domingo. At the same time the enemy silently evacuated the Forts El Diablo, El Libertad, and—with the exception of the citadel—the entire lines on the northern and eastern fronts of the city; and were busily engaged in strengthening the interior

[1] Gen. Worth's Report, Sept. 28, 1846; Gen. Taylor's Dispatch, No. 94, Oct. 9, 1846; Campaign in Northern Mexico, p. 195.

[1] Gen. Worth's Report, Sept. 28, 1846; Notes for the History, p. 79; Campaign in Northern Mexico, pp. 195, 196. Some writers have confounded Col. Francisco Barras, the commander of this post, with Gen. Torrejon, and made the former command the sortie.

[2] Gen. Worth's Report, Sept. 28, 1846.

works of defence, and in concentrating the troops behind them.[1]

The movement of the enemy, in his evacuation of the exterior works of the city, having been reported to General Taylor at an early hour on the twenty-third, he sent instructions to General Quitman, leaving it to his discretion to enter the city, covering his men by the houses and walls, and to advance carefully as far as he might deem prudent; and, at the same time, General Twiggs was ordered, with his brigade, to act as a *corps de reserve*. Immediately afterwards General Taylor joined General Quitman, who was steadily, but slowly, moving into the city; and, under his own eye, the operations were continued. A company of riflemen under Lieutenant Graves, supported by Captain McMurray's company of Tennessee infantry, had been sent forward to reconnoitre; and, subsequently, Colonel Jefferson Davis, with two companies of Mississippi rifles, and two of Tennessee infantry, had been sent forward against the enemy's works. It soon became necessary to strengthen this detachment, and "a brisk firing was opened on both sides—the enemy from the house tops and parapets attempting to drive the Americans from the lodgment they had effected." General Quitman had also considered it his duty to order all the effective troops of his command, who could be spared from the lines on the eastern front of the city, to support his storming parties; and when General Taylor came up he ordered Captain Bragg's battery—which had been throwing a steady fire on the Mexican headquarters in the cathedral—with the Third infantry and the Second Texan Rangers, dismounted, to co-operate in the assault. The troops steadily pressed forward; the enemy, meanwhile, contending manfully for the possession, and contesting, inch by inch, as the assailants advanced. Entering the houses which the enemy occupied, the Americans passed from roof to roof, or, by knocking holes through the walls, from house to house; and they fought, hand-to-hand, for possession of the buildings, while the batteries scoured the streets, and scattered destruction among all those who showed themselves outside the dwellings. Thus, from house to house, and from square to square, the Volunteers gallantly, but slowly, forced their way, until they reached a street which was but one square in rear of the principal plaza, in and around which the enemy had mainly concentrated his forces. At this time, victorious and in the heart of the city, for some cause which has not been fully explained, the troops were withdrawn to the Forts El Teneria, El Diablo, and El Libertad, and to the lines on the eastern front of the city; while General Taylor determined to "concert with General Worth a combined attack upon the town."[1]

The gallant Worth, from his elevated position on the Obispado, was an interested spectator of the exciting scene which was spread before him; and, with his characteristic promptitude, he hastened to participate in the struggle. Two columns of attack, composed of light troops, in open order, were organized to move along the two principal streets which led from his position towards the great square of the city, with orders to mask the men wherever practicable; to avoid the points which were swept by the Mexican batteries; to press forward to the first square (*San Antonio*); to seize the end of the streets beyond; to enter the buildings, and, by means of picks and crowbars, to break through the walls; to work from house to house and from square to square, without exposing the men to the enfilading fire in the streets; and, by ascending to the roofs of the houses, to place themselves upon the same breast-height with the enemy. These assaulting parties were supported by the

[1] Gen. Taylor's Dispatch, No. 94, Oct. 9, 1846; Notes for the History, pp. 75, 76; Gen. Quitman's Report, Sept. 28, 1846; Campaign in Northern Mexico, p. 198.

[1] Gen. Taylor's Dispatch, No. 94, Oct. 9, 1846; Gen. Quitman's Report, Sept. 28, 1846; Notes for the Hist., p. 76.

J. A. Quitman

From the original Painting by Chappel in the possession of the Publishers

Johnson, Fry & Co. Publishers New York

light batteries under Lieutenant-colonel Duncan, Captain Roland, and Lieutenants Mackall, Martin, Hays, Irons, Clarke, and Curd, with reserves to guard the pieces; and the most careful attention was paid, not only to secure the streets, but to protect the troops in their movements.[1]

From the complication of these precautions, and the absence of previous preparations, however, the troops were not ready to move before three o'clock in the afternoon,—at which time the assailants under General Taylor had been withdrawn, and the full force of the enemy was concentrated on the western, as it had been, previously, on the eastern front,—and the same desperate and powerful opposition which had been experienced by Generals Taylor and Quitman was met by General Worth. Notwithstanding this opposition, however, the troops worked, steadily, through the walls, from house to house, driving the Mexicans before them, and pouring from the flat roofs of the houses a heavy fire into the streets below. By a singular coincidence the troops had also worked their way, before dark, to within a single square from the principal Plaza—the same distance at which General Taylor had suspended his operations; but, for some reason, which does not appear, while the latter had withdrawn his victorious troops, and fallen back on the forts which had been captured on the twenty-first, General Worth maintained his position, with a covered way—the perforated houses through which he had passed—in his rear; and had carried a large building, the roof of which commanded the principal defences of the enemy, while, at the same time, it afforded a shelter to his men.[2]

In these positions the night of the twenty-third was passed—General Worth (as at a subsequent date, in another city) occupying the post of honor in the heart of the city, ready to seize, with the earliest dawn, the full honors which legitimately belonged to him; the First brigade of Volunteers was holding El Teneria, El Diablo, and the exterior lines on the eastern front of the city;[1] while General Quitman, with his gallant and victorious command, withdrawn from his line of operations, and the main body of the army, were reposing in the camp at El Bosque de Santa Domingo.

During the evening the ten-inch mortar—which had been sent around from the northern front of the city—was mounted in the Plaza San Antonio, and opened its fire, with great effect, on the masses within the great square of the city; while, with great labor, soon afterwards, two howitzers and a six-pounder were carried from the camp, and raised to the roof of the large building near the same place, from which, not only the square itself, but the defences with which it was surrounded, were completely and entirely commanded.[2] Within an hour after this mortar opened its fire General Ampudia addressed a letter to General Taylor proposing "to evacuate the city and its fort, taking with him the *personnel* and *materiel* which have remained, and under the assurance that no harm shall ensue to the inhabitants who have taken a part in the defence;"[3] but the latter, on the morning of the twenty-fourth, replied "that his duty compelled him to decline acceding to it." A complete surrender of the town and garrison, the latter as prisoners of war, was then demanded, although "terms" were offered; and hostilities were suspended, and twelve o'clock, at the quarters of General Worth, was the time designated for the delivery of an answer.[4] At eleven o'clock General Ampudia, in person,

[1] Gen. Worth's Report, Sept. 28, 1846; Campaign in Northern Mexico, pp. 199, 200; Thorpe, pp. 78, 79; Notes for the History, p. 77.—[2] Gen. Worth's Report, Sept. 28, 1846; Notes for the History, p. 77; Ripley, i. 234–237.

[1] Gen. Quitman's Report, Sept. 28; Gen. Hamer's Report, Sept. 28, 1846; Thorpe, p. 80.

[2] Gen. Worth's Report, Sept. 28, 1846; Furber, p. 110; Thorpe, pp. 79, 80.

[3] Gen. Ampudia to Gen. Taylor, 9 P. M., Sept. 23.

[4] Gen. Taylor to Gen. Ampudia, Sept. 24.

met General Taylor;[1] and, soon afterwards, a capitulation was agreed to, the terms of which were subsequently drawn up by commissioners of both nations[2]—the city, works, and the greater part of the public property being surrendered to the Americans; the Mexican officers retaining their side-arms, the cavalry and infantry their arms and accoutrements, and the artillery a battery of six pieces with twenty-one rounds of ammunition; the Mexican troops, within seven days, agreeing to retire from the city; the citadel to be evacuated and occupied by the Americans at ten o'clock the next day; an armistice of eight weeks being agreed to; and the Mexican flag, when struck at the citadel, to be saluted by its own battery[3]—and, at the appointed time, two companies from each regiment of the Second division (*General Worth's*) and one section of each battery in the same command, under General Smith, took possession of the citadel.[1]

In this memorable siege and defence the Americans lost Lieutenant-colonel Watson, Major Barbour, Captains Morris, Field, McKavett, and Allen, Lieutenants Woods, Irwin, Hazlett, Hoskins, Hett, and Putnam, and one hundred and eighteen men *killed;* General Butler, Colonel Mitchell, Lieutenant-colonel McClung, Majors Mansfield, Abercrombie, Lear, and Alexander, Captains Williams, Lamotte, Bainbridge, Catlin, George, Downing, and Gillespie, Lieutenants Terrett, Dilworth, Graham, Russell, Potter, Wainwright, Armstrong, Matter, McCarty, Niles, Scudder, Nixon, Allen, Cook, Arthur, Reese, and Howard, and three hundred and thirty-seven men *wounded*, and two men *missing;*[2] that of the enemy is not known.

¹ Gen. Taylor's Dispatch, No. 94, Oct. 9, 1846; Furber, p. 110.—² Memoranda of the transactions in connection with the capitulation, by Col. Jefferson Davis.

³ Articles of Capitulation, &c.—⁴ Vide Chap. CII.

⁵ Vide p. 459; Gen. Kearney's "*General Orders*," No. 30.

¹ Gen. Worth's Report, Sept. 28, 1846.

² Gen. Taylor's Dispatch, No. 94, Oct. 9, 1846. The names of *all* the killed and wounded, with their regiments and companies, appear in Thorpe's *Monterey*.

CHAPTER CIV.

December 14, 1846, to March 3, 1847.

THE EXPEDITION AGAINST CHIHUAHUA.

Reference has been made, in a preceding chapter of this volume, to the expedition commanded by General Kearney, to its conquest of New Mexico, to its subsequent division into three separate commands, and to the operations of one of the three parties in the conquest of California.[4] As was seen in that place, a detachment from General Kearney's command was left at Santa Fé, under Colonel Doniphan, with orders to proceed to Chihuahua, and to report to General Wool for duty;[5] and, after the necessary preparations had been made, before proceeding to Chihuahua, it moved from Santa Fé against the Navajo Indians, whose depredations had been very severely felt by the people of New Mexico.[3]

At length, in December, 1846, the troops destined for Chihuahua rendezvoused at Valverde; and on the fourteenth of that month Major Gilpin moved towards El Paso with three hundred men; on the sixteenth, Lieutenant-colonel Jackson followed with two hundred; and on the nineteenth, Colonel Doniphan, with the remainder of his command, about three hundred and fifty men, the provision and part of the baggage train, moved in the same direction. In marching over the Great Desert the men suffered very

³ Col. Doniphan's Dispatch to Adj.-Gen. (no date); Cutts' Conquest of New Mexico and California, p. 76.

severely, both from the cold and from want of water; and on the twenty-second, the three divisions united, and encamped near a small town named Doña Ana, where plenty of the necessaries of life were readily procured. On the following day the army moved again; and on the afternoon of the twenty-fifth it had proceeded as far as Brazito (*the Little Arm*), where, on the eastern bank of the River Rio Grande del Norte, on an open, level prairie, bordered by chaparral, it had commenced to form an encampment for the night.[1]

The advance-guard had halted, and the men were scattered in every direction in search of wood and water, for cooking purposes, and of fodder for their animals; while the trains—both of provisions and baggage—were scattered along the road, in the rear, for many miles.[2] It is said by the enemy that no precautions had been taken to insure the safety of the expedition, and that Don Antonio Ponce[3]—the commandant of the Lancers—had reconnoitred "to his satisfaction, and unobserved;"[4] while it is admitted, by a friend, "that Colonel Doniphan and several of his officers and men," even at that early hour, while the camp was still incomplete, and the trains still exposed, "were, at this moment, engaged in playing a game of *three-trick-loo*."[5] The operations of the Mexicans, so auspiciously commenced, were carried on with no less success; and, by adroit management, the enemy's column had reached the immediate front of the American position before it was discovered.[6]

The Mexicans were formed in order of battle—the infantry of El Paso, seventy in number, being in the centre; the company of Collame, part of that of Chihuahua, and the auxiliary squadrons of El Paso, on the left; and a picket of the Second cavalry, the companies of the North and of San Elceario, and the remainder of that of Chihuahua, on the right; the howitzer, which accompanied the party, remaining with the rear-guard.[1] The Americans, having no time to take their animals, so suddenly had the enemy sprung upon them, rallied on foot, under any flag which they first came to,[2]—the left being composed, nominally, of companies F and A, with Lieutenant-colonel Mitchell's command of Second regiment of Missouri Mounted Volunteers; the centre, of companies D, H, and G; and the right of companies B, C, and E,—and, for the protection of the flanks, they were thrown back, at a slight angle, from the main body.[3]

Before the engagement opened, Lieutenant-colonel Ponce dispatched a messenger with a *black* flag, demanding that the commander of the American troops should appear before him for a conference, declaring, at the same time, that, unless it was complied with, *he would charge and take him, neither asking or giving quarter*. As Colonel Doniphan justly remarks, the reply to this insolent demand—"Charge and be d—d" —"was more abrupt than decorous."[4]

The action immediately commenced by the enemy throwing forward his entire line —the infantry in the centre deploying as skirmishers as it advanced, the howitzer, from the rear, at the same time, opening its fire. The Americans returned the fire, at long distance, with their rifles, and produced a serious impression on the ranks of the enemy; yet he appears to have moved forward with considerable coolness. His right wing, led by Lieutenant-colonel Ponce in person, was pushed "into the closest fire;" but, although "the charge was a handsome one," he was driven back, and a counter-charge,

[1] Col. Doniphan to Adj.-Gen., No. 1, March 4, 1847; Lieut. Kribben's Letter, Dec. 26, 1846.—[2] Col. Doniphan to Adj.-Gen., No. 1, March 4, 1847; Hughes' Doniphan's Campaign, p. 260.—[3] Not *General* Ponce de Leon, as many have supposed.—[4] Notes for the History, &c., p. 169.

[5] Hughes, p. 260 —[6] Notes for the History, p. 169; Hughes, p. 260.

[1] Notes for the History, p. 170.—[2] Hughes, p. 261; Ripley, i. p. 457.—[3] Col. Doniphan to Adj.-Gen., No. 1, March 4, 1847; Map in Hughes' "*Doniphan's Expedition*," p. 263.—[4] Col. Doniphan to Adj.-Gen., No. 1, March 4, 1847; Hughes, p. 262; Ripley, i. p. 458.

by some eighteen or twenty men, under Captain Reid, after a warm engagement of twenty minutes, effectually dispersed it. At the same time his left was engaged, with no more success, against the American right, where his charge had been met with equal gallantry; and the centre, also, had been driven back by company G, with the loss of the howitzer.[1]

While the several divisions of the enemy's force were thus driven back, a section of his right wing dashed forward and attacked the wagons; but the teamsters, also, were prepared for his reception, and this movement was not successful.[2]

Thus, defeated on every hand, the enemy fell back, leaving his provisions, a number of carbines, and other property, on the field of action; while the Americans, with the provisions which they had captured, and the wine which was found among the stores of the enemy, spent a merry Christmas-night on the field of battle.[3]

The Americans, as before stated, numbered eight hundred and fifty-six men; the Mexicans are said to have numbered twelve hundred and twenty, of whom five hundred and thirty-seven were cavalry.[4] The loss of the former was, "none killed, seven wounded, all since recovered;"[5] that of the latter was forty-three killed, and about one hundred and fifty wounded, of whom a large number died subsequently.[6]

The enemy's main body immediately abandoned El Paso,—a fine town, in the vicinity of the battle-field,—and, on the twenty-seventh, it was occupied by the Americans without opposition, the authorities and inhabitants seeking, at the hands of the latter, the protection which had not been afforded by their own countrymen.[1]

At this place Colonel Doniphan remained until the eighth of February, 1847, when, having been reinforced by the arrival of Major Clark's artillery, from Santa Fé, at the head of nine hundred and twenty-four effective men, he resumed his march towards Chihuahua.[2] Nothing occurred, which requires especial notice, until the evening of the twenty-seventh, when information was received that the enemy had fortified the pass of the Sacramento,—about fifteen miles in advance, and about the same distance from Chihuahua,—where he appeared to be preparing to resist the farther progress of the detachment.

At sunrise on the twenty-eighth, after forming the wagon-trains into four columns, for safety, and masking the force between the trains, the detachment moved forward, through an open prairie valley, towards the enemy.[3]

This valley, or plain, is bounded on either hand by chains of sterile mountains, and is about seven miles wide. From the westernmost range a spur, upwards of three miles in length, projects; while, from the opposite side, also, a similar, but lower, spur rises up and intersects the valley, a short distance above the former. Between these two spurs flows the Rio de Sacramento; while the road, along which the army moved, after crossing the latter spur or high ground, wound around the former and passed along the valley. The slopes and summit of the latter spur, or high ground, over which the road passed, were the sites on which the enemy had thrown up his works; and they appear to have been well calculated, by an enfilading fire, to command the road and secure the pass. Upwards of thirty distinct

1 Col. Doniphan to Adj. Gen., No. 1, March 4, 1847; Hughes, pp. 262-266.

2 Hughes, p. 265.—3 Ibid., p. 267.

4 Col. Doniphan to Adj.-Gen., No. 1, March 4, 1847.

5 Ibid.; Ripley, i. p. 459. Mr. Hughes (p. 266) says *eight* were wounded.

6 Col. Doniphan to Adj.-Gen., No. 1, March 4, 1847; Ripley, i. p. 459. Mr. Hughes (p. 266) says *seventy-one* were killed.

1 Col. Doniphan to Adj.-Gen., No. 1, March 4, 1847; Hughes, p. 269; Notes for the History, p. 171.

2 Col. Doniphan to Adj.-Gen., No. 2, March 4, 1847; Hughes, pp. 286, 287.—3 Col. Doniphan to Adj.-Gen., No. 2, March 4, 1847; Hughes, p. 301; Maj. Gilpin's Report, March 2, 1847.

batteries appear to have been constructed at the more commanding points; and, through the exertions of the inhabitants of Chihuahua, these works, and their vicinity, had been manned with large bodies of well-appointed troops, under Generals Heredia and Garcia Conde—the infantry occupying the defences, the cavalry, four deep, between the batteries, or, two deep, in front of and masking them.[1]

When the American column had come within a mile and a half of the enemy's position, it diverged to the right, in order to avail itself of the peculiarity of the ground in that direction. Perceiving this movement, General Heredia ordered his cavalry, with four field-pieces, to move in that direction, under the command of General Garcia Conde, and to check the progress of the Americans; while, soon afterwards, in person, with the infantry and artillery, he moved in the same direction, and formed in line on the right of the cavalry. In the mean time, the head of the American column had gained the crest of the lower spur, on which the enemy was posted; and as soon as the cavalry had come within range of the American battery the pieces were rapidly unlimbered, and opened a destructive fire; while the Mexicans, also, opened a fire from their battery, but without much effect, immediately afterwards.[2]

The Mexican historian thus relates the effect of this cannonade: "The first discharges from their (*the American*) batteries produced the natural effect. Our (*the Mexican*) cavalry, chiefly composed of soldiers who had never heard the sound of a cannon, and so placed as to be unable to perform any manœuvre, exposed to a fire which produced considerable slaughter, could not long stand their ground, without showing, by the undulations in their line, symptoms of that disorder which their chiefs and officers strove, unsuccessfully, to prevent. Our artillery, also, opened their fire upon the enemy in vain. The cavalry soon lost all order, and many of them dispersed, involving the infantry in the confusion, *in which force the same circumstances happened.* This had a decisive effect on the result of the action. The enthusiasm of our troops, exposed to so unfortunate a trial, suffered a terrible blow in that dismay and confusion, which revealed to them their weakness and misfortune. The ineffectual efforts of the chiefs and officers to restore the line of battle, demonstrated that the confidence of the soldiers was lost. The firing being now, for a few moments, suspended on both sides, General Heredia gave orders to retire to the intrenchments, and this being done, the dead and wounded were taken from the field. One piece of artillery, which they had dismounted for us, and every thing on the field, were abandoned."[1]

The result of this first movement, thus impartially recorded by the Mexican authorities, was truly disastrous to the Mexican arms; and the American column immediately resumed its march. By inclining still farther to the right, Colonel Doniphan endeavored to avoid the batteries on the enemy's right; and when he had advanced in that direction as far as he could with safety, without coming within range of a heavy battery on the opposite spur, on his right, he ordered Captain Weightman, with his battery of two twelve-pound howitzers, to charge on the enemy's left, while Captains Reid, Parsons, and Hudson, with their troops of cavalry, were ordered to support the movement. Through some misunderstanding on the part of the Adjutant, the covering party moved without concert; and, while Captain Weightman, with his battery, and Captains Reid and Hudson, separately, dashed down against the Mexican left, Captain Parsons engaged the enemy nearer the

[1] Notes for the History, pp. 173, 174; Col. Doniphan to Adj.-Gen., No. 2, March 4, 1847; Ripley, i. pp. 459–461.

[2] Col. Doniphan to Adj.-Gen., No. 2, March 4, 1847; Notes for the History, p. 175; Hughes, pp. 305, 306.

[1] Notes for the History, p. 175.

centre—Captain Reid being the first of the party, however, who was successful in securing a foothold within the lines. Soon afterwards the enemy rallied, however, and drove Captain Reid from his position,—on the extreme left of the Mexican centre,—in which he succeeded in killing Major Owens, the only American who was killed in the action.[1]

Within a few minutes the entire company commanded by Captain Reid concentrated its strength, and gallantly recaptured the battery from which he had been driven; and, almost at the same moment, Captains Weightman, Parsons, and Hudson carried the battery which covered Captain Reid's left flank.[2]

The main body, also, had come up within one hundred and fifty yards of the Mexican works; and, having been dismounted,—the fourth man of every seven holding the horses of his six associates,—the entire line was vigorously assaulted; while Major Clark, with his battery of four six-pounders, opened his fire on a body of cavalry, which, from the extreme right of the Mexican centre, was threatening the wagons on the rear of the American column of attack. This body of cavalry was quickly dispersed, by the very efficient fire of Major Clark's battery; while, with equal success, the several companies, in their places in the line, pressed forward, drove the enemy from his intrenchments, and occupied the works. The Mexicans defended their works with great obstinacy, yet the assailants, with a determination which could not be withstood, dashed in with their sabres, after having discharged their rifles, and the enemy fled in great confusion.[3]

During the entire period of the action the heavy battery on the opposite side of the valley, near the Rancheria Sacramento, to which reference has been made, continued to annoy the Americans with a heavy cross-fire; and no sooner had the lines been taken than the attention of Colonel Doniphan was directed to it. A movement of part of the troops, and Captain Weightman's howitzers, was immediately ordered, while Major Clark opened on it, with his battery, from one of the heights on the battle-field. The first fire of the latter silenced one of the guns, the third cut one of the ammunition-wagons in two, and the enemy became satisfied that farther resistance was useless. Without any delay, therefore, he abandoned the position, and "*The Battle of the Sacramento*" was ended.[1]

The strength of the Americans was nine hundred and twenty-four men; that of the Mexicans, four thousand two hundred and twenty-three.[2] The loss of the former was Major Owen *killed* and eleven men *wounded;* that of the latter was three hundred and four men *killed*, a larger number *wounded*, and forty prisoners, while the spoils of victory included vast quantities of provisions, six thousand dollars in specie, and arms and ammunition of great value.[3]

The army occupied the field of battle during the night; on the following day (*March* 1) the advance-guard, under Lieutenant-colonel Mitchell, occupied Chihuahua, without opposition; and on the second, Colonel Doniphan, with the main body, also entered the city in triumph.[4]

The great purpose of the campaign had now been accomplished, and the capital of Central Mexico had fallen. The heaviest blow which Mexico had experienced had now fallen on her; and never before had so marked an evidence of her weakness been exhibited to the world. A mere handful of undisciplined Volunteers had marched triumphantly through her northern provinces; some of her most accomplished generals, and the most intelligent of her troops, had been met and overcome; and the colors of her enemy floated in triumph over the capitals of New Mexico, Alta California, and Chihuahua.

---

[1] Col. Doniphan to Adj.-Gen., No. 2, March 4, 1847; Hughes, p. 308; Lieut.-Col. Mitchell's Report, March 5, 1847; Maj. Gilpin's Report, March 2, 1847.

[2] Hughes, pp. 308–311.—[3] Col. Doniphan to Adj.-Gen., No. 2, March 4, 1847; Lieut.-Col. Mitchell's Report, March 5, 1847; Maj. Gilpin's Report, March 2, 1847.

[1] Col. Doniphan to Adj.-Gen., No. 2, March 4, 1847; Lieut.-Col. Mitchell's Report, March 5, 1847; Maj. Clark's Report, March 2, 1847.—[2] Col. Doniphan to Adj.-Gen., No. 2, March 4, 1847.—[3] Hughes, p. 313.—[4] Ibid., pp. 313–316.

CHAPTER CV.

January 23 to February 5, 1847.

THE INSURRECTION IN NEW MEXICO.

The march, from Santa Fé, of the main body of "The Army of the West," under General Kearney; and, subsequently, that of the detachment under Colonel Doniphan, have been noticed in preceding chapters of this volume; and the movements of the troops who were left at that place, under Colonel Sterling Price, require a passing notice.

The command of Colonel Price embraced the Second regiment of Missouri Mounted Volunteers, the battalion of Missouri Mounted Volunteers, under Lieutenant-colonel Willock, two companies of infantry, under Captains Angney and Murphy, one of light-artillery, under Captain Fischer, "The La Clede Rangers," under Lieutenant Elliott, a detachment of the First regiment of dragoons, under Captain Burgwin, and some smaller bodies of troops, under Lieutenants Dyer and Wilson—the whole numbering about two thousand men. The dragoons were posted at Albuquerque to maintain tranquillity on the Rio Grande; two hundred men of the Second Volunteers, under Major Edmondson, were near Cebolleta; Captain Hendley, with a small party, was in the valley of the Mora; and the remainder of the force was in Santa Fé.[1]

The natives in New Mexico, like those in California, had witnessed the change of government with impatience; and they watched for an opportunity to throw it off at the earliest possible moment. With this purpose they had held secret meetings, and had organized an insurrection; and on the nineteenth of December outbreaks had been made at Don Fernando de Taos, at the Arroya Honda, and on the Rio Colorado—the Governor of the Territory, the sheriff, the circuit-attorney, the prefect, and two friendly Mexicans having been killed at Taos, seven Americans at Arroya Honda, and two on the Rio Colorado.

As it was evident that the object of the insurgents was "to put to death every American and every Mexican who had accepted office under the American government," Colonel Price promptly concentrated his forces in Santa Fé; and on the twenty-third of January he marched against them from that city with companies D, K, L, M, and N, of the Second regiment of Missouri Mounted Volunteers, the battalion of infantry under Captain Angney, a company of Santa Fé Volunteers, under Captain St. Vrain, and four mounted howitzers—three hundred and fifty-three rank and file, and all, except the Santa Fé Volunteers, dismounted. Orders were left for company A, of the Second Volunteers, and Captain Burgwin, with one of his troops, to join the expedition.

Soon after noon, on the twenty-fourth, Captain St. Vrain, who led the column, discovered the insurgents in position near the town of Cañada, and preparations were immediately made to attack them, before they could escape or occupy more commanding positions. For this purpose the troops hastened forward, leaving the wagons in the rear, to come up at their leisure; and, hastily forming his men, Colonel Price approached the enemy.

The Rio Chicito, near which the insurgents were posted, flows through a narrow valley, on either hand of which are high grounds; and the road from Santa Fé to Cañada passes this valley and the river nearly at right angles, after which it inclines to the west, and runs parallel with the heights until it enters the town. The high grounds referred to, on the northern bank of the stream, command not only the ford, but the road between the ford and the town; and it was on these heights, and

[1] Hughes' Doniphan's Expedition, pp. 387, 388.

under cover of three strong houses at their base, that the insurgents awaited the arrival of Colonel Price.

The action commenced at about two o'clock, by the artillery which Colonel Price had thrown forward, beyond the creek, and against the insurgents' right flank—the main body awaiting the arrival of the wagons, under cover of the high bluff bank on the northern side of the stream. The howitzers opened their fire on the houses, as well as upon the heights beyond, but it appears to have done but little damage; and the enemy reciprocated, by attempting, at that time, to cut off the wagons which were slowly coming up, in the rear. The latter movement was checked by Captain St. Vrain, who was ordered back from the front for that purpose; the former was kept up, although comparatively harmless, until the wagons had advanced beyond all danger, when more energetic measures were adopted.

As the house which the enemy occupied, opposite the right flank of Colonel Price's line, sheltered a considerable force, whose fire was somewhat annoying, Captain Angney was ordered to move against it with his battalion; and, after a short struggle, the charge was crowned with success. A charge was next ordered on all the points occupied by the enemy in any force; when Captain Angney, with his battalion, supported by company K, of the Volunteers, and, subsequently, by company M, of the same regiment, and Captain St. Vrain's Santa Fé Volunteers, moved against the principal position of the enemy on the heights in the rear, while, by a simultaneous movement, the artillery, supported by companies D, L, and N, of the Volunteers, moved against the other houses in which the enemy had found shelter, and against the high grounds in their rear.

After a short, but severe, struggle, the insurgents gave way in all directions, and fled into the hills beyond the reach of their victors, the lateness of the hour, and the character of the ground among which they had found refuge, rendering pursuit both hopeless and hazardous.

In this engagement,—"The Battle of Cañada,"—as before stated, the Americans numbered three hundred and fifty-three men, exclusive of officers; the enemy is said to have numbered fifteen hundred. The loss of the former was two *killed*, and Lieutenant Irvine and five men *wounded;* of the latter, thirty-six were *killed*, forty-five were taken *prisoners*, and many were *wounded.*

On the twenty-seventh, Colonel Price left Cañada; and, on the next day, was joined by Captain Burgwin, with company G, First regiment of dragoons, company A, of the Second Missouri Mounted Volunteers, and a six-pounder; and, on the twenty-ninth, he marched to La Joya, where he learned that the insurgents had rallied at the Pass of Embudo, where they intended to dispute his passage.

Finding that the road was impracticable for artillery or wagons, Colonel Price halted at La Joya, while a detachment—embracing companies G, of the First dragoons, and K, of the Missouri Mounted Volunteers, and the Santa Fé Volunteers, one hundred and eighty in number, the whole under Captain Burgwin—was sent forward to attack the enemy.

The detachment pushed forward, through the rugged defile along which the road to Embudo winds its course among the mountains, until it came within sight of the pass where the enemy was posted. At that spot the defile becomes so contracted that scarcely three men can march abreast; while the abrupt slopes of the mountains, on either hand —rendered still more defensible by the dense masses of thick cedars and the large fragments of rock which everywhere cluster along the mountain sides—afforded shelter for the opposing forces which could not have been easily improved. When the head of the little column had reached the immediate vicinity of the pass, Captain St. Vrain dismounted his command and ascended the mountain on his left, "doing much execution." At the same time heavy flanking parties were thrown out, on either hand, under the command, respectively, of Lieutenants White and McIlvaine, while Captain Burgwin moved through the defile, on the road, with the main body. As these parties advanced, simultaneously, the insurgents fell back in the direction of Embudo, "bounding along the steep and rugged sides of the mountains with a speed that defied pursuit."

While the engagement was still pending, Captain Slack, of company L, was pushed forward from La Joya, and relieved Lieutenant White's flanking party, while Lieutenant Ingalls, at the same time, relieved Lieutenant McIlvaine; and, with renewed energy, the pursuit was continued, although without inflicting any serious injury on the fugitives.

Soon afterwards, Captain Burgwin and his entire command debouched into the open valley in which Embudo is situated, when his flanking parties were called in, "The Battle of the Pass of Embudo" ended, and the village was occupied without any opposition.

In this action, one man was *killed* and one severely *wounded*, among the Americans; while of the Mexicans, about twenty were *killed* and sixty wounded.

Colonel Price and his command steadily advancing into the enemy's country,—although the severity of the weather rendered the march a tedious and difficult one,—on the third of February, 1847, they entered Don Fernando de Taos; and, on the same day, the Pueblo de Taos—the stronghold of the insurgents—was reconnoitred. It was found to be a position of considerable strength, being surrounded by adobe walls and strong pickets, while within the inclosure two large and unusually high buildings,—each capable of sheltering five or six hundred men,—the parish church, and many of the smaller buildings, furnished means of defence.

After having reconnoitred the enemy's position and his several defences, Colonel Price determined to attack the western front of the Pueblo, where the church stands; and at two o'clock Lieutenant Dyer was ordered to open his fire, with the howitzers and six-pounder, at two hundred and fifty yards distance; but, after it had been continued two hours and a half, it was discontinued for the want of ammunition, and the troops returned to Don Fernando.

At an early hour the next day (*Feb.* 4), the troops were put in motion a second time; but a different plan of attack had been adopted by the Colonel in command. On the eastern front of the city were posted the Santa Fé Volunteers (*Captain St. Vrain's*) and company L (*Captain Slack's*), of the Missouri Volunteers, for the purpose of cutting off the retreat of any of the insurgents who might attempt to escape to the mountains; on the northern front, three hundred yards from the wall, was posted the main body of the detachment, with Lieutenant Dyer, the six-pounder, and two of the howitzers; and on the western front were posted Captain Burgwin, with his company of the First dragoons, company D (*Captain McMillan's*), of the Missouri Volunteers, and Lieutenant Hassandaubel, with two howitzers.

At nine o'clock the batteries opened on the town, but after two hours' steady fire it was found impossible to breach the walls of the church, against which it had, principally, been directed, and the fire was suspended, in order that the Pueblo might be stormed. Soon afterwards, by simultaneous movements, the northern front was assaulted by Captains Angney and Barber, and Lieutenant Boone, with the infantry battalion and companies N and A, of the Missouri Volunteers; and the western front by Captains Burgwin and McMillan. In the face of a heavy fire of small-arms, thrown through loop-holes in the walls, the former established themselves under the western front of the church, and with axes attempted to breach its walls; while, at the same time, the roof was fired, by means of a temporary ladder, by one of their party; the latter, in front of the church, at the same time, attempted to force the doors, in the face of a fire not less destructive than the other. The latter party, after making desperate efforts, was compelled to retire from the doorway of the church, with the loss of its gallant leader, Captain Burgwin, who was mortally wounded; the former, against a defence which was not less determined, succeeded in cutting several small holes through the wall, and in throwing several hand-grenades into the interior of the building, "doing good execution" among its defenders. Encouraged by this success the six-pounder was carried around, and poured a heavy fire of grape into the town until half-past three o'clock, when it was run up within sixty yards of the church, and ten rounds were poured into the breach, making it wide enough for the purpose of the assault. The gun was then advanced within *ten yards* of the breach, and a shell and three rounds of grape were thrown among the occupants of the building; after which the storming-party entered, without opposition, and completed the work.

There appears to have been no farther opposition, and the insurgents fled from the works on the western front of the town, taking refuge in the large buildings on the eastern front, or, in vain, attempting to escape to the mountains. The latter were intercepted by Captains Slack and St. Vrain, and fifty-one were killed, only two or three of them escaping; the former remained in the town, and, in the end, surrendered.

The night of the fourth was passed by the troops in the buildings which had been evacuated by the insurgents; and on the morning of the fifth, at the solicitations of the enemy, seconded by the appeals of the women and the aged people, the submission of the insurgents was received, on the condition that Tomas, one of their principal chiefs, should be surrendered—a condition which was complied with.

In this obstinate affair,—"The Battle of the Pueblo de Taos,"—the Americans lost seven *killed* and forty-five *wounded*, many of whom afterwards died; the insurgents lost about one hundred and fifty *killed*, besides those who were *wounded*.

With this affair the insurrection was quelled; and no farther trouble, worth notice, occurred in New Mexico.

[This chapter has been wholly based on the Report of Col. Price to the Adjutant-general of the Army, and on the maps which accompanied it; no other original authority having been found on the subject.]

CHAPTER CVI.

February 22 and 23, 1847.

THE BATTLE OF BUENA VISTA.

The siege and the surrender of the city of Monterey have been heretofore referred to, in a preceding chapter of this volume; and immediately after the flag of Mexico had been lowered on the citadel, the garrison began its retreat, falling back on Saltillo, from which place, soon afterwards, it was ordered to march to San Luis de Potosi, where "it formed the base of a new army," under Santa Anna, which met, and was defeated by, General Taylor, at Buena Vista.[1]

A revolution in the government of Mexico had overturned Paredes, and restored the exiled Santa Anna to power; and the latter, with the assistance of a loan from the Church, had organized a strong force against the "Army of Occupation" commanded by General Taylor. For this purpose the forces were moved from Mexico, Saltillo, Guadalajara, Guanajuato, and other parts of the country, until twenty-two thousand five hundred and fifty-three men were concentrated at that point, under Generals Mora y Villamil, Micheltorena, Vanderlinden, Blanco, Corona, Pacheco, Lombardini, Guzman, Miñon, Juvera, Torrejon, Andrade, Parrodi, Vazquez, and Urrea, with General Santa Anna at the head of the army.[1]

During this interval, General Taylor and the Secretary of War were engaged in an unpleasant correspondence, showing ill-feeling on both sides;[2] and on the thirteenth of November, the former, in pursuance of his design to move on Mexico, from the north,

[1] Notes for the History, pp. 79, 80; Gen. Taylor's Dispatch, No. 98, Oct. 15, 1846.

[1] Notes for the History, pp. 81, 82.—[2] Gen. Taylor's Dispatches, No. 98, Oct. 15; No. 107, Nov. 8.

John E. Wool

moved to Saltillo with General Worth's division and a small party of the Second dragoons, entering that place, without opposition, on the sixteenth.[1] General Worth was left in command of that position, while General Taylor returned to Monterey,[2] and on the thirteenth of December he detached General Twiggs to Victoria,—still farther in advance than Saltillo,—while, on the fourteenth, General Quitman, with the Volunteers, marched for the same place.[3] On the seventeenth, the Second regiment of infantry and Second regiment of Tennessee (foot) Volunteers, from Camargo, joined the column;[4] while General Patterson, with the Illinois brigade of Volunteers and the Tennessee regiment of cavalry, was also ordered to move towards Victoria.[5] On the twenty-ninth, General Quitman occupied, without opposition, the city of Victoria—a strong body of the enemy's cavalry retiring before him; and on the fourth of January, 1847, General Taylor, with General Twiggs' division, and General Patterson, with the Illinois and Tennessee troops, also reached the same place.[6]

It was while this column was moving from Monterey towards Victoria, that the well-known "Worth stampede"—so called—took place. Intelligence had reached General Worth, at Saltillo, that General Santa Anna, taking advantage of the division of the American army, "designed to strike a heavy blow at that place; and, if successful, then at General Wool's force at Parras;"[7] and he had dispatched the intelligence to General Taylor, then, with the main body, at Montemorelos, *en route* for Victoria; to General Butler, commanding at Monterey; and to General Wool, who, with a strong body of troops, had moved through the southwestern wilderness, from Port Lavacca, in Texas, towards Chihuahua, and had taken post at Parras.[8] By forced marches, each of these Generals moved to the relief of the gallant commander of the Second division, at Saltillo;[1] and it was while thus *en route* from Parras that General Wool first perceived the superior facilities for defence which the Pass of Angostura afforded,[2] and which he employed so advantageously, at a subsequent date, in checking the progress of General Santa Anna, in the well-known action which is the subject of this chapter.

The subsequent discovery of the untruth of the reports referred to, produced corresponding changes in the disposition of the forces,—General Taylor resuming his march towards Victoria, where he arrived on the fourth of January, 1847;[3] General Butler taking the command at Saltillo, while his troops returned to Monterey;[4] and General Wool encamping between the Pass of Angostura and the hacienda of Buena Vista,[5]—General Santa Anna, in the mean time, remaining at San Luis de Potosi, drilling his troops and preparing for more active and important operations.[6]

Soon afterwards orders were issued by General Scott for the withdrawal of the greater part of General Taylor's command, for the purposes of the campaign which the former officer had opened against the city of Mexico;[7] and General Taylor was compelled to fall back from Victoria on Monterey, leaving General Wool at Buena Vista, in command of the advance.[8] This reduction—General Scott having taken the greater part of the regulars, Duncan's and Taylor's batteries, and "the best" of the Volunteer forces—left General Taylor at the head of two squadrons of regular dragoons, four batteries (in all sixteen guns) of regular artil-

[1] Gen. Taylor's Dispatches, No. 111, Nov. 16; No. 113, Nov. 24, 1846.—[2] Ibid., No. 112, Nov. 23.—[3] Ibid., No. 122, Dec. 14.—[4] Ibid., No. 123, Dec. 22.—[5] Maj. Bliss, A. A. G., to Gen. Patterson, Nov. 28.—[6] Gen. Taylor's Dispatch, No. 1, Jan. 7, 1847.—[7] Ibid., No. 123, Dec. 22, 1846.—[8] Baylie's Campaign in Mexico, p. 19.

[1] Gen. Taylor's Dispatch, No. 123, Dec. 22, 1846.

[2] This interesting fact—involving the successful resistance of the Mexican army by the fragments of the American Army of Occupation—is fully set forth in a letter from Capt. J. H. Carlton to Gen. Wool, dated "*Buena Vista, Mexico, July* 27, 1847," as well as in the valuable little work, by Capt. Carlton, on "*The Battle of Buena Vista.*"—[3] Gen. Taylor's Dispatches, No. 123, Dec. 22; No. 124, Dec. 26; No. 125, Dec. 26, 1846; No. 1, Jan. 7, 1847.—[4] Campaign in Northern Mexico, pp. 273, 274.

[5] Baylie's Campaign in Mexico, p. 24.

[6] Notes for the History, pp. 89–93.—[7] Gen. Scott to Gen. Taylor, No. 1, Dec. 20, 1846; Same to same, Jan. 3, 1847; Same to Gen. Butler, Jan. 3 and 8, 1847.

[8] Gen. Taylor's Dispatch, No. 5, Jan. 26, 1847.

lery, one company of regular artillery, the Kentucky and Arkansas regiments of Mounted Volunteers, eight regiments of Volunteer infantry, and two pieces of Volunteer artillery;[1] and rendered it utterly impossible for the latter to make any movement, if, indeed, he was strong enough to defend his positions at Saltillo and Monterey.

In the mean time,—while General Santa Anna occupied San Luis de Potosi, and General Taylor was at Victoria,—the orders from General Scott were sent through General Butler at Saltillo, and by the latter were transmitted to head-quarters at Victoria by special messengers. One of these messengers, Lieutenant John A. Richey, who was bearing to General Taylor the "Confidential" letter of General Scott to General Butler, dated January 3, 1847,—in which the former had communicated to the latter the entire plan of operations, the withdrawal of the troops from the "Army of Occupation," and other important information,—was murdered on his way, and his papers were carried to Santa Anna.[2] By this means the enemy became fully acquainted with the designs of the General-in-chief, the weakness of the Army of Occupation, and the movements of the latter which would be necessary to insure its safety; and he appears to have arranged his own plans to conform to this new and important state of affairs. Scouts were sent out in front of his army in greater numbers and with stronger force than usual, and several parties of Americans were cut off and taken prisoners; strong bodies of troops moved towards Saltillo, and appeared to threaten the American position; and other evidences were manifested of the change of policy which influenced the enemy's movements. Yet a remarkable degree of ignorance prevailed, concerning the real purposes of General Santa Anna, notwithstanding General Taylor assumed the personal command of the troops at Saltillo, and removed his head-quarters thither on the second of February;[3] and it is said that, almost up to the very moment when General Wool opened the action of Buena Vista, General Taylor disbelieved the report that General Santa Anna had moved against him.[1] In addition to this ignorance of the purposes of the enemy, General Taylor appears to have felt disposed to act offensively; and he advanced, with his small personal command, to Agua Nueva,—eighteen miles from Saltillo,—on the fifth of February;[2] and within the following week he was joined, at that place, by General Wool and the greater part of the troops;[3] but having subsequently discovered the weakness of the new position, and the enemy having assembled, in a very heavy force, at Encarnacion, thirty miles in front of Agua Nueva, on the twenty-first of February he fell back on Buena Vista, leaving a small covering party of cavalry at Agua Nueva.[4]

It appears that General Santa Anna, soon after the capture of the American dispatches, resolved to take advantage of the weakness of General Taylor's command, and to crush it before moving against General Scott; and his troops were moved from San Luis de Potosi with that object. First General Torrejon moved to Bocas, with the Third brigade of cavalry, eight hundred and eight in number; and he was followed by the Second, one thousand and ninety-four in number, to the Verrado, under General Juvera; by the Fourth, three hundred and ninety in number, to the Cedral, under General Andrade; and by the First, fourteen hundred and eighteen in number, to Encarnacion, under General Miñon. These were followed, on the twenty-eighth of January, by the artillery, five hundred and eighty-four in number, with the trains and *materiel* of war, the Sappers and Miners, and the company of organized American deserters, known as that of St. Patrick; on the twenty-ninth, by the First division, four thousand eight hundred and thirty-nine in number, under General Pacheco; on the thirtieth, by

[1] Gen. Taylor's Dispatch, No. 5, Jan. 26, 1847.

[2] Ibid., No. 6, Jan. 26, 1847.—[3] Ibid., No. 12, Feb. 4, 1847.

[1] Gen. Taylor's Dispatch, No. 14, Feb. 14, 1847; Baylie's Campaign in Mexico, pp. 26, 27.—[2] Gen. Taylor's Dispatch, No. 13, Feb. 7, 1847; Ripley, i. p. 381.

[3] Gen. Taylor's Dispatch, No. 14, Feb 14, 1847.

[4] Ibid., No. 18, March 6, 1847; Ripley, i. pp. 385, 386.

the Second division, four thousand three hundred in number, under General Lombardini; and on the thirty-first, by the Third division, three thousand one hundred and ninety-seven in number, under General Ortega—General Santa Anna following on the second of February. During the march the Mexicans suffered severely from the extreme cold; and, when at Matehuala, they were strengthened by the junction of General Parrodi's brigade—one thousand strong. Between the seventeenth and twenty-first of February, this army rendezvoused at Encarnacion: at one o'clock on that day, the light corps and Hussars, under General Ampudia, led the way to Agua Nueva, followed by the main body; and at night it halted at the Pass of the Carnero. On the twenty-second, it moved forward to Agua Nueva, driving thence a small party of American cavalry; and during the forenoon it appeared before the American lines at Buena Vista,[1] to which place, as already stated, General Taylor had retreated.

The Pass of Angostura—or, as the Americans call it, of *Buena Vista*—is a position of great strength. The lofty chain of mountains which separates the plain north of Saltillo from that of La Encantada, is broken by a narrow valley of irregular width, through which pass the road and a small stream, which flows to the northward. This small valley differs in width, from a mile and a half to four miles, and is bounded, on either hand, by rugged mountains, which are some two to three thousand feet in height, and inaccessible, except for light troops. From Saltillo, the northern extremity of this valley, to the hacienda San Juan de la Buena Vista, a distance of five miles, the road continues along the eastern side of the little stream, on which the ground—forming a plateau or table—is some sixty or seventy feet higher than that on the western bank. The next mile the road runs over a series of dry ravines, which cross it diagonally from the mountains on the left, when it descends to the bottom of the valley, and follows a narrow strip of land which extends between the stream and several abrupt spurs of the mountains, or of the upper plateau, which juts out upon it, and which are separated from each other, at unequal distances, by ravines, which are much broader and deeper than the former, and parallel with them. Thence it winds gradually up to the plain of La Encantada. One of these spurs referred to extends so near to the stream that there is scarcely sufficient room left for the passage of the road; while the abrupt sides of the spur, its commanding position,—completely controlling the road, to the southward, for a great distance,—and the complicated network of gullies which the stream has made on the opposite side of the road,—presenting, in themselves, a formidable obstacle to the progress of any species of troops whatever, from that direction,—all tend to make the Pass of Angostura, as that spot is called, "the Thermopylæ of Mexico."[1]

The American army had been placed under the command of General Wool on the preceding evening,—General Taylor having proceeded to Saltillo, with a small force, "to provide against the attack meditated by General Miñon," with the First brigade of Mexican cavalry, who had threatened that place by way of the Pass of Palomas Adentro and a narrow and winding pathway over the mountains,[2]—and on the evening of the twenty-first he had posted the First Illinois regiment (*Colonel Hardin's*) on the top of the spur which forms the eastern bounds of the pass, with orders to throw up a parapet on its crest, and to dig a ditch and throw up a parapet on the opposite side of the road and around the edge of the gully. Knowing the vital importance of that part of the position, at eight o'clock on the morning of the twenty-second, General Wool had also ordered a section of Captain Washington's battery to occupy the pass; and orders were given to the Illinois regiment, at the same time, to dig a ditch and make a parapet across the road, for the protection of

[1] Notes for the History, pp. 94, 114–122; Ripley, i. pp. 375–377.

[1] Carlton's Buena Vista, pp. 5–9; Baylie's Campaign in Mexico, pp. 27, 28; Ripley, i. pp. 389–391.

[2] Gen. Wool's Report, March 4; Carlton, pp. 27, 28.

the artillery. At nine o'clock the enemy came within sight of the pickets stationed at La Encantada, three and a half miles in front of the pass; and while messengers hastened to Saltillo with the intelligence, General Wool moved his command to the immediate vicinity of the pass, and prepared for the reception of the enemy.[1]

He had posted Captain Washington's battery of eight pieces across the road at the pass, its left resting on the spur of the mountain, while its right was covered by two companies of the First Illinois regiment, under Lieutenant-colonel Weatherford; and six companies of the same regiment, under Colonel Hardin, occupied the summit of the spur on the left of the artillery; the Second Kentucky regiment, under Colonel McKee, was posted on a spur covering the rear of the pass, and supporting the battery; and the Second Illinois regiment (*Colonel Bissell's*) was posted on Colonel McKee's left; the Arkansas and Kentucky regiments of Mounted Volunteers, under Colonels Yell and Marshall, were posted on the extreme left, on the upper plateau, near the base of the mountains; and the Second and Third Indiana regiments, under Colonels Bowles and Lane, and Captain Stein's squadron of dragoons, were posted on a ridge immediately in the rear of the front line, as a reserve.[2]

At this time General Taylor reached the pass, and the Mississippi Rifles, under Colonel Davis, Lieutenant-colonel May's dragoons, and the light batteries of Captains Sherman and Bragg—the troops which General Taylor brought with him from Saltillo—were added to the reserve.[3]

At eleven o'clock General Taylor was summoned to surrender at discretion, at which time General Santa Anna informed him that the American army was surrounded by twenty thousand men, and that "it could not, in any human probability, avoid suffering a rout and being cut to pieces;" and the General, with great composure, returned the well-known answer, in which he "declined acceding to the request" of his opponent.[1]

The Mexican advance had halted just beyond cannon-shot from the pass, and appears to have awaited the arrival of his main body; while he deployed his forces on either side of the road, as they came up, and made demonstrations of a desire to turn the left of the American position. To counteract any similar movement which might be made on the right flank,—without being aware that such a movement could not be successful, in consequence of an impassable marsh, which is in front of that position,—before he left, at the close of the day, for Saltillo, General Taylor ordered the Second Kentucky regiment of infantry (*Colonel McKee's*), and Captain Bragg's battery, with a detachment of mounted men, from the reserve to the west side of the stream, on the right and somewhat in advance of the pass; while, for the purpose of checking the movement on the left, the Kentucky and Arkansas regiments of cavalry, dismounted, were moved up the slope of the mountain, supported by the Indiana rifle battalion, under Major Gorman; while three of Captain Washington's pieces, under Lieutenant O'Brian, supported by the Second Indiana regiment, under Colonel Bowles, for the same purpose, were ordered to move to the head of the plateau, on the left of the pass, for the purpose of preventing the enemy from coming around the base of the mountains, up the ravine, and to the plateau, on the left of the battery, which was, in reality, the key of the position.[2]

At this time,—about three o'clock,—the action was opened on the upper plateau by the Mexican artillery; and immediately afterwards the Mexican light troops, under General Ampudia, who had crept up the slope of the mountains, opened their fire on the American riflemen, while in both cases the recipients of the fire returned it with great spirit and much effect.[3]

[1] Gen. Wool's Report, March 4; Ripley, i. p. 392.
[2] Gen. Wool's Report, March 4.—[3] Ibid.

[1] The correspondence of both Generals was inclosed in Gen. Taylor's Dispatch, No. 15, Feb. 24, 1847. Capt. Carlton says the flag through which Gen. Santa Anna sent this summons was borne by the Surgeon-general of the army, a German, named *Vanderlinden*.
[2] Gen. Wool's Report, March 4; Ripley, i. pp. 393, 394.
[3] Gen. Wool's Report, March 4; Ripley, i. p. 395.

During the remainder of the day the contending parties contented themselves with the operations of these light troops, on the side and at the foot of the mountains, without opening a fire from any other part of the lines; and at dark a shell was thrown up by the enemy as a signal for the suspension of the fire, when the action was entirely discontinued, both parties bivouacking on the field;[1] while General Taylor, with the Mississippi Rifles and Lieutenant-colonel May's dragoons, returned to his quarters at Saltillo, where he spent the night.[2]

When the action had terminated on the twenty-second, General Santa Anna is said to have addressed his troops in a pertinent speech, in which "he referred to the wrongs which had been inflicted upon their country by the barbarians of the North—wrongs which could not be submitted to without eternal disgrace, and which could be redressed only by the last resort of nations. The United States of the North had, cowardlike, presumed on their strength alone, and wantonly set at defiance every principle of right. They had provoked this war," he said, "under the cover of other objects to be gained, but really for their own aggrandizement, and the acquisition of territory clearly the property of the United States of the South. The one country aimed only at the entire destruction of the nationality of the other. He wished to call their whole attention to that single fact; and not only to that, but to a thousand others, which, like that, would make them burn to take terrible vengeance on the mercenary invaders of their soil. He called upon them to look upon their country. What met their sight? Its possessions wrested away; its dignity insulted; its fair fields ravaged; its citizens slaughtered; its hearths and homes made desolate. Others had gone forth to vindicate these wrongs, but they had fallen; and now their blood, which had drenched the fields of Palo Alto, Resaca de la Palma, and Monterey, called on them, their brethren, with an eloquence that must reach their hearts, to avenge their death. He reminded them that they had crossed deserts, had suffered hunger, and thirst, and fatigue, without a murmur. Long and weary had been their march; but now they should be rewarded with repose, and the enjoyment of the abundance which filled the ample granaries of the murderers of their brethren. He concluded by saying that the Americans were but a handful, and at his mercy; that he had magnanimously offered to spare their lives, and even to treat them with consideration; that they had vain-gloriously rejected his clemency, leaving, as the only alternative, their utter extermination, *without pity or quarter*."[1]

This speech was received with loud cries of "*Viva Santanna*," "*Viva la Republica*," and "*Libertad ó Muerta;*" while the fine military band which belonged to the Mexican general's guard played some of the finest of the Mexican national airs—both the cheers and the music being distinctly heard within the American lines.[2]

With the close of this exciting scene—not less so in the American camp than in that of the enemy, under the influence of excited imaginations, while the sounds of the applause and the music swept through the valley—the most sullen silence took most absolute possession of the entire surrounding country; and, for a time, the most dreary and unrelieved darkness added horrors to the cheerless and foreboding night. The dark forms of the mountains, on either hand of the valley, under any circumstances, would have shut out the light and made the night more unpleasant, yet even this power was increased by the black and storm-bearing clouds which drifted across the scene, and by the cold winds and the drizzling rain which chilled the bodies, if they did not check the confidence, of the thousands who were exposed to their influence. So intense, indeed, was the cold, that the Americans built fires along the sides of the mountains, and sought a temporary relief from the uncertain warmth which they sent out.[3]

[1] Gen. Wool's Report, March 4.
[2] Gen. Taylor's Dispatch, No. 18, March 6, 1847; Ripley, i. p. 397.

[1] Carlton, pp. 45–47. See also Baylie's Campaign in Mexico, pp. 30, 31.—[2] Carlton, p. 47.—[3] Baylie's Campaign in Mexico, p. 31; Notes for the History, p. 123.

During the night, with great good judgment, General Santa Anna had strengthened General Ampudia's light troops in the mountains on the left of the American line, by ordering the Fourth regiment of the line for his support;[1] and, at the dawn of day, after having driven in the American pickets,[2] the Mexicans renewed the contest at the same place, which they, correctly, knew "was extremely important in deciding the action."[3] At the same time, with equal vigilance, General Wool had strengthened Colonel Marshall with a battalion of riflemen from the Second Illinois regiment, under Major Trail; and, as soon as it was light enough, they were ordered forward to renew the action. The light troops which were thus intended to hold General Ampudia in check, were the dismounted Kentucky riflemen, under Captains Shawham, Beard, Milan, and Pennington, and Lieutenant Field; the Indiana rifle battalion, under Major Gorman; and the four Illinois rifle companies, under Major Trail; and, notwithstanding the overpowering numbers of the enemy which were opposed to them, it is said "they stood as firm as the rocks of the mountain." "They were but a handful, as compared with the enemy," says Colonel Marshall, "but they yielded not an inch of ground for at least two hours, during which I was gratified to observe that they kept *their front* clear within rifle-shot, though the enemy was enabled to turn their left flank, and another regiment pressed down the mountain to their right, with the view of cutting off the whole from the main body."[4]

The movements of the enemy indicating his intention to make a bold push on the left flank of the American line, General Wool provided for its defence; and while the light troops were contesting for the possession of the slopes of the mountains, both the Generals in command—Santa Anna and Wool—formed the respective armies for the approaching contest. In the American lines, the Second Kentucky Volunteers (*Colonel McKee's*), Captain Bragg's battery, and Captain Pike's squadron of Arkansas Volunteer Cavalry, were ordered from the extreme right,—opposite to, and in advance of, the pass, where they had been posted by General Taylor, on the preceding evening; while Captain Sherman's battery, and six companies of the Second Illinois regiment of Volunteers (*Colonel Bissell's*), were sent to the left, on the plateau, to support Lieutenant O'Brian's battery, and the Second Indiana regiment (*Colonel Bowles'*), with orders to General Lane, who commanded there, to defend the position to the last extremity. At the same time, Captain Washington's battery and Colonel Hardin's regiment of Illinois Volunteers defended the pass, supported by the Third Indiana regiment of Volunteers (*Colonel Lane's*); the Arkansas and Kentucky Mounted Volunteers—except those of them who were engaged, on foot, in the mountains, under Colonel Marshall, and Captain Pike's squadron—were posted near the head of a broad ravine which covered the rear of the plateau, to support the riflemen, should they be driven from the mountains; and two troops of the First dragoons, under Captain Stein, and Major McCulloch's Texans, were held in readiness to support either the riflemen in the mountains, or the troops on the left of the centre, as circumstances might require.[1]

Against this handful of troops, thus posted, the hosts of the enemy moved at an early hour, in four dense columns. That on his right, against the American left,—at the head of the plateau, and on the slope of the mountain,—commanded by General Ampudia, has been noticed already. The second was "the Centre of the Army," under General Lombardini, which was directed to move up one of the ravines, on the eastern side of the road, against the head of the plateau; while the third,—"the Vanguard of the Army," under General Pacheco,—moving up another of the ravines, was ordered to unite with the second, at the head of the plateau, and, with it, to break through the American left, where

---

[1] Notes for the History, p. 124; Gen. Wool's Report, March 4.—[2] Gen. Wool's Report, March 4, 1847.

[3] Notes for the History, p. 122.—[4] Gen. Wool's Report, March 4; Col. Marshall's Report, March 1; Notes for the History, p. 124; Gen. Taylor's Dispatch, No. 18, March 6.

[1] Gen. Wool's Memoranda, May 21, 1860.

Lieutenant O'Brian's and Captain Sherman's batteries, and the regiments of Volunteers, under Colonels Bowles and Bissell, had been posted. At the same time, General D. Santiago Blanco, of the Engineers, at the head of the regiment of Engineers, the mixed regiment of Tampico, that known as the "Fijo de Mejico," and the body-guard of General Santa Anna,—the regiment of Hussars,—supported by a heavy battery, under General Mora y Villamil, moved along the valley against the pass of Angostura, which was the key of the American position; and General Ortega, with the remainder of the troops, was held in reserve, in the extreme rear of the enemy's line.[1]

Between seven and eight o'clock in the morning of the twenty-third of February, General Blanco moved down the valley, towards the pass, against Captain Washington's battery;[2] and, with a degree of modesty which is honorable to that gallant officer, the Captain thus narrates the result:—"The rapidity and precision of our fire scattered and dispersed this force in a few minutes, with considerable loss on his side, and little or none on our own."[3] The compact column of the enemy could not withstand the terrible effect of this fire; and, after wavering a moment, it halted, and, finally sought shelter, in confusion, in the mouth of one of the ravines, behind the spur which projected into the valley.[4]

In the mean time, Captain Washington had notified General Wool of the movement of General Blanco; and the former had hastened to the pass to superintend the defence of that very important position. During this temporary absence of the General from the plateau, the columns of the enemy, under Generals Lombardini and Pacheco,—in conjunction with a battery of three eight-pounders, on the right and rear of their line of march,—attacked the left of the American centre, where, as before stated, had been posted General Lane, with Lieutenant O'Brian's and Captain Duncan's batteries, and the Second Illinois and the Second Indiana regiments of Volunteers. This attack was resisted with great spirit and success; and Lieutenant O'Brian's guns, "which were admirably served, swept down whole platoons of the enemy at every discharge." The head of the Mexican columns was quickly thrown into disorder, and suffered severely from this fire,—the fine corps of Guanajuato, which was in front, having been nearly annihilated,—and as they had gradually fallen back, General Lane ordered Lieutenant O'Brian and Colonel Bowles to advance, notwithstanding the disparity appeared too great to promise a permanent success. The gallant Lieutenant promptly obeyed the order, and limbering up his pieces, he advanced some fifty or sixty yards down the spur, placed his pieces in battery, and renewed his fire. It was not so, however, with the Second Indiana regiment, which,—from some unexplained cause, in which the regiment appears to have had no share,—had been ordered by its Colonel (*Bowles*) to *retreat*, notwithstanding the firmness with which it had withstood the shock of the enemy's first advance, a few minutes before. By this defection—which no effort of General Lane and his staff, or of General Wool, who had returned to the plateau in season to witness the disastrous flight of the regiment, could remedy—the unflinching Lieutenant O'Brian was left with no immediate support; while General Santa Anna was not slow in taking advantage of the disaster, and in returning to the attack. In the language of the Mexican Engineers, "new columns were organized, and successfully charged, with extraordinary firmness;" and Lieutenant O'Brian, with the loss of one of his four-pounders,—the horses and cannoniers of which had been either killed or disabled,—the Second Illinois regiment, and Captain Sherman's battery, were compelled to change their position, and to fall back nearer to the head of the plateau.[1]

The Mexicans now appeared in great force

[1] Notes for the History, p. 124.—[2] Gen. Wool's Report, March 4.—[3] Capt. Washington's Report, Feb. 28.

[4] Gen. Taylor's Dispatch, No. 18, March 6; Gen. Wool's Report, March 4; Carlton, pp. 67, 68.

[1] Gen. Wool's Report, March 4; Lieutenant O'Brian's Report, Feb. 28; Scribner's Camp-life of a Volunteer (*Second Indiana regiment*), p. 60; Gen. Wool's Memoranda, May 21, 1860; Lieut. O'Brian's Report, Feb. 28.

on the plateau, and commenced the descent towards the height which covered the left of Captain Washington's position at the pass; but, at this moment, Major Mansfield came up, with the Second Kentucky regiment (*Colonel McKee's*), and Captain Bragg's battery, which General Wool had ordered up from the extreme right, on the opposite side of the valley, where General Taylor had posted them the preceding afternoon; while, at the same time, General Blanco's command having been repulsed at the pass, as before stated, Colonel Hardin was also ordered up the plateau, with the First Illinois regiment, which had covered Captain Washington's left at the pass. These, with O'Brian's and Sherman's batteries, and the Second Illinois regiment, were quickly formed in line, extending entirely across the head of the plateau, from near the head of the gorge on its front, to the brink of the ravine in its rear; and once more, from the entire line, Sherman, Bragg, and O'Brian—a glorious trio—hurled their well-directed and terribly-destructive fire into the dense masses of the Mexican columns. For a short time this terrible cannonade was withstood by the Mexicans; and it was returned with great spirit.[1]

While this spirited engagement was going on,—both parties contending manfully for the possession of the plateau,—the heavy masses of Mexican cavalry (finding no opposition to their progress, since the three regiments of Volunteers and the three batteries were actively engaged with the infantry and artillery of the divisions of Generals Lombardini and Pacheco) swept across the head of the plateau, between the Mexican columns and the foot of the mountain;[2] while the light troops which were engaged in the mountain, with General Ampudia, fearing that they might be cut off from the main body, fell back, across the gorge which covered the rear of the American line, towards the hacienda of Buena Vista; and General Ampudia pressing forward after them, the entire face of the mountain, and the upper part of the plateau, together with the upper part of the gorge in front and rear of it, were occupied by the Mexicans—the small body of cavalry which had been posted in the rear of the left flank having, in the mean time, also been swept away with the current towards the hacienda.[1]

¹ Gen. Wool's Report, March 4, 1847; Gen. Wool's Memoranda, May 21, 1860.—² Ibid.; Carlton, p. 70.

As has been already stated, the advance of Generals Lombardini and Pacheco, at the upper part of the plateau, was resisted with great spirit by the Second Illinois regiment (*Colonel Bissell's*), the Second Kentucky regiment (*Colonel McKee's*), the six companies of the First Illinois regiment (*Colonel Hardin's*), and the batteries under Captains Sherman and Bragg and Lieutenant O'Brian,—which had formed a line across the head of the plateau for that purpose,—and, notwithstanding the determination of General Santa Anna and his movement of reinforcements, both of men and artillery, he was driven back, in confusion, to the base of the mountains, and the entire plateau was again in the undisputed possession of the Americans.[2]

At this moment both the armies were greatly scattered—Generals Torrejon and Ampudia, with the Mexican cavalry and light troops which they commanded, had succeeded in turning the extreme left of the American line, and were moving towards the rear, with the American light troops, the Arkansas and Kentucky cavalry (*Colonels Yell and Marshall*), and the *debris* of the Second Indiana regiment of Volunteers (*Colonel Bowles*), retiring before them; General Santa Anna, with the divisions of Generals Lombardini and Pacheco, had been driven from the plateau, in front of the American centre,—which still occupied its position,—and had sought refuge in the ravines and gorges at the base of the mountains; the Mexican reserves, under General Ortega, still occupied their position in the rear of their lines; Generals Blanco and Villamil, with their commands, had been driven from before the pass by the gallant

¹ Gen. Taylor's Dispatch, No. 18, March 6; Gen. Wool's Report, March 4; Carlton, pp. 70, 71.

² Gen. Wool's Report, March 4; Gen. Wool's Memoranda, May 21, 1860; Carlton, pp. 71-73; Baylie, p. 33.

Captain Washington and his battery, and had found refuge in the neighboring gorges; and Colonel May's squadron of dragoons, and the Mississippi riflemen,—General Taylor's body-guard,—were not on the field.

Immediately afterwards,—after the repulse of the Mexicans,—while the armies were thus situated, General Taylor, accompanied by Colonel May's dragoons, reached the plateau, from Saltillo, where he had spent the night, and assumed the command—the Mississippi Rifles following him, some three miles distant; and General Wool thus relieved from duty on the plateau, after a short conversation with the commanding general, hastened to the left and rear, for the purpose of remedying the mischief which had befallen the army in that direction, and to arrest the progress of the enemy towards the rear of the position.[1]

Thus relieved from the responsibility of the chief command, as well as the more immediate command on the plateau, General Wool, as before stated, hastened to the left and rear, in pursuit of the Second Indiana regiment, in order to rally them, and with them and the other regiments which had retired before the Mexican cavalry and light troops, to arrest the progress of the enemy to the rear of the position. He overtook General Lane, Colonel Bowles, and Major Gorman—the first and last wounded—in the deep and broad ravine which bounded the rear of the American position, and after giving such orders as he deemed necessary, he continued the pursuit of the enemy. About midway between the Hacienda of Buena Vista and the plateau, he met the Mississippi riflemen, under Colonel Jefferson Davis, who had left the road, and were taking a diagonal course towards the plateau. Colonel Davis, also, was busily engaged in a laudable attempt to rally the fugitives who were retreating before the Mexicans, and he appealed to them to return with him and renew the fight, pointing to his noble regiment as a mass of men behind whom they might form in security. With here and there an honorable exception, Colonel Davis's appeal was disregarded.[1]

General Wool next directed the attention of Colonel Davis to a body of Mexicans which was coming down from the foot of the mountains; and the latter moved to oppose its progress, while the General, in person, hastened to bring up a regiment to support the riflemen.[2]

During the General's absence, and while the Mississippians were thus engaged, a large body of lancers, under General Torrejon, had passed along the base of the mountains, on the left of Colonel Davis, and had moved against the Hacienda of Buena Vista. Here it was met by the Kentucky and Arkansas Volunteer cavalry, under Colonels Marshall and Yell, and the riflemen under Majors Gorman and Trail; and, after a spirited skirmish, he was compelled to retire, with considerable loss—a part of the fugitives retreating right and left, while the greater part of them joined the party with which Colonel Davis had engaged. In this gallant defence, Colonel Yell and Captain Porter, of the Arkansas regiment, and Adjutant Vaughn, of the Kentucky regiment, were killed.[3]

By this time General Wool had joined the Mississippi riflemen, with the Third Indiana Volunteers (*Colonel Lane's*), and with these regiments, a small party of the fugitive Second Indiana regiment, under Colonel Bowles, and a field-piece, under Lieutenant Kilburn; and subsequently, with the batteries under Captains Sherman and Bragg (which had been sent from the plateau for that purpose by General Taylor), he moved against the columns of the Mexicans who had turned the extreme left of the line, and, after a series of most brilliant engagements, he succeeded

[1] Gen. Taylor's Dispatch, No. 18, March 6; Gen. Wool's Report, March 4; Gen. Wool's Memoranda, May 21 and 24, 1860.

[1] Gen. Wool's Memoranda, May 21 and 24, 1860; Baylie, pp. 33, 34; Col. Davis' Report, March 1, 1847; Carlton, pp. 76, 77.—[2] Gen. Wool's Memoranda, May 21 and 24, 1860; Col. Davis' Report, March 1, 1847; Baylie, p. 34.—[3] Gen. Taylor's Dispatch, No. 18, March 6; Gen. Wool's Report, March 4, 1847; Gen. Wool's Memoranda, May 21 and 24, 1860; Col. Marshall's Report, March 1, 1847; Lieut.-Col. Roane's Report, Feb. 27; Scribner, pp. 65, 66.

in driving them back on their main body, with great loss.[1]

It was during this retreat that two thousand Mexicans, anxious to escape the fire in their rear, as well as a destructive fire on their flank from the troops on the plateau, had sought shelter in the recesses of the mountains, and were huddled together in a helpless, disorderly mass. At this moment the goodness of General Taylor's heart interceded in their behalf, notwithstanding they were enemies; and he hesitated before sacrificing a single life—even that of an enemy—unnecessarily. With the merciful desire of saving life, therefore, he dispatched Lieutenant Crittenden, his Aid-de-camp, with a flag, and demanded the surrender of this party; but instead of complying with the demand, the Mexicans availed themselves of the opportunity afforded them, and marched out of the gorge, while the troops under General Wool, under orders from General Taylor, silently looked on, without being permitted to fire a shot, or take a step to prevent their escape.[2]

Immediately after General Taylor had dispatched this flag by Lieutenant Crittenden, and after having ordered Colonel Hardin to attack a Mexican battery which was on the plateau, directing its fire against General Wool,—who was busily engaged with the Mexicans whom he had driven from the left and rear, as already related,—he left the plateau. In accordance with this order, Colonel Hardin moved with his regiment,—the First Illinois,—the Second Illinois (*Colonel Bissell's*), and the Second Kentucky (*Colonel McKee's*) regiments; but he had scarcely left his position when he met the Mexicans whom General Wool had driven from the rear, and he, too, commenced to harass the disordered columns of the fugitives. Perceiving the result of the movements of his troops to the left and rear of the American position, and properly supposing that the good-fortune of the morning was no longer attending the banners of Generals Ampudia and Torrejon, General Santa Anna determined, by a bold movement, to rescue his apparently lost columns by another movement against the plateau, and, at the same time, to venture, on that final movement, the fortunes of the day. Accordingly, with all his reserves, and the remains of his scattered forces, he moved forward without attracting the attention of General Taylor,—who commanded in person on the plateau,—and, during the temporary absence of the latter, he poured the masses of his entire army on the handful of men who had remained to defend that part of the field.[1] Lieutenant O'Brian was the first to feel the force of this inundation; and his two remaining pieces were taken from him. Next, the First and Second Illinois and the Second Kentucky regiments of Volunteers (*Colonels Hardin's, Bissell's, and McKee's*) were met and overpowered, with great loss;[2] and the most triumphant success appeared to be within reach of the enemy. Unfortunately for him, however, the master-spirit of the little army—he who had selected the position, formed the line of battle, and commenced the contest, and under whose personal direction, a few minutes before, the triumphant progress of the Mexican columns had been arrested and turned back in disgraceful defeat—at that moment hurried forward with the batteries of Captains Sherman and Bragg, the Mississippi Rifles, and the Third and part of the Second Indiana regiments. On their arrival on the plateau the batteries met General Taylor returning from his temporary absence, who ordered them into battery, when they opened a destructive fire on the head of the enemy's columns, first checking, and, finally, repulsing them. At the same time, the rifles and the Indianians gallantly poured a heavy fire into the right flank of the assailants, and contributed to their repulse; and the latter,

[1] Gen. Taylor's Dispatch, No. 18, March 6; Gen. Wool's Report, March 4, 1847; His Memoranda, May 21 and 24, 1860; Col. Davis' Report, March 1, 1847.

[2] Gen. Taylor's Dispatch, No. 18, March 6; Gen. Wool's Report, March 4, 1847; His Memoranda, May 21 and 24, 1860; Baylie, p. 35; Carlton, pp. 80, 81.

[1] Gen. Wool's Report, March 4; Gen. Taylor's Dispatch, No. 18, March 6, 1847.—[2] Gen. Taylor's Dispatch, No. 18, March 6, 1847; Lieut. O'Brian's Report, Feb. 28; Maj. Fry's Report, March 3; Lieut.-Col. Washington's Report, Feb. 26.

subsequently, drove a body of Lancers into the mountains.[1]

Soon afterwards General Santa Anna made a second demonstration, and threatened to renew his assault on the plateau; while General Wool concentrated the troops on the plateau, and General Taylor ordered Lieutenant-colonel May to cover the left and rear of the position with the regular dragoons of his command.[2] The enemy did not return, however, and THE BATTLE OF BUENA VISTA, or, as the Mexicans call it, *The Battle of Angostura*, ended.

A gallant officer, who mingled in the thickest of the fight, thus closes his excellent and detailed account of the action:—"As the sun sank lower and lower, the occasional rattle of musketry gave place to dropping shot, which, in turn, became less and less frequent, and at length entirely ceased. The fire of the artillery on both sides had gradually subsided; the sun went down; the heavy and reverberated report of cannon had longer and more uncertain intervals; finally it was hushed, and a profound and painful silence succeeded, and again the cold, deepening shadows of evening began silently to steal over the field. The two armies were still there, and were still sternly regarding each other, face to face. *They were standing almost upon the same ground where they had respectively stood the night before.* But in the Mexican lines we could hear no animated harangue, no responding *vivas*, nor approving cheers; and the night wind brought not to our ears again the witchery of that sweet music. One could hardly realize, as he now looked upon the dark masses of the two armies, that they had been so mingled in bloody strife since he last saw them similarly situated; all was now so calm. Indeed, hardly a sound could be heard, save the occasional dismal flapping of the wings of the fierce zapalotes,[3] now hovering over the pass, or the distant and almost human yell of the hungry wolf, answered by others away in the gloomy recesses of the surrounding mountains. They were already beginning to gather in to their horrible repast. And now, scarcely an evidence of the conflict could be seen, except when one took a closer survey of the ground about him. There, scattered on every hand, how many and many were the dark forms which met his eye of what had been stalwart men and powerful steeds! some lying as if asleep, and some in strange, unnatural postures, with the moonlight resting steadily and coldly on the bright points of uniforms and trappings, all still and firm as if they were belted to stone—not tremulous and moving, as when on breathing, animated beings. These were fearful proofs of the desperate struggle which had gone by. These ghastly figures, with the immovable luminous points resting upon them, were the solemn characters, the terrible hieroglyphics, traced upon the field, which, being deciphered amid the obscurity of night, told in mute but eloquent language how dreadful a day had passed."

In the battle of Buena Vista there is but little doubt of the correctness of General Santa Anna's statement respecting the strength of the Mexican forces—that it numbered twenty thousand effective men;[1] the American army, including officers, numbered four thousand seven hundred and fifty-nine, of whom three hundred and eighty-two were sick or disabled.[2] The loss of the former is not known, although General Taylor estimated it to be about fifteen hundred, but he said would "probably reach two thousand;"[3] that of the Americans was Colonels Hardin, Yell, and McKee, Lieutenant-colonel Henry Clay, jr., and one adjutant, eight captains, fifteen lieutenants, and two hundred and thirty-nine non-commissioned officers and privates *killed;* General Lane, Colonel Jefferson Davis, one major, eleven

[1] Gen. Taylor's Dispatch, No. 18, March 6, 1847; Gen. Wool's Memoranda, May 21 and 24, 1860.

[2] Carlton, pp. 117-119; Baylie, p. 37.

[3] A species of vulture, which flies by night as well as by day, and is very fierce.

[1] General Santa Anna to General Taylor, Feb. 22, 1847.

[2] "Returns of the troops engaged," &c., appended to Gen. Taylor's Dispatch, No. 18, March 6, 1847.

[3] Gen. Taylor's Dispatch, No. 18, March 6, 1847.

captains, twenty-seven lieutenants, and four hundred and fifteen non-commissioned officers and privates *wounded;* and twenty-three non-commissioned officers and privates *missing.*[1]

During the dreary night of the twenty-third the Mexican army precipitately abandoned its position, and fell back to Agua Nueva, and thence, on the twenty-seventh, to San Luis de Potosi.[1]

Thenceforth a new scene of operations was opened, in a different part of Mexico, under other commanders; and the military services of the gallant Taylor and Wool were confined to less active but not less responsible duties of camp-life.

CHAPTER CVII.

March 9 to September 14, 1847.

THE CAMPAIGN UNDER GENERAL SCOTT:

Including the Siege and Capture of Vera Cruz; the Actions at Puenta del Medio and Medellin; the Capture of Alvarado, Tuspan, Perote, Puebla, La Haya, and Tobasco; the Actions at Cerro Gordo, Amozoque, Paso de Ovegas, National Bridge, San Juan de los Llanos, Mira Flores, Oka Laka, Contreras, San Antonio, Churubusco, Molino del Rey, Chapultepec, Mexico; the Second Actions at Paso de Ovegas, the National Bridge, and Cerro Gordo; the Siege of Puebla and the Battle of Huantla; and the Affairs at Atlixco and Matamoras.

As has been stated in a preceding chapter of this volume, General Scott was ordered to organize, and to take the command of, an army which was designed to move against the city of Mexico by way of Vera Cruz; and he had withdrawn, for this purpose, the greater part of the regular troops, and many of the Volunteers, from General Taylor's command.[2]

In conformity with the orders referred to, on the thirtieth of November, 1846, General Scott had sailed from the city of New York,[3] and on the nineteenth of December, he reached New Orleans.[4] On the twenty-third he had left the latter place,[5] and on the thirtieth he had reached Matamoras, from which place he had gone up the Rio Grande, as far as Camargo, apparently undetermined whether to take command of the victorious "Army of Occupation,"—superseding General Taylor,—or to proceed to "the new and more distant theatre."[6] On the seventh of January, 1847,—after having issued the orders for the withdrawal of General Taylor's troops, giving him a detailed statement of his purposes,[2]—he returned to the mouth of the Rio Grande;[3] and on the twenty-second of the same month, General Worth, with the head of his division of regular troops, had reached the same place.[4] On the fifteenth of February the General left Brazos Santa Iago; on the twentieth, Tampico; and on the twenty-first he reached the rendezvous at Lobos, where the First and Second Pennsylvania, the South Carolina, two-thirds of the Louisiana, and detachments from the Massachusetts and the New York regiments had arrived before him.[5]

On the sixth of March General Scott arrived off Vera Cruz;[6] on the seventh, in company with Commodore Conner, who commanded the naval auxiliary forces, he proceeded in the steamer *Petrita*, and reconnoitred the city and the castle of San Juan de Ulloa, and the adjacent shores;[7] and on the ninth the debarkation was effected, in entire safety.[8]

The spot which had been selected as the landing-place of the troops was the beach of

[1] Returns of killed, wounded, and missing, appended to Gen. Taylor's Dispatch, No. 18.—[2] Vide Chap. CVI.

[3] Mansfield, p. 364.—[4] Gen. Scott to Sec. of War, No. 2, Dec. 21, 1846; Same to Gen. Taylor, Dec. 20, 1846.

[5] Gen. Scott to Sec. of War, No. 3, Dec. 23, 1846.

[6] Gen. Scott to Sec. of War, No. 4, Dec. 30, 1846.

[1] Carlton, pp. 129–132, 142, 143.—[2] Gen. Scott to Gen. Butler, "Confidential, Camargo, Jan. 3, 1847."

[3] Gen. Scott to Gen. Butler, "Mouth of Rio Grande, Jan. 8, 1847."—[4] Gen. Scott to Sec. of War, No. 6, Jan. 24, 1847.—[5] Gen. Scott to Sec. of War, No. 12, Feb. 28, 1847.—[6] Semmes, p. 125.—[7] Ibid.; Mansfield, p. 367.

[8] Gen. Scott to Sec. of War, No. 13, March 12.

Collado,[1] abreast of the Island of Sacrificios,[2] and about three or four miles from Vera Cruz.[3] On the morning of the ninth the men were furnished with two days' provisions in their haversacks, and were ordered to sling their canteens, filled with water.[4] Soon afterwards they were transferred from the transports to the decks of the ships of war and the steamers; and, between eleven and twelve o'clock, the fleet—led by Commodore Conner, in the *Raritan*, and followed by General Scott, in the *Massachusetts*—got under way, in gallant style; filed, one by one, out of the narrow pass which leads from the anchorage at Anton Lizardo; and within two hours approached that at the Sacrificios—"each dropping her anchor and swinging into her appropriated place without the least confusion, and with the most admirable precision."[5]

The successful management of this debarkation having been the subject of general admiration, it cannot be passed without a more extended notice than such movements generally receive; and the graphic description which has been given by an intelligent eye-witness,—a gallant participant in the toils and dangers, as well as the glories of the war,—will best convey to the reader a correct idea of the splendor of the scene. "The surf-boats," he says, "sixty-seven in number, and each one manned by experienced seamen of the navy, were hauled alongside of the ships; the soldiers, with their arms and accoutrements, were passed into them; and as each boat received her complement, she shoved off, and laid on her oars, at a little distance, until the others should be ready. The post of honor, on this memorable occasion, was given to Brevet Brigadier-general Worth, who had so recently distinguished himself before Monterey—it being decided by the General-in-chief, that his division (the First of regulars, which afterwards became so celebrated in the valley of Mexico) should be the first to flout our flag in the enemy's face. Accordingly, when all was ready, the General, whose fine military person and bearing had already won the hearts of such of the officers of the navy as had come in contact with him, descended into one of the man-of-war's boats, prepared for him, and placing himself at the head of his troops, the latter moved, in a semicircle, towards the shore. Commodore Conner had previously directed two steamers, the *Spitfire*, Commander Tattnal, and the *Vixen*, Commander Sands, with five gun-schooners, to anchor in line, abreast of the beach, to cover the landing, in case any opposition should be made. This part of the movement had already been handsomely executed. Nothing could exceed the beauty of this spectacle, as viewed from the poop of the flag-ship. It was just before sunset, an hour at which all the beauties of the Mexican coast are wont to stand out in bold and beautiful relief. The day had continued as clear as it had begun, and the sea-breeze, as it died gradually away, had left behind it a glazed and unruffled sea. The magnificent mountain of Orizaba, with its snow-clad summit, which had been hidden from view most of the day, suddenly revealed itself with startling distinctness and grandeur; the distant Cofre of Perote loomed up, also, in blue and mystic beauty; and the bold and rugged outline of the coast seemed more bold and rugged still, from the refracting power of the atmosphere.

"The walls of the town and castle, the domes of the churches, and the rigging and mast-heads of the foreign men-of-war, anchored at Sacrificios, all filled with curious and eager spectators, completed a scene which made a lively impression upon the minds of all beholders. The boats reaching the shore, in fine style, the troops debarked in good order; and, in a few minutes afterwards, a detachment, which had wound its way up one of the sand-hills, unfurled the American flag, and waving it proudly, planted it in the land of Cortez. By common consent, a shout, such as seamen only can give, arose at this moment from the decks of all the ships of war present, which was joined in, and prolonged, by such portions of the army as had not yet landed. The

[1] Notes for the History, p. 181.—[2] Semmes, p. 125.
[3] Ripley, ii. p. 18.—[4] Autobiography of an English soldier in the American army, p. 144
[5] Semmes, p. 126.

debarkation now went briskly forward,[1] and before ten o'clock P. M., the whole force present, consisting of about twelve thousand men, was safely landed, without the occurrence of a single mistake or accident; an event unparalleled in the history of similar operations, and of which any naval commander might well be proud."[2]

"The environs of the city outside the fire of its guns, and those of the castle, being broken into innumerable hills of loose sand, from twenty to two hundred and fifty feet in height, with almost impassable forests of chaparral between," and the scarcity of carts and pack-mules, which made the transportation of subsistence along the entire proposed line of investment a work of great difficulty, the entire line was not occupied on the night of the ninth, or until the twelfth; and at that time, even, it was only accomplished with great difficulty and labor, and with some loss, both of officers and men.[3]

At this time General Worth's command occupied a position immediately southeast from the city, and this was considered the *front* of the attack. The centre was occupied by the Volunteers under General Patterson—under whose command were Generals Quitman, Pillow, and Shields. The Second division of regulars, under General Twiggs, completed the line, on the north;[4] and some firing had taken place, with loss on both sides.[5]

At the same time the garrison of Vera Cruz consisted of three thousand three hundred and sixty men, that of the castle of San Juan of one thousand and thirty men;[6]

[1] "Brevet Brig.-Gen. Worth's brigade of regulars led the descent, quickly followed by the division of United States Volunteers under Maj.-Gen. Patterson and Brig.-Gen. Twigg's reserve brigade of regulars. The whole army reached the shore in fine style, and without direct opposition, accident, or loss, driving the enemy from the ground to be occupied."—*Gen. Scott's Dispatch, No.* 13, *March* 12, 1847.—[2] Semmes' Afloat and Ashore, pp. 127, 128. See also Ripley, ii. pp. 21–23; Notes for the Hist., p. 181; Autobiog. of English Soldier, pp. 144–150; Mansfield's Scott, pp. 369–372; MS. Diary of an Officer, March 9, 1847.—[3] Gen. Scott to Sec. of War, No. 13, March 12, 1847; Semmes, pp. 128, 129.—[4] Gen. Scott to Sec. of War, No. 13, March 12, 1847; Mansfield, pp. 372, 373.

[5] MS. Diary, March 11.—[6] Notes for the History, pp. 182. 183.

and, although a commendable degree of enthusiasm existed in the ranks of both, the scarcity of provisions speedily checked their ardor.[1]

The enemy harassed the besiegers with small parties of light troops, and a series of heavy storms ("northers," as they are termed) prevented the debarkation of supplies and artillery in sufficient quantities.[2] It was not until the twenty-second, therefore, that the engineers reported that the batteries were sufficiently advanced to receive seven mortars, when Colonel Bankhead, the "Chief of Artillery," placed that number in battery.[3]

At two o'clock, the mortars being ready, and "the labors for planting the remainder of the heavy metal being in progress," General Scott addressed a summons to General Morales, the Governor of Vera Cruz,[4] and within two hours the latter replied, declining to lower his flag, and inviting the former to "commence his operations of war in the manner which he may consider most advantageous."[5]

At a quarter-past four o'clock the fire was opened from three batteries (*Numbers One, Two, and Three*), with great animation and apparent effect, and without any material diminution, until the surrender of the city. During the twenty-second the batteries were commanded by Captain Brooks, Lieutenant Shackelford, and Captain Vinton—the latter of whom was killed by a cannon-shot at about four o'clock.[6] On the twenty-third, Captains McKenzie, Anderson, and Taylor commanded; and battery *Number Four* was completed with three twenty-four pounders.[7] On the night of the twenty-fourth, another twenty-four pounder and an eight-inch howitzer were added to *Number Four;* and on the morning of the twenty-fifth, three more

[1] Notes for the Hist., p. 182; MS. Diary, ———

[2] Gen. Scott to Sec. of War, No. 13, March 12; No. 14, March 14; No. 15, March 17; No. 16, March 18.

[3] Col. Bankhead's Report, March 24.—[4] Gen. Scott to Gen. Morales, March 22, appended to Gen. Scott's Dispatch, No. 18, March 23; Notes for the History, p. 183.

[5] Gen. Morales to Gen. Scott, March 22, 1847, appended to same dispatch.—[6] Col. Bankhead's Report, March 24; Notes for the History, p. 184.—[7] Col. Bankhead's Report, March 25.

twenty-four pounders and another eight-inch howitzer were added to the same battery. On the twenty-sixth, additional mortar-platforms were finished, and four large mortars were placed in battery.[1]

During the same time, while the batteries under Colonel Bankhead were pouring in their murderous missiles from the rear of the town, two steamers and five small vessels[2] approached within about a mile and a half of the shore, and, "according to previous arrangement with Commodore Perry," they also opened a brisk fire upon the city;[3] while Captain Aulick, on the twenty-fourth, was permitted to land with about twelve hundred seamen and six pieces of heavy artillery, to join, as "a Naval Battery," in the dangers and the honors of the contest.[4]

The fire continued, on both sides, with great spirit, until the twenty-sixth, when overtures were received from General Landero, on whom General Morales had devolved the chief command;[5] and on the twenty-sixth, Generals Worth and Pillow and Colonel Totten were appointed Commissioners from the American army to adjust the terms of capitulation.[6] After considerable discussion, terms were agreed to, and articles signed, on the twenty-seventh of March, by which the garrisons of the city and castle surrendered as prisoners of war;[7] and at ten o'clock on the twenty-ninth, the American colors were hoisted, with all the honors, on the works of both the city and the castle.[8]

In this memorable siege the army threw about two thousand five hundred shot and shells,[9] while the naval battery threw one thousand Paixhan shells and eight hundred round-shot[1] into the city and its defences.

The loss of the Mexicans was very severe, both in life and property. It is said, by the Mexican historians, that four or five hundred of the inhabitants of the city "had perished," and that "six hundred soldiers had shed their blood, and four hundred of them had been killed;"[2] while "the condition of the place was frightful. From the gate of La Merced to the Parish, not a single house was uninjured. The greater part of them was destroyed, and the streets were impassable, from the rubbish. From the Parish to the Caleta, although not on the same level, all the houses were damaged. There was no light, and there was no passing by the sidewalks, for fear the balconies would fall."[3] The same authorities depict, in most glowing colors, the misery which had been entailed on the inhabitants,—especially on the aged, the women, and the children,—and the recital of the affliction of these—"groups of women, of all classes, were to be seen carrying little bundles of clothes, running about the streets, terrified, and out of breath, with distress depicted in their countenances, and everywhere that kind of dread prevailed which arises from the memory of a past danger, when a future is expected; the mother, with her tender children in her arms, hastened along in search of a secure asylum, which sad reality denied her; the young daughter, guiding the steps of the aged man, raised her eyes to heaven, streaming with tears, imploring a retreat, to save the life of the author of her being; the little boy, terrified by the dismay of his mother, hardly able to keep up, following her"—brings a sad account against the "glories" of the war.

In the American camp but little loss was experienced. Midshipman Shubrick, of the navy, and four seamen were killed at the Naval Battery;[4] and Captains Vinton and Alburtis and nine men were *killed;* and Lieutenant-colonel Dickenson, of the South Carolina Volunteers, Lieutenant Niell, of the Second dragoons, and fifty-three men

---

[1] Col. Bankhead's Report, March 28.—[2] The steamers *Spitfire*, Com. Tattnal, and *Vixen*, Com. Sands; and the schooners *Bonita*, Lieut. Benham; *Reefer*, Lieut. Sterrett; *Petrel*, Lieut. Shaw; *Falcon*, Lieut. Glassin; and *Tampico*, Lieut. Griffin.—[3] Gen. Scott to Sec. of War, No. 18, March 23; Semmes, pp. 130, 131; Notes for the Hist., pp. 184, 185.—[4] Gen. Scott to Sec. of War, No. 18, March 24; Semmes, pp. 132–141; Notes for the History, p. 185.

[5] Gen. Scott to Sec. of War, No. 19, March 29.

[6] Credentials of Commissioners, &c., appended to Gen. Scott's Dispatch, No. 19.—[7] Articles of Capitulation; Notes for the History, p. 194.

[8] Gen. Scott to Secretary of War, No. 19, March 19; Notes for the History, p. 196.

[9] Col. Bankhead's Report, March 28.

[1] Semmes, pp. 140, 141.—[2] Notes for the History, p. 195.—[3] Ibid., pp. 189, 190.—[4] Semmes, p. 141.

wounded, in all the operations attending the siege, including the skirmishes.[1]

General Worth was placed in command of the city and castle—a position which justly belonged to him, as his division had "performed most of the duties at the batteries;" and, soon afterwards, Captain Backus, of the First infantry, and his company,—the heroes of El Teneria, at Monterey,—were detached to the castle of San Juan de Ulloa.[2]

Immediately after the surrender of Vera Cruz, the celebrated expedition to Alvarado, of which the world has heard so much, was planned and put into execution. The naval forces had made two attempts, on the same place, at an earlier date, without success;[3] and with great show of power the third expedition left Vera Cruz on the thirtieth of March—the army being represented by the South Carolina, Georgia, and Alabama regiments of Volunteers, a squadron of cavalry, under Major Beale, and a section of light artillery, under Lieutenant Judd, the whole under General Quitman;[4] while the navy was represented by the frigate *Potomac* and steamer *Mississippi*, the sloop of war *St. Mary's*, the steamers *Spitfire*, *Vixen*, and *Water Witch*, the brig *Porpoise*, one bomb-ketch, and the five small gun-schooners,[5] and by the sloop of war *Albany* and the steamer *Scourge*, which, as an advance, had been dispatched some days earlier.[6] On the approach of the joint expeditions, messengers met them with the intelligence that the positions which had twice overcome the efforts of the navy, and which had now called forth the powerful demonstration which was approaching the town, had surrendered to the cool daring of Lieutenant Hunter, of the steamer *Scourge*, without loss or damage![7] and the laurels which would otherwise have graced the brows of a Commodore and a General—to say nothing of the subordinate officers of the army and the navy—were already reposing on that of a junior officer, without inflicting any injury or disquieting any nerves. Unfortunately, they were not long allowed to remain there. The unfortunate Lieutenant—who, single-handed, had accomplished successfully what his Commodore, with all his power, had failed to perform—had exhibited, too plainly, the inefficiency of the latter, and he was subjected to an arrest, a court-martial, and a virtual dismissal from the service!—a course of treatment which the President, prompted by the voice of the people, promptly and effectually remedied.[1]

On the eighth of April, having made all necessary preparations for that purpose, General Scott moved the Second division of regular troops (*Gen. Twiggs'*) from the city towards Mexico;[2] and on the following day, the Volunteers under General Patterson, except General Quitman's brigade and the Tennessee regiment, followed.[3]

While General Scott had been operating against Vera Cruz, the President of the Republic, General Santa Anna, had hastened down from San Luis de Potosi,—whither he had retired after the battle of Buena Vista,—and had prepared to resist the progress of the army towards Mexico. With this purpose he had established his head-quarters at his hacienda of Encero, on the fifth of April; and, having added to the army the fragments of the veteran regiments which had met General Taylor at the Pass of Angostura, and forced many of the dispersed soldiers, who had given their parol at Vera Cruz, to re-enter the service, he fortified the strong pass of Cerro Gordo, and awaited, at that place, the approach of the American columns.[4]

The position which the Mexicans occupied was one of peculiar strength. It was, in fact, a mountain gorge, through which the National Road, on which the army marched, wound its way up the mountains. The left is flanked and commanded, for two miles before reaching the hill of El Telégrafo, by an almost inaccessible ridge, rising to the

---

[1] Report of killed, &c., signed "Winfield Scott," and dated, "*Head-quarters of the Army, Vera Cruz, April* 6, 1847."—[2] MS. Diary of an Officer, March 29.

[3] Ripley, ii. p. 54; Thurber, p. 565.—[4] Gen. Quitman's Report, April 7, 1847.—[5] Thurber, p. 565.

[6] Semmes, p. 147.—[7] Gen. Quitman's Report, April 7; Ripley, ii. pp. 54, 55.

[1] Thurber, p. 565; Ripley, ii. p. 55.—[2] MS. Diary; Gen. Scott to Sec. of War, No. 22, April 11.—[3] Gen. Scott to Sec. of War, No. 22, April 11.—[4] Notes for the History, pp. 198, 199.

BATTLE OF CERRO GORDO.

height of nearly eight hundred feet; while the right, also, is alternately shut in by the heights and skirted by what was considered, by the enemy, an impenetrable chaparral. On the left of this road, and nearly at right angles with it, three nearly parallel ridges presented their abrupt fronts, and descended gradually, to the rear, into rugged ground, broken into rocky ravines, and covered by thick chaparral. These three bluffs, as they may be called, were the first line of defences; and while their summits were crowned with batteries of unusual strength, their sides, in front and flank, were defended by abatis and other obstructions, which had been thrown in the way of an attacking party.[1] They had been strengthened under the direction of the well-known Lieutenant-colonel of Engineers, Robles; and on the southernmost of the three—which was flanked on the right by the precipitous banks of the Rio del Plan—was posted General Pinzon, with the battalion of Atlixco and the Fifth regiment of infantry, more than five hundred rank and file, with seven pieces of artillery. The next work on its left—the centre of the right, which commanded most of the approaches to each of the three works on the right of the enemy's line—was manned by Captain Araujo, of the navy, with the battalion Libertad (four hundred rank and file), and that of Zacapoastla (three hundred rank and file), with eight pieces of artillery. The northernmost of the three—next to the road—was occupied by Colonel Badillo, with two hundred and fifty rank and file of the companies of the National Guard from Jalapa, Coatepec, and Teusitlan, with nine pieces of artillery. Besides these local garrisons, "the camp of Matamoras" was posted in the ravine, between the northernmost and the central positions; and General Jarero,—the general commander of the "camp" and the two posts on its flanks—with four hundred and fifty men from the battalion of Matamoras and Tepeaca, and an eight-pounder, was in

[1] Maps in "Notes for the History," "War with Mexico," and Mansfield's "Scott," and that appended to Gen. Scott's Dispatches; Ripley, ii. p. 58.

position at that place.[1] On the right of the National Road, and some distance in the rear of the line of defences last referred to, the heights projected so far to the southward that but a very limited space remained for the passage of the road between the foot of the heights on the right and precipitous bank of the Rio del Plan on its left; and at this spot — sweeping the road, on either hand, for a long distance, as well as the paths which led to the batteries last referred to[2]—was a battery of seven heavy pieces, manned with the Sixth regiment of infantry, nine hundred rank and file, under General de la Vega, under whose command, also, was the reserve of the grenadiers, four hundred and sixty rank and file, which had been posted for this and the battery in front, which General Pinzon commanded.[3] On the left, and slightly in the rear, of the Pass of Cerro Gordo, and of the work which defended it, rises the bald and abrupt conical hill known to the Mexicans as El Telégrafo, while in front of it, as abrupt and bare a cone as the other, but less lofty, rises that known as El Atalaya.[4] On the summit of El Telégrafo, a thousand feet above the pass, —where had been posted the Third regiment of infantry, under Generals Vasquez and Uraga,[5]—was a strong work, mounting six heavy guns; and these commanded not only the pass, but all the works in front of it, and rendered the possession of any of the works in front exceedingly hazardous, even should they be taken.[6] In the rear of El Telégrafo is the hacienda of Cerro Gordo, which gives a name to the pass and the action which occurred there;[7] and at that place was encamped the Mexican General-in-chief, with the reserves of the army, embracing the First, Second, Third, and Fourth battalions of light troops, seventeen hundred rank and file, the Fourth and Eleventh regiments of infantry, seven hundred and eighty rank and file, and the hospital, baggage, and store trains; while at Corral Falso were posted,

[1] Notes for the History, pp. 199–201; Ripley, ii. pp. 58, 59.—[2] Ripley, ii. p. 59.—[3] Notes for the History, pp. 201, 202.—[4] Ibid., p. 199; Ripley, ii. p. 59.—[5] Notes for the History, p. 202.—[6] Ripley, ii. pp. 59, 60.—[7] Map by Maj. Turnbull and the Engineers of the army.

in reserve, the cavalry of the army,—including the squadrons of Jalapa, Húzares, Chalchicomula, and Orizava, the regiments of Morelia and Coraceros, and the Fifth and Ninth regiments of the line,—under General Canalizo.[1]

Against this force, thus posted, as before stated, Generals Twiggs and Patterson had moved from Vera Cruz. The command of the former embraced the regiment of Mounted Rifles, under Colonel Harney, the First regiment of artillery, under Brevet-colonel Childs, and the Seventh regiment of infantry, under Lieutenant-colonel Plimpton — forming a brigade, under Colonel Harney; and the Second and Third regiments of infantry, under Captains Morris and Alexander, the Fourth regiment of artillery, under Major Gardner, and the company of rocketeers, under Major Talcott—the whole forming a brigade, under General Riley: that of the latter, the Third and Fourth regiments of Illinois Volunteers, under Colonels Baker and Foreman, and the Second regiment of New York Volunteers, under Colonel Burnett—the whole forming a brigade, under General Shields; the First and Second Tennessee regiments of Volunteers, one company of Kentucky Mounted Volunteers, under Captain Williams, one of Tennessee horse, under Captain Caldwell, and the First and Second regiments of Pennsylvania Volunteers—the whole forming a brigade, under General Pillow.[2]

The head of the column reached the Plan del Rio—about four miles from the Pass of Cerro Gordo—on the eleventh of April, and at that place the enemy first showed himself —Colonel Harney driving from it a body of Mexican Lancers, before the division encamped for the night. On the following day (*April* 12), General Twiggs—who commanded the advance—moved forward with his entire division to within half a mile from the enemy's line of batteries, on the southern side of the road, for the purpose of covering a thorough reconnoissance of the ground.[3] During this movement, his Adjutant-general, Lieutenant W. T. H. Brooks, discovered, and, to some extent, explored, a trail, which, diverging to the right, from the road, lead to the flank and rear of the works on El Telégrafo;[1] and General Twiggs resolved to move forward, on the following morning (*April* 13), and to assault the enemy's lines. On the same day on which the reconnoissance was made, however, two brigades of Volunteers, under Generals Pillow and Shields, reached the camp, from Vera Cruz; and, although "they were much broken down from the recent march," they urgently requested permission to join in the assault; and, for the purpose of gratifying their request, and in order to give them a short rest, the movement was postponed until the fourteenth.[2]

Major-general Patterson, of the Volunteer service, who had been reported sick, and who was in the rear, hearing of the projected movement, and desiring, also, to participate in the action, on the evening of the thirteenth he issued an order to suspend all farther offensive operations until the arrival of the General-in-chief, or until ordered by himself (*General Patterson*).[3]

On the fourteenth of April General Scott arrived at the camp at Plan del Rio, and on the evening of the sixteenth he ordered General Twiggs to move to the right of the enemy's position, for the purpose of turning the left of his lines, agreeably to his original plan of operations.[4] At eight o'clock on the morning of the seventeenth, in conformity with this order, General Twiggs advanced with his division,—the regiment of Mounted Rifles, dismounted, under Major Sumner, and the First artillery, under Colonel Thomas Childs, being at the head of the column,—and at eleven o'clock he occupied the position assigned to him, his right resting about seven hundred yards from the enemy's main work. Soon afterwards Lieutenant Gardner, of the Seventh infantry, was ordered to move with his company to a high ground on the

[1] Notes for the History, pp. 202-204.—[2] Returns appended to Gen. Scott's Dispatch.—[3] Gen. Twiggs' Report, April 19.

[1] Semmes, p. 177—[2] Ripley, ii. p. 62.—[3] Gen. Twiggs' Report, April 19; Autobiog. of English Soldier, p. 175. [4] Gen. Twiggs' Report, April 19; Ripley, ii. p. 63.

left of the route, for the purpose of observing the enemy; and, at the same time, evidently ignorant of the nature of the American movement, General Alcorta, with a strong party, moved from the Mexican lines, to the same place, for the same purpose. The heads of these columns came in contact,—apparently the first intimation either party had of the approach of the other,—and while Colonel Harney moved to support Lieutenant Gardner, with the Mounted Rifles (dismounted) and the First artillery, and, subsequently, with the Seventh infantry, General Santa Anna moved the Third regiment from El Telégrafo to support General Alcorta; while, at the same time, he sent several corps down from Cerro Gordo, after ordering the reserve column to form on the road. "He subsequently placed the several light battalions on the declivity of the Telégrafo, in several lines, *en echelon*, from the centre of that position, and the Fourth regiment of the line towards the left, where the Americans were advancing with great resolution; while at the summit, on the parapets, remained a portion of the Third regiment of the line and the Eleventh regiment of infantry; and the Sixth regiment of infantry moved to the right, under General Vega, to prevent the turning of the position."[1]

Between the two detachments of observation and their respective supporting parties, therefore, the action was warmly contested—the artillery on the summit of El Telégrafo, under Lieutenant Olzinger, on the one side, doing great execution; while a portion of the First Artillery, under Colonel Childs, on the other, swept over El Atalaya and the intervening valleys to the foot of El Telégrafo, driving before it the Mexican troops, and commenced, without any support, to ascend the rugged slope of the latter, for the purpose of assaulting the main works of the Mexicans on its summit. As it was not the purpose of the General to attack the lines at that time, these troops were recalled, and joined the main body under General Twiggs. The remainder of the detachment, embracing

[1] Gen. Twiggs' Report, April 19; Notes for the History, pp. 205, 206; Col. Harney's Report, April 21, 1847.

the Rifles and the Seventh regiment of infantry, bivouacked on El Atalaya, to which position were brought, in the night, a twenty-four-pounder and two twenty-four-pound howitzers; and, under the direction of Captain Lee, of the Engineers, and Lieutenant Hagner, of the Ordnance Department, they were placed in battery at an early hour in the morning.[1]

In the mean time, the Second infantry moved to the heights in front of El Atalaya, and, subsequently, to the main road near the batteries, where it remained all night; the Fourth artillery, at the same time, covering the batteries of Captain Taylor and Major Talcott; the Third infantry conducting the twenty-four-pounder and howitzer battery over the rugged trail over which the division had moved; and the remainder of the forces occupying the camp at Plan del Rio.[2]

During the night of the seventeenth, as before stated, the battery was planted on El Atalaya; an eight-inch howitzer, under Lieutenant Towers, of the Engineers, and Laidley, of the Ordnance Department, was put in position on the south bank of the Rio del Plan—opposite to, and within range of, the batteries on the extreme right of the Mexican lines—by companies C, F, G, and H, of the New York Volunteers, under Major James C. Burnham;[3] General Shields, with the Third and Fourth regiments of Illinois Volunteers, and the New York regiment of Volunteers, was sent to strengthen General Twiggs;[4] and four companies of the First regiment of artillery, under Colonel Childs, and six companies of the Third regiment of infantry, under Captain Alexander, were sent by General Twiggs to strengthen Colonel Harney on El Atalaya.[5]

General Scott had issued a General Order,

[1] Gen. Scott's Dispatch, No. 24, April 23; Gen. Twiggs' Report, April 19; Semmes, p. 177; Autobiog. of English Soldier, pp. 178–184; Notes for the History, pp. 206, 207; Ripley, ii. pp. 64–66; Col. Harney's Report, April 21.

[2] Gen. Twiggs' Report, April 19; Col. Riley's Report, April 20.—[3] Gen. Twiggs' Report, April 19; Gen. Scott's Dispatch, No. 24, April 19; Personal information from Col. J. C. Burnham.—[4] Gen. Twiggs' Report, April 19; Gen. Scott's Dispatch, No. 24, April 23; Ripley, ii. p. 66.

[5] Ripley, ii. pp. 66, 67; Col. Harney's Report, April 21.

in which, while the great features of the proposed movements were briefly set forth, the details were left to the discretion of his subordinates;[1] and the result proved that if the army had an able Commander-in-chief, that Commander was not less favored in the concentration of skill, prudence, energy, and gallantry which his subordinate officers displayed, or in the untiring energy and the unflinching firmness which were displayed by his troops.

At an early hour on the morning of the eighteenth, the troops were formed, for the purpose of storming the Mexican batteries; while the battery on El Atalaya opened its fire on the Mexican lines with good effect, and not only prepared the way of the storming party, by scattering the bodies of troops which were thrown out to oppose its ascent up the slopes of El Telégrafo, but, at the same time, it appears to have broken the spirit of the artillerists at the summit of that hill, and to have produced a cessation of their fire, at that important period.[2] As already stated, Colonel Harney had been reinforced during the early part of the morning; and he had detached the regiment of Mounted Riflemen (dismounted) to the left, with orders to dislodge the enemy from the ravine in that quarter; while, with the remainder of his force, he had prepared to move against the front of the position, which was the stronghold of the Mexican lines, as soon as the Rifles were engaged. Accordingly two columns were formed,—the Seventh regiment of infantry on the right, and the Third regiment on the left,—while the detachment from the First regiment of artillery was formed, as a reserve, in the rear, with orders to support the infantry. The movements of the enemy subsequently led Colonel Harney to change his plan of attack, so far as to charge without waiting for the co-operation of the riflemen; and, notwithstanding the abruptness of the ascent, the intervening lines of defence, and the warmth of the Mexican fire, his command moved forward, surmounting all obstacles and overcoming all enemies, until the works on the summit of the hill had been taken, the Mexican colors lowered,[1] and those of the Seventh infantry and First artillery raised in their place—the Rifles, meanwhile, agreeably to instructions, moving to the left, and engaging with "a succoring force, which they held in check, notwithstanding a most galling fire from the enemy's intrenchments and from the musketry in front.[2]

In the mean time, while Colonel Harney advanced against the front of El Telégrafo, as already related, the Second brigade, under Colonel Riley, and the brigade of Volunteers, under General Shields, moved to the right, around the foot of the hill, and turned the Mexican left flank;[3] while, at the same time, General Pillow, with his brigade, moved against the batteries on the south side of the road.[4]

The Second brigade,—embracing the Second infantry and Fourth artillery, the Third infantry being with Colonel Harney's command,—under the guidance of Captain Lee, of the Engineers, was moved around the northern base of the hill El Telégrafo, under a heavy fire from the enemy's lines; and companies A, B, H, and I, of the Second infantry,—and, subsequently, the Fourth artillery and the remaining companies of the Second infantry,—were moved against the works on its summit. The four companies first named attacked the enemy in reverse, simultaneously with the attack, under Colonel Harney, on his front; and, with the First brigade, were participants in the glory of that encounter. The supporting parties which Colonel Riley sent out subsequently, although they encountered the fire of the Mexicans, reached the crest of the hill after

[1] General Orders, No. 111, April 17, 1847.

[2] Col. Harney's Report, April 21, 1847; Semmes, p. 180; Autobiography of an English Soldier, p. 187.

[1] "The enemy's flag was taken down by the intrepid and gallant Quartermaster-sergeant Henry (*of the Seventh infantry*), and the flag and standard of the Seventh infantry were raised and floated in its place by the brave Color-sergeants Bradford, Brady, and Murphy."—*Lieut.-Col. Plympton's Report, April* 20, 1847.

[2] Col. Harney's Report, April 21; Maj. Loring's Report, April 23; Col. Childs' Report, April 20; Lieut.-Col. Plympton's Report, April 20, 1847; Semmes, pp. 179–181.

[3] Col. Riley's Report, April 20; Col. Baker's Report, April 21, 1847; Semmes, p. 181.—[4] Gen. Pillow's Report, April 18, 1847; Semmes, pp. 181, 182.

the works had been carried, and were not among the victors in that conflict. Colonel Riley having accompanied his command up the hill, soon discovered, from its summit, that the enemy's batteries, on the plain in the rear of the hill, could be turned on the right and carried, he ordered the advance of the Second infantry, guided by Assistant Adjutant-general Canby, to move down, attack, and carry them; while the entire brigade was moved down to cover the movement. Some delay in the delivery of the order, and in the concentration of the scattered forces of the brigade, led to the loss of the credit of sharing with the Volunteers in the capture of the works referred to, although one of the evacuated batteries was first occupied by the Second infantry, the pursuit was maintained by company D, of the same regiment, and company E was established as a guard over the property found in the enemy's camp.[1]

The Third Volunteer brigade, under General Shields, — embracing the Third and Fourth Illinois and the Second New York regiments of Volunteers,—as already stated, was pushed forward around the northern base of El Telégrafo, for the purpose of turning the extreme left of the Mexican lines, resting upon the Jalapa road. This was accomplished with great spirit and success, notwithstanding it encountered a heavy battery of five guns, supported by a large body of lancers, in which General Shields was very severely wounded; and the rout of the enemy being complete, his camp, with his guns, baggage, a large amount of specie, and his stores, were taken possession of and retained by this brigade.[2]

While the movements, just related, on the north side of the road, were rapidly throwing, not only the enemy's position, but his troops and his appointments into the hands of the Americans, and while the retreat of the forces in front was being rapidly cut off by the movement of Generals Shields and Riley, and their occupation of the Jalapa road in the rear of the pass, General Pillow, with the First division of Volunteers,—embracing the First and Second Tennessee and First and Second Pennsylvania regiments, one company (*Captain Caswell's*) of Tennessee horse, and one of Kentucky foot, under Captain Williams,—moved against the right of the Mexican lines—the three batteries on the south side of the road, near the bank of the Rio del Plan. The serious obstacles which this command encountered, both from the chaparral and the weight of the enemy's fire, and its heavy loss of men, led the General in command to suspend his operations—after part of his division had been compelled to retire from before one of the batteries—until the capture of the works on the summit of the hill (*El Telégrafo*) rendered farther movements unnecessary.[1]

The defeat of the enemy was complete, and the cavalry, with Captains Taylor and Wall's field-batteries, followed by the infantry, pushed after the fugitives, towards Jalapa, killing and capturing many, "before the men and the horses were exhausted by the heat and the distance."[2] General Worth, with the First division, however, did not stop until not only Jalapa and La Hoya, but the fortress of Perote,—second only to San Juan de Ulloa,—with an armament of sixty-six guns and mortars, and large supplies of materiel, had fallen into his hands.[3]

The strength of the Americans, in action and in reserve, was eight thousand five hundred men;[4] that of the enemy is said to have been "estimated at twelve thousand or more."[5] The loss of the former was three officers and sixty rank and file *killed*, thirty officers and three hundred and thirty-six rank and file *wounded*, and one private *missing*;[6] that of the former is computed at from one thousand to one thousand two hundred, besides which, about three thousand prisoners, four or five thousand stands

[1] Col Riley's Report, April 20; Maj. Gardner's Report, April 19: Capt. Morris' Report, April 20.—[2] Col. Baker's Report, April 21, 1847; Semmes, p. 181; Ripley, ii. p. 70.

[1] Gen. Pillow's Report, April 18; Autobiog. of English Soldier, p. 187; Ripley, ii. pp. 72, 73.

[2] Gen. Scott's Dispatch, No. 24, Jalapa, April 23.

[3] Gen. Worth's Report, April 23; Ripley, ii. pp. 76, 77.

[4] Gen. Scott's Dispatch, No. 24, April 23. Maj. Ripley (ii. p. 73) says it "did not exceed 9000 men."

[5] Gen. Scott's Dispatch, No. 24, April 23.

[6] Return of killed, &c., appended to Gen. Scott's Dispatch, No. 24, April 23, 1847.

of arms, and forty-three pieces of artillery were taken.[1]

Immediately after the action at Cerro Gordo, General Scott moved forward and fixed his head-quarters at Jalapa;[2] and on the eighth of May General Worth advanced from Perote, followed, on the ninth, by General Quitman.[3] With the exception of a small, but interesting affair at Amozoque, General Worth encountered no opposition; and on the fifteenth of May he entered and occupied Puebla.[4]

In the mean time, the naval forces had moved against the garrisoned port of Tuspan, on the Gulf; and on the seventeenth of April it was taken, with the loss, to the assailants, of two killed and eleven wounded.[5]

On the twenty-first of May General Scott advanced towards Puebla; and on the twenty-eighth, he fixed his head-quarters at that place;[6] while General Santa Anna, previous to that time, had returned to Mexico, and soon afterwards, encouraged by the constant movement of small detachments between the base of operations at Vera Cruz and head-quarters at Puebla, a system of guerrilla warfare was instituted, for the purpose of cutting off the supplies and the reinforcements of the Americans.[7]

One of these detachments, commanded by Brevet-colonel McIntosh, escorting one hundred and twenty-eight wagons, laden with specie and other property of great value, was attacked on the sixth of June, near El Paso de Ovejas, and twenty-four soldiers, exclusive of teamsters, were killed or wounded.[8] Reinforcements of the escort were sent forward from Vera Cruz, on the requisition of Colonel McIntosh, and the train moved forward to the National Bridge, where it was attacked a second time, and thirty-two of the escort, besides a large number of the teamsters and other employees, were killed or wounded.[1] When the train reached Jalapa the escort was strengthened a second time, and on the eighteenth it left that place. On the nineteenth, when it had reached La Hoya, it was attacked a third time, and suffered severely; and it was rescued from its dangerous situation only by great exertions.[2]

About this time the squadron proceeded to the port of Tobasco, and after a slight opposition, in which two men were killed and seven wounded, on the fifteenth of June, it was taken and occupied by the American forces.[3]

Soon afterwards another detachment of three thousand men, under General Franklin Pierce, left Vera Cruz for head-quarters; and his flanks were constantly harassed by the irregular troops which appeared at every turn of the road. The substantial bridges, which spanned the several streams on his route, were broken down by the Mexicans, and he was obliged either to ford the streams or to march by other and more difficult routes.[4]

In order to assist in the protection of this detachment, General Smith was detached from Puebla to meet General Pierce; and while on his way, on the thirtieth of July, when near the hacienda of San Juan de los Llanos, about midway between Ojo del Agua and Tepeahualco, he encountered a small body of the enemy. A brisk engagement ensued, notwithstanding the small force of the enemy, and the latter was driven off, with a reported loss of forty killed and fifty wounded, and on the sixth of August General Pierce entered Puebla.[5]

A considerable time was spent in reconnoitring, and it was not until the seventh of August that any portion of the main body of the army was advanced from Puebla. On that day Colonel Harney's brigade of cavalry, followed by the Second

---

[1] Gen. Scott's Dispatch, No. 24, April 23; Same to Gen. Taylor, April 24, 1847.—[2] Ripley, ii. p. 76.

[3] Ibid., pp. 107, 108.—[4] Gen. Scott's Dispatch, No. 28, May 20; Gen. Worth's Report, May 15; Ripley, ii. pp. 108–111.—[5] Com. Perry to Sec. of Navy, April 24, 1847; Ripley, ii. p. 88.—[6] Gen. Scott's Dispatch, No. 29, June 4.

[7] Ibid., No. 25, April 28; José Mariana Salas to the Mexicans, April 21; Ripley, ii. pp. 104, 105; Notes for the History, pp. 439–442.—[8] Col. McIntosh to Col. Scott, July 9; Ripley, ii. pp. 130–132.

[1] Gen. Cadwallader's Report, July 12; Ripley, ii. pp. 133–136.—[2] Gen. Cadwallader's Report, July 12; Col. Child's Report, July 12.—[3] Com. Perry to Sec. of Navy, June 24, 1847; Notes for the History, pp. 443, 444.

[4] Gen. Pierce to Gen. Scott, Aug. 1, 1847.

[5] Gen. Smith to Capt. Scott, A. A. A. G., Aug. 2, 1847.

division, under General Twiggs, moved forward; on the eighth, General Quitman's division of Volunteers (*the Fourth*), and a detachment of marines, followed; on the ninth, General Worth's division (*the First*) was moved forward; and on the tenth, General Pillow, with the Third division, brought up the rear. These divisions were concentrated in the valley of Mexico; and on the twelfth and thirteenth, reconnoissances were pushed upon the Peñon and upon Mexicalcingo—the latter within eight miles from the city of Mexico.[1]

During this time General Scott's head-quarters, with those of General Twiggs, were at Ayotla, General Quitman's at Buena Vista, General Worth's at Chalco, and General Pillow's at Chimalpa; and no enemy had opposed them.[2] The country in front was but imperfectly known, and the reconnoissances had not been remarkably successful, notwithstanding the daring which had been displayed in carrying them on. Two routes to the capital were before the army,—each possessing peculiarities of access or of obstruction,—and General Scott appeared to have selected for the march of the army that on the eastern side of Lake Chalco,—the National road,—by which the capital would have been approached on its eastern front; and in that direction all the reconnoissances *of the engineers* appeared to have been pushed. It appears, however, that notwithstanding these movements, they were only *feints;* and that even at that early day, General Scott had fully determined to move on the southern and western sides of Lake Chalco; and he had communicated that purpose, *in confidence*, to his military family, to General Worth, and the Chief of Engineers, with the most stringent injunctions of privacy. Although the appearances indicated, both to the enemy and to his own army, an intention to move towards El Peñon or Mexicalcingo, the capabilities of the route on the opposite side of the lake were generally known to the General and Captain Lee, of the Engineers, and that was the route which was really designated for the movement of the army.[1]

While the troops were thus resting on their arms, almost within sight of the city, one of the most remarkable exploits of the war was performed by a young officer,—an aid-de-camp of the General-in-chief,—Lieutenant Schuyler Hamilton.[2] It has been modestly related by the gallant young officer himself; and no language can be used, with more propriety than his own, in describing it:

"The first affair between the Mexican and American forces in the valley of the city of Mexico, in which blood was shed on both sides, was that of Mira Flores. At a convocation of officers, August 13, 1847, at Chalco, where General Worth's head-quarters were then established, in sight of the city of Mexico, General Scott, while 'thinking aloud,' as he termed it, expressed a regret that, owing to the want of a larger supply of shot and shell, some combinations which might be made, possibly with advantage to the army, must, owing to this want, be foregone. At this point in the conversation, Lieutenant Schuyler Hamilton, one of the aids of General Scott, suggested to the General-in-chief that the foundry of San Raphael, at which shot and shell had been cast for the Mexicans, the calibres of whose great guns corresponded, though under different denominations, with those of the Americans, was only three leagues distant; that possibly the moulds used by the Mexicans might still be there; that he knew a person who could act as a guide to that point, and, with fifteen dragoons, would undertake to ascertain if the moulds were still there, and the state of the roads.

"General Worth immediately represented that three thousand men had the day before retreated, on his approach, into the mountains towards San Raphael, and that such an attempt would be certain destruction.

[1] Gen. Scott's Dispatch, No. 31, Aug. 19, 1847; Ripley, ii. pp. 187–189; Semmes, pp. 320, 321.

[2] Ripley, ii. p. 187; Semmes, pp. 325, 326.

[1] Gen. E. A. Hitchcock to the Author, July 18, 1860.

[2] This young gentleman is a son of John C. Hamilton, Esq., of the city of New York, grandson of Gen. Alexander Hamilton, and great-grandson of Gen. Philip Schuyler, of the Revolutionary Army.

General Scott, however, conceived it of sufficient importance to give the order that the attempt should be made, and the necessary instructions, and directed General Worth to detail such a force as he should deem proper for the success of the expedition. About fifty dragoons, with a supporting force of one hundred infantry, under Captain (now Colonel) Hoffman, Sixth infantry, were detailed for this service. The infantry halted at three leagues from Chalco—to the foundry it was nearly three leagues more. It was, however, reached, the moulds were found to be there, and all the needed information obtained. The road lay through a narrow mountain defile. The ravine, forming the bed of a stream, at one time fell off abruptly from the roadway, dug out of the face of the steep hills; at other points the terrace of the roadway widened to a few hundred feet. The sun was sinking in the west, and already the tall mountains threw their shadows on the pathway of the returning cavalcade. At a turn of the road, near Halmanalco, a hamlet near the factory of Mira Flores, the advanced guard reported the enemy in force. After a moment's examination of the ground, it was determined to force a passage, sword in hand. The bugle sounded the charge. Lieutenant George W. Adde, Third dragoons, gallantly led the advance, but a portion of his men were thrown into disorder, and retreated. Rallied by the commander, Lieutenant Hamilton, they returned to the charge. The ranks of the enemy were broken. The impression made upon them being gallantly seconded by Lieutenant Lorimer Graham, they fled in disorder. After being engaged in personal conflict with several of the enemy, by whom, at one time, he was surrounded, the commander was fearfully wounded with a lance, which traversed his chest and lungs. He, however, was enabled to collect the wounded about him, after directing the pursuit of the enemy, and led them to the command under Colonel Hoffman, who mentions, 'When I directed Lieutenant Hamilton, whose conduct is spoken of in the highest terms, to be assisted, as he could with difficulty sustain himself on his horse, he gallantly said,' "Don't mind me, sir, but go to the assistance of my party."'

"To the fifty Americans were opposed some two hundred and fifty of the enemy, whose flag, bearing the device of a death's head and cross-bones, and the motto, 'No doy Quartel'—'*I give no quarter*,' was captured. The flag afterwards attracted much notice in the office of Mr. Marcy, Secretary of War. On a report, intended for the files of the War Department, Washington, General Scott indorsed: 'The within report, made by my desire (long after the event to which it refers), for the records of the War Department, modestly describes the conduct of the Commander (Brevet-captain Schuyler Hamilton) in an affair of great daring and brilliancy. It won for him, at the time, the esteem and admiration of the whole army.'"[1]

Without entering into the unfortunate dispute in which the General-in-chief and General Worth became involved, it may be remarked, that after the southern and western route had been examined by Colonel Duncan, under orders from General Worth, and after the report of that reconnoissance had been sent to head-quarters by the latter officer,—Captain Lee having, almost at the same moment, reported the impracticability of the route by way of Mexicalcingo, which he had before supposed to have been available for a movement on the north and east of Lake Chalco,—orders were issued, directing the advance by the opposite, or southern and western, route.[2]

In accordance with this new order of affairs, on the afternoon of the fifteenth, the army moved—Colonel Harney's brigade of cavalry and General Worth's division leading the column, followed by those under Generals Pillow and Quitman, and, on the next day, by that of General Twiggs.[3] The

[1] MS. Narrative to the Author. See also Capt. Hoffman's Report, Aug. 14, 1847; Gen. Scott's Dispatch, No. 32, Aug. 28, 1847; Ripley, ii. pp. 191–193.

[2] Gen. Scott's Dispatch, No. 31, Aug. 19, 1847; Mr. Trist to Mr. Buchanan, Aug. 22, 1847; Gen. Worth to Gen. Scott, Aug. 14, 1847; Gen. E. A. Hitchcock to the Author, July 18, 1860.—[3] Gen. Scott's Dispatch, No. 31, Aug. 19; Ripley, ii. p. 104; Semmes, pp. 370, 371.

latter, on the morning of the sixteenth, while moving from Ayotla, had been threatened by a large body of Mexican troops, under General Alvarez, posted near Oka Lake. The enemy was formed in order of battle, and evidently intended to fall on the American rear, to cut it off; but General Twiggs promptly formed in front of the Mexicans and moved forward. As the former approached, the latter retired; and after a brisk cannonade, in which several were killed and wounded, and a pursuit of two miles, the Americans resumed their march.[1]

On the night of the sixteenth, General Worth encamped at San Gregorio; General Pillow, at Tulancingo, some four miles in the rear of General Worth; and Generals Quitman and Twiggs, at Tetelco, three miles farther in the rear;[2] and, on the following day, after encountering many obstructions, which the enemy had thrown in the road,[3] General Worth occupied San Augustine, which had been selected as the base of the new line of operations.[4]

In the mean time, General Santa Anna had become fully acquainted with the purposes of General Scott; and he, also, had changed his plan of operations. Leaving El Peñon under the command of Generals Herrera and Leon,[5] he hastened to intercept the progress of the Americans on the southern and eastern sides of the lake; fixing his head-quarters at the hacienda of San Antonio, and laboring with great zeal to finish the several lines of defence in that vicinity.[6] On the morning of the eighteenth, the brigade of General Anaya left El Peñon, and took post at Churubusco; and on the nineteenth, the battalions of Victoria and Hidalgo were advanced to San Antonio;[7] while, at the same time, the "*Army of the North*"—the shattered fragments of the army which had met Generals Taylor and

[1] Gen. Twiggs to Capt. H. L. Scott, Aug. 16, 1847; Gen. Scott's Dispatch, No. 31, Aug. 19, 1847.

[2] "G. W. K." to the *N. O. Picayune*, Aug. 22, 1847; Semmes, pp. 373, 374.—[3] G. W. K. to *N. O. Picayune*, Aug. 22, 1847; Letter from Tacubaya to Washington *Union*, Aug. 22, 1847; Semmes, p. 374; Ripley, ii. p. 206.—[4] Mansfield, p. 409; Semmes, p. 375.

[5] Notes for the History, p. 256.—[6] Ripley, ii. p. 206.

[7] Notes for the History, p. 258.

Wool at Buena Vista—had occupied San Angel, under General Valencia.[1] Subsequently, General Valencia was ordered to fall back on Coyoacan, and to send his artillery to Churubusco, whence he might move to check the advance of the Americans, whether they moved by way of San Angel or San Antonio.[2]

While the enemy was thus arraying his forces for the defence of the capital, General Pillow advanced to San Augustine, and General Twiggs and Quitman approached it; and on the eighteenth, General Scott moved his head-quarters to the same town.[3] Immediately afterwards General Worth's division and Colonel Harney's cavalry were pushed forward, about a league, to reconnoitre,[4] when that gallant General seized on a hacienda named Coapa,—about fifteen hundred yards in front of San Antonio,—and established his head-quarters there.[5]

While this reconnoissance was being made, the enemy opened his fire on the covering party,—the first fire in the valley of Mexico,—and, by a singular coincidence, the first shot killed Captain Thornton, of the Second dragoons[6]—he who first felt the weight of the Mexican opposition in the valley of the Rio Grande.[7]

While the reconnoissance in front of San Antonio was progressing, others were made on the left of San Augustine, towards Contreras, under Major Smith, Captain Lee, and Lieutenants Beauregard and Tower; and on the nineteenth, Generals Pillow and Twiggs were thrown forward to open a road for heavy artillery.

At this time the main body of the American army was at San Augustine, north from which place, and in a direct line with the city of Mexico, was a large Pedregal, or field of lava—an impassable bed of volcanic matter, which extended, to the eastward, as far as the mountains. From this place, on either hand, extended a road—that on the

[1] Notes for the History, p. 267.—[2] Ibid., p. 272; Ripley, ii. p. 208.—[3] Gen. Scott's Dispatch, No. 31, Aug. 19; Ripley, ii. p. 210.—[4] Gen. Scott's Dispatch, No. 31, Aug. 19; Semmes, p. 377.—[5] Semmes, p. 377; Gen. Worth's Report, Aug. 28, 1847.—[6] Gen. Scott's Dispatch, No. 31, Aug. 19; Ripley, ii. pp. 210, 211.—[7] Vide Chap. XCIX.

left only to the edge of the Pedregal, whence, by a mere trail, it wound its way among the irregularities of that remarkable plain into the village of Contreras, near which it debouched into a well-beaten road, which, by way of San Angel, Coyoacan, and Churubusco, led to the city of Mexico.[1] On this road had been advanced the divisions of Generals Twiggs and Pillow, as already stated, for the purpose of opening a road towards the main road at Contreras.[2] To the *right* of San Augustine extended a causeway, by way of San Antonio and Churubusco,—where the road from Contreras, before referred to, united with it,—to the city of Mexico;[3] and, advanced on this road, to Cuapa, was the splendid division under General Worth.[4]

Opposed to these operations General Santa Anna had made a skilful disposition of his forces. On the heights of Contreras—or of Pelon Cuanlititla, as the Mexicans call them—were twenty-two pieces of artillery; supporting which, on the left, was the corps of San Luis de Potosi, and on the right were "the auxiliaries and the actives of Celaya, Guanjuato, and Querétaro, under Lieutenant-colonel Cabrera." A second line embraced the Tenth and Twelfth battalions, and those known as the "*Fijo of Mexico*," and the "*Costa Guarda of Tampico*." In front of this force, near the rancho of Padierna,—at the edge of the Pedregal,—were two regiments of infantry and one of cavalry; supporting the right of the position were the Seventh regiment of the line and that of San Luis; while, near Anzaldo, under General Salas, was the reserve, embracing the regiment of sappers, those known as the Mixto de Santa Anna and Aguascalientes, the Second, Third, and Eighth regiments of cavalry, and the active of Guanajuato. A heavy force was also stationed for the defence of San Antonio, and of the bridge of Churubusco, while General Santa Anna, with twelve thousand men, occupied the high ground between Anzaldo and San Angel.[1]

In the prosecution of his assigned duty,—that of opening the road,—General Pillow moved, on the morning of the nineteenth; and, notwithstanding the menaces of the enemy, he pushed forward into the mass of lava; but he was quickly opposed by the enemy's pickets and advanced parties, and he was compelled to throw forward the rifle regiment, commanded by Major Loring, to clear the ground, while the batteries under Captain Magruder and Lieutenant Callender were, soon afterwards, pushed forward and placed in position, within three hundred yards of the enemy's works.[2]

General Pillow—the senior in rank—had ordered General Twiggs, with his finely-disciplined division, to advance and give the enemy battle; and that veteran commander had pushed forward, in advance of the working parties, for that purpose. Ordering General Persifer F. Smith, with his brigade, to assault the front of the enemy's position, and Colonel Riley, with his brigade, by inclining to the right, to turn the enemy's left flank, and gain his rear, the General moved steadily onward in the execution of his orders. Colonel Riley's path was difficult and tedious,—having to "pass over volcanic rocks and crossing large fissures, barely narrow enough to permit the men to get over by leaping,"—besides which, he was opposed, first, by a large body of the enemy's lancers, who were driven back, and afterwards by two other bodies of Mexicans,—one of them ten or twelve thousand in number, on his rear; the other, two or three thousand in number, on his right flank,—both of which he withstood and held in check. General Twiggs immediately ordered General Smith to support Colonel Riley; while the brigades of Generals Pierce, Shields, and Cadwallader, and, subsequently, the Fifteenth infantry, under Col-

[1] Map of the Line of Operations, by Maj. Turnbull and the Engineers of the army.—[2] Gen. Scott's Dispatch, No. 31, Aug. 19, 1847; Gens. Twiggs and Smith's Report, Aug. 23, 1847.

[3] Map of the Line, &c.; Semmes, p. 377.

[4] Gen. Scott's Dispatch, No. 31, Aug. 19, 1847; Gen. Worth's Report, Aug. 23, 1847; Semmes, p. 377.

[1] Notes for the History, p. 273.

[2] Gen. Scott's Dispatch, No. 31, Aug. 19, 1847; Gen. Twiggs' Report, Aug. 23, 1847.

onel Morgan, were sent forward, for the same purpose, by General Scott.[1]

The battle raged furiously, and for more than three hours the entire force was under a heavy fire of artillery and musketry along the almost impassable ravine in front and on the right of the Mexican position. Night at length put an end to the conflict; and a cold rain which, soon afterwards, began to fall in torrents upon the unsheltered and unfed troops, rendered their repose, during the night, an unsatisfactory one, notwithstanding the village of Anzaldo was occupied by the American forces.[2]

At this time the relative positions of the two armies were as follows:—On the extreme right of the Mexican lines—on the heights of Contreras—was General Valencia and the troops composing "the army of the North," as before described. On his left flank, separating him from the great body of the Mexican army, under General Santa Anna, were the brigades of Generals Smith, Cadwallader, and Riley. On his front were General Pierce's brigade and the American light batteries; and still farther in front, at the foot of the hill of Zacatepec, was the cavalry under Colonel Harney. General Santa Anna still occupied the high ground in the vicinity of Anzaldo,—the hill of the Olivar of the Carmelites,—with his reserve, and Churubusco. General Quitman, with the remainder of his division, was held in reserve at San Augustine; and General Worth, with his division, was on the extreme right of the American line at San Antonio.

As will be seen, the American troops at Anzaldo were detached from the main body, and were between the enemy's main body, under General Santa Anna, in their rear, and his veteran "*Army of the North*," under General Valencia, on their front; and it was well considered, both by General Scott and by themselves, a position of great hazard. They had in their front and on their left flank, eighteen thousand Mexicans, with between twenty-five and thirty guns. Among the troops, six or seven thousand were cavalry. They were, at most, three thousand three hundred strong, without cavalry or artillery; and as it was evident that they could maintain their position only by the most prompt and energetic measures, General Smith—to whom the command was given by his associates, in command of other brigades—decided to assault the heights of Contreras during the night.[1]

As a preliminary to this movement, Captain Lee was sent to General Scott to inform him of the position of the troops, and of the purpose of General Smith, with a request that the former would favor the attack with any movement which he might consider expedient; and, at about the same time, General Shields, with the New York and South Carolina Volunteers,—who had been sent by General Scott, while the action was still pending, during the afternoon, to strengthen the Americans who were in action,—arrived in the village, and reported to General Smith.[2]

After ordering General Shields to hold Anzaldo, "and cut off the retreat of the troops from Contreras (*General Valencia's*) or take his large reserve (*General Santa Anna*) in flank, if it changed front to the right to attack him," General Smith, at precisely three o'clock in the morning, moved against the enemy's intrenched camp on the heights of Contreras. The men had laid in the mud, exposed to a pelting rain, without fire, all night, and were suffering from cold; and as they groped their way, unable to see any object which might be six feet from them,—the several files keeping within touch of each other, to prevent the rear from going astray,—the duty of surprising the enemy's lines appeared to be a hopeless one. Lieutenant Tower, of the Engineers, led the column, where Colonel Riley's brigade had been placed; Lieutenants Brooks and Beauregard, also of the Engineers, led General Cadwallader's brigade, which formed the centre of the column of attack; and Lieutenant G. W. Smith led General Smith's

[1] Gen. Scott's Dispatch, No. 31, Aug. 19; Gen. Pillow's Report, Aug. 24; Gen. Twiggs' Report, Aug. 23.

[2] Gen. Scott's Dispatch, No. 31, Aug. 19; Gen. Twiggs' Report, Aug. 23.

[1] Gen. Smith's Report, Aug. 23; Ripley, ii. p. 236.

[2] Gen. Shields' Report, Aug. 24; Ripley, ii. p. 241.

brigade, commanded by Major Dimmick, which brought up the rear. The narrow path, obstructed by rocks and mud, afforded but a sorry route for the long line of assailants; and it was full daylight when Colonel Riley—at a sufficient distance up the ravine, along which the troops had filed, to turn the enemy's position—had formed his brigade into two columns, and prepared for the desperate charge. Advancing but little farther up the ravine, he turned to his left and mounted the high bank of the mountain-stream which runs at the bottom of the gully, and stood fronting the rear of the work, but somewhat sheltered by a high ground in his front. Here he reformed his ranks, and ascended the slope which commanded the enemy's intrenchments, when the Mexicans opened a heavy fire, not only from their works in front, but from a covering party on his right flank. With as little delay as possible, therefore, Colonel Riley threw out his first two divisions as skirmishers; and, after a single noisy fire, and a shout, with his entire strength, he rushed down the slope to the works which were occupied by the enemy. General Cadwallader followed closely after Colonel Riley, and, as fast as his men came up, he formed his columns and pushed forward for the support of the leading brigade; while Major Dimmick, with General Smith's brigade, was directed into a foot-path on his left, and moving along that to the heights, attacked a large body of Mexicans which was posted on the north side of the intrenchments, just as Colonel Riley's brigade was pouring into the works themselves.[1]

Thus suddenly assailed, both in front and rear, by an enemy whom they supposed to be still in the hamlet of Anzaldo and its neighborhood, the Mexicans appeared to have been seized with the most unaccountable terror, and, led by their General (*Valencia*), they fled in the wildest disorder. Colonel Riley quickly cleared the work, and planted his regimental colors on it; and, strange to say, the first pieces of artillery which fell into the hands of the victors—among whom was the Fourth artillery—were the two guns which were lost by Lieutenant O'Brian, of that regiment, with so much honor, at Buena Vista.[1]

The fugitives, harassed by Colonel Ransom,—who, with the Ninth and Twelfth infantry, had occupied a position at the edge of the Pedregal,—broke and fled in all directions. The greater part of them, however, fled down the road towards San Angel, and were intercepted by Major Dimmick, with General Smith's brigade, and were roughly handled; while those who passed through this second ordeal were again intercepted by General Shields, who, with his brigade, had moved from Anzaldo for that purpose. Here they threw down their arms; and, after the series of disasters, in the North and in the centre, the celebrated "*Army of the North*" ceased to exist. Near two thousand of its number, it is said, fell on this eventful morning; Generals Valencia and Torrejon fled, and were lost to their country; and Generals Salas, Blanco, Garcia, and Mendoza, eighty-four other officers, and seven hundred and twenty-five privates, several stands of colors, twenty-two pieces of brass artillery, the military chest, thousands of small arms and accoutrements, an immense quantity of shot, shells, powder, and cartridges, seven hundred pack-mules, a number of horses, &c., were among the trophies of the victors. Not more than sixty were killed or wounded in this gallant exploit.[2]

Leaving a small force to guard the captured ordnance, General Smith prepared to press forward after the fugitives; and was forming his men, when General Twiggs came on the heights and assumed the command. Under this veteran's directions, therefore, the victors of Contreras moved forward; and as he advanced towards San Angel, General Santa Anna broke up his encampment and fell back on his works at

[1] Gen. Smith's Report, Aug. 23; Col. Riley's Report, Aug. 24; Gen. Cadwallader's Report, Aug. 22; Maj. Dimmick's Report, Aug. 23.

[1] Gen. Scott's Dispatch, No. 32, Aug. 28; Gen. Smith's Report, Aug. 23; Col. Riley's Report, Aug. 24.

[2] Gen. Scott's Dispatch, No. 32, Aug. 28; Gen. Shield's Report, Aug. 24.

Painted by Chappel

Engraved by Phillibrown.

BATTLE OF CHURUBUSCO . . CAPTURE OF THE *TÊTE DE PONT.*

From the original picture in the possession of the Publishers.

Churubusco, with the Americans at his heels.[1]

While these important operations were going on at Contreras, General Scott—to whom the purpose of General Smith was known—had ordered General Pillow to go over to the scene of action and take the command; while General Worth was ordered to move from Cuapa with one of his brigades, and General Quitman, with his division, from San Augustine, both for the purpose of supporting the assault. When General Pillow had reached the hill of Zacatepec he was informed of the result of the engagement; and, after sending word back to General Scott,—who, in turn, ordered Generals Worth and Quitman to resume their former positions,—General Pillow pushed forward, and, at San Angel, he came up with the victorious columns and assumed the chief command.[2]

The design of General Pillow was to push around the Pedregal, and by way of Ayoacan, to turn the Mexican position of San Antonio, advancing against that post in reserve; but General Scott, after sending orders for a halt, joined the columns at the former place, and ordered Captain Lee to reconnoitre San Antonio, and Lieutenant Stevens to reconnoitre the fortified convent of San Pablo, near the bridge of Churubusco. Immediately afterwards General Pillow, with General Cadwallader's brigade, was ordered to move against the rear of San Antonio; General Twiggs, with General Smith's and Colonel Riley's brigades, against the convent of San Pablo; General Pierce, with his brigade, farther to the left, also against the convent, and to cut off the enemy's retreat to the capital; and General Shields, with his command,—the New York and South Carolina Volunteers,—to support General Pierce and take command of the left wing; and "the battle now raged from the right to the left of our whole line."[3]

[1] Gen. Smith's Report, Aug. 23; Gen. Twiggs' Report, Aug. 23.—[2] Gen. Scott's Dispatch, No. 32, Aug. 28; Gen. Pillow's Report, Aug. 24; Gen. Worth's Report, Aug. 23.

[3] Gen. Scott's Dispatch, No. 32, Aug. 28; Gen. Pillow's Report, Aug. 24; Gen. Twigg's Report, Aug. 23; Gen. Shield's Report, Aug. 24.

In the mean time, General Worth, by a series of skilful and daring movements upon the front and right of the position, had turned and forced San Antonio—its garrison being either driven to Dolores or joining the great body of the enemy, concentrated at Churubusco.[1]

Having thus secured the post of San Antonio, and opened another road to the city of Mexico, without the aid of General Pillow, General Worth pressed, by way of the causeway, towards Churubusco. On his approach the head of his column was received with a heavy discharge of artillery, by the Mexicans, and "*The Battle of Churubusco*" commenced.[2]

The positions of the respective armies, at this time, may be thus defined. The hamlet of Churubusco, which is intersected by the causeway which leads from San Antonio to the city of Mexico, is composed of a small cluster of adobe houses, and the massive stone convent and church, known as San Pablo, and it is situated on the south bank of the Rio de Churubusco, over which the great road is carried on a fine stone bridge. This bridge is defended by a field-work, known as a *tête-de-pont;* and it had been constructed with great care, with bastions, curtains, and a wet ditch—four guns, two in front and two on the left flank, having been placed in battery for its defence. The convent of San Pablo was a strong stone edifice, and had been strengthened with two walls, one within the other, and of great strength. The outer wall was a regular field-work, pierced with embrasures, and defended with five guns, although it was still incomplete. In these two works, behind the Rio de Churubusco,—sheltered by its high banks, on the causeway still nearer to the capital, or within supporting distance of some portion of the works,—were not only the reserve of the army, under General Santa Anna; the garrisons of San Antonio, El Peñon, and Mexicalcingo, the fragments from Contreras; and the floating forces of the

[1] Gen. Scott's Dispatch, No. 32, Aug. 28; Gen. Worth's Report, Aug. 23; Semmes, pp. 393–395; Ripley, ii. pp. 252–255.—[2] Gen. Scott's Dispatch, No. 32, Aug. 28; Gen. Worth's Report, Aug. 23; Semmes, p. 398.

National Guard; but the reserves from the city of Mexico—not less than from twenty-seven to thirty thousand in the aggregate. In the convent were Generals Rincon and Anaya, with the National Guard, the Independencia, and the Bravos. In the bridge-head were the battalions of San Patricio and of Tlapa, to which was subsequently added the First light battalion. On the left of the bridge were posted the Third, Fourth, and Eleventh battalions; while under cover of the northern bank or levee of the Rio de Churubusco, was the main body of the army of Mexico.[1]

In front of the *tête-de-pont* were Generals Worth and Pillow, with the First division and General Cadwallader's brigade; in front, or on the right flank of the convent, were General Twiggs, with his division, General Pierce, with his brigade, and General Shields, with his brigade; and at San Augustin,—far in the rear,—was General Quitman, keeping guard over the trains.

When General Worth had come within gunshot of the *tête-de-pont*, Colonel Garland, with his brigade, was thrown out to the right of, and in line of columns obliquely to, the causeway, the light battalion, under Colonel Smith, covering his right; the Second brigade, except the Sixth infantry, was also ordered to move to the right, and by a flank parallel with the causeway; and the Sixth infantry, in front, moved steadily along the causeway, for the purpose of storming the *tête-de-pont* in front. Colonels Garland and Clarke, with their brigades, moved through fields of standing corn, suffering very severely in their march; and Lieutenant-colonel Duncan's noble battery, in consequence of the difficulties of the march, was withdrawn and held in reserve.

It was not long before the Mexican flanking parties, on the left of the bridge,—the Third, Fourth, and Eleventh battalions,—fell back to and strengthened the bridge-head; and General Worth's command was quickly engaged with them. The fire of the enemy was very warm, and the Sixth infantry was momentarily checked in its advance upon the *tête-de-pont;* but the other regiments of Colonel Clarke's brigade—the Fifth and Eighth infantry—"more favorably situated to effect results, but under a terrible fire, dashed past the deep and wet ditch that entirely surrounded the work, *carried it by the bayonet*, and as quick as thought, turned the captured cannon upon that portion of enemy stationed in the town, and which was combating our troops approaching from the direction of Contreras, occasionally reversing their fire upon our left flank." When it is remembered that this bridge-head was the key of the position; that the loss of it dispirited the masses of the Mexicans, and filled their officers with "horror;" and that it was captured by the Americans, at the point of the bayonet, with only two regiments, the character of the exploit will be fully understood.[1]

While Generals Worth and Pillow were thus employed, at the *tête-de-pont*, General Twiggs was engaged with the convent, and Generals Shields and Pierce with the reserves on the opposite bank of the river. The former had suffered very severely, when the loss of the bridge-head enabled Captain Smith and Lieutenant Snelling, of the Eighth infantry, to turn one of its guns on the convent, with great success; and General Worth to bring up Lieutenant-colonel Duncan's battery, with his usual effect, forcing the enemy to hasten his desire for quarters by surrendering his post.[2]

General Shields having suffered very severely, the Rifles (General Twiggs' reserve) and Captain Sibley's troops of the Second dragoons, had been sent by General Scott to reinforce him. Having four thousand Mexican infantry and three thousand cavalry as its opponents, this small party—embracing the fragments of the Ninth, Twelfth, and Fifteenth regiments of infantry, the New York and South Carolina regiments of Volunteers, and the mountain-howitzer battery, under Lieutenant Reno—had been most se-

[1] Semmes, pp. 396, 397; Ripley, ii. pp. 255–257.

[1] Gen. Scott's Dispatch, No. 32, Aug. 28; Gen. Worth's Report, Aug. 23; Semmes, pp. 399, 400; Ripley, ii. pp. 267–273.—[2] Gen. Scott's Dispatch, No. 32, Aug. 28; Gen. Worth's Report, Aug. 23; Gen. Twiggs' Report, Aug. 23; Gen. Shields' Report, Aug. 24.

verely handled; and the battle was long, hot, and varied. When the *tête-de-pont* had been taken, however, and the enemy's main body had given way, victory crowned its labors, and its shattered platoons joined with the gallant Worth in his pursuit of the fugitives towards the gates of Mexico.[1]

Thus ended the operations of this eventful day. *Five several actions had been fought and won*, and the American troops, surfeited with victory, sought repose. Thirty-two thousand men had been met and defeated; three thousand prisoners had been taken—eight of the number being generals and two hundred and five other officers; about four thousand had been killed or wounded—besides whole armies dissolved and dispersed; thirty-seven pieces of artillery had also been taken, with large numbers of small arms, a full supply of ammunition of every kind, &c., &c.[2]

Of the American army, sixteen officers and one hundred and twenty-three men had been *killed*, and sixty officers and eight hundred and sixteen men *wounded*. Of the Mexicans, it is said that upwards of four thousand men were killed or wounded, three thousand more were prisoners, and six thousand one hundred and fifty were "missing."[3]

On the day after the battle (*August* 21) the army moved to Tacubaya, whence advances were made by General Scott for a suspension of hostilities;[4] both he and Mr. Trist—the latter a civil officer, who had been sent out to Mexico as a floating, contingent representative of the Federal government, to catch and preserve the first symptoms of a desire for peace which the enemy might manifest—having been beguiled into the error of desiring such an armistice, under a profession of a desire for peace, which was conveyed to them by several "*intelligent neutrals*," who were tools of General Santa Anna, and who favored the desire of that wily but talented officer "to give his troops *rest*, re-establish their *morale*, and enable him to collect the dispersed, and adopt other measures to insure a reaction."[1]

Strange as it may appear the victorious march of the army of the United States—before whom no serious obstacle was interposed to prevent its triumphant entry into the city of Mexico—was arrested by its own General-in-chief, at the instance of known instruments of the enemy; and that General, at the head of his veteran and victorious troops, became a suppliant for peace. The differences between the two belligerent nations—with the evident hope of conciliating the prostrate enemy and of favoring the suit of the suppliant victor—were declared by General Scott to be "*unnatural;*" and, in his "impatience" for peace, regardless of the declarations of his country, through her official authorities, at every period of the war, he acquiesced in the declaration of the enemy that the shedding of blood in this war was "in consequence of the disregard of the rights of the Mexican republic" by the United States.

Desiring only to secure the repose which his armies required, and the opportunity for repairing the mischief, among the people, which the disasters of the preceding day had produced, General Santa Anna *assented* to the armistice, and nominally observed it during a very short period. A series of infractions, on the part of the enemy, however, soon led General Scott to declare this armistice at an end, and at noon, on the seventh of September, hostilities were renewed.[2]

About the same time information was received that the enemy was busily employed in the manufacture of cannon at a foundry which was said to have been within the King's Mill (*Molino del Rey*), and the bells of the churches within the city, it was also said, had been taken to supply the material for that purpose. This foundry—if such an establishment existed—was covered by the batteries at Chapultepec, and was not more than three-quarters of a mile from the Bishop's Palace, at Tacubaya, where General Scott had taken

1 Gen. Scott's Dispatch, No. 32, Aug. 28; Gen. Worth's Report, Aug. 23; Gen. Shields' Report, Aug. 24.

2 Gen. Scott's Dispatch, No. 32, Aug. 28; Ripley, ii. pp. 282, 283.—3 Gen. Scott's Dispatch, No. 32, Aug. 28.

4 Gen. Scott to Gen. Santa Anna, Aug. 21, 1847.

1 Gen. Santa Anna, cited by Semmes, p. 423.

2 Gen. Scott to Gen. Santa Anna, Sept. 6, 1847.

up his quarters. Proceeding to the top of the building, the General was no longer in doubt on the subject of the communication —as from the spot where he then stood, even to the naked eye the evidence of there being some kind of a furnace in the "Mill," was distinctly visible in the bright red flame which rose above its roof. This was regarded by General Scott as a full confirmation of what he had heard. After looking some little time towards the "Mill," he stepped down upon a sort of *banqueta*, on which he had been standing, and, as he folded up his glass, he remarked, "*I must destroy that place.*"[1]

In accordance with this determination, General Worth was ordered to hold himself in readiness with the division under his command; and as the enemy was covering the position with a heavy force, at General Worth's request, a strong reinforcement—embracing three squadrons of dragoons and one company of mounted riflemen, under Major Sumner; a battery of three field-pieces, under Captain Drum; two twenty-four-pound battering-guns, under Captain Huger; and the regiment of Voltigeurs, and the Eleventh and Fourteenth regiments of infantry, under General Cadwallader—was added to the attacking force.[2]

The King's Mill is a long range of stone buildings, which forms the western front of the inclosure, within which are the groves, rocks, and castle of Chapultepec; and, as before stated, they are covered by the batteries of the latter. This range is some fifteen hundred feet in length; and it is subdivided into various subdivisions, among which are a flour-mill and the old powder-mill, from which it derives its name. Nearly five hundred yards distant from the northern extremity of the Mills is another strong stone building,—which, at the period in question, had been very carefully strengthened,—originally designed for a storehouse, or magazine for the gunpowder manufactured at Molino del Rey, and known as the *Casa Mata*. Westward from the Casa Mata, about three hundred yards distant, is a ravine of considerable depth and width, beyond which is the hacienda of Morales. This range of ground—from the King's Mill, on the left, to the high ground west from the ravine, on the right—was the position occupied by the Mexican forces.[1]

[1] Gen. Hitchcock's MS. Reminiscences, folio 93. See also Ripley, ii. pp. 357, 358. It is proper to remark that some have denied that there was any evidence, whatever, of the existence of a foundry at that place.

[2] Gen. Worth's Report, Sept. 10.

In the Mills, on the extreme left of their line, were the National Guards of Liberty, Union, Querétaro, and Mina, under General Leon, and the brigade of troops commanded by General Rangel; between the Mills and the Casa Mata were the Second light battalion, that of the Fijo de Mejico, and the First and Second regiments of the line, with six pieces of artillery, under General Ramirez; in the Casa Mata were the Fourth light battalion and the Eleventh regiment of the line, under General Perez; in the grove of Chapultepec, in the rear of the Mills, as a reserve, were the First and Third light battalions; and west of the ravine, towards Morales, were four thousand cavalry. General Santa Anna was confident of victory; and his troops were equally sanguine of success. During the night of the seventh some slight alterations were made in this arrangement, it is said, but the strength remained about the same.[2]

Against this force, at three o'clock in the morning of the eighth, General Worth moved with the troops under his command. Colonel Garland's brigade (*the First*), with two field-pieces, moved against the extreme left of the Mills; on his left were Captain Huger, with two heavy guns, and Major Wright, with a storming party of five hundred picked men, moving against the centre of the Mills; the Second brigade, under Colonel McIntosh, and Duncan's battery, in the rear of the storming party, also moved against the enemy's centre — the space between the Mills and the Casa Mata; General Cadwallader's brigade was left in reserve, in the rear of the line; and the cavalry, under Major Sumner, was posted on

[1] Ripley, ii. pp. 359–361; Semmes, p. 436; Notes for the History, pp. 333–335.

[2] Notes for the History, pp. 335, 336.

BATTLE OF MOLINO DEL RAY.

From the original Painting by Chappel in the possession of the Publishers

the extreme left, to act as circumstances might require.[1]

The action commenced with the heavy guns, under Captain Huger, which opened a fire on the Mills; and it was thus continued until this point of the enemy's line became sensibly shaken, when Major Wright dashed forward, with the storming party, at a charge. The Mexican artillery,—which had taken a position on the flank of the column,—and the infantry on the flat roof of the Mills, also in flank, as well as in front, threw in a terrible fire on the little party, killing or wounding eleven out of fourteen officers who were with it, and scattering destruction among the gallant party of which it was composed. With an almost unparalleled degree of bravery, however, it kept its face to the enemy, driving him from his guns; and the light battalion (*C. F. Smith's*) and the right wing of General Cadwallader's division moving forward to the support of the storming party, the triumph of the latter was established, and that portion of the enemy's line was occupied by the assailants.[2]

While the centre of the American line was thus adding fresh laurels to the trophies of the army in Mexico, Colonel Garland and the First brigade on the right were gallantly seconding it. In conjunction with Captain Drum's battery, they also drove the enemy from his position, and occupied it, notwithstanding the guns of Chapultepec were immediately over them.[3]

On the left, Colonel McIntosh led his brigade gallantly up to the Casa Mata, under a most murderous fire from that work; and, at one time, it was compelled to fall back on Duncan's battery for support; when that noble officer and his unsurpassed command opened their fire, scattering the heavy columns of Mexicans which were moving down to support those who were engaged, and, finally, compelling the occupants of Casa Mata to retire from the work, when the entire line of the enemy's position was at the will of the victors.[1]

After blowing up the Casa Mata, and destroying the moulds and other property in the Mills, the assailants returned to Tacubaya, carrying with them three of the enemy's guns, large quantities of small arms and ammunition, and eight hundred prisoners.[2]

In this sanguinary conflict—the bloodiest of the war—the enemy numbered upwards of fourteen thousand men, under General Santa Anna in person; the Americans, all told, numbered only three thousand one hundred. The loss of the former was Generals Valdarez and Leon, and upwards of three thousand men; that of the latter was Lieutenant-colonel Scott, Major Graham, Captains Merrill and Ayres, Lieutenants Johnston, Armstrong, Strong, Burwell, and Farry, *killed*, forty-nine officers *wounded*, and seven hundred and twenty-nine men *killed* and *wounded*.[3]

It will thus be seen that, "with three thousand one hundred men, General Worth advanced against a position selected by the enemy, commanded by the fortress of Chapultepec, defended by twelve thousand troops, protected behind stone walls and ditches, the ground swept by artillery, on a dead level with the American line, and threatened with a charge of four thousand cavalry. It was the most decisive victory ever gained in Mexico, or on the continent of America; but it is a picture too blood-stained for any portion of the American army or people yet to look upon, except in grief and sorrow."[4]

Immediately after the close of the engagement such articles as served for the purposes of a foundry were broken up, and the gunpowder which was in the Casa Mata was either carried away or destroyed;[5] when,

[1] Gen. Worth's Report, Sept. 10; Reports of Garland, Huger, Duncan, McIntosh, Drum, Cadwallader, and Wright.—[2] Gen. Worth's Report, Sept. 10; Reports of Capt. Huger, Maj. Wright, Gen. Cadwallader, Maj. Hunter, and Capt. Reeve.—[3] Gen. Worth's Report, Sept. 10; Reports of Col. Garland, Capts. Drum, McKenzie, and Burke, Maj. Lee, Lieut.-Col. Belton, and Col. Andrews.

[1] Gen. Worth's Report, Sept. 10; Reports of Col. McIntosh, Capt. Chapman, Maj. Bonneville, Capt. Hoffman, and Maj. Montgomery.—[2] Gen. Worth's Report, Sept. 10.

[3] Ibid.; Report of casualties, &c., appended to the latter report.—[4] Col. Ramsay, 11th infantry, U. S. A.

[5] Gen. Worth's Report, Sept. 10; Ripley, ii. pp. 378–380.

having collected his killed and wounded, and the trophies of his victory, General Worth then returned to Tacubaya, in accordance with the commands of the General-in-chief.[1]

During the afternoon of the eighth, and on the ninth and tenth of September, Captain Lee and his associates, of the Engineers, made daring reconnoissances, which were directed mainly against the gates of Piedad, San Angel, San Antonio, and the Paseo de la Viga; and on the eleventh General Scott "determined to avoid the network of obstacles" which the southern front of the city presented, and to turn his attention against the southwestern and western fronts, where less difficulties intervened. For this purpose measures were taken to deceive the enemy; and while Generals Pillow and Quitman were ordered to move, *by daylight*, towards the southern gates of the city, they were ordered, at the same time, to return to Tacubaya *by night*—leaving General Twiggs, with Colonel Riley's brigade and two batteries, "in front of those gates to manœuvre, to threaten, or to make false attacks, in order to occupy and deceive the enemy;" while General Smith's brigade was at supporting distance in the rear, covering, at the same time, the general depot at Mixcoac.[2]

During the eleventh, twelfth, and part of the thirteenth, the masking operations of the army were continued; while, during the night of the eleventh, four heavy batteries were in course of construction; and, on the following morning, they opened their fire on the castle of Chapultepec. With the demonstrations, under General Twiggs, before the gates of the city, on the one hand; and the cannonade of the castle on the other, many of the Mexicans were entirely deceived respecting the purposes of the assailants. It was not so, however, with the able General-in-chief of the Mexican army; and while he exercised proper care of that portion of his lines in front of General Twiggs, he carefully concentrated his strength in front of General Scott.

[1] Gen. Worth's Report, Sept. 10; Semmes, pp. 442, 443; Ripley, ii. p. 380.—[2] Gen. Scott's Dispatch, No. 34, Sept. 18; Ripley, ii. pp. 391, 392.

The fire continued steadily until evening; while the most active preparations were made for assaulting the works, by the collection of ladders, fascines, and other materiel necessary for that purpose. The divisions of Generals Pillow and Quitman having been in position since the preceding evening, General Worth was ordered to hold his division in readiness near El Molino del Rey, to support General Pillow; and General Smith, with the brigade under his command,—the heroes of Contreras,—was moved from Piedad to support General Quitman; the former, at the same time, supplying a storming party of two hundred and fifty men, under Captain McKenzie, to lead General Pillow's column; while the latter supplied a similar party, under Captain Casey, to the column under General Quitman.[1]

The castle and rock of Chapultepec—the objects of the intended attack—are at the head of one of the causeways which extend across the marsh by which the city of Mexico is surrounded, and within range of the American artillery at Tacubaya. The rock rises abruptly from the level "valley of Mexico" to the height of a hundred and fifty feet; and while its western and southwestern fronts—towards the Molino del Rey and Tacubaya—although "savagely rugged and precipitous," were yet practicable for infantry, the northern, eastern, and southeastern fronts were so precipitous as to be inaccessible. On the summit of this precipice is the "castle," surrounded by defensive works—the northern front being defended by a parapet wall of heavy masonry, with a semicircular bastion, on which were mounted several pieces of artillery; the eastern front had no defensive work, the perpendicular rock in its front rendering such a defence unnecessary; on the southern front a parapet, with bastions, was presented to the assailants; and on the narrow western front, besides the parapet, it was also defended with a ditch. Within this line of defences was the "castle,"—a strong stone building, used as a military college, the West Point

[1] Gen. Scott's Dispatch, No. 34, Sept. 18; Reports of Gens. Pillow, Smith, and Quitman.

of Mexico,—which had been strengthened with great care; and supplied with sand-bags on its *azotea*, for the purpose of enabling its garrison to defend itself with musketry, as a last resort.[1]

Eleven pieces of artillery and a strong garrison, under Generals Bravo, Monterde, Norrega, Dosamantes, and Perez, defended these works; besides which, the declivity of the rock, on its southern and western fronts, was abundantly protected with breastworks, redans, mines, &c., where also were large bodies of troops under Generals Barragan and Rangel.[2]

At about eight o'clock in the morning of the thirteenth, notice was given to both Generals Quitman and Pillow that the signal for the attack was about to be given, and both columns "pressed forward with an alacrity which gave assurance of prompt success"—General Pillow moving against the western front of the rock, and General Quitman on its southern and southeastern front.[3]

The former having thrown forward eight companies of Voltigeurs, under Colonel Andrews and Lieutenant-colonel Johnstone, and Lieutenant Reno, with the mountain howitzer-battery, for the purpose of brushing the enemy's light troops from the grove which is at the foot of the rock of Chapultepec, he followed closely after them with Captain McKenzie's storming party, and the Ninth and Fifteenth regiments of infantry, as a support, and by the Fifth, Sixth, and Eighth regiments of infantry, which General Worth had detached as a cover to the column of assault. At the same time the Eleventh and Fourteenth regiments of infantry, under Colonel Trousdale, and one section of Captain Magruder's battery, under Lieutenant Jackson, were posted on the road leading to the left of Chapultepec,—near the northwestern angle of El Molino del Rey,—for the purpose of observing General Alvarez, who had moved from Morales towards Chapultepec with a heavy body of cavalry, and General Barragan, who was posted on the road which leads to the north from Chapultepec, to hold them in check; and to give battle in case a movement should be made to throw in succors to the garrison.[1]

The grove was quickly cleared; and the storming party under Captain McKenzie, the Voltigeurs, and the infantry,—forlorn-hope, light-infantry, and supporting party,—apparently intermingled, pushed forward up the rugged slope, "over rocks, chasms, and mines, and under the hottest fire of cannon and musketry." Their progress was necessarily slow; and the officers cheered on their men, as they approached one of the advanced redoubts, while the Mexicans who occupied it were brushed away by the ascending column in its steady progress towards the crest of the hill. As the assailants approached the summit the artillery on the parapet of the castle, and the infantry on the roof of the buildings, hurled destruction into their ranks. The storming party, however, is said to have been left behind in the general rush; and these, inspirited by the example of their supporting parties, had thrown down the scaling-ladders on the slope and hastened after those who had passed them in the race for glory. The delay which was occasioned by this circumstance afforded the enemy an opportunity to commit serious havoc in the exposed ranks of the assailants; while it also afforded an opportunity for portions of the reserve, which General Worth had ordered to the support of the assaulting column, together with a detachment of fifty men from the New York Volunteers, under Captain Samuel S. Gallagher, and a company of marines,—both belonging to General Quitman's command,—to join the column and participate in the honors and dangers of the assault.[2]

[1] Ripley, ii. pp. 398–400; Semmes, p. 450; Mansfield's Scott, pp. 446, 447.

[2] Notes for the History, pp. 355, 356.

[3] Gen. Scott's Dispatch, No. 34, Sept. 18; Reports of Gens. Pillow and Quitman.

[1] Reports of Gen. Pillow, Col. Andrews, Lieut.-Col. Johnstone, Capt. McKenzie, Maj. Seymour, Lieut.-Col. Howard, Capt. Chapman, Majs. Bonneville and Montgomery, Col. Trousdale, Lieut.-Col. Hebert, and Capt. Magruder.

[2] Gen. Scott's Dispatch, No. 34, Sept. 18; Reports of Gen. Pillow, Capt. McKenzie, Col. Andrews, Lieut.-Col. Johnstone, and Gens. Quitman and Shields.

At length the ladders were brought up, and some of all parties dashed forward to scale the walls of the fortress. Lieutenant Selden is said to have been the first to mount the parapet, but with a few soldiers who immediately followed him, he was stricken down. Captain Howard, of the Voltigeurs, and Lieutenant Mayne Reid, of the New York Volunteers, each with the colors of his regiment, were among the first who succeeded in establishing their foothold; and it is claimed by each that his colors first bowed the tricolor of Mexico into retirement, as one was raised and the other lowered from the flag-staff of Chapultepec.[1]

While part of the Voltigeurs were thus struggling with their fellows for the honors, as well as the rewards of victory, on the western front, Lieutenant-colonel Johnstone led another portion around the southern front of the castle, expelled the Mexicans who opposed him, and cleared the lower works, in that direction, of the enemy who occupied them.[2]

In the mean time the second column of assault, under General Quitman, was actively employed. After adding a select party to the original storming-party, and ordering General Smith, with his covering brigade, to move on the right flank of the column of assault, the order to advance was given. With great enthusiasm this order was obeyed in the face of a terribly destructive cross-fire from the castle and from a battery on the Tacubaya road; and the column sought shelter under cover of some old buildings and of the low meadow which extended on the flank of its line of march.[3]

At this time General Shields, with the New York and South Carolina regiments, was directed to move obliquely to the left, towards the castle; and it was while thus employed that Lieutenant-colonel Charles Baxter and Captain Van O'Linda, of the New York Volunteers, fell at the head of their respective commands.[4]

As the assailants approached the works the covering brigade drove back the light troops of the enemy; while Lieutenant Hunt, with a section of Captain Duncan's battery, having obtained a commanding position in the rear of the storming parties, "threw shells and shrapnell-shot into the works with good effect;" and a short struggle ensued in this part of the field. Part of this division, as already seen, by moving farther to the left, was enabled to unite with General Pillow's command and to be among the first of those who entered the castle—the early display of the colors of the New York regiment on the castle, and the surrender of General Bravo, the commander of the castle, to Lieutenant Charles Brower, of the same regiment, showing, conclusively, the activity, no less than the bravery, of that portion of General Quitman's command. At the same time the batteries on the Tacubaya road were stormed and carried, after desperate opposition, by other portions of the division.[1]

While the divisions of Generals Quitman and Pillow were thus engaged, the single brigade commanded by Colonel Garland, the light battalion, under Lieutenant-colonel Smith, Captain Duncan's light battery, and three squadrons of dragoons, under Major Sumner—the whole under General Worth, were directed "to turn Chapultepec and proceed cautiously by the road at its northern base, in order, if not met by very superior numbers, to threaten or to attack in rear," a large body of troops which had been sent out from the city, and which had formed with their right on the Tacubaya road, threatening General Quitman's flank. In accordance with this order, they were put in motion around the northeastern base of the hill of Chapultepec, and moved, in operation, upon the San Cosmé causeway and aqueduct—one of the routes to the city from the rock of Chapultepec.[2]

In the execution of this order, General Worth soon came to and assisted in the cap-

---

[1] Reports of Gens. Pillow, Quitman, and Shields, and Col. Andrews.—[2] Reports of Gen. Pillow and Lieut.-Col. Johnstone.—[3] Gen. Scott's Dispatch, No. 34, Sept. 18; Reports of Gens. Quitman, Smith, and Shields.—[4] Reports of Gens. Quitman and Shields; Ripley, ii. p. 425.

[1] Reports of Gens. Quitman and Smith, and Lieut. Hunt; Ripley, ii. pp. 424–427.

[2] Gen. Scott's Dispatch, No. 34, Sept. 18; Reports of Gen. Worth, Cols. Garland, Trousdale, and Duncan, and Maj. Sumner.

ture of the battery before which General Quitman's column had battled with such heavy loss; and he also fell on the right of the enemy's line, where the reinforcements from the city were opposing the progress of General Quitman, scattering that body also, and greatly facilitating the operations of the day.[1]

After the capture of the castle, both General Worth and General Quitman pressed forward towards the city—the former, over the causeway of Veronica, by way of Campo Santo and the San Cosmé gate; the latter by way of the causeway of Belen and the Belen Gate.[2]

The former had not proceeded more than three-quarters of a mile when he discovered an arched passage through the aqueduct, on which he was moving towards Campo Santo, with a cross-road, practicable for artillery, for a considerable distance, over the meadows which flanked his line of march; and he immediately detached a section of Lieutenant-colonel Duncan's battery and the light battalion commanded by Lieutenant-colonel Smith, to his right, for the purpose of assisting General Quitman, who had been "*battling* and *advancing*" on the causeway in that direction; and whose progress was, at that moment, opposed by the battalion of Morelia, which was posted in a battery which intersected his route, and by another battery, in the meadows, which commanded his left flank. The gallant officers who commanded the detachment advanced to a point within four hundred yards of the enemy's positions, and from that place opened an effective fire on the enemy's flank, driving him from his position, under an equally effective fire from Duncan's battery, which cut down great numbers of the terror-stricken fugitives in their hurried flight towards the city.[3]

Having thus cleared the front of General Quitman's column, and, to this extent, facilitated his advance towards the gate of the city, General Worth withdrew his detachment; and having been joined by his Second brigade (*Colonel Clark's*),—which had been detached to support General Pillow's column of attack on the western front of Chapultepec,—he continued his march towards Campo Santo. Two strong batteries, each enfilading the line of march, were successively attacked and carried; and he reached Campo Santo soon afterwards, without material opposition.[1]

At this place the causeway and aqueduct, along which General Worth had moved, connected with the great road from Western Mexico; here General Scott and his suite joined the column; and here, also, soon afterwards, by order of the General-in-chief, General Cadwallader, with his brigade, came up to support the veterans which General Worth was thus triumphantly leading towards the city.[2]

Leaving General Cadwallader at Campo Santo to maintain that very important position, and to keep open a communication with the other portions of the army, General Worth pressed forward towards the city; and fully and entirely sympathizing with their General in his anxiety to win the glorious prize which was before him,—the honor of taking the National Palace in the city of Mexico,—the battle-scathed veterans, whom he had led over so many fields of carnage, hastened to accomplish his wishes and to share with him the honors which were in reserve for the victors.[3]

The causeway, between Campo Santo and the city of Mexico,—the route which laid before General Worth,—passes through the once celebrated suburb of Tlaletolco; and the houses and churches along the margin of the roadway were filled with troops, for the purpose of harassing the troops with small-arms, and of resisting their progress, inch by inch. In addition to this means of defence, a battery had been erected across the cause-

[1] Reports of Gens. Worth and Quitman; Semmes, p. 456.
[2] Gen. Scott's Dispatch, No. 34, Sept. 18; Reports of Gens. Worth and Quitman; Notes for the History, p. 368.
[3] Reports of Gens. Worth and Quitman, Cols. Duncan and Smith; Semmes, p. 457; Ripley, ii. p. 433; Notes for the History, p. 368.

[1] Gen. Scott's Dispatch, No. 34, Sept. 18; Reports of Gen. Worth and Col. Clark; Ripley, ii. pp. 436, 437; Semmes, pp. 457, 458.—[2] Gen. Scott's Dispatch, No. 34, Sept. 18; Gen. Worth's Report.—[3] Reports of Gens. Worth and Cadwallader; Semmes, p. 458.

way, at about one hundred and fifty yards distant from Campo Santo; while at the gate of San Cosmé,—two hundred and fifty yards in the rear of the latter, and sustaining it,—a heavy gun and howitzer had been put in battery, and literally swept the line of march with grape, canister, and shells.[1]

In consequence of the unusual character of the opposition, General Worth immediately adapted his plan of operations to suit the circumstances. Two mountain-howitzers, from General Cadwallader's brigade, were ordered to the front, and mounted *on the tops of two high buildings*,—one on the roof of the church of San Cosmé, on the right of the causeway, and the other on the roof of a commanding building on the opposite side of the way,—and from their elevated positions each poured *down* upon the heads of those who occupied the roofs of the houses by the road-side, and upon those who were on the road itself, an unexpected, but terrible and effective fire. At the same time the First brigade (*Colonel Garland's*) was supplied with crow-bars and pickaxes, and thrown into the buildings on the right of the roadway, with orders to force through the side-walls of the houses; and, *by burrowing*, as had been done so successfully at Monterey, to approach the enemy's batteries *under cover of his own defences*. Colonel Clark, with the Second brigade, was thrown out to the left, with similar orders.[2]

Slowly, but surely, the assailants thus insidiously approached the gate—the enemy, meanwhile, abandoning the battery on his front, and concentrating his forces behind the defences of San Cosmé. At five o'clock in the afternoon the sappers had reached those points on either flank of the gate, from which, it was seen, the gate itself would be commanded, and (while Lieutenant Hunt, with a field-piece, gallantly pushed forward and occupied the deserted battery—losing five men out of nine who accompanied him in the movement) the men "sprang, as if by magic, to the tops of the houses, into which they had patiently and quietly made their way with the bar and pick, and, to the utter surprise and consternation of the enemy, opened on him, within easy range, a destructive fire of musketry." At the same time, Lieutenant Hunt, in front, opened a fire from his battery; and it was apparent to all that the moment had come when the question was to be solved whether the invaders or the Mexicans should occupy the capital of the Mexican republic.[1]

General Santa Anna, in person, appeared on the ground to direct and encourage his troops in their hopeless duty of defending the gate; while the latter,—demoralized by the series of disasters to which they had been subjected, by the sudden appearance of the Americans on the roofs of the buildings on either flank, and by the fall of many of their comrades, from the American small-arms, *while serving their guns within the gate*,—were thrown into hopeless confusion before a second fire could be made.[2]

The moment had now arrived for a final and combined attack upon the last stronghold of the enemy which stood between General Worth and the city; and, at about sunset, as the enemy retreated from the gate, the shouts of the veterans on the roadway, and on the housetops, announced to the General-in-chief, and to their comrades in the rear, that the *garita* of San Cosmé had been carried, and that the city of Mexico was already within reach of the victors.[3]

Among the prisoners who were taken at this post were Captain Castanara—Aid-de-camp of General Santa Anna—and several other prominent officers; and "a well-prepared supper," which awaited the presence of that General himself, fell into the hands of, and was enjoyed by, "one of the most gallant and leading subalterns" of the American army.[4]

Immediately afterwards the entire division,

[1] Report of Gen. Worth; Semmes, p. 458; Ripley, ii. pp. 438, 439.—[2] Gen. Scott's Dispatch, No. 34, Sept. 18; Reports of Gen. Worth, Cols. Clark, Garland, and Duncan; Semmes, pp. 458, 459; Ripley, ii. p. 440; Notes for the History, p. 370.

[1] Gen. Scott's Dispatch, No. 34, Sept. 18; Reports of Gen. Worth, Cols. Garland and Clark; Semmes, pp. 459, 460.—[2] Gen. Worth's Report; Semmes, p. 469; Notes for the History, p. 370.—[3] Gen. Worth's Report; Semmes, p. 460; Ripley, ii. p. 440; Notes for the History, p. 370.

[4] Gen. Worth's Report.

with Colonel Riley's brigade,—which had been sent forward by General Scott to support General Worth, should it be necessary, —was marched into the city; and Captain Huger was ordered to advance a twenty-four-pounder and a ten-inch mortar, place them in battery at the gate, obtain the direction, and open a few shot and shells upon the grand plaza and palace—about sixteen hundred yards distant. At nine o'clock this fire was opened, and five shells and three shot were thrown, with such admirable effect that, as will be seen hereafter, the Mexican troops were withdrawn from the city; the Mayor—Don Leandro Estrada—and the Regidors Fonseca and Zaldivar, in the name of the Ayuntamiento,[1] sought the quarters of General Worth, to ask security, and were sent to the rear, where General Scott was quartered; and the enemy's capital—the city of Mexico —was *added to the trophies* which then increased the previously well-earned fame of the First division and of General Worth, its gallant commander.[2]

While General Worth was thus nobly sustaining the honor of the army on the causeway of Veronica and the San Cosmé, General Quitman and his command were as gallantly sustaining it on the Belen causeway and at the *garita Belen.*

The movement, by General Worth, of Duncan's battery and the light battalion, to open the route of General Quitman at "the Bridge of the Insurgents," where the enemy had thrown up two batteries, has been already referred to; and at the same time that General Cadwallader had been sent on a similar errand after General Worth, as already related, General Pierce had been ordered to the support of General Quitman, on the causeway of Belen.[3]

Knowing the difficulties which the latter route presented, General Scott had intended that General Quitman should only manœuvre and threaten the Belen gate, in order to favor the main attack by General Worth; and he had repeatedly communicated those views, in the course of the day, to General Quitman; but the impetuosity of both officers and men, and the flattering prospect of success which was presented to them, lured them forward, and induced them to take a more important part in the great drama of that eventful day.[1]

After passing "the Bridge of the Insurgents,"—where the batteries were,—General Quitman reorganized his column for an assault on the gate, from whence, and from the Piedad road on the right, a steady and galling fire was maintained. He advanced the regiment of Rifles and the South Carolina Volunteers in advance,—three rifles and three volunteers under each arch of the aqueduct,—and supported them with the remainder of his command. In this order the column resolutely advanced from arch to arch of the aqueduct, under a tremendous fire of artillery and small-arms from the batteries at the gate, the Paseo, and a large body of the enemy on the Piedad road, to the right of his line of march, extending from the left of the gate. At the same time Captain Drum and Lieutenant Benjamin had kept up a constant and destructive fire from a sixteen-pound field-piece and an eight-inch howitzer; and a few rounds of canister from these soon afterwards scattered the troops which had occupied the Piedad road.[2]

Notwithstanding the severity of the opposition, the whole column moved forward steadily and firmly; and at twenty minutes past one o'clock in the afternoon the gate was carried by assault. In a few minutes afterwards nearly the whole command was within the gate, *and the city of Mexico, for the first time, had been entered by the hostile forces of the United States.*[3]

Although General Quitman and his command were really the first to enter the limits of the city of Mexico, the citadel of the city was between them and the city proper, and checked their progress. From that defence,

[1] The Council of the city.—[2] Reports of Gen. Worth, Col. Riley, Capt. Huger; Semmes, p. 463; Ripley, ii. pp. 442, 443; Notes for the History, pp. 373, 375.

[3] Gen. Scott's Dispatch, No. 34, Sept. 18; Report of Gens. Pierce and Quitman.

[1] Gen. Scott's Dispatch, No. 34, Sept. 18.

[2] Reports of Gens. Quitman, Smith, and Shields; Ripley, ii. p. 434.—[3] Gen. Scott's Dispatch, No. 34, Sept. 18; Reports of Gens. Quitman and Shields; Ripley, ii. p. 434; Notes for the History, pp. 368, 369.

from the batteries on the Paseo, and from the houses on their right and front, "an iron shower swept the road on both sides of the aqueduct, and rendered it impossible to bring forward ammunition for their artillery;" and several times the enemy sallied from the citadel and from the buildings in front of it, and endeavored, unsuccessfully, to drive the assailants from their position. Notwithstanding this serious and unsurmountable opposition, which held General Quitman in a mortifying and useless position *within* the gate, but *without* the city, *the enemy was unable to expel him;* and when night closed the efforts of the Mexicans, he was still within the gate and before the citadel. During the night, "by the indefatigable energy of his Acting-assistant-adjutant-general Lieutenant Mansfield Lovell, his volunteer aid, Captain Davis, and Lieutenant Brown, of the Third artillery," sand-bags and ammunition were brought forward; and, "by the persevering exertions of Captains Morton Fairchild and Jay P. Taylor, of the New York Volunteers,—who directed the working parties,"—two batteries were constructed for his heavy guns, on which, before the morning of the fourteenth, Captain Steptoe had mounted a twenty-four-pounder, an eighteen-pounder, and an eight-inch howitzer.[1] The spirited preparation for battering the citadel, which these works indicated, was gallantly seconded by the entire body of General Quitman's command; and General Pierce is especially mentioned in the dispatches for "his prompt attention" to the important duties of that eventful night.[2]

While the night was thus spent, with two columns of the American army within the gates of the city, the General-in-chief of the Mexican army, with his officers, and many members of the civil government of the city, were sitting in council in "the pavilion of the citadel;" and they determined to withdraw the troops from the city, and to throw the municipality at the feet of the victor. With this intent, as before stated, the civil officers, headed by the Mayor, sought the quarters of General Worth, and tendered their submission; and, at the same time, General Lombardini — to whom General Santa Anna had surrendered the command of the fragments of the army—led the troops from the city, by way of the gate of Peralvillo, towards the villa of Guadalupe, to which place General Santa Anna had retired earlier in the night.[1]

At the break of day, on the fourteenth, General Quitman was surprised with the sight of a white flag, which came from the citadel, with intelligence of the surrender of the city and the withdrawal of the Mexican forces; and immediately afterwards the column moved forward—the South Carolina Volunteers occupying the works at the gate, and the Second Pennsylvania regiment those at the citadel, while the remainder of the command entered the city.[2]

Soon after daylight—after the withdrawal of the deputation from the *Ayuntamiento*—General Scott sent orders to both Generals Worth and Quitman to advance slowly and cautiously towards the heart of the city, and to occupy its stronger and more commanding points. At the same time, however, for some strange and *unexplained* reason—savoring strongly of injustice, and boldly and continually declared to be such, by General Worth and those who enjoyed his confidence, as well as by those who had struggled, with him, for the honors of which they were thus deprived—"express orders" were sent to the latter officer, from the General-in-chief, "halting" the column which he had led into the city, and at the head of which he had received the tenders of its submission from its municipal authorities, "at the head of the *Alameda* (a green park), within three squares of that goal of general ambition," the National Palace of Mexico. By this means "the grateful service" of "planting guards and hoisting the colors of the United States on the National Palace—containing the halls of Congress and executive apartments of federal Mexico"—was thrown, un-

[1] Reports of Gens. Quitman and Shields; Ripley, ii. pp. 435, 436.—[2] Report of Gen. Quitman.

[1] Notes for the History, pp. 371–375, 383–385.
[2] Gen. Quitman's Report.

solicited, and with apparent injustice, into the hands of General Quitman and his gallant division; while the officers and the men to whom, by military usage and justice, that "grateful service" belonged, were compelled to occupy a position "three squares from that goal of general ambition," and to witness—at a distance, and under the iron rod of military law—the wrong to which they had been subjected by the General whose crowning glory *they* had secured for him only a few hours before.[1]

As has been said, General Quitman and his command occupied the palace; and to Captain Roberts, of the Rifles, who commanded the advance, was assigned the agreeable duty of raising the "star-spangled banner of his country" on the flag-staff of that building. At about eight o'clock General Scott, escorted by Colonel Harney's dragoons, entered the Grand Plaza amidst the cheers of the troops by whom he was surrounded.[2]

Immediately afterwards a shot, aimed at General Worth, was fired from the store of one Lopez, on the Plaza;[3] and, although it failed to reach the officer against whom it had been aimed, Colonel Garland received it in his leg, and suffered severely. This appears to have been a signal for the commencement of a series of similar assassin-like attempts, extending through two days and over the entire city; and the free use of heavy battering-guns upon every building from which such a fire proceeded, together with musketry from some of our men, thrown out as skirmishers, were found necessary to secure the lives of the troops and the quiet of the city.[4]

The strength of the American force, with which the last series of exploits was accomplished, exclusive of those who were in the rear, protecting the stores, &c., did not exceed, in the aggregate, seven thousand one hundred and eighty men;[5] and when it is borne in mind that even this small force was divided between General Twiggs—at the southern gates, General Worth—on the east and north of Chapultepec, General Quitman—south and west of it, and General Pillow—on its rocky front, the result was truly wonderful.

The loss of the Americans, during the same eventful period (*Sept.* 12, 13, *and* 14), was ten officers and one hundred and twenty men *killed*, sixty-eight officers and six hundred and thirty-five men *wounded*, and twenty-nine men *missing*—making a total of eight hundred and sixty-two.[1]

The strength and the loss of the enemy are equally unknown.

With the fall of the city of Mexico a new and not less determined line of policy appears to have been adopted by General Santa Anna and the Mexican authorities. Dividing the forces which remained under his command, General Santa Anna moved down to Puebla, where had been left a small garrison of two hundred and forty-seven men, under Colonel Thomas Childs, of the First artillery, to keep open the communication and to protect a hospital, filled with eighteen hundred sick or disabled soldiers, which had been established in that city. Withdrawing the hospitals within a tenable position (*San José*), when the first appearance of hostilities was manifested, Colonel Childs was enabled to defend his interesting charge with greater success, and to resist every conceivable attempt which was made by the inhabitants of the city, from the thirteenth of September to the twenty-second of the same month, when General Santa Anna arrived, with a heavy reinforcement, and was greeted with the ringing of bells and every manifestation of delight by the inhabitants. On the twenty-fifth Colonel Childs was summoned to surrender, but refused to do so; and on the twenty-seventh the operations were resumed by the Mexicans, under the directions of their General-in-chief. On the first of October, General Santa Anna withdrew, with four thousand men; yet the siege was actively sustained by the town's-people and

[1] Gen. Scott's Dispatch, No. 34, Sept. 18.—[2] Gen. Quitman's Report.—[3] Notes for the History, pp. 375, 376.
[4] Gen. Worth's Report; Semmes, pp. 464–466; Ripley, ii. pp. 444, 445; Notes for the History, pp. 375–381.
[5] Gen. Scott's Dispatch, No. 34, Sept. 18.

[1] Returns appended to Gen. Scott's Dispatch, No. 34, Sept. 18.

the remainder of the troops until the eleventh of October, when the enemy's fire ceased, and on the following day he decamped.[1]

When the ardor of the besiegers and their overpowering numbers are considered, together with the weakness of the garrison and the disadvantages under which it labored, this siege—extending through twenty-eight days—will be acknowledged to have been one of the most remarkable on record; and the honors which everywhere awaited the gallant Colonel and his command will be fully approved. Nineteen of the garrison had been killed and fifty-three wounded during the period of the investiture. The loss of the enemy is not known.[2]

While the series of movements in "the valley of Mexico" and at Puebla, to which reference has been made, was prostrating the power of Mexico, recruits from the United States, and reinforcements from the army under General Taylor, were sent forward to take the places of those who had fallen, and were landed at Vera Cruz during the summer of 1847. Of the first of these, eleven companies of infantry and two of cavalry, under the command of Major Lally, moved from Vera Cruz on the sixth of August; and he was not interrupted until he reached the Paso de Ovejas, four days afterwards. When near that place the column was attacked by General Soto and two thousand men, posted among the ruins of a strong stone house; while, at the same moment, strong parties attacked the rear of the column. An effective fire from the field-pieces, followed by a disorderly, but well-intended and successful charge, repulsed the enemy, —two officers and nine men having been wounded in the operation,—and the march was resumed until the column reached the Paso, where it halted.[3]

On the twelfth of August, when Major Lally had reached the National Bridge, he found that important pass in possession of the enemy; and it was only after a warm engagement—in which one officer and ten men were *killed*, and four officers and thirty-six men were *wounded*—that the passage was effected.[1]

Reinforcements having been asked for, the progress was a slow one; and it was not until the fifteenth that Major Lally reached Cerro Gordo. This difficult pass had also been occupied by the enemy, who had fallen back from Paso de Ovejas and the National Bridge; and a third time the raw troops, composing the Major's command, were compelled to force their way through their persevering opposers. A judicious disposition of the troops, and an energetic and simultaneous charge on both sides of the road, brushed away the opposition,—three Americans having been killed and ten wounded in the operation,—and on the nineteenth the column reached Jalapa.[2]

Soon afterwards the detachment from the northern army, already referred to, reached Vera Cruz; and General Lane, at the head of one regiment of Indiana and one of Ohio Volunteers, two battalions of recruits, five companies of volunteer horse, and two pieces of artillery,—in all about two thousand five hundred men,—marched from that city on the twentieth of September. The column was considerably harassed on its march, and several minor affairs with the guerillas added to the interest of the otherwise monotonous journey to Jalapa; at which place a junction was formed with the command of Major Lally.[3]

In the mean time reports had reached Jalapa of the troubles at Puebla; and the entire force, after a very short halt, was moved forward towards that place. Reports had also been received of the movement of General Santa Anna to arrest the progress of the column, and of the concentration of his force near the pass of El Piñal; and the force had been increased by the addition of a company of mounted rifles and four of in-

[1] Col. Childs' Report, Oct. 13; Reports of Lieut.-Col. Black, Maj. Gwynne, and Capt. Moorehead.

[2] Returns, &c., inclosed in Col. Childs' Report of Sept. 18.

[3] Maj. Lally's Dispatch to the Adj.-Gen. of the Army, Aug. 27, 1847; Reports of Lieuts. Sears and Ridgely; Ripley, ii. pp. 499, 500.

[1] Maj. Lally's Dispatch to the Adj.-Gen. of the Army, Aug. 27, 1847; Reports of Lieuts. Sears and Ridgely; Ripley, ii. pp. 499, 500.—[2] Ibid.

[3] Gen. Lane to Adj.-Gen., Oct. 18, 1847; Ripley, ii. pp. 504, 505.

fantry, with three field-pieces, from the castle of Perote.[1]

As General Lane advanced he ascertained that the enemy, instead of occupying the pass of El Piñal, as had been reported, had taken post at Huamantla,—a town some miles north of the line of march, and east from it,—evidently with the intention of falling on the rear of the column while it passed through the defile. To prevent this, General Lane resolved to move against and attack him in his position, before his forces could be formed for battle. Accordingly, after parking his train, and mounting an ample guard for its protection, on the morning of the ninth of October, General Lane moved towards Huamantla; and his approach was not discovered by the enemy until the head of his column had arrived within three miles of the town. At this moment several parties of horsemen were seen making their way across the fields to the city; and Captain Walker, with his company of mounted rifles, and the volunteer cavalry, was sent in pursuit of them. With that reckless daring which too frequently characterized the cavalry of the American army, the Captain pressed forward at a gallop; and, without waiting for a support, he entered the town with his little party; attacked a body of five hundred lances, which was posted, with two pieces of artillery, in the Plaza; drove it from the position it occupied, and dispersed the greater part of the force. As might have been expected, however, the enemy was reinforced, and rallied before the infantry could come up to the support of the Captain and his party; and the assailants were driven back with heavy loss—the Captain and thirteen men having been *killed*, and eleven men been *wounded*. Soon afterwards the main body came up, and General Lane so disposed his troops that the town would be assaulted at three points, at the same time, while Major Lally and his recruits were held in reserve.[2]

By a judicious disposition of his troops, General Lane secured the town without much effort, and the enemy fell back upon Atlixco, the temporary seat of the State government.[1] Thither General Lane pursued him; and on the nineteenth of October an action took place near that town, in which the enemy, after suffering severely, again fell back, with his artillery and equipments, as far as Matamoras, a small village, eleven leagues in his rear.[2]

With the exception of some minor operations, in the course of which skirmishes were fought at Matamoras and Galaxara,[3] at Orizaba and Cordova,[4] at Sequalteplan,[5] at San José and La Paz,[6] and at Santa Cruz de Rosales,[7]—for a description of which our space is too limited,—the military operations of the war ended.

A treaty of peace, so called, was accepted as such by the President and the Senate of the United States, and the peaceful relations of the two countries were restored.

Originating in dishonor, in violation of the law of nations, this war had been thrown upon the United States, by their Executive, without the formalities of legislation, required by the Federal Constitution; and it had been acquiesced in, as a necessity, by the Congress and the people. The fine discipline of the army then in the field, directed by a body of the most accomplished and gallant subordinate officers, had secured for the Commanding-general, and for the war, a degree of popularity, immediately afterwards, which the negative qualities of the former, and the positive injustice of the latter, could not otherwise have secured; and that popularity—renewed, and subsequently increased, by the genius of him who had planned and principally conducted the defence of the pass of Angostura and the rugged field of Buena Vista—bore the Gen-

[1] Gen. Lane to Adj.-Gen., Oct. 18.—[2] Ibid.

[1] Gen. Lane to Adj.-Gen., Oct. 18, 1847; Ripley, ii. pp. 506, 507.—[2] Gen. Lane to Adj.-Gen., Oct. 22, 1847; Ripley, ii. pp. 508, 509.—[3] Gen. Lane to Adj.-Gen., Dec. 1, 1847.—[4] Gen. Lane to Gen. Scott, Feb. 10, 1848.

[5] Gen. Lane to Adj.-Gen., March 2, 1848; Reports of Col. John C. Hays and Majors Polk and Turett.

[6] Col. Mason to Adj.-Gen., April 12, 1848; Lieut.-Col. Burton's and Lieut. Heywood's Reports.

[7] Gen. Pierce to Adj.-Gen., March 31, 1848; Reports of Lieut. Col. Lane, Majors Beale and Walker, Capt. Hassendeibel, and Lieut. Love.

eral-in-chief in safety, from Vera Cruz to Mexico, notwithstanding the discordant elements with which he had surrounded himself.

Dreading the effects of that reaction, in the Congress and among the people,—that "sober second thought," which politicians seldom feel willing to encounter,—the Executive gladly availed itself of the unauthorized agreement of a degraded former secret agent of its Department of State,—no longer a representative of the United States, in any capacity,—with the equally questionable representatives of as questionable a government of the Mexican republic; and with a degree of effrontery which fully became the author of the surreptitious war, it became the abettor of equally as surreptitious a peace.

Amity was thus restored between the nations; the troops of the United States—regulars and volunteers—returned to their barracks or to the frontier posts, or to their respective homes among the people, with shattered frames or with the seeds of disease or premature decay rooted in their systems. Many of them have already sunk into unhonored graves; others still linger among us, and with tottering steps and emaciated forms, bear mournful testimony to the hardships they have endured, and to the insidious enemy they have encountered in every breeze. Others, few in number, have been spared, in the Providence of God, in apparent health,—as monuments of the past,—to whom we may also turn to refresh our recollections, and to receive lessons of the solemn realities of war; and may the day be far distant when our children may not be taught, from the lips of the living witness, the inestimable value of peace, and the equally inestimable evil of an "unnatural" and an unrighteous war.